NEW! Careers in Criminal Justice Website

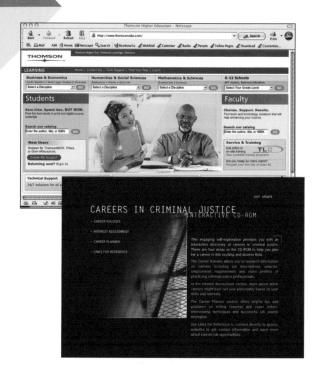

This new site helps you investigate and focus on the criminal justice career choices that are right for you. The site explores dozens of criminal justice-related careers, including:

- Cyber crime investigator
- FBI terrorism specialist
- Crime scene technician
- Criminologist
- Explosives enforcement specialist
- Federal security director/assistant
- Immigration enforcement agent
- Transportation security screener
- *And many more*

The Careers in Criminal Justice Website also includes:

- **Video Testimonials** from practicing professionals in the field
- **Interest Assessment** to help you decide which careers best suit your personality and interests
- **A Career Planner** that includes helpful tips and worksheets for resumé writing and successful job search strategies
- **Links for Reference,** featuring quick access to federal, state, and local agencies where you can get contact information and learn more about current job opportunities

The Careers in Criminal Justice Website is available at www.thomsonedu.com.

INTRODUCTION TO
Criminal Justice

ELEVENTH EDITION

LARRY J. SIEGEL
University of Massachusetts, Lowell

JOSEPH J. SENNA

THOMSON

WADSWORTH

Australia · Brazil · Canada · Mexico · Singapore
Spain · United Kingdom · United States

THOMSON
★
™
WADSWORTH

Introduction to Criminal Justice, **Eleventh Edition**
Larry J. Siegel, Joseph J. Senna

Senior Acquisitions Editor, Criminal Justice: Carolyn
Henderson Meier
Development Editor: Shelley Murphy
Assistant Editor: Rebecca Johnson
Editorial Assistant: Beth McMurray
Technology Project Manager: Amanda Kaufmann
Marketing Manager: Terra Schultz
Marketing Assistant: Emily Elrod
Marketing Communications Manager: Tami Strang
Project Manager, Editorial Production: Jennie Redwitz
Creative Director: Rob Hugel
Art Director: Vernon Boes

Print Buyer: Becky Cross
Permissions Editor: Writers Research Group
Production Service: Melanie Field, Strawberry Field Publishing
Text Designer: Adriane Bosworth
Photo Researcher: Linda Rill
Copy Editor: Donald Pharr
Illustrator: Matt Perry, Laura Murray Productions
Cover Designer: Yvo
Cover Image: Police car in city: © Paul Colangelo/Corbis; paint,
stop sign, and police tape images: istockphoto.com
Compositor: Pre-Press Company, Inc.
Text and Cover Printer: Transcontinental Printing/Interglobe

Library of Congress Control Number: 2006936558

ISBN-13: 978-0-495-09541-5
ISBN-10: 0-495-09541-9

Thomson Higher Education
10 Davis Drive
Belmont, CA 94002-3098
USA

For more information about our products, contact us at:
Thomson Learning Academic Resource Center
1-800-423-0563

For permission to use material from this text or product,
submit a request online at
http://www.thomsonrights.com
Any additional questions about permissions can be submitted
by e-mail to **thomsonrights@thomson.com**.

Brief Contents

Contents

CHAPTER 12
The Criminal Trial   380

CHAPTER 13
Punishment and Sentencing   412

PART FIVE

THE HISTORY AND NATURE OF THE
JUVENILE JUSTICE SYSTEM   571

CHAPTER 17

The Juvenile Justice
System   572

CAREERS

Spotlighted in the 11th Edition

Preface

According to a U.S. Department of Justice press release, in July 2006 law enforcement authorities across the United States arrested 30 members of an international criminal organization led by drug traffickers Bashi Muse, Ali Awad, Abdi Emil Moge, and Osman Osman, who were involved in a worldwide khat distribution ring. Khat is a plant cultivated in Kenya and Ethiopia, whose leaves contain stimulants banned by U.S. drug law. Khat users chew the leaves to experience euphoria and stimulation, but the side effects include anorexia, heart disease, hypertension, and cancer of the mouth, among other problems.

The khat smugglers send the plants from the Horn of Africa, where it is cultivated, to users in the United States and Europe. Before the arrests, the cartel had smuggled 25 tons of khat—worth more than $10 million—into the United States. The cartel imported khat from Africa to Europe, then to New York, either by using human couriers flying on commercial airlines or by sending commercial express mail packages from the United Kingdom, Italy, the Netherlands, Germany, Austria, and other countries in Western Europe. Once in New York, the khat was retrieved and sent by land to other states to be sold on the streets. The traffickers then used "hawalas"—informal networks of money remitters commonly found in Africa and the Middle East—to transfer money and "launder" the khat proceeds. After receiving millions in proceeds, the hawaladars worked with co-conspirators in Europe, Africa, and Dubai (United Arab Emirates) to transfer a portion of the khat proceeds from bank accounts in the United States to bank accounts in Dubai for the benefit of the khat suppliers.

◆ INTRODUCTION TO CRIMINAL JUSTICE

The khat smuggling case illustrates the wide range of human behavior that falls under the jurisdiction of agencies within the criminal justice system. Each year the criminal justice system routinely processes millions of cases involving theft, violence, drug trafficking, and other crimes that are rarely reviewed on TV or in the newspapers. Some involve petty thefts from the neighborhood grocery store. Others—like the smuggling case just described—involve complex international schemes that net the conspirators millions of dollars. Agents of the justice system, then, must be able to contend with crimes involving neighborhood teens out on a shoplifting spree as well as international drug cartels that use sophisticated technology to launder money in overseas capitals.

The justice system has become an enterprise costing more than $100 billion each year. It employs millions of people in law enforcement, courts, and correctional agencies. Justice agencies are engaged in an ongoing effort to improve their efficiency and effectiveness. We have written *Introduction to Criminal Justice* to help students better understand this enormous and complex system, and to aid their journey in introductory-level criminal justice courses. The text analyzes and describes the agencies of justice and the variety of procedures they use to apprehend, adjudicate, and treat criminal offenders. It covers what most experts believe are the critical issues in criminal justice and analyzes their impact on the justice system. Our primary goals in writing this, the Eleventh Edition, remain as they have been for the previous ten:

1. To provide students with a thorough knowledge of criminal justice agencies, procedures, and policies.
2. To be as thorough and up-to-date as possible.
3. To be objective and unbiased.
4. To challenge students to think critically about justice.

Every attempt has been made to present the material in an interesting, balanced, and objective manner, making sure that no single political or theoretical position dominates the text. Instead, the many diverse views that shape the contemporary criminal justice system and characterize its interdisciplinary nature are presented. Diversity of opinion is what the study of criminal justice is all about and is the central focus of the text. We have tried to provide a text that is scholarly and informative, comprehensive yet interesting, and well organized and objective while at the same time provocative and thought-provoking.

♦ ORGANIZATION OF THE TEXT

The Eleventh Edition has been thoroughly revised. We have made a concerted effort to make the text more concise, "student friendly," and accessible than ever before. Great care has been taken to organize the text to reflect the structure and process of justice. Each chapter attempts to be comprehensive, self-contained, and orderly.

Part One gives the student a basic introduction to crime, law, and justice. The first chapter briefly describes the history of criminal justice, the agencies of justice, and the formal justice process, and introduces students to the concept of the informal justice system, which involves discretion, deal making, and plea bargains. The major perspectives or philosophies of justice are also described. Chapter 1 now includes a discussion of some of the most recent challenges facing the justice system, including cyber crime and terrorism, and discusses the ethical dilemmas that these and other issues present to justice system personnel. Chapter 2 discusses the nature and extent of crime and victimization: How is crime measured? Where and when does it occur? Who commits crime? Who are its victims? What social factors influence the crime rate? Chapter 3 covers crime patterns and addresses this critical question: Why do people commit crime, and why do some people become the victims of criminal acts? Chapter 4 provides a discussion of the criminal law and its relationship to criminal justice. It focuses on critical issues in both substantive and procedural law.

Part Two provides an overview of the law enforcement field. Four chapters cover the history and development of law enforcement; the role, organization, and function of police in modern society; issues in policing; and the police and the rule of law. In the Eleventh Edition we have added a significant amount of new material to this section to address recent changes in contemporary U.S. police organizations and the ways in which they are more focused on responding to the threat of terrorism. New sections describing the goals and organization of the Department of Homeland Security and the recent growth of the private security industry are also included.

Part Three is devoted to the adjudication process, from pretrial indictment to the sentencing of criminal offenders. These chapters focus on organization of the court system, an analysis of the prosecution and defense functions, pretrial procedures, the criminal trial, and sentencing. Topics included here range from court structure to sentencing policies to capital punishment. There are also sections on the processing of felony cases, indigent defense systems, attorney competence, legal ethics, pretrial services, and bail reform.

Part Four focuses on the correctional system, including probation, intermediate sanctions, and restorative justice. The traditional correctional system of jails, prisons, community-based corrections, and parole is also discussed in depth. Issues such as techno-corrections and the problem of prisoner reentry are analyzed.

Part Five explores the juvenile justice system. There is information on preventive detention of youths, waiving juveniles to the adult court, and recent changes in the death penalty for children.

◆ WHAT'S NEW IN THIS EDITION

Because the study of criminal justice is a dynamic, ever-changing field of scientific inquiry and because the concepts and processes of justice are constantly changing and evolving, we have updated *Introduction to Criminal Justice* to reflect the field's most recent structural and procedural changes, critical legal cases, research studies, and policy initiatives. The updated edition also identifies emerging programs and policy issues in the criminal justice system, ranging from cyber crime to ethics, from biometrics to homeland security and terrorism. Additionally, we have incorporated a stronger comparative/cross-cultural thread into the Eleventh Edition and dramatically enhanced our coverage of career opportunities in the field by including a new **Careers in Criminal Justice** box in every chapter. (For a complete list of these new career profiles, see page xii.)

Chapter-by-Chapter Changes

Chapter 1, "Crime and Criminal Justice," begins with a new vignette focusing on NSA surveillance on U.S. citizens in the post-9/11 world. We ask the reader to consider the question "Should personal privacy be sacrificed for the war on terrorism?" The chapter includes substantial new material on recent challenges facing the justice system, including terrorism and cyber crime, as well as a new section on ethical issues in criminal justice. We have included a new Careers in Criminal Justice box that describes the work of police officers.

Chapter 2, "The Nature and Extent of Crime," has been updated with the most recent crime data available. It contains two new International Justice boxes, "Child Prostitution on the German–Czech Border" and "International Crime Trends." A new Careers in Criminal Justice box features statisticians in the field of criminal justice.

Chapter 3, "Understanding Crime and Victimization," opens with a new vignette on the topic of Medicare fraud. There is new material on categories of situational crime prevention, a new Careers in Criminal Justice box focusing on criminologists, and a new International Justice feature on "Organized Crime in Russia."

Chapter 4, "Criminal Law: Substance and Procedure," begins with a new vignette describing another interesting case of fraud, a "work at home" fraud that bilked thousands of people out of millions of dollars. We have added a new Careers in Criminal Justice feature on attorneys, and a great deal of material has been added to describe the ways the criminal law responded to changing social and technological conditions, including cyber and environmental crimes. At the request of our reviewers, we have also expanded the sections on constitutional law and constitutional criminal procedure.

Chapter 5, "Police in Society: History and Organization," now opens with an example of a recent collaborative law enforcement effort known as Operation Valley SCAR, which targeted criminal street gangs in Stanislaus County, California. The collaboration provides a compelling illustration of how law enforcement agents today use interagency cooperation to be effective against challenges ranging from gang activity to international terrorism. We have reorganized and expanded our coverage of contemporary police organizations to include new material on how the various levels of law enforcement agencies in the United States have restructured and evolved to more effectively respond to the threat of terrorism. Included is a substantial new section describing the goals and organization of the Department of Homeland Security, as well as a new section focused on the recent growth of the private security industry in the post-9/11 era. The new Careers in Criminal Justice feature details the nature of the job of private security guard.

Chapter 6, "The Police: Organization, Role, Function," begins with a recent case involving the illegal sale of permanent residence documents, or "green cards," to illegal aliens, and how the scam was busted by law enforcement agents. This new vignette highlights the rather complex criminal conspiracies that law enforcement agents must confront on a daily basis. The section on the patrol function includes a new discussion of how police departments rely on technology, such as Compstat, to help guide patrol efforts. A new Analyzing Criminal Justice Issues box features the book *Street Stories—The World of Police Detectives*, a fascinating look at the factors shaping the meaning of detectives' work, their images of the world, and their own self-images. We have added new information on investigative techniques employed by detectives, and a new Careers in Criminal Justice feature on the employment of investigators by private detective agencies and security companies. The sections on community policing have been revised and expanded, and a new International Justice box, "Neighborhood Policing in England," shows that community and neighborhood policing models are not unique to the United States.

Chapter 7, "Issues in Policing," introduces the reader to the Gambino "mob detectives," two New York cops who are alleged to have served as hit men for the mob. This new vignette highlights the critical and controversial role that police play in the justice system and the need for developing a professional, competent police force. We have reorganized and expanded our coverage of the changing composition of the nation's police forces, police education and training, and women and minorities in policing. Coverage of police discretion has been expanded and includes new research findings on racial profiling and the use of discretion in policing. The section on violence and use of force has been revised and expanded. And we have added a new International Justice feature, "When the Cops Are Robbers," on police problems in Nigeria, showing that police corruption is not a uniquely U.S. phenomenon.

Chapter 8, "Police and the Rule of Law," introduces the Hudson case, in which the Supreme Court loosened restrictions on "no knock" entries, illustrating how the Court must balance the greater needs of society with the more narrow rights of a criminal defendant, and how the Court's interpretation of such abstract legal concepts as "privacy" and "inevitable discovery" shapes the scope of police behavior. The section on search and seizure has been significantly revised and updated, and the discussion of the concept of reasonableness in search warrants has been expanded. A new Careers in Criminal Justice feature describes the job of an FBI agent. The issue of vehicle searches is highlighted in a new Law in Review box on *United States v. Thornton*, and we have included new coverage of *Georgia v. Randolph*, which defines the concept of second-party consent to search. To conclude this chapter, we have added a new section on the future of the exclusionary rule.

Chapter 9, "The Courts and the Judiciary," opens with a vignette on Mumia Abu-Jamal, a man who has spent many years in prison and death row for a murder that many supporters believe he did not commit. We have revised and updated the discussion of court organization and case flow data, added a new Criminal Justice and Technology feature on the use of virtual reality technology in the modern courtroom, and provided a profile of judges in a new Careers in Criminal Justice box.

Chapter 10, "The Prosecution and Defense," begins with a new chapter-opening profile of the career of Eliot Spitzer, the hard-charging New York Attorney General who has taken on Wall Street tycoons, a timely example of one of the two adversaries who face each other every day in the criminal trial process.

Sections on prosecutorial discretion and decision making have been updated, and we have expanded the discussion of the role of ethics in criminal defense.

Chapter 11, "Pretrial Procedures," includes a new Careers in Criminal Justice box on becoming a bail bondsman. The sections on bail and bail reform have been revised and expanded to include more coverage of legal rights pertaining to bail, how bail decisions are made, types of bail, and bail reform. In this chapter we have also included new material on the extent of plea bargaining and the effect of plea bargains on case outcomes.

Chapter 12, "The Criminal Trial," has a new Law in Review box featuring *Crawford v. Washington*, a case that defines the confrontation clause and the use of evidence at trials. A new Analyzing Criminal Justice Issues box examines the controversies surrounding jury nullification. The job of court reporter is highlighted in the Careers in Criminal Justice feature. And the chapter analyzes the case of *House v. Bell*, in which the U.S. Supreme Court expanded the ability of death row inmates to challenge their convictions in federal court based on DNA evidence produced long after their trials.

Chapter 13, "Punishment and Sentencing," thoroughly updates the material on sentencing and capital punishment, including the use of the death penalty in other countries. We have added a Careers in Criminal Justice box on becoming a forensic psychologist. And the sections on sentencing guidelines have been revised in the aftermath of the *Blakely* ruling, which mandates that juries and not judges be the decider of facts in cases involving sentencing enhancements.

Chapter 14, "Community Sentences: Probation, Intermediate Sanctions, and Restorative Justice," begins with a new vignette on Elizabeth Stowe, a teacher given probation after being convicted on charges that she was sexually involved with her underage students. There is a new International Justice box, "Restorative Cautioning in England." A Careers in Criminal Justice box highlights the job of probation officers. And the sections on alternative sanctions in the United States and abroad have been revised and updated.

Chapter 15, "Corrections: History, Institutions, and Populations," includes new sections on supermax prisons and the effectiveness of private corrections, and expands our coverage of jails. A new Careers in Criminal Justice box focuses on correctional counseling, a field that has been growing due to the expansion of the U.S. prison system.

Chapter 16, "Prison Life: Living in and Leaving Prison," has been revised and updated to include new information on inmates' rights, parole, and reentry. We have added a new Analyzing Criminal Justice Issues feature discussing therapeutic communities and the "TC" approach to substance abuse treatment, and a new Race, Gender, and Ethnicity in Criminal Justice feature that looks at life in a women's prison. The new Careers in Criminal Justice feature provides information about becoming a correctional officer.

Chapter 17, "The Juvenile Justice System," contains new data on trends in the juvenile justice system, including detention and incarceration. We have revised the section on status offenders, and a new Careers in Criminal Justice feature on social workers has been added for this edition.

◆ SPECIAL FEATURES

We have created a comprehensive, proven learning system designed to help students get the most out of their first course in criminal justice. In addition to the many changes already mentioned, we have included a wealth of new photographs to appeal to visual learners and make material more relevant and meaningful. Carefully updated tables and completely redrawn figures highlight key chapter concepts. Marginal definitions of key terms; concise, bulleted end-of-chapter summaries; and a comprehensive end-of-book glossary all help students master the material, and Internet research links appearing in the text's margins let students explore topics further via the web.

Boxed Features

We have also included a number of thematic boxes to introduce students to some of the field's most crucial programs, policies, and issues, providing them with an opportunity to analyze material in greater depth.

- ♦ **Careers in Criminal Justice** We have added this new feature to the Eleventh Edition to provide up-to-date information on career paths for criminal justice students, ranging from statistician to forensic psychologist. These boxes contain detailed information on salaries, educational requirements, and future prospects for employment.

- ♦ **International Justice** Crime in the twenty-first century is increasingly global in nature and characterized by a need for international cooperation. As such, it is necessary for today's student to be aware of justice issues and institutions in other countries. What's more, students in the United States can gain perspective on our system of criminal justice by comparing it with other countries' systems. The International Justice boxes, which have been expanded in the Eleventh Edition, enable students to look at criminal justice issues around the world from a comparative perspective. In Chapter 2, for example, "Child Prostitution on the German–Czech Border" discusses the serious social problem of commercial sexual exploitation of children.

- ♦ **Images of Justice** These boxes show how the criminal justice system is portrayed in the media, on television, in films, and in books, and also how the media influence crime and justice. For example, in Chapter 12, the Images of Justice box ("Should Criminal Trials Be Televised?") looks at the advantages—and disadvantages—of broadcasting criminal trials.

- ♦ **Race, Gender, and Ethnicity in Criminal Justice** These boxes are aimed at helping students better understand the problems of women and minorities in the U.S. justice system. For example, Chapter 16 includes "World Apart—Life in a Female Prison," which reveals what it is like to be an inmate in a women's prison.

- ♦ **Criminal Justice and Technology** These boxed features focus on some of the latest efforts to modernize the criminal justice system by using contemporary technology. For example, "Using Virtual Reality in the Courtroom," a feature in Chapter 9, looks at how technology is shaping trial practices.

- ♦ **Analyzing Criminal Justice Issues** This feature helps students to learn and to think critically about current justice issues and practices. For example, a Chapter 12 Analyzing Criminal Justice Issues feature on jury nullification discusses how defense lawyers use tactics to appeal to jurors' emotions in order to get a favorable verdict.

- ♦ **Law in Review** This feature gives the facts, decision, and significance of critical legal cases. In Chapter 8, *United States v. Thornton* discusses a recent Supreme Court decision covering the right of police officers to search people in an automobile stop who leave the car before police arrive.

Other Important Chapter Features

We have included numerous learning tools in every chapter to aid student mastery of the material. A few of the most valuable study aids we have provided are the following:

- ♦ **Ethical Challenges in Criminal Justice Writing Assignment** As a new addition to *Introduction to Criminal Justice*, each chapter now has a writing assignment that challenges students to solve an ethical dilemma that they may someday confront while working within the justice system. Chapter 2's ethical dilemma, for example, poses the issue of whether it is fair and just to punish more severely someone who commits a crime motivated by hate than one motivated by greed, jealousy, or revenge—a dilemma that students are asked to explore in essay format.

♦ **Perspectives on Justice** Running throughout the book are Perspectives on Justice insets that link chapter material to the various competing viewpoints on what criminal justice is and what it should be directed to accomplish. For example, some people believe that the primary mission of the justice system is punishing criminals, whereas others focus more on treatment and rehabilitation. The Perspectives on Justice boxes show how each of these competing views has influenced the way the system of justice operates and identify programs and polices to which they are linked.

♦ **ThomsonNOW™** Integrated through marginal references in the text is ThomsonNOW, a unique assessment and study tool that determines each student's precise learning needs via a Pre-Test and then offers him or her a Personalized Study plan that focuses study time on the concepts that the student needs to master. Personalized Study includes ABC® News clips with questions, career profile videos, concept learning modules with assessments, integrated simulations, interactive diagrams, animations, Microsoft® Power-Point® lectures, topic reviews, an e-book, and more. Once the student has completed the Personalized Study plan, a Post-Test evaluates his or her improved comprehension of chapter content.

♦ **Web Links** These are designed to guide students to websites that will provide them with additional information if they want to conduct further research on the topics covered in the text.

♦ **Concept Summaries** Concept Summary charts appear throughout the chapters to summarize important concepts so students can compare and contrast ideas, views, cases, and findings. For example, in Chapter 2 a Concept Summary reviews concepts and theories of criminology.

♦ ANCILLARY MATERIALS

An extensive package of supplemental aids accompanies this edition of *Introduction to Criminal Justice*. Supplements are available to qualified adopters. Please consult your local sales representative for details.

For the Instructor

INSTRUCTOR'S RESOURCE MANUAL The fully updated and revised *Instructor's Resource Manual* for this edition, prepared by Lisa Anne Zilney of Montclair State University, includes learning objectives, detailed chapter outlines, key terms and figures, class discussion exercises, lecture suggestions, and a complete test bank. Each chapter's test bank contains approximately 80 multiple-choice, true–false, fill-in-the-blank, and essay questions, which are coded according to difficulty level; a full answer key completes the test bank. Each question in the Test Bank has been carefully reviewed by experienced criminal justice instructors for quality, accuracy, and content coverage. Our Instructor Approved seal, which appears on the front cover, is our assurance that you are working with an assessment and grading resource of the highest caliber. Also included is a Resource Integration Guide, which will help you make maximum use of the rich supplement package available for this text by integrating media, Internet, video, and other resources into each chapter. Finally, a detailed transition guide is provided to make it easier to change from your current text to *Introduction to Criminal Justice*.

EXAMVIEW® COMPUTERIZED TESTING The comprehensive *Instructor's Resource Manual* described above is backed up by ExamView, a computerized test bank available for PC compatibles and Macintosh computers. With ExamView you can create, deliver, and customize tests and study guides (both print and online) in minutes. You can easily edit and import your own questions and graphics, change test layouts, and reorganize questions. And using ExamView's complete word processing capabilities, you can enter an unlimited number of new questions or edit existing questions.

JOININ™ ON TURNING POINT® Spark discussion and assess your students' comprehension of chapter concepts with interactive classroom quizzes and background polls developed specifically for use with this edition of *Introduction to Criminal Justice.* Also available are polling/quiz questions that enable you to maximize the educational benefits of the ABC News video clips we custom selected to accompany this textbook. Thomson Wadsworth's exclusive agreement with TurningPoint software lets you run our tailor-made Microsoft® PowerPoint® slides in conjunction with the "clicker" hardware of your choice. Enhance how your students interact with you, your lecture, and each other. *For college and university adopters only. Contact your local Thomson representative to learn more.*

THOMSON POWERLECTURE CD This instructor resource includes Microsoft® PowerPoint® lecture slides with graphics from the text, making it easy for you to assemble, edit, publish, and present custom lectures for your course. The PowerLecture CD also includes video-based polling and quiz questions that can be used with the JoinIn on TurningPoint personal response system, and integrates ExamView testing software for customizing tests of up to 250 items that can be delivered in print or online. Finally, all of your media teaching resources in one place!

WEBTUTOR™ TOOLBOX ON BLACKBOARD® AND WEBCT® A powerful combination: easy-to-use course management tools for whichever program you use (WebCT or Blackboard) with content from this text's rich companion website all in one place. You can use ToolBox as is, from the moment you log on—or, if you prefer, customize the program with web links, images, and other resources.

THE WADSWORTH CRIMINAL JUSTICE VIDEO LIBRARY So many exciting new videos—so many great ways to enrich your lectures and spark discussion of the material in this text! A list of our unique and expansive video program follows. Or visit **www.thomsonedu.com/criminaljustice/media_center/index.html** for a complete, up-to-the-minute list of all of Wadsworth's video offerings—many of which are also available in DVD format—as well as clip lists and running times. The library includes these selections and many others:

- *ABC Videos*: Featuring short, high-interest clips from current news events specially developed for courses in introduction to criminal justice, criminology, corrections, terrorism, and white-collar crime, these videos are perfect for use as discussion starters or lecture launchers to spark student interest. The brief video clips provide students with a new lens through which to view the past and present, one that will greatly enhance their knowledge and understanding of significant events and open up to them new dimensions in learning. Clips are drawn from programs such as *World News Tonight, Good Morning America, This Week, PrimeTime Live, 20/20,* and *Nightline,* as well as numerous ABC News specials and material from the Associated Press Television News and British Movietone News collections.

- *The Wadsworth Custom Videos for Criminal Justice*: Produced by Wadsworth and Films for the Humanities, these videos include short (5- to 10-minute) segments that encourage classroom discussion. Topics include white-collar crime, domestic violence, forensics, suicide and the police officer, the court process, the history of corrections, prison society, and juvenile justice.

- *Court TV Videos*: One-hour videos presenting seminal and high-profile cases, such as the interrogation of Michael Crowe and serial killer Ted

Bundy, as well as crucial and current issues such as cyber crime, double jeopardy, and the management of the prison on Riker's Island.

♦ *A&E American Justice*: Forty videos to choose from, on topics such as deadly force, women on death row, juvenile justice, strange defenses, and Alcatraz.

♦ *Films for the Humanities*: Nearly 200 videos to choose from on a variety of topics such as elder abuse, supermax prisons, suicide and the police officer, the making of an FBI agent, and domestic violence.

♦ *Oral History Project*: Developed in association with the American Society of Criminology, the Academy of Criminal Justice Society, and the National Institute of Justice, these videos will help you introduce your students to the scholars who have developed the criminal justice discipline. Compiled over the last several years, each video features a set of guest lecturers—scholars whose thinking has helped to build the foundation of present ideas in the discipline.

CLASSROOM ACTIVITIES FOR CRIMINAL JUSTICE This valuable booklet, available to adopters of any Wadsworth criminal justice text, offers instructors the best of the best in criminal justice classroom activities. Containing both tried-and-true favorites and exciting new projects, its activities are drawn from across the spectrum of criminal justice subjects, including introduction to criminal justice, criminology, corrections, criminal law, policing, and juvenile justice, and can be customized to fit any course. Novice and seasoned instructors alike will find it a powerful tool to stimulate classroom engagement.

INTERNET ACTIVITIES FOR CRIMINAL JUSTICE, THIRD EDITION This is the resource that no introductory criminal justice instructor should be without! The user-friendly booklet allows instructors to send their students far beyond the classroom, guiding them online to conduct research and retrieve information. Its URLs and virtual projects, drawn from all foundational criminal justice areas, have been completely revised and expanded for 2008.

THE WADSWORTH CRIMINAL JUSTICE RESOURCE CENTER (WWW.THOMSONEDU. COM/CRIMINALJUSTICE) Designed with the instructor in mind, this website features information about Thomson Wadsworth's technology and teaching solutions, as well as several features created specifically for today's criminal justice student. Supreme Court updates, timelines, and hot-topic polling can all be used to supplement in-class assignments and discussions. You'll also find a wealth of links to careers and news in criminal justice, book-specific sites, and much more.

For the Student

THOMSONNOW™ This unique, interactive online resource is the most exciting assessment-centered student learning tool ever offered for this course. ThomsonNOW determines each student's unique study needs by having him or her take a chapter Pre-Test and then offers a Personalized Study plan that focuses study time on the concepts that the student needs to master. Personalized Study includes ABC News clips with questions, career profile videos, concept learning modules with assessments, integrated simulations, interactive diagrams, animations, Microsoft® PowerPoint® lectures, topic reviews, an e-book, and more. Once the student has completed the Personalized Study plan, a Post-Test evaluates his or her improved comprehension of chapter content. At any time the student can view his or her Pre-Test or Post-Test scores, and all scores and gradable assignments flow directly into the instructor's grade book.

STUDY GUIDE The already extensive student study guide that accompanies *Introduction to Criminal Justice* has been thoroughly revised and updated for the latest edition by Debra Heath-Thornton of Messiah College. Because students learn in different ways, the guide includes a variety of pedagogical aids. Each chapter is outlined and summarized, major terms and figures are defined, and worksheets and self-tests are provided.

THOMSON AUDIO STUDY Students can finally study anytime and anywhere they want using Thomson Audio Study for *Introduction to Criminal Justice*, Eleventh Edition. Our exclusive audio content, which can be downloaded to any MP3 player, includes a review of all key terms and concepts, as well as a summary of the chapter. With this unique supplement, students can quiz themselves on each chapter's vocabulary and key concepts as they go or review important material before tests—even if they don't have their textbook on hand or aren't at their desk.

COMPANION WEBSITE (WWW.THOMSONEDU.COM/CRIMINALJUSTICE/SIEGEL) The companion website provides many chapter-specific resources, including chapter outlines, learning objectives, glossary, flash cards, crossword puzzles, web links, and tutorial quizzing.

CAREERS IN CRIMINAL JUSTICE WEBSITE (WWW.THOMSONEDU.COM/LOGIN) This unique website helps students investigate the criminal justice career choices that are right for them with the help of several important tools:

♦ *Career Profiles*: Video testimonials from a variety of practicing professionals in the field as well as information on many criminal justice careers, including job descriptions, requirements, training, salary and benefits, and the application process.

♦ *Interest Assessment*: Self-assessment tool to help students decide which careers suit their personalities and interests.

♦ *Career Planner*: Résumé-writing tips and worksheets, interviewing techniques, and successful job search strategies.

♦ *Links for Reference*: Direct links to federal, state, and local agencies where students can get contact information and learn more about current job opportunities.

WADSWORTH'S GUIDE TO CAREERS IN CRIMINAL JUSTICE, THIRD EDITION This handy guide, compiled by Caridad Sanchez-Leguelinel of John Jay College of Criminal Justice, gives students information on a wide variety of career paths, including requirements, salaries, training, contact information for key agencies, and employment outlooks.

WRITING AND COMMUNICATING FOR CRIMINAL JUSTICE This book contains articles on writing skills—along with basic grammar review and a survey of verbal communication on the job—that will give students an introduction to academic, professional, and research writing in criminal justice. The voices of professionals who have used these techniques on the job will help students see the relevance of these skills to their future careers.

HANDBOOK OF SELECTED SUPREME COURT CASES, THIRD EDITION This supplementary handbook covers almost 40 landmark cases, each of which includes a full case citation, an introduction, a summary from WestLaw, excerpts from the case, and the decision. The updated edition includes *Hamdi v. Rumsfeld, Roper v. Simmons, Ring v. Arizona, Atkins v. Virginia, Illinois v. Caballes*, and much more.

CURRENT PERSPECTIVES: READINGS FROM INFOTRAC® COLLEGE EDITION
These readers, designed to give students a deeper taste of special topics in criminal justice, include free access to InfoTrac College Edition. The timely articles are selected by experts in each topic from within InfoTrac College Edition and are available for free when bundled with the text. Topics include the following:

♦ Terrorism and Homeland Security

♦ Juvenile Justice

♦ Public Policy and Criminal Justice

♦ Crisis Management and National Emergency Response

♦ Racial Profiling

♦ New Technologies and Criminal Justice

♦ White-Collar Crime

TERRORISM: AN INTERDISCIPLINARY PERSPECTIVE Available for bundling with each copy of *Introduction to Criminal Justice*, Eleventh Edition, this 80-page booklet discusses terrorism in general and the issues surrounding the events of September 11, 2001. This information-packed booklet examines the origins of terrorism in the Middle East, focusing on Osama bin Laden in particular, as well as issues involving bioterrorism, the specific role played by religion in Middle Eastern terrorism, globalization as it relates to terrorism, and the reactions to and repercussions of terrorist attacks.

CRIME SCENES 2.0: AN INTERACTIVE CRIMINAL JUSTICE CD-ROM Recipient of several *New Media Magazine* Invision Awards, this interactive CD-ROM allows your students to take on the roles of investigating officer, lawyer, parole officer, and judge in excitingly realistic scenarios. Available FREE when bundled with every copy of *Introduction to Criminal Justice*, Eleventh Edition. An online instructor's manual is also available for the CD-ROM.

MIND OF A KILLER CD-ROM (BUNDLE VERSION) Voted one of the top 100 CD-ROMs by an annual *PC Magazine* survey, *Mind of a Killer* gives students a chilling glimpse into the realm of serial killers, with over 80 minutes of video *and* 3D simulations, and extensive mapping system, a library, and much more.

INTERNET GUIDE FOR CRIMINAL JUSTICE, SECOND EDITION Intended for the novice user, this guide provides students with the background and vocabulary necessary to navigate and understand the web, then provides them with a wealth of criminal justice websites and Internet project ideas.

♦ ACKNOWLEDGMENTS

Many people helped make this book possible. A complete list of all those who have reviewed the text and provided feedback over the years can be found on page xxiv. The form and content of this new edition were directed by our marvelous editor Carolyn Henderson Meier, who is an unofficial co-author. A lot of credit for getting this book out must go to our patient, competent, and fabulous development editor Shelley Murphy. Special thanks to our incredible production manager Jennie Redwitz, fantastic production editor Melanie Field, our special friend and outstanding photo editor Linda Rill, and our incredible marketing manager Terra Schultz, all of whom do great and magnificent jobs.

Larry Siegel
Joseph Senna

Reviewers

About the Authors

LARRY J. SIEGEL was born in the Bronx in 1947. While attending City College of New York in the 1960s, he was swept up in the social and political currents of the time. He became intrigued with the influence contemporary culture had on individual behavior: Did people shape society or did society shape people? He applied his interest in social forces and human behavior to the study of crime and justice. After graduating CCNY, he attended the newly opened program in criminal justice at the State University of New York at Albany, earning both his M.A. and Ph.D. degrees there. After completing his graduate work, Dr. Siegel began his teaching career at Northeastern University, where he was a faculty member for nine years. He has also held teaching positions at the University of Nebraska–Omaha and Saint Anselm College in New Hampshire. He is currently a professor at the University of Massachusetts–Lowell. Dr. Siegel has written extensively in the area of crime and justice, including books on juvenile law, delinquency, criminology, and criminal procedure. He is a court certified expert on police conduct and has testified in numerous legal cases. The father of four and grandfather of three, Larry Siegel and his wife, Terry, now reside in Bedford, New Hampshire, with their two cockapoos, Watson and Cody.

JOSEPH J. SENNA was born in Brooklyn, New York. He graduated from Brooklyn College, Fordham University Graduate School of Social Service, and Suffolk University Law School. Mr. Senna spent over sixteen years teaching law and justice courses at Northeastern University. In addition, he served as an assistant district attorney, director of Harvard Law School Prosecutorial Program, and consultant to numerous criminal justice organizations. His academic specialties include areas of criminal law, Constitutional due process, criminal justice, and juvenile law. Mr. Senna lives with his wife and sons outside of Boston.

The Nature of Crime, Law, and Criminal Justice

©AP Images/Peter Cosgrove

*O*n September 3, 2003, Paul Hill was executed in Florida for the murders of Dr. John Bayard Britton and his bodyguard, retired Air Force Lieutenant Colonel James Herman Barrett. The killings had taken place in Pensacola, outside the Ladies Center, an abortion clinic. Although members of the anti-abortion movement dismissed Hill as a fringe character, soon after his execution Florida abortion clinics and police were put on alert for reprisals. Several officials connected to the case received threatening letters, accompanied by rifle bullets.

Why do people kill or commit violent acts instead of finding peaceful solutions to their problems? And what should be done to those who commit criminal acts? A great deal of irony can be found in the Hill case: Society chose to kill someone who chose to kill someone because he considered that person a killer. What is the process of justice, and how are people such as Hill tried, convicted, and sentenced to death? Are such murders common, and is the United States an especially violent society? ◆

THESE QUESTIONS are addressed in Part One of this text. Chapter 1 covers the justice process and the organizations that are entrusted with conducting its operations: the police, courts, and corrections. Chapter 2 looks at the nature and extent of crime, and Chapter 3 tries to answer an important question: Why do people commit crime? Finally, Chapter 4 covers the criminal law, analyzing both its substantive and procedural components.

Crime and Criminal Justice

Chapter Outline

Chapter Objectives

After reading this chapter, you should be able to:

1. Describe the development of crime in the United States.
2. Tell how the criminal justice system was created.
3. Describe the origins of federal involvement in criminal justice.
4. List three main types of criminal justice agencies.
5. Know the critical decision points in the criminal justice process.
6. Identify the interrelationship between criminal justice process and agencies.
7. Analyze the importance of the informal justice system.
8. List the four basic stages of the criminal justice "wedding cake."
9. Describe the six most important perspectives on contemporary criminal justice.
10. Analyze how each perspective influences criminal justice policy in the war on drugs.

A few months after the September 11, 2001 attacks, President Bush secretly authorized the National Security Agency (NSA) to eavesdrop on people in and outside the United States to search for evidence of terrorist activity.[1] The NSA is the nation's cryptologic (hidden, disguised, or encrypted communications) organization that is charged with protecting classified government information systems and monitoring foreign intelligence information. Normally, the NSA must obtain a court-approved warrant before it can engage in domestic spying.

Under a presidential order signed in 2002, the intelligence agency began, without warrants, to monitor the international telephone calls and international e-mail messages of people inside the United States in an effort to track possible numbers linked to Al-Qaeda. This decision to permit some eavesdropping inside the country without court approval was a major shift in U.S. intelligence-gathering practices. As a result, some critics questioned whether the surveillance violated constitutional limits on legal searches. The president forcefully defended his actions as being crucial to national security, stating that he was merely responding to the American people's expectation that he protect them as long as there was a continuing threat from Al-Qaeda.[2] The administration's view was that the president had the authority under the "Authorization for Use of Military Force Against September 11 Terrorists" ("AUMF") and by his constitutional powers to authorize the NSA surveillance programs. The AUMF states "[t]hat the President is authorized to use all necessary and appropriate force against those nations, organizations, or persons he determines planned, authorized, committed, or aided the terrorist attacks that occurred on September 11, 2001, or harbored such organizations or persons, in order to prevent any future acts of international terrorism against the United States by such nations, organizations or persons."[3]

While unusual, the NSA case illustrates one of the dilemmas facing the justice system in contemporary society: Is it possible to provide security and protection in an age of uncertainty without compromising the personal privacy and civil liberties of the average citizen? As technology improves, agencies of the justice system can use it to monitor areas (e.g., with closed-circuit video) and people (e.g., monitoring e-mails and Internet connections). Such applications of technology may help the justice system become a more effective instrument of crime control, yet there may be a price to be paid when the government eavesdrops on our conversations and monitors our whereabouts. How can we balance the need to maintain security with the desire to uphold civil liberties? Is it worth the risk? ◆

criminal justice system
The various sequential stages through which offenders pass, from initial contact with the law to final disposition, and the agencies charged with enforcing the law at each of these stages.

The public relies on the agencies of the **criminal justice system** to provide solutions to the crime problem and to shape the direction of crime policy. This loosely organized collection of agencies is charged with, among other matters, protecting the public, maintaining order, enforcing the law, identifying transgressors, bringing the guilty to justice, and treating criminal behavior. The public depends on this vast system, employing more than 2 million people and costing taxpayers more than $150 billion per year, to protect them from evildoers and to bring justice to their lives. The criminal justice system is now expanding and taking on new duties, including protecting the country from terrorists and cyber criminals, groups that were almost unknown a decade ago. Consequently, the justice system is constantly evolving to meet these new challenges.

This text serves as an introduction to the study of criminal justice. This chapter covers some basic issues and concepts, beginning with a discussion of the concept and the study of criminal justice. The major processes of the criminal justice system are then examined so that you can develop an overview of how the system functions. Because no single view exists of the underlying goals that help shape criminal justice, the varying perspectives on what criminal justice really is or should be are set out in some detail.

◆ IS CRIME A RECENT DEVELOPMENT?

Older people often say, "Crime is getting worse every day" and "I can remember when it was safe to walk the streets at night," but their memories may be colored by wishful thinking. Crime and violence have existed in the United States for more than two hundred years. In fact, the crime rate may have been much higher in the nineteenth and early twentieth centuries than it is today.

Crime and violence have been common since the nation was first formed.[4] Guerilla activity was frequent before, during, and after the Revolutionary War. Bands supporting the British (Tories) and the American revolutionaries engaged in savage attacks on each other, using hit-and-run tactics, burning, and looting.

The struggle over slavery during the mid-nineteenth century generated decades of conflict, crime, and violence, including a civil war. **Slave patrols** were made up of small groups of white men who enforced discipline upon slaves. Their duties included searching slave quarters for weapons that might be used in insurrections and breaking up clandestine slave meetings. They hunted down fugitive slaves and used brutal punishments on the escapees, which could

slave patrols
Vigilante groups that enforced discipline on slaves and apprehended runaway slaves seeking freedom.

include both maiming and killing them, a practice that horrified even some plantation owners.[5]

After the war, night riders and Ku Klux Klan members were active in the South, using vigilante methods to maintain the status quo and terrorize former slaves. The violence also spilled over into bloody local feuds in the hill country of southern Appalachia. Factional hatreds, magnified by the lack of formal law enforcement and grinding poverty, gave rise to violent attacks and family feuding. Some former Union and Confederate soldiers, heading west with the dream of finding gold or starting a cattle ranch, resorted to theft and robbery.

Crime in the Old West

Some western lawmen developed reputations that have persisted for more than a century. Of these, none is more famous than Wyatt Earp. In 1876 he became chief deputy marshal of Dodge City, Kansas, a lawless frontier town, and he later moved on to Deadwood, in the Dakota Territory. In 1879 Earp and his brothers Morgan and Virgil journeyed to Tombstone, Arizona, where he eventually was appointed acting deputy U.S. marshal for the Arizona Territory. The Earps, along with their gunslinging dentist friend, Doc Holliday, participated in the famous OK Corral gunfight in 1881, during which they killed Frank McLaury, Tom McLaury, and Billy Clanton, members of a rustler gang known as the Cowboys, whose members also included the notorious Curly Bill Brocius and Johnny Ringo. The Cowboys were not the only gang that plied its trade in the old west. Train robbery was popularized by the Reno brothers of Indiana and bank robbery by the James–Younger gang of Missouri.

Crime in the Cities

The old west was not the only area where gang activity flourished. In New York City, gangs bearing colorful monikers such as the Hudson Dusters and the Shirttails played a major role in the city's political power struggles.

The Civil War also produced widespread business crime. The great robber barons bribed government officials and intrigued to corner markets and obtain concessions for railroads, favorable land deals, and mining and mineral rights on government land. The administration of President Ulysses S. Grant was tainted by numerous corruption scandals.

From 1900 to 1935, the nation experienced a sustained increase in criminal activity. This period was dominated by Depression-era outlaws who later became mythic figures. Charles "Pretty Boy" Floyd was a folk hero among the sharecroppers of eastern Oklahoma, while the nation eagerly followed the exploits of its premier bank robber, John Dillinger, until he was killed in front of a Chicago movie house. The infamous "Ma" Barker and her sons Lloyd, Herman, Fred, and Arthur are credited with killing more than 10 people, while Bonnie Parker and Clyde Barrow killed more than 13 before they were slain in a shootout with federal agents.

The crime problem, then, is not a recent phenomenon; it has been evolving along with the nation itself. Crime has provided a mechanism for the frustrated to vent their anger, for business leaders to maintain their position of wealth and power, and for those outside the economic mainstream to take a shortcut to the American dream. To protect itself from this ongoing assault, the public has supported the development of a great array of government agencies whose stated purpose is to control and prevent crime; identify, apprehend, and bring to trial those who choose to violate the law; and devise effective methods of criminal correction. These agencies make up what is commonly referred to today as the criminal justice system.

Creating Criminal Justice

The debate over the proper course for effective crime control can be traced back to the publication in 1764 of Cesare Beccaria's famous treatise *On Crime and Punishments*. Beccaria, an Italian social philosopher, made a persuasive argument

At the turn of the last century, rural outlaws became mythic figures. At the left are photos of the FBI's six most wanted men in 1934. Charles "Pretty Boy" Floyd (left photos, top right) was a folk hero among the sharecroppers of eastern Oklahoma. Floyd robbed as many as thirty banks, filing a notch in his pocket watch for each of the ten men he killed. Floyd was shot dead by police on October 19, 1934. John Dillinger (left photos: top left; right photo) became the nation's premier bank robber until he was killed in front of a Chicago movie house on July 22, 1934. After his death, his body was put on view at the morgue. Hordes of people came to view America's most notorious criminal.

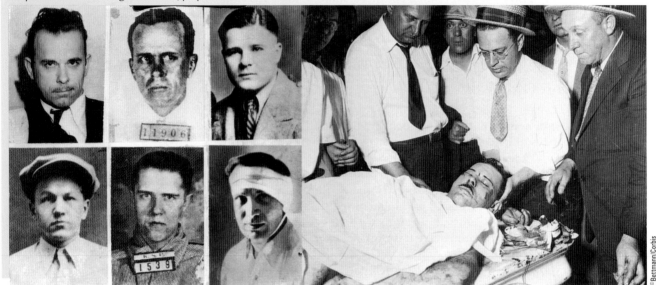

©Bettmann/Corbis

against the use of torture and capital punishment, common practices in the eighteenth century. He argued that only the minimum amount of punishment was needed to control crime if criminals could be convinced that their law violations were certain to be discovered and punished.[6] Beccaria's work provides a blueprint for criminal justice: Potential law violators would most certainly be deterred if agencies of government were created that could swiftly detect, try, and punish anyone foolish enough to violate the criminal law.

However, it was not until 1829 that the first police agency, the London Metropolitan Police, was created both to keep the peace and identify and apprehend criminal suspects. A huge success in England, police agencies began to appear in the United States during the mid-nineteenth century. Another nineteenth-century innovation, the penitentiary, or prison, was considered a liberal reform that replaced physical punishments.

Although significant and far reaching, these changes were isolated developments. As criminal justice developed over the next century, these fledgling agencies of justice rarely worked together in a systematic fashion. It was not until 1919—when the Chicago Crime Commission, a professional association funded by private contributions, was created—that the work of the criminal justice system began to be recognized.[7] The Chicago Crime Commission acted as a citizens' advocate group and kept track of the activities of local justice agencies. The commission still carries out its work today and is active in administering anticrime programs.[8]

In 1931 President Herbert Hoover appointed the National Commission of Law Observance and Enforcement, which is commonly known as the Wickersham Commission. This national study group made a detailed analysis of the U.S. justice system and helped usher in the era of treatment and rehabilitation. Its final report found that thousands of rules and regulations govern the system, making it difficult for justice personnel to keep track of the system's legal and administrative complexity. Some of the problems they encountered are still with us today: controlling illegal substances, the risk of compromising individual liberties, limiting the costs of justice, and recognizing cultural differences within society.[9]

The Modern Era of Justice

The modern era of criminal justice can be traced to a series of research projects, first begun in the 1950s, under the sponsorship of the American Bar Foundation (ABF).[10] Originally designed to provide in-depth analysis of the organization, administration, and operation of criminal justice agencies, the ABF project discovered that the justice system contained many procedures that heretofore had been kept hidden from the public view. The research focus then shifted to an examination of these previously obscure processes and their interrelationship—investigation, arrest, prosecution, and plea negotiations. Justice professionals used a great deal of personal choice in decision making, and how this discretion was used became a prime focus of the research effort. For the first time, the term *criminal justice system* began to be used, reflecting a view that justice agencies could be connected in an intricate yet often unobserved network of decision-making processes.

FEDERAL INVOLVEMENT In 1967 the President's Commission on Law Enforcement and Administration of Justice (Crime Commission), which had been appointed by President Lyndon B. Johnson, published its final report, *The Challenge of Crime in a Free Society*.[11] This group of practitioners, educators, and attorneys was charged with creating a comprehensive view of the criminal justice process and recommending reforms. Concomitantly, Congress passed the Safe Streets and Crime Control Act of 1968, providing for the expenditure of federal funds for state and local crime control efforts.[12] This act helped launch a massive campaign to restructure the justice system. It funded the National Institute of Law Enforcement and Criminal Justice, which encouraged research and development in criminal justice. Renamed the National Institute of Justice in 1979, it has continued its mission as a major source of funding for the implementation and evaluation of innovative experimental and demonstration projects in the criminal justice system.[13]

The Safe Streets Act provided funding for the **Law Enforcement Assistance Administration (LEAA)**, which granted hundreds of millions of dollars in aid to local and state justice agencies. Throughout its 14-year history, the LEAA provided the majority of federal funds to states for criminal justice activities. On April 15, 1982, the program came to an end when Congress ceased funding it. Although the LEAA suffered its share of criticism, it supported many worthwhile programs, including the development of a vast number of criminal justice departments in colleges and universities and the use of technology in the criminal justice system.

The federal government continues to fund the National Institute of Justice, the Office of Juvenile Justice and Delinquency Prevention, and the Bureau of Justice Statistics. These agencies carry out a more limited role in supporting criminal justice research and development and in publishing valuable data and research findings. (See Figure 1.1 for the criminal justice system time line.)

The National Institute of Justice is the research and development agency of the U.S. Department of Justice and is the only federal agency solely dedicated to researching crime control and justice issues. To reach the NIJ website, go to the Siegel/Senna Introduction to Criminal Justice 11e website: www.thomsonedu .com/criminaljustice/siegel.

Law Enforcement Assistance Administration (LEAA)
Federal agency that granted hundreds of millions of dollars in aid to local and state justice agencies between 1968 and 1982.

ThomsonNOW Improve your grade on the exam with Personalized Study! For reinforcement resources and a mastery check of crime in the United States, go to www.thomsonedu.com/ thomsonnow.

FIGURE 1.1
Criminal Justice Time Line

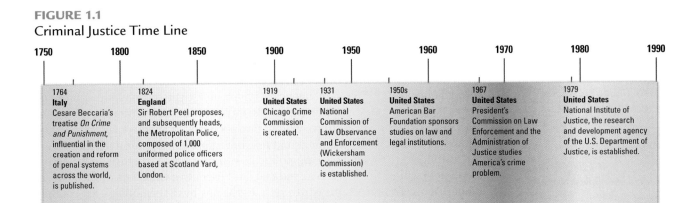

1764 **Italy** Cesare Beccaria's treatise *On Crime and Punishment*, influential in the creation and reform of penal systems across the world, is published.	**1824** **England** Sir Robert Peel proposes, and subsequently heads, the Metropolitan Police, composed of 1,000 uniformed police officers based at Scotland Yard, London.	**1919** **United States** Chicago Crime Commission is created.	**1931** **United States** National Commission of Law Observance and Enforcement (Wickersham Commission) is established.	**1950s** **United States** American Bar Foundation sponsors studies on law and legal institutions.	**1967** **United States** President's Commission on Law Enforcement and the Administration of Justice studies America's crime problem.	**1979** **United States** National Institute of Justice, the research and development agency of the U.S. Department of Justice, is established.

1750 1800 1850 1900 1950 1960 1970 1980 1990

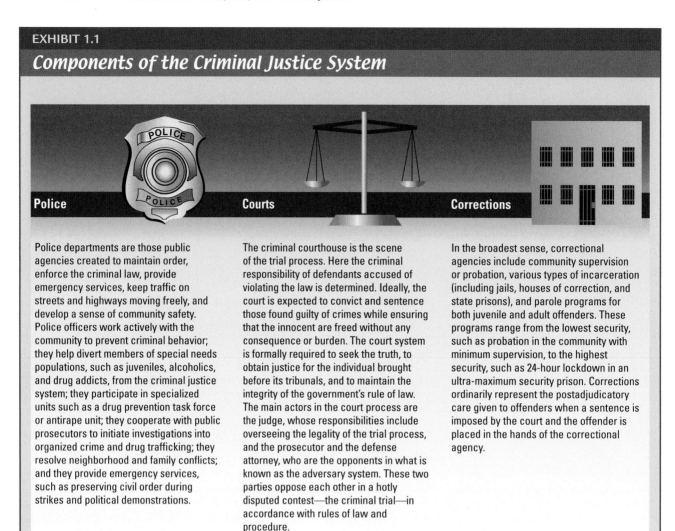

EXHIBIT 1.1

Components of the Criminal Justice System

Police | **Courts** | **Corrections**

Police departments are those public agencies created to maintain order, enforce the criminal law, provide emergency services, keep traffic on streets and highways moving freely, and develop a sense of community safety. Police officers work actively with the community to prevent criminal behavior; they help divert members of special needs populations, such as juveniles, alcoholics, and drug addicts, from the criminal justice system; they participate in specialized units such as a drug prevention task force or antirape unit; they cooperate with public prosecutors to initiate investigations into organized crime and drug trafficking; they resolve neighborhood and family conflicts; and they provide emergency services, such as preserving civil order during strikes and political demonstrations.

The criminal courthouse is the scene of the trial process. Here the criminal responsibility of defendants accused of violating the law is determined. Ideally, the court is expected to convict and sentence those found guilty of crimes while ensuring that the innocent are freed without any consequence or burden. The court system is formally required to seek the truth, to obtain justice for the individual brought before its tribunals, and to maintain the integrity of the government's rule of law. The main actors in the court process are the judge, whose responsibilities include overseeing the legality of the trial process, and the prosecutor and the defense attorney, who are the opponents in what is known as the adversary system. These two parties oppose each other in a hotly disputed contest—the criminal trial—in accordance with rules of law and procedure.

In the broadest sense, correctional agencies include community supervision or probation, various types of incarceration (including jails, houses of correction, and state prisons), and parole programs for both juvenile and adult offenders. These programs range from the lowest security, such as probation in the community with minimum supervision, to the highest security, such as 24-hour lockdown in an ultra-maximum security prison. Corrections ordinarily represent the postadjudicatory care given to offenders when a sentence is imposed by the court and the offender is placed in the hands of the correctional agency.

♦ THE CRIMINAL JUSTICE SYSTEM TODAY

social control
The ability of society and its institutions to control, manage, restrain, or direct human behavior.

The White House web page has useful links to federal efforts in the criminal justice system. To reach it, go to the Siegel/Senna Introduction to Criminal Justice 11e website: www.thomsonedu.com/criminaljustice/siegel.

legislature
The branch of state government invested with power to make and repeal laws.

The contemporary criminal justice system is society's instrument of **social control**: Some behaviors are considered so dangerous that they must be either strictly controlled or outlawed outright; some people are so destructive that they must be monitored or even confined. The agencies of justice seek to prevent or deter outlawed behavior by apprehending, adjudicating, and sanctioning lawbreakers. Society maintains other forms of informal social control, such as parental and school discipline, but these are designed to deal with moral—not legal—misbehavior. Only the criminal justice system maintains the power to control crime and punish outlawed behavior through the arm of the criminal law.

The contemporary criminal justice system can be divided into three main components: law enforcement agencies, which investigate crimes and apprehend suspects; the court system, which charges, indicts, tries, and sentences offenders; and the correctional system, which incapacitates convicted offenders and attempts to aid in their treatment and rehabilitation (see Exhibit 1.1).

Criminal justice agencies are political entities whose structure and function are lodged within the legislative, judicial, and executive branches of the government (Figure 1.2). The **legislature** defines the law by determining what conduct is prohibited and establishes criminal penalties for those who violate the law.

FIGURE 1.2

The Interrelationship among the Three Branches of Government

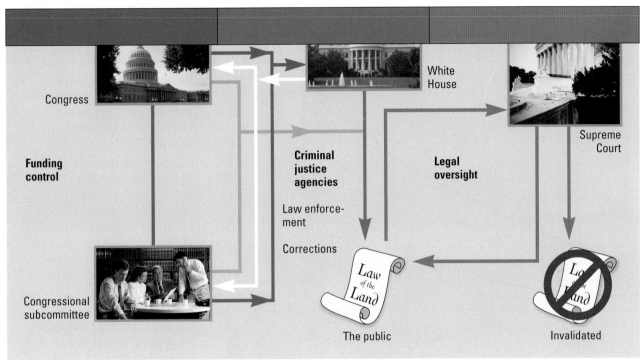

Source: *The United States Government Manual 1981/82* (Washington D.C.: Government Printing Office, 1981); *The United States Government Manual 1982/83* (Washington D.C.: Government Printing Office, 1982).

The legislative branch of government helps shape justice policy by creating appropriations for criminal justice agencies and acting as a forum for the public expression of views on criminal justice issues.

The judiciary interprets the existing law and determines whether it meets constitutional requirements. It also oversees criminal justice practices and has the power to determine whether existing operations fall within the ambit of the state constitution and ultimately the U.S. Constitution. The courts have the right to overturn or ban policies that are in conflict with constitutional rights.

Scope of the System

The contemporary criminal justice system in the United States is monumental in size. It consists of more than 55,000 public agencies and costs federal, state, and local governments about $150 billion per year for civil and criminal justice, which is an increase of more than 300 percent since 1982 (see Exhibit 1.2).

One reason the justice system is so expensive to run is that it employs more than 2.4 million people. The nation's 16,000 law enforcement agencies employ almost 1 million people: about 600,000 on the local level, 330,000 by county sheriffs' offices, and more than 80,000 by state police. Of these, about two-thirds are sworn officers, and one-third are civilian employees.[14]

In addition to the thousands of law enforcement agencies, there are nearly 17,000 courts, more than 8,000 prosecutorial agencies, about 6,000 correctional institutions, and more than 3,500 probation and parole departments.

As a result of the enormous number of people processed each year, the correctional system population is at an all-time high. As Figure 1.3 shows, the correctional population has been consistently increasing, and today more than 7 million people are under the control of the correctional system, including about 2 million behind bars in **prison** or **jail**, another 4 million on **probation** or some other form of community supervision, and another 700,000-plus being

The Sourcebook of Criminal Justice Statistics is a useful tool for finding data on the criminal justice system. To reach it, go to the Siegel/Senna Introduction to Criminal Justice 11e website: www.thomsonedu.com/criminaljustice/siegel.

prison
A state or federal correctional facility that houses convicted criminals who have been sentenced to a period of confinement that is typically more than one year.

jail
A county correctional facility that holds people pending trial, awaiting sentencing, serving a sentence that is usually less than one year, or awaiting transfer to other facilities after conviction.

probation
Court-ordered community supervision of convicted offenders by a probation agency. Probationers are required to obey specific rules of conduct while in the community.

EXHIBIT 1.2

Expenditures on Criminal Justice by Level of Government and Criminal Justice Function

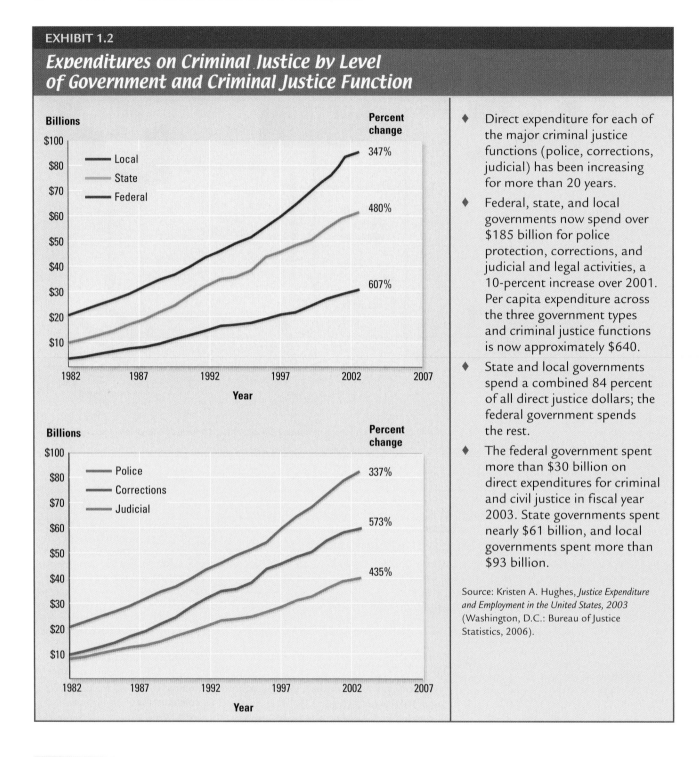

◆ Direct expenditure for each of the major criminal justice functions (police, corrections, judicial) has been increasing for more than 20 years.

◆ Federal, state, and local governments now spend over $185 billion for police protection, corrections, and judicial and legal activities, a 10-percent increase over 2001. Per capita expenditure across the three government types and criminal justice functions is now approximately $640.

◆ State and local governments spend a combined 84 percent of all direct justice dollars; the federal government spends the rest.

◆ The federal government spent more than $30 billion on direct expenditures for criminal and civil justice in fiscal year 2003. State governments spent nearly $61 billion, and local governments spent more than $93 billion.

Source: Kristen A. Hughes, *Justice Expenditure and Employment in the United States, 2003* (Washington, D.C.: Bureau of Justice Statistics, 2006).

parole
Community supervision after a period of incarceration.

supervised on **parole** in the community after the completion of their prison sentence. The correctional population has substantially increased since 1990 despite a decade-long drop in the crime rate.

◆ THE FORMAL CRIMINAL JUSTICE PROCESS

ThomsonNOW Improve your grade on the exam with Personalized Study! For reinforcement resources and a mastery check of contemporary criminal justice, go to www.thomsonedu.com/thomsonnow.

Another way of understanding criminal justice is to view it as a process that takes an offender through a series of decision points, beginning with arrest and concluding with reentry into society. During this process, key decision makers resolve whether to maintain the offender in the system or to discharge the suspect without further action. This decision making is often a matter of individual discretion, based upon a variety of factors and perceptions. Legal factors, including the seriousness of the charges, available evidence, and the suspect's prior record, are usually considered legitimate influences on decision making. Troubling is the fact that such extralegal factors as the suspect's race, gender, class, and age may also influence decision outcomes. A significant debate is ongoing over the impact of extralegal factors in the decision to arrest, convict, and sentence a suspect. Critics believe that a suspect's race, class, and gender can often determine the direction a case will take and what sentence those convicted will receive, whereas supporters argue that the system is relatively fair and unbiased.[15]

In reality, few cases are processed through the entire formal justice system. Most are handled informally and with dispatch. The system has been roundly criticized for its backroom deals and "bargain justice." Although informality and deal making are the rule, the concept of the formal justice process is important because it implies that every criminal defendant charged with a serious crime is entitled to a full range of rights under law. Central to the U.S. concept of liberty is that every individual is entitled to his or her day in court, to be represented by competent counsel in a fair trial before an impartial jury, and with trial procedures subject to review by a higher authority. Secret ("kangaroo") courts and summary punishment are elements of political systems that most Americans fear and despise. The fact that most criminal suspects are treated informally may be less important than the fact that all criminal defendants are entitled to a full range of legal rights and constitutional protections.

A comprehensive view of the formal criminal process would normally include the following stages:

Police Procedures

The police are the *gatekeepers* of the formal justice process. In this role they are given the responsibility for maintaining order, enforcing the law, preventing crime, and responding to calls for assistance. They are permitted to use their professional judgment to decide whether a suspicious act amounts to a violation of the criminal law. Even if they believe a crime has occurred, they may use their discretion to issue a warning, make a formal arrest, or take some other course of action. This gatekeeper role involves police officers in the first four stages of decision making:

INITIAL CONTACT In most instances, the initial contact with the criminal justice system takes place as a result of a police action (see the Careers in Criminal Justice feature). Contact may take place in a number of different ways:

◆ While on routine patrol, police officers observe a person acting suspiciously, conclude that a crime been committed, and take the suspect into custody.

◆ Police officers are contacted by a victim who reports a crime; they respond by going to the scene and apprehending the suspect.

◆ An informer tells police about some ongoing criminal activity to receive favorable treatment.

FIGURE 1.3

The Number of Adults in the Correctional Population

Adult correctional populations (millions)

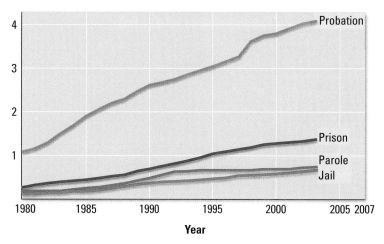

Source: Bureau of Justice Statistics Correctional Surveys (The Annual Probation Survey, National Prisoner Statistics, Survey of Jails, and The Annual Parole Survey) as presented in *Correctional Populations in the United States*, Annual, Prisoners in 2004, and *Probation and Parole in the United States, 2004.*

The National Center for State Courts (NCSC) is an independent, nonprofit organization dedicated to the improvement of justice. NCSC activities include developing policies to enhance state courts, advancing state courts' interests within the federal government, fostering state court adaptation to future changes, securing sufficient resources for state courts, strengthening state court leadership, helping with state court collaboration, and providing a model for organizational administration. To reach the NCSC website, go to the Siegel/Senna Introduction to Criminal Justice 11e website: www.thomsonedu.com/criminaljustice/siegel.

Municipal Police Officer

Duties and Characteristics of the Job

Police officers are responsible for enforcing the written laws and ordinances of their jurisdiction. Police officers will patrol within their jurisdiction and will respond to calls wherever police attention is needed. Police officers' duties can be routine, such as writing a speeding ticket, or more involved, such as responding to a domestic disturbance or investigating a robbery. Their nonpatrol duties include testifying in court and writing reports of their law enforcement actions. Some officers will choose or be chosen to work in specialized units such as the well-known special weapons and tactics (SWAT) or canine corps (K9).

Police officers patrol jurisdictions of various sizes and have varying duties based on the nature of their jurisdiction. For example, sheriffs and their deputies enforce the laws within a county. State police primarily patrol state highways and respond to calls for backup from police units across their respective state. Institutions such as colleges and universities often have their own police forces as well, which enforce laws and rules in this specific area.

Police work can be an intense and stressful job; it sometimes entails encounters with hostile and potentially violent people. Police are asked to put their lives on the line to preserve order and safety. Their actions are watched closely and reflect upon their entire department. Because the places that police protect must be watched at all times, police work shifts that may fall on weekends and holidays. Quite often it is the younger police officers who take these less desirable shifts. Additionally, police officers will often have to work overtime; 45-hour workweeks are common.

Job Outlook

Government spending ultimately determines how many officers a department has. In general, opportunities for employment are expected to grow at an average rate. However, in most departments positions will open regularly because of those leaving the job and those retiring.

Most police officers are employed at the local level, so this is where a majority of the jobs will be found. Additionally, there are generally more opportunities for more employment in larger departments, usually in larger urban or suburban areas. Not surprisingly, most opportunities exist in areas with comparatively higher crime rates or lower salaries.

Salary

Police officers and sheriffs' patrol officers have a median annual salary of $47,270. The majority of police officers earn between $35,140 and $57,690. At the extremes, a small percentage of police officers will

♦ On its own initiative, a police department may investigate an ongoing social problem such as gang activity or prostitution. Police officers may go undercover to buy narcotics from a drug-dealing gang or pose as underage minors to trap an Internet predator.

♦ A person calls police headquarters and confesses to a crime—for example, he stabbed his wife during a domestic dispute.

INVESTIGATION The purpose of the investigatory stage of justice is to gather sufficient evidence to identify a suspect and support a legal arrest. An investigation can take but a few minutes, as when a police officer sees a crime in progress and can apprehend the suspect at the scene. Or it can take many months and involve hundreds of law enforcement agents, such as the Federal Bureau of Investigation's pursuit of the so-called Unabomber, which led to the arrest of Ted Kaczynski. Investigations may be conducted at the local, state, or federal level and involve coordinated teams of law enforcement agents, prosecutors, and other justice officials.

arrest
Taking a person into legal custody for the purpose of restraining the accused until he or she can be held accountable for the offense at court proceedings.

ARREST The **arrest** power of the police involves taking a person into custody in accordance with lawful authority and holding that person to answer for a violation of the criminal law. A legal arrest occurs when the following conditions exist:

earn around $27,150, and the highest paid will earn more than $57,690. Those who ascend the ranks of their police department to police lieutenant or go into a specialization will see increases in their income.

Opportunities

Police work is often appealing to many because of the good benefits and retirement policies. However, these factors may contribute to the fact that at the better-paying positions such as state police, there may be more applicants than available positions. This competition means that those with qualities such as a college education will have better chances of being hired. After several years, those with a reputation for good work as well as the proper education can rise in the ranks of their department or be assigned to other desirable positions such as detective or investigator.

Qualifications

To be a police officer, one must be in good shape mentally and physically, as well as meet certain education requirements and pass written tests. New police officers go through rigorous training and testing before they are allowed on the streets, normally in the form of a local police academy for 12–14 weeks. During this time, new officers learn diverse skills that will be necessary for their job, such as knowledge of laws and individual rights, self-defense, and first aid.

Applicants can also expect to be asked to pass lie detector and drug tests.

Because of the enormous responsibility associated with being a police officer, certain personal qualities are considered key for future police officers, such as responsibility, good communications skills, good judgment, and the ability to make quick decisions.

Education and Training

In most cases, a high school diploma is required to be a police officer. However, more and more jurisdictions are requiring at least some college education. Although some college credits are enough for one to obtain a position on the police force, in order to be promoted and move up in rank, more education, generally in the form of a bachelor's degree in a relevant field, especially criminal justice, is necessary.

Sources: "Police and Detectives," *Occupational Outlook Handbook*, 2006–2007 edition (Bureau of Labor Statistics, U.S. Department of Labor), retrieved June 16, 2006, from http://www.bls.gov/oco/ocos160.htm; "Occupational Employment and Wages, May 2005: Police and Sheriff's Patrol Officers" (Bureau of Labor Statistics, U.S. Department of Labor), retrieved June 27, 2006, from http://www.bls.gov/oes/current/oes333051.htm, last modified date: May 24, 2006; "Police Officer," *Princeton Review*, retrieved June 16, 2006, from http://www.princetonreview.com/cte/profiles/dayInLife.asp?careerID=120.

1. The police officer believes that sufficient evidence of a crime exists to restrain the suspect. The officer has *probable cause* to believe that a crime has occurred and that the person he seeks to arrest is the culprit.

2. The officer deprives the individual of her freedom.

3. The suspect believes that she is in the custody of the officer and cannot voluntarily leave. She has lost her *liberty*.

The police officer is not required to exclaim "You're under arrest!" as is usually presented in TV dramas, and the officer does not first have to haul the suspect to the station house. Basically, a person who has been deprived of liberty is under arrest.

An arrest can be made if a police officer personally witnesses the guilty act, if he has probable cause based on a witness or victim statement, or if an **arrest warrant** has been issued by a court. The arrest warrant is a court order that empowers any police officer to arrest the suspect and bring the named person before the court. An arrest warrant must be based on probable cause that the person to be arrested has committed or is attempting to commit a crime. Police officers will ordinarily go before a judge and obtain a warrant when no danger exists that the suspect will leave the area, when a long-term investigation of a crime is under way, or when they can produce probable cause to arrest the

arrest warrant
Written court order authorizing and directing that an individual be taken into custody to answer criminal charges.

suspect even though they did not directly witness the crime—that is, they have some physical evidence such as fingerprints or a DNA sample.

Most arrests are made without a warrant. The decision to arrest often comes from the police officer during contact with the suspect. In the case of a felony, most jurisdictions provide that police officers may arrest a suspect without a warrant when probable cause exists, even if the officers did not see the crime being committed. In the case of a misdemeanor, officers traditionally needed to observe the crime firsthand before a warrantless arrest could be made, known as the **in presence requirement**. However, many states have recently eliminated this requirement in order to better enforce such crimes as domestic violence, shoplifting, or cases in which the suspect will escape if not arrested immediately. As a general rule, if the police make an arrest without a warrant, the arrestee must be brought promptly (within 48 hours) before a magistrate for a **probable cause hearing**.[16]

CUSTODY The moment after an arrest is made, the detained suspect is considered in police custody. The police may wish to search the suspect for weapons or contraband, interrogate the suspect to gain more information, find out if the person had any accomplices, or even encourage the suspect to confess to the crime. The police may wish to enter the suspect's home, car, or office to look for further evidence. Similarly, the police may want to bring witnesses to view the suspect in a lineup or in a one-to-one confrontation. Personal information will also be taken from the suspect, including name, address, fingerprints, and photo. Because these procedures are so crucial and can have a great impact at trial, the U.S. Supreme Court has granted suspects in police custody protection from the unconstitutional abuse of police power, such as illegal searches and intimidating interrogations.

The Prosecutorial Stage

If the arresting officers or their superiors believe that sufficient evidence exists to charge a person with a crime, the case will be turned over to the prosecutor's office. The prosecutor maintains great discretion in deciding what charges to bring, how to process the case, and whether to negotiate a deal or bring the case to trial.

CHARGING Minor crimes—misdemeanors—are generally handled with a complaint being filed before the court that will try the case. For serious crimes—felonies—the prosecutor must decide to either bring the case before a grand jury or conduct a preliminary hearing (depending on the procedures used in the jurisdiction—see the following section). In either event, the decision to charge the suspect with a specific criminal act involves many factors, including evidence sufficiency, crime seriousness, case pressure, and political issues, as well as personal factors such as a prosecutor's own specific interests and biases. For example, in some jurisdictions obscenity charges may be vigorously pursued, whereas in another they are all but ignored. After conducting a preliminary investigation of the legal merits of a case, prosecutors may decide to take no further action, referred to as a **nolle prosequi**.

PRELIMINARY HEARING/GRAND JURY Because a criminal suspect faces great financial and personal costs when forced to stand trial for a felony, the U.S. Constitution mandates that before a trial can take place, the government must first prove probable cause that the accused committed the crime with which he is being charged. In about half the states and in the federal system, this decision is rendered by a group of citizens brought together to form a grand jury, which considers the merits of the case—presented by the prosecutor only—in a closed hearing. If the evidence is sufficient, the grand jury will issue a bill of indictment, which specifies the charges on which the accused must stand trial. In the remaining states, the grand jury has been replaced with a preliminary hearing. In these jurisdictions, a charging document called an *information* is filed before a lower trial

---

in presence requirement
A police officer cannot arrest someone for a misdemeanor unless the officer sees the crime occur. To make an arrest for a crime he did not witness, the officer must obtain a warrant.

probable cause hearing
If a person is taken into custody for a misdemeanor, a hearing is held to determine if probable cause exists that he committed the crime.

nolle prosequi
The decision by a prosecutor to drop a case after a complaint has been made because of, for example, insufficient evidence, witness reluctance to testify, police error, or office policy.

The role of the grand jury is to evaluate evidence presented by the prosecution and decide whether there is sufficient cause to bring a case to trial. Here, 23-year-old Duke University lacrosse player David Evans proclaims his innocence as he addresses the media after being indicted by a grand jury on sexual assault charges on May 15, 2006, in Durham, North Carolina. Evans was the third player to be indicted for the sexual assault of a woman hired as a private dancer for a party attended by the lacrosse team members.

court, which then conducts an open hearing on the merits of the case. During this procedure, sometimes referred to as a *probable cause hearing*, the defendant and her attorney may appear and dispute the prosecutor's charges. The suspect will be called to stand trial if the presiding magistrate or judge accepts the prosecutor's evidence as factual and sufficient. In some states, such as California, the prosecutor can choose either a preliminary hearing or a grand jury.

ARRAIGNMENT Before the trial begins, the defendant will be arraigned, or brought before the court that will hear the case. At the arraignment, formal charges are read, the defendant is informed of his constitutional rights (e.g., the right to be represented by legal counsel), an initial plea is entered in the case (e.g., not guilty or guilty), a trial date is set, and bail issues are considered.

BAIL/DETENTION Bail is a money bond levied to ensure the return of a criminal defendant for trial, while allowing the person pretrial freedom to prepare her defense. Defendants who do not show up for trial forfeit their bail. Those people who cannot afford to put up bail or who cannot borrow sufficient funds for it will remain in state custody prior to trial. In most instances, this means an extended stay in a county jail or house of correction. Most jurisdictions allow defendants awaiting trial to be released on their own recognizance (promise to the court), without bail, if they are stable members of the community and have been charged with committing nonviolent crimes.

PLEA BARGAINING Soon after an arraignment, if not before, defense counsel will meet with the prosecution to see if the case can be brought to a conclusion without a trial. In some instances, this can involve filing the case while the defendant participates in a community-based treatment program for substance abuse or receives psychiatric care. Most commonly, the defense and prosecution will discuss a possible guilty plea in exchange for reducing or dropping some of the charges or agreeing to a request for a more lenient sentence. Almost 90 percent of all cases end in a plea bargain instead of a criminal trial.

The Trial Stage

If an agreement cannot be reached or if the prosecution does not wish to arrange a negotiated settlement of the case, a criminal trial will be held. The criminal trial is the focal point of the criminal justice process because it represents the very concept of justice to the public: Regardless of power, position, and status, every citizen is entitled to a fair and evenhanded trial before the law.

TRIAL/ADJUDICATION   A criminal trial is held before a judge (bench trial) or jury, whose duty is to decide whether the prosecution's evidence against the defendant is sufficient beyond a reasonable doubt to prove guilt. If a jury cannot reach a decision—in other words, it is deadlocked—the case is left unresolved. The prosecution then decides whether it should be retried at a later date.

SENTENCING/DISPOSITION   If after a criminal trial the accused has been found guilty as charged, he will be returned to court for sentencing. Possible dispositions include a fine, probation, a period of incarceration in a penal institution, or some combination of these. In cases involving first-degree murder, more than 35 states and the federal government allow the death penalty. Sentencing is a key decision point in the criminal justice system because in many jurisdictions judicial discretion can result in people receiving vastly different sentences even though they have committed the same crime. Some may be released on community supervision, whereas others committing the same crime can receive long prison sentences.

APPEAL/POSTCONVICTION REMEDIES   After conviction, the defense attorney can ask the trial judge to set aside the jury's verdict because she believes there has been a mistake of law. In a well known 1997 case, Louise Woodward, a young British au pair, was convicted on the charge of second-degree murder when a Massachusetts jury found her responsible for the death of Matthew Eappen, an infant boy placed in her care. Woodward allegedly shook Eappen, causing his death. The verdict was soon set aside by the trial judge, Hiller Zobel, because he believed that the facts of the case did not substantiate the charge of second-degree murder. He instead reduced the charge to manslaughter and sentenced Woodward to time already served while she was awaiting trial.[17]

An appeal may be filed if after conviction the defendant believes that he has not received fair treatment or that his constitutional rights were violated. Appellate courts review such issues as whether evidence was used properly, a judge conducted the trial in an approved fashion, jury selection was properly done, and the attorneys in the case acted appropriately. If the court rules that the appeal has merit, it can hold that the defendant be given a new trial or, in some instances, be set free. Outright release can be ordered, for example, when the state prosecutes the case in violation of the double jeopardy clause (Fifth Amendment) or when it violates the defendant's right to a speedy trial (Sixth Amendment).

Correctional Procedures

After sentencing, custody of the convicted defendant is transferred to state or federal correctional authorities, who must determine where the defendant should be placed and how he should be treated.

CORRECTIONAL TREATMENT   Correctional treatment corresponds to the judge's sentencing decision. An offender may be ordered to serve a period of secure confinement or serve a probationary term. Secure confinement may be served in a community correctional facility, in a county jail, or in a prison. During this stage of the criminal justice process, the offender may be asked to participate in rehabilitation programs designed to help her make a successful readjustment to society.

RELEASE   Upon completion of his sentence and period of correction, the offender will be free to return to society. Most inmates do not serve the full term of their sentence but are freed via an early-release mechanism, such as parole or pardon or by earning time off for good behavior. Offenders sentenced to community supervision simply finish their term and resume their lives in the community.

POSTRELEASE After termination of their correctional treatment, offenders may be asked to spend some time in a community correctional center, which acts as a bridge between a secure treatment facility and absolute freedom. Offenders may find that their conviction has cost them some personal privileges, such as the right to hold certain kinds of employment. These may be returned by court order once the offenders have proven their trustworthiness and willingness to adjust to society's rules. Reentry is often a difficult process and poses significant risk for the offender, his family, and the community in which he resides. As millions of former offenders filter back into their communities, they create a destabilizing force that unsettles neighbors and increases crime rates. The topic of reentry will be discussed further in Chapter 16.

The Criminal Justice Assembly Line

The image that comes to mind when considering the criminal justice process described above is an assembly-line conveyor belt that moves an endless stream of cases, never stopping, carrying them to workers who stand at fixed stations and who perform on each case as it comes by the same small but essential operation that brings it one step closer to being a finished product or, to exchange the metaphor for the reality, a closed file. Criminal justice is seen as a screening process in which each successive stage—prearrest investigation, arrest, postarrest investigation, preparation for trial or entry of plea, conviction, disposition—involves a series of routinized operations whose success is gauged primarily by its ability to pass the case along to a successful conclusion.[18]

According to this view, each of the stages described previously is a decision point through which cases flow. At the investigatory stage, police must decide whether to pursue the case or terminate involvement because insufficient evidence exists to identify a suspect, because the case is considered trivial, because the victim decides not to press charges, and so on. At the bail stage, a decision must be made whether to set so high a bail that the defendant remains in custody, set a reasonable bail, or release the defendant on her own recognizance. Each of these decisions can have a critical effect on the defendant, the justice system, and society. If an error is made, an innocent person may suffer or, conversely, a dangerous individual may be released to continue to prey upon the community.

Figure 1.4 illustrates the approximate number of offenders removed from the criminal justice system at each stage of the process. Most people who commit crime escape detection, and of those who do not, relatively few are bound over for trial, convicted, and eventually sentenced to prison. About 30 percent of people arrested on felony charges are eventually convicted in criminal court. However, about 30 percent of convictees are released back into the community without having to do time in prison.[19]

In practice, many suspects are released before trial because of a procedural error, evidence problems, or other reasons that result in a case dismissal by the prosecutor (nolle prosequi). Although most cases that go to trial wind up in a conviction, others are dismissed by the presiding judge because of a witness or complainant's failure to appear or because of procedural irregularities. So the justice process can be viewed as a funnel that holds many cases at its mouth and relatively few at its end.

Theoretically, nearly every part of the process requires that individual cases be disposed of as quickly as possible. However, the criminal justice process is slower and more tedious than desired because of congestion, inadequate facilities, limited resources, inefficiency, and the nature of governmental bureaucracy. When defendants are not processed smoothly, often because of the large caseloads and inadequate facilities that exist in many urban jurisdictions, the

FIGURE 1.4
The Criminal Justice Funnel

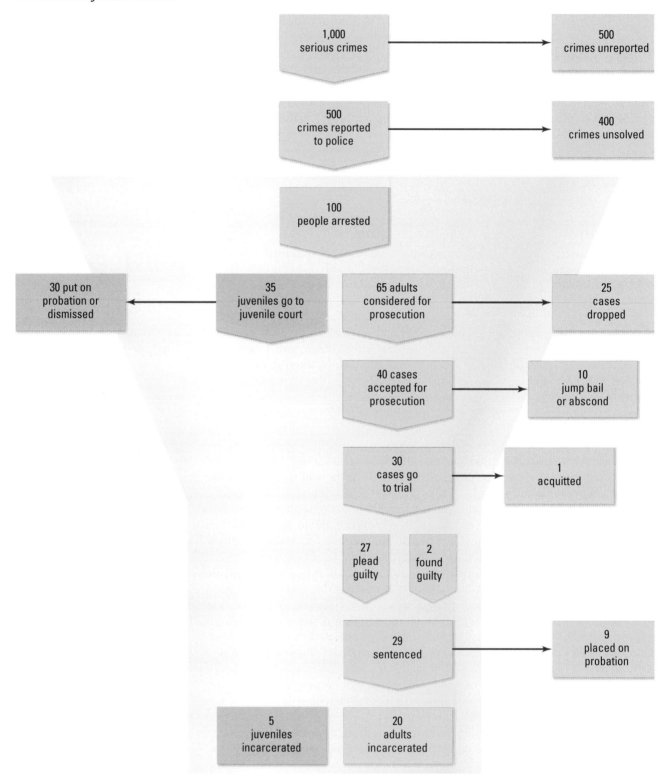

Source: Thomas Cohen and Brian Reaves, *Felony Defendants in Large Urban Counties, 2002* (Washington, D.C.: Bureau of Justice Statistics, 2006).
Matthew Durose and Patrick Langan, *Felony Sentences in State Courts, 2002* (Washington, D.C.: Bureau of Justice Statistics, 2004).

EXHIBIT 1.3	
The Interrelationship of the Criminal Justice System and the Criminal Justice Process	
The System: **Agencies of crime control**	**The Process**
1. Police	1. Contact
	2. Investigation
	3. Arrest
	4. Custody
2. Prosecution and defense	5. Complaint/charging
	6. Grand jury/preliminary hearing
	7. Arraignment
	8. Bail/detention
	9. Plea negotiations
3. Court	10. Adjudication
	11. Disposition
	12. Appeal/postconviction remedies
4. Corrections	13. Correction
	14. Release
	15. Postrelease

procedure breaks down, the process within the system fails, and the ultimate goal of a fair and efficient justice system cannot be achieved. Exhibit 1.3 shows the interrelationship of the component agencies of the criminal justice system and the criminal justice process.

◆ THE INFORMAL CRIMINAL JUSTICE SYSTEM

The traditional model of the criminal justice system depicts the legal process as a series of decision points through which cases flow. Each stage of the system, beginning with investigation and arrest and ending after a sentence has been served, is defined by time-honored administrative procedures and controlled by the rule of law. The public's perception of the system, fueled by the media, is that it is composed of daredevil, crime-fighting police officers who never ask for over-time or sick leave, crusading district attorneys who stop at nothing to send the mob boss up the river, wily defense attorneys who neither ask clients for up-front cash nor cut short office visits to play golf, no-nonsense judges who are never inept political appointees, and tough wardens who rule the yard with an iron hand. It would be overly simplistic to assume that the system works this way for every case. Although a few cases receive a full measure of rights and procedures, many are settled in an informal pattern of cooperation between the major actors in the justice process. For example, police may be willing to make a deal with a suspect to gain his cooperation, and the prosecutor may bargain with the defense attorney to get a plea of guilty as charged in return for a promise of leniency. Law enforcement agents and court officers are allowed tremendous discretion in their decision to make an arrest, bring formal charges, handle a case informally, substitute charges, and so on. Crowded courts operate in a spirit of getting the matter settled quickly and cleanly, instead of engaging in long, drawn-out criminal proceedings with an uncertain outcome.

The recognition of the informal justice process has spurred development of two concepts—the courtroom work group and the wedding cake model—that help us better understand how U.S. justice really operates.

The Courtroom Work Group

Whereas the traditional model regards the justice process as an adversary proceeding in which the prosecution and defense are combatants, the majority of criminal cases are cooperative ventures in which all parties get together to work out a deal. This has been called the **courtroom work group**.

This group, made up of the prosecutor, defense attorney, judge, and other court personnel, functions to streamline the process of justice through the extensive use of plea bargaining and other trial alternatives. Instead of looking to provide a spirited defense or prosecution, these legal agents, who have often attended the same schools, know one another, and have worked together for many years, try to work out a case to their own professional advantage. Their goal is to remove "unnecessary" delays and avoid formal trials at all costs. Because most defendants who have gotten this far in the system are assumed to be guilty, the goal is to process cases efficiently rather than seek justice.

Political Scientist David Neubauer has identified five essential ingredients that identify the courtroom work group:

1. *Shared decision making.* The legal process provides the trial judge with formal authority over the outcome of court proceedings. However, the judge's reliance on other members for information about the case results in a shared decision-making process. Shared decision making allows the judge to remain the informal leader of the work group and also serves to diffuse blame for mistakes.

2. *Shared norms.* Each of the members of the work group agrees to behave in a predictable manner. The most important shared norm is shielding the work group from nonmembers; the greatest uncertainty comes from outsider contributions (e.g., witnesses, jurors) that work group members cannot control. There are standards of professional conduct (e.g., be firm in your decisions) and policy (e.g., all members agree on the seriousness of certain cases).

3. *Socialization.* Newcomers are taught the informal expectations of the work group as part of their orientation. Senior members who possess great formal authority, such as judges, may be oriented to work group methods by those with less authority, such as deputy clerks. The socialization process shapes the overall behavior of the group by limiting the use of judicial authority and by communicating the group's informal work rules.

4. *Reward and sanction.* To be meaningful, group rules must be enforced. Group members who abide by the norms are rewarded; those who do not are sanctioned. Conformity to group norms is secured by both extending rewards and leveling sanctions.

5. *Goal modification.* Although all members share the goal of "doing justice," its definition is often cloudy because it is difficult to define justice and/or measure whether it has been achieved. As a result, members pursue organizational objectives, such as disposing of cases efficiently rather than worrying about effectiveness.[20]

In most criminal cases, cooperation, not conflict, between prosecution and defense appears to be the norm. The adversarial process is called into play in only a few widely publicized criminal cases involving rape or murder. Consequently, upward of 80 percent of all felony cases and over 90 percent of misdemeanors are settled without trial.

What has developed is a system in which criminal court experiences can be viewed as a training ground for young defense attorneys looking for seasoning

courtroom work group
All parties in the adversary process working together in a cooperative effort to settle cases with the least amount of effort and conflict.

and practice. It provides a means for newly established lawyers to receive government compensation for cases taken to get their practice going or an arena in which established firms can place their new associates for experience before they are assigned to paying clients. Similarly, successful prosecutors can look forward to a political career or a highly paid partnership in a private firm. To further their career aspirations, prosecutors must develop and maintain a winning track record in criminal cases. Although the courtroom work group limits the constitutional rights of defendants, it may be essential for keeping the overburdened justice system afloat. Moreover, though informal justice exists, it is not absolutely certain that it is inherently unfair to both the victim and the offender. Evidence shows that the defendants who benefit the most from informal court procedures commit the least serious crimes, whereas the more chronic offender gains relatively little.[21]

The National Association of Attorneys General (NAAG) provides useful information about ethics and the role of the prosecutor. You can reach this website by going to the Siegel/Senna Introduction to Criminal Justice 11e website: www.thomsonedu.com/criminaljustice/siegel.

The "Wedding Cake" Model of Justice

Samuel Walker, a justice historian and scholar, has come up with a dramatic way of describing this informal justice process. He compares it with a four-layer cake, as depicted in Figure 1.5.[22]

LEVEL 1 The first layer of Walker's model is made up of the celebrated cases involving the wealthy and famous, such as media figure O. J. Simpson, style guru Martha Stewart, and Enron executive Jeff Skilling, or the not so powerful who victimize a famous person—John Hinckley, Jr., who shot President Ronald Reagan, might fall into this category. Other cases fall into the first layer because they are widely reported in the media and become the subject of a TV investigation. The media usually focus on hideous or unusual cases, such as the disappearance of 18-year-old Natalee Holloway while on holiday in Aruba or the kidnapping of Utah teen Elizabeth Smart.

"wedding cake" model of justice
A view of justice that divides the criminal process into four layers based on the seriousness and notoriety of the crime. The top layer gets the full interest of the law, whereas the bottom layer receives only superficial attention.

FIGURE 1.5
The Criminal Justice "Wedding Cake"

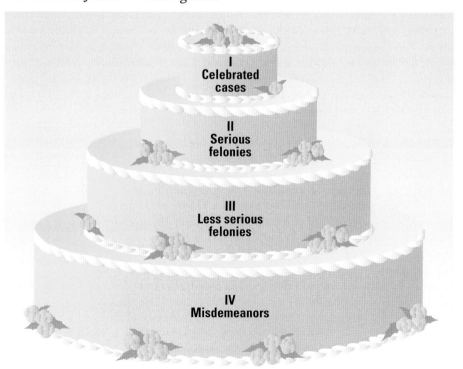

Source: Based on Samuel Walker, *Sense and Nonsense about Crime* (Monterey, Calif.: Brooks/Cole, 1983).

Cases that capture wide media attention represent the top level of the criminal justice wedding cake. One such case was the disappearance of Natalee Holloway on a class trip to Aruba. Here her mother Beth Holloway Twitty (left) leaves a restaurant where she has passed out prayer cards and bracelets in hopes of raising awareness about her missing daughter. Police devote more attention to these cases and sometimes make arrests years after the crime occurred.

Cases in the first layer of the criminal justice "wedding cake" usually receive the full array of criminal justice procedures, including competent defense attorneys, expert witnesses, jury trials, and elaborate appeals. The media typically focus on Level I cases, and the TV-watching public is given the impression that most criminals are sober, intelligent people and most victims are members of the upper classes, a patently false impression.

LEVEL II In the second layer are the serious felonies—rapes, robberies, and burglaries—which have become all too routine in U.S. society. They are in the second layer because they are serious crimes committed by experienced offenders. Burglaries are included if the amount stolen is high and the techniques used indicate the suspect is a pro. Violent crimes, such as rape and assault, are vicious incidents against an innocent victim and may involve a weapon and extreme violence. Robberies involve large amounts of money and suspects who brandish handguns or other weapons and are considered career criminals. Police, prosecutors, and judges all agree that these are serious cases, worthy of the full attention of the justice system. Offenders in such Level II cases receive a full jury trial and, if convicted, can look forward to a prison sentence.

LEVEL III Although they can also be felonies, crimes that fall in the third layer of the wedding cake are less serious offenses committed by young or first-time offenders or involving people who knew each other or were otherwise related: An inebriated teenager committed a burglary and netted $50; the rape victim had gone on a few dates with her assailant before he attacked her; the robbery involved members of rival gangs and no weapons; the assault was the result of a personal dispute, and some question arises as to who hit whom first. Agents of the criminal justice system relegate these cases to the third level because they see them as less important and less deserving of attention. Level III crimes may be dealt with by an outright dismissal, a plea bargain, reduction in charges, or, most typically, a probationary sentence or intermediate sanction, such as victim restitution.

LEVEL IV The fourth layer of the cake is made up of the millions of misdemeanors, such as disorderly conduct, shoplifting, public drunkenness, and minor assault. The lower criminal courts handle these cases in assembly-line fashion.

Few defendants insist on exercising their constitutional rights because the delay would cost them valuable time and money. Because the typical penalty is a small fine, everyone wants to get the case over with.[23]

The wedding cake model of informal justice is an intriguing alternative to the traditional criminal justice flowchart. Criminal justice officials handle individual cases differently, yet a high degree of consistency is found with the way in which particular types or classes of cases are dealt with in every legal jurisdiction. For example, police and prosecutors in Los Angeles and Boston will each handle the murder of a prominent citizen in similar fashion. They will also deal with the death of an unemployed street person killed in a brawl in a similar manner. Yet in each jurisdiction, the two cases will be handled very differently. The bigwig's killer will receive a full-blown jury trial (with details on the 6 o'clock news); the drifter's killer will get a quick plea bargain. The model is useful because it shows that all too often, public opinion about criminal justice is formed on the basis of what happened in an atypical case.

ThomsonNOW™ Improve your grade on the exam with Personalized Study! For reinforcement resources and a mastery check of the criminal justice process, go to www.thomsonedu.com/thomsonnow.

◆ PERSPECTIVES ON JUSTICE

Almost 40 years have passed since the field of criminal justice began to be the subject of both serious academic study and attempts at unified policy formation, significant debate continues over the meaning of the term *criminal justice* and how the problem of crime control should be approached. After decades of research and policy analysis, criminal justice is still far from a unified field. Practitioners, academics, and commentators alike have expressed irreconcilable differences concerning its goals, purpose, and direction. Some conservatives believe the solution to the crime problem is to increase the number of police, apprehend more criminals, and give them long sentences in maximum-security prisons. In contrast, liberals call for increased spending on social services and community organization. Others worry about giving the government too much power to regulate and control behavior and to interfere with individual liberty and freedom.

Given the multitude of problems facing the justice system, this lack of consensus is particularly vexing. The agencies of justice must attempt to eradicate such seemingly diverse social problems as substance abuse, gang violence, pornography, cyber crime, and terrorism while at the same time respecting individual liberties and civil rights. The agencies of the justice system also presumably have adequate resources and knowledge to carry out their complex tasks in an efficient and effective manner, something that so far seems to be wishful thinking. Experts are still searching for the right combination of policies and actions that will significantly reduce crime and increase public safety while maintaining individual freedom and social justice.

Considering the complexity of criminal justice, it is not surprising that no single view, perspective, or philosophy dominates the field. What are the dominant views of the criminal justice system today? What is the role of the justice system, and how should it approach its tasks?

The Crime Control Perspective

More than 20 years ago, political scientist James Q. Wilson made the persuasive argument that most criminals are not poor unfortunates who commit crime to survive but are greedy people who choose theft or drug dealing for quick and easy profits.[24] Criminals, he argued, lack inhibition against misconduct, value the excitement and thrills of breaking the law, have a low stake in conformity, and are willing to take greater chances than the average person. If they could be convinced that their actions will bring severe punishment, only the irrational would be willing to engage in crime. Restraining offenders and preventing their future misdeeds, he argued, is a much more practical goal of the criminal justice system

One popular crime control strategy is a police crackdown during which law enforcement agencies aggressively focus on a particular crime pattern in an effort to achieve its control or elimination. Here, Ludwig "Ninny" Bruschi stands in Superior Court during his arraignment on organized crime charges in Freehold, New Jersey. Bruschi, a reputed capo with the Genovese crime family, and sixteen others were indicted on charges they operated loansharking, gambling, and drug distribution businesses in central and northern New Jersey. The 68-year-old Bruschi was charged with running the operation out of a bar in Union County.

than trying to eradicate the root causes of crime: poverty, poor schools, racism, and family breakup. He made this famous observation:

> Wicked people exist. Nothing avails except to set them apart from innocent people. And many people, neither wicked nor innocent, but watchful, dissembling, and calculating of their chances, ponder our reaction to wickedness as a clue to what they might profitably do.[25]

crime control perspective
A model of criminal justice that emphasizes the control of dangerous offenders and the protection of society through harsh punishment as a deterrent to crime.

Wilson's views helped define the **crime control perspective** of criminal justice. According to this view, the proper role of the justice system is to prevent crime through the judicious use of criminal sanctions. People want protection from dangerous criminals and expect the government to do what is necessary—i.e., punish criminals—to make them feel secure; crime control is part of the democratic process.[26] Because the public is outraged by such crimes as mass school shootings (e.g., at Columbine High School in Colorado), it demands an efficient justice system that hands out tough sanctions to those who choose to violate the law.[27]

According to the crime control philosophy, if the justice system operated in an effective manner, most potential criminals would be deterred from crime, while the few who dared would be apprehended, tried, and punished so that they would never again risk committing crime. Crime rates trend upward, the argument goes, when criminals do not sufficiently fear apprehension and punishment. If the efficiency of the system could be increased and the criminal law could be toughened, crime rates would decline. Effective law enforcement, strict mandatory punishment, and expanding the use of prison are the keys to reduce crime rates. Although crime control may be expensive, reducing the gains of criminal activity is well worth the price.

EFFECTIVENESS AND EFFICIENCY According to the crime control perspective, the focus of justice should be on the victim of crime, not the criminal, so that innocent people can be protected from the ravages of crime. This objective can be achieved through more effective police protection, tough sentences (including liberal use of the death penalty), and the construction of prisons designed to safely incapacitate hardened criminals. If the system could be made more efficient, few would be tempted to break the law, and its effectiveness would improve.

Crime control advocates do not want legal technicalities to help the guilty go free and tie the hands of justice. They lobby for the abolition of legal restrictions that control a police officer's ability to search for evidence and interrogate suspects. Police departments would be more effective crime fighters, they argue, if administrators employed a proactive, aggressive law enforcement style without having to worry about charges that their forceful tactics violated the right of criminal defendants.[28] The police may sometimes be forced to use tactics that sacrifice civil liberties for the sake of effectiveness, such as **profiling** people at an airport based on their race or ethnic origin in order to identify and apprehend suspected terrorists. Civil libertarians are wary of racial profiling, but crime control advocates would argue that we are in the midst of a national emergency and that the ends justify the means.

ABOLISHING LEGAL ROADBLOCKS One impediment to effective crime control is the legal roadblocks set up by the courts to protect the due process rights of criminal defendants. Several hundred thousand criminals go free every year in cases dropped because courts find that police have violated the suspects' *Miranda* **rights**.[29] Crime control advocates lobby for abolition of the **exclusionary rule**, which requires that illegally seized evidence be barred from criminal proceedings. Their voices have been heard: A more conservative Supreme Court has given police greater latitude to search for and seize evidence and has eased restrictions on how police operate. However, even in this permissive environment, research shows that police routinely violate suspects' rights when searching for evidence and that the majority of these incidents are never reviewed by the courts because the search was not followed up by arrest or citation.[30]

Crime control advocates also question the criminal justice system's ability to rehabilitate offenders. Most treatment programs are ineffective because the justice system is simply not equipped to treat people who have a long history of antisocial behavior. Even when agents of the system attempt to prevent crime by working with young people, the results are unsatisfactory. For example, evaluations of the highly touted Drug Abuse Resistance Education (DARE) antidrug program indicate that it has had little impact on students.[31] From both a moral and a practical standpoint, the role of criminal justice should be the control of antisocial people. If not to the justice system, then to whom can the average citizen turn for protection from society's criminal elements?

The Rehabilitation Perspective

If the crime control perspective views the justice system in terms of protecting the public and controlling criminal elements, then advocates of the **rehabilitation perspective** may be said to see the justice system as a means of caring for and treating people who cannot manage themselves. They view crime as an expression of frustration and anger created by social inequality. Crime can be controlled by giving people the means to improve their lifestyle through conventional endeavors.

The rehabilitation concept assumes that people are at the mercy of social, economic, and interpersonal conditions and interactions. Criminals themselves are the victims of racism, poverty, strain, blocked opportunities, alienation, family disruption, and other social problems. They live in socially disorganized neighborhoods that are incapable of providing proper education, health care, or civil services. Society must help them compensate for their social problems.

ALTERNATIVES TO CRIME Rehabilitation advocates believe that government programs can help reduce crime on both a societal (macro) and individual (micro) level. On the macro, or societal, level, research shows that as the number of legitimate opportunities to succeed declines, people are more likely to turn to criminal behaviors, such as drug dealing, to survive. Increasing economic opportunities through job training, family counseling, educational services, and crisis

profile (profiling)
The practice of police targeting members of particular racial or ethnic groups for traffic and other stops because they believe that members of that group are more likely to be engaged in criminal activity even though the individual being stopped has not engaged in any improper behavior.

***Miranda* rights**
According to the case of *Miranda v. Arizona*, the right of a suspect to refuse to answer questions after an arrest and to have an attorney provided to protect civil rights and liberties.

exclusionary rule
The legal doctrine that any Evidence illegally seized by police cannot be used against a suspect in a court of law.

rehabilitation perspective
A model of criminal justice that sees crime as an expression of frustration and anger created by social inequality that can be controlled by giving people the means to improve their lifestyle through conventional endeavors.

intervention is a more effective crime reducer than prisons and jails. As legitimate opportunities increase, violence rates decline.[32]

On a micro or individual level, rehabilitation programs can help at-risk youths avoid entry into criminal careers by providing them with legitimate alternatives to crime and the counseling to enable them to grasp opportunities. Drug offenders, a population known to be resistant to change, have shown marked improvement given the proper course of treatment.[33]

Even if preventive measures have not worked, incarcerating offenders without proper treatment is not the right course of action. Given the proper therapy, incarcerated offenders can significantly lower their rates of recidivism.[34] Within correctional settings, programs that develop interpersonal skills, induce a prosocial change in attitudes, and improve cognitive thinking patterns have been shown to significantly reduce recidivism rates.[35]

Society has a choice: Pay now, by funding treatment and educational programs, or pay later, when troubled youths enter costly correctional facilities over and over again. This view is certainly not lost on the public. Although the public may want to get tough on crime, many are willing to make exceptions, for example, by advocating leniency for younger offenders.[36]

The Due Process Perspective

due process perspective
A model of criminal justice that emphasizes individual rights and constitutional safeguards against arbitrary or unfair judicial or administrative proceedings.

Advocates of the **due process perspective** argue that the greatest concern of the justice system should be providing fair and equitable treatment to those accused of crime.[37] This means providing impartial hearings, competent legal counsel, equitable treatment, and reasonable sanctions. The use of discretion within the justice system should be strictly monitored to ensure that no one suffers from racial, religious, or ethnic discrimination. The system must be attuned to the civil rights afforded every citizen by the U.S. Constitution. Therefore, it is vexing to due process advocates when the Supreme Court extends the scope of law enforcement's reach, enabling police agencies to monitor and control citizens at the expense of their right to privacy.

Although many views exist of what the true goals of justice should be, the system undoubtedly must be expected to operate in a fair and unbiased manner. Those who advocate the due process orientation point out that the justice system remains an adversary process that pits the forces of an all-powerful state against those of a solitary individual accused of a crime. If concern for justice and fairness did not exist, the defendant who lacked resources could easily be overwhelmed.

Miscarriages of justice are common. Numerous criminal convictions have been overturned because newly developed DNA evidence later showed that the accused could not have committed the crimes. Many of the falsely convicted spent years in prison before their release.[38] Evidence also shows that many innocent people have been executed for crimes they did not commit. From 1976 to 1999, 566 people were executed. During that same period of time, 82 convicts awaiting execution were exonerated—a ratio of one freed for every seven put to death.[39] Because such mistakes can happen, even the most apparently guilty offender deserves all the protection the justice system can offer. Having a competent attorney who puts on a spirited defense may mean the difference between life and death. Recent research (2005) by Talia Roitberg Harmon and William Lofquist compared people who had been (a) falsely convicted of murder and later exonerated with those who were (b) most likely innocent but executed. The research showed that those convicted but later exonerated employed private defense attorneys who were better prepared to put on a robust defense at trial.[40] Is it fair that a life versus death outcome may rest on the ability to afford private counsel?

Those who question the due process perspective claim that the legal privileges afforded criminal suspects have gone too far and that the effort to protect individual rights now interferes with public safety. Is it fair, they argue, for evidence to be suppressed if it is obtained in violation of the constitutional right to be free from an illegal search and seizure, even if it means that a dangerous person goes free? Is it better to free a guilty person than trample on the civil rights of citizens, even those who commit criminal acts? But what about the rights of actual or potential victims of crime? Should the needs of the victim take precedence over those of criminal offenders? Those who advocate the due process perspective believe firmly that legal principles of fairness and due process must be upheld, even if it means that on occasion a patently guilty person is freed. Preserving the democratic ideals of U.S. society takes precedence over the need to punish the guilty.

The Nonintervention Perspective

Supporters of the **nonintervention perspective** believe that justice agencies should limit their involvement with criminal defendants. Regardless of whether intervention is designed to punish or treat people, the ultimate effect of any involvement is harmful. Whatever their goals or design, programs that involve people with a social control agency—such as the police, a mental health department, the correctional system, or a criminal court—will have long-term negative effects. Once involved with such an agency, criminal defendants may be watched, people might consider them dangerous and untrustworthy, and they can develop a lasting record that has negative connotations. Bearing an official label disrupts their personal and family life and harms parent–child relationships. Eventually, they may even come to believe what their official record suggests; they may view themselves as bad, evil, outcasts, troublemakers, or crazy. Thus, official labels promote rather than reduce the tendency to engage in antisocial activities.[41]

Noninterventionists are concerned about the effect of the stigma that criminal suspects bear when they are given negative labels such as "rapist" or "child abuser." These labels will stick with them forever. Once labeled, people may find it difficult to be accepted back into society, even after they have completed their sentence. It is not surprising, considering these effects of stigma and labeling, that recidivism rates are so high. When people are given less stigmatized forms of punishment such as probation, they are less likely to become repeat offenders.[42]

Fearing the harmful effects of stigma and labels, noninterventionists have tried to place limitations on the government's ability to control people's lives. They have called for the **decriminalization** (reduction of penalties) and legalization of nonserious **victimless crimes**, such as the possession of small amounts of marijuana, public drunkenness, and vagrancy.

Noninterventionists demand the removal of nonviolent offenders from the nation's correctional system, a policy referred to as **deinstitutionalization**. First offenders who commit minor crimes should instead be placed in informal, community-based treatment programs, a process referred to as **pretrial diversion**.

Sometimes the passage of new criminal laws can stigmatize offenders beyond the scope of their offense, referred to as **widening the net** of justice. For example, a person who purchases pornography on the Internet is labeled a dangerous sex offender, or someone caught for a second time with marijuana is considered a habitual drug abuser. Noninterventionists have fought implementation of community notification–type laws that require convicted sex offenders to register with state law enforcement officials and allow officials to publicly disclose when a registrant moves into a community. Their efforts have resulted in rulings stating that these laws can be damaging to the reputation and future of offenders who have not been given an opportunity to defend themselves from the charge that they are chronic criminal sex offenders.[43] As a group, noninterventionist initiatives have been implemented to help people avoid the stigma associated with contact with the criminal justice system.

nonintervention perspective
A model of criminal justice that favors the least intrusive treatment possible: decarceration, diversion, and decriminalization.

decriminalization
Reducing the penalty for a criminal act without legalizing it.

victimless crime
A crime typically involving behavior considered immoral or in violation of public decency that has no specific victim, such as public drunkenness, vagrancy, or public nudity.

deinstitutionalization
The movement to remove as many offenders as possible from secure confinement and treat them in the community.

pretrial diversion
Informal, community-based treatment programs that are used in lieu of the formal criminal process.

widening the net
Enmeshing more offenders for longer periods in the criminal justice system—a criticism of pretrial diversion programs.

The Justice Perspective

The core of the justice perspective is that all people should receive the same treatment under the law. Any effort to distinguish between criminal offenders will create a sense of unfairness that can interfere with readjustment to society. Frustration arises when two people commit the same crime but receive different sentences or punishments. The resulting anger and a sense of unfairness will increase the likelihood of recidivism.

To remedy this situation, the criminal justice system must reduce discretion and unequal treatment. Law violators should be evaluated on the basis of their current behavior, not on what they have done in the past (they have already paid for their behavior) or on what they may do in the future (because future behavior cannot be accurately predicted). The treatment of criminal offenders must be based solely on present behavior: Punishment must be equitably administered and based on just deserts.

The justice perspective has had considerable influence in molding the nation's sentencing policy. An ongoing effort has been made to reduce discretion and guarantee that every offender convicted of a particular crime receives equal punishment. This change has been particularly welcome, given the charges of racial discrimination that have beset the sentencing process. A number of initiatives have been designed to achieve this result, including mandatory sentences requiring that all people convicted of a crime receive the same prison sentence. *Truth-in-sentencing laws* require offenders to serve a substantial portion of their prison sentence behind bars, thus limiting their eligibility for early release on parole.[44]

The Restorative Justice Perspective

restorative justice
The view that the purpose of justice is to restore offenders back into society through reconciliation rather than punishment.

According to the concept of **restorative justice**, the true purpose of the criminal justice system is to promote a peaceful and just society; the justice system should aim for peacemaking, not punishment.[45] The restorative justice perspective draws its inspiration from religious and philosophical teachings ranging from Quakerism to Zen. Advocates of restorative justice view the efforts of the state to punish and control as "crime encouraging" rather than "crime discouraging." The violent punishing acts of the state, they claim, are not dissimilar from the violent acts of individuals.[46] Therefore, mutual aid, not coercive punishment, is the key to a harmonious society. Without the capacity to restore damaged social relations, society's response to crime has been almost exclusively punitive.

According to restorative justice, resolution of the conflict between criminal and victim should take place in the community in which it originated and not in some far-off prison. The victim should be given a chance to voice his story, and the offender can directly communicate her need for social reintegration and treatment. The goal is to enable the offender to appreciate the damage she has caused, to make amends, and to be reintegrated back into society.

Restorative justice programs are now being geared to these principles. Mediation and conflict-resolution programs are now common in efforts to resolve harmful human interactions ranging from domestic violence to hate crimes.[47] Police officers, as elements of community policing programs, are beginning to use mediation techniques to settle disputes instead of resorting to formal arrest.[48] Financial and community service restitution programs as an alternative to imprisonment have been in operation for more than two decades. The perspectives are summarized in Figure 1.6.

Perspectives in Perspective

The variety of tactics being used to combat crime today aptly illustrates the impact of the various perspectives on justice on the operations of the criminal justice system. Advocates of each view have attempted to promote their vision of what justice is all about and how it should be applied. During the past decade,

FIGURE 1.6
Perspectives on Justice: Key Concerns and Concepts

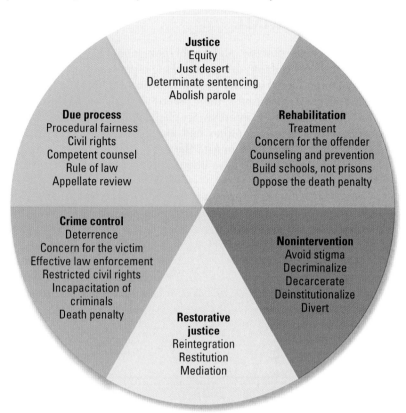

the crime control and justice models have dominated. Laws have been toughened and the rights of the accused curtailed, the prison population has grown, and the death penalty has been employed against convicted murderers. Because the crime rate has been dropping, these policies seem to be effective. They may be questioned if crime rates once again begin to rise. At the same time, efforts to rehabilitate offenders, to provide them with elements of due process, and to give them the least intrusive treatment have not been abandoned. Police, courts, and correctional agencies supply a wide range of treatment and rehabilitation programs to offenders in all stages of the criminal justice system. Whenever possible, those accused of a crime are treated informally in nonrestrictive, community-based programs, and the effects of stigma are guarded against.

Although the legal rights of offenders are being closely scrutinized by the courts, the basic constitutional rights of the accused remain inviolate. Guardians of the process have made sure that defendants are allowed the maximum protection possible under the law. For example, criminal defendants have been awarded the right to competent legal counsel at trial; merely having a lawyer to defend them is not considered sufficient legal protection.

In sum, understanding the justice system today requires analyzing a variety of occupational roles, institutional processes, legal rules, and administrative doctrines. Each predominant view of criminal justice provides a vantage point for understanding and interpreting these complex issues. No single view is the right or correct one. Each individual must choose the perspective that best fits his or her ideas and judgment—or they can all be discarded and the individual's own view substituted.

ThomsonNOW Improve your grade on the exam with Personalized Study! For reinforcement resources and a mastery check of perspectives on justice, go to www.thomsonedu.com/thomsonnow.

PERSPECTIVES ON JUSTICE

Introduction

Throughout the remainder of the book we will link the various perspectives on justice to the practices of the contemporary justice system. This feature will allow you to assess the impact of the various schools of thought on justice policy and their impact in guiding the system's efforts to reduce the frequency of criminal behaviors.

◆ NEW CHALLENGES FOR THE JUSTICE SYSTEM: TERRORISM AND CYBER CRIME

terrorism
Premeditated, politically motivated violence perpetrated against noncombatant targets by subnational groups or clandestine agents.

cyber crime
Illegal behavior that targets the security of computer systems and/or the data accessed and processed by computer networks.

cyber terrorism
Internet attacks against an enemy nation's technological infrastructure.

For useful links on terrorism, go to the website of the Constitutional Rights Foundation. You can reach it by going to the Siegel/Senna Introduction to Criminal Justice 11e website: www.thomsonedu.com/criminaljustice/siegel.

As debate over the most effective philosophy/perspective to control traditional crimes—murder, rape, robbery, drug trafficking—continues, newly emerging forms of criminal and illegal activity pose a significant challenge to the justice system. Because of their seriousness, their potential for damage, and their effect on public morale, two of these contemporary challenges stand out in importance: **terrorism** and **cyber crime**. Neither had much of an impact on the justice system 20 years ago; today, they dominate the news. Criminal justice agencies at the federal, state, and local levels have been forced to adapt to the threats they present.

One reason cyber crime and terrorism present formidable challenges for the justice system is that both have been evolving in complexity and seriousness. Although at first glance cyber criminals seem to present a far different challenge to law enforcement officials than terrorists, there is actually some common ground. Both groups rely on stealth and secrecy. Cyberspace may become an avenue for terrorist activity. Using the Internet as an operational theater, cyber terrorists can mount attacks against an enemy nation's technological infrastructure, an action referred to as **cyber terrorism**. What forms do these crimes now take, and how is the justice system responding to the challenge?

Criminal Justice and Terrorism

Terrorism involves the illegal use of force against innocent people to achieve a political objective. According to the U.S. State Department, the term *terrorism* means "premeditated, politically motivated violence perpetrated against noncombatant targets by sub-national groups or clandestine agents."[49] The term *international terrorism* means terrorism involving citizens or the territory of more than one country. A *terrorist group* is any group practicing, or that has significant subgroups that practice, international terrorism.[50]

Confronting terrorism is also critical because of the lethal tactics now being used—bombings, killing hostages, chemical warfare, spreading toxic biological

The threat of terrorism is felt all over the world. At London's Gatwick airport, armed police walk through crowds of people on August 10, 2006, after MI5, Britain's Intelligence Service, upgraded the National Security level to "critical" because Scotland Yard Police arrested 21 people they believed were planning to detonate explosive devices on transatlantic flights to the United States. Air passengers in both the United States and Great Britain were restricted to a minimum of carry-on items, and cancellations and long delays to flights occurred in both countries.

agents. Because they or their group do not share in its benefits, terrorists not only are uninterested in maintaining the economic, social, and political structure, but they may be actively planning its destruction as well. They obey few rules of combat and will use any tactic, no matter how violent, to achieve their goals.[51] Agencies of the justice system have little experience in dealing with such ruthlessness.

The Contemporary Terrorist

The criminal justice system is now confronting a new breed of terrorists, whose motivations are varied and whose sponsors are diverse. Rather than being motivated by nationalism or by the creation of a separate state or nation (see Exhibit 1.4), these groups, most importantly **Al-Qaeda** (Arabic for "the foundation" or "the base"), are motivated by religious and cultural values.[52] They view their cause as a global war against their enemies' values and traditions. Consequently, contemporary terrorism may produce higher casualties: Violence is a divine duty, justified by scripture, and the terrorists are absolved from guilt because their targets are blasphemers.[53]

Rather than having a unified central command, these new terrorists are organized in far-flung nets or cells. Not located in any particular nation or area, they have no identifiable address.[54] They are capable of attacking anyone at any time with great destructive force. They may employ an arsenal of weapons of mass destruction—chemical, biological, nuclear—without fear of contaminating their own homeland, because in reality they may not actually have one.

Contemporary terrorists use technology—computers and the Internet—to attack their targets' economic infrastructure and actually profit from the resulting economic chaos by buying and/or selling securities in advance of their own attack![55] They may want to bankrupt their opponents by forcing them to spend billions on terror defense.[56]

Al-Qaeda
Arabic for "the base"—an international fundamentalist Islamist organization comprising independent and collaborative cells whose goal is reducing Western influence upon Islamic affairs.

The Criminal Justice Response to Terrorism

After the 9/11 attacks, agencies of the criminal justice system began to focus their attention on combating the threat of terror. Even local police agencies created antiterror programs designed to protect their communities from the threat of attack. How should the nation best prepare itself to thwart potential attacks?

FEDERAL RESPONSE The National Commission on Terrorist Attacks upon the United States (also known as the 9/11 Commission), an independent, bipartisan commission, was created in late 2002 and was given the mission of preparing an in-depth report on the events leading up to the 9/11 attacks. To monitor the more than 500 million people who cross into the United States, the commission recommended that a single agency should be created to screen border crossings. It also recommended creation of an investigative agency to monitor all aliens in the United States and to gather intelligence on the way that terrorists travel across borders. The commission suggested that people who wanted passports be tagged with biometric measures to make them easily identifiable.

In response to the commission report, the position of the **Director of National Intelligence (DNI)**, charged with coordinating data from the nation's primary intelligence gathering agencies, was created. The DNI serves as the principal intelligence advisor to the president and the statutory intelligence advisor to the National Security Council. On February 17, 2005, President George W. Bush named U.S. Ambassador to Iraq John Negroponte to be the first person to hold the post; he was confirmed on April 21, 2005. Also reporting to the DNI is the staff of the newly created National Counterterrorism Center (NCTC), which is staffed by terrorism experts from the CIA, the FBI, and the Pentagon;

Director of National Intelligence (DNI)
Government official charged with coordinating data from the nation's primary intelligence-gathering agencies.

EXHIBIT 1.4

Contemporary Forms of Terrorism

REVOLUTIONARY TERRORISM

Revolutionary terrorists aim to replace the existing government with a regime that holds acceptable political or religious views. In Egypt, groups such as Jamaat al-Islamiyya Jihad, which is also known as Al-Gama'a al-Islamiyya (the Islamic Group), and Egyptian Islamic Jihad have attacked foreigners in an effort to sabotage the tourist industry, topple the secular government, and turn Egypt into an Islamic state. On July 23, 2005, two car bombs and a bomb in a knapsack ripped through a hotel and beach promenade in Sharm el-Sheik, killing 64 people, mainly tourists, and again on April 24, 2006, three bombings hit the Sinai seaside city of Dahab, killing at least 23 people and wounding more than 60.

POLITICAL TERRORISM

Political terrorists engage in a campaign of violence designed to suppress or destroy those people or groups who oppose the terrorists' political ideology or whom the terrorists define as a threat to their social and religious views and political leanings within their own homeland. In the United States, political terrorists tend to be heavily armed groups organized around such themes as white supremacy, militant tax resistance, and religious revisionism. These groups include the Aryan Republican Army, Fourth Reich, Aryan Revolutionary Front, and Aryan Nation. Their actions are aimed at curtailing the rights of people and groups they oppose—for example, racial and religious minorities and immigrants.

NATIONALIST TERRORISM

Nationalist terrorists promote the interests of a minority ethnic or religious group that believes it has been persecuted under majority rule and wishes to carve out its own independent homeland. In the Middle East, terrorist activities have been linked to the Palestinians' desire to wrest their former homeland from Israel. In India, Sikh radicals have used violence to recover what they believe to be lost homelands in Kashmir. The Tamil Tigers are fighting for a separate homeland for minority Tamils in the north and east of Sri Lanka.

Basque rebels have conducted terror attacks against the Spanish government.

CAUSE-BASED TERRORISM

Some terrorist organizations direct their activities against individuals and governments to whom they object on economic, social, or religious grounds. They do not wish to carve out a homeland or replace the existing government of their own nation but simply to destroy all those who oppose their view anywhere in the world.

ENVIRONMENTAL TERRORISM

Environmental terrorists carry out raids against those whom they consider to be a threat to the ecosystem. They seek to inflict economic damage on those profiting from the destruction and exploitation of the natural environment; to reveal to and educate the public on the atrocities committed against the earth and the species that populate it; and to take all necessary precautions against harming any animal, human or nonhuman.

STATE-SPONSORED TERRORISM

State-sponsored terrorism occurs when a repressive governmental regime forces its citizens into obedience, oppresses minorities, and stifles political dissent. Death squads and the use of government troops to destroy political opposition parties are common tactics.

CRIMINAL TERRORISM

Terrorist groups sometimes become involved in common-law crimes such as drug dealing and kidnapping to fund their activities. These illegal activities may on occasion become so profitable that they replace the group's original focus. In some instances the line between being a terrorist organization with political support and vast resources and an organized criminal group engaging in illicit activities for profit becomes blurred. The greatest threat from criminal terrorism is the theft of nuclear material and its subsequent sale to other terrorist groups that will not hesitate to build and use weapons of mass destruction.

the Privacy and Civil Liberties Board; and the National Counterproliferation Center. The NCTC serves as the primary organization in the U.S. government for analyzing and integrating all intelligence possessed or acquired by the government pertaining to terrorism and counterterrorism, excepting purely domestic counterterrorism information.

Another significant change has been a realignment of the Federal Bureau of Investigation (FBI), the federal government's main law enforcement agency (see Chapter 5 for more on the FBI). The FBI has already announced a reformulation of its priorities, making protecting the United States from terrorist attack its number-one commitment. It is now charged with coordinating intelligence collection with the Border Patrol, the Secret Service, and the CIA. The FBI must also work with and share intelligence with the National Counterterrorism Center (NCTC).

In addition to reorienting the FBI mission, soon after the 2001 attack President Bush proposed the creation of a new cabinet-level agency called the **Department of Homeland Security (DHS)** and assigned it the following mission:

◆ Preventing terrorist attacks within the United States.

◆ Reducing the nation's vulnerability to terrorism.

◆ Minimizing the damage and recovering from attacks that do occur.

The organization and role of the DHS will be discussed further and in greater detail in Chapter 5.

Law enforcement agencies around the country have realigned their resources to combat future terrorist attacks. In response to 9/11, law enforcement agencies have taken a number of steps: increasing the number of personnel engaged in emergency response planning; updating response plans for chemical, biological, or radiological attacks; and reallocating internal resources or increasing departmental spending to focus on terrorism preparedness.[57] The threat of terror attacks has transformed the justice system. Police, courts, and corrections have had to respond to this new threat. How they have done so will be discussed throughout the remainder of the text.

Cyber Crime

Controlling and eliminating cyber crime, the second contemporary challenge facing the justice system, is defined as "any illegal behavior that targets the security of computer systems and/or the data accessed and processed by computer networks."

Why has cyber crime become so important? Information technology (IT) has become an intrinsic part of daily life in most industrialized societies. It is the key to the economic system and will become more important as major industries shift their manufacturing plants to areas of the world where production is much cheaper. IT is responsible for the **globalization** phenomenon, the process of creating transnational markets, politics, and legal systems—in other words, creating a global economy. The Internet, coupled with ever more powerful computers, is now the chosen medium to provide a wide range of global services, ranging from entertainment and communication to research and education.

The cyber age has also generated an enormous amount of revenue. Spending on IT and telecommunications will grow by more than 6 percent each year, soon reaching about $2 trillion.[58] Today, more than 1 billion people are using e-mail, and 240 million are mobile Internet users. Magnifying the importance of the Internet is the fact that many critical infrastructure functions are now being conducted online, ranging from banking to control of shipping on the Mississippi River.[59]

Cyber crime presents a compelling challenge for the criminal justice system because (1) it is rapidly evolving with new schemes being created daily, (2) it is difficult to detect through traditional law enforcement channels, and (3) its control demands that agents of the justice system develop technical skills that match those of the perpetrators.[60] The new computer-based technology allows criminals to operate in a more efficient and effective manner. Cyber thieves now have the luxury of remaining anonymous, living in any part of the planet, conducting their business during the day or in the evening, working alone or in a group, and at the same time reaching a much wider number of potential victims

Department of Homeland Security (DHS)
Federal agency responsible for preventing terrorist attacks within the United States, reducing the nation's vulnerability to terrorism, and minimizing the damage and recovering from attacks that do occur.

globalization
The process of creating transnational markets, politics, and legal systems in order to develop a global economy.

EXHIBIT 1.5
Examples of Computer Fraud

THEFT OF INFORMATION

The unauthorized obtaining of information from a computer ("hacking"), including software that is copied for profit.

THE "SALAMI" FRAUD

With this type of fraud the perpetrator carefully "skims" small sums from the balances of a large number of accounts in order to bypass internal controls and escape detection.

SOFTWARE THEFT

The comparative ease of making copies of computer software has led to a huge illegal market, depriving authors of very significant revenues.

MANIPULATION OF ACCOUNTS/BANKING SYSTEMS

Similar to a "salami" but on a much larger and usually more complex scale. The number of variations is as long as the imagination of the criminal mind.

CORPORATE ESPIONAGE

Trade secrets are stolen by a company's competitors, which can be either domestic or foreign. The goal is to increase the rival company's (or nation's) competitive edge in the global marketplace.

Source: VoGon International (http://www.vogon-international.com/index.htm), accessed on April 22, 2006.

than ever before. No longer is the con artist or criminal entrepreneur limited to fleecing victims in a particular geographic locale; the whole world can be his target. And the technology revolution has opened novel methods for cyber theft—ranging from the unlawful distribution of computer software to Internet security fraud—that heretofore were nonexistent. Not all cyber criminals seek profit; some are intent on causing damage and destroying computer networks for malicious reasons. But the rapid growth of cyber theft schemes now makes them a serious new entry into the world of enterprise crime. Some of the most common methods are set out following.

COMPUTER FRAUD Computer fraud is not a unique offense but rather a common-law crime committed using contemporary technology. Consequently, many computer crimes are prosecuted under such traditional criminal statutes as larceny or fraud. However, not all computer crimes fall under common-law statutes because the property stolen may be intangible—e.g., electronic and/or magnetic impulse. Some of these crimes are listed in Exhibit 1.5.

DISTRIBUTING ILLEGAL SEXUAL MATERIAL The Internet is an ideal venue for selling and distributing obscene material; the computer is an ideal device for storing and viewing pornography. It is difficult to estimate the number of websites featuring sexual content, including nude photos, videos, live sex acts, and web-cam strip sessions among other forms of "adult entertainment."[61] N2H2, a Seattle-based web-filtering company, estimates that the number of pornographic web pages has soared during the past six years and that there are now over 1.3 million sites containing about 260 million pages of erotic content—all hoping to cash in on the billions in revenue spent on Internet porn annually.[62] The number of visits to pornographic sites surpasses those made to Internet search engines; some individual sites report as many as 50 million hits per year.

denial-of-service attack
Extorting money from an Internet service user by threatening to prevent the user from having access to the service.

DENIAL-OF-SERVICE ATTACK A **denial-of-service attack** is characterized as an attempt to extort money from legitimate users of an Internet service by threatening to prevent the user from having access to the service.[63] Examples include attempts to "flood" a computer network with spam or e-mails, thereby preventing legitimate network traffic. Denial of service may also involve attempts to disrupt connections within a computer network, thereby preventing access by authorized users. Retail firms such as Amazon and eBay that rely solely on the net are particularly vulnerable to these attacks, as are offshore gambling sites that have few legal alternatives for protection or reimbursement.

ILLEGAL COPYRIGHT INFRINGEMENT For the past decade, groups of individuals have been working together to illegally obtain software and then "crack" or "rip" its copyright protections before posting it on the Internet for other members of the group to use; this is called **warez**.

Frequently, these newly pirated copies reach the Internet days or weeks before the legitimate product is commercially available. The government has actively pursued members of the warez community, and some have been charged and convicted under the Computer Fraud and Abuse Act (CFAA), which criminalizes accessing computer systems without authorization to obtain information,[64] and the Digital Millennium Copyright Act (DMCA), which makes it a crime to circumvent the antipiracy measures built into most commercial software and also outlaws the manufacture, sale, or distribution of code-cracking devices used to illegally copy software.[65]

Another form of illegal copyright infringement involves file-sharing programs that allow Internet users to download music and other copyrighted material without paying the artists and record producers their rightful royalties.

INTERNET SECURITIES FRAUD Some cyber criminals intentionally use the Internet to manipulate the securities marketplace for profit. Some cyber criminals create websites specifically designed to sell fraudulent securities. To make the offerings look more attractive than they are, assets may be inflated, expected returns overstated, and risks understated. In these schemes, investors are promised abnormally high profits on their investments. No investment is actually made. Another form of securities fraud, *illegal touting*, involves making securities recommendations on the Internet (and elsewhere) and failing to disclose payment for the dissemination of favorable opinions. Section 17(b) of the Securities Act of 1933 requires that paid touters disclose the nature, source, and amount of their compensation. If those who tout stocks fail to disclose their relationship with the company, information misleads investors into believing that the speaker is objective and credible rather than bought and paid for.

ETAILING FRAUD New fraud schemes are evolving to reflect the fact that billions of dollars of goods are sold on the Internet each year. **Etailing fraud** can involve both illegally buying and selling merchandise on the net.

Some etailing scams involve failure to deliver on promised purchases or services, whereas others involve the substitution of cheaper or used material for higher-quality purchases. So, for example, a person buys expensive jewelry on an Internet site and receives a somewhat less valuable piece than she expected. The online auction site eBay is fertile ground for such fraud.[66]

IDENTITY THEFT **Identity theft** occurs when a person uses the Internet to steal someone's identity and/or impersonate the victim to open a new credit card account or conduct some other financial transaction. It is a type of cyber crime that has grown at surprising rates over the past few years.[67]

Some identity thieves create false e-mails and/or websites that look legitimate but are designed to gain illegal access to a victim's personal information; this is called **phishing** (also known as *carding* and *spoofing*).

Some phishers send out e-mails that look like they come from a credit card company or online store, telling victims about a "problem" with their credit account or balance. To fix the problem and update their account, they are asked

warez
The efforts of organized groups to download and sell copyrighted software in violation of its license.

Interested in cyber crime? Go to the the Internet Crime Complaint Center (IC3). You can reach this site by going to the Siegel/Senna Introduction to Criminal Justice 11e website: www.thomsonedu.com/criminaljustice/siegel.

etailing fraud
Illegally buying or selling merchandise on the Internet.

identity theft
Using the Internet to steal someone's identity and/or impersonate the victim in order to conduct illicit transactions such as committing fraud using the victim's name and identity.

phishing (also known as carding and spoofing)
Illegally acquiring personal information, such as bank passwords and credit card numbers, by masquerading as a trustworthy person or business in what appears to be an official electronic communication, such as an e-mail or an instant message. The term *phishing* comes from the lures used to "fish" for financial information and passwords.

EXHIBIT 1.6

Cyber Vandalism

♦ *Computer viruses* are a type of malicious software program (also called *malware*) that disrupts or destroys existing programs and networks, causing them to perform the task for which the virus was designed. The virus is then spread from one computer to another when a user sends out an infected file through e-mail, a network, or a disk.

♦ *Computer worms* are similar to viruses but use computer networks or the Internet to self-replicate and "send themselves" to other users, generally via e-mail and without the aid of the operator.

♦ *Trojan horses* look like benign applications but contain illicit codes that can damage the system's operations. Although trojan horses do not replicate themselves like viruses, they can be just as destructive.

♦ *Logic bombs* are programs that secretly attach to computer systems. They monitor the network's work output and wait for a particular signal such as a date to appear. Also called a *slag code*,

it is a type of delayed-action virus that may be set off when a program user makes certain input that sets it in motion. A logic bomb may cause a variety of problems, ranging from displaying or printing a spurious message to deleting or corrupting data.

♦ *Spam* is an unsolicited advertisement or promotional material, and it typically comes in the form of an unwanted e-mail message; *spammers* use electronic communications to send unsolicited messages in bulk.

♦ *Web defacement* occurs when computer hackers damage or deface another person's website by inserting or substituting codes that expose visitors to misleading or provocative information. Defacement can range from installing humorous graffiti to sabotaging or corrupting the site.

Sources: Heather Jacobson and Rebecca Green, "Computer Crimes," *American Criminal Law Review* 39 (2002): 272–326; Symantec, Internet Security Threat Report, 2006 (https://enterprise.symantec.com/enterprise/whitepaper.cfm?id=2238).

to submit their name, address, phone numbers, personal information, credit card account numbers, and Social Security number.

CYBER VANDALISM Some cyber criminals may not be motivated by greed or profit but by the desire for revenge, destruction, and/or other malicious intent. Their motivations vary:

♦ Some are seeking revenge for some perceived wrong.

♦ Some desire to exhibit their technical prowess and superiority.

♦ Some wish to highlight the vulnerability of computer security systems.

♦ Some desire to spy on other people's private financial and personal information ("computer voyeurism").

♦ Some want to destroy computer security because they believe in a philosophy of open access to all systems and programs.

Exhibit 1.6 illustrates the various forms that cyber vandalism can take.

Controlling Cyber Crime

The proliferation of cyber crime and its cost to the economy have created the need for new laws and enforcement processes specifically aimed at controlling its new and emerging formulations. Because technology evolves so rapidly, the enforcement challenges are particularly vexing. Numerous organizations have been set up to provide training and support for law enforcement agents. In addition, new federal and state laws have been aimed at particular areas of high-tech crimes.

Congress has treated computer-related crime as a distinct federal offense since the passage of the Counterfeit Access Device and Computer Fraud and Abuse Law in 1984.[68] The 1984 act protected classified U.S. defense and foreign relations information, financial institution and consumer reporting agency files, and access to computers operated for the government. The act was supplemented in 1996 by the National Information Infrastructure Protection Act (NIIPA), which significantly broadened the scope of the law. Since then, legislation has evolved with the scope of cyber crime in an ongoing effort to protect the public from this new breed of offense. For example, before October 30, 1998, when the Identity Theft and Assumption Act of 1998 became law, there was no federal statute that made identity theft a crime. Today, federal prosecutors are making substantial use of the 1998 statute and are actively prosecuting cases of identity theft.[69] The states have followed suit, and at present, all states except Vermont have passed laws regulating identity theft.

To enforce these laws, the federal government is now operating a number of organizations to control cyber fraud. One approach is to create working groups that coordinate the activities of numerous agencies involved in investigating cyber crime. For example, the Interagency Telemarketing and Internet Fraud Working Group brings together representatives of numerous U.S. attorneys' offices, the FBI, the Secret Service, the Postal Inspection Service, the Federal Trade Commission, the Securities and Exchange Commission, and other law enforcement and regulatory agencies to share information about trends and patterns in Internet fraud schemes.[70]

Specialized enforcement agencies have been created. The Internet Fraud Complaint Center, based in Fairmont, West Virginia, is run by the FBI and the National White-Collar Crime Center. It brings together about 1,000 state and local law enforcement officials and regulators. Its goal is to analyze fraud-related complaints in order to find distinct patterns, develop information on particular cases, and send investigative packages to law enforcement authorities in the jurisdictions that appear likely to have the greatest investigative interest in the matter. Today, the center receives more than 200,000 complaints per year.[71] Over the last several years, law enforcement has made remarkable strides in dealing with identity theft as a crime problem.

ThomsonNOW* Improve your grade on the exam with Personalized Study! For reinforcement resources and a mastery check of terrorism and cyber crime, go to www.thomsonedu.com/thomsonnow.

◆ ETHICS IN CRIMINAL JUSTICE

Cyber crime and terrorism, as well as the enforcement of "traditional" crimes such as murder and rape, present ethical challenges for the criminal justice system. Both the general public and criminal justice professionals are concerned with the application of ethics.[72] Both would like every police officer on the street, every district attorney in court, and every correctional administrator in prison to be able to discern what is right, proper, and moral; to be committed to ethical standards; and to apply equal and fair justice. These demands are difficult because justice system personnel are often forced to work in an environment where moral ambiguity is the norm. Should a police officer be forced to arrest, a prosecutor charge, and a correctional official punish a woman who for many years was the victim of domestic abuse and in desperation retaliated against her abusive spouse? Who is the victim here, and who is the aggressor? And what about the parent who attacks the man who has sexually abused her young child? Should she be prosecuted as a felon? But what happens if the parent mistakenly attacks and injures the wrong person? Can a clear line be drawn between righteous retribution and vigilante justice? As students of justice, we are concerned with identifying the behavioral standards that should govern each of the elements of justice. And if these can be identified, is it possible to find ways to spread these standards to police, court, and correctional agencies around the nation?

Ethics in criminal justice is an especially important topic today, considering the power granted to those who work in, operate, and control the justice system. We rely on the justice system to exert power over people's lives and to be society's instrument of social control, so we thereby grant the system and its agents the authority to deny people their personal liberty on a routine basis. A police officer's ability to arrest and use force, a judge's power to sentence, and a correctional administrator's ability to punish an inmate give them considerable personal power, which must governed by ethical considerations. Without ethical decision making, it is possible that individual civil rights will suffer and personal liberties guaranteed by the U.S. Constitution will be trampled upon. The need for an ethical criminal justice system is further enhanced by cyber-age advances in record keeping and data recording. Agents of the criminal justice system now have immediate access to our most personal information, ranging from arrest record to medical history. Issues of privacy and confidentiality, which can have enormous economic, social, and political consequences, are now more critical than ever.

Ethical issues transcend all elements of the justice system. Yet each branch has specific issues that shape its ethical standards.

Ethics and Law Enforcement

Ethical behavior is particularly important in law enforcement because, quite simply, police officers have the authority to deprive people of their liberty. And in carrying out their daily activities, they also have the right to use physical and even deadly force.

Depriving people of liberty and using force are not the only police behaviors that require ethical consideration. Police officers maintain considerable discretion when they choose whom to investigate and how far the investigation should go and how much effort is required—e.g., undercover work, listening devices, surveillance. While carrying out their duties, police officers must be responsive to the public's demand for protection and at the same time remain sensitive to the rights and liberties of those they must deter and/or control. In this capacity, they serve as the interface between the power of the state and the citizens it governs. This duality creates many ethical dilemmas. Consider the following:

1. Should law enforcement agents target groups whom they suspect are heavily involved in crime and violence, or does this practice lead to racial/ethnic profiling? Is it unethical for a security agent to pay closer attention to a young Arab male getting on an airline flight than she gives to a clean-cut American soldier from upstate New York? After all, there have been no terrorist activities among Army personnel, and the 9/11 terrorists were of Arab descent. But don't forget that Tim McVeigh, who grew up in rural Pendleton, New York, and spent more than three years in the Army, went on to become the Oklahoma City Bomber. How can police officers balance their need to protect public security with the ethical requirement that they protect citizens' legal rights?

2. Should police officers tell the truth even if it means that a guilty person will go free? Let's say that a police officer stops a car for a traffic violation and searches it illegally. He finds a weapon used in a particularly heinous shooting in which three children were killed. Would it be ethical for the officer to lie on the witness stand and say the gun was lying on the car seat in plain sight (thereby rendering its seizure legal and proper), or should he tell the truth and risk having the charges dismissed, leaving the offender free to kill again?

3. Should police officers be loyal to their peers even when they know they have violated the law? A new officer soon becomes aware that his partner is taking gratuities from local gangsters in return for looking the other way and allowing their prostitution and bookmaking operations to flourish. Should the rookie file a complaint and turn in his partner? Will she be labeled a "rat" and lose the respect of her fellow officers? After all, gambling and prostitution are not violent crimes and do not really hurt anyone. Or do they?

How can law enforcement officers be aided in making ethical decisions? Various national organizations have produced model codes of conduct that can serve as behavioral guides. One well-known document created by the International Association of Chiefs of Police says in part:[73]

> As a Law Enforcement Officer my fundamental duty is to serve mankind; to safeguard lives and property; to protect the innocent against deception, the weak against oppression or intimidation, and the peaceful against violence or disorder; and to respect the Constitutional Rights of all men to liberty, equality and justice. . . .

Ethics and the Court Process

Ethical concerns do not stop with an arrest. As an officer of the court and the "people's attorney," the prosecutor must seek justice for all parties in a criminal matter and should not merely be hunting a conviction. To be fair, prosecutors must share evidence with the defense, not use scare tactics or intimidation, and represent the public interest. It would be inexcusable and illegal for prosecutors to suppress critical evidence, a practice that might mean that the guilty walk free and the innocent are convicted.

Prosecutorial ethics become tested when the dual role of a prosecutor causes her to experience role conflict. On the one hand, she represents the people and has an obligation to present evidence, uphold the law, and obtain convictions as vigorously as possible. In the adversary system, it is the prosecutor who takes the side of the victims and upon whom they count for justice.

But as a fair and impartial officer of the court, the prosecutor must oversee the investigation of crime and make sure that all aspects of the investigation meet constitutional standards. If during the investigation it appears that the police have violated the constitutional rights of suspects—for example, by extracting an illegal confession or conducting an illegal search—then the prosecutor has an ethical obligation to take whatever action is necessary and appropriate to remedy legal or technical errors, even if it means rejecting a case in which the defendant's rights have been violated. Moreover, the canon of legal ethics in most states forbids the prosecutor from pursuing charges when there is no probable cause and mandates that all evidence that might mitigate guilt or reduce the punishment be turned over to the defense.

THE DEFENSE ATTORNEY As an officer of the court, along with the judge, prosecutors, and other trial participants, the defense attorney seeks to uncover the basic facts and elements of the criminal act. In this dual capacity of being both a defensive advocate and an officer of the court, the attorney is often confronted with conflicting obligations to his client and profession. Suppose, for example, a client confides that she is planning to commit a crime. What are the defense attorney's ethical responsibilities in this case? Obviously, the lawyer would have to counsel the client to obey the law; if the lawyer assisted the client in engaging in illegal behavior, the lawyer would be subject to charges of unprofessional conduct and even criminal liability.

Ethics and Corrections

Ethical issues do not stop once a defendant has been convicted. The ethical issues in punishment are too vast to discuss here, but a few include the following:

1. Is it fair and ethical to execute a criminal? Can capital punishment ever be considered as a moral choice?

2. Should people be given different punishments for the same criminal law violation? Is it fair and just when some convicted murderers and rapists receive probation only for their crimes and others are sentenced to prison for the same offense?

3. Is it fair to grant leniency to criminals who agree to testify against their co-conspirators and therefore allow them to benefit for their perfidy while

Interested in criminal justice ethics? Check out the American Civil Liberties Union website. To reach it, go to the Siegel/Senna Introduction to Criminal Justice 11e website: www.thomsonedu.com/criminaljustice/siegel.

ThomsonNOW™ Improve your grade on the exam with Personalized Study! For reinforcement resources and a mastery check of ethics in criminal justice, go to www.thomsonedu.com/thomsonnow.

others not given the opportunity to "squeal" are forced to bear the full brunt of the law?

4. Should some criminal inmates be granted early release because they can persuade the parole board they have been rehabilitated while others, not as glib, convincing, or well spoken, are forced to serve their entire sentence behind bars?

Ethics are also challenged by the discretion that is afforded to correctional workers and administrators. Discretion is involved when a correctional officer decides to report an inmate for disorderly conduct, which might jeopardize the inmate's future parole. And although the U.S. Supreme Court has issued many rulings relating to prisoners' rights, the Justices are not at the scene of the prison to make sure that their mandates are carried out in an orderly fashion.

Correctional officers have significant coercive power over offenders. They are under a legal and professional obligation not to use unnecessary force or to take advantage of inmate powerlessness. Examples of unethical behavior would be an officer who beats an inmate or a psychologist who coerces sex from an inmate. These are abuses of power, and the possibility for them exists because of the powerlessness of the offender relative to the correctional professional. Sensitivity to ethical issues involves the recognition and respect that one has for this element of the profession.

Ethical considerations transcend all elements of the justice system. Making ethical decisions is an increasingly important task in a society that is becoming more diverse, pluralistic, and complex every day.

ETHICAL CHALLENGES IN CRIMINAL JUSTICE: A WRITING ASSIGNMENT

Some experts believe that the justice system could operate more effectively if drugs were legalized and their trade controlled so that they could not fall into the hands of adolescents. This would be similar to the way we now regulate the sale of alcohol and cigarettes. Write an essay addressing this issue. Remember to consider such topics as the consequences of regulating the sale of drugs: If juveniles, criminals, and members of other at-risk groups were forbidden to buy drugs, who would be the customers? Noncriminal, nonabusing, middle-aged adults? And would not those adolescents prohibited from legally buying drugs create an underground market almost as vast as the one for illegal alcohol?

Doing Research on the Web

Before you write your essay, you might want to go to the Students Against Drunk Driving (SADD) website. To reach this site, go to the Siegel/Senna Introduction to Criminal Justice 11e website: www.thomsonedu.com/criminaljustice/siegel.

The Drug Policy Alliance is the nation's leading organization working to end the war on drugs. It envisions new drug policies based on "science, compassion, health and human rights and a just society in which the fears, prejudices and punitive prohibitions of today are no more." Visit its website by going to the Siegel/Senna Introduction to Criminal Justice 11e website: www.thomsonedu.com/criminaljustice/siegel.

To view the government's take on drug control, examine the website of the Office of National Drug Control Policy. You can reach this site by going to the Siegel/Senna Introduction to Criminal Justice 11e website: www.thomsonedu.com/criminaljustice/siegel.

SUMMARY

◆ The United States has experienced crime throughout its history.

◆ In the old west, justice was administered by legendary lawmen such as Wyatt Earp. There was little in the way of a formal criminal justice system.

◆ The term *criminal justice* became prominent around 1967, when the President's Commission on Law Enforcement and the Administration of Justice began a study of the nation's crime problem. Since then, a field of study has emerged that uses knowledge from various disciplines in an attempt to understand what causes people to commit crimes and how to deal with the crime problem. Criminal justice, then, consists of the study of crime and of the agencies concerned with its prevention and control.

◆ The contemporary criminal justice system functions as a cooperative effort among the primary agencies—police, courts, and corrections.

◆ The criminal justice process consists of the steps the offender takes from the initial investigation through trial, sentencing, and appeal.

◆ In many instances, the criminal justice system works informally to expedite the disposal of cases. Criminal acts that are very serious or notorious may receive the full complement of criminal justice processes, from arrest to trial. However, less serious cases are often settled when a bargain is reached between the prosecution and the defense. The process has been described by Samuel Walker as the "wedding cake" model of justice.

◆ There are a number of different perspectives on criminal justice today.

◆ The crime control perspective is oriented toward deterring criminal behavior and incapacitating serious criminal offenders.

◆ The rehabilitation model views the justice system as a treatment agency focused on helping offenders. Counseling programs are stressed over punishment and deterrence strategies.

◆ The due process perspective sees the justice system as a legal process. The concern here is that every defendant receive the full share of legal rights granted under law.

◆ The justice model is concerned with making the system equitable. The arrest, sentencing, and correctional process should be structured so that every person is treated equally.

◆ The nonintervention model is concerned about stigma and helping defendants avoid the net of justice. Advocates call for the least intrusive methods possible.

◆ The restorative justice model focuses on finding peaceful and humanitarian solutions to crime.

◆ The various perspectives on justice are visible in the way the nation has sought to control substance abuse. Some programs rely on a strict crime control policy featuring the detection and arrest of drug traffickers, whereas others seek the rehabilitation of known offenders. The justice model has influenced the development of sentencing policies that emphasize mandatory punishments. Another approach is to legalize drugs, thereby reducing abusers' incentive to commit crimes, a policy that reflects the nonintervention perspective.

◆ The criminal justice system is now responding to two new threats: cyber crime and terrorism.

◆ Federal agencies such as the FBI are reorienting their priorities to fight terrorists.

◆ There are many ethical issues facing agents of the justice system.

KEY TERMS

criminal justice system, 4
slave patrols, 4
Law Enforcement Assistance
    Administration (LEAA), 7
social control, 8
legislature, 8
prison, 9
jail, 9
probation, 9
parole, 10
arrest, 12
arrest warrant, 13
in presence requirement, 14
probable cause hearing, 14
nolle prosequi, 14

courtroom work group, 20
wedding cake model of justice, 21
crime control perspective, 24
profile (profiling), 25
Miranda rights, 25
exclusionary rule, 25
rehabilitation perspective, 25
due process perspective, 26
nonintervention perspective, 27
decriminalization, 27
victimless crime, 27
deinstitutionalization, 27
pretrial diversion, 27
widening the net, 27
restorative justice, 28

terrorism, 30
cyber crime, 30
cyber terrorism, 30
Al-Qaeda, 31
Director of National Intelligence
    (DNI), 31
Department of Homeland Security
    (DHS), 33
globalization, 33
denial-of-service attack, 34
warez, 35
etailing fraud, 35
identity theft, 35
phishing, 35

ThomsonNOW™   Maximize your study time by using ThomsonNOW's diagnostic study plan to help you review this chapter. The Study Plan will

◆   help you identify areas on which you should concentrate;

◆   provide interactive exercises to help you master the chapter concepts; and

◆   provide a post-test to confirm you are ready to move on to the next chapter.

CRITICAL THINKING QUESTIONS

1. Which criminal behavior patterns pose the greatest threat to the public? Should the justice system devote greater resources to combating these crimes? If so, which crime patterns should be deemphasized?

2. Describe the differences between the formal and informal justice systems. Is it fair to treat some offenders informally?

3. What are the layers of the criminal justice "wedding cake"? Give an example of a crime for each layer.

4. What are the basic elements of each model or perspective on justice? Which best represents your own point of view?

5. How would each perspective on criminal justice consider the use of the death penalty as a sanction for first-degree murder?

6. Can the criminal justice system effectively deal with cyber crime and/or terrorism, or should new agencies be created that specialize in these problems?

NOTES

1. James Risen and Eric Lichtblau, "Bush Lets U.S. Spy on Callers Without Courts," *New York Times*, December 16, 2005.

2. Lowell Bergman, Eric Lichtblau, Scott Shane, and Don Van Natta, Jr., "Domestic Surveillance: The Program; Spy Agency Data After Sept. 11 Led F.B.I. to Dead Ends," *New York Times*, January 17, 2006, p. 1.

3. "Authorization for Use of Military Force Against Iraq Resolution of 2002," Pub. L. 107–243, Oct. 16, 2002, 116 Stat. 1498 (http://www4.law.cornell.edu/uscode/html/uscode50/usc_sec_50_0 0001541—000-notes.html).

4. This section leans heavily on Ted Robert Gurr, "Historical Trends in Violent Crime: A Critical Review of the Evidence," in *Crime and Justice: An Annual Review of Research*, vol. 3, ed. Michael Tonry and Norval Morris (Chicago: University of Chicago Press, 1981); Richard Maxwell Brown, "Historical Patterns of American Violence," in *Violence in America: Historical and Comparative Perspectives*, ed. Hugh Davis Graham and Ted Robert Gurr (Beverly Hills, Calif.: Sage, 1979).

5. Sally Hadden, *Slave Patrols: Law and Violence in Virginia and the Carolinas* (Cambridge, Mass.: Harvard University Press, 2001).

6. Cesare Beccaria, *On Crimes and Punishments* (1764; reprint, Indianapolis: Bobbs-Merrill, 1963).

7. Samuel Walker, *Popular Justice* (New York: Oxford University Press, 1980).

8. Visit the commission's website (http://www.chicagocrimecommission.org/about.html), accessed on May 2, 2006.

9. Lexis/Nexis, "Records of the Wickersham Commission on Law Observance and Enforcement" (http://www.lexisnexis.com/academic/2upa/Allh/WickershamComm.asp).

10. For an insightful analysis of this effort, see Samuel Walker, "Origins of the Contemporary Criminal Justice Paradigm: The American Bar Foundation Survey, 1953–1969," *Justice Quarterly* 9 (1992): 47–76.

11. President's Commission on Law Enforcement and the Administration of Justice, *The Challenge of Crime in a Free Society* (Washington, D.C.: Government Printing Office, 1967).

12. See Public Law 90–351, Title I—Omnibus Crime Control Safe Streets Act of 1968, 90th Congress, June 19, 1968.

13. For a review, see Kevin Wright, "Twenty-Two Years of Federal Investment in Criminal Justice Research: The National Institute of Justice, 1968–1989," *Journal of Criminal Justice* 22 (1994): 27–40.

14. Matthew J. Hickman and Brian A. Reaves, *Local Police Departments 2003* (Washington, D.C.: Bureau of Justice Statistics, 2006).

15. Sara Steen, Rodney Engen, and Randy Gainey, "Images of Danger and Culpability: Racial Stereotyping, Case Processing, and Criminal Sentencing," *Criminology* 43 (2005): 435–68; Stephanie Bontrager, William Bales, and Ted Chiricos, "Race, Ethnicity, Threat, and the Labeling of Convicted Felons," *Criminology* 43 (2005): 589–622.

16. *Riverside County v. McLaughlin*, 500 U.S. 44, 111 S.Ct. 1661, 114 L.Ed.2d 49 (1991).

17. Middlesex SS Superior Court Criminal No. 97–0433, Commonwealth Memorandum, and *Order v. Louise Woodward*, 1997.

18. Herbert L. Packer, *The Limits of the Criminal Sanction* (Stanford, Calif.: Stanford University Press, 1975), p. 21.

19. Jacob Perez, *Tracking Offenders, 1990* (Washington, D.C.: Bureau of Justice Statistics, 1994), p. 2.

20. David W. Neubauer, *America's Courts and the Criminal Justice System* (Pacific Grove, Calif.: Brooks/Cole, 1996), pp. 72–75.

21. Douglas Smith, "The Plea Bargaining Controversy," *Journal of Criminal Law and Criminology* 77 (1986): 949–67.

22. Samuel Walker, *Sense and Nonsense About Crime* (Belmont, Calif.: Wadsworth, 1985).

23. Malcolm Feeley, *The Process Is the Punishment* (New York: Russell Sage, 1979).

24. James Q. Wilson, *Thinking About Crime* (New York: Vintage, 1983).

25. Ibid., p. 128.

26. Vanessa Barker, "The Politics of Punishing," *Punishment & Society* 8 (2006): 5–32.

27. John DiIulio, *No Escape: The Future of American Corrections* (New York: Basic Books, 1991).

28. Richard Timothy Coupe and Laurence Blake, "The Effects of Patrol Workloads and Response Strength on Arrests at Burglary Emergencies," *Journal of Criminal Justice* 33 (2005): 239–55.

29. Paul Cassell, "How Many Criminals Has Miranda Set Free?" *Wall Street Journal,* March 1, 1995, p. A15.

30. Jon Gould and Stephen Mastrofski, "Suspect Searches: Assessing Police Behavior Under the U.S. Constitution," *Criminology & Public Policy* 3 (2004): 315–62.

31. Dennis Rosenbaum and Gordon Hanson, "Assessing the Effects of School-Based Drug Education: A Six-Year Multilevel Analysis of Project DARE," *Journal of Research in Crime and Delinquency* 35 (1998): 381–412.

32. Karen Parker and Patricia McCall, "Structural Conditions and Racial Homicide Patterns: A Look at the Multiple Disadvantages in Urban Areas," *Criminology* 37 (1999): 447–48.

33. Denise Gottfredson, "Participation in Drug Treatment Court and Time to Rearrest," *Justice Quarterly* 21 (2004): 637–58.

34. John Hepburn, "Recidivism Among Drug Offenders Following Exposure to Treatment," *Criminal Justice Policy Review* 16 (2005): 237–59.

35. Francis Cullen, John Paul Wright, and Mitchell Chamlin, "Social Support and Social Reform: A Progressive Crime Control Agenda," *Crime and Delinquency* 45 (1999): 188–207.

36. Jane Sprott, "Are Members of the Public Tough on Crime? The Dimensions of Public 'Punitiveness,'" *Journal of Criminal Justice* 27 (1999): 467–74.

37. Packer, *The Limits of the Criminal Sanction,* p. 175.

38. "DNA Testing Has Exonerated 28 Prison Inmates, Study Finds," *Criminal Justice Newsletter,* June 17, 1996, p. 2.

39. Caitlin Lovinger, "Death Row's Living Alumni," *New York Times,* August 22, 1999, p. 1.

40. Talia Roitberg Harmon and William S. Lofquist. "Too Late for Luck: A Comparison of Post-Furman Exonerations and Executions of the Innocent," *Crime and Delinquency* 51 (2005): 498–520.

41. Eric Stewart, Ronald Simons, Rand Conger, and Laura Scaramella, "Beyond the Interactional Relationship Between Delinquency and Parenting Practices: The Contribution of Legal Sanctions," *Journal of Research in Crime and Delinquency* 39 (2002): 36–60.

42. Cassia Spohn and David Holleran, "The Effect of Imprisonment on Recidivism Rates of Felony Offenders: A Focus on Drug Offenders," *Criminology* 40 (2002): 329–59.

43. *Doe v. Pryor M.D. Ala,* Civ. No. 99-T-730-N, J. Thompson, August 16, 1999.

44. This section is based on Paula M. Ditton and Doris James Wilson, *Truth in Sentencing in State Prisons* (Washington, D.C.: Bureau of Justice Statistics, 1999).

45. Herbert Bianchi, *Justice as Sanctuary* (Bloomington: Indiana University Press, 1994); Nils Christie, "Conflicts as Property," *British Journal of Criminology* 17 (1977): 1–15; L. Hulsman, "Critical Criminology and the Concept of Crime," *Contemporary Crises* 10 (1986): 63–80.

46. Larry Tifft, "Foreword," in Dennis Sullivan, *The Mask of Love* (Port Washington, N.Y.: Kennikat Press, 1980), p. 6.

47. Robert Coates, Mark Umbreit, and Betty Vos, "Responding to Hate Crimes Through Restorative Justice Dialogue," *Contemporary Justice Review* 9 (2006): 7–21; Kathleen Daly and Julie Stubbs, "Feminist Engagement with Restorative Justice," *Theoretical Criminology* 10 (2006): 9–28.

48. Christopher Cooper, "Patrol Police Officer Conflict Resolution Processes," *Journal of Criminal Justice* 25 (1997): 87–101.

49. United States State Department, "Country Reports on Terrorism April 2005" (www.state.gov/documents/organization/45313.pdf), accessed on July 12, 2005.

50. Title 22 of the United States Code section 2656f(d) (1999).

51. Thomas P. M. Barnett, *The Pentagon's New Map: War and Peace in the Twenty-First Century*. (New York: Putnam, 2004), pp. 43–46.

52. Michael Scott Doran, "Somebody Else's Civil War," *Foreign Affairs* 81 (January–February 2002): 22–25; Bruce Hoffman, "Change and Continuity in Terrorism," *Studies in Conflict and Terrorism* 24 (2001).

53. Ian Lesser, Bruce Hoffman, John Arquilla, David Ronfeldt, and Michele Zanini, *Countering the New Terrorism* (Washington, D.C.: Rand, 1999); Jessica Stern, *The Ultimate Terrorists* (Cambridge, Mass.: Harvard University Press, 1999).

54. Doran, "Somebody Else's Civil War"; Hoffman, "Change and Continuity in Terrorism."

55. Andrew Chen and Thomas Siems, "Effects of Terrorism on Global Capital Markets," *European Journal of Political Economy* 20 (2004): 349–56.

56. Sanjeev Gupta, Benedict Clements, Rina Bhattacharya, and Shamit Chakravarti, "Fiscal Consequences of Armed Conflict and Terrorism in Low- and Middle-Income Countries," *European Journal of Political Economy* 20 (2004): 403–21.

57. Rand Corporation, "How Prepared Are State and Local Law Enforcement for Terrorism?" (www.rand.org/publications/RB/RB9093), accessed on June 28, 2005.

58. Ed Frauenheim, "IDC: Cyberterror and Other Prophecies," CNET News.com, December 12, 2002, accessed on August 14, 2005.

59. Giles Trendle, "An E-Jihad Against Government?" *EGOV Monitor,* September 2002.

60. Statement of Michael A. Vatis, Director, National Infrastructure Protection Center, Federal Bureau of Investigation, on Cybercrime before the Senate Judiciary Committee, Criminal Justice Oversight Subcommittee and House Judiciary Committee, Crime Subcommittee, Washington, D.C., February 29, 2000 (www.cybercrime.gov/vatis.htm), accessed on July 12, 2005.

61. Andreas Philaretou, "Sexuality and the Internet," *Journal of Sex Research* 42 (2005): 180–81.

62. N2H2 communication (http://www.n2h2.com/index.php).

63. This section relies heavily on "CERT® Coordination Center Denial of Service Attacks" (http://www.cert.org/tech_tips/denial_of_service.html), accessed on September 8, 2005.

64. The Computer Fraud and Abuse Act (CFAA), 18 U.S.C. §1030 (1998).

65. The Digital Millennium Copyright Act, Public Law 105-304 (1998).

66. Saul Hansell, "U.S. Tally in Online-Crime Sweep: 150 Charged," *New York Times,* August 27, 2004, p. C1.

67. These sections rely on "Phishing Activity Trends Report," June 2005, Anti-Phishing Working Group (http://www.ncjrs.org/spotlight/identity_theft/publications.html#phishing), retrieved August 30, 2005; "Special Report of 'Phishing,'" 2004, U.S. Department of Justice Criminal Division (http://www.ncjrs.org/spotlight/identity_theft/publications.html#phishing), retrieved on August 30, 2005.

68. Public Law 98-473, Title H, Chapter XXI, [sections] 2102(a), 98 Stat. 1837, 2190 (1984).

69. Heather Jacobson and Rebecca Green, "Computer Crimes," *American Criminal Law Review* 39 (2002): 273–326; Identity Theft and Assumption Act of 1998 (18 U.S.C. S 1028(a)(7)).

70. Bruce Swartz, Deputy Assistant General, Criminal Division, Justice Department, "Internet Fraud Testimony Before the House Energy and Commerce Committee," May 23, 2001.

71. "IC3 Annual Internet Fraud Report, January 1, 2004–December 31, 2004" (http://www.ifccfbi.gov/strategy/2004_IC3Report.pdf).

72. This section leans heavily on Jocelyn M. Pollock, *Ethics in Crime and Justice, Dilemmas and Decisions,* 4th ed. (Belmont, Calif.: Wadsworth, 2004).

73. International Association of Chiefs of Police (2005).

The Nature and Extent of Crime

Chapter Objectives

After reading this chapter, you should be able to:
1. Name the three major sources of crime data.
2. Know the similarities and differences among the Uniform Crime Reports, National Crime Victimization Survey, and self-report data.
3. Recognize the problems associated with each data form.
4. Describe the factors that explain the rise and fall of crime rates in the United States.
5. Discuss crime trends around the world.
6. Recognize that there are stable patterns in the crime rate.
7. Describe the ecological patterns in crime.
8. Discuss the social, gender, age, and racial differences in the crime rate.
9. Argue the pro and con positions on gun control.
10. Identify the factors that produce chronic offenders.
11. Explain how chronic offending has influenced crime policy.

©Erik S. Lesser/Getty Images

*O*n May 31, 2003, Eric Rudolph was arrested behind a grocery store in rural western North Carolina after five years on the run. He was accused of detonating a bomb outside a Birmingham, Alabama, abortion clinic on January 29, 1998, killing a police officer and critically injuring a nurse. He was also charged with setting off a bomb that killed one person and injured 150 others in a park in downtown Atlanta, Georgia, during the 1996 Olympics. There is also evidence that Rudolph was involved in the 1997 bombings of a gay nightclub and a building that housed an abortion clinic.

Rudolph came under suspicion when someone saw a man believed to be Rudolph leaving the scene of the Birmingham bombing. A truck registered to Rudolph was spotted moments later. In the days following the bombing, law enforcement agents searched a storage locker rented by Rudolph and found nails like those in the devices used to bomb the clinic and an Atlanta building that housed an abortion clinic. Similarities also linked the nails to the bomb set off during the Olympics.

Rudolph's crime spree was motivated by his extreme political beliefs. He was a member of a white supremacist group called the Army of God. His relatives told authorities that Rudolph was an ardent anti-Semite who claimed that the Holocaust never happened and that the Jews control the media and the government. Ironically, soon after he was arrested, the court appointed attorney Richard S. Jaffe, a practicing Jew, to lead Rudolph's defense team.[1] On April 8, 2005, Rudolph agreed to plead guilty in all the attacks he was accused of committing in order to avoid the death penalty; he was sentenced to four consecutive life terms.[2] ◆

The Rudolph case illustrates the undercurrent of violence that is still all too common on the American landscape. But although the Rudolph case is a shocking reminder of the damage that a single person can inflict on the public, the overall crime rate seems to be in decline. And although the United States has the reputation of being an extremely violent nation, violence rates here are dropping while they are increasing abroad. This chapter reviews major crime problems facing the justice system. It also discusses how crime is measured and what we know about criminal conduct. What causes the rise and fall in crime rates? Who commits crime, and what are the crime patterns that the criminal justice system must confront on a daily basis?

◆ CRIME IN THE UNITED STATES

Crimes such as the ones committed by Eric Rudolph have become an all-too-familiar and disturbing aspect of life in the United States. Both the poor and the affluent engage in criminal activity. Crime cuts across racial, class, and gender lines. It involves some acts that shock the conscience such as Rudolph's violent spree, but others may seem to be relatively harmless human foibles. Some involve strangers, so-called predatory criminals who care little for the lives of their victims, whereas others—including date rape and spouse, child, elderly, and sexual abuse—involve family members, friends, or trusted associates. Such acts are referred to as intimate violence.

In Chapter 1 we discussed terrorism and cyber crime, two newly emerging crimes that challenge the justice system. Although these new crimes represent critical issues, the criminal justice system must still confront traditional criminal conduct involving violence, theft, and breaches of the public order. What are some of the most significant of these crimes that concern most Americans?

Violent Crime

Americans are bombarded with television news stories and newspaper articles featuring grisly accounts of violent gangs, serial murder, child abuse, and rape. Although rates of violent crime have declined significantly, violence rates in the United States still exceed those of most other industrialized nations. What are the forms of violence that most people fear?

GANG VIOLENCE After remaining dormant for many years, organized youth gangs today terrorize neighborhoods in urban communities around the United States. From Boston to Los Angeles, gangs have become actively involved in drug distribution, extortion, and violence.

Whereas youth gangs once relied on group loyalty and emotional involvement with neighborhood turf to encourage membership, modern gangs seem more motivated by the quest for drug profits and street power. It is common for drug cliques to form within gangs or for established drug dealers to make use of "gang bangers" for protection and distribution services. As a consequence, gang-related killings have become so commonplace that the term *gang homicide* is now recognized as a separate and unique category of criminal behavior.[3]

At one time, gang activity was restricted to the nation's largest cities, especially Philadelphia, New York, Detroit, Los Angeles, and Chicago. These cities still have large gang populations, but today smaller and medium-size cities—such as Cleveland and Columbus, Ohio, and Milwaukee, Wisconsin—have also been the locus of gang activity. One reason that gang populations are swelling is that established urban gang members migrate to other locales to set up local branches.

The most recent surveys indicate that active in the United States are more than 24,000 gangs, with more than 760,000 gang members. About 80 percent of larger cities with a population of more than 50,000 reported persistent gang activity; towns (28 percent) and rural areas (12 percent) are less likely to experience gangs.[4]

MULTIPLE MURDER On April 20, 1999, the nation's most deadly school shooting occurred at Columbine High School in Littleton, Colorado. Two heavily armed students, Eric Harris, 18, and Dylan Klebold, 17, members of a secretive student group called the "Trenchcoat Mafia," went on a shooting spree that claimed the lives of 12 students and 1 teacher and wounded 24 others, many seriously. As police SWAT (special weapons and tactics) teams closed in, the two boys committed suicide in the school library, leaving authorities to puzzle over the cause of their deadly act. Later, their friends described Harris and Klebold as outsiders whose behavior may have been triggered by their perceived victimization at the hands of school athletes.[5]

There are three different types of multiple killers:

♦ *Mass murderers* kill many victims in a single violent outburst.

♦ *Spree killers* spread their murderous outburst over a few days or weeks.

♦ *Serial killers* kill over a long period of time but typically assume a "normal" identity between murders.

Mass murderers such as Harris and Klebold, serial killers such as Jeffrey Dahmer of Milwaukee, and spree killers such as John Allen Muhammed (the D.C. sniper) have become familiar to the U.S. public.[6] The threat of the unknown, random, and deranged assailant has become a part of modern reality.

There is no single explanation for serial, spree, or mass murder. Such widely disparate factors as mental illness, sexual frustration, neurological damage, child abuse and neglect, smothering maternal relationships, and childhood anxiety have been suggested as possible causes. However, most experts view multiple murderers as sociopaths who from early childhood demonstrate bizarre behavior (such as torturing animals), enjoy killing, are immune to their victims' suffering, and bask in the media limelight when caught.[7]

INTIMATE VIOLENCE Although violent attacks by strangers produce the most fear and create the most graphic headlines, Americans face greater physical danger from people with whom they are in close and intimate contact: spouses, other relatives, and dating partners.

One area of intimate violence that has received a great deal of media attention is child abuse, which is any physical or emotional trauma to a child for which no reasonable explanation, such as an accident or ordinary disciplinary practices, can be found. Child abuse can result from physical beatings administered by hands, feet, weapons, belts, or sticks, or from burning.

The last data available indicate that an estimated 3 million children were alleged to have been abused or neglected and received investigations or assessments by state and local child protective services (CPS) agencies. Approximately 870,000 children were determined to be actual victims of child maltreatment. Although the rate of reported child abuse has been in a decline, the problem has not been eliminated: About 12 children for every 1,000 children in the population were victims of some form of abuse or neglect.[8]

Regardless of how it is defined, the effects of abuse can be devastating. Children who have experienced some form of maltreatment have a devalued sense of self, a mistrust of others, a tendency toward attributing hostility toward others in situations where the intentions of others are ambiguous, a tendency to generate antagonistic solutions to social problems, and a suspicion of close relationships.[9]

Hate Crimes

Hate crimes or bias crimes are criminal acts directed toward a particular person or members of a group merely because the targets share a discernible racial, ethnic, religious, or gender characteristic.[10] Hate crimes can include the desecration of a house of worship or cemetery, harassment of a minority-group family that has moved into a previously all-white neighborhood, or a racially motivated murder.

hate crimes
Criminal acts directed toward a particular person or members of a group targeted because of their racial, ethnic, religious, or gender characteristics.

Child Prostitution on the German-Czech Border

Cathrin Schauer, a social worker with the KARO social project, has been working since 1994 on both sides of the German–Czech border as part of a group that looks after women and children involved in prostitution. She helps the kids on the streets, distributes birth control supplies, goes to brothels to hand out information on AIDS prevention, and supports women and children who seek a way out of prostitution. Since 1996, she has gathered information from a variety of sources, including prostitutes, social workers, and police, on the scale of child prostitution in the German–Czech border region in the district of Karlovy Vary (Karlsbad). In addition to close observation of around 500 sexually exploited children and youth, she has conducted more than 200 interviews with people involved in the sex trade. The interviewees included 40 children and young people between the ages of 6 and 17 years, 100 adults in prostitution in the region, 11 staff members of social institutions, 10 police officers, as well as 50 people at the border checkpoints.

Child Prostitution at the German–Czech Border: The Dimensions

The commercial sexual exploitation of children in the German–Czech border districts began to flourish in 1996 and has increased substantially in the years since. A key reason for the increasing demand is that larger numbers of tourists specifically request children. The children have been observed mainly along the Europastrasse E48 and E49 and near the small connecting roads to the German border checkpoints, as well as in the Czech towns near the border. The girls and boys hang out near petrol stations, bus stops, and restaurants. Within towns, they are found in parks, in front of supermarkets, at the entrances of gambling halls and houses, and at the railway station. In one small town, children were observed showing themselves in the windows of a brothel-like institution. In some areas, the children wait for tourists in cars or by windows. Women holding babies and small children have also been seen touting for pedosexuals from Germany.

Small babies and children up to six years of age are usually offered to tourists by women. Children older than seven years are usually accompanied by a male adolescent or an adult. In parking lots and in front of supermarkets, one frequently sees small children who address only German men ("Can you take me with you for a while?") or who beg for money or food ("Can you buy me an ice cream?"). Many of the children get inside the cars of German tourists and drive away with them. Older children, from eight years on, negotiate prices and sexual services. They offer themselves with questions such as "Do you want sex?"

The men usually drive with their victim to a place they are familiar with, where they will not be

Hate crimes usually involve convenient, vulnerable targets who are incapable of fighting back. For example, there have been numerous reported incidents of teenagers attacking vagrants and the homeless in an effort to rid their town or neighborhood of people they consider undesirable.[11] Another group targeted for hate crimes is gay men and women: Gay bashing has become common in U.S. cities.

Currently, the FBI annually records about 8,000 hate crime incidents—motivated by bias against a race, religion, disability, ethnicity, or sexual orientation—that involve more than 9,000 victims and 7,000 offenders.[12]

Public Order Crimes

public order crimes
Behaviors considered illegal because they run counter to existing moral standards. Obscenity and prostitution are considered public order crimes.

Societies have long banned or limited behaviors that are believed to run contrary to social norms, customs, and values. These behaviors are commonly referred to as **public order crimes** or victimless crimes, although the latter term can be misleading.[13] Public order crimes involve acts that interfere with how society operates and functions. These acts are criminalized because those who shape the law believe that they conflict with social norms, prevailing moral rules, and current public opinion. Public order crimes are those that disrupt the "public order" and the ability of people to function efficiently. Included within this category are sexually related crimes such as prostitution, trafficking in pornography, and trafficking in illegal substances. As the International Justice feature shows, these problems are certainly not unique to the United States.

observed. These places may be on the outskirts of a town, in nearby forests or parks, in isolated garages, or in empty side streets. Or the abusers go with their victims—sometimes accompanied by a pimp—to a nearby apartment.

The Victims

Many of the children were raped or sexually abused before they became involved in commercial sexual exploitation. Poverty, sexual abuse, and family obligation are the main reasons given by children for entering into prostitution. The children usually receive between 5 to 25 euros in payment. Sometimes they just receive sweets. Some sex tourists take the children for a meal or give financial support to their families.

The Trafficking and Sale of Children

The study gave clear indications that organized trafficking in children exists. Children from other regions of the Czech Republic and from Central and Eastern European states are trafficked to the border regions, or from there to Germany, in order to be sexually exploited. Children from remote areas of the Czech Republic, the Slovak Republic, and other countries such as Moldova, Ukraine, Lithuania, and the Russian Federation were observed and questioned. Their statements and, in particular, the interviews with adult prostitutes made it clear

that gangs of pimps systematically drag minors to the German–Czech border regions and force them into prostitution.

Some of the prostitutes have already worked in several European countries. One girl from North Bohemia was sold into prostitution when she was 14 years old. First, she worked in a brothel in a Czech city, then moved on to several different places, finally to end up in the German–Czech border region. Later, she and some other girls crossed the border into Germany by taxi and went on to Strasbourg, where pimps forced her into street prostitution.

Critical Thinking

1. Devise a plan to limit the international trafficking of women and children. In your plan, would you focus on punishing traffickers, helping victims, or controlling people who serve as customers?

2. If prostitution were legalized, would international trafficking be terminated?

 InfoTrac College Edition Research

Use the key words "sex trafficking" in a subject search.

Source: Cathrin Schauer, *Children in Street Prostitution—Report from the German–Czech Border* (ECPAT Germany, UNICEF Germany, Horlemann Editors, Bad Honnef, 2003), http://www.childcentre.info/projects/exploitation/germany/dbatile11447.doc.

SUBSTANCE ABUSE The United States has been waging a "war on drugs" for some time. There are indications that at least among teens, drug use has stabilized and/or declined. The most recent Centers for Disease Control and Prevention's Youth Risk Behavior Survey (YRBS) found that youth use of drugs, including marijuana, methamphetamine, and steroids, has declined significantly:[14]

◆ 38.4 percent of high school students had used marijuana at least once in their lifetimes, compared to 42.4 percent in 2001 (a 9.4-percent reduction).

◆ 20.2 percent of high school students reported using marijuana at least once in the 30 days prior to taking the survey, down from 23.9 percent in 2001 (a 15.4-percent reduction).

◆ 6.2 percent reported lifetime methamphetamine use in 2005, versus 9.8 percent in 2001 (a 36.7-percent reduction).

◆ 4 percent of students reported using steroids at least once in their lifetimes, down from 5.0 percent in 2003 (a 20-percent reduction).

◆ 25.5 percent of students reported binge drinking in the past 30 days, down from 29.9 percent in 2001 (a 14.7-percent reduction).

Although most of the focus is on drugs such as cocaine and heroin, the most commonly abused substance, alcohol, is legal, easily obtained, and suspected of being involved in half of all U.S. murders, suicides, and accidental deaths. Alcohol-related

EXHIBIT 2.1

The Association Between Drug Abuse and Crime

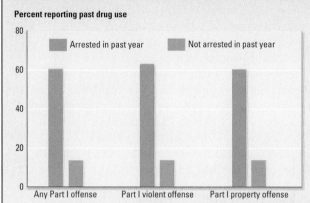

Percent reporting past drug use

Legend: ■ Arrested in past year   ■ Not arrested in past year

X-axis categories: Any Part I offense | Part I violent offense | Part I property offense

◆ Based on annual averages from the 2002–2004 National Surveys on Drug Use and Health, an estimated 1.2 million adults aged 18 or older are arrested for serious violent or property offense each year.

◆ Adults who were arrested in the past year for any serious offense were more likely to have used an illicit drug in the past year than those who were not arrested (60.1 versus 13.6 percent).

◆ Of adults who had been arrested for serious offenses in the past year, 46.5 percent had used marijuana in the past year compared with 10.0 percent of those who had not been arrested for any serious offense.

Source: National Survey on Drug Use and Health, "Illicit Drug Use Among Persons Arrested for Serious Crimes (2005)" (http://oas.samhsa.gov/2k5/arrests/arrests.htm), accessed on May 5, 2006.

deaths number 100,000 a year, far more than deaths by all illegal drugs combined. Strong links are found between alcohol abuse and violent crime and other antisocial behaviors, including episodes of assaultive behavior and vandalism.[15] Strong links also exist between alcohol consumption and certain types of homicide, especially those that occur during robberies and other criminal offenses.[16]

The association between alcohol and crime is strong, but there are indications that people who use illicit drugs are also more likely to engage in criminal acts. The Department of Health and Human Services' most recent annual survey on youth and violence found that about half of the adolescents who used marijuana in the past year also engaged in violent behavior and that more than two-thirds (69 percent) of the adolescents who used methamphetamine in the past year engaged in violent behavior.[17] National surveys of people who have been arrested for serious crimes find that drug abuse is quite common (Exhibit 2.1).

Although the drug–crime connection is powerful, the true relationship between them is still uncertain because many users have had a history of criminal activity before the onset of their substance abuse.[18] It is possible that

Alcohol, legal and easily obtained, is related to half of all U.S. murders, suicides, and accidental deaths. Alcohol-related deaths number 100,000 a year—far more than deaths related to all illegal drugs combined.

©Andrew Lichtenstein/The Image Works

◆ Chronic criminal offenders begin to abuse drugs and alcohol after they have engaged in crime; that is, crime causes drug abuse.

◆ Substance abusers turn to a life of crime to support their habits; that is, drug abuse causes crime.

◆ Drug use and crime co-occur in individuals; that is, both crime and drug abuse are caused by some other common factor—e.g., risk takers use drugs and also commit crime.[19]

◆ Drug users suffer social problems—e.g., heavy drinking and/or mental instability—that are linked to crime.[20]

Economic Crimes

Millions of property- and theft-related crimes occur each year. Most are the work of amateur or occasional criminals whose decision to steal is spontaneous and whose acts are unskilled, unplanned, and haphazard. Many thefts, ranging in seriousness from shoplifting to burglary, are committed by school-age youths who are unlikely to enter into a criminal career.

Added to the pool of amateur thieves are the millions of adults whose behavior may occasionally violate the criminal law—shoplifters, pilferers, tax cheats—but whose main source of income comes from conventional means and whose self-identity is noncriminal. Most of these property crimes occur when an immediate opportunity, or *situational inducement*, arises to commit crime.[21]

Some thieves take advantage of social disorder to ply their trade. Taking no chances, this shopkeeper posted a hand-painted sign outside his New Orleans business to warn away looters in the wake of Hurricane Katrina in September 2005.

Professional thieves, in contrast, derive a significant portion of their income from crime. Professionals do not delude themselves that their acts are impulsive, one-time efforts. They also do not employ elaborate rationalizations to excuse the harmfulness of their action ("Shoplifting doesn't really hurt anyone"). Professionals pursue their craft with vigor, attempting to learn from older, experienced criminals the techniques that will earn them the most money with the least risk. Their numbers are relatively few, but professionals engage in crimes that produce greater losses to society and perhaps cause more significant social harm. Typical forms include pickpocketing, burglary, shoplifting, forgery and counterfeiting, extortion, and swindling.[22]

WHITE-COLLAR CRIME Some criminal activities involve people and institutions whose purpose is illegal profit in the course of their occupation and/or business transactions. Included within the category of **white-collar crime** are such acts as income tax evasion, credit card fraud, and bank fraud. Some white-collar criminals also use their positions of trust in business or government to commit crimes. Their activities might include soliciting bribes or kickbacks as well as embezzlement. Other white-collar criminals set up businesses for the sole purpose of victimizing the general public. They engage in land swindles, securities theft, medical fraud, and so on. And, in addition to acting as individuals, white-collar crimes include criminal conspiracies designed to improve the market share or profitability of corporations. This type of white-collar crime, which includes antitrust violations, price fixing, and false advertising, is known as **corporate crime**. Violations of safety standards, pollution of the environment, and industrial accidents due to negligence can be classified as corporate violence.

It is difficult to estimate the extent and influence of white-collar crime because it is common to ignore the victims who suffer the consequences of such crime. Some experts place its total monetary value in the hundreds of billions of dollars. Beyond their monetary cost, white-collar crimes often damage property and kill people. White-collar crime also destroys confidence, saps the integrity of commercial life, and has the potential for devastating destruction.

ORGANIZED CRIME Organized crime involves the criminal activity of people and organizations whose acknowledged purpose is economic gain through illegal enterprise.[23] These criminal cartels provide the outlawed goods and services demanded by the general public: prostitution, narcotics, gambling, loan sharking, pornography, and untaxed liquor and cigarettes. In addition, organized criminals infiltrate legitimate organizations, such as unions, to drain off their funds and profits for illegal purposes.

Federal and state agencies have been dedicated to wiping out organized crime, and some well-publicized arrests have resulted in the imprisonment of important leaders. The membership of the traditional Italian and Irish crime

white-collar crime
White-collar crimes involve the violation of rules that control business enterprise. They can include employee pilferage, bribery, commodities law violations, mail fraud, computer fraud, environmental law violations, embezzlement, Internet scams, extortion, forgery, insurance fraud, price fixing, and environmental pollution.

corporate crime
Crimes committed by a corporation or by individuals who control the corporation or other business entity for such purposes as illegally increasing market share, avoiding taxes, or thwarting competition.

Statistician

Duties and Characteristics of the Job

Statisticians use numerical data to examine, understand, and predict various phenomena. In the criminal justice system they use their skills to study crime rates and trends and to create more accurate methods of crime measurement. Usually, statisticians focus on demographic information to analyze people's behaviors and trends within a society. A statistician's job includes designing surveys, deciding which methods should be used to analyze the data collected, and making predictions based on patterns within the data. Once this analysis is complete, statisticians will present these data, often in the form of written reports or scholarly articles. Although the concepts and mathematical calculations they perform may be abstract, the knowledge they produce is often used to describe events in the real world and used to impel action on the part of those who read the findings of the researcher.

Statisticians will generally work normal hours in a comfortable office setting. However, certain projects may require longer hours and travel to sites where data are being collected. Statisticians may earn a master's or doctorate degree, but their education is never fully complete because they need to keep up-to-date on the latest findings in their field and be knowledgeable of the newest methods of analysis. Statisticians must also attend conferences to learn the latest developments in their field and the findings of other statisticians. They can work for a variety of employers, including private companies involved in security, and for private research institutes such as the Rand Corporation, although most work for the government or at colleges and universities. Like other academics, statisticians will research, publish, and teach. It should be noted that the skills a statistician has are useful beyond their pure mathematical purposes and can be adapted for work in various fields such as criminology and criminal justice.

Job Outlook

Steady growth is predicted in the number of opportunities for employment as a statistician in the near future. However, there is expected to be faster growth of jobs that will most often not present themselves under the title of "statistician," but under different titles in various fields requiring the skills of a statistician. For example, criminologists and psychologists who

---

families has dropped an estimated 50 percent over a 20-year period. However, new groups—including Russian and Eastern European, Hispanic, and African American gangs—have filled the vacuum created by federal prosecutors. For example, more than 2,000 Russian immigrants are believed to be involved in criminal activity, primarily in Russian enclaves in New York City. Beyond extortion from fellow Eastern European immigrants, Russian organized crime groups have engaged in narcotics trafficking, fencing stolen property, money laundering, and other traditional organized crime schemes.[24]

◆ HOW MUCH CRIME IS THERE? HOW DO WE MEASURE IT?

You can access the Uniform Crime Reports at the FBI website. To reach this website, go to the Siegel/Senna Introduction to Criminal Justice 11e website: www.thomsonedu.com/criminaljustice/siegel.

In order to plan effective crime control policies, it is important to understand how many crimes take place every year, what the trends and patterns in crime are, and who commits crimes. Without such knowledge it would be impossible to know if policies were effective and whether they were worth the cost. For example, although many people advocate the use of the death penalty to deter murder, it would be impossible to know whether capital punishment is indeed an effective deterrent unless murder rates and trends could be calculated. Capital punishment might be justified if murder rates fell dramatically soon after the death penalty was imposed. If, however, imposition of the death penalty had little if any effect on murder rates, then justifications for its use would be

conduct research will need the strong analytical skills and statistical knowledge possessed by statisticians.

Statisticians are increasingly being employed in the private sector as market analysts who look at purchasing trends, but statisticians are still employed primarily by state, local, and federal agencies and by colleges and universities.

Salary

Statisticians have a median annual salary of $58,620. The majority of statisticians earn between $42,770 and $80,690. At the extremes, a small percentage of statisticians will earn around $32,870, and the highest paid will earn more than $100,000. Those with master's and doctorate degrees will have increasingly higher salaries than those with a bachelor's degree.

Opportunities

Opportunities will be best for those whose training is not purely statistics based, but combined with another disciplinary focus such as sociology or criminology.

Qualifications

Statisticians' primary requirements for employment are educational. A bachelor's degree in statistics or

mathematics sets a solid base for more education, either in further study of math or in another area of interest. Employment in this field requires an interest and skill with numbers and analytical thinking. Statisticians must not only collect and interpret potentially complex data; they must also be able to explain their findings and predictions to nonstatisticians. Finally, there are multiple computer programs that can be used to collect and examine data, and it will be beneficial for future statisticians to be familiar with the ones most commonly used in their field of interest.

Education and Training

Although a bachelor's degree in the appropriate field can gain a statistician entry into this field, in order to advance, further education in the form of a master's or doctorate is necessary.

Sources: "Statisticians," *Occupational Outlook Handbook*, 2006–2007 edition (Bureau of Labor Statistics, U.S. Department of Labor), retrieved June 19, 2006, from http://www.bls.gov/oco/ocos045.htm; "Princeton Review Career Profiles: Statistician," retrieved June 16, 2006, from http://www.princetonreview.com/cte/profiles/dayInLife.asp?careerID=47.

damaged. Because obtaining accurate crime data statistics is so essential, there are many career opportunities for statisticians in the criminal justice system (see the Careers in Criminal Justice feature).

Today, three significant methods are used to measure the nature and extent of crime: official data, victim data, and self-report data.

Official Data: Uniform Crime Reports

Official data on crime refer to those crimes known to and recorded by the nation's police departments. The **Uniform Crime Reports (UCRs)**, issued by the Federal Bureau of Investigation (FBI), are the best known and most widely cited source of official criminal statistics.[25] The FBI receives and compiles records from more than 17,000 police departments that serve a majority of the U.S. population. The report's major unit of analysis involves **Part I crimes**: murder and non-negligent manslaughter, forcible rape, robbery, aggravated assault, burglary, larceny/theft, motor vehicle theft, and arson. Exhibit 2.2 defines these crimes.

The FBI tallies and annually publishes the number of reported offenses by city, county, standard metropolitan statistical area, and geographical divisions of the United States. In addition to these statistics, the UCR shows the number and characteristics (age, race, and gender) of individuals who have been arrested for these and all other crimes (**Part II crimes**), except traffic violations.

COLLECTING DATA FOR THE UNIFORM CRIME REPORTS The methods used to compile the UCR are complex. Each month, law enforcement agencies report the

Uniform Crime Reports (UCRs)
The official crime data collected by the FBI from local police departments.

Part I crimes
Those crimes in the FBI's Uniform Crime Report that are considered the most prevalent and serious. The offenses included are the violent crimes of murder and non-negligent manslaughter, forcible rape, robbery, and aggravated assault and the property crimes of burglary, larceny/theft, motor vehicle theft, and arson.

Part II crimes
All other crimes reported to the FBI. These are less serious crimes and misdemeanors, excluding traffic violations.

EXHIBIT 2.2

FBI Part I Crimes

CRIMINAL HOMICIDE

1. *Murder and non-negligent manslaughter:* the willful (non-negligent) killing of one human being by another. Deaths caused by negligence, attempts to kill, assaults to kill, suicides, accidental deaths, and justifiable homicides are excluded. Justifiable homicides are limited to the killing of a felon by a law enforcement officer in the line of duty and the killing of a felon by a private citizen.

2. *Manslaughter by negligence:* the killing of another person through gross negligence. Traffic fatalities are excluded.

FORCIBLE RAPE

The carnal knowledge of a female forcibly and against her will. Included are rapes by force and attempts or assaults to rape. Statutory offenses (no force used—victim under age of consent) are excluded.

ROBBERY

The taking or attempting to take anything of value from the care, custody, or control of a person or persons by force, by threat of force or violence, or by putting the victim in fear.

AGGRAVATED ASSAULT

An unlawful attack by one person on another for the purpose of inflicting severe or aggravated bodily injury. This type of assault is usually accompanied by the use of a weapon or by means likely to produce death or great bodily harm. Simple assaults are excluded.

BURGLARY

Breaking or entering. The unlawful entry of a structure to commit a felony or a theft. Attempted forcible entry is included.

LARCENY/THEFT

The unlawful taking, carrying, leading, or riding away of property from the possession or constructive possession of another. Examples are thefts of bicycles or automobile accessories, shoplifting, pickpocketing, or the stealing of any property or article that is not taken by force and violence or by fraud. Attempted larcenies are included. Embezzlement, con games, forgery, worthless checks, and so on are excluded.

MOTOR VEHICLE THEFT

The theft or attempted theft of a motor vehicle. A motor vehicle is self-propelled and runs on the surface and not on rails. Specifically excluded from this category are motorboats, construction equipment, airplanes, and farming equipment.

ARSON

Any willful or malicious burning or attempt to burn, with or without intent to defraud, a dwelling, house, public building, motor vehicle or aircraft, personal property of another, and so on.

Source: Federal Bureau of Investigation, *Crime in the United States, 2005* (Washington, D.C.: Government Printing Office, 2006).

---

number of index crimes known to them. These data are collected from records of all crime complaints that victims, officers who discovered the infractions, or other sources reported to these agencies.

Whenever criminal complaints are found through investigation to be unfounded or false, they are eliminated from the count. However, the number of offenses known is reported to the FBI whether or not anyone is arrested for the crime, the stolen property is recovered, or prosecution ensues.

In addition, each month law enforcement agencies report how many crimes were **cleared**. Crimes are cleared in two ways: (1) when at least one person is arrested, charged, and turned over to the court for prosecution; or (2) by exceptional means, when some element beyond police control precludes the physical arrest of an offender (for example, he leaves the country). Data on the number of clearances involving the arrest of only juvenile offenders, data on the value of property stolen and recovered in connection with Part I offenses, and detailed information pertaining to criminal homicide are also reported. Traditionally, slightly more than 20 percent of all reported Part I crimes are cleared by arrest each year (see Figure 2.1).

FIGURE 2.1

Percentage of Crimes Cleared by Arrest

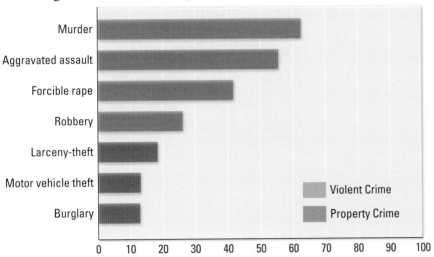

Source: Federal Bureau of Investigation, *Crime in the United States, 2005* (Washington, D.C.: Government Printing Office, 2006), http://www.fbi.gov/ucr/05cius/offenses/clearances/index.html.

cleared
An offense is cleared by arrest or solved when at least one person is arrested or charged with the commission of the offense and is turned over to the court for prosecution. If the following questions can all be answered "yes," the offense can then be cleared "exceptionally": (1) Has the investigation definitely established the identity of the offender? (2) Is there enough information to support an arrest, charge, and turning over to the court for prosecution? (3) Is the exact location of the offender known so that the subject can be taken into custody now? (4) Is there some reason outside law enforcement control that precludes arresting, charging, and prosecuting the offender?

Violent crimes are more likely to be solved than property crimes because police devote more resources to these more serious acts. For these types of crime, witnesses (including the victim) are frequently available to identify offenders, and in many instances the victim and offender were previously acquainted.

The UCR uses three methods to express crime data. First, the number of crimes reported to the police and arrests made are expressed as raw figures (for example, 16,137 murders occurred in 2005). Second, crime rates per 100,000 people are computed. That is, when the UCR indicates that the murder rate was 5.5 in 2005, it means that almost 6 people in every 100,000 were murdered between January 1 and December 31, 2005. This is the equation used:

$$\frac{\text{number of reported crimes}}{\text{total U.S. population}} \times 100{,}000 = \text{rate per } 100{,}000$$

Third, the FBI computes changes in the number and rate of crime over time. The murder rate increased 4.8 percent between 2004 and 2005.

HOW ACCURATE ARE THE UNIFORM CRIME REPORTS? Despite crime experts' continued reliance on the UCR, its accuracy has been suspect. The three main areas of concern are reporting practices, law enforcement practices, and methodological problems.

Reporting Practices Some crime experts claim that victims of many serious crimes do not report these incidents to police; therefore, these crimes do not become part of the UCR. The reasons for not reporting vary. Some victims do not trust the police or do not have confidence in their ability to solve crimes. Others do not have property insurance and therefore believe it is useless to report theft. In other cases, victims fear reprisals from an offender's friends or family or, in the case of family violence, from their spouse, boyfriend, or girlfriend.[26]

According to surveys of crime victims, less than 40 percent of all criminal incidents are reported to the police. Some of these victims justify nonreporting by stating that the incident was "a private matter," that "nothing could be done," or that the victimization was "not important enough."[27] These findings indicate that the UCR data may significantly underrepresent the total number of annual criminal events.

EXHIBIT 2.3

Factors Affecting the Validity of the Uniform Crime Reports

1. No federal crimes are reported.

2. Reports are voluntary and vary in accuracy and completeness.

3. Not all police departments submit reports.

4. The FBI uses estimates in its total crime projections.

5. If an offender commits multiple crimes, only the most serious is recorded. Thus, if a narcotics addict rapes, robs, and murders a victim, only the murder is recorded. Consequently, many lesser crimes go unreported.

6. Each act is listed as a single offense for some crimes but not for others. If a man robbed six people in a bar, the offense would be listed as one robbery, but if he assaulted or murdered them, it would be listed as six assaults or six murders.

7. Incomplete acts are lumped together with completed ones.

8. Important differences exist between the FBI's definition of certain crimes and those used in a number of states.

9. Victimless crimes often go undetected.

10. Many cases of child abuse and family violence are unreported.

Source: Leonard Savitz, "Official Statistics," in *Contemporary Criminology*, ed. Leonard Savitz and Norman Johnston (New York: Wiley, 1982), pp. 3–15, updated 2006.

Law Enforcement Practices The way that police departments record and report criminal and delinquent activity also affects the validity of UCR statistics. How law enforcement agencies interpret the definitions of crimes may also affect reporting practices. Some departments define crimes loosely—for example, reporting a trespass as a burglary or an assault on a woman as an attempted rape—whereas others pay strict attention to FBI guidelines.[28] For example, arson may be seriously underreported because many fire departments do not report to the FBI, and those that do define as "accidental" or "spontaneous" many fires that may have been set by arsonists.[29]

Ironically, boosting police efficiency and professionalism may help increase crime rates. As people develop confidence in the police, they may be more motivated to report crime. Higher crime rates may occur as departments adopt more sophisticated computer technology and hire better-educated, better-trained employees. Crime rates may also be altered based on the way that law enforcement agencies process UCR data. As the number of employees assigned to dispatching, record keeping, and criminal incident reporting increases, so, too, will national crime rates. What appears to be a rising crime rate may be simply an artifact of improved police record-keeping ability.[30]

Methodological Issues The way data is collected may also influence the validity of the Uniform Crime Reports. The most frequent issues are listed in Exhibit 2.3. The complex scoring procedure means that many serious crimes are not counted. For example, during an armed bank robbery, the offender strikes a teller with the butt of a handgun. The robber runs from the bank and steals an automobile at the curb. Although the offender has technically committed robbery, aggravated assault, and motor vehicle theft, which are three Part I offenses, because robbery is the most serious, it would be the only one recorded in the UCR.[31]

NIBRS: The Future of the Uniform Crime Reports

Clearly, there must be a more reliable source for crime statistics than the UCR as it stands today. Beginning in 1982, a five-year redesign effort was undertaken to provide more comprehensive and detailed crime statistics. The effort resulted in the **National Incident-Based Reporting System (NIBRS)**, a program that collects data on each reported crime incident. Instead of submitting statements of the kinds of crime that individual citizens report to the police and summary

National Incident-Based Reporting System (NIBRS)
A new form of crime data collection created by the FBI requiring local police agencies to provide at least a brief account of each incident and arrest within 22 crime patterns, including incident, victim, and offender information.

statements of resulting arrests, the new program requires local police agencies to provide at least a brief account of each incident and arrest, including incident, victim, and offender information.

Under NIBRS, law enforcement authorities provide information to the FBI on each criminal incident involving 46 specific offenses, including the 8 Part I crimes, that occur in their jurisdiction; arrest information on the 46 offenses plus 11 lesser offenses is also provided in NIBRS. These expanded crime categories include numerous additional crimes, such as blackmail, embezzlement, drug offenses, and bribery; this allows a national database on the nature of crime, victims, and criminals to be developed. Other collected information includes statistics gathered by federal law enforcement agencies, as well as data on hate or bias crimes. Thus far, more than 20 states have implemented their NIBRS program, and 12 others are in the process of finalizing their data collections. When this program is fully implemented and adopted across the nation, it should bring about greater uniformity in cross-jurisdictional reporting and improve the accuracy of official crime data.[32]

Victim Surveys: The National Crime Victimization Survey

The second source of crime data is surveys that ask crime victims about their encounters with criminals. Because many victims do not report their experiences to the police, victim surveys are considered a method of getting at the unknown figures of crime. Some surveys are conducted with relatively small groups in an effort to find out if personal status influences victimization risk. One recent survey of gang members found that gang youths not only commit a great number of crimes but that they are also more likely to experience violent victimization than are nongang members. Although many youths claim that they joined gangs for protection, in reality gang membership offers little in the way of security and much in the way of danger.[33]

The most important and widely used victim survey—the **National Crime Victimization Survey (NCVS)**—is sponsored by the Bureau of Justice Statistics of the U.S. Department of Justice. In these national surveys, housing units are selected using a complex, multistage sampling technique. Each year, data are obtained from a large nationally representative sample; in 2005, more than 77,000 households representing a total of more than 134,000 people age 12 or older were interviewed.[34] People are asked to report their experiences with such crimes as rape, sexual assault, robbery, assault, theft, household burglary, and motor vehicle theft. Due to the care with which the samples are drawn and the high completion rate, NCVS data are considered a relatively unbiased, valid estimate of all victimizations for the target crimes included in the survey.

The NCVS finds that many crimes go unreported to police. The UCR shows that slightly more than 90,000 rapes or attempted rapes occur each year, but the NCVS estimates that almost 200,000 actually occur. The reason for such discrepancies is that fewer than half of violent crimes, fewer than one-third of personal theft crimes (such as pickpocketing), and fewer than half of household thefts are reported to police. Victims seem to report to the police only crimes that involve considerable loss or injury. If we are to believe NCVS findings, the official UCR statistics do not provide an accurate picture of the crime problem because many crimes go unreported to the police.

Like the UCR, the NCVS may also suffer from some problems.[35] These are listed in Exhibit 2.4.

Self-Report Surveys

The problems associated with official statistics have led many crime experts to seek alternative sources of information in assessing the true extent of crime patterns. The data provided by the NCVS are important, but they cannot reveal much about the personality, attitudes, and behavior of individual offenders. Neither the NCVS

Read more about the National Incident-Based Reporting System. You can reach this information by going to the Siegel/Senna Introduction to Criminal Justice 11e website: www.thomsonedu.com/criminaljustice/siegel.

National Crime Victimization Survey (NCVS)
The nation's primary source of information on criminal victimization. Each year, data are obtained from a national sample that measures the frequency, characteristics, and consequences of criminal victimization by such crimes as rape, sexual assault, robbery, assault, theft, household burglary, and motor vehicle theft.

You can access the most recent National Crime Victimization Survey data by going to the Siegel/Senna Introduction to Criminal Justice 11e website: www.thomsonedu.com/criminaljustice/siegel.

EXHIBIT 2.4

Validity Issues in the NCVS

- ◆ Overreporting due to victims' misinterpretation of events. A lost wallet may be reported as stolen, or an open door may be viewed as a burglary attempt.

- ◆ Underreporting due to the embarrassment of reporting crime to interviewers, fear of getting in trouble, or simply forgetting an incident.

- ◆ Inability to record the personal criminal activity of those interviewed, such as drug use or gambling; murder is also not included, for obvious reasons.

- ◆ Sampling errors, which produce a group of respondents who do not represent the nation as a whole.

- ◆ Inadequate question format that invalidates responses. Some groups, such as adolescents, may be particularly susceptible to error because of question format and wording.

---

self-report survey
A research approach that questions large groups of subjects, typically high school students, about their own participation in delinquent or criminal acts.

nor UCR is of much value in charting the extent of one of the nation's most important social problems—substance abuse in the teenage population. To address these issues, crime experts have developed the **self-report survey**.

Most often, self-report surveys are administered to groups of subjects through a mass distribution of questionnaires. Although some surveys are able to identify the subjects, most are given anonymously so that respondents feel freer to tell the truth about their behaviors. The basic assumption of self-report studies is that because anonymity and confidentiality are assured, people will be encouraged to accurately describe their illegal activities.

Because most self-report instruments contain items measuring subjects' attitudes, values, personal characteristics, and behaviors, the data obtained from them can be used for various purposes. These include testing theories, measuring attitudes toward crime, and computing the association between crime and important social variables, such as family relations, educational attainment, and income. Statistical analysis of the responses can be used to determine such issues as (a) are people who report being abused as children also more likely to use drugs as adults and (b) does school failure lead to delinquency?[36]

ARE SELF-REPORTS ACCURATE? Critics of self-report studies frequently suggest that it is unreasonable to expect people to candidly admit illegal acts. They have nothing to gain, and the ones taking the greatest risk are the ones with official records who may be engaging in the most criminality. In addition, some people may exaggerate their criminal acts, forget some of them, or be confused about what is being asked. Some surveys contain an overabundance of trivial offenses, such as shoplifting small amounts of items or using false identification, which are often lumped together with serious crimes to form a total crime index. Consequently, comparisons between groups can be highly misleading.

Various techniques have been used to verify self-report data.[37] The "known group" method compares youths who are known to be offenders with those who are not to see whether the former report more delinquency.[38] Research shows that when kids are asked if they have ever been arrested or sent to court, their responses accurately reflect their true life experiences.[39]

Another approach is to use peer informants who can verify the honesty of a subject's answers. Subjects can also be tested twice to see if their answers remain stable. Sometimes questions are designed to reveal respondents who are lying; for example, an item might say, "I have never done anything wrong in my life."

Polygraphs, commonly known as lie detectors, have also been used to verify the responses given on self-report surveys. The results often validate the accuracy of self-report survey data.[40] Research studies also indicate a substantial association between official processing and self-reported crime.[41]

Although these findings are encouraging, nagging questions still remain about the validity of self-reports:

♦ Research indicates that offenders with the most extensive prior criminality are also the ones most likely to falsify their behavior.[42]

♦ Serious chronic offenders are usually unwilling to cooperate with self-report tests.[43]

♦ Institutionalized youths are not generally represented in the self-report surveys. They are not only more delinquent than the general population but are also considerably more misbehaving than the most delinquent youths identified in the typical self-report survey.[44]

♦ Self-reports may measure only nonserious, occasional delinquents while ignoring hard-core chronic offenders who may be institutionalized and unavailable for self-reports.

Compatibility of Crime Statistics Sources

Are the various sources of crime statistics compatible? Each has strengths and weaknesses. The FBI survey is carefully tallied and contains data on the number of murders and people arrested, information that the other data sources lack. However, this survey omits the many crimes that victims choose not to report to police, and it is subject to the reporting caprices of individual police departments.

The NCVS contains unreported crimes and important information on the personal characteristics of victims, but the data consist of estimates made from relatively limited samples of the total U.S. population. Because of this, even narrow fluctuations in the rates of some crimes can have a major impact on findings. It also relies on personal recollections that may be inaccurate. The NCVS does not include data on important crime patterns, including murder and drug abuse.

Self-report surveys can provide information on the personal characteristics of offenders, such as their attitudes, values, beliefs, and psychological profiles, which is unavailable from any other source. Yet at their core, self-reports rely on the honesty of criminal offenders and drug abusers, a population not generally known for accuracy and integrity.

Despite these differences, a number of prominent crime experts have concluded that the data sources are more compatible than was first believed. Although their tallies of crimes are certainly not in sync, the crime patterns and trends they record are often similar.[45] All three sources generally agree about the personal characteristics of serious criminals (such as age and gender) and where and when crime occurs (such as urban areas, nighttime, and summer months). Therefore, what do these data sources tell us about crime rates, patterns, and trends?

ThomsonNOW Improve your grade on the exam with Personalized Study! For reinforcement resources and a mastery check of crime statistics, go to www.thomsonedu.com/thomsonnow.

♦ OFFICIAL CRIME TRENDS

Crime is not a new phenomenon.[46] Studies have indicated that a gradual increase in the crime rate, especially in violent crime, occurred from 1830 to 1860. Following the Civil War, this rate increased significantly for about 15 years. Then, from 1880 up to the time of World War I, with the possible exception of the years immediately preceding and following the war, the number of reported crimes decreased. After a period of readjustment, the crime rate steadily declined until the Great Depression (about 1930), when another crime wave was recorded. As measured by the UCR, crime rates increased gradually following the 1930s until the 1960s, when the growth rate became much greater.

The homicide rate, which had actually declined from the 1930s to the 1960s, also began a sharp increase that continued through the 1970s.

In 1984 police recorded 11 million crimes. By the following year, however, the number of crimes once again began an upward trend so that by 1991, police recorded almost 15 million crimes. Since then, the number of crimes has been in decline. Even teenage criminality, a source of national concern, has been in decline during this period, decreasing by about one-third over the past 20 years. The teen murder rate, which had remained stubbornly high, has also declined during the past few years.[47] In 2005 slightly less than 12 million Part I crimes were reported to police. Figure 2.2 illustrates the Part I crime rate trend between 1960 and 2005. The factors that help explain the upward and downward movement in crime rates are discussed in the Analyzing Criminal Justice Issues feature.

Trends in Violent Crime

The violent crimes reported by the FBI include murder, rape, assault, and robbery. In 2005, about 1.5 million violent crimes were reported to police, a rate of more than 465 per 100,000 Americans. Although violence in the United States decreased about 24 percent during the past decade (1995–2005), the number of violent crimes increased 2.5 percent between 2004 and 2005. Whether this increase portends a new trend in U.S. violence or is simply a one-year aberration remains to be seen.

Murder statistics are generally regarded as the most accurate aspect of the UCR. Therefore, it is particularly troubling that the murder rate increased more than 3 percent between 2004 and 2005. This increase comes after a decade that had witnessed a significant decrease in the number and rate of murders. Figure 2.3 illustrates homicide rate trends since 1900. Note that the rate peaked around 1930, then held relatively steady at about 4 to 5 per 100,000 population from 1950 through the mid-1960s, at which point it started rising to a peak of 10.2 per 100,000 population in 1980. By 1991, the number of murders topped 24,000 for the first time in the nation's history. Then, between 1991 and 2004, homicide rates dropped more than 40 percent. Although it is premature to assume that this recent one-year increase in murder indicates a new trend, any increase in the number of homicides is quite troubling.

Trends in Property Crime

The property crimes reported in the UCR include larceny, motor vehicle theft, and arson. In 2005, about 10 million property crimes were reported, a rate of about 3,500 per 100,000 population. Property crime rates have declined in recent years, although the drop has not been as dramatic as that experienced by the violent crime rate. Between 1995 and 2005, the total number of property crimes declined about 15 percent, and the property crime rate declined almost 25 percent. Importantly, unlike violent crimes, the property crime rates declined almost 2 percent between 2004 and 2005.

Victimization (NCVS) Trends

According to the National Crime Victimization Survey (NCVS), at last count (2005) residents age 12 or older experienced about 23 million violent and property victimizations. Similar to UCR trends, reported victimizations have also declined significantly during the 30 years since an estimated 44 million victimizations were recorded in 1973. Between 1993 and 2005, the violent crime rate decreased more than

Robyn Ramsey, 25, is arrested after a police chase in Lancaster, California, on March 2, 2006. Ramsey, detained in a car theft case, stole a sheriff's sport utility vehicle and led deputies on a two-hour pursuit through the Antelope Valley before being captured. Despite such news-making incidents, property crime rates have been in a decade-long decline.

©Associated Press/AP Photo/Antelope Valley Press, Kelly Lacefield

FIGURE 2.2
Crime Rate Trends

Rate per 100,000 population

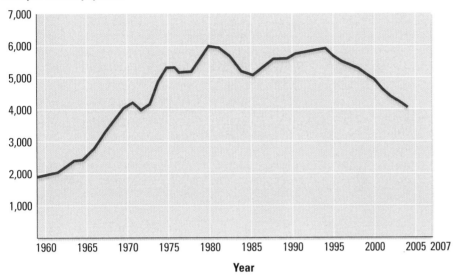

Year

Source: FBI, *Crime in the United States*, 2004, updated.

FIGURE 2.3
Homicide Rate Trends

Rate per 100,000 population

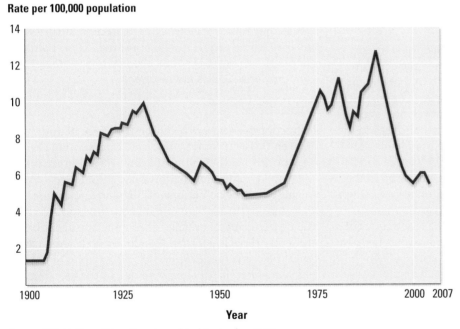

Year

Source: FBI, Uniform Crime Report, updated September 2005.

50 percent, from 50 to 21 victimizations per 1,000 persons age 12 or older, and the property crime rate declined at about the same rate (from 319 to 154 crimes per 1,000 households). The main findings of the most recent NCVS survey are as follows:

◆ Of the 23 million victimizations, more than three quarters (18 million) were property crimes, about 20 percent (5.4 million) were crimes of violence, and 1 percent were personal thefts. (*continued on page 64*)

The Forces That Shape Crime Trends

Crime experts have identified a variety of social, economic, personal, and demographic factors that influence crime rate trends. Although crime experts are still uncertain about how these factors affect these trends, directional change seems to be associated with changes in crime rates.

Age

Because teenagers have extremely high crime rates, crime experts view changes in the population age distribution as having the greatest influence on crime trends: As a general rule, the crime rate follows the proportion of young males in the population. Kids who commit a lot of crime early in childhood are also likely to continue to commit crime in their adolescence and into adulthood. The more teens in the population, the higher the crime rate. The number of juveniles should be increasing over the next decade, and some crime experts fear that this will signal a return to escalating crime rates. However, the number of senior citizens is also expanding, and their presence in the population may have a moderating effect on crime rates (seniors do not commit much crime), offsetting the effect of teens.

Economy/Jobs

There is debate over the effect the economy has on crime rates. It seems logical that when the economy turns down, people (especially those who are unemployed) will become more motivated to commit theft crimes. As the economy heats up, crime rates should decline because people can secure good jobs; why risk crime when there are legitimate opportunities? Recent (2006) research by Thomas Arvanites and Robert Defina found that the crime rate drop in the 1990s could be linked to the strong economy's effect on criminal motivation.

However, some criminologists believe that a poor economy may actually help lower crime rates because it limits the opportunity to commit crime: Unemployed parents are at home to supervise children and guard their possessions, and because there is less money to spend, people have fewer valuables worth stealing. Moreover, law-abiding, middle-age workers do not turn to a life of crime when they lose their jobs during an economic downturn.

Although the effect of the economy on crime rates is still in question, it is possible that over the long haul, a strong economy will help lower crime rates, whereas long periods of sustained economic weakness and unemployment may eventually lead to increased rates. Crime skyrocketed in the 1930s during the Great Depression; crime rates fell when the economy surged for almost a decade during the 1990s. Also, economic effects may be very localized: People in one area of the city are doing well, but people living in another part of town may be suffering unemployment. The economic effect on the crime rates may vary by neighborhood or even by street.

Social Malaise

As the level of social problems increases—such as single-parent families, dropout rates, racial conflict, and teen pregnancies—so do crime rates. Crime rates are correlated with the number of unwed mothers in the population. It is possible that children of unwed mothers need more social services than children in two-parent families. As the number of kids born to single mothers increases, the child welfare system will be taxed and services depleted. The teenage birth rate has trended downward in recent years, and so have crime rates.

Racial conflict may also increase crime rates. Areas undergoing racial change, especially those experiencing a migration of minorities into predominantly white neighborhoods, seem prone to significant increases in their crime rate. Whites in these areas may be using violence to protect what they view as their home turf. Racially motivated crimes actually diminish as neighborhoods become more integrated and power struggles are resolved.

Abortion

In a controversial work, John J. Donohue III and Steven D. Levitt found empirical evidence that the recent drop in the crime rate can be attributed to the availability of legalized abortion. In 1973, *Roe* v. *Wade* legalized abortion nationwide. Within a few years of *Roe* v. *Wade*, more than one million abortions were being performed annually, or roughly one abortion for every three live births. Donohue and Levitt suggest that the crime rate drop, which began approximately 18 years later, in 1991, can be tied to the fact that at that point the first groups of potential offenders affected by the abortion decision began reaching the peak age of criminal activity. The researchers found that states that legalized abortion before the rest of the nation were the first to experience decreasing crime rates and that states with high abortion rates have seen a greater drop in crime since 1985. According to Donohue and Levitt, if abortion were illegal, crime rates might increase by 10 to 20 percent. If these estimates are correct, legalized abortion can explain about half of the recent decrease in crime.

Guns

The availability of firearms may influence the crime rate, especially the proliferation of weapons in the hands of teens. Surveys of high school students indicate that between 6 and 10 percent carry guns at least some of the time. Guns also cause escalation in the seriousness of crime. As the number of gun-toting students increases, so does the seriousness of violent crime: A schoolyard fight may well turn into murder.

Gangs

Another factor that affects crime rates is the explosive growth in teenage gangs. Surveys indicate that there are about 760,000 gang members in the United States. Boys who are members of gangs are far more likely to possess guns than nongang members; criminal activity increases when kids join gangs.

Drug Use

Some experts tie increases in the violent crime rate between 1980 and 1990 to the crack epidemic, which swept the nation's largest cities, and to drug-trafficking gangs that fought over drug turf. These well-armed gangs did not hesitate to use violence to control territory, intimidate rivals, and increase market share. As the crack epidemic has subsided, so has the violence in New York City and other metropolitan areas where crack use was rampant. A sudden increase in drug use, on the other hand, may be a harbinger of future increases in the crime rate.

Media

Some experts argue that violent media can influence the direction of crime rates. As the availability of media with a violent theme skyrocketed with the introduction of home video players, DVDs, cable TV, computer and video games, and so on, so did teen violence rates. Watching violence on TV is correlated to aggressive behaviors, especially when viewers have a preexisting tendency toward crime and violence. Research shows that the more often kids watch TV, the more often they get into violent encounters.

Justice Policy

Some law enforcement experts have suggested that a reduction in crime rates may be attributed to adding large numbers of police officers and using them in aggressive police practices that target "quality of life" crimes such as panhandling, graffiti, petty drug dealing, and loitering. By showing that even the smallest infractions will be dealt with seriously, aggressive police departments may be able to discourage potential criminals from committing more serious crimes.

Michael White and his associates have recently shown that cities employing aggressive, focused police work may be able to lower homicide rates in the area.

It is also possible that tough laws imposing lengthy prison terms on drug dealers and repeat offenders can affect crime rates. The fear of punishment may inhibit some would-be criminals, and tough laws place a significant number of potentially high-rate offenders behind bars, lowering crime rates. As the nation's prison population has expanded, the crime rate has fallen.

Critical Thinking

Although crime rates have been declining in the United States, they have been increasing in Europe. Is it possible that factors that correlate with crime rate changes in the United States have little utility in predicting changes in other cultures? What other factors may increase or reduce crime rates?

InfoTrac College Edition Research

Gang activity may have a big impact on crime rates. To find out the influence of gangs in other nations, read this article: Rob White and Ron Mason, "Youth Gangs and Youth Violence: Charting the Key Dimensions," *Australian and New Zealand Journal of Criminology* 39 (2006): 54–70.

Sources: Thomas Arvanites and Robert Defina, "Business Cycles and Street Crime," *Criminology* 44 (2006): 139–64; David Fergusson, L. John Horwood, and Elizabeth Ridder, "Show Me the Child at Seven: The Consequences of Conduct Problems in Childhood for Psychosocial Functioning in Adulthood," *Journal of Child Psychology & Psychiatry & Allied Disciplines* 46 (2005): 837–49; Fahui Wang, "Job Access and Homicide Patterns in Chicago: An Analysis at Multiple Geographic Levels Based on Scale-Space Theory," *Journal of Quantitative Criminology* 21 (2005): 195–217; Gary Kleck and Ted Chiricos, "Unemployment and Property Crime: A Target-Specific Assessment of Opportunity and Motivation as Mediating Factors," *Criminology* 40 (2002): 649–80; Steven Levitt, "Understanding Why Crime Fell in the 1990s: Four Factors That Explain the Decline and Six That Do Not," *Journal of Economic Perspectives* 18 (2004): 163–90; Michael White, James Fyfe, Suzanne Campbell, and John Goldkamp, "The Police Role in Preventing Homicide: Considering the Impact of Problem-Oriented Policing on the Prevalence of Murder," *Journal of Research in Crime and Delinquency* 40 (2003): 194–226; Jeffrey Johnson, Patricia Cohen, Elizabeth Smailes, Stephanie Kasen, and Judith Brook, "Television Viewing and Aggressive Behavior During Adolescence and Adulthood," *Science* 295 (2002): 2468–71; Brad Bushman and Craig Anderson, "Media Violence and the American Public," *American Psychologist* 56 (2001): 477–89; Steven Messner, Lawrence Raffalovich, and Richard McMillan, "Economic Deprivation and Changes in Homicide Arrest Rates for White and Black Youths, 1967–1998: A National Time-Series Analysis," *Criminology* 39 (2001): 591–614; John Laub, "Review of the Crime Drop in America," *American Journal of Sociology* 106 (2001): 1820–22; John J. Donohue III and Steven D. Levitt, "The Impact of Legalized Abortion on Crime," *Quarterly Journal of Economics* 116 (2001): 379–420; Robert O'Brien, Jean Stockard, and Lynne Isaacson, "The Enduring Effects of Cohort Characteristics on Age-Specific Homicide Rates, 1960–1995," *American Journal of Sociology* 104 (1999): 1061–95.

FIGURE 2.4
Violent Crime Rates

Victimization rate per 1,000 persons age 12 and over

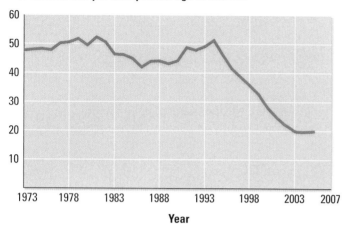

Year

FIGURE 2.5
Property Crime Rates

Victimization rate per 1,000 households

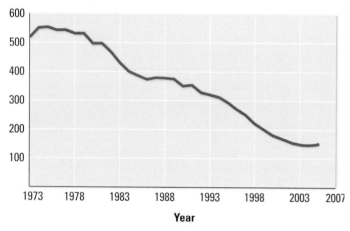

Year

ThomsonNOW™ Improve your grade on the exam with Personalized Study! For reinforcement resources and a mastery check of crime trends, go to www.thomsonedu.com/thomsonnow.

◆ For every 1,000 persons age 12 or older, there occurred 1 rape or sexual assault, 1 assault with injury, and 2 robberies.

◆ About 24 percent of all violent crime incidents were committed by an armed offender and 7 percent by an offender with a firearm.

◆ Males, African Americans, and youths are more likely to be victimized than are members of other groups/statuses.[48]

As Figures 2.4 and 2.5 show, victim rates have seen an almost steady decline for the past decade. Whether the recent increase in UCR violence rates will be matched by the NCVS remains to be seen.

Trends in Self-Reporting

Self-report results appear to be more stable than the UCR. When the results of recent self-report surveys are compared with various studies conducted over a 20-year period, a uniform pattern emerges: The use of drugs and alcohol increased markedly in the 1970s, leveled off in the 1980s, and then began to increase in the mid-1990s until 1997, when the use of most drugs began to decline. The level of theft, violence, and damage-related crimes seems more stable. Although a self-reported crime wave has not occurred, neither has there been any visible reduction in self-reported criminality. Table 2.1 contains data from the most recent Monitoring the Future (MTF) survey. A surprising number of these *typical* teenagers reported involvement in serious criminal behavior: About 13 percent reported hurting someone badly enough that the victim needed medical care (7 percent said they did it more than once); about 27 percent reported stealing something worth less than $50, and another 9 percent stole something worth more than $50; 28 percent reported shoplifting; 13 percent had damaged school property.

The MTF study is also used to measure teen drug use. Data suggest that drug use has declined during the past two decades (with a few exceptions, such as inhalants and oxycontin).[49] But the MTF findings show that drug use has certainly not disappeared: Today, about 15 percent of eighth graders, 31 percent of tenth graders, and 39 percent of twelfth graders have used drugs in the past year; about half of all twelfth graders have used drugs at least once in their lifetime.

◆ WHAT THE FUTURE HOLDS

It is risky to speculate about the future of crime trends because current conditions can change rapidly, but some crime experts have tried to predict future patterns. For example, criminologist James A. Fox predicts a significant increase in teen violence if current trends persist. The United States has approximately 50 million school-age children, and many are under age 10. This is more than there have been for decades. Many lack stable families and adequate supervision. These children will soon enter their prime crime years. As a result, there may be an increase in youth violence.[50] The recent uptick in murders gives support to Fox's projections.

Fox's predictions are persuasive, but not all crime experts believe that an age-driven crime wave is forthcoming. Some, such as Steven Levitt, dispute the fact that the population's age makeup contributes as much to the crime

TABLE 2.1

Self-Reported Delinquent Activity, High School Seniors, During Past 12 Months

Type of Crime	Total %	Committed Only Once (%)	Committed More Than Once (%)
Set fire on purpose	4	2	2
Damaged school property	13	6	7
Damaged work property	7	3	4
Auto theft	5	2	3
Auto-part theft	6	3	3
Breaking and entering	23	10	13
Theft of less than $50	27	13	14
Theft of more than $50	9	4	5
Shoplifting	28	12	15
Gang fight	19	10	9
Hurt someone badly enough so that the victim needed medical care	13	6	7
Used force to steal	4	2	2
Hit teacher or supervisor	3	1	2
Got into serious fight	14	7	7

Source: *Monitoring the Future, 2005* (Ann Arbor, MI: Institute for Social Research, 2005).

rate as has been suggested by Fox and others.[51] Even if teens commit more crime in the future, Levitt finds that their contribution may be offset by the aging of the population, which will produce a large number of senior citizens and elderly, a group with a relatively low crime rate.

Such prognostication is reassuring, but there is no telling what changes are in store that may influence crime rates either up or down. Technological developments such as the rapid expansion of Internet e-commerce have created new classes of crime. Terrorists present a continuing threat. Although crime rates have trended downward, it is too early to predict that this trend will continue into the foreseeable future.

Although crime has declined and stabilized for the moment in the United States, it seems to be increasing around the world. The recent boom in crime rates overseas is the subject of the International Justice feature.

♦ CRIME PATTERNS

Crime experts look for stable crime rate patterns to gain insight into the nature of crime. If crime rates are consistently higher at certain times, in certain areas, and among certain groups, this knowledge might help explain the onset or cause of crime. For example, if criminal statistics show that crime rates are consistently higher in poor neighborhoods in large urban areas, then crime may be a function of poverty and neighborhood decline. If, in contrast, crime rates are spread evenly across society, this would provide little evidence that crime has an economic basis. Instead, crime might be linked to socialization, personality, intelligence, or some other trait unrelated to class position or income.

©AP Images/Saurabh Das

Rape and sexual assault are not unique to the U.S. Supporters of the youth wing of the Communist Party of India Marxist listen to a leader while protesting the inability of police to curb a rising rate of sexual abuse of women in New Delhi, India on July 12, 2005. The recent increase in incidents of abuse has shown women of all ages being targeted for sexual assault. The placard reads "Women."

International Crime Trends

India has experienced a shocking form of violence against women known as bride burning: A woman may be burned to death if her family fails to provide the expected dowry to the groom's family or if she is suspected of premarital infidelity; as well, many Indian women commit suicide to escape the brutality of their situation.

The danger from various forms of violent behavior, such as bride burning in India, has become a worldwide epidemic. Although crime rates are trending downward in the United States, they seem to be increasing abroad. The United States in 1980 clearly led the Western world in overall crime, but there has been a marked decline in U.S. crime rates, a trend that has now placed crime rates in the United States below those of other industrial nations, including England and Wales, Denmark, and Finland. And contrary to the common assumption that the United States is the most heavily armed nation on earth, there is new evidence that people around the world are arming themselves in record numbers: Residents in the 15 countries of the European Union have an estimated 84 million firearms. Of that total, 67 million (80 percent) are in civilian hands. With a total European Union population of 375 million people, this amounts to 17.4 guns for every 100 people.

Although these trends are alarming, making international comparisons is often difficult because the legal definitions of *crime* vary from country to country. There are also differences in the way crime is measured. For example, in the United States crime may be measured by counting criminal acts reported to the police or by using victim surveys, but many European countries measure crime by the number of cases solved by the police. Despite these problems, valid comparisons can still be made about crime across different countries by using a number of reliable data sources. For example, the United Nations Survey of Crime Trends and Operations of Criminal Justice Systems (UNCJS) is the most well-known source of information on cross-national data. The International Crime Victims Survey (ICVS) is conducted in 60 countries and is managed by the Ministry of Justice of the Netherlands, the Home Office of the United Kingdom, and the United Nations Interregional Crime and Justice Research Institute. There is also the United Nations International Study on the Regulation of Firearms. Interpol, the international police agency, collects data from police agencies in 179 countries. The World Health Organization (WHO) has conducted surveys on global violence. The *European Sourcebook of Crime and Criminal Justice Statistics* provides data from police agencies in 36 European nations.

What do these various sources tell us about international crime rates?

Homicide

Many nations, especially those experiencing social or economic upheaval, have murder rates much higher than the U.S. rate. Colombia has about 63 homicides per 100,000 people and South Africa 51, compared to less than 6 in the United States. During the 1990s there were more homicides in Brazil than in the United States, Canada, Italy, Japan, Australia, Portugal, Britain, Austria, and Germany taken together. Why are murder rates so high in nations such as Brazil? Law enforcement officials link the upsurge in violence to drug trafficking, gang feuds, vigilantism, and disputes over trivial matters, in which young, unmarried, uneducated males are involved.

Rape

Until 1990, U.S. rape rates were higher than those of any other Western nation, but by 2000, Canada took the lead. Generally, violence against women is related to economic hardship and the social status of women. Rates are high in poor nations in which women are oppressed. Where women are more emancipated, the rates of violence against women are lower.

For many women, sexual violence starts in childhood and adolescence and may occur in the home, school, and community. Studies conducted in a wide variety of nations, ranging from Cameroon to New Zealand, found high rates of reported forced sexual initiation. In some nations, as many as 46 percent of adolescent women and 20 percent of adolescent men report sexual coercion at the hands of family members, teachers, boyfriends, or strangers.

Sexual violence has significant health consequences, including suicide, stress, mental illnesses, unwanted pregnancy, sexually transmitted diseases, HIV/AIDS, self-inflicted injuries, and, in the case of child sexual abuse, adoption of high-risk behaviors such as multiple sexual partners and drug use.

Robbery

Countries with more reported robberies than the United States included England and Wales, Portugal, and Spain. Countries with fewer reported robberies included Germany, Italy, and France, as well as Middle Eastern and Asian nations.

Burglary

The United States had lower burglary rates than Australia, Denmark, Finland, England and Wales, and Canada. It had higher reported burglary rates than Spain, South Korea, and Saudi Arabia.

Vehicle Theft

Australia, England and Wales, Denmark, Norway, Canada, France, and Italy now have higher rates of vehicle theft than the United States.

Child Abuse

A World Health Organization report found that child physical and sexual abuse takes a significant toll around the world. In a single year, about 57,000 children under 15 years are murdered. The homicide rates for children aged 0 to 4 years were more than twice as high as rates among children aged 5 to 14 years. Many more children are subjected to nonfatal abuse and neglect; 8 percent of male and 25 percent of female children up to age 18 experience sexual abuse of some kind.

Why the Change?

Why are crime rates increasing around the world while leveling off in the United States? In some developing nations, crime rates may be spiraling upward because these nations are undergoing rapid changes in their social and economic makeup. In Eastern Europe, the fall of communism has brought about a transformation of the family, religion, education, and the economy. These changes increase social pressures and result in crime rate increases. Some Asian societies, such as China, are undergoing rapid industrialization, urbanization, and social change. The shift from agricultural to industrial and service economies has produced political turmoil and a surge in their crime rates. For example, the island of Hong Kong, long a British possession but now part of the People's Republic of China, is experiencing an upsurge in club drugs. Tied to the local dance scene, ecstasy and ketamine use has skyrocketed and is in synch with the traditional drug of choice, heroin. The problems that we experience at home are not unique to the United States.

Critical Thinking

1. Although risk factors at all levels of social and personal life contribute to youth violence, youths in all nations who experience change in societal-level factors—such as economic inequalities, rapid social change, and the availability of firearms, alcohol, and drugs—seem the most likely to get involved in violence. Can anything be done to help alleviate these social problems?

2. The United States is notorious for employing much tougher penal measures than Europe. Do you believe our tougher measures explain why crime is declining in the United States while increasing abroad?

InfoTrac College Edition Research

To find out more about violence around the world, use "violence Europe," "violence Asia," and "violence Africa" as key words in InfoTrac College Edition.

Sources: Jan Grijpink, "Criminal Records in the European Union: The Challenge of Large-Scale Information Exchange," *European Journal of Crime, Criminal Law & Criminal Justice* 14 (2006): 1–19; Karen Joe Laidler, "The Rise of Club Drugs in a Heroin Society: The Case of Hong Kong," *Substance Use & Misuse* 40 (2005): 1257–79; Virendra Kumar and Sarita Kanth, "Bride Burning," *Lancet* 364 (2004): 18–19; Etienne Krug, Linda Dahlberg, James Mercy, Anthony Zwi, and Rafael Lozano, *World Report on Violence and Health* (Geneva: World Health Organization, 2002); Gene Stephens, "Global Trends in Crime: Crime Varies Greatly Around the World, Statistics Show, But New Tactics Have Proved Effective in the United States. To Keep Crime in Check in the Twenty-First Century, We'll All Need to Get Smarter, Not Just Tougher," *Futurist* 37 (2003): 40–47; Graeme Newman, *Global Report on Crime and Justice* (New York: Oxford University Press, 1999); Gary Lafree and Kriss Drass, "Counting Crime Booms Among Nations: Evidence for Homicide Victimization Rates, 1956–1998," *Criminology* 40 (2002): 769–801; *The Small Arms Survey, 2004* (http://www.smallarmssurvey.org/publications/yb_2004.htm), accessed on July 10, 2005; Pedro Scuro, *World Factbook of Criminal Justice Systems: "Brazil"* (Washington, D.C.: Bureau of Justice Statistics, 2003).

The Ecology of Crime

Crime is not spread equally across society, and specific patterns in the crime rate seem to be linked to temporal and ecological factors. These factors are stable and unchanging.

DAY, SEASON, AND CLIMATE   Most reported crimes occur during the warm summer months of July and August. During the summer, teenagers, who usually have the highest crime levels, are out of school and have greater opportunity to commit crime. People spend more time outdoors during warm weather, making themselves easier targets. Similarly, homes are left vacant more often during the summer vacation months, making them more vulnerable to property crimes. Two exceptions to this trend are murders and robberies, which occur frequently in December and January (although rates are also high during the summer).

Crime rates may also be higher on the first day of the month than at any other time. Government welfare and Social Security checks arrive at this time, and with them come increases in such activities as breaking into mailboxes and accosting recipients on the streets. Also, people may have more disposable income at this time, and the availability of extra money may relate to behaviors associated with crime such as drinking, partying, and gambling.[52]

TEMPERATURE   Weather effects (such as temperature swings) have an impact on crime rates. The human body generates stress hormones (adrenaline and testosterone) in response to excessive heat, an activity that has been linked to aggression.[53]

There is agreement that temperature influences crime rates, but there are a number of alternative explanations for the association:

♦   The association between temperature and crime resembles an inverted U-shaped curve: Crime rates increase with rising temperatures and then begin to decline at some point (85 degrees) when it may be too hot for any physical exertion.[54]

♦   Crime rates rise with temperature (the hotter the day, the higher the crime rate).[55]

♦   Rising temperature increases some crimes (e.g., domestic assault), but the rate of others (e.g., rape) declines as temperatures rise.[56]

POPULATION DENSITY   Large urban areas have by far the highest violence rates. Areas with low per capita crime rates tend to be rural. These findings are also supported by victim data. Exceptions to this trend are low-population resort areas with large transient or seasonal populations—such as Atlantic City, New Jersey, and Nantucket, Massachusetts.

Crime rates vary by region. For many years, southern states have had consistently higher crime rates in almost all crime categories than those found in other regions of the country. These data convinced some crime experts that there was a "southern subculture of violence." Although the lead has flip-flopped in recent years between the South and the West, the latest UCR data, illustrated in Figure 2.6, indicate that southern crime rates are once again the highest in the nation.

Firearms and Crime

Firearms play a dominant role in criminal activity. According to the NCVS, firearms are typically involved in about 20 percent of robberies, 10 percent of assaults, and more than 5 percent of rapes. According to the UCR, about two-thirds of all murders involve firearms; most of these weapons are handguns. Criminals of all races and ethnic backgrounds are equally likely to use guns in violent attack, and the presence of a weapon increases the likelihood that a violent incident will result in serious injury and/or death.[57]

Because of the association between guns and crime, there have been numerous efforts to restrict gun ownership, the most important being the Brady Handgun

FIGURE 2.6
Regional Crime Rates

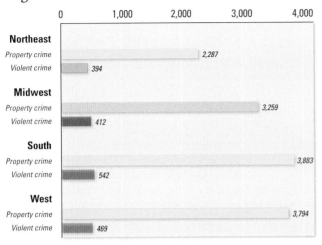

Source: FBI, *Crime in the United States, 2005* (http://www.fbi.gov/ucr/05cius/figures/regcrimefig.html).

Violence Prevention Act, enacted on November 30, 1993. Named after press secretary James Brady, shot in the attack on President Ronald Reagan, the Brady Law imposes a waiting period of five days before a licensed importer, manufacturer, or dealer may sell, deliver, or transfer a handgun to an unlicensed individual. The waiting period applies only in states without an acceptable alternate system of conducting background checks on handgun purchasers. Beginning November 30, 1998, the Brady Law changed, providing an instant check on whether a prospective buyer is prohibited from purchasing a weapon. Federal law bans gun purchases by people convicted of or under indictment for felony charges, fugitives, the mentally ill, those with dishonorable military discharges, those who have renounced U.S. citizenship, illegal aliens, illegal drug users, and those convicted of domestic violence misdemeanors or who are under domestic violence restraining orders (individual state laws may create other restrictions). The Brady Law now requires background approval not just for handgun buyers but also for those who buy rifles and shotguns. In addition, the Federal Violent Crime Control and Law Enforcement Act of 1994 banned a group of military-style semiautomatic firearms (that is, assault weapons). However, this ban on assault weapons was allowed to lapse in 2004.

DEBATING GUNS There is an ongoing debate over gun control. Some experts believe that personal gun use can actually be a deterrent to crime.[58] Gary Kleck and Marc Gertz have found that as many as 400,000 people per year use guns in situations in which they later claim that the guns almost "certainly" saved lives. Even if these estimates are off by a factor of 10, it means that armed citizens may save 40,000 lives annually. Although Kleck and Gertz recognize that guns are involved in murders, suicides, and accidents, which claim more than 30,000 lives per year, they believe their benefit as a crime prevention device should not be overlooked.[59]

Guns have other uses. In many assaults, the aggressor does not wish to kill but only scare the victim. Possessing a gun gives aggressors enough killing power so that they may actually be inhibited from attacking. Research by Kleck and Karen McElrath found that during a robbery, guns can control the situation without the need for illegal force.[60] Guns may also help victims escape serious injury. Victims may be inhibited from fighting back without losing face; it is socially acceptable to back down from a challenge if the opponent is armed with a gun. Therefore, guns can deescalate a potentially violent situation. Kleck, along with Michael Hogan, finds that people who own guns are only slightly more likely

The Small Arms Survey is an independent research project located at the Graduate Institute of International Studies, Geneva, Switzerland. It serves as the principal international source of public information on all aspects of small arms and as a resource center for governments, policy makers, researchers, and activists. You can access it by going to the Siegel/Senna Introduction to Criminal Justice 11e website: www.thomsonedu.com/criminaljustice/siegel.

to commit homicide than nonowners.[61] The benefits of gun ownership, Kleck concludes, outweigh the costs.

Although Kleck's arguments are persuasive, numerous experts disagree with his position and staunchly favor gun control.[62] Franklin Zimring and Gordon Hawkins believe that the proliferation of handguns and the high rate of lethal violence they cause is the single most significant factor separating the crime problem in the United States from the rest of the developed world.[63] Differences between the United States and Europe in nonlethal crimes are only modest at best and getting smaller over time.[64]

Empirical research also supports the gun-control view.[65] Tomislav Kovandzic and his colleagues used data for all large (population over 100,000) U.S. cities to examine the impact of "right to carry" concealed handgun laws on violent crime rates from the period 1980 to 2000 and found that carry laws have little effect on local crime rates.[66] And although Kleck's research touts the benefits of defensive gun use, other researchers find that it may have a more limited effect than he believes.[67]

Social Class and Crime

A still-unresolved issue in criminological literature is the relationship between social class and crime. Traditionally, crime has been thought of as a lower-class phenomenon. After all, people at the lowest rungs of the social structure have the greatest incentive to commit crimes. Those unable to obtain desired goods and services through conventional means may consequently resort to theft and other illegal activities—such as selling narcotics—to obtain them. These activities are referred to as **instrumental crimes**. Those living in poverty are also believed to engage in disproportionate amounts of **expressive crimes**, such as rape and assault, as a means of venting their rage and frustration against society. Alcohol and drug abuse, common in impoverished areas, help fuel violent episodes.[68]

instrumental crimes
Criminal acts intended to improve the financial or social position of the criminal.

expressive crimes
Criminal acts that serve to vent rage or frustration.

When measured with UCR data, official statistics indicate that crime rates in inner-city, high-poverty areas are generally higher than those in suburban or wealthier areas.[69] Surveys of prison inmates consistently show that prisoners were members of the lower class and unemployed or underemployed in the years before their incarceration.

An alternative explanation for these findings is that the relationship between official crime and social class is a function of law enforcement practices, not criminal behavior patterns. Police may devote more resources to poor areas; consequently, apprehension rates may be higher there. Similarly, police may be more likely to formally arrest and prosecute lower-class citizens than those in the middle and upper classes, which may account for the lower class's overrepresentation in official statistics and the prison population.

CLASS AND SELF-REPORTS Self-report data have been used extensively to test the class–crime relationship. If people in all social classes self-report similar crime patterns, but only those in the lower class are formally arrested, that would explain higher crime rates in lower-class neighborhoods. However, if lower-class people report greater criminal activity than their middle- and upper-class peers, it would indicate that official statistics accurately represent the crime problem. Surprisingly, early self-report studies conducted in the 1950s, specifically those by James Short and F. Ivan Nye, did not find a direct relationship between social class and youth crime.[70] They found that socioeconomic class was related to official processing by police, courts, and correctional agencies but not to the commission of crimes. In other words, although lower- and middle-class youths self-reported equal amounts of crime, the lower-class youths had a greater chance of being arrested, convicted, and incarcerated and becoming official delinquents. In addition, factors generally associated with lower-class membership, such as broken homes, were found to be related to institutionalization but not to admissions of delinquency. Other studies of this period reached similar conclusions.[71]

For more than 20 years after the use of self-reports became widespread, a majority of self-report studies concluded that a class–crime relationship did not exist. If the poor possessed more extensive criminal records than the wealthy, this difference was attributed to differential law enforcement and not to class-based behavior differences. That is, police may be more likely to arrest lower-class offenders and treat the affluent more leniently.

Almost 30 years ago, Charles Tittle, Wayne Villemez, and Douglas Smith wrote what is still considered the definitive review of the relationship between class and crime.[72] They concluded that little if any support exists for the contention that crime is primarily a lower-class phenomenon. Consequently, Tittle and his associates argued that official statistics probably reflect class bias in processing lower-class offenders. In a subsequent article written with Robert Meier, Tittle once again reviewed existing data on the class–crime relationship and found little evidence of a consistent association between class and crime.[73] More recent self-report studies generally support Tittle's conclusions: No direct relationship exists between social class and crime.[74]

Tittle's findings have sparked significant debate in the criminological community. Many self-report instruments include trivial offenses such as using a false ID or drinking alcohol, which may invalidate findings. Affluent youths could frequently engage in trivial offenses such as petty larceny, using drugs, and simple assault but rarely escalate their criminal involvement. Those who support a class–crime relationship suggest that a significant association can be observed if only serious felony offenses are considered.[75] Some studies find that when only serious crimes, such as burglary and assault, are considered, lower-class youths are significantly more delinquent.[76]

THE CLASS–CRIME CONTROVERSY The relationship between class and crime is an important one for criminological theory. If crime is related to social class, then it follows that economic and social factors, such as poverty and neighborhood disorganization, cause criminal behavior.

One reason that a true measure of the class–crime relationship has so far eluded crime experts is that the methods employed to determine social class vary widely. For example, the father's occupation and education are only weakly related to self-reported crime, but unemployment or receiving welfare is a more significant predictor of criminality.[77]

The association between class and crime could also be more complex than a simple linear relationship (that is, the poorer you are, the more crime you commit).[78] Class may affect some subgroups in the population (e.g., women, African Americans) more than it does others (e.g., males, whites).[79] Sally Simpson and Lori Elis found that white females are more likely to be influenced by social class than are minority females. They speculate that white females have had their financial expectations significantly raised because of the women's movement, which had less effect on minority women. Therefore, white females are more likely to turn to crime when their expectations of wealth are not achieved.[80] In light of these findings, it is not surprising that the true relationship between class and crime is difficult to determine. The effect may be obscured because its impact varies within and between groups.

Like so many other criminological controversies, the debate over the true relationship between class and crime will most likely persist. The weight of recent evidence seems to suggest that serious, official crime is more prevalent among the lower classes, whereas less serious and self-reported crime is spread more evenly throughout the social structure.[81] Income inequality, poverty, and resource deprivation are all associated with the most serious violent crimes, including homicide and assault.[82] Members of the lower class are more likely to suffer psychological

PERSPECTIVES ON JUSTICE

Rehabilitation

Rehabilitation advocates believe that social class is correlated with crime and that the key to reducing crime rates is not punishment but programs that emphasize jobs, counseling, and opportunity.

abnormality, including high rates of anxiety and conduct disorders, conditions that may promote criminality.[83]

Age and Crime

General agreement exists that age is inversely related to criminality.[84] Regardless of economic status, marital status, race, sex, and so on, younger people commit crime more often than older people. Research indicates that this relationship has been stable across time periods ranging from 1935 to the present.[85] Official statistics reveal that young people are arrested at a disproportionate rate to their numbers in the population. Victim surveys generate similar findings for crimes in which assailant age can be determined. Whereas youths aged 13 to 17 collectively make up about 6 percent of the total U.S. population, they account for about 25 percent of Part I crime arrests and 17 percent of arrests for all crimes. As a general rule, the peak age for property crime is believed to be 16, and for violence, 18 (see Figure 2.7). In contrast, adults 45 and over, who make up 32 percent of the population, account for only 7 percent of Part I crime arrests. The elderly are particularly resistant to the temptations of crime. They make up more than 12 percent of the population and less than 1 percent of arrests. Elderly males 65 and over are predominantly arrested for alcohol-related matters (public drunkenness and drunk driving) and elderly females for larceny (shoplifting). The elderly crime rate has remained stable for the past 20 years.[86]

Gender and Crime

The three data-gathering criminal statistics tools support the theory that male crime rates are much higher than those of females. Victims report that their assailant was male in more than 80 percent of all violent personal crimes. According to the Uniform Crime Reports arrest statistics, the overall male–female arrest ratio is about 3.5 male offenders to 1 female offender; for serious violent crimes, the ratio is closer to 5 males to 1 female; murder arrests are 8:1 male. Recent self-report data collected by the Institute for Social Research at the University of Michigan also show that males commit more serious crimes, such as robbery, assault, and burglary, than females do. However, although the patterns in self-reports parallel official data, the ratios are smaller. In other words, males self-report more criminal behavior than females—but not to the degree suggested by official data.

TRAITS AND TEMPERAMENT   Early crime experts pointed to emotional, physical, and psychological differences between males and females to explain the differences in crime rates. Cesare Lombroso's 1895 book, *The Female Offender*, argued that a small group of female criminals lacked "typical" female traits of "piety, maternity, undeveloped intelligence, and weakness."[87] In physical appearance as well as in their emotional makeup, delinquent females appeared closer to men than to other women. Lombroso's theory became known as the **masculinity hypothesis**; in essence, a few "masculine" females were responsible for the handful of crimes that women commit.

Another early view of female crime focused on the supposed dynamics of sexual relationships. Female criminals were viewed as either sexually controlling or sexually naive, either manipulating men for profit or being manipulated by them. The female's criminality was often masked because criminal justice authorities were reluctant to take action against a woman.[88] This perspective is known as the **chivalry hypothesis**, which holds that much female criminality is hidden because of U.S. culture's generally protective and benevolent attitude toward women.[89] In other words, police are less likely to arrest, juries are less likely to convict, and judges are less likely to incarcerate female offenders.

Although these early writings are no longer taken seriously, some crime experts still consider trait differences a key determinant of crime rate differences. For example, some crime experts link antisocial behavior to hormonal

masculinity hypothesis
The view that women who commit crimes have biological and psychological traits similar to those of men.

chivalry hypothesis
The idea that female defendants are treated more leniently in sentencing (and are less likely to be arrested and prosecuted in the first place) because the criminal justice system is dominated by men who have a paternalistic or protective attitude toward women.

FIGURE 2.7

The Relationship Between Age and Serious Crime Arrests

Arrest rate per 100,000 persons

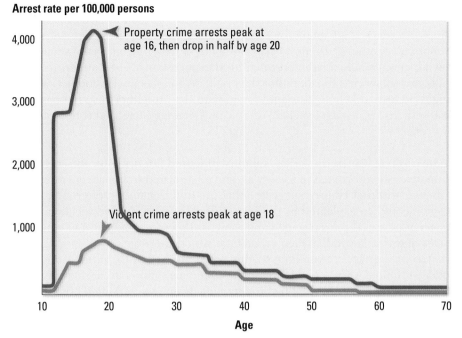

Source: FBI, *Crime in the United States, 2005* (Washington, D.C.: Government Printing Office, 2006).

influences by arguing that male sex hormones (androgens) account for more aggressive male behavior and that gender-related hormonal differences can also explain the gender gap in the crime rate.[90]

SOCIALIZATION AND DEVELOPMENT Another view is that, unlike boys, a majority of young girls are socialized to avoid being violent and aggressive and are supervised more closely by parents. It comes as no surprise when research shows that most girls develop moral values that strongly discourage antisocial behavior.[91] The few female criminals are troubled individuals, alienated at home, who pursue crime as a means of compensating for their disrupted personal lives.[92] The streets are a second home to girls whose physical and emotional adjustment was hampered by a strained home life marked by such conditions as absent fathers and overly competitive mothers.

For example, Emily Gaarder and Joanne Belknap have found that many delinquent girls sent to adult prisons had troubled lives that set them on a criminal career path.[93] One girl told them how her father had attacked her, yet her mother shortly let him return home:

> I told her I'd leave if he came back, but she let him anyway. I was thinking, you know, she should be worrying about me. I left and went to my cousin's house. Nobody even called me. Mom didn't talk to me for two weeks, and Dad said to me "Don't call." It was like they didn't care. I started smoking weed a lot then, drinking, skipping school, and shoplifting . . . I had no [delinquency] record before this happened.

Some experts explain these differences in socialization by pointing to gender-based differences in human development that help shape behavior choices. Girls are believed to have cognitive traits that shield them from criminal behaviors.

COGNITIVE DIFFERENCES Psychologists note significant cognitive differences between boys and girls that may affect their antisocial behaviors. Girls have been found to be superior to boys in verbal ability, yet boys test higher in visual–spatial performance. Girls acquire language faster, learning to speak earlier and with better pronunciation. Girls are far less likely to have reading problems than boys, whereas boys do much better on standardized math tests. (This difference is attributed by some experts to boys' receiving more attention from math teachers.) In most cases these cognitive differences are small, narrowing, and usually attributed to cultural expectations. Their superior verbal skills may allow girls to talk rather than fight. When faced with conflict, women might be more likely to attempt to negotiate than to either respond passively or to physically resist, especially when they perceive increased threat of harm or death.[94]

liberal feminist theory
An ideology holding that women suffer oppression, discrimination, and disadvantage as a result of their sex and calling for gender equality in pay, opportunity, child care, and education.

FEMINIST VIEWS In the 1970s, feminists focused attention on the social and economic role of women in society and its relationship to female crime rates.[95] **Liberal feminist theory** suggested that the traditionally lower crime rate for women could be explained by their second-class economic and social position. As women's social roles changed and their lifestyles became more like those of males, it was believed that their crime rates would converge.

Crime experts, responding to this research, began to refer to the "new female criminal." The rapid increase in the female crime rate during the 1960s and 1970s, especially in what had traditionally been male-oriented crimes (such as burglary and larceny), supported the feminist view. In addition, self-report studies seem to indicate that the pattern of female criminality, if not its frequency, is similar to that of male criminality and that the factors predisposing male criminals to crime have an equal impact on female criminals.[96] Crime experts began to assess the association among economic issues, gender roles, and criminality.

IS CONVERGENCE LIKELY? In sum, gender differences in the crime rate have been explained by such statements as these:

◆ Males are stronger and better able to commit violent crime.

◆ Hormonal differences make males more aggressive.

◆ Girls are socialized to be less aggressive than boys.[97]

◆ Girls have better verbal skills and use them to diffuse conflict.

◆ Boys are granted greater personal freedom; girls are subject to greater parental control.

However, these views are now being challenged by the rapid rise in the female crime rate.[98] As gender role differences at home, school, and the workplace have narrowed, so have crime rates. As a result, there has been a rise in female participation in traditionally male-oriented forms of criminality such as violent crime and juvenile gang membership.[99]

Will the gender differences in the crime rate eventually dissolve? Some crime experts find that gender-based crime rate differences remain significant and argue that the emancipation of women has had relatively little influence on female crime rates.[100] They dispute the idea that increases in the female arrest rate reflect economic or social change brought about by the women's movement. For one thing, many female criminals come from the socioeconomic class least affected by the women's movement. Their crimes seem more a function of economic inequality than women's rights. For another, the offense patterns of women are still quite different from those of men, who commit a disproportionate share of serious crimes, such as robbery, burglary, murder, and assault.[101] According to Darrell Steffensmeier and his associates, recent trends may be explained more by changes in police activity than in criminal activity: Police today may be more willing to arrest girls for crimes.[102] Police may be abandoning their traditional deference toward women in an effort to be "gender neutral."

In addition, new laws such as dual arrest laws in domestic cases, which mandate that both parties be taken into custody, result in more women suffering arrest in domestic incidents.[103] Whether male and female crime rates will eventually converge remains to be seen.

Race and Crime

Official crime data indicate that minority-group members are involved in a disproportionate share of criminal activity. According to UCR reports, African Americans make up about 12 percent of the general population, yet they account for about 39 percent of Part I violent crime arrests and 29 percent of property crime arrests. They also are responsible for a disproportionate number of Part II arrests (except for alcohol-related arrests, which detain primarily white offenders).

These data could reflect racial differences in the crime rate, but they could also reflect police bias in the arrest process. This issue can be evaluated by comparing racial differences in self-report data with those found in official delinquency records. Charges of racial discrimination in the arrest process would be substantiated if whites and blacks self-reported equal numbers of crimes but minorities were arrested far more often.

Early efforts found virtually no relationship between race and self-reported delinquency.[104] These research efforts supported a case for police bias in the arrest decision. Other, more recent self-report studies that use large national samples of youths have also found little evidence of racial disparity in crimes committed. The Monitoring the Future self-report survey found that, if anything, black youths self-report less delinquent behavior and substance abuse than whites.[105] These and other self-report studies seem to indicate that the delinquent behavior rates of black and white teenagers are generally similar and that differences in arrest statistics may indicate a differential selection policy by police.[106]

Racial differences in the crime rate remain an extremely sensitive issue. Although official arrest records indicate that African Americans are arrested at a higher rate than members of other racial groups, some question whether this is a function of crime rate differences, racism by police, or faulty data collection.[107] Research shows that suspects who are poor, minority, and male are more likely to be formally arrested than suspects who are white, affluent, and female.[108] Some critics charge that police officers routinely use racial profiling to stop African Americans and search their cars without probable cause or reasonable suspicion. Some cynics have gone so far as to suggest that police officers have created a new form of traffic offense called DWB, "driving while black."[109]

Although the UCR may reflect discriminatory police practices, African Americans are arrested for a disproportionate amount of violent crime, such as robbery and murder, and police discretion alone is unlikely to account for these proportions. It is doubtful that police routinely ignore white killers, robbers, and rapists while arresting violent black offenders. Recent research by Stewart J. D'Alessio and Lisa Stolzenberg, using data from the National Incident-Based Reporting System, found that the odds of arrest for white offenders is approximately 22 percent higher for robbery, 13 percent higher for aggravated assault, and 9 percent higher for simple assault than they are for black offenders; race is not related to rape arrests. Their findings suggest that the fact that African Americans account for a disproportionately high percentage of serious crime arrests is most likely attributable to differential involvement in reported crime, not to racially biased law enforcement practices. If these findings are accurate, how can the racial differences in the crime rate be explained?[110]

PERSPECTIVES ON JUSTICE

Due Process

Advocates of the due process perspective are especially sensitive to charges of race bias and have drawn attention to the practice of racial profiling.

RACISM AND DISCRIMINATION Most crime experts focus on the impact of economic deprivation and the legacy of racism and discrimination on personality and behavior.[111] The fact that U.S. culture influences African American crime rates is underscored by the fact that black violence rates are much lower in other nations—both those that are predominantly white, such as Canada, and those that are predominantly black, such as Nigeria.[112]

Some crime experts view black crime as a function of socialization in a society where the black family was torn apart and black culture destroyed by slavery in such a way that recovery has proved impossible. Early experiences have left a wound that has been deepened by racism and lack of opportunity.[113] Children of the slave society were thrust into a system of forced dependency and ambivalence and antagonism toward oneself and one's group. Today, the cohesiveness of the African American family is affected by the low employment rates among African American males, which places a strain on marriages. The relatively large number of single, female-headed households in these communities may be tied to the high mortality rate among African American males due in part to their increased risk of early death by disease and violence.[114] When families are weakened or disrupted, their social control is compromised. Therefore, it is not surprising that divorce and separation rates are significantly associated with homicide rates in the African American community.[115] However, even among at-risk African American kids growing up in communities categorized by poverty, high unemployment levels, and single-parent households, those who manage to live in stable families with sufficient income and educational achievement are much less likely to engage in violent behaviors than those lacking family support.[116]

INSTITUTIONAL RACISM Racism is still an element of daily life in the African American community, a factor that undermines faith in social and political institutions and weakens confidence in the justice system. Such fears are supported by empirical evidence that, at least in some jurisdictions, young African American males are treated more harshly by the criminal and juvenile justice systems than are members of any other group.[117] According to the **racial threat theory**, as the percentage of African Americans in the population increases, so does the amount of social control that police direct at blacks.[118]

racial threat theory
The view that young minority males are subject to greater police control—e.g., formal arrest—when their numbers increase within the population.

The racial threat theory has received only mixed support, but a significant body of research shows that the justice system may be racially biased.[119] Police are more likely to formally arrest minority-group members, and because African Americans are more likely to become the focus of unwarranted police attention, they are more likely to obtain a prior criminal record and, consequently, be eligible for more severe punishments than Caucasian youths if they are re-arrested.[120] Research shows that black and Latino adults are less likely to receive bail in violent crime cases than whites and that minority juveniles are more likely to be kept in detention pending trial in juvenile court.[121] African Americans, especially those who are indigent or unemployed, receive longer prison sentences than whites with the same employment status. Judges could be imposing harsher punishments on unemployed African Americans because they view them as "social dynamite," considering them more dangerous and more likely to recidivate than white offenders.[122] Yet when African Americans are victims of crime, their predicament receives less public concern and media attention than that afforded white victims.[123]

Differential enforcement practices take their toll on the African American community. One national survey found that more than 13 percent of all African American males have lost the right to vote; that in seven states, 25 percent have been disenfranchised; and that in two states, Florida and Alabama, 33 percent of African American males have lost their voting privileges.[124] So it is not surprising that African Americans of all social classes hold negative attitudes toward the justice system and view it as an arbitrary and unfair institution.[125]

ECONOMIC AND SOCIAL DISPARITY Racial differentials in crime rates may also be tied to economic disparity. Blacks and whites face different economic and social realities. African Americans typically have higher unemployment rates and lower incomes than whites. They face a greater degree of social isolation and economic deprivation, a condition that has been linked by empirical research to high murder rates.[126] Many black youths are forced to attend essentially segregated schools that are underfunded and deteriorated, a condition that elevates the likelihood of their being incarcerated in adulthood.[127] Not helping the situation is that during tough economic times, blacks and whites may find themselves competing for shrinking job opportunities. As economic competition between the races grows, interracial homicides do likewise. Economic and political rivalries lead to greater levels of interracial violence.[128]

Even during times of economic growth, lower-class African Americans are left out of the economic mainstream, a fact that meets with a growing sense of frustration and failure.[129] As a result of being shut out of educational and economic opportunities enjoyed by the rest of society, this population may be prone, some believe, to the lure of illegitimate gain and criminality. Young African American males in the inner city often are resigned to a lifetime of little if any social and economic opportunity. Even when economic data say they are doing better, news accounts of "protests, riots, and acts of civil disobedience" tell them otherwise.[130] African Americans living in slums may be disproportionately violent because they are exposed to more violence in their daily lives than are other racial and economic groups. This exposure is a significant risk factor for violent behavior.[131]

In sum, many African American families are forced to reside in some of the nation's poorest communities, which cannot provide economic opportunities. The resulting economic inequality increases the incentive to commit crime. African American crime is motivated more by economic necessity than by anger, strain, and rage.[132]

IS CONVERGENCE POSSIBLE? Considering these overwhelming social problems, is it possible that racial crime rates will soon converge? One argument is that if economic conditions improve in the minority community, then differences in crime rates will eventually disappear.[133] Sociologist Julie Phillips found that if whites were subjected to the same economic and social disabilities as minorities, interracial homicide rate differences would be dramatically reduced: All of the white–Latino homicide differential and about half of the white–black homicide gap would evaporate if the social and economic characteristics of minorities were improved to levels currently enjoyed by whites.[134] A trend toward residential integration, under way since 1980, may also help reduce crime rate differentials.[135] Despite economic disparity, few racial differences are evident in attitudes toward crime and justice today. Convergence in crime rates will occur if economic and social obstacles can be removed.

In sum, the weight of the evidence shows that although little difference exists in the self-reported crime rates of racial groups, African Americans are more likely to be arrested for serious violent crimes. The causes of minority crime have been linked to poverty, racism, hopelessness, lack of opportunity, and urban problems experienced by all too many African American citizens.

Careers and Crime

Crime data show that most offenders commit a single criminal act and upon arrest discontinue their antisocial activity. Others commit a few less serious crimes. However, a small group of criminal offenders accounts for a majority of all criminal offenses. These persistent offenders are referred to as **career criminals** or **chronic offenders**.

career criminals
Persistent repeat offenders who organize their lifestyle around criminality.

chronic offenders
As defined by Marvin Wolfgang, Robert Figlio, and Thorsten Sellin, delinquents who are arrested 5 or more times before the age of 18 and who commit a disproportionate amount of all criminal offenses.

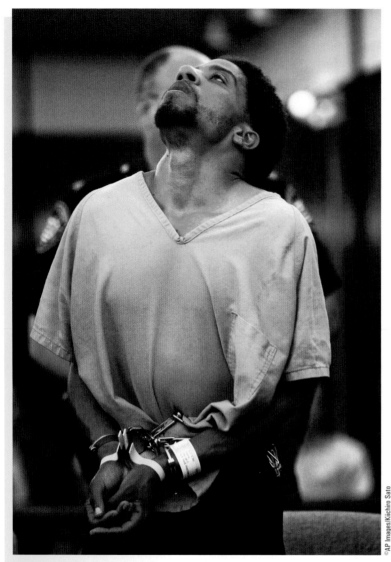

Career criminals are responsible for a significant portion of the total crime rate. Here, George Hyatte, 34, appears in a courtroom on August 12, 2005, for an extradition hearing in Columbus, Ohio. George and his wife, Jennifer Hyatte, were arrested at the America's Best Value Inn in Columbus after a cab driver tipped off authorities that he had driven them there. Hyatte, a career-criminal inmate serving a 41-year sentence for robbery and related charges, killed a guard during a daring escape attempt—a crime that might bring him the death penalty.

The concept of the chronic or career offender is most closely associated with the research efforts of Marvin Wolfgang, Robert Figlio, and Thorsten Sellin.[136] In their landmark 1972 study, *Delinquency in a Birth Cohort*, they used official records to follow the criminal careers of a cohort of 9,945 boys from the time of their birth in Philadelphia in 1945 until they reached 18 years of age in 1963. Official police records were used to identify delinquents. About one-third of the boys (3,475) had some police contact. The remaining two-thirds (6,470) had none. Each delinquent was given a seriousness weight score for every delinquent act.[137] The weighting of delinquent acts allowed the researchers to differentiate, for example, between a simple assault requiring no medical attention for the victim and serious battery in which the victim needed hospitalization.

The best-known discovery of Wolfgang and his associates was that of the so-called chronic offender. The cohort data indicated that 54 percent (1,862) of the sample's delinquent youths were repeat offenders, whereas the remaining 46 percent (1,613) were one-time offenders. The repeaters could be further categorized as nonchronic recidivists and chronic recidivists. The former consisted of 1,235 youths who had been arrested more than once but fewer than five times and who made up 35.6 percent of all delinquents. The latter was a group of 627 boys arrested five times or more, who accounted for 18 percent of the delinquents and 6 percent of the total sample of 9,945. The chronic career criminals (known today as "the chronic 6 percent") were involved in the most dramatic amounts of delinquent behavior. They were responsible for 5,305 offenses, or 51.9 percent of all the offenses committed by the cohort. Even more striking was the involvement of chronic offenders in serious criminal acts. Of the entire sample, they committed 71 percent of the homicides, 73 percent of the rapes, 82 percent of the robberies, and 69 percent of the aggravated assaults (see Exhibit 2.5).

Wolfgang and his associates found that arrests and court experiences did little to deter the chronic offender. In fact, punishment was inversely related to chronic offending: The more stringent the sanction chronic offenders received, the more likely they would be to engage in repeated criminal behavior.

In a second cohort study, Wolfgang and his associates selected a new, larger birth cohort, born in Philadelphia in 1958, which contained both male and female subjects.[138] Although the proportion of delinquent youths was about the same as that in the 1945 cohort, the researchers found a similar pattern of chronic offending. Chronic female delinquency was relatively rare—only 1 percent of the females in the survey were chronic offenders. Wolfgang's pioneering effort to identify the chronic career offender has been replicated by a number of other researchers in a variety of locations in the United States.[139] The chronic offender has also been found abroad.[140]

©AP Images/Kiichiro Sato

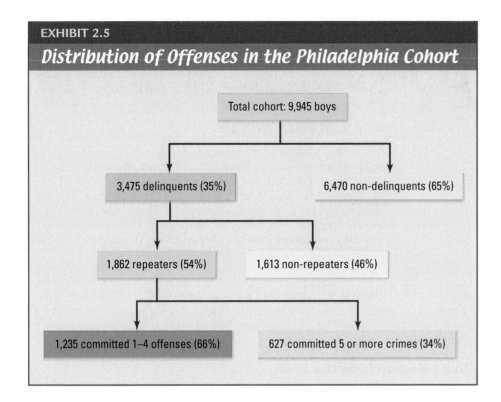

EXHIBIT 2.5

Distribution of Offenses in the Philadelphia Cohort

Total cohort: 9,945 boys

3,475 delinquents (35%) → 6,470 non-delinquents (65%)

1,862 repeaters (54%) → 1,613 non-repeaters (46%)

1,235 committed 1–4 offenses (66%) → 627 committed 5 or more crimes (34%)

WHO ARE CAREER CRIMINALS? Who is at risk of becoming a career criminal? As might be expected, youths who have been exposed to a variety of personal and social problems at an early age are the most at risk for repeat offending. Other research studies have found that involvement in criminal activity (for example, getting arrested before age 15), relatively low intellectual development, and parental drug involvement were key predictive factors for chronicity.[141] Children who are found to be disruptive and antisocial as early as age 5 or 6 are the most likely to exhibit stable, long-term patterns of disruptive behavior throughout adolescence.[142] They have measurable behavior problems in areas such as learning and motor skills, cognitive abilities, family relations, and other areas of social, psychological, and physical functioning.[143] Youthful offenders who persist are more likely to abuse alcohol, become economically dependent, have lower aspirations, and have a weak employment record.[144] They do not specialize in one type of crime; instead, they engage in a variety of criminal acts, including theft, drugs, and violent offenses.

IMPLICATIONS OF THE CAREER CRIMINAL CONCEPT Concern about repeat offenders has been translated into programs at various stages of the justice process. To meet the challenge, police departments and district attorneys' offices around the nation have set up programs to focus resources on capturing and prosecuting dangerous or repeat offenders.[145] Legal jurisdictions are developing sentencing policies designed to incapacitate chronic offenders for long periods of time without hope of probation or parole. Among the policies spurred by the chronic offender concept are mandatory sentences for violent or drug-related crimes and **three strikes laws**, which require people convicted of a third felony offense to serve a mandatory life sentence. Whether such policies can reduce crime rates or are merely get-tough measures designed to placate conservative voters remains to be seen.

PERSPECTIVES ON JUSTICE

Crime Control

The discovery of the chronic offender was a key element in the development of sentences that provide extended terms for repeat offenders. It stands to reason that if only a few hard-core offenders commit most crimes, locking them up for life can have a dramatic effect on the crime rate. This is a cornerstone of the crime control model.

ThomsonNOW™ Improve your grade on the exam with Personalized Study! For reinforcement resources and a mastery check of crime patterns, go to www.thomsonedu.com/thomsonnow.

three strikes laws
Sentencing codes which require that an offender receive a life sentence after conviction for a third felony. Some states allow parole after a lengthy prison stay—for example, 25 years.

ETHICAL CHALLENGES IN CRIMINAL JUSTICE: A WRITING ASSIGNMENT

Eric Rudolph's criminal acts might be classified as hate crimes. Each state defines this type of crime differently. Here is a section of California's hate crime statute, which states in part:

California PENAL CODE SECTION 422.6

> 422.6. (a) No person, whether or not acting under color of law, shall by force or threat of force, willfully injure, intimidate, interfere with, oppress, or threaten any other person in the free exercise or enjoyment of any right or privilege secured to him or her by the Constitution or laws of this state or by the Constitution or laws of the United States because of the other person's race, color, religion, ancestry, national origin, disability, gender, or sexual orientation, or because he or she perceives that the other person has one or more of those characteristics.

Write an essay discussing the issue of whether it is fair and just to punish more severely someone who commits a crime motivated by hate than one motivated by greed, jealousy, or revenge. Consider such issues as morality, legality, and practicality. For example, how can we "prove" that someone was motivated by hate and not anger?

Doing Research on the Web

Search the web for sites that discuss hate crimes. The Religious Freedom Watch contains the laws of most states and other information. You can reach it by going to the Siegel/Senna Introduction to Criminal Justice 11e website: www.thomsonedu.com/criminaljustice/siegel.

The Hate Crimes Research Network provides general information and many links. You can reach this site by going to the Siegel/Senna Introduction to Criminal Justice 11e website: www.thomsonedu.com/criminaljustice/siegel.

You might also use "hate crime" as a subject guide on InfoTrac College Edition.

SUMMARY

♦ The three primary sources of crime statistics are the Uniform Crime Reports, based on police data accumulated by the FBI; self-reports from criminal behavior surveys; and victim surveys.

♦ These sources reveal significant levels of crime in the United States, although the amount of violent crime is decreasing.

♦ Each data source has its strengths and weaknesses, and although different from one another, the sources agree on the nature of criminal behavior.

♦ The data sources show stable patterns in the crime rate. Ecological patterns show that some areas of the country are more crime prone than others, that there are seasons and times for crime, and that these patterns are stable.

♦ Evidence also exists of gender and age gaps in the crime rate: Men commit more crime than

women, and young people commit more crime than the elderly.

♦ Crime data show that people commit less crime as they age, but the significance and cause of this pattern are still not completely understood.

♦ Racial and class patterns appear in the crime rate. However, whether these are true differences or a function of discriminatory law enforcement remains unclear.

♦ One of the most important findings in the crime statistics is the existence of the chronic offender, a repeat career criminal responsible for a significant share of all law violations. Career criminals begin their careers early in life and, instead of aging out of crime, persist into adulthood.

KEY TERMS

hate crimes, 47
public order crimes, 48
white-collar crime, 51
corporate crime, 51
Uniform Crime Reports
(UCRs), 53
Part I crimes, 53
Part II crimes, 53

cleared, 54
National Incident-Based Reporting
System (NIBRS), 56
National Crime Victimization
Survey (NCVS), 57
self-report survey, 58
instrumental crimes, 70
expressive crimes, 70

masculinity hypothesis, 72
chivalry hypothesis, 72
liberal feminist theory, 74
racial threat theory, 76
career criminals, 77
chronic offenders, 77
three strikes law, 79

ThomsonNOW Maximize your study time by using ThomsonNOW's diagnostic study plan to help you review this chapter. The Study Plan will

◆ help you identify areas on which you should concentrate;

◆ provide interactive exercises to help you master the chapter concepts; and

◆ provide a post-test to confirm you are ready to move on to the next chapter.

CRITICAL THINKING QUESTIONS

1. Would you answer honestly if a national crime survey asked you about your criminal behavior, including drinking and drug use? If not, why not? If you said "no," do you question the accuracy of self-report surveys?

2. How would you explain gender differences in the crime rate? Why do you think males are more violent than females?

3. Assuming that males are more violent than females, does that mean crime has a biological as opposed to a social basis (because males and females share a similar environment)?

4. The UCR states that crime rates are higher in large cities than in small towns. What does that say about the effects of TV, films, and music on teenage behavior?

5. What social and environmental factors do you believe influence the crime rate? For example, do you think a national emergency such as the September 11, 2001, terrorist attacks would increase or decrease crime rates?

6. If the characteristics of chronic offenders could be determined, should people with those traits be monitored from birth?

NOTES

1. Information on the Rudolph case can be obtained at http://www.cnn.com/2003/US/ 05/31/rudolph.arrest/ http://www.belleville.com/mld/newsdemocrat/6027216.htm.

2. Cited on http://en.wikipedia.org/wiki/Eric_Rudolph, accessed on August 17, 2005.

3. Gary Bailey and N. Prabha Unnithan, "Gang Homicides in California: A Discriminant Analysis," *Journal of Criminal Justice* 22 (1994): 267–75.

4. Arlen Egley, Jr., and Christina Ritz, *Highlights of the 2004 National Youth Gang Survey* (Washington, D.C.: Office of Juvenile Justice and Delinquency Prevention, 2006).

5. "Special Report: The Columbine Tapes," *Time*, December 20, 1999, p. 23.

6. James Alan Fox and Jack Levin, "Multiple Homicide: Patterns of Serial and Mass Murder," in *Crime and Justice: An Annual Edition*, vol. 23, ed. Michael Tonry (Chicago: University of Chicago Press, 1998), pp. 407–55.

7. Ibid.

8. U.S. Department of Health and Human Services, Children's Bureau, *Child Maltreatment 2004* (Washington, D.C.: Government Printing Office, 2006).

9. Joseph Price and Kathy Glad, "Hostile Attributional Tendencies in Maltreated Children," *Journal of Abnormal Child Psychology* 31 (2003): 329–44.

10. James Garofalo, "Bias and Non-Bias Crimes in New York City: Preliminary Findings." Paper presented at the annual meeting of the American Society of Criminology, Baltimore, November 1990.

11. "Boy Gets 18 Years in Fatal Park Beating of Transient," *Los Angeles Times*, December 24, 1987, p. 9B.

12. FBI, *Hate Crime Statistics, 2004* (http://www.fbi.gov/ucr/hc2004/ section1.htm), accessed on April 11, 2006.

13. Edwin Schur, *Crimes Without Victims* (Englewood Cliffs, N.J.: Prentice-Hall, 1965).

14. *The Centers for Disease Control and Prevention's Youth Risk Behavior Survey 2006* (http://www.whitehousedrugpolicy.gov/ news/press06/060806.html), accessed on June 12, 2006.

15. Ruth Engs and David Hanson, "Boozing and Brawling on Campus: A National Study of Violent Problems Associated with Drinking Over the Past Decade," *Journal of Criminal Justice* 22 (1994): 171–80.

16. Robert Nash Parker, "Bringing 'Booze' Back In: The Relationship Between Alcohol and Homicide," *Journal of Research in Crime and Delinquency* 32 (1993): 3–38.

17. *Department of Health and Human Services National Survey on Drug Youth and Health, National Survey on Youth Violence and Illicit Drug Use,* Issue 5 (2006) (http://oas.samhsa.gov/2k6/youthViolence/youthViolence.htm).

18. George Speckart and M. Douglas Anglin, "Narcotics Use and Crime: An Overview of Recent Research Advances," *Contemporary Drug Problems* 13 (1986): 741–69.

19. Evelyn Wei, Rolf Loeber, and Helene Raskin White, "Teasing Apart the Developmental Associations Between Alcohol and Marijuana Use and Violence," *Journal of Contemporary Criminal Justice* 20 (2004): 166–83.

20. Susan Martin, Christopher Maxwell, Helene Raskin White, and Yan Zhang, "Trends in Alcohol Use, Cocaine Use, and Crime," *Journal of Drug Issues* 34 (2004): 333–60.

21. John Hepburn, "Occasional Criminals," in *Major Forms of Crime,* ed. Robert Meier (Beverly Hills, Calif.: Sage, 1984), pp. 73–94.

22. James Inciardi, "Professional Crime," in *Major Forms of Crime,* ed. Robert Meier (Beverly Hills, Calif.: Sage, 1984), p. 223.

23. See, generally, Jay Albanese, *Organized Crime in America,* 2nd ed. (Cincinnati, Ohio: Anderson, 1989), p. 68.

24. James O. Finckenauer and Yuri A. Voronin, *The Threat of Russian Organized Crime* (Washington, D.C.: National Institute of Justice, 2001).

25. Federal Bureau of Investigation, *Crime in the United States, 2005* (Washington, D.C.: Government Printing Office, 2006). http://www.fbi.gov/ucr/05cius/index.html

26. Richard Felson, Steven Messner, Anthony Hoskin, and Glenn Deane, "Reasons for Reporting and Not Reporting Domestic Violence to the Police," *Criminology* 40 (2002): 617–48.

27. Callie Marie Rennison and Michael Rand, *Criminal Victimization 2002* (Washington, D.C.: Bureau of Justice Statistics, 2003).

28. Duncan Chappell, Gilbert Geis, Stephen Schafer, and Larry Siegel, "Forcible Rape: A Comparative Study of Offenses Known to the Police in Boston and Los Angeles," in *Studies in the Sociology of Sex,* ed. James Henslin (New York: Appleton Century Crofts, 1971), pp. 169–93.

29. Patrick Jackson, "Assessing the Validity of Official Data on Arson," *Criminology* 26 (1988): 181–95.

30. Robert O'Brien, "Police Productivity and Crime Rates: 1973–1992," *Criminology* 34 (1996): 183–207.

31. FBI, *UCR Handbook* (Washington, D.C.: Government Printing Office, 1998), p. 33.

32. Lynn Addington, "The Effect of NIBRS Reporting on Item Missing Data in Murder Cases," *Homicide Studies* 8 (2004): 193–213.

33. Dana Peterson, Terrance Taylor, and Finn-Aage Esbensen, "Gang Membership and Violent Victimization," *Justice Quarterly* 21 (2004): 793–816.

34. Shannan Catalano, *Criminal Victimization 2005* (Washington, DC: Bureau of Justice Statistics, 2006). Data in this section come from this report.

35. L. Edward Wells and Joseph Rankin, "Juvenile Victimization: Convergent Validation of Alternative Measurements," *Journal of Research in Crime and Delinquency* 32 (1995): 287–307.

36. Christiane Brems, Mark Johnson, David Neal, and Melinda Freemon, "Childhood Abuse History and Substance Use Among Men and Women Receiving Detoxification Services," *American Journal of Drug & Alcohol Abuse* 30 (2004): 799–821.

37. See, for example, Spencer Rathus and Larry Siegel, "Crime and Personality Revisited: Effects of MMPI Sets on Self-Report Studies," *Criminology* 18 (1980): 245–51; John Clark and Larry Tifft, "Polygraph and Interview Validation of Self-Reported Deviant Behavior," *American Sociological Review* 31 (1966): 516–23.

38. Charles Katz, Vincent Webb, and Scott Decker, "Using the Arrestee Drug Abuse Monitoring (ADAM) Program to Further Understand the Relationship Between Drug Use and Gang Membership," *Justice Quarterly* 22 (2005): 58–88.

39. Mallie Paschall, Miriam Ornstein, and Robert Flewelling, "African-American Male Adolescents' Involvement in the Criminal Justice System: The Criterion Validity of Self-Report Measures in Prospective Study," *Journal of Research in Crime and Delinquency* 38 (2001): 174–87.

40. Clark and Tifft, "Polygraph and Interview Validation of Self-Reported Deviant Behavior."

41. David Farrington, Rolf Loeber, Magda Stouthamer-Loeber, Welmoet Van Kammen, and Laura Schmidt, "Self-Reported Delinquency and a Combined Delinquency Seriousness Scale Based on Boys, Mothers, and Teachers: Concurrent and Predictive Validity for African Americans and Caucasians," *Criminology* 34 (1996): 501–25.

42. Leonore Simon, "Validity and Reliability of Violent Juveniles: A Comparison of Juvenile Self-Reports with Adult Self-Reports Incarcerated in Adult Prisons," paper presented at the annual meeting of the American Society of Criminology, Boston, November 1995, p. 26.

43. Stephen Cernkovich, Peggy Giordano, and Meredith Pugh, "Chronic Offenders: The Missing Cases in Self-Report Delinquency Research," *Journal of Criminal Law and Criminology* 76 (1985): 705–32.

44. Terence Thornberry, Beth Bjerregaard, and William Miles, "The Consequences of Respondent Attrition in Panel Studies: A Simulation Based on the Rochester Youth Development Study," *Journal of Quantitative Criminology* 9 (1993): 127–58.

45. Alfred Blumstein, Jacqueline Cohen, and Richard Rosenfeld, "Trend and Deviation in Crime Rates: A Comparison of UCR and NCVS Data for Burglary and Robbery," *Criminology* 29 (1991): 237–48. See also Michael Hindelang, Travis Hirschi, and Joseph Weis, *Measuring Delinquency* (Beverly Hills, Calif.: Sage, 1981).

46. Clarence Schrag, *Crime and Justice: American Style* (Washington, D.C.: U.S. Government Printing Office, 1971), p. 17.

47. Thomas Bernard, "Juvenile Crime and the Transformation of Juvenile Justice: Is There a Juvenile Crime Wave?" *Justice Quarterly* 16 (1999): 336–56.

48. Shannan M. Catalano, *Criminal Victimization, 2003* (Washington, D.C.: Bureau of Justice Statistics, 2004).

49. Lloyd Johnston, Patrick O'Malley, Jerald Bachman, and J. E. Schulenberg, "Overall Teen Drug Use Continues Gradual Decline; But Use of Inhalants Rises." Press release, University of Michigan News and Information Services, Ann Arbor, Dec. 21, 2004.

50. James A. Fox, *Trends in Juvenile Violence: A Report to the United States Attorney General on Current and Future Rates of Juvenile Offending* (Boston, Mass.: Northeastern University Press, 1996).

51. Steven Levitt, "The Limited Role of Changing Age Structure in Explaining Aggregate Crime Rates," *Criminology* 37 (1999): 581–99.

52. Ellen Cohn, "The Effect of Weather and Temporal Variations on Calls for Police Service," *American Journal of Police* 15 (1996): 23–43.

53. John Simister and Cary Cooper, "Thermal Stress in the U.S.A.: Effects on Violence and on Employee Behaviour," *Stress and Health* 21 (2005): 3–15.

54. Paul Bell, "Reanalysis and Perspective in the Heat–Aggression Debate," *Journal of Personality & Social Psychology* 89 (2005): 71–73; R. A. Baron, "Aggression as a Function of Ambient Temperature and Prior Anger Arousal," *Journal of Personality and Social Psychology* 21 (1972): 183–89.

55. Brad Bushman, Morgan Wang, and Craig Anderson, "Is the Curve Relating Temperature to Aggression Linear or Curvilinear? Assaults and Temperature in Minneapolis Reexamined," *Journal of Personality & Social Psychology* 89 (2005): 62–66.

56. Ellen Cohn, "The Prediction of Police Calls for Service: The Influence of Weather and Temporal Variables on Rape and Domestic Violence," *Journal of Environmental Psychology* 13 (1993): 71–83.

57. Amie Nielsen, Ramiro Martinez, and Richard Rosenfeld, "Firearm Use, Injury, and Lethality in Assaultive Violence: An Examination of Ethnic Differences," *Homicide Studies* 9 (2005): 83–108.

58. John Lott, *More Guns, Less Crime: Understanding Crime and Gun-Control Laws,* 2nd ed. (Chicago: University of Chicago Press, 2000); John Lott, Jr., "More Guns, Less Crime: Understanding Crime and Gun-Control Laws," in *Studies in Law and Economics,* 2nd ed. (Chicago: University of Chicago Press, 2001); John Lott, Jr., and David Mustard, "Crime, Deterrence, and Right-to-Carry Concealed Handguns," *Journal of Legal Studies* 26 (1997): 1–68.

59. Gary Kleck and Marc Gertz, "Armed Resistance to Crime: The Prevalence and Nature of Self-Defense with a Gun," *Journal of Criminal Law and Criminology* 86 (1995): 219–49.

60. Gary Kleck and Karen McElrath, "The Effects of Weaponry on Human Violence," *Social Forces* 69 (1991): 669–92.

61. Gary Kleck and Michael Hogan, "A National Case-Control Study of Homicide Offending and Gun Ownership," *Social Problems* 46 (1999): 275–93.

62. Stephen Schnebly, "An Examination of the Impact of Victim, Offender, and Situational Attributes on the Deterrent Effect of Gun Use: A Research Note," *Justice Quarterly* 19 (2002): 377–99.

63. See, generally, Franklin Zimring and Gordon Hawkins, *Crime Is Not the Problem: Lethal Violence in America* (New York Oxford University Press, 1997).

64. Ibid., p. 36.

65. Anthony A. Braga and David M. Kennedy, "The Illicit Acquisition of Firearms by Youth and Juveniles," *Journal of Criminal Justice* 29 (2001): 379–88; Anthony Hoskin, "Armed Americans: The Impact of Firearm Availability on National Homicide Rates," *Justice Quarterly* 18 (2001): 569–92.

66. Tomislav Kovandzic, Thomas Marvell, and Lynne Vieraitis, "The Impact of 'Shall-Issue' Concealed Handgun Laws on Violent Crime Rates: Evidence from Panel Data for Large Urban Cities," *Homicide Studies* 9 (2005): 292–323; Tomislav Kovandzic and Thomas Marvell, "Right-to-Carry Concealed Handguns and Violent Crime: Crime Control Through Gun Control?" *Criminology & Public Policy* 2 (2003): 363–96.

67. Robert Martin and Richard Legault, "Systematic Measurement Error with State-Level Crime Data: Evidence from the 'More Guns, Less Crime' Debate," *Journal of Research in Crime and Delinquency* 42 (2005): 187–210.

68. Parker, "Bringing 'Booze' Back In."

69. Victoria Brewer and M. Dwayne Smith, "Gender Inequality and Rates of Female Homicide Victimization Across U.S. Cities," *Journal of Research in Crime and Delinquency* 32 (1995): 175–90.

70. James Short and F. Ivan Nye, "Reported Behavior as a Criterion of Deviant Behavior," *Social Problems* 5 (1957): 207–13; James Short and F. Ivan Nye, "Extent of Unrecorded Juvenile Delinquency, Tentative Conclusions," *Journal of Criminal Law, Criminology, and Police Science* 49 (1958): 296–302.

71. Ivan Nye, James Short, and Virgil Olsen, "Socioeconomic Status and Delinquent Behavior," *American Journal of Sociology* 63 (1958): 381–89; Robert Dentler and Lawrence Monroe, "Social Correlates of Early Adolescent Theft," *American Sociological Review* 63 (1961): 733–43. See also Terence Thornberry and Margaret Farnworth, "Social Correlates of Criminal Involvement: Further Evidence of the Relationship Between Social Status and Criminal Behavior," *American Sociological Review* 47 (1982): 505–18.

72. Charles Tittle, Wayne Villemez, and Douglas Smith, "The Myth of Social Class and Criminality: An Empirical Assessment of the Empirical Evidence," *American Sociological Review* 43 (1978): 643–56.

73. Charles Tittle and Robert Meier, "Specifying the SES/Delinquency Relationship," *Criminology* 28 (1990): 271–301.

74. R. Gregory Dunaway, Francis Cullen, Velmer Burton, and T. David Evans, "The Myth of Social Class and Crime Revisited: An Examination of Class and Adult Criminality," *Criminology* 38 (2000): 589–632.

75. Delbert Elliott and Suzanne Ageton, "Reconciling Race and Class Differences in Self-Reported and Official Estimates of Delinquency," *American Sociological Review* 45 (1980): 95–110.

76. See also Delbert Elliott and David Huizinga, "Social Class and Delinquent Behavior in a National Youth Panel: 1976–1980," *Criminology* 21 (1983): 149–77. For a similar view, see John Braithwaite, "The Myth of Social Class and Criminality Reconsidered," *American Sociological Review* 46 (1981): 35–58; Hindelang, Hirschi, and Weis, *Measuring Delinquency,* p. 196.

77. David Brownfield, "Social Class and Violent Behavior," *Criminology* 24 (1986): 421–39.

78. Douglas Smith and Laura Davidson, "Interfacing Indicators and Constructs in Criminological Research: A Note on the Comparability of Self-Report Violence Data for Race and Sex Groups," *Criminology* 24 (1986): 473–88.

79. Dunaway, Cullen, Burton, and Evans, "The Myth of Social Class and Crime Revisited."

80. Sally Simpson and Lori Elis, "Doing Gender: Sorting Out the Case and Crime Conundrum," *Criminology* 33 (1995): 47–81.

81. Judith Blau and Peter Blau, "The Cost of Inequality: Metropolitan Structure and Violent Crime," *American Sociological Review* 147 (1982): 114–29; Richard Block, "Community Environment and Violent Crime," *Criminology* 17 (1979): 46–57; Robert Sampson, "Structural Sources of Variation in Race-Age-Specific Rates of Offending Across Major U.S. Cities," *Criminology* 23 (1985): 647–73.

82. Chin-Chi Hsieh and M. D. Pugh, "Poverty, Income Inequality, and Violent Crime: A Meta-Analysis of Recent Aggregate Data Studies," *Criminal Justice Review* 18 (1993): 182–99.

83. Richard Miech, Avshalom Caspi, Terrie Moffitt, Bradley Entner Wright, and Phil Silva, "Low Socioeconomic Status and Mental Disorders: A Longitudinal Study of Selection and Causation During Young Adulthood," *American Journal of Sociology* 104 (1999): 1096–1131; Marvin Krohn, Alan Lizotte, and Cynthia Perez, "The Interrelationship Between Substance Use and Precocious Transitions to Adult Sexuality," *Journal of Health and Social Behavior* 38 (1997): 87–103, at 88; Richard Jessor, "Risk Behavior in Adolescence: A Psychosocial Framework for Understanding and Action," in *Adolescents at Risk: Medical and Social Perspectives,* ed. D. E. Rogers and E. Ginzburg (Boulder, Colo.: Westview, 1992).

84. Travis Hirschi and Michael Gottfredson, "Age and the Explanation of Crime," *American Journal of Sociology* 89 (1983): 552–84, at 581.

85. Darrell Steffensmeier and Cathy Streifel, "Age, Gender, and Crime Across Three Historical Periods: 1935, 1960, and 1985," *Social Forces* 69 (1991): 869–94.

86. For a comprehensive review of crime and the elderly, see Kyle Kercher, "Causes and Correlates of Crime Committed by the Elderly," in *Critical Issues in Aging Policy,* ed. E. Borgatta and R. Montgomery (Beverly Hills, Calif.: Sage, 1987), pp. 254–306; Darrell Steffensmeier, "The Invention of the 'New' Senior Citizen Criminal," *Research on Aging* 9 (1987): 281–311.

87. Cesare Lombroso, *The Female Offender* (New York: Appleton, 1920), p. 122.

88. Otto Pollack, *The Criminality of Women* (Philadelphia: University of Pennsylvania Press, 1950).

89. For a review of this issue, see Darrell Steffensmeier, "Assessing the Impact of the Women's Movement on Sex-Based Differences in the Handling of Adult Criminal Defendants," *Crime and Delinquency* 26 (1980): 344–57.

90. Alan Booth and D. Wayne Osgood, "The Influence of Testosterone on Deviance in Adulthood: Assessing and Explaining the Relationship," *Criminology* 31 (1993): 93–118.

91. Daniel Mears, Matthew Ploeger, and Mark Warr, "Explaining the Gender Gap in Delinquency: Peer Influence and Moral

Evaluations of Behavior," *Journal of Research in Crime and Delinquency* 35 (1998): 251–66.

92. Gisela Konopka, *The Adolescent Girl in Conflict* (Englewood Cliffs, N.J.: Prentice-Hall, 1966); Clyde Vedder and Dora Somerville, *The Delinquent Girl* (Springfield, Ill.: Charles C. Thomas, 1970).

93. Emily Gaarder and Joanne Belknap, "Tenuous Borders: Girls Transferred to Adult Court," *Criminology* 40 (2002): 481–517.

94. Debra Kaysen, Miranda Morris, Shireen Rizvi, and Patricia Resick, "Peritraumatic Responses and Their Relationship to Perceptions of Threat in Female Crime Victims," *Violence Against Women* 11 (2005): 1515–35.

95. Freda Adler, *Sisters in Crime* (New York: McGraw-Hill, 1975); Rita James Simon, *The Contemporary Woman and Crime* (Washington, D.C.: Government Printing Office, 1975).

96. David Rowe, Alexander Vazsonyi, and Daniel Flannery, "Sex Differences in Crime: Do Mean and Within-Sex Variation Have Similar Causes?" *Journal of Research in Crime and Delinquency* 32 (1995): 84–100; Michael Hindelang, "Age, Sex, and the Versatility of Delinquency Involvements," *Social Forces* 14 (1971): 525–34; Martin Gold, *Delinquent Behavior in an American City* (Belmont, Calif.: Brooks/Cole, 1970); Gary Jensen and Raymond Eve, "Sex Differences in Delinquency: An Examination of Popular Sociological Explanations," *Criminology* 13 (1976): 427–48.

97. Mears, Ploeger, and Warr, "Explaining the Gender Gap in Delinquency."

98. Adler, *Sisters in Crime;* Simon, *The Contemporary Woman and Crime.*

99. Finn-Aage Esbensen and Elizabeth Piper Deschenes, "A Multisite Examination of Youth Gang Membership: Does Gender Matter?" *Criminology* 36 (1998): 799–828.

100. Darrell Steffensmeier and Renee Hoffman Steffensmeier, "Trends in Female Delinquency," *Criminology* 18 (1980): 62–85. See also Darrell Steffensmeier and Renee Hoffman Steffensmeier, "Crime and the Contemporary Woman: An Analysis of Changing Levels of Female Property Crime, 1960–1975," *Social Forces* 57 (1978): 566–84; Joseph Weis, "Liberation and Crime: The Invention of the New Female Criminal," *Crime and Social Justice* 1 (1976): 17–27; Carol Smart, "The New Female Offender: Reality or Myth," *British Journal of Criminology* 19 (1979): 50–59; Steven Box and Chris Hale, "Liberation/Emancipation, Economic Marginalization or Less Chivalry," *Criminology* 22 (1984): 473–78.

101. Meda Chesney-Lind, "Female Offenders: Paternalism Reexamined," in *Women, the Courts and Equality,* ed. Laura Crites and Winifred Hepperle (Newbury Park, Calif.: Sage, 1987), pp. 114–39, at 115.

102. Darrell Steffensmeier, Jennifer Schwartz, Hua Zhong, and Jeff Ackerman, "An Assessment of Recent Trends in Girls' Violence Using Diverse Longitudinal Sources: Is the Gender Gap Closing?" *Criminology* 43 (2005): 355–406.

103. Susan Miller, Carol Gregory, and Leeann Iovanni, "One Size Fits All? A Gender-Neutral Approach to a Gender-Specific Problem: Contrasting Batterer Treatment Programs for Male and Female Offenders," *Criminal Justice Policy Review* 16 (2005): 336–59.

104. Leroy Gould, "Who Defines Delinquency: A Comparison of Self-Report and Officially Reported Indices of Delinquency for Three Racial Groups," *Social Problems* 16 (1969): 325–36; Harwin Voss, "Ethnic Differentials in Delinquency in Honolulu," *Journal of Criminal Law, Criminology, and Police Science* 54 (1963): 322–27; Ronald Akers, Marvin Krohn, Marcia Radosevich, and Lonn Lanza-Kaduce, "Social Characteristics and Self-Reported Delinquency," in *Sociology of Delinquency,* ed. Gary Jensen (Beverly Hills, Calif.: Sage, 1981), pp. 48–62.

105. Institute for Social Research, *Monitoring the Future* (Ann Arbor, Mich.: 2000).

106. Paul Tracy, "Race and Class Differences in Official and Self-Reported Delinquency," in *From Boy to Man, from Delinquency to Crime,* ed. Marvin Wolfgang, Terence Thornberry, and Robert Figlio (Chicago: University of Chicago Press, 1987), p. 120.

107. Phillipe Rushton, "Race and Crime: An International Dilemma," *Society* 32 (1995): 37–42; for a rebuttal, see Jerome Neapolitan, "Cross-National Variation in Homicides: Is Race a Factor?" *Criminology* 36 (1998): 139–56.

108. Miriam Sealock and Sally Simpson, "Unraveling Bias in Arrest Decisions: The Role of Juvenile Offender Type-Scripts," *Justice Quarterly* 15 (1998): 427–57.

109. "Law Enforcement Seeks Answers to 'Racial Profiling' Complaints," *Criminal Justice Newsletter* 29 (1998): 5.

110. Stewart J. D'Alessio and Lisa Stolzenberg, "Race and the Probability of Arrest," *Social Forces* 81 (2003): 1381–97.

111. Barry Sample and Michael Philip, "Perspectives on Race and Crime in Research and Planning," in *The Criminal Justice System and Blacks,* ed. D. Georges-Abeyie (New York: Clark Boardman, 1984), pp. 21–36.

112. Candace Kruttschnitt, "Violence by and Against Women: A Comparative and Cross-National Analysis," *Violence and Victims* 8 (1994): 4.

113. James Comer, "Black Violence and Public Policy," in *American Violence and Public Policy,* ed. Lynn Curtis (New Haven: Yale University Press, 1985), pp. 63–86.

114. R. Kelly Raley, "A Shortage of Marriageable Men? A Note on the Role of Cohabitation in Black–White Differences in Marriage Rates," *American Sociological Review* 61 (1996): 973–83.

115. Julie Phillips, "Variation in African American Homicide Rates: An Assessment of Potential Explanations," *Criminology* 35 (1997): 527–59.

116. Thomas Mcnulty and Paul Bellair, "Explaining Racial and Ethnic Differences in Adolescent Violence: Structural Disadvantage, Family Well-Being, and Social Capital," *Justice Quarterly* 20 (2003): 1–32.

117. Michael Leiber and Jayne Stairs, "Race, Contexts, and the Use of Intake Diversion," *Journal of Research in Crime and Delinquency* 36 (1999): 56–86; Darrell Steffensmeier, Jeffery Ulmer, and John Kramer, "The Interaction of Race, Gender, and Age in Criminal Sentencing: The Punishment Cost of Being Young, Black, and Male," *Criminology* 36 (1998): 763–98.

118. Hurbert Blalock, Jr., *Toward a Theory of Minority-Group Relations* (New York: Capricorn, 1967).

119. Karen Parker, Briam Stults, and Stephen Rice, "Racial Threat, Concentrated Disadvantage and Social Control: Considering the Macro-Level Sources of Variation in Arrests," *Criminology* 43 (2005): 1111–34; Lisa Stolzenberg, J. Stewart D'Alessio, and David. Eitle, "A Multilevel Test of Racial Threat Theory," *Criminology* 42 (2004): 673–98.

120. Rodney Engen, Sara Steen, and George Bridges, "Racial Disparities in the Punishment of Youth: A Theoretical and Empirical Assessment of the Literature," *Social Problems* 49 (2002): 194–221.

121. Michael Leiber and Kristan Fox, "Race and the Impact of Detention on Juvenile Justice Decision Making," *Crime and Delinquency* 51 (2005): 470–97; Traci Schlesinger, "Racial and Ethnic Disparity in Pretrial Criminal Processing," *Justice Quarterly* 22 (2005): 170–92.

122. Tracy Nobiling, Cassia Spohn, and Miriam DeLone, "A Tale of Two Counties: Unemployment and Sentence Severity," *Justice Quarterly* 15 (1998): 459–86.

123. Alexander Weiss and Steven Chermak, "The News Value of African American Victims: An Examination of the Media's Presentation of Homicide," *Journal of Crime and Justice* 21 (1998): 71–84.

124. *The Sentencing Project, Losing the Vote: The Impact of Felony Disenfranchisement Laws in the United States* (Washington, D.C.: Sentencing Project, 1998).

125. Ronald Weitzer and Steven Tuch, "Race, Class, and Perceptions of Discrimination by the Police," *Crime and Delinquency* 45 (1999): 494–507.

126. Karen Parker and Patricia McCall, "Structural Conditions and Racial Homicide Patterns: A Look at the Multiple Disadvantages in Urban Areas," *Criminology* 37 (1999): 447–69.

127. Gary LaFree and Richard Arum, "The Impact of Racially Inclusive Schooling on Adult Incarceration Rates Among U.S. Cohorts of African Americans and Whites Since 1930," *Criminology* 44 (2006): 73–103.

128. David Jacobs and Katherine Woods, "Interracial Conflict and Interracial Homicide: Do Political and Economic Rivalries Explain White Killings of Blacks or Black Killings of Whites?" *American Journal of Sociology* 105 (1999): 157–90.

129. Melvin Thomas, "Race, Class, and Personal Income: An Empirical Test of the Declining Significance of Race Thesis, 1968–1988," *Social Problems* 40 (1993): 328–39.

130. Gary LaFree, Kriss Drass, and Patrick O'Day, "Race and Crime in Postwar America: Determinants of African American and White Rates, 1957–1988," *Criminology* 30 (1992): 157–88.

131. Mallie Paschall, Robert Flewelling, and Susan Ennett, "Racial Differences in Violent Behavior Among Young Adults: Moderating and Confounding Effects," *Journal of Research in Crime and Delinquency* 35 (1998): 148–65.

132. Tim Wadsworth and Charis Kubrin, "Structural Factors and Black Interracial Homicide: A New Examination of the Causal Process," *Criminology* 42 (2004): 647–72.

133. Roy Austin, "Progress Toward Racial Equality and Reduction of Black Criminal Violence," *Journal of Criminal Justice* 15 (1987): 437–59.

134. Julie Phillips, "White, Black, and Latino Homicide Rates: Why the Difference?" *Social Problems* 49 (2002): 349–74.

135. Reynolds Farley and William Frey, "Changes in the Segregation of Whites from Blacks During the 1980s: Small Steps Toward a More Integrated Society," *American Sociological Review* 59 (1994): 23–45.

136. Marvin Wolfgang, Robert Figlio, and Thorsten Sellin, *Delinquency in a Birth Cohort* (Chicago: University of Chicago Press, 1972).

137. See Thorsten Sellin and Marvin Wolfgang, *The Measurement of Delinquency* (New York: Wiley, 1964), p. 120.

138. The following sections rely heavily on Paul Tracy and Robert Figlio, "Chronic Recidivism in the 1958 Birth Cohort," paper presented at the annual meeting of the American Society of Criminology, Toronto, Canada, October 1982; Marvin Wolfgang, "Delinquency in Two Birth Cohorts," in *Perspective Studies of Crime and Delinquency*, ed. Katherine Teilmann Van Dusen and Sarnoff Mednick (Boston: Kluwer-Nijhoff, 1983), pp. 7–17.

139. Lyle Shannon, *Criminal Career Opportunity* (New York: Human Sciences Press, 1988).

140. D. J. West and David P. Farrington, *The Delinquent Way of Life* (London: Hienemann, 1977).

141. Peter Jones, Philip Harris, James Fader, and Lori Grubstein, "Identifying Chronic Juvenile Offenders," *Justice Quarterly* 18 (2001): 478–507.

142. R. Tremblay, R. Loeber, C. Gagnon, P. Charlebois, S. Larivee, and M. LeBlanc, "Disruptive Boys with Stable and Unstable High Fighting Behavior Patterns During Junior Elementary School," *Journal of Abnormal Child Psychology* 19 (1991): 285–300.

143. Jennifer White, Terrie Moffitt, Felton Earls, Lee Robins, and Phil Silva, "How Early Can We Tell? Predictors of Childhood Conduct Disorder and Adolescent Delinquency," *Criminology* 28 (1990): 507–35.

144. Kimberly Kempf-Leonard, Paul Tracy, and James Howell, "Serious, Violent, and Chronic Juvenile Offenders: The Relationship of Delinquency Career Types to Adult Criminality," *Justice Quarterly* 18 (2001): 449–78.

145. Susan Martin, "Policing Career Criminals: An Examination of an Innovative Crime Control Program," *Journal of Criminal Law and Criminology* 77 (1986): 1159–82.

CHAPTER 3

Understanding Crime and Victimization

Chapter Outline

Chapter Objectives

After reading this chapter, you should be able to:
1. Describe the problems of violent and economic crimes and substance abuse.
2. Know the reasons that crime seems rational.
3. Recognize the differences between general deterrence and specific deterrence.
4. Understand the concept of situational crime prevention.
5. Discuss the biological factors linked to crime.
6. Recognize that psychological factors are related to crime.
7. Describe the relationship between media and violence.
8. Discuss why social and economic factors influence the crime rate.
9. Recognize the sociocultural factors associated with crime.
10. Identify the socialization factors related to crime.
11. Explain how social conflict leads to crime.
12. Understand the concept of human development and crime.
13. Discuss the behavior patterns that increase the chances of becoming a crime victim.

$20,000,000

O n March 21, 2006, Konstantin Grigoryan, his wife Mayya Leonidovna Grigoryan, Eduard Gersheli, Aleksandr Treynker, and Haroutyun Gulderyan were all arrested on charges related to a long-running Medicare fraud scheme that netted them at least $20 million. The scheme involved getting Medicare to pay for tests that were either unnecessary or never performed. The group recruited patients and submitted fraudulent billing to Medicare on behalf of medical service providers such as medical clinics and diagnostic testing centers. The scheme, commonly referred to as "beneficiary sharing" or "patient rotating," involved "marketers" who obtain data about Medicare beneficiaries and sell the information to Medicare providers who engage in fraudulent billings. Some marketers, known as "cappers," recruit patients with Medicare coverage to travel to clinics and receive services that are medically unnecessary, whereas others receive no medical services at all.

Grigoryan conducted fraudulent activity through 12 Los Angeles–area medical providers that he controlled. They purportedly conducted diagnostic tests, such as ultrasound examinations and blood tests, on people who were brought in by car, van, and bus. Once the patients came into a physician's office, the medical providers allegedly billed the patients' Medicare numbers on the dates of their visits and on many other dates—whether or not any services were in fact provided to the beneficiaries. The conspirators would fabricate the tests so that the patients' files could withstand an audit by Medicare. The criminal scheme caused Medicare to pay out at least $20 million in fraudulent claims from 2000 until 2005. Much of the money was deposited into a maze of bank accounts of "management" and "consulting" companies, including a Panamanian shell corporation with a Swiss bank account.[1] ◆

Criminologist

Duties and Characteristics of the Job

Criminologists are academics who analyze patterns in criminal activity and attempt to determine the causes of, future trends in, and potential solutions to crime in society. Criminologists are concerned with questions such as how to effectively deter crime, who will commit crime and why, and how to predict and prevent criminal behavior. Like statisticians, criminologists will often design and carry out research projects to collect and analyze data with the intention of answering some aspect of these larger questions. Their ideas are written up into reports or articles for various agencies and publications and are used for academic, law enforcement, and policy purposes.

Criminologists will often work with law enforcement at the local, state, or federal level. In these positions, they might do research on problems specific to the district they are working with, or they might examine case files and attend crime scenes to help determine whether a suspect's profile is accurate. Other criminologists seek positions at universities and colleges, where they conduct research, write books and articles, and teach courses about crime and criminal justice. In general, criminologists work normal 40-hour weeks in office-type settings.

Job Outlook

The demand for criminologists is expected to reflect the general demand for sociologists, which at present is expected to grow slowly at the government and law enforcement level. There is much greater demand for criminologists working in the university setting, however. Those with more education can expect better job opportunities and higher salaries.

Salary

Criminologists' median annual earnings are $57,870. However, salaries will vary widely depending upon employer. A doctorate-level criminologist working at a college or university can expect pay comparable to other faculty. Starting pay for an assistant professor ranges from $45,000 to $60,000, depending on the institution. A full professor has an average annual salary of about $100,000. Pay will vary depending upon the individual institution and personal level of advancement.

Opportunities

Those entering the field of criminology should be aware that they will face competition from other qualified candidates for a limited number of jobs,

◆ THE CAUSE OF CRIME

How can we explain the convoluted crimes of someone like Konstantin Grigoryan and his co-conspirators? Was his illegal behavior a product of a disturbed childhood? Poverty? An impulsive personality? Despite years of study and research, crime experts are still uncertain about why people commit crime or why some people become crime victims. One of the enduring goals of **criminology**—the scientific study of the nature, extent, cause, and control of criminal behavior—is to develop an understanding of the nature and cause of crime and victimization. Without knowing why crime occurs, it would be difficult to create effective crime reduction programs. No one could be sure if efforts were being aimed at the proper audience or, if they were, whether the prevention efforts were the ones most likely to cause positive change. A crime prevention program based on providing jobs for unemployed teenagers would be effective only if crime is, in fact, linked to unemployment. Similarly, a plan to reduce prison riots by eliminating the sugar intake of inmates is feasible only if research shows a link between diet and violence. Criminologists help study these crime patterns so that agents of the criminal justice system can plan and construct programs to reduce crime. If you are interested in becoming a criminologist, you may want to read the Careers in Criminal Justice feature.

In the sections following, the most important theories of crime causation are discussed in some detail. We then look at the concept of victimization and

criminology
The scientific study of the nature, extent, cause, and control of criminal behavior.

especially at the more financially rewarding positions with the federal government. However, the predicted increase in retirement in the near future will most likely open up new positions. There is more opportunity in the university setting for criminologists than for psychologists or sociologists.

Many individuals who get a degree in criminology or work as criminologists can use their education and experience and successfully launch careers in related jobs, such as police officer, federal agent, or psychologist.

Qualifications

Due to the academic nature of criminology, the primary requirement for a career in this field is proper academic training. Educational requirements usually include courses on human behavior and the criminal justice system, and should involve developing skills in statistics and writing. Training should also include familiarity with computer programs that are used for statistical analysis, such as SAS or SPSS. Because criminology requires collecting and examining data, conducting research, and presenting these ideas to others, personal qualities such as intellectual curiosity and strong communicative and analytical skills are important. Those

who want to be involved in law enforcement in a "hands-on" manner or do not like math and writing reports may not be interested in this career.

Certain states require potential criminologists to pass a written test in order to become licensed before they can work. Additionally, those working with law enforcement agencies will have to pass background and security checks.

Education and Training

Although some criminologists will enter the field with a bachelor's degree, a majority will pursue postgraduate education. Typically, this means a master's degree in criminology and/or criminal justice. Other social science degrees can be acceptable. This is generally enough for those desiring work at law enforcement agencies. However, some positions—for example, teaching at the university level—will require a doctorate in one of the previously mentioned fields.

Sources: "Social Scientists, Other," *Occupational Outlook Handbook,* 2006–2007 edition (Bureau of Labor Statistics, U.S. Department of Labor), retrieved June 19, 2006, from http://www.bls.gov/oco/ocos054 .htm; J. Pope, "Report: Some College Faculty Salaries Rise," Associated Press Online Domestic News; "Princeton Review Career Profiles: Criminologist" (April 24, 2006), retrieved June 16, 2006, from http:// www.princetonreview.com/cte/profiles/dayInLife.asp?careerID=47.

discuss theories that attempt to explain why some people are likely to be victimized while others remain crime free.

◆ BECAUSE THEY WANT TO: CHOICE THEORY

One prominent view of criminality is that people choose to commit crime after weighing the potential benefits and consequences of their criminal act. People like Konstantin Grigoryan commit a crime if they believe it will provide immediate benefits without the threat of long-term risks. Drug trafficking fits this pattern. Before concluding a drug sale, experienced traffickers will mentally balance the chances of making a large profit against the probability of being apprehended and punished for drug dealing. They know that most drug deals are not detected and that the potential for enormous, untaxed profits is great. They evaluate their lifestyle and determine how much cash they need to maintain their standard of living, which is usually extravagant. They may have borrowed to finance the drug deal, and their creditors are not usually reasonable if loans cannot be repaid promptly. They also realize that they could be the target of a sting operation by undercover agents and, if caught, will get a long mandatory sentence in a forbidding federal penitentiary. If the greedy culprits conclude that the potential for profits is great enough, their need for cash urgent, and the chances of apprehension minimal, they will carry out the deal. If, however, they believe that the transaction will bring them only a small profit and a large

ThomsonNOW Improve your grade on the exam with Personalized Study! For reinforcement resources and a mastery check of causes of crime, go to www.thomsonedu. com/thomsonnow.

Criminals are believed to be rational decision makers because they learn illicit skills, use apprehension avoidance techniques, and plan crimes carefully. Some crimes are so complex that they seem inherently "rational." Police and reporters look at the tunnel where highly sophisticated thieves spent three months digging under a busy city avenue to break into a central bank in Fortaleza, Brazil on August 8, 2005. The crime, which netted 150 million reais ($65 million), was the biggest robbery ever in Brazil.

©AP Images/Turo de Vieira, Diario do Nordeste

deterrent
Preventing crime before it occurs by means of the threat of criminal sanctions.

risk of apprehension and punishment, they may forgo the deal, believing it too risky.

According to this vision, crime is a matter of rational choice, involving a calculated decision made after a motivated offender weighs the potential costs and benefits of illegal activity. To deter crime, punishment must be sufficiently strict, sure, and swift to outweigh any benefits of law violation. A 30-year prison sentence should deter potential bank robbers, regardless of the amount of money in the bank's vault. However, no matter how severely the law punishes a criminal act, it will have little **deterrent** effect if potential law violators believe they have little chance of being caught or that the wheels of justice are slow and inefficient.

Rational Criminals

The decision to commit a specific crime, then, is a matter of personal decision based on the evaluation of available information. Criminals are likely to desist from crime if they believe that their future illegal earnings will be relatively low and that attractive and legal opportunities to generate income are available.[2] In contrast, criminals may be motivated when they know people who have made big scores and are successful at crime. Although the prevailing wisdom is that "crime does not pay," a small but significant subset of criminals earn close to $50,000 a year from crime, and their success may help motivate other would-be offenders.[3] In this sense, rational choice is a function of a person's perception of conventional alternatives and opportunities.

The rational criminal may also decide to forgo or desist from illegal behaviors. Such criminals may fear apprehension and punishment—a target appears too well protected, the police in the area are very active, local judges have vowed to crack down on crime, or they simply cannot find a safe site to break the law.[4]

Rational Crimes

That crime is rational can be observed in a wide variety of criminal events. As noted previously, white-collar and organized crime figures engage in elaborate and well-planned conspiracies, ranging from international drug deals to the looting of savings and loan institutions (see the International Justice feature for more on these deals).

Organized Crime in Russia

If rational choice theory is valid, its principles should apply to criminals around the world. The dealings of the Russian organized crime cartels certainly seem to validate the theory. James Finckenauer, one of the nation's leading authorities on Russian organized crime, finds that mobsters have been able to use their cunning to penetrate Russian business and government enterprises. By exploiting corrupt government officials, their influence extends to a degree that is far beyond what is experienced in most other countries of the world.

Today, the Russian mob maintains protection rackets that are operated by local *kryshas*, or "roofs." Nearly every business in cities such as Moscow and St. Petersburg must make payments for "protection" by a *krysha*. This protection sometimes comes in the form of acquiring unwanted partners who use their muscle to grab shares of businesses. Gangsters use violence to enforce contracts and otherwise ensure that business transactions are carried out. Organized criminals also engage in sophisticated economic and Internet crime. Russian criminals have also set up shop around the world, not only in the United States but as far away as Australia. The globalization and transnational nature of Russian crime is evident in such activities as worldwide money laundering and in the trafficking of a variety of goods and of persons. Who is attracted to Russian organized crime? These violent entrepreneurs are made up of former prison (gulag) inmates, sportsmen, Afghan war veterans, ex-soldiers, ex-security agents, and so on. They represent a volatile combination of persons who are physically intimidating, who are trained in the use of weapons and killing methods, and who are otherwise unemployed.

Government corruption has hindered the fight against Russian organized crime. As the former Soviet Union has moved to privatize its vast state holdings—that is, sell to private owners what was previously owned by the central government—organized crime in partnership with corrupt officials has engaged in a wholesale rape of the privatization process. Criminals and corrupt officials have collaborated to buy up valuable properties at fire-sale prices via insider information. They have demonstrated their greed in carving up the body of the old Soviet state. They

cooperate in drug smuggling, arms trafficking, and human trafficking. Corruption and violence are widespread. Business or political rivals are frequently the victims of contract killings that are carried out by the violent entrepreneurs.

Russia does not have effective legal tools for fighting organized crime, nor does it have an effective law enforcement system. The police are outmanned, outgunned, and underresourced. They are also hobbled by corruption. This means that law enforcement officials in other countries must be very careful about sharing intelligence information with Russian authorities. The former should recognize that some of this intelligence will be lost—i.e., sold to criminals. It is questionable whether the benefits of collaboration outweigh the intelligence losses. There is the absence of a viable, independent, and professional civil service. The symbiotic relationship among business, crime, and government presents an enormous challenge that so far shows no signs of being overcome. Until these fundamental problems are solved, Russia will not be able to effectively excise its organized crime.

Critical Thinking

1. Russian organized crime seems to be an example of rational criminal decision making. People who cannot find work but have developed skills, albeit criminal ones, choose a criminal vocation supported by government corruption. Their acts are not random but well thought out, calculating, and highly profitable. Do you agree that their behavior is a "rational choice," or could it be the product of some other forces?

2. If Russian organized crime were not a product of rational choice but occurred because of economic desperation, then how would you explain the existence of similar groups in wealthier nations such as Japan and the United States?

 InfoTrac College Edition Research
Use "Russian organized crime" and "organized crime" in a subject search on InfoTrac.

Source: James Finckenauer, "The Russian 'Mafia,'" *Society* 41 (2004): 61–64.

But even predatory street criminals exhibit stealth and planning in their criminal acts. Burglars may try to determine which homes are easy targets by reading newspaper stories about weddings or social events that mean the attendees' homes will be unguarded. They choose houses that are easily accessible and

FIGURE 3.1
Preventing Crime

screened from public view and offer good escape routes—for example, at the end of a cul-de-sac abutting a wooded area. They target high-value homes that do not have burglar alarms or other security devices.[5] Burglars seem to prefer working between 9 A.M. and 11 A.M. and in midafternoon, when parents are either working or dropping off or picking up children at school. Burglars appear to monitor car and pedestrian traffic and avoid selecting targets on heavily traveled streets.[6]

Even violent criminals exhibit elements of rationality. Research shows that armed robbers choose targets close to their homes or in areas that they routinely travel. Familiarity with the area gives them knowledge of escape routes; this is referred to as their awareness space.[7] Robbers also report being wary of people who are watching the community for signs of trouble. Robbery levels are relatively low in neighborhoods where residents keep a watchful eye on their neighbors' property.[8] Robbers avoid freestanding buildings because they can more easily be surrounded by police. Others select targets that are known to do a primarily cash business, such as bars, supermarkets, and restaurants.[9] If crime is a rational choice, how can it be prevented or controlled? See Figure 3.1.

Make 'Em Afraid I: The Concept of General Deterrence

If crime is a matter of choice, it follows that it can be controlled by convincing criminals that breaking the law is a bad or dangerous choice to make. If people believe that they are certain to be apprehended by the police, quickly tried, and severely penalized, they will most likely forgo any thought of breaking the law.[10] In other words, people will not choose crime if they fear legal punishment. This principle is referred to as **general deterrence**.

If the justice system could be made more effective, those who care little for the rights of others would be deterred by fear of the law's sanctioning power.[11] Only by reducing the benefits of crime through sure, swift, and certain punishment can society be sure that a group of new criminals will not emerge to replace the ones who have already been dealt with.[12]

Research shows that some people who report that they fear punishment will be deterred from committing certain crimes.[13] The prevailing wisdom is that the certainty of being punished is a greater deterrent to crime than the severity of punishment. In other words, people will more likely be deterred from crime if they believe that they will get caught. What happens to them after apprehension seems to have a lesser impact.[14]

Although certain, not severe, punishment has some influence on crime, little hard evidence is yet available that fear of the law alone can be a general deterrent to crime.[15] Even the harshest punishment, the death penalty, appears to have little effect on the murder rate.[16]

What factors inhibit the sanctioning power of the criminal law? One is the lack of efficiency of the justice system. About 20 percent of serious reported crimes result in an arrest. Relatively few criminals are eventually tried, convicted, and sentenced to prison. Chronic offenders and career criminals may believe that the risk of apprehension and imprisonment is limited and conclude that the certainty of punishment, a key element in deterrence, is minimal. Even if they do fear punishment, their anxiety may be neutralized by the belief that a crime gives them a significant chance for large profit. When criminologists Alex Piquero and George Rengert interviewed active burglars, they were told that fear

general deterrence
A crime control policy that depends on the fear of criminal penalties.

According to the deterrence approach, if people fear the consequences of crime, they will be deterred from criminal involvement. Here, Sam Waksal leaves a Federal court after being sentenced to more than seven years in prison and a $4 million fine for his involvement in insider trading on his company stock. Do you think that such a harsh sentence for a business-related crime will deter other businesspeople from violating securities laws?

of capture and punishment was usually neutralized by the hope of making a big score; greed overcomes fear.[17]

The concept of general deterrence assumes a rational criminal—that is, an offender who carefully weighs and balances the pains and benefits of the criminal act. However, a majority of arrested criminals are under the influence of drugs or alcohol at the time of their arrest. Therefore, many offenders may be incapable of having the rational thought patterns upon which the concept of general deterrence rests. Relatively high rates of substance abuse, including alcohol and illegal drugs, may render even the harshest criminal penalties for violent crimes ineffective deterrents.[18]

In sum, the theory of rational choice predicts that criminals are calculating individuals who can be deterred by the threat of punishment. Research has so far failed to turn up clear and convincing evidence that the threat of punishment or its implementation can deter would-be criminals.

Make 'Em Afraid II: Specific Deterrence

Even if the threat of punishment cannot deter would-be criminals, actual punishment at the hands of the justice system should be sufficient to convince arrested offenders never to repeat their criminal acts. If punishment were severe enough, a convicted criminal would never dare repeat his or her offense. What rational person would? This view is called **specific deterrence**. Prior to the twentieth century, specific deterrence was a motive for the extreme tortures and physical punishments commonly used on convicted criminals. By breaking the convicts physically, legal authorities hoped to control their spirit and behavior.[19]

Although the more enlightened society in America today no longer uses such cruel and unusual punishments, it imposes long sentences in dangerous and forbidding prisons. Yet such measures do not seem to deliver the promise of crime control inherent in the specific deterrence concept. A majority of inmates repeat their criminal acts soon after returning to society, and most inmates have served time previously.[20]

PERSPECTIVES ON JUSTICE

Crime Control

Rational choice theory is the philosophical cornerstone of the crime control perspective of justice. It has been used to justify the get-tough law-and-order approach that is predominant today. If criminals choose crime, then it follows that increasing the level of criminal punishment should deter and reduce crime. Law enforcement agencies now establish task forces to locate and apprehend chronic offenders, prosecutors target career criminals, and state legislatures enact laws providing lengthy prison sentences for recidivists. Long prison sentences are believed to be the best way to keep repeaters out of circulation, to convince prospective offenders that crime does not pay, and to teach those who decide to commit crimes a lesson not soon forgotten.

specific deterrence
Punishment severe enough to convince convicted offenders never to repeat their criminal activity.

Associated Press/AP Images

Why have these punishments failed as a specific deterrent? Specific deterrence also assumes a rational criminal, someone who learns from experience. Many offenders have impulsive personalities that interfere with their ability to learn from experience. And if they do learn while incarcerated, the lessons may be from more experienced offenders who encourage them to commit crime once they are released. A majority of criminal offenders have lifestyles marked by heavy substance abuse, lack of formal education, and disturbed home lives, which inhibit conventional behavior. The pains of imprisonment and the stigma of a prison record do little to help an already troubled person readjust to society. Rather than deter crime, a prison sentence may encourage future law violations.

Make It Difficult: Situational Crime Prevention

Some advocates of rational choice theory argue that crime prevention can be achieved by reducing the opportunities people have to commit particular crimes, a technique known as *situational crime prevention.* Situational crime prevention was first popularized in the United States in the early 1970s by Oscar Newman, who coined the term *defensible space.* The idea is that crime can be prevented or displaced through the use of residential architectural designs that reduce criminal opportunity, such as well-lit housing projects that maximize surveillance.[21]

Contemporary choice theorists maintain that situational crime prevention can be achieved by creating a strategy or overall plan to reduce specific crimes and then developing specific tactics to achieve those goals. Ronald Clarke has set out the main types of crime prevention tactics in use today:[22]

1. *Increase the effort needed to commit the crime.* Increasing the effort needed to commit crimes involves using target-hardening techniques and access control: placing steering locks on cars, putting unbreakable glass on storefronts, locking gates and fencing yards, having owners' photos on credit cards, controlling the sale of spray paint (to reduce graffiti), and installing caller ID (a device that displays the telephone number of the party placing the call, which can reduce the number of obscene or crank calls).

2. *Increase the risks of committing the crime.* It is also possible to increase the risks of committing a crime by improving surveillance lighting, creating neighborhood watch programs, controlling building entrances and exits, putting in burglar alarms and security systems, and increasing the number and effectiveness of private security officers and police patrols. Research shows that crime rates are reduced when police officers use aggressive crime reduction techniques and promote community safety by increasing lighting and cleaning up vacant lots.[23]

3. *Reduce the rewards for committing the crime.* Reward-reduction strategies include making car radios removable so they can be taken into the home at night, marking property so that it is more difficult to sell when stolen, and having gender-neutral phone lists to discourage obscene phone calls.

4. *Induce shame or guilt.* Inducing guilt or shame might include such techniques as embarrassing offenders (for example, publishing "John lists" in the newspaper to punish those arrested for soliciting prostitutes) or improving compliance by providing trash bins whose easy access might shame chronic litterers into using them. When caller ID was installed in New Jersey, the number of obscene phone calls reported to police declined significantly because of the threat of exposure.[24]

5. *Reduce provocation.* Some crimes are the result of extreme provocation—e.g., road rage. It might be possible to reduce provocation by creating programs that reduce conflict. Creating an early closing time in local bars and pubs might limit assaults that are the result of late-night drinking and conflicts in pubs at closing time. Posting guards outside schools at closing time might prevent childish taunts from escalating into full-blown brawls.

6. *Remove excuses.* Crime may be reduced by making it difficult for people to excuse their criminal behavior by saying things like "I didn't know that was illegal" or "I had no choice." To achieve this goal, municipalities have set up roadside displays that electronically flash a car's speed as it passes, eliminating the driver's excuse that she did not know how fast she was going when stopped by police. Litter boxes, brightly displayed, can eliminate the claim that "I just didn't know where to throw my trash."

At their core, situational crime prevention efforts seek clearly defined solutions to specific crime problems. Instead of changing criminals, they seek to change the environment so that criminality becomes more difficult and consequently less profitable.

ThomsonNOW Improve your grade on the exam with Personalized Study! For reinforcement resources and a mastery check of choice theory, go to www.thomsonedu.com/ thomsonnow.

◆ BECAUSE THEY ARE DIFFERENT: BIOLOGICAL THEORIES

As the nineteenth century came to a close, some criminologists began to suggest that crime was caused not so much by human choice but by inherited and uncontrollable biological and psychological traits: intelligence, body build, personality, biomedical makeup. The newly developed scientific method was applied to the study of social relations, including criminal behavior.

The origin of scientific criminology is usually traced to the research of Cesare Lombroso (1836–1909). Lombroso, an Italian army physician fascinated by human anatomy, became interested in finding out what motivated criminals to commit crimes. He physically examined hundreds of prison inmates and other criminals to discover any similarities among them. On the basis of his research, Lombroso proposed that criminals manifest *atavistic anomalies:* primitive, animal-like physical qualities such as an asymmetric face or excessive jaw, eye defects, large eyes, a receding forehead, prominent cheekbones, long arms, a twisted nose, and swollen lips.[25]

Lombroso's views were discredited in the twentieth century, and biological explanations of crime were abandoned. Today, the biology of crime has gained a resurgence of interest, and a number of criminologists are looking once again at the biological underpinnings of crime. Biological theories assume that variation in human physical traits can explain behavior. Instead of being born equal and influenced by social and environmental conditions, each person possesses a unique biochemical, neurological, and genetic makeup. People may develop physical or mental traits at birth, or soon after, that affect their social functioning over the life course and influence their behavior choices. For example, low-birth-weight babies have been found to suffer poor educational achievement later in life; academic deficiency has been linked to delinquency and drug abuse.[26] Because they recognize social influences, these are often referred to as biosocial theories.

Biocriminologists are attempting to link physical traits with tendencies toward violence, aggression, and other antisocial behavior. Their work, which is still in the early stages of development, can be divided into three broad areas of focus: biochemical factors, neurological problems, and genetic influence.

In the Blood: Biochemical Factors

Biocriminologists sometimes focus on the influence of biochemical factors on criminal behavior. Some research efforts have linked antisocial behavior to vitamin and mineral deficiencies, food additives, improper diet, environmental contaminants, and allergies. Exposure to environmental contaminants such as the now-banned PCB (polychlorinated biphenyls), a chemical that was once used in insulation materials, has been shown to influence brain functioning and intelligence levels.[27] Ingestion of common food additives such as calcium propionate, used to preserve bread, has been linked to problem behaviors.[28] Another suspected biochemical hazard is high levels of lead ingestion, which has been linked to antisocial behaviors.[29] In some cases, the association between chemical and mineral imbalance and crime is indirect. Research shows that high levels of mercury may lead to cognitive and learning dysfunctions, factors associated with antisocial behaviors.[30]

Another area of biological research focuses on hypoglycemia, a condition that occurs when blood glucose (sugar) falls below levels necessary for normal and efficient brain functioning. Symptoms of hypoglycemia include irritability, anxiety, depression, crying spells, headaches, and confusion. Research shows that persistent abnormality in the way the brain metabolizes glucose is linked to substance abuse.[31]

Hormonal imbalance has been linked to aggressive behavior. Children who have low levels of the stress hormone cortisol tend to be more violent and antisocial than those with normal levels.[32] A growing body of evidence suggests that hormonal changes are also related to mood and behavior and that adolescents experience more intense mood swings, anxiety, and restlessness than their elders, explaining in part the high violence rates found among teenage males.[33]

In sum, biochemical studies suggest that criminal offenders have abnormal levels of organic or inorganic substances that influence their behavior and in some way make them prone to antisocial behavior.

The Abnormal Brain: Neurological Problems

Another area of interest to biocriminologists is the relationship of brain activity to behavior. Electroencephalograms (EEGs) have been used to record the electrical impulses given off by the brain. Psychologist Dorothy Otnow Lewis and her associates found that murderous youths suffer signs of major neurological impairment (such as abnormal EEGs, multiple psychomotor impairment, and severe seizures).[34] In her book *Guilty by Reason of Insanity,* Lewis reports that death row inmates have a history of mental impairment and intellectual dysfunction.[35] Other research efforts show that spouse abusers exhibit a variety of neuropsychological disorders and cognitive deficits; many suffered brain injuries in youth.[36]

neurotransmitters
Chemical substances that carry impulses from one nerve cell to another. Neurotransmitters are found in the space (synapse) that separates the transmitting neuron's terminal (axon) from the receiving neuron's terminal (dendrite).

Another cause of abnormal neurological function is impairment in **neurotransmitters**, which are chemical compounds that influence or activate brain functions. Those studied in relation to aggression include dopamine, serotonin, monoamine oxidase, and gamma-aminobutryic acid. Evidence exists that abnormal levels of these chemicals are associated with aggression.[37] Studies of habitually violent criminals show that low serotonin levels are linked with poor impulse control and hyperactivity, increased irritability, and sensation seeking.[38]

People with an abnormal cerebral structure referred to as minimal brain dysfunction may experience periods of explosive rage. Brain dysfunction is sometimes manifested as an attention-deficit hyperactivity disorder (ADHD), another suspected cause of antisocial behavior. Several studies have shown that children with attention problems experience increased levels of antisocial behavior and aggression during childhood, adolescence, and adulthood.[39] Boys and girls who suffer from ADHD are impaired both academically and socially, factors that are related to long-term antisocial behaviors.[40]

The National Attention Deficit Disorder Association disseminates information and policy updates. To reach this site, go to the Siegel/Senna Introduction to Criminal Justice 11e website: www.thomsonedu.com/criminaljustice/siegel.

The condition may cause poor school performance, bullying, stubbornness, and a lack of response to discipline. Although the origin of ADHD is still unknown, suspected causes include neurological damage, prenatal stress, and even food additives and chemical allergies. Research shows that youths with ADHD who grow up in a dysfunctional family are the most vulnerable to chronic delinquency that continues into their adulthood.[41]

The Bad Seed: Genetic Factors

Although the earliest biological studies of crime tried and failed to discover a genetic basis for criminality, modern biocriminologists are still concerned with the role of heredity in producing crime-prone people.

If inherited traits are related to criminality, twins should be more similar in their antisocial activities than other sibling pairs. However, because most twins are brought up together, determining whether behavioral similarities are a function of environmental influences or genetics is difficult. To overcome this problem, biocriminologists usually compare identical, or monozygotic (MZ), twins with fraternal, or dizygotic (DZ), twins of the same sex. MZ twins are genetically identical, so their behavior would be expected to be more similar than that of DZ twins. Preliminary studies have shown that this is true.[42] Some evidence exists that genetic makeup is a better predictor of criminality than either social or environmental variables.[43]

Another approach has been to evaluate the behavior of adopted children. If an adopted child's behavior patterns run parallel to those of his or her biological parents, it would be strong evidence to support a genetic basis for crime. Preliminary studies conducted in Europe have indicated that the criminality of the biological father is a strong predictor of a child's antisocial behavior.[44] The probability that a youth will engage in crime is significantly enhanced when both biological and adoptive parents exhibit criminal tendencies.

ThomsonNOW™ Improve your grade on the exam with Personalized Study! For reinforcement resources and a mastery check of biological theories of crime, go to www. thomsonedu.com/thomsonnow.

◆ IN THEIR HEADS: PSYCHOLOGICAL THEORIES

The view that criminals may be suffering from psychological abnormality or stress has also had a long history.

The Disturbed Mind: Psychodynamic Theory

Psychodynamic theory, the creation of Viennese physician Sigmund Freud (1856–1939), still holds a prominent position in psychological thought.[45] According to the psychodynamic view, some people encounter problems during their early development that cause an imbalance in their personality. Some have mood disorders and are extremely anxious, fearful, and impulsive. *Psychotics* are people whose primitive impulses have broken through and actually control their personality; they may hear voices telling them what to do or see visions. One type of psychosis is *schizophrenia*, a condition marked by incoherent thought processes, a lack of insight, hallucinations, and feelings of persecution.

Psychodynamic theorists believe that law violators may have suffered damage to their egos or superegos early in their development that renders them powerless to control their impulses. They may suffer delusions and feel persecuted, worthless, and alienated.[46] Psychosis is often associated with violent episodes, but even nonviolent criminals may be motivated by a lack of insight and control caused by personality disorders.[47] As a result, they seek immediate gratification of their needs without considering right and wrong or the needs of others.

MENTAL ILLNESS AND CRIME Although a link between mental instability and criminality seems logical (and a popular topic in horror movies), the evidence associating the two conditions is still inconclusive.

Those who believe in an association between mental illness and crime suggest that certain symptoms of mental illness are connected to violence—for example, the feeling that others wish the person harm, that the person's mind is dominated by forces beyond his or her control, or that thoughts are being put into the person's head by others.[48] Research also demonstrates a linkage between mental instability and criminal behavior patterns.[49] Studies of adolescent males accused of murder have found that 75 percent could be classified as having some mental illness, including schizophrenia.[50] Abusive mothers have been found to have mood and personality disorders and a history of psychiatric diagnoses.[51] The diagnosed mentally ill appear in arrest and court statistics at a rate disproportionate to their presence in the population.[52] In some bizarre cases, people who commit murder hope to be executed for their crimes, a form of suicide-murder.[53]

Nor is the association between mental illness and crime restricted to the United States. Forensic criminologist Henrik Belfrage studied mental patients in Sweden and found that 28 percent of those who were still alive 10 years after being discharged from mental hospitals were found to be registered for a criminal offense. Among those who were 40 years old or younger at the time of discharge, nearly 40 percent had a criminal record, as compared with less than 10 percent of the general public.[54] Another study, conducted with samples of Australian men with schizophrenia, has shown them to be four times more likely than the general population to be convicted for serious violence.[55]

Despite this evidence, some doubt remains as to whether the mentally ill commit more crime than the mentally sound. Studies focusing on the criminal activity of the mentally ill have failed to establish a clear link between crime and psychiatrically diagnosed problems.[56] The mentally ill may be more likely to withdraw or harm themselves than to act aggressively toward others.[57] Research shows that after release, prisoners with prior histories of hospitalization for mental disorders are less likely to be re-arrested than those who have never been hospitalized.[58] And even if the mentally ill have a higher arrest and conviction rate than the mentally sound, in any given year only 0.2 percent of patients with schizophrenia were convicted of crimes. So although a link between mental illness and crime seems plausible, the association has been the subject of much debate.

Learning to Commit Crime: Behavioral Theory

A second branch of psychological theory views behavior as learned through interactions with others. Behavior that is rewarded becomes habitual; behavior that is punished becomes extinguished. One branch of behavioral theory of particular relevance to criminology is **social learning theory**. According to social learning theorists, people act aggressively because, as children, they modeled their behavior after the violent acts of adults.[59] Later in life, antisocial behavioral patterns are reinforced by peers and other acquaintances.[60]

Social learning theorists conclude that the antisocial behavior of potentially violent people can be triggered by a number of different influences: verbal taunts and threats; the experience of direct pain; and perceptions of relative social disability, such as poverty and racial discrimination. Those who have learned violence and have seen it rewarded are more likely to react violently under these stimuli than those who have not.

One area of particular interest to social learning theorists is whether the entertainment media can influence violence. This topic is discussed in the Images of Justice feature on page 100.

Developing Criminal Ideas: Cognitive Theory

Cognitive psychologists are concerned with the way that people perceive and mentally represent the world in which they live. Some focus on how people process and store information, viewing the operation of human intellect as similar to the way that computers analyze available information; the emphasis is on *information processing*. Aggressive people may base their behavior on faulty information. They perceive other people to be more aggressive than they really are. Consequently, they are more likely to be vigilant, on edge, or suspicious. When they attack victims, they may believe they are defending themselves, when they are simply misreading the situation.[61] The college student who rapes his date may have a cognitive problem, rendering him incapable of distinguishing behavioral cues. He misidentifies rejection as a come-on or as playing hard to get.

social learning theory
The view that human behavior is learned through observation of human social interactions, either directly from those in close proximity or indirectly from the media.

Another area of cognitive psychology is *moral development theory.* According to this theory, people go through a series of stages beginning early in childhood and continuing through their adult years.[62] Each stage is marked by a different view of right and wrong. For example, a child may do what is right simply to avoid punishment and censure. Later in life, the same person will develop a sensitivity to others' needs and do what is right to avoid hurting others. On reaching a higher level of maturity, the same person may behave in accordance with his or her perception of universal principles of justice, equality, and fairness.

According to developmental psychologists, criminals may lack the ability to make moral judgments. Criminals report that their outlooks are characterized by self-interest and impaired moral development. They are unlikely to consider the rights of others, and they are not concerned with maintaining the rules of society.[63]

Personality and Crime: The Psychopath

Some psychologists view criminal behavior as a function of a disturbed personality structure. Personality can be defined as the reasonably stable patterns of behavior, including thoughts and emotions, that distinguish one person from another.[64] An individual's personality reflects characteristic ways of adapting to life's demands and problems. The way you behave is a function of how your personality enables you to interpret life events and make appropriate behavioral choices.

Psychologists have explored the link between personality and crime. Evidence suggests that aggressive youths have unstable personality structures,

Psychopaths are predators who use charm, manipulation, intimidation, and violence to control others and to seek personal gratification. Dennis L. Rader, the "BTK" serial killer, is escorted into the El Dorado Correctional Facility on August 19, 2005, in El Dorado, Kansas. Rader pleaded guilty to 10 killings dating back to 1974, and he received 10 life terms for his crimes. Psychopaths like Rader lack concern for others and feel little guilt for their crimes.

© Larry W. Smith/AFP/Getty Images

The Media and Violence

Does the media influence behavior? Does broadcast violence cause aggressive behavior in viewers? This has become a hot topic because of the persistent theme of violence on television, in films, and in popular music. Critics have called for drastic measures, ranging from the banning of TV violence to putting warning labels on heavy metal albums, because of a fear that listening to hard-rock lyrics produces delinquency.

If a TV–violence link exists, the problem is indeed alarming. Systematic viewing of TV begins at 2.5 years of age and continues at a high level during the preschool and early school years. It has been estimated that children age 2 to 5 watch TV for 27.8 hours each week, children age 6 to 11 watch 24.3 hours per week, and teens watch 23 hours per week. Marketing research indicates that adolescents age 11 to 14 rent violent horror movies at a higher rate than any other age group. Children this age use older peers and siblings and apathetic parents to gain access to R-rated films. More than 40 percent of U.S. households now have cable TV, which features violent films and shows. Even children's programming is saturated with violence.

Numerous anecdotal cases of violence linked to TV and films can be cited. For example, in a famous incident, John Hinckley, Jr., shot President Ronald Reagan because of his obsession with actress Jodie Foster, which developed after he watched her play a prostitute in the film *Taxi Driver*. Hinckley viewed the film at least 15 times.

A national survey found that almost 80 percent of the general public believe that violence on TV can cause violence in "real life." However, psychologists believe that media violence does not in itself cause violent behavior because if it did, there would be millions of daily incidents in which viewers imitated the aggression they watched on TV or in movies. But most psychologists agree that media violence contributes to aggression. There are several explanations for the effects of television and film violence on behavior:

◆ Media violence can provide aggressive scripts that children store in memory. Repeated exposure to these scripts can increase their retention and lead to changes in attitudes.

◆ Children learn from what they observe. In the same way they learn cognitive and social skills from their parents and friends, children learn to be violent from television.

◆ Television violence increases the arousal levels of viewers and makes them more prone to act aggressively. Studies measuring the galvanic skin response of subjects—a physical indication of arousal based on the amount of electricity conducted across the palm of the hand—show that viewing violent television shows led to increased arousal levels in young children.

◆ Watching television violence promotes such negative attitudes as suspiciousness and the expectation that the viewer will become involved in violence. Those who watch television frequently come to view aggression and violence as common and socially acceptable behavior.

◆ Television violence allows aggressive youths to justify their behavior. Instead of causing violence, television could help violent youths rationalize their behavior as a socially acceptable and common activity.

◆ Television violence may disinhibit aggressive behavior, which is normally controlled by other learning processes. **Disinhibition** takes place when adults are viewed as being rewarded for violence and when violence is seen as socially acceptable. This contradicts previous learning experiences in which violent behavior was viewed as wrong.

Such distinguished bodies as the American Psychological Association, the National Institute of Mental Health, and the National Research Council support the TV–violence link. They base their conclusion on research efforts which indicate that watching violence on TV leads to increased levels of violence in the laboratory settings as well as in natural settings. A number of experimental approaches have been used, including the following:

◆ Having groups of subjects exposed to violent TV shows in a laboratory setting, then monitoring their behavior afterward and comparing it with

disinhibition
Unrestricted behavior resulting from a loss of inhibition produced by an external influence, such as drugs or alcohol, or from a brain injury.

often marked by hyperactivity, impulsiveness, and instability. Suspected traits include impulsivity, hostility, and aggressiveness.[65] There is also a demonstrated linkage between depression and delinquent behavior patterns.[66]

One area of particular interest to criminologists is the identification of the *psychopathic* (also called *antisocial* or *sociopathic*) personality. **Psychopaths**

the behavior of control groups who viewed nonviolent programming.

♦ Observing subjects on playgrounds, athletic fields, and residences after they have been exposed to violent television programs.

♦ Requiring subjects to answer attitude surveys after watching violent TV shows.

♦ Using aggregate measures of TV viewing—for example, tracking the number of violent TV shows on the air during a given time period and comparing it with crime rates during the same period.

According to a recent analysis of available scientific data since 1975, Brad Bushman and Craig Anderson found that the weight of the evidence indicates that watching violence on TV is correlated to aggressive behaviors and that the newest and most methodologically sophisticated works show the greatest amount of association.

In one of the most important recent studies, L. Rowell Huesmann and his associates at the University of Michigan contacted 329 adults 15 years after they had participated as 6- to 9-year-olds in a study indicating that youths who watched more violent television shows also displayed more aggressive behavior than their peers. As adults, those same children who had viewed violent shows in their adolescence continued to behave in a violent and aggressive manner. Boys who liked violent television grew into men who were significantly more likely to have pushed, grabbed, or shoved their wives and attacked others whom they found insulting. They were also much more likely to be convicted of a crime. Ironically, women who watched violent shows as children reported being punched, beaten, or choked as adults at a rate over four times the rate of nonviolence-watching women.

Although this research is persuasive, not all criminologists accept that watching TV or movies and listening to heavy metal music eventually lead to violent and antisocial behavior. For example, little evidence is available that residential areas that experience the highest levels of violent TV viewing also have rates of violent crime that are above the norm. If violent TV shows did cause interpersonal violence, then there should be few

ecological and regional patterns in the crime rate, of which there are many. Put another way, how can regional differences in the violence rate be explained considering the fact that people all across the nation watch the same TV shows and films? Finally, millions of children watch violence every night, but they do not become violent criminals. Despite the increased availability of violent TV shows, films, and video games, the violence rate among teens has been in a significant decline.

Critical Thinking

1. Should the government control the content of TV shows and limit the amount of weekly violence? How could the national news be shown if violence were omitted? What about boxing matches or hockey games?

2. How do you explain the fact that millions of kids watch violent TV shows and remain nonviolent? If there is a TV–violence link, how do you explain the fact that violence rates may have been higher in the old west than they are today? Do you think that violent gang kids stay home and watch TV?

InfoTrac College Edition Research

Is the presence of violence on TV increasing or in decline? To find out, check out Nancy Signorielli's "Prime-Time Violence 1993–2001: Has the Picture Really Changed?" *Journal of Broadcasting and Electronic Media* 47 (March 2003): 36.

Sources: René Weber, Ute Ritterfeld, and Klaus Mathiak, "Does Playing Violent Video Games Induce Aggression? Empirical Evidence of a Functional Magnetic Resonance Imaging Study," *Media Psychology* 8 (2006): 39–60; John Murray et al., "Children's Brain Activations While Viewing Televised Violence Revealed by fMRI," *Media Psychology* 8 (2006): 25–37; Dimitri Christakis, Frederick Zimmerman, David DiGiuseppe, and Carolyn McCarty, "Early Television Exposure and Subsequent Attentional Problems in Children," *Pediatrics* 113 (2004): 708–13; L. Rowell Heusmann, Jessica Moise-Titus, Cheryl-Lynn Podolski, and Leonard Eron, "Longitudinal Relations Between Children's Exposure to TV Violence and Their Aggressive and Violent Behavior in Young Adulthood: 1977–1992," *Developmental Psychology* 39 (2003): 201–21; Brad Bushman and Craig Anderson, "Media Violence and the American Public," *American Psychologist* 56 (2001): 477–89; Garland White, Janet Katz, and Kathryn Scarborough, "The Impact of Professional Football Games upon Violent Assaults on Women," *Violence and Victims* 7 (1992): 157–71; Albert Reiss and Jeffrey Roth, eds., *Understanding and Preventing Violence* (Washington, D.C.: National Academy Press, 1993).

are believed to be dangerous, aggressive, antisocial individuals who act in a callous manner. They neither learn from their mistakes nor are deterred by punishments.[67] Although they may appear charming and have at least average intelligence, psychopaths lack emotional depth, are incapable of caring for others, and maintain an abnormally low level of anxiety. They are likely to be persistent

psychopath
A person whose personality is characterized by a lack of warmth and feeling, inappropriate behavioral responses, and an inability to learn from experience—also called a sociopath or an antisocial personality.

While some research shows that people who act aggressively in social settings also have lower IQ scores than their peers, other findings suggest that the association between intelligence and crime is insignificant. Should mentally challenged offenders be punished in the same manner as those who are nonintellectually impaired? Daryl Atkins walks into the York-Poquoson Courtroom in York, Virginia, on July 25, 2005. Atkins, whose case led the U.S. Supreme Court to bar execution of the mentally retarded as unconstitutionally cruel, remained on death row, years after the landmark ruling.

ThomsonNOW™ Improve your grade on the exam with Personalized Study! For reinforcement resources and a mastery check of psychological theories of crime, go to www.thomsonedu.com/thomsonnow.

alcohol and drug abusers.[68] Violent offenders often display psychopathic tendencies such as impulsivity, aggression, dishonesty, pathological lying, and lack of remorse.[69] Psychopathy has also been linked to chronic recidivism and serial murder.[70] A high proportion of serial rapists and re-peat sexual offenders exhibit psychopathic personality structures.[71]

A number of factors are believed to contribute to the development of a psychopathic personality.[72] Some factors are related to improper socialization and include having a psychopathic parent, parental rejection and lack of love during childhood, and inconsistent discipline.

Others suspect that psychopaths suffer from a low level of arousal as measured by the activity of their autonomic nervous system.[73] Therefore, psychopaths could be thrill seekers who engage in high-risk antisocial activities to raise their general neurological arousal level.

Some psychologists believe that antisocial personality traits can be linked to brain dysfunction or damage.[74] Research shows that psychopaths may have brain-related physical anomalies that cause them to process emotional input differently than do nonpsychopaths.[75]

IQ and Crime

One of the most enduring controversies in the psychology of crime is the relationship between intelligence, as measured by standardized intelligence quotient (IQ) tests, and violent or criminal behavior. Numerous studies link low IQ to violent and aggressive behavior and crime.[76] Some research examines samples of people to determine whether those with low IQ are also more aggressive in social settings. Evidence shows that people who act aggressively in social settings also have lower IQ scores than their peers.[77] Some studies have found a direct IQ–delinquency link among samples of adolescent boys.[78]

Although this evidence is persuasive, many experts dispute that an IQ–crime relationship exists. It has been suggested that any association is a function of bias in the testing procedures. Furthermore, a number of studies have found that IQ level has negligible influence on criminal behavior.[79] Also, a recent evaluation of existing knowledge on intelligence conducted by the American Psychological Association concluded that the strength of an IQ–crime link was "very low."[80] However, it is unlikely that the IQ–criminality debate will be settled in the near future.

◆ BLAME SOCIETY: SOCIOLOGICAL THEORIES

Official, self-report, and victim data all indicate social patterns in the crime rate.[81] Some regions are more crime prone than others. Distinct differences are found in crime rates across states, cities, and neighborhoods. If crime rates are higher in California than Vermont, it is probably not because Californians are more likely to suffer personality defects or eat more sugar than Vermonters. Crime rates are higher in large urban areas that house concentrations of the poor than they are in sparsely populated rural areas in which residents are relatively affluent. Prisons are filled with the poor and the hopeless, not the rich and the famous. Because crime patterns have a decidedly social orientation, sociological explanations of crime have predominated in criminology.

Sociological criminology is usually traced to the pioneering work of sociologist Émile Durkheim (1858–1917), who viewed crime as a social phenomenon.[82] In formulating his theory of **anomie**, Durkheim held that crime is an essential part of society and a function of its internal conflict. As he used the term, *anomie* means the absence or weakness of rules and social norms in any person or group; without these rules or norms, an individual may lose the ability to distinguish between right and wrong.

As the field of sociological criminology emerged in the twentieth century, greater emphasis was placed on environmental conditions, whereas the relationship between crime and physical or mental traits (or both) was neglected. Equating the cause of criminal behavior with social factors, such as poverty and unemployment, was instrumental in the development of treatment-oriented crime prevention techniques. If criminals are made and not born—if they are forged in the crucible of societal action—then it logically follows that crime can be eradicated by the elimination of the social elements responsible for crime. The focus of crime prevention shifted from punishing criminals to treatment and rehabilitation.

anomie
The absence or weakness of rules, norms, or guidelines on what is socially or morally acceptable.

Because They Are Poor: Social Structure Theory

According to **social structure** theory, the United States is a stratified society. Social strata are created by the unequal distribution of wealth, power, and prestige. Social classes are segments of the population whose members have relatively similar attitudes, values, and norms and have an identifiable lifestyle.

In U.S. society, it is common to identify people as upper-, middle-, and lower-class citizens, with a broad range of economic variations existing within each group. The upper-upper class is reserved for a small number of exceptionally well-to-do families who maintain enormous financial and social resources. The government estimates that there are now 37 million Americans living in poverty, defined as a family of four earning about $20,000 per year, who have scant, if any, resources and suffer socially and economically as a result. Today, the poorest fifth (20 percent) of all U.S. households receives only 3.5 percent of the country's aggregate income, the smallest share ever. In contrast, the top fifth (20 percent) of households receives more than 50 percent of all income, a record high; the top 5 percent collects more than 20 percent of all household income, the most in history.[83]

About 20 million high school dropouts face dead-end jobs, unemployment, and social failure. Because of their meager economic resources, lower-class citizens are often forced to live in slum areas marked by substandard housing, inadequate health care, poor educational opportunities, underemployment, and despair. They live in areas with deteriorated housing and abandoned buildings, which research shows are magnets for crime, drug dealing, and prostitution.[84] Violence and crime have been found to spread in these areas in a pattern similar to a contagious disease epidemic.[85] When lower-class youths are exposed to a continual stream of violence, they are more likely to engage in violent acts themselves.[86]

social structure
The stratifications, classes, institutions, and groups that characterize a society.

RACIAL DISPARITY The problems of lower-class culture are particularly acute for racial and ethnic minorities. Research indicates that their disproportionate representation in the poverty class may be a result of negative racial stereotyping among potential employers, which leads to both lower employment opportunities and greater income inequality.[87] Among recent findings about the plight suffered by young minority males:

◆ The share of young black men without jobs has climbed relentlessly, with only a slight pause during the economic peak of the late 1990s. In 2000, 65 percent of black male high school dropouts in their twenties were jobless—that is, unable to find work, not seeking it, or incarcerated. By 2004, the share had grown to 72 percent, compared with 34 percent of white and 19 percent of Hispanic dropouts. Even when high school graduates were included, half of black men in their twenties were jobless in 2004, up from 46 percent in 2000.

◆   Incarceration rates climbed in the 1990s and reached historic highs in the past few years. In 1995, 16 percent of black men in their twenties who did not attend college were in jail or prison; 10 years later, 21 percent were incarcerated. By their mid-thirties, 6 in 10 black men who had dropped out of school had spent time in prison.

◆   In the inner cities, more than half of all black men do not finish high school.[88]

These economic and social disparities continually haunt members of the minority underclass and their children. Even if they value education and other middle-class norms, their desperate life circumstances (including high unemployment and nontraditional family structures) may prevent them from developing the skills, habits, and styles that lead first to educational success and later to success in the workplace; these deficits have been linked to crime and drug abuse.[89]

culture of poverty
The view that people in the lower class of society form a separate culture with its own values and norms that are in conflict with those of conventional society.

The crushing burden of urban poverty brings on the development of a **culture of poverty**.[90] This subculture is marked by apathy, cynicism, helplessness, and distrust. The culture is passed from one generation to the next, creating a permanent underclass, referred to as the "truly disadvantaged."[91]

Considering the social disability suffered by the lower class, it is not surprising that some people turn to crime as a means of support and survival. According to the social structure approach, a significant majority of people who commit violent crimes and serious theft offenses live in the lower-class culture, and a majority of all serious crimes occur in inner-city areas. The social forces operating in lower-class, inner-city areas produce high crime rates. What are these forces, and how do they produce crime?

The Disorganized Neighborhood

Some crime experts believe that crime is a product of neighborhoods that are characterized by physical deterioration and by conflicting values and social systems. Disorganized neighborhoods are undergoing the disintegration of their existing culture and services, the diffusion of cultural standards, and successive changes from purely residential to a mixture of commercial, industrial, transient, and residential populations. In these areas, the major sources of informal social control—family, school, neighborhood, civil service—are broken and ineffective.

Urban areas are believed to be crime prone because their most important social institutions cannot function properly. These neighborhoods are unable to realize the common values of their residents or to solve commonly experienced problems.[92] Disorganized neighborhoods have high population density, large numbers of single-parent households, unrelated people living together, and a lack of employment opportunities.[93] Because they experience a daily barrage of violence, residents live in fear; as perceptions of fear increase, quality of life deteriorates.[94] Fear is often based on experience. Residents who have already been victimized are more fearful of the future than those who have escaped crime.[95] People become afraid when they are approached by someone in the neighborhood selling drugs. They may fear that their children will also be approached and seduced into the drug life.[96] The presence of such incivilities, especially when accompanied by relatively high crime rates, convinces residents that their neighborhood is dangerous; becoming a crime victim seems inevitable.[97]

Disorganized neighborhoods also experience rapid population turnover.[98] Changes in racial and economic composition seem to destabilize neighborhoods and elevate their crime rates.[99] In contrast, stable neighborhoods, even those with a high rate of poverty, experience relatively low crime rates and have the strength to restrict substance abuse and criminal activity.[100] As areas decline, residents flee to safer, more stable localities. Those who can move to more-affluent neighborhoods find that their lifestyles and life chances improve immediately and continue to do so over their lifespan.[101] As the more-affluent residents flee, leaving behind a neighborhood with nonexistent employment opportunities, inferior housing patterns, and unequal access to health care, poverty becomes concentrated in these areas.[102] Urban areas marked by concentrated poverty become isolated and insulated from the social mainstream and more prone to criminal activity, violence, and homicide.[103]

Those who cannot leave because they cannot afford to live in more-affluent communities face an increased risk of victimization. Because of racial differences in economic well-being, those "left behind" are all too often minority citizens.[104] Whites may feel threatened as the number of minorities in the population increases, producing competition for jobs and political power.[105] As racial prejudice increases, the call for "law and order" aimed at controlling the minority population grows louder.[106]

In contrast to areas plagued by poverty concentration, cohesive communities with high levels of social control and social integration, where people know one another and develop interpersonal ties, may also develop **collective efficacy**: mutual trust, a willingness to intervene in the supervision of children, and the maintenance of public order.[107] It is the cohesion among neighborhood residents combined with shared expectations for informal social control of public space that promotes collective efficacy.[108] Residents in these areas are able to enjoy a better life because the fruits of cohesiveness can be better education, health care, and housing opportunities.[109]

The crime-producing influences of these economic disadvantages are felt by all residents.[110] However, minority-group members living in these areas suffer the added disadvantages of race-based income inequality and institutional racism.[111] The fact that significant numbers of African Americans are forced to live under these conditions can help explain the distinct racial patterns in the official crime statistics.

Unfortunately, the problems found in disorganized areas are stubborn and difficult to overcome. Even when an attempt is made to revitalize a neighborhood—for example, by creating institutional support programs such as community centers and better schools—the effort may be countered by the enduring lack of economic and social resources.[112]

DEVIANT VALUES AND CULTURES Living in deteriorated inner-city neighborhoods, forced to endure substandard housing and schools, and cut off from conventional society, slum dwellers are faced with a constant assault on their self-image and sense of worth. Although the media bombard them with images glorifying a materialistic lifestyle, they cannot purchase fine clothes, a luxury automobile, or their own home. Residents may become resentful and angry when they realize that they are falling further and further behind the social mainstream.[113] Residents who live in these high-crime areas, where drug abuse is common, also suffer. Because they believe that their neighbors lack ties to conventional cultural values, their own ability to maintain social ties in the neighborhood becomes weak and attenuated. This may further reduce already weakened levels of informal social control.[114]

How is it possible for them to adjust and satisfy their needs? One method of adjusting is to create an independent value system. Whereas middle-class values favor education, hard work, sexual abstinence,

collective efficacy
A condition of mutual trust and cooperation that develops in neighborhoods that have a high level of formal and informal social control.

PERSPECTIVES ON JUSTICE

Rehabilitation

Social structure theory is linked to the rehabilitation perspective of justice. If poverty and strain cause crime, then efforts to improve economic opportunity can help reduce crime rates. Job and social welfare programs are part of the government's effort to give members of the lower class opportunities to succeed legitimately. Efforts to reduce crime rates by revitalizing a community's social and economic health are extremely difficult to achieve because the problems of decayed, transitional neighborhoods are overwhelming. Rehabilitation efforts are dwarfed by the social problems ingrained in these areas.

focal concerns
Central values and goals that, according to Walter Miller, differ by social class.

honesty, and sobriety, lower-class values in slum areas applaud goals that are realistically obtainable in a disorganized society: being cool, promiscuous, intemperate, and fearless. Thus, lower-class **focal concerns** include scorning authority, living for today, seeking excitement, and scoffing at formal education.[115]

Some people living in disorganized areas band together to form an independent lower-class subculture—small reference groups that provide members with a unique set of values, beliefs, and traditions distinct from those of conventional society. Within this subculture, lower-class youths can achieve success unobtainable within the larger culture while also gaining a sense of identity and achievement. Members of the criminal subculture adopt a set of norms and principles in direct opposition to middle-class society. They engage in short-run hedonism, living for today by taking drugs, drinking, and engaging in unsafe sex. They resist efforts by family members and other authority figures to control their behavior and instead join autonomous peer groups and gangs.[116] Members may be prone to violence, for example, because the routine activities of their subculture require them to frequent locations, such as bars and dance clubs, where aggressive behavior is the norm and where they are exposed to other violence-prone people.[117] Cultural values might include excluding police officers from social conflicts and handling problems personally. When Charis Kubrin and Ronald Weitzer examined the ecological and socioeconomic correlates of homicide in St. Louis, they found that a certain type of homicide (what they call "cultural retaliatory homicide") is more common in some neighborhoods than in others.[118] Residents in these communities often solve problems informally, without calling the police, even if it means having to kill someone in retaliation for a perceived or actual slight or provocation. The neighborhood culture codes support this type of problem solving, even if it leads to violence and death. In sum, in lower-class areas, social, cultural, and economic forces interact to produce a violent environment.

strain
The emotional turmoil and conflict caused when people believe that they cannot achieve their desires and goals through legitimate means.

STRAIN In lower-class neighborhoods, **strain**, or status frustration, occurs because legitimate avenues for success are all but closed. Frustrated and angry, with no acceptable means of achieving success, people may use deviant methods, such as theft or violence, to achieve their goals.

The concept of strain can be traced to the pioneering work of famed sociologist Robert Merton, who recognized that members of the lower class experience

According to strain theory, people who want to experience the American Dream of wealth, success, and happiness will be frustrated and angry if they lack the means of achieving their goals.

FIGURE 3.2
Agnew's Sources of Strain and Their Consequences

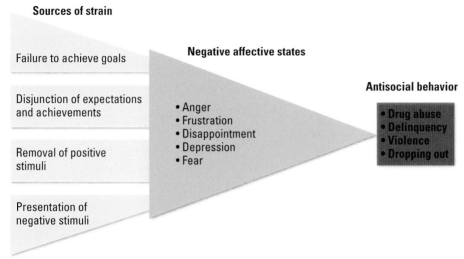

anomie, or normlessness, when the means they have for achieving culturally de-fined goals, mainly wealth and financial success, are insufficient.[119] As a result, people will begin to seek alternative solutions to meet their need for success: They will steal, sell drugs, or extort money. Merton referred to this method of adaptation as *innovation*—the use of innovative but illegal means to achieve suc-cess in the absence of legitimate means. Other youths, faced with the same dilemma, might reject conventional goals and choose to live as drug users, alco-holics, and wanderers; Merton referred to this as *retreatism*. Still others might join revolutionary political groups and work to change the system to one of their liking; Merton refers to this as *rebellion*.

Criminologist Robert Agnew has expanded anomie theory by recognizing other sources of strain in addition to failure to meet goals. These include both negative experiences, such as child abuse, and the loss of positive supports, such as the end of a stable romantic relationship (see Figure 3.2).[120] Some people, es-pecially those with an explosive temperament, those with low tolerance for ad-versity, those with poor problem-solving skills, and those who are overly sensitive or emotional, are less likely to cope well with strain.[121] As their perceptions of strain increase, so does their involvement in antisocial behaviors.[122]

Socialized to Crime: Social Process Theories

Not all criminologists agree that the root cause of crime can be found solely within the culture of poverty.[123] After all, self-report studies indicate that many middle- and upper-class youths take drugs and commit serious criminal acts. As adults, they commit white-collar and corporate crimes. Conversely, the majority of people living in the poorest areas hold conventional values and forgo criminal activity. Simply living in a violent neighborhood does not produce violent peo-ple. Research shows that family, peer, and individual characteristics play a large role in predicting violence.[124] These patterns indicate that forces must be oper-ating in all strata of society that influence individual involvement in criminal activity.

If crime is spread throughout the social structure, then it follows that the fac-tors that cause crime should be found within all social and economic groups. People commit crimes as a result of the experiences they have while they are be-ing socialized by the various organizations, institutions, and processes of society.

People are most strongly influenced toward criminal behavior by poor family relationships, destructive peer-group relations, educational failure, and labeling by agents of the justice system. Although lower-class citizens have the added burdens of poverty, strain, and blocked opportunities, middle- or upper-class citizens also may turn to crime if their socialization is poor or destructive.

Social process theorists point to research efforts linking family problems to crime as evidence that socialization, not social structure, is the key to understanding the onset of criminality:

parental efficacy
Parenting that is supportive, effective, and noncoercive.

♦ Parents who are supportive and effectively control their children in a noncoercive fashion are more likely to raise children who refrain from delinquency; this is called **parental efficacy**.[125]

♦ Delinquency will be reduced if parents provide the type of structure that integrates children into families while giving them the ability to assert their individuality and regulate their own behavior.[126]

♦ Kids who report having troubled home lives also exhibit lower levels of self-esteem and are more prone to antisocial behaviors.[127]

♦ Adolescents who do not receive affection from their parents during childhood are more likely to use illicit drugs and be more aggressive as they mature.[128]

♦ Children whose parents abuse drugs are more likely to become persistent substance abusers than the children of nonabusers.[129]

♦ Children who experience abuse, neglect, or sexual abuse are believed to be more crime prone and suffer from other social problems such as depression, suicide attempts, and self-injurious behaviors.[130] Children who grow up in homes where parents use severe discipline yet lack warmth and involvement in their lives are prone to antisocial behavior.[131] Links have been found among corporal punishment, delinquency, anger, spousal abuse, depression, and adult crime.[132]

Educational experience has also been found to have a significant impact on behavioral choices. Schools contribute to fostering criminality when they set problem youths apart by creating a track system that labels some as college-bound and others as academic underachievers. Studies show that chronic delinquents do poorly in school, lack educational motivation, and are frequently held back.[133] Research indicates that high school dropouts are more likely to become involved in crime than those who complete their education.[134] School climate may be the culprit: Many students are also subject to violence and intimidation on school grounds; school crime surveys estimate that about 1.5 million violent incidents occur in public elementary and secondary schools each year.[135] Bullying is a sad but common occurrence in the U.S. educational system; more than 15 percent of U.S. schoolchildren say they have been bullied by other students during the current school term.[136]

Associating with deviant peers also exerts tremendous influence on behavior, attitudes, and beliefs.[137] Some kids consider themselves "social outcasts" and then hook up with friends who are dangerous and get them into trouble.[138] Those who acquire delinquent friends may find that peer influence is a powerful determinant of behavior. Once acquired, deviant peers may sustain or amplify antisocial behavior trends—e.g., riding around, staying out late, and partying—and amplify delinquent careers.[139] Because delinquent friends tend to be "sticky" (once acquired, they are not easily lost), peer influence may continue through the life span.[140] In contrast, nondelinquent friends help moderate delinquency.[141] Having prosocial friends who are committed to conventional success may help shield youths from crime-producing inducements in their environment.[142]

In sum, significant evidence exists that the direction and quality of interpersonal interactions and relationships influence behavior throughout the life span. However, disagreement arises over the direction this influence takes:

♦ *Social learning theory* suggests that people learn the techniques and attitudes of crime from close relationships with criminal peers. Crime is a learned behavior.

♦ *Social control theory* maintains that everyone has the potential to become a criminal but that most people are controlled by their bonds to society. Crime occurs when the forces that bind people to society are weakened or broken.

♦ *Social reaction (labeling) theory* says that people become criminals when significant members of society label them as such and they accept those labels as a personal identity.

STUDENTS OF CRIME: LEARNING THEORIES Those who advocate learning theories hold that people enter into a life of crime when, as adolescents, they are taught the attitudes, values, and behaviors that support a criminal career. They may learn the techniques of crime from a variety of intimates, including parents and family members.[143]

The best-known example of the learning perspective is Edwin Sutherland's **differential association theory**.[144] Sutherland, considered by many to be the preeminent American criminologist, believed that the attitudes and behaviors that cause crime are learned in close and intimate relationships with significant others. People learn to commit crime in the same way that they learn any other behavior. Children learn to ride a bike by observing more experienced riders, practicing riding techniques, and hearing how much fun it is to ride. In the same fashion, some kids may meet and associate with criminal "mentors" who teach them how to be successful criminals and gain the greatest benefits from their criminal activities.[145] Adolescents who are exposed to an excess of attitudes ("definitions") in support of deviant behavior will eventually view those behaviors as attractive, appropriate, and suitable, and then engage in a life of crime.

Testing the principles of differential association theory is difficult, but several notable research efforts have supported its core assumptions:

♦ Crime appears to be intergenerational. Youths whose parents are deviant and criminal are more likely to become criminal themselves. This finding suggests that children learn crime from their parents.[146]

♦ People who report having attitudes that support deviant behavior are also likely to engage in deviant behavior.[147]

♦ Association with deviant peers has been found to sustain the deviant attitudes.[148]

♦ Romantic partners influence each other's behavior; partners may "learn" from each other.[149]

♦ Youths who associate with and presumably learn from aggressive peers are more likely to behave aggressively themselves.[150]

♦ Scales measuring differential association have been significantly correlated with criminal behaviors among samples taken in other nations and cultures.[151]

OUT OF CONTROL: CONTROL THEORIES When they were in high school, most students knew a few people who seemed detached and alienated from almost everything and everyone. They did not care about school, they had poor relationships

differential association theory
The view that criminal acts are related to a person's exposure to antisocial attitudes and values.

at home, and although they may have belonged to a tough crowd, their relationships with their peers were superficial and often violent. Very often these same people got into trouble at school, had run-ins with the police, and were involved in drugs and antisocial behaviors.

These observations form the nucleus of **social control theory**. This approach to understanding crime holds that all people may have the inclination to violate the law but that most are held in check by their relationships to conventional institutions and individuals, such as family, school, and peer group. For some people, when these relationships are strained or broken, they become free to engage in deviant acts that otherwise would be avoided. Crime occurs when the influence of official and informal sources of social control is weakened or absent.

social control theory
The view that most people do not violate the law because of their social bonds to family, peer group, school, and other institutions. If these bonds are weakened or absent, they become free to commit crime.

The most influential advocate of control theory is sociologist Travis Hirschi, who suggests that people's social bonds are formed from a number of different elements (see Figure 3.3). According to Hirschi, people whose bond to society is secure are unlikely to engage in criminal misconduct because they have a strong stake in society. Those who find their social bond weakened are much more likely to succumb to the temptations of criminal activity. After all, crime does have rewards, such as excitement, action, material goods, and pleasures. Hirschi does not give a definitive reason for what causes a person's social bond to weaken, but the process has two likely main sources: disrupted home life and poor school ability (leading to subsequent school failure and dislike of school).

Ongoing research efforts have attempted to test Hirschi's theory about social control and crime. Although results vary, a number of studies have supplied

PERSPECTIVES ON JUSTICE

Rehabilitation

Control theory has been linked to the rehabilitation perspective. Programs have been designed to present alternative values and lifestyles to youths who have bought into a delinquent way of life. These programs often use group process and counseling to attack the criminal behavior orientations of their clients and help them learn conventional values and beliefs. Rehabilitation advocates suggest that community-based programs designed to strengthen young people's bonds to society will insulate them from crime. Family development, counseling programs, and school-based prevention programs are often employed. In addition, various state youth and adult correctional authorities maintain inmate treatment programs that stress career development, work and educational furloughs, and self-help groups, all designed to help reestablish social bonds.

What would Travis Hirschi have to say about singer Courtney Love, shown here exiting a New York courtroom following a hearing where she pleaded guilty to disorderly conduct for throwing a microphone stand and striking a man in the head at a New York City nightclub? Would he conclude that her behavior was a function of her frayed bonds to society?

©AP Images/Louis Lanzano

FIGURE 3.3
Elements of the Social Bond

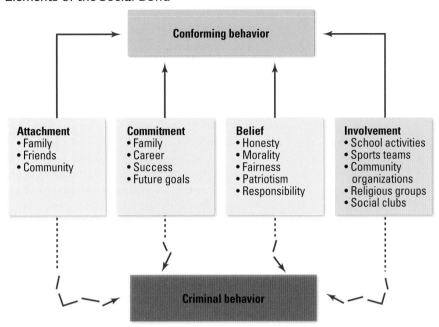

data that support Hirschi's view.[152] For example, youths who maintain positive attachments with others also report low rates of delinquency.[153] Those adolescents who are committed to school are less likely to engage in delinquent acts than youths who fail at school and are detached from the educational experience.[154]

THE OUTSIDER: SOCIAL REACTION THEORY According to **social reaction (labeling) theory**, officially designating people as "troublemakers," stigmatizing them with a permanent deviant label, leads them to criminality. People who commit undetected antisocial acts are called "secret deviants" or "primary deviants." Their illegal act has little influence or impact on their lifestyle or behavior. However, if another person commits the same act and his or her behavior is discovered by social control agents, the labeling process may be initiated. That person may be given a deviant label, such as "mentally ill" or "criminal." The deviant label transforms him or her into an outsider, shunned by the rest of society. In time, the stigmatized person may believe that the deviant label is valid and assume it as a personal identity. For example, the student placed in special education classes begins to view himself as "stupid" or "backward," the mental patient accepts society's view of her as "crazy," and the convicted criminal considers himself "dangerous" or "wicked."

Accompanying the deviant label are a variety of degrading social and physical restraints—handcuffs, trials, incarceration, bars, cells, and a criminal record—that leave an everlasting impression on the accused. These sanctions are designed to humiliate and are applied in what labeling experts call *degradation ceremonies*, in which the target is made to feel unworthy and despised.

Labels and sanctions work to define the whole person, meaning that a label evokes stereotypes that are used to forecast other aspects of the labeled

social reaction (labeling) theory
The view that society produces criminals by stigmatizing certain individuals as deviants, a label that they come to accept as a personal identity.

PERSPECTIVES ON JUSTICE

Noninterventionism

Labeling theory principles support the noninterventionist view that an offender's contacts with the criminal justice system should be limited. Among the most prominent policy initiatives based on labeling theory are efforts to divert first offenders from the normal justice process and to shepherd them into treatment programs, to order offenders to pay victim restitution instead of entering them into the justice process, and to deinstitutionalize nonviolent offenders (that is, remove them from the prison system).

FIGURE 3.4
The Labeling Process

Initial criminal act
People commit crimes for a number of reasons.

Detection by the justice system
Arrest is influenced by racial, economic, and power relations.

Decision to label
Some are labeled "official" criminals by police and court authorities.

Creation of a new identity
Those labeled are known as troublemakers, criminals, and so on, and they are shunned by conventional society.

Acceptance of labels
Labeled people begin to see themselves as outsiders. Secondary deviance. Self-labeling.

Deviance amplificaton
Stigmatized offenders are now locked into criminal careers.

ThomsonNOW Improve your grade on the exam with Personalized Study! For reinforcement resources and a mastery check of sociological theories of crime, go to www.thomsonedu.com/thomsonnow.

critical criminology
The view that crime results from the imposition by the rich and powerful of their own moral standards and economic interests on the rest of society.

person's character. A person labeled "mentally ill" is assumed to be dangerous, evil, cruel, or untrustworthy, even though he or she has exhibited none of these characteristics.

Faced with such condemnation, negatively labeled people may begin to adopt their new, degraded identity. They may find no alternative but to seek others who are similarly stigmatized and form a deviant subculture. They are likely to make deviant friends and join gangs, associations that escalate their involvement in criminal activities.[155] Instead of deterring crime, labeling begins a deviance amplification process. If apprehended and subjected to even more severe negative labels, the offender may be transformed into a real deviant—one whose view of self is in direct opposition to conventional society. The deviant label may become a more comfortable and personally acceptable social status than any other. The individual whose original crime may have been relatively harmless is transformed by social action into a career deviant, a process referred to as *secondary deviance*. The entire labeling process is illustrated in Figure 3.4.

Labeling theorists also believe that the labeling process includes racial, gender, and economic discrimination. For example, judges may sympathize with white defendants and help them avoid criminal labels, especially if they seem to come from "good families," whereas minority youths are not afforded that luxury.[156] This may help explain racial and economic differences in the crime rate.

◆ MONEY, POWER, AND POLITICS: CRITICAL CRIMINOLOGY

Critical criminology views the economic and political forces operating in society as the fundamental cause of criminality. The criminal law and criminal justice system are seen as vehicles for controlling the poor. The criminal justice system helps the powerful and rich impose their own morality and standards of good behavior on the entire society, while protecting their property and physical safety from the have-nots, even though the cost may be the legal rights of the lower class. Those in power control the content and direction of the law and the legal system. Crimes are defined in a way that meets the needs of the ruling classes. Thus, the theft of property worth five dollars by a poor person can be punished much more severely than the misappropriation of millions by a large corporation. Those in the middle class are drawn into this pattern of control because they are led to believe that they, too, have a stake in maintaining the status quo and should support the views of the upper-class owners of production.[157]

Critical criminologists often take a broad view of deviant behavior, opposing racism, sexism, and genocide, rather than focusing on burglary, robbery, and rape.[158] They trace the history of criminal sanctions to show how those sanctions have corresponded to the needs of the wealthy. They attempt to show how police, courts, and correctional agencies have served as tools of the powerful members of society. Critical theorists maintain that because of social and economic inequality, members of the lower class are forced to commit larceny and burglary, take part in robberies, and sell drugs as a means of social and economic survival. In some instances, the disenfranchised will engage in rape, assault, and senseless homicides as a means of expressing their rage, frustration, and anger.

A considerable body of research supports critical criminology. Criminologists routinely have found evidence that measures of social inequality, such as income level, deteriorated living conditions, and relative economic deprivation are highly associated with crime rates, especially the felony murders that typically accompany robberies and burglaries.[159] The conclusion is that as people become economically marginalized, they will turn to violent crime for survival, producing an inevitable upswing in the number of street crimes and a corresponding spike in the murder rate.

Another area of critical research involves examining the criminal justice system to see if it operates as an instrument of class oppression or as a fair, evenhanded social control agency. Research has found that jurisdictions with significant levels of economic disparity are also the most likely to have large numbers of people killed by police officers. Police may act more forcefully in areas where class conflict creates the perception that extreme forms of social control are needed to maintain order.[160] There is also evidence of racial discrimination. Analysis of national population trends and imprisonment rates shows that as the percentage of minority-group members increases in a population, the imprisonment rate does likewise.[161]

Critical criminology has evolved over the past two decades, and a number of new sub-branches have been developed. **Left realism** attempts to reconcile critical views with the social realities of crime and its impact on the lower class. Left realists recognize that predatory crimes are not revolutionary acts and that crime is an overwhelming problem for the poor. Regardless of its origins, according to left realists, crime must be dealt with by the police and courts.[162] **Radical feminism** has tried to explain how capitalism places particular stress on women and to explicate the role of male dominance in female criminality.[163] **Peacemaking criminology** views crime as just one form of violence among others, such as war and genocide. Peacemakers call for universal social justice as a means of eliminating antisocial acts.[164] They argue that the old methods of punishment are failures and that new, less punitive methods must be discovered. When conservatives scoff at their ideas and claim that the crime rate dropped in the 1990s because the number of people in prison was at an all-time high, peacemakers counter by citing studies showing that imprisonment rates are not related to crime rates, that no consistent finding has been reached that locking people up helps reduce crimes, and that upward of two-thirds of all prison inmates recidivate soon after their release.[165]

> ### PERSPECTIVES ON JUSTICE
> ### *Restorative Justice*
>
> Peacemaking criminology serves as the basis of the restorative justice perspective. Rather than being adversarial and punitive, the justice system should strive to restore damaged social relations. Harsh punishments have become the norm. Alternatives would be mediation, arbitration, restitution, and forgiveness. This call for social justice has helped focus attention on the plight of the poor, women, and minority groups when they confront the agencies of the justice system. Programs that have been developed as a result include free legal services for indigent offenders, civilian review boards to oversee police, laws protecting battered women, and shelters for victims of domestic abuse.

left realism
A branch of conflict theory that accepts the reality of crime as a social problem and stresses its impact on the poor.

radical feminism
A branch of conflict theory that focuses on the role of capitalist male dominance in female criminality and victimization.

peacemaking criminology
A branch of conflict theory that stresses humanism, mediation, and conflict resolution as means to end crime.

developmental theories
A view of crime holding that as people travel through the life course, their experiences along the way influence behavior patterns. Behavior changes at each stage of the human experience.

◆ THE PATH TO CRIME: DEVELOPMENTAL THEORIES

Developmental theories seek to identify, describe, and understand the developmental factors that explain the onset and continuation of a criminal career. As a group, they do not ask the relatively simple question: Why do people commit crime? Instead, they focus on more complex issues: Why do some offenders persist in criminal careers, whereas others desist from or alter their criminal activity as they mature? Why do some people continually escalate their criminal involvement, whereas others slow down and turn their lives around? Are all criminals similar in their offending patterns, or are there different types of offenders and paths to offending? Developmental theories not only want to know why people enter a criminal way of life but also whether, once they do, they are able to alter the trajectory of their criminal involvement. Developmental theories seem to fall into two distinct groups: latent trait theory and life course theory.

FIGURE 3.5
General Theory of Crime

Criminal offender

Impulsive personality
• Physical
• Insensitive
• Risk-taking
• Shortsighted
• Nonverbal

Low self-control
• Poor parenting
• Deviant parents
• Lack of supervision
• Active
• Self-centered

Criminal opportunity
• Gangs
• Free time
• Drugs
• Suitable targets

Criminal act
• Delinquency
• Smoking
• Drinking
• Sex
• Crime

Weakening of social bonds
• Attachment
• Involvement
• Commitment
• Belief

Latent Trait Theory

latent trait theories
A view that human behavior is controlled by a master trait, present at birth or soon after, that influences and directs behavior.

Latent trait theories hold that human development is controlled by a master trait, present at birth or soon after. Some criminologists believe that this master trait remains stable and unchanging throughout a person's lifetime, whereas others suggest that it can be later altered or influenced by experience. In either event, as people travel through their life course this trait is always there, influencing decisions and directing their behavior. Because this master trait is enduring, the ebb and flow of criminal behavior are directed by the impact of external forces such as criminal opportunity and the reactions of others.[166] Suspected latent traits include defective intelligence, impulsive personality, and genetic makeup—characteristics that may be present at birth or established early in life and remain stable over time.[167] People who are antisocial during adolescence are the ones most likely to remain criminals throughout their life span because the latent trait controlling their behavior in youth also does so in adulthood.

The best-known latent trait theory is Michael Gottfredson and Travis Hirschi's general theory of crime (see Figure 3.5).[168] In the general theory, Gottfredson and Hirschi argue that individual differences in the tendency to commit criminal acts can be found in a person's level of self-control. People with limited self-control tend to be impulsive, insensitive, physical (rather than mental), risk-taking, shortsighted, and nonverbal. They have a here-and-now orientation and refuse to work for distant goals. They lack diligence, tenacity, and persistence in a course of action. People lacking self-control tend to be adventuresome, active, physical, and self-centered. As they mature, they have unstable marriages, jobs, and friendships.

Criminal acts are attractive to such individuals because they provide easy and immediate gratification—or, as Gottfredson and Hirschi put it, "money without work, sex without courtship, revenge without court delays." Given the opportunity to commit crime, they will readily violate the law. Under the same set of circumstances, nonimpulsive people will refrain from antisocial behavior.

Criminal activity diminishes when the opportunity to commit crime is limited. People age out of crime because the opportunity to commit crimes diminishes with age. Teenagers simply have more opportunity to commit crimes than the elderly, regardless of their intelligence. Here the general theory integrates the concepts of latent traits and criminal opportunity: Possessing a particular trait + having the opportunity to commit crime = the choice to commit crime.

Life Course Theory

In contrast to this view, the **life course** branch views criminality as a dynamic process, influenced by a multitude of individual characteristics, traits, and social experiences. As people travel through the life course, they are constantly bombarded by changing perceptions and experiences. As a result, their behavior will change directions, sometimes for the better and sometimes for the worse (see Figure 3.6).

Criminals start their journey at different times. Some are precocious, beginning their criminal careers early and persisting into adulthood, whereas others stay out of trouble in their early adolescence and do not violate the law until late in their teenage years.[169] Early-onset criminals seem to get involved in such behaviors as truancy, cruelty to animals, lying, and theft; they also appear to be more violent than their less precocious peers.[170] In contrast, late starters are more likely to be involved in nonviolent crimes such as theft.[171]

There are also differences in the types of crimes people commit. *Specialists* limit their criminal activities to a cluster of crime such as theft offenses, including burglary and shoplifting.[172] On the other hand, *generalists* engage in a garden variety of criminal activity ranging from drug abuse and burglary to rape, depending on the opportunity to commit crime and the likelihood of success.[173]

Life course theorists dispute the existence of an unchanging master trait that controls human development. Instead, they suggest that as people mature, the factors that influence their behavior also undergo change. At first, family relations may be most influential; in later adolescence, school and peer relations predominate; in adulthood, marital relations may be the most critical influence. Some antisocial youths who are in trouble throughout their adolescence may be able to find stable work and maintain intact marriages as adults. These life events help them desist from crime. In contrast, those who develop arrest records, get involved with the wrong crowd, and can find only menial jobs are at risk for

life course
The course of social and developmental changes through which an individual passes as he or she travels from birth through childhood, adolescence, adulthood, and finally old age.

FIGURE 3.6
Life Course Theories

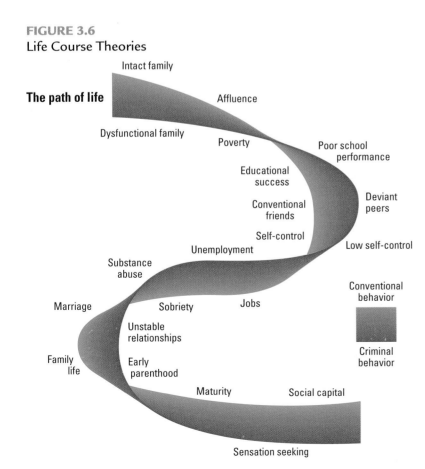

criminal careers. Social forces that are critical at one stage of life may have little meaning or influence at another.

Life course theorists believe that crime is one among a group of antisocial behaviors that cluster together and typically involve family dysfunction, sexual and physical abuse, substance abuse, smoking, precocious sexuality and early pregnancy, educational underachievement, suicide attempts, sensation seeking, and unemployment.[174] According to this view, crime is a type of social problem rather than the product of other social problems.[175] People who suffer from one of these conditions typically exhibit many symptoms of the rest.[176] They find themselves with a range of personal dilemmas, from drug abuse to being accident prone, to requiring more health care and hospitalization, to becoming teenage parents, to having mental health problems.[177] Problem behaviors have a cumulative effect: The more risk factors a person suffers in childhood, the greater the likelihood that these will carry over into adulthood.[178] The psychic scars of childhood are hard to erase.[179]

AGE-GRADED THEORY   Two of the leading life course theorists, criminologists Robert Sampson and John Laub, have formulated what they call *age-graded theory*.[180] According to Sampson and Laub, "turning points" in a criminal career are life events that enable people to "knife off" from a criminal career path into one of conventional and legitimate activities. As they mature, people who have had significant problems with the law are able to desist from crime if they can become attached to a spouse who supports and sustains them. They may encounter employers who are willing to give them a chance despite their record. People who cannot sustain secure marital relations or are failures in the labor market are less likely to desist from crime. Getting arrested can help sustain a criminal career because it reduces the chances of marriage, employment, and job stability, factors that are directly related to crime.

According to Sampson and Laub, these life events help people build **social capital**—positive relations with individuals and institutions that are life-sustaining. Building social capital, which includes acquiring personal connections and relationships, is critical if a person hopes to obtain his or her life's objectives.[181] For example, a successful marriage creates social capital when it improves a person's stature, creates feelings of self-worth, and encourages people to give him a chance.[182] Getting a good job inhibits crime by creating a stake in conformity—why commit crimes when you are doing well at your job? The relationship is reciprocal: Persons chosen as employees return the favor by doing the best job possible; those chosen as spouses blossom into devoted partners. Building social capital and strong social bonds reduces the likelihood of long-term deviance. According to research by Alex Piquero and his associates, even people who have long histories of criminal activity and have been convicted of serious offenses reduce the frequency of their offending if they get married and fall into a domestic lifestyle.[183] People who are married often have schedules where they work 9-to-5 jobs, come home for dinner, take care of children if they have them, watch television, go to bed, and repeat the cycle over and over again. People who are not married have free rein to do what they want, especially if they are not employed. Crossing the line of getting married helps these men stay away from crime. If they do not cross that line, they can continue their lifestyles, which are erratic.[184]

social capital
Positive relations with individuals and institutions that foster self-worth and inhibit crime.

ThomsonNOW⁺ Improve your grade on the exam with Personalized Study! For reinforcement resources and a mastery check of developmental theories of crime, go to www. thomsonedu.com/thomsonnow.

◆ IT'S HOW YOU LIVE: THEORIES OF VICTIMIZATION

For many years, criminological theory focused on the actions of the criminal offender. The role of the victim was virtually ignored. Then a number of scholars found that the victim is not a passive target in crime but someone whose behavior can influence his or her own fate. Hans Von Hentig portrayed the crime victim as

CONCEPT SUMMARY 3.1

Concepts and Theories of Criminology: A Review

Theory	Major premise
CHOICE THEORY	People commit crime when they perceive that the benefits of law violation outweigh the threat and pain of punishment.
BIOSOCIAL THEORY	
BIOCHEMICAL	Crime, especially violence, is a function of diet, vitamin intake, hormonal imbalance, or food allergies.
NEUROLOGICAL	Criminals and delinquents often suffer brain impairment. Attention deficit disorder and minimum brain dysfunction are related to antisocial behavior.
GENETIC	Delinquent traits and predispositions are inherited. The criminality of parents can predict the delinquency of children.
PSYCHOLOGICAL THEORY	
PSYCHODYNAMIC	The development of personality early in childhood influences behavior for the rest of a person's life. Criminals have weak egos and damaged personalities.
SOCIAL LEARNING	People commit crime when they model their behavior after others whom they see being rewarded for the same acts. Behavior is enforced by rewards and extinguished by punishment.
SOCIAL STRUCTURE THEORY	
SOCIAL DISORGANIZATION	The conflicts and problems of urban social life and communities control the crime rate. Crime is a product of transitional neighborhoods that manifest social disorganization and value conflict.
STRAIN	People who adopt the goals of society but lack the means to attain them seek alternatives such as crime.
SOCIAL PROCESS THEORY	
LEARNING THEORY	People learn to commit crime from exposure to antisocial behaviors. Criminal behavior depends on the person's experiences with rewards for conventional behaviors and punishments for deviant ones. Being rewarded for deviance leads to crime.
SOCIAL CONTROL THEORY	A person's bond to society prevents him or her from violating social rules. If the bond weakens, the person is free to commit crime.
CRITICAL THEORY	
CRITICAL CRIMINOLOGY	People commit crimes when the law, controlled by the rich and powerful, defines their behavior as illegal. The immoral actions of the powerful go unpunished.
LEFT REALISM	Crime is a function of relative deprivation. Criminals prey on the poor.
RADICAL FEMINISM	The capital system creates patriarchy, which oppresses women. Male dominance explains gender bias, violence against women, and repression.
PEACEMAKING	Peace and humanism can reduce crime. Conflict-resolution strategies can work.
DEVELOPMENTAL THEORY	
AGE-GRADED THEORY	Early in life, people begin relationships that determine their behavior through their life course. Life transitions control the probability of offending.
SELF-CONTROL THEORY	Crime and criminality are separate concepts. People choose to commit crime when they lack self-control. People lacking self-control will seize criminal opportunities.

victim precipitation
The role of the victim in provoking or encouraging criminal behavior.

someone who "shapes and molds the criminal."[185] The criminal may be a predator, but the victim may help the criminal by becoming a willing prey. Stephen Schafer extended this approach by focusing on the victim's responsibility in the "genesis of crime."[186] Schafer accused some victims of provoking or encouraging criminal behavior, a concept now referred to as **victim precipitation**. These early works helped focus attention on the role of the victim in the crime problem and led to further research efforts that have sharpened the image of the crime victim.

Victim Precipitation

The concept of victim precipitation was popularized by Marvin Wolfgang's 1958 study of criminal homicide. Wolfgang found that crime victims were often intimately involved in their demise and that as many as 25 percent of all homicides could be classified as victim-precipitated.[187]

There are two types of victim precipitation. *Active precipitation* occurs when victims act provocatively, use threats or fighting words, or even attack first.[188] For example, some experts have suggested that female rape victims contribute to their attacks by their manner of dress or by pursuing a relationship with the rapist.[189] Although this finding has been disputed, courts have continued to return not-guilty verdicts in rape cases if a victim's actions can in any way be construed as consenting to sexual intimacy.[190]

Passive precipitation occurs when the victim exhibits some personal characteristic that unintentionally either threatens or encourages the attacker. The crime may occur because of personal conflict. For example, a woman may become the target of intimate violence when she increases her job status and her success results in a backlash from a jealous spouse or partner.[191] Passive precipitation may also occur when the victim belongs to a group whose mere presence threatens the attacker's reputation, status, or economic well-being. For example, hate crime violence may be precipitated by immigrants arriving in the community and competing for jobs and housing.[192]

Lifestyle Theory

Some criminologists believe that people may become crime victims because their lifestyle increases their exposure to criminal offenders. Victimization risk is increased by such behaviors as associating with violent young men, going out in public places late at night, and living in an urban area. Those who have histories of engaging in serious delinquency, getting involved in gangs, carrying guns, and selling drugs have an increased chance of being shot and killed themselves.[193] One way for young males to avoid victimization: Limit their male friends and hang out with girls! The greater the number of girls in their peer group, the lower their chances of victimization.[194] Those who have a history of engaging in serious delinquency, getting involved in gangs, carrying guns, and selling drugs have an increased chance of being shot and killed.[195]

Having a risky lifestyle increases victimization risk across the life course. College students who spend several nights each week partying and who take recreational drugs are much more likely to suffer violent crime than those who avoid such risky behavior.[196] As adults, those who commit crimes increase their chances of becoming the victims of homicide.[197]

Lifestyle theory suggests that a person can reduce the chances of victimization by reducing risk-taking behavior: staying home at night, moving to a rural area, staying out of public places, earning more money, and getting married. The basis of this theory is that crime is not a random occurrence but a function of the victim's lifestyle.

routine activities theory
The view that crime is a product of three everyday factors: motivated offenders, suitable targets, and a lack of capable guardians.

Routine Activities Theory

Routine activities theory, a variation on the lifestyle model, holds that the incidence of criminal activity and victimization is related to the nature of normal, everyday patterns of human behavior. According to this view, predatory crime

FIGURE 3.7
Routine Activities Theory

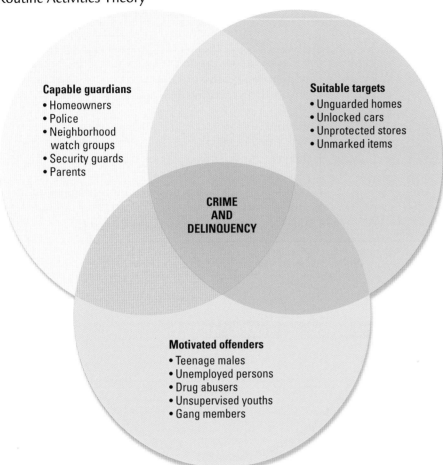

Capable guardians
- Homeowners
- Police
- Neighborhood watch groups
- Security guards
- Parents

Suitable targets
- Unguarded homes
- Unlocked cars
- Unprotected stores
- Unmarked items

CRIME AND DELINQUENCY

Motivated offenders
- Teenage males
- Unemployed persons
- Drug abusers
- Unsupervised youths
- Gang members

rates can be explained by three factors (see Figure 3.7): the supply of *motivated offenders* (such as large numbers of unemployed teenagers), *suitable targets* (goods that have value and can be easily transported, such as DVD players), and the absence of *effective guardians* (protections such as police and security forces or home security devices).[198]

The presence of these components increases the likelihood that a predatory crime will take place. Targets are more likely to be victimized if they are poorly guarded and exposed to a large group of motivated offenders such as teenage boys.[199] Increasing the number of motivated offenders and placing them in close proximity to valuable goods will increase property victimizations. Even after-school programs, designed to reduce criminal activity, may produce higher crime rates because they lump together motivated offenders—e.g., teenage boys—with vulnerable victims—e.g., teenage boys.[200]

According to this approach, the likelihood of victimization is a function of both criminal motivation and the behavior of potential victims. For example, if average family income increases because of an increase in the number of working mothers, and consequently the average family is able to afford more luxury goods such as portable computers and digital cameras, a comparable increase in the crime rate might be expected because the number of suitable targets has expanded while the number of capable guardians left to protect the home has been reduced.[201] In contrast, crime rates may go down during times of high unemployment because there is less to steal and more people are at home to guard their possessions. The routine activities approach seems a promising way of understanding crime and victimization patterns and predicting victim risk.

ThomsonNOW™ Improve your grade on the exam with Personalized Study! For reinforcement resources and a mastery check of victimization theories, go to www.thomsonedu.com/thomsonnow.

CONCEPT SUMMARY 3.2

Victimization Theories

VICTIM PRECIPITATION	Victims trigger criminal acts by their provocative behavior. Active precipitation involves fighting words or gestures. Passive precipitation occurs when victims unknowingly threaten their attackers.
LIFESTYLE	Victimization risk is increased when people have a high-risk lifestyle. Placing oneself at risk by going to dangerous places results in increased victimization.
ROUTINE ACTIVITIES	Crime rates can be explained by the availability of suitable targets, the absence of capable guardians, and the presence of motivated offenders.

ETHICAL CHALLENGES IN CRIMINAL JUSTICE: A WRITING ASSIGNMENT

A criminologist proposes a research project to test the association between IQ and crime. To carry out the project, she wants to conduct IQ tests with K–12 students in the local school district, use a self-report instrument, and gather arrest data from local police. She guarantees that all data will be kept confidential. Take the role of the school board member who must approve of the project. Would you grant her permission to conduct the research? Explain your answer in detail. What possible harm could be done by her project, and to whom?

Doing Research on the Web

Before you answer, you might want to look at the website of Professor Gary Marx, who is quite concerned with privacy issues. To reach this site, go to the Siegel/Senna Introduction to Criminal Justice 11e website: www.thomsonedu.com/criminaljustice/siegel.

The Office for Human Research Protections (OHRP) of the United States Department of Health and Human Services also has important information on protecting human subjects. To reach this site, go to the Siegel/Senna Introduction to Criminal Justice 11e website: www.thomsonedu.com/criminaljustice/siegel.

SUMMARY

◆ Crime in the United States comes in a number of diverse forms.

◆ Violent crimes range from gang warfare to serial killing to family violence.

◆ Substance abuse continues to be a significant social problem.

◆ Property crimes now include high-tech crimes, which involve the use of computers and the Internet.

◆ More than one approach can be taken to understanding the cause of crime and its consequences (see Concept Summary 3.1).

◆ Debate continues over whether crime is a social, economic, psychological, biological, or personal problem; whether it is a matter of free choice or the product of uncontrollable social and personal forces; and whether it can be controlled by the fear of punishment or the application of rehabilitative treatment. Consequently, there are a number of different and diverse schools of criminological theory—some focusing on the individual and others viewing social factors as the most important element in producing crime.

◆ Choice theories assume that criminals carefully choose whether to commit criminal acts. Evidence shows that crime is a rational event and criminals are rational decision makers.

◆ According to the general deterrence concept, people are influenced by their fear of the criminal penalties associated with being caught and convicted for law violations. The more severe, certain, and swift the punishment, the more likely it is to control crime. Deterrence theory holds that if criminals are rational, then an inverse relationship should exist between punishment and crime.

◆ Specific deterrence theory holds that the crime rate can be reduced if known offenders are punished so severely that they never commit crimes again.

◆ According to the situational crime prevention approach, because criminals are rational, taking steps to reduce their opportunity to commit crimes will result in lower crime rates.

◆ Biological theories hold that human traits and conditions such as biochemical makeup, neurological deficits, and genetic abnormalities control crime.

◆ Psychological theories suggest that crime may be a function of mental abnormality, learned behavior, or deficient cognitive ability.

◆ Sociologists believe that crime is a product of environmental influences.

◆ Some argue that people living in disorganized inner-city neighborhoods are at risk of committing crime because their environment gives them little hope of achieving success through conventional means. They may become angry and frustrated.

◆ Another view is that people become socialized to crime because of their upbringing and social learning. Some learn to commit crime. Others may commit crime because their socialization has weakened their bond to society.

◆ Still another view is that the conflict inherent in a capitalist society is a direct cause of antisocial behavior.

◆ Some theorists believe that crime is a function of human development. Within this group are those who believe that an underlying master trait directs human behavior. Others believe that criminal careers are part of a developmental process and that the conditions that cause criminal behavior at one point in the life cycle change radically as people mature.

◆ There are also a number of theories of victimization (see Concept Summary 3.2). One view, called victim precipitation, is that victims provoke criminals and are at least partially responsible for their victimization.

◆ Lifestyle theories suggest that victims put themselves in danger by engaging in high-risk activities, such as going out late at night, living in a high-crime area, and associating with high-risk peers.

◆ The routine activities theory maintains that a pool of motivated offenders exists and that these offenders will take advantage of suitable, unguarded targets.

KEY TERMS

ThomsonNOW Maximize your study time by using ThomsonNOW's diagnostic study plan to help you review this chapter. The Study Plan will

♦ help you identify areas on which you should concentrate;

♦ provide interactive exercises to help you master the chapter concepts; and

♦ provide a post-test to confirm you are ready to move on to the next chapter.

CRITICAL THINKING QUESTIONS

1. In a disorganized urban area, what factors are present that produce high crime rates?

2. If research could show that the tendency to commit crime is inherited, what should be done with the young children of violence-prone criminals?

3. It seems logical that biological and psychological factors might explain why some people commit crime. Why would these factors fail to explain crime patterns and trends?

4. Are criminals impulsive? How could impulsivity be used to explain white-collar and organized crime?

5. If crime is a routine activity, what steps should you take to avoid becoming a crime victim?

NOTES

1. Department of Justice Press Release, "Five Arrested in Health Care Fraud Scheme That Collected at Least $20 Million from Medicare Program," March 21, 2006 (http://losangeles.fbi.gov/dojpressrel/pressrel06/la032106usa.htm), accessed on March 31, 2006.

2. Liliana Pezzin, "Earnings Prospects, Matching Effects, and the Decision to Terminate a Criminal Career," *Journal of Quantitative Criminology* 11 (1995): 29–50.

3. Pierre Tremblay and Carlo Morselli, "Patterns in Criminal Achievement: Wilson and Abrahamse Revisited," *Criminology* 38 (2000): 633–60.

4. Gordon Knowles, "Deception, Detection, and Evasion: A Trade Craft Analysis of Honolulu, Hawaii's Street Crack Cocaine Traffickers," *Journal of Criminal Justice* 27 (1999): 443–55.

5. Andrew Buck, Simon Hakim, and George Rengert, "Burglar Alarms and the Choice Behavior of Burglars: A Suburban Phenomenon," *Journal of Criminal Justice* 21 (1993): 497–507; Julia MacDonald and Robert Gifford, "Territorial Cues and Defensible Space Theory: The Burglar's Point of View," *Journal of Environmental Psychology* 9 (1989): 193–205; Paul Cromwell, James Olson, and D'Aunn Wester Avary, *Breaking and Entering: An Ethnographic Analysis of Burglary* (Newbury Park, Calif.: Sage, 1991), pp. 48–51.

6. Matthew Robinson, "Lifestyles, Routine Activities, and Residential Burglary Victimization," *Journal of Criminal Justice* 22 (1999): 27–52.

7. William Smith, Sharon Glave Frazee, and Elizabeth Davison, "Furthering the Integration of Routine Activity and Social Disorganization Theories: Small Units of Analysis and the Study of Street Robbery as a Diffusion Process," *Criminology* 38 (2000): 489–521.

8. Paul Bellair, "Informal Surveillance and Street Crime: A Complex Relationship," *Criminology* 38 (2000): 137–67.

9. John Gibbs and Peggy Shelly, "Life in the Fast Lane: A Retrospective View by Commercial Thieves," *Journal of Research in Crime and Delinquency* 19 (1982): 229–30.

10. James Q. Wilson, *Thinking About Crime* (New York: Basic Books, 1975); Ernest Van den Haag, *Punishing Criminals* (New York: Basic Books, 1975).

11. Herbert Packer, *The Limits of the Criminal Sanction* (Stanford, Calif.: Stanford University Press, 1968).

12. Ernest Van den Haag, "Could Successful Rehabilitation Reduce the Crime Rate?" *Journal of Criminal Law and Criminology* 73 (1985): 1022–35.

13. Steven Klepper and Daniel Nagin, "Tax Compliance and Perceptions of the Risks of Detection and Criminal Prosecution," *Law and Society Review* 23 (1989): 209–40.

14. Daniel Nagin and Greg Pogarsky, "An Experimental Investigation of Deterrence: Cheating, Self-Serving Bias, and Impulsivity," *Criminology* 41 (2003): 167–95.

15. Raymond Paternoster, "Decisions to Participate in and Desist from Four Types of Common Delinquency: Deterrence and the Rational Choice Perspective," *Law and Society Review* 23 (1989): 7–29.

16. Jon Sorenson, Robert Wrinkle, Victoria Brewer, and James Marquart, "Capital Punishment and Deterrence: Examining the Effect of Executions on Murder in Texas," *Crime and Delinquency* 45 (1999): 481–93.

17. Alex Piquero and George Rengert, "Studying Deterrence with Active Residential Burglars," *Justice Quarterly* 16 (1999): 451–62.

18. Robert Nash Parker, "Bringing 'Booze' Back In: The Relationship Between Alcohol and Homicide," *Journal of Research in Crime and Delinquency* 32 (1993): 3–38.

19. Michel Foucault, *Discipline and Punishment* (New York: Random House, 1978).

20. David J. Levin, Patrick A. Langan, and Jodi M. Brown, *State Court Sentencing of Convicted Felons, 1996* (Washington, D.C.: Bureau of Justice Statistics, 2000); Allen Beck and Bernard Shipley, *Recidivism of Young Parolees* (Washington, D.C.: Bureau of Justice Statistics, 1987).

21. Oscar Newman, *Defensible Space: Crime Prevention Through Urban Design* (New York: Macmillan, 1972).

22. Ronald Clarke, *Situational Crime Prevention* (Albany, N.Y.: Harrow and Heston, 1992).

23. Anthony Braga, David Weisburd, Elin Waring, Lorraine Green Mazerolle, William Spelman, and Francis Gajewski, "Problem-Oriented Policing in Violent Crime Places: A Randomized Controlled Experiment," *Criminology* 37 (1999): 541–80.

24. Ronald Clarke, "Deterring Obscene Phone Callers: The New Jersey Experience," *Situational Crime Prevention,* ed. Ronald Clarke (Albany, N.Y.: Harrow and Heston, 1992), pp. 124–32.

25. Cesare Lombroso, *Crime: Its Causes and Remedies* (Montclair, N.J.: Patterson Smith, 1968).

26. Dalton Conley and Neil Bennett, "Is Biology Destiny? Birth Weight and Life Chances," *American Sociological Review* 654 (2000): 458–67.

27. Jens Walkowiak, Jörg-A Wiener, Annemarie Fastabend, Birger Heinzow, Ursula Krämer, Eberhard Schmidt, Hans-J Steingürber, Sabine Wundram, and Gerhard Winneke, "Environmental Exposure to Polychlorinated Biphenyls and Quality of the Home Environment: Effects on Psychodevelopment in Early Childhood," *Lancet* 358 (2001): 92–93.

28. S. Dengate and A. Ruben, "Controlled Trial of Cumulative Behavioural Effects of a Common Bread Preservative," *Journal of Pediatrics and Child Health* 38 (2002): 373–76.

29. Herbert Needleman, Christine McFarland, Roberta Ness, Stephen Fienberg, and Michael Tobin, "Bone Lead Levels in Adjudicated Delinquents: A Case Control Study," *Neurotoxicology and Teratology* 24 (2002): 711–17.

30. G. B. Ramirez, O. Pagulayan, H. Akagi, A. Francisco Rivera, L. V. Lee, A. Berroya, M. C. Vince Cruz, and D. Casintahan, "Tagum Study II: Follow-Up Study at Two Years of Age After Prenatal Exposure to Mercury," *Pediatrics* 111 (2003): 289–95.

31. Diana Fishbein, "Neuropsychological Function, Drug Abuse, and Violence: A Conceptual Framework," *Criminal Justice and Behavior* 27 (2000): 139–59.

32. Keith McBurnett and others, "Aggressive Symptoms and Salivary Cortisol in Clinic-Referred Boys with Conduct Disorder," *Annals of the New York Academy of Sciences* 794 (1996): 169–77.

33. Christy Miller Buchanan, Jacquelynne Eccles, and Jill Becker, "Are Adolescents the Victims of Raging Hormones? Evidence for Activational Effects of Hormones on Moods and Behavior at Adolescence," *Psychological Bulletin* 111 (1992): 62–107.

34. Dorothy Otnow Lewis, Ernest Moy, Lori Jackson, Robert Aaronson, Nicholas Restifo, Susan Serra, and Alexander Simos, "Biopsychosocial Characteristics of Children Who Later Murder," *American Journal of Psychiatry* 142 (1985): 1161–67.

35. Dorothy Otnow Lewis, *Guilty by Reason of Insanity* (New York: Fawcett Columbine, 1998).

36. Ronald Cohen, Alan Rosenbaum, Robert Kane, William Warneken, and Sheldon Benjamin, "Neuropsychological Correlates of Domestic Violence," *Violence and Victims* 15 (2000): 397–410.

37. Susan Young, Andrew Smolen, Robin Corley, Kenneth Krauter, John DeFries, Thomas Crowley, and John Hewitt, "Dopamine Transporter Polymorphism Associated with Externalizing Behavior Problems in Children," *American Journal of Medical Genetics* 114 (2002): 144–49.

38. Matti Virkkunen, David Goldman, and Markku Linnoila, "Serotonin in Alcoholic Violent Offenders," *The Ciba Foundation Symposium: Genetics of Criminal and Antisocial Behavior* (Chichester, England: Wiley, 1995).

39. Rolf Loeber and Dale Hay, "Key Issues in the Development of Aggression and Violence from Childhood to Early Adulthood," *Annual Review of Psychology* 48 (1997): 371–410.

40. D. R. Blachman and S. P. Hinshaw, "Patterns of Friendship Among Girls with and Without Attention-Deficit/Hyperactivity Disorder," *Journal of Abnormal Child Psychology* 30 (2002): 625–40.

41. Terrie Moffitt and Phil Silva, "Self-Reported Delinquency, Neuropsychological Deficit, and History of Attention Deficit Disorder," *Journal of Abnormal Child Psychology* 16 (1988): 553–69.

42. See S. A. Mednick and Karl O. Christiansen, eds., *Biosocial Bases of Criminal Behavior* (New York: Gardner, 1977).

43. David Rowe and D. Wayne Osgood, "Heredity and Sociological Theories of Delinquency: A Reconsideration," *American Sociological Review* 49 (1984): 526–40.

44. B. Hutchings and S. A. Mednick, "Criminality in Adoptees and Their Adoptive and Biological Parents: A Pilot Study," in *Biosocial Bases of Criminal Behavior,* ed. S. A. Mednick and Karl O. Christiansen (New York: Gardner, 1977), pp. 83–105.

45. For an analysis of Sigmund Freud, see Spencer Rathus, *Psychology* (New York: Holt, Rinehart, and Winston, 1990), pp. 412–20.

46. August Aichorn, *Wayward Youth* (New York: Viking, 1965).

47. Seymour Halleck, *Psychiatry and the Dilemmas of Crime* (New York: Harper and Row, 1967), pp. 99–115.

48. John Monahan, *Mental Illness and Violent Crime* (Washington, D.C.: National Institute of Justice, 1996).

49. Jennifer Beyers and Rolf Loeber, "Untangling Developmental Relations Between Depressed Mood and Delinquency in Male Adolescents," *Journal of Abnormal Child Psychology* 31 (2003): 247–67.

50. Richard Rosner, "Adolescents Accused of Murder and Manslaughter: A Five-Year Descriptive Study," *Bulletin of the American Academy of Psychiatry and the Law* 7 (1979): 342–51.

51. Richard Famularo, Robert Kinscherff, and Terence Fenton, "Psychiatric Diagnoses of Abusive Mothers: A Preliminary Report," *Journal of Nervous and Mental Disease* 180 (1992): 658–60.

52. Bruce Link, Howard Andrews, and Francis Cullen, "The Violent and Illegal Behavior of Mental Patients Reconsidered," *American Sociological Review* 57 (1992): 275–92; Ellen Hochstedler Steury, "Criminal Defendants with Psychiatric Impairment: Prevalence, Probabilities and Rates," *Journal of Criminal Law and Criminology* 84 (1993): 354–74.

53. Katherine Van Wormer and Chuk Odiah, "The Psychology of Suicide-Murder and the Death Penalty," *Journal of Criminal Justice* 27 (1999): 361–70.

54. Henrik Belfrage, "A Ten-Year Follow-up of Criminality in Stockholm Mental Patients: New Evidence for a Relation Between Mental Disorder and Crime," *British Journal of Criminology* 38 (1998): 145–55.

55. C. Wallace, P. Mullen, P. Burgess, S. Palmer, D. Ruschena, and C. Browne, "Serious Criminal Offending and Mental Disorder: Case Linkage Study," *British Journal of Psychiatry* 174 (1998): 477–84.

56. John Monahan and Henry Steadman, *Crime and Mental Disorder* (Washington, D.C.: National Institute of Justice, September 1984); David Tennenbaum, "Research Studies of Personality and Criminality," *Journal of Criminal Justice* 5 (1977): 1–19.

57. Marc Hillbrand, John Krystal, Kimberly Sharpe, and Hilliard Foster, "Clinical Predictors of Self-Mutilation in Hospitalized Patients," *Journal of Nervous and Mental Disease* 182 (1994): 9–13.

58. Carmen Cirincione, Henry Steadman, Pamela Clark Robbins, and John Monahan, *Mental Illness as a Factor in Criminality: A Study of Prisoners and Mental Patients* (Delmar, N.Y.: Policy Research Associates, 1991); see also Carmen Cirincione, Henry Steadman, Pamela Clark Robbins, and John Monahan, *Schizophrenia as a Contingent Risk Factor for Criminal Violence* (Delmar, N.Y.: Policy Research Associates, 1991).

59. This discussion is based on three works by Albert Bandura: *Aggression: A Social Learning Analysis* (Englewood Cliffs, N.J.: Prentice-Hall, 1973); *Social Learning Theory* (Englewood Cliffs, N.J.: Prentice-Hall, 1977); and "The Social Learning Perspective: Mechanisms of Aggression," in *The Psychology of Crime and Criminal Justice,* ed. H. Toch (New York: Holt, Rinehart, and Winston, 1979), pp. 198–226.

60. Mark Warr and Mark Stafford, "The Influence of Delinquent Peers: What They Think or What They Do?" *Criminology* 29 (1991): 851–66.

61. J. E. Lockman, "Self and Peer Perception and Attributional Biases of Aggressive and Nonaggressive Boys in Dyadic Interactions," *Journal of Consulting and Clinical Psychology* 55 (1987): 404–10.

62. Jean Piaget, *The Moral Judgement of the Child* (London: Kegan Paul, 1932).

63. Lawrence Kohlberg and others, *The Just Community Approach in Corrections: A Manual* (Niantic, Conn.: Connecticut Department of Corrections, 1973).

64. Walter Mischel, *Introduction to Personality*, 4th ed. (New York: Holt, Rinehart, and Winston, 1986), p. 1.

65. Edelyn Verona and Joyce Carbonell, "Female Violence and Personality," *Criminal Justice and Behavior* 27 (2000): 176–95.

66. Jennifer Beyers and Rolf Loeber, "Untangling Developmental Relations Between Depressed Mood and Delinquency in Male Adolescents," *Journal of Abnormal Child Psychology* 31 (2003): 247–67.

67. Albert Rabin, "The Antisocial Personality: Psychopathy and Sociopathy," in *The Psychology of Crime and Criminal Justice*, ed. H. Toch (New York: Holt, Rinehart, and Winston, 1979), pp. 236–51.

68. Steven Smith and Joseph Newman, "Alcohol and Drug Abuse: Dependence Disorders in Psychopathic and Nonpsychopathic Criminal Offenders," *Journal of Abnormal Psychology* 99 (1990): 430–39.

69. Richard Rogers, Randall Salekin, Kenneth Sewell, and Keith Cruise, "Prototypical Analysis of Antisocial Personality Disorder," *Criminal Justice and Behavior* 27 (2000): 234–55.

70. Jack Levin and James Alan Fox, *Mass Murder* (New York: Plenum, 1985).

71. Stephen Porter, David Fairweather, Jeff Drugge, Huues Herve, Angela Birt, and Douglas Boer, "Profiles of Psychopathy in Incarcerated Sexual Offenders," *Criminal Justice and Behavior* 27 (2000): 216–33.

72. David Lykken, "Psychopathy, Sociopathy, and Crime," *Society* 34 (1996): 30–38.

73. Christopher J. Patrick, "Emotion and Psychopathy: Startling New Insights," *Psychophysiology* 31 (1994): 319–30.

74. Adrian Raine, Todd Lencz, Susan Bihrle, Lori LaCasse, and Patrick Colletti, "Reduced Prefrontal Gray Matter Volume and Reduced Autonomic Activity in Antisocial Personality Disorder," *Archives of General Psychiatry* 57 (2000): 119–27.

75. Kent Kiehl, Andra Smith, Robert Hare, Adrianna Mendrek, Bruce Forster, Johann Brink, and Peter F. Liddle, "Limbic Abnormalities in Affective Processing by Criminal Psychopaths as Revealed by Functional Magnetic Resonance Imaging," *Biological Psychiatry* 5 (2001): 677–84.

76. Deborah Denno, "Sociological and Human Developmental Explanations of Crime: Conflict or Consensus," *Criminology* 23 (1985): 711–41; Christine Ward and Richard McFall, "Further Validation of the Problem Inventory for Adolescent Girls: Comparing Caucasian and Black Delinquents and Nondelinquents," *Journal of Consulting and Clinical Psychology* 54 (1986): 732–33; L. Hubble and M. Groff, "Magnitude and Direction of WISC-R Verbal Performance IQ Discrepancies Among Adjudicated Male Delinquents," *Journal of Youth and Adolescence* 10 (1981): 179–83.

77. Peter R. Giancola and Amos Zeichner, "Intellectual Ability and Aggressive Behavior in Nonclinical-Nonforensic Males," *Journal of Psychopathology and Behavioral Assessment* 16 (1994): 20–32.

78. Donald Lynam, Terrie Moffitt, and Magda Stouthamer-Loeber, "Explaining the Relation Between IQ and Delinquency: Class, Race, Test Motivation, School Failure, or Self-Control," *Journal of Abnormal Psychology* 102 (1993): 187–96; Alex Piquero, "Frequency, Specialization, and Violence in Offending Careers," *Journal of Research in Crime and Delinquency* 37 (2000): 392–418.

79. H. D. Day, J. M. Franklin, and D. D. Marshall, "Predictors of Aggression in Hospitalized Adolescents," *Journal of Psychology* 132 (1998): 427–35; Scott Menard and Barbara Morse, "A Structuralist Critique of the IQ–Delinquency Hypothesis: Theory and Evidence," *American Journal of Sociology* 89 (1984): 1347–78; Denno, "Sociological and Human Developmental Explanations of Crime."

80. Ulric Neisser and others, "Intelligence: Knowns and Unknowns," *American Psychologist* 51 (1996): 77–101, at 83.

81. Terance Miethe and Robert Meier, *Crime and Its Social Context: Toward an Integrated Theory of Offenders, Victims, and Situations* (Albany, N.Y.: State University of New York Press, 1994).

82. Émile Durkheim, *The Division of Labor in Society* (New York: Free Press, 1964); Émile Durkheim, *Rules of the Sociological Method*, trans. S. A. Solvay and J. H. Mueller, ed. G. Catlin (New York: Free Press, 1966).

83. Sam Roberts, *Who We Are Now: The Changing Face of America in the Twenty-First Century* (New York: Times Books, Henry Holt, 2004).

84. William Spelman, "Abandoned Buildings: Magnets for Crime," *Journal of Criminal Justice* 21 (1993): 481–95.

85. Jeffrey Fagan and Garth Davies, "The Natural History of Neighborhood Violence," *Journal of Contemporary Criminal Justice* 20 (2004): 127–47.

86. Justin Patchin, Beth Huebner, John McCluskey, Sean Varano, and Timothy Bynum, "Exposure to Community Violence and Childhood Delinquency," *Crime & Delinquency* 2006 (52): 307–32.

87. William Julius Wilson, "Poverty, Joblessness, and Family Structure in the Inner City: A Comparative Perspective," paper presented at the annual meeting of the American Society of Criminology, San Francisco, November 1991.

88. Ronald Mincy, ed., *Black Males Left Behind* (Washington, D.C.: Urban Institute, 2006); Erik Eckholm, "Plight Deepens for Black Men, Studies Warn," *New York Times*, March 20, 2006.

89. James Ainsworth-Darnell and Douglas Downey, "Assessing the Oppositional Culture Explanation for Racial/Ethnic Differences in School Performances," *American Sociological Review* 63 (1998): 536–53.

90. Oscar Lewis, "The Culture of Poverty," *Scientific American* 215 (1966): 19–25.

91. William Julius Wilson, *The Truly Disadvantaged* (Chicago: University of Chicago Press, 1987).

92. Robert Bursik, "Social Disorganization and Theories of Crime and Delinquency: Problems and Prospects," *Criminology* 26 (1988): 519–51, at 521.

93. Robert Sampson, "Structural Sources of Variation in Race-Age-Specific Rates of Offending Across Major U.S. Cities," *Criminology* 23 (1985): 647–73; Janet Heitgerd and Robert Bursik, Jr., "Extracommunity Dynamics and the Ecology of Delinquency," *American Journal of Sociology* 92 (1987): 775–87; Ora Simcha-Fagan and Joseph Schwartz, "Neighborhood and Delinquency: An Assessment of Contextual Effects," *Criminology* 24 (1986): 667–703.

94. Yili Xu, Mora Fiedler, and Karl Flaming, "Discovering the Impact of Community Policing: The Broken Windows Thesis, Collective Efficacy, and Citizens' Judgment," *Journal of Research in Crime and Delinquency* 42 (2005): 147–86.

95. Stephanie Greenberg, "Fear and Its Relationship to Crime, Neighborhood Deterioration, and Informal Social Control," in *The Social Ecology of Crime*, eds. James Byrne and Robert Sampson (New York: Springer Verlag, 1985), pp. 47–62.

96. C. L. Storr, C.-Y. Chen, and J. C. Anthony, " 'Unequal Opportunity': Neighborhood Disadvantage and the Chance to Buy Illegal Drugs," *Journal of Epidemiology and Community Health* 58 (2004): 231–38.

97. Pamela Wilcox Rountree and Kenneth Land, "Burglary Victimization, Perceptions of Crime Risk, and Routine Activities: A Multilevel Analysis Across Seattle Neighborhoods and Census Tracts," *Journal of Research in Crime and Delinquency* 33 (1996): 147–80.

98. E. Britt Patterson, "Poverty, Income Inequality, and Community Crime Rates," *Criminology* 29 (1991): 755–76.

99. Karen Parker, Brian Stults, and Stephen Rice, "Racial Threat, Concentrated Disadvantage and Social Control: Considering the Macro-Level Sources of Variation in Arrests," *Criminology* 43 (2005): 1111–34.

100. Bridget Freisthler, Elizabeth Lascala, Paul Gruenewald, and Andrew Treno, "An Examination of Drug Activity: Effects of Neighborhood Social Organization on the Development of Drug Distribution Systems," *Substance Use & Misuse* 40 (2005): 671–86.

101. Micere Keels, Greg Duncan, Stefanie Deluca, Ruby Mendenhall, and James Rosenbaum, "Fifteen Years Later: Can Residential Mobility Programs Provide a Long-term Escape from Neighborhood Segregation, Crime, and Poverty?" *Demography* 42 (2005): 51–72.

102. Gregory Squires and Charis Kubrin, "Privileged Places: Race, Uneven Development and the Geography of Opportunity in Urban America," *Urban Studies* 42 (2005): 47–68; Matthew Lee, Michael Maume, and Graham Ousey, "Social Isolation and Lethal Violence Across the Metro/Nonmetro Divide: The Effects of Socioeconomic Disadvantage and Poverty Concentration on Homicide," *Rural Sociology* 68 (2003): 107–31.

103. Lee, Maume, and Ousey, "Social Isolation and Lethal Violence Across the Metro/Nonmetro Divide"; Charis E. Kubrin, "Structural Covariates of Homicide Rates: Does Type of Homicide Matter?" *Journal of Research in Crime and Delinquency* 40 (2003): 139–70; Darrell Steffensmeier and Dana Haynie, "Gender, Structural Disadvantage, and Urban Crime: Do Macrosocial Variables Also Explain Female Offending Rates?" *Criminology* 38 (2000): 403–38.

104. Allen Liska and Paul Bellair, "Violent-Crime Rates and Racial Composition: Convergence Over Time," *American Journal of Sociology* 101 (1995): 578–610.

105. Patricia McCall and Karen Parker, "A Dynamic Model of Racial Competition, Racial Inequality, and Interracial Violence," *Sociological Inquiry* 75 (2005): 273–94.

106. Steven Barkan and Steven Cohn, "Why Whites Favor Spending More Money to Fight Crime: The Role of Racial Prejudice," *Social Problems* 52 (2005): 300–14.

107. Jeffrey Michael Cancino, "The Utility of Social Capital and Collective Efficacy: Social Control Policy in Nonmetropolitan Settings," *Criminal Justice Policy Review* 16 (2005): 287–318; Chris Gibson, Jihong Zhao, Nicholas Lovrich, and Michael Gaffney, "Social Integration, Individual Perceptions of Collective Efficacy, and Fear of Crime in Three Cities," *Justice Quarterly* 19 (2002): 537–64; Felton Earls, *Linking Community Factors and Individual Development* (Washington, D.C.: National Institute of Justice, 1998).

108. Robert J. Sampson and Stephen W. Raudenbush, *Disorder in Urban Neighborhoods: Does It Lead to Crime?* (Washington, D.C.: National Institute of Justice, 2001).

109. Andrea Altschuler, Carol Somkin, and Nancy Adler, "Local Services and Amenities, Neighborhood Social Capital, and Health," *Social Science and Medicine* 59 (2004): 1219–30.

110. Steffensmeier and Haynie, "Gender, Structural Disadvantage, and Urban Crime."

111. Karen Parker and Matthew Pruitt, "Poverty, Poverty Concentration, and Homicide," *Social Science Quarterly* 81 (2000): 555–82.

112. Ruth Peterson, Lauren Krivo, and Mark Harris, "Disadvantage and Neighborhood Violent Crime: Do Local Institutions Matter?" *Journal of Research in Crime and Delinquency* 37 (2000): 31–63.

113. Beverly Stiles, Xiaoru Liu, and Howard Kaplan, "Relative Deprivation and Deviant Adaptations: The Mediating Effects of Negative Self-Feelings," *Journal of Research in Crime and Delinquency* 37 (2000): 64–90.

114. Barbara Warner, "The Role of Attenuated Culture in Social Disorganization Theory," *Criminology* 41 (2003): 73–97.

115. Walter Miller, "Lower Class Culture as a Generating Milieu of Gang Delinquency," *Journal of Social Issues* 14 (1958): 5–19; see also Thorsten Sellin, *Culture Conflict and Crime*, bulletin no. 41 (New York: Social Science Research Council, 1938).

116. Richard Cloward and Lloyd Ohlin, *Delinquency and Opportunity* (Glencoe, Ill.: Free Press, 1960).

117. Leslie Kennedy and Stephen Baron, "Routine Activities and a Subculture of Violence: A Study of Violence on the Street," *Journal of Research in Crime and Delinquency* 30 (1993): 88–112.

118. Charis Kubrin and Ronald Weitzer, "Retaliatory Homicide: Concentrated Disadvantage and Neighborhood Culture," *Social Problems* 50 (2003): 157–81.

119. Robert Merton, "Social Structure and Anomie," *American Sociological Review* 3 (1938): 672–82.

120. Robert Agnew, "Foundation for a General Strain Theory of Crime and Delinquency," *Criminology* 30 (1992): 47–87; Robert Agnew, "Stability and Change in Crime Over the Life Course: A Strain Theory Explanation," in *Advances in Criminological Theory*, vol. 7, *Developmental Theories of Crime and Delinquency*, ed. Terence Thornberry (New Brunswick, N.J.: Transaction, 1994).

121. Robert Agnew, Timothy Brezina, John Paul Wright, and Francis T. Cullen, "Strain, Personality Traits, and Delinquency: Extending General Strain Theory," *Criminology* 40 (2002): 43–71.

122. Lee Ann Slocum, Sally Simpson, and Douglas Smith, "Strained Lives and Crime: Examining Intra-individual Variation in Strain and Offending in a Sample of Incarcerated Women," *Criminology* 43 (2005): 1067–1110.

123. Charles Tittle, Wayne Villemez, and Douglas Smith, "The Myth of Social Class and Criminality: An Empirical Assessment of the Evidence," *American Sociological Review* 43 (1978): 643–56.

124. Eric Stewart, Ronald Simons, and Rand Conger, "Assessing Neighborhood and Social Psychological Influences on Childhood Violence in an African American Sample," *Criminology* 40 (2002): 801–30.

125. John Paul Wright and Francis Cullen, "Parental Efficacy and Delinquent Behavior: Do Control and Support Matter?" *Criminology* 39 (2001): 677–706.

126. Carter Hay, "Parenting, Self-Control, and Delinquency: A Test of Self-Control Theory," *Criminology* 39 (2001): 707–36.

127. Robert Vermeiren, Jef Bogaerts, Vladislav Ruchkin, Dirk Deboutte, and Mary Schwab-Stone, "Subtypes of Self-Esteem and Self-Concept in Adolescent Violent and Property Offenders," *Journal of Child Psychology and Psychiatry* 45 (2004): 405–11.

128. Tiffany Field, "Violence and Touch Deprivation in Adolescents," *Adolescence* 37 (2002): 735–49.

129. Thomas Ashby Wills, Donato Vaccaro, Grace McNamara, and A. Elizabeth Hirky, "Escalated Substance Use: A Longitudinal Grouping Analysis from Early to Middle Adolescence," *Journal of Abnormal Psychology* 105 (1996): 166–80.

130. Kristi Holsinger and Alexander Holsinger, "Differential Pathways to Violence and Self-Injurious Behavior: African American and White Girls in the Juvenile Justice System," *Journal of Research in Crime and Delinquency* 42 (2005): 211–42; Fred Rogosch and Dante Cicchetti, "Child Maltreatment and Emergent Personality Organization: Perspectives from the Five-Factor Model," *Journal of Abnormal Child Psychology* 32 (2004): 123–45.

131. Eric Slade and Lawrence Wissow, "Spanking in Early Childhood and Later Behavior Problems: A Prospective Study of Infants and Young Toddlers," *Pediatrics* 113 (2004): 1321–30; Ronald Simons, Chyi-In Wu, Kuei-Hsiu Lin, Leslie Gordon, and Rand Conger, "A Cross-Cultural Examination of the Link Between Corporal Punishment and Adolescent Antisocial Behavior," *Criminology* 38 (2000): 47–79.

132. Murray A. Straus, "Spanking and the Making of a Violent Society: The Short- and Long-Term Consequences of Corporal Punishment," *Pediatrics* 98 (1996): 837–43.

133. Lyle Shannon, *Assessing the Relationship of Adult Criminal Careers to Juvenile Careers: A Summary* (Washington, D.C.: Government Printing Office, 1982); Donald J. West and David P. Farrington, *The Delinquent Way of Life* (London: Heineman, 1977); Marvin Wolfgang, Robert Figlio, and Thorsten Sellin, *Delinquency in a Birth Cohort* (Chicago: University of Chicago Press, 1972).

134. Terence Thornberry, Melanie Moore, and R. L. Christenson, "The Effect of Dropping Out of High School on Subsequent Criminal Behavior," *Criminology* 23 (1985): 3–18.

135. Jill DeVoe, Katharin Peter, Sally Ruddy, Amanda Miller, Mike Planty, Thomas Snyder, and Michael Rand, *Indicators of School*

Crime and Safety, 2003 (Washington, D.C.: U.S. Department of Education and Bureau of Justice Statistics, 2004).

136. Catherine Dulmus, Matthew Theriot, Karen Sowers, and James Blackburn, "Student Reports of Peer Bullying Victimization in a Rural School," *Stress, Trauma & Crisis* 7 (2004): 1–15; Tonja Nansel, Mary Overpeck, and Ramani Pilla, "Bullying Behaviors Among U.S. Youth: Prevalence and Association with Psychosocial Adjustment," *Journal of the American Medical Association* 285 (2001): 2094–3100.

137. Scott Menard, "Demographic and Theoretical Variables in the Age-Period Cohort Analysis of Illegal Behavior," *Journal of Research in Crime and Delinquency* 29 (1992): 178–99.

138. Daneen Deptula and Robert Cohen, "Aggressive, Rejected, and Delinquent Children and Adolescents: A Comparison of Their Friendships," *Aggression & Violent Behavior* 9 (2004): 75–104; Stephen W. Baron, "Self-Control, Social Consequences, and Criminal Behavior: Street Youth and the General Theory of Crime," *Journal of Research in Crime and Delinquency* 40 (2003): 403–25.

139. Sylive Mrug, Betsy Hoza, and William Bukowski, "Choosing or Being Chosen by Aggressive-Disruptive Peers: Do They Contribute to Children's Externalizing and Internalizing Problems?" *Journal of Abnormal Child Psychology* 32 (2004): 53–66; Terence Thornberry and Marvin Krohn, "Peers, Drug Use and Delinquency," in David Stoff, James Breiling, and Jack Maser, eds., *Handbook of Antisocial Behavior* (New York: Wiley, 1997), pp. 218–33.

140. Mark Warr, "Age, Peers, and Delinquency," *Criminology* 31 (1993): 17–40.

141. Sara Battin, Karl Hill, Robert Abbott, Richard Catalano, and J. David Hawkins, "The Contribution of Gang Membership to Delinquency Beyond Delinquent Friends," *Criminology* 36 (1998): 93–116.

142. John Paul Wright and Francis Cullen, "Employment, Peers, and Life-Course Transitions," *Justice Quarterly* 21 (2004): 183–205.

143. Denise Kandel and Mark Davies, "Friendship Networks, Intimacy, and Illicit Drug Use in Young Adulthood: A Comparison of Two Competing Theories," *Criminology* 29 (1991): 441–67.

144. Edwin Sutherland and Donald Cressey, *Criminology* (Philadelphia: J. B. Lippincott, 1970), pp. 71–91.

145. Carlo Morselli, Pierre Tremblay, and Bill McCarthy, "Mentors and Criminal Achievement," *Criminology* 44 (2006): 17–43.

146. Terence Thornberry, Adrienne Freeman-Gallant, Alan Lizotte, Marvin Krohn, and Carolyn Smith, "Linked Lives: The Intergenerational Transmission of Antisocial Behavior," *Journal of Abnormal Child Psychology* 31 (2003): 171–84.

147. Paul Vowell and Jieming Chen, "Predicting Academic Misconduct: A Comparative Test of Four Sociological Explanations," *Sociological Inquiry* 74 (2004): 226–49.

148. Andy Hochstetler, Heith Copes, and Matt DeLisi, "Differential Association in Group and Solo Offending," *Journal of Criminal Justice* 30 (2002): 559–66.

149. Dana Haynie, Peggy Giordano, Wendy Manning, and Monica Longmore," Adolescent Romantic Relationships and Delinquency Involvement," *Criminology* 43 (2005): 177–210.

150. Joel Hektner, Gerald August, and George Realmuto, "Effects of Pairing Aggressive and Nonaggressive Children in Strategic Peer Affiliation," *Journal of Abnormal Child Psychology* 31 (2003): 399–412; Matthew Ploeger, "Youth Employment and Delinquency: Reconsidering a Problematic Relationship," *Criminology* 35 (1997): 659–75; William Skinner and Anne Fream, "A Social Learning Theory Analysis of Computer Crime Among College Students," *Journal of Research in Crime and Delinquency* 34 (1997): 495–518; Denise Kandel and Mark Davies, "Friendship Networks, Intimacy, and Illicit Drug Use in Young Adulthood: A Comparison of Two Competing Theories," *Criminology* 29 (1991): 441–67.

151. Clayton Hartjen and S. Priyadarsini, "Gender, Peers, and Delinquency," *Youth & Society* 34 (2003): 387–414.

152. See, for example, Randy La Grange and Helene Raskin White, "Age Differences in Delinquency: A Test of Theory," *Criminology* 23 (1985): 19–45; Marvin Krohn and James Massey, "Social Control and Delinquent Behavior: An Examination of the Elements of the Social Bond," *Sociological Quarterly* 21 (1980): 529–44.

153. Bobbi Jo Anderson, Malcolm Holmes, and Erik Ostresh, "Male and Female Delinquents' Attachments and Effects of Attachments on Severity of Self-Reported Delinquency," *Criminal Justice and Behavior* 26 (1999): 435–52.

154. Patricia Jenkins, "School Delinquency and the School Social Bond," *Journal of Research in Crime and Delinquency* 34 (1997): 337–67.

155. Jón Gunnar Bernburg, Marvin Krohn, and Craig Rivera, "Official Labeling, Criminal Embeddedness, and Subsequent Delinquency: A Longitudinal Test of Labeling Theory," *Journal of Research in Crime and Delinquency* 43 (2006): 67–88.

156. Christina DeJong and Kenneth Jackson, "Putting Race into Context: Race, Juvenile Justice Processing, and Urbanization," *Justice Quarterly* 15 (1998): 487–504.

157. W. Byron Groves and Robert Sampson, "Critical Theory and Criminology," *Social Problems* 33 (1986): 58–80.

158. Andrew Woolford, "Making Genocide Unthinkable: Three Guidelines for a Critical Criminology of Genocide," *Critical Criminology* 14 (2006): 87–106.

159. Travis Pratt and Christopher Lowenkamp, "Conflict Theory, Economic Conditions, and Homicide: A Time-Series Analysis," *Homicide Studies* 6 (2002): 61–84.

160. David Jacobs and David Britt, "Inequality and Police Use of Deadly Force: An Empirical Assessment of a Conflict Hypothesis," *Social Problems* 26 (1979): 403–12.

161. Thomas Arvanites, "Increasing Imprisonment: A Function of Crime or Socioeconomic Factors?" *American Journal of Criminal Justice* 17 (1992): 19–38.

162. See, generally, Jock Young, *Realist Criminology* (London: Sage, 1989).

163. Kathleen Daly and Meda Chesney-Lind, "Feminism and Criminology," *Justice Quarterly* 5 (1988): 438–97.

164. Kevin Anderson, "Richard Quinney's Journey: The Marxist Dimension," *Crime and Delinquency* 48 (2002): 232–43; Harold Pepinsky, "Violence as Unresponsiveness: Toward a New Conception of Crime," *Justice Quarterly* 5 (1988): 539–87.

165. Robert DeFina and Thomas Arvanites, "The Weak Effect of Imprisonment on Crime: 1971–1998," *Social Science Quarterly* 83 (2002): 635–54.

166. David Rowe, D. Wayne Osgood, and W. Alan Nicewander, "A Latent Trait Approach to Unifying Criminal Careers," *Criminology* 28 (1990): 237–70.

167. David Rowe and Daniel Flannery, "An Examination of Environmental and Trait Influences on Adolescent Delinquency," *Journal of Research in Crime and Delinquency* 31 (1994): 374–89.

168. Michael Gottfredson and Travis Hirschi, *A General Theory of Crime* (Stanford, Calif.: Stanford University Press, 1990).

169. Ick-Joong Chung, Karl G Hill, J. David Hawkins, Lewayne Gilchrist, and Daniel Nagin, "Childhood Predictors of Offense Trajectories," *Journal of Research in Crime and Delinquency* 39 (2002): 60–91; Amy D'Unger, Kenneth Land, Patricia McCall, and Daniel Nagin, "How Many Latent Classes of Delinquent/Criminal Careers? Results from Mixed Poisson Regression Analyses," *American Journal of Sociology* 103 (1998): 1593–1630.

170. W. Alex Mason, Rick Kosterman, J. David Hawkins, Todd Herrenkohi, Liliana Lengua, and Elizabeth McCauley, "Predicting Depression, Social Phobia, and Violence in Early Adulthood from Childhood Behavior Problems," *Journal of the American Academy of Child & Adolescent Psychiatry* 43 (2004): 307–15; Rolf Loeber and David Farrington, "Young Children Who Commit Crime: Epidemiology, Developmental Origins, Risk Factors, Early Interven-

tions, and Policy Implications," *Development and Psychopathology* 12 (2000): 737–62; Patrick Lussier, Jean Proulx, and Marc Leblanc, "Criminal Propensity, Deviant Sexual Interests and Criminal Activity of Sexual Aggressors Against Women: A Comparison of Explanatory Models," *Criminology* 43 (2005): 249–81.

171. Dawn Jeglum Bartusch, Donald Lynam, Terrie Moffitt, and Phil Silva, "Is Age Important? Testing a General Versus a Developmental Theory of Antisocial Behavior," *Criminology* 35 (1997): 13–48.

172. Jacqueline Schneider, "The Link Between Shoplifting and Burglary: The Booster Burglar," *British Journal of Criminology* 45 (2005): 395–401.

173. Glenn Deane, Richard Felson, and David Armstrong, "An Examination of Offense Specialization Using Marginal Logit Models," *Criminology* 43 (2005): 955–88; Christopher Sullivan, Jean Marie McGloin, Travis Pratt, and Alex Piquero, "Rethinking The 'Norm' of Offender Generality: Investigating Specialization in the Short-Term," *Criminology* 44 (2006): 199–233.

174. Helene Raskin White, Peter Tice, Rolf Loeber, and Magda Stouthamer-Loeber, "Illegal Acts Committed by Adolescents Under the Influence of Alcohol and Drugs," *Journal of Research in Crime & Delinquency* 39 (2002): 131–53; Xavier Coll, Fergus Law, Aurelio Tobias, Keith Hawton, and Josep Tomas, "Abuse and Deliberate Self-Poisoning in Women: A Matched Case-Control Study," *Child Abuse and Neglect* 25 (2001): 1291–93.

175. David Fergusson, L. John Horwood, and Elizabeth Ridder, "Show Me the Child at Seven II: Childhood Intelligence and Later Outcomes in Adolescence and Young Adulthood," *Journal of Child Psychology & Psychiatry & Allied Disciplines* 46 (2005): 850–59.

176. Richard Miech, Avshalom Caspi, Terrie Moffitt, Bradley Entner Wright, and Phil Silva, "Low Socioeconomic Status and Mental Disorders: A Longitudinal Study of Selection and Causation During Young Adulthood," *American Journal of Sociology* 104 (1999): 1096–1131; Marvin Krohn, Alan Lizotte, and Cynthia Perez, "The Interrelationship Between Substance Use and Precocious Transitions to Adult Sexuality," *Journal of Health and Social Behavior* 38 (1997): 87–103.

177. Rolf Loeber, David Farrington, Magda Stouthamer-Loeber, Terrie Moffitt, Avshalom Caspi, and Don Lynam, "Male Mental Health Problems, Psychopathy, and Personality Traits: Key Findings from the First 14 Years of the Pittsburgh Youth Study," *Clinical Child and Family Psychology Review* 4 (2002): 273–97.

178. Rolf Loeber, Dustin Pardini, D. Lynn Homish, Evelyn Wei, Anne Crawford, David Farrington, Magda Stouthamer-Loeber, Judith Creemers, Steven Koehler, and Richard Rosenfeld, "The Prediction of Violence and Homicide in Young Men," *Journal of Consulting and Clinical Psychology* 73 (2005): 1074–88.

179. David Gadd and Stephen Farrall, "Criminal Careers, Desistance and Subjectivity: Interpreting Men's Narratives of Change," *Theoretical Criminology* 8 (2004): 123–56.

180. Robert Sampson and John Laub, *Crime in the Making: Pathways and Turning Points Through Life* (Cambridge, Mass.: Harvard University Press, 1993).

181. Nan Lin, *Social Capital: A Theory of Social Structure and Action* (Cambridge, England: Cambridge University Press, 2002).

182. Doris Layton MacKenzie and Spencer De Li, "The Impact of Formal and Informal Social Controls on the Criminal Activities of Probationers," *Journal of Research in Crime and Delinquency* 39 (2002): 243–78.

183. Alex Piquero, John MacDonald, and Karen Parker, "Race, Local Life Circumstances, and Criminal Activity Over the Life Course," *Social Science Quarterly* 83 (2002): 654–71.

184. Personal communication with Alex Piquero, September 24, 2002.

185. Hans Von Hentig, *The Criminal and His Victim: Studies in the Sociobiology of Crime* (New Haven, Conn.: Yale University Press, 1948), p. 384.

186. Stephen Schafer, *The Victim and His Criminal* (New York: Random House, 1968), p. 152.

187. Marvin Wolfgang, *Patterns of Criminal Homicide* (Philadelphia: University of Pennsylvania Press, 1958).

188. Ibid.

189. Menachem Amir, *Patterns in Forcible Rape* (Chicago: University of Chicago Press, 1971).

190. Susan Estrich, *Real Rape* (Cambridge, Mass.: Harvard University Press, 1987).

191. Edem Avakame, "Females' Labor Force Participation and Intimate Femicide: An Empirical Assessment of the Backlash Hypothesis," *Violence and Victims* 14 (1999): 277–83.

192. Rosemary Gartner and Bill McCarthy, "The Social Distribution of Femicide in Urban Canada, 1921–1988," *Law and Society Review* 25 (1991): 287–311.

193. Rolf Loeber, Mary DeLamatre, George Tita, Jacqueline Cohen, Magda Stouthamer-Loeber, and David Farrington, "Gun Injury and Mortality: The Delinquent Backgrounds of Juvenile Offenders," *Violence and Victims* 14 (1999): 339–51.

194. Dana Haynie and Alex Piquero, "Pubertal Development and Physical Victimization in Adolescence," *Journal of Research in Crime and Delinquency* 43 (2006): 3–35.

195. Loeber, DeLamatre, Tita, Cohen, Stouthamer-Loeber, and Farrington, "Gun Injury and Mortality."

196. Bonnie Fisher, John Sloan, Francis Cullen, and Chunmeng Lu, "Crime in the Ivory Tower: The Level and Sources of Student Victimization," *Criminology* 36 (1998): 671–710.

197. Adam Dobrin, "The Risk of Offending on Homicide Victimization: A Case Control Study," *Journal of Research in Crime and Delinquency* 38 (2001): 154–73.

198. Lawrence Cohen and Marcus Felson, "Social Change and Crime Rate Trends: A Routine Activities Approach," *American Sociological Review* 44 (1979): 588–608; Lawrence Cohen, Marcus Felson, and Kenneth Land, "Property Crime Rates in the United States: A Macrodynamic Analysis, 1947–1977, with Ex-Ante Forecasts for the Mid-1980s," *American Journal of Sociology* 86 (1980): 90–118; for a review, see James LeBeau and Thomas Castellano, "The Routine Activities Approach: An Inventory and Critique," Center for the Studies of Crime, Delinquency, and Corrections, Southern Illinois University, Carbondale, Illinois, 1987.

199. Teresa LaGrange, "The Impact of Neighborhoods, Schools, and Malls on the Spatial Distribution of Property Damage," *Journal of Research in Crime and Delinquency* 36 (1999): 393–422.

200. Denise Gottfredson and David Soulé, "The Timing of Property Crime, Violent Crime, and Substance Use Among Juveniles," *Journal of Research in Crime & Delinquency* 42 (2005): 110–20.

201. Cohen, Felson, and Land, "Property Crime Rates in the United States."

CHAPTER 4

Criminal Law: Substance and Procedure

Chapter Outline

Chapter Objectives

After reading this chapter, you should be able to:

1. Understand the concept of substantive criminal law and its history.
2. Know the similarities and differences between criminal law and civil law.
3. Recognize the differences between felonies and misdemeanors.
4. Name the various elements of a crime.
5. Discuss the concept of criminal intent.
6. Recognize the recent changes in the criminal law.
7. Describe the role of the Bill of Rights.
8. Know which constitutional amendments are the most important to the justice system.
9. List the elements of due process of law.
10. Show how interpretations of due process affect civil rights.

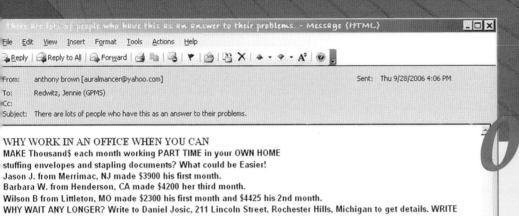

WHY WORK IN AN OFFICE WHEN YOU CAN
MAKE Thousand$ each month working PART TIME in your OWN HOME
stuffing envelopes and stapling documents? What could be Easier!
Jason J. from Merrimac, NJ made $3900 his first month.
Barbara W. from Henderson, CA made $4200 her third month.
Wilson B from Littleton, MO made $2300 his first month and $4425 his 2nd month.
WHY WAIT ANY LONGER? Write to Daniel Josic, 211 Lincoln Street, Rochester Hills, Michigan to get details. WRITE TODA! Y!'

All-new Yahoo! Mail - Fire up a more powerful email and get things done faster.

On June 1, 2006, Daniel Josic, of Rochester Hills, Michigan, entered pleas of guilty to all 18 counts in an indictment that had charged him with conspiracy, mail fraud, and money laundering.[1] What did Josic do? From approximately March 1999 to about June 2003, Josic and his co-conspirators engaged in a scheme to defraud thousands of people from all across the United States by falsely offering to pay individuals for a "work at home" business involving stuffing envelopes or stapling booklets for advertising to be mailed. The defendants promised to pay participants $5 to $10 for each envelope stuffed or booklet stapled. To get in the program, the victims were told they had to pay a $29 to $169 "application fee" that would later be refunded. Unfortunately for them, Josic never intended to pay anyone for stuffing envelopes, and the only purpose of the defendants' purported business was to collect application fees.

Would anyone fall for such a scheme? Josic victimized over 20,000 individuals across the country and collected at least $2 million from application fees. Conspiracies like Josic's are a clear violation of the criminal law. ♦

criminal law
The body of rules that defines crimes, sets out their punishments, and mandates the procedures for carrying out the criminal justice process.

substantive criminal law
A body of specific rules that declare what conduct is criminal and prescribe the punishment to be imposed for such conduct.

procedural criminal law
The rules and laws that define the operation of the criminal proceedings. Procedural law describes the methods that must be followed in obtaining warrants, investigating offenses, effecting lawful arrests, conducting trials, introducing evidence, sentencing convicted offenders, and reviewing cases by appellate courts.

civil law
All law that is not criminal, including tort, contract, personal property, maritime, and commercial law.

torts
The law of personal injuries.

In modern U.S. society, the criminal law governs almost all phases of human enterprise, including commerce, family life, property transfer, and the regulation of interpersonal conflict. It contains elements that control personal relationships between individuals and public relationships between individuals and the government. The former is known as *civil law*, and the latter is called **criminal law**. The law then can generally be divided into three broad categories:

◆   **Substantive criminal law**: the branch of the law that defines crimes and their punishment. It involves such issues as the mental and physical elements of crime, crime categories, and criminal defenses.

◆   **Procedural criminal law**: those laws that set out the basic rules of practice in the criminal justice system. Some elements of the law of criminal procedure are the rules of evidence, the law of arrest, the law of search and seizure, questions of appeal, jury selection, and the right to counsel.

◆   **Civil law**: the set of rules governing relations between private parties, including both individuals and organizations (such as business enterprises and/or corporations). The civil law is used to resolve, control, and shape such personal interactions as contracts, wills and trusts, property ownership, and commerce. The element of civil law that is most relevant to criminal justice is **torts**, the law of personal injuries (see Exhibit 4.1).

The three elements of the law can be interrelated: a crime victim may also sue the perpetrator for damages in a civil court; some crime victims may forgo criminal action and choose to file a tort claim alone. It is also possible to seek civil damages from a perpetrator even if he is found not guilty of crime (e.g., the families of Nicole Brown and Ron Goldman sucessfully sued O. J. Simpson for damages) because the evidentiary standard in a tort action is less than is needed for a criminal conviction (preponderance of the evidence versus beyond a reasonable doubt).

In some instances, the government has the option to pursue a legal matter through the criminal process or file a tort action. White-collar crimes, such as Josic's, often involve both criminal and civil penalties, giving the government the choice of pursuing one type of action or both. Josic agreed to forfeit $500,000 to the government and pay a fine of $250,000.

Concept Summary 4.1 summarizes the main similarities and differences between criminal law and tort law. If you are interested in becoming involved in this process and want to become an attorney, read the Careers in Criminal Justice feature on page 132.

Although civil law is certainly an important area for study, the focus of this text is on criminal law. We begin with an analysis of the substantive criminal law.

◆ THE SUBSTANTIVE CRIMINAL LAW

The substantive criminal law defines crime and punishment in U.S. society. Each state government and the federal government has its own criminal code, developed over many generations and incorporating moral beliefs, social values, and political, economic, and other societal concerns. The criminal law is a living document, constantly evolving to keep pace with society and its needs. The rules designed to implement the substantive law are known as procedural law. In contrast to the substantive law, the procedural law is concerned with the criminal process—the legal steps through which an offender passes—commencing with the initial criminal investigation and concluding with the release of the offender. Some elements of the law of criminal procedure such as the rules of evidence, the right to notice of charges, questions of appeal, and the right to counsel, impact on the substantive law. Many of the rights that have been extended to offenders over the past two decades lie within procedural law.

EXHIBIT 4.1

Three Categories of Torts

1. *Intentional torts:* injury that the person knew or should have known would occur through his or her actions—e.g., a person attacks and injures another (assault and battery) after a dispute.
2. *Negligent torts:* injuries caused because a person's actions were unreasonably unsafe or careless—e.g., a traffic accident is caused by a reckless driver.
3. *Strict liability torts:* a particular action causes damage prohibited by statute—e.g., a victim is injured because a manufacturer made a defective product.

CONCEPT SUMMARY 4.1

A Comparison of Criminal and Tort Law

Similarities	Differences
♦ Goal of controlling behavior.	♦ Crime is a public offense. Tort is a civil or private wrong.
♦ Imposition of sanctions.	♦ The sanction associated with tort law is monetary damages. Only a violation of criminal law can result in incarceration or even death.
♦ Some common areas of legal action—for example, personal assault and control of white-collar offenses such as environmental pollution.	♦ In criminal law, the right of enforcement belongs to the state. The individual brings the action in civil law.
♦ The payment of damages to the victim in a tort case serves some of the same purposes as the payment of a fine in a criminal case.	♦ In criminal law, monetary damages (fines) go to the state. In civil law, the individual receives damages as compensation for harm done.
♦ Some acts, including rape, assault and battery, larceny, and corporate crimes, can be the basis for both criminal and civil actions.	

Because the law defines crime, punishment, and procedure, which are the basic concerns of the criminal justice system, it is essential for students to know something of the nature, purpose, and content of the substantive and procedural criminal law.

The Historical Development of Criminal Law

The roots of the criminal codes used in the United States can be traced back to such early legal charters as the Babylonian Code of Hammurabi (2000 BCE), the Mosaic Code of the Israelites (1200 BCE), and the Roman Twelve Tables (451 BCE), which were formulated by a special commission of ten noble Roman men in response to pressure from the lower classes, who complained that the existing, unwritten legal code gave arbitrary and unlimited power to the wealthy classes. The original code was written on bronze plaques, which have been lost, but records of sections, which were memorized by every Roman male, survive. The remaining laws deal with debt, family relations, property, and other daily matters.

To read some of the statutes in the Justinian code, go to "Medieval Sourcebook: The Institutes, 535 CE." To read some of the original elements of the Roman Twelve Tables, go to "The Law of the Twelve Tables." To reach this site, go to the Siegel/Senna Introduction to Criminal Justice 11e website: www.thomsonedu.com/criminaljustice/siegel.

Attorney

Duties and Characteristics of the Job

Attorneys use their experience and extensive knowledge of the law and the legal system to defend the rights of their clients. They can fulfill this role by representing the best interests of their clients in a legal setting by defending them during a trial or settling their grievances in or out of court. However, lawyers will also act as a legal advisor and engage in such activities as drawing up and/or interpreting a legal document or contract. They will act as advisors to inform their clients about changes in existing laws. Attorneys will often choose a field of specialization such as tax law or intellectual property.

Attorneys typically work in firms, organizations of lawyers who pool their resources on legal cases. Some attorneys will gain experience within existing firms and then leave to start their own practice. Some work for the federal, state, or local governments, whereas others will take advantage of increasing opportunities for employment within businesses.

Attorneys generally work in offices and courtrooms, though at times they may have to travel to meet clients at their homes or even in prison. Quite often, they will work long hours; especially if a case goes to trial, a 60+ hour workweek is not uncommon for an attorney.

Job Outlook

Job opportunities are expected to grow at an average rate for the next several years. Competition for education and professional positions will be considerable, especially at prestigious institutions and law firms. A good academic record from a prestigious law school, as well as work experience, mobility, and additional education in a field of specialty, will be especially helpful. Jobs will be most plentiful in urban areas, where there tend to be more law firms, big businesses, and government offices.

Salary

Attorneys have a median annual salary of $94,930. The majority of attorneys earn between $64,620 and $143,620. Partners in large national firms in Chicago or New York may have an annual salary in the millions. An attorney's salary will depend on type of employer, experience, region, and type of law being practiced. For example, lawyers employed by the federal government will tend to make more than state-employed lawyers. Extremely successful sole practitioners can win millions in tort actions.

Opportunities

Gaining entrance into law school can be challenging; there are many talented applicants applying for a limited number of spots. This competition for jobs with prestigious firms is fierce because there are more

Criminal law has a long and rich history dating back to ancient Babylonia. Courts and the law have played an important role in every civilization. Here is a scene of justice from fifteenth-century Paris.

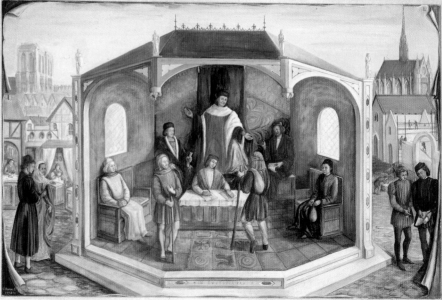

graduating lawyers than there are job positions. Making the law review, publishing law review articles while in school, and obtaining prestigious internships can be helpful in securing coveted jobs.

Training and practice as a lawyer can be a personally and financially rewarding career in itself. However, many lawyers will use their education and experience as a means of launching into other careers. It is not uncommon for lawyers to have successful careers as business administrators, politicians, law professors, or judges.

Qualifications

The primary qualification for a career as an attorney is a legal education. A bachelor's degree in a program that gives one strong analytical and writing skills is recommended for preparation for law school.

Becoming a successful lawyer can be challenging and requires personality traits such as discipline, commitment, and the ability to work hard. Additionally, those who like an intellectual challenge and communicate well will more likely enjoy being an attorney and be successful.

Education and Training

The primary requirements for a career as an attorney begin with proper educational training. Potential attorneys must have a bachelor's degree in order to obtain entrance into an American Bar Association–accredited law school, which will prepare them for legal practice. After graduating from law school, young attorneys must become certified before they can practice. Certification can be obtained through passing the state bar exam. Completing these requirements can be challenging. It not only takes hard work and discipline to gain entrance into a law school, but also good grades and a desirable score on the Law School Admissions Test (LSAT).

Even after obtaining a position, an attorney's education is not complete. Attorneys must stay informed of the latest developments in law and will often attend conferences, and many states have continuing legal education (CLE) requirements that must be met.

For certain positions, such as law school professor and specialties such as patent law, further experience and education will be needed.

Sources: "Lawyers," *Occupational Outlook Handbook,* 2006–2007 edition (Bureau of Labor Statistics, U.S. Department of Labor), retrieved June 22, 2006, from http://www.bls.gov/oco/ocos053.htm; "Princeton Review Career Profiles: Attorney," retrieved June 19, 2006, from http://www.princetonreview.com/cte/profiles/dayInLife.asp?careerID=149.

Although the early formal legal codes were lost during the Dark Ages, German and Anglo-Saxon societies developed legal systems featuring monetary compensation, called wergild (*wer* means "worth" and refers to what the person, and therefore the crime, was worth), for criminal violations. Guilt was determined by two methods: compurgation, which involved having the accused person swear an oath of innocence while being backed up by a group of 12 to 25 oath helpers, who would attest to his or her character, and claims of innocence and ordeal, which were based on the principle that divine forces would not allow an innocent person to be harmed.

Determining guilt by ordeal involved such measures as having the accused place his or her hand in boiling water or hold a hot iron. If the wound healed, the person was found innocent; if the wound did not heal, the accused was deemed guilty. Trial by combat allowed the accused to challenge his accuser to a duel, with the outcome determining the legitimacy of the accusation. Punishments included public flogging, branding, beheading, and burning.

The Development of Common Law

After the Norman Conquest of England in 1066, royal judges began to travel throughout the land,

PERSPECTIVES ON JUSTICE

Justice Perspective

Wergild was the forerunner of the modern fine. Efforts are being made to gear fines to a person's income, a procedure that is in sync with the justice perspective.

holding court in each county several times a year. When court was in session, the royal administrator, or judge, would summon a number of citizens who would, on their oath, tell of the crimes and serious breaches of the peace that had occurred since the judge's last visit. The royal judge would then decide what to do in each case, using local custom and rules of conduct as his guide—a system known as **stare decisis** (Latin for "to stand by decided cases"). Courts were bound to follow the law established in previous cases unless a higher authority, such as the king or the pope, overruled the law.

The present English system of law came into existence during the reign of Henry II (1154–1189), when royal judges began to publish their decisions in local cases. Judges began to use these written decisions as a basis for their decision making, and eventually a fixed body of legal rules and principles was produced. If the new rules were successfully applied in a number of different cases, they would become precedents, which would then be commonly applied in all similar cases—hence the term *common law*. Crimes such as murder, burglary, arson, and rape are common-law crimes whose elements were initially defined by judges. They are referred to as **mala in se**, inherently evil and depraved. When the situation required it, the English Parliament enacted legislation to supplement the judge-made common law. These were referred to as statutory or mala prohibitum crimes, which reflected existing social conditions. English common law evolved constantly to fit specific incidents that the judges encountered.

Before the American Revolution, the colonies, then under British rule, were subject to the common law. After the colonies won their independence, state legislatures standardized common-law crimes such as murder, burglary, arson, and rape by putting them into statutory form in criminal codes. As in England, whenever common law proved inadequate to deal with changing social and moral issues, the states and Congress supplemented it with legislative statutes. Similarly, statutes prohibiting such offenses as the sale and possession of narcotics or the pirating of DVDs have been passed to control human behavior unknown at the time the common law was formulated. Today, criminal behavior is defined primarily by statute. With few exceptions, crimes are removed, added, or modified by the legislature of a particular jurisdiction.

◆ SOURCES OF THE CRIMINAL LAW

The contemporary U.S. legal system is codified by the state legislatures and the U.S. Congress. Each jurisdiction precisely defines *crime* in its legal code and sets out the appropriate punishments. However, like its English common-law roots, U.S. criminal law is not static and is constantly evolving. A state statute based on common law may define first-degree murder as the "unlawful killing, with malice and premeditation, of one human being by another." Over time, state court decisions might help explain the meaning of the term *malice* or clarify whether *human being* refers only to someone "born and alive" or whether it can refer to an unborn fetus. More than half the states have expanded their legal codes to include *feticide law*, which declares the killing of an unborn fetus to be murder (see Exhibit 4.2 for Louisiana's statute).

The content of the law may also be influenced by judicial decision making. A criminal statute may be no longer enforceable when an appellate judge rules that it is vague, deals with an act no longer of interest to the public, or is an unfair exercise of state control over an individual. Conversely, a judicial ruling may expand the scope of an existing criminal law, thereby allowing control over behaviors that heretofore were beyond its reach. In a famous 1990 case, 2 Live Crew (made up of Luther Campbell, Christopher Wong-Won, Mark Ross, and DJ Mr. Mixx), a prominent rap group, found its sales restricted in Florida as police began arresting children under 18 for purchasing the band's sexually explicit CD *As Nasty As They Want to Be*. The hit single "Me So Horny" was

---

EXHIBIT 4.2

Louisiana: Feticide in the First Degree

First degree feticide is:

The killing of an unborn child when the offender has a specific intent to kill or to inflict great bodily harm.

The killing of an unborn child when the offender is engaged in the perpetration or attempted perpetration of aggravated rape, forcible rape, aggravated arson, aggravated burglary, aggravated kidnapping, second degree kidnapping, assault by drive-by shooting, aggravated escape, armed robbery, first degree robbery, or simple robbery, even though he has no intent to kill or inflict great bodily harm.

Whoever commits the crime of first degree feticide shall be imprisoned at hard labor for not more than fifteen years.

Source: Louisiana First Degree Feticide Law, La. Rev. Stat. Ann. §§14:32.5–14.32.8, read with §§14:2(1), (7), (11) (West 1997).

---

banned from local radio stations. Prosecutors tried but failed to get a conviction after group members were arrested at a concert. If members of the Crew had in fact been found guilty and the conviction had been upheld by the state's highest appellate court, obscenity laws would have been expanded to cover people singing (or rapping) objectionable music lyrics.

Constitutional Limits

Regardless of its source, all criminal law in the United States must conform to the rules and dictates of the U.S. Constitution.[2] Any criminal law that even appears to conflict with the various provisions and articles of the Constitution must reflect a compelling need to protect public safety or morals.[3]

Criminal laws have been interpreted as violating constitutional principles if they are too vague or overbroad to give clear meaning of their intent. A law forbidding adults to engage in "immoral behavior" could not be enforced because it does not use clear and precise language or give adequate notice as to which conduct is forbidden.[4] The Constitution also prohibits laws that make a person's status a crime. Becoming or being a heroin addict is not a crime, although laws can forbid the sale, possession, and manufacture of heroin. The Constitution limits laws that are overly cruel and/or capricious. Whereas the use of the death penalty may be constitutionally approved, capital punishment would be forbidden if it were used for lesser crimes such as rape or employed in a random, haphazard fashion.[5] Cruel ways of executing criminals that cause excessive pain are likewise forbidden.

The Constitution also forbids *bills of attainder:* legislative acts that inflict punishment without a judicial trial. This device, used by the English kings to punish rebels and seize their property, was particularly troublesome to American colonials when it was used to seize the property of people considered disloyal to the Crown; hence, attainder is forbidden in the Constitution. Nor does the Constitution permit the government to pass **ex post facto laws**, defined as the following:

1. A law that makes an action, done before the passing of the law, and which was innocent when done, criminal; and punishes such action.

ex post facto laws
Laws that retroactively punish people.

PERSPECTIVES ON JUSTICE

Due Process

Constitutional control over the substantive criminal law is a cornerstone of the due process model. Laws that may erode such personal rights as notice of charges or the right to a hearing raise red flags. Efforts to control terrorism through legislation may create a conflict between constitutional rights and national security issues.

2. A law that makes a crime more serious after the fact, than it was when first committed.

3. A law inflicts a greater punishment than was available when the crime was committed.

4. A law which makes it easier to convict the offender than was present at the time she committed the crime.[6]

◆ CLASSIFYING CRIMES

The decision of how a crime should be classified rests with the individual jurisdiction. Each state has developed its own body of criminal law and consequently determines its own penalties for the various crimes. Thus, the criminal law of a given state defines and grades offenses, sets levels of punishment, and classifies crimes into categories. Over the years, crimes have been generally grouped into (1) felonies, misdemeanors, and violations and (2) other statutory classifications, such as juvenile delinquency, sex offender categories, and multiple- or first-offender classifications. In general terms, felonies are considered serious crimes, misdemeanors are seen as less serious crimes, and violations may be noncriminal offenses such as traffic offenses and public drunkenness. Some states consider violations civil matters, whereas others classify them as crimes.

Felonies and Misdemeanors

The most common classification in the United States is the division between felonies and misdemeanors.[7] This distinction is based primarily on the degree of seriousness of the crime. Distinguishing between a felony and a misdemeanor is sometimes difficult. *Black's Law Dictionary* defines the two terms as follows:

> A felony is a crime of a graver or more atrocious nature than those designated as misdemeanors. Generally it is an offense punishable by death or imprisonment in a penitentiary. A misdemeanor is lower than a felony and is generally punishable by fine or imprisonment otherwise than in a penitentiary.[8]

Serious crimes are known as felonies, petty ones are categorized as misdemeanors. Would you consider the following a felony or a misdemeanor? Constables Adam Loomis (left) and Jerold Loomis (right) detain Stephen Burns at McMaster Funeral Home in Braintree, Massachusetts, on June 27, 2006. Burns owed $250,000 in child support payments stretching back 15 years when he was arrested at his mother's wake after authorities were tipped off by his ex-wife. The Child Support Recovery Act of 1992 makes a willful failure to pay a past due support obligation, with respect to a child residing in another state, a federal offense. The intent of the statute was to prevent noncustodial parents from fleeing across state lines to avoid paying their child support obligations and to facilitate recovery of unpaid child support. A first offense is a misdemeanor; a second offense is a felony punishable by up to two years in prison.

© AP Images/*The Patriot Ledger*/Amelia Kunhardt

Each jurisdiction in the United States determines by statute what types of conduct constitute felonies or misdemeanors. The most common definition of a *felony* is a crime punishable in the statute by death or by imprisonment in a state or federal prison. Another way of determining what category an offense falls into is by providing in the statute that a *felony* is any crime punishable by imprisonment for more than one year. In the former method, the place of imprisonment is critical; in the latter, the length of the prison sentence distinguishes a felony from a misdemeanor.

In the United States today, felonies include serious crimes against the person, such as criminal homicide, robbery, and rape, as well as such crimes against property as burglary and larceny. Misdemeanors include petit (or petty) larceny, assault and battery, and the unlawful possession of marijuana.

The least serious, or petty, offenses, which often involve criminal traffic violations, are called infractions or violations. The felony–misdemeanor classification has a direct effect on the offender charged with the crime. A person convicted of a felony may be barred from certain fields of employment or some professions, such as law and medicine. A felony offender's status as an alien in the United States might also be affected, or the offender might be denied the right to hold public office, vote, or serve on a jury.[9] These and other civil liabilities exist only when a person is convicted of a felony offense, not a misdemeanor.

Whether the offender is charged with a felony or a misdemeanor also makes a difference at the time of arrest. Normally, the law of arrest requires that if the crime is a misdemeanor and has not been committed in the presence of a police officer, the officer cannot make an arrest. This is known as the *in presence requirement*. However, the police officer does have the legal authority to arrest a suspect for a misdemeanor at a subsequent time by the use of a validly obtained arrest warrant. In contrast, an arrest for a felony may be made regardless of whether the crime was committed in the officer's presence, as long as the officer has reasonable grounds to believe that the person has committed the felony.

The Legal Definition of a Crime

Occasionally, people admit at trial that they committed the act of which they are accused, yet they are not found guilty of the crime. There was little question that John Hinckley, Jr., attempted to assassinate President Ronald Reagan in 1981; the shooting and Hinckley's capture were captured on film and broadcast on national TV. Yet Hinckley was not found guilty of a crime because he lacked one of the legal requirements needed to prove his guilt—mental competency. Therefore, the jury found him not guilty by reason of insanity. In this case, federal prosecutors failed to prove that Hinckley's behavior fell within the legal definition of a crime. To fulfill the legal definition, all elements of the crime must be proven, including these:

◆ The accused engaged in the guilty act (**actus reus**).

◆ The accused had the intent to commit the act (**mens rea**).

◆ Both the actus reus and the mens rea were concurrently present.

◆ The defendant's actions were the proximate cause of the crime.

◆ Actual harm was caused. Thoughts of committing an act do not alone constitute a crime.

Each of these elements is discussed following in greater detail.

ACTUS REUS The actus reus is an aggressive act, such as taking someone's money, burning a building, or shooting someone. The action must be voluntary for an act to be considered illegal. An accident or involuntary act would not be considered criminal. For example, if while walking down the street, a person has a seizure and as a result strikes another person in the face, he cannot be held criminally liable for assault. But if he had known beforehand that he could have a seizure and unreasonably put himself in a position where he was likely to harm others—for instance, by driving a car—he would be criminally liable for his behavior.

In addition, the failure or omission to act can be considered a crime on some occasions:

1. *Failure to perform a legally required duty that is based on relationship or status.* These relationships include parent and child and husband and wife. If a husband finds his wife unconscious because she took an overdose of sleeping pills, he is obligated to seek medical aid. If he fails to do so and she dies, he can be held responsible for her death. Parents are required to look after the welfare of their children; failure to provide adequate care can be a criminal offense.

actus reus
An illegal act, or failure to act, when legally required.

mens rea
A guilty mind, the intent to commit a criminal act.

Actus reus *refers to the guilty or evil act: shooting a victim, selling drugs, robbing a bank. Here a series of bank surveillance photos show bank robber William Ginglen during a holdup of the Bank of Kenney in Kenney, Illinois on July 8, 2005. Ginglen pleaded guilty to robbing five central Illinois banks. He was arrested after his sons saw the photos, recognized him, and contacted authorities.*

2. *Imposition by statute.* Some states have passed laws that require a person who observes an automobile accident to stop and help the other parties involved.

3. *A contractual relationship.* These relationships include lifeguard and swimmer, doctor and patient, and baby-sitter or au pair and child. Because lifeguards have been hired to ensure the safety of swimmers, they have a legal duty to come to the aid of drowning persons. If a lifeguard knows a swimmer is in danger and does nothing about it and the swimmer drowns, the lifeguard is legally responsible for the swimmer's death.

The duty to act is a legal and not a moral duty. The obligation arises from the relationship between the parties or from explicit legal requirements. For example, a private citizen who sees a person drowning is under no legal obligation to save that person. Although it may be considered morally reprehensible, the private citizen could walk away and let the swimmer drown without facing legal sanctions.

MENS REA Under common law, for an act to constitute a crime, the actor must have criminal intent or mens rea. To intend to commit a crime, the person must have clear knowledge of the consequences of his actions and desire those consequences/outcomes to occur. A person who enters a store with a gun and shouts at the clerk to open the cash register is signaling his intent to commit a robbery. Criminal intent is implied if the results of an action, though originally unintended, are certain to occur. When Mohammed Atta and his terrorist band crashed airplanes into the World Trade Center on September 11, 2001, they did not intend to kill any particular person in the buildings. Yet the law would hold that anyone would be substantially certain that people in the building would be killed in the blast; therefore, the terrorists had the criminal intent to commit the crime of first-degree murder. Mens rea is legally present when a person's reckless and/or negligent act produces social harm. Recklessness occurs when a person is or should be aware of the potentially harmful consequences of his planned behavior but goes ahead anyway, knowing that his actions may expose someone to risk or suffering. Even though he may not desire to hurt the eventual victim, his act is considered intentional because he was willing to gamble with the safety of others rather than take precautions to avoid injury. It would be considered

EXHIBIT 4.3

New York State Law: § 270.10, Creating a Hazard

A person is guilty of creating a hazard when:

1. Having discarded in any place where it might attract children, a container which has a compartment of more than one and one-half cubic feet capacity and a door or lid which locks or fastens automatically when closed and which cannot easily be opened from the inside, he fails to remove the door, lid, locking or fastening device; or

2. Being the owner or otherwise having possession of property upon which an abandoned well or cesspool is located, he fails to cover the same with suitable protective construction.

Creating a hazard is a class B misdemeanor.

Source: New York State Consolidated Laws, Article 270, Other Offenses Relating to Public Safety, Section 270.10, Creating a Hazard (2002).

reckless for a disgruntled student to set a fire in a dormitory supply closet to protest new restrictions on visitation rights. If some of her classmates were killed in the blaze, she might be charged with manslaughter even though she did not intend to cause injury. Her actions would be considered reckless because she went ahead with her plan despite the fact that she surely knew that a fire could spread and cause harm.

In contrast, **criminal negligence**, another form of mens rea, occurs when a person's careless and inattentive actions cause harm. If a student who stayed up for three days studying for a test and then drove home fell asleep at the wheel, thereby causing a fatal accident, his behavior might be considered negligent because driving while in a drowsy state creates a condition that a reasonable person can assume will lead to injury. Negligence differs from recklessness, and is considered less serious, because the person did not knowingly gamble with another's safety but simply failed to foresee possible dangers.

criminal negligence
Liability that can occur when a person's careless and inattentive actions cause harm.

STRICT LIABILITY Certain statutory offenses exist in which mens rea is not essential. These offenses fall within a category known as a **public safety** or **strict liability crime**. A person can be held responsible for such a violation independent of the existence of intent to commit the offense. Strict liability criminal statutes generally include narcotics control laws, traffic laws, health and safety regulations, sanitation laws, and other regulatory statutes. For example, a driver could not defend herself against a speeding ticket by claiming that she was unaware of how fast she was going and did not intend to speed, and a bartender could not claim that a juvenile to whom he sold liquor looked older. No state of mind is generally required where a strict liability statute is violated.[10] Consider the New York state law § 270.10, about creating a hazard, which is set out in Exhibit 4.3.[11] Intent to commit is not required for a person to be found guilty on charges of creating a hazardous condition.

public safety or **strict liability crime**
A criminal violation—usually one that endangers the public welfare—that is defined by the act itself, irrespective of intent.

Examine the public safety statutes in New York. To reach this government website, go to the Siegel/Senna Introduction to Criminal Justice 11e website: www.thomsonedu.com/criminaljustice/siegel.

THE CONCURRENCE OF MENS REA AND ACTUS REUS The third element needed to prove that a crime was committed is the immediate relationship or concurrence of the act to the criminal intent or result. The law requires that the offender's conduct be the proximate cause of any injury resulting from the criminal act. If, for example, a man chases a victim into the street intending to assault him and the victim is struck and killed by a car, the accused could be convicted of murder if the court felt that his actions made him responsible for the victim's death. In other words, the victim would not have run into the street on his own accord and therefore would not have been killed. If, however, a victim dies from a completely unrelated illness after being assaulted, the court must determine whether the death was a probable consequence of the defendant's illegal conduct or whether it would have resulted even if the assault had not occurred.

CRIMINAL HARM Thought alone is not a crime. To be considered a crime, some act is required to prove the actor's willingness to cause harm. It is the nature of the harm that ultimately determines what crime the person committed. If someone trips another with the intent of making the person fall down and be embarrassed in public, he has committed the crime of battery. If by some chance the victim dies from the fall, the harm caused elevates the crime to manslaughter even if that was not the intended result.

In the crime of robbery, the actus reus is taking the property from the person or presence of another. In order to satisfy the harm requirement, the robber must acquire the victim's possessions, referred to as *asportation*. The legal definition of robbery is satisfied when even for a brief moment possession of the property is transferred to the robber. If a robber removes a victim's wallet from his pocket and immediately tosses it over a fence when he spies a police officer approaching, the robbery is complete because even the slightest change in possession of the property is sufficient to cause harm. Nor is the value of the property important: Actual value is unimportant as long as the property had some value to the victim.

ThomsonNOW™ Improve your grade on the exam with Personalized Study! For reinforcement resources and a mastery check of crime classifications, go to www.thomsonedu.com/thomsonnow.

♦ CRIMINAL DEFENSES

In 1884 two British sailors, desperate after being shipwrecked for days, made the decision to kill and eat a suffering cabin boy. Four days later, they were rescued by a passing ship and returned to England. In the case of *Regina* v. *Dudley and Stephens*, English authorities, wanting to end the practice of shipwreck cannibalism, tried the two men for murder and convicted them. Clemency was considered, and a reluctant Queen Victoria commuted the death sentences to six months.[12] Were the seamen justified in killing a shipmate to save their lives? If they had not done so, they likely would have died. Can there ever be a good reason to take a life? Can the killing of another ever be justified? Before you answer, remember that people can kill in self-defense, to prevent lethal crimes, or in times of war. The passengers aboard United Airlines Flight 93 are considered heroes for attacking the hijackers on September 11, 2001. Certainly no rational person would condemn their acts even though they may have resulted in the death of others. Often, the quality of the act is not most important; the way society defines and reacts to it determines whether a crime has been committed.

When people defend themselves against criminal charges, they must refute one or more of the elements of the crime of which they have been accused. Defendants may deny the actus reus by arguing that they were falsely accused and the real culprit has yet to be identified. Defendants may also claim that although they did engage in the criminal act they are accused of, they lacked the mens rea, or mental intent, needed to be found guilty of the crime. If a person whose mental state is impaired commits a criminal act, the person could be excused of his or her criminal actions by claiming that he or she lacked the capacity to form sufficient intent to be held criminally responsible. Insanity, intoxication, ignorance, age, and entrapment are among the types of **excuse defenses**.

Another type of defense is **justification**. Here, the individual usually admits committing the criminal act but maintains that the act was justified under the circumstances and that he or she, therefore, should not be held criminally liable. Among the justification defenses are consent, necessity, duress, and self-defense. Persons standing trial for criminal offenses may defend themselves by claiming either that their actions were justified under the circumstances or that their behavior should be excused by their lack of mens rea. If either the physical or mental elements of a crime cannot be proven, then the defendant cannot be convicted.

excuse defenses
A defense in which a person states that his or her mental state was so impaired that he or she lacked the capacity to form sufficient intent to be held criminally responsible.

justification
A defense for a criminal act claiming that the criminal act was reasonable or necessary under the circumstances.

Ignorance or Mistake

Ignorance or mistake can be an excuse if it negates an element of a crime. As a general rule, however, ignorance of the law is no excuse. Some courts have had to accept this excuse in cases in which the government failed to make enactment of a new law public. It is also a viable justification when the offender relies on an official statement of the law that is later deemed incorrect. Barring that, even immigrants and other new arrivals to the United States are required to be aware of the content of the law. For example, on October 7, 1998, Chris Ahamefule Iheduru, a Nigerian immigrant, was convicted of sexual assault on the grounds that he had intimate relations with his 14-year-old stepdaughter after signing a contract with the girl to bear him a son (she gave birth to a daughter in September 1998).[13] At trial, Iheduru testified that it is not illegal in his native country to have sex with a juvenile and that he did not know it was against the law in the United States. However, his ignorance of U.S. law did not shield him from conviction.

Insanity

Insanity is a defense to criminal prosecution in which the defendant's state of mind negates his or her criminal responsibility. A successful insanity defense results in a verdict of "not guilty by reason of insanity." Insanity, in this case, is a legal category. As used in U.S. courts, it does not necessarily mean that everyone who suffers from a form of mental illness can be excused from legal responsibility. Many people who are depressed, suffer mood disorders, or have a psychopathic personality can be found legally sane. Instead, *insanity* means that the defendant's state of mind at the time the crime was committed made it impossible for her to have the necessary mens rea to satisfy the legal definition of a crime. Thus, a person can be undergoing treatment for a psychological disorder but still be judged legally sane if it can be proven that at the time she committed the crime she had the capacity to understand the wrongfulness of her actions.

If a defendant uses the insanity plea, it is usually left to psychiatric testimony to prove that a person understood the wrongfulness of her actions and was therefore legally sane or, conversely, was mentally incapable of forming intent. The jury must then weigh the evidence in light of the test for sanity currently used in the jurisdiction. These tests vary throughout the United States. The commonly used ones are listed in Concept Summary 4.2.

Intoxication

As a general rule, intoxication, which may include drunkenness or being under the influence of drugs, is not considered a defense. However, a defendant who becomes involuntarily intoxicated under duress or by mistake may be excused for crimes committed. Involuntary intoxication may also lessen the degree of the crime. For example, a judgment may be decreased from first- to second-degree murder because the defendant uses intoxication to prove the lack of the critical element of mens rea, or mental intent. Thus, the effect of intoxication on criminal liability depends on whether the defendant uses alcohol or drugs voluntarily. For example, a defendant who enters a bar for a few drinks, becomes intoxicated, and strikes someone can be convicted of assault and battery. If, however, the defendant ordered a nonalcoholic drink that was subsequently spiked by someone else, the defendant may have a legitimate legal defense.

Because of the frequency of crime-related offenses involving drugs and alcohol, the impact of intoxication on criminal liability is a persistent issue in the criminal justice system.

The American Psychiatric Association is a medical specialty society dedicated to the humane care and effective treatment for all persons with mental disorders, including mental retardation and substance-related disorders. To read its take on the insanity plea, go to its website, which you can access by going to the Siegel/Senna Introduction to Criminal Justice 11e website: www.thomsonedu.com/criminaljustice/siegel.

While willful intoxication is not generally a defense to crime, it can be used to mitigate the intent to commit crime. On July 13, 2006, in Oshkosh, Wisconsin, Lorinda Hawkins hears her sentence for felony child neglect. Hawkins was accused of smothering her 4-month-old daughter when she passed out drunk while nursing the child. Would you consider her intoxication when deciding on a sentence? Hawkins was sentenced to seven years in prison for her crime.

©AP Images/*The Northwestern*/Shu-Ling Zhou

CONCEPT SUMMARY 4.2

Various Insanity Defense Standards

The *M'Naghten* Rule	The M'Naghten rule, first formulated in England in 1843, defines a person as insane if at the time she committed the act she stands accused of, she was laboring under such a defect of reason, arising from a disease of the mind, that she could not tell or know the nature and quality of the act or, if she did know it, that she did not know what she was doing was wrong. In other words, she could not tell "right from wrong." The M'Naghten rule is used in the majority of the states.
The Irresistible Impulse	The irresistible impulse test was formulated in Ohio in 1834. It is used quite often in conjunction with M'Naghten and defines a person as insane if he should or did know that his actions were illegal but, because of a mental impairment, he couldn't control his behavior. His act was a result of an uncontrollable or irresistible impulse. A person who commits a crime during a "fit of passion" would be considered insane under this test. The most famous use of this defense occurred in 1994, when Lorena Bobbitt successfully defended herself against charges that she cut off the penis of her husband, John, after suffering abuse at his hands.
The *Durham* Rule	The Durham rule or "product test" was set forth by the U.S. Court of Appeals for the District of Columbia Circuit in 1954 and states that ". . . an accused is not criminally responsible if her unlawful act was the product of mental disease or defect." It was used for some time in the state of New Hampshire.
The Insanity Defense Reform Act	The Insanity Defense Reform Act, Title 18, U.S. Code, Section 17, was enacted by Congress in 1984 and states that a person accused of a crime can be judged not guilty by reason of insanity if "the defendant, as a result of a severe mental disease or defect, was unable to appreciate the nature and quality or the wrongfulness of her acts."
The Substantial Capacity Test	The substantial capacity test was defined by the American Law Institute in its Model Penal Code. This argues that insanity should be defined as a lack of substantial capacity to control one's behavior. Substantial capacity is defined as "the mental capacity needed to understand the wrongfulness of [an] act, or to conform . . . behavior to the . . . law." This rule combines elements of the M'Naghten rule with the concept of "irresistible impulse."

The connection among drug use, alcoholism, and violent street crime has been well documented. Although those in law enforcement and the judiciary tend to emphasize the use of the penal process in dealing with problems of chronic alcoholism and drug use, others in corrections and crime prevention favor approaches that depend more on behavioral theories and the social sciences. For example, in the case of *Robinson* v. *California,* the U.S. Supreme Court struck down a California statute making addiction to narcotics a crime, on the ground that it violated the defendant's rights under the Eighth and Fourteenth amendments to the Constitution.[14] However, the landmark decision in *Powell* v. *Texas* placed severe limitations on the behavioral science approach in *Robinson* when it rejected the defense of chronic alcoholism of a defendant charged with the crime of public drunkenness.[15]

Age

The law holds that a child is not criminally responsible for actions committed at an age that precludes a full realization of the gravity of certain types of behavior. Under common law, there is generally a conclusive presumption of incapacity for a child under age 7, a reliable presumption for a child between the ages of 7 and 14, and no presumption for a child over the age of 14. This generally means that a child under age 7 who commits a crime will not be held criminally responsible for these actions and that a child between ages 7 and 14 may be held responsible. These common-law rules have been changed by statute in most jurisdictions. Today, the maximum age of criminal responsibility for children ranges from ages 14 to 17 or 18, whereas the minimum age may be set by statute at age 7 or under age 14.[16] In addition, every jurisdiction has established a juvenile court system to deal with juvenile offenders and children in need of court and societal supervision. Thus, the mandate of the juvenile justice system is to provide for the care and protection of children under a given age, established by state statute. In certain situations, a juvenile court may transfer a more serious chronic youthful offender to the adult criminal court.

Entrapment

Under the rule of law, a defendant may be excused from criminal liability if he can convince the jury that law enforcement agents used traps, decoys, and deception to induce criminal action. Law enforcement officers can legitimately set traps for criminals by getting information about crimes from informers, undercover agents, and codefendants. Police officers are allowed to use ordinary opportunities for defendants to commit crime and to create these opportunities without excessive inducement. However, when the police instigate the crime, implant criminal ideas, and coerce individuals into bringing about crime, defendants can claim to have been entrapped.

Entrapment then must be viewed within the context of the defendant's predisposition to commit a crime. A defendant with a criminal record would have a tougher time using this defense successfully than one who had never been in trouble. However, in one of the most important entrapment cases, *Jacobson* v. *United States* (1992), the Supreme Court ruled that a defendant with a past history of child pornography had been entrapped by the government into purchasing more. Keith Jacobson had ordered *Bare Boys* magazines depicting nude children. When his name came up in their *Bare Boys* files, government agents sent him mailings for more than two and one-half years in an effort to get him to purchase more kiddie porn. Such purchases are a violation of the Child Protection Act of 1984. Jacobson was arrested after he gave in to the inducements and ordered a magazine showing young boys engaged in sexual activities. A search of his house revealed no materials other than those sent by the government (and the original *Bare Boys* magazines). On appeal, the Court held that Jacobson was entrapped because the state could not prove a predisposition to break the law and the purchase of the sexually charged magazines was the result of government coaxing.[17]

Justification Defenses

Criminal defenses may be based on the concepts of justification. In these instances, defendants normally acknowledge that they committed the act but claim that they cannot be prosecuted because they were justified in doing so.

Major types of criminal defenses involving justification or excuse are consent, self-defense, duress, and necessity.

CONSENT As a general rule, the victim's consent to a crime does not justify or excuse the defendant who commits the action. The type of crime involved generally determines the validity of consent as an appropriate legal defense. Such crimes as common-law rape and larceny require lack of consent on the part of the victim. In other words, a rape does not occur if the victim consents to sexual relations. In the same way, a larceny cannot occur if the owner voluntarily consents to the taking of property. Consequently, in such crimes, consent is an essential element of the crime, and it is a valid defense where it can be proven or shown that it existed at the time the crime was committed. But in other crimes, such as sexual relations with a minor child, consent cannot be a defense because the state presumes that young people are not capable of providing adequate or mature consent. Nor can consent be used to justify the crime of incest or bigamy.

One controversial area of consent is the crime of assisted suicide; it is still against the law to help someone commit suicide even if the person consented to the procedure. The issue became prominent because of the involvement of Michigan doctor Jack Kevorkian in numerous physician-assisted suicides. Kevorkian was convicted in 1999 on charges of second-degree murder after the death of Thomas Youk, a man he helped commit suicide. It is today illegal for a doctor to write or fill a prescription for medications sufficient for a patient to commit suicide, or personally give medications sufficient to cause death, in every state except Oregon, which passed a "death with dignity act" in 1994. A number of other nations, including Belgium, Switzerland, and the Netherlands, allow at least some forms of assisted suicide.[18]

SELF-DEFENSE A criminal defendant can claim to be not guilty because he or she acted in self-defense. To establish self-defense, the defendant must prove he acted with a reasonable belief that he was in imminent danger of death or harm and had no reasonable means of escape from the assailant. In some instances, a woman (or man) may kill his or her mate after years of abuse; this is known as *battered-wife syndrome* (or in cases involving child abuse, *battered-child syndrome*). Although a history of battering can be used to mitigate the seriousness of the crime, a finding of not guilty most often requires the presence of imminent danger and the inability of the accused to escape from the assailant.

As a general legal rule, a person defending herself may use only such force as is reasonably necessary to prevent personal harm. A person who is assaulted by another with no weapon is ordinarily not justified in hitting the assailant with a baseball bat. A person verbally threatened by another is not justified in striking the other party with his fists. If a woman hits a larger man, the man would not generally be justified in striking the woman and causing her physical harm. In other words, to exercise the self-defense privilege, the danger to the defendant must be immediate. And even in cases where the victim was the one who initiated the fray and pummeled his opponent first, an imbalance in weaponry (e.g., gun versus fist) would mitigate a finding of self-defense.[19]

STAND YOUR GROUND Most self-defense statutes require a duty to retreat before reacting to a threat with physical violence. An exception is one's own home. According to the "castle exception" (from the old saying "every man's home is his castle"), a person is not obligated to retreat within his or her residence before fighting back. Some states, most notably Florida, now have "stand your ground" laws, which allow people to use force in a wide variety of circumstances and eliminate or curtail the need to retreat.

Florida's law, enacted on October 1, 2005, allows the use of deadly force when a person reasonably believes it necessary to prevent the commission of a "forcible felony," including carjacking, robbery, and assault.

The traditional "castle doctrine" allowed people to use deadly force only when they reasonably believed that their lives were in danger. The new law allows average citizens to use deadly force when they reasonably believe that their homes or vehicles have been illegally invaded. The Florida law authorizes the use of defensive force by anyone "who is not engaged in an unlawful activity and who is attacked in any other place where he or she has a right to be." Furthermore, under the law, such a person has no duty to retreat and can stand his or her ground and meet force with force. The statute also grants civil and criminal immunity to anyone found to have had such a reasonable belief.[20]

DURESS A duress (also called compulsion or coercion) defense may be used when the defendant claims he was forced to commit a crime as the only means of preventing death or serious harm to himself or others. For example, a bank employee might be excused from taking bank funds if she can prove that her family was being threatened and that consequently she was acting under duress. But widespread general agreement exists that duress is no defense for an intentional killing.

A famous, albeit unsuccessful, duress defense was launched by Patty Hearst, the young daughter of wealthy newspaper owners, who on February 4, 1974, was kidnapped by the Symbionese Liberation Army (SLA), a heavily armed radical group. While in captivity she began to sympathize with her kidnappers and actually joined with them in a series of bank robberies. After the group was captured, Hearst's lawyers argued that her participation in the crimes was caused by the duress of her ordeal. Hearst testified that she feared for her life if she did not cooperate. Her performance on the stand did not convince jurors because she refused to answer many questions posed by the prosecution; she was convicted and sentenced to seven years in prison. (President Jimmy Carter commuted her sentence on February 1, 1979, and ordered her release.)

NECESSITY The defense of necessity is used when a crime was committed under extreme circumstances and could not be avoided. Unlike the duress defense, which involves threats made by another person, people act out of necessity according to their own judgment. Typically, to prove necessity, the burden is on the defendant to show that he acted to prevent imminent harm and that there were no legal alternatives to violating the law. Using these criteria, a successful necessity defense could be launched if a woman in labor, fearing that she was about to give birth, stole a car in order to get to the hospital for an emergency delivery. It might also be considered necessity if a hunter shot an animal of an endangered species that was about to attack his child. However, defendants must prove that their actions were "the lesser of two evils." Unlike the case of the pregnant woman above, a defendant could not claim necessity for stealing a car because he was late for a soccer game.

Changing Defenses

Criminal defenses are undergoing rapid change. As society becomes more aware of existing social problems that may in part produce crime, it has become commonplace for defense counsels to defend their clients by raising a variety of new defenses based on preexisting conditions or syndromes with which their clients were afflicted. Examples might include "battered woman syndrome," "Vietnam syndrome," "child sexual abuse syndrome," "Holocaust survivor syndrome," and "adopted child syndrome." In using these defenses, attorneys are asking judges either to recognize a new excuse for crime or to fit these conditions into pre-existing defenses. For example, a person who used lethal violence in self-defense may argue that the trauma of serving in the Vietnam War caused him to over-react to provocation. Or a victim of child abuse may use her experiences to miti-gate her culpability in a crime, asking a jury to consider her background when making a death penalty decision. In some instances, exotic criminal defenses have been gender-specific. Attorneys have argued that their female clients' behavior was a result of their premenstrual syndrome (PMS) and that male clients were aggressive because of an imbalance in their testosterone levels. These defenses have achieved relatively little success in the United States.[21] Others contend that prosecutors can turn the tables and use these defenses against the defendant. For example, some commentators have suggested that courts will ultimately view PMS as an aggravating condition in a crime, prompt-ing harsher penalties.

Although criminal law reform may be guided by good intentions, it is some-times difficult to put the changes into actual operation. Law reform may require new enforcement agencies to be created or severely tax existing ones. As a result, the system becomes strained, and cases are backlogged.

♦ REFORMING THE CRIMINAL LAW

In recent years, many states and the federal government have been examining their substantive criminal law. Because the law, in part, reflects public opinion and morality regarding various forms of behavior, what was considered crimi-nal 40 years ago may not be considered so today. In some cases, states have reassessed their laws and reduced the penalties on some common practices such as public intoxication; this is referred to as **decriminalization**. Such crimes, which in the past might have resulted in a prison sentence, may now be punished with a fine. In other instances, what was once considered a crim-inal act may be declared noncriminal or legalized. Sexual activity between consenting same-sex adults was punished as a serious felony under sodomy statutes in a number of states until the U.S. Supreme Court ruled such statutes illegal in 2003.

States may take action to decriminalize or legalize some crimes because the general public simply ignores the laws and law enforcement agents are reluctant to press charges even when they apprehend violators. Legal scholar Margaret Raymond calls these **penumbral crimes**—criminal acts defined by a high level of noncompliance with the stated legal standard, an absence of stigma associated with violation of the stated standard, and a low level of law enforcement or public sanction.[22] Because otherwise law-abiding people routinely violate these laws, they may be targets for penalty reduction and eventual legalization. For example, given that the 55-mile-per-hour speed limit has been so widely ignored, states have increased limits to 65 and even 70 miles per hour.

What are some other reasons that new laws are created or old ones eliminated?

Protecting Special Classes

In some instances, new criminal laws have been created to protect special classes of victims who were ignored by existing statutes. More than 25 states have enacted **stalking** statutes, which prohibit and punish acts described typically as "the willful, malicious and repeated following and harassing of another person."[23] Stalking laws were originally formulated to protect women terrorized by former husbands and boyfriends, although celebrities are often plagued by stalkers as well. In celebrity cases, these laws often apply to stalkers who are strangers or casual acquaintances of their victims.

ThomsonNOW Improve your grade on the exam with Personalized Study! For reinforcement re-sources and a mastery check of criminal defenses, go to www.thomsonedu.com/thomsonnow.

decriminalization
Reducing the seriousness of and subsequent penalties for a criminal offense.

penumbral crimes
Criminal acts defined by a high level of noncompliance with the stated legal standard, an absence of stigma associated with violation of the stated standard, and a low level of law enforcement or public sanction.

stalking
The willful, malicious, and repeated following, harassing, or contacting of another person. It becomes a criminal act when it causes the victim to feel fear for his or her safety or the safety of others.

One change in the criminal law allows for the registration of convicted sex offenders. Is this fair? After all, we do not register muggers or arsonists, though they may be dangerous offenders. Recently released from prison, Kerry Skora sits on a couch inside a friend's home where he is staying in Villa Park, Illinois. Skora was looking forward to getting his life back together after spending 15 years in prison for a murder he says he didn't commit. Skora found out a few months ago that because the victim was 16, he would have to register as a sex offender when released even though the crime did not involve sex. This prompted Skora to urge Illinois lawmakers to create a unique new registry for people who commit violent but nonsexual crimes against youths.

Responding to Public Opinion

Some laws are created when public opinion turns against a previously legal practice. Physician-assisted suicide became the subject of a national debate when Dr. Jack Kevorkian began practicing what he calls **obitiatry**, helping people take their lives.[24] In an attempt to stop Kevorkian, Michigan passed a statutory ban on assisted suicide, reflecting what lawmakers believed to be prevailing public opinion.[25]

obitiatry
Helping people take their own lives: assisted suicide.

Some legal changes have been prompted by public outrage over a particularly heinous crime. One of the most well-known is Megan's Law, named after seven-year-old Megan Kanka of Hamilton Township, New Jersey, who was killed in 1994. Charged with the crime was a convicted sex offender, who, unknown to the Kankas, lived across the street. On May 17, 1996, President Bill Clinton signed Megan's Law, which contained two components:

1. *Sex offender registration:* a revision of the 1994 Jacob Wetterling Act, which had required the states to register individuals convicted of sex crimes against children, to also establish a community notification system.

2. *Community notification:* compels the states to make private and personal information on registered sex offenders available to the public.

Variations of Megan's Law have been adopted by most state jurisdictions. Although civil libertarians have expressed concern that notification laws may interfere with an offender's postrelease privacy rights, recent research indicates that registered offenders find value in Megan's Law because is helps deter future abuse. When DNA collection is included in the law, it helps reduce false accusations and convictions.[26]

Clarifying Existing Laws

Sometimes laws are changed to clarify the definition of crime and to quell public debate over the boundaries of the law. When does bad behavior cross the line into criminality, and when does it remain merely bad behavior? An example of the former can be found in changes to the law of rape. In seven states, including California, it is now considered rape if (a) the woman consents to sex, (b) the sex

> **EXHIBIT 4.4**
>
> ## HB 2304, Computer crimes; gathering personal information by deception (phishing), penalty
>
> COMPUTER CRIMES; PHISHING; PENALTY
>
> Makes it a Class 6 felony to fraudulently obtain, record, or access from a computer the following identifying information of another: (i) Social Security number; (ii) driver's license number; (iii) bank account numbers; (iv) credit or debit card numbers; (v) personal identification numbers (PIN); (vi) electronic identification codes; (vii) automated or electronic signatures; (viii) biometric data; (ix) fingerprints; (x) passwords; or
>
> (xi) any other numbers or information that can be used to access a person's financial resources, obtain identification, act as identification, or obtain goods or services. Any person who sells or distributes such information or uses it to commit another crime is guilty of a Class 5 felony.
>
> Source: HB 2304, Computer crimes; gathering personal information by deception (phishing), penalty (http://leg1.state.va.us/cgi-bin/legp504.exe?051+sum+HB2304), accessed on May 12, 2006.

act begins, (c) she changes her mind during the act and tells her partner to stop, and (d) he refuses and continues. Before the legal change, such a circumstance was not considered rape but merely aggressive sex.[27]

Responding to Technology

Changing technology and the ever-increasing role of technology in people's daily lives will require modifications of the criminal law. Such technologies as automatic teller machines and cellular phones have already spawned a new generation of criminal acts involving theft of access numbers and software piracy. For example, a modification to Virginia's Computer Crimes Act (Exhibit 4.4) that took effect in 2005 makes *phishing*—sending out bulk e-mail messages designed to trick consumers into revealing bank account passwords, Social Security numbers, and other personal information—a felony. Those convicted of selling the data or using the data to commit another crime, such as identity theft, now face twice the prison time.

Protecting the Environment

In response to the concerns of environmentalists, the federal government has passed numerous acts designed to protect the nation's well-being. Some of the most important are listed in Exhibit 4.5.

The Environmental Protection Agency has successfully prosecuted significant violations of these and other new laws, including data fraud cases (e.g., private laboratories submitting false environmental data to state and federal environmental agencies); indiscriminate hazardous waste dumping that resulted in serious injuries and death; industry-wide ocean dumping by cruise ships; oil spills that caused significant damage to waterways, wetlands, and beaches; and illegal handling of hazardous substances such as pesticides and asbestos that exposed children, the poor, and other especially vulnerable groups to potentially serious illness.[28]

Responding to Terrorism

The criminal law has also undergone extensive change in both substance and procedure in the aftermath of the September 11, 2001, terrorist attacks.

ThomsonNOW™ Improve your grade on the exam with Personalized Study! For reinforcement resources and a mastery check of criminal law reform, go to www.thomsonedu.com/thomsonnow.

EXHIBIT 4.5

Environmental Protection Laws

Federal Insecticide, Fungicide and Rodenticide Act (FIFRA), 7 USC §§ 136–136y

Energy Supply and Environmental Coordination Act, 15 USC §§ 791–798

Toxic Substances Control Act (TSCA), 15 USC §§ 2601–2692

Federal Water Pollution Control Act (also known as the Clean Water Act), 33 USC §§ 1251–1387

Safe Drinking Water Act, 42 USC §§ 300f–300j–26

Noise Control Act, 42 USC §§ 4901–4918, 42 USC § 4910 (criminal provision)

Solid Waste Disposal Act (including, in Subchapter III, the Resource Conservation and Recovery Act [RCRA]), 42 USC §§ 6901–6992k

Clean Air Act, 42 USC §§ 7401–7671

Federal Hazardous Material Transportation Statute, 49 USC §§ 5101–5127

Source: http://www.usdoj.gov/usao/eousa/foia_reading_room/usam/title5/11menv.htm.

♦ CONSTITUTIONAL CRIMINAL PROCEDURE

Whereas substantive criminal law primarily defines crimes, the law of criminal procedure consists of the rules and procedures that govern the processing of criminal suspects and the conduct of criminal trials. The right to remain silent, the right to an attorney, and the right to a speedy and fair trial are all critical elements of criminal procedure. The main source of the procedural law is the 10 amendments added to the U.S. Constitution on December 15, 1791, collectively known as the Bill of Rights. These amendments were added to the Constitution to quell fears among some of the Founding Fathers such as George Mason that, as drafted, the Constitution did not offer protections from the tyrannical exercise of power by an all-powerful central government.[29] The British violation of the colonists' civil rights before and during the Revolution was still fresh in their minds when they demanded a "bill of rights" that would spell out the rights and privileges of individual citizens. On September 25, 1789, the First Congress of the United States therefore proposed to the state legislatures 12 amendments to the Constitution that met arguments most frequently advanced against it. The first two proposed amendments, which concerned the number of constituents for each representative and the compensation of congressmen, were not ratified. Articles 3 to 12, however, ratified by three-fourths of the state legislatures, constitute the first 10 amendments of the Constitution, known as the Bill of Rights.[30]

The purpose of these amendments was to prevent the government from usurping the personal freedoms of citizens. The U.S. Supreme Court's interpretation of these amendments has served as the basis for the creation of legal rights of the accused. Of primary concern to the law of criminal procedure are the Fourth, Fifth, Sixth, and Eighth amendments, which limit and control the manner in which the federal government operates the justice system. In addition, the due process clause of the Fourteenth Amendment has been interpreted to apply limits on governmental action on the state and local level.

♦ The Fourth Amendment bars illegal "searches and seizures," a right especially important for the criminal justice system because it means that police officers cannot indiscriminately use their authority to investigate a possible crime or arrest a suspect. Stopping, questioning, or searching an individual without legal justification represents a serious violation of the Fourth Amendment right to personal privacy.

♦ The Fifth Amendment limits the admissibility of confessions that have been obtained unfairly. In 1966, in the landmark case of *Miranda v. Arizona*, the Supreme Court held that a person accused of a crime has

Criminal Law and Terrorism

Soon after the September 11, 2001, terrorist attacks, the federal government enacted several laws focused on preventing further acts of violence against the United States. President George W. Bush signed the USA Patriot Act (USAPA, short for the "Uniting and Strengthening America by Providing Appropriate Tools Required to Intercept and Obstruct Terrorism" Act of 2001) into law on October 26, 2001. The bill was more than 342 pages long, created new laws, and made changes to more than 15 different existing statutes. Its aim was to give sweeping new powers to domestic law enforcement and international intelligence agencies in an effort to fight terrorism, to expand the definition of terrorist activities, and to alter sanctions for violent terrorism.

Among its provisions, USAPA expands all four traditional tools of surveillance—wiretaps, search warrants, pen/trap orders (installing devices that record phone calls), and subpoenas. The Foreign Intelligence Surveillance Act, which allows domestic operations by intelligence agencies, was also expanded. USAPA gave greater power to the FBI to check and monitor phone, Internet, and computer records without first needing to demonstrate that the devices were being used by a suspect or target of a court order.

The government may now serve a single wire tap or pen/trap order on any person regardless of whether that person or entity is named in a court order. Prior to the act, telephone companies could be ordered to install pen/trap devices on their networks, which would monitor calls coming to a surveillance target and calls that the surveillance target made. The USAPA extends this monitoring to the Internet. Law enforcement agencies may now obtain the e-mail addresses and websites visited by a target as well as the e-mails of those people with whom the target

communicates. An Internet service provider can be required to install a device that records e-mail and other electronic communications on its servers, looking for communications initiated or received by the target of an investigation. Under USAPA, the government does not need to show a court that the information or communication is relevant to a criminal investigation, and it does not have to report where it served the order or what information it received.

The act also allows enforcement agencies to monitor cable television operators and obtain access to cable operators' records and systems. Before the act, the cable company had to give prior notice to the customer, even if that person was a target of an investigation. Information can be obtained about people with whom the cable subscriber communicates, the content of the communications, and the person's subscription records. Prior notice is still required if law enforcement agencies want to learn what television programming a subscriber purchases.

As well, the act expands the definition of terrorism and enables the government to monitor more closely those people suspected of "harboring" and giving "material support" to terrorists. It further increases the authority of the attorney general to detain and deport noncitizens with little or no judicial review. The attorney general can certify that he has "reasonable grounds to believe" that a noncitizen endangers national security and therefore is eligible for deportation. The attorney general and secretary of state are also given the authority to designate domestic groups as terrorist organizations and deport any noncitizen who is a member.

Under section 224, portions of the act were originally to expire on December 31, 2005. However, after a great deal of debate the act was renewed by Congress and signed into law by President Bush on

---

the right to refuse to answer questions when placed in police custody.[31] The Fifth Amendment also guarantees defendants the right to a grand jury and not to be tried twice for the same crime—that is, they are protected from double jeopardy. Its due process clause guarantees defendants the right to fundamental fairness and the expectation of fair trials, fair hearings, and similar procedural safeguards.

♦ The Sixth Amendment guarantees the defendant the right to a speedy and public trial by an impartial jury, the right to be informed of the nature of the charges, and the right to confront any prosecution witnesses. It also contains the right of a defendant to be represented by an attorney, a privilege that has been extended to numerous stages of the criminal justice process, including

March 9, 2006. Two of its provisions (authority to conduct "roving" surveillance under the Foreign Intelligence Surveillance Act [FISA] and the authority to request production of business records under FISA [USA PATRIOT Act sections 206 and 215, respectively]) will end in 2010.

Although law enforcement agencies may applaud these new laws, civil libertarians are troubled because they view the Patriot Act as eroding civil rights. Some political commentators have complained that provisions in the law permit the government to share with intelligence agencies information from grand jury proceedings and from criminal wiretaps. One of the most controversial sections of the act allows FBI agents to obtain a warrant from the United States Foreign Intelligence Surveillance Court to look at library or bookstore records of anyone suspected of international terrorism or spying. Should the government be allowed to find out what books we took out of the library even if we have committed no crime? Another controversial element (Section 213) expands law enforcement's ability to conduct secret "sneak and peek" searches of people's homes. The FBI can now enter a home or office, take pictures, and seize items without informing the owner that a warrant was issued. Section 216 lets the government get records that show the subject lines of e-mails and details about web surfing habits, including recent research, all without probable cause.

Although supporters believe that such powers are necessary in the war against terrorism, critics claim that this new and sweeping authority is not limited to true terrorism investigations but covers a much broader range of activity involving reasonable political protest. The USAPA will also be used against common-law criminals such as drug traffickers and members of organized crime. The American Civil Liberties Union, perhaps the most vocal critic of USAPA, summed its opposition as follows:

> There has never been a more urgent need to preserve fundamental privacy protections and our system of checks and balances than the need we face today, as illegal government spying, provisions of the Patriot Act and government-sponsored torture programs transcend the bounds of law and our most treasured values in the name of national security.

Critical Thinking

1. Are you concerned that the government's efforts to control terrorism have produced a reduction in civil liberties? Does the danger presented by future September 11–type attacks justify erosion of the law of personal privacy?

2. Should noncitizens residing in the United States enjoy the same rights, liberties, and protections as citizens?

InfoTrac College Edition Research

Use "USA Patriot Act" as a key term to find out more about its scope and provisions.

Sources: Douglas A. Kash, "Hunting Terrorists Using Confidential Informant Reward Programs," *FBI Law Enforcement Bulletin* 71 (2002): 26–28; Sara Sun Beale and James Felman, "The Consequences of Enlisting Federal Grand Juries in the War on Terrorism: Assessing the USA Patriot Act's Changes to Grand Jury Secrecy," *Harvard Journal of Law and Public Policy* 25 (2002): 699–721; Morton Halperin, "Less Secure, Less Free: Striking Terror at Civil Liberty," *American Prospect* 12 (November 19, 2001): 10–13; American Civil Liberties Union, "USA Patriot Act" (http://www.aclu.org/safefree/resources/17343res20031114.html); "Uniting and Strengthening America by Providing Appropriate Tools Required to Intercept and Obstruct Terrorism (USA Patriot Act)" (http://www.epic.org/privacy/terrorism/hr3162.html).

pretrial custody, identification and lineup procedures, preliminary hearing, submission of a guilty plea, trial, sentencing, and postconviction appeal.

♦ According to the Eighth Amendment, "Excessive bail shall not be required, nor excessive fines imposed, nor cruel and unusual punishments inflicted." Bail is a money bond put up by the accused to attain freedom between arrest and trial. Bail is meant to ensure a trial appearance, because the bail money is forfeited if the defendant misses the trial date. The Eighth Amendment does not guarantee a constitutional right to bail but instead prohibits the use of excessive bail, which is typically defined as an amount far greater than that imposed on similar defendants who are accused of committing similar crimes. The Eighth Amendment also forbids the use of cruel and unusual punishment. This prohibition protects both the accused and convicted offenders from actions regarded as unacceptable by a civilized society, including corporal punishment and torture.

◆ The Fourteenth Amendment is the vehicle used to apply the protection of the Bill of Rights to the states. It affirms that no state shall "deprive any person of life, liberty, or property, without due process of law." In essence, the same general constitutional restrictions previously applicable to the federal government can be imposed on the states.

Due Process of Law

The concept of due process, found in both the Fifth and Fourteenth amendments, has been used to evaluate the constitutionality of legal statutes and to set standards and guidelines for fair procedures in the criminal justice system. In seeking to define the meaning of the term, most legal experts believe that it refers to the essential elements of fairness under law.[32] This definition basically refers to the legal system's need for rules and regulations that protect individual rights.

Due process can be divided into two distinct categories: substantive and procedural. Substantive due process refers to the citizen's right to be protected from criminal laws that may be biased, discriminatory, or otherwise unfair. These laws may be vague or may apply unfairly to one group over another. For example, in an important 2003 case, *Lawrence et al. v. Texas*, the U.S. Supreme Court declared that laws banning sodomy were unconstitutional in that they violated the due process rights of citizens because of their sexual orientation. A neighbor in 1998 had reported a "weapons disturbance" at the home of John G. Lawrence, and when police arrived they found Lawrence and another man, Tyron Garner, having sex. The two were held overnight in jail and later fined $200 each for violating the state's homosexual conduct law. In its decision, the Court said the following:

> Although the laws involved . . . here . . . do not do more than prohibit a particular sexual act, their penalties and purposes have more far-reaching consequences, touching upon the most private human conduct, sexual behavior, and in the most private of places, the home. They seek to control a personal relationship that, whether or not entitled to formal recognition in the law, is within the liberty of persons to choose without being punished as criminals. The liberty protected by the Constitution allows homosexual persons the right to choose to enter upon relationships in the confines of their homes and their own private lives and still retain their dignity as free persons.

As a result of the decision, all sodomy laws in the United States are now unconstitutional and unenforceable.[33]

In contrast, procedural due process seeks to ensure that no person will be deprived of life, liberty, or property without proper and legal criminal process. Basically, procedural due process is intended to guarantee that fundamental fairness exists in each individual case. Specific due process procedures include the following:

PERSPECTIVES ON JUSTICE

Due Process

The *Lawrence v. Texas* case is a milestone in the ongoing effort to grant due process rights to all Americans. No one, according to the due process perspective, should be denied the protection of the law simply because of his or her personal status—race, religion, ethnicity, or sexual orientation.

◆ Prompt notice of charges

◆ A formal hearing

◆ The right to counsel or some other representation

◆ The opportunity to respond to charges

◆ The opportunity to confront and cross-examine witnesses and accusers

♦ The privilege to be free from self-incrimination

♦ The opportunity to present one's own witnesses

♦ A decision made on the basis of substantial evidence and facts produced at the hearing

♦ A written statement of the reasons for the decision

♦ An appellate review procedure

These concepts, which protect basic freedoms, are not unique to the United States.

The Meaning of Due Process

Exactly what constitutes due process in a specific case depends on the facts of the case, the federal and state constitutional and statutory provisions, previous court decisions, and the ideas and principles that society considers important at a given time and in a given place.[34] Justice Felix Frankfurter emphasized this point in *Rochin v. California* (1952):

> Due process of law requires an evaluation based on a disinterested inquiry pursued in the spirit of science on a balanced order of facts, exactly and clearly stated, on the detached consideration of conflicting claims[,] . . . on a judgment not ad hoc and episodic but duly mindful of reconciling the needs both of continuity and of change in a progressive society.[35]

The interpretations of due process of law are not fixed but reflect what society deems fair and just at a particular time and place. The degree of loss suffered by the individual (victim or offender) balanced against the state's interests also determines which and how many due process requirements are ordinarily applied. When the Supreme Court Justices are conservative, as they are now, they are less likely to create new rights and privileges under the guise of due process.

ThomsonNOW Improve your grade on the exam with Personalized Study! For reinforcement resources and a mastery check of constitutional criminal, go to www.thomsonedu.com/thomsonnow.

©AP Images/Brennan Linsley

Should terrorists enjoy the same due process protections as U.S. citizens if they are held by U.S. authorities and incarcerated under U.S. law? Here, an inmate prays inside the compound of Camp Delta Detention Center at the Guantanamo Bay U.S. Naval Base in Cuba. While providing legal counsel and civil rights for people who want to destroy the U.S. may disturb some people, not providing such protections is alien to the U.S. view of justice and equally disturbing to others.

ETHICAL CHALLENGES IN CRIMINAL JUSTICE: A WRITING ASSIGNMENT

*I*n 1997 Louise Woodward, a teenage British nanny, was accused in Massachusetts of first-degree murder for allegedly shaking to death Matthew Eappen, the infant she was baby-sitting. Prosecutors claimed that Woodward was so frustrated by the crying child that she first shook him and then slammed the infant against a hard surface to silence him. Woodward's defense claimed that the nanny did not cause Eappen's death and that a prior incident must have caused the baby's skull fracture.

After the jury found Woodward guilty of second-degree murder, Hiller B. Zobel, the trial judge, reduced Woodward's sentence to manslaughter because he concluded that the intent to do bodily harm or act with malice was not present. Involuntary manslaughter is a killing with no intention to cause serious bodily harm, such as acting without proper caution. Write an essay commenting on the judge's decision: Is it fair for a trial judge to overturn a jury verdict and impose his will on the people? Does that allow a single person to control the content of the law? What are some possible harmful outcomes if this became a common practice? What are some of the benefits?

Doing Research on the Web

Before you answer, read more about the Woodward case at Court TV Online. You can access this case by going to the Siegel/Senna Introduction to Criminal Justice 11e website: www.thomsonedu.com/criminaljustice/siegel.

Trish Wilson wrote an essay reviewing the case. You can access this essay by going to the Siegel/Senna Introduction to Criminal Justice 11e website: www.thomsonedu.com/criminaljustice/siegel.

The judge's decision is also available online. You can access this document by going to the Siegel/Senna Introduction to Criminal Justice 11e website: www.thomsonedu.com/criminaljustice/siegel.

SUMMARY

♦ The criminal justice system is basically a legal system. Its foundation is the criminal law, which is concerned with people's conduct.

♦ The purpose of criminal law is to regulate behavior and maintain order in society. What constitutes a crime is defined primarily by the state and federal legislatures and reviewed by the courts. What is considered criminal conduct changes from one period to another. Social norms, values, and community beliefs play major roles in determining what conduct is antisocial.

♦ Crimes are generally classified as felonies or misdemeanors, depending on their seriousness.

♦ There are different elements, both mental and physical, in a crime.

♦ Crimes have a mental element known as mens rea, or intent.

♦ The actus reus is the physical element of the crime. Thought alone is not enough; a crime must involve action.

♦ The law does not hold an individual blameworthy unless that person is capable of intending to commit the crime of which he is accused and that intent causes him to commit an illegal action.

♦ A person can defend himself against crime by denying he committed the act.

♦ Defendants can also deny their intent to commit crime. They may claim that they were intoxicated, acted under duress or out of necessity, or acted in self-defense. They can argue that the police entrapped them into committing crime. Such factors as insanity, a mental defect, or age mitigate a person's criminal responsibility.

◆ States periodically revise and update the substantive criminal law. The definitions of crime and criminal defense shift to reflect existing social and cultural change. For example, recent changes in the law to control terrorism reflect the public condemnation of the September 11, 2001, terrorist attacks.

◆ Procedural laws set out the rules for processing the offender from arrest through trial, sentencing, and release. An accused must be provided with the guarantees of due process under the Fifth and Fourteenth amendments to the U.S. Constitution.

KEY TERMS

criminal law, 130
substantive criminal law, 130
procedure criminal law, 130
civil law, 130
torts, 130
stare decisis, 134
mala in se, 134

ex post facto laws, 135
actus reus, 137
mens rea, 137
criminal negligence, 139
public safety or strict liability
   crime, 139
excuse defenses, 140

justification, 140
decriminalization, 146
penumbral crimes, 146
stalking, 146
obitiatry, 147

ThomsonNOW Maximize your study time by using ThomsonNOW's diagnostic study plan to help you review this chapter. The Study Plan will

◆ help you identify areas on which you should concentrate;

◆ provide interactive exercises to help you master the chapter concepts; and

◆ provide a post-test to confirm you are ready to move on to the next chapter.

CRITICAL THINKING QUESTIONS

1. What are the specific aims and purposes of the criminal law? To what extent does the criminal law control behavior?

2. What kinds of activities should be labeled criminal in contemporary society? Why?

3. What is a criminal act? What is a criminal state of mind? When are individuals liable for their actions?

4. Discuss the various kinds of crime classifications. To what extent or degree are they distinguishable?

5. Numerous states are revising their penal codes. Which major categories of substantive crimes do you think should be revised?

6. Entrapment is a defense used when the defendant was lured into committing the crime. To what extent should law enforcement personnel induce the commission of an offense?

7. What legal principles can be used to justify self-defense? Because the law seeks to prevent, not promote, crime, are such principles sound?

8. What are the minimum standards of criminal procedure required in the criminal justice system?

NOTES

1. Department of Justice News Release, "Work at Home Program Scheme," June 9, 2006 (http://cleveland.fbi.gov/dojpressrel/2006/moneylaundering060906.htm).
2. See John Weaver, *Warren—The Man, the Court, the Era* (Boston: Little, Brown, 1967); see also "We the People," *Time*, July 6, 1987, p. 6.
3. *Kansas v. Hendricks*, 117 S.Ct. 2072 (1997); *Chicago v. Morales*, 119 S.Ct. 246 (1999).
4. *City of Chicago v. Morales et al.*, 527 U.S. 41 (1999).

5. Daniel Suleiman, "The Capital Punishment Exception: A Case for Constitutionalizing the Substantive Criminal Law," *Columbia Law Review* 104 (2004): 426–58.
6. *Calder v. Bull*, 3 U.S. 386 (1798).
7. See American Law Institute, Model Penal Code, Sec. 104.
8. Henry Black, *Black's Law Dictionary*, rev. 5th ed. (St. Paul, Minn.: West, 1979), pp. 744, 1150.
9. Sheldon Krantz, *Law of Corrections and Prisoners' Rights, Cases, and Materials*, 3d ed. (St. Paul, Minn.: West, 1986), p. 702; Barbara

Knight and Stephen Early, Jr., *Prisoners' Rights in America* (Chicago: Nelson-Hall, 1986), Chapter 1; see also Fred Cohen, "The Law of Prisoners' Rights—An Overview," *Criminal Law Bulletin* 24 (1988): 321–49.

10. See *United States v. Balint*, 258 U.S. 250, 42 S.Ct. 301, 66 L.Ed. 604 (1922); see also *Morissette v. United States*, 342 U.S. 246, 72 S.Ct. 240, 96 L.Ed. 288 (1952).

11. New York State Consolidated Laws, Article 270, Other Offenses Relating to Public Safety, Section 270.10, Creating a Hazard (2002).

12. *Regina v. Dudley and Stephens*, 14 Q.B.D. 273 (1884).

13. Associated Press, "Nigerian Used Stepdaughter, 14, for a Son, Jury Finds," *Boston Globe*, October 8, 1998, p. 9.

14. 370 U.S. 660, 82 S.Ct. 1417, 8 L.Ed.2d 758 (1962).

15. 392 U.S. 514, 88 S.Ct. 2145, 20 L.Ed.2d 1254 (1968).

16. Samuel M. Davis, *Rights of Juveniles: The Juvenile Justice System* (New York: Boardman, 1974; updated 1993), Chapter 2; Larry Siegel and Joseph Senna, *Juvenile Delinquency: Theory, Practice, and Law* (St. Paul, Minn.: West, 1996).

17. 503 U.S. 540, 112 S.Ct. 1535, 118 L.Ed.2d 174 (1992).

18. ERGO (Euthanasia Research & Guidance Organization) (http://www.finalexit.org), accessed on May 11, 2006.

19. "Criminal Law—Mutual Combat Mitigation—Appellate Court of Illinois Holds That Disproportionate Reaction to Provocation Negates Mutual Combat Mitigation.—*People v. Thompson*, 821 N.E. 2d 664 (Ill. App. Ct. 2004)," *Harvard Law Review* 118 (2005): 2437–44.

20. Patrik Jonsson, "Is Self-Defense Law Vigilante Justice? Some Say Proposed Laws Can Help Deter Gun Violence. Others Worry About Deadly Confrontations," *Christian Science Monitor*, February 24, 2006.

21. Deborah W. Denno, "Gender, Crime, and the Criminal Law Defenses," *Journal of Criminal Law and Criminology* 85 (Summer 1994): 80–180.

22. Margaret Raymond, "Penumbral Crimes," *American Criminal Law Review* 39 (2002): 1395–1440.

23. National Institute of Justice, *Project to Develop a Model Anti-Stalking Statute* (Washington, D.C.: National Institute of Justice, 1994).

24. Marvin Zalman, John Strate, Denis Hunter, and James Sellars, "Michigan Assisted Suicide Three Ring Circus: The Intersection of Law and Politics," *Ohio Northern Law Review* 23 (1997): 863–903.

25. 1992 P.A. 270, as amended by 1993 P.A.3, M.C. L. ss. 752.1021 to 752. 1027.

26. Sarah Welchans, "Megan's Law: Evaluations of Sexual Offender Registries," *Criminal Justice Policy Review* 16 (2005): 123–40.

27. Matthew Lyon, "No Means No? Withdrawal of Consent During Intercourse and the Continuing Evolution of the Definition of Rape," *Journal of Criminal Law & Criminology* 95 (2004): 277–314.

28. Environmental Protection Agency, Criminal Enforcement Division (http://www.epa.gov/compliance/criminal/index.html), accessed on May 8, 2005.

29. National Archives (http://www.archives.gov/national-archives-experience/charters/bill_of_rights.html), accessed on May 12, 2006.

30. Ibid.

31. 384 U.S. 436, 86 S.Ct. 1602, 16 L.Ed.2d 694 (1966).

32. James MacGregor Burns and Steward Burns, *The Pursuit of Rights in America* (New York: Knopf, 1991).

33. *Lawrence et al. v. Texas*, No. 02–102, June 26, 2003.

34. 342 U.S. 165, 72 S.Ct. 205, 95 L.Ed. 183 (1952).

35. Ibid., at 172, 72 S.Ct. at 209.

The Police and Law Enforcement

©AP Images/Joseph Kaczmarek

R ecently, the FBI announced it had formed an art squad. This group of eight agents was assigned to work in major art markets around the country—New York, Los Angeles, Philadelphia, San Francisco, Indianapolis, St. Louis, and Salt Lake City. The team is supported by two assistant U.S. attorneys and several FBI analysts. Their goal is to break up crime rings that steal and smuggle priceless works of art, loot archaeological sites, and churn out fakes and forgeries. They have the expertise in art that allows them to know a Monet from a Manet, a Rembrandt from a Rubens. They know the dealers, appraisers, collectors, curators, and auction houses as well as the markets and the unique laws that apply to art theft.

The FBI's decision to form an art squad is indicative of the varied roles played by law enforcement personnel. In today's complex world, policing is no longer a matter of patrolling the streets and protecting the public. ♦

THE FOLLOWING four chapters serve as an introduction and overview of policing and law enforcement in contemporary society. Chapter 5 discusses the history of law enforcement and the various contemporary agencies, Chapter 6 covers the role and function of police agencies, Chapter 7 analyzes the most pressing issues facing police agencies, and Chapter 8 is

CHAPTER 5

Police in Society: History and Organization

Chapter Objectives

After reading this chapter, you should be able to:

1. Recount the early development of the police in England.
2. Know the reasons that police departments were created in the United States.
3. Recognize the problems of the early police agencies.
4. Identify the various levels of law enforcement.
5. Discuss the differences among local, county, state, and federal law enforcement agencies.
6. Know how law enforcement agencies are addressing the problem of terrorism.
7. Be familiar with the concept of private policing.
8. Know what is meant by the term *biometric technology*.
9. Identify the different types of DNA testing and tell how they are used.
10. Explain how some critics fear the spread of police technology.

Over the course of two days in June 2006, officers from more than a dozen federal, state, and local agencies fanned out across Stanislaus County, California, and arrested more than 45 gang members who had outstanding arrest warrants, had administrative warrants issued by U.S. Immigration and Customs Enforcement (ICE), and/or had violated the terms of their parole or probation. This multi-agency action, dubbed Operation Valley SCAR (Serious Criminal Apprehension and Removal), was a collaborative law enforcement effort targeting members of criminal street gangs and their associates. The goal of the operation was to reduce gang-related crime and violence in the area. The targets were documented gang members with criminal histories who had violated the terms of their probation and/or parole, making them subject to arrest. In addition, the operation resulted in the arrests of foreign national gang members on immigration violations. Those subjects now face deportation from the United States. Task Force SCAR was made up of teams from the United States Attorney's Office; the FBI; Immigration and Customs; the Modesto, California, Police Department; the U.S. Marshals Service; the Bureau of Alcohol, Tobacco, Firearms and Explosives; the California Department of Correction and Rehabilitation; the Stanislaus County District Attorney's Office; the Stanislaus County Sheriff's Department; the Stanislaus County Probation Department; and the Ceres, Turlock, and Oakdale police departments.[1] ♦

Operation SCAR illustrates a cooperative law enforcement effort to neutralize a growing public safety problem, namely gang activity. SCAR is unusual if not unique because so many diverse agencies cooperated in the program. But interagency cooperation is needed today if law enforcement agencies are going to be effective against contemporary challenges ranging from gang activity to international terrorism. Fifty years ago, gangs were restricted to large metropolitan areas such as Los Angeles, New York, and Chicago. Now that gangs can be found in small towns and rural areas, law enforcement agencies have to be up to the challenge they present.[2]

The public may applaud police efforts that confront these challenges and have helped bring the crime rate down. But they are also concerned by media reports of law enforcement officers who abuse their power by using unnecessary force and brutality or by violating the civil rights of suspects. Even when community members believe that police officers are competent and dependable, some question their priorities and often consider them disrespectful.[3] Some critics charge that police officers have induced or forced confessions from criminal suspects. If true, such a confession could influence jurors at a subsequent trial, even if the confession seems inconsistent with the facts of the case.[4] Another concern is that police are racially and ethnically biased and use racial profiling to routinely stop African Americans and search their cars. Some have suggested that police have created a new form of crime: DWB, "driving while black."[5]

Police officers are frustrated because they feel that they get little credit when they do a good job but get slammed when thing go awry. Their perceptions may be correct. Recent research by Wesley Skogan shows that the impact on the average citizen of having what he or she considers to be a bad experience with police is four to fourteen times as great as that of having a positive experience. Members of the public do not seem to respond to police when they are treated fairly, treated politely, and receive good service; however, they are quick to condemn officers who are rude or overly aggressive.[6]

Despite these concerns, the majority of citizens give their police force high marks. Citizens are especially likely to value local police if they view their neighborhood as safe and believe that the efficiency of the local police is a key to its protection.[7] Metropolitan police departments are attracting applicants who value an exciting, well-paid job that also holds the opportunity to provide valuable community service. Salaries in municipal police agencies are becoming more competitive; therefore, many people are considering a career in policing and law enforcement.

This chapter, the first of four on policing and law enforcement, covers the history of the police, the various police agencies, and how technology is now being used to improve police operations. The evolution of policing has been dramatic and somewhat ironic. One thousand years ago, during tribal times, the people appointed villagers to protect them from outside marauders who wanted to destroy their society. Now, one thousand years later, we expect law enforcement agents to protect us from outside marauders who want to destroy our society. The only difference is the size and power of their weapons and the dangers that we face.

♦ THE HISTORY OF POLICE

The origin of U.S. police agencies, like that of criminal law, can be traced to early English society.[8] England had no regular police force before the Norman Conquest. Every person living in the villages scattered throughout the countryside was responsible for aiding neighbors and protecting the settlement from thieves and marauders. This was known as the pledge system. People were grouped in collectives of 10 families, called **tythings** (or **tithings**), and were entrusted with policing their own minor problems such as dealing with disturbances, fire, wild animals, or other threats. The leader was called the tythingman. When trouble

tything (tithing)
In medieval England, a collective group of 10 families that pledged to help one another and provide mutual aid.

occurred, he was expected to make a **hue and cry** to assemble his helpers and warn the village. Ten tythings were grouped into a **hundred**, whose affairs were supervised by a hundredman appointed by the local nobleman. The hundredman (later to be called the parish **constable**) might be considered the first real police officer, and he dealt with more serious breaches of the law.[9]

Shires, which resembled the counties of today, were controlled by the shire reeve, who was appointed by the Crown or local landowner to supervise the territory and ensure that order would be kept. The **shire reeve**, a forerunner of today's sheriff, soon began to pursue and apprehend law violators as part of his duties.

In the thirteenth century, the **watch system** was created to help protect property in England's larger cities and towns. Watchmen patrolled at night and helped protect against robberies, fires, and disturbances. They reported to the area constable, who became the primary metropolitan law enforcement agent. In larger cities, such as London, the watchmen were organized within church parishes and were usually members of the parish they protected.

In 1326 the office of **justice of the peace** was created to assist the shire reeve in controlling the county. Eventually, these justices took on judicial functions in addition to their primary role as peacekeeper. The local constable became the operational assistant to the justice of the peace, supervising the night watchmen, investigating offenses, serving summonses, executing warrants, and securing prisoners. This system helped delineate the relationship between police and the judiciary, which has continued for more than 600 years.

Private Police and Thief Takers

As the eighteenth century began, rising crime rates in the cities encouraged a new form of private, monied police, who were able to profit both legally and criminally from the lack of formal police departments. These private police agents, referred to as *thief takers,* were universally corrupt, taking profits not only from catching and informing on criminals but also from theft, receiving stolen property, intimidation, perjury, and blackmail. They often relieved their prisoners of money and stolen goods and made more income by accepting hush money, giving perjured evidence, swearing false oaths, and operating extortion rackets. Petty debtors were especially easy targets for those who combined thief taking with the keeping of alehouses and taverns. While prisoners were incarcerated, their health and safety were entirely at the whim of the keepers, or thief takers, who were virtually free to charge what they wanted for board and other necessities. Court bailiffs who also acted as thief takers were the most passionately detested legal profiteers. They seized debtors and held them in small lockups, where they forced their victims to pay exorbitant prices for food and lodging.

The thief takers' use of violence was notorious. They went armed and were prepared to maim or kill in order to gain their objectives. Before he was hanged in 1725, Jack Wild, the most notorious thief taker, "had two fractures in his skull and his bald head was covered with silver plates. He had seventeen wounds in various parts of his body from swords, daggers, and gunshots, [and] . . . his throat had been cut in the course of his duties."[10]

Henry Fielding, famed author of *Tom Jones,* along with Saunders Welch and Sir John Fielding (Henry's brother), sought to clean up the thief-taking system. Appointed a city magistrate in 1748, Fielding operated his own group of monied police out of Bow Street in London, directing and deploying them throughout the city and its environs, deciding which cases to investigate and what streets to protect. His agents were carefully instructed on their legitimate powers and duties. Fielding's Bow Street Runners were a marked improvement over the earlier monied police because they actually had an administrative structure that improved record-keeping and investigative procedures.

Although an improvement, Fielding's forces were not adequate, and by the nineteenth century, state police officers were needed. Ironically, almost 200 years later, private policing is now considered essential. Private police forces are

hue and cry
In medieval England, a call for mutual aid against trouble or danger.

hundred
In medieval England, a group of 100 families responsible for maintaining order and trying minor offenses.

constable
In early English towns, an appointed peacekeeper who organized citizens for protection and supervised the night watch.

shire reeve
In early England, the chief law enforcement official in a county, forerunner of today's sheriff.

watch system
In medieval England, men who organized in church parishes to guard at night against disturbances and breaches of the peace under the direction of the local constable.

justice of the peace
Official appointed to act as the judicial officer in a county.

Modern policing began in England. This nineteenth-century photo shows Tom Smith, a well known "peeler." English policemen became known as peelers in reference to Home Secretary Sir Robert Peel, who organized the Police Force in 1829. They were also referred to as "bobbies" after their creator—a name that has stuck to the present day.

Metropolitan Police Act
Sir Robert Peel's legislation that established the first organized police force in London.

sheriff
The chief law enforcement officer in a county.

To read about Sir Robert Peel's life and political career, go to the Robert Peel website. You can access this site by going to the Siegel/Senna Introduction to Criminal Justice 11e website: www.thomsonedu.com/criminaljustice/siegel.

a rapidly growing entity, and in many instances local police forces work closely with private security firms and similar entities. In some gated communities and special tax assessment districts, property owners pay a special levy, in addition to their tax dollars, to hire additional private police, who may work in partnership with local law enforcement to investigate criminal activities.[11]

The London Metropolitan Police

In 1829 Sir Robert Peel, England's home secretary, guided through Parliament an "Act for Improving the Police in and near the Metropolis." The **Metropolitan Police Act** established the first organized police force in London. Composed of more than 1,000 men, the London police force was structured along military lines. Its members would be known from then on as *bobbies*, after their creator. They wore a distinctive uniform and were led by two magistrates, who were later given the title of commissioner. However, the ultimate responsibility for the police fell to the home secretary and consequently Parliament.

The early bobbies suffered many problems. Many were corrupt, they were unsuccessful at stopping crime, and they were influenced by the wealthy. Owners of houses of ill repute who in the past had guaranteed their undisturbed operations by bribing watchmen now turned their attention to the bobbies. Metropolitan police administrators fought constantly to terminate cowardly, corrupt, and alcoholic officers, dismissing in the beginning about one-third of the bobbies each year.

Despite its recognized shortcomings, the London experiment proved a vast improvement over what had come before. It was considered so successful that the metropolitan police soon began providing law enforcement assistance to outlying areas that requested it. Another act of Parliament allowed justices of the peace to establish local police forces, and by 1856 every borough and county in England was required to form its own police force.

Law Enforcement in Colonial America

Law enforcement in colonial America paralleled the British model. In the colonies, the county **sheriff** became the most important law enforcement agent. In addition to keeping the peace and fighting crime, sheriffs collected taxes, supervised elections, and handled a great deal of other legal business.

The colonial sheriff did not patrol or seek out crime. Instead, he reacted to citizens' complaints and investigated crimes that had occurred. His salary, related to his effectiveness, was paid on a fee system. Sheriffs received a fixed amount for every arrest made. Unfortunately, their tax-collecting chores were more lucrative than fighting crime, so law enforcement was not one of their primary concerns.

In the cities, law enforcement was the province of the town marshal, who was aided, often unwillingly, by a variety of constables, night watchmen, police justices, and city council members. However, local governments had little power of administration, and enforcement of the criminal law was largely an individual or community responsibility. After the American Revolution, larger cities relied on elected or appointed officials to serve warrants and recover stolen property, sometimes in cooperation with the thieves themselves. Night watchmen, referred to as *leatherheads* because of the leather helmets they wore, patrolled the streets calling the hour while equipped with a rattle to summon help and a nightstick to ward off lawbreakers. Watchmen were not widely respected. Rowdy young men enjoyed tipping over watch houses with a leatherhead inside, and a favorite saying in New York was "While the city sleeps the watchmen do too."[12]

In rural areas in the South, "slave patrols" charged with recapturing escaped slaves were an early, if loathsome, form of law enforcement.[13] In the western territories, individual initiative was encouraged by the practice of offering rewards for the capture of felons. If trouble arose, the town vigilance committee might form a posse to chase offenders. These **vigilantes** were called on to eradicate such social problems as theft of livestock, through force or intimidation. For example, the San Francisco Vigilance Committee actively pursued criminals in the mid-nineteenth century.

As cities grew, it became exceedingly difficult for local leaders to organize ad hoc citizen vigilante groups. Moreover, the early nineteenth century was an era of widespread urban unrest and mob violence. Local leaders began to realize that a more structured police function was needed to control demonstrators and keep the peace.

vigilantes
In the old west, members of a vigilance committee or posse called upon to capture cattle thieves or other felons.

Early Police Agencies

The modern police department was born out of the urban mob violence that wracked the nation's cities in the nineteenth century. Boston created the first formal U.S. police department in 1838. New York formed its police department in 1844; Philadelphia did so in 1854. The new police departments replaced the night watch system and relegated constables and sheriffs to serving court orders and running jails.

At first, the urban police departments inherited the functions of the institutions they replaced. For example, Boston police were charged with maintaining public health until 1853, and in New York, the police were responsible for street sweeping until 1881. Politics dominated the departments and determined the recruitment of new officers and the promotion of supervisors. An individual with the right connections could be hired despite a lack of qualifications. Early police agencies were corrupt, brutal, and inefficient.[14]

In the late nineteenth century, police work was highly desirable because it paid more than most other blue-collar jobs. By 1880, the average factory worker earned $450 per year, while a metropolitan police officer made double that amount. For immigrant groups, having enough political clout to be appointed to the police department was an important step up the social ladder.[15] However, job security was uncertain because it depended on the local political machine's staying in power.

Police work itself was primitive. Few of even the simplest technological innovations common today, such as call boxes or centralized record keeping, were in place. Most officers patrolled on foot, without backup or the ability to call for help. Officers were commonly taunted by local toughs and responded with force and brutality. The long-standing conflict between police and the public was born in the difficulty that untrained, unprofessional officers had in patrolling the streets of nineteenth-century U.S. cities and in breaking up and controlling labor disputes. Police were not crime fighters as they are known today. Their major role was maintaining order, and their power was almost unchecked. The average officer had little training, no education in the law, and a minimum of supervision, yet the police became virtual judges of law and fact, with the ability to exercise unlimited discretion.[16]

At mid-nineteenth century, the detective bureau was set up as part of the Boston police. Until then, thief taking had been the province of amateur bounty hunters who hired themselves out to victims for a price. When professional police departments replaced bounty hunters, the close working relationships that developed between police detectives and their underworld informants produced many scandals and, consequently, high personnel turnover.

Police during the nineteenth century were regarded as incompetent and corrupt, and they were disliked by the people whom they served. The police role was only minimally directed at law enforcement. Its primary function was serving as the enforcement arm of the reigning political power, protecting

One of the few policemen who stayed at work during the Boston police strike of 1919. Police earned about twenty-five cents an hour and were expected to work up to ninety-eight hours a week!

private property, and keeping control of the ever-rising numbers of foreign immigrants.

Police agencies evolved slowly in the second half of the nineteenth century. Uniforms were introduced in 1853 in New York. The first technological breakthroughs in police operations came in the area of communications. The linking of precincts to central headquarters by telegraph began in the 1850s. In 1867 the first telegraph police boxes were installed. An officer could turn a key in a box, and his location and number would automatically register at headquarters. Additional technological advances were made in transportation. The Detroit Police Department outfitted some of its patrol officers with bicycles in 1897. By 1913, the motorcycle was being used by departments in the eastern part of the nation. The first police car was used in Akron, Ohio, in 1910, and the police wagon became popular in Cincinnati in 1912.[17] Nonpolice functions, such as care of the streets, began to be abandoned after the Civil War.

Big-city police were still disrespected by the public, unsuccessful in their role as crime stoppers, and uninvolved in progressive activities. The control of police departments by local politicians impeded effective law enforcement and fostered an atmosphere of graft and corruption.

Twentieth-Century Reform

In an effort to reduce police corruption, civic leaders in a number of jurisdictions created police administrative boards to lessen local officials' control over the police. These tribunals were responsible for appointing police administrators and controlling police affairs. In many instances, these measures failed because the private citizens appointed to the review boards lacked expertise in the intricacies of police work.

Another reform movement was the takeover of some big-city police agencies by state legislators. Although police budgets were financed through local taxes, control of police was usurped by rural politicians in the state capitals. New York City temporarily lost authority over its police force in 1857. It was not until the first decades of the twentieth century that cities regained control of their police forces.

The Boston police strike of 1919 heightened interest in police reform. The strike came about basically because police officers were dissatisfied with their status in society. Other professions were unionizing and increasing their standards of living, but police salaries lagged behind. The Boston police officers organization, the Boston Social Club, voted to become a union affiliated with the American Federation of Labor. The police officers struck on September 9, 1919. Rioting and looting broke out, resulting in Governor Calvin Coolidge's mobilization of the state militia to take over the city. Public support turned against the police, and the strike was broken. Eventually, all the striking officers were fired and replaced by new recruits. The Boston police strike ended police unionism for decades and solidified power in the hands of reactionary, autocratic police administrators. In the aftermath of the strike, various local, state, and federal crime commissions began to investigate the extent of crime and the ability of the justice system to deal with it and made recommendations to improve police effectiveness.[18] However, with the onset of the Great Depression, justice reform became a less important issue than economic revival, and for many years, little changed in the nature of policing.

The Emergence of Professionalism

Around the turn of the century, a number of nationally recognized leaders called for measures to help improve and professionalize the police. In 1893 the International Association of Chiefs of Police (IACP), a professional society, was

What effect did the Boston police strike have on police labor unions? To find out, go to "Disorganized Labor." You can reach this site by going to the Siegel/Senna Introduction to Criminal Justice 11e website: www.thomsonedu.com/criminaljustice/siegel.

©Associated Press/AP Images

formed. Under the direction of its first president (District of Columbia Chief of Police Richard Sylvester), the IACP became the leading voice for police reform during the first two decades of the twentieth century. The IACP called for creating a civil service police force and for removing political influence and control. It also advocated centralized organizational structure and record keeping to curb the power of politically aligned precinct captains. Still another professional reform the IACP fostered was the creation of specialized units, such as delinquency control squads.

The most famous police reformer of the time was August Vollmer. While serving as police chief of Berkeley, California, Vollmer instituted university training for young officers. He also helped develop the School of Criminology at the University of California at Berkeley, which became the model for justice-related programs around the United States. Vollmer's disciples included O. W. Wilson, who pioneered the use of advanced training for officers when he took over and reformed the Wichita (Kansas) Police Department in 1928. Wilson was also instrumental in applying modern management and administrative techniques to policing. His text, *Police Administration*, became the single most influential work on the subject.

During this period, police professionalism was equated with an incorruptible, tough, highly trained, rule-oriented department organized along militaristic lines. The most respected department was that in Los Angeles, which emphasized police as incorruptible crime fighters who would not question the authority of the central command.

> **PERSPECTIVES ON JUSTICE**
>
> ### Restorative Justice
>
> The fact that police agencies grew out of the desire of the upper classes to suppress the social behavior and economic aspirations of the lower classes agrees with the restorative justice vision that U.S. justice is traditionally coercive and must be changed to become humanistic.

ThomsonNOW Improve your grade on the exam with Personalized Study! For reinforcement resources and a mastery check of the history of police, go to www.thomsonedu.com/thomsonnow.

◆ THE MODERN ERA OF POLICING: 1960 TO THE PRESENT

The modern era of policing can be traced from 1960 to the present day. What are the major events that occurred during this period?

Policing in the 1960s

Turmoil and crisis were the hallmarks of policing during the 1960s. Throughout this decade, the U.S. Supreme Court handed down a number of decisions designed to control police operations and procedures. Police officers were now required to obey strict legal guidelines when questioning suspects, conducting searches and wiretapping, and so on. As the civil rights of suspects were significantly expanded, police complained that they were being "handcuffed by the courts."

Also during this time, civil unrest produced a growing tension between police and the public. African Americans, who were battling for increased rights and freedoms in the civil rights movement, found themselves confronting police lines. When riots broke out in New York, Detroit, Los Angeles, and other cities between 1964 and 1968, the spark that ignited conflict often involved the police. When students across the nation began marching in anti–Vietnam War demonstrations, local police departments were called on to keep order. Police forces were ill equipped and poorly trained to deal with these social problems. Not surprisingly, the 1960s were marked by a number of bloody confrontations between the police and the public.

Compounding these problems was a rapidly growing crime rate. The number of violent and property crimes increased dramatically. Drug addiction and

The 60's were a time of social ferment. This photo shows Chicago policemen with nightsticks in hand confronting a demonstrator on the ground in Grant Park, Chicago, on August 26, 1968. The police force converged at Grant Park when protesters opposing the Vietnam War climbed on the statue of Civil War general John Logan. Conflict such as this between police and the public inspired the creation of university-based criminal justice programs.

©Associated Press/AP Images

abuse grew to be national concerns, common in all social classes. Urban police departments could not control the crime rate, and police officers resented the demands placed on them by dissatisfied citizens.

Policing in the 1970s

The 1970s witnessed many structural changes in police agencies themselves. The end of the Vietnam War significantly reduced tensions between students and police. However, the relationship between police and minorities was still rocky. Local fears and distrust, combined with conservative federal policies, encouraged police departments to control what was perceived as an emerging minority-group "threat."[19]

Increased federal government support for criminal justice greatly influenced police operations. During the decade, the Law Enforcement Assistance Administration (LEAA) devoted a significant portion of its funds to police agencies. Although a number of police departments used this money to purchase little-used hardware, such as anti-riot gear, most of it went to supporting innovative research on police work and advanced training of police officers. Perhaps most significant, LEAA's Law Enforcement Education Program helped thousands of officers further their college education. Hundreds of criminal justice programs were developed on college campuses around the country, providing a pool of highly educated police recruits. LEAA funds were also used to import or transfer technology originally developed in other fields into law enforcement. Technological innovations involving computers transformed the way police kept records, investigated crimes, and communicated with one another. State training academies improved the way police learned to deal with such issues as job stress, community conflict, and interpersonal relations.

More women and minorities were recruited to police work. Affirmative action programs helped, albeit slowly, alter the ethnic, racial, and gender composition of U.S. policing.

Policing in the 1980s

As the 1980s began, the police role seemed to be changing significantly. A number of experts acknowledged that the police were not simply crime fighters and called for police to develop a greater awareness of community issues, which resulted in the emergence of the community policing concept.[20]

Police unions, which began to grow in the late 1960s, continued to have a great impact on departmental administration in the 1980s. Unions fought for and won increased salaries and benefits for their members. In many instances, unions eroded the power of the police chief to make unquestioned policy and personnel decisions. During the decade, chiefs of police commonly consulted with union leaders before making major decisions concerning departmental operations.

Although police operations improved markedly during this time, police departments were also beset by problems that impeded their effectiveness. State and local budgets were cut back during the Reagan administration, and federal support for innovative police programs was severely curtailed with the demise of the LEAA.

Police–community relations continued to be a major problem. Riots and incidents of urban conflict occurred in some of the nation's largest cities.[21] They triggered continual concern about what the police role should be, especially in inner-city neighborhoods.

Policing in the 1990s

The 1990s began on a sour note and ended with an air of optimism. The incident that helped change the face of U.S. policing occurred on March 3, 1991, when two African American men, Rodney King and Bryant Allen, were driving in Los Angeles. They refused to stop when signaled by a police car, instead increasing their speed. King, who was driving, was apparently drunk or on drugs. When police finally stopped the car, they delivered 56 baton blows and 6 kicks to King in a period of 2 minutes, producing 11 skull fractures, brain damage, and kidney damage. They did not realize that their actions were being videotaped by an observer, who later gave the tape to the media. The officers involved were tried and acquitted in a suburban court by an all-white jury. The acquittal set off 6 days of rioting in South Central Los Angeles, which was brought under control by the California National Guard. In total, 54 people were killed, 2,383 were known to have been injured, and 13,212 people were arrested.[22] The police officers involved in the beatings were later tried and convicted in federal court.

The King case prompted an era of reform. Several police experts decreed that the nation's police forces should be evaluated not on their crime-fighting ability but on their courteousness, deportment, and helpfulness. Interest renewed in reviving an earlier style of police work featuring foot patrols and increased citizen contact. Police departments began to embrace new forms of policing that stressed cooperation with the community and problem solving; this is referred to as the **community policing** model. Ironically, urban police departments began to shift their focus to becoming community organizers at a time when technological improvements increased the ability to identify suspects.

An ongoing effort was made to bring diversity to police departments, and African Americans began to be hired as chiefs of police, particularly in Los Angeles. As a result of the reform efforts, the intellectual caliber of the police rose dramatically, and they became smarter, better informed, and more sophisticated than ever before. Management skills became more sophisticated, and senior police managers began to implement sophisticated information technology systems. As a result, policing became intellectually more demanding, requiring specialized knowledge about technology, forensic analysis, and crime. Although a few notorious cases of police corruption and violence made headlines, by and large the police began to treat the public more fairly and more equitably than ever before.[23]

community policing
A law enforcement program that seeks to integrate officers into the local community to reduce crime and gain good community relations. It typically involves personalized service and decentralized policing, citizen empowerment, and an effort to reduce community fear of crime, disorder, and decay.

ThomsonNOW Improve your grade on the exam with Personalized Study! For reinforcement resources and a mastery check of modern era of policing, go to www.thomsonedu.com/thomsonnow.

♦ POLICING AND LAW ENFORCEMENT TODAY

Policing and law enforcement today are organized into four broad categories: federal, state, county, and local policing agencies (and many subcategories within).

The federal government has a number of law enforcement agencies designed to protect the rights and privileges of U.S. citizens. No single agency has unlimited jurisdiction, and each has been created to enforce specific laws and cope with particular situations. Federal police agencies have no particular rank order or hierarchy of command or responsibility, and each reports to a specific department or bureau.

The United States Justice Department

The U.S. Department of Justice is the legal arm of the federal government. Headed by the attorney general, it is empowered to enforce all federal laws, represent the United States when it is party to court action, and conduct independent investigations through its law enforcement services.

The Department of Justice maintains several separate divisions that are responsible for enforcing federal laws and protecting U.S. citizens. The Civil Rights Division proceeds legally against violations of federal civil rights laws that protect citizens from discrimination on the basis of their race, creed, ethnic background, age, or sex. Areas of greatest concern include discrimination in education, housing, and employment, including affirmative action cases. The Tax Division brings legal actions against tax violators. The Criminal Division prosecutes violations of the Federal Criminal Code. Its responsibility includes enforcing statutes relating to bank robbery (because bank deposits are federally insured), kidnapping, mail fraud, interstate transportation of stolen vehicles, and narcotics and drug trafficking.

Federal Bureau of Investigation (FBI)
The arm of the Justice Department that investigates violations of federal law, gathers crime statistics, runs a comprehensive crime laboratory, and helps train local law enforcement officers.

THE FEDERAL BUREAU OF INVESTIGATION The Justice Department first became involved in law enforcement when the attorney general hired investigators to enforce the Mann Act (forbidding the transportation of women between states for immoral purposes). These investigators were formalized in 1908 into a distinct branch of the government, the Bureau of Investigation. The agency was later reorganized into the **Federal Bureau of Investigation (FBI)**, under the direction of J. Edgar Hoover from its creation in 1924 until his death in 1972.

Today's FBI is not a police agency but an investigative agency with jurisdiction over all law enforcement matters in which the United States is or may be an interested party. However, its jurisdiction is limited to federal laws, including all federal statutes not specifically assigned to other agencies. Areas covered by these laws include espionage, sabotage, treason, civil rights violations, murder and assault of federal officers, mail fraud, robbery and burglary of federally insured banks, kidnapping, and interstate transportation of stolen vehicles and property. The FBI headquarters in Washington, D.C., oversees more than 50 field offices, approximately 400 satellite offices known as resident agencies, 4 specialized field installations, and more than 40 foreign liaison posts. The foreign liaison offices, each of which is headed by a legal attaché or legal liaison officer, work abroad with U.S. and local authorities on criminal matters within FBI jurisdiction. In all, the FBI has approximately 30,000 employees, including more than 12,000 special agents and 17,000 support personnel, who perform professional, administrative, technical, clerical, craft, trade, or maintenance operations.

The FBI offers a number of important services to local law enforcement agencies. Its identification division, established in 1924, collects and maintains a vast fingerprint file that can be used by local police agencies. Its sophisticated crime laboratory, established in 1932, aids local police in testing and identifying such evidence as hairs, fibers, blood, tire tracks, and drugs. The Uniform Crime Reports (UCR) is another service of the FBI. The UCR is an annual compilation of crimes reported to local police agencies, arrests, police killed or wounded in action, and other information. Finally, the FBI's National Crime Information Center is a computerized network linked to local police departments that provides ready information on stolen vehicles, wanted persons, stolen guns, and so on. The major activities of the FBI are described in Exhibit 5.1.

The FBI is a key element in the war against terrorism, but that is not all they do. FBI agents gather at Hidden Dreams Farm in Milford Township, Michigan on May 19, 2006, where they, along with archaeologists and anthropologists, searched for the body of former Teamsters labor union leader Jimmy Hoffa. It is believed that Hoffa, who disappeared in 1975, was murdered by Mafia leaders who did not want him to regain his leadership position. The FBI did not find any remains at the site, and the disappearance remains unsolved.

©AP Images/John M. Galloway

EXHIBIT 5.1

Divisions of the FBI

♦ The *National Security Division* coordinates investigative matters concerning foreign counter-intelligence and counterterrorism. Activities include investigations into espionage, overseas homicide, protection of foreign officials and guests, domestic security, and nuclear extortion.

♦ The *Criminal Investigative Division* coordinates investigations into illegal activities, including organized crime, violent crimes and property crimes of an interstate nature, crime on Native American reservations, crimes against U.S. citizens overseas, theft of government property, and white-collar crime.

♦ The *FBI Laboratory*, established in 1932, is one of the largest and most comprehensive crime laboratories in the world. Laboratory activities include crime scene searches, special surveillance photography, latent-fingerprint examinations, forensic examinations of evidence (including DNA testing), court testimony, and other scientific and technical services.

♦ The *Criminal Justice Information Services (CJIS) Division*, established in 1924, serves as the central repository for criminal justice information services in the FBI. The CJIS Division includes the Fingerprint Identification Program, the National Crime Information Center Program, the Uniform Crime Reporting Program, and the development of the Integrated Automated Fingerprint Identification System (IAFIS)—a new, computer-based system that can store, process, analyze, and

retrieve millions of fingerprints in a relatively short period of time.

♦ The *Information Resources Division (IRD)* provides centralized management and planning for information resources within the FBI. The IRD is responsible for the development of the National Crime Information Center (NCIC) 2000 project. The NCIC 2000 will enhance the existing NCIC system, which is used by federal, state, and local law enforcement agencies to locate wanted and missing persons, vehicles, boats, guns, and so on.

♦ The *Training Division* manages the FBI Academy and trains FBI special agents and professional support staff as well as local, state, federal, and international law enforcement personnel.

♦ The *Administrative Services Division* manages FBI and non-FBI background investigations. This division is responsible for the management and security of all FBI facilities, in addition to managing and providing executive direction in all aspects of FBI personnel management matters, including but not limited to personnel assistance, personnel benefits, and personnel selection.

♦ The *Critical Incident Response Group (CIRG)* provides rapid assistance to incidents in a crisis such as terrorist activities, hostage taking, barricaded persons, and other critical incidents. The CIRG comprises eight diverse units that provide operational support and training.

Source: FBI, "Organization" (http://www.fas.org/irp/agency/doj/fbi/org.htm), accessed on May 25, 2006.

The FBI mission has been evolving to keep pace with world events. With the end of the cold war and the reduction of East–West tension, the FBI's mission to investigate European-based spy rings has diminished. In some offices, agents have been reassigned to antiterror, antigang, and drug control efforts.[24]

Since the September 11, 2001, terrorist attacks, the FBI has dedicated itself to combating terrorism. The FBI has announced a reformulation of its priorities (see Exhibit 5.2), which makes protecting the United States from terrorist attack its number-one commitment. At the center of this initiative, the Counterterrorism Division collects, analyzes, and shares critical information and intelligence on (1) international terrorism operations both within the United States and in support of extraterritorial investigations, (2) domestic terrorism operations, and 3) counterterrorism relating to both international and domestic terrorism. Based in Washington, the Counterterrorism Division

♦ Manages a team of analysts who work to put together information gathered by the field offices.

EXHIBIT 5.2

Reformulated FBI Priorities

1. Protect the United States from terrorist attack.
2. Protect the United States against foreign intelligence operations and espionage.
3. Protect the United States against cyber-based attacks and high-technology crimes.
4. Combat public corruption at all levels.
5. Protect civil rights.
6. Combat transnational and national criminal organizations and enterprises.
7. Combat major white-collar crime.
8. Combat significant violent crime.
9. Support federal, state, local, and international partners.
10. Upgrade technology to successfully perform the FBI's mission.

Source: FBI (http://www.fbi.gov/priorities/priorities.htm).

♦ Operates a national threat warning system that allows the FBI to instantly distribute important terrorism alert bulletins to law enforcement agencies and public safety departments.

♦ Sends out "flying squads" of specially trained officers to provide counterterrorism knowledge and experience, language capabilities, and analytical support as needed to FBI field offices.

♦ Maintains the Joint Terrorism Task Force (JTTF), which includes representatives from the Department of Defense, Department of Energy, Federal Emergency Management Agency, Central Intelligence Agency, Customs Service, Secret Service, and the Immigration and Naturalization Service. Additionally, there are 66 local joint terrorism task forces in which representatives from federal agencies, state and local law enforcement personnel, and first responders work together to track down terrorists and prevent acts of terrorism in the United States.

Exhibit 5.3 describes some of the other actions the FBI has undertaken to combat terrorist activities.

BUREAU OF ALCOHOL, TOBACCO AND FIREARMS (ATF) The ATF helps control sales of untaxed liquor and cigarettes, and, through the Gun Control Act of 1968 and the Organized Crime Control Act of 1970, has jurisdiction over the illegal sale, importation, and criminal misuse of firearms and explosives. On January 24, 2003, ATF's law enforcement functions were transferred to the Department of Justice (DOJ), and ATF became the Bureau of Alcohol, Tobacco, Firearms and Explosives (ATF). ATF's strategic plan is currently being revised to reflect the agency's new name and mission and function within DOJ.

U.S. MARSHALS The Marshals Service is the nation's oldest federal law enforcement agency. Among its duties are the following:

♦ *Judicial security.* Protection of federal judicial officials, which includes judges, attorneys, and jurors. The Marshals Service also oversees each aspect of courthouse construction, from design through completion, to ensure the safety of federal judges, court personnel, and the public.

♦ *Fugitive investigations.* Working with law enforcement authorities at federal, state, local, and international levels, the Marshals Service apprehends thousands of dangerous felons each year. The Marshals Service is the primary agency responsible for tracking and extraditing fugitives who are apprehended in foreign countries and wanted for prosecution in the United States.

EXHIBIT 5.3

Key Near-Term Actions to Combat Terrorism

1. Restructure the Counterterrorism Division at FBI headquarters.
   - ◆ Redefine relationship between headquarters and field offices.
   - ◆ Shift from reactive to proactive orientation.
2. Establish "flying squads" to coordinate national and international investigations.
3. Establish national Joint Terrorism Task Force.
4. Substantially enhance analytical capabilities with personnel and technology.
   - ◆ Expand use of data mining, financial record analysis, and communications analysis to combat terrorism.

- ◆ Establish the Office of Intelligence.
5. Build a national terrorism response capability that is more mobile, agile, and flexible—for example, the use of flying squads and regional assets.
6. Permanently shift additional resources to the Counterterrorism Division.
7. Augment overseas capabilities and partnerships.
8. Target recruitment to acquire agents, analysts, translators, and others with specialized skills and backgrounds.
9. Enhance counterterrorism training for FBI and law enforcement partners.

Source: http://www.fas.org/irp/news/2002/05/fbi052902b.html.

- ◆ *Witness security.* The Marshals Service Witness Security Program ensures the safety of witnesses who risk their lives testifying for the government in cases involving organized crime and other significant criminal activity. Since 1970, the Marshals Service has protected, relocated, and given new identities to more than 7,500 witnesses.

- ◆ *Prisoner services.* The Marshals Service houses more than 47,000 federal unsentenced prisoners each day in federal, state, and local jails.

- ◆ *Justice prisoner and alien transportation system (JPATS).* In 1995 the air fleets of the Marshals Service and the Immigration and Naturalization Service merged to form a more efficient and effective system for transporting prisoners and criminal aliens.

- ◆ *Asset forfeiture program.* The Marshals Service is responsible for managing and disposing seized and forfeited properties acquired by criminals through illegal activities.

The Department of Homeland Security (DHS)

Following the September 11, 2001, attacks, a new cabinet-level agency called the **Department of Homeland Security (DHS)** received congressional approval and was assigned the mission of preventing terrorist attacks within the United States, reducing America's vulnerability to terrorism, and minimizing the damage and aiding the recovery from attacks that do occur. The DHS has a number of independent branches and bureaus:[25]

Department of Homeland Security (DHS)
A federal agency created to coordinate national efforts to prevent terrorist attacks from occurring within the United States, to respond if an attack takes place, and to reduce or minimize the damage from attacks that do happen.

1. The *Directorate for Preparedness* works with state, local, and private-sector partners to identify threats, determine vulnerabilities, and target resources where risk is greatest, thereby safeguarding our borders, seaports, bridges, highways, and critical information systems.

2. The *Directorate for Science and Technology* is the primary research and development arm of the department. It provides federal, state, and local officials with the technology and capabilities to protect the homeland.

3. The *Directorate for Management* is responsible for department budgets and appropriations, expenditure of funds, accounting and finance, procurement, human resources, information technology systems, facilities and equipment, and the identification and tracking of performance measurements.

President George W. Bush views a demonstration of a mock-attack on a bus while visiting the Northeastern Illinois Public Safety Training Academy in Glenview, Illinois. Homeland security and anti-terror preparedness is now being practiced by law enforcement agencies on the federal, state, county, and local levels.

4. The *Office of Intelligence and Analysis* is responsible for using information and intelligence from multiple sources to identify and assess current and future threats to the United States.

5. The *Office of Operations Coordination* is responsible for monitoring the security of the United States on a daily basis and coordinating activities within the department and with governors, Homeland Security advisors, law enforcement partners, and critical infrastructure operators in all 50 states and more than 50 major urban areas nationwide.

6. The *Directorate for Policy* is the primary policy formulation and coordination component for the Department of Homeland Security. It provides a centralized, coordinated focus to the development of department-wide, long-range planning to protect the United States.

7. The *Domestic Nuclear Detection Office* works to enhance the nuclear detection efforts of federal, state, territorial, tribal, and local governments, and the private sector, and to ensure a coordinated response to such threats.

8. The *Federal Emergency Management Agency (FEMA)* prepares the nation for hazards, manages federal response and recovery efforts following any national incident, and administers the National Flood Insurance Program.

9. The *Transportation Security Administration (TSA)* protects the nation's transportation systems to ensure freedom of movement for people and commerce.

10. *Customs and Border Protection* is responsible for protecting our nation's borders in order to prevent terrorists and terrorist weapons from entering the United States, while improving the flow of legitimate trade and travel.

11. *Immigration and Customs Enforcement (ICE)*, the largest investigative arm of the Department of Homeland Security, is responsible for identifying and shutting down vulnerabilities in the nation's border, economic, transportation, and infrastructure security.

12. *Federal Law Enforcement Training Center* provides career-long training to law enforcement professionals to help them fulfill their responsibilities safely and proficiently.

13. *Citizenship and Immigration Services* is responsible for the administration of immigration and naturalization adjudication functions and establishing immigration services, policies, and priorities.

14. The *U.S. Coast Guard* protects the public, the environment, and U.S. economic interests in the nation's ports and waterways, along the coast, on international waters, or in any maritime region as required to support national security.

15. The *U.S. Secret Service* protects the president and other high-level officials and investigates counterfeiting and other financial crimes, including financial institution fraud, identity theft, computer fraud, and computer-based attacks on our nation's financial, banking, and telecommunications infrastructure.

DHS is the third-largest cabinet department in the U.S. federal government after the Department of Defense and Department of Veterans Affairs. It has approximately 180,000 employees.

State Law Enforcement Agencies

Unlike municipal police departments, state police were legislatively created to deal with the growing incidence of crime in nonurban areas, a consequence of the increase in population mobility and the advent of personalized mass transportation in the form of the automobile. County sheriffs—elected officials with occasionally corrupt or questionable motives—had proven to be ineffective in dealing with the wide-ranging criminal activities that developed during the latter half of the nineteenth century. In addition, most local police agencies were unable to effectively protect against highly mobile lawbreakers who randomly struck at cities and towns throughout a state. In response to citizens' demands for effective and efficient law enforcement, state governors began to develop plans for police agencies that would be responsible to the state, instead of being tied to local politics and possible corruption.

The Texas Rangers, created in 1835, was one of the first state police agencies formed. Essentially a military outfit that patrolled the Mexican border, it was followed by the Massachusetts state constables in 1865 and the Arizona Rangers in 1901. Pennsylvania formed the first truly modern state police in 1905.[26]

Today, about 23 state police agencies have the same general police powers as municipal police and are territorially limited in their exercise of law enforcement regulations only by the state's boundaries. The remaining state police agencies are primarily responsible for highway patrol and traffic law enforcement. Some state police, such as those in California, direct most of their attention to the enforcement of traffic laws. Most state police organizations are restricted by legislation from becoming involved in the enforcement of certain areas of the law. For example, in some jurisdictions, state police are prohibited from becoming involved in strikes or other labor disputes, unless violence erupts.

The nation's 80,000 state police employees (55,000 officers and 25,000 civilians) are not only involved in law enforcement and highway safety but also carry out a variety of functions, including maintaining a training academy and providing emergency medical services. State police crime laboratories aid local departments in investigating crime scenes and analyzing evidence. State police also provide special services and technical expertise in such areas as bomb-site analysis and homicide investigation. Other state police departments, such as California's, are involved in highly sophisticated traffic and highway safety programs, including the use of helicopters for patrol and rescue, the testing of safety devices for cars, and the conducting of postmortem examinations to determine the causes of fatal accidents.

State-Level Antiterror Activities

In the wake of the 9/11 attacks, a number of states have created antiterror agencies to beef up their intelligence-gathering capabilities and aimed them directly at homeland security. California has introduced the California Anti-Terrorism Information Center (CATIC), a statewide intelligence system designed to combat terrorism. It divides the state into five zones and links federal, state, and local information services in one system. Trained intelligence analysts operate within civil rights guidelines and use information in a secure communications system; information is analyzed daily.[27] CATIC combines machine intelligence with information coming from a variety of police agencies. The information is correlated and organized by analysts looking for trends. Rather than simply operating as an information-gathering unit, CATIC is a synthesizing process. It combines open-source public information with data on criminal trends and possible terrorist activities. Processed intelligence is designed to produce threat assessments for each area and to project trends outside the jurisdiction. The CATIC system attempts to process multiple sources of information to predict threats. By centralizing the collection and analytical sections of a statewide system, California's Department of Justice may have developed a method for moving offensively against terrorism.

California is not alone in implementing antiterror legislation. Alabama is the first state in the nation to create its own legislatively enacted cabinet-level Department of Homeland Security. Its mission is to protect lives, safeguard property, and, if required, to respond to any acts of terrorism occurring in Alabama. To accomplish this mission, the Alabama Department of Homeland Security works closely with both public and private sector stakeholders in a wide range of disciplines: law enforcement, emergency management, emergency medical, fire services, public works, agriculture, public health, public safety communications, environmental management, military, transportation, and more. Since its inception, the Alabama Department of Homeland Security has administered more than $100 million in federally appropriated homeland security grants.[28]

County Law Enforcement Agencies

The county sheriff's role has evolved from that of the early English shire reeve, whose primary duty was to assist the royal judges in trying prisoners and enforcing sentences. From the time of the westward expansion in the United States until municipal departments were developed, the sheriff was often the sole legal authority over vast territories.

Today, more than 3,000 sheriffs' offices operate nationwide, employing more than 330,000 full-time staffers, including about 155,000 sworn personnel.[29] Nearly all sheriffs' offices provide basic law enforcement services such as routine patrol (97 percent), responding to citizen calls for service (95 percent), and investigating crimes (92 percent).[30]

The duties of a county sheriff's department vary according to the size and degree of development of the county. The standard tasks of a typical sheriff's department are serving civil process (summons and court orders), providing court security, operating the county jail, and investigating crimes. Less commonly, sheriffs' departments may serve as coroners, tax collectors, overseers of highways and bridges, custodians of the county treasury, and providers of fire, animal control, and emergency medical services. In years past, sheriffs' offices also conducted executions. Typically, a sheriff department's law enforcement functions are restricted to unincorporated areas within a county, unless a city or town police department requests its help.

Some sheriffs' departments are exclusively law enforcement oriented; some carry out only court-related duties; some are involved solely in correctional and judicial matters and not in law enforcement. However, a majority are full-service programs that carry out judicial, correctional, and law enforcement activities. As a rule, agencies serving large population areas (more than one million people) are devoted to maintaining county correctional facilities, whereas those in smaller population areas are focused on law enforcement.

In the past, sheriffs' salaries were almost always based on the fees they received for the performance of official acts. They received fees for every summons, warrant, subpoena, writ, or other process they served. They were also compensated for summoning juries or locking prisoners in cells. Today, sheriffs are salaried to avoid conflict of interest.

COUNTY ANTITERROR ACTIVITIES In addition to traditional law enforcement, some counties are now engaging in antiterror and homeland security activities. For example, the Harris County Office of Homeland Security & Emergency Management (OHSEM) in Texas is responsible for an emergency management plan that prepares for public recovery in the event of natural or manmade disasters, catastrophes, or attacks. It works in conjunction with federal, state, and local authorities, including the city of Houston and other municipalities in the surrounding Harris County area when required. If needed, OHSEM activates an emergency operations center to allow coordination of all support agencies and provide continuity of services to the public. OHSEM is responsible for advisement, notification, and assembly of services that are in the best interest of the citizens of Harris County. It prepares and distributes information and procedures governing the same.[31] Similarly, in Maryland, Montgomery County's Homeland Security Department plans for, prevents, and protects against major threats that may harm, disrupt, or destroy the community, its commerce, and its institutions. The mission is to effectively manage and coordinate the county's unified response, mitigation, and recovery from the consequences of such disasters or events should they occur. It also serves to educate the public on emergency preparedness for all hazards, and it conducts outreach to diverse and special populations to protect, secure, and sustain critical infrastructures to ensure the continuity of essential services.[32]

Metropolitan Law Enforcement Agencies

Local police make up the majority of the nation's authorized law enforcement personnel. Metropolitan police departments range in size from the New York City Police Department, with almost 40,000 full-time officers and 10,000 civilian employees, to rural police departments, which may have only a single part-time officer. Today, local police departments have more than 450,000 sworn personnel.[33] In addition to sworn personnel, many police agencies hire civilian employees who bring special skills to the department. For example, in this computer age, departments often employ information resource managers, who are charged with improving data processing, integrating the department's computer information database with others in the state, operating computer-based fingerprint identification systems and other high-tech investigative devices, and linking with national computer systems such as the FBI's national crime information system, which holds the records of millions of criminal offenders. To carry out these tasks, local departments employ an additional 130,000 civilians, bringing the entire number to more than 580,000 people.

Most TV police shows feature the work of big-city police officers, but an overwhelming number of departments have fewer than 50 officers and serve a population of less than 25,000. About 70 law enforcement agencies employ 1,000 or more full-time sworn personnel, including 48 local police departments with 1,000 or more officers. These agencies account for about one-third of all local police officers. In contrast, nearly 800 departments employ just one officer.

Regardless of their size, most individual metropolitan police departments perform a standard set of functions and tasks and provide similar services to the community. These include the following:

- ◆ Traffic enforcement
- ◆ Narcotics and vice control
- ◆ Accident investigation
- ◆ Radio communications
- ◆ Patrol and peacekeeping
- ◆ Crime prevention
- ◆ Property and violent crime investigation
- ◆ Fingerprint processing
- ◆ Death investigation
- ◆ Search and rescue

The police role is expanding, so procedures must be developed to aid special-needs populations, including AIDS-infected suspects, the homeless, and victims of domestic and child abuse.

These are only a few examples of the multiplicity of roles and duties assumed today in some of the larger urban police agencies around the nation. Smaller agencies can have trouble carrying out these tasks effectively. The hundreds of small police agencies in each state often provide duplicative services. Whether unifying smaller police agencies into superagencies would improve services is often debated among police experts. Smaller municipal agencies can

PERSPECTIVES ON JUSTICE

Crime Control Versus Restorative Justice

Police departments are evolving because leaders recognize that traditional crime control–oriented models have not been effective. In the future, the police role may shift to a more restorative justice emphasis, moving away from a legalistic style that isolates officers from the public to a service orientation that holds officers accountable to the community and encourages them to learn from the people they serve. This means that the police must actively create a sense of community where none has existed and recruit neighborhood cooperation for crime prevention activities.

provide important specialized services that might have to be relinquished if they were combined and incorporated into larger departments. Another approach has been to maintain smaller departments but to link them via computerized information-sharing and resource-management networks.[34]

MUNICIPAL-LEVEL ANTITERROR ACTIVITIES   Since 9/11, a number of local law enforcement agencies have responded to the threat of terrorism by creating special antiterror programs. New York City, one of the main targets of the 9/11 attacks, has established a new Counterterrorism Bureau.[35] Teams within the bureau have been trained to examine potential targets in the city and are now attempting to insulate them from possible attack. Viewed as prime targets are the city's bridges, the Empire State Building, the Rockefeller Center, and the United Nations building. Bureau detectives are assigned overseas to work with the police in several foreign cities, including ones in Canada and Israel. Detectives have been assigned as liaisons with the FBI and with Interpol, in Lyon, France. The city is now recruiting detectives with language skills from Pashtun and Urdu to Arabic, Fujianese, and other dialects. The existing New York City Police Intelligence Division has been revamped, and agents are examining foreign newspapers and monitoring Internet sites. The department is also setting up several backup command centers in different parts of the city in case a terror attack puts headquarters out of operation. Several backup senior command teams have been created so that if people at the highest levels of the department are killed, individuals will already have been tapped to step into their jobs.

The Counterterrorism Bureau has assigned more than 100 city police detectives to work with FBI agents as part of a Joint Terrorist Task Force. In addition, the Intelligence Division's 700 investigators now devote 35 to 40 percent of their resources to counterterrorism, up from about 2 percent before January 2002. The department is also drawing on the expertise of other institutions around the city. For example, medical specialists have been enlisted to monitor daily developments in the city's hospitals to detect any suspicious outbreaks of illness that might reflect a biological attack. And the police are now conducting joint drills with the New York Fire Department to avoid the problems in communication and coordination that marked the emergency response on September 11, 2001.

ThomsonNOW Improve your grade on the exam with Personalized Study! For reinforcement resources and a mastery check of today's law enforcement, go to www. thomsonedu.com/thomsonnow.

◆ PRIVATE POLICING

Supplementing local police forces is a burgeoning private security industry. Private security service has become a multi-billion-dollar industry with 10,000 firms and 1.5 million employees. Even federal police services have been privatized to cut expenses.

Some private security firms have become billion-dollar companies. The Wackenhut Corporation is the U.S.-based division of Group 4 Securicor, the world's second-largest provider of security services. Among its clients are a number of Fortune 500 companies. It has several subsidiaries that work for the federal government. For example, Wackenhut Services Incorporated (WSI) is a primary contractor to NASA and the Army. Wackenhut also provides security and emergency response services to local governments—for example, helping them guard their public transport systems. Wackenhut helps the U.S. government protect nuclear reactors, guards the Trans-Alaska Pipeline System, and maintains security in closed government facilities. It maintains a Custom Protection Officer Division, made up of highly trained uniformed security officers who are assigned to highly critical or complex facilities or situations requiring special skills in such places as government buildings, banks, and other special situations. (The Careers in Criminal Justice feature discusses a career in the private security area.)

There will be more legal scrutiny as the private security business blossoms. A number of questions remain to be answered. One important issue is whether security guards are subject to the same search and seizure standards as police officers. The U.S. Supreme Court has repeatedly stated that purely private search activities do not violate the Fourth Amendment's prohibitions. Might security guards be subject to Fourth Amendment requirements if they are performing services that are traditionally reserved for the police, such as guarding communities?

ThomsonNOW Improve your grade on the exam with Personalized Study! For reinforcement resources and a mastery check of private policing, go to www.thomsonedu.com/thomsonnow.

◆ TECHNOLOGY AND LAW ENFORCEMENT

Budget realities demand that police leaders make the most effective use of their forces, and technology seems to be an important method of increasing productivity at a relatively low cost. The introduction of technology has already been explosive. In 1964, only one city, St. Louis, had a police computer system; by 1968, 10 states and 50 cities had state-level criminal justice information systems; today, almost every city of more than 50,000 people has some sort of computer-support services.[36] Local police departments, even in the smallest jurisdictions, now rely on computers in the field to link patrol officers with law enforcement databases (see Figure 5.1), and this capability has grown considerably during the past decade.

Police officers now trained to prevent burglaries may someday have to learn to create high-tech forensic labs that can identify suspects involved in the theft of genetically engineered cultures from biomedical labs.[37] Criminal investigation will be enhanced by the application of sophisticated electronic gadgetry: computers, cellular phones, and digital communication devices. Where else has technology affected law enforcement?

For news about police technology and other related issues, go to the Police Officer Internet Directory. You can reach this site by going to the Siegel/Senna Introduction to Criminal Justice 11e website: www.thomsonedu.com/criminaljustice/siegel.

Identifying Criminals

Police are becoming more sophisticated in their use of computer software to identify and convict criminals. One of the most important computer-aided tasks is the identification of criminal suspects. Computers now link neighboring agencies so they can share information on cases, suspects, and warrants. On a broader jurisdictional level, the FBI implemented the National Crime Information Center in 1967. This system provides rapid collection and retrieval of data about persons wanted for crimes anywhere in the 50 states.

Some police departments are using computerized imaging systems to replace mug books. Photos or sketches are stored in computer memory and are easily retrieved for viewing. Several software companies have developed identification programs that help witnesses create a composite picture of the perpetrator. A vast library of photographed or drawn facial features can be stored in computer files and accessed on a terminal screen. Witnesses can scan through thousands of noses, eyes, and lips until they find those that match the suspect's. Eyeglasses, mustaches, and beards can be added; skin tones can be altered. When the composite is created, an attached camera prints a hard copy for distribution.

In an effort to identify crime patterns and link them to suspects, some departments have begun to use computer software to conduct analysis of behavior patterns, a process called

FIGURE 5.1

Trends in the Percentage of Police Departments Using Computers in the Field

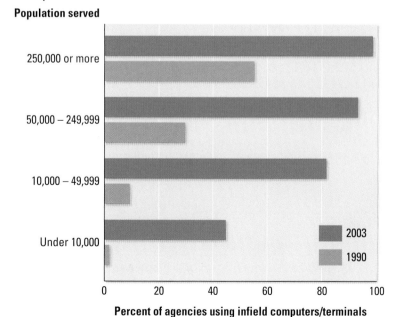

Population served

Percent of agencies using infield computers/terminals

Legend: 2003, 1990

Source: Matthew Hickman and Brian Reaves, *Local Police Departments, 2003* (http://www.ojp.usdoj.gov.bjs/pub/pdf/1pd03.pdf), accessed on June 15, 2006.

Private Security Guard

Duties and Characteristics of the Job

Private security guards or security officers are hired by companies to protect goods, people, and/or places against illegal acts. Depending on exactly where they work, their job may be to deter crimes that threaten the safety and comfort of people and their surroundings, such as trespassing, theft, or even terrorism. They may also prevent the theft or destruction of items belonging to public and private businesses and organizations. Private security guards also ensure that entertainment events such as sporting events and concerts run smoothly and safely.

The actual duties that private security guards perform depend on where they work. They may patrol grounds, restrict access to buildings, or use security equipment to monitor facilities and enforce rules. For example, if weapons are not permitted at their site, they may use a metal detector to ensure that potential visitors are not carrying weapons.

Private security guards may be asked to write reports of illegal events that occurred during their shift or take part in legal actions resulting from illegal behavior they observed. Finally, preventing and/or leading a response to events such as fires or other emergencies is also a common job responsibility.

A typical private security guard will work five 8-hour shifts for a total of 40 hours a week. Because many places need security around the clock, nighttime and weekend hours may be an option.

Job Outlook

Security has become and continues to be a growing concern for schools, apartments, large businesses, museums, and important government buildings. This concern is especially present in urban and suburban areas. Because of this, job opportunities will be most plentiful there.

Salary

Median annual salary for security guards is $20,320. The majority of security guards earn between $16,640 and $25,510 per year. At the extremes, a small percentage of security guards will earn around $14,390, and the highest paid will earn more than $33,270. In general, armed guards will enjoy higher pay,

---

data mining
Using sophisticated computer software to conduct analysis of behavior patterns in an effort to identify crime patterns and link them to suspects.

data mining.[38] By discovering patterns in crimes such as burglary, especially those involving multiple offenders, computer programs can be programmed to recognize a particular way of working at crime and thereby identify suspects most likely to fit the working profile.

Crime Scene Investigation

Using advanced technology to analyze crime scenes has caught the public interest now that *CSI*-type programs are routine TV fare. But in truth, CSI technology is now undergoing considerable change as cyber capabilities are being added to the investigator's bag of tricks.[39]

Traditionally, to investigate and evaluate a crime scene, detectives relied on photographic evidence and two-dimensional drawings. However, it can be difficult to visualize the positional relationships of evidence with two-dimensional tools. Now, through a combination of laser and computer technology, high-definition surveying (HDS) creates a virtual crime scene that allows investigators to maneuver every piece of evidence.

High-definition surveying gives law enforcement a complete picture of a crime scene. HDS reflects a laser light off objects in the crime scene and back to a digital sensor, creating three-dimensional spatial coordinates that are calculated and stored using algebraic equations. An HDS device projects light in the form of a laser in a 360-degree horizontal circumference, measuring millions of points and creating a "point cloud." The data points are bounced back to the receiver, collected, converted, and used to create a virtual image of any location. A personal computer can now take the data file and project that site onto any screen.

benefits, greater job security, and more opportunities for advancement.

Opportunities

Due to a growing demand for security services and high turnover rates, the outlook for those who aim to be career security guards is favorable both in opportunities for employment and advancement. Despite this, those seeking more desirable positions, such as those that pay better and require more training, should be aware that they will face competition for these coveted jobs. Additionally, many individuals, especially from the law enforcement field, take part-time security positions to supplement their salary or after retiring.

Qualifications

In most states, a security guard will need to be licensed in order to work. This means that an individual will need to be at least 18 years old, pass a background check, and complete relevant educational training. A potential security guard may also be continually expected to pass drug tests. Qualifications may be stricter depending upon the level of risk and responsibility associated with the position. In general, a high school diploma is necessary for these positions. Security guards should possess certain characteristics, such as responsibility, good physical and mental health, and also communications skills if they will interact with the public. They must be willing to follow and enforce the rules of their employer.

Education and Training

The amount and type of training a future security guard will receive vary greatly, depending upon the specific duties and the environment in which the guard will work. In some states, in order to be a licensed guard some educational training on job-relevant issues such as property rights must be completed. Armed guards will need to be licensed and may receive some police training.

Source: "Security Guards and Gaming Surveillance Officers," *Occupational Outlook Handbook,* 2006–2007 edition (Bureau of Labor Statistics, United States Department of Labor), retrieved May 25, 2006, from http://www.bls.gov/oco/ocos159.htm.

Not only does HDS technology allow the crime scene to be preserved exactly, but the perspective can also be manipulated to provide additional clues. For instance, if the crime scene is the front room of an apartment, the three-dimensional image allows the investigator to move around and examine different points of view. Or, if a victim was found seated, an investigator can see and show a jury what the victim might have seen just before the crime occurred. If witnesses outside said that they looked in a living room window, an investigator can zoom around and view what the witnesses could or could not have seen through that window.

HDS technology can also limit crime scene contamination. Investigators may inadvertently touch an object at a crime scene, leaving their fingerprints, or they may move or take evidence from the scene, perhaps by picking up fibers on their shoes. Evidence is compromised if moved or disturbed from its resting place, which may contaminate the scene and undermine the case. HDS technology is a "stand-off" device, allowing investigators to approach the scene in stages by scanning from the outer perimeter and moving inward, reducing the chances of contamination. The investigative and prosecutorial value of virtual crime scenes is evident. If an HDS device is used at the scene, detectives, prosecutors, and juries can return to a crime scene in its preserved state. Showing a jury exactly what a witness could or could not have seen can be very valuable.

Crime Mapping

It is now recognized that there are geographic "hot spots" where a majority of predatory crimes are concentrated.[40] Computer mapping programs that can

Technology is becoming commonplace in law enforcement not only in big cities, but also in suburban and rural areas. Here, Lake County, Ohio, Sheriff Deputy Keith Rohrbaugh views a map from the county's Geographical Information System, which provides detailed address information on residents living within 1,000 feet of a school. He will use this information to notify residents of any registered sex offenders in the area.

translate addresses into map coordinates allow departments to identify problem areas for particular crimes, such as drug dealing. Computer maps allow police to identify the location, time of day, and linkage among criminal events and to concentrate their forces accordingly. Figure 5.2 illustrates a typical crime map that is now being used in Providence, Rhode Island.

Crime maps offer police administrators graphic representations of where crimes are occurring in their jurisdiction. Computerized crime mapping gives the police the power to analyze and correlate a wide array of data to create immediate, detailed visuals of crime patterns. The simplest maps display crime locations or concentrations and can be used to help direct patrols to the places they are most needed. More-complex maps can be used to chart trends in criminal activity, and some have even proven valuable in solving individual criminal cases. For example, a serial rapist may be caught by observing and understanding the patterns of his crime so that detectives may predict where he will strike next and stake out the area with police decoys.

Crime mapping makes use of new computer technology. Instead of archaic pin maps, computerized crime mappings let the police detect crime patterns and pathologies of related problems. It enables them to work with multiple layers of information and scenarios, and thus identify emerging hot spots of criminal activity far more successfully and target resources accordingly.

A number of the nation's largest departments are now using mapping techniques. The New York City Police Department's CompStat process relies on computerized crime mapping to identify crime hot spots. The Chicago Police Department has developed ICAM (Information Collection for Automated Mapping), designed to help police officers in analyzing and solving neighborhood crime problems. ICAM, operational in all of the department's 25 police districts, lets beat officers and other police personnel quickly and easily generate maps of timely, accurate crime data for their beats and larger units. The police use the information they develop to support the department's community policing philosophy.

Some mapping efforts cross jurisdictional boundaries. Examples of this approach include the Regional Crime Analysis System in the greater Baltimore–Washington area and the multijurisdictional efforts of the Greater Atlanta PACT Data Center. The Charlotte–Mecklenburg Police Department (North Carolina) uses data collected by other city and county agencies in its crime mapping efforts. By coordinating the tax assessor's, public works, planning, and sanitation departments, these police department analysts have made links between disorder and crime that have been instrumental in supporting the department's community policing philosophy.

Crime maps alone may not be a panacea that allows police agencies to significantly improve their effectiveness. Many officers are uncertain about how to read maps and assess their data. To maximize the potential of this new technique, police agencies need to invest in training and infrastructure to allow the full capabilities of crime mapping to have an impact on their service efficiency.

ALTERNATIVE MAPPING INITIATIVES Mapping may soon serve other purposes than resource allocation. Law enforcement officials in the state of Washington are now developing a new Internet-based mapping system that will provide critical information about public infrastructures to help them handle terrorist or emergency situations. The new initiative, known as the Critical Incident Planning and Mapping System, is expected to provide access to tactical response

FIGURE 5.2
Violent Crime in Providence, Rhode Island

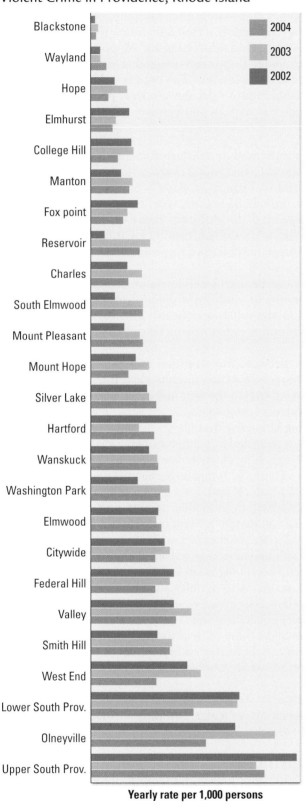

Yearly rate per 1,000 persons

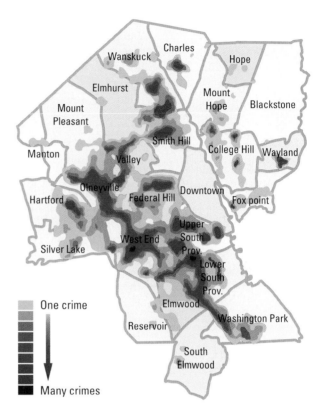

Source: Provident Plan (www.provplan.org).

plans, satellite imagery, photos, floor plans, and hazardous chemical locations.[41] In West Virginia, local and state government entities are working with private firms to develop an emergency 911 system that can pinpoint the location of callers if they are unable to speak English, if they are unconscious, or even if they hang up. The West Virginia Statewide Addressing and Mapping Board is using geospatial information technology to produce maps that show a caller's exact locations by a given number and street name. The project is designed to reduce emergency response times and improve disaster recovery planning, floodplain mapping, security, evacuation routing, counterterrorism efforts, crime analysis, and more.[42]

biometrics
Automated methods of recognizing a person based on a physiological or behavioral characteristic.

BIOMETRICS **Biometrics** is defined as automated methods of recognizing a person based on a physiological or behavioral characteristic.[43] Some biometric measures, such as fingerprint identification, have been used for years by law enforcement to identify criminals. However, recent improvements in computer technology have expanded the different types of measures that can be used for identification. Biometrics is now used to identify individuals based on voice, retina, facial features, and handwriting identification, just to name a few.

The field of biometrics can be used by all levels of government, including the military and law enforcement, and is also helpful in private businesses. Financial institutions, retail shopping, and health and social fields can all use biometrics as a way to limit access to financial information or to secure Internet sites.

As opposed to current personal identification methods such as personal identification numbers (PINs) used for bank machines and Internet transactions, biometric authenticators are unique to the user and as a result cannot be stolen and used without that individual's knowledge.

The process of recording biometric data occurs in four steps. First, the raw biometric data is captured or recorded by a video camera or a fingerprint reading device. Second, the distinguishing characteristics of the raw data are used to create a biometric template. Third, the template is changed into a mathematical representation of the biometric sample and is stored in a database. Finally, a verification process will occur when an individual attempts to gain access to a restricted site. The individual will have to present his or her fingerprint or retina to be read and then matched to the biometric sample on record. Once verification is made, the individual will have access to restricted areas. Currently, a number of programs are in effect. The Immigration and Naturalization Service (INS, now ICE) has been using hand geometry systems at major U.S. airports to check frequent international travelers. Law enforcement agencies now have access to the automatic fingerprint identification system (AFIS), which can match a sample fingerprint with a national database of fingerprints with no human interaction. Casinos around the country have started to implement facial recognition software into their buildings to notify them when a known cheater has entered their premises.

The field of biometrics appears to be growing every day in response to breaches in security in major industries and in government. Biometrics is further discussed in the Criminal Justice and Technology feature on page 186.

Automated Fingerprint Identification Systems

The use of computerized automated fingerprint identification systems (AFIS) is growing in the United States. Using mathematical models, AFIS can classify fingerprints and identify up to 250 characteristics (minutiae) of the print. These automated systems use high-speed silicon chips to plot each point of minutiae and count the number of ridge lines between that point and its four nearest neighbors, which substantially improves their speed and accuracy over earlier systems.

Some police departments report that computerized fingerprint systems are allowing them to make over 100 identifications per month from fingerprints taken at crime scenes. AFIS files have been regionalized. For example, the Western Identification Network (WIN) consists of eight central site members (Alaska, Idaho, Montana, Nevada, Oregon, Utah, Wyoming, and Portland Police Bureau), two interface members (California and Washington), multiple local members, and six federal members (Drug Enforcement Administration, Federal Bureau of Investigation, Immigration and Naturalization Service, Internal Revenue Service, Postal Inspection Service, and Secret Service).[44] When it first began, the system had a centralized automated database of 900,000 fingerprint records; today, with the addition of new jurisdictions (Alaska, California, and Washington), the system's number of searchable fingerprint records has increased to more than 14,000,000. Technology is constantly improving the effectiveness and reliability of the AFIS system, making it easier to use and more efficient in identifying suspects.[45]

DNA Testing

DNA profiling, a procedure that gained national attention during the O. J. Simpson trial, allows suspects to be identified on the basis of the genetic material found in hair, blood, and other bodily tissues and fluids. When DNA is used as evidence in a rape trial, DNA segments are taken from the victim, the suspect, and blood and semen found on the victim. A DNA match indicates a four-billion-to-one likelihood that the suspect is the offender.

Every U.S. state and nearly every industrialized country now maintains DNA databases of convicted offenders.[46] These databases allow comparison of crime scene DNA to samples taken at other crime scenes and to known offenders. The United States has more than three million samples of offenders/arrestees in its state and federal DNA databases. The United States is not alone in gathering this material: Great Britain requires that almost any violation of law enforcement result in the collection of DNA of the violator.[47]

Two methods of DNA matching are used. The most popular technique, known as *RFLP* (restriction fragment length polymorphism), uses radioactive material to produce a DNA image on an X-ray film. The second method, *PCR* (polymerase chain reaction), amplifies DNA samples through molecular photocopying.[48]

DNA fingerprinting is now used as evidence in criminal trials in more than 20 states.[49] The use of DNA evidence to gain convictions has also been upheld on appeal.[50] Its use in criminal trials received a boost in 1997, when the FBI announced that the evidence has become so precise that experts no longer have to supply a statistical estimate of accuracy while testifying at trial ("The odds are a billion to one that this is the culprit"); they can now state in court that there exists "a reasonable degree of scientific certainty" that the evidence came from a single suspect.[51]

Leading the way in the development of the most advanced forensic techniques is the Forensic Science Research and Training Center, operated by the FBI in Washington, D.C., and Quantico, Virginia. The lab provides information and services to hundreds of crime labs throughout the United States. The National Institute of Justice is also sponsoring research to identify a wider variety of DNA segments for testing and is involved in developing a PCR-based DNA-profiling examination using fluorescent detection that will reduce the time required for DNA profiling. The FBI is now operating the DNA Index System (NDIS), a computerized database that will allow DNA taken at a crime scene to be searched electronically to find matches against samples taken from convicted offenders and from other crime scenes. The first database will allow suspects to be identified, and the second will allow investigators to establish links between crimes, such as those involving serial killers or rapists. In 1999 the FBI announced that the system made its first "cold hit" by linking evidence taken from crime scenes in Jacksonville, Florida, to ones in Washington, D.C.,

www Check out the Western Identification Network website. You can access this site by going to the Siegel/Senna Introduction to Criminal Justice 11e website: www.thomsonedu.com/criminaljustice/siegel.

www Want to work with automated fingerprint identification system files? Go to AFIS, which has links to numerous information pages. You can reach it by going to the Siegel/Senna Introduction to Criminal Justice 11e website: www.thomsonedu.com/criminaljustice/siegel.

DNA profiling
The identification of criminal suspects by matching DNA samples taken from their person with specimens found at the crime scene.

Using Biometrics to Fight Terrorism

Since the terrorist attacks of September 11, 2001, added security measurements have been installed to help protect the country's citizens. Biometrics, the science of using digital technology to identify individuals, has been implemented in many facets of the country's security system. Biometric technology has been installed in both airports and immigration centers to ensure that people are not using fake identities for illegal behavior.

Airports

Airports have started to implement the use of biometrics into their systems to prevent nonemployees from entering secured locations, and biometrics also allows for the control of access of passengers onto airplanes. For example, the most popular type of biometrics being used within airports is iris scanning. While you are looking into a camera, a computer scans your eye, records information regarding your iris, and stores the information into a database. Once your eye has been scanned, you are then permitted onto the plane. In order to depart from the plane at your destination, your iris scan must match the one in the database to ensure that you are the person who is supposed to be departing the plane. For those who travel frequently, this procedure has proved effective, not requiring the individual to continuously stop at checkpoints and have identification examined; the person simply looks into a camera and within seconds is permitted to pass through all the checkpoints.

In addition, an airport in Charlotte, North Carolina, has used the system to keep unwanted individuals from entering secure facilities. When swipe cards and/or codes were used, people could sneak in behind personnel to gain entry into an area; however, this is no longer a problem with the use of biometrics. Employees of the Charlotte airport have their irises scanned, and the information remains in a database. In order to access the secured areas, personnel must look into a tube and have their match confirmed. Although fingerprints have also been used for this purpose, an iris scan can match more than 400 different points of identification, compared to the only 60–70 points of a fingerprint.

Other airports have incorporated another type of biometric technology within their security system: facial recognition. Facial recognition systems measure facial features of people, noting the distance of one feature from another, along with sizes of features, etc. An airport in Florida uses a facial recognition system that contains the images of the FBI's Top Ten Most Wanted, along with other sought-after individuals. Passengers are required to look into cameras to verify that they do not match any of the images in the system. If no matches are found, passengers are permitted to pass through and board their airplane. There is hope that with the continued success of this system, facial recognition systems will help locate fugitives, terrorists, and abducted children who are passing through transportation terminals.

Immigration

The Department of Homeland Security has implemented the United States Visitor and Immigrant Status Indicator Technology (US-Visit). US-Visit was developed to provide more security to the nation's airports while keeping transportation into and out

If you want to read more about the science of DNA testing, go to "DNA Testing." You can access this site by going to the Siegel/Senna Introduction to Criminal Justice 11e website: www.thomsonedu.com/criminaljustice/siegel.

thereby tying nine crimes to a single offender.[52] When Timothy Spence was executed in Virginia on April 27, 1994, he was the first person convicted and executed almost entirely on the basis of DNA evidence.[53]

Communications

Computer technology is now commonplace in policing. Officers routinely and effectively use mobile-computer systems and other information technology (IT) devices to gather information from and transmit information about criminal incidents to local, state, and national criminal information systems (Figure 5.3).[54]

Many larger departments have equipped officers with portable computers, which significantly cut down the time needed to write and duplicate reports. Police can now use terminals to draw accident diagrams, communicate with city traffic engineers, and merge their incident reports into other databases.

Future Technology

New investigation techniques are constantly being developed. Here are three examples:

of the country open. This is accomplished by using biometric scans to determine the identity of all travelers from foreign countries who attempt to enter the United States.

Almost all foreign citizens, regardless of country of origin, who wish to travel into the United States must comply with US-Visit requirements. The process of registering for travel into the United States under the new US-Visit program starts far from U.S. soil. Individuals who wish to travel to the United States must first visit the U.S. consular office in their country and apply for a visa. When they apply for the visa, they will have their biometrics collected in two separate ways. First, photographs will be taken of every applicant, and those photographs will be entered into the US-Visit database, along with digital finger scans. The digital finger scans will be taken of both the right and left index fingers of the applicant. This information will be loaded into a database and then checked to see if the individual matches any criminal or suspected terrorist already in the system.

Once an applicant passes the database check, she can be issued a visa to travel to the United States. Upon arrival at a U.S. point of entry, the traveler will be required to scan her left and right index fingers to determine if she is the same person who applied for the visa. Entry procedures were started in 115 airports at the beginning of 2004, and by the end of 2005 all airports that receive international flights were scheduled to have US-Visit capabilities.

Currently, there are also 12 U.S. airports that are taking part in the US-Visit exit procedures and two seaports that are testing the exit procedures for US-Visit. The exit procedure requires every traveler to scan his or her fingers before leaving the country to determine the identity of the individual.

Homeland Security believes that implementing these new security features will result in fewer criminals or terrorists entering the country and also reduce the incidence of identity theft and fraud that may occur upon entry to or exit from the country. However, there are critics who say that the information available to U.S. Customs and Immigration provides too much personal information about travelers and U.S. citizens. Despite privacy concerns, the Department of Homeland Security is set on using the US-Visit program in conjunction with other government programs to increase the security of the United States.

Critical Thinking

1. Are you afraid that futuristic security methods such as biometric technology will lead to the loss of personal privacy and the erosion of civil liberties?

2. Would you want your personal medical information to be posted on a computer network where it could potentially be accessed by future employers and others?

InfoTrac College Edition Research

To learn more about the subject, use "biometric technology" as a key word on InfoTrac College Edition.

Sources: "United States Visitor and Immigrant Status Indicator Technology" (Electronic Privacy Information Center) (http://www.epic.org/privacy/us-visit), accessed on September 1, 2005; "US-Visit" (Travel and Transportation, U.S. Department of Homeland Security) (http://www.dhs.gov/dhspublic/interapp/content_multi_image/content_multi_image_0006.xml), accessed on September 1, 2005.

◆ *Genetic algorithms.* Using these mathematical models, a computerized composite image of a suspect's face will be constructed from relatively little information. Digitization of photographs will enable the reconstruction of blurred images. Videotapes of bank robbers or blurred photos of license plates—even bite marks—can be digitized using highly advanced mathematical models.

◆ *Automatic Biometric Identification System (ABIS).* ABIS can be used by law enforcement agencies in facial searches or in matching suspects who use false identities to their mug shots from past crimes.[55] ABIS may one day be mated to closed-circuit TV (CCTV) surveillance systems. Today, second-generation CCTV can be positioned to observe environments, such as harbors, airports, or freeways, and then link the recorded images to a computer system that can detect unusual behavior, unauthorized traffic, or surprising and unexpected changes, and then alert a human operator.[56] Closed-circuit surveillance cameras armed with ABIS technology will be able to pick out and track wanted felons and terrorists by using computer-recorded facial recognition patterns. Big Brother will be watching you!

 To learn more about ABIS, go to the Identix website. You can reach it by going to the Siegel/Senna Introduction to Criminal Justice 11e website: www.thomsonedu.com/criminaljustice/siegel.

ThomsonNOW™ Improve your grade on the exam with Personalized Study! For reinforcement resources and a mastery check of technology and law enforcement, go to www.thomsonedu.com/thomsonnow.

FIGURE 5.3

Trends in the Percentage of Police Departments Using IT to Transmit Reports

Population served

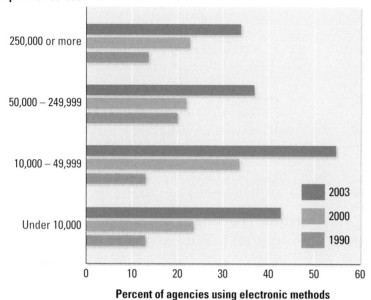

Percent of agencies using electronic methods

Source: Matthew Hickman and Brian Reaves, *Local Police Departments, 2003*
(http://www.ojp.usdoj.gov/bjs/pub/pdf/lpd03.pdf), accessed on June 15, 2006.

♦ *Augmented reality (AR) technology.* Now in the development stage, AR technology will supply wearable components that will give computer-generated virtual information to police. AR technology displays information in real time, in a way that enhances the individual abilities of people operating in the real world. (An example of AR technology is the virtual lines drawn by broadcasters on football fields to show the first-down marker.) Uniformed patrol officers will have many potential uses for AR, ranging from real-time language translation to the immediate display of real-time intelligence about crimes to facial and voice recognition data, which will tell them if a suspect is wanted for another crime.[57]

ETHICAL CHALLENGES IN CRIMINAL JUSTICE: A WRITING ASSIGNMENT

FBI officials say that they have developed surveillance cameras that can instantly compare people's "faceprints" against those of suspected terrorists and known criminals in a computerized database. This biometric facial recognition system uses measurable facial features, such as the distances and angles between geometric points on the face, to recognize a specific individual. This highly automated, computerized process can be installed at airports and train stations in order to constantly monitor people using transportation. Those who match photos can be called out, detained, and questioned.

Write an essay on the ethics of using this system. Is this use of this technology cause for alarm? Is it an undesirable invasion of individual privacy, or does it represent a positive advance in security measures that generates benefits for society?

Doing Research on the Web

To read more about biometric recognition patterns, go to the Face Recognition Home Page. You can reach this site by going to the Siegel/Senna Introduction to Criminal Justice 11e website: www.thomsonedu.com/criminaljustice/siegel.

To read more about the issue of privacy in a world of technological innovation, check out Privacy International. You can access this site by going to the Siegel/Senna Introduction to Criminal Justice 11e website: www.thomsonedu.com/criminaljustice/siegel.

SUMMARY

- Early in British history, law enforcement was a personal matter.

- Tythings and hundreds (10 tythings) were early forms of law enforcement.

- In the Middle Ages, constables were appointed to keep peace among groups of 100 families. This rudimentary beginning was the seed of today's police departments.

- In 1838 the first true U.S. police department was born in Boston.

- The first U.S. police departments were created because of the need to control mob violence, which was common during the nineteenth century.

- The early police were viewed as being dominated by political bosses who controlled their hiring practices and policies.

- Reform movements begun during the 1920s culminated in the concept of professionalism in the 1950s and 1960s. Police professionalism was interpreted to mean tough, rule-oriented police work featuring advanced technology and hardware. However, the view that these measures would quickly reduce crime proved incorrect.

- Between 1960 and the 1990s, police were beset by many problems, including their treatment of minorities and their lack of effectiveness.

- This paved the way for a radical change in policing and the development of community policing.

- There are several major law enforcement agencies in the Justice Department, including the FBI, the Drug Enforcement Administration, and the U.S. Marshals.

- After September 11, 2001, Congress approved the formation of the Department of Homeland Security to coordinate protection of the nation from terrorists and other threats.

- County-level law enforcement is provided by sheriffs' departments, and most states, except Hawaii, maintain state police agencies. Some of these agencies specialize in traffic control, whereas others are full-fledged law enforcement departments.

- Most law enforcement is conducted by local police agencies, which carry out patrol, investigative, and traffic functions, as well as many support activities.

- State, county, and local law enforcement agencies are now becoming involved in antiterror activity.

- Today, most police departments rely on advanced computer-based technology to identify suspects and collate evidence.

- Automated fingerprint systems and computerized identification systems have become widespread. Some believe that technology may make police overly intrusive and interfere with civil liberties.

KEY TERMS

tything (tithing), 160
hue and cry, 161
hundred, 161
constable, 161
shire reeve, 161
watch system, 161
justice of the peace, 161

Metropolitan Police
   Act, 162
sheriff, 162
vigilantes, 163
community policing, 167
Federal Bureau of Investigation
   (FBI), 168

Department of Homeland
   Security (DHS), 171
data mining, 178
biometrics, 182
DNA profiling, 183

ThomsonNOW Maximize your study time by using ThomsonNOW's diagnostic study plan to help you review this chapter. The Study Plan will

- help you identify areas on which you should concentrate;

- provide interactive exercises to help you master the chapter concepts; and

- provide a post-test to confirm you are ready to move on to the next chapter.

CRITICAL THINKING QUESTIONS

1. List the problems faced by today's police departments that were also present during the early days of policing.

2. Distinguish among the duties of the state police, sheriffs' departments, and local police departments.

3. What is the Department of Homeland Security? What are its component agencies?

4. What are some of the technological advances that should help the police solve more crimes? What are the dangers of these advances?

5. Discuss the trends that may influence policing during the coming decade. What are some other social factors that may affect police?

NOTES

1. FBI News Release, "Local, State, and Federal Agencies Join Forces to Arrest Over 45 Gang Members and Gang Associates in Stanislaus County Two-Day, Multi-Agency Enforcement Effort Dubbed 'Operation Valley SCAR,'" June 14, 2006 (http://sacramento.fbi.gov/dojpressrel/pressrel06/gang_arrests061406.htm).

2. Ralph Weisheit and L. Edward Wells, "Youth Gangs in Rural America," *NIJ Journal* 251 (2004): 1–5.

3. Sara Stoutland, "The Multiple Dimensions of Trust in Resident/Police Relations in Boston," *Journal of Research in Crime and Delinquency* 38 (2001): 226–56.

4. Richard A. Leo and Richard J. Ofshe, "The Consequences of False Confessions: Deprivations of Liberty and Miscarriages of Justice in the Age of Psychological Interrogation," *Journal of Criminal Law and Criminology* 88 (1998): 429–96.

5. "Law Enforcement Seeks Answers to 'Racial Profiling' Complaints," *Criminal Justice Newsletter* 29 (1998): 5.

6. Wesley Skogan, "Asymmetry in the Impact of Encounters with Police," *Policing & Society* 16 (2006): 99–126.

7. Thomas Priest and Deborah Brown Carter, "Evaluations of Police Performance in an African American Sample," *Journal of Criminal Justice* 27 (1999): 457–65.

8. This section relies heavily on such sources as Malcolm Sparrow, Mark Moore, and David Kennedy, *Beyond 911: A New Era for Policing* (New York: Basic Books, 1990); Daniel Devlin, *Police Procedure, Administration, and Organization* (London: Butterworth, 1966); Robert Fogelson, *Big-City Police* (Cambridge, Mass.: Harvard University Press, 1977); Roger Lane, *Policing the City, Boston 1822–1885* (Cambridge, Mass.: Harvard University Press, 1967); J. J. Tobias, *Crime and Industrial Society in the Nineteenth Century* (New York: Schocken, 1967); Samuel Walker, *A Critical History of Police Reform: The Emergence of Professionalism* (Lexington, Mass.: Lexington, 1977); Samuel Walker, *Popular Justice* (New York: Oxford University Press, 1980); John McMullan, "The New Improved Monied Police: Reform Crime Control and Commodification of Policing in London," *British Journal of Criminology* 36 (1996): 85–108.

9. Devlin, *Police Procedure,* p. 3.

10. John L. McMullan, "The New Improved Monied Police," at 92.

11. Elizabeth Joh, "The Paradox of Private Policing," *Journal of Criminal Law & Criminology* 95 (2004): 49–132.

12. Wilbur Miller, "The Good, the Bad, and the Ugly: Policing America," *History Today* 50 (2000): 29–32.

13. Phillip Reichel, "Southern Slave Patrols as a Transitional Type," *American Journal of Police* 7 (1988): 51–78.

14. Walker, *Popular Justice,* p. 61.

15. Ibid., p. 8.

16. Dennis Rousey, "Cops and Guns: Police Use of Deadly Force in Nineteenth-Century New Orleans," *American Journal of Legal History* 28 (1984): 41–66.

17. Law Enforcement Assistance Administration, *Two Hundred Years of American Criminal Justice* (Washington, D.C.: Government Printing Office, 1976).

18. National Commission on Law Observance and Enforcement, *Report on the Police* (Washington, D.C.: Government Printing Office, 1931), pp. 5–7.

19. Pamela Irving Jackson, *Minority Group Threat, Crime, and Policing* (New York: Praeger, 1989).

20. James Q. Wilson and George Kelling, "Broken Windows," *Atlantic Monthly,* March 1982, pp. 29–38.

21. Frank Tippett, "It Looks Just Like a War Zone," *Time,* May 27, 1985, pp. 16–22; "San Francisco, New York Police Troubled by Series of Scandals," *Criminal Justice Newsletter* 16 (1985): 2–4; Karen Polk, "New York Police: Caught in the Middle and Losing Faith," *Boston Globe,* December 28, 1988, p. 3.

22. The Staff of the Los Angeles Times, *Understanding the Riots: Los Angeles Before and After the Rodney King Case* (Los Angeles, Calif.: Los Angeles Times, 1992).

23. David H. Bayley, "Policing in America," *Society* 36 (December 1998): 16–20.

24. Kathleen Grubb, "Cold War to Gang War," *Boston Globe,* January 22, 1992, p. 1.

25. Department of Homeland Security (http://www.dhs.gov/dhspublic/display?theme=9).

26. Bruce Smith, *Police Systems in the United States* (New York: Harper and Row, 1960).

27. California Anti-Terrorism Information Center (CATIC) (http://ag.ca.gov/antiterrorism/index.htm), accessed on June 7, 2006.

28. Alabama Department of Homeland Security (http://www.dhs.alabama.gov/department.htm), accessed on June 8, 2006.

29. Matthew Hickman and Brian Reaves, *Sheriffs' Offices, 2003* (Washington, D.C.: Bureau of Justice Statistics, 2006).

30. Matthew Hickman and Brian Reaves, *Local Police Departments 2003* (Washington, D.C.: Bureau of Justice Statistics, 2006).

31. Harris County Homeland Security (http://www.hcoem.org/homeland.php).

32. Montgomery County, Maryland, Homeland Security (http://www.montgomerycountymd.gov/mcgtmpl.asp?url=/content/homelandsecurity/index.asp), accessed on June 7, 2006.

33. Hickman and Reaves, *Local Police Departments 2003.*

34. See, for example, Robert Keppel and Joseph Weis, *Improving the Investigation of Violent Crime: The Homicide Investigation and Tracking System* (Washington, D.C.: National Institute of Justice, 1993).

35. William K. Rashbaum, "Terror Makes All the World a Beat for New York Police," *New York Times,* July 15, 2002, p. B1; Al Baker, "Leader Sees New York Police in Vanguard of Terror Fight," *New York Times,* August 6, 2002, p. A2; Stephen Flynn, "America the Vulnerable," *Foreign Affairs* 81 (January–February 2002): 60.

36. Lois Pliant, "Information Management," *Police Chief* 61 (1994): 31–35.

37. Larry Coutorie, "The Future of High-Technology Crime: A Parallel Delphi Study," *Journal of Criminal Justice* 23 (1995): 13–27.

38. Bill Goodwin, "Burglars Captured by Police Data Mining Kit," *Computer Weekly*, August 8, 2002, p. 3.

39. Raymond E. Foster, "Crime Scene Investigation," *Government Technology* (March 2005) (http://www.govtech.net/magazine/story.php?id=93225&issue=3:2005), accessed on September 17, 2005.

40. This section is based on Derek Paulsen, "To Map or Not to Map: Assessing the Impact of Crime Maps on Police Officer Perceptions of Crime," *International Journal of Police Science & Management* 6 (2004): 234–46; William W. Bratton and Peter Knobler, *Turnaround: How America's Top Cop Reversed the Crime Epidemic* (New York: Random House, 1998), p. 289; and Jeremy Travis, "Computerized Crime Mapping," *NIJ News* (National Institute of Justice), January 1999.

41. U.S. Department of Justice, Office of Justice Programs, Information Technology Initiatives, "Washington State Develops Mapping System" (http://it.ojp.gov/index.jsp), accessed on September 18, 2005.

42. U.S. Department of Justice, Office of Justice Programs, Information Technology Initiatives, "Where's the Emergency?" (http://it.ojp.gov/index.jsp), accessed on September 18, 2005.

43. "Introduction to Biometrics" (http://www.biometrics.org), accessed on August 25, 2005; Fernando L. Podio, "Biometrics—Technologies for Highly Secure Personal Authentication," *ITL Bulletin* (National Institute of Standards and Technology).

44. Laura Moriarty and David Carter, *Criminal Justice Technology in the Twenty-First Century* (Springfield, Ill.: Charles C. Thomas, 1998).

45. Weipeng Zhang, Yan Yuan Tang, and Xinge You, "Fingerprint Enhancement Using Wavelet Transform Combined with Gabor Filter," *International Journal of Pattern Recognition & Artificial Intelligence* 18 (2004): 1391–1406.

46. Frederick Bieber, Charles Brenner, and David Lazer, "Finding Criminals Through DNA of Their Relatives," *Science* 312 (2006): 1315–16.

47. Ibid.

48. Ronald Reinstein, *Postconviction DNA Testing: Recommendations for Handling Requests* (Philadelphia: Diane, 1999).

49. "California Attorney General Endorses DNA Fingerprinting," *Criminal Justice Newsletter* 1 (1989): 1.

50. *State v. Ford*, 301 S.C. 485, 392 S.E.2d 781 (1990).

51. "Under New Policy, FBI Examiners Testify to Absolute DNA Matches," *Criminal Justice Newsletter* 28 (1997): 1–2.

52. "FBI's DNA Profile Clearinghouse Announce First 'Cold Hit,'" *Criminal Justice Newsletter* 16 (1999): 5.

53. "South Side Strangler's Execution Cited as DNA Evidence Landmark," *Criminal Justice Newsletter* 2 (1994): 3.

54. Ralph Ioimo and Jay Aronson, "Police Field Mobile Computing: Applying the Theory of Task–Technology Fit," *Police Quarterly* 7 (2004): 403–28.

55. "Facial AFIS Launched by Identix," *Biometric Technology Today* 11 (2003): 4.

56. Ray Surette, "The Thinking Eye: Pros and Cons of Second Generation CCTV Surveillance Systems," *Policing* 28 (2005): 152–73.

57. Thomas Cowper, "Improving the View of the World: Law Enforcement and Augmented Reality Technology," *FBI Law Enforcement Bulletin* 74 (2004): 11–14.

CHAPTER 6

The Police: Organization, Role, Function

Chapter Objectives

After reading this chapter, you should be able to:
1. Understand the organization of police departments.
2. Know the similarities and differences between patrol and detective operations.
3. Recognize the problems associated with the time-in-rank system.
4. Describe the efforts being made to improve patrol effectiveness.
5. Discuss the organization of police detectives.
6. Understand the concept of community policing.
7. Describe various community policing strategies.
8. Discuss the concept of problem-oriented policing.
9. Explain the various police subsystems.
10. Identify the factors that may be used to improve police productivity.

© Julia Gaines/NewsDay. Reprinted by permission of *Los Angeles Times.*

O n June 7, 2006, Beverly Mozer-Browne was arrested for fraud in a case involving the illegal sale of permanent residence documents, or "green cards," to illegal aliens. Mozer-Browne owned and operated a business called Help Preparers Professional Services (HPPS), which offered its customers assistance in a variety of financial and legal matters. It was actually a front for her scheme to supply fraudulent green cards. According to authorities, in exchange for fees ranging from $8,000 to $16,000, Mozer-Browne and her employees arranged for U.S. citizens to enter into sham marriages with HPPS applicants. In some instances, HPPS is alleged to have produced phony documentation indicating that a marriage to a U.S. citizen had occurred. Once the HPPS applicant had documentation of marriage to a U.S. citizen, HPPS employees prepared a green card application package and submitted it to the government. According to authorities, after the application was made, Beverly's brother Phillip would take over. Phillip worked as district adjudication officer for Citizenship and Immigration Services (CIS), a position that allowed him to approve the applications without requiring the HPPS applicant to appear for the interview. According to law enforcement officials, Beverly and her co-conspirators made millions in the scheme and then laundered the cash through a complex web of bank deposits and real estate ventures.[1] ◆

This scheme highlights the rather complex criminal conspiracies that law enforcement agents must confront on a daily basis. There is no question that the job can be challenging. The law enforcement role is extremely varied and complex, ranging from penetrating elaborate criminal conspiracies to providing emergency medical care to a woman giving birth. Law enforcement officers serve in suburban communities, rural towns, and some of the toughest urban streets in the United States. Their roles can be quite different. Although rural/suburban police tend to be generalists who focus on social problems ranging from public disorder to family dysfunction, urban cops may be asked to confront heavily armed drug-dealing gangs.[2] However, in all settings, the public demands that the police "make them feel safe" and lose confidence in them if they fear crime in the streets.[3] The reaction can have a terrific impact on police officers, deeply affecting their professional and personal lives. One day they may be considered "heroes" who risk their lives to protect citizens from danger, but the next day they are accused of practicing "racial profiling."

◆ THE POLICE ORGANIZATION

Most municipal police departments in the United States are independent agencies within the executive branch of government. On occasion, police agencies in two independent jurisdictions will cooperate and participate in mutually beneficial enterprises, such as sharing information on known criminals, or they may work with joint task forces of state, county, and federal agencies to investigate ongoing criminal cases (see Operation SCAR in Chapter 5). Aside from such cooperative efforts, police departments tend to be functionally independent organizations with unique sets of rules, policies, procedures, norms, budgets, and so on. In other words, no two are exactly alike. Although many police agencies are today in the process of rethinking their organization and goals, the majority are still organized in a hierarchical manner, as illustrated in Figure 6.1. Within this organizational model, each element of the department normally has its own chain of command and rank system. New York City ranks include the following:[4]

◆   Patrolman

◆   Sergeant (symbol of rank: 3 chevrons)

◆   Lieutenant (symbol of rank: 1 gold bar)

◆   Captain (symbol of rank: 2 gold bars)

◆   Deputy inspector (symbol of rank: gold oak leaf)

◆   Inspector (symbol of rank: gold eagle)

◆   Deputy chief (symbol of rank: 1 gold star)

◆   Assistant chief (symbol of rank: 2 gold stars)

◆   Bureau chief (symbol of rank: 3 gold stars)

◆   Chief of department (symbol of rank: 4 gold stars)

◆   Deputy commissioner (symbol of rank: 3 gold stars)

◆   First deputy commissioner (symbol of rank: 4 gold stars)

◆   Police commissioner (symbol of rank: 5 gold stars)

Many police departments operate a website designed to provide basic information about the department and its duties. You can access the one for the New York City Police Department by going to the Siegel/Senna Introduction to Criminal Justice 11e website: www.thomsonedu.com/criminaljustice/siegel.

In a large municipal department, there may be a number of independent units headed by a bureau chief who serves as the senior administrator, a captain who oversees regional or precinct units and acts as liaison with other police agencies, a lieutenant who manages daily activities, and sergeants and patrol officers who carry out field work. Smaller departments may have a captain or lieutenant as a unit head. At the head of the organization is the police chief, who sets policy and has general administrative control over all the department's various operating branches.

Problems regarding a police department's organizational structure are not uncommon, nor are they unique to policing agencies, as anyone who has ever dealt with any governmental bureaucracy is aware. Most often they are attributable to

FIGURE 6.1

Organization of a Traditional Metropolitan Police Department

Civilian advisory board	Chief of police / Assistant chief	Planning and research / Crime mapping / Program evaluation

Personnel
Affirmative action officer
Recruitment and promotion

Internal affairs
Trial board

Equipment
- Repairs
- Station, grounds
- Uniforms
- Squad cars
- Computers

Chief clerk
- Payroll
- Property
- Supplies
- Purchasing
- Printing
- Statistics
- Budget and finance

Special services
- Ambulance
- Records, communications
- Morgue
- Radio
- Psychologist
- Computer programmer
- Court liaison
- Lockup

Training
- Academy
- In-service training
- Pistol range
- Physical fitness
- Stress-control program

Vice
- Gambling
- Liquor
- Prostitution
- Obscenity

Detectives
- Bunko (checks, fraud)
- Homicide
- Robbery
- Sex
- Fugitives
- Autos
- Narcotics

Patrol
- 1st district
- 2nd district
- 3rd district
- 4th district
- Foot patrol
- Canine corps
- SWAT (Special Weapons and Tactics)

Community police unit
- Neighborhood newsletter
- Ministations
  Station 1
  Station 2
  Station 3
- Community coordinating council liaison

Traffic
- Control
- Accidents
- Public vehicles
- Violator's school

Prevention
- Community relations
- Athletic league
- Project DARE
- Officer-friendly

Juveniles
- Detectives
- Juvenile court prosecutor
- School liaison
- Gang control unit

personnel changes (due to retirements, promotions, transfers, or resignations) or simply to a periodic internal reorganization. As a result, citizens may sometimes have difficulty determining who is responsible for a particular police function or operational policy, or two divisions may unknowingly compete with each other over jurisdiction on a particular case. The large number of operating divisions and the lack of any clear relationship among them almost guarantee that the decision-making practices of one branch will be unknown to another. These are common management problems that are not insurmountable, and they are typically resolved over time.

Most departments also follow a system in promoting personnel called the **time-in-rank system.** This means that before moving up the administrative ladder, an officer must spend a certain amount of time in the next lowest rank. A sergeant cannot become a captain without serving an appropriate amount of time as a lieutenant. In New York City, for example, promotion from patrolman to sergeant, sergeant to lieutenant, and lieutenant to captain all occur via a civil service formula that involves such criteria as performance on a civil service written examination, length of service, citations awarded, and optional physical fitness test (for extra points). Promotion beyond the rank of captain is discretionary. Unlike the private sector, where people can be hired away from another company and given an immediate promotion and boost in pay, the time-in-rank system prohibits departments from allowing officers to skip ranks and prevents them from hiring an officer from another department and awarding her a higher rank.

time-in-rank system
The promotion system in which a police officer can advance in rank only after spending a prescribed amount of time in the preceding rank.

Copsonline is a police Internet resource. It provides information on how to become a police officer and on the latest books, training, and jobs. You can access it by going to the Siegel/Senna Introduction to Criminal Justice 11e website: www.thomsonedu.com/criminaljustice/siegel.

Although this system is designed to promote fairness and stability in police agencies and limit favoritism, it may restrict administrative flexibility.

♦ THE POLICE ROLE

In countless books, movies, and TV shows, the public has been presented with a view of policing that romanticizes police officers as fearless crime fighters who

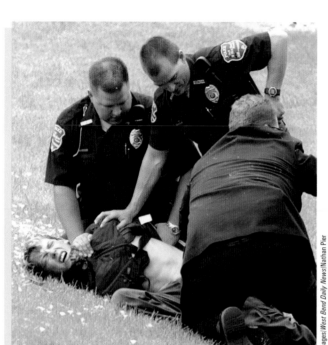

think little of their own safety as they engage in daily shoot-outs with Uzi-toting drug runners, psychopathic serial killers, and organized-crime hit men. Occasionally, but not often, fictional patrol officers and detectives seem aware of departmental rules, legal decisions, citizens' groups, civil suits, or physical danger. They are rarely faced with the economic necessity of moonlighting as security guards, taking on extra details, caring about an annual pay raise, or griping when someone less deserving gets a choice assignment for political reasons.

How close is this portrayal of a selfless crime fighter to real life? Not very, according to most research efforts. Police officers are asked to deal with hundreds of incidents each year, and crime fighting is only a small part of the daily routine. Studies of police work indicate that a significant portion of an officer's time is spent handling minor disturbances, service calls, and administrative duties. Police work, then, involves much more than catching criminals. Figure 6.2 shows the results of a national survey of police behavior.[5] This survey found that about 20 percent of all Americans (about 45 million people) have contacts with the police each year. Most involve some form of motor vehicle or traffic-related issues. About 5 million annual contacts involve citizens asking

©AP Images/West Bend Daily News/Nathan Pier

While the role of the police involves activities ranging from emergency medical care to traffic control, law enforcement and crime control are critical (and often misunderstood) elements of policing. Here a suspect in the robbery of a U.S. Bank branch on July 1, 2005, in West Bend, Wisconsin is being subdued by patrol officers. The suspect was only able to make it across the street from the bank before being apprehended.

for assistance—responding to a complaint about music being too loud during a party, warning kids not to shoot fireworks, and so on. This survey indicates that the police role is both varied and complex.

These results are not surprising when Uniform Crime Report (UCR) arrest data are considered. Each year, about 700,000 local, county, and state police officers make about 14 million arrests, or about 20 each. Of these, about 2 million are for serious crimes (Part I), or about 3 per officer. Given an even distribution of arrests, it is evident that the average police officer makes fewer than 2 arrests per month and fewer than 1 felony arrest every four months.

These figures should be interpreted with caution because not all police officers are engaged in activities that allow them to make arrests, such as patrol or detective work, and many work in rural and suburban departments in areas with very low crime rates. About one-third of all sworn officers in the nation's largest police departments are in such units as communications, antiterrorism, administration, and personnel. Even if the number of arrests per officer were adjusted by one-third, it would still amount to about 4 serious crime arrests per officer per year, and these figure include such crimes as shoplifting and other minor larce-

PERSPECTIVES ON JUSTICE

Rehabilitation

Rehabilitation advocates would suggest that the police role should be reconsidered because a majority of police activities involve community activities instead of crime control. Police might better serve by preventing crime than catching criminals after a crime occurs.

nies. So although police handle thousands of calls each year, relatively few result in an arrest for a serious crime such as a robbery and burglary; in suburban and rural areas, years may go by before a police officer makes a felony arrest.

The evidence, then, shows that unlike the TV/film portrayal, the police role involves many non-crime-related activities. Although the media depict police officers busting criminals and engaging in high-speed

FIGURE 6.2
Police Encounters with Citizens

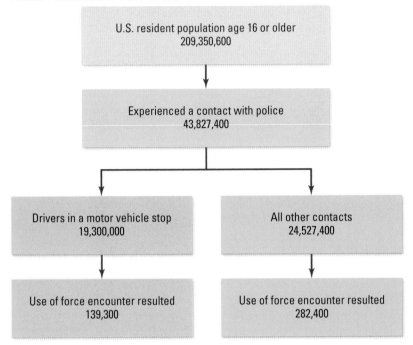

Sources: Matthew Durose, Erica Schmitt, and Patrick Langan, *Contacts Between Police and the Public: Findings from the 2002 National Survey* (Washington, D.C.: Bureau of Justice Statistics, 2005).

chases, the true police role is much more complex. Police officers function in a variety of roles, ranging from dispensers of emergency medical care to keepers of the peace on school grounds. Although officers in large urban departments may be called on to handle more felony cases than those in small towns, they too will probably find that most of their daily activities are not crime related. What are some of the most important functions of police?

ThomsonNOW Improve your grade on the exam with Personalized Study! For reinforcement resources and a mastery check of the role of the police, go to www.thomsonedu.com/thomsonnow.

♦ THE PATROL FUNCTION

Regardless of style of policing, uniformed patrol officers are the backbone of the police department, usually accounting for about two-thirds of a department's personnel.[6] Patrol officers are the most highly visible components of the entire criminal justice system. They are charged with supervising specific areas of their jurisdiction, called **beats**, whether in a patrol car, or by motorcycle, horse, helicopter, boat or even on foot in some community-oriented departments. Each beat, or patrol area, is covered 24 hours a day by different shifts. The major purpose of patrol is to

beats
Designated police patrol areas.

♦ Deter crime by maintaining a visible police presence.

♦ Maintain public order (peacekeeping) within the patrol area.

♦ Enable the police department to respond quickly to law violations or other emergencies.

♦ Identify and apprehend law violators.

♦ Aid individuals and care for those who cannot help themselves.

♦ Facilitate the movement of traffic and people.

♦ Create a feeling of security in the community.[7]

Patrol officers' responsibilities are immense. They may suddenly be faced with an angry mob, an armed felon, or a suicidal teenager and be forced to make split-second decisions on what action to take. At the same time, they must be sensitive to the needs of citizens who are often of diverse racial and ethnic backgrounds. When police are present and visible, a sense of security is created in a neighborhood, and residents' opinions of the police improve.[8]

Patrol Activities

Most experts agree that the great bulk of patrol effort is devoted to what has been described as **order maintenance**, or **peacekeeping**: maintaining order and civility within their assigned jurisdiction.[9] Order-maintenance functions fall on the border between criminal and noncriminal behavior. The patrol officer's discretion often determines whether a noisy neighborhood dispute involves the crime of disturbing the peace or whether it can be controlled with street-corner diplomacy and the combatants sent on their way. Similarly, teenagers milling around in the shopping center parking lot can be brought in and turned over to the juvenile authorities or handled in a less formal and often more efficient manner.

The major role of police seems to be handling the situation. Police encounter many troubling incidents that need some sort of fixing up.[10] Enforcing the law might be one tool a patrol officer uses; threats, coercion, sympathy, understanding, and apathy might be others. Most important is keeping things under control so that no complaints arise that the officer is doing nothing or doing too much. The real police role, then, may be as a community problem solver.

Police officers practice a policy of selective enforcement, concentrating on some crimes but handling the majority in an informal manner. A police officer is supposed to know when to take action and when not to, whom to arrest and whom to deal with by issuing a warning or some other informal action. If a mistake is made, the officer can come under fire from his peers and superiors, as well as from the general public. Consequently, the patrol officer's job is extremely demanding and often unrewarding and unappreciated. The attitudes of police officers toward the public, not surprisingly, are sometimes characterized as being ambivalent and cynical.[11]

Does Patrol Deter Crime?

For many years, preventive police patrol was considered one of the greatest deterrents to criminal behavior. The visible presence of patrol cars on the street and the rapid deployment of police officers to the scene of the crime were viewed as particularly effective law enforcement techniques.

However, research efforts have questioned the basic assumptions of patrol. The most widely heralded attempt at measuring patrol effectiveness was undertaken during the early 1970s in Kansas City, Missouri, under sponsorship of the Police Foundation, a private institute that studies police behavior.[12]

To evaluate the effectiveness of patrol, the researchers divided 15 police districts into 3 groups: One group retained normal patrol, the second (proactive) set of districts was supplied with two to three times the normal amount of patrol forces, and the third (reactive) group had its preventive patrol eliminated, with police officers responding only when summoned by citizens to the scene of a particular crime.

Data from the Kansas City study indicated that these variations in patrol techniques had little effect on the crime patterns in the 15 districts. The presence or absence of patrol did not seem to affect residential or business burglaries, motor vehicle thefts, larcenies involving auto accessories, robberies, vandalism, or other criminal behavior.[13] Moreover, variations in patrol techniques appeared to have little influence on citizens' attitudes toward the police, their satisfaction with police, or their fear of future criminal behavior.[14]

Although the Kansas City study found little evidence that police patrol could deter crime, police in a number of jurisdictions have attempted to test the effectiveness of patrol by targeting areas for increased police presence. A police task force might target street-level narcotics dealers by using undercover agents and surveillance cameras in known drug-dealing locales. Or the police may actively enforce public nuisance laws in an effort to demonstrate the department's crime-fighting resolve. These efforts have not proven to be successful mechanisms for lowering crime rates.[15] In addition, there is the problem of **displacement**: Criminals move from an area targeted for increased police presence to another that is less well protected. When the police leave, the criminals return to business as usual.

Improving Patrol

Due to the aforementioned issues, police departments have initiated a number of programs and policies to try to improve patrol effectiveness:

AGGRESSIVE PATROL The Kansas City study, although subject to criticism because of its research design, greatly influenced the way that police experts viewed the effectiveness of patrol. Its lukewarm findings set the stage for community and problem-oriented policing models, which stress social service over crime deterrence. However, it may be too soon to dismiss police patrol as a crime-fighting technique. Although the mere presence of police may not be sufficient to deter crime, the manner in which they approach their task may make a difference. Evidence shows that cities with larger police departments, which have more officers per capita than the norm, also experience lower levels of violent crimes.[16] Police departments that use a proactive, aggressive law enforcement style may also help reduce crime rates. Jurisdictions that encourage patrol officers to stop motor vehicles to issue citations and to aggressively arrest and detain suspicious persons also experience lower crime rates than jurisdictions that do not follow such proactive policies.[17] Improving response time and increasing the number of patrol cars that respond per crime may be one way of increasing police efficiency.[18] Departments that more actively enforce minor regulations, such as disorderly conduct and traffic laws, are also more likely to experience lower felony rates.[19]

Pinpointing why proactive policing works so effectively is difficult. It may have a deterrent effect: Aggressive policing increases the community perception that police arrest many criminals and that most violators get caught. Therefore, criminals are scared to commit crimes in a town that has such an active police force. **Proactive policing** may also help control crime because it results in conviction of more criminals. Because aggressive police arrest more suspects, fewer criminals are left on the street to commit crime, and fewer criminals produce lower crime rates.

Aggressive police patrol efforts have been a critical success. The downturn in the New York City violent crime rate during the 1990s has been attributed to aggressive police work aimed at lifestyle crimes: vandalism, panhandling, and graffiti.[20] Some commentators fear that aggressive policing will result in antagonism between proactive cops and a fearful general public. However, research indicates that precinct-level efforts to ensure that officers are respectful of citizens can help lower the number of complaints and improve community relations.[21] Aggressive police can take steps to improve their public image.

displacement
An effect that occurs when criminals move from an area targeted for increased police presence to another that is less well protected.

proactive policing
An aggressive law enforcement style in which patrol officers take the initiative against crime instead of waiting for criminal acts to occur. For example, they stop motor vehicles to issue citations and aggressively arrest and detain suspicious persons.

PERSPECTIVES ON JUSTICE

Crime Control

The results of proactive policing are encouraging to crime control enthusiasts, but the downside of aggressive tactics must be considered before a general policy of vigorous police work can be adopted. Proactive police strategies may cause resentment in minority areas where citizens believe they are being unfairly targeted by police. Aggressive police tactics such as stopping, frisking, and rousting teenagers who congregate on street corners may be the seeds from which racial conflict grows. Overly aggressive police may also be the ones who are continually involved in incidents of unnecessary brutality. Due process advocates are troubled by these side effects and demand review boards to oversee police activities. Despite such reservations, many large police jurisdictions have adopted a crime control philosophy by having patrol officers become more aggressive and concentrate on investigating and deterring crimes.

TARGETING CRIMES Evidence also shows that targeting specific crimes can be successful. One aggressive patrol program, known as the Kansas City Gun Experiment, was directed at restricting the carrying of guns in high-risk places at high-risk times. Working with academics from the University of Maryland, the Kansas City Police Department focused extra patrol attention on a hot-spot high-crime area identified by computer analysis of all gun crimes. Over a 29-week period, the gun patrol officers made thousands of car and pedestrian checks and traffic stops, and they made more than 600 arrests. Using frisks and

Alcohol, Tobacco, Firearms and Explosives (ATF) officers arrange a display of weapons seized in a raid on a gang suspected in the shooting deaths of two police officers. The raid on June 21, 2005, targeted 42 members of the Vineland Boys gang and netted 19 arrests. Aggressive law enforcement can have a long-term impact: As word gets out that police will not tolerate crime, a general deterrent effect may occur, and people contemplating violent crime become convinced that apprehension risks are unacceptably high.

searches, they found 29 guns, and an additional 47 weapons were seized by other officers in the experimental area. There were 169 gun crimes in the target beat in the 29 weeks prior to the gun patrol but only 86 while the experiment was under way, a decrease of 49 percent. Drive-by shootings dropped significantly, as did homicides, without any displacement to other areas in the city. The weapons seized could have been taken from high-rate offenders who were among the most likely perpetrators of gun-related crimes. Their lost opportunity to commit violent crimes may have resulted in an overall rate decrease. The gun sweeps also could have caused some of the most violent criminals to be taken off the streets. And, as word of the patrol got out, there may have been a general deterrent effect: People contemplating violent crime may have been convinced that apprehension risks were unacceptably high.[22]

While the Kansas City Gun Experiment appears successful, a number of lingering questions remain: Does targeting a crime in one area merely shift it to another? If one crime is targeted, e.g. burglary, do criminals simply shift to another (e.g. car theft)?

MAKING ARRESTS Can more formal police action, such as an arrest, reduce crime? Research studies show that contact with the police may cause some offenders to forgo repeat criminal behavior and deter future criminality.[23] For example, an arrest for drunk driving has been shown to reduce the likelihood of further driving while intoxicated because arrestees are afraid that they will be re-arrested if they drink and drive.[24] The effect of arrest may be immediate: As the number of arrests increase, reported crimes decrease substantially the following day.[25] News of increased and aggressive police activity could be rapidly diffused through the population and have an immediate impact that translates into lower crime rates. Some cities have adopted a zero-tolerance approach, making arrests for even nuisance crimes—for example, panhandling—to deter repeat offenders and give citizens the impression that crime will not be tolerated.

ADDING PATROL OFFICERS One reason that patrol activity may be less effective than desired is the lack of adequate resources. Does adding more police help bring down the crime rate? The evidence is mixed. Some reviews find that the number of law enforcement officers in a jurisdiction seems to have little effect on area crimes.[26] Comparisons of police expenditures in U.S. cities indicate that cities with the highest crime rates also spend the most on police services.[27] Although these results are disappointing, a number of recent studies, using different methodologies, have found that police presence may reduce crime levels and that adding police may bring crime levels down.[28] In addition, increasing the size of the local police force may have other benefits for the overall effectiveness of the justice system. Adding police and bolstering resources can increase prosecution and conviction rates.[29] Inadequate resources make it difficult to gather sufficient evidence to ensure a conviction, and prosecutors are likely to drop these cases. Adding police resources helps increase prosecutorial effectiveness.

USING TECHNOLOGY Police departments have also relied on technology to help guide patrol efforts. The most well-known program, Compstat, was begun in New York City as a means of directing police efforts in a more productive fashion.[30]

CONCEPT SUMMARY 6.1

Improving Patrol

Strategy	Tactic	Goal
Aggressive patrol	Enforce law vigorously	Give message that crime will not be tolerated
Target specific crimes	Crack down on persistent problems such as gun possession	Stopping one type of crime may have spillover effect
Make arrests	Arrest even minor offenders; zero-tolerance approach	Convince people that crime does not pay
Add police	Increase number of officers on the street	Improve system efficiency
Use technology	Employ latest communications and mapping technologies	Efficiently identify criminals and target crimes

William Bratton, who had been appointed as the New York City police chief, wanted to revitalize the department and break through its antiquated bureaucratic structures. He installed Compstat, a computerized system that gave local precinct commanders up-to-date information about where and when crime was occurring in their jurisdictions. Part of the Compstat program, twice-weekly "crime-control strategy meetings," brought precinct commanders together with the department's top administrators, who asked them to report on crime problems in their precincts and tell what they were doing to turn things around. Those involved in the strategy sessions had both detailed data and electronic pin maps that showed how crime clustered geographically in the precinct and how patrol officers were being deployed. The Compstat program required local commanders to demonstrate both their intimate knowledge of crime trends and to develop strategies to address them effectively. When ideas were presented by the assembled police administrators, the local commander was required to demonstrate in follow-up sessions how he or she had incorporated the new strategies in the local patrol plan. Compstat proved extremely successful and is generally credited with being a big part of why New York City's crime rate fell dramatically during the past decade. Concept Summary 6.1 summarizes efforts to improve patrol effectiveness.

ThomsonNOW Improve your grade on the exam with Personalized Study! For reinforcement resources and a mastery check of the police function, go to www.thomsonedu.com/thomsonnow.

◆ THE INVESTIGATION FUNCTION

Since the first independent detective bureau was established by the London Metropolitan Police in 1841, criminal investigators have been romantic figures vividly portrayed in novels, such as Detective Alex Cross in James Patterson's widely read books (such as *Kiss the Girls* and *Along Came a Spider*), in movies such as Eddie Murphy's portrayal of Axel Foley in *Beverly Hills Cop* and Clint Eastwood's role as Dirty Harry, and in television shows such as *CSI: Crime Scene Investigation* and *Law & Order*.[31] The fictional police detective is usually depicted as a loner who is willing to break departmental rules, perhaps even violate the law, to capture the suspect. The average fictional detective views departmental policies and U.S. Supreme Court decisions as unfortunate roadblocks to police efficiency. Civil rights are either ignored or actively scorned.[32]

Although every police department probably has a few aggressive detectives who may take matters into their own hands at the expense of citizens' rights, the modern criminal investigator is most likely an experienced civil servant, trained

Street Stories—The World of Police Detectives

In his book *Street Stories,* sociologist Robert Jackall narrates the stories and insights he gathered while interviewing and hanging with New York City detectives. Jackall formed close associations with veteran detectives and observed them in action as they controlled a crime scene, canvassed for witnesses, interviewed suspects, gathered evidence, and honed their interrogation techniques.

He found that detectives get great satisfaction from solving crimes and putting criminals behind bars. But they also see themselves caught in a bureaucratic and moral dilemma: They are outsiders because they must play the game of the streets and work amid the mayhem caused by the city's most dangerous criminals and then bring the case to the organized and controlled processing unit that is the criminal court. Detectives believe that the court rules victimize them and all too often neutralize their hard work. They get to know the suspect and his or her entire recorded criminal history. Talking with the suspect for hours on end, they form ironclad beliefs based on their assessment of the suspect's character and record. Because the reliability of these assessments may be questionable, even the best detectives are sometimes dead wrong. Partly to guard against

such errors of judgment, the law deliberately ignores individuals' criminal histories and allows no consideration at trial of the police detectives' assessment of the suspect's moral character. Of course, these rules conflict with the detectives' views of the case and of the culpability of the suspect.

Detectives also find themselves regularly competing with other agencies such as the FBI and with other detective branches for cases. They resent the federal agencies for their large budgets, their agents' lack of understanding of how the city works, and especially agents' unwillingness to share information about criminal groups. Some detective squads regularly hide important information from other units even within their own departments so that they won't steal the case or get credit for its solution. Borough-wide homicide squads steal good cases from precinct detectives, and bosses regularly appropriate credit for their subordinates' work on the streets.

Detectives have the privilege of seeing the underside of life, even the lives of the rich and famous. As Jackall puts it,

> Detectives' work regularly takes them behind respectable public faces, where they glimpse messy, sometimes tumultuous, sometimes sad, sometimes ironic, sometimes

in investigatory techniques, knowledgeable about legal rules of evidence and procedure, and at least somewhat cautious about the legal and administrative consequences of her actions (see the Criminal Justice and the Media feature).[33]

CSI's Gil Grissom, head of the crime scene investigation team in Las Vegas, may be a more realistic portrayal of the modern investigator than Dirty Harry. Although detectives are often handicapped by limited time, money, and resources, they are certainly aware of how their actions will one day be interpreted in a court of law.

Investigative services can be organized in a variety of different ways. In New York City, each borough or district has its own detective division that supervises investigators assigned to neighborhood police precincts (stations). Local squad detectives work closely with patrol officers in order to provide an immediate investigative response to crimes and incidents. New York City also maintains specialized borough squads—homicide, robbery, and special victims—to give aid to local squads and help identify suspects whose crimes may have occurred in multiple locations. There are also specialty squads that help in areas such as forensics. Other departments maintain special divisions with prime responsibility over specific types of crimes. Some jurisdictions maintain **vice squads**, which are usually staffed by plainclothes officers or detectives specializing in victimless crimes, such as prostitution or gambling. Vice squad officers may set themselves up as customers for illicit activities to make arrests. For example, male undercover detectives may frequent public men's rooms and make advances toward other men. Those who respond are arrested for homosexual soliciting. In other instances, female police officers may pose as prostitutes. These covert police activities have often been criticized as violating the personal rights of citizens, and their appropriateness and fairness have been questioned.

vice squads
Police officers assigned to enforce morality-based laws, such as those addressing prostitution, gambling, and pornography.

tragic, sometimes comic, sometimes despairing, sometimes vice-filled private lives. (p. 343)

They watch as a man walks into the squad room clad only in his underwear, claiming that he and a friend were just having a quiet conversation in his parked car when a robber reached through the window and snatched their clothes. They come across otherwise respectable professionals addicted to narcotics. In one case, while investigating the murder of a man dressed up in women's clothes, they uncover a genteel "butterfly society" of established professional men who cross-dress for Friday evening cocktails. These journeys behind respectable public façades stir prurient interests in some detectives but profound class resentments in most. Police officers come overwhelmingly from the working class. They are the sons and daughters of police officers and firefighters, and they are appalled at the antics of the rich and their ability to get away with crimes for which the poor would be sent to prison.

Because detectives are agents of the state, symbols of authority, ultimate insiders with privileged access to hidden social arenas and forbidden knowledge, they become objects of fear, anger, and resentment. This double-sided role, Jackall concludes, shapes the meanings of detectives' work, their images of the world, and their self-images.

Critical Thinking

1. Should detectives use deception and coercion to gather evidence, or do these practices reduce their credibility in the eyes of the community?

2. Should detectives be selected, trained, and promoted in the same fashion as patrol officers, or should investigations be carried out by a totally independent agency that focuses on the scientific gathering of evidence?

 InfoTrac College Edition Research

Use "police detectives" and "police investigators" in a key word search on InfoTrac.

Source: Robert Jackall, *Street Stories: The World of Police Detectives* (Cambridge, Mass.: Harvard University Press, 2005).

How Do Detectives Detect?

Detectives investigate the causes of crime and attempt to identify the individuals or groups responsible for committing particular offenses. They may enter a case after patrol officers have made the initial contact, such as when a patrol car interrupts a crime in progress and the offenders flee before they can be apprehended. They can investigate a case entirely on their own, sometimes by following up on leads provided by informants. Sometimes detectives go undercover in order to investigate crime: A lone agent can infiltrate a criminal group or organization to gather information on future criminal activity. Undercover officers can also pose as victims to capture predatory criminals who have been conducting street robberies and muggings.[34]

In his recent study of investigation techniques, Martin Innes found that police detectives rely heavily on interviews and forensic evidence to create or manufacture a narrative of the crime, creating in a sense the "story" that sets out how, where, and why the incident took place.[35] To create their story, contemporary detectives typically use a three-pronged approach:[36]

SPECIFIC FOCUS Detectives interview witnesses, gather evidence, record events, and collect facts that are at the immediate crime scene.

GENERAL COVERAGE This process involves detectives who (a) canvass the neighborhood and make observations; (b) conduct interviews with friends, families, and associates; (c) contact coworkers or employers for information regarding victims and suspects; and (d) construct victim/suspect time lines to outline their whereabouts prior to the incident.

EXHIBIT 6.1

Investigative Techniques

Immediate Specific Focus	Immediate General Coverage	Pending Informative
Specific witnesses Specific evidence	Neighborhood canvass Friends, family, and associates (victimology)	Cell phone records Computer hard drives
Specific events Specific facts	Coworkers Victim/suspect time lines	Other records Private papers

INFORMATIVE Detectives use modern technology to collect records of cell phones and pagers, computer hard drives (e.g., palm pilots, laptops, notebooks, desktops, and servers), diaries, notes, and documents. Informative includes data that persons of interest in the investigation use that, in turn, tell about their lives, interactions with others, and geographic connections (see Exhibit 6.1). Detectives may successfully identify a criminal suspect if these methods pan out. But that is only the beginning of building an airtight case. Next, the detectives will attempt to gain as much information as possible from their suspect, perhaps even getting him to confess.

Sting Operations

sting operation
Organized groups of detectives who deceive criminals into openly committing illegal acts or conspiring to engage in criminal activity.

Another approach to detective work, commonly referred to as a **sting operation**, involves organized groups of detectives who deceive criminals into openly committing illegal acts or conspiring to engage in criminal activity. Numerous sting operations have been aimed at capturing professional thieves and seizing stolen merchandise. Undercover detectives pose as fences, set up ongoing fencing operations, and encourage thieves interested in selling stolen merchandise. Transactions are videotaped to provide prosecutors with strong cases. Sting operations have netted millions of dollars in recovered property and resulted in the arrests of many criminals.

These results seem impressive, but sting operations have drawbacks. By its very nature, a sting involves deceit by police agents that often comes close to entrapment.[37] Covert police activities have often been criticized as violating the personal rights of citizens while forcing officers into demeaning roles, such as having female officers act like prostitutes. (Ironically, recent [2005] research by Mary Dodge and her associates found that rather than considering it demeaning, female officers find their sting work as make-believe prostitutes exciting; they consider it a stepping-stone for promotion.[38])

Sting operations may encourage criminals to commit new crimes because they have a new source for fencing stolen goods. Innocent people may hurt their reputations by buying merchandise from a sting operation when they had no idea that the items had been stolen. By putting the government in the fencing business, such operations blur the line between law enforcement and criminal activity.

Undercover Work

Sometimes detectives go undercover to investigate crime.[39] Undercover work can take a number of forms. A lone agent can infiltrate a criminal group or organization to gather information on future criminal activity. Or a Drug Enforcement Administration agent may go undercover to gather intelligence on drug smugglers. Undercover officers can also pose as victims to capture predatory criminals who have been conducting street robberies and muggings.

Undercover work is considered a necessary element of police work, although it can prove dangerous for the agent. Police officers may be forced to engage in

Undercover agents may target known criminals in order to locate their whereabouts. Norman Porter, who was at the top of the Massachusetts State Police's Most Wanted list, is escorted to a car on March 23, 2005, in Chicago. In Massachusetts, he was a twice-convicted murderer who vanished after escaping from prison. In Illinois, he was a poet and an anti-war protester devoted to his local Unitarian church. The two lives of Porter collided when undercover police investigators arrested the man who 20 years ago fled from justice and built a new life in Chicago.

illegal or immoral behavior to maintain their cover. They also face significant physical danger in playing the role of a criminal and dealing with mobsters, terrorists, and drug dealers. In far too many cases, undercover officers are mistaken for real criminals and are injured by other law enforcement officers or private citizens trying to stop a crime. Arrest situations involving undercover officers may also provoke violence when suspects do not realize they are in the presence of police and therefore violently resist arrest.

Undercover officers may also experience psychological problems. Being away from home, keeping late hours, and always worrying that their identity will be uncovered can create enormous stress. Officers have experienced post-undercover strain, resulting in trouble at work and, in many instances, ruined marriages and botched prosecutions. Hanging around with criminals for a long period of time, making friends with them, and earning their trust can also have a damaging psychological impact.

Evaluating Investigations

Serious criticism has been leveled at the nation's detective forces for being bogged down in paperwork and being relatively inefficient in clearing cases. One famous study of 153 detective bureaus found that a great deal of a detective's time was spent in nonproductive work and that investigative expertise did little to solve cases. Half of all detectives could be replaced without negatively influencing crime clearance rates.[40]

Although some question remains about the effectiveness of investigations, police detectives do make a valuable contribution to police work because their skilled interrogation and case-processing techniques are essential to eventual criminal conviction.[41] Nonetheless, a majority of cases that are solved are done so when the perpetrator is identified at the scene of the crime by patrol officers. Research by the Police Executive Research Forum shows that if a crime is reported while in progress, the police have about a 33-percent chance of making an arrest; the arrest probability declines to about 10 percent if the crime is reported 1 minute later, and to 5 percent if more than 15 minutes has elapsed. As the time between the crime and the arrest grows, the chances of a conviction are also reduced, probably because the ability to recover evidence is lost. Put another way, the longer the gap between completion of the crime and the placing of the investigation into the hands of detectives, the lower the odds that the perpetrator will be identified and arrested.[42]

Improving Investigations

A number of efforts have been made to revamp and improve investigation procedures. One practice has been to give patrol officers greater responsibility for conducting preliminary investigations at the scene of the crime. In addition, specialized units, such as homicide or burglary squads, now operate over larger areas and can bring specific expertise to bear. Technological advances in DNA and fingerprint identification have also aided investigation effectiveness. The Images of Justice feature highlights how advances are being portrayed on one popular TV series.

One reason for investigation ineffectiveness is that detectives often lack sufficient resources to carry out a lengthy ongoing probe of any but the most serious cases. Research shows the following:[43]

UNSOLVED CASES Almost 50 percent of burglary cases are screened out by supervisors before assignment to a detective for a follow-up investigation. Of those assigned, 75 percent are dropped after the first day of the follow-up investigation. Although robbery cases are more likely to be assigned to detectives, 75 percent of them are also dropped after one day of investigation.

LENGTH OF INVESTIGATION The vast majority of cases are investigated for no more than 4 hours stretching over 3 days. An average of 11 days elapses between the initial report of a crime and the suspension of the investigation.

SOURCES OF INFORMATION Early in an investigation, the focus is on the victim; as the investigation is pursued, emphasis shifts to the suspect. The most critical information for determining case outcome is the name and description of the suspect and related crime information. Victims are most often the source of information. Unfortunately, witnesses, informants, and members of the police department are consulted far less often. However, when these sources are tapped, they are likely to produce useful information.

EFFECTIVENESS Preliminary investigations by patrol officers are critical. In situations in which the suspect's identity is not known immediately after the crime is committed, detectives make an arrest in less than 10 percent of all cases.

A Los Angeles police officer interviews witnesses and suspects after a gang shooting in Boyle Heights, East Los Angeles. Boyle Heights has one of the city's highest gang shooting rates. The probability of successfully settling a case is improved if patrol officers gather evidence at the scene of a crime and effectively communicate it to detectives working the case.

© Gilles Mingasson/Getty Images

CSI: Crime Scene Investigation

When *CSI: Crime Scene Investigation* debuted, it was a surprise television hit. Instead of relying on shoot-outs and car chases, it pit criminals against a dedicated team of forensic scientists who work for the Las Vegas, Nevada, Police Department. Instead of using their brawn, the CSI investigators relied on their wits and scientific training.

The team is led by Gil Grissom, played by William Peterson. The character is a trained scientist whose specialty is forensic entomology, which is the study of insects found on or near a crime scene. He searches for clues within victims' bodies, outside their bodies, or in any other way that can provide evidence to identify the suspect or solve the crime. For example, he can test the waste products from an insect found in the body of the deceased to determine the time of death, whether the body has been moved, and so on. The opposite of a hard-drinking, two-fisted crime fighter, Grissom is a shy, quiet guy who, when not working, can be found doing crossword puzzles.

Although not all CSI members were trained as scientists, most have the skills and education that make them formidable forensic specialists. For example, Sara Sidle, played by Jorja Fox, holds a B.S. degree in physics from Harvard. Brought in specifically by Grissom, she is dedicated to her work and seems to spend her free time studying forensics.

Each show revolves around a seemingly unsolvable crime. In some instances, a leading suspect is exonerated when the team uses its skills to show that, despite appearances, he or she could not have committed the crime. For example, in "Sex, Lies, and Larvae," the team investigates the shooting death of a young woman whose bloodied and bug-infested body is found on a nearby mountain. At first glance, it seems that the woman's abusive husband is the killer. But Grissom's analysis of the bugs found on the woman's body indicates that the victim had been killed three days earlier, when her husband was out of town. The *CSI* series has proven so popular that a second version set in Miami, Florida, premiered in 2002, and a New York *CSI* began in 2004.

The *CSI* series draws attention to the developing field of forensics in police work. *Forensic* means "pertaining to the law," and forensic scientists perform comprehensive chemical and physical analyses on evidence submitted by law enforcement agencies. Although most forensic scientists focus on criminal cases (they are sometimes referred to as criminalists), others work in the civil justice system—for example, performing handwriting comparisons to determine the validity of a signature on a will. Nevertheless, their analyses involve a variety of sciences, mathematical principles, and problem-solving methods, including the use of complex instruments and chemical, physical, and microscopic examining techniques. In addition to analyzing crime scene investigations, forensic scientists provide testimony in a court of law when the case is brought to trial. Some forensic scientists are generalists, but others, such as Gil Grissom, specialize in a particular scientific area, including the following:

1. *Controlled substances and toxicology.* Crime lab professionals specializing in this area examine blood and other body fluids and tissues for the presence of alcohol, drugs, and poisons.

2. *Biology.* Crime lab professionals compare body fluids and hair for typing factors, including DNA analysis. Analysis of a hair found at a crime scene can determine factors such as whether the hair belongs to a human or animal, the body area that a hair came from, diseases that the person or animal has, and, sometimes, race.

3. *Chemistry.* Forensic scientists analyze trace physical evidence such as blood spatters, paint, soil, and glass. For example, blood spatters help reconstruct a crime scene. The patterns of spatters and the shapes of blood droplets tell how the crime was committed.

4. *Document examination.* Document examination includes many areas of expertise, including forgery, document dating, and analysis of handwriting, typewriting, computer printing, and photocopying.

5. *Firearms and toolmark identification.* Firearms examination involves matching identifying characteristics between a firearm and a projectile and between a projectile and a target. Typically, this includes matching bullets to the gun that fired them. Toolmark identification involves matching some identifying characteristics of a tool, such as a pry bar, to the object on which it was used, such as a door frame. It also includes explosives and imprint evidence.

Critical Thinking

It is said that life imitates art. As the popularity of the *CSI* series grows, more students will likely be drawn into forensics, and more police and law enforcement agencies are likely to use forensic specialists in their daily operations. Do you think that crime is better solved in the lab or on the beat?

InfoTrac College Edition Research

How accurate is *CSI*? To find out, read Michael Lipton and Lorenzo Benet, "Getting Dead Right: Forensics Expert Elizabeth Devine Makes Sure *CSI*'s Corpses Are Ready for Their Close-Ups," *People*, April 22, 2002, p. 77. Use "*Crime Scene Investigation*" as a subject guide on InfoTrac College Edition to learn more about the show.

Source: Hall Dillon, "Forensic Scientists: A Career in the Crime Lab," *Occupational Outlook Quarterly* 43 (1999): 2–5.

Private Detectives and Investigators

Duties and Characteristics of the Job

Private detectives' and investigators' work comes in a variety of forms, but they primarily collect information for a client. Most often this will involve interviewing individuals, conducting surveillance, and conducting searches for information. Private investigators often specialize in a certain type of case, such as corporate, financial, or legal investigation. Loss-prevention agents, commonly known as store detectives, prevent the loss, theft, or destruction of store merchandise at the hands of shoplifters, employees, and delivery persons. The kinds of cases that private investigators take on might include locating missing persons, computer-based crimes, uncovering fraud, or conducting background checks. Because their work often involves legal issues, private detectives and investigators may be asked to prepare materials for a trial by producing evidence or writing reports, aiding attorneys, or testifying in court.

Private detectives and investigators often have to work irregular hours, including nights and weekends, when conducting surveillance, interviews, or other forms of research. Investigators who own their own

detective agency are exceptions to this tendency because they can send other investigators to do this work. Likewise, work settings can vary from safe places such as offices and homes to more dangerous settings.

Job Outlook

The outlook is good for those seeking a career in this field. The best opportunities will be for those seeking entry-level positions at detective agencies or as part-time store detectives. Larger discount and retail chains have the most opportunities for those who seek store detective positions.

Salary

Private detectives and investigators who have full-time positions earn a median annual salary of $32,110. For investigators who are paid on a case-by-case basis, pay will depend upon the number and pay rate for cases they choose to take or are assigned. However, it should be noted that earnings vary greatly upon factors such as geographical region and employer.

Considering these findings, detective work may be improved if greater emphasis is placed on collecting physical evidence at the scene of the crime, identifying witnesses, checking departmental records, and using informants. The probability of successfully settling a case is improved if patrol officers gather evidence at the scene of a crime and effectively communicate it to detectives working the case. Also recommended is the use of targeted investigations that direct attention at a few individuals, such as career criminals, who are known to have engaged in the behavior under investigation.

As the private security industry grows, a great many investigators are being employed by private detective agencies or security companies. Sound like an interesting career? Read the Careers in Criminal Justice feature.

Using Technology

Police departments are now employing advanced technology in all facets of their operations, from assigning patrol routes to gathering evidence. Similarly, investigators are starting to use advanced technology to streamline and enhance the investigation process. Gathering evidence at a crime scene and linking clues to a list of suspects can be a tedious job for many investigators. Yet linkage is critical if suspects are to be quickly apprehended before they are able to leave the jurisdiction, intimidate witnesses, or cover up any clues they may have left behind.

One innovative use of technology allows investigators to compare evidence found at the crime scene with material collected from similar crimes by other police agencies. Police agencies are using a program called Coplink to help with this time-consuming task. Coplink integrates information from different jurisdictions

Opportunities

Job opportunities within the field are expected to grow in the coming years for numerous reasons, including the need to replace those who retire or change careers and increasing litigation. Candidates entering the field should expect healthy competition from other applicants with degrees and relevant law enforcement experience. Opportunities for advancement may be limited, so after several years of experience, many private detectives and investigators will start their own agencies.

Qualifications

In many states, a private investigator needs a license in order to work. The strictness of the licensing requirements will vary by state. Personality and work characteristics that will serve a potential applicant well when applying for positions include determination, responsibility, assertiveness, good communications skills, and the ability to handle confrontations. If a detective or investigator wants to specialize in a certain field, such as corporate investigating, relevant education and personal experience in that field may

be necessary. In general, detectives and investigators are not armed; however, certain jobs may require proper licensing and training to be armed.

Education and Training

Although there is no explicit educational minimum for this type of work, many applicants in this field will have undergraduate degrees in a related field such as criminal justice or some previous law enforcement or military experience. Education gives those who do not have such experience an advantage. Knowledge of how to conduct searches and surveillance techniques is also helpful.

Sources: "Private Detectives and Investigators," *Occupational Outlook Handbook,* 2006–2007 edition (Bureau of Labor Statistics, United States Department of Labor), retrieved May 25, 2006, from http://www.bls.gov/oco/ocos157.htm; S. E. Lambert and D. Regan, "Private Investigators," in *Great Jobs for Criminal Justice Majors* (New York: McGraw-Hill, 2001), pp. 252–53, 255; "Monster Career Advice: Private Detective/Investigator," retrieved June 15, 2006, from http://jobprofiles.monster.com/Content/job_content/JC_Military/JSC_PrivateSecurity/copy_of_JOB_PrivateDetectiveandInvestigator/jobzilla_html?jobprofiles=1.

into a single database that detectives can access when working investigations.[44] The Coplink program allows investigators to search the entire database of past criminal records and compute a list of possible suspects even if only partial data are available, such as first or last name, partial license plate numbers, vehicle type, vehicle color, location of crime, or weapon used. The Coplink program allows police to access data from other police agencies in minutes, a process that normally could take days or weeks. The Coplink system allows for easy information sharing between law enforcement agencies, a task that has been problematic in the past. It is one of the new breed of computer-aided investigation techniques that are beginning to have a significant impact on capture ratios in the nation's police departments.

Community Policing

For more than 30 years, police agencies have been trying to gain the cooperation and respect of the communities that they serve. At first, efforts at improving the relationships between police departments and the public involved programs with the general title of police–community relations (PCR). Developed at the station house and departmental levels, these initial PCR programs were designed to make citizens more aware of police activities, alert them to methods of self-protection, and improve general attitudes toward policing.

Although PCR efforts showed a willingness for police agencies to cooperate with the public, some experts believed that law enforcement agencies needed to undergo a significant transformation to create meaningful partnerships with the public. These views were articulated in a critical 1982 paper by two justice policy

The most successful community-oriented policing programs give officers time to meet with local residents to talk about crime in the neighborhood and the ability to use personal initiative to solve problems. Police officer Kurt Indehar (right) mixes lemonade for local Minneapolis children on June 29, 2006. Police set up the lemonade stand and a basketball hoop to take a step toward establishing connections with citizens in hopes of deterring crime.

broken windows model
The role of the police as maintainers of community order and safety.

The School of Criminal Justice at Michigan State University maintains a comprehensive website devoted to community policing. It contains an extensive collection of full-text papers on all aspects of this subject. You can access it by going to the Siegel/Senna Introduction to Criminal Justice 11e website: www .thomsonedu.com/criminaljustice/ siegel.

experts, George Kelling and James Q. Wilson, who espoused a new approach to improving police relations in the community, which has come to be known as the **broken windows model**.[45] Kelling and Wilson made three points:

1. Neighborhood disorder creates fear. Urban areas filled with street people, youth gangs, prostitutes, and the mentally disturbed are the ones most likely to maintain a high degree of crime.

2. Neighborhoods give out crime-promoting signals. A neighborhood filled with deteriorated housing, unrepaired broken windows, and untended disorderly behavior gives out crime-promoting signals. Honest citizens live in fear in these areas, and predatory criminals are attracted to them.

3. Police need citizen cooperation. If police are to reduce fear and successfully combat crime in these urban areas, they must have the cooperation, support, and assistance of the citizens.[46]

According to the broken windows approach, community relations and crime control effectiveness cannot be the province of a few specialized units housed within a traditional police department. Instead, the core police role must be altered if community involvement is to be won and maintained. To accomplish this goal, urban police departments should return to an earlier style of policing, in which officers on the beat had intimate contact with the people they served. Modern police departments generally rely on motorized patrol to cover wide areas, to maintain a visible police presence, and to ensure rapid response time. Although effective and economical, the patrol car removes officers from the mainstream of the community, alienating people who might otherwise be potential sources of information and help to the police.

PERSPECTIVES ON JUSTICE

Rehabilitation and Restorative Justice

According to the broken windows model, police administrators would best be served by deploying their forces where they can encourage public confidence, strengthen feelings of safety, and elicit cooperation from citizens. Community preservation, public safety, and order maintenance—not crime fighting—should become the primary focus of patrol. Just as physicians and dentists practice preventive medicine and dentistry, police should help maintain an intact community structure, not simply fight crime. Broken windows policing has shifted police from a purely crime control model to one that embraces elements of rehabilitation and restorative justice.

Implementing Community Policing

The community policing concept was originally implemented through a number of innovative demonstration projects.[47] Among the most publicized were experiments in foot patrol, which took officers out of cars and had them walking beats in the neighborhood. Foot patrol efforts were aimed at forming a bond with community residents by acquainting them with the individual officers who patrolled their neighborhood, letting them know that police were caring and available. The first **foot patrol** experiments were conducted in cities in Michigan and New Jersey. An evaluation of foot patrol indicated that although it did not bring down the crime rate, residents in areas where foot patrol was added perceived greater safety and were less afraid of crime.[48]

Since the advent of these programs, the federal government has encouraged the growth of community policing by providing millions of dollars to hire and train officers.[49] Hundreds of communities have adopted innovative forms of decentralized, neighborhood-based community policing models. Recent surveys indicate that a significant increase is evident in community policing activities in recent years and that certain core programs such as crime prevention activities have become embedded in the police role.[50]

Community-oriented policing (COP) programs have been implemented in large cities, suburban areas, and rural communities.[51] The most successful programs give officers the time to meet with local residents to talk about crime in the neighborhood and to use personal initiative to solve problems (see Exhibit 6.2).

Although not all programs work (police–community newsletters and cleanup campaigns do not seem to do much good), the overall impression has been that patrol officers can reduce the level of fear in the community. Some COP programs assign officers to neighborhoods, organize training programs for community leaders, and feature a bottom-up approach to deal with community problems—that is, decision making involves the officer on the scene, not a directive from central headquarters. Programs have also been created for juveniles who might ordinarily have little to do besides get involved in gangs but are now included in such activities as neighborhood cleanup efforts.[52] In Spokane, Washington, "Cops and Kids" is a weekend event that brings police officers and young people together as a reward for staying out of summer trouble. Events include show cars, car competitions, demonstrations by the SWAT and K-9 Units, and other activities.[53]

Neighborhood Policing

Community policing means more than implementing direct-action programs. It also refers to a philosophy of policing that requires departments to reconsider their recruitment, organization, and operating procedures. What are some of the most important community policing concepts? First, community policing emphasizes results, not bureaucratic process. Instead of reacting to problems in the community, police departments take the initiative in identifying issues and actively treating their cause. Problem-solving and analysis techniques replace emphasis on bureaucratic detail. There is less concern with playing by the book and more with getting the job done.

To achieve the goals of COP, some agencies have tried to decentralize, an approach sometimes referred to as innovative **neighborhood-oriented policing (NOP)**.[54] Problem solving is best done at the neighborhood level where issues originate, not at a far-off central headquarters. Because each neighborhood has its own particular needs, police decision making must be flexible and adaptive. For example, neighborhoods undergoing changes in racial composition all experience high levels of racially motivated violence.[55] Police must be able to distinguish these neighborhood characteristics and allocate resources to meet their needs.

The neighborhood concept is not only being used here but is also catching on in Europe. The International Justice feature on page 212 describes the British version of the program.

Changing the Police Role

Community policing also stresses sharing power with local groups and individuals. A key element of the community policing philosophy is that citizens must

foot patrol
Police patrol that takes officers out of cars and puts them on a walking beat to strengthen ties with the community.

community-oriented policing (COP)
Programs designed to bring police and the public closer together and create a more cooperative working environment between them.

neighborhood-oriented policing (NOP)
A police philosophy suggesting that problem solving is best done at the neighborhood level, where issues originate, not at a far-off central headquarters.

The Community Policing Consortium was created and funded in 1993 by the Bureau of Justice Assistance of the U.S. Department of Justice to deliver community policing training and technical assistance to police departments and sheriffs' offices that receive federal grant money. You can access its website by going to the Siegel/Senna Introduction to Criminal Justice 11e website: www.thomsonedu.com/criminaljustice/siegel.

EXHIBIT 6.2

The Elements of Community Policing

ORGANIZATIONAL ELEMENTS

1. *Philosophy adopted organization-wide.* Police departments must integrate community policing concepts within the core of the organization and not treat community policing as a special program or add-on. Department-wide adoption of community policing is evidenced by the integration of the philosophy into mission statements, policies and procedures, performance evaluations and hiring and promotional practices, training programs, and other systems and activities that define organizational culture and activities.

2. *Decentralized decision making and accountability.* In community policing, individual line officers are given the authority to solve problems and make operational decisions suitable to their roles, both individually and collectively. Leadership is required and rewarded at every level, with managers, supervisors, and officers held accountable for decisions and the effects of their efforts at solving problems and reducing crime and disorder within the community.

3. *Fixed geographic accountability and generalist responsibilities.* In community policing, the majority of staffing is geographically based. Appropriate personnel are assigned to fixed geographic areas for extended periods of time in order to foster communication and partnerships between individual officers and their community, and are accountable for reducing crime and disorder within their assigned area.

4. *Use of volunteer resources.* Community policing encourages the use of non-law-enforcement resources within a law enforcement agency. Examples of such resources are police reserves, volunteers, Explorer Scouts, service organizations, and citizen or youth police academies.

5. *Enhancers.* There are a number of enhancers and facilitators that may assist departments in their transition to community policing. For example, updated technology and information systems can aid community policing by providing officers access to crime and incident data that support problem analysis or increase uncommitted officer time by reducing time spent on administrative duties.

TACTICAL ELEMENTS

1. *Enforcement of laws.* Although community policing complements the use of proven and established enforcement strategies, emphasis is placed on being active partners in identifying laws that need to be amended or enacted, then working with lawmakers and organizing citizen support efforts to change them.

2. *Proactive, crime prevention oriented.* Under community policing, law enforcement focuses on crime prevention and proactively addressing the root causes of crime and disorder. The community actively engages in collaborating on prevention and problem-solving activities, with a goal of reducing victimization and fear of crime.

3. *Problem solving.* Police, community members, and other public and private entities work together to address the underlying problems that contribute to crime and disorder by identifying and analyzing problems, developing suitable responses, and assessing the effectiveness of these responses.

EXTERNAL ELEMENTS

1. *Public involvement and community partnerships.* Citizens serve as partners who share responsibility for identifying priorities and developing and implementing responses. The public has "ownership" of the problem-solving process.

2. *Government, other agency partnerships.* Under community policing, other government agencies are called upon and recognized for their abilities to respond to and address crime and social disorder issues.

Source: Office of Community Oriented Policing Services (http://www.cops.usdoj.gov/Default.asp?Item=36).

actively participate with police to fight crime.[56] This participation might involve providing information in area-wide crime investigations or helping police reach out to troubled youths.

Community policing also means the eventual redesign of police departments. Management's role must be reordered to focus on the problems of the community, not the needs of the police department. The traditional vertical police organizational chart must be altered so that top-down management gives way to bottom-up decision making. The patrol officer becomes the manager of his beat and a key decision maker.

Community policing requires that police departments alter their recruitment and training requirements. Future officers must develop community-organizing and problem-solving skills, along with traditional police skills. Their training must prepare them to succeed less on their ability to make arrests or issue citations and more on their ability to solve problems effectively.

ThomsonNOW Improve your grade on the exam with Personalized Study! For reinforcement resources and a mastery check of police investigations and community policing, go to www.thomsonedu.com/thomsonnow.

◆ PROBLEM-ORIENTED POLICING (POP)

Closely associated with, yet independent from, the community policing concept are **problem-oriented policing (POP)** strategies. Traditional police models focus on responding to calls for help in the fastest possible time, dealing with the situation, and then getting on the street again as soon as possible.[57] In contrast, the core of problem-oriented policing is a proactive orientation.

Problem-oriented policing strategies require police agencies to identify particular long-term community problems—street-level drug dealers, prostitution rings, gang hangouts—and to develop strategies to eliminate them.[58] As with community policing, being problem solvers requires that police departments rely on local residents and private resources. This means that police managers must learn how to develop community resources, design efficient and cost-effective solutions to problems, and become advocates as well as agents of reform.[59]

A significant portion of police departments are using special units to confront specific social problems. For example, departments may employ special units devoted to youth issues ranging from child abuse to gangs.

Problem-oriented policing models are supported by the fact that a great deal of urban crime is concentrated in a few hot spots.[60] A large number of all police calls in metropolitan areas typically radiate from a relatively few locations: bars, malls, the bus depot, hotels, and certain apartment buildings.[61] By implication, concentrating police resources on these **hot spots of crime** could appreciably reduce crime.[62]

problem-oriented policing (POP)
A style of police management that stresses proactive problem solving instead of reactive crime fighting.

hot spots of crime
The view that a significant portion of all police calls in metropolitan areas typically radiate from a relatively few locations: bars, malls, the bus depot, hotels, and certain apartment buildings.

Criminal Acts, Criminal Places

Problem-oriented strategies are being developed that focus on specific criminal problem areas, specific criminal acts, or both. One POP effort in Sarasota, Florida, aimed at reducing prostitution involved intensive, focused, and/or high-visibility patrols to discourage prostitutes and their customers, undercover work to arrest prostitutes and drug dealers, and collaboration with hotel and motel owners to identify and arrest pimps and drug dealers.[63] Some other efforts include the following:

COMBATING AUTO THEFT Because of problem-oriented approaches (combined with advanced technology), car thieves in many jurisdictions are no longer able to steal cars with as much ease as before. To reduce the high number of car thefts occurring each year, some police departments have invested in bait cars, which are parked in high-theft areas and are equipped with technology that alerts law enforcement personnel when someone has stolen a vehicle. A signal goes off when either a door is opened or the engine starts. Then, equipped with global positioning satellite (GPS) technology, police officers are able to watch the movement of the car. Some cars are also equipped with microscopic videos and audio recorders, which allow officers to see and hear the suspect(s) within the car, and remote engine and door locks, which can trap the thief inside. The technology has been used in conjunction with an advertising campaign to warn potential car thieves about the program. The system has been instituted in Vancouver, Canada, and Minneapolis, Minnesota, with impressive results. Motor vehicle theft dropped over 40 percent in Minneapolis over a three-year period in which bait cars were used and 30 percent in Vancouver within six months of being

INTERNATIONAL JUSTICE

Neighborhood Policing in England

Community and neighborhood policing models are not unique to the United States. Similar programs are being used in France, the Netherlands, and other European countries. In England, community policing models have attempted to identify crime problems at the neighborhood level. The English model calls for services being delivered by mixed policing teams that are assigned to neighborhoods on a permanent basis. Typically, the teams include the following:

♦ *Uniformed police officers.* Teams leaders who act as community leaders and tackle crimes that require the full range of police officer powers.

♦ *Police community support officers (PCSOs).* Uniformed members of the police team who provide a high-visibility, reassuring presence in communities and do follow-up with victims of crime. They can be designated with a range of powers by their chief constable (such as confiscating alcohol), which can have an immediate impact on dealing with problems of nuisance behavior and disorder. The British government is currently legislating for a set of standard powers for all PCSOs, although a small number of powers will remain at the discretion of the chief officer.

♦ *Special constables.* Volunteers with full police powers. They play an important role in tackling crime and in providing a visible, reassuring presence in communities.

♦ *Neighborhood wardens.* Employed by local authorities, housing associations, and community groups, wardens play a vital role in neighborhoods, particularly in deprived areas. They can be the first point of contact for people on issues of local concern, such as littering or abandoned vehicles. They are working as part of joint teams with the police in some areas.

♦ *Local authority figures.* They are not employed directly by the police but work within communities

to help improve people's safety and quality of life—for example, security guards, park rangers, housing association employees, and environmental officers. They provide additional "eyes and ears" for the police and are important for forging links, improving communication, and delivering effective policing to neighborhoods.

The size of teams varies according to local decision. For example, the London Metropolitan Police operates with teams of one sergeant, two constables, and three PCSOs, with phone and e-mail contacts through the department's website. Other forces are configuring their teams differently, in accordance with local needs.

The Purpose of Neighborhood Policing in England

Neighborhood policing in England is aimed at reducing both the amount of crime and fear of crime and bringing the police closer to communities. Here are its key principles:

♦ *Visible and accessible police.* Local people seeing and having regular contact with the same officers—week in and week out—who stay in the job long enough to build lasting and trusting relationships with the communities they serve.

♦ *Influence.* Reflects community safety priorities in their communities, which might be dealing with persistent burglaries, clearing up graffiti and vandalism, or tackling open drug dealing or gun crime. Local people who are closest to the problems in their communities are often best placed to help shape and participate in the solutions to them.

♦ *Interventions.* Joint action with communities and partners to solve problems and harness everyone's strengths.

♦ *Answers.* Sustainable solutions to problems and feedback on results. People will know the

---

instituted. In addition to cutting down on auto theft, the system, which costs roughly $3,500 per car, seems to decrease the chance of danger of high-speed pursuits because police officers can put obstacles on the road to stop the car.[64]

gang tactical detail
A police unit created to combat neighborhood gang problems by targeting known offenders who have shown a propensity toward gang violence or criminal activity.

REDUCING VIOLENCE A number of efforts have been made to reduce violence by using problem-oriented community policing techniques. Police in Richmond, California, successfully applied such techniques, including citizen involvement, to help reduce murder rates.[65] Problem-oriented techniques have also been directed at combating gang-related violence. For example, the Tucson, Arizona, Police Department has created a **gang tactical detail** unit, which is aimed at proactively attacking neighborhood gang problems by targeting known offenders

names, numbers, and e-mail addresses of their neighborhood policing teams. They will also know who is responsible for what in terms of reducing crime, tackling antisocial behavior, and keeping the areas where they live and work safe. The government is legislating to make it possible for local people, through the Community Call for Action, to trigger action by the police and other partners to address acute or persistent problems of crime or antisocial behavior.

The British government's goal is that police forces should be able to guarantee that neighborhood police teams will stay in neighborhoods and will not be taken away to deal with other events. This is one reason for restructuring police forces so that they have the capacity to deal with major events without having to divert neighborhood teams.

Neighborhood Policing in Action: Two Case Studies

◆ *Leicestershire.* Neighborhood beat officers and police community support officers in Leicestershire worked with the local community, the Leicester City Council, and the local Joint Action Group to tackle a specific example of antisocial behavior. A gang of youths was vandalizing a derelict toilet block, a focal point for drug users, in a park opposite a Hindu temple. Bricks were thrown at people using the park and were also used to break the windows of the temple, causing thousands of pounds worth of damage. The police, working with their partners, identified key individuals involved and issued warnings that stopped the damage in the short term. A long-term solution was also sought, and the council agreed to demolish the toilet block. A PCSO has maintained the links developed with the users of the temple and makes regular visits.

◆ *Northumbria.* A demonstration project in Northumbria involved close partnership between the police and two rural communities. Participatory appraisal methods were used to build community capacity and involvement in local problem solving. Action planning meetings were held where community beat managers, local residents, partner agencies, and community groups all came together to highlight problems and plan achievable, jointly delivered solutions. Local residents in one area were trained to undertake their own surveys on local problems and experiences of crime. Community beat managers and sergeants in Northumbria felt that the project had been a success, especially in relation to greater opportunities to share information and intelligence with the public. The sector inspector has extended the project to neighboring areas.

Critical Thinking

1. Can community policing be used in the fight against terrorism? How might it be more effective than traditional police operations?

2. What can be the downside of community policing? For example, does it put neighborhood residents at risk?

⌕ InfoTrac College Edition Research

To read about community policing programs in other nations, go to Erin Gibbs Van Brunschot, "Community Policing and 'John Schools,'" *Canadian Review of Sociology and Anthropology* 40 (2003): 215–32.

Source: British Home Office, *Neighbourhood Policing, Progress Report, May 2006* (London, British Home Office, 2006) (http://police.homeoffice.gov.uk/news-and-publications/publication/community-policing/neighbourhood_booklet_170506.pdf?view=Binary).

who have shown a propensity toward gang violence or criminal activity. Members of the tactical unit work directly with neighborhood community groups to identify specific gang problems within individual neighborhoods. Once the problem is identified, the unit helps devise a working solution combining community involvement, intergovernmental assistance, and law enforcement intervention. The officers of the Gang Tactical Detail attend meetings with community groups to identify gang-related problems. They assist with gang-awareness presentations for schools and civic groups.[66]

Another well-known program, Operation Ceasefire, is a problem-oriented policing intervention aimed at reducing youth homicide and youth firearms violence in Boston. Evaluations of the program found that Ceasefire produced significant reductions in youth homicide victimization and gun assault incidents in Boston that were not experienced in other communities in New England or elsewhere in the nation.[67] The Jersey City, New Jersey, police recently applied a variety of aggressive crime-reducing techniques in some of the city's gang-ridden areas. Evaluations of the program show that crime rates were reduced when police officers used aggressive problem solving (e.g., drug enforcement) and community improvement techniques (e.g., increased lighting and cleaned vacant lots) in high-crime areas.[68] Another recent initiative by the Dallas Police Department assigned officers to aggressively pursue truancy and curfew enforcement, a tactic that resulted in lower rates of gang violence.[69]

Although programs such as these seem successful, the effectiveness of any street-level problem-solving efforts must be interpreted with caution.[70] Criminals could be displaced to other, safer areas of the city and could return shortly after the program is called a success and the additional police forces have been pulled from the area.[71] Nonetheless, evidence shows that merely saturating an area with police may not deter crime but that focusing efforts at a particular problem may have a crime-reducing effect.

◆ THE CHALLENGES OF COMMUNITY POLICING

The core concepts of police work are changing as administrators recognize the limitations and realities of police work in modern society. If they are to be successful, community policing strategies must be able to react effectively to some significant administrative problems:

1. *Defining community.* Police administrators must be able to define the concept of community as an ecological area defined by common norms, shared values, and interpersonal bonds.[72] After all, the main focus of community policing is to activate the community norms that make neighborhoods more crime resistant. If, in contrast, community policing projects cross the boundaries of many different neighborhoods, any hope of learning and accessing community norms, strengths, and standards will be lost.[73] And even if natural community structures

In Anderson, South Carolina, police officer Art Jones talks with Drek Pratt, age 12, as he makes his rounds on foot through the neighborhood on April 3, 2006. For the past two years, Jones, a reserve officer with the Anderson Police Department, has been walking his beat—a practice that in some areas is a critical element of community-oriented policing.

©AP Images/*Independent Mail*/Sefton Ipock

can be identified, it will be necessary for policing agencies to continually monitor the changing norms, values, and attitudes of the community they serve, a process that has the side effect of creating positive interactions between the community and the police.[74]

2. *Defining roles.* Police administrators must also establish the exact role of community police agents. How should they integrate their activities with those of regular patrol forces? For example, should foot patrols have primary responsibility for policing in an area, or should they coordinate their activities with officers assigned to patrol cars? Should community police officers be solely problem identifiers and neighborhood organizers, or should they also be expected to be law enforcement agents who get to the crime scene rapidly and later do investigative work? Can community police teams and regular patrols work together, or must a department abandon traditional police roles and become purely community policing oriented?

3. *Changing supervisor attitudes.* Some supervisors are wary of community policing because it supports a decentralized command structure. This would mean fewer supervisors and, consequently, less chance for promotion and a potential loss of authority.[75] It is not surprising, considering these misgivings, that more than a decade after the COP initiative began many police commanders still focus on the core values of order maintenance, crime fighting, and service at the expense of community policing.[76] They still use performance measures such as arrest and response time to evaluate subordinates, which makes it difficult for line-level officers to change their approach toward policing and embrace community policing goals.[77] Conversely, those supervisors who learn to actively embrace community policing concepts are the ones best able to encourage patrol officers to engage in self-initiated activities, including community policing and problem solving.[78]

4. *Reorienting police values.* Research shows that police officers who have a traditional crime control orientation are less satisfied with community policing efforts than those who are public service oriented.[79] In some instances, officers holding traditional values may go as far as looking down upon their own comrades assigned to community policing, who as a result feel "stigmatized" and penalized by lack of agency support.[80] Although this finding comes as no surprise, it is indicative of the difficulty that police managers will face in convincing experienced officers, many of whom hold traditional law-and-order values, to embrace community policing models. Yet it is unlikely that community policing activities can be successful unless police line officers are able to form a commitment to the values of community policing.[81]

5. *Revising training.* Because the community policing model calls for a revision of the police role from law enforcer to community organizer, police training must be revised to reflect this new mandate. If community policing is to be adopted on a wide scale, a whole new type of police officer must be recruited and trained in a whole new way. Retraining and reorienting police from their traditional roles into a more social service orientation may also be difficult. Most police officers do not have the social service skills required of effective community agents. Thus, community policing requires that police departments alter their training requirements. Future officers must develop community-organizing and problem-solving skills, along with traditional police skills. Their training must prepare them to succeed less on their ability to make arrests or issue citations and more on their ability to solve problems, prevent crime effectively, and deal with neighborhood diversity and cultural values.[82]

6. *Reorienting recruitment.* To make community policing successful, mid-level managers must be recruited and trained who are receptive to and can implement community-change strategies.[83] The selection of new recruits must be guided by a desire to find individuals with the skills and attitudes that support community policing. They must be open to the fact that community policing will

To find a website dedicated to providing the latest information, training, advice, and discussion on community policing, go to Policing.com. Its view is that community policing is a philosophy based on the recognition that nothing can outperform dedicated people working together to make their communities better and safer places in which to live and work and raise children. You can access it by going to the Siegel/Senna Introduction to Criminal Justice 11e website: www.thomsonedu.com/criminaljustice/siegel.

help them gain knowledge of the community, give them opportunities to gain skill and experience, and help them engage in proactive problem solving.[84] Selecting people who find these values attractive and then providing training that accentuates the community vision of policing are essential to the success of the COP model.

7. *Reaching out to every community.* Because each neighborhood has its own particular needs, community policing must become flexible and adaptive. In neighborhoods undergoing change in racial composition, special initiatives to reduce tensions may be required.[85] Some neighborhoods are cohesive and highly organized, and residents work together to solve problems. These neighborhoods are said to have collective efficacy; others are fragmented and disorganized (anomic). The police must be able to distinguish between these situations and provide appropriate services. In the strong, organized area they might want to work with existing neighborhood groups, whereas in the anomic area they might want to use aggressive tactics to reduce crime and "take back the streets" before building relations with community leaders.[86] If crime rates can drop in these areas, especially youth crime, community policing will be viewed by residents as creating cohesiveness where none existed before.[87]

Overcoming Obstacles

Although there are formidable obstacles to overcome, growing evidence suggests that community- and problem-oriented policing can work and fit well with traditional forms of policing.[88] Many police experts and administrators have embraced these concepts as revolutionary revisions of the basic police role. Community policing efforts have been credited with helping reduce crime rates in large cities such as New York and Boston. The most professional and highly motivated officers are the ones most likely to support community policing efforts.[89]

These results are encouraging, but there is no clear-cut evidence that community policing is highly successful at reducing crime or changing the traditional values and attitudes of police officers involved in the programs.[90] Some research does show that the arrest rate actually increases after COP programs have been implemented.[91] However, crime rate reductions in cities that have used COP may be the result of an overall downturn in the nation's crime rate rather than a result of community policing efforts.

Despite these professional obstacles, community policing has become a common part of municipal police departments. The concept is also being exported around the world, with varying degrees of success; some nations do not seem to have the stability necessary to support community policing.[92] Where it is used, citizens seem to like community policing initiatives, and those who volunteer and get involved in community crime prevention programs report higher confidence in the police force and its ability to create a secure environment.[93]

ThomsonNOW Improve your grade on the exam with Personalized Study! For reinforcement resources and a mastery check of the challenges of community policing, go to www.thomsonedu.com/thomsonnow.

◆ SUPPORT FUNCTIONS

As the model of a typical police department indicates (Figure 6.1), not all members of a department engage in what the general public regards as real police work—patrol, detection, and traffic control. Even in departments that are embracing community and problem-oriented policing, a great deal of police resources are devoted to support and administrative functions.

Many police departments maintain their own personnel service, which carries out such functions as recruiting new police officers, creating exams to determine the most qualified applicants, and handling promotions and transfers.

Innovative selection techniques are constantly being developed and tested. For example, the Behavioral–Personnel Assessment Device (B-PAD) requires police applicants to view videotaped scenarios and respond as if they were officers handling the situation. Reviews indicate that this procedure may be a reliable and unbiased method of choosing new recruits.[94]

Larger police departments often maintain an internal affairs branch, which is charged with policing the police. The **internal affairs** division processes citizen complaints of police corruption, investigates allegations of unnecessary use of force by police officers, and even probes allegations of police participation in criminal activity, such as burglaries or narcotics violations. In addition, the internal affairs division may assist police managers when disciplinary action is brought against individual officers. Internal affairs is a controversial function given that investigators are feared and distrusted by fellow police officers. Nonetheless, rigorous self-scrutiny is the only way that police departments can earn the respect of citizens. Because of these concerns, it has become commonplace for police departments to institute citizen oversight of police practices and institute civilian review boards that have the power to listen to complaints and conduct investigations.

Most police departments are responsible for the administration and control of their own budgets. This task includes administering payroll, purchasing equipment and services, planning budgets for future expenditures, and auditing departmental financial records.

Police departments maintain separate units that are charged with maintaining and disseminating information on wanted offenders, stolen merchandise, traffic violators, and so on. Modern data-management systems enable police to use their records in a highly sophisticated fashion. For example, officers in a patrol car who spot a suspicious-looking vehicle can instantly receive a computerized rundown on whether it has been stolen. Or, if property is recovered during an arrest, police using this sort of system can determine who reported the loss of the merchandise and arrange for its return.

Another important function of police communication is the effective and efficient dispatching of patrol cars. Again, modern computer technologies have been used to make the most of available resources.[95]

In many departments, training is continuous throughout an officer's career. Training usually begins at a police academy, which may be run exclusively for larger departments or be part of a regional training center that services smaller and varied governmental units. More than 90 percent of all police departments require preservice training, including almost all departments in larger cities (population over 100,000). The average officer receives more than 600 hours of preservice training, including 400 hours in the classroom and the rest in field training. Police in large cities receive more than 1,000 hours of instruction divided almost evenly between classroom and field instruction.[96] Among the topics usually covered are law and civil rights, firearms handling, emergency medical care, and restraint techniques.[97]

After assuming their police duties, new recruits are assigned to field-training officers who break them in on the job. However, training does not stop here. On-the-job training is a continuous process in the modern police department and covers such areas as weapons skills, first aid, crowd control, and community relations. Some departments use roll-call training, in which superior officers or outside experts address police officers at the beginning of the workday. Other departments allow police officers time off to attend annual training sessions to sharpen their skills and learn new policing techniques.

Police departments provide emergency aid to the ill, counsel youngsters, speak to school and community agencies on safety and drug abuse, and provide countless other services designed to improve citizen–police interactions.

Larger police departments maintain specialized units that help citizens protect themselves from criminal activity. For example, they advise citizens on

internal affairs
The unit that investigates allegations of police misconduct.

effective home security techniques or conduct Project ID campaigns—engraving valuables with an identifying number so that they can be returned if recovered after a burglary. Police also work in schools teaching youths how to avoid drug use.[98]

Police agencies maintain (or have access to) forensic laboratories that enable them to identify substances to be used as evidence and to classify fingerprints.

Planning and research functions include designing programs to increase police efficiency and strategies to test program effectiveness. Police planners monitor recent technological developments and institute programs to adapt them to police services.

◆ IMPROVING POLICE PRODUCTIVITY

Police administrators have sought to increase the productivity of their line, support, and administrative staff. As used today, the term *police productivity* refers to the amount of order, maintenance, crime control, and other law enforcement activities provided by individual police officers and concomitantly by police departments as a whole. By improving police productivity, a department can keep the peace, deter crime, apprehend criminals, and provide useful public services without necessarily increasing its costs. This goal is accomplished by having each police officer operate with greater efficiency, thus using fewer resources to achieve greater effectiveness.

Police departments are now experimenting with cost-saving reforms that maximize effectiveness while saving taxpayer dollars. David Hirschel and Charles Dean describe how a program to summon offenders to court via a field citation is considerably cheaper than a formal arrest. Factoring in the cost of re-arresting offenders who fail to appear in court, a citation program would save about $72 per case. Considering the millions of arrests made each year, the adoption of a citation policy could produce considerable savings, not to mention the positive effects on the overcrowded jail system.[99] Other cost-saving productivity measures include consolidation, informal arrangements, sharing, pooling, contracting, police service districts, using civilian employees, multiple tasking, special assignment programs, and differential police responses.[100]

CONSOLIDATION One way to increase police efficiency is to consolidate police services. This means combining small departments (usually with under 10 employees) in adjoining areas into a superagency that services the previously fragmented jurisdictions. Consolidation has the benefit of creating departments large enough to use expanded services, such as crime labs, training centers, communications centers, and emergency units, that are not cost-effective in smaller departments. This procedure is controversial because it demands that existing lines of political and administrative authority be drastically changed.

INFORMAL ARRANGEMENTS Unwritten cooperative agreements may be made between localities to perform a task collectively that would be mutually beneficial (such as monitoring neighboring radio frequencies so that needed backup can be provided).

SHARING Sharing is the provision or reception of services that aid in the execution of a law enforcement function (such as the sharing of a communications system by several local agencies). Some agencies form mutual-aid pacts so that they can share infrequently used emergency services such as SWAT (special weapons and tactics) and emergency response teams.[101] Some states have gone as far as setting up centralized data services that connect most local police agencies into a statewide information net.[102]

POOLING Some police agencies combine the resources of two or more agencies to perform a specified function under a predetermined, often formalized arrangement with direct involvement by all parties. An example is the use of a city–county law enforcement building or training academy or the establishment of a crime task force.

CONTRACTING Another productivity measure is a limited and voluntary approach in which one government enters into a formal binding agreement to provide all or certain specified law enforcement services (such as communications or patrol service) to another government for an established fee. Many communities that contract for full law enforcement service do so at the time they incorporate to avoid the costs of establishing their own police capability. For example, five small towns in Florida (Pembroke Park, Lauderdale Lakes, Tamarac, Dania, and Deerfield Beach) contract with the Broward County Sheriff's Department to provide law enforcement for their communities. Contracting saves each town millions of dollars.[103]

SERVICE DISTRICTS Some jurisdictions have set aside areas, usually within an individual county, where a special level of service is provided and financed through a special tax or assessment. In California, residents of an unincorporated portion of a county may petition to form such a district to provide more intensive patrol coverage than is available through existing systems. Such service may be provided by a sheriff, another police department, or a private person or agency. This system is used in Contra Costa and San Mateo counties in California and Suffolk and Nassau counties in New York.

CIVILIAN EMPLOYEES One common cost-saving method is to use civilians in administrative support or even in some line activities. Civilians' duties have included operating communications gear; performing clerical work, planning, and doing research; and staffing traffic control (meter monitors). Using civilian employees can be a real savings to taxpayers because civilian salaries are considerably lower than those of regular police officers. In addition, trained, experienced officers are then allowed to spend more time on direct crime control and enforcement activities.

MULTIPLE TASKING Some police officers are trained to carry out other functions of municipal government. For example, in a number of smaller departments, the roles of firefighters and police officers have been merged into a job called a public safety officer. The idea is to increase the number of people trained in both areas to have the potential for putting more police at the scene of a crime or more firefighters at a blaze than was possible when the two tasks were separated. The system provides greater coverage at far less cost.

SPECIAL ASSIGNMENTS Some departments train officers for special assignments that are required only occasionally, such as radar operation, crowd control, and security.

DIFFERENTIAL POLICE RESPONSE These strategies maximize resources by differentiating among police requests for services in terms of the form that the police response takes. Some calls will result in the dispatch of a sworn officer, others in the dispatching of a less highly trained civilian. Calls considered low priority are handled by asking citizens to walk in or to mail in their requests.[104]

In sum, police departments are now implementing a variety of administrative models designed to stretch resources while still providing effective police services.

ETHICAL CHALLENGES IN CRIMINAL JUSTICE: A WRITING ASSIGNMENT

*T*he Middle City police force has created crime control teams—decentralized units relieved of routine, noncriminal duties and given responsibility for controlling serious crime, apprehending offenders, conducting investigations, and increasing clearance rates on a neighborhood basis. Two team members, officers Donald Libby and Karen Johnson, each of whom has more than 15 years on the force, were part of a team given the assignment to displace gangs of local teenagers who were constantly causing problems in the neighborhood, After a few months on the job, Libby and Johnson were the targets of numerous complaints that centered on their treatment of neighborhood youths. They were charged with roughing up neighborhood kids, slapping some of them around, and being disrespectful. In the most serious incident, they used a nightstick on the head of a 15-year-old who they claim had resisted arrest after they found him smoking marijuana in the park. The youth suffered a broken arm and a concussion and required hospitalization. When interviewed by the Internal Affairs Bureau, the officers admitted that they scuffled with the boy but claimed that they were "only doing their job." Besides, they argued, community leaders had demanded results, and their aggressive style had helped lower the crime rate in the area by more than 20 percent. The boy and his parents have filed suit, claiming that the amount of force used was unnecessary and violated his civil rights.

As their defense attorney, you are asked to write an essay outlining their defense. Don't worry about legal rules. How would you defend the two officers?

Doing Research on the Web

The Rand Corporation, a private think tank, has an interesting monograph on police effectiveness titled *Police Effectiveness: Measurement and Incentives.* You can access it by going to the Siegel/Senna Introduction to Criminal Justice 11e website: www.thomsonedu.com/criminaljustice/siegel.

Can aggressive police tactics control crime? Read the following article by Edmund McGarrell and his associates: "Reducing Firearms Violence Through Directed Police Patrol." You can access it by going to the Siegel/Senna Introduction to Criminal Justice 11e website: www.thomsonedu.com/criminaljustice/siegel.

SUMMARY

♦ Today's police departments operate in a military-like fashion. Policy generally emanates from the top of the hierarchy.

♦ Most police officers use a great deal of discretion when making on-the-job decisions.

♦ The most common law enforcement agencies are local police departments, which carry out patrol and investigative functions, as well as many support activities.

♦ Many questions have been raised about the effectiveness of police work, and although some research efforts seem to indicate that police are not effective crime fighters, evidence shows that aggressive police work, the threat of formal action,

and cooperation between departments can have a measurable impact on crime.

♦ Recent research indicates that adding police can help reduce crime rates.

♦ For some crimes, making arrests can help reduce criminal activity.

♦ To improve effectiveness, police departments have developed new methods of policing that stress community involvement and problem solving.

♦ Community policing typically involves programs with law enforcement and community involvement.

♦ Police agencies face many challenges in transforming themselves into community-based problem solvers.

◆ Police departments contain many subareas, including training, communications, personnel, and other administrative systems.

◆ Police agencies are constantly trying to improve their productivity because of budget demands.

They have learned how to share tasks, perform multiple tasks, and pool resources with other agencies.

KEY TERMS

time-in-rank system, 192
beats, 195
order maintenance (peacekeeping), 196
displacement, 197
proactive policing, 197
vice squads, 200

sting operation, 202
broken windows model, 208
foot patrol, 209
community-oriented policing (COP), 209
neighborhood-oriented policing (NOP), 209

problem-oriented policing (POP), 211
hot spots of crime, 211
gang tactical detail, 212
internal affairs, 217

ThomsonNOW Maximize your study time by using ThomsonNOW's diagnostic study plan to help you review this chapter. The Study Plan will

◆ help you identify areas on which you should concentrate;

◆ provide interactive exercises to help you master the chapter concepts; and

◆ provide a post-test to confirm you are ready to move on to the next chapter.

CRITICAL THINKING QUESTIONS

1. Should the primary police role be law enforcement or community service? Explain.

2. Should a police chief be permitted to promote an officer with special skills to a supervisory position, or should all officers be forced to spend time in rank? Why or why not?

3. Do the advantages of proactive policing outweigh the disadvantages? Explain.

4. Should all police recruits take the same physical tests, or are different requirements permissible for male and female applicants? Explain.

5. Can the police and the community ever form a partnership to fight crime? Why or why not? Does the community policing model remind you of early forms of policing? Explain.

NOTES

1. United States Attorney's Office for the Southern District of New York, "U.S. Announces Arrests on Charges of Using Sham Marriages to Obtain Immigration Documents" (http://newyork.fbi.gov/dojpressrel/pressrel06/marriagefraud060706.pdf), accessed on June 7, 2006.

2. Brian Payne, Bruce Berg, and Ivan Sun, "Policing in Small Town America: Dogs, Drunks, Disorder, and Dysfunction," *Journal of Criminal Justice* 33 (2005): 31–41.

3. Stacey Nofziger and Susan Williams, "Perceptions of Police and Safety in a Small Town," *Police Quarterly* 8 (2005): 248–70.

4. The first 10 ranks are sworn officers. Deputy commissioners are administrators appointed by the police commissioner and specialize in an area of great importance to the department, such as counterterrorism, training, or community affairs. The commissioner is appointed by the mayor.

5. Matthew Durose, Erica Schmitt, and Patrick Langan, *Contacts Between Police and the Public: Findings from the 2002 National Survey* (Washington, D.C.: Bureau of Justice Statistics, 2005).

6. Brian Reaves and Pheny Smith, *Law Enforcement Management and Administrative Statistics, 1993: Data for Individual State and Local Agencies with 100 or More Officers* (Washington, D.C.: Bureau of Justice Statistics, 1995).

7. American Bar Association, *Standards Relating to Urban Police Function* (New York: Institute of Judicial Administration, 1974), Standard 2.2.

8. James Hawdon and John Ryan, "Police–Resident Interactions and Satisfaction with Police: An Empirical Test of Community Policing Assertions," *Criminal Justice Policy Review* 14 (2003): 55–74.

9. Albert J. Reiss, *The Police and the Public* (New Haven, Conn.: Yale University Press, 1971), p. 19.

10. James Q. Wilson, *Varieties of Police Behavior: The Management of Law and Order in Eight Communities* (Cambridge, Mass.: Harvard University Press, 1968).

11. See Harlan Hahn, "A Profile of Urban Police," in *The Ambivalent Force*, ed. A. Niederhoffer and A. Blumberg (Hinsdale, Ill.: Dryden, 1976), p. 59.

12. George Kelling, Tony Pate, Duane Dieckman, and Charles Brown, *The Kansas City Preventive Patrol Experiment: A Summary Report* (Washington, D.C.: Police Foundation, 1974).

13. Ibid., pp. 3–4.

14. Ibid.

15. Kenneth Novak, Jennifer Hartman, Alexander Holsinger, and Michael Turner, "The Effects of Aggressive Policing of Disorder on Serious Crime," *Policing* 22 (1999): 171–90.

16. David Jacobs and Katherine Woods, "Interracial Conflict and Interracial Homicide: Do Political and Economic Rivalries Explain White Killings of Blacks or Black Killings of Whites?" *American Journal of Sociology* 105 (1999): 157–90.

17. James Q. Wilson and Barbara Boland, "The Effect of Police on Crime," *Law and Society Review* 12 (1978): 367–84.

18. Richard Timothy Coupe and Laurence Blake, "The Effects of Patrol Workloads and Response Strength on Arrests at Burglary Emergencies," *Journal of Criminal Justice* 33 (2005): 239–55.

19. Robert Sampson, "Deterrent Effects of the Police on Crime: A Replication and Theoretical Extension," *Law and Society Review* 22 (1988): 163–91.

20. For a thorough review of this issue, see Andrew Karmen, *Why Is New York City's Murder Rate Dropping So Sharply?* (New York: John Jay College, 1996).

21. Robert Davis, Pedro Mateu-Gelabert, and Joel Miller, "Can Effective Policing Also Be Respectful? Two Examples in the South Bronx," *Police Quarterly* 8 (2005): 229–47.

22. Lawrence Sherman, James Shaw, and Dennis Rogan, *The Kansas City Gun Experiment* (Washington, D.C.: National Institute of Justice, 1994).

23. Mitchell Chamlin, "Crime and Arrests: An Autoregressive Integrated Moving Average (ARIMA) Approach," *Journal of Quantitative Criminology* 4 (1988): 247–55.

24. Perry Shapiro and Harold Votey, "Deterrence and Subjective Probabilities of Arrest: Modeling Individual Decisions to Drink and Drive in Sweden," *Law and Society Review* 18 (1984): 111–49.

25. Stewart D'Alessio and Lisa Stolzenberg, "Crime, Arrests, and Pretrial Jail Incarceration: An Examination of the Deterrence Thesis," *Criminology* 36 (1998): 735–61.

26. Thomas Marvell and Carlysle Moody, "Specification Problems, Police Levels, and Crime Rates," *Criminology* 34 (1996): 609–46; Colin Loftin and David McDowall, "The Police, Crime, and Economic Theory: An Assessment," *American Sociological Review* 47 (1982): 393–401.

27. Craig Uchida and Robert Goldberg, *Police Employment and Expenditure Trends* (Washington, D.C.: Bureau of Justice Statistics, 1986).

28. Tomislav V. Kovandzic and John J. Sloan, "Police Levels and Crime Rates Revisited: A County-Level Analysis from Florida (1980–1998)," *Journal of Criminal Justice* 30 (2002): 65–75; Steven Levitt, "Using Electoral Cycles in Police Hiring to Estimate the Effect of Police on Crime," *American Economic Review* 87 (1997): 270–91.

29. Joan Petersilia, Allan Abrahamse, and James Q. Wilson, "A Summary of RAND's Research on Police Performance, Community Characteristics, and Case Attrition," *Journal of Police Science and Administration* 17 (1990): 219–29.

30. William Bratton, *Turnaround: How America's Top Cop Reversed the Crime Epidemic* (New York: Random House, 1998).

31. See Belton Cobb, *The First Detectives* (London: Faber and Faber, 1957).

32. See, for example, James Q. Wilson, "Movie Cops—Romantic vs. Real," *New York Magazine*, August 19, 1968, pp. 38–41.

33. For a view of the modern detective, see William Sanders, *Detective Work: A Study of Criminal Investigations* (New York: Free Press, 1977).

34. Mark Pogrebin and Eric Poole, "Vice Isn't Nice: A Look at the Effects of Working Undercover," *Journal of Criminal Justice* 21 (1993): 385–96; Gary Marx, *Undercover: Police Surveillance in America* (Berkeley: University of California Press, 1988).

35. Martin Innes, *Investigating Murder: Detective Work and the Police Response to Criminal Homicide* (Clarendon Studies in Criminology) (London, England: Oxford University Press, 2003).

36. John B. Edwards, "Homicide Investigative Strategies," *FBI Law Enforcement Bulletin* 74 (2005): 11–21.

37. Robert Langworthy, "Do Stings Control Crime? An Evaluation of a Police Fencing Operation," *Justice Quarterly* 6 (1989): 27–45.

38. Mary Dodge, Donna Starr-Gimeno, and Thomas Williams, "Puttin' on the Sting: Women Police Officers' Perspectives on Reverse Prostitution Assignments," *International Journal of Police Science & Management* 7 (2005): 71–85.

39. Porgebin and Poole, "Vice Isn't Nice"; Marx, *Undercover*.

40. Peter Greenwood and Joan Petersilia, *The Criminal Investigation Process: Summary and Policy Implications*, ed. Peter Greenwood and others (Santa Monica, Calif.: Rand Corporation, 1975).

41. Mark Willman and John Snortum, "Detective Work: The Criminal Investigation Process in a Medium-Size Police Department," *Criminal Justice Review* 9 (1984): 33–39.

42. Police Executive Research Forum, *Calling the Police: Citizen Reporting of Serious Crime* (Washington, D.C.: Police Executive Research Forum, 1981).

43. John Eck, *Solving Crimes: The Investigation of Burglary and Robbery* (Washington, D.C.: Police Executive Research Forum, 1984).

44. A. Fischer, "Coplink Nabs Criminals Faster," *Arizona Daily Star*, January 7, 2001, p. 1; Alexandra Robbins, "A. I. Cop on the Beat," *PC Magazine*, 22 (2002); M. Sink, "An Electronic Cop That Plays Hunches," *New York Times*, November 2, 2002, p. B1.

45. George Kelling and James Q. Wilson, "Broken Windows: The Police and Neighborhood Safety," *Atlantic Monthly* 249 (March 1982): 29–38.

46. Ibid.

47. For a general review, see Robert Trojanowicz and Bonnie Bucqueroux, *Community Policing: A Contemporary Perspective* (Cincinnati, Ohio: Anderson, 1990).

48. Police Foundation, *The Newark Foot Patrol Experiment* (Washington, D.C.: Police Foundation, 1981).

49. John Worrall and Jihong Zhao, "The Role of the COPS Office in Community Policing," *Policing* 26 (2003): 64–87.

50. Jihong Zhao, Nicholas Lovrich, and Quint Thurman, "The Status of Community Policing in American Cities," *Policing* 22 (1999): 74–92.

51. Albert Cardarelli, Jack McDevitt, and Katrina Baum, "The Rhetoric and Reality of Community Policing in Small and Medium-Sized Cities and Towns," *Policing* 21 (1998): 397–415.

52. Quint Thurman, Andrew Giacomazzi, and Phil Bogen, "Research Note: Cops, Kids, and Community Policing—An Assessment of a Community Policing Demonstration Project," *Crime and Delinquency* 39 (1993): 554–64.

53. Spokane, Washington Police Department (http://www.spokanepolice.org/other_programs.htm), accessed on October 6, 2006.

54. Susan Sadd and Randolph Grinc, *Implementation Challenges in Community Policing* (Washington, D.C.: National Institute of Justice, 1996).

55. Donald Green, Dara Strolovitch, and Janelle Wong, "Defended Neighborhoods, Integration, and Racially Motivated Crime," *American Journal of Sociology* 104 (1998): 372–403.

56. Walter Baranyk, "Making a Difference in a Public Housing Project," *Police Chief* 61 (1994): 31–35.

57. Ibid., p. 17.

58. Herman Goldstein, "Improving Policing: A Problem-Oriented Approach," *Crime and Delinquency* 25 (1979): 236–58.

59. Jerome Skolnick and David Bayley, *Community Policing: Issues and Practices Around the World* (Washington, D.C.: National Institute of Justice, 1988), p. 12.

60. Lawrence Sherman, Patrick Gartin, and Michael Buerger, "Hot Spots of Predatory Crime: Routine Activities and the Criminology of Place," *Criminology* 27 (1989): 27–55.

61. Ibid., p. 45.

62. Dennis Roncek and Pamela Maier, "Bars, Blocks, and Crimes Revisited: Linking the Theory of Routine Activities to the Empiricism of 'Hot Spots,' " *Criminology* 29 (1991): 725–53.

63. Sherry Plaster Carter, Stanley Carter, and Andrew Dannenberg, "Zoning Out Crime and Improving Community Health in Sarasota, Florida: 'Crime Prevention Through Environmental Design,' " *American Journal of Public Health* 93 (2003): 1442–45.

64. C. Jewett, "Police Use Bait Cars to Reduce Theft," *Knight Ridder/Tribune Business News*, March 3, 2003, p. 1.

65. Michael White, James Fyfe, Suzanne Campbell, and John Goldkamp, "The Police Role in Preventing Homicide: Considering the Impact of Problem-Oriented Policing on the Prevalence of Murder," *Journal of Research in Crime and Delinquency* 40 (2003): 194–226.

66. Tucson Police Department, "Gang Tactical Detail" (http://www.ci .tucson.az.us/police/ Organization/Investigative_Services_/Violent_ Crimes_Section/Gang_Tactical_ Detail/gang_tactical_detail.html), accessed on July 18, 2003.

67. Anthony Braga, David Kennedy, Elin Waring, and Anne Morrison Piehl, "Problem-Oriented Policing, Deterrence, and Youth Violence: An Evaluation of Boston's Operation Ceasefire," *Journal of Research in Crime and Delinquency* 38 (2001): 195–225.

68. Anthony Braga, David Weisburd, Elin Waring, Lorraine Green Mazerolle, William Spelman, and Francis Gajewski, "Problem-Oriented Policing in Violent Crime Places: A Randomized Controlled Experiment," *Criminology* 37 (1999): 541–80.

69. Eric Fritsch, Tory Caeti, and Robert Taylor, "Gang Suppression Through Saturation Patrol, Aggressive Curfew, and Truancy Enforcement: A Quasi-Experimental Test of the Dallas Anti-Gang Initiative," *Crime and Delinquency* 45 (1999): 122–39.

70. Bureau of Justice Assistance, *Problem-Oriented Drug Enforcement: A Community-Based Approach for Effective Policing* (Washington, D.C.: National Institute of Justice, 1993).

71. Ibid., pp. 64–65.

72. Jack R. Greene, "The Effects of Community Policing on American Law Enforcement: A Look at the Evidence" (paper presented at the International Congress on Criminology, Hamburg, Germany, September 1988), p. 19.

73. Roger Dunham and Geoffrey Alpert, "Neighborhood Differences in Attitudes Toward Policing: Evidence for a Mixed-Strategy Model of Policing in a Multi-Ethnic Setting," *Journal of Criminal Law and Criminology* 79 (1988): 504–22.

74. Mark E. Correia, "The Conceptual Ambiguity of Community in Community Policing: Filtering the Muddy Waters," *Policing* 23 (2000): 218–33.

75. Scott Lewis, Helen Rosenberg, and Robert Sigler, "Acceptance of Community Policing Among Police Officers and Police Administrators," *Policing* 22 (1999): 567–88.

76. Jihong Zhao, Ni He, and Nicholas Lovrich, "Community Policing: Did It Change the Basic Functions of Policing in the 1990s? A National Follow-Up Study," *Justice Quarterly* 20 (2003): 697–724.

77. Mark Moore and Anthony Braga, "Measuring and Improving Police Performance: The Lessons of Compstat and Its Progeny," *Policing* 26 (2003): 439–53.

78. Robin Shepard Engel, *How Police Supervisory Styles Influence Patrol Officer Behavior* (Washington, D.C.: National Institute of Justice, 2003).

79. Amy Halsted, Max Bromley, and John Cochran, "The Effects of Work Orientations on Job Satisfaction Among Sheriffs' Deputies Practicing Community-Oriented Policing," *Policing* 23 (2000): 82–104.

80. Venessa Garcia, "Constructing the 'Other' Within Police Culture: An Analysis of a Deviant Unit Within the Police Organization," *Police Practice and Research* 6 (2005): 65–80.

81. Kevin Ford, Daniel Weissbein, and Kevin Plamondon, "Distinguishing Organizational from Strategy Commitment: Linking Officers' Commitment to Community Policing to Job Behaviors and Satisfaction," *Justice Quarterly* 20 (2003): 159–86.

82. Michael Palmiotto, Michael Birzer, and N. Prabha Unnithan, "Training in Community Policing: A Suggested Curriculum," *Policing* 23 (2000): 8–21.

83. Lisa Riechers and Roy Roberg, "Community Policing: A Critical Review of Underlying Assumptions," *Journal of Police Science and Administration* 17 (1990): 112–13.

84. John Riley, "Community-Policing: Utilizing the Knowledge of Organizational Personnel," *Policing* 22 (1999): 618–33.

85. Donald Green, Dara Strolovitch, and Janelle Wong, "Defended Neighborhoods: Integration and Racially Motivated Crime," *American Journal of Sociology* 104 (1998): 372–403.

86. James Nolan, Norman Conti, and Jack McDevitt, "Situational Policing: Neighbourhood Development and Crime Control," *Policing & Society* 14 (2004): 99–118.

87. James Forman, "Community Policing and Youth as Assets," *Journal of Criminal Law & Criminology* 95 (2004): 1–48.

88. David Kessler, "Integrating Calls for Service with Community- and Problem-Oriented Policing: A Case Study," *Crime and Delinquency* 39 (1993): 485–508.

89. L. Thomas Winfree, Gregory Bartku, and George Seibel, "Support for Community Policing Versus Traditional Policing Among Nonmetropolitan Police Officers: A Survey of Four New Mexico Police Departments," *American Journal of Police* 15 (1996): 23–47.

90. Jihong Zhao, Ni He, and Nicholas Lovrich, "Value Change Among Police Officers at a Time of Organizational Reform: A Follow-Up Study of Rokeach Values," *Policing* 22 (1999): 152–70.

91. Jihong Zhao, Matthew Scheider, and Quint Thurman, "A National Evaluation of the Effect of COPs Grants on Police Productivity (Arrests) 1995–1999," *Police Quarterly* 6 (2003): 387–410.

92. Mike Brogden, "'Horses for Courses' and 'Thin Blue Lines': Community Policing in Transitional Society," *Police Quarterly* 8 (2005): 64–99.

93. Ling Ren, Liqun Cao, Nicholas Lovrich, and Michael Gaffney, "Linking Confidence in the Police with the Performance of the Police: Community Policing Can Make a Difference," *Journal of Criminal Justice* 33 (2005): 55–66.

94. William Boerner and Terry Nowell, "The Reliability of the Behavioral Personnel Assessment Device (B-PAD) in Selecting Police Recruits," *Policing* 22 (1999): 343–52.

95. See, for example, Richard Larson, *Urban Police Patrol Analysis* (Cambridge, Mass.: MIT Press, 1972).

96. Brian Reaves, *State and Local Police Departments, 1990* (Washington, D.C.: Bureau of Justice Statistics, 1992), p. 6.

97. Philip Ash, Karen Slora, and Cynthia Britton, "Police Agency Officer Selection Practices," *Journal of Police Science and Administration* 17 (1990): 258–69.

98. Dennis Rosenbaum, Robert Flewelling, Susan Bailey, Chris Ringwalt, and Deanna Wilkinson, "Cops in the Classroom: A Longitudinal Evaluation of Drug Abuse Resistance Education (DARE)," *Journal of Research in Crime and Delinquency* 31 (1994): 3–31.

99. J. David Hirschel and Charles Dean, "The Relative Cost-Effectiveness of Citation and Arrest," *Journal of Criminal Justice* 23 (1995): 1–12.

100. Adapted from Terry Koepsell and Charles Gerard, *Small Police Agency Consolidation: Suggested Approaches* (Washington, D.C.: Government Printing Office, 1979).

101. Mike D'Alessandro and Charles Hoffman, "Mutual Aid Pacts," *Law and Order* 43 (1995): 90–93.

102. Leonard Sipes, Jr., "Maryland's High-Tech Approach to Crime Fighting," *Police Chief* 61 (1994): 18–20.

103. Nick Navarro, "Six Broward County Cities Turn to the Green and Gold," *Police Chief* 59 (1992): 60.

104. Robert Worden, "Toward Equity and Efficiency in Law Enforcement: Differential Police Response," *American Journal of Police* 12 (1993): 1–24.

Issues in Policing

Chapter Outline

Chapter Objectives

After reading this chapter, you should be able to:

1. Describe how the role of women in local police agencies has evolved over time.
2. Discuss some of the problems of minority police officers.
3. Explain the concept of a police culture.
4. Know the reasons that experts believe police have a unique personality.
5. Recognize the different types of police officer style.
6. Understand how police use discretion.
7. Discuss the issue of racial profiling.
8. Know what is meant by police stress.
9. Identify the different methods used to control the police use of force.
10. Explain the concept of police corruption.

O n November 7, 1990, the bullet-riddled corpse of Edward Lino was found in Brooklyn, New York, on the front seat of an abandoned car.[1] Lino, a member of the Gambino mob, was believed to have been involved in numerous killings, so his untimely death came as no surprise. Although a mob killing is nothing new in New York City, the case became a top priority when four years later an informer made the scandalous claim that two New York City police detectives, Louis Eppolito (above left) and Stephen Caracappa (right), had carried out the hit. It took another 10 years before the two were indicted, in 2004.

Both detectives had interesting backgrounds. Eppolito's father, Ralph, was a Gambino family soldier known in the underworld as Fat the Gangster. His uncle James was a Gambino captain who went by Jimmy the Clam. Although Eppolito loved being on the police force, he also maintained Mafia ties and associations. He would sometimes get in trouble for showing up in FBI surveillance tapes associating with mobsters. Caracappa met Eppolito while working at the Brooklyn Robbery Squad. He eventually moved on to the Major Case Squad, where he helped form the Organized Crime Homicide Unit and had access to a flood of secret information on mob investigations.

By 1985, the two detectives had developed a business relationship with Anthony (Gaspipe) Casso, the Luchese family underboss. They helped him take control of the family and were on Casso's payroll to the tune of $4,000 per month. For this they supplied names of informants and the timing of arrests. Additional services, including the killing of rivals, were extra. They were paid $65,000 for the hit on Edward Lino. On April 6, 2006, Eppolito and Caracappa were convicted on all charges. On June 30, 2006, a judge threw out a racketeering murder conviction against the two detectives on a technicality: The five-year statute of limitations had expired on the key charge of racketeering conspiracy. Had the two been tried in state court rather than federal court, the charges would have prevailed because there is no statute of limitations for murder in the state of New York. ◆

Incidents such as those involving the "Mafia cops" highlight the critical and controversial role that police play in the justice system and the need for developing a professional, competent police force. The police are the gatekeepers of the criminal justice process. They initiate contact with law violators and decide whether to formally arrest them and start their journey through the criminal justice system, settle the issue in an informal way (such as by issuing a warning), or simply take no action at all. The strategic position of police officers, their visibility and contact with the public, and their use of weapons and arrest power have kept them in the forefront of public thought about law enforcement. A great deal of progress has been made in improving the public's opinion of the police. Progress is sometimes difficult to achieve because police agencies tend to be traditional organizations and resistant to change at the whim of public perceptions and attitudes.[2] Public concern over police behavior, fed by intense media scrutiny of police departments as well as individual police officers, has forced commanders to become more sensitive to their public image. Programs have been created to improve relations between police and community—to help police officers on the beat be more sensitive to the needs of the public and cope more effectively with the stress of their jobs. Police officers have also become better educated and are now attending programs in criminology and criminal justice in large numbers. After graduation, they seem willing to stay on the job and contribute their academic experiences to improve police performance and enhance police–community relationships.[3]

Because of these efforts, most citizens today seem to approve of their local law enforcement agents. About 60 percent say they have a "great deal of confidence" in the police.[4] Although this is encouraging, approval is often skewed along racial lines.[5] It may not be surprising that minority citizens report having less confidence in the police compared with Caucasians and are less likely to report crime to police agencies.[6] To combat these perceptions, police departments have gone to great lengths to improve relationships with minorities, and these efforts may have begun to pay off. Surveys show improvement in the African American community's view of the local police: Minority groups value police services, welcome the presence of both white and African American police officers, and are generally supportive of the local police.[7]

The general public is not the only group concerned about police attitudes and behavior. Police administrators and other law enforcement experts have focused their attention on issues that may influence the effectiveness and efficiency of police performance in the field. Some of their concerns are outgrowths of the development of policing as a profession: Does an independent police culture exist, and what are its characteristics? Do police officers develop a unique working personality, and, if so, does it influence their job performance? Are there police officer styles that make some police officers too aggressive and others inert and passive? Is policing too stressful an occupation?

Important questions are also being raised about the problems that police departments face while interacting with the society they are entrusted with supervising: Are police officers too forceful and brutal, and do they discriminate in their use of deadly force? Are police officers corrupt, and how can police deviance be controlled? There is evidence that police officers are all too often involved in marital disputes and even incidents of domestic violence, which may be linked to anxiety and strain.[8] Stress and burnout become part of the job.[9] This chapter focuses on these and other problems facing police officers in contemporary society. It looks at issues that police face on the job and in society. We begin with a discussion of the makeup of the police and the police profession.

◆ WHO ARE THE POLICE?

The composition of the nation's police forces is changing. Traditionally, police agencies were composed of white males with a high school education who viewed policing as a secure position that brought them the respect of family and friends and a step up the social ladder. It was not uncommon to see police families in which one member of each new generation would enter the force. This picture has been changing and will continue to change. As criminal justice programs turn out thousands of graduates every year, an increasing number of police officers have at least some college education. In addition, affirmative action programs have helped slowly change the racial and gender composition of police departments to reflect community makeup.

Police and Education

In recent years, many police experts have argued that police recruits should have a college education. This development is not unexpected, considering that higher education for police officers has been recommended by national commissions since 1931.[10]

Although most law enforcement agencies still do not require recruits to have an advanced degree, the number requiring some higher education in the hiring and promotion process is growing. Today, nearly all (98 percent) of local police departments have an education requirement for new officer recruits:

◆ About 18 percent of departments have some type of college requirement.

◆ About 9 percent require a two-year degree.

◆ About one-third of all officers work in departments that have some type of college requirement, more than three times as high as in 1990.[11]

◆ When asked, most departments express a preference for criminal justice majors, usually because of their enhanced knowledge of the entire criminal justice system and issues in policing.[12]

Another promising trend is that, although not requiring college credits for promotion, most police departments recognize that college education is an important element in promotion decisions. The United States is not alone in this regard; police departments around the world are now encouraging recruits and in-service officers to gain college credits.[13]

What are the benefits of higher education for police officers? Better communication with the public, especially minority and ethnic groups, is believed to be one benefit. Educated officers write better and more clearly and are more likely to be promoted. Police administrators believe that education enables officers to perform more effectively, generate fewer citizen complaints, show more initiative in performing police tasks, and generally act more professionally.[14] In addition, educated officers are less likely to have disciplinary problems and are viewed as better decision makers.[15] Studies have shown that college-educated police officers generate fewer citizen complaints and have better behavioral and performance characteristics than their less educated peers. Research indicates that educated officers are more likely to rate themselves higher on most performance indicators, indicating that, if nothing else, higher education is associated with greater self-confidence and assurance.[16]

Although education has its benefits, little conclusive evidence has been found that educated officers are more effective crime fighters.[17] The diversity of the police role, the need for split-second decision making, and the often boring and mundane tasks that police are required to do are all considered reasons that formal education may not improve performance on the street.[18] Nonetheless, because police administrators value educated officers and citizens find them to be exceptional in the use of good judgment and problem solving, the trend toward having a more educated police force will likely continue.[19]

Minorities in Policing

For the past two decades, U.S. police departments have made a concerted effort to attract minority police officers, and there have been some impressive gains.

Police departments have made a determined effort to increase diversity. As a result, the percentage of minority officers in many departments is closer to representing community makeup. Here Laos-born Sacramento, California police officer Chou Vang plays basketball with a neighborhood youth. Vang's beat includes some of the city's most poverty-stricken neighborhoods. What are the benefits of diversity in policing? Are there any drawbacks?

As might be expected, cities with large minority populations are the ones having a higher proportion of minority officers in their police departments.[20]

The reasons for this effort are varied. Ideally, police departments recruit minority citizens to field a more balanced force that truly represents the communities they serve. African Americans generally have less confidence in the police than whites and are skeptical of their ability to protect them from harm.[21] African Americans also seem to be more adversely affected than whites when well-publicized incidents of police misconduct occur.[22] Therefore, it comes as no surprise that public opinion polls and research surveys show that African American citizens report having less confidence in the police when compared with both Hispanics and Caucasians.[23] African American juveniles seem particularly suspicious of police even when they deny having had negative encounters with them.[24] A heterogeneous police force can be instrumental in gaining the confidence of the minority community by helping dispel the view that police departments are generally bigoted or biased organizations. Furthermore, minority police officers possess special qualities that can serve to improve police performance. Spanish-speaking officers can help with investigations in Hispanic neighborhoods, and Asian officers are essential for undercover or surveillance work with Asian gangs and drug importers.

Minority Police Officers

It is disturbing that recent (2005) research by Stephen Rice and Alex Piquero found that African Americans living in New York City were three times more likely than Caucasians to perceive that (a) police are racially biased, (b) discrimination is widespread and unjustified, and (c) they had personally experienced police bias.[25] To combat these perceptions, police departments have actively recruited minority police officers.

The earliest known date when an African American was hired as a police officer was 1861 in Washington, D.C.; Chicago hired its first African American officer in 1872.[26] By 1890, an estimated 2,000 minority police officers were employed in the United States. At first, African American officers suffered a great deal of discrimination. Their work assignments were restricted, as were their chances for promotion. Minority officers were often assigned solely to the patrol of African American neighborhoods, and in some cities they were required to call a white officer to make an arrest. White officers held highly prejudicial attitudes, and as late as the 1950s some refused to ride with African Americans in patrol cars.[27]

The experience of African American police officers has not been an easy one. In his classic book, *Black in Blue*, written almost 40 years ago, Nicholas Alex pointed out that African American officers of the time suffered from what he called **double marginality**.[28] On the one hand, African American officers had to deal with the expectation that they would give members of their own race a break. On the other hand, they often experienced overt racism from their police colleagues. Alex found that African American officers' adaptation to these pressures ranged from denying that African American suspects should be treated differently from whites to treating African American offenders more harshly than white offenders (to prove their lack of bias). Alex offered several reasons why some African American officers' are tougher on African American offenders: They desire acceptance from their white colleagues, they were particularly sensitive to any disrespect given them by African American teenagers, and they viewed themselves as protectors of the African American community. Ironically, minority citizens may be more likely to accuse a minority officer of misconduct than they are white officers, a circumstance that underscores the difficult position of the minority officer in contemporary society.[29]

These conflicts have become more muted as the number of minority officers has increased. Figure 7.1 illustrates the increase in minority representation. Today, almost 25 percent of local police officers are African American, Hispanic, or other races.

Minority police officers now seem more aggressive and self-assured, and less willing to accept any discriminatory practices by the police department.[30] If anything, they are more willing to use their authority to take official action than white officers: The higher the percentage of black officers on the force, the higher the arrest rate for crimes such as assault.[31] Nor do black officers hesitate to use their arrest powers on African American suspects. Using observational data on police–citizen encounters in Cincinnati, Robert Brown and James Frank found that although white officers were more likely to arrest suspects than black officers were, black suspects were more likely to be arrested when the decision maker was a black officer.[32]

As their numbers increase, minority officers appear to be experiencing some of the same problems and issues encountered by white officers.[33] They report feeling similar rates of job-related stress and strain as white officers, stemming from the same type of stressors—e.g., family conflict.[34] Minority officers do report more stress when they consider themselves "tokens," marginalized within the department. They also report high levels of stress.[35] They may also deal with stress in a somewhat different fashion: They are more likely to seek aid from fellow minority officers, whereas white officers are more likely to try to express their feelings to others, form social bonds, and try to get others to like them more.[36]

African American and white police officers share similar attitudes toward community policing (although minority officers report being even more favorable toward it than white officers).[37] African American officers may today be far less detached and alienated from the local community than white or Hispanic officers.[38] Also helping is the fact that the number of African American officers in some of the nation's largest cities is now proportionate to minority representation in the population. So, although minority officers report feeling somewhat

double marginality
According to Nicholas Alex, the social burden that African American police officers carry by being both minority-group members and law enforcement officers.

FIGURE 7.1

Minority Representation on Local Police Departments
Percent of full-time sworn personnel

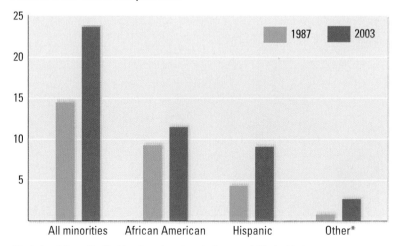

*Includes Asians, Pacific Islanders, American Indians, and Alaska Natives.
Source: Matthew Hickman and Brian Reaves, *Local Police Departments, 2003* (Washington D.C.: Bureau of Justice Statistics, 2006), p. iii.

more job-related stress and strain than white officers do, they appear to be on the path to overcoming the problems of double marginality.[39]

When affirmative action was first instituted, white police officers viewed it as a threat to their job security.[40] As more minorities have joined U.S. police forces, their situation seems to be changing. Caucasian officers are more likely to appreciate the contribution of minority officers. When Charles Katz examined the formation of a police gang unit in a midwestern city, he found that commanders chose minority officers so that the unit could be representative of the community they served.[41] As one Hispanic officer told Katz, "When you talk to Hispanics, you have to know and be familiar with their culture. . . . [Y]ou always talk to the man of the house, never presenting your position to the kid or to the mother."[42] These benefits are not lost on citizens either, and research shows that the general public cares little about the racial or ethnic makeup of the police officers in their neighborhood and more about their effectiveness.[43]

Women in Policing

In 1910 Alice Stebbins Wells became the first woman to hold the title of police officer (in Los Angeles) and to have arrest powers.[44] Today, about 16 percent of all sworn officers in larger cities (over 250,000) are women; in all, about 11 percent of sworn officers are female (Figure 7.2).[45]

The road to success in police work has not been easy for women. For more than half a century, female officers endured separate criteria for selection, were given menial tasks, and were denied the opportunity for advancement.[46] Some relief was gained with the passage of the 1964 Civil Rights Act and its subsequent amendments. Courts have consistently supported the addition of women to police forces by striking down entrance requirements that eliminated almost all female candidates but that could not be proven to predict job performance (such as height and upper-body strength).[47] Women do not perform as well as men on strength tests and are much more likely to fail the entrance physical than male recruits. Critics contend that many of these tests do not reflect the actual tasks that police do on the job.[48] Nonetheless, the role of women in police work is still restricted by social and administrative barriers that have been difficult to remove.

Studies of policewomen indicate that they are still struggling for acceptance, believe that they do not receive equal credit for their job performance, and report that it is common for them to be sexually harassed by their coworkers.[49] One reason may be that many male police officers tend to view policing as an overtly masculine profession not appropriate for women. For example, officers in the Los Angeles Police Department make an important distinction between two models of officers—"hard chargers" and "station queens." The former display such characteristics as courage and aggressiveness; they are willing to place themselves in danger and handle the most hazardous calls.[50] The latter like to work in the station house doing paperwork or other administrative tasks. The term *queen* is designed as a pejorative to indicate that these officers are overly feminine.[51]

Female police officers may also be targeted for more disciplinary actions by administrators and, if cited, are more likely to receive harsher punishments than male officers. That is, a larger percentage receive punishment greater than a reprimand.[52] Considering the sometimes hostile

FIGURE 7.2

Percentage of Women on Local Police Departments

Percent of full-time sworn personnel

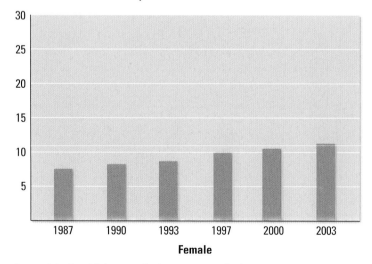

Source: Matthew Hickman and Brian Reaves, *Local Police Departments, 2003* (Washington D.C.: Bureau of Justice Statistics, 2006), p. iii.

reception they get from male colleagues and supervisors, it is not surprising that female officers report significantly higher levels of job-related stress than male officers do.[53]

JOB PERFORMANCE Gender bias is certainly not supported by existing research, which indicated that female officers are highly successful police officers.[54] In an important study of recruits in the Metropolitan Police Department of Washington, D.C., policewomen were found to display extremely satisfactory work performances.[55] Compared with male officers, women were found to respond to similar types of calls, and the arrests they made were as likely to result in conviction. Women were more likely than their male colleagues to receive support from the community and were less likely to be charged with improper conduct.

Research also shows that female officers are less likely to use force than male officers.[56] Because female officers seem to have the ability to avoid violent encounters with citizens and to deescalate potentially violent arrest situations, they are typically the target of fewer citizen complaints.[57]

GENDER CONFLICTS Despite the overwhelming evidence supporting their performance, policewomen have not always been fully accepted by their male peers or the general public.[58] Surveys of male officers show that only one-third accept a woman on patrol and that more than half do not think that women can handle the physical requirements of the job as well as men.[59] This form of bias is not unique to the United States. Research shows that policewomen working in northern England report being excluded from full membership in the force, based on gender inequality. Although policewomen in England are enthusiastic about crime-related work, their aspirations are frequently frustrated in favor of male officers.[60]

Women working in this male-dominated culture can experience stress and anxiety.[61] Not surprisingly, then, significantly more female than male officers report being the victim of discrimination on the job. And the male officers who claim to have experienced gender-based discrimination suggest that it comes at the hands of policewomen who use their sexuality for job-related benefits.[62]

Female officers are frequently caught in the classic catch-22 dilemma: If they are physically weak, male partners view them as a risk in street confrontations; if they are more powerful and aggressive than their male partners, they are regarded as an affront to a male officer's manhood. Ironically, to adapt to this paternalistic culture they may develop values and attitudes that support traditional concepts of police work instead of the new community policing models, which are viewed as taking a more humanistic, people-oriented approach.[63]

MINORITY FEMALE OFFICERS African American women, who account for less than 5 percent of police officers, occupy a unique status. In a study of African American policewomen serving in five large municipal departments, Susan Martin found that they perceive significantly more racial discrimination than both other female officers and African American male officers.[64] However, white policewomen were significantly more likely to perceive sexual discrimination than African American policewomen were.

Martin found that African American policewomen often incur the hostility of both white women and African American men, who feel that they will take their place. On patrol, African American policewomen are treated differently by male officers than white policewomen are. Neither group of women is viewed as equals. White policewomen are protected and coddled, whereas African American policewomen are viewed as passive, lazy, and unequal. In the station house, male officers show little respect for African American women, who face "widespread racial stereotypes as well as outright racial harassment."[65] African American women also report having difficult relationships with African American male officers. Their relationships are strained by tensions and dilemmas "associated with sexuality and

The Police Foundation is a nonprofit organization dedicated to conducting research on law enforcement. To check out its activities and publications, go to the Siegel/Senna Introduction to Criminal Justice 11e website: www.thomsonedu.com/criminaljustice/siegel.

competition for desirable assignments and promotions."[66] Surprisingly, little unity is found among the female officers. As Martin concludes, "Despite changes in the past two decades, the idealized image of the representative of the forces of 'law and order' and protector who maintains 'the thin blue line' between 'them' and 'us' remains white and male."[67]

Despite these problems, the future of women in policing grows continually brighter.[68] Female officers want to remain in policing because it pays a good salary, offers job security, and is a challenging and exciting occupation.[69] These factors should continue to bring women to policing for years to come.

ThomsonNOW™ Improve your grade on the exam with Personalized Study! For reinforcement resources and a mastery check of the demographic makeup of the police, go to www.thomsonedu.com/thomsonnow.

◆ THE POLICE PROFESSION

All professions have unique characteristics that distinguish them from other occupations and institutions. Policing is no exception. Police experts have long sought to understand the unique nature of the police experience and to determine how the challenges of police work shape the field and its employees.

Police Culture

Police experts have found that the experience of becoming a police officer and the nature of the job itself cause most officers to band together in a police subculture, characterized by cynicism, clannishness, secrecy, and insulation from others in society—the so-called **blue curtain**. Police officers tend to socialize together and believe that their occupation cuts them off from relationships with civilians. Police officers perceive their working environment to be laden with danger or the risk of danger, and they become preoccupied with the danger and violence that surround them, always anticipating both.[70] Perceptions of danger have a unifying effect on officers and work to separate them from the chief source of danger—the public—and help create the boundaries of a police subculture. Joining the police subculture means always having to stick up for fellow officers against outsiders; maintaining a tough, macho exterior personality; and distrusting the motives and behavior of outsiders.[71] Six core beliefs are viewed as being at the heart of the police culture:

blue curtain
The secretive, insulated police culture that isolates officers from the rest of society.

1. Police are the only real crime fighters. The public wants the police officer to fight crime; other agencies, both public and private, only play at crime fighting.

Police officers stand at attention as they wait outside the Mount Olive Baptist Church in Jersey City, New Jersey at the funeral service for police officer Shawn Carson on December 30, 2005. Carson and fellow officer Robert Nguyen died Christmas night when their emergency services vehicle plummeted 45 feet off an open drawbridge in blinding rain and fog into the frigid Hackensack River. The police culture requires solidarity with fellow officers both on duty and off.

2. No one else understands the real nature of police work. Lawyers, academics, politicians, and the public in general have little concept of what it means to be a police officer.

3. Loyalty to colleagues counts above everything else. Police officers have to stick together because everyone is out to get the police and make the job more difficult.

4. The war against crime cannot be won without bending the rules. Courts have awarded criminal defendants too many civil rights.

5. Members of the public are basically unsupportive and unreasonably demanding. People are quick to criticize police unless they need police help themselves.

6. Patrol work is the pits. Detective work is glamorous and exciting.[72]

The forces that support a police culture are generally believed to develop out of on-the-job experiences. Most officers originally join the police force because they want to help people, fight crime, and have an interesting, exciting, prestigious career with a high degree of job security.[73] Recruits often find that the social reality of police work does not mesh with their original career goals. They are unprepared for the emotional turmoil and conflict that accompany police work today.

Membership in the police culture helps recruits adjust to the rigors of police work and provides the emotional support needed for survival.[74] The culture encourages decisiveness in the face of uncertainty and the ability to make split-second judgments that may later be subject to extreme criticism. Officers who view themselves as crime fighters are the ones most likely to value solidarity and depend on the support and camaraderie of their fellow officers.[75] The police subculture encourages its members to draw a sharp distinction between good and evil. Officers, more than mere enforcers of the law, are warriors in the age-old battle between right and wrong.[76] In contrast, criminals are referred to as "terrorists" and "predators," terms that convey the fact that they are evil individuals ready to prey upon the poor and vulnerable. Because the predators represent a real danger, the police culture demands that its members be both competent and concerned with the safety of their peers and partners. Competence is often translated into respect and authority, and citizens must obey lest they face payback.[77]

In sum, the police culture has developed in response to the insulated, dangerous lifestyle of police officers. Policing is a hazardous occupation, and the availability of the unquestioned support and loyalty of their peers is not something officers could readily do without.[78] Nonetheless, some experts fear that the police culture will divide officers from the people they serve and create an "us against the world" mentality.[79]

Police Personality

Along with an independent police culture, some experts believe that police officers develop a unique set of personality traits that distinguish them from the average citizen.[80] To some commentators, the typical police personality can be described as dogmatic, authoritarian, and suspicious.[81] **Cynicism** has been found on all levels of policing, including chiefs of police, and throughout all stages of a police career.[82] Maintenance of these negative values and attitudes is believed to cause police officers to be secretive and isolated from the rest of society, producing the blue curtain.[83]

cynicism
The belief that most people's actions are motivated solely by personal needs and selfishness.

The police officer's working personality is shaped by constant exposure to danger and the need to use force and authority to reduce and control threatening situations.[84] Police feel suspicious of the public they serve and defensive about the actions of their fellow officers. There are two opposing viewpoints on the cause of this phenomenon. One position holds that police departments attract recruits who are by nature cynical, authoritarian, secretive, and so on.[85] Other experts maintain that socialization and experience on the police force itself cause these character traits to develop.

Since the first research measuring police personality was published, numerous efforts have been made to determine whether the typical police recruit possesses a unique personality that sets her apart from the average citizen. The results have been mixed.[86] Although some research concludes that police values are different from those of the general adult population, other efforts reach an opposing conclusion. Some have found that police officers are more psychologically healthy than the general population, less depressed and anxious, and more social and assertive.[87] Still other research on police personality found that police officers highly value such personality traits as warmth, flexibility, and emotion. These traits are far removed from rigidity and cynicism.[88] Given that research has found evidence supportive of both viewpoints, no one position dominates on the issue of how the police personality develops, or even if one exists.

In his classic study of police personality, *Behind the Shield* (1967), Arthur Neiderhoffer examined the assumption that most police officers develop into cynics as a function of their daily duties.[89] Among his most important findings were that police cynicism increased with length of service and that military-like police academy training caused new recruits to quickly become cynical about themselves.[90]

Police Style

Policing encompasses a multitude of diverse tasks, including peacekeeping, criminal investigation, traffic control, and providing emergency medical service. Part of the socialization as a police officer is developing a working attitude, or style, through which he approaches policing. For example, some police officers may view their job as a well-paid civil service position that stresses careful compliance with written departmental rules and procedures. Other officers may see themselves as part of the "thin blue line" that protects the public from wrongdoers. They will use any means to get the culprit, even if it involves such cheating as planting evidence on an obviously guilty person who so far has escaped arrest. Should the police bend the rules to protect the public? This has been referred to as the "Dirty Harry problem," after the popular Clint Eastwood film character who routinely (and successfully) violated all known standards of police work.[91]

police styles
The working personalities adopted by police officers that can range from being a social worker in blue to a hard-charging crime fighter.

Several studies have attempted to define and classify **police styles** into behavioral clusters. These classifications, called typologies, attempt to categorize law enforcement agents by groups, each of which has a unique approach to police work. The purpose of such classifications is to demonstrate that the police are not a cohesive, homogeneous group, as many believe, but individuals with differing approaches to their work.[92] The way that police take on their task and their attitude toward the police role, as well as their peers and superior officers, have been shown to affect their work.[93]

An examination of the literature suggests that four styles of police work seem to fit the current behavior patterns of most police agents: the crime fighter, the social agent, the law enforcer, and the watchman, which are described in Exhibit 7.1.

POLICE PERSONALITY, CULTURE, STYLES Although some experts have found that a unique police personality and culture do exist, others have challenged that assumption. No clear-cut agreement has been reached on the matter. In either event, changes in contemporary police agencies likely will have a significant impact on police culture and personality, if they have not done so already. Police departments have become diverse, attracting women and minorities in growing numbers. Police are becoming more educated and technologically sophisticated. The vision of a monolithic department whose employees share similar and uniform values, culture, and personality traits seems somewhat naïve in the presence of such diversity.

Furthermore, today's police officer is unlikely to be able to choose to embrace a particular style of policing while excluding others. Although some police

---

EXHIBIT 7.1

The Four Basic Styles of Policing

THE CRIME FIGHTER

To crime fighters, the most important aspect of police work is investigating serious crimes and apprehending criminals. Their focus is on the victim, and they view effective police work as the only force that can keep society's "dangerous classes" in check. They are the "thin blue line" protecting society from murderers and rapists. They consider property crimes to be less significant, and they believe that such matters as misdemeanors, traffic control, and social service functions would be better handled by other agencies of government. The ability to investigate criminal behavior that poses a serious threat to life and safety, combined with the power to arrest criminals, separates a police department from other municipal agencies. They see diluting these functions with minor social service and nonenforcement duties as harmful to police efforts to create a secure society.

THE SOCIAL AGENT

Social agents believe that police should be involved in a wide range of activities without regard for their connection to law enforcement. Instead of viewing themselves as criminal catchers, the social agents consider themselves community problem solvers. They are troubleshooters who patch the holes that appear where the social fabric wears thin. They are happy to work with special-needs populations, such as the homeless, school kids, and those who require emergency services. Social agents fit well within a community policing unit.

THE LAW ENFORCER

According to this view, duty is clearly set out in law, and law enforcers stress playing it "by the book."

Because the police are specifically charged with apprehending all types of lawbreakers, they see themselves as generalized law enforcement agents. Although law enforcers may prefer working on serious crimes—which are more intriguing and rewarding in terms of achievement, prestige, and status—they see the police role as one of enforcing all statutes and ordinances. They perceive themselves as neither community social workers nor vengeance-seeking vigilantes. Simply put, they are professional law enforcement officers who perform the functions of detecting violations, identifying culprits, and taking the lawbreakers before a court. Law enforcers are devoted to the profession of police work and are the officers most likely to aspire to command rank.

THE WATCHMAN

The watchman style is characterized by an emphasis on the maintenance of public order as the police goal, not on law enforcement or general service. Watchmen choose to ignore many infractions and requests for service unless they believe that the social or political order is jeopardized. Juveniles are expected to misbehave and are best ignored or treated informally. Motorists will often be left alone if their driving does not endanger or annoy others. Vice and gambling are problems only when the currently accepted standards of public order are violated. Like the watchmen of old, these officers take action only if and when a problem arises. Watchmen are the most passive officers, more concerned with retirement benefits than crime rates.

Sources: William Muir, *Police: Streetcorner Politicians* (Chicago: University of Chicago Press, 1977); James Q. Wilson, *Varieties of Police Behavior* (Cambridge, Mass.: Harvard University Press, 1968).

---

officers may emphasize one area of law enforcement over another, their daily activities most likely require them to engage in a wide variety of duties. A contemporary police officer probably cannot choose to concentrate on crime fighting and ignore his other duties. Police departments are today seeking public support through community police models and are reorienting the police role toward community outreach.[94]

♦ POLICE DISCRETION

A critical aspect of a police officer's professional responsibility is the personal discretion each officer has in carrying out his daily activities. **Discretion** can involve the selective enforcement of the law, as when a vice-squad plainclothes officer decides not to take action against a tavern that is serving drinks afterhours. Patrol officers use discretion when they decide to arrest one suspect for disorderly

discretion
The use of personal decision making and choice in carrying out operations in the criminal justice system.

FBI Agent

Duties and Characteristics of the Job

Federal Bureau of Investigation special agents work for the federal government. Their primary duty is to conduct investigations of federal crimes and threats to national security. Their primary areas of investigation include white-collar crime, drug trafficking, and espionage. They may also lend aid, services, and training to other law enforcement organizations. The actual law enforcement role of an agent is limited; apprehension and arrest are often delegated to local authorities.

Working as a federal agent is a challenging occupation. Federal agents may be required to travel to conduct investigations and can be away for long periods of time. Special agents often work overtime; a 45-hour workweek is the average for an agent. Finally, some find it troubling that they have to maintain secrecy about their work, even with their family.

Job Outlook

Factors such as the high pay, good benefits, generous retirement policy (full retirement at age 55), and the prestige associated the position make this career highly desirable and thus very competitive. However,

the early retirement policy ensures that there will always be job openings. Recruitment is ongoing, and the FBI is always accepting applications.

Salary

New special agents have a salary of between $61,100 and $69,900 a year. Salary varies according to the amount of overtime pay and where the agent is located. Agents promoted to supervisory positions will earn higher pay, as will those who work in a geographical area where pay is higher in general.

Opportunities

The FBI does not put forth specific recommendations for what skills or specialties it is seeking. However, strong analytical and research skills are always desirable, and law, accounting, and engineering degrees are also sought after for their usefulness in federal investigations.

Qualifications

Being a federal agent can be a demanding job, and the qualifications to become one are just as demanding.

---

low-visibility decision making
Decision making by police officers that is not subject to administrative review—for example, when a decision is made not to arrest someone or not to stop a speeding vehicle.

conduct but escort another home. Because police have the ability to deprive people of their liberty, arrest them, take them away in handcuffs, and even use deadly force to subdue them, their use of discretion is a vital concern.

The majority of police officers use a high degree of personal discretion in carrying out daily tasks, sometimes referred to in criminal justice as **low-visibility decision making**.[95] This terminology suggests that unlike members of almost every other criminal justice agency, police are neither regulated in their daily procedures by administrative scrutiny nor subject to judicial review (except when their behavior clearly violates an offender's constitutional rights). As a result, the exercise of discretion by police may sometimes deteriorate into discrimination, violence, and other abusive practices. Nonetheless, the public recognizes the right of police to use their discretion even if it means using force to control an unruly suspect while treating a more respectful one with deference and respect.[96]

A number of factors influence police discretion.

Legal Factors

Police discretion is inversely related to the severity of the offense. There is relatively little, if any, discretion used for the most serious crimes such as murder and aggravated assault.[97] Far more personal discretion is available when police confront a suspect in a minor case involving a simple assault or trespass.

Therefore, the likelihood of a police officer taking legal action may depend on how the individual officer views offense severity. Some police officers may treat all drug-related crimes as serious and deserving of formal action, whereas other officers, less concerned about the drug problem, may confiscate illegal

There are seven steps in the process of being hired as an agent. In order to even apply to be an agent, one must be a U.S. citizen, be at least 23 but younger than 37, hold a valid driver's license, and have earned a bachelor's degree. A potential federal agent must first qualify in one of five categories representing the different entry programs: accounting/finance, computer science/information technology, language, law, and diversified (a miscellaneous-type category). Once a candidate qualifies for one of these larger categories, he will need certain skills and/or experience that the agency currently desires within that category, and the skills desired can change over time. Candidates must also be willing to travel wherever their assignments take them and also be willing to move, because an agent can be asked to relocate at any time.

Certain personality characteristics and skills are important for potential special agents. Because a special agent's job is primarily investigative, strong research and analytical skills are very important.

Education and Training

As a general rule, potential agents do not move directly from schooling into a federal position. Some entry programs require previous work experience before one can even apply. A bachelor's degree is the minimum education requirement; however, graduate study makes an application more likely to be accepted. Depending on the category of entry program, the degree should be in certain relevant fields. If accepted, then the applicant spends several weeks at a training program in Quantico, Virginia, where he learns investigative procedures and other necessary skills. After completion of training, new special agents are paired with more experienced ones to observe how the knowledge they gained is to be applied in real-life settings.

Sources: "Police and Detectives," *Occupational Outlook Handbook*, 2006–2007 edition (Bureau of Labor Statistics, U.S. Department of Labor), retrieved June 30, 2006, from http://www.bls.gov/oco/ocos160.htm; "Careers" (Federal Bureau of Investigation), retrieved June 30, 2006, from http://www.fbijobs.gov/031.asp; "Princeton Review Career Profiles: FBI Agent," retrieved June 30, 2006, from: http:// www.princetonreview.com/cte/profiles/dayInLife.asp?careerID=64.

substances and let the perpetrator off with a warning. Police may view some offenders as being undesirable or a nuisance rather than a danger. Rather than formally arrest these "troublemakers"—e.g., homeless people or alcoholics—they may use informal measures to deal with the problem: take them to another jurisdiction and "dump" them off![98]

Victim Factors

The relationship between the parties involved influences decision making and discretion. An altercation between two friends or relatives may be handled differently than an assault on a stranger. A case in point is policing domestic violence cases. Research indicates that police are reluctant to even respond to these kinds of cases because they are a constant source of frustration and futility.[99] Police sometimes intentionally delay responding to domestic disputes, hoping that by the time they get there the problem will be settled.[100] Victims, they believe, often fail to get help or change their abusive situation.[101] Even when they are summoned, police are likely to treat domestic violence cases more casually than other assault cases. If, however, domestic abuse involves extreme violence, especially if a weapon is brandished or used, police are much more likely to respond with a formal arrest.[102] Therefore, police use their discretion to separate what they consider nuisance cases from those serious enough to demand police action.

Environmental Factors

The degree of discretion that an officer will exercise is at least partially defined by the living and working environment.[103] Police officers may work or dwell within a community culture that either tolerates eccentricities and personal freedoms or expects extremely conservative, professional, no-nonsense behavior on the part of its civil servants. Communities that are proactive and contain progressive governmental institutions also may influence the direction of a police officer's discretion. Police who are assigned to communities that provide training in domestic violence prevention and maintain local shelters are more likely to take action in cases involving spousal abuse.[104]

An officer who lives in the community she serves is probably strongly influenced by and shares a large part of the community's beliefs and values and is likely to be sensitive to and respect the wishes of neighbors, friends, and relatives. However, conflict may arise when the police officer commutes to an assigned area of jurisdiction, as is often the case in inner-city precincts. The officer who holds personal values in opposition to those of the community can exercise discretion in ways that conflict with the community's values and result in ineffective law enforcement.[105]

According to the **overload hypothesis**, community crime rates may shape officer discretion. As local crime rates increase, police resources become strained to the breaking point; officers are forced to give less time and attention to each new case. The amount of attention they can devote to less serious crimes decreases, and they begin to treat petty offenders more leniently than officers in less crime-ridden neighborhoods might have done.[106]

A police officer's perception of community alternatives to police intervention may also influence discretion. A police officer may exercise discretion to arrest an individual in a particular circumstance if it seems that nothing else can be done, even if the officer does not believe that an arrest is the best possible option. In an environment that has a proliferation of social agencies—detoxification units, drug control centers, and child-care services, for example—a police officer will have more alternatives to choose from in deciding whether to make an arrest. Referring cases to these alternative agencies saves the officer both time and effort, for records do not have to be filled out and court appearances can be avoided. Thus, social agencies offer police greater latitude in decision making.

Departmental Factors

Where the department operates and its budget may shape police practices. Officers are more likely to be proactive and use their arrest powers if they work in departments located in high-crime areas but have relatively few personnel.[107]

The policies, practices, and customs of the local police department are another influence on discretion. These conditions vary from department to department and strongly depend on the judgment of the chief and others in the organizational hierarchy. Efforts by the administration to limit or shape the behavior of the officer on patrol may prompt it to issue directives aimed at influencing police conduct. In an effort to crack down on a particular crime—e.g., adolescent drug abuse—the department can create a strict arrest and referral policy for those engaging in that crime. In other words, all juveniles who violate the law must be arrested and sent to court.[108] Some departments have created mandatory arrest policies in domestic violence cases in effort to get officers to take action because of public demand to crack down on spousal abuse.[109]

Patrol officers may be asked to issue more traffic tickets and make more arrests, sometimes called "the numbers game." In other instances they may be told to refrain from arresting under certain circumstances, or limit their hot pursuits to avoid accidents. Occasionally, a directive will instruct officers to be particularly alert for certain types of violations or to make some sort of interagency referral when specific events occur. Administrators may order patrol officers to crack down on street panhandlers or to take formal action in domestic violence cases.[110] Some departments may organize special units to crack down on particular social problems—e.g., public intoxication—and officers in these units may approach their job quite differently than they would had they been assigned to regular patrol duties.[111]

overload hypothesis
The theory that police workload influences discretion so that as workload increases, less time and attention can be devoted to new cases, especially petty crimes.

Most experts believe that written rules either directing or prohibiting action can be highly effective at controlling police discretion and a valuable administrative tool.[112] Many departments now rely on written rules to control discretion in violent confrontations. More than 90 percent have strict rules governing such activities as controlling domestic abuse and using lethal force.

Supervisory Factors

Along with departmental policy, a patrol officer's supervisor can influence discretion. The ratio of supervisory personnel to subordinates may also influence discretion. Departments with a high ratio of sergeants to patrol officers may experience fewer officer-initiated actions than ones in which fewer eyes are observing the action in the streets. Supervisory style may also have an influence on how police use discretion. Robin Shepard Engel found that patrol officers supervised by sergeants who are take-charge types and like to participate in high levels of activity in the field themselves spend significantly more time per shift engaging in self-initiated and community policing or problem-solving activities than they do in administrative activities. In contrast, officers with supervisors whose style involves spending time mentoring and coaching subordinates are more likely to devote significantly more attention to engaging in administrative tasks.[113] The size of the department may also determine the level of officer discretion. In larger departments, looser control by supervisors seems to encourage a level of discretion unknown in smaller, more tightly run police agencies.

Peer Factors

Police discretion is also subject to peer pressure.[114] Police officers suffer a degree of social isolation because the job involves strange working conditions and hours, including being on 24-hour call, and their authority and responsibility to enforce the law may cause embarrassment during social encounters. At the same time, officers must handle irregular and emotionally demanding encounters involving the most personal and private aspects of people's lives. As a result, police officers turn to their peers for both on-the-job advice and off-the-job companionship, essentially forming a subculture to provide a source of status, prestige, and reward.

The peer group affects how police officers exercise discretion on two distinct levels. First, in an obvious, direct manner, other police officers dictate acceptable responses to street-level problems by displaying or withholding approval in office discussions. Second, the officer who takes the job seriously and desires the respect and friendship of others will take their advice, abide by their norms, and seek out the most experienced and most influential patrol officers on the force and follow their behavioral models.

Situational Factors

Regardless of departmental or peer influences, the officer's immediate interaction with a criminal act, offender, citizen, or victim will weigh heavily on the use of discretionary powers.[115]

Some early research efforts found that a police officer relies heavily on suspect **demeanor** (the attitude and appearance of the offender) when making decisions. If an offender is surly, talks back, or otherwise challenges the officer's authority, formal action is more likely to be taken.[116] According to this view, a negative demeanor will result in formal police action.[117] When Joseph Schafer and Stephen Mastrofski surveyed police officers on the factors that influenced their decision to issue traffic citations, they found that motorists who behaved in a civil manner, accepted responsibility for their offense, and admitted their guilt were less likely to receive a ticket than those who displayed a less courteous demeanor. Of course, even the most well-mannered motorist was not immune from citation if he committed what was considered to be a very serious offense—e.g., speeding near a school shortly after classes had been dismissed.[118]

demeanor
The way in which a person outwardly manifests his or her personality.

A police officer turns a taxi away as it tries to enter the 59th Street Bridge during the transit strike in New York City on December 20, 2005 because it was not carrying the four passengers required from 5 a.m. to 11 a.m. New Yorkers struggled to work on foot, by bike, and in cars shared with strangers after subway and bus workers walked off the job, stranding millions during a peak holiday shopping and tourist season. Police behavior and their use of discretion is shaped by emergency situations such as the transit strike.

In a series of research studies, however, David Klinger has challenged the long-held belief that bad demeanor has a significant influence on police decision making. Klinger, a police officer turned criminologist, suggests that it is criminal behavior and actions (touching, hitting, or grappling with an officer) occurring during police detention, not negative attitudes, that influence the police decision to take formal action. Police officers are unimpressed by a bad attitude; they have seen it all before.[119] Research in support of Klinger's views indicates that suspects who offer physical resistance are much more likely to receive some form of physical coercion in return but that those who offer verbal disrespect are not likely to be physically coerced.[120] Therefore, police officers' response to a suspect's challenge to their authority is dependent on the way the challenge is delivered. Verbal challenges are met with verbal responses, and physical with physical.[121]

Another set of situational influences on police discretion concerns the manner in which a crime or situation is encountered. If, for example, a police officer stumbles on an altercation or break-in, the discretionary response may be different from a situation in which the officer is summoned by police radio. If an act has received official police recognition, such as the dispatch of a patrol car, police action must be taken, or an explanation made as to why it was not. Or if a matter is brought to an officer's attention by a citizen observer, the officer can either ignore the request and risk a complaint or take discretionary action. When an officer chooses to become involved in a situation without benefit of a summons or complaint, maximum discretion can be used. Even in this circumstance, however, the presence of a crowd or of witnesses may influence the officer's decision making.

The officer who acts alone is also affected by personal matters—physical condition, mental state, police style, and whether she has other duties to perform. Other factors that might influence police are the use of a weapon, seriousness of injury, and the presence of alcohol or drugs.

Extralegal Factors and Discretion

Amadou Bailo Diallo was a 23-year-old African immigrant living in New York City when he was shot by four police officers assigned to NYPD's Street Crime Unit, whose task was apprehending the most dangerous violent criminals. On February 4, 1999, Diallo was standing near his building after returning from a meal when he was noticed by police officers who believed that he fit the description of a serial rapist.

When he was approached by the officers, Diallo ran up the outside steps, ignoring their orders to stop and "show his hands." He reached into his pocket and drew out an object that the officers believed was a gun. They began to fire, and during the melee, one of the officers tripped and fell, appearing to be shot. The four officers fired 41 shots, hitting Diallo 19 times. Diallo did not have a weapon. He had pulled out his wallet in order to show the police his identification card. The officers were tried on charges of second-degree murder and reckless endangerment and were acquitted of all charges on February 25, 2000.[122]

The Diallo case highlights one of the most critical issues in law enforcement: Do police take race into account when using their discretion? Many experts believe that they do. In his *No Equal Justice: Race and Class in the American Criminal Justice System*, constitutional scholar David Cole argues that despite efforts to create racial neutrality, a race-based double standard operates in virtually every aspect of criminal justice.[123] These disparities allow the privileged to enjoy constitutional protections from police power without extending these protections across the board to minorities and the poor.

Is Cole correct? Is racial bias/profiling normative? The research so far has produced sketchy results: Some efforts do show that the offender's racial characteristics are key determinants that shape the police use of discretion; others find that situational and legal factors are more important.[124] One reason for the inconclusive findings may be that race plays a role in some police procedures but not in others. When Greg Ridgeway studied police practices in Oakland, California, he found that minorities were no more likely to be issued traffic citations than white drivers. However, police officers were more than twice as likely to do searches of black drivers than nonblack drivers. Race also influenced the time or duration of the traffic stop: African American drivers were much more likely than white drivers to be involved in stops lasting 10 minutes or longer.[125]

Regardless of the truth, minority-group members believe that police may be racially and ethnically biased. When Ronald Weitzer and Steven Tuch analyzed national survey data, they found that African Americans and Hispanics are more likely than whites to believe that racially biased policing exists:

◆ A majority of African American (75 percent) and Hispanics (54 percent) believe that police in their city treat African Americans worse than whites, and virtually the same proportions also believe that Hispanics are treated worse than whites (74 percent and 53 percent, respectively).

◆ The overwhelming majority of whites (75–77 percent) believe that police in their city treat whites and the two minority groups "equally."

◆ A majority of African Americans and Hispanics—but just one-third of whites—believe that police provide "worse" services to African American and Hispanic neighborhoods (in comparison to white neighborhoods) throughout the United States. The majority of whites believe that police treat neighborhoods similarly.

◆ African Americans and Hispanics are also much more likely than whites to believe that police prejudice is a problem. Three times as many African Americans as whites believe that police prejudice is "very common" throughout the United States, and African Americans are about six times as likely as whites to believe it is very common in their own city (Hispanics take an intermediate position).[126] Because this issue is so important, it is the topic of the Race, Gender, and Ethnicity in Criminal Justice feature.

Police discretion is one of the most often debated issues in criminal justice (see Concept Summary 7.1 on page 244). On its face, the unequal enforcement of the law smacks of unfairness and violates the Constitution's doctrines of due process and equal protection. Yet if some discretion were not exercised, police would be forced to function as robots merely following the book. Administrators have sought to control discretion so that its exercise may be both beneficial to citizens and nondiscriminatory.[127]

RACE, GENDER, AND ETHNICITY IN CRIMINAL JUSTICE

Racial Profiling

In the late summer of 1997, New Yorkers were shocked as an astounding case of police brutality began to unfold in the daily newspapers. Abner Louima, 33, a Haitian immigrant, had been arrested outside Club Rendez-vous, a Brooklyn nightclub, on August 9 after a fight had broken out. Louima later claimed that the arresting officers had become furious when he protested his arrest, twice stopping the patrol car to beat him with their fists. When they arrived at the station house, two officers, apparently angry because some of the club-goers had fought with the police, led Louima to the men's room, removed his trousers, and attacked him with the handle of a toilet plunger, first shoving it into his rectum and then into his mouth, breaking teeth, while Louima screamed: "Why are you doing this to me? Why? Why?" The officers also shouted racial slurs at Louima, who was rushed to a hospital for emergency surgery to repair a puncture in his small intestine and injuries to his bladder. Louima, who witnesses said had no bruises or injuries when officers took him into custody, arrived at the hospital three hours later bleeding profusely.

In the aftermath of the case, NYPD investigators granted departmental immunity to nearly 100 officers in order to gain information. Cracking the "blue curtain" of silence allowed a number of police officers to be given long prison sentences on charges of sexual abuse and first-degree assault.

The Louima case and other incidents involving the police and the minority community reignited the long debate over whether police use race as a factor in making decisions such as stopping and questioning a suspect or deciding to make an arrest. The term *racial profiling* has been coined to describe the racial influence over police discretion. A number of empirical research studies have found evidence that racial profiling exists: State and local police officers routinely stop African American motorists at a rate far greater than their representation in the driving pool:

♦ Brian Withrow looked at police practices in Wichita, Kansas, and found that African American citizens are stopped at disproportionately higher rates than non–African American citizens and that African American and Hispanic citizens are more likely to be searched and arrested than non–African American and non-Hispanic citizens.

♦ Researchers at Northeastern University in Boston used four statistical tests to analyze 1.6 million traffic citations issued between April 1, 2001, and June 30, 2003, in towns across Massachusetts and found the following: ticketing resident minorities disproportionately more than whites, ticketing all minorities disproportionately more than whites, searching minorities more often than whites, and

issuing warnings to whites more often than to minorities. According to the study, 15 police departments failed all four tests, 42 failed three tests, 87 failed two tests, and 105 failed one.

♦ Richard Lundman's analysis of citizen encounters with police indicates that minority citizens are (a) more likely to be stopped than whites but that (b) searches of minority-driven vehicles are no more likely to yield drugs or contraband than searches of vehicles driven by whites.

Does Race Matter?

Some experts question whether profiling and racial discrimination are as widespread as currently feared. One approach has been to measure the attitudes that minority citizens hold toward police. When Ronald Weitzer surveyed residents in three Washington, D.C., neighborhoods, he found that African Americans value racially integrated police services and welcome the presence of both white and African American police officers, a finding that would seem improbable if most white officers were racially biased. The African American community is generally supportive of the local police, especially when officers respond quickly to calls for service. It is unlikely that African Americans would appreciate rapid responses from racist police.

Another approach is to directly measure whether police treat minority and majority citizens differently —that is, use racial profiling in making decisions. Some research efforts show little evidence that police use racial profiling:

1. David Eitle, Lisa Stolzenberg, and Stewart J. D'Alessio found that whites are more likely to be arrested for assaults than African Americans and that as the percentage of African American police officers in a department increases, this racial gap actually widens.

2. Matt DeLisi and Bob Regoli found that whites are nine times more likely to suffer DWI arrests than African Americans, a finding that would be unlikely if racial profiling was routine.

3. Jon Gould and Stephen Mastrofski studied illegal police searches and found that race has little influence on police conduct. Although police may routinely conduct illegal searches, the suspect's race does not influence their tactics.

4. Joseph Schafer, David Carter, and Andra Katz-Bannister found that although race plays some role in traffic stops, age and gender actually have a greater influence over police decision making.

5. James Lange, Mark Johnson, and Robert Voas surveyed drivers on the New Jersey Turnpike and found that the racial makeup of speeders differed

from that of nonspeeding drivers. The proportion of speeding drivers who were identified as African American coincided with the proportion of African American drivers stopped by police. Their findings suggest that police are less likely to engage in racial profiling today and that efforts to control profiling have been successful.

6. The National Survey of Police Contacts found that most drivers, regardless of race, who experienced a traffic stop said that they felt the officer had a legitimate reason for making the stop. Nearly nine out of ten white drivers and three out of four African American drivers described the officer as having had a legitimate reason. Both African American and white drivers maintained these perceptions regardless of the race of the officer making the stop. The survey found that although whites were more likely to say they were stopped for a "legitimate reason," a clear majority of members of both racial groups believe that the police officer acted in a forthright fashion, that they were not the victim of profiling, and that the race of the police officer had no influence on the situation.

These studies suggest that efforts to control profiling may have achieved their desired results. According to legal experts Dan Kahan and Tracey Meares, racial discrimination may be on the decline because minorities now possess sufficient political status to protect themselves from abuses within the justice system. And in the event that political influence is insufficient to control profiling, members of the minority community have used the court system to seek legal redress. In a 2003 settlement, the city of Cincinnati was forced to establish a $4.5-million settlement fund to compensate 16 people for instances of racial profiling. One plaintiff was held at gunpoint after being stopped for a traffic infraction, and another had been shot in the back while running away, unarmed. Community policing efforts may also be helping police officers become more sensitive to issues that concern the public, such as profiling.

Can Racial Profiling Be Justified?

Whereas most experts condemn any form of racial profiling, two Harvard scholars, Mathias Risse and Richard Zeckhauser, have argued that profiling may have utility as a crime control tactic. First, they suggest that there is a significant correlation between membership in certain racial groups and the propensity to commit certain crimes. This justifies why profiling takes place. Second, they suggest that given such a propensity, stopping, searching, or investigating members of such groups differentially will help curb crime. That is, racial profiling has utility because it can eliminate more crime than other law enforcement practices for equivalent expenditures of resources and disruption. If these assumptions are true, then racial profiling is morally justified in a broad range of cases, including many cases that tend to be controversial. Some people consider profiling abusive, but Risse and Zeckhauser believe that police abuse is a separate issue and should not be considered an aspect of profiling.

A key element of Risse and Zeckhauser's position is that racial profiling is not as harmful as crime and therefore not too big a price to pay in order to achieve reductions in crime rates. Most stops are not abusive, and police try to act as civilly as possible under the circumstances. But as legal scholars Samuel Gross and Katherine Barnes point out, the assumption that a stop and search is intrinsically a minor inconvenience is questionable. Its effect can be corrosive:

> As the level of the police officer's interest increases, the cost to the innocent citizen escalates rapidly. It's one thing to get a speeding ticket and an annoying lecture . . . it's quite another to be told to step out of the car and to be questioned. . . . The questions may seem intrusive and out of line, but you can hardly refuse to answer an armed cop. At some point you realize you are not just another law-abiding citizen who's being checked out . . . like everyone else. You've been targeted. The trooper is not going through a routine so he can let you go . . . he wants to find drugs on you. . . . Those of us who have not been through this sort of experience probably underestimate its impact. To be treated as a criminal is a basic insult to a person's self-image and his position in society. It cannot easily be shrugged off. . . . (pp. 745–46)

In other words, although some may argue that profiling can reduce some forms of criminal behavior such as drug trafficking, the social costs it brings are too big a price to pay for modest crime reductions.

Critical Thinking

1. What, if anything, can be done to reduce racial bias on the part of police? Would adding minority officers help? Would it be a form of racism to assign minority officers to minority neighborhoods?

2. Would research showing that police are more likely to make arrests in interracial incidents than intraracial incidents constitute evidence of racism?

3. Police spot three men of Middle Eastern descent carrying a large, heavy box into a crowded building. Should they stop and question them and demand to look into the carton? Is this racial profiling?

(continued)

InfoTrac College Edition Research

Use "racial profiling" as a key word to review articles on the use of race as a determining factor in the police use of discretion.

Sources: Kasper Lippert-Rasmussen, "Racial Profiling Versus Community," *Journal of Applied Philosophy* 23 (2006): 191–205; James Lange, Mark Johnson, and Robert Voas, "Testing the Racial Profiling Hypothesis for Seemingly Disparate Traffic Stops on the New Jersey Turnpike," *Justice Quarterly* 22 (2005): 193–223; Mathias Risse and Richard Zeckhauser, "Racial Profiling," *Philosophy and Public Affairs* 32 (2004): 131–70; Samuel Gross and Katherine Barnes, "Road Work: Racial Profiling and Drug Interdiction on the Highway," *Michigan Law Review* 101 (2003): 651–754; Illya Lichtenberg, "Driving While Black (DWB): Examining Race as a Tool in the War on Drugs," *Police Practice & Research* 7 (2006): 49–60; Richard Lundman, "Driver Race, Ethnicity, and Gender and Citizen Reports of Vehicle Searches by Police and Vehicle Search Hits," *Journal of Criminal Law & Criminology* 94 (2004): 309–50; Stephen Rice and Alex Piquero, "Perceptions of Discrimination and Justice in New York City," *Policing* 28 (2005): 98–117; Joseph Schafer, David Carter, and Andra Katz-Bannister, "Studying Traffic Stop Encounters," *Journal of Criminal Justice* 32 (2004): 159–70; Candice Batton and Colleen Kadleck, "Theoretical and Methodological Issues in Racial Profiling Research," *Police Quarterly* 7 (2004): 30–64; David Eitle, Lisa Stolzenberg, and Stewart J. D'Alessio, "Police Organizational Factors, the Racial Composition of the Police, and the Probability of Arrest," *Justice Quarterly* 22 (2005): 30–57; Brian Withrow, "Race-Based Policing: A Descriptive Analysis of the Wichita Stop Study," *Police Practice & Research* 5 (2004): 223–40; Amy Farrell, Jack McDevitt, Lisa Bailey, Carsten Andresen, and Erica Pierce, "Massachusetts Racial and Gender Profiling Final Report" (Boston: Northeastern University, 2004) (http://www.racialprofilinganalysis.neu.edu/IRJsite_docs/finalreport.pdf), accessed on September 13, 2004; Tom Tyler and Cheryl Wakslak, "Profiling and Police Legitimacy: Procedural Justice, Attributions of Motive, and Acceptance of Police Authority," *Criminology* 42 (2004): 253–81; Jon Gould and Stephen Mastrofski, "Suspect Searches: Assessing Police Behavior Under the U.S. Constitution," *Criminology & Public Policy* 3 (2004): 315–62; Andrew E. Taslit, "Racial Auditors and the Fourth Amendment: Data with the Power to Inspire Political Action," *Law and Contemporary Problems* 66 (2003): 221–99; *In re Cincinnati Policing*, No. C-1-99-3170 (S.D. Ohio, 2003); Patrick A. Langan, Lawrence A. Greenfeld, Steven K. Smith, Matthew R. Durose, and David J. Levin, *Contacts Between Police and the Public: Findings from the 1999 National Survey* (Washington, D.C.: Bureau of Justice Statistics, 2001); Ronald Weitzer, "White, Black, or Blue Cops? Race and Citizen Assessments of Police Officers," *Journal of Criminal Justice* 28 (2000): 313–24; Matt DeLisi and Robert Regoli, "Race, Conventional Crime, and Criminal Justice: The Declining Importance of Skin Color," *Journal of Criminal Justice* 27 (1999): 549–57; Randall Kennedy, *Race, Crime, and the Law* (New York: Vintage, 1998); Dan M. Kahan and Tracey L. Meares, "The Coming Crisis of Criminal Procedure," *Georgetown Law Journal* 86 (1998): 1153–84.

ThomsonNOW Improve your grade on the exam with Personalized Study! For reinforcement resources and a mastery check of the police profession, go to www.thomsonedu.com/thomsonnow.

CONCEPT SUMMARY 7.1
Police Discretion

Factors influencing discretion	Individual influences
Legal factors	Crime seriousness; prior record
Victim factors	Victim–criminal relationship
Environmental factors	Community culture and values
Departmental factors	Policies and orders
Supervision factors	Supervisor's style and control
Peer factors	Peer influence and culture
Situational factors	Suspect demeanor
Extralegal factors	Race, gender, age

◆ PROBLEMS OF POLICING

Law enforcement is not an easy job. The role ambiguity, social isolation, and threat of danger present in working the streets are the police officer's constant companions. What effects do these strains have on police? Three of the most significant problems are job stress, violence, and corruption.

Job Stress

The complexity of their role, the need to exercise prudent discretion, the threat of using violence and having violence used against them, and isolation from the rest of society all take a toll on law enforcement officers. Police officer stress leads to negative attitudes, burnout, loss of enthusiasm and commitment (cynicism), increased apathy, substance abuse problems, divorce, health problems, and many other social, personal, and job-related problematic behaviors.[128] Evidence suggests that police officers are often involved in marital disputes and even incidents of domestic violence, which may be linked to stress.[129] Stress may not be constant, but at some time during their career (usually the middle years), most officers will feel its effects.[130]

CAUSES OF STRESS A number of factors have been associated with job stress.[131] Some are related to the difficulties that police officers have in maintaining social and family relationships, considering their schedule and workload.[132] Police suffer stress in their personal lives when they bring the job home or when their work hours are shifted, causing family disruptions.[133] Those who perceive being alienated from family and friends at home are more likely to feel stress on the job.[134]

Some stressors are job-related. The pressure of being on duty 24 hours per day leads to stress and emotional detachment from both work and public needs. Policing is a dangerous profession, and officers are at risk of many forms of job-related accidental deaths (see Table 7.1). On the other hand, law enforcement officers contemplating retirement also report high stress levels. So although the job may be dangerous, many officers are reluctant to leave it.[135]

Stress has been related to internal conflict with administrative policies that deny officers support and a meaningful role in decision making.[136] Stress may result when officers are forced to adapt to a department's new methods of policing, such as community-oriented policing, and they are skeptical about the change in policy.[137] Other stressors include poor training, substandard equipment, inadequate pay, lack of opportunity, job dissatisfaction, role conflict, exposure to brutality, and fears about competence, success, and safety.[138] Some officers may feel stress because they believe that the court system favors the rights of the criminal and handcuffs the police; others might be sensitive to a perceived lack of support from governmental officials and the general public.[139] Others believe that their superiors care little about their welfare.[140]

Police psychologists have divided these stressors into four distinct categories:

1. External stressors, such as verbal abuse from the public, justice system inefficiency, and liberal court decisions that favor the criminal. What are

TABLE 7.1
Circumstances of Accidental Police Deaths, 1995–2004

Circumstance	Total	1995	1996	1997	1998	1999	2000	2001	2002	2003	2004
Total	717	59	52	63	81	65	83	76	75	81	82
Automobile accidents	404	33	33	33	48	41	42	36	40	50	48
Motorcycle accidents	60	3	4	4	3	6	6	7	7	10	10
Aircraft accidents	43	8	1	4	4	4	7	5	6	1	3
Struck by vehicles	120	10	7	15	14	9	14	19	12	10	10
Accidental shootings	28	2	2	1	3	3	3	5	3	2	4
Drownings	21	1	0	0	6	0	3	1	3	4	3
Falls	20	2	2	5	1	1	3	2	1	2	1
Other accidents	21	0	3	1	2	1	5	1	3	2	3

Source: Federal Bureau of Investigation (http://www.fbi.gov/ucr/killed/2004/table59.htm), accessed on August 20, 2006.

perceived to be antipolice judicial decisions may alienate police and reduce their perceptions of their own competence.[141]

2. Organizational stressors, such as low pay, excessive paperwork, arbitrary rules, and limited opportunity for advancement.

3. Duty stressors, such as rotating shifts, work overload, boredom, fear, and danger.

4. Individual stressors, such as discrimination, marital difficulties, and personality problems.[142]

The effects of stress can be shocking. Police work has been related to both physical and psychological ailments. Police have a significantly high rate of premature death caused by such conditions as heart disease and diabetes. They also experience a disproportionate number of divorces and other marital problems. Research indicates that police officers in some departments, but not all, have higher suicide rates than the general public. (Recent research shows that New York City police have equal or lower suicide rates than the general public and that some researchers have found a lower than average police suicide rate in other areas of the country.[143]) Police who feel stress may not be open to adopting new ideas and programs such as community policing.[144]

COMBATING STRESS   Research efforts have shown that the more support police officers get in the workplace, the lower their feelings of stress and anxiety.[145] Consequently, departments have attempted to fight job-related stress by training officers to cope with its effects. Today, stress training includes diet information, biofeedback, relaxation and meditation, and exercise. Many departments include stress management as part of an overall wellness program, also designed to promote physical and mental health, fitness, and good nutrition.[146] Some programs have included family members: They may be better able to help the officer cope if they have more knowledge about the difficulties of police work. Still other efforts promote total wellness programming, which enhances the physical and emotional well-being of officers by emphasizing preventive physical and psychological measures.[147] Research also shows that because police perceive many benefits of their job and enjoy the quality of life it provides, stress-reduction programs might help officers focus on the positive aspects of police work.[148]

Stress is a critically important aspect of police work. Further research is needed to create valid methods of identifying police officers under considerable stress and to devise effective stress-reduction programs.[149]

Violence

The Louima case, discussed in the Race, Gender, and Ethnicity feature, and other incidents involving the police illustrate the persistent problems police departments have in regulating violent contacts with citizens. Police officers are empowered to use force and violence in pursuit of their daily tasks. Some scholars argue that the use of violent measures is the core of the police role.[150]

Since their creation, U.S. police departments have wrestled with the charge that they are brutal, physically violent organizations. Early police officers resorted to violence and intimidation to gain the respect that was not freely given by citizens. In the 1920s, the Wickersham Commission detailed numerous instances of police brutality, including the use of the "third degree" to extract confessions.

Today, **police brutality** continues to be a concern, especially when police use excessive violence against members of the minority community. The nation looked on in disgust when a videotape was aired on network newscasts showing members of the Los Angeles Police Department beating, kicking, and using electric stun guns on Rodney King. Earlier, Los Angeles police stopped using a restraining choke hold, which cuts off blood circulation to the brain, after minority

police brutality
Actions such as using abusive language, making threats, using force or coercion unnecessarily, prodding with nightsticks, and stopping and searching people to harass them.

While research shows that police officers use force only sparingly, violence is still a part of police work. This January 30, 2006 video taken by KTVI-TV shows Maplewood, Missouri police officers kicking and punching Edmond Burns after three police cruisers rammed his van. Burns refused to stop following a high-speed chase through the streets of St. Louis—police were initially watching him case a gas station. When should police use force? Should the standard be the same as that which applies to civilians?

citizens complained that it caused permanent damage and may have killed as many as 17 people. Three-quarters of all complaints filed against the police for misconduct tend to be by nonwhite males under the age of 30.[151]

HOW COMMON IS THE USE OF FORCE TODAY? How much force is being used by the police today?[152] Despite some highly publicized incidents that get a lot of media attention, the research data show that the use of force is not a very common event. The national (2005) survey on police contacts with civilians sponsored by the federal government found that in a single year, of the 45 million people who had one or more police contacts, about 1.5 percent (664,500 persons) reported that an officer used or threatened to use force.[153] African Americans (3.5 percent) and Hispanics (2.5 percent) were more likely than whites (1.1 percent) to experience police threat or use of force during the contact; young people (ages 16–29) were almost three times more likely to experience force than people over 29. When force was applied, however, it was most likely to be "pushing" or "grabbing." In 19 percent of the 664,500 force incidents, a police officer pointed a gun at the individual, and 14 percent resulted in injury to the citizen. And although 24 percent of the combatants cursed at, insulted, or verbally threatened the officer(s) during the incident, three-quarters claimed that the force was excessive, and more than 80 percent believed the officer acted improperly. So 45 million people were contacted by police, but only 90,000 or so were injured. Is that far too many or relatively few?

These data indicate that the police use of force may not be as common as previously believed, but it still remains a central part of the police role. Although getting an accurate figure is difficult, at least 6,600 civilians have been killed by the police since 1976, and the true number is probably much higher.[154] Considering these numbers, police use of force is an important topic for study.

RACE AND FORCE The routine use of force may be diminishing, but there is still debate over whether police are more likely to get rough with minority suspects. The national survey on police contacts with civilians found that African Americans and Hispanics were more likely than whites to experience police threat or use of force as a consequence of police contact. Cities with large African American populations also experience the highest amount of lethal violence by police.[155]

Considering this evidence, it is not surprising that surveys of minority-group members show they are more likely to disapprove of the police view of force than majority-group members.[156] Minority citizens are much more likely to claim that police "hassle them"—stop them or watch them closely when they have done nothing wrong.[157] Race may be only one element of the factors that determine the outcome of police–citizen encounters, but it is certainly not the only one. Joel Garner's study of police encounters with citizens, using a wide variety of samples taken in different locales, found that race actually played an insignificant role in the decision to use force.[158] The Garner research and similar efforts indicate that a suspect's behavior is a much more powerful determinant of police response than age or race. William Terrill studied 3,544 police–suspect encounters and found that situational factors often influence the extent to which force is applied. Use of force seems to escalate when a police officer gives a suspect a second chance (e.g., "Dump the beer out of your car, and I'll let you go") but the suspect hesitates or defies the order.[159] People who resist police orders or actually grapple with officers are much more likely to be the target of force than those who are respectful, passive, and noncombative. Members of certain sub-populations such as intravenous drug users may be more likely to perceive or experience police coercion and violence than the general population.[160] The general public seems to understand the situational use of force: Even people who condemn police violence—e.g., racial minorities—are more supportive of its use if the officer is in danger or a suspect is confrontational.[161] So the evidence suggests that whether African American or white, suspect behavior may be a more important determinant of force than race or ethnicity.

WHO ARE THE PROBLEM COPS? Evidence shows that only a small proportion of officers are continually involved in use-of-force incidents.[162] What kind of police officer gets involved in problem behavior? Aggressive cops may be ones who overreact to the stress of police work while at the same time feel socially isolated. They believe that the true sources of their frustration—e.g., corrupt politicians and/or liberal judges—are shielded from their anger, so they take their frustrations out on readily available targets: vulnerable people in their immediate environment.[163] Some officers are chronic offenders. Research conducted in a southeastern city by Kim Michelle Lersch and Tom Mieczkowski found that a few officers (7 percent) were chronic offenders who accounted for a significant portion of all citizen complaints (33 percent). Those officers receiving the bulk of the complaints tended to be younger and less experienced, and had been accused of harassment or violence after a proactive encounter that they had initiated. Although repeat offenders were more likely to be accused of misconduct by minority citizens, little evidence existed that attacks were racially motivated.[164]

Efforts to deal with these problem cops are now being undertaken in police departments around the nation. A number of departments have instituted early-warning systems to change the behavior of individual officers who have been identified as having performance problems. The basic intervention strategy involves a combination of deterrence and education. According to the deterrence strategy, officers who are subject to intervention will presumably change their behavior in response to a perceived threat of punishment. Early-warning systems operate on the assumption that training, as part of the intervention, can help officers improve their performance. Evaluations show that early-warning systems appear to have a dramatic effect on reducing citizen complaints and other indicators of problematic police performance among those officers subject to intervention.[165]

Research into police violence and its relation to calls for service usually focuses on so-called dangerous encounters. The dangerous encounters, based on rankings on assaults and injuries to police officers, are almost exclusively considered to be traffic stops, domestic disturbances, or violent crime calls.

Urban police departments are implementing or considering implementing neighborhood and community policing models to improve relations with the public. In addition, detailed rules of engagement that limit the use of force are common in major cities. However, the creation of departmental rules limiting behavior is often haphazard and is usually a reaction to a crisis situation (for example, a citizen is seriously injured) instead of part of a systematic effort to improve police–citizen interactions.[166] Some departments have developed administrative policies that stress limiting the use of **deadly force** and containing armed offenders until specially trained backup teams are sent to take charge of the situation. Administrative policies have been found to be an effective control on deadly force, and their influence can be enhanced if given the proper support by the chief of police.[167]

Some cities are taking an aggressive, proactive stance to curb violent cops. Since 1977, the New York City Police Department has been operating a force-related integrity testing program in which undercover officers pose as angry citizens in elaborate sting operations intended to weed out officers with a propensity for violence. In a typical encounter, officers responding to a radio call about a domestic dispute confront an aggressive husband who spews hatred at everyone around, including the police. The husband is actually an undercover officer from the Internal Affairs Bureau who is testing whether the officers, one of whom has had a history of civilian complaints, will respond to verbal abuse with threats or violence. The NYPD conducts about 600 sting operations each year to test the integrity of its officers, including several dozen devoted to evaluating the conduct of officers with a history of abuse complaints.[168]

What may be the most significant factors that can control the use of police brutality are the threat of civil judgments against individual officers who use excessive force, police chiefs who ignore or condone violent behavior, and the cities and towns in which they are employed. Civilians routinely file civil actions against police departments when they believe that officers have violated their civil rights. Police may be sued when a victim believes that excessive force was used during his or her arrest or custody. Civilians may collect damages if they can show that the force used was unreasonable, considering all the circumstances known to the officer at the time he or she acted. Excessive force suits commonly occur when police use a weapon, such as a gun or baton, to subdue an unarmed person who is protesting his or her treatment. The U.S. Supreme Court in 1978 (*Monell v. Department of Social Services*) ruled that local agencies could be held liable under the federal Civil Rights Act (42 U.S.C. 1983) for actions of their employees if such actions were part of an official custom or practice.[169]

> **deadly force**
> Police killing of a suspect who resists arrest or presents a danger to an officer or the community.

Deadly Force

As commonly used, the term *deadly force* refers to the actions of a police officer who shoots and kills a suspect who is fleeing from arrest, assaulting a victim, or attacking an officer.[170] The justification for the use of deadly force can be traced to English common law, in which almost every criminal offense was a felony and bore the death penalty. The use of deadly force in the course of arresting a felon was considered expedient, saving the state the burden of trial (the "fleeing felon" rule).[171]

Although the media depict hero cops in a constant stream of deadly shootouts in which scores of bad guys are killed, the number of people killed by the police each year is most likely between 250 and 300.[172] Although these data are encouraging, some researchers believe that the actual number of police shootings is far greater and may be hidden or masked by a number of factors. For example, coroners may be intentionally or accidentally underreporting police homicides by almost half.[173]

FACTORS RELATED TO POLICE SHOOTINGS Is police use of deadly force a random occurrence, or are there social, legal, and environmental factors associated with its use? The following seven patterns have been related to police shootings:

1. *Local and national violence levels.* The higher the levels of violence in a community, the more likely police in the area will use deadly force.[174] A number

of studies have found that fatal police shootings were closely related to reported national violent crime rates and criminal homicide rates. Police officers kill civilians at a higher rate in years when the general level of violence in the nation is higher. The perception of danger may contribute to the use of violent means for self-protection.[175]

2. *Exposure to violence.* Police officers may become exposed to violence when they are forced to confront the emotionally disturbed. Some distraught people attack police as a form of suicide.[176] This tragic event has become so common that the term *suicide by cop* has been coined to denote victim-precipitated killings by police. For example, during an 11-year period (1988–1998) more than 10 percent of the shootings by police officers in Los Angeles involved suicidal people intentionally provoking police.[177]

3. *Workload.* A relationship exists among police violence and the number of police on the street, the number of calls for service, the number and nature of police dispatches, the number of arrests made in a given jurisdiction, and police exposure to stressful situations.

4. *Firearms availability.* Cities that experience a large number of crimes committed with firearms are also likely to have high police violence rates. A strong association has been found between police use of force and gun density (the proportion of suicides and murders committed with a gun).[178]

5. *Social conflict: the threat hypothesis.* According to the *threat hypothesis*, more police are killed in cities with a large underclass.[179] The greatest number of police shootings occurs in areas that have significant disparities in economic opportunity and high levels of income inequality.[180] One conflict-reduction approach is to add minority police officers. However, recent research by Brad Smith shows that the mere addition of minority officers to a department is not a sufficient way to reduce levels of police violence.[181] However, David Jacobs and Jason Carmichael found that the presence of an African American mayor significantly reduces the likelihood of police–citizen violence.[182] They conclude that economic disadvantage within the minority community coupled with political alienation leads to a climate in which police–citizen conflict is sharpened. Politically excluded groups may turn to violence to gain ends that those not excluded can acquire with conventional tactics. The presence of an African American mayor may reduce feelings of powerlessness in the minority community, which in turn reduces anger against the state, of which the police are the most visible officials.

6. *Administrative policies.* The philosophy, policies, and practices of individual police chiefs and departments significantly influence the police use of deadly force.[183] Departments that stress restrictive policies on the use of force generally have lower shooting rates than those that favor tough law enforcement and encourage officers to shoot when necessary. Poorly written or ambivalent policies encourage shootings because they allow the officer at the scene to decide when deadly force is warranted, often under conditions of high stress and tension.

7. *Race.* No other issue is as important to the study of the police use of deadly force as that of racial discrimination. A number of critics have claimed that police are more likely to shoot and kill minority offenders than they are whites. In a famous statement, sociologist Paul Takagi charged that police have "one trigger finger for whites and another for African-Americans."[184] Takagi's complaint was supported by a number of research studies which showed that a disproportionate number of police killings involved minority citizens—almost 80 percent in some of the cities surveyed.[185]

Do these findings alone indicate that police discriminate in the use of deadly force? Some pioneering research by James Fyfe helps provide an answer to this question. In his study of New York City shootings over a five-year period, Fyfe found that police officers were most likely to shoot suspects who were armed and with whom they became involved in violent confrontations. Once such factors as being armed with a weapon, being involved in a violent crime, and attacking an officer were considered, the racial differences in the police use of force ceased to be significant. Fyfe found that African American officers were almost twice as likely as white officers to have shot citizens. Fyfe attributes this finding to the fact that African American officers work and live in high-crime, high-violence areas where shootings are more common and that African American officers hold proportionately more line positions and fewer administrative posts than white officers, which would place them more often on the street and less often behind a desk.[186]

CONTROLLING DEADLY FORCE Given that the police use of deadly force is such a serious problem, ongoing efforts have been made to control it.

One of the most difficult problems that influenced its control was the continued use of the fleeing felon rule in a number of states. However, in 1985 the U.S. Supreme Court outlawed the indiscriminate use of deadly force with its decision in the case of *Tennessee v. Garner*. In this case, the Court ruled that the use of deadly force against apparently unarmed and nondangerous fleeing felons is an illegal seizure of their person under the Fourth Amendment. Deadly force may not be used unless it is necessary to prevent escape and the officer has probable cause to believe that the suspect poses a significant threat of death or serious injury to the officer or others. The majority opinion stated that when the suspect poses no immediate threat to the officer and no threat to others, the harm resulting from failing to apprehend the suspect does not justify the use of deadly force to do so: "A police officer may not seize an unarmed, nondangerous suspect by shooting him dead."[187]

With *Garner*, the Supreme Court effectively put an end to any local police policy that allowed officers to shoot unarmed or otherwise nondangerous offenders if they resisted arrest or attempted to flee from police custody. However, the Court did not ban the use of deadly force or otherwise control police shooting policy. Consequently, in *Graham v. Connor*, the Court created a reasonableness standard for the use of force: Force is excessive when, considering all the circumstances known to the officer at the time he acted, the force used was unreasonable.[188] For example, an officer is approached in a threatening manner by someone wielding a knife. The assailant fails to stop when warned and is killed by the officer. The officer would not be held liable if it turns out that the shooting victim was deaf and could not hear the officer's command and if the officer at the time of the incident had no way of knowing the person's disability.

Individual state jurisdictions still control police shooting policy. Some states have adopted statutory policies that restrict the police use of violence. Others have upgraded training in the use of force. The Federal Law Enforcement Training Center (FLETC) has developed the FLETC use-of-force model, illustrated in Figure 7.3, to teach officers the proper method to escalate force in response to the threat they face. As the figure shows, resistance ranges from compliant and cooperative to assaultive with the threat of serious bodily harm or death. Officers are taught via lecture, demonstration, computer-based instruction, and training scenarios to assess a suspect's behavior and apply an appropriate and corresponding amount of force.[189]

Another method of controlling police shootings is through internal review and policy making by police administrative review boards. For example, New York's Firearm Discharge Review Board was established to investigate and adjudicate all police firearm discharges. Among the dispositions available to the board are the following:

◆ The discharge was in accordance with law and departmental policy.

◆ The discharge was justifiable, but the officer should be given additional training in the use of firearms or in the law and departmental policy.

FIGURE 7.3

The Federal Law Enforcement Training Center's Use-of-Force Model

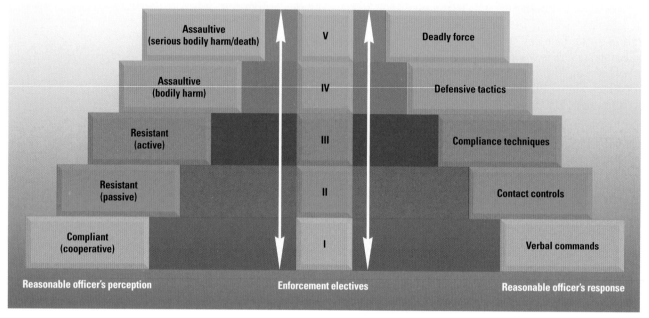

Source: Franklin Graves and Gregory Connor, Federal Law Enforcement Training Center, Glynco, Georgia.

◆   The shooting was justifiable under law but violated departmental policy and warrants departmental disciplinary action.

◆   The shooting was in apparent violation of law and should be referred to the appropriate prosecutor if criminal charges have not already been filed.

◆   The officer involved should be transferred (or offered the opportunity to transfer) to a less sensitive assignment.

◆   The officer involved should receive testing or alcoholism counseling.[190]

The review board approach is controversial because it can mean that the department recommends that one of its own officers be turned over for criminal prosecution.[191]

NONLETHAL WEAPONS In the last few years, about 1,000 local police forces have started using some sort of less-than-lethal weapon designed to subdue suspects. The most widely used nonlethal weapons are wood, rubber, or polyurethane bullets shot out of modified 37-mm pistols or 12-gauge shotguns. At short distances, officers use pepper spray and tasers, which deliver electric shocks from long wire tentacles, producing intense muscle spasms. Other technologies still in development include guns that shoot giant nets, guns that squirt sticky glue, and lights that can temporarily blind a suspect. Some shoot bags filled with lead pellets, which have a range of 100 feet and pack the wallop of a pro boxer's punch.[192]

Recent research efforts indicate that nonlethal weapons may help reduce police use of force.[193] However, greater effort must be made to regulate these nonlethal weapons and create effective policies for their use.[194] See the Criminal Justice and Technology feature on page 254.

POLICE AS VICTIMS Police use of force continues to be an important issue, but control measures seem to be working. Fewer people are being killed by police, and fewer officers are being killed in the line of duty than ever before—about 50 each year. The number rose dramatically in 2001 because 23 officers were killed

A New York City police officer is assisted by colleagues after being injured while trying to control a union protest march. Policing is a dangerous profession, and death and injury are part of the job.

in the September 11 terrorist attacks, along with 343 firefighters. Before the 2001 spike, the number of officers slain in the line of duty had been trending downward for the previous decade.[195] In 2004, the last year for which data are available, 57 law enforcement officers were feloniously killed in 50 separate incidents. What were the circumstances surrounding their deaths? Of the 57 officers slain, 17 were killed in arrest situations, including 7 officers who were murdered while responding to robberies in progress or pursuing robbery suspects, and 2 who were killed while responding to burglaries in progress or pursuing burglary suspects. Eight officers died while attempting other types of arrest. Another 12 officers were ambushed by their assailants, and of these, 6 were victims of unprovoked attacks, and 6 were entrapped or victims of premeditation. Ten officers died while investigating disturbance calls, most of which were family quarrels. Six officers were murdered while investigating suspicious persons or circumstances, and 6 were slain in the course of stopping vehicles for traffic violations or the resulting vehicle pursuits. Three officers were killed while working to resolve hostage situations or other high-risk tactical situations, and 2 were slain while handling mentally deranged individuals. One officer was killed while handling a prisoner.[196]

One long-cherished myth is that police officers who answer domestic violence calls are at risk for violent victimization. The scenario goes that, when confronted, one of the two battling parties turns on the outsider who dares interfere in a private matter. However, research conducted in Charlotte, North Carolina, indicates that domestic violence calls may be no more dangerous than many other routine police interactions.[197] So although police officers should be on their guard when investigating a call for assistance from an abused spouse, the risk of violence against them may be no greater than when they answer a call for a burglary or car theft.

Corruption

In July 1996 the elite antigang unit from the Los Angeles Police Department's Rampart Division raided gang-infested apartments at Shatto Place. Their target was the notorious 18th Street Gang, one of Los Angeles's most violent. During the raid, police officers killed one gang member and wounded another. A departmental investigation found nothing wrong and exonerated the police involved. Then, in 1999, Rafael A. Perez, an officer who took part in the raid, was caught

Less-Than-Lethal Weapons

After the U.S. Supreme Court ruling in *Tennessee v. Garner*, law enforcement officers were prohibited from using deadly force to capture a fleeing, non-violent, unarmed suspect. Because an alternative to deadly force was needed, police departments around the country turned to nonlethal weapons for use in many incidents.

Pepper Spray

One of the most popular less-than-lethal weapons being used by law enforcement personnel is oleoresin capsicum, also known as pepper spray. The product, which is made from peppers, is so strong that when suspects are sprayed, their eyes will automatically shut and they will experience shortness of breath. Pepper spray is used in a variety of scenarios, ranging from the subduing of an agitated individual to subduing groups that are uncooperative and causing problems.

Some law enforcement agencies have adopted more high-powered pepper spray models, including the PepperBall System, which is a semiautomatic high-pressure launcher which fires projectiles that contain the strongest form of oleoresin capsicum and that are built to burst on impact. The launcher is accurate up to 30 feet and can saturate an area up to 100 feet, which allows police officers to safely stand back while incapacitating suspects. Now used by 1,200 different agencies, including law enforcement, corrections, security, and other government agencies, the PepperBall System projectiles explode with 8–10 foot-pounds of force to stop suspects without causing permanent injury. The PepperBall System is used for handling violent suspects who may have barricaded themselves in a hard-to-get-at area as well as for riot control and hostage rescue.

Although it is billed as a nonlethal weapon, some critics fear that pepper spray is dangerous. After 63 people died after being exposed to pepper spray in three North Carolina counties, the federal government sponsored research to determine whether this nonlethal weapon was more lethal than previously believed. The research cleared use of the spray, finding that only 2 of the 63 deaths could be blamed on it; the other fatalities were attributed to drug use, illness, or a combination of the two. As a result, police are continuing to use incapacitating sprays, and new ones are being developed.

Bean Bag Gun

Some law enforcement agencies are using the bean bag gun, which delivers a projectile the size of a tea bag filled with lead birdshot. Once an assailant is hit by the projectile, he will experience a muscle spasm that will either drop him in his tracks or at least slow him down so he can easily be subdued by law enforcement agents.

Although effective, bean bag guns have also caused injuries and deaths. Approximately 12 people

stealing eight pounds of cocaine from police evidence lockers. After pleading guilty in September 1999, he bargained for a lighter sentence by telling departmental investigators about police brutality, perjury, planted evidence, drug corruption, and attempted murder within the Rampart Division and its antigang unit, known as CRASH (Community Resources Against Street Hoodlums). Perez told authorities that during the Shatto raid, the victims may have been unarmed, so the raiding officers resorted to a "throwdown"—slang for a weapon being planted to make a shooting legally justifiable. Perez's testimony resulted in at least 12 Rampart cops being fired or relieved from duty. But Perez was not done. He also said that he and his partner, Nino Durden, shot an unarmed 18th Street Gang member named Javier Ovando, then planted a semiautomatic rifle on the unconscious suspect and claimed that Ovando had tried to shoot them during a stakeout. Their original testimony helped get Ovando, confined to a wheelchair for life because of the shooting, a 23-year sentence for assault. Ovando has since been freed from prison and is suing the city for more than $20 million.[198] Perez was sentenced to two years in prison for violating Ovando's civil rights and three more for stealing cocaine from LAPD evidence lockers. Durden received a five-year prison sentence and was released in 2005.[199]

From their creation, U.S. police departments have wrestled with the problem of controlling illegal and unprofessional behavior by their officers. Corruption pervaded the U.S. police when the early departments were first formed.

have been killed in the United States and Canada after being struck by the bean bags. Although the projectiles are supposed to unfold once they are released from the gun, when they malfunction, they can rip through the skin, resulting in devastating effects, especially when discharged too close to the target. Because of these concerns, bean bag guns are being used less frequently while new versions, lacking the sharp edges of previous projectiles, are being developed.

Tasers

Tasers fire electrified darts at fleeing individuals who, when hit, can experience up to 50,000 volts of electricity. The darts can travel approximately 20 feet and can pierce through two inches of clothing, attack the individual's central nervous system, and cause muscle contractions and temporary paralysis. Currently, 2,400 law enforcement agencies in the country are using Tasers, and little evidence exists that they cause permanent injury or death. The biggest complaint is that they have less effect on extremely large or overweight people, whose muscles are not located as close to the skin surface as the average person.

Other weapons, such as net launchers and sticky glues, two products that would also help capture fleeing offenders, are still being developed. So far, safety issues regarding these products have deterred them from being used frequently.

Critical Thinking

1. Would the easy availability of nonlethal weapons encourage their use by police officers, thus increasing the risk of civilian injuries?

2. Would you prohibit most police officers from carrying firearms and ask them to rely more on nonlethal weapons? Should police in non-death-penalty states be allowed to shoot and kill criminal suspects even though they would not face death if they were caught, tried, and convicted?

InfoTrac College Edition Research

To read about the PepperBall System in more detail, go to "Law Enforcement Across the Nation Uses PepperBall to Save Lives: Non-Lethal Weapon Helps Police and Civilians Avoid Death, Serious Injury," *PR Newswire*, June 9, 2003.

Sources: National Institute of Justice, *The Effectiveness and Safety of Pepper Spray* (Washington, D.C.: Department of Justice, 2003); Patricia Biggs, "Officers Take to Shock, Awe of Taser Guns," *Arizona Republic*, May 13, 2003, pp. 1–2; Tamara Lush, "Deputies to Test 50,000-Volt Weapon," *St. Petersburg Times*, March 17, 2003, pp. 1–2; Jennifer LeClaire, "Police Now Carry Guns, Badges . . . Beanbags," *Christian Science Monitor*, December 18, 2001, pp. 1–3; Jack Leonard, "Police Dropping 'Non-Lethal' Bean Bags as Too Dangerous," *Nation*, June 3, 2002, pp. 1–5; Terry Flynn, "Ft. Thomas Police Get Non-Lethal Weapons," *Cincinnati Enquirer*, June 15, 2001, pp. 1–2.

In the nineteenth century, police officers systematically ignored violations of laws related to drinking, gambling, and prostitution in return for regular payoffs. Some entered into relationships with professional criminals, especially pickpockets. Illegal behavior was tolerated in return for goods or information. Police officers helped politicians gain office by allowing electoral fraud to flourish. Some senior officers sold promotions to higher rank within the police department.[200]

Since the early nineteenth century, scandals involving police abuse of power have occurred in many urban cities, and elaborate methods had been devised to control or eliminate the problem. Although most police officers are not corrupt, the few who are dishonest bring discredit to the entire profession. And corruption is often hard to combat because the police code of silence demands that officers never turn in their peers even if they engage in corrupt or illegal practices.[201] Nor, as the International Justice feature shows, is police corruption a uniquely American phenomenon.

VARIETIES OF CORRUPTION Police deviance can include a number of activities. In a general sense, it involves misuse of authority by police officers in a manner designed to produce personal gain for themselves or others.[202] However, debate continues over whether a desire for personal gain is an essential part of corruption. Some experts argue that police misconduct also involves such issues as the

INTERNATIONAL JUSTICE

When the Cops Are Robbers

Nigeria is one of the largest nations in Africa and one of the wealthiest because of its vast oil reserves. But it is also known as a nation that suffers from a great deal of governmental corruption, especially by police officers. Despite the end of military rule in 1999, ill-paid police officers have engaged in torture, beatings, and extrajudicial killings to suppress political opponents or to further their criminal enterprise.

A report by Human Rights Watch quotes Nigerian's own police data, which acknowledge that policemen killed more than 3,000 suspected armed robbers in 2003 alone; in 2002, more than 2,000 were killed. This increase in killings may be part of a crackdown on crime called "Operation Fire for Fire." Especially violent is the anti-riot unit, known as "Mopol" (mobile police), causing it to be nicknamed "Kill and Go."

Despite national and international law prohibiting their use, torture and other cruel, inhuman, and degrading treatment are routinely used by the Nigerian Police Force. The Human Rights Watch conducted interviews in the cities of Enugu, Lagos, and Kano with some 50 victims and witnesses and heard that terrible tortures, which resulted in dozens of deaths, were perpetrated by and with the knowledge of senior police officers, including inspectors, divisional police officers, a deputy superintendent of police, and a chief superintendent of police. So routine is the use of torture on prisoners that some of these senior officers are known within the ranks by the nickname "Officer in Charge of Torture." The abuse is carried out in local and state police stations, often in interrogation rooms that witnesses and victims said appeared to be especially equipped for the purpose. Interviews with witnesses documented dozens of deaths as a result of injuries sustained during torture or after summary executions. Four detainees in Kano estimated that between 20 and 40 people had died in the state police headquarters alone between early 2003 and early 2005. One witness described how police officers in Lagos shouted "rest in pieces" after shooting suspects in their custody. He explained that this was a common euphemism used by the police to signify the death of a detainee.

The majority of the victims are ordinary criminal suspects, arrested for crimes ranging from petty theft to armed robbery. Many of these arrests were unlawful and arbitrary because the police failed to inform the suspects of their reasons for arrest or produce evidence against them. Suspects who claimed to be innocent said that they were arbitrarily apprehended at police checkpoints or during anticrime patrols, either because they happened to be in the wrong place at the wrong time or on the basis of what the police later told them was a tip-off.

Nigeria now spends more on its 300,000 policemen than on its armed forces. Yet many claim to be poorly paid and as a result are forced to resort to robbery. They routinely stake out checkpoints on major highways and demand payment from drivers to pass through. Those who refuse to pay may be beaten or locked up. These same officers have no interest in protecting the motorists from the roving bands of robbers that plague the country. As soon as they get a hint about armed robbery on any part of the road, the policemen temporarily disappear, only to reappear after the robbers have successfully maimed or killed innocent passengers and car owners and robbed them of their belongings.

Critical Thinking

1. Would raising police officer pay reduce corruption, or are corrupt officers never satisfied no matter how high their pay?

2. What do you consider "real" police corruption? Armed robbery obviously qualifies. But what about racial profiling or accepting a free cup of coffee from a local merchant?

InfoTrac College Edition Research

Use "police corruption" in a subject search on InfoTrac. To read an article on ethics and corruption, go to Stephen Coleman, "When Police Should Say 'No!' to Gratuities," *Criminal Justice Ethics* 23 (2004): 33–45.

Sources: Human Rights Watch, "'Rest in Pieces': Police Torture and Deaths in Custody in Nigeria" (http://hrw.org/reports/2005/nigeria0705); "When the Cops Are Robbers," *Economist* 376 (2005): 37; African Citizens Development Foundation, "Reforming the Nigerian Police" (http://www.acdf-assefad.org/police.htm).

Knapp Commission
A public body that conducted an investigation into police corruption in New York City in the early 1970s and uncovered a widespread network of payoffs and bribes.

unnecessary use of force, unreasonable searches, or an immoral personal life and that these should be considered as serious as corruption devoted to economic gain.

Scholars have attempted to create typologies categorizing the forms that the abuse of police powers can take. For example, the **Knapp Commission**, a public body set up to investigate the New York City police in the 1970s, classified abusers into two categories: **meat eaters** and **grass eaters**.[203] Meat eaters aggressively misuse police power for personal gain by demanding bribes, threatening legal action, or cooperating with criminals. Across the country, police officers have been accused, indicted, and convicted of shaking down club owners and other businesspeople.[204] In contrast, grass eaters accept payoffs when their everyday duties place them in a position to be solicited by the public. For example, police officers have been investigated for taking bribes to look the other way while neighborhood bookmakers ply their trade.[205] The Knapp Commission concluded that the vast majority of police officers on the take are grass eaters, although the few meat eaters who are caught capture all the headlines. In 1993 another police scandal prompted formation of the **Mollen Commission**, which found that some New York cops were actively involved in violence and drug dealing.

Other police experts have attempted to create models to better understand police corruption. Police corruption can be divided into four major categories:[206]

1. *Internal corruption.* This corruption takes place among police officers themselves, involving both the bending of departmental rules and the outright performance of illegal acts. For example, Chicago police officers conspired to sell relatively new police cars to other officers at cut-rate prices, forcing the department to purchase new cars unnecessarily. A major scandal hit the Boston Police Department when a captain was indicted in an exam-tampering-and-selling scheme. Numerous officers bought promotion exams from the captain, and others had him lower the scores of rivals who were competing for the same job.[207]

2. *Selective enforcement or nonenforcement.* This form occurs when police officers abuse or exploit their discretion. If an officer frees a drug dealer in return for valuable information, that is considered a legitimate use of discretion; if the officer does so for money, that is an abuse of police power.

3. *Active criminality.* This is participation by police in serious criminal behavior. Police may use their positions of trust and power to commit the very crimes they are entrusted with controlling. The case of officers Louis Eppolito and Stephen Caracappa, discussed in the opening vignette, is perhaps the most shocking example of police criminality in recent history. Eppolito and Caracappa sold police files on key witnesses to the mob and were convicted on charges linking them to 11 mob hits.[208]

4. *Bribery and extortion.* This includes practices in which law enforcement roles are exploited specifically to raise money. Bribery is initiated by the citizen; extortion is initiated by the officer. Bribery or extortion can be a one-shot transaction, as when a traffic violator offers a police officer $500 to forget about issuing a summons. Or the relationship can be an ongoing one, in which the officer solicits (or is offered) regular payoffs to ignore criminal activities, such as gambling or narcotics dealing. This is known as "being on the pad." Sometimes police officers accept routine bribes and engage in petty extortion without considering themselves corrupt. They consider these payments as some of the unwritten benefits of police work. For example, mooching involves receiving free gifts of coffee, cigarettes, meals, and so on in exchange for possible future acts of favoritism. Chiseling occurs when officers demand admission to entertainment events or price discounts. And shopping involves taking small items, such as cigarettes, from a store whose door was accidentally left unlocked after business hours.[209]

THE CAUSES OF CORRUPTION No single explanation satisfactorily accounts for the various forms that the abuse of power takes:

1. *Police personality.* One view puts the blame on the type of person who becomes a police officer. This position holds that policing tends to attract

meat eater
A term used to describe a police officer who actively solicits bribes and vigorously engages in corrupt practices.

grass eater
A term used for a police officer who accepts payoffs when everyday duties place him or her in a position to be solicited by the public.

Mollen Commission
An investigative unit set up to inquire into police corruption in New York City in the 1990s.

How do police feel about the abuse of power? To find out, you can read the findings of a national survey on police attitudes toward abuse of authority. To reach the article, go to the Siegel/Senna Introduction to Criminal Justice 11e website: www.thomsonedu.com/criminaljustice/siegel.

lower-class individuals who do not have the financial means to maintain a coveted middle-class lifestyle. As they develop the cynical, authoritarian police personality, accepting graft seems an all-too-easy method of achieving financial security.

2. *Institutions and practices.* A second view is that the wide discretion police enjoy, coupled with the low visibility they maintain with the public and their own supervisors, makes them likely candidates for corruption. In addition, the code of secrecy maintained by the police subculture helps insulate corrupt officers from the law. Similarly, police managers, most of whom have risen through the ranks, are reluctant to investigate corruption or punish wrongdoers. Thus, corruption may also be viewed as a function of police institutions and practices.[210]

3. *Moral ambivalence.* A third position holds that corruption is a function of society's ambivalence toward many forms of vice-related criminal behavior that police officers are sworn to control. Unenforceable laws governing moral standards promote corruption because they create large groups with an interest in undermining law enforcement. These include consumers—people who gamble, wish to drink after the legal closing hour, or patronize a prostitute—who do not want to be deprived of their chosen form of recreation. Even though the consumers may not actively corrupt police officers, their existence creates a climate that tolerates active corruption by others.[211] Because vice cannot be controlled and the public apparently wants it to continue, the officer may have little resistance to inducements for monetary gain offered by law violators.

4. *Environmental conditions.* A fourth position is that corruption may be linked to specific environmental and social conditions which enhance the likelihood that police officers may become involved in misconduct. For example, in some areas a rapid increase in the minority residential population may be viewed as a threat to dominant-group interests. Police in these areas may become overly aggressive and routinely use coercive strategies. The conflict produced by these outcomes may lead to antagonism between the police and the minority public, and eventual police misconduct of all types. One recent study, in which social ecological conditions in New York City police precincts and divisions were associated with patterns of police misconduct from 1975 to 1996, found that misconduct cases involving bribery, extortion, excessive force, and other abuses of police authority were linked to trends in neighborhood structural disadvantage, increasing population mobility, and increases in the Latino population. It is possible that neighborhood disorganization reduced informal social control mechanisms, population mobility disrupted neighborhood bonds and networks, and the rapidly increasing Latino population was regarded as a threat to the existing social order. These factors provided a source of conflict necessary to encourage police misconduct. Ironically, the communities most in need of protection by the police because of environmental conditions were also the ones in need of the greatest protection from the police because of conditions favoring deviance.[212]

5. *Corrupt departments.* It has also been suggested that police corruption is generated at the departmental level and that conditions within the department produce and nurture deviance.[213] In some departments, corrupt officers band together and form what is called a "rotten pocket."[214] Rotten pockets help institutionalize corruption because their members expect newcomers to conform to their illegal practices and to a code of secrecy.

CONTROLLING CORRUPTION How can police misconduct be controlled? One approach is to strengthen the internal administrative review process within police departments. A strong and well-supported internal affairs division has been linked to lowered corruption rates.[215] However, asking police to police themselves is not a simple task. Officers are often reluctant to discipline their peers. One review of disciplinary files of New York City police officers found that many miscreants escaped punishment when their cases were summarily dismissed by the police department without ever interviewing victims or witnesses or making any other efforts to examine the strength of the evidence.[216] One reason may be the "blue curtain" mentality that inhibits police from taking action against their fellow officers. Surveys indicate that police officers are reluctant to report unethical behavior unless they suspect that a colleague is engaged in actual criminality such as theft. Engaging in illegal brutality or bending the rules of procedure falls under the code of silence.[217]

Another approach, instituted by then New York Commissioner Patrick Murphy in the wake of the Knapp Commission, is the **accountability system**. This holds that supervisors at each level are directly accountable for the illegal behaviors of the officers under them. Consequently, a commander can be demoted or forced to resign if one of her command officers is found guilty of corruption.[218] However, close scrutiny by a department can lower officer morale and create the suspicion that the officers' own supervisors distrust them.

Some departments have set up guidelines to help reduce corruption. The city of Philadelphia agreed to implement a set of reforms to combat corruption and settle a lawsuit brought by civil rights organizations. The following were among the measures taken to reduce corruption:

♦ A policy mandating that all citizens' complaints be forwarded for investigation by the Internal Affairs Division.

♦ Development of computer files that contain all types of complaints and suits against individual officers that could be easily accessed during investigations.

♦ A policy requiring that Internal Affairs give a high priority to any officer's claim that another officer was corrupt or used excessive force.

♦ Mandatory reporting and recording of all incidents in which an officer used more than incidental force.

♦ Training of officers to treat citizens without racial bias; assigning a deputy commissioner to monitor charges of race discrimination.

♦ Reviewing all policies and practices to ensure they do not involve or have the potential for race bias.[219]

Police departments have also organized outside review boards or special prosecutors to investigate reported incidents of corruption. However, outside investigators and special prosecutors are often limited by their lack of intimate knowledge of day-to-day operations. As a result, they depend on the testimony of a few officers who are willing to cooperate, either to save themselves from prosecution or because they have a compelling moral commitment. Outside evaluators also face the problem of the blue curtain, which is quickly closed when police officers feel that their department is under scrutiny. A more realistic solution to corruption, albeit a difficult one, might be to change the social context of policing. Police operations must be made more visible, and the public must be given freer access to police operations. All too often, the public finds out about police problems only when a scandal hits the newspaper.

Some of the vice-related crimes the police now deal with might be decriminalized or referred to other agencies. Although decriminalization of vice cannot in itself end the problem, it could lower the pressure placed on individual police officers and help eliminate their moral dilemmas.

accountability system
A system that makes police supervisors responsible for the behavior of the officers in their command.

ThomsonNOW™ Improve your grade on the exam with Personalized Study! For reinforcement resources and a mastery check of problems of policing, go to www.thomsonedu.com/thomsonnow.

ETHICAL CHALLENGES IN CRIMINAL JUSTICE: A WRITING ASSIGNMENT

Sergeant Steven Jones is an eight-year veteran of the Midcity police force. On the morning of November 5, 2006, Paul Bessey, a city councilman, spots Jones leaving a local restaurant without paying the check. When he queries the restaurant owner, she laughingly states that "Steve" has been coming there for breakfast for two years and that it's "always on the house." It is a mutual understanding they have because Jones has been very helpful in keeping "riffraff" out of the place. In fact, she tells the councilman that she once called for him at the station house, and Steve drove all the way across town to tell a troublemaker to leave.

The town has a strict policy prohibiting police officers from accepting or soliciting bribes or gratuities, so Councilman Bessey files a complaint against Jones with the city's Civilian Review Board. A hearing on the matter is scheduled, and if he is found liable, Jones faces three possible penalties: suspension, suspension and loss of rank, or dismissal. Jones asks you to act as his representative at the meeting. Write an essay on how you would defend his actions before the board.

Doing Research on the Web

To read about police corruption, go to the Drug Policy Alliance website and check out "Drugs, Police & the Law." You can reach this report by going to the Siegel/Senna Introduction to Criminal Justice 11e website: www.thomsonedu.com/criminaljustice/siegel.

The New York City Commission to Combat Police Corruption (CCPC) was created in 1995 as a permanent board to monitor and evaluate the anti-corruption programs, activities, commitment, and efforts of the New York City Police Department. The commission is completely independent of the NYPD and comprises commissioners, appointed by the mayor, who direct a full-time staff, including a number of attorneys. You can read more about the commission by going to the Siegel/Senna Introduction to Criminal Justice 11e website: www.thomsonedu.com/criminaljustice/siegel.

SUMMARY

◆ Police departments today are faced with many critical problems in their development and their relationship with the public.

◆ One area of concern is the existence of an independent and unique police culture, which insulates police officers from the rest of society. This culture has distinct rules and loyalties.

◆ Some experts hold that police officers have distinct personality characteristics marked by authoritarianism and cynicism.

◆ Police officers may develop a unique working style. Four distinct police styles have been identified, and each influences police decision making.

◆ Today, many police officers are seeking higher education. The jury is still out on whether educated officers are more effective.

◆ Women and minorities are being recruited into the police in increasing numbers. Research indicates that, with few exceptions, they perform as well or even better than male or white officers.

◆ In some larger departments, the percentage of minorities on police forces now reflects their representation in the general population.

◆ The number of female officers still lags behind the number of male officers.

◆ Women and minorities still lag behind white males in supervisory positions.

◆ The complexity and danger of the police role produce an enormous amount of stress that harms police effectiveness. Police departments have tried a variety of techniques designed to limit police stress.

♦ Police have been charged with being brutal and have worked hard to reduce their use of force through training and rule making. Surveys indicate that today the police use of force seems limited, indicating that these techniques may be working.

♦ One critical concern is the police use of deadly force. Research indicates that anti-shooting policies can limit deaths resulting from police action. The U.S. Supreme Court has ruled that police cannot shoot unarmed fleeing felons.

♦ Another effort has been to identify and eliminate police corruption, which still mars the reputation of police forces.

KEY TERMS

double marginality, 229
blue curtain, 232
cynicism, 233
police styles, 234
discretion, 235

low-visibility decision making, 236
overload hypothesis, 238
demeanor, 239
police brutality, 246
deadly force, 249

Knapp Commission, 256
meat eater, 257
grass eater, 257
Mollen Commission, 257
accountability system, 259

ThomsonNOW Maximize your study time by using ThomsonNOW's diagnostic study plan to help you review this chapter. The Study Plan will

♦ help you identify areas on which you should concentrate;

♦ provide interactive exercises to help you master the chapter concepts; and

♦ provide a post-test to confirm you are ready to move on to the next chapter.

CRITICAL THINKING QUESTIONS

1. Should male and female officers have exactly the same duties in a police department? If not, why not?

2. Do you think that an officer's working the street will eventually produce a cynical personality and distrust for civilians? Explain.

3. How can education help police officers?

4. Should a police officer who accepts a free meal from a restaurant owner be dismissed from the force? Why or why not?

5. A police officer orders an unarmed person running away from a burglary to stop; the suspect keeps running and is shot and killed by the officer. Has the officer committed a crime? Explain.

6. Would you like to live in a society that abolished police discretion and used a full enforcement policy? Why or why not?

NOTES

1. John Marzulli, "2 Cops Who Killed for Mafia: Feds Say Retired Detective Pals Are Linked to at Least 8 Murders," *New York Daily News*, March 10, 2005; Alan Feuer and William K. Rashbaum, "Blood Ties: 2 Officers' Long Path to Mob Murder Indictments," *New York Times*, March 12, 2005, p. A1; *BBC News*, "NY Police Guilty of Mafia Murders" (http://news.bbc.co.uk/1/hi/world/americas/4885674.stm).

2. William Wells, Julie Horney, and Edward Maguire, "Patrol Officer Responses to Citizen Feedback: An Experimental Analysis," *Police Quarterly* 8 (2005): 171–205.

3. David Jones, Liz Jones, and Tim Prenzler, "Tertiary Education, Commitment, and Turnover in Police Work," *Police Practice and Research* 6 (2005): 49–63.

4. Kathleen Maguire and Ann Pastore, eds., *Sourcebook of Criminal Justice Statistics*, online version (http://www.albany.edu/sourcebook/1995/pdf/t216.pdf), accessed on October 25, 2003.

5. Steven Tuch and Ronald Weitzer, "The Polls: Trends, Racial Differences in Attitudes Toward the Police," *Public Opinion Quarterly* 61 (1997): 642–63.

6. Robert Sigler and Ida Johnson, "Reporting Violent Acts to the Police: A Difference by Race," *Policing* 25 (2002): 274–93.

7. Thomas Priest and Deborah Brown Carter, "Evaluations of Police Performance in an African American Sample," *Journal of Criminal Justice* 27 (1999): 457–65; Ronald Weitzer, "White, Black, or Blue Cops? Race and Citizen Assessments of Police Officers," *Journal of Criminal Justice* 28 (2000): 313–24.

8. Karen Kruger and Nicholas Valltos, "Dealing with Domestic Violence in Law Enforcement Relationships," *FBI Law Enforcement Bulletin* 71 (2002): 1–7.

9. Robert Loo, "A Typology of Burnout Types Among Police Managers," *Policing* 27 (2004): 156–65.

10. See Larry Hoover, *Police Educational Characteristics and Curricula* (Washington, D.C.: Government Printing Office, 1975).

11. Matthew Hickman and Brian Reaves, *Local Police Departments, 2003* (Washington, D.C.: Bureau of Justice Statistics, 2006).

12. Brian Reaves and Matthew J. Hickman, *Police Departments in Large Cities, 1990–2000* (Washington, D.C.: Bureau of Justice Statistics, 2002).

13. Maggy Lee and Maurice Punch, "Policing by Degrees: Police Officers' Experience of University Education," *Policing & Society* 14 (2004): 233–49.

14. Bruce Berg, "Who Should Teach Police: A Typology and Assessment of Police Academy Instructors," *American Journal of Police* 9 (1990): 79–100.

15. David Carter and Allen Sapp, *The State of Police Education: Critical Findings* (Washington, D.C.: Police Executive Research Forum, 1988), p. 6.

16. John Krimmel, "The Performance of College-Educated Police: A Study of Self-Rated Police Performance Measures," *American Journal of Police* 15 (1996): 85–95.

17. Robert Worden, "A Badge and a Baccalaureate: Policies, Hypotheses, and Further Evidence," *Justice Quarterly* 7 (1990): 565–92.

18. See Lawrence Sherman and Warren Bennis, "Higher Education for Police Officers: The Central Issues," *Police Chief* 44 (1977): 32.

19. Worden, "A Badge and a Baccalaureate," 587–89.

20. Jihong Zhao and Nicholas Lovrich, "Determinants of Minority Employment in American Municipal Police Agencies: The Representation of African American Officers," *Journal of Criminal Justice* 26 (1998): 267–78.

21. David Murphy and John Worrall, "Residency Requirements and Public Perceptions of the Police in Large Municipalities," *Policing* 22 (1999): 327–42.

22. Tuch and Weitzer, "The Polls," 62; Sutham Cheurprakobkit, "Police–Citizen Contact and Police Performance: Attitudinal Differences Between Hispanics and Non-Hispanics," *Journal of Criminal Justice* 28 (2000): 325–36; Maguire and Pastore, eds., *Sourcebook of Criminal Justice Statistics.*

23. Cheurprakobkit, "Police–Citizen Contact and Police Performance"; Maguire and Pastore, eds., *Sourcebook of Criminal Justice Statistics.*

24. Yolander G. Hurst, James Frank, and Sandra Lee Browning, "The Attitudes of Juveniles Toward the Police: A Comparison of African-American and White Youth," *Policing* 23 (2000): 37–53.

25. Stephen Rice and Alex Piquero, "Perceptions of Discrimination and Justice in New York City," *Policing* 28 (2005): 98–117.

26. Jack Kuykendall and David Burns, "The African-American Police Officer: An Historical Perspective," *Journal of Contemporary Criminal Justice* 1 (1980): 4–13.

27. Ibid.

28. Nicholas Alex, *Black in Blue: A Study of the Negro Policeman* (New York: Appleton-Century-Crofts, 1969).

29. Kim Michelle Lersch, "Predicting Citizen's Race in Allegations of Misconduct Against the Police," *Journal of Criminal Justice* 26 (1998): 87–99.

30. Nicholas Alex, *New York Cops Talk Back* (New York: Wiley, 1976).

31. David Eitle, Lisa Stolzenberg, and Stewart J. D'Alessio, "Police Organizational Factors, the Racial Composition of the Police, and the Probability of Arrest," *Justice Quarterly* 22 (2005): 30–57.

32. Robert Brown and James Frank, "Race and Officer Decision Making: Examining Differences in Arrest Outcomes Between Black and White Officers," *Justice Quarterly* 23 (2006): 96–126.

33. Stephen Leinen, *African-American Police, White Society* (New York: New York University Press, 1984).

34. Ni He, Jihong Zhao, and Ling Ren, "Do Race and Gender Matter in Police Stress? A Preliminary Assessment of the Interactive Effects," *Journal of Criminal Justice* 33 (2005): 535–47.

35. Merry Morash, Robin Haarr, and Dae-Hoon Kwak, "Multilevel Influences on Police Stress," *Journal of Contemporary Criminal Justice* 22 (2006): 26–43.

36. Robin Haarr and Merry Morash, "Gender, Race, and Strategies of Coping with Occupational Stress in Policing," *Justice Quarterly* 16 (1999): 303–36.

37. Kenneth Novak, Leanne Fiftal Alarid, and Wayne Lucas, "Exploring Officers' Acceptance of Community Policing: Implications for Policy Implementation," *Journal of Criminal Justice* 31 (2003): 57–71; Donald Yates and Vijayan Pillai, "Race and Police Commitment to Community Policing," *Journal of Intergroup Relations* 19 (1993): 14–23.

38. Bruce Berg, Edmond True, and Marc Gertz, "Police, Riots, and Alienation," *Journal of Police Science and Administration* 12 (1984): 186–90.

39. D. L. Yates and V. K. Pillai, "Frustration and Strain Among Fort Worth Police Officers," *Sociology and Social Research* 76 (1992): 145–49.

40. James Jacobs and Jay Cohen, "The Impact of Racial Integration on the Police," *Journal of Police Science and Administration* 6 (1978): 182.

41. Charles Katz, "The Establishment of a Police Gang Unit: An Examination of Organizational and Environmental Factors," *Criminology* 39 (2001): 37–73.

42. Ibid., p. 61.

43. Weitzer, "White, Black, or Blue Cops?"

44. For a review of the history of women in policing, see Dorothy Moses Schulz, "From Policewoman to Police Officer: An Unfinished Revolution," *Police Studies* 16 (1993): 90–99; Cathryn House, "The Changing Role of Women in Law Enforcement," *Police Chief* 60 (1993): 139–44.

45. Reaves and Hickman, *Police Departments in Large Cities.*

46. Susan Martin, "Female Officers on the Move? A Status Report on Women in Policing," in *Critical Issues in Policing,* ed. Roger Dunham and Geoffery Alpert (Grove Park, Ill.: Waveland, 1988), pp. 312–31.

47. *Le Bouef v. Ramsey,* 26 FEP Cases 884 (September 16, 1980).

48. Michael Birzer and Delores Craig, "Gender Differences in Police Physical Ability Test Performance," *American Journal of Police* 15 (1996): 93–106.

49. James Daum and Cindy Johns, "Police Work from a Woman's Perspective," *Police Chief* 61 (1994): 46–49.

50. Steve Herbert, "'Hard Charger' or 'Station Queen'? Policing and the Masculinist State," *Gender Place and Culture: A Journal of Feminist Geography* 8 (2001): 55–72.

51. Ibid., p. 58.

52. Matthew Hickman, Alex Piquero, and Jack Greene, "Discretion and Gender Disproportionality in Police Disciplinary Systems," *Policing* 23 (2000): 105–16.

53. Haarr and Morash, "Gender, Race, and Strategies."

54. Merry Morash and Jack Greene, "Evaluating Women on Patrol: A Critique of Contemporary Wisdom," *Evaluation Review* 10 (1986): 230–55.

55. Peter Bloch and Deborah Anderson, *Policewomen on Patrol: Final Report* (Washington, D.C.: Police Foundation, 1974).

56. Joel Garner, Christopher Maxwell, and Cederick Heraux, "Characteristics Associated with the Prevalence and Severity of Force Used by the Police," *Justice Quarterly* 19 (2002): 705–47.

57. Steven Brandl, Meghan Stroshine, and James Frank, "Who Are the Complaint-Prone Officers? An Examination of the Relationship Between Police Officers' Attributes, Arrest Activity, Assignment, and Citizens' Complaints About Excessive Force," *Journal of Criminal Justice* 29 (2001): 521–29.

58. Daum and Johns, "Police Work from a Woman's Perspective."

59. Mary Brown, "The Plight of Female Police: A Survey of NW Patrolmen," *Police Chief* 61 (1994): 50–53.

60. Simon Holdaway and Sharon K. Parker, "Policing Women Police: Uniform Patrol, Promotion, and Representation in the CID," *British Journal of Criminology* 38 (1998): 40–48.

61. Curt Bartol, George Bergen, Julie Seager Volckens, and Kathleen Knoras, "Women in Small-Town Policing, Job Performance, and Stress," *Criminal Justice and Behavior* 19 (1992): 245–59.

62. Susan Martin, "Outsider Within the Station House: The Impact of Race and Gender on African-American Women Police," *Social Problems* 41 (1994): 383–400.

63. Michael Birzer and Robert Nolan, "Learning Strategies of Selected Urban Police Related to Community Policing," *Policing* 25 (2002): 242–55.

64. Martin, "Outsider Within the Station House," p. 387.

65. Ibid., p. 392.

66. Ibid., p. 394.

67. Ibid., p. 397.

68. Ibid.

69. Eric Poole and Mark Pogrebin, "Factors Affecting the Decision to Remain in Policing: A Study of Women Officers," *Journal of Police Science and Administration* 16 (1988): 49–55.

70. Eugene Paoline, "Taking Stock: Toward a Richer Understanding of Police Culture," *Journal of Criminal Justice* 31 (2003): 199–214.

71. See, for example, Richard Harris, *The Police Academy: An Inside View* (New York: Wiley, 1973); John Van Maanen, "Observations on the Making of a Policeman," in *Order Under Law*, ed. R. Culbertson and M. Tezak (Prospect Heights, Ill.: Waveland, 1981), pp. 111–26; Jonathan Rubenstein, *City Police* (New York: Ballantine, 1973); John Broderick, *Police in a Time of Change* (Morristown, N.J.: General Learning Press, 1977).

72. Malcolm Sparrow, Mark Moore, and David Kennedy, *Beyond 911: A New Era for Policing* (New York: Basic Books, 1990), p. 51.

73. M. Steven Meagher and Nancy Yentes, "Choosing a Career in Policing: A Comparison of Male and Female Perceptions," *Journal of Police Science and Administration* 16 (1986): 320–27.

74. Michael K. Brown, *Working the Street* (New York: Russell Sage, 1981), p. 82.

75. Stan Shernock, "An Empirical Examination of the Relationship Between Police Solidarity and Community Orientation," *Journal of Police Science and Administration* 18 (1988): 182–98.

76. Ibid., p. 360.

77. Ibid., p. 359.

78. Egon Bittner, *The Functions of Police in Modern Society* (Cambridge, Mass.: Oelgeschlager, Gunn, and Hain, 1980), p. 63.

79. Venessa Garcia, "Constructing the 'Other' Within Police Culture: An Analysis of a Deviant Unit Within the Police Organization," *Police Practice and Research* 6 (2005): 65–80.

80. Wallace Graves, "Police Cynicism: Causes and Cures," *FBI Law Enforcement Bulletin* 65 (1996): 16–21.

81. Richard Lundman, *Police and Policing* (New York: Holt, Rinehart, and Winston, 1980). See also Jerome Skolnick, *Justice Without Trial* (New York: Wiley, 1966).

82. Robert Regoli, Robert Culbertson, John Crank, and James Powell, "Career Stage and Cynicism Among Police Chiefs," *Justice Quarterly* 7 (1990): 592–614.

83. William Westly, *Violence and the Police: A Sociological Study of Law, Custom, and Morality* (Cambridge, Mass.: MIT Press, 1970).

84. Skolnick, *Justice Without Trial*, pp. 42–68.

85. Milton Rokeach, Martin Miller, and John Snyder, "The Value Gap Between Police and Policed," *Journal of Social Issues* 27 (1971): 155–71.

86. Bruce Carpenter and Susan Raza, "Personality Characteristics of Police Applicants: Comparisons Across Subgroups and with Other Populations," *Journal of Police Science and Administration* 15 (1987): 10–17.

87. Larry Tifft, "The 'Cop Personality' Reconsidered," *Journal of Police Science and Administration* 2 (1974): 268; David Bayley and Harold Mendelsohn, *Minorities and the Police* (New York: Free Press, 1969); Robert Balch, "The Police Personality: Fact or Fiction?" *Journal of Criminal Law, Criminology, and Police Science* 63 (1972): 117.

88. Lowell Storms, Nolan Penn, and James Tenzell, "Policemen's Perception of Real and Ideal Policemen," *Journal of Police Science and Administration* 17 (1990): 40–43.

89. Arthur Niederhoffer, *Behind the Shield: The Police in Urban Society* (Garden City, N.Y.: Doubleday, 1967).

90. Ibid., pp. 216–20.

91. Carl Klockars, "The Dirty Harry Problem," *Annals* 452 (1980): 33–47.

92. Jack Kuykendall and Roy Roberg, "Police Manager's Perceptions of Employee Types: A Conceptual Model," *Journal of Criminal Justice* 16 (1988): 131–35.

93. Stephen Matrofski, R. Richard Ritti, and Jeffrey Snipes, "Expectancy Theory and Police Productivity in DUI Enforcement," *Law and Society Review* 28 (1994): 113–38.

94. Paoline, "Taking Stock."

95. Skolnick, *Justice Without Trial*.

96. Carroll Seron, Joseph Pereira, and Jean Kovath, "Judging Police Misconduct: 'Street-Level' Versus Professional Policing," *Law & Society Review* 38 (2004): 665–710.

97. Kenneth Litwin, "A Multilevel Multivariate Analysis of Factors Affecting Homicide Clearances," *Journal of Research in Crime & Delinquency* 41 (2004): 327–51.

98. William King and Thomas Dunn, "Dumping: Police-Initiated Transjurisdictional Transport of Troublesome Persons," *Police Quarterly* 7 (2004): 339–58.

99. Helen Eigenberg, Kathryn Scarborough, and Victor Kappeler, "Contributory Factors Affecting Arrest in Domestic and Non-domestic Assaults," *American Journal of Police* 15 (1996): 27–51.

100. Leonore Simon, "A Therapeutic Jurisprudence Approach to the Legal Processing of Domestic Violence Cases," *Psychology, Public Policy, and Law* 1 (1995): 43–79.

101. Peter Sinden and B. Joyce Stephens, "Police Perceptions of Domestic Violence: The Nexus of Victim, Perpetrator, Event, Self and Law," *Policing* 22 (1999): 313–26.

102. Robert Kane, "Patterns of Arrest in Domestic Violence Encounters: Identifying a Police Decision-Making Model," *Journal of Criminal Justice* 27 (1999): 65–79.

103. Gregory Howard Williams, *The Law and Politics of Police Discretion* (Westport, Conn.: Greenwood, 1984).

104. Dana Jones and Joanne Belknap, "Police Responses to Battering in a Progressive Pro-Arrest Jurisdiction," *Justice Quarterly* 16 (1999): 249–73.

105. Douglas Smith and Jody Klein, "Police Control of Interpersonal Disputes," *Social Problems* 31 (1984): 468–81.

106. David Klinger, "Negotiating Order in Patrol Work: An Ecological Theory of Police Response to Deviance," *Criminology* 35 (1997): 277–306.

107. Allison Chappell, John Macdonald, and Patrick Manz, "The Organizational Determinants of Police Arrest Decisions," *Crime and Delinquency* 52 (2006): 287–306.

108. John McCluskey, Sean Varano, Beth Huebner, and Timothy Bynum, "Who Do You Refer? The Effects of a Policy Change on Juvenile Referrals," *Criminal Justice Policy Review* 15 (2004): 437–61.

109. David Eitle, "The Influence of Mandatory Arrest Policies, Police Organizational Characteristics, and Situational Variables on the Probability of Arrest in Domestic Violence Cases," *Crime and Delinquency* 51 (2005): 573–97.

110. Jones and Belknap, "Police Responses to Battering," 249–73.

111. Joseph Schafer, "Negotiating Order in the Policing of Youth Drinking," *Policing* 28 (2005): 279–300.

112. Wendy L. Hicks, "Police Vehicular Pursuits: An Overview of Research and Legal Conceptualizations for Police Administrators," *Criminal Justice Policy Review* 14 (2003): 75–95.

113. Robin Shepard Engel, "Patrol Officer Supervision in the Community Policing Era," *Journal of Criminal Justice* 30 (2002): 51–64.

114. Westly, *Violence and the Police*.

115. John McCluskey, William Terrill, and Eugene Paoline III, "Peer Group Aggressiveness and the Use of Coercion in Police–Suspect Encounters," *Police Practice & Research* 6 (2005): 19–37.

116. Nathan Goldman, *The Differential Selection of Juvenile Offenders for Court Appearance* (New York: National Council on Crime and Delinquency, 1963).

117. Schafer, "Negotiating Order in the Policing of Youth Drinking"; Richard Lundman, "Demeanor or Crime? The Midwest City Police–Citizen Encounters Study," *Criminology* 32 (1994): 631–53; Robert Worden and Robin Shepard, "On the Meaning, Measurement, and Estimated Effects of Suspects' Demeanor Toward the Police," paper presented at the annual meeting of the American Society of Criminology, Miami, November 1994.

118. Joseph Schafer and Stephen Mastrofski, "Police Leniency in Traffic Enforcement Encounters: Exploratory Findings from Observations and Interviews," *Journal of Criminal Justice* 33 (2005): 225–38.

119. David Klinger, "Bringing Crime Back in: Toward a Better Understanding of Police Arrest Decisions," *Journal of Research in Crime and Delinquency* 33 (1996): 333–36; David Klinger, "More on Demeanor and Arrest in Dade County," *Criminology* 34 (1996): 61–79; David Klinger, "Demeanor or Crime? Why 'Hostile' Citizens Are More Likely to Be Arrested," *Criminology* 32 (1994): 475–93.

120. William Terrill and Stephen Mastrofski, "Situational and Officer-Based Determinants of Police Coercion," *Justice Quarterly* 19 (2002): 215–48.

121. William Terrill, *Police Coercion: Application of the Force Continuum* (New York: LFB Scholarly Publishing, 2001).

122. Benjamin Weiser, "Federal Inquiry Finds Racial Profiling in Street Searches," *New York Times*, October 5, 2000, p. 1.

123. David Cole, *No Equal Justice: Race and Class in the American Criminal Justice System* (New York: New Press, 2000).

124. For a thorough review of this issue, see Samuel Walker, Cassia Spohn, and Miriam DeLone, *The Color of Justice: Race, Ethnicity and Crime in America* (Belmont, Cal: Wadsworth, 1996), p. 115.

125. Greg Ridgeway, "Assessing the Effect of Race Bias in Post-Traffic Stop Outcomes Using Propensity Scores," *Journal of Quantitative Criminology* 22 (2006): 1–29.

126. Ronald Weitzer and Steven Tuch, "Racially Biased Policing: Determinants of Citizen Perceptions," *Social Forces* 83 (2005): 1009–30.

127. Brown, *Working the Street*, 290.

128. Richard Lumb and Ronald Breazeale, "Police Officer Attitudes and Community Policing Implementation: Developing Strategies for Durable Organizational Change," *Policing and Society* 13 (2003): 91–107.

129. Karen Kruger and Nicholas Valltos, "Dealing with Domestic Violence in Law Enforcement Relationships," *FBI Law Enforcement Bulletin* 71 (2002): 1–7.

130. Yates and Pillai, "Frustration and Strain Among Fort Worth Police Officers."

131. Richard Farmer, "Clinical and Managerial Implications of Stress Research on the Police," *Journal of Police Science and Administration* 17 (1990): 205–17.

132. Ni He, Jihong Zhao, and Carol Archbold, "Gender and Police Stress: The Convergent and Divergent Impact of Work Environment, Work–Family Conflict, and Stress Coping Mechanisms of Female and Male Police Officers," *Policing* 25 (2002): 687–709.

133. Francis Cullen, Terrence Lemming, Bruce Link, and John Wozniak, "The Impact of Social Supports on Police Stress," *Criminology* 23 (1985): 503–22.

134. Morash, Haarr, and Kwak, "Multilevel Influences on Police Stress."

135. Deborah Wilkins Newman and LeeAnne Rucker-Reed, "Police Stress, State-Trait Anxiety, and Stressors Among U.S. Marshals," *Journal of Criminal Justice* 32 (2004): 631–41.

136. Jihong Zhao, Ni He, and Nicholas Lovrich, "Predicting Five Dimensions of Police Officer Stress: Looking More Deeply into Organizational Settings for Sources of Police Stress," *Police Quarterly* 5 (2002): 43–63.

137. Lawrence Travis III and Craig Winston, "Dissension in the Ranks: Officer Resistance to Community Policing and Support for the Organization," *Journal of Crime and Justice* 21 (1998): 139–55.

138. Farmer, "Clinical and Managerial Implications of Stress Research on the Police"; Nancy Norvell, Dale Belles, and Holly Hills, "Perceived Stress Levels and Physical Symptoms in Supervisory Law Enforcement Personnel," *Journal of Police Science and Administration* 16 (1988): 75–79.

139. Donald Yates and Vijayan Pillai, "Attitudes Toward Community Policing: A Causal Analysis," *Social Science Journal* 33 (1996): 193–209.

140. Harvey McMurray, "Attitudes of Assaulted Police Officers and Their Policy Implications," *Journal of Police Science and Administration* 17 (1990): 44–48.

141. Robert Ankony and Thomas Kelly, "The Impact of Perceived Alienation of Police Officers' Sense of Mastery and Subsequent Motivation for Proactive Enforcement," *Policing* 22 (1999): 120–32.

142. John Blackmore, "Police Stress," in *Policing Society*, ed. Clinton Terry (New York: Wiley, 1985), p. 395.

143. Stephen Curran, "Separating Fact from Fiction About Police Stress," *Behavioral Health Management* 23 (2003): 38–40; Peter Marzuk, Matthew Nock, Andrew Leon, Laura Portera, and Kenneth Tardiff, "Suicide Among New York City Police Officers, 1977–1996," *American Journal of Psychiatry* 159 (2002): 2069–72; Rose Lee Josephson and Martin Reiser, "Officer Suicide in the Los Angeles Police Department: A Twelve-Year Follow-Up," *Journal of Police Science and Administration* 17 (1990): 227–30.

144. Yates and Pillai, "Attitudes Toward Community Policing," 205–06.

145. Ibid.

146. Rosanna Church and Naomi Robertson, "How State Police Agencies Are Addressing the Issue of Wellness," *Policing* 22 (1999): 304–12.

147. Farmer, "Clinical and Managerial Implications of Stress Research on the Police," 215.

148. Peter Hart, Alexander Wearing, and Bruce Headey, "Assessing Police Work Experiences: Development of the Police Daily Hassles and Uplifts Scales," *Journal of Criminal Justice* 21 (1993): 553–73.

149. Vivian Lord, Denis Gray, and Samuel Pond, "The Police Stress Inventory: Does It Measure Stress?" *Journal of Criminal Justice* 19 (1991): 139–49.

150. Bittner, *The Functions of Police in Modern Society*, p. 46.

151. Richard R. Johnson, "Citizen Complaints: What the Police Should Know," *FBI Law Enforcement Bulletin* 67 (1998): 1–6.

152. For a general review, see Tom McEwen, *National Data Collection on Police Use of Force* (Washington, D.C.: National Institute of Justice, 1996).

153. Matthew Durose, Erica Schmitt, and Patrick Langan, *Contacts Between Police and the Public: Findings from the 2002 National Survey* (Washington, D.C.: Bureau of Justice Statistics, 2005).

154. Colin Loftin, David McDowall, Brian Wiersema, and Adam Dobrin, "Underreporting of Justifiable Homicides Committed by Police Officers in the United States, 1976–1998," *American Journal of Public Health* 93 (2003): 1117–21.

155. Brad Smith, "The Impact of Police Officer Diversity on Police-Caused Homicides," *Policy Studies Journal* 31 (2003): 147–62.

156. Brian Thompson and James Daniel Lee, "Who Cares If Police Become Violent? Explaining Approval of Police Use of Force Using a National Sample," *Sociological Inquiry* 74 (2004): 381–410.

157. Sandra Lee Browning, Francis Cullen, Liqun Cao, Renee Kopache, and Thomas Stevenson, "Race and Getting Hassled by the Police: A Research Note," *Police Studies* 17 (1994): 1–11.

158. Joel Garner, Christopher Maxwell, and Cederick Heraux, "Characteristics Associated with the Prevalence and Severity of Force Used by the Police," *Justice Quarterly* 19 (2002): 705–47.

159. William Terrill, "Police Use of Force: A Transactional Approach," *Justice Quarterly* 22 (2005): 107–38.

160. Hannah Cooper, Lisa Moore, Sofia Gruskin, and Nancy Krieger, "Characterizing Perceived Police Violence: Implications for Public Health," *American Journal of Public Health* 94 (2004): 1109–1119.

161. Thompson and Lee, "Who Cares If Police Become Violent?"

162. Ibid.

163. Sean Griffin and Thomas Bernard, "Angry Aggression Among Police Officers," *Police Quarterly* 6 (2003): 3–21.

164. Kim Michelle Lersch and Tom Mieczkowski, "Who Are the Problem-Prone Officers? An Analysis of Citizen Complaints," *American Journal of Police* 15 (1996): 23–42.

165. Samuel Walker, Geoffrey P. Alpert, and Dennis J. Kenney, *Early Warning Systems: Responding to the Problem Police Officer, Research in Brief* (Washington, D.C.: National Institute of Justice, 2001).

166. Samuel Walker, "The Rule Revolution: Reflections on the Transformation of American Criminal Justice, 1950–1988," Working Papers, Series 3 (Madison: University of Wisconsin Law School, Institute for Legal Studies, December 1988).

167. Michael D. White, "Controlling Police Decisions to Use Deadly Force: Reexamining the Importance of Administrative Policy," *Crime and Delinquency* 47 (2001): 131.

168. Kevin Flynn, "New York Police Sting Tries to Weed Out Brutal Officers," *New York Times,* September 24, 1999, p. 2.

169. Victor Kappeler, Stephen Kappeler, and Rolando Del Carmen, "A Content Analysis of Police Civil Liability Cases: Decisions of the Federal District Courts, 1978–1990," *Journal of Criminal Justice* 21 (1993): 325–37.

170. Lawrence Sherman and Robert Langworthy, "Measuring Homicide by Police Officers," *Journal of Criminal Law and Criminology* 4 (1979): 546–60.

171. Ibid.

172. James Fyfe, "Police Use of Deadly Force: Research and Reform," *Justice Quarterly* 5 (1988): 165–205.

173. Sherman and Langworthy, "Measuring Homicide by Police Officers."

174. Brad Smith, "The Impact of Police Officer Diversity on Police-Caused Violence," *Policy Studies Journal* 31 (2003): 147–63.

175. John MacDonald, Geoffrey Alpert, and Abraham Tennenbaum, "Justifiable Homicide by Police and Criminal Homicide: A Research Note," *Journal of Crime and Justice* 22 (1999): 153–64.

176. Richard Parent and Simon Verdun-Jones, "Victim-Precipitated Homicide: Police Use of Deadly Force in British Columbia," *Policing* 21 (1998): 432–49.

177. "10% of Police Shootings Found to Be 'Suicide by Cop,'" *Criminal Justice Newsletter* 29 (1998): 1.

178. Sherman and Langworthy, "Measuring Homicide by Police Officers."

179. Brad Smith, "Structural and Organizational Predictors of Homicide by Police," *Policing* 27 (2004): 539–57.

180. Jonathan Sorenson, James Marquart, and Deon Brock, "Factors Related to Killings of Felons by Police Officers: A Test of the Community Violence and Conflict Hypotheses," *Justice Quarterly* 10 (1993): 417–40; David Jacobs and David Britt, "Inequality and Police Use of Deadly Force: An Empirical Assessment of a Conflict Hypothesis," *Social Problems* 26 (1979): 403–12.

181. Smith, "The Impact of Police Officer Diversity on Police-Caused Violence."

182. David Jacobs and Jason Carmichael, "Subordination and Violence Against State Control Agents: Testing Political Explanations for Lethal Assaults Against the Police," *Social Forces* 80 (2002): 1223–52.

183. Fyfe, "Police Use of Deadly Force," p. 181.

184. Paul Takagi, "A Garrison State in a 'Democratic' Society," *Crime and Social Justice* 5 (1974): 34–43.

185. Mark Blumberg, "Race and Police Shootings: An Analysis in Two Cities," in *Contemporary Issues in Law Enforcement,* ed. James Fyfe (Beverly Hills, Calif.: Sage, 1981), pp. 152–66.

186. James Fyfe, "Shots Fired," Ph.D. dissertation, State University of New York, Albany, 1978.

187. *Tennessee v. Garner,* 471 U.S. 1, 105 S.Ct. 1694, 85 L.Ed.2d 889 (1985).

188. *Graham v. Connor,* 490 U.S. 386, 109 S.Ct. 1865, 104 L.Ed.2d 443 (1989).

189. Franklin Graves and Gregory Connor, "The FLETC Use-of-Force Model," *Police Chief* 59 (1992): 56–58.

190. See James Fyfe, "Administrative Interventions on Police Shooting Discretion: An Empirical Examination," *Journal of Criminal Justice* 7 (1979): 313–25.

191. Frank Zarb, "Police Liability for Creating the Need to Use Deadly Force in Self-Defense," *Michigan Law Review* 86 (1988): 1982–2009.

192. Warren Cohen, "When Lethal Force Won't Do," *U.S. News and World Report,* June 23, 1997, p. 12.

193. Richard Lumb and Paul Friday, "Impact of Pepper Spray Availability on Police Officer Use-of-Force Decisions," *Policing* 20 (1997): 136–49.

194. Tom McEwen, "Policies on Less-Than-Lethal Force in Law Enforcement Agencies," *Policing* 20 (1997): 39–60.

195. Federal Bureau of Investigation, "Law Enforcement Officers Killed and Assaulted, 2000," press release, November 26, 2001.

196. Federal Bureau of Investigation, "Law Enforcement Officers Killed and Assaulted, 2004" (http://www.fbi.gov/ucr/killed/2004/section1felonkilled.htm).

197. J. David Hirschel, Charles Dean, and Richard Lumb, "The Relative Contribution of Domestic Violence to Assault and Injury of Police Officers," *Justice Quarterly* 11 (1994): 99–118.

198. John Cloud, "L.A. Confidential, for Real: Street Cops Accused of Frame-Ups in Widening Scandal," *Time,* September 27, 1999, p. 44; "L.A.'s Dirty War on Gangs: A Trail of Corruption Leads to Some of the City's Toughest Cops," *Newsweek,* October 11, 1999, p. 72.

199. Andrew Blankstein, "Jury Awards $6.5 Million in Frame-Up," *Los Angeles Times,* May 26, 2005 (http://www.latimes.com/news/local/la-me-rampart26may26,1,7864390.story?ctrack=1&cset=true), accessed on May 29, 2005.

200. Samuel Walker, *Popular Justice* (New York: Oxford University Press, 1980), p. 64.

201. Louise Westmarland, "Police Ethics and Integrity: Breaking the Blue Code of Silence," *Policing & Society* 15 (2005): 145–65.

202. Herman Goldstein, *Police Corruption* (Washington, D.C.: Police Foundation, 1975), p. 3.

203. Knapp Commission, *Report on Police Corruption* (New York: Braziller, 1973), pp. 1–34.

204. Elizabeth Neuffer, "Seven Additional Detectives Linked to Extortion Scheme," *Boston Globe,* October 25, 1988, p. 60.

205. Kevin Cullen, "U.S. Probe Eyes Bookie Protection," *Boston Globe,* October 25, 1988, p. 1.

206. Michael Johnston, *Political Corruption and Public Policy in America* (Monterey, Calif.: Brooks/Cole, 1982), p. 75.

207. William Doherty, "Ex-Sergeant Says He Aided Bid to Sell Exam," *Boston Globe,* February 26, 1987, p. 61.

208. Feuer and Rashbaum, "Blood Ties"; Lisa Stein, "Cops Gone Wild," *U.S. News & World Report* 138 (March 21, 2005): 14.

209. Ellwyn Stoddard, "Blue Coat Crime," in *Thinking About Police,* ed. Carl Klockars (New York: McGraw-Hill, 1983), pp. 338–49.

210. Lawrence Sherman, *Police Corruption: A Sociological Perspective* (Garden City, N.Y.: Doubleday, 1974), pp. 40–41.

211. Samuel Walker, *Police in Society* (New York: McGraw-Hill, 1983), p. 181.

212. Robert Kane, "The Social Ecology of Police Misconduct," *Criminology* 40 (2002): 867–97.

213. Sherman, *Police Corruption.*

214. Robert Daley, *Prince of the City* (New York: Houghton Mifflin, 1978).

215. Sherman, *Police Corruption,* p. 194.

216. Kevin Flynn, "Police Dept. Routinely Drops Cases of Officer Misconduct, Report Says," *New York Times,* September 15, 1999, p. 1.

217. Louise Westmarland, "Police Ethics and Integrity."

218. Barbara Gelb, *Tarnished Brass: The Decade After Serpico* (New York: Putnam, 1983); Candace McCoy, "Lawsuits Against Police: What Impact Do They Have?" *Criminal Law Bulletin* 20 (1984): 49–56.

219. "Philadelphia Police Corruption Brings Major Reform Initiative," *Criminal Justice Newsletter* 27 (1996): 4–5.

Police and the Rule of Law

Chapter Objectives

After reading this chapter, you should be able to:
1. Understand the concept of legal control over police activity.
2. Know what is meant by the term *search and seizure*.
3. Recognize the controls the courts have placed on the use of informers to get warrants.
4. Explain the term *totality of the circumstances*.
5. Recognize that searches can occur without a warrant.
6. Know the term *stop and frisk*.
7. Describe the postarrest warrantless search.
8. Discuss the instances in which police can search a car without a warrant.
9. Explain the *Miranda v. Arizona* decision.
10. Identify the ways that incriminating statements can be used in the absence of a *Miranda* warning.
11. Understand the concept of the lineup.

©Reuters/Carlos Barria/Landov

©AP Images/Detroit Police Department

W hen Michigan police, armed with a search warrant, came to the home of Booker T. Hudson, Jr., they knocked on the door, waited less than five seconds, and broke into the apartment. They found crack cocaine in his pockets and a gun wedged in a chair nearby. Hudson was convicted on drug charges despite the fact that state law required that police announce their presence during raids and give occupants a chance to come to the door; this is the so-called "knock and announce rule." After his conviction, Hudson appealed, arguing that his rights had been violated by this "no knock" search.

Should the police be forced to knock, wait, and give a wanted criminal such as Hudson the opportunity to arm himself and shoot first? On the other hand, should police officers have the right to burst unannounced into someone's home even if their purpose is to serve a search warrant? Doesn't such an unexpected entrance violate a person's right to privacy and dignity? And should the evidence seized in such a raid—in this case, crack cocaine—be excluded from trial because the police violated a rule governing proper procedure? What is fair? What is just? ◆

The Hudson case and those like it are critical to the operation of the justice system because police are charged with preventing crime before it occurs and identifying and arresting criminals who have already broken the law. To carry out these tasks, police officers want a free hand to search for evidence, to seize contraband such as guns and drugs, to interrogate suspects, and to have witnesses and victims identify suspects. They know their investigation must be thorough. At trial, they will need to provide the prosecutor with sufficient evidence to prove guilt "beyond a reasonable doubt." Therefore, soon after the crime is committed, they must make every effort to gather physical evidence, obtain confessions, and take witness statements that will be adequate to prove the case in court. Police officers also realize that evidence the prosecutor is counting on to prove the case, such as the testimony of a witness or co-conspirator, may evaporate before the trial begins. Then the case outcome may depend on some piece of physical evidence or a suspect's statement taken early in the investigation.

The need for police officers to gather conclusive evidence can conflict with the constitutional rights of citizens. Although police want a free hand to search homes and cars for evidence, the Constitution's Fourth Amendment restricts police activities by requiring that they obtain a warrant before conducting a search. When police want to vigorously interrogate a suspect, they must honor the Fifth Amendment's prohibition against forcing people to incriminate themselves.

◆ POLICE AND THE COURTS

Once a crime has been committed and an investigation begun, the police may use various means to collect the evidence needed for criminal prosecution. A number of critical decisions must take place:

◆ Should surveillance techniques be employed to secure information?

◆ How can information be gathered to support a request for a search warrant?

◆ If the suspect is driving a vehicle, can the car be searched without a warrant?

◆ Can a suspect's phone be tapped or her conversations recorded?

◆ Is there reasonable suspicion to justify stopping and frisking a suspect?

◆ Can a legal arrest be made?

◆ If a suspect has been detained, what constitutes an appropriate interrogation?

◆ Can witnesses be brought in to identify the suspect?

The U.S. Supreme Court has taken an active role in answering these questions concerning police procedure and activities. Of primary concern has been to balance the law enforcement agent's need for a free hand to investigate crimes with the citizen's constitutional right to be free from illegal searches and interrogations. In some instances, the Supreme Court has expanded police power—for example, by increasing the occasions when police can search without a warrant. In other cases, the Supreme Court has restricted police operations—for example, by ruling that every criminal suspect has a right to an attorney when being interrogated by police. Changes in the law often reflect such factors as the Justices' legal philosophy and their concern about the ability of police to control crime, their views on the need to maintain public safety versus their commitment to the civil liberties of criminal defendants, and current events such as the September 11, 2001, terrorist attacks.

The ruling in the *Hudson* case reflects this dynamic.[1] The Court found that the search was constitutional and allowed Hudson's conviction to stand. The majority concluded that whether the premature entry had occurred or not, the police would have executed the warrant they had obtained and would have discovered the gun and drugs inside the house. Therefore, the discovery of the contraband was inevitable and should be allowed. The Court seemed to fear that if the "knock and announce" rule was inflexible, patently guilty defendants might go free because otherwise valid evidence would have to be thrown out of court. The "social cost" of freeing a dangerous drug dealer was too high, in the Court's opinion, when compared to the loss of Hudson's privacy. Here we can see how the Supreme Court must balance the greater need of society with the more narrow rights of a criminal defendant. The Court's interpretations of such legal abstract concepts as "privacy" and "inevitable discovery" shape the scope of police behavior. Before *Hudson*, police executing a search warrant had to worry that evidence might be excluded if they did not first knock on the door, announce themselves, and wait a reasonable time for a response before forcing their way in. Now they can act first and ask later.

What are the key areas of court involvement with police activities, and how have they been shaped by legal authority? That is the subject of the following sections.

ThomsonNOW Improve your grade on the exam with Personalized Study! For reinforcement resources and a mastery check of police and the courts, go to www.thomsonedu.com/thomsonnow.

◆ SEARCH AND SEIZURE

One of the key elements of police investigation is the search for incriminating evidence, the seizure of that evidence, and its use during a criminal trial. The Fourth Amendment protects criminal suspects against unreasonable searches and seizures by requiring that evidence cannot be seized without a lawful **search warrant** issued only after police agents can show in court that they had probable cause to believe that an offense has been or is being committed.

A search warrant is an order from a court authorizing and directing the police to search a designated place for property stated in the order and to bring that property to court. To obtain a warrant, a police officer must offer sworn testimony that the facts on which the request for the search warrant is made are trustworthy and true. If the judge issues the warrant, it will authorize police officers to search for particular objects, at a specific location, at a certain time. A warrant may authorize the search of "the premises at 221 Third Avenue, Apt. 6B, between the hours of 8 A.M. to 6 P.M." and direct the police to search for and seize "substances, contraband, paraphernalia, scales, and other items used in connection with the sale of illegal substances." Generally, warrants allow the seizure of a variety of types of evidence, as described in Exhibit 8.1.

search warrant
An order, issued by a judge, directing officers to conduct a search of specified premises for specified objects or persons and to bring these before the court.

Warrants are required when police officers want to search a home for evidence or contraband. Brenda Depetris, sister of Pennsylvania state Senator Robert Regoli, talks on a cell phone as she looks over a search warrant that is being served at Regoli's home on August 9, 2006. During the search, police seized a safe and a computer as part of an investigation into the shooting death of a teenage neighbor who was killed with Regoli's 9-mm gun. Regoli had given the slain 14-year-old, a friend of his son's who lived next door, a key to his home so he could care for Regoli's pets while the lawmaker was out of town.

Search Warrant Requirements

The Fourth Amendment contains three elements that protect members of the public against intrusions of their privacy and shape the issuance of warrants: reasonableness, particularity, and probable cause.

REASONABLENESS Searches must be reasonable. Typically, the concept of reasonableness has two dimensions:

1. The police officer must have a reasonable suspicion that a person has violated a law before searching his person or property.

2. The scope of the search must be reasonably related to its objectives and not excessively intrusive. Searches are considered unreasonable if the police did not have sufficient information to justify the search and not merely because they used unreasonable force or coercion to gain

© AP Images| *Tribune-Review*/Sean Stipp

EXHIBIT 8.1

Categories of Evidence

Warrants are typically issued to search for and seize a variety of evidence.

♦ Property that represents evidence of the commission of a criminal offense; for example, a bloody glove or shirt.

♦ Contraband, the fruits of crime, smuggled goods, illegal material, or anything else that is of a criminal nature.

♦ Property intended for use or which has been used as the means of committing a criminal offense; for example, burglary tools, safecracking equipment, and drug paraphernalia.

♦ People may be seized when there is probable cause for their arrest.

♦ Conversation involving criminal conspiracy and other illegalities can be seized via tape recordings and wiretaps.

A great site for U.S. Supreme Court decisions on criminal procedure is the Cornell Law School website. You can reach it by going to the Siegel/Senna Introduction to Criminal Justice 11e website: www.thomsonedu.com/criminaljustice/siegel.

particularity
The requirement that a search warrant state precisely where the search is to take place and what items are to be seized.

probable cause
The evidentiary criterion necessary to sustain an arrest or the issuance of an arrest or search warrant: a set of facts, information, circumstances, or conditions that would lead a reasonable person to believe that an offense was committed and that the accused committed that offense.

evidence. Any attempt to gather evidence would be held invalid if it relied on stealth, deception, or disguise to gain admittance to a home or business or to fool a suspect into allowing a more extensive search than the warrant demanded. It would be considered unreasonable, for example, for police officers holding a valid warrant to disguise themselves as building inspectors to fool a home owner into granting them greater opportunity to search than the warrant specified. This protective envelope extends to any area in which individuals have a reasonable expectation of privacy, including their homes, possessions, and persons. So if police have a warrant to search a home for illegal weapons, it would be unreasonable for them to search a car parked out in front of the home.

PARTICULARITY When the Fourth Amendment was created, the **particularity** requirement was created to counteract the use of general warrants by government agents. This was a device used against the colonists by the English crown. British officials had obtained general warrants empowering them to search any suspected places for smuggled goods, placing the liberty of every man in the hands of government officials.[2]

This requirement is designed to curtail potential abuse that may result from an officer being allowed to conduct a search with unbridled discretion. If a warrant is issued in violation of the particularity clause, the ensuing search is invalid even if the officers actually exercise proper restraint in executing their search. What and whom are to be searched must be clearly spelled out. The police cannot search the basement of a house if the warrant specifies the attic; they cannot look in a desk drawer if the warrant specifies a search for a missing piano. However, this does not mean that police officers can seize only those items listed in the warrant. If, during the course of their search, police officers come across contraband or evidence of a crime that is not listed in the warrant, they can lawfully seize the unlisted items. This is referred to as the *plain sight* exception. But they cannot look in places that are off-limits within the scope of the warrant. For more on search warrants, see Concept Summary 8.1.

PROBABLE CAUSE A search cannot be conducted unless a warrant is issued by a magistrate based upon **probable cause**, typically defined as a reasonable belief, based on fact, that a crime has been committed and that the person, place, or object to be searched and/or seized is linked to the crime with a reasonable degree of certainty.

CONCEPT SUMMARY 8.1

The Elements of a Search Warrant

Reasonableness	The warrant must not violate what society considers a reasonable intrusion of privacy under the circumstances. Pumping the stomach of someone to seize cocaine she swallowed would not be a reasonable search. Searching the glove compartment of a car for a missing rifle would be unreasonable.
Particularity	The warrant must set forth and precisely specify the places to be searched and items to be seized so that it can provide reasonable guidance to the police officers and prevent them from having unregulated and unrestricted discretion to search for evidence.
Probable cause	Probable cause is determined by whether a police officer, based on fact, has objective, reasonable, and reliable information that the person under investigation has committed or was committing an offense.

EXHIBIT 8.2

Sources for a Warrant

- ◆ A police informant whose reliability has been established because he has provided information in the past.
- ◆ Someone who has firsthand knowledge of illegal activities.
- ◆ A co-conspirator who implicates herself as well as the suspect.
- ◆ An informant whose information can be partially verified by the police.
- ◆ A victim of a crime who offers information.
- ◆ A witness to the crime related to the search.
- ◆ A fellow law enforcement officer.

Under normal circumstances, a search warrant cannot be obtained unless the request for it is supported by facts, supplied under oath by a law enforcement officer, that are sufficient to convince the court that a crime has been or is being committed.

To establish probable cause, the police must provide the judge or magistrate with information in the form of written affidavits, which report either their own observations or those of private citizens or police undercover informants. If the magistrate believes that the information is sufficient to establish probable cause to conduct a search, he or she will issue a warrant. Although the suspect is not present when the warrant is issued and therefore cannot contest its issuance, he can later challenge the validity of the warrant before trial.

The Fourth Amendment does not explicitly define probable cause, and its precise meaning still remains unclear. However, the police officers have to provide factual evidence to define and identify suspicious activities, not simply offer the officers' beliefs or suspicions. In addition, the officers must show how they obtained the information and provide evidence of its reliability. Some common sources are listed in Exhibit 8.2.

Obtaining a Warrant

Police can obtain a warrant if their investigation turns up sufficient evidence to convince a judge that a crime likely has been committed and that the person or place the police wish to search is probably involved materially in that crime. Because this can be an extremely time-consuming procedure that involves carefully collecting physical evidence, taking photos, and interviewing witnesses, police often rely on informers, who may be trying to avoid criminal charges. Informers are often acting out of self-interest instead of civic duty, and the reliability of the evidence they provide may be questionable. Moreover, their statements reflect only what they have seen and heard, are not substantiated by hard evidence, and thus are defined as **hearsay evidence**.

hearsay evidence
Testimony that is not firsthand but relates information told by a second party.

For answers to frequently asked questions about search and seizure, go to LawInfo.com. You can reach it by going to the Siegel/Senna Introduction to Criminal Justice 11e website: www.thomsonedu.com/criminaljustice/siegel.

The U.S. Supreme Court has been concerned about the reliability of evidence obtained from informers. The Court has determined that hearsay evidence must be corroborated to serve as a basis for probable cause and thereby justify the issuance of a warrant. In the case of *Aguilar* v. *Texas* (1964), the Court articulated a two-part test for issuing a warrant on the word of an informant. The police had to show (1) why they believed the informant and (2) how the informant acquired personal knowledge of the crime.[3] This ruling restricted informant testimony to people who were in direct contact with police and whose information could be verified.

Anonymous Tips

Because the *Aguilar* case required that an informer be known and that his or her information be proven knowledgeable, it all but ruled out using anonymous tips to secure a search warrant. This was changed in a critical 1983 ruling, *Illinois v. Gates*, in which the Court eased the process of obtaining search warrants by developing a *totality of the circumstances* test to determine probable cause for issuing a search warrant. In *Gates*, the police received a knowledgeable and detailed anonymous letter describing the drug-dealing activities of Lance and Sue Gates. Based on that tip, the police began a surveillance and eventually obtained a warrant to search their home. The search was later challenged on the grounds that it would be impossible to determine the accuracy of information provided by an anonymous letter, a condition required by the *Aguilar* case. However, the Court ruled that to obtain a warrant, the police must prove to a judge that, considering *the totality of the circumstances*, an informant has relevant and factual knowledge that a fair probability exists that evidence of a crime will be found in a certain place.[4] The anonymous letter, rich in details, satisfied that demand.

TELEPHONE TIPS Can the police conduct a search based on an anonymous tip, such as one that is given via telephone? In *Alabama v. White*, the police received an anonymous tip that a woman was carrying cocaine.[5] Only after police observation showed that the tip had accurately predicted the woman's movements did it become reasonable to believe the tipster had inside knowledge about the suspect and was truthful in his assertion about the cocaine. The Supreme Court ruled that the search based on the tip was legal because it was corroborated by independent police work. In its ruling, the Court stated the following:

> Standing alone, the tip here is completely lacking in the necessary indicia of reliability, since it provides virtually nothing from which one might conclude that the caller is honest or his information reliable and gives no indication of the basis for his predictions regarding [Vannesa] White's criminal activities. However, although it is a close question, the totality of the circumstances demonstrates that significant aspects of the informant's story were sufficiently corroborated by the police to furnish reasonable suspicion. . . . Thus, there was reason to believe that the caller was honest and well informed, and to impart some degree of reliability to his allegation that White was engaged in criminal activity.[6]

The *White* case seemed to give police powers to search someone after corroborating an anonymous tip. However, in *Florida v. J. L.*, the Court narrowed that right. In *J. L.*, an anonymous caller reported to the Miami-Dade police that a young, black male standing at a particular bus stop, wearing a plaid shirt, was carrying a gun.[7] The tip was not recorded, and no information was known about the caller. Two officers went to the bus stop and spotted three black males. One of them, the 15-year-old J. L., was wearing a plaid shirt. Apart from the anonymous tip, the officers had no reason to suspect that any of the males were involved in any criminal activity. The officers did not see a firearm, and J. L. made no threatening or unusual movements. One officer approached J. L., frisked him, and seized a gun from his pocket. The Court disallowed the search, ruling that a police officer must have reasonable suspicion that criminal activity is being conducted prior to stopping a person. Because anonymous tips are generally considered less reliable than tips from known informants, they can be used to search only if they include specific information that shows they are reliable. Unlike the *White* case, the police in *J. L.* failed to provide independent corroboration of the tipster's information.

◆ WARRANTLESS SEARCHES

Under normal circumstances, the police must obtain a warrant to conduct a search. However, the Supreme Court has over the years carved out some significant exceptions to the search warrant requirement of the Fourth Amendment. Most of these involve **exigent** or emergency situations in which police are allowed to search without a warrant being issued to protect their lives or to ensure that evidence is not moved or destroyed. Let's say that police officers become involved in a shoot-out with three suspects who then run into a house. After arresting the suspects, the police would be allowed to search without a warrant the area they had been in to look for weapons or contraband. The search would be allowed because the police were in **hot pursuit** of the suspects and because failure to search could put citizens in danger, a condition that courts typically view as "exigent."

The definition of *exigency* is not written in stone, and situations that a police officer considers exigent may be later disputed in the courts. In *Kirk v. Louisiana* (2002), police officers observed a suspect engaging in what they considered to be drug deals. Without a warrant, they entered his home, arrested him, frisked him, found a drug vial in his underwear, and seized contraband that was in plain view in the apartment. Only after these actions did the officers obtain a warrant. The Supreme Court ruled that police officers need either a warrant or probable cause plus exigent circumstances to make a lawful entry into a home. Although the Court left unclear the factors that define *exigent circumstances*, the facts of the Kirk case indicate that merely observing a suspect committing what appears to be a nonviolent crime is not enough to justify a warrantless entry of a person's home.[8]

The Reasonableness Doctrine

Even under exigent circumstances the police must adhere to the reasonableness doctrine: A warrantless search must also be reasonable. A search would also be considered unreasonable if, for example, it was conducted simply because of an offender's prior behavior or status. Police officers cannot stop and search a vehicle driven by a known drug dealer unless some other factors support the search. Unless there was something discernible to a police officer that indicated a crime was then being committed, the suspect's past history would not justify an officer

exigent
Emergency or immediate circumstance.

hot pursuit
A legal doctrine that allows police to search premises where they suspect a crime has been committed without a warrant when delay would endanger their lives or the lives of others and lead to the escape of the alleged perpetrator.

ThomsonNOW™ Improve your grade on the exam with Personalized Study! For reinforcement resources and a mastery check of search and seizure, go to www.thomsonedu.com/thomsonnow.

Police may conduct a warrantless search under exigent or emergency circumstances if they have probable cause. Here a police officer holsters his gun before attempting to ram the door of a motel as a sheriff's department officer looks on during a door-to-door search on May 31, 2006. Authorities were searching for Sandra Eubank Gregory, an attorney who was abducted from a parking lot in Birmingham, Alabama, by a gunman who forced her back into the vehicle she had been driving and then drove off. Gregory was successfully rescued from her abductor.

©AP Images/Rainier Ehrhardt

Postal Inspector

Duties and Characteristics of the Job

The Postal Inspection Service is a law enforcement body of the U.S. government. Postal inspectors investigate crimes that break postal laws, and they ensure the security of the U.S. Postal Service. The duties of postal inspectors include general law enforcement tasks such as executing warrants, arresting offenders, and testifying in court. However, a large part of a postal inspector's job is investigating crimes perpetrated through the mail such as mail theft, mail fraud, drug trafficking, child pornography, and identity theft. Postal inspectors conduct investigations using a combination of advanced technology and forensic skills. They investigate harassment and threats against postal employees and the postal service itself. Postal inspectors are also responsible for any threat that involves the mail as a medium. For example, postal inspectors were involved in the 2001 investigation into the envelopes containing anthrax that had been mailed to government and news offices.

Postal inspectors are responsible for ensuring that the entire postal service is safe and dependable. Being a postal inspector can be a demanding job—irregular hours and working over 40 hours per week are common.

Job Outlook

Unfortunately, opportunities for employment as a postal inspector open at irregular intervals. However, when the postal service is hiring, a diversity of skills and backgrounds is desirable in potential postal inspectors.

Salary

As with other federal employees, salaries for postal inspectors are determined by the General Pay Scale, and various factors, such as employment qualifications, are used to determine position on the scale. Base pay for these positions does not vary by locality, but postal inspectors can earn overtime pay. The average salary for a postal inspector is between $48,295 and $88,105.

Opportunities

Because of the good pay, benefits, prestige, and opportunities that these positions offer, applicants should expect competition. Accounting experience,

to stop and search the vehicle. Nor would it be considered reasonable if police decided to search someone simply because he was seen engaging in a pattern of behavior that seemed similar or comparable to the activity of known criminals. A person could not be searched because he was seen driving a flashy new car and making routine stops at the same places each day merely because that is a pattern of behavior common to drug dealing.

Because police are now confronting such significant social problems as drug trafficking and terrorist activity, the Supreme Court has given them some leeway on the reasonableness rule. In the 2002 case *United States v. Arvizu*, the Court allowed a search of a vehicle based on a pattern of suspicious behavior:

1. A vehicle registration check showing that the vehicle was registered to an address in an area notorious for alien and narcotics smuggling.
2. The patrol officer's personal experience and his knowledge that the suspect had taken a route frequently used by drug smugglers.
3. The driver's route having been designed to pass through the area during a border patrol shift change.

Although each fact alone was insufficient to form reasonable suspicion, taken together they sufficed to allow the officer to stop the vehicle.[9]

The Supreme Court has identified a number of exigent circumstances in which a search warrant might have normally been required but because of some

computer skills, and a law degree are helpful when applying for a position. Law enforcement experience as a detective or even a patrol officer will also be helpful. Finally, good students who earned a bachelor's or an advanced degree with a 3.0 average or higher can qualify for the academic achievement track with or without full-time job experience.

Qualifications

Candidates must be U.S. citizens 21 or over, but younger than 36½, have a four-year degree, have no felonies or domestic violence convictions, and have a driver's license. A candidate must also be in sound mental and physical health, including passing a hearing test. Qualities such as good communications skills (written and oral), sound decision-making skills, and the ability to follow instructions are also highly valued. Once satisfying the general requirements, a candidate must qualify for training under one of several tracks offered: language skills, postal experience, specialized nonpostal experience (includes those with law degrees, certification in auditing or computer systems, law enforcement experience, and others), or academic achievement.

Additionally, applicants must also undergo a background check, pass a polygraph, and be interviewed. After completing the proper training, a postal inspector may be relocated, so a willingness to move is also necessary.

Education and Training

In order to even apply for a position, a potential candidate must have a four-year degree. After successfully moving through the application process and being hired, new employees will be sent to Basic Inspector Training in Potomac, Maryland, where they will learn about the responsibilities of their organization, investigative techniques, firearms proficiency, and physical defense. Those with no postal experience will then be on a six-month probation period before becoming full-time employees.

Sources: *2002 Annual Report of Investigations of the United States Postal Inspection Service* (Washington, D.C.: U.S. Postal Inspection Service); "Employment" (U.S. Postal Inspection Service), retrieved July 6, 2006, from http://www.usps.com/postalinspectors/recruit/whoweare.html.

immediate emergency police officers can search suspects and places without benefit of a warrant. These include stop-and-frisk searches, searches incident to a lawful arrest, automobile searches, and consent searches.

Field Interrogation: Stop and Frisk

One important exception to the rule requiring a search warrant is the **threshold inquiry**, or the **stop-and-frisk** procedure. This type of search typically occurs when a police officer encounters a suspicious person on the street and frisks or pats down his outer garments to determine if he is in possession of a concealed weapon. The police officer need not have probable cause to arrest the suspect but simply must be reasonably suspicious based on the circumstances of the case—that is, time and place, and her experience as a police officer. The stop-and-frisk search consists of two distinct components:

1. The *stop*, in which a police officer wishes to briefly detain a suspicious person in an effort to effect crime prevention and detection.

2. The *frisk*, in which an officer pats down or frisks a person who is stopped, in order to check for weapons. The purpose of the frisk is the protection of the officer making the stop.

Therefore, the stop and the frisk are separate actions, and each requires its own factual basis. Stopping a suspect allows for brief questioning, and frisking affords the officer an opportunity to avoid the possibility of attack. For instance, a police officer patrolling a high-crime area observes two young men loitering outside

threshold inquiry
A term used to describe a stop and frisk.

stop and frisk
The situation in which police officers who are suspicious of an individual run their hands lightly over the suspect's outer garments to determine if the person is carrying a concealed weapon, also called a threshold inquiry or pat-down.

a liquor store after dark. The two men confer several times and stop to talk to a third person who pulls up alongside the curb in an automobile. From this observation, the officer may conclude that the men are casing the store for a possible burglary. He can then stop the suspects and ask them for some identification and an explanation of their conduct. However, the facts that support a stop do not automatically allow a frisk. The officer must have reason to believe that the suspect is armed or dangerous. In this instance, if the three men identify themselves as security guards and produce identification, a frisk would not be justified. If they seem nervous and secretive and the officer concludes that they are planning a crime, the suspicion would be enough to justify a pat-down.

The landmark case of *Terry v. Ohio* (1968) shaped the contours of the stop and frisk.[10] In *Terry,* a police officer found a gun in the coat pocket of one of three men he frisked when their suspicious behavior convinced him that they were planning a robbery. At trial, the defendants futilely moved to suppress the gun on the grounds that it was the product of an illegal search. On appeal, the Supreme Court ruled that if a reasonably prudent police officer believes that her safety or that of others is endangered, she may make a reasonable search for weapons of the person regardless of whether she has probable cause to arrest that individual for a crime or the absolute certainty that the individual is armed. The *Terry* case illustrates the principle that although the police officer, whenever possible, must secure a warrant to make a search and seizure, when swift action, based upon on-the-spot observations, is called for, the need for the warrant is removed.

What kind of behavior can trigger a *Terry* search? How suspicious does a person have to look before the police can legally stop him and pat him down? In *Illinois v. Wardlow,* the defendant was walking on the street in an area known for narcotics trafficking. When he made eye contact with a police officer riding in a marked police car, he ran away. The officer caught up with the defendant on the street, stopped him, and conducted a protective pat-down search for weapons. A handgun was discovered in the frisk, and the defendant was convicted of unlawful use of a weapon by a felon. The Illinois Supreme Court ruled that the frisk violated *Terry v. Ohio* because flight may simply be an exercise of the right to "go on one's way" and does not constitute reasonable suspicion. However, on appeal, the U.S. Supreme Court reversed the state court ruling that a person's presence in a "high crime area," in and of itself, is not enough to support a reasonable, particularized suspicion of criminal activity.[11] It held that a location's characteristics are sufficiently suspicious to warrant further investigation and that, in this case, the additional factor of the defendant's unprovoked flight added up to reasonable suspicion. The officers found that the defendant possessed a handgun, and as a result of the pat-down and search, they had probable cause to arrest him for violation of a state law. The frisk and arrest were thus proper under *Terry v. Ohio.*

Search Incident to a Lawful Arrest

Traditionally, a search without a warrant is permissible if it is made incident to a lawful arrest. The police officer who searches a suspect incident to a lawful arrest must generally observe two rules: (1) the search must be conducted at the time of or immediately following the arrest, and (2) the police may search only the suspect and the area within the suspect's immediate control. The search may not legally go beyond the area where the person can reach for a weapon or destroy any evidence. For example, if shortly after the armed robbery of a grocery store, officers arrest a suspect with a briefcase hiding in the basement, a search of the suspect's person and of the briefcase would be a proper **search incident to a lawful arrest** without a warrant. The legality of this type of search depends almost entirely on the lawfulness of the arrest. The arrest will be upheld if the police officer observed the crime being committed or had probable cause to believe that the suspect committed the offense. If the arrest is found to have

search incident to a lawful arrest
An exception to the search warrant rule, limited to the immediate surrounding area.

been invalid, then any warrantless search made incident to the arrest would be considered illegal, and the evidence obtained from the search would be excluded from trial.

The U.S. Supreme Court defined the permissible scope of a search incident to a lawful arrest in *Chimel v. California*.[12] According to the *Chimel* doctrine, the police can search a suspect without a warrant after a lawful arrest to protect themselves from danger and to secure evidence. But a search of his home is illegal even if the police find contraband or evidence during the course of that search and if the police would otherwise be forced to obtain a warrant to search the premises.

Automobile Searches

The U.S. Supreme Court has also established that certain situations justify the warrantless search of an automobile on a public street or highway. Evidence can be seized from an automobile when a suspect is taken into custody in a lawful arrest. In *Carroll v. United States*, which was decided in 1925, the Supreme Court ruled that distinctions should be made among searches of automobiles, persons, and homes. The Court also concluded that a warrantless search of an automobile is valid if the police have probable cause to believe that the car contains evidence they are seeking.[13]

The legality of searching automobiles without a warrant has always been a trouble spot for police and the courts. Should the search be limited to the interior of the car, or can the police search the trunk? What about a suitcase in the trunk? What about the glove compartment? Does a traffic citation give the police the right to search an automobile? These questions have produced significant litigation over the years. To clear up the matter, the Supreme Court decided the landmark case of *United States v. Ross* in 1982.[14] The Court held that if probable cause exists to believe that an automobile contains criminal evidence, a warrantless search by the police is permissible, including a search of closed containers in the vehicle.

In sum, the most important requirement for a warrantless search of an automobile is that it must be based on the legal standard of probable cause that a crime related to the vehicle has been or is being committed. Under such conditions, the car may be stopped and searched, the contraband seized, and the occupant arrested.

ROADBLOCK SEARCHES Police departments often wish to set up roadblocks to check drivers' licenses or the condition of drivers. Is such a stop an illegal search and seizure? In *Delaware v. Prouse* (1979), the Supreme Court forbade the practice of random stops in the absence of any reasonable suspicion that some traffic or motor vehicle law has been violated.[15] Unless there is at least reasonable belief that a motorist is unlicensed, that an automobile is not registered, or that the occupant is subject to seizure for violation of the law, stopping and detaining a driver to check his or her license violates the Fourth Amendment. In *City of Indianapolis v. Edmund*, the Court ruled that the police may not routinely stop all motorists in the hope of finding a few drug criminals.[16] The general rule is that any seizure must be accompanied by individualized suspicion; the random stopping of cars to search for drugs is illegal.

Although random stops are forbidden, a police department can set up a roadblock to stop cars in some systematic fashion to ensure public safety. As long as the police can demonstrate that the checkpoints are conducted in a uniform manner and that the operating procedures have been determined by someone other than the officer at the scene, roadblocks can be used to uncover violators of even minor traffic regulations. In *Michigan Dept. of State Police v. Sitz*, the Court held that brief, suspicionless seizures at highway checkpoints for the purposes of combating drunk driving were constitutional.[17]

Roadblocks have recently become popular for combating drunk driving. Courts have ruled that police can stop a predetermined number of cars at a checkpoint and can request each motorist to produce his or her license, registration, and insurance card. While doing so, they can check for outward signs of intoxication.

SEARCHING DRIVERS AND PASSENGERS Can police officers search drivers and passengers during routine traffic stops? In 1977 the Supreme Court ruled in *Pennsylvania v. Mimms* that officers could order drivers out of their cars and frisk them during routine traffic stops. Officers' safety outweighed the intrusion on individual rights.[18] In 1997 the Court held in *Maryland v. Wilson* that the police had the same authority with respect to passengers.[19] In the Wilson case, a state patrol officer lawfully stopped a vehicle for speeding. While the driver was producing his license, the front-seat passenger, Jerry Lee Wilson, was ordered out of the vehicle. As he exited, crack cocaine dropped to the ground. Wilson was arrested and convicted of drug possession. His attorney moved to suppress the evidence, but the U.S. Supreme Court disagreed and extended the *Mimms* rule to passengers. The Court noted that lawful traffic stops had become progressively more dangerous to police officers and that thousands of officers were assaulted and even killed during such stops. The decision means that passengers must comply when ordered out of a lawfully stopped vehicle.

The Scope of the Automobile Search Generally, police can search a suspect after he has exited a vehicle to determine if he has a weapon. They can also search the area in the car, such as the driver's seat, where the suspect was sitting or that was under his control. But can police officers search a car even though their initial contact with the suspect occurs after he is no longer a driver or passenger? The case of *Thornton v. United States*, discussed in the Law in Review feature, addresses this issue.

"FREE TO GO" Must police officers inform detained drivers that they are "free to go" before asking consent to search the vehicle? In *Ohio v. Robinette* (1996), the Court concluded that no such warning is needed to make consent to a search reasonable. Robert D. Robinette was stopped for speeding. After checking his license, the officer asked if Robinette was carrying any illegal contraband in the car. When the defendant answered in the negative, the officer asked for and received permission to search the car. The search turned up illegal drugs. The Supreme Court ruled that police officers do not have to inform a driver that he is "free to go" before asking if they can search the car. According to the Court, the touchstone of the Fourth Amendment is reasonableness, which is assessed by examining the totality of the circumstances.[20] In this case the search was ruled a reasonable exercise of discretion.

PRETEXT STOPS A pretext stop is one in which police officers stop a car because they suspect the driver is involved in a crime such as drug trafficking, but, lacking probable cause, they use a pretext such as a minor traffic violation to stop the car and search its interior. The legality of pretext stops was challenged in *Whren v. United States* (1996).[21] Two defendants claimed that plainclothes police officers used relatively minor traffic violations as an excuse or pretext to stop their vehicle because the officers lacked objective evidence that they were drug couriers. However, the Supreme Court ruled that if probable cause exists to stop a person for a traffic violation, the actual motivation of the officers is irrelevant; therefore, the search was legal. This point was reiterated in *Arkansas v. Sullivan*, in which the Court ruled that if an officer has a legal basis for making a custodial arrest for a particular crime, it does not matter if he has suspicions that the suspect is involved in any other criminal activity.[22] Thus, as long as there is a legal basis for making an arrest, officers may do so, even in cases in which they are motivated by a desire to gather evidence of other suspected crimes.

Consent Searches

Police officers may also undertake warrantless searches when the person in control of the area or object consents to the search. Those who consent to a search essentially waive their constitutional rights under the Fourth Amendment. Ordinarily, courts are reluctant to accept such waivers and require the state to prove that the consent was voluntarily given. In addition, the consent must be given intelligently, and in some jurisdictions, consent searches are valid only after the suspect is informed of the option to refuse consent.

VOLUNTARINESS The major legal issue in most consent searches is whether the police can prove that consent was given voluntarily. For example, in the case of *Bumper v. North Carolina* (1968), police officers searched the home of an elderly woman after informing her that they possessed a search warrant.[23] At the trial, the prosecutor informed the court that the search was valid because the woman had given her consent. When the government was unable to produce the warrant, the court decided that the search was invalid because the woman's consent was not given voluntarily. On appeal, the U.S. Supreme Court upheld the lower court's finding that the consent had been illegally obtained by the false claim that the police had a search warrant.

In most consent searches, however, voluntariness is a question of fact to be determined from all the circumstances of the case. In *Schneckloth v. Bustamonte* (1973), the defendant helped the police by opening the trunk and glove compartment of the car. The Court said this action demonstrated that the consent was voluntarily given.[24] Furthermore, the police are usually under no obligation to inform a suspect of the right to refuse consent. Failure to tell a suspect of this right does not make the search illegal, but it may be a factor used by the courts to decide if the suspect gave consent voluntarily.

SECOND-PARTY CONSENT Can a person give consent for someone else? In *United States v. Matlock*, the Court ruled that it is permissible for one co-occupant of an apartment to give consent to the police to search the premises in the absence of the other occupant, as long as the person giving consent shares common authority over the property and no present co-tenant objects.[25] What happens if one party gives consent to a search while another interested party refuses? This is what happened in the recent (2006) case of *Georgia v. Randolph*. Police were called to Scott Randolph's home because of a domestic dispute. His wife told police that Randolph had been using a lot of cocaine and that drugs were on the premises. One officer asked Randolph if he could conduct a search of the home, and Randolph said no. Another officer asked his wife for permission, and she not only said yes, but also led the officer upstairs to a bedroom where he allegedly found cocaine residue. The Supreme Court held that because Randolph was present when the police came to his home, they were required by the Fourth Amendment to heed his objection to the search; the seizure of the drugs was ruled illegal.[26]

BUS SWEEPS Today, consent searches have additional significance because of their use in drug control programs. On June 20, 1991, the U.S. Supreme Court, in *Florida v. Bostick*, upheld the drug interdiction technique known as the **bus sweep**, in which police board buses and, without suspicion of illegal activity, question passengers, ask for identification, and request permission to search luggage.[27] Police in the *Bostick* case boarded a bus bound from Miami to Atlanta during a stopover in Fort Lauderdale. Without suspicion, the officers picked out the defendant and asked to inspect his ticket and identification. After identifying themselves as narcotics officers looking for illegal drugs, they asked to inspect the defendant's luggage. Although there was some uncertainty about whether the defendant consented to the search in which contraband was found and whether he was informed of his right to refuse consent, the defendant was convicted.

bus sweep
Police investigation technique in which officers board a bus or train without suspicion of illegal activity and question passengers, asking for identification and seeking permission to search their baggage.

United States v. Thornton

Officer Deion Nichols of the Norfolk, Virginia, Police Department was in uniform but driving an unmarked police car when he spotted Marcus Thornton in the next lane slow down. Officer Nichols assumed that Thornton knew he was a police officer and for some reason did not want to drive next to him. His suspicions aroused, Nichols pulled off onto a side street, and when Thornton passed him, Nichols ran a check on his license tags, which revealed that the plates had been issued to another car. Before Nichols had an opportunity to pull him over, Thornton drove into a parking lot and got out of the vehicle. Nichols parked the patrol car, stopped Thornton, and asked him for his driver's license. He also told him that his license tags did not match the vehicle he was driving.

Thornton appeared nervous. He began rambling and licking his lips; he was sweating. Concerned for his safety, Nichols asked him if he had any narcotics or weapons on him or in his vehicle. When Thornton said no, Officer Nichols asked him if he could pat him down, to which Thornton agreed. Nichols felt a bulge in Thornton's left front pocket and again asked him if he had any illegal narcotics on him. This time, Thornton stated that he did, and he reached into his pocket and pulled out two individual bags, one containing three bags of marijuana and the other containing a large amount of crack cocaine. Nichols handcuffed Thornton, informed him that he was under arrest, and placed him in the back seat of the patrol car. He then searched Thornton's car and found a BryCo .9-millimeter handgun under the driver's seat.

Thornton was charged with federal drug and firearms violations. He appealed on the grounds that the search of the car was illegal because at the time of his arrest he was no longer in the vehicle.

The U.S. Supreme Court held the search of the car and seizure of the firearm were legal. It relied on its previous decision in *New York v. Belton*, 453 U.S. 454 (1981), which held that after a police officer makes a lawful custodial arrest of an automobile's occupant, the Fourth Amendment allows the officer to search the vehicle's passenger compartment as a contemporaneous incident of arrest even if the driver

The Supreme Court was faced with deciding whether consent was freely given or whether the nature of the bus sweep negated the defendant's consent. The Court concluded that drug enforcement officers, after obtaining consent, may search luggage on a crowded bus without meeting the Fourth Amendment requirements for a search warrant or probable cause.

This case raises fundamental questions about the legality of techniques used to discourage drug trafficking. Are they inherently coercive? In *Bostick*, when the officers entered the bus, the driver exited and closed the door, leaving the defendant and passengers alone with two officers. Furthermore, Terrance Bostick was seated in the rear of the bus, and officers blocked him from exiting. Finally, one of the officers was clearly holding his handgun in full view. In light of these circumstances, was this a consensual or coercive search? The Supreme Court ruled, despite the coercive circumstances, that it was in fact appropriate because consent had been given voluntarily.

Plain View

The Supreme Court has also ruled that police can search for and seize evidence without benefit of a warrant if it is in plain view. For example, if a police officer is conducting an investigation and notices while questioning some individuals that one has drugs in her pocket, the officer can seize the evidence and arrest the suspect. Or if the police are conducting a search under a warrant authorizing them to look for narcotics in a person's home and they come upon a gun, the police can seize the gun, even though it is not mentioned in the warrant. The 1986 case of *New York v. Class* illustrates the **plain view doctrine**.[28] A police officer stopped a car for a traffic violation. Wishing to check the vehicle identification number (VIN) on the dashboard, he reached into the car to clear away material that was obstructing his view. While clearing the dash, he

plain view doctrine
The principle that evidence in plain view of police officers may be seized without a search warrant.

is no longer in the vehicle. In the *Belton* case, the officer arrested the driver while he was standing outside the vehicle on a highway, handcuffed him, and then conducted the vehicle search. The Court ruled that the search was permissible because Belton was a "recent occupant" of the car. In *Thornton*, the Court ruled that a search is permissible even when an officer does not make contact until the person arrested has left the vehicle. There is simply no basis to conclude, the Court ruled, that the span of the area generally within the arrestee's immediate control is determined by whether the arrestee exited the vehicle at the officer's direction or whether the officer initiated contact with him while he was in the car. In all relevant aspects, the arrest of a suspect who is next to a vehicle presents identical concerns regarding officer safety and evidence destruction as the arrest of a suspect who is inside a vehicle. This way, an officer who decides that it may be safer and more effective to conceal her presence until a suspect has left his car would be able to search the passenger compartment in the event of an arrest. This decision places officer safety and the retention of evidence as primary objectives.

Critical Thinking

1. Although *Thornton* expands police search powers, it remains to be seen how long a passenger may leave the vehicle before he is arrested and the vehicle searched. Would it have made a difference if he had gone to a restaurant, had lunch, and was then arrested an hour later?

2. If the police officer found a gun under the seat, should he be allowed to search the trunk of the car and a suitcase found in the spare tire compartment?

InfoTrac College Edition Research

To read an analysis of *Thornton*, go to Craig M. Bradley, "Just One Cheer for the Court," *Trial* 40 (2004): 62–64.

Source: *Thornton v. United States*, 541 U.S. 615 (2004).

---

noticed a gun under the seat—in plain view. The U.S. Supreme Court upheld the seizure of the gun as evidence because the police officer had the right to check the VIN; therefore, the sighting of the gun was legal.

The doctrine of plain view was applied and further developed in *Arizona v. Hicks* (1987).[29] Here, the Court held that moving a stereo component in plain view a few inches to record the serial number constituted a search under the Fourth Amendment. When a check with police headquarters revealed that the item had been stolen, the equipment was seized and offered for evidence at James Hicks's trial. The Court held that a plain view search and seizure could be justified only by probable cause, not reasonable suspicion, and suppressed the evidence against the defendant. In this case, the Court decided to take a firm stance on protecting Fourth Amendment rights. The *Hicks* decision is uncharacteristic in an era when most decisions have tended to expand the exceptions to the search warrant requirement.

CURTILAGE An issue long associated with plain view is whether police can search open fields that are fenced in but otherwise open to view. In *Oliver v. United States* (1984), the U.S. Supreme Court distinguished between the privacy granted persons in their own home or its adjacent grounds and fields (**curtilage**). The Court ruled that police can use airplane surveillance to spot marijuana fields and then send in squads to seize the crops, or they can peer into fields from cars for the same purpose.[30]

In *California v. Ciraola* (1986), the Court expanded the police ability to spy on criminal offenders. In this case, the police received a tip that marijuana was growing in the defendant's backyard.[31] The yard was surrounded by fences, one of which was 10 feet high. The officers flew over the yard in a private plane at an altitude of 1,000 feet to ascertain whether it contained marijuana plants. On the basis of this information, a search warrant was obtained

curtilage
Grounds or fields attached to a house.

and executed, and with the evidence against him, the defendant was convicted on drug charges. On appeal, the Supreme Court found that his privacy had not been violated.

This holding was expanded in 1989 in *Florida v. Riley*, when the Court ruled that police do not need a search warrant to conduct even low-altitude helicopter searches of private property.[32] The Court allowed Florida prosecutors to use evidence obtained by a police helicopter that flew 400 feet over a greenhouse in which defendants were growing marijuana plants. The Court said the search was constitutionally permissible because the flight was within airspace legally available to helicopters under federal regulations.

These cases illustrate how the concepts of curtilage and open fields have added significance in defining the scope of the Fourth Amendment in terms of the doctrine of plain view.

PLAIN TOUCH   If the police touch contraband, can they seize it legally? Is "plain touch" like "plain view"? In the 1993 case of *Minnesota v. Dickerson*, two Minneapolis police officers noticed the defendant acting suspiciously after leaving an apartment building they believed to be a crack house. The officers briefly stopped Timothy Dickerson to question him and conducted a pat-down search for weapons. The search revealed no weapons, but one officer felt a small lump in the pocket of Dickerson's nylon jacket. The lump turned out to be one-fifth of a gram of crack cocaine, and Dickerson was arrested and charged with drug possession. In its decision, the Court added to its "plain view" doctrine a "plain touch" or "plain feel" corollary. However, the pat-down must be limited to a search for weapons, and the officer may not extend the "feel" beyond that necessary to determine if it is a weapon.[33]

Although *Dickerson* created the plain feel doctrine, the Supreme Court limited its scope in *Bond v. United States*.[34] Here a federal border patrol agent boarded a bus near the Texas–Mexico border to check the immigration status of the passengers. As he was leaving the bus, he squeezed the soft luggage that passengers had placed in the overhead storage space. When he squeezed a canvas bag belonging to the defendant, he noticed that it contained a "brick-like" object. The defendant consented to a search of the bag, the agent discovered a "brick" of methamphetamine, and the defendant was charged with and convicted of possession. The court of appeals ruled that the agent's manipulation of the bag was not a search under the Fourth Amendment. On appeal, however, the Supreme Court held that the agent's manipulation of the bag violated the Fourth Amendment's rule against unreasonable searches. Personal luggage, according to the Court, is protected under the Fourth Amendment. The defendant had a privacy interest in his bag, and his right to privacy was violated by the police search.

Electronic Surveillance

The use of wiretapping to intercept conversations between parties has significantly affected police investigative procedures. Electronic devices allow people to listen to and record the private conversations of other people over telephones, through walls and windows, and even over long-distance phone lines. Using these devices, police are able to intercept communications secretly and obtain information related to criminal activity.

The oldest and most widely used form of electronic surveillance is wiretapping. With approval from the court and a search warrant, law enforcement officers place listening devices on telephones to overhear oral communications of suspects. Such devices are also often placed in homes and automobiles. The evidence collected is admissible and can be used in the defendant's trial.

The use of surveillance cameras and videos is growing. Some civil libertarians see them as a threat to personal privacy, but police view them as important law enforcement tools. Here, a surveillance video released during a Phoenix press conference on Tuesday, June 24, 2003, of Arizona Cardinals' Dennis McKinley (left) and Robert Lee puts them at the scene of a south Phoenix warehouse that was the site of a drug bust. McKinley and three other men were arrested as suspects in an investigation of a drug ring based in Phoenix.

D.M. AND R.L. SEEN TOGETHER AT WAREHOUSE ON 2/28/03

©AP Images/East Valley Tribune

CONCEPT SUMMARY 8.2

Warrantless Searches

Action	Scope of search
Stop and frisk	Pat-down of a suspect's outer garments.
Search incident to arrest	Full body search after a legal arrest.
Automobile search	If probable cause exists, full search of car including driver, passengers, and closed containers found in trunk. Search must be reasonable.
Consent search	Warrantless search of person or place is justified if the suspect knowingly and voluntarily consents to a search.
Plain view	Suspicious objects seen in plain view can be seized without a warrant.
Electronic surveillance	Material can be seized electronically without a warrant if the suspect has no expectation of privacy.

Many citizens believe that electronic eavesdropping through hidden microphones, radio transmitters, telephone taps, and bugs represents a grave threat to personal privacy.[35] Although the use of such devices is controversial, the police are generally convinced of their value in investigating criminal activity. However, opponents believe that these techniques are often used beyond their lawful intent to monitor political figures, harass suspects, or investigate cases involving questionable issues of national security.

In response to concerns about invasions of privacy, the U.S. Supreme Court has increasingly limited the use of electronic eavesdropping in the criminal justice system. In *Katz v. United States* (1967), the Court ruled that when federal agents eavesdropped on a phone conversation using a listening device that could penetrate the walls of a phone booth, they had conducted an illegal search and seizure.[36] The *Katz* doctrine is usually interpreted to mean that the government must obtain a court order if it wishes to listen in on conversations in which the parties have a reasonable expectation of privacy, such as in their own homes or on the telephone. Meanwhile, public utterances or actions are fair game. *Katz* concluded that electronic eavesdropping is a search, even though there is no actual trespass. Therefore, it is unreasonable, and a warrant is needed.

More sophisticated devices have come into use in recent years. A pen register, for instance, is a mechanical device that records the numbers dialed on a telephone. Trap and tracer devices ascertain the number from which calls are placed to a particular telephone. Law enforcement agencies also obtain criminal evidence through electronic communication devices, such as e-mail, video surveillance, and computer data transmissions, and even through thermal imaging devices that can do infrared searches of dwellings. The Supreme Court has examined the impact of these devices on privacy and in some instances has limited the ability of law enforcement agencies to use them for investigatory purposes. The future development of technology that can go around, through, and between walls should create new areas of conflict between the police who want to use them to observe criminals and the courts that are interested in maintaining personal privacy. The Law in Review feature examines the important case of *Kyllo v. United States*, which deals with electronic snooping and helps set the boundaries for this future clash.

For more about warrantless searches, see Concept Summary 8.2.

ThomsonNOW Improve your grade on the exam with Personalized Study! For reinforcement resources and a mastery check of warrantless searches, go to www.thomsonedu.com/thomsonnow.

Kyllo v. United States

In 1991, Agent William Elliott of the U.S. Department of the Interior came to suspect that marijuana was being grown in Danny Kyllo's home, which was part of a triplex on Rhododendron Drive in Florence, Oregon. Indoor marijuana growth typically requires high-intensity lamps. In order to determine whether an amount of heat was emanating from Kyllo's home consistent with the use of such lamps, at 3:20 A.M. on January 16, 1992, Agent Elliott and Dan Haas used an Agema Thermovision 210 thermal imager to scan the triplex. Thermal imagers detect infrared radiation, which virtually all objects emit but which is not visible to the naked eye. The scan of Kyllo's home took only a few minutes and was performed from the passenger seat of Agent Elliott's vehicle across the street from the front of the house and also from the street in back of the house. The scan showed that the roof over the garage and a side wall of Kyllo's home were relatively hot compared to the rest of the home and substantially warmer than neighboring homes in the triplex. Agent Elliott concluded that Kyllo was using halide lights to grow marijuana in

his house, which indeed he was. Based on tips from informants, utility bills, and the thermal imaging, a federal magistrate judge issued a warrant authorizing a search of Kyllo's home, and the agents found an indoor growing operation involving more than 100 plants. After Kyllo was indicted on a federal drug charge, he unsuccessfully tried to suppress the evidence seized from his home and then entered a conditional guilty plea. On appeal, the Ninth Circuit Court upheld the conviction, ruling that use of the thermal imaging was permissible on the grounds that Kyllo had shown no subjective expectation of privacy because he had made no attempt to conceal the heat escaping from his home. Even if he had, the appeals court ruled, there was no objectively reasonable expectation of privacy because the thermal imager did not expose any intimate details of Kyllo's life, only amorphous hot spots on his home's exterior.

On further appeal, the U.S. Supreme Court reversed that decision. The Court ruled that without a warrant, the use of thermal imaging (infrared) scanners to look at homes for evidence of crimes is

◆ ARREST

The arrest power of the police involves taking a person into custody in accordance with lawful authority and holding that person to answer for a violation of the criminal law. Police officers have complete law enforcement responsibility and unrestricted powers of arrest in their jurisdictions. Private citizens also have the right to make an arrest, generally when a crime is committed in their presence.

An arrest occurs when a police officer takes a person into custody or deprives a person of freedom for having allegedly committed a criminal offense. The police stop unlimited numbers of people each day for a variety of reasons, so the time when an arrest occurs may be hard to pinpoint. Some persons are stopped for short periods of questioning, others are informally detained and released, and still others are formally placed under arrest. However, a legal arrest occurs when the following conditions exist:

◆   The police officer believes that sufficient legal evidence—that is, probable cause—exists that a crime is being or has been committed and intends to restrain the suspect.

◆   The police officer deprives the individual of freedom.

◆   The suspect believes that he is in the custody of the police officer and cannot voluntarily leave. He has lost his liberty.

Arrests can be initiated when an officer observes a crime or otherwise develops sufficient probable cause to take a suspect into custody or when an arrest warrant, a writ that directs the police to bring the named person before the court, has been issued. In either case, an arrest must be based on probable cause that the person has committed or is attempting to commit a crime.

unconstitutional. This landmark decision suggests that the warrantless use of other high-tech gear that reduces privacy in the home would also be disallowed.

Kyllo was an unusual case because the majority included the most conservative judges (Thomas and Scalia) and the most liberal (Ginsburg, Breyer, and Souter), who expressed fears that technology has advanced to a point that it threatens the privacy of average citizens: "The question we confront today is what limits there are upon this power of technology to shrink the realm of guaranteed privacy. To withdraw protection of this minimum expectation would be to permit police technology to erode the privacy guaranteed by the Fourth Amendment." Rejecting the government's case that the use of scanners does not require a warrant because the thing it looks at is in public view, the majority stated the following:

> We think that obtaining by sense-enhancing technology any information regarding the interior of the home that could not otherwise have been obtained without physical "intrusion into a constitutionally protected area" constitutes a search—at least where (as here) the technology in question is not in general public use.

Critical Thinking

1. If you were a Supreme Court Justice, what would you have decided in the *Kyllo* case? Were there actually real damage and invasion of privacy caused by "looking" into a suspect's house with a heat-sensing device? Was the Court being oversensitive to the defendant's privacy rights?

2. Would it be different if the agents had listened in with a recording device that could "hear" through walls? Do you distinguish between sight and sound?

InfoTrac College Edition Research

To read an extensive analysis of *Kyllo* and the issue of electronic eavesdropping, go to Orin S. Kerr, "The Fourth Amendment and New Technologies: Constitutional Myths and the Case for Caution," *Michigan Law Review* 102 (2004): 801–88.

Source: *Kyllo v. United States*, 533 U.S. 27 (2001).

The decision to arrest is often made by the police officer during contact with the suspect and does not rely on a warrant being used. In the case of a felony, most jurisdictions provide that a police officer may arrest a suspect without a warrant when probable cause exists, even though the officer was not present when the offense was committed. The arrest can be based on statements made by victims and witnesses. In the case of a misdemeanor, probable cause and the officer's presence at the time of the offense are required to make an arrest in most offenses; this is referred to as the in presence requirement. In some jurisdictions, the in presence requirement has been waived for some crimes such as domestic violence in order to better protect victims from further abuse.

As a general rule, if the police make an arrest without a warrant, the arrestee must be promptly brought before a magistrate for a probable cause hearing. The U.S. Supreme Court dealt with the meaning of *promptly* in the 1991 case of *Riverside County* v. *McLaughlin*.[37] The Court said that the police may detain an individual arrested without a warrant for up to 48 hours without a court hearing to determine whether the arrest was justified.

Arrest in Noncriminal Acts

Can police arrest someone for a noncriminal act such as a traffic violation? This issue was decided in the case of *Atwater et al. v. City of Lago Vista et al.*[38] Gail Atwater was stopped for failing to wear a seat belt as she drove her two children home from soccer practice in Lago Vista, near Austin, Texas. She unbuckled for just a moment, she said, to look for a toy that had fallen from the pickup truck onto the street. The Lago Vista patrolman pulled her over, berated her, and arrested her. Under Texas law, she had committed a misdemeanor. Atwater subsequently was found to be driving without a license and to lack proof of insurance.

ThomsonNOW˙ Improve your grade on the exam with Personalized Study! For reinforcement resources and a mastery check of arrest, go to www.thomsonedu.com/ thomsonnow.

The standard for determining whether a police action was reasonable under the circumstances in this case is difficult. Some might argue that Atwater's traffic violation was not a breach of the peace, but others might suggest that Atwater's arrest was legal because she had violated a state statute. Whatever your opinion is, in April 2001 the U.S. Supreme Court upheld the right to arrest a suspect for a traffic violation.

◆ CUSTODIAL INTERROGATION

After a suspect is taken into custody, it is routine to question her about her involvement in the crime. The police may hope to find out about co-conspirators or even if the suspect was involved in similar crimes. This is a particularly unsettling time, and the arrestee may feel disoriented, alone, and afraid. Consequently, she may give police harmful information that can be used against her in a court of law. Exacerbating the situation is the fact that the interrogating officers may sometimes use extreme pressure to get suspects to talk or to name their accomplices. Because of these concerns, the Supreme Court has issued rulings that protect criminal suspects from police intimidation, the most important of which was set down in the 1966 case of *Miranda v. Arizona*.

The *Miranda* Warning

In the landmark case of *Miranda v. Arizona* (1966), the Supreme Court held that the police must give the *Miranda* warning to a person in custody before questioning begins.[39] Suspects in custody must be told that they have the following rights:

◆   They have the right to remain silent.

◆   If they decide to make a statement, the statement can and will be used against them in a court of law.

◆   They have the right to have an attorney present at the time of the interrogation, or they will have an opportunity to consult with an attorney.

◆   If they cannot afford an attorney, one will be appointed for them by the state.

Some suspects choose to remain silent, and because oral as well as written statements are admissible in court, police officers often do not elicit any statements without making certain that a defense attorney is present. If an accused decides to answer any questions, he or she may also stop at any time and refuse to answer further questions.

A suspect's constitutional rights under *Miranda* can be given up (waived). A suspect can choose to talk to the police or sign a confession. However, for the waiver to be effective, the state must first show that it was voluntary and that the defendant was aware of all of his *Miranda* rights. People who cannot understand the *Miranda* warning because of their age, mental handicaps, or language problems may not be legally questioned absent an attorney. If they can understand their rights, they may be questioned.[40]

The purpose of the Miranda *rule is to protect criminal defendants during police interrogations, even if it means dismissing cases involving patently guilty people because of procedural error or mistake. In one such case, a group of boys were wrestling near a canal when one of them, 5-year-old Jordan Payne, fell into the water and drowned. Broward County, Florida, police investigators zeroed in on Gorman Roberts, a mentally challenged 17-year-old, who admitted his involvement soon after he was read his* Miranda *rights. But in one of dozens of similar Broward County cases, including several high-profile murders, the manslaughter conviction against Roberts was tossed out by an appellate court because the* Miranda *rights form used by the sheriff's office failed to advise that defendants had the right to an attorney during police questioning, not just before the interrogation began.*

Once the suspect asks for an attorney, all questioning must stop until the attorney is present. And if the criminal suspect has invoked his or her *Miranda* rights, police officials cannot reinitiate interrogation in the absence of counsel even if the accused has consulted with an attorney in the meantime.[41] However, even if the suspect has invoked his *Miranda* rights and demanded an attorney, the police can question the offender about another separate crime (as long as they give the *Miranda* warning for the second crime as well). For example, a person is arrested on burglary charges and requests an attorney. The next day, police question him about a murder after reading the suspect his *Miranda* rights. He decides to waive his rights and confesses to the murder without a lawyer being present. The murder confession would be legal even though the suspect had requested an attorney in the burglary case because they are two separate legal matters.[42]

The *Miranda* Rule Today

The Supreme Court has used case law to define the boundaries of the *Miranda* warning since its inception. Although statements made by a suspect who was not given the *Miranda* warning or received it improperly cannot be used against him in a court of law, it is possible to use illegally gained statements and the evidence they produce in some well-defined instances:

◆ If a defendant perjures himself, evidence obtained in violation of the *Miranda* warning can be used by the government to impeach his testimony during trial.[43]

◆ At trial, the testimony of a witness is permissible even though her identity was revealed by the defendant in violation of the *Miranda* rule.[44]

◆ Initial errors by police in getting statements do not make subsequent statements inadmissible. A subsequent *Miranda* warning that is properly given can cure the condition that made the initial statements inadmissible.[45] However, if police intentionally mislead suspects by questioning them before giving them a *Miranda* warning, their statements made after the warning is given are inadmissable in court. The "*Miranda* rule would be frustrated were the police permitted to undermine its meaning and effect."[46]

◆ A voluntary statement given in the absence of a *Miranda* warning can be used to obtain evidence that can be used at trial. Failure to give the warning does not make seizure of evidence illegal per se.[47]

◆ The admissions of mentally impaired defendants can be admitted in evidence as long as the police acted properly and there is a preponderance of the evidence that they understood the meaning of *Miranda*.[48]

◆ The erroneous admission of a coerced confession at trial can be ruled a harmless error that would not automatically result in overturning a conviction.[49] The Supreme Court has also ruled that in some instances the *Miranda* warning may not have to be given before a suspect is questioned and has also narrowed the scope of *Miranda*—for example, by restricting with whom a suspect may ask to consult.

◆ The *Miranda* warning applies only to the right to have an attorney present. The suspect cannot demand to speak to a priest, probation officer, or any other official.[50]

◆ A suspect can be questioned in the field without a *Miranda* warning if the information the police seek is needed to protect public safety. For example, in an emergency, suspects can be asked where they hid their weapons.[51] This is known as the **public safety doctrine**.

◆ Suspects need not be aware of all the possible outcomes of waiving their rights for the *Miranda* warning to be considered properly given.[52]

◆ An attorney's request to see the defendant does not affect the validity of the defendant's waiver of the right to counsel. Police misinformation to an attorney does not affect waiver of *Miranda* rights.[53] For example, a suspect's statements may be used if they are given voluntarily even though his family has hired an attorney and the statements were made before the attorney arrived. Only the suspect can request an attorney, not his friends or family.

◆ A suspect who makes an ambiguous reference to an attorney during questioning, such as "Maybe I should talk to an attorney," is not protected under *Miranda*. The police may continue their questioning.[54]

Read the full text of the *Miranda v. Arizona* opinion at FindLaw.com. You can reach it by going to the Siegel/Senna Introduction to Criminal Justice 11e website: www.thomsonedu.com/criminaljustice/siegel.

public safety doctrine
The principle that a suspect can be questioned in the field without a *Miranda* warning if the information the police seek is needed to protect public safety.

♦   Failure to give a suspect a *Miranda* warning is not illegal unless the case becomes a criminal issue. In *Chavez v. Martinez,* the Supreme Court ruled that a *Miranda* warning applies only to criminal matters.[55] While Oliverio Martinez was being treated for gunshot wounds received during a fight with police, he was interrogated without a *Miranda* warning being administered by a patrol supervisor and admitted to having engaged in criminal acts. He was never charged with a crime, and his answers were never used against him in any criminal proceeding. Later, however, Martinez filed a civil rights suit charging that his Fifth Amendment and Fourteenth Amendment rights had been violated by the coercive questioning. The Court ruled that Martinez could not sue because a police officer is entitled to immunity from lawsuits if his alleged misconduct did not violate a constitutional right and that the interrogation did not violate a constitutional right because the confession was never used in a criminal case. The Court stated that a criminal case at the very least requires the initiation of legal proceedings, and police questioning by itself does not constitute such a case. Statements compelled by police interrogation may not be used against a defendant in a criminal case, but it is not until such use that the self-incrimination clause is violated.

The Impact of *Miranda*

After *Miranda* was decided, law enforcement officials became concerned that the Supreme Court had gone too far in providing procedural protections to defendants. Subsequent research indicates that the decision has had little effect on the number of confessions obtained by the police and that it has not affected the rate of convictions.[56] It now seems apparent that the police formerly relied too heavily on confessions to prove a defendant's guilt. Other forms of evidence, such as witness statements, physical evidence, and expert testimony, have generally proved adequate to win the prosecution's case. Blaming *Miranda* for increased crime rates in the 1970s and 1980s now seems problematic given that rates are down and *Miranda* is still the law.[57]

Critics have called the *Miranda* decision incomprehensible and difficult to administer. How can one tell when a confession is truly voluntary or when it has been produced by pressure and coercion? Aren't all police interrogations essentially coercive?[58] These criticisms aside, the Supreme Court is unlikely to ever reverse course. In the critical case *Dickerson v. United States,* the Court made it clear that the *Miranda* ruling is here to stay and has become enmeshed in the prevailing legal system.[59] Not surprisingly, police administrators who in the past might have been wary of the restrictions forced by *Miranda* now favor its use.[60] One recent survey found that nearly 60 percent of police chiefs believe that the *Miranda* warning should be retained, and the same number report that abolishing *Miranda* would change the way the police function.[61] To ensure that *Miranda* rules are being followed, many departments now routinely videotape interrogations, although research shows that this procedure is not a surefire cure for police intimidation.[62]

With the ongoing war on terrorism, law enforcement officers may find themselves in unique situations involving national security and forced to make an immediate decision as to whether the *Miranda* rule applies.

♦ PRETRIAL IDENTIFICATION

After the accused is arrested, he or she is ordinarily brought to the police station, where the police list the possible criminal charges. At the same time, they obtain other information, such as a description of the offender and the circumstances of the offense, for booking purposes. The **booking** process is a police administrative procedure in which generally the date and time of the arrest are recorded; arrangements are made for bail, detention, or removal to court; and any other information needed for identification is obtained. The defendant may be fingerprinted, photographed, and required to participate in a lineup.

---

www The Library of Congress contains more than 121 million items. Some of these are designated "treasures." One of them is Chief Justice Earl Warren's handwritten notes on the *Miranda* case. You can view these notes by going to the Siegel/Senna Introduction to Criminal Justice 11e website: www.thomsonedu .com/criminaljustice/siegel.

ThomsonNOW Improve your grade on the exam with Personalized Study! For reinforcement resources and a mastery check of custodial interrogation, go to www. thomsonedu.com/thomsonnow.

booking
The administrative record of an arrest, listing the offender's name, address, physical description, date of birth, employer, time of arrest, offense, and name of arresting officer; it also includes photographing and fingerprinting of the offender.

In a **lineup**, a suspect is placed in a group for the purpose of being viewed and identified by a witness. Lineups are one of the primary means that the police have of identifying suspects. Others are show-ups, which occur at the crime scene, and photo displays or mug shots of possible suspects. In accordance with the U.S. Supreme Court decisions in *United States v. Wade* (1967) and *Kirby v. Illinois* (1972), the accused has the right to have counsel present at this postindictment lineup or identification procedure.[63]

In the *Wade* case, the Supreme Court held that a defendant has a right to counsel if the lineup takes place after the suspect has been formally charged with a crime. This decision was based on the Court's belief that the postindictment lineup procedure is a critical stage of the criminal justice process. In contrast, the suspect does not have a comparable right to counsel at a pretrial lineup when a complaint or indictment has not been issued. Right to counsel does not apply until judicial proceedings have begun and the defendant is formally charged with a crime. When the right to counsel is violated, the evidence of any pretrial identification must be excluded from the trial.

One of the most difficult legal issues in this area is determining if the identification procedure is suggestive and consequently in violation of the due process clause of the Fifth and Fourteenth amendments.[64] In *Simmons v. United States* (1968), the Supreme Court said that "The primary evil to be avoided is a very substantial likelihood of irreparable misidentification."[65] In its decision in *Neil v. Biggers* (1972), the Court established the following general criteria to judge the suggestiveness of a pretrial identification procedure:

◆ The opportunity of the witness to view the criminal at the time of the crime.

◆ The degree of attention by the witness and the accuracy of the prior description by the witness.

◆ The level of certainty demonstrated by the witness.

◆ The length of time between the crime and the confrontation.[66]

Weighing all these factors, the Court determines the substantial likelihood of misidentification.

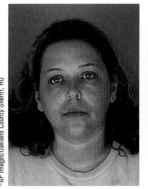

Michael Carter and his wife Aretha Carter, suspected of robbing two banks and using their four children as a cover for their getaways. The Carters were arraigned on August 1, 2006, in two separate courts in Oakland, California, and were charged with armed robbery, bank robbery, and attempted armed robbery. The courts protect criminal defendants during pretrial identifications because once an identification is made early in a case it will provide powerful testimony later during trial. Witnesses can be shown photos of the suspects repeatedly until the suspects' faces and identities become embedded in their psyche, regardless of whether they are the actual culprits. Do you think you would remember the Carter's once shown their photos? Would such viewing bias your judgement?

◆ THE EXCLUSIONARY RULE

No review of the legal aspects of policing would be complete without a discussion of the **exclusionary rule**, the principal means used to restrain police conduct. The Fourth Amendment guarantees individuals the right to be secure in their persons, homes, papers, and effects against unreasonable searches and seizures. The exclusionary rule provides that all evidence obtained by illegal searches and seizures is inadmissible in criminal trials. Similarly, it excludes the use of illegal confessions under Fifth Amendment prohibitions.

For many years, evidence obtained by unreasonable searches and seizures that consequently should have been considered illegal was admitted by state and federal governments in criminal trials. The only criteria for admissibility were whether the evidence was incriminating and whether it would assist the judge or jury in ascertaining the innocence or guilt of the defendant. How the evidence was obtained was unimportant; its admissibility was determined by its relevance to the criminal case.

In 1914, however, the rules on the admissibility of evidence underwent a change of direction when the Supreme Court decided the case of *Weeks v. United States*.[67] The defendant, Freemont Weeks, was accused by federal law enforcement authorities of using the mail for illegal purposes. After his arrest, the home in which Weeks was staying was searched without a valid search

lineup
Placing a suspect in a group for the purpose of his or her being viewed and identified by a witness.

exclusionary rule
The principle that prohibits using illegally obtained evidence in a trial.

warrant. Evidence in the form of letters and other materials was found in his room and admitted at the trial. Weeks was then convicted of the federal offense based on the incriminating evidence. On appeal, the Supreme Court held that evidence obtained by unreasonable search and seizure must be excluded in a federal criminal trial.

Thus, for the first time, the Court held that the Fourth Amendment barred the use of evidence obtained through illegal search and seizure in a federal prosecution. With this ruling, the Court established the exclusionary rule. The rule was based not on legislation but on judicial decision making. Can the criminal go free because the constable blunders? That became the question.

In 1961 the Supreme Court made the exclusionary rule applicable to the state courts in the landmark decision of *Mapp v. Ohio.* In *Mapp*, police officers forcibly searched a home while using a fake warrant. The Court held that although the search had turned up contraband, it violated the Fourth Amendment's prohibition against unreasonable searches and seizures, so the illegally seized evidence could not be used in court. Justice Tom Clark, delivering the majority opinion of the Court, made clear the importance of this constitutional right in the administration of criminal justice:

> There are those who say, as did Justice [then Judge Benjamin] Cardozo, that under our constitutional exclusionary doctrine "[t]he criminal is to go free because the constable has blundered." In some cases this will undoubtedly be the result. But . . . there is another consideration—the imperative of judicial integrity. . . . The criminal goes free, if he must, but it is the law that sets him free. Nothing can destroy a government more quickly than its failure to observe its own laws, or worse its disregard of the charter of its own existence.[68]

Read the full text of the *Mapp v. Ohio* decision at FindLaw.com. You can reach it by going to the Siegel/Senna Introduction to Criminal Justice 11e website: www.thomsonedu.com/criminaljustice/siegel.

Current Status

In the 1980s, a more conservative U.S. Supreme Court gradually began to limit the scope of the exclusionary rule. It has created three major exceptions:

1. *Independent source exception.* This rule allows admission of evidence that has been discovered by means wholly independent of any constitutional violation. So if police enter a drug dealer's home with an arrest warrant and while arresting him illegally search for and seize evidence such as drug paraphernalia, the illegally seized material may be allowed in court if, independently, a warrant had been issued to search the apartment for the same evidence but had not yet arrived at the scene.

2. *Good faith exception.* In *United States v. Leon* (1984), the Court ruled that evidence seized by police relying on a warrant issued by a detached and neutral magistrate can be used in a court proceeding, even if the judge who issued the warrant may have erred in drawing up the document.[69] In this case, the Court articulated a **good faith exception** to the exclusionary rule: Evidence obtained with a less than adequate search warrant may be admissible in court if the police officers acted in good faith when obtaining court approval for their search. However, deliberately misleading a judge or using a warrant that the police know is unreasonably deficient would be grounds to invoke the exclusionary rule. Although prosecutors initially applauded the *Leon* decision and defense lawyers feared that police would be inclined to secure warrants from sympathetic judges, both groups agree that *Leon* has had little practical effect on the processing of criminal cases. Further, most experts believe that no important data exist to prove that the exclusionary rule has had a direct impact on police behavior. In a subsequent case, *Arizona v. Evans*, the Court ruled that the exclusionary rule was designed as a means of deterring police misconduct, not to punish police for honest mistakes; it does not apply when they have acted in objectively reasonable reliance on an apparently valid warrant but later find out it was technically faulty.[70]

good faith exception
The principle that evidence may be used in a criminal trial even though the search warrant used to obtain it was technically faulty, as long as the police acted in good faith when they sought the warrant from a judge.

3. *Inevitable discovery rule.* This rule holds that evidence obtained through an unlawful search or seizure is admissible in court if it can be established, to a very high degree of probability, that police investigation would be expected to lead to the discovery of the evidence. In the case that established the rule, *Nix v. Williams*, police illegally interrogated a suspect and found the location of his victim's body. The evidence obtained was allowed at trial when the Court ruled that because the body was lying in plain sight and many police officers were searching for the body, it would have been obtained anyway even without the information provided by the illegal interrogation; this is now referred to as the **inevitable discovery rule**.[71]

In these and other cases, the Supreme Court has made it easier for the police to conduct searches of criminal suspects and their possessions and then use the seized evidence in court proceedings. The Court has indicated that, as a general rule, the protection afforded the individual by the Fourth Amendment may take a backseat to concerns about public safety if criminal actions pose a clear threat to society.

The Future of the Exclusionary Rule

Should the exclusionary rule be retained? Those who favor retention of the exclusionary rule believe it is justified because it deters illegal searches and seizures. However, the rule appears to result in relatively few case dismissals.

Yet the public wants to be protected from overzealous police officers and are concerned with reports that police routinely violate suspects' rights when searching for evidence. Jon Gould and Stephen Mastrofski made direct observations of police searches in a medium-sized U.S. city and found that nearly one-third of searches performed were unconstitutional and that almost none of these illegal searches were recognized as such by the courts. Surprisingly, the majority of illegal searches were made by a relatively small number of otherwise conscientious officers who may have become overzealous in their attempts to enforce the municipality's crackdown on drug offenders.[72]

Supporters believe the rule is fundamentally sound and can be justified on the basis of such legal principles as checks and balances and separation of power. When agents of the executive branch (the police) disregard or sidestep the terms of court-issued search warrants, the judicial branch can respond by overruling the misbehavior. Judges can also react when executive branch prosecutors attempt to introduce illegally seized evidence in court.[73] This power is especially important for warrantless searches because the judge is not on the scene when a search takes place and becomes aware of the circumstances surrounding the search only when prosecutors are in court seeking to present the evidence that the police acquired. The rule gives the judge the opportunity to correct executive branch excesses before they can influence the outcome of the proceedings.[74]

How can the rule be improved? Suggested approaches to dealing with violations of the exclusionary rule include criminal prosecution of police officers who violate constitutional rights, internal police control, civil lawsuits against state or municipal police officers, and federal lawsuits against the government under the Federal Tort Claims Act.

Law professor Donald Dripps has derived a novel approach for modifying the exclusionary rule.[75] The contingent exclusionary rule would apply when a judge who finds police testimony questionable concludes that the release of the guilty would be unpleasant and unwarranted. Instead of excluding the evidence, she could request that the prosecution or police pay a fee, similar in form to a fine, to use the evidence in court. Exclusion of the evidence would be contingent on the failure of the police department to pay the damages set by the court. Thereby, the judge could uphold the Constitution without freeing the guilty.

inevitable discovery rule
The principle that evidence can be used in court even though the information that led to its discovery was obtained in violation of the *Miranda* rule if a judge finds it would have been discovered anyway by other means or sources.

To learn more about the exclusionary rule, read C. Maureen Stinger's "*Arizona v. Evans*: Adapting the Exclusionary Rule to Advancing Computer Technology." You can reach it by going to the Siegel/Senna Introduction to Criminal Justice 11e website: www.thomsonedu.com/criminaljustice/siegel.

PERSPECTIVES ON JUSTICE

Crime Control

Throughout the past decade, the U.S. Congress has tried to loosen the admissibility of evidence from illegal searches and seizures. Curtailing the use of the exclusionary rule would widen the scope of justice and favor the crime control perspective.

The contingent exclusionary rule would force the prosecution to decide whether justice was worth the damages.

The United States is the only nation that applies an exclusionary rule to protect individuals from illegal searches and seizures. Whether the U.S. Supreme Court or legislative bodies adopt any further significant changes to the rule remains to be seen. However, like the *Miranda* warning, the exclusionary rule has been incorporated in modern police procedure and seems to be a permanent fixture.

ETHICAL CHALLENGES IN CRIMINAL JUSTICE: A WRITING ASSIGNMENT

Write an essay addressing the following issue: For much of the past three decades, the U.S. Supreme Court has given police more power to stop motorists, search homes, and put defendants in jail. The Justices seem intent on giving police the power to crack down on crime and expand their power. Considering the cases discussed in this chapter, do you believe that the Court will eventually limit the reach of the exclusionary rule to the extent that it is essentially neutralized, or has it become an essential part of the U.S. legal system?

Doing Research on the Web

To read more about the exclusionary rule, go to FindLaw.com. You can reach it by going to the Siegel/Senna Introduction to Criminal Justice 11e website: www.thomsonedu.com/criminaljustice/siegel.

Find out more about the future of *Miranda* and the exclusionary rule at the Federalist Society website. You can reach it by going to the Siegel/Senna Introduction to Criminal Justice 11e website: www.thomsonedu.com/criminaljustice/siegel.

See what the American Civil Liberties Union has to say about the exclusionary rule. You can read this essay by going to the Siegel/Senna Introduction to Criminal Justice 11e website: www.thomsonedu.com/criminaljustice/siegel.

SUMMARY

◆ Law enforcement officers use many different investigatory techniques to detect and apprehend criminal offenders, including searches, electronic eavesdropping, interrogation, informants, surveillance, and witness identification procedures.

◆ Over the past three decades, the U.S. Supreme Court has placed constitutional limitations on the police ability to conduct investigations.

◆ A more conservative Court may now be giving police more leeway. A recent case allows police entering homes with a warrant not to have to knock and wait for an answer.

◆ Under interpretations of the Fourth Amendment, police are required to use warrants to conduct searches except in some clearly defined situations.

◆ Police are required to have probable cause to obtain a warrant.

◆ Many warrants are obtained with the help of informants. The Court has ruled that the informant's information must, considering the totality of the circumstances, be valid and factual.

◆ The exceptions to the search warrant rule include searches of automobiles used in a crime, stop and frisk, searches incident to an arrest, consent searches, and searches of material in plain view.

◆ The Supreme Court now allows a search to be conducted if only one party consents. However, a search cannot be conducted if one party allows a search and another party living in the same premises refuses.

♦ In the future, the Court will have to deal with the use of technology to conduct "virtual searches." It recently ruled that law enforcement agents cannot "peek" into a person's home with sensors unless they have a warrant.

♦ If police violate the legal rule controlling search and seizure, then the evidence they collect cannot be used in court.

♦ Through the *Miranda* rule, the Supreme Court established a procedure required for all custodial interrogations that focuses on the need to warn criminal suspects of their right to remain silent and be advised by an attorney.

♦ Many issues concerning *Miranda* continue to be litigated. The Supreme Court has shaped *Miranda* protections, increasing them in some instances and reducing them in others.

♦ Statements made without a *Miranda* warning being given can now be used in court under some circumstances such as an emergency situation or to impeach a witness who is committing perjury.

♦ Lineups and other suspect identification practices have been subject to court review. Police cannot manipulate lineups. Defendants in postindictment lineups are entitled to the presence of their counsel.

♦ The exclusionary rule continues to be one of the most controversial issues in the criminal justice system. Even though the courts have curtailed its application in recent years, it still generally prohibits the admission of evidence obtained in violation of a defendant's constitutional rights.

♦ Some critics have called for the abolition of the exclusionary rule, but others believe that it can be successfully modified.

KEY TERMS

search warrant, 269
particularity, 270
probable cause, 270
hearsay evidence, 272
exigent, 273
hot pursuit, 273
threshold inquiry, 275

stop and frisk, 275
search incident to a lawful arrest, 276
bus sweep, 279
plain view doctrine, 280
curtilage, 281
public safety doctrine, 287

booking, 288
lineup, 289
exclusionary rule, 289
good faith exception, 290
inevitable discovery rule, 291

ThomsonNOW Maximize your study time by using ThomsonNOW's diagnostic study plan to help you review this chapter. The Study Plan will

♦ help you identify areas on which you should concentrate;

♦ provide interactive exercises to help you master the chapter concepts; and

♦ provide a post-test to confirm you are ready to move on to the next chapter.

CRITICAL THINKING QUESTIONS

1. Should obviously guilty persons go free because police originally arrested them with less than probable cause?

2. Should illegally seized evidence be excluded from trial, even though it is conclusive proof of a person's criminal acts?

3. Should a person be put in a lineup without the benefit of counsel?

4. Have criminals been given too many rights? Should courts be more concerned with the rights of the victims or the rights of offenders?

5. Can a search and seizure be reasonable if it is not authorized by a warrant?

6. What is the purpose of the *Miranda* warning?

7. What is a pretext traffic stop? Does it violate a citizen's civil rights?

NOTES

1. *Hudson v. Michigan,* No. 04–1360 (2006).
2. Mark I. Koffsky, "Choppy Waters in the Surveillance Data Stream: The Clipper Scheme and the Particularity Clause," *Berkeley Technology Law Journal* 9 (1994) (http://btlj.boalt.org/data/articles/9-1_spring-1994_koffsky.pdf).
3. 378 U.S. 108, 84 S.Ct. 1509, 12 L.Ed.2d 723 (1964).
4. 462 U.S. 213, 103 S.Ct. 2317, 76 L.Ed.2d 527 (1983).
5. *Alabama v. White,* 496 U.S. 325 (1990).
6. *Alabama v. White,* 496 U.S. 325, 326.
7. *Florida v. J. L.,* No. 98–1993 (2000).
8. *Kirk v. Louisiana,* No. 01–8419, U.S. Supreme Court, per curiam opinion, decided June 24, 2002.
9. *United States v. Arvizu,* No. 00–1519 (2002).
10. 392 U.S. 1, 88 S.Ct. 1868, 20 L.Ed.2d 899 (1968).
11. 120 S.Ct. 673 (2000).
12. 395 U.S. 752, 89 S.Ct. 2034, 23 L.Ed.2d 685 (1969).
13. 267 U.S. 132, 45 S.Ct. 280, 69 L.Ed.2d 543 (1925). See also James Rodgers, "Poisoned Fruit: Quest for Consistent Rule on Traffic Stop Searches," *American Bar Association Journal* 81 (1995): 50–51.
14. 456 U.S. 798, 102 S.Ct. 2157, 72 L.Ed.2d 572 (1982). See also Barry Latzer, "Searching Cars and Their Contents: *U.S. v. Ross,*" *Criminal Law Bulletin* 6 (1982): 220; Joseph Grano, "Rethinking the Fourth Amendment Warrant Requirements," *Criminal Law Review* 19 (1982): 603.
15. 440 U.S. 648, 99 S.Ct. 1391, 59 L.Ed.2d 660 (1979). See also Lance Rogers, "The Drunk-Driving Roadblock: Random Seizure or Minimal Intrusion?" *Criminal Law Bulletin* 21 (1985): 197–217.
16. No. 99–1030, U.S. Supreme Court, 2000–2001.
17. *Michigan v. Sitz,* 496 U.S. 444 (1990).
18. 434 U.S. 106, 98 S.Ct. 330, 54 L.Ed.2d 331 (1977).
19. *Maryland v. Wilson,* 65 U.S.L.W. 4124 (February 19, 1997).
20. *Ohio v. Robinette,* 117 S.Ct. 417 (1996).
21. *Whren v. United States,* 116 S.Ct. 1769 (1996); Mark Hansen, "Rousting Miss Daisy?" *American Bar Association Journal* 83 (1997): 22; *Wyoming v. Houghton,* 199 S.Ct. (1999).
22. 121 S.Ct. 1876, 149 L.Ed.2d 994 (2001).
23. 391 U.S. 543, 88 S.Ct. 1788, 20 L.Ed.2d 797 (1968).
24. 412 U.S. 218, 93 S.Ct. 2041, 36 L.Ed.2d 854 (1973).
25. *United States v. Matlock,* 415 U.S. 164 (1974).
26. *Georgia v. Randolph,* No. 04–1067 (2006).
27. *Florida v. Bostick,* 501 U.S. 429, 111 S.Ct. 2382, 115 L.Ed.2d 389 (1991).
28. 475 U.S. 106, 106 S.Ct. 960, 89 L.Ed.2d 81 (1986).
29. 480 U.S. 321, 107 S.Ct. 1149, 94 L.Ed.2d 347 (1987).
30. 466 U.S. 170, 104 S.Ct. 1735, 80 L.Ed.2d 214 (1984).
31. 476 U.S. 207, 106 S.Ct. 1809, 90 L.Ed.2d 210 (1986).
32. 488 U.S. 445, 109 S.Ct. 693, 102 L.Ed.2d 835 (1989).
33. 508 U.S. 366, 113 S.Ct. 2130, 124 L.Ed.2d 334 (1993).
34. *Bond v. United States,* 120 S.Ct. 1462 (2000).
35. Gary T. Marx, *Undercover: Police Surveillance in America* (Berkeley: University of California Press, 1988).
36. 389 U.S. 347, 88 S.Ct. 507, 19 L.Ed.2d 576 (1967).
37. 500 U.S. 44, 111 S.Ct. 1661, 114 L.Ed.2d 49 (1991).
38. No. 99–1408, April 24, 2001.
39. 384 U.S. 436, 86 S.Ct. 1602, 16 L.Ed.2d 694 (1966).
40. *Colorado v. Connelly,* 107 S.Ct. 515 (1986).
41. *Minnick v. Miss.,* 498 U.S. 46; 111 S.Ct. 486; 112 L.Ed. 2d. 489 (1990).
42. *Texas v. Cobb,* No. 99–1702 (2001).
43. *Harris v. New York,* 401 U.S. 222 (1971).
44. *Michigan v. Tucker,* 417 U.S. 433 (1974).
45. *Oregon v. Elstad,* 105 S.Ct. 1285 (1985).
46. *Missouri v. Seibert,* No. 02–1371 (2004).
47. *United States v. Patane,* No. 02–1183 (2004).
48. *Colorado v. Connelly,* 107 S.Ct. 515 (1986).
49. *Arizona v. Fulminante,* 499 U.S. 279, 111 S.Ct. 1246; 113 L.Ed. 2d. 302 (1991).
50. *Fare v. Michael C.,* 439 U.S. 1310 (1978).
51. *New York v. Quarles,* 104 S.Ct. 2626 (1984).
52. *Colorado v. Spring,* 107 S.Ct. 851 (1987).
53. *Moran v. Burbine,* 106 S.Ct. 1135 (1986).
54. *Davis v. United States,* 114 S.Ct. 2350 (1994).
55. *Chavez v. Martinez,* No. 01–1444, decided May 27, 2003.
56. Michael Wald and others, "Interrogations in New Haven: The Impact of *Miranda,*" *Yale Law Journal* 76 (1967): 1519. See also Walter Lippman, "*Miranda v. Arizona*—Twenty Years Later," *Criminal Justice Journal* 9 (1987): 241; Stephen J. Schulhofer, "Reconsidering *Miranda,*" *University of Chicago Law Review* 54 (1987): 435–461; Paul Cassell, "How Many Criminals Has *Miranda* Set Free?" *Wall Street Journal,* March 1, 1995, p. A12.
57. "Don't Blame *Miranda,*" *Washington Post,* December 2, 1988, p. A26. See also Scott Lewis, "*Miranda* Today: Death of a Talisman," *Prosecutor* 28 (1994): 18–25; Richard Leo, "The Impact of *Miranda* Revisited," *Journal of Criminal Law and Criminology* 86 (1996): 621–48.
58. Ronald Allen, "*Miranda's* Hollow Core," *Northwestern University Law Review* 100 (2006): 71–85.
59. *Dickerson v. United States,* 530 U.S. 428 (2000).
60. Victoria Time and Brian Payne, "Police Chiefs' Perceptions About *Miranda:* An Analysis of Survey Data," *Journal of Criminal Justice* 30 (2002): 77–86.
61. Ibid.
62. G. Daniel Lassiter, Jennifer Ratcliff, Lezlee Ware, and Clinton Irvin, "Videotaped Confessions: Panacea or Pandora's Box?" *Law & Policy* 28 (2006): 192–210.
63. 388 U.S. 218, 87 S.Ct. 1926, 18 L.Ed.2d 1149 (1967); 406 U.S. 682, 92 S.Ct. 1877, 32 L.Ed.2d 40 (1972).
64. Marvin Zalman and Larry Siegel, *Key Cases and Comments on Criminal Procedure* (St. Paul, Minn.: West, 1994).
65. 390 U.S. 377, 88 S.Ct. 967, 19 L.Ed.2d 1247 (1968).
66. 409 U.S. 188, 93 S.Ct. 375, 34 L.Ed.2d 401 (1972).
67. 232 U.S. 383, 34 S.Ct. 341, 58 L.Ed. 652 (1914).
68. *Mapp v. Ohio,* 367 U.S. 643 (1961).
69. 468 U.S. 897, 104 S.Ct. 3405, 82 L.Ed.2d 677 (1984).
70. *Arizona v. Evans,* 514 U.S. 260, 115 S.Ct. 1185, 131 L.Ed.2d 34 (1995).
71. *Nix v. Williams,* 104 S.Ct. 2501 (1984).
72. Jon Gould and Stephen Mastrofski, "Suspect Searches: Assessing Police Behavior Under the U.S. Constitution," *Criminology & Public Policy* 3 (2004): 315–62.
73. Timothy Lynch, *In Defense of the Exclusionary Rule* (Washington, D.C.: Cato Institute, Center for Constitutional Studies, 1998).
74. Ibid.
75. Donald Dripps, "The Case for the Contingent Exclusionary Rule," *American Criminal Law Review* 38 (2001): 1–47.

Courts and Adjudication

PART THREE

©Denver Rocky Mountain/Corbis Sygma

*A*lex Hunter was the district attorney of Boulder County, Colorado, when six-year-old JonBenet Ramsey was found murdered in her home in 1997. The case drew instant national attention because of the age of the victim, the fact that she was a beauty contest winner, and the many confusing aspects of the crime.

A great deal of pressure was placed on Hunter to prosecute Jon-Benet's parents for the murder. The media coverage was widespread, and the prosecutors would have liked to hand down indictments. But in the U.S. system of justice, an individual is innocent until proven guilty, and the government must be able to prove beyond a reasonable doubt that the defendant committed the crime. The results of DNA and lie detector tests raised serious doubts regarding the sufficiency of the evidence against the parents, and Hunter refused to indict the Ramseys. In 2006, John Mark Karr confessed to killing JonBenet, but DNA evidence indicated that he could not have committed the crime and he was not prosecuted. ◆

THE JONBENET RAMSEY murder is one of a number of notorious cases that the U.S. court system handles each year. In some instances, defendants receive the full course of rights and processes guaranteed by the U.S. Constitution. In others, the prosecutor curtails his or her actions for lack of evidence or because a plea bargain has been struck. The chapters in this section cover the court process. Chapter 9 reviews the structure of the courts and the role of the judge. Chapter 10 covers the prosecution and defense. Chapter 11 analyzes the pretrial stage, including bail and plea bargaining. Chapter 12 covers the process of the criminal trial and the legal rules that structure its process. Chapter 13 looks at criminal sentencing, including capital punishment.

The Courts and the Judiciary

Chapter Outline

Chapter Objectives

After reading this chapter, you should be able to:
1. Understand the state and federal court structure.
2. Know the differences between limited and general courts.
3. Recognize the function of the appellate court system.
4. Explain the various levels of federal courts.
5. Describe how a case gets to the U.S. Supreme Court.
6. Know the problems associated with case overload.
7. Discuss the duties of a judge.
8. Know what the Missouri Plan is.
9. Identify the different types of judicial selection.
10. Explain how technology is changing the trial process.

©April Saul/The Philadelphia Inquirer

*M*umia Abu-Jamal (born Wesley Cook on April 24, 1954) began his career as a journalist and broadcaster, winning a Peabody Award for his coverage of the pope's visit to the United States; he also became president of the Philadelphia Association of Black Journalists.[1] His life was turned upside down when he was charged with first-degree murder in the killing of Philadelphia police officer Daniel Faulkner, who had been shot during a routine traffic stop. According to prosecutors, Abu-Jamal, the driver's older brother, had observed the stop from across the street, approached Officer Faulkner, and shot him in the back. While Faulkner lay helpless, Abu-Jamal stood over him and shot him numerous times at close range, killing him instantly.

At trial, four eyewitnesses testified that they saw Abu-Jamal kill Faulkner, experts testified that the gun that killed Faulkner was Abu-Jamal's, and jurors heard that a wounded Abu-Jamal was found at the scene of the crime. He was convicted and sentenced to death. Despite the conviction, the case became a cause célèbre because supporters claim that Abu-Jamal was targeted and framed because of his radical political activities. He was denied a fair trial, they charge, because the prosecution hid evidence, intimidated witnesses, and illegally excused potential African American jurors.

Abu-Jamal has now been in prison for more than 20 years, and his future is still in doubt (though his death sentence was overturned in 2001). While serving time, Abu-Jamal completed B.A. and M.A. degrees and has made frequent radio broadcasts. The French made him an honorary citizen of Paris, and organizations including Amnesty International, Human Rights Watch, the European Parliament, and the Japanese Diet have demanded that he be awarded a new trial because of the problems in the original case. ◆

The Abu-Jamal case is but one of many controversial trials that must be decided by the court system. Within the confines of the court, those accused of crime (defendants) call on the tools of the legal system to provide them with a fair and just hearing, with the burden of proof resting on the state; crime victims ask the government to provide them with justice for the wrongs done them and the injuries they have suffered; and agents of the criminal justice system attempt to find solutions that benefit the victim, the defendant, and society in general. The court process is designed to provide an open and impartial forum for deciding the truth of the matter and reaching a solution that, although punitive, is fairly arrived at and satisfies the rule of law.

The court process must render fair, impartial justice in deciding the outcome of a conflict between criminal and victim, law enforcement agents and violators of the law, parent and child, the federal government and violators of governmental regulations, or other parties. Regardless of the issues involved, the court process must guarantee that hearings will be conducted under rules of procedure in an atmosphere of fair play and objectivity and that the outcome of the hearing will be clear. If the ground rules have been violated, the case may be taken to a higher appellate court, where the procedures of the original trial will be reexamined. If a violation of legal rights has occurred, the appellate court may deem the findings of the original trial improper and either order a new hearing or hold that some other remedy be provided.

The court is a complex social agency with many independent but interrelated subsystems—clerk, prosecutor, defense attorney, judge, and probation department—each having a role in the adjudicatory process. Ideally, the entire process, from filing the initial complaint to final sentencing of the defendant, is governed by precise rules of law designed to ensure fairness. No defendant tried before a U.S. court should suffer or benefit because of his or her personal characteristics, beliefs, or affiliations.

However, in today's crowded court system, such abstract goals are often impossible to achieve. Discretion accompanies defendants through every step of the process, determining what will happen to them and how their cases will be resolved. Discretion means that two people committing similar crimes will receive highly dissimilar treatment. For example, most people convicted of homicide receive a prison sentence, but about 4 percent receive probation as a sole sentence. More murderers get probation than the death penalty.[2]

The dual curses of overcrowding and underfunding have become standard features of the court system. The nation's court system is chronically underbudgeted, and recent economic downturns have not helped matters.[3] Tax cutting has become a U.S. way of life and has restricted the state and federal budgets that fund the courts. These constraints have a significant impact on the way that courts do justice. The U.S. court system is often the scene of accommodation and "working things out," instead of an arena for a vigorous criminal defense. **Plea negotiations/plea bargaining** and other nonjudicial alternatives, such as diversion, are far more common than the formal trial process.

◆ THE CRIMINAL COURT PROCESS

The U.S. court system has evolved over the years into an intricately balanced legal process that has recently come under siege because of the sheer numbers of cases it must consider and the ways in which it is forced to handle such overcrowding.

Overloaded court dockets have given rise to charges of "assembly-line justice," in which a majority of defendants are induced to plead guilty, jury trials are rare, and the speedy trial is highly desired but unattainable. Overcrowding

PERSPECTIVES ON JUSTICE

Noninterventionism

Such abstract goals as fairness can be impossible to reach in the crowded U.S. court system. The players in the system often seek accommodation, not a vigorous criminal defense. Plea negotiations and other nonjudicial alternatives, such as diversion, are far more common than the formal trial process. In a sense, caseload pressure interferes with due process and in many cases makes the court system an instrument of nonintervention.

plea negotiations/plea bargaining
Discussions between defense counsel and prosecution in which the accused agrees to plead guilty in exchange for certain considerations, such as reduced charges or a lenient sentence.

causes the poor to languish in detention while the wealthier go free on bail. An innocent person can be frightened into pleading guilty; conversely, a guilty person can be released because a trial has been delayed too long.[4] Whether providing more judges or new or enlarged courts will solve the problem of over-crowding remains to be seen. Trial alternatives such as mediation, diversion, and bail reform provide other avenues of possible relief. Making court management and administration more efficient is also seen as a step that might ease the congestion of the courts. The introduction of professional trial court managers—administrators, clerks, and judges with management skills—has had a significant influence on court efficiency.

♦ STATE COURT SYSTEMS

To house this complex process, each state maintains its own state court organization and structure. There are 50 state trial and appellate systems, with separate courts for the District of Columbia and the Commonwealth of Puerto Rico. Usually three (or more) separate court systems exist within each state jurisdiction. States are free to create as many courts as they wish, name courts what they like (in New York, felony courts are known as Supreme Courts!), and establish specialized courts that handle a single legal matter, such as drug courts and/or domestic courts. Consequently, no two court organizations are exactly alike. State courts handle a wide variety of cases and regulate numerous personal behaviors, ranging from homicide to property maintenance. The various state court systems are described below.

Courts of Limited Jurisdiction

Depending on the jurisdiction in which they are located, state **courts of limited jurisdiction** are known by a variety of names—municipal courts, county courts, district courts, and metropolitan courts—to mention but a few. The term derives from the fact that the jurisdiction of these courts is limited to minor or less serious civil and criminal cases.

    Courts of limited jurisdiction are restricted in the types of cases they may hear. Usually, they will handle misdemeanor criminal infractions, violations of municipal ordinances, traffic violations, and civil suits where the damages involve less than a certain amount of money (usually $1,000). In criminal matters, they hear misdemeanors such as shoplifting, disorderly conduct, or simple assault. Their sanctioning power is also limited. In criminal matters, punishments may be limited to fines, community sentencing, or incarceration in the county jail for up to a year. In addition to their trial work, limited-jurisdiction courts conduct arraignments, preliminary hearings, and bail hearings in felony cases (before they are transferred to superior courts).

    Some states separate limited courts into those that handle civil cases only and those that settle criminal cases. Included in the category of courts of limited jurisdiction are special courts, such as juvenile, family, and probate (divorce, estate issues, and custody) courts. State lawmakers may respond to a particular social problem, such as drug use, by creating specialized courts that focus on treatment and care for these special-needs offenders. One of the most common is the family or juvenile court, which handles custody cases, delinquency, and other issues involving children (juvenile courts will be discussed further in Chapter 17). Some recent types of specialty courts are discussed in the Analyzing Criminal Justice Issues feature.

    The nation's approximately 13,500 independent courts of limited jurisdiction are the ones most often accused of providing assembly-line justice. Because the matters they decide involve minor personal confrontations and conflicts—family disputes, divorces, landlord–tenant conflicts, barroom brawls—the rule of the day is "handling the situation" and resolving the dispute.

court of limited jurisdiction
A generic term referring to a court that has jurisdiction over misdemeanors and conducts preliminary investigations of felony charges.

The National Center for State Courts (NCSC) is an independent, nonprofit organization dedicated to the improvement of justice. NCSC activities include developing policies to enhance state courts, advancing state courts' interests within the federal government, fostering state court adaptation to future changes, securing sufficient resources for state courts, strengthening state court leadership, aiding state court collaboration, and providing a model for organizational administration. To reach the NSCS website, go to the Siegel/Senna Introduction to Criminal Justice 11e website: www.thomsonedu.com/criminaljustice/siegel.

Specialized Courts—Drugs and Mental Health

A growing phenomenon in the United States is the creation of specialty courts that focus on one type of criminal act—for example, drug courts and gun courts. All cases within the jurisdiction that involve this particular type of crime are funneled to the specialty court, where presumably they will get prompt resolution.

Drug Courts

The **drug court** movement began in Florida to address the growing problem of prison overcrowding due in large part to an influx of drug-involved offenders. Drug courts were created to have primary jurisdiction over cases involving substance abuse and drug trafficking. The aim is to place nonviolent first offenders into intensive treatment programs rather than place them in jail or prison. Today, there are more than 300 drug courts across 43 states, the District of Columbia, and Puerto Rico. Drug courts address the overlap between the public health threats of drug abuse and crime: Crimes are often drug related, and drug abusers are frequently involved with the criminal justice system. Drug courts provide an ideal setting to address these problems by linking the justice system with health services and drug treatment providers while easing the burden on the already overtaxed correctional system.

Although some recent research finds that drug courts may not be as effective as originally believed, research by Denise Gottfredson and her associates conducted in the Baltimore City Drug Treatment Court (BCDTC) found that drug courts did seem to work for reducing crime in a population of offenders who were severely drug addicted. In one study conducted with Lyn Exum, Gottfredson used a carefully designed experimental model in which cases were randomly sent either to the drug court or a traditional court. The researchers found that drug court judges actually impose harsher sentences but that they suspended these sentences conditional to compliance with the drug court regimen in drug testing and treatment and attending status hearings. Most importantly, within a 12-month period, 48 percent of drug treatment court clients were arrested for new offenses, compared to 64 percent of the people handled in traditional courts. Among the more serious cases heard, 32 percent of drug court clients versus 57 percent of controls were re-arrested. All things considered, defendants sentenced in a traditional court suffered re-arrest at a rate nearly three times that of drug treatment court clients.

This research finding is not unique. Although methodological issues often make analysis difficult, reviews of drug court success have found that on balance this approach can help reduce recidivism rates.

Mental Health Courts

Based largely on the organization of drug courts, mental health courts focus their attention on mental health treatment to help people with emotional problems reduce their chances of reoffending. By focusing on the need for treatment, along with providing supervision and support from the community, mental health courts provide a venue for those dealing with mental health issues to avoid the trauma of jail or prison, where they will have little if any access to treatment.

Although mental health courts tend to vary in their approach, most share a few basic operating procedures:

◆ Most demand active participation by the defendant.

◆ The participant must be diagnosed with a mental illness, and a direct link must be established between the illness and the crime committed.

◆ Intervention must occur quickly; individuals must be screened and referred to the program either immediately after arrest or within three weeks.

◆ Once in the program, participants are closely monitored by case managers.

Program supervisor Jeff Schultz (left) presents Brad Zeroni with his diploma after Zeroni completed the Polk County Adult Drug Court program in Des Moines, Iowa. Drug courts are now commonplace in the criminal justice system and appear to be an effective alternative to the traditional court model.

©AP Image/Steve Pope

- Most provide voluntary outpatient or inpatient mental health treatment, in the least-restrictive manner appropriate as determined by the court, that carries with it the possibility of dismissal of charges or reduced sentencing on successful completion of treatment.

- Centralized case management involves the consolidation of cases that include mentally ill or mentally disabled defendants (including probation violators) and the coordination of mental health treatment plans and social services, including life skills training, placement, health care, and relapse prevention for each participant who requires such services.

- Supervision of treatment plan compliance continues for a term not to exceed the maximum allowable sentence or probation for the charged or relevant offense, and, to the extent practicable, psychiatric care continues at the end of the supervised period.

Although programs vary, most require that defendants plead guilty in exchange for entering the program. After "guilt" is established, participants are sent to live in a residential treatment facility where, with help from counselors, they develop a treatment plan, which is rigorous at first and then gradually less restrictive if improvement is shown. Most programs involve the use of medication to help overcome symptoms of the individual's illness.

The mental health court concept seems beneficial, but it has encountered a few operational difficulties. It is difficult to get community support for programs and institutions treating mentally ill offenders, nor do residents want treatment centers to be located close to where they live—the "not in my neighborhood" syndrome. Most programs accept only the nonviolent mentally ill; those who are violence prone are still lost in the correctional system without receiving the proper treatment.

It is also difficult to assess the benefits of having specialized mental health courts. With other specialized courts, measuring offender improvement is relatively easy. For example, people sent to drug court programs must simply prove they can remain drug free. However, those involved with mental health court programs suffer from complex mental issues, and case managers must ensure that these individuals have gained control over their illness, which can be difficult to determine. A thorough evaluation of mental health courts in 20 jurisdictions conducted by the nonprofit Bazelon Center found the following:

- There is no single "model" of a mental health court; each court operates under its own, mostly unwritten rules and procedures and has its own way of addressing service issues.

- Many of the existing courts include practices that are unnecessarily burdensome to defendants, that make it harder for them to reintegrate into the community, and that may compromise their rights.

- Few of the courts are part of any comprehensive plan to address the underlying failure of the service system to reach and effectively address the needs of people at risk of arrest. Substantial numbers of mental health court participants are people who should not have been arrested in the first place. However, some courts are beginning to accept defendants who are more appropriate for such a program, such as people who have committed serious felonies.

The mental health court movement has prompted the development of juvenile mental health courts to treat troubled adolescents who have been accused of committing nonviolent crimes. Juvenile mental health court programs typically involve collaboration among the justice system, mental health professionals, and the parents of the young offender to devise a treatment plan to treat the child, helping him or her avoid the standard juvenile justice system process.

Critical Thinking

1. Do you believe that specialized courts are needed for other crime types, such as sex offenses and/or domestic violence?

2. Should a judge preside over a specialized court, or should it be administered by treatment personnel?

InfoTrac College Edition Research

To learn more about the drug court movement, use it as a subject guide on InfoTrac College Edition.

Sources: Robert Bernstein and Tammy Seltzer, "The Role of Mental Health Courts in System Reform," Bazelon Center (http://www.bazelon.org/issues/criminalization/publications/mentalhealthcourts/#_ftnref1); Bureau of Justice Assistance, "Mental Health Courts" (http://www.ojp.usdoj.gov/BJA/grant/mentalhealth.html), accessed on May 20, 2006; J. Scott Sanford and Bruce Arrigo, "Lifting the Cover on Drug Courts: Evaluation Findings and Policy Concerns," *International Journal of Offender Therapy and Comparative Criminology* 49 (2005): 239–59; John Goldkamp, "The Impact of Drug Courts," *Criminology & Public Policy* 2 (2003): 197–206; Denise Gottfredson, Stacy Najaka, and Brook Kearley, "Effectiveness of Drug Treatment Courts: Evidence from a Randomized Trial," *Criminology & Public Policy* 2 (2003): 171–97; Denise Gottfredson and Lyn Exum, "The Baltimore City Drug Treatment Court: One-Year Results from a Randomized Study," *Journal of Research in Crime & Delinquency* 39 (2002): 337–57.

Courts of General Jurisdiction

Approximately 2,000 **courts of general jurisdiction** exist in the United States, variously called felony, superior, supreme, county, or circuit courts. Courts of general jurisdiction handle the more serious felony cases (e.g., murder, rape, robbery) and civil cases where damages are over a specified amount, such as $10,000. Courts of general jurisdiction may also be responsible for reviewing cases on appeal from courts of limited jurisdiction. In some instances they will base their decision on a review of the transcript of the case, whereas in others they can actually grant a new trial; this latter procedure is known as the *trial de novo process.* Changes in the courts of general jurisdiction, such as increases in felony filing rates, are watched closely because serious crime is of great public concern.

Courts of general jurisdiction are typically organized in judicial districts or circuits, based on a political division such as a county or a group of counties ("Superior Court for the Southern Tier"). They then receive cases from the various limited courts located within the county/jurisdiction. Some general courts separate criminal and civil cases so that some specialize in civil matters whereas others maintain a caseload that is exclusively criminal. In 10 states, Washington, D.C., and Puerto Rico, general and limited courts have unified their jurisdictional differences, creating a unified court system.

State criminal appeals are heard in one of the **appellate courts** in the 50 states and the District of Columbia. Each state has at least one court of last resort, usually called a state supreme court, which reviews issues of law and fact appealed from the trial courts. A few states have two high courts, one for civil appeals and the other for criminal cases. In addition, many states have established intermediate appellate courts (IACs) to review decisions by trial courts and administrative agencies before they reach the supreme court stage. Currently, 39 states have at least one permanent IAC. Mississippi was the last state to create an IAC, which began operations in 1995.

Many people believe that criminal appeals clog the nation's court system because so many convicted criminals try to "beat the rap" on a technicality. Actually, criminal appeals represent a small percentage of the total number of cases processed by the nation's appellate courts. All types of appeals, including criminal ones, continue to inundate the courts, so most courts are having problems processing cases expeditiously.

State courts have witnessed an increase in the number of appellate cases each year. In the meantime, the number of judges and support staff has not kept pace. The resulting imbalance has led to the increased use of intermediate courts to screen cases.

In sum, most states have at least two trial courts and two appellate courts, but they differ about where jurisdiction over such matters as juvenile cases and felony versus misdemeanor offenses is found. Such matters vary from state to state and between the state courts and the federal system.

Model State Court Structure

Figure 9.1 illustrates the interrelationship of appellate and trial courts in a typical state court structure. Each state's court organization varies from this standard pattern. Every state has a tiered court organization (lower, upper, and appellate courts), but states differ in the way they have delegated responsibility to a particular court system. For example, the court organizations of Texas and New York are complex in comparison with the model court structure (Figures 9.2 and 9.3). Texas separates its highest appellate divisions into civil and criminal courts. The Texas Supreme Court hears civil, administrative, and juvenile cases, and an independent court of criminal appeals has the final say on criminal matters.

FIGURE 9.1

A Model of a State Judicial System

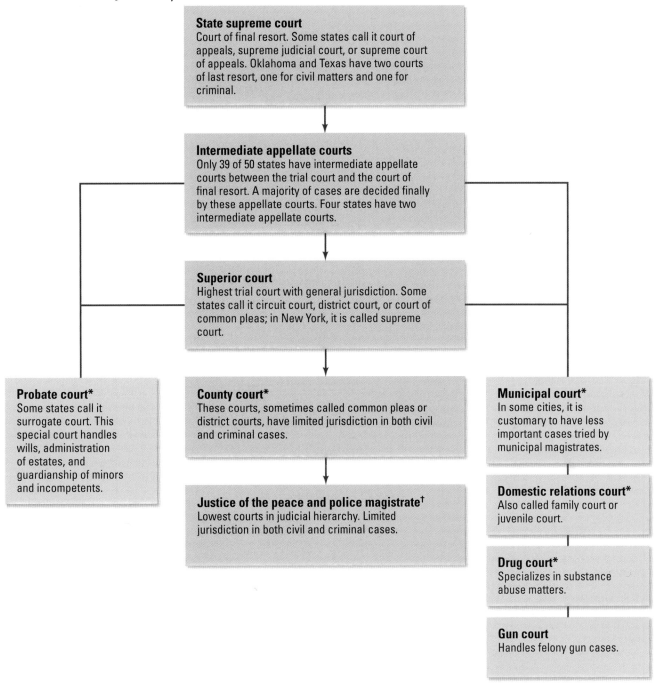

State supreme court
Court of final resort. Some states call it court of appeals, supreme judicial court, or supreme court of appeals. Oklahoma and Texas have two courts of last resort, one for civil matters and one for criminal.

Intermediate appellate courts
Only 39 of 50 states have intermediate appellate courts between the trial court and the court of final resort. A majority of cases are decided finally by these appellate courts. Four states have two intermediate appellate courts.

Superior court
Highest trial court with general jurisdiction. Some states call it circuit court, district court, or court of common pleas; in New York, it is called supreme court.

Probate court*
Some states call it surrogate court. This special court handles wills, administration of estates, and guardianship of minors and incompetents.

County court*
These courts, sometimes called common pleas or district courts, have limited jurisdiction in both civil and criminal cases.

Municipal court*
In some cities, it is customary to have less important cases tried by municipal magistrates.

Justice of the peace and police magistrate†
Lowest courts in judicial hierarchy. Limited jurisdiction in both civil and criminal cases.

Domestic relations court*
Also called family court or juvenile court.

Drug court*
Specializes in substance abuse matters.

Gun court
Handles felony gun cases.

Courts of special jurisdictions, such as probate, family, or juvenile courts, and the so-called inferior courts, such as common pleas or municipal courts, may be separate courts or part of the trial court of general jurisdiction.

†*Justices of the peace do not exist in all states. Where they do exist, their jurisdictions vary greatly from state to state.*

Source: American Bar Association, *Law and the Courts* (Chicago 1974), p. 20; Bureau of Justice Statistics, *State Court Organization 1998* (Washington, D.C.: Department of Justice, 2000).

New York's unique structure features two separate intermediate appellate courts with different geographic jurisdictions and an independent family court, which handles both domestic relations (such as guardianship and custody, neglect, and abuse) and juvenile delinquency. Surrogates' court handles adoptions and settles disagreements over estate transfers. The court of claims handles civil matters in

FIGURE 9.2

Texas Court Structure

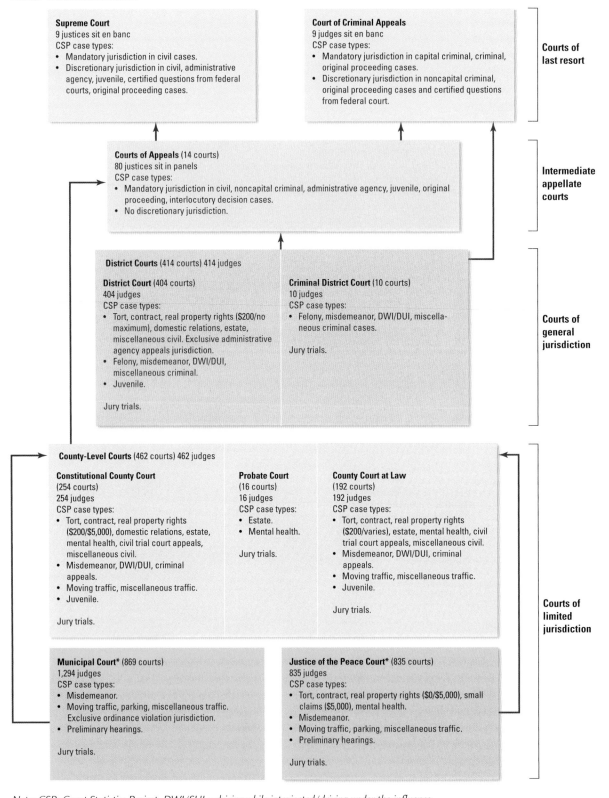

Supreme Court
9 justices sit en banc
CSP case types:
• Mandatory jurisdiction in civil cases.
• Discretionary jurisdiction in civil, administrative agency, juvenile, certified questions from federal courts, original proceeding cases.

Court of Criminal Appeals
9 judges sit en banc
CSP case types:
• Mandatory jurisdiction in capital criminal, criminal, original proceeding cases.
• Discretionary jurisdiction in noncapital criminal, original proceeding cases and certified questions from federal court.

Courts of last resort

Courts of Appeals (14 courts)
80 justices sit in panels
CSP case types:
• Mandatory jurisdiction in civil, noncapital criminal, administrative agency, juvenile, original proceeding, interlocutory decision cases.
• No discretionary jurisdiction.

Intermediate appellate courts

District Courts (414 courts) 414 judges

District Court (404 courts)
404 judges
CSP case types:
• Tort, contract, real property rights ($200/no maximum), domestic relations, estate, miscellaneous civil. Exclusive administrative agency appeals jurisdiction.
• Felony, misdemeanor, DWI/DUI, miscellaneous criminal.
• Juvenile.

Jury trials.

Criminal District Court (10 courts)
10 judges
CSP case types:
• Felony, misdemeanor, DWI/DUI, miscellaneous criminal cases.

Jury trials.

Courts of general jurisdiction

County-Level Courts (462 courts) 462 judges

Constitutional County Court
(254 courts)
254 judges
CSP case types:
• Tort, contract, real property rights ($200/$5,000), domestic relations, estate, mental health, civil trial court appeals, miscellaneous civil.
• Misdemeanor, DWI/DUI, criminal appeals.
• Moving traffic, miscellaneous traffic.
• Juvenile.

Jury trials.

Probate Court
(16 courts)
16 judges
CSP case types:
• Estate.
• Mental health.

Jury trials.

County Court at Law
(192 courts)
192 judges
CSP case types:
• Tort, contract, real property rights ($200/varies), estate, mental health, civil trial court appeals, miscellaneous civil.
• Misdemeanor, DWI/DUI, criminal appeals.
• Moving traffic, miscellaneous traffic.
• Juvenile.

Jury trials.

Municipal Court* (869 courts)
1,294 judges
CSP case types:
• Misdemeanor.
• Moving traffic, parking, miscellaneous traffic. Exclusive ordinance violation jurisdiction.
• Preliminary hearings.

Jury trials.

Justice of the Peace Court* (835 courts)
835 judges
CSP case types:
• Tort, contract, real property rights ($0/$5,000), small claims ($5,000), mental health.
• Misdemeanor.
• Moving traffic, parking, miscellaneous traffic.
• Preliminary hearings.

Jury trials.

Courts of limited jurisdiction

Note: CSP=Court Statistics Project. DWI/SUI = driving while intoxicated/driving under the influence.
*Some municipal and justice of the peace courts may appeal to the district court.

Source: Brian Ostrom, Neal Kauder, and Robert LaFountain, *Examining the Works of State Courts, 2002* (Williamsburg, Va.: National Center for State Courts, 2003), p. 52.

FIGURE 9.3
New York Court Structure

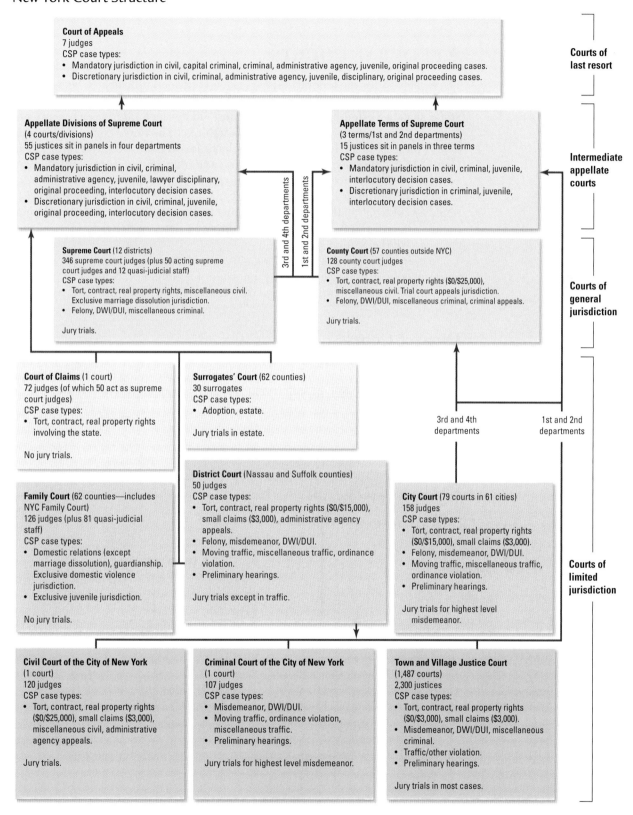

Note: Unless otherwise noted, numbers reflect statutory authorization. Many judges sit in more than one court so the number of judgeships indicated in this chart does not reflect the actual number of judges in the system. Fifty County Court judges also serve Surrogates' Court and six County Court judges also serve Family Court. CSP = Court Statistics Project. DWI/DUE = driving while intoxicated/driving under the influence.

Source: Brian Ostrom, Neal Kauder, and Robert LaFountain, *Examining the Works of State Courts, 2002* (Williamsburg, Va.: National Center for State Courts, 2003), p. 40.

ThomsonNOW Improve your grade on the exam with Personalized Study! For reinforcement resources and a mastery check of state court systems, go to www.thomsonedu. com/thomsonnow.

which the state is a party. In contrast to New York, which has 10 independent courts, six states (Idaho, Illinois, Iowa, Massachusetts, Minnesota, and South Dakota) have unified their trial courts into a single system.

◆ FEDERAL COURTS

The legal basis for the federal court system is contained in Article 3, Section 1, of the U.S. Constitution, which provides that "the judicial power of the United States shall be vested in one Supreme Court, and in such inferior courts as Congress may from time to time ordain and establish." The important clauses in Article 3 indicate that the federal courts have jurisdiction over the laws of the United States, treaties, and cases involving admiralty and maritime jurisdiction, as well as over controversies between two or more states and citizens of different states.[5] This complex language generally means that state courts have jurisdiction over all legal matters, unless they involve a violation of a federal criminal statute or a civil suit between citizens of different states or between a citizen and an agency of the federal government.

Within this authority, the federal government has established a three-tiered hierarchy of court jurisdiction that, in order of ascendancy, consists of the U.S. district courts, U.S. courts of appeals (circuit courts), and the U.S. Supreme Court (Figure 9.4).

District Courts

U.S. district courts are the trial courts of the federal system. They have jurisdiction over cases involving violations of federal laws, including civil rights abuses, interstate transportation of stolen vehicles, and kidnappings. They may also hear

FIGURE 9.4
The Federal Judicial System

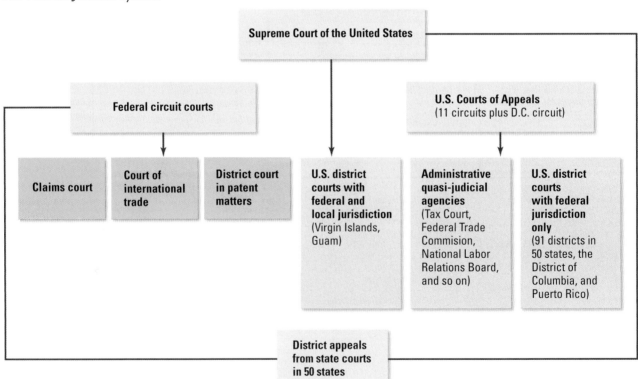

Source: American Bar Association, *Law and the Courts* (Chicago: 1974), p. 21. Updated information provided by the Federal Courts Improvement Act of 1982 and West Publishing Company, St. Paul, Minnesota.

Artist rendering of Zacarias Moussaoui with his lawyers before U.S. District Judge Leonie M. Brinkema during a pretrial hearing, February 14, 2006, in Alexandria, Virginia. Federal district courts handle criminal matters such as the terrorist activities of Moussaoui, who is known as the "20th Hijacker" for his involvement in the 9/11 plot.

cases on questions involving citizenship and the rights of aliens. The jurisdiction of the U.S. district court will occasionally overlap that of state courts. For example, citizens who reside in separate states and are involved in litigation of an amount in excess of $10,000 may choose to have their cases heard in either of the states or in the federal court. Finally, federal district courts hear cases in which one state sues a resident (or firm) in another state, where one state sues another, or where the federal government is a party in a suit. A single judge ordinarily presides over criminal trials; a defendant may also request a jury trial.

Federal district courts were organized by Congress in the Judicial Act of 1789, and today 94 independent courts are in operation. Originally, each state was allowed one court. As the population grew, however, so did the need for courts. Now each state has from one to four district courts, and the District of Columbia has one for itself.

Federal Appeals Courts

Approximately 40,000 appeals from the district courts are heard each year in the 12 federal courts of appeals, sometimes referred to as U.S. circuit courts. This name is derived from the historical practice of having judges ride the circuit and regularly hear cases in the judicial seats of their various jurisdictions. Today, appellate judges are not required to travel (although some may sit in more than one court), and each federal appellate court jurisdiction contains a number of associate justices who share the caseload. Circuit court offices are usually located in major cities, such as San Francisco and New York, and cases to be heard must be brought to these locations by attorneys.

The circuit court is empowered to review federal and state appellate court cases on substantive and procedural issues involving rights guaranteed by the Constitution. Circuit courts neither retry cases nor determine whether the facts brought out during trial support conviction or dismissal. Instead, they analyze judicial interpretations of the law, such as the charge (or instructions) to the jury, and reflect on the constitutional issues involved in each case they hear.

The Supreme Court selects cases to hear because of their legal importance, not because they necessarily involve serious or notorious crimes. Anna Nicole Smith and her lawyer Howard K. Stern leave the U.S. Supreme Court on February 28, 2006, in Washington, D.C. A Texas state court had ruled that Smith should be cut out of her late husband's $1.6 billion estate, with the primary inheritance falling to his son, E. Pierce Marshall. At issue in the Supreme Court case was whether a federal appeals court ruled correctly in determining that only state (and not federal) courts have authority over disputed estates. Smith encountered a sympathetic audience at the Supreme Court, who ruled in her favor, allowing her to pursue her claim to the inheritance in federal court.

Although federal court criminal cases make up only a small percentage of appellate cases, they are still of concern to the judiciary. Steps have been taken to make the appeal process more difficult. For example, the U.S. Supreme Court has tried to limit the number of appeals being filed by prison inmates, which often represent a significant number of cases appealed in the federal criminal justice system.

The U.S. Supreme Court

court of last resort
A court that handles the final appeal on a matter—in the federal system, the U.S. Supreme Court.

The U.S. Supreme Court is the nation's highest appellate body and the **court of last resort** for all cases tried in the various federal and state courts. The Supreme Court is composed of nine members appointed for lifetime terms by the president, with the approval of Congress. (The size of the Court is set by statute.) The Court has discretion over most of the cases it will consider and may choose to hear only those it deems important, appropriate, and worthy of its attention. The Court chooses around 300 of the 5,000 cases that are appealed each year; less than half of these typically receive full opinions.

When the Supreme Court decides to hear a case, it grants a writ of certiorari, requesting a transcript of the proceedings of the case for review. However, the Court is required to hear cases in a few instances, such as decisions from a three-judge federal district court on reapportionment or cases involving the Voting Rights Act.

When the Supreme Court rules on a case, usually by majority decision (at least five votes), the outcome becomes a precedent that must be honored by all lower courts. For example, if the Court grants a particular litigant the right to counsel at a police lineup, all similarly situated clients must be given the same right. This type of ruling is usually referred to as a landmark decision. The use of precedent in the legal system gives the Supreme Court power to influence and mold the everyday operating procedures of the police, trial courts, and corrections agencies. This influence became particularly pronounced during the tenure of Chief Justices

Earl Warren (1953–1969) and Warren Burger (1969–1986), who greatly amplified and extended the power of the Court to influence criminal justice policies. Under William H. Rehnquist, who was elevated to Chief Justice in 1986, the Court continued to influence criminal justice matters, ranging from the investigation of crimes to the execution of criminals. The newest Chief Justice, John Roberts, is expected to bring a conservative approach to criminal justice matters. The personal legal philosophy of the Justices and their orientation toward the civil and personal rights of victims and criminals significantly affect the daily operations of the justice system.

HOW A CASE GETS TO THE SUPREME COURT The Supreme Court is unique in several ways. First, it is the only court established by constitutional mandate instead of federal legislation. Second, it decides basic social and political issues of grave consequence and importance to the nation. Third, the Justices shape the future meaning of the U.S. Constitution. Their decisions identify the rights and liberties of citizens throughout the United States.

When the nation was first established, the Supreme Court did not review state court decisions involving issues of federal law. Even though Congress had given the Supreme Court jurisdiction to review state decisions, much resistance and controversy surrounded the relationship between the states and the federal government. However, in a famous decision, *Martin v. Hunter's Lessee* (1816), the Court reaffirmed the legitimacy of its jurisdiction over state court decisions when such courts handled issues of federal or constitutional law.[6] This decision allowed the Court to actively review actions by states and their courts and reinforced the Court's power to make the supreme law of the land. Since that time, a defendant who indicates that governmental action—whether state or federal—violates a constitutional law is in a position to have the Court review such action.

To carry out its responsibilities, the Supreme Court had to develop a method for dealing with the large volume of cases coming from the state and federal courts for final review. In the early years of its history, the Court sought to review every case brought before it. Since the middle of the twentieth century, however, the Court has used the **writ of certiorari** to decide what cases it should hear. (*Certiorari* is a Latin term meaning "to bring the record of a case from a lower court up to a higher court for immediate review.") When applied, it means that an accused in a criminal case is requesting that the U.S. Supreme Court hear the case. More than 90 percent of the cases heard by the Court are brought by petition for a writ of certiorari. Under this procedure, the Justices have discretion to select the cases they will review for a decision. Of the thousands of cases filed before the Court every year, less than 100 typically receive a full opinion. Four of the nine Justices sitting on the Court must vote to hear a case brought by a writ of certiorari for review. Generally, these votes are cast in a secret meeting attended only by the Justices.

After the Supreme Court decides to hear a case, it reviews written and oral arguments. The written materials are referred to as legal briefs, and oral arguments are normally presented to the Justices at the Court in Washington, D.C.

After the material is reviewed and the oral arguments heard, the Justices normally meet in what is known as a case conference. At this case conference, they discuss the case and vote to reach a decision. The cases voted on by the Court generally come from the judicial systems of the various states or the U.S. courts of appeals, and they represent the entire spectrum of law.

In reaching a decision, the Supreme Court reevaluates and reinterprets state statutes, the U.S. Constitution, and previous case decisions. Based on a review of the case, the Court either affirms or reverses the decision of the lower court. When the Justices reach a decision, the Chief Justice of the Court assigns someone of the majority group to write the opinion. Another Justice normally writes a dissent, or minority, opinion. When the case is finished, it is submitted to the public and becomes the law of the land. The decision represents the legal precedents that add to the existing body of law on a given subject, change it, and guide its future development (Figure 9.5).

The Supreme Court maintains a website that has a wealth of information on its history, judges, procedures, case filings, rules, handling guides, opinions, and other relevant Court-related material. To access the site, go to the Siegel/Senna Introduction to Criminal Justice 11e website: www.thomsonedu.com/criminaljustice/siegel.

writ of certiorari
An order of a superior court requesting that a record of an inferior court (or administrative body) be brought forward for review or inspection.

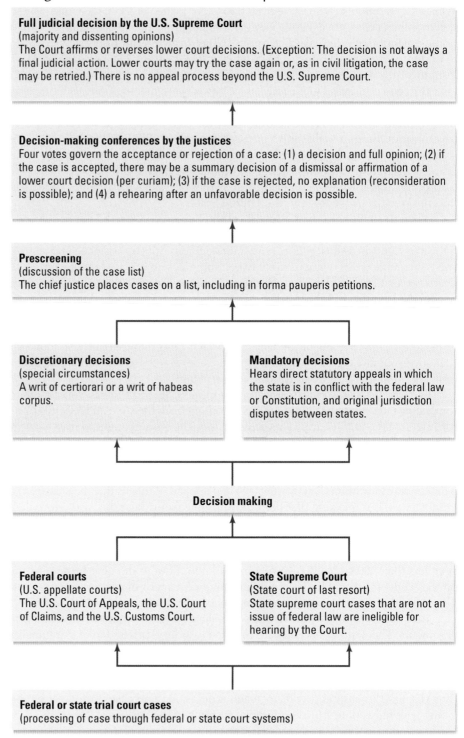

FIGURE 9.5
Tracing the Course of a Case to the U.S. Supreme Court

In the area of criminal justice, the decisions of the U.S. Supreme Court have had the broadest impact on the reform of the system. The Court's action is the final step in settling constitutional criminal disputes throughout the nation. By discretionary review through a petition for certiorari, the Court requires state courts to accept its interpretation of the Constitution. In doing so, the Court has changed the day-by-day operations of the criminal justice system.

♦ COURT CONGESTION

The vast U.S. court system has been overloaded by the millions of cases that are brought each year. State court systems now handle about one hundred million new cases annually. That total includes the following:

♦ About twenty million civil and domestic cases.

♦ More than fifteen million criminal cases.

♦ Two million juvenile cases.

♦ More than fifty-seven million traffic and ordinance violations.

The number of cases in all courts has been increasing at a steady pace for more than a decade (see Figure 9.6).

Though smaller, federal courts are equally burdened:

♦ Criminal cases have increased 55 percent since 1994. There are now more than 530 cases filed each year per judge, up from 339 in 1969.

♦ The circuit courts now hear more than 60,000 appeals per year, an increase of more than 25 percent in a decade. In 1969 the same number of circuit courts heard 10,000 appeals. Appeals have grown from 123 per judge per year to more than 380.[7] See Figure 9.7.

Both federal and state court caseloads have grown significantly for the past two decades, increasing more than 50 percent since 1984.

Why has the court system become so congested? There are numerous factors that produce trial delay and court congestion:

♦ Rapidly increasing populations in some states such as Nevada have outpaced growth in the court system.

♦ Some communities have attempted to control crime by aggressively prosecuting petty offenses and nuisance crimes such as panhandling or vagrancy.

♦ As the law becomes more complex, and involves such technological issues as intellectual property rights concerning computer programs, the need for a more involved court process has escalated.

♦ Ironically, efforts being made to reform the criminal law may also be helping to overload the courts. The increase of mandatory prison sentences for some crimes may reduce the use of plea bargaining and increase the number of jury trials because defendants fear that a conviction will lead to incarceration and thus must be avoided at all costs.

♦ Civil litigation has exploded as people view the court process as a means of redressing all kinds of personal wrongs. This can result in *frivolous lawsuits*— for example, when overweight people file suit against manufacturers,

The courts now handle over 100 million cases each year, causing congestion and inhibiting case processing. Criminal defendants chained together are ushered into a Whatcom County courtroom for hearings in Bellingham, Washington on June 1, 2006. Thanks to a practice that has been routine for nearly 30 years in this county on the Canadian border, federal agents dump scores of drug cases on local officials, clogging the courts and crowding the jails.

©AP Images/Elaine Thompson

FIGURE 9.6
Court Caseload Trends

Millions

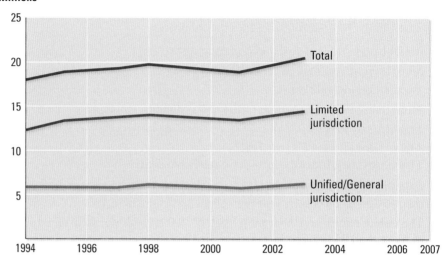

Source: National Center for State Courts

FIGURE 9.7
Federal Court Caseloads

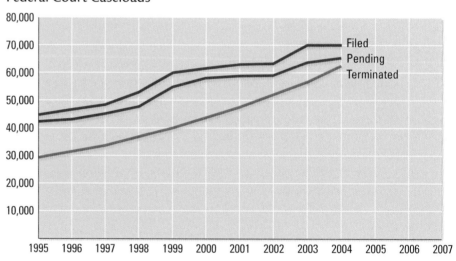

Source: http://www.uscourts.gov/caseload2004/front/judbus03.pdf.

distributors, or sellers of food products, charging them with responsibility for their obesity.[8] Increased civil litigation can add to the backlog because most courts handle both criminal and civil matters.

If relief is to be found, it will probably be in the form of better administrative and management techniques that improve the use of existing resources. Another possible method of creating a more efficient court system is to unify existing state courts into a single administrative structure using modern management principles.

◆ THE JUDICIARY

The judge is the senior officer in a court of criminal law. A judge's duties are varied and far more extensive than might be expected. During trials, the judge rules on the appropriateness of conduct, settles questions of evidence and

ThomsonNOW Improve your grade on the exam with Personalized Study! For reinforcement resources and a mastery check of court congestion, go to www.thomsonedu.com/thomsonnow.

procedure, and guides the questioning of witnesses. In a jury trial, the judge must instruct jurors on which evidence is proper to examine and which should be ignored. The judge also formally charges the jury by instructing its members on what points of law and evidence they must consider to reach a verdict of either guilty or not guilty. When a jury trial is waived, the judge must decide whether to hold for the complainant or the defendant. Finally, if a defendant is found guilty, the judge must decide on the sentence (in some cases, this is legislatively determined), which includes choosing the type of sentence and its length as well as the conditions under which probation may be revoked.

While carrying out her duties, the judge must be wary of the legal controls placed on the trial process by the appellate court system. If an error is made, the judge's decision may be reversed, causing at the minimum personal embarrassment. Although some experts believe that fear of reversal may shape judicial decision making, recent research by David Klein and Robert Hume indicates that judges may be more independent than previously believed, especially if they can use their judicial power as a policy-making tool to influence important social policies such as affirmative action or privacy.[9]

Other Judicial Functions

Beyond these stated duties, the trial judge has extensive control and influence over the other agencies of the court: probation, the court clerk, court reporters, the police, and the district attorney's office. Probation and the clerk may be under the judge's explicit control. In some courts, the operations, philosophy, and procedures of these agencies are within the magistrate's administrative domain. In others—for example, where a state agency controls the probation department—the attitudes of the county or district court judge greatly influence the way a probation department is run and how its decisions are made. Judges often consult with probation staff on treatment decisions, and many judges are interested in providing the most innovative and up-to-date care possible.

Police and prosecutors are also directly influenced by the judge, whose sentencing discretion affects the arrest and charging processes. For example, if a judge usually chooses minimal sentences—such as a fine for a particular offense—the police may be reluctant to arrest offenders for that crime, knowing that doing so will basically be a waste of time. Similarly, if a judge is known to have an open attitude toward police discretion, the local department may be more inclined to engage in practices that border on entrapment or to pursue cases through easily obtained wiretaps. However, a magistrate oriented toward strict use of due process guarantees would stifle such activities by dismissing all cases involving apparent police abuses of personal freedoms. The district attorney's office may also be sensitive to judicial attitudes. The district attorney might forgo indictments in cases that the presiding magistrate expressly considers trivial or quasi-criminal and in which the judge has been known to take only token action, such as the prosecution of pornographers.

Finally, the judge considers requests by police and prosecutors for leniency (or severity) in sentencing. The judge's reaction to these requests is important if the police and the district attorney are to honor the bargains they may have made with defendants to secure information, cooperation, or guilty pleas. For example, when police tell informers that they will try to convince the judge to go easy on them to secure required information, they will often discuss the terms of the promised leniency with representatives of the court. If a judge ignores police demands, the department's bargaining power is severely diminished, and communication within the criminal justice system is impaired.

There is always concern that judges will discriminate against defendants on the basis of their gender, race, or class. Although this issue is of great social concern, most research efforts have failed to find consistent bias in judicial decision making. Judges tend to dismiss cases that they consider weak and less serious.[10]

The American Judges Association seeks to improve the effective and impartial administration of justice, to enhance the independence and status of the judiciary, to provide for continuing education of its members, and to promote the interchange of ideas of a judicial nature among judges, court organizations, and the public. You can access its website by going to the Siegel/Senna Introduction to Criminal Justice 11e website: www.thomsonedu.com/criminaljustice/siegel.

The National Summit on Improving Judicial Selection was convened on January 25, 2001, under the leadership of Texas Supreme Court Chief Justice Thomas R. Phillips and Texas State Senator Rodney Ellis. The participants discussed how to best improve judicial selection processes, focusing on those states in which judicial selection is subject to popular election. You can access their findings by going to the Siegel/Senna Introduction to Criminal Justice 11e website: www.thomsonedu.com/criminaljustice/siegel.

Court Reporter

Duties and Characteristics of the Job

Court reporters create the official transcripts of legal proceedings such as trials and depositions. These transcripts include all the dialogue as well as other important details such as emotional reactions. The court reporter records these events as they occur in real time.

Court reporters use three different methods of transcription: voice writing, electronic, and stenography. Voice writers make an audio record of the proceedings. When making their recording, they speak into a microphone surrounded by a soundproof mask so that the report cannot be heard by others. Electronic court reporters will use audio equipment to tape an event, then supplement this recording later with notes taken during the proceedings. The commonly used recording method in legal and courtroom settings is stenography. A modern stenographic court reporter uses a computerized stenotype machine to transcribe spoken words. A court reporter can press multiple keys simultaneously to represent words, sounds, or even phrases. The court reporter will go over the record later to ensure that it is clear, thorough, and accurate. The correctness of this record is important because it will be the only official record of the event and may be used in future judgments, for trial preparation by attorneys, and during appeals.

Although the court reporter's primary purpose is to record courtroom legal proceedings and depositions, at times a court reporter may do more than just transcription. For example, when a request is made to review the transcript, the court reporter will provide the information from the official record. Court reporters may also advise lawyers on legal procedure when necessary. Outside of a strictly legal setting, a court reporter will often also use his or her skills to create real-time translated or closed-captioned transcription for the hearing impaired.

Job Outlook

The number of jobs available for court reporters is greater than the number of trained professionals entering the field. This means that the job prospects are good and the outlook is favorable for entry-level court reporters, especially those who are certified.

Salary

A court reporter's pay will depend on several factors, including method of transcription, region of the United States, type of employer, amount of previous work experience, and level of certification.

Median annual salary for court reporters is $42,920. The majority of court reporters earn between $30,680 and $60,760. At the extremes, a small percentage of court reporters will earn around $23,690, and the highest paid will earn more than $80,000.

Judicial Qualifications

The qualifications for appointment to one of the existing 30,000 judgeships vary from state to state and court to court. Most typically, the potential judge must be a resident of the state, licensed to practice law, a member of the state bar association, and at least 25 and less than 70 years of age. However, a significant degree of diversity exists in the basic qualification, depending on the level of court jurisdiction. Although almost every state requires judges to have a law degree if they are to serve on appellate courts or courts of general jurisdiction, it is not uncommon for municipal or town court judges to lack a legal background, even though they maintain the power to incarcerate criminal defendants.

Judges are held in high esteem, but they must sacrifice many financial benefits if they shift careers from lucrative private practices to low-paid government positions. Table 9.1 shows the average salaries of judges in state courts. Although an average of $138,000 for the chief of the highest court seems substantial, it is relatively modest when compared to corporate salaries and what partners in top law firms earn. The *starting pay* in some high-powered New York City law firms—e.g., Goodwin Proctor—is now more than what the Chief Justice of the state's highest court makes![11]

Opportunities

The opportunities for employment as a court reporter are expected to grow at a moderate pace in the next several years. Court reporters are always needed in courtrooms and lawyers' offices across the country, although jobs may be more plentiful in urban areas.

A majority of court reporters work for state and local governments. However, salaried workers such as these will often freelance for extra income at attorneys' offices or as closed captioners/real-time translators. Other court reporters work for court reporting agencies or freelance full time. Agency workers and freelancers enjoy the flexibility of setting their own schedules.

Qualifications

The qualifications necessary to be a practicing court reporter vary by state. In some states, court reporters are required to be notary publics. In others, an individual will have to become a certified court reporter (CCR) by passing a state certification test. The National Court Reporters Association has several designated levels of certification that a court reporter can achieve, each connoting a higher level of experience and achievement.

Court reporters must continually study and practice their skills. Accuracy is of the utmost importance, and small mistakes can threaten future job opportunities. Because a court reporter must create a record of events as they occur, the ability to listen carefully and work quickly is key. Familiarity with legal terms and practices is necessary, as is a thorough knowledge of grammar, spelling, and vocabulary.

Education and Training

At minimum a court reporter needs an associate's degree, although a bachelor's degree is more common. A bachelor's degree is useful because it can substitute for several years of work experience when the court reporter is attempting to obtain increasingly higher levels of certification.

In addition to general education, training programs are available at vocational or technical schools. There are seventy National Court Reporters Association–approved programs in the United States and Canada. These programs prepare future court reporters to work with the appropriate technology and meet the standards necessary for certification, such as the minimum 225-words-per-minute capture rate.

Sources: S. E. Lambert and D. Regan, "Court Reporter." In *Great Careers for Criminal Justice Majors* (New York: McGraw-Hill, 2001), pp. 159–61; "Court Reporters" (U.S. Department of Labor: Bureau of Labor Statistics), retrieved May 31, 2006, from http://www.bls.gov/oco/ocos152.htm.

A great deal of concern has been raised about the qualifications of judges. In most states, people appointed to the bench have had little or no training in how to be a judge. Others may have held administrative posts and may not have appeared before a court in years. The relatively low level of judicial salaries may make it difficult to attract the most competent attorneys to the bench.

A number of agencies have been created to improve the quality of the judiciary. The National Conference of State Court Judges and the National College of Juvenile Justice both operate judicial training seminars and publish manuals and guides on state-of-the-art judicial technologies. Their ongoing efforts are designed to improve the quality of the nation's judges.

Judicial Alternatives

Increased judicial caseloads have prompted the use of alternatives to the traditional judge. For example, to expedite matters in civil cases, it has become common for both parties to agree to hire a retired judge and abide by his or her decision. Jurisdictions have set up dispute-resolution systems for settling minor complaints informally upon the agreement of both parties. An estimated 700 dispute-resolution programs are now handling domestic conflicts, landlord–tenant cases, misdemeanors, consumer–merchant disputes, and so on.[12]

TABLE 9.1
Judicial Salaries

	Mean	Median	Range	Average Annual % Change 1997–2006
Chief, Highest Court	$138,234	$133,600	$102,466 to 193,567	3.1%
Associate Justice, Court of Last Resort	133,602	128,018	100,884 to 182,071	3.1%
Judge, Intermediate Appelate Courts	128,695	125,000	101,612 to 107,694	3.0%
Judge, Genearl Jurisdiction Trial Courts	119,630	116,100	94,093 to 165,200	3.2%
State Court Administrators	118,834	115,384	69,100 to 175,728	3.1%

Source: National Center for State Courts.

PERSPECTIVES ON JUSTICE

Restorative Justice

The use of mediation is one of the key components of the restorative justice perspective. By removing cases from the court setting, mediation is designed to be both a money-saving device and a forum in which conflicts can be solved in a nonadversarial manner.

Other jurisdictions have created new quasijudicial officers, such as referees or magistrates, to relieve the traditional judge of time-consuming responsibilities. The Magistrate Act of 1968 created a new type of judicial officer in the federal district court system to handle pretrial duties.[13] Federal magistrates also handle civil trials if both parties agree to the arrangement.[14]

Some jurisdictions use part-time judges. Many of these are attorneys who carry out their duties pro bono—for no or limited compensation. These judicial adjuncts assist the courts on a temporary basis while maintaining an active law practice.[15] The use of alternative court mechanisms should continue to grow as court congestion increases.

Selecting Judges

Many methods are used to select judges. In some jurisdictions, the governor appoints judges. It is common for the governor's recommendations to be confirmed by the state senate, the governor's council, a special confirmation committee, an executive council elected by the state assembly, or an elected review board. Some states employ a judicial nominating commission that submits names to the governor for approval.

Another form of judicial selection is popular election. In some jurisdictions, judges run as members of the Republican, Democratic, or other parties; in others, they run without party affiliation. In 13 states, partisan elections are used for selecting judges in courts of general jurisdiction; in 17 states, nonpartisan elections are used; and in the remainder, upper-trial-court judges are appointed by the governor or the legislature. Of state judges, 87 percent face elections of some type, with 53 percent of appellate judges and 77 percent of trial judges (general jurisdiction) facing contestable elections. However, each judge may face a different election experience because each has a different term of appointment. About 39 percent of state supreme court justices have terms of 10–15 years, but 45 percent have only 6 years; 19 percent of trial judges have terms of 10–15 years, compared to the 18 percent with only 3–4 years, and 56 percent with 6 years.[16] For a review of judicial selection, see Concept Summary 9.1.

Judicial elections are troubling to some because they involve partisan politics in a process to select people who must be nonpolitical and objective. The process itself has been tainted by charges of scandal—for example, when political parties

CONCEPT SUMMARY 9.1

Judicial Selection

Type	Process
Appointment	Governor selects candidate, confirmed by state senate or other official body.
Election	Potential judge runs as partisan politician during regular election.
Missouri Plan	Bar committee searches for qualified candidates, governor chooses among them, judge runs for reappointment in nonpartisan election.

©*Syracuse Newspaper*/The Image Works

In many states, judges are selected by partisan elections and campaigning is part of their routine. Here Cliff English, the father of city court candidate Mark J. English, posts a campaign sign for his son.

insist that judicial candidates hire favored people or firms to run their campaigns or have them make contributions to the party to obtain an endorsement.[17]

To avoid this problem, a number of states have adopted some form of what is known as the **Missouri Plan** to select appellate court judges, and six states also use it to select trial court judges. This plan consists of three parts: (1) a judicial nominating commission to nominate candidates for the bench, (2) an elected official (usually from the executive branch) to make appointments from the list submitted by the commission, and (3) subsequent nonpartisan and noncompetitive elections in which incumbent judges run on their records and voters can choose either their retention or dismissal.[18]

The quality of the judiciary is a concern. Although merit plans, screening committees, and popular elections are designed to ensure a competent judiciary,

Missouri Plan
A method of judicial selection that combines a judicial nominating commission, executive appointment, and nonpartisan confirmation elections.

it has often been charged that many judicial appointments are made to pay off political debts or to reward cronies and loyal friends. Also not uncommon are charges that those desiring to be nominated for judgeships are required to make significant political contributions.

Judicial Overload

Great concern has arisen about the stress placed on judges by case pressure. Once they are appointed to the bench, judges are given an overwhelming amount of work that has grown dramatically over the years. The number of civil and criminal filings per state court judge has increased significantly since 1985. Annually, there are about 1,500 civil and criminal case filings per state court judge and 450 per federal judge.[19] State court judges deal with far more cases, but federal cases may be more complex and demand more judicial time. In any event, the number of civil and criminal cases, especially in state courts, seems to be outstripping the ability of states to create new judgeships.

♦ COURT ADMINISTRATION AND MANAGEMENT

In addition to qualified personnel, the judicial system needs efficient management. Improved court administration may serve as a way to relieve court congestion. Management goals include improving organization and scheduling of cases, devising methods to allocate court resources efficiently, administering fines and monies due the court, preparing budgets, and overseeing personnel.

The federal courts have led the way in creating and organizing court administration. In 1939 Congress passed the Administrative Office Act, which established the Administrative Office of the United States Courts. Its director was charged with gathering statistics on the work of the federal courts and preparing the judicial budget for approval by the Conference of Senior Circuit Judges. One clause of the act created a judicial council with general supervisory responsibilities for the district and circuit courts.

Unlike the federal government, the states have experienced a slow and uneven growth in the development and application of court management principles. The first state to establish an administrative office was North Dakota, in 1927. Today, all states employ some form of central administration.

The federal government has encouraged the development of state court management through funding assistance to court managers. In addition, the federal judiciary has provided the philosophical impetus for better and more effective court management.

Despite the multitude of problems in reforming court management, some progress is being made. In most jurisdictions today, centralized court administrative services perform numerous functions with the help of sophisticated computers that free the judiciary to fulfill their roles as arbiters of justice.

Technology and Court Management

As trial reconvenes, the participants blink into existence on the computer monitors that supply the only commonality applicable to them. Judge, counsel, parties, witnesses, and jury appear in virtual form on each person's monitor. Necessary evidentiary foundations are laid by witnesses with distant counsel's questions; documentary evidence is not seen by the jury until received by the court. A real-time, multi-media record (transcript with digital audio, video, and evidence) is available instantly. Sidebar conferences are accomplished simply by switching the jury out of circuit. During the interim, the jurors can head for their kitchens or for restroom breaks. The public can follow the proceedings on the Internet. Should critical interlocutory motions be argued, the appellate court can directly monitor the proceedings.[20]

ThomsonNOW™ Improve your grade on the exam with Personalized Study! For reinforcement resources and a mastery check of the judiciary, go to www.thomsonedu.com/thomsonnow.

This is how court technology expert Fredric I. Lederer foresees the court of the future. His projections may not be too far off. Computers are becoming an important aid in the administration and management of courts. Rapid retrieval and organization of data are now being used for such functions as

◆ Maintaining case histories and statistical reporting.

◆ Monitoring and scheduling of cases.

◆ Preparing documents.

◆ Indexing cases.

◆ Issuing summonses.

◆ Notifying witnesses, attorneys, and others of required appearances.

◆ Selecting and notifying jurors.

◆ Preparing and administering budgets and payrolls.

Information technology (IT) is also being applied in the courts in such areas as videotaped testimonies, new court-reporting devices, information systems, and data processing systems to handle such functions as court docketing and jury management.[21]

In 1968, only 10 states had state-level automated information systems; today, all states employ such systems for a mix of tasks and duties. A survey of Georgia courts found that 84 percent used computers for three or more court administration applications. What are some other developing areas of court technology?

CASE MANAGEMENT In the 1970s, municipal courts installed tracking systems, which used databases to manage court data. These older systems were limited and could not process the complex interrelationships of information pertaining to persons, cases, time, and financial matters that occur in court cases.

Contemporary relational databases now provide the flexibility to handle complex case management. To help programmers define the multiplicity of relationships that occur in a court setting, the National Center for State Courts in Williamsburg, Virginia, has developed a methodology for structuring a case management system that tracks a person to the case or cases in which he is a defendant, the scheduling of the cases to avoid any conflicts, and (of increasing importance) the fines that have been levied and the accounts to which the money goes. One of the more advanced current approaches to statewide court system automation has been undertaken by Wisconsin, which has developed and implemented an information system called the Circuit Court Automation Program (CCAP), used to improve day-to-day operations of courts, such as case records management and court calendaring, as well as jury selection and financial management.[22]

COMMUNICATIONS Court jurisdictions are cooperating with police departments in the installation of communications gear that allows defendants to be arraigned via closed-circuit television while they are in police custody. Closed-circuit television has been used for judicial conferences and scheduling meetings. Courts are using voice-activated cameras to record all testimony during trials; these are the sole means of keeping trial records.

About 400 courts across the country have videoconferencing capability. It is now being employed for juvenile detention hearings, expert witness testimony at trial, oral arguments on appeal, and parole hearings. More than 150 courts are using two-way live, televised remote linkups for first appearance and arraignment. In the usual arrangement, the defendant appears from a special location in the jail where he or she is able to see and hear and be seen and heard by the presiding magistrate. Such appearances are now being authorized by state statute. Televised appearances minimize delays in prisoner transfer, effect large cost savings through the elimination of transportation and security costs, and reduce escape and assault risks.

CRIMINAL JUSTICE AND TECHNOLOGY

Using Virtual Reality in the Courtroom

Just on the horizon is the use of virtual environments (VEs), immersive virtual environments (IVEs), and collaborative virtual environments (CVEs) in the courtroom. What does this mean? These processes employ digital computers to generate images that enable real-time interaction between a user and the VE. In principle, people can interact with a VE in these modes: visual (by wearing a head-mounted display with digital displays that project objects in the VE), auditory (by wearing earphones that are conducive toward playing sounds that seem to emanate from a specific point in space in the VE), haptic (by wearing gloves that use mechanical feedback or air blasts toward the hands when a person makes contact with an object in the VE), or olfactory (by wearing a nosepiece that releases different smells when a person approaches different objects in a VE). An immersive virtual environment (IVE) is one that perceptually surrounds the user of the system. It allows people to be at the center of the virtual world and to control movement, perception, and so on. An IVE in which multiple people interact with one another inside the same virtual reality is called a collaborative virtual environment (CVE); an Internet chat room is a form of CVE.

Current software makes it quite easy to produce digital virtual worlds; consequently, digital VE simulations can be produced to fit almost any specific application effort. So in a courtroom, instead of using maps, charts, and cardboard cutouts, VEs are using computers. Attorneys could employ VEs for a number of tasks, including presenting evidence to the triers of fact (judge or jury) and preparing expert or nonexpert witnesses for the trial process.

VEs can be used to put the trier of fact in the position of the parties and the witnesses to the events surrounding the crime—for example, by re-creating crime and accident scenes. Lawyers can create an extremely realistic presentation of the exact site on which a crime or accident occurred, including inanimate objects from the scene; witnesses, victims, and suspects from the scene; atmospheric conditions from the scene such as bright light or fog; background noise such as traffic sounds; and literally any sensory information. Currently, researchers are also exploring the use of IVEs as a mechanism to demonstrate witnesses' identification of suspects in lineups. The use of these technologies in identifying suspects improves upon earlier technology by making it possible to gauge degrees of certainty and better understand the subjective perspective of the witness.

Critical Thinking

1. VE technology allows for people who would be unable to attend the trial to still provide useful testimony. Do you believe that virtual trials will someday be conducted, relegating the physical courtroom to a thing of the past?

2. What constitutional principles conflict with the use of VE technology in the courtroom?

InfoTrac College Edition Research

What are the issues in court administration and technology? To find out, use "court administration" and "court management" as key words on InfoTrac College Edition.

Source: Jeremy Bailenson, Jim Blascovich, Andrew Beall, and Beth Noveck, "Courtroom Applications of Virtual Environments, Immersive Virtual Environments, and Collaborative Virtual Environments," *Law & Policy* 28 (2006): 249–70.

EVIDENCE PRESENTATION Many high-tech courtrooms are now equipped for real-time transcription and translation, audio–video preservation of the court record, remote witness participation, computer graphics displays, television monitors for jurors, and computers for counsel and judge. For example, the Harris County Criminal Justice Center in Texas now has the largest evidence display and courtroom video distribution project in the history of the U.S. court system. The facility-wide, hub-based videoconferencing system supports a total of 105 rooms, with conferencing ability among multiple parties from various locations throughout the building. This system was designed to allow witnesses to testify without having contact with criminal defendants. The technology includes the following:

♦ A digital evidence presentation system.

♦ Simultaneous evidence viewing via high-resolution 52-inch monitors.

♦ Annotation capabilities.

♦ Flat-panel display for judges' viewing.

♦ Under-carpet cable installation.

♦ Remote participation via videoconferencing.[23]

INTERNET RECORDS The Internet has become increasingly involved in the court system. For example, in the federal system, J-Net is the judiciary's website, making it easier for judges and court personnel to receive important information in a timely fashion. The federal court's administrative office has begun sending official correspondence by e-mail, a method that provides instantaneous communication of important information. In 1999 an automated library management system was developed, which meant that judges could access a web-based virtual law library. An electronic network providing the public with access to court records and other information via the Internet was also implemented. In 2002, 11 federal courts announced that they would allow Internet access to criminal case files. This was the first time the public could gain access to such files.

The U.S. Supreme Court's Public Access to Court Electronic Records (PACER) offers an inexpensive, fast, and comprehensive case information service to any individual with a personal computer and Internet access. The PACER system permits people to request information about a particular individual or case. The data are displayed instantly and are simple enough that little user training or documentation is required.[24]

The Criminal Justice Technology Feature on the previous page discusses an innovative technique that may be used in the courtrooms of the future.

ThomsonNOW™ Improve your grade on the exam with Personalized Study! For reinforcement resources and a mastery check of court administration and management, go to www.thomsonedu.com/thomsonnow.

ETHICAL CHALLENGES IN CRIMINAL JUSTICE: A WRITING ASSIGNMENT

Court congestion is a major threat to the trial process and the criminal justice system in general. Write an essay proposing radical ideas to limit overcrowding. Think outside the box. For instance, what about privatizing trials?

Doing Research on the Web

Numerous websites can help you with your court-focused research. Foremost among them is the one provided by the National Center for State Courts. As well, the federal judiciary maintains its own site. Each state system maintains numerous sites for individual courts or the general court system. Colorado's is a good one to explore. You can link to all of these sites by going to the Siegel/Senna Introduction to Criminal Justice 11e website: www.thomsonedu.com/criminaljustice/siegel.

SUMMARY

♦ The U.S. court system is a complex social institution.

♦ There is no set pattern of court organization. Courts are organized on federal, state, county, and local levels of government.

♦ Courts of general jurisdiction hear felony cases and larger civil trials.

♦ Courts of limited jurisdiction hear misdemeanors and more limited civil cases.

♦ Specialty courts have been developed to focus on particular crime problems such as drug abuse.

♦ Appellate courts review trials if there is a complaint about the process.

♦ The U.S. Supreme Court is the highest court in the land and has final jurisdiction over federal and state cases.

♦ Courts today must deal with almost 100 million cases each year. The heavy caseload leads to congestion and delays.

♦ A judge's duties include approving plea bargains, trying cases, and determining the sentence given the offender.

♦ Judges can be selected via executive appointment, election, or the Missouri Plan, which combines both approaches.

♦ Many judges are overworked and underpaid.

♦ The trial process is undergoing significant change through the introduction of technology and modern court management.

♦ Caseloads are being more effectively managed, and modern communications allow many aspects of the court process to be conducted in cyberspace.

♦ Some experts believe that the United States is at the threshold of a new form of trial in which the courthouse of old will be supplanted by the computer, the Internet, and wireless communications.

KEY TERMS

plea negotiations/plea bargaining, 298
courts of limited jurisdiction, 299

drug courts, 302
courts of general jurisdiction, 302
appellate courts, 302

court of last resort, 308
writ of certiorari, 309
Missouri Plan, 317

ThomsonNOW Maximize your study time by using ThomsonNOW's diagnostic study plan to help you review this chapter. The Study Plan will

♦ help you identify areas on which you should concentrate;

♦ provide interactive exercises to help you master the chapter concepts; and

♦ provide a post-test to confirm you are ready to move on to the next chapter.

CRITICAL THINKING QUESTIONS

1. What are the benefits and drawbacks of selecting judges through popular elections? Can a judge who considers himself a Republican or a Democrat render fair and impartial justice?

2. Should more specialized courts be created and, if so, for what?

3. Should all judges be trained as attorneys? If not, what other professions are suitable for consideration?

4. Should a defendant have to be present in the courtroom, or would a virtual courtroom suffice? What about witnesses?

5. What is the Missouri Plan? Do you consider it an ideal way to select judges?

6. The Judiciary Act of 1869 increased the U.S. Supreme Court membership to nine. The judicial workload in the aftermath of the Civil War proved more than the seven sitting Justices could handle. Considering that the population is now approaching 300 million, do you think the number of Justices should be increased once again?

NOTES

1. Daniel R. Williams, *Executing Justice: An Inside Account of the Case of Mumia Abu-Jamal* (New York: St. Martin's, 2002).

2. Matthew Durose and Patrick A. Langan, *State Court Sentencing of Convicted Felons, 1998* (Washington, D.C.: Bureau of Justice Statistics, February 2001).

3. "Courts Hit by Budget Cuts," *State Government News* 45 (June–July 2002): 6.

4. Thomas Henderson, *The Significance of Judicial Structure: The Effect of Unification on Trial Court Operations* (Washington, D.C.: National Institute of Justice, 1984).

5. U.S. Constitution, Article 3, Sections 1 and 2.

6. 1 Wharton 304, 4 L.Ed. 97 (1816).

7. American Bar Association, "Federal Judicial Pay, 2003" (http://www.uscourts.gov/newsroom/judgespayaction.pdf).

8. Jason Perez-Dormitzer, "Bill Safeguards Restaurants in Obesity-Related Lawsuits," *Providence Business News,* March 22, 2004, pp. 5–7.

9. David Klein and Robert Hume, "Fear of Reversal as an Explanation of Lower Court Compliance," *Law and Society Review* 37 (2003): 579–607.

10. Huey-Tsyh Chen, "Dropping In and Dropping Out: Judicial Decisionmaking in the Disposition of Felony Arrests," *Journal of Criminal Justice* 19 (1991): 1–17.

11. Starting salaries at New York City firms can be found at http://www.infirmation.com/shared/search/payscale-compare.tcl?city=New%20York (accessed on May 20, 2006). For New York judicial salaries, see http://www.ncsconline.org/WC/Publications/KIS_JudComJudSal040105Pub.pdf.

12. "State Adoption of Alternative Dispute Resolution," *State Court Journal* 12 (1988): 11–15.

13. Public Law 90–578, Title I, Sec. 101, 82 Stat. 1113 (1968), amended; Public Law 94–577, Sec. 1, Stat. 2729 (1976); Public Law 96–82, Sec. 2, 93 Stat. 643 (1979).

14. See, generally, Carroll Seron, "The Professional Project of Parajudges: The Case of U.S. Magistrates," *Law and Society Review* 22 (1988): 557–75.

15. Alex Aikman, "Volunteer Lawyer–Judges Bolster Court Resources," *NIJ Report* (January 1986): 2–6.

16. Roy Schotland, "2002 Judicial Elections," *Spectrum: The Journal of State Government* 76 (2003): 18–20.

17. Daniel Wise, "Making a Criminal Case Over Selection of Judges in Brooklyn," *New York Law Journal* (July 23, 2003): 1.

18. Sari Escovitz with Fred Kurland and Nan Gold, *Judicial Selection and Tenure* (Chicago: American Judicature Society, 1974), pp. 3–16.

19. Richard Schauffler, Robert LaFountain, Neal Kauder, and Shauna Strickland, *Examining the Work of State Courts, 2004* (Williamsburg, Va.: National Center for State Courts, 2006) (http://www.ncsconline.org/D_Research/csp/2004_Files/EWFront%20_final_2.pdf).

20. Fredric I. Lederer, "The Road to the Virtual Courtroom? Consideration of Today's—and Tomorrow's—High Technology Courtrooms," *South Carolina Law Review* 50 (1999): 799.

21. The following sections rely heavily on Elizabeth Wiggins, "The Courtroom of the Future Is Here: Introduction to Emerging Technologies in the Legal System," *Law & Policy* 28 (2006): 182–91; "Criminal Court Records Go Online," *Quill* 90 (2002): 39; Donald C. Dilworth, "New Court Technology Will Affect How Attorneys Present Trials," *Trial* 33 (1997): 100–14.

22. Wisconsin Circuit Court Access (WCCA), "Access to the Public Records of the Consolidated Court Automation Programs (CCAP)" (http://wcca.wicourts.gov), accessed on May 30, 2006.

23. Harris County Criminal Justice Center (http://aceav.com/cases/index.php?case_id=29), accessed on June 25, 2006.

24. Find out more about the PACER system at http://pacer.psc.uscourts.gov (accessed on June 25, 2006).

CHAPTER 10

The Prosecution and the Defense

Chapter Outline

Chapter Objectives

After reading this chapter, you should be able to:

1. Understand the role of the prosecutor.
2. Know the similarities and differences between different types of prosecutors.
3. Recognize the role of prosecutorial discretion in the justice system.
4. Explain the political influences on prosecutorial discretion.
5. Discuss the concept of right to counsel.
6. Recognize the different types of defender services.
7. Know the cases that mandate the right to counsel at trial.
8. Describe the role of the defense attorney in the trial process.
9. Understand the issues involved in legal ethics.
10. Explain what it means to be a legally competent attorney.

ince Eliot Spitzer took office in 1999, he has made quite a name for himself as attorney general of the state of New York. His ongoing investigations into white-collar crime have made national news. He has directed investigations aimed at conflicts of interest by investment banks, illegal trading practices by mutual funds, and bid rigging in the insurance industry. His office has recovered billions of dollars for small investors and other consumers in these cases and has been the catalyst for industry-wide reforms. He sued midwestern power plants and achieved significant reductions in the emissions that are responsible for acid rain and smog in the Northeast. He directed investigations into pharmaceutical companies that were engaged in the dangerous practice of concealing information about the clinical trials of drugs, and he helped develop new disclosure policies for the industry. As a result of these and other actions, he has won national acclaim. He was named "Crusader of the Year" by Time, the "Sheriff of Wall Street" by 60 Minutes, and "The Enforcer" by People. Reader's Digest called him America's "Best Public Servant."

Spitzer went to Princeton University and Harvard Law School, where he was an editor of the Harvard Law Review. He began his career in public service as a clerk to U.S. District Court Judge Robert Sweet and from 1986 to 1992 served as an assistant district attorney in Manhattan. His biggest case came in 1992, when his investigation ended the Gambino organized crime family's control of Manhattan's trucking and garment industries. He also spent time in private practice as an attorney with mega-firm Skadden, Arps, Slate, Meagher and Flom. At the time of this writing, Spitzer is running for governor of New York, a position he expects to win.[1] ◆

prosecutor
An appointed or elected member of the practicing bar who is responsible for bringing the state's case against the accused.

The American Bar Association (ABA) has published a set of *Standards for Criminal Justice*—a compilation of more than 20 volumes dealing with every aspect of justice. Go to the ABA home page and review the standards for prosecution and defense. You can reach it by going to the Siegel/Senna Introduction to Criminal Justice 11e website: www.thomsonedu.com/criminaljustice/siegel.

Eliot Spitzer is the paradigm of the hard-charging criminal prosecutor, one of the two adversaries who face each other every day in the criminal trial process: the **prosecutor**, who represents the state's interest and serves as the "people's attorney," and the defense attorney, who represents the accused. Although the judge manages the trial process, ensuring that the rules of evidence are obeyed, the prosecution and defense attorneys control the substance of the criminal process. They both share the goal and burden of protecting the civil rights of the criminal defendant while they conduct the trial process in a fair and even-handed manner, a difficult task in the current era of vast media coverage and national fascination with high-profile cases.

♦ THE PROSECUTOR

Depending on the level of government and the jurisdiction in which the prosecutor functions, he or she may be known as a district attorney, a county attorney, a state's attorney, or a U.S. attorney. Whatever the title, the prosecutor is ordinarily a member of the practicing bar who has been appointed or elected to be a public prosecutor responsible for bringing the state's case against the accused. He or she focuses the power of the state on those who disobey the law by charging them with a crime and eventually bringing them to trial or, conversely, releasing them after deciding that the evidence at hand does not constitute proof of a crime.

Although the prosecutor's primary duty is to enforce the criminal law, his or her fundamental obligation as an attorney is to seek justice as well as convict those who are guilty. If, for example, the prosecutor discovers facts suggesting that the accused is innocent, he or she must bring this information to the attention of the court. The American Bar Association's *Model Code of Professional Responsibility* requires that prosecutors a)never bring false or unsupported charges, and b)disclose all relevant evidence to the defense.

The senior prosecutor must make policy decisions on the exercise of prosecutorial enforcement powers in a wide range of cases in criminal law, consumer protection, housing, and other areas. In so doing, the prosecutor determines and ultimately shapes the manner in which justice is exercised in society.[2] Although these decisions should be rendered in a fair and objective manner, the prosecutor remains a political figure who has a party affiliation, a constituency of voters and supporters, and a need to respond to community pressures and interest groups.

The political nature of the prosecutor's office can heavily influence decision making. When deciding if, when, and how to handle a case, the prosecutor cannot forget that he or she may be up for election soon and may have to answer to an electorate that will scrutinize those decisions. In a murder trial involving a highly charged issue such as child killing, the prosecutor's decision to ask for the death penalty may hinge on his or her perception of the public's will. Individual prosecutors are often caught between being compelled by their supervisors to do everything possible to obtain a guilty verdict and acting as a concerned public official to ensure that justice is done. Sometimes this conflict can lead to prosecutorial misconduct. According to some legal authorities, unethical prosecutorial behavior is often motivated by the desire to obtain a conviction and by the fact that prosecutorial misbehavior is rarely punished by the courts.[3] Some prosecutors may conceal evidence, misrepresent it, or influence juries by impugning the character of opposing witnesses. Even when a court may instruct a jury to ignore certain evidence, a prosecutor may attempt to sway the jury or the judge by simply mentioning the tainted evidence. Appellate courts generally uphold convictions when such misconduct is not considered serious (the *harmless error doctrine*), so prosecutors are not penalized for their behavior. They are also not held personally liable for their conduct. Overzealous, excessive, and even cruel prosecutors, motivated by political gain or notoriety, produce wrongful convictions, thereby abusing their office and the public trust.[4]

CONCEPT SUMMARY 10.1

Prosecutorial Duties

1. Investigating possible violations of the law.
2. Cooperating with police in investigating a crime.
3. Determining what the charge will be.
4. Interviewing witnesses in criminal cases.
5. Reviewing applications for arrest and search warrants.
6. Subpoenaing witnesses.

7. Representing the government in pretrial hearings and in motion procedures.
8. Entering into plea-bargaining negotiations.
9. Trying criminal cases.
10. Recommending sentences to courts upon conviction.
11. Representing the government in appeals.

According to legal expert Stanley Fisher, prosecutorial excesses appear when the government

◆   Always seeks the highest charges.

◆   Interprets the criminal law expansively.

◆   Wins as many convictions as possible.

◆   Obtains the most severe penalties.[5]

Today, there are more than 2,300 state court prosecutors' offices employing over 79,000 attorneys, investigators, and support staff, which represents a 39-percent increase from 1992 and a 13-percent increase from 1996. Most of these offices are relatively small. Half employ nine or fewer people and have a budget of about $300,000 or less.

The Duties of the Prosecutor

The prosecutor is the chief law enforcement officer of a particular jurisdiction. His or her participation spans the entire gamut of the justice system, from the time that search and arrest warrants are issued or a grand jury is impaneled to the final sentencing decision and appeal (Concept Summary 10.1). General duties of a prosecutor include enforcing the law, representing the government, maintaining proper standards of conduct as an attorney and court officer, developing programs and legislation for law and criminal justice reform, and being a public spokesperson for the field of law. Of these, representing the government while presenting the state's case to the court is the prosecutor's central activity.

REPEAT OFFENDER PROSECUTION   Because they are political figures, prosecutors may respond to the public's demand for action on particular social problems. Sometimes they respond to media campaigns that focus attention on specific crime problems ranging from corporate wrongdoing to drug abuse. In response, many jurisdictions have established special programs aimed at seeking indictments and convictions of those committing major felonies. Career criminal prosecution programs involve identifying dangerous adult and juvenile offenders who commit a high number of crimes so that prosecutors can target them for swift prosecution. Many jurisdictions have developed protection programs so that victims of domestic violence can obtain temporary and then, after a hearing, more permanent court orders protecting them from an abusive spouse; research indicates that protection orders can reduce the incidence of repeat violence.[6]

WHITE-COLLAR CRIME   Well-publicized corporate scandals involving billion-dollar companies such as Enron and WorldCom may be prompting prosecutorial action. In a national survey of prosecutorial practices, Michael Benson and his colleagues found an apparent increase in local prosecution of corporate offenders.[7] According to the research, the federal government historically played a dominant role in controlling white-collar crime, but an increased willingness to prosecute corporate misconduct is evident on a local level if an offense causes substantial harm.

HIGH-TECH CRIMES   The federal government is operating a number of organizations that are coordinating efforts to prosecute high-tech crime, including cyber crime. For example, the Interagency Telemarketing and Internet Fraud Working Group brings together representatives of numerous U.S. attorneys' offices, the FBI, the Secret Service, the Postal Inspection Service, the Federal Trade Commission, the Securities and Exchange Commission, and other law enforcement and regulatory agencies to share information about trends and patterns in Internet fraud schemes and open the door for prosecutions. Because cyber crime is so new, existing laws are sometimes inadequate to address the problem. Therefore, legislation is being drafted to protect the public from this new threat. The Identity Theft and Assumption Act of 1998 was created to help control this emerging form of crime.[8]

ENVIRONMENTAL CRIMES   Environmental crime prosecution—a field that mixes elements of law, public health, and science—has also emerged as a new area of specialization. Not only federal prosecutions but also local environmental crime prosecutions have increased dramatically.[9] Approximately half of all U.S. jurisdictions operate special environmental units.

The most common environmental offenses being prosecuted center around waste disposal. Such cases, often involving the illegal disposal of hazardous wastes, are referred to the prosecutor by local law enforcement and environmental regulatory agencies. The two most important factors in deciding to prosecute these crimes are the degree of harm posed by the offense and the criminal intent of the offender. If the prosecutor decides not to prosecute, it is usually because of a lack of evidence or problems with evidentiary standards and the use of expert witnesses.

The National District Attorneys Association has responded to the concerns of prosecutors faced with the need to enforce complex environmental laws by creating the National Environmental Crime Prosecution Center. This center, modeled after the National Center for Prosecution of Child Abuse, lends assistance to district attorneys who are prosecuting environmental crimes.[10]

CAREER CRIMINALS   Another area of priority prosecutions in many jurisdictions is the *career criminal prosecution program*. Such programs involve identifying those dangerous offenders who commit a high proportion of crime so that prosecutors can target them for swift prosecution.[11]

RAPE AND SEXUAL ASSAULT   Local prosecutors' handling of rape crimes continues to undergo changes. In the 1980s, most states imposed a heavy burden on rape victims, such as prompt reporting of the crime to police, corroboration by witnesses, and the need to prove physical resistance. In recent years, many states have removed these restrictions and have also made the victims' sexual history inadmissible as evidence at trial. In addition, the definition of rape has been expanded to include other forms of penetration of the person, and laws now exist making the rape of a woman by her husband a crime. Other areas in which the justice system is expanding its sexual assault prosecution capabilities are the following: more vigorous prosecution of acquaintance rape, testing of defendants for the AIDS virus and for DNA profiling, and improved coordination among police, prosecutors, rape crisis centers, and hospitals.[12]

PUBLIC HEALTH   Prosecutors have also assumed the role of protector of the public health.[13] They are responsible for such areas as prosecution of physician-assisted suicide, cases in which AIDS transmission is used as a weapon, violence

Check out the National District Attorneys Association website. You can reach it by going to the Siegel/Senna Introduction to Criminal Justice 11e website: www.thomsonedu.com/criminaljustice/siegel.

The American Prosecutors Research Institute of the National District Attorneys Association conducts research and provides consultation to state and local prosecutors. To learn more about current research on prosecutorial issues, visit its website by going to the Siegel/Senna Introduction to Criminal Justice 11e website: www.thomsonedu.com/criminaljustice/siegel.

against the elderly, cases in which pregnant women are known drug abusers, and health care fraud cases. Prosecutors are paying special attention to the illegal practices of physicians and other health care professionals who abuse their position of trust. One health-related prosecution that made recent headlines involved a dentist named Michael Mastromarino and three other men who were charged with running a multi-million-dollar body-snatching business. They looted bones and tissue from more than a thousand corpses and sold the body parts to legitimate companies that supplied hospitals around the United States. The tainted tissue was used in such procedures as joint and heart-valve replacements, back surgery, dental implants, and skin grafts.[14]

Types of Prosecutors

In the federal system, prosecutors are known as U.S. attorneys and are appointed by the president. They are responsible for representing the government in federal district court. The chief prosecutor is usually an administrator, whereas assistants normally handle the preparation and trial work. Federal prosecutors are professional civil service employees with reasonable salaries and job security.

On the state and county levels, the **attorney general** and the **district attorney**, respectively, are the chief prosecutorial officers. Again, the bulk of the criminal prosecution and staff work is performed by scores of full- and part-time attorneys, police investigators, and clerical personnel. Most attorneys who work for prosecutors on the state and county levels are political appointees who earn low salaries, handle many cases, and in some jurisdictions maintain private law practices. Many young lawyers take these staff positions to gain the trial experience that will qualify them for better opportunities. In most state, county, and municipal jurisdictions, however, the attorneys working within the office of the prosecutor can be described as having the proper standards of professional skill, personal integrity, and adequate working conditions.

In urban jurisdictions, the structure of the district attorney's office is often specialized, with separate divisions for felonies, misdemeanors, and trial and appeal assignments. In rural offices, chief prosecutors handle many of the criminal cases themselves. When assistant prosecutors are employed in such areas, they often work part time, have limited professional opportunities, and

attorney general
The chief legal officer and prosecutor of each state and of the United States.

district attorney
The county prosecutor who is charged with bringing offenders to justice and enforcing the criminal laws of the state.

Assistant prosecutors conduct investigations into activities that endanger the public health. Though these typically involve environmental crimes, this is not always the case. Here Brooklyn, New York Assistant District Attorney Josh Hanshaft holds a photograph of an x-ray showing the pelvic area of a deceased person with PVC plumbing pipe inserted where bones should have been at a news conference on February 23, 2006, announcing the indictment of four individuals, including Michael Mastromarino, head of Biomedical Tissue Services. It is alleged that Mastromarino was involved in taking body parts from deceased individuals and selling them for profit. On the table are pieces of PVC piping illustrating the type of material used to replace the bone in cadavers that were looted for body parts.

FIGURE 10.1
County District Attorney's Office

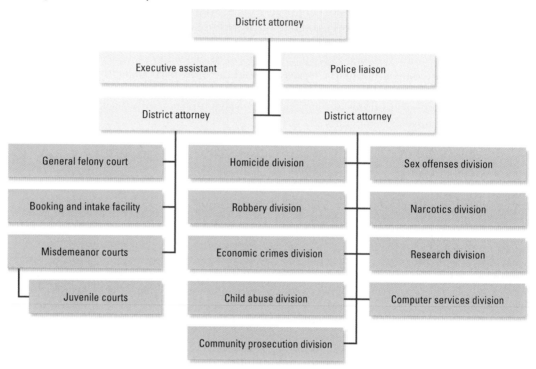

depend on the political patronage of chief prosecutors for their positions. See Figure 10.1 for an organizational chart of a county district attorney's office.

The Prosecutor Within Society

Prosecutors are routinely criticized for bargaining justice away, for using their positions as a stepping-stone to higher political office, and for failing to investigate or simply dismissing criminal cases.

In response to this criticism, during the past decade local, state, and federal prosecutors have become extremely aggressive in attacking particular crime problems. Federal prosecutors have made extraordinary progress in the war against insider trading and securities fraud on Wall Street, using information, wiretaps, and the federal racketeering laws. Some commentators now argue that the government may be going overboard in its efforts to punish white-collar criminals, especially for crimes that are the result of negligent business practices, not intentional criminal conspiracy.[15] Both fines and penalties have been increasing. And even such notorious white-collar criminals as Tyco's Dennis Kozlowski (8–25 years in prison) and WorldCom's Bernie Ebbers (25-year sentence) have received sympathy because of the severity of their criminal sentences.[16]

In addition, prosecutors are now sharpening their working relationships with both the law enforcement community and the general public. These relationships are key to greater prosecutorial effectiveness.

PROSECUTORS AND LAW ENFORCEMENT One of the most important of the prosecutor's many functions involves the relationship between the prosecutor and law enforcement agents. When it comes to processing everyday offenses and minor crimes, the prosecutor often relies on law enforcement officers to provide and initiate the formal complaint. With more serious offenses, such as some felonies, the prosecutor's office may become directly involved in the criminal investigation. Some district attorneys' offices carry out special investigations of organized crime, corruption of public officials, and corporate and white-collar crime, as well as vice and drug offenses. Much of the investigative work is handled by police personnel directly assigned to the prosecutor.

Police and prosecutorial relationships vary from one jurisdiction to another and often depend on whether the police agency is supplying the charge or the district attorney is investigating the matter. In either case, the prosecutor is required to maintain regular contact with the police department to develop the criminal prosecution properly. Some of the areas in which the police officer and the prosecutor work together include the following:

◆ *The police investigation report.* This report is one of the most important documents in the prosecutor's file. It is basically a statement by the police of the details of the crime, including all the evidence needed to support each element of the offense. It is a critical first step in developing the government's case against a suspect.

◆ *Providing legal advice.* Often the prosecutor advises the police officer about the legal issues in a given case. The prosecutor may also assist the officer by limiting unnecessary court appearances, informing the officer of the disposition of the case, and preparing the officer for pretrial appearances. As an officer of the court, the prosecutor enjoys civil immunity when assisting the police in criminal cases. This means that he or she is not liable to a criminal defendant in a civil suit.

◆ *Training police personnel.* In many jurisdictions, prosecutors help train police officers in securing warrants, making legal arrests, interrogating persons in custody, and conducting legal lineups. Some police departments have police legal advisors who work with the prosecutor in training new and experienced police personnel in legal matters.[17]

THE PROSECUTOR AND THE COMMUNITY Today, many prosecutors' offices are improving their working relationship with the community. The concept of **community prosecution** recognizes that crime reduction is built on community partnerships.[18] It is not just a program, but also a new strategy for prosecutors to do their job. Just as police officers no longer simply make arrests, prosecutors need to do more than try cases. They become problem solvers looking to improve the overall safety and well-being of the communities over which they have jurisdiction.

The traditional prosecutorial model is case oriented and reactive to crime, not problem oriented and proactive. Prosecutors are centrally located and assigned to teams focusing on specific types of crime (homicide, narcotics, sex offenses, misdemeanors, and so on), with the most senior prosecutors handling the most serious felonies. Most prosecutions are arrest-generated. There is not much direct interaction among prosecutors, police, and members of the community outside of specific cases.

The lack of direct involvement by prosecutors in the community, when combined with an arrest-generated, case-oriented approach, often leads to an inefficient allocation of criminal justice resources. Frequently, no effort is made to allocate resources on a geographical basis or to assign prosecutors where they are needed. To align resources with community needs, some prosecutors must be in the community daily. In this way, the prosecutors can gauge the seriousness of the crime problem and play a positive role in its solution, along with other law enforcement and community groups. Community prosecution requires that field prosecutors work directly with the police to improve public safety in a particular district.

The main components of such a program include placing prosecutors in selected communities to work at police stations; increasing communication with police and with community groups, schools, and other organizations so prosecutors can be made aware of which cases and problems need the most attention;

community prosecution
A prosecutorial philosophy that emphasizes community support and cooperation with other agencies in preventing crime as well as a less centralized and more proactive role for local prosecutors.

Community prosecution is considered community policing's legal partner. The Chicago Police Department recently launched a website granting users public access to a wide range of crime information. Can the same concept be applied to community prosecution? To find out, access the Chicago website. You can reach it by going to the Siegel/Senna Introduction to Criminal Justice 11e website: www.thomsonedu.com/ criminaljustice/siegel.

and using prosecutorial resources to solve community problems, not just to prosecute individual cases.

What is the role of community prosecutors? They meet with the police daily to discuss law enforcement problems, strategize about the methods used to approach criminal behaviors, attend community meetings to learn about criminal incidents ranging from nuisances to felonies, and screen citizen complaints by diverting those cases that should not be in the criminal justice system. In short, field prosecutors build partnerships with the police, citizen groups, schools, and businesses to ensure public safety for the community.

Community prosecution programs have been started in many jurisdictions, with notable accomplishments. For example, prosecutors working with police and business leaders reduced the incidence of robberies near a local theater by implementing measures to make the area less attractive to criminals (better lighting, removal of pay phones, stricter enforcement of trespass laws, and increased police surveillance). In another example, community prosecutors, police, and housing inspectors closed and condemned a drug house where illegal drug activities were consistently taking place.[19]

Establishing partnerships with the community and law enforcement, as well as strong working relationships with other public and private agencies, is the key to a successful community prosecution approach. Community prosecution is not a new program, but rather an important new philosophy. It is the result of efforts, similar to those involved in community policing, to provide better criminal justice service to the community.

Finally, one of the greatest challenges facing community prosecution is the task of evaluating its effectiveness. What is the best measure of success for a prosecutor? Is it the number of prosecutions? What about the percentage of cases won in court? Is it how many offenders are given prison time? Or is it whether crime is reduced in the community? Each of these factors provides a useful measure for determining the success or failure of community prosecution efforts.

◆ PROSECUTORIAL DISCRETION

One might expect that after the police arrest and bring a suspect to court, the entire criminal court process would be mobilized. This is often not the case, however. For a variety of reasons, a substantial percentage of defendants are never brought to trial. The prosecutor decides whether to bring a case to trial or to dismiss it outright. Even if the prosecutor decides to pursue a case, the charges may later be dropped, in a process called nolle prosequi, if conditions are not favorable for a conviction.

Even in felony cases, the prosecutor ordinarily exercises considerable discretion in deciding whether to charge the accused with a crime.[20] After a police investigation, the prosecutor may be asked to review the sufficiency of the evidence to determine if a criminal complaint should be filed. In some jurisdictions, this may involve presenting the evidence at a preliminary hearing. In other cases, the prosecutor may decide to seek a criminal complaint through a **grand jury** or other information procedure. These procedures, representing the formal methods of charging the accused with a felony offense, are discussed in Chapter 11.

Prosecutors exercise a great deal of discretion in even the most serious cases. In a classic study of prosecutorial discretion in three counties, Barbara Boland found that prosecutors used their discretion to dismiss a high percentage of the cases before trial.[21] However, when cases were forwarded for trial, few defendants were acquitted, indicating that prosecutorial

grand jury
A group of citizens chosen to hear charges against persons accused of crime and to determine whether there is sufficient evidence to bring the persons to trial.

Prosecutors have discretion to either move forward on cases or discontinue their involvement. Here, Martha Stewart waves to supporters on June 19, 2003, as she leaves a federal courthouse. Stewart was indicted on charges stemming from her trading of ImClone Systems stock, which federal prosecutors considered in violation of insider trading laws. Prosecutors had the choice of seeking an indictment in the case or concluding that Stewart was merely a sharp stock trader who had broken no laws. They decided to prosecute.

©Stephen Chernin/Getty Images

Common Reasons for Rejection or Dismissal of a Criminal Case

Many criminal cases are rejected or dismissed because of

◆ *Insufficient evidence*—a failure to find sufficient physical evidence linking the defendant to the offense.

◆ *Witness problems*—for example, when a witness fails to appear, gives unclear or inconsistent statements, is reluctant to testify, or is unsure of the identity of the offender, or when a prior relationship exists between the victim or witness and the offender.

◆ *The interests of justice*—deciding not to prosecute certain types of offenses, particularly those that violate the letter but not the spirit of the law (for example, offenses involving insignificant amounts of property damage).

◆ *Due process problems*—violations of the constitutional requirements for seizing evidence and for questioning the accused.

◆ *A plea on another case*—for example, when the accused is charged in several cases and the prosecutor agrees to drop one or more of the cases in exchange for a plea of guilty in another case.

◆ *Pretrial diversion*—agreeing to drop charges when the accused successfully meets the conditions for diversion, such as completion of a treatment program.

◆ *Referral for other prosecution*—when there are other offenses, perhaps of a more serious nature, in a different jurisdiction, or deferring to a federal prosecution.

---

discretion was exercised to screen out the weakest cases. The reasons that some cases are rejected or dismissed are summarized in Concept Summary 10.2. Evidence problems are the most common reason for rejecting cases; many other cases are dropped because defendants plead guilty to lesser crimes.

The Exercise of Discretion

The power to institute or discontinue formal charges against the defendant is the key to the prosecutorial function, representing the control and power that the prosecutor has over an individual's liberty. The prosecutor has broad discretion in the exercise of his or her duties. This discretion is subject to few limitations and often puts the prosecutor in the position of making difficult decisions without appropriate policies and guidelines. Prosecutorial discretion is rarely reviewed by the courts, unless the prosecutor specifically violates a defendant's constitutional rights.[22] As the U.S. Supreme Court stated in *United States v. Armstrong*,

> The Attorney General and the United States Attorneys retain "broad discretion" to enforce the Nation's criminal laws. They have this latitude because they are designated by statute as the President's delegates to help him discharge his constitutional responsibility to "take Care that the Laws be faithfully executed."[23]

As a result, prosecutorial decisions to drop cases are rarely reviewed. More than 70 years ago, legal scholar Newman Baker commented on the problems of prosecutorial decision making:

> "To prosecute or not to prosecute?" is a question which comes to mind of this official scores of times each day. A law has been contravened and the statute says he is bound to commence proceedings. His legal duty is clear. But what will be the result? Will it be a waste of time? Will it be expensive to the state? Will it be unfair to the defendant (the prosecutor applying his own ideas of justice)? Will it serve any good purpose to society in general? Will it have good publicity value? Will it cause a political squabble? Will it prevent the prosecutor from carrying the offender's home precinct when he, the prosecutor, runs for Congress after his term as prosecutor? Was the law violated a foolish piece of legislation? If the offender is a friend, is it the square thing to do to reward

friendship by initiating criminal proceedings? These and many similar considerations are bound to come to the mind of the man responsible for setting the wheels of criminal justice in motion.[24]

Once involved in a case, the prosecutor must also determine the formal charge. Deciding whether or not to charge a person with a crime is not easy—nor is determining the appropriate charge. Should a 16-year-old boy be charged with burglary or handled as a juvenile offender in the juvenile court? Would it be more appropriate to reduce a drug charge from the sale of marijuana to mere possession? Should an offense be considered mayhem, battery, or simply assault?

What, then, are the factors that influence prosecutorial decision making?

SYSTEM FACTORS In determining what course of action to take, the prosecutor has a significant effect on the criminal justice system. Initiating formal charges against all defendants arrested by the police would clog the courts with numerous petty crimes and cases with little chance of conviction. In dealing with minor cases, the prosecutor would waste time that could have been better spent on the investigation and prosecution of more serious crimes. Effective screening by prosecutors can eliminate from the judicial system many cases in which convictions cannot reasonably be obtained or that may be inappropriate for criminal action, such as petty thefts, minor crimes by first offenders, and criminal acts involving offenders in need of special services (such as emotionally disturbed or mentally challenged offenders). The prosecutor can then concentrate on bringing to trial offenders who commit serious personal and property crimes, such as homicide, burglary, rape, and robbery. In meeting this goal, the prosecutor may decide not to press charges in the current case but rely on such mechanisms as revoking the client's probation or, if appropriate, turning the case over to correctional authorities for a parole revocation hearing. As a result, many cases that may look as if they were dropped by the prosecutor conclude with the incarceration of the defendant.[25]

CASE FACTORS Because they are ultimately responsible for deciding whether to prosecute, prosecutors must be aware of the wide variety of circumstances that affect their decisions. Frank Miller, in his classic work *Prosecution: The Decision to Charge a Suspect with a Crime*, identified the factors that affect discretion and the charging decision. Among these factors are the attitude of the victim, the cost of prosecution to the criminal justice system, the avoidance of undue harm to the suspect, the availability of alternative procedures, the availability of civil sanctions, and the willingness of the suspect to cooperate with law enforcement authorities.[26]

Evidence also indicates that the relationship between the victim and the criminal may greatly influence whether a prosecutor wishes to pursue a case. Barbara Boland found that conviction rates were much lower in cases involving friends (30 percent) or relatives (19 percent) than they were in cases involving strangers (48 percent).[27] Prosecutors who are aware of the lower conviction probability in friend and relative cases may be reluctant to pursue them unless they involve serious offenses. Recent (2006) research by John Worrall and his associates finds that case seriousness shapes prosecutorial discretion in domestic violence cases: Charges are more likely to occur if the victim is both a female and is injured in the assault. In some of the cases they studied, police officers could not easily identify a victim and/or a suspect. When the assault seemed to be mutual, prosecutors were much less likely to bring charges than in cases where there was a case with a clear victim and/or suspect. How can this finding be explained? Prosecutors do not move forward if they cannot identify who is responsible.[28]

"Convictability" is another factor that shapes prosecutorial discretion. Prosecutors know that the victim's character and background will be attacked in court and must conclude that their witness and supporting evidence can withstand the attack. When Cassia Spohn and David Holleran studied prosecutors' decisions in rape cases, they found that perception of the victim's character was still a critical factor in prosecutors' decision to file charges. In cases involving an acquaintance, prosecutors were reluctant to file charges when the victim's character was questioned—for example, when police reports described the victim as sexually active or as being engaged in sexually oriented occupations such as exotic dancing. In cases involving strangers, prosecutors were more likely to take action if a gun or a knife was used. Spohn and Holleran conclude that prosecutors are still influenced by perceptions of what constitutes "real rape" and who are "real victims."

DISPOSITION FACTORS In determining which cases should be eliminated from the criminal process or brought to trial, the prosecutor has the opportunity to select alternative actions if they are more appropriate. Some offenders may be alcoholics or narcotic addicts, they may be mentally ill, or they may have been led into crime by their family situation or their inability to get a job. If they are not helped, they may return to crime. In many cases, only minimal intrusions on defendants' liberty seem necessary. Often it will be enough simply to refer offenders to the appropriate agency in the community and hope that they will take advantage of the help offered. The prosecutor might, for example, be willing to drop charges if a man goes to an employment agency and makes a bona fide effort to get a job, seeks help from a social service agency, or resumes his education. The prosecutor retains legal power to file a charge until the period of limitations has expired, but as a practical matter, unless the offense is repeated, reviewing the initial charge would be unusual.

Today, particularly in those jurisdictions where alternative programs exist, prosecutors are identifying and diverting offenders to community agencies in cases in which the full criminal process does not appear necessary. This may occur in certain juvenile cases, with alcoholic and drug offenders, and in nonsupport paternity, prostitution, and gambling offenses. The American Bar Association recommends the use of social service programs as an appropriate alternative to prosecution.[29]

Dealing with the accused in such a way has come to be known as pretrial **diversion**. In this process, the prosecutor postpones or eliminates criminal prosecution in exchange for the alleged offender's participation in a rehabilitation program.[30] In recent years, the reduced cost and general utility of such programs have made them an important factor in prosecutorial discretion and a major part of the criminal justice system. A more detailed discussion of pretrial diversion is found in Chapter XI.

diversion
The use of an alternative to trial, such as referral to treatment or employment programs.

POLITICAL FACTORS The prosecutor is a political figure, typically elected to office, whose discretion may be shaped by prevailing political necessities. If the public is outraged by school shootings, the prosecutor may be under media pressure to do something about kids who carry guns to school. Similarly, public interest groups that are interested in curbing particular behaviors, such as domestic violence or possession of handguns, may lobby prosecutors to devote more attention to these social problems. If too successful, however, lobbying efforts may dilute resources and overextend the prosecutor's office. When prosecutors in Milwaukee, Wisconsin, substantially increased the prosecution of domestic violence cases, the time taken to process the cases doubled, convictions declined, pretrial crimes increased, and victim satisfaction with the justice process decreased.[31]

The Role of Prosecutorial Discretion

The proper exercise of prosecutorial discretion can improve the criminal justice process, preventing unnecessarily rigid implementation of the criminal law. Discretion allows the prosecutor to consider alternative decisions and humanize the operation of the criminal justice system. If prosecutors had little or no discretion, they would be forced to prosecute all cases brought to their attention. According to Judge Charles Breitel, "If every policeman, every prosecutor, every court, and

Prosecutor

Duties and Characteristics of the Job

Prosecutors represent the public in criminal trials and are responsible for proving in court that the accused is guilty of the charges brought against him. Prosecutors work at municipal, state, and federal levels of government. During a trial, a prosecutor is opposed by a defense attorney, who is trying to maintain the innocence of the accused offender. In order to convince the judge or jury of the defendant's guilt, the prosecutor will question witnesses and give statements using evidence collected during the investigative phase of the case. Prosecutors also decide which cases to bring to trial and have the authority to settle cases out of court. Even though they represent the people, prosecutors will often meet with victims of crime and present the case from that point of view when in court.

This job comes with many responsibilities and pressures. Prosecutors must be mindful of their actions and words as representatives of the government body for which they work. Victims of crime and their families, community members, and law enforcement are depending on the prosecutor to prove the guilt of an alleged offender to a jury or judge and gain a conviction. Prosecutors may work long hours, especially during trials. In general, prosecutors may tend to be paid less than their counterparts in private practice; however, many report high personal satisfaction from seeing that justice is served.

Job Outlook

Crime rates and budgets will dictate the number of job openings. However, job opportunities open up on a regular basis because the position has a high turnover rate. Positions should be more available in smaller communities and at lower levels of government.

Salary

Prosecutors working in federal and state offices will tend to earn more than those working at the county and municipal levels. In larger cities, pay will also be higher. Entering prosecutors earn an average of $34,000. After 11 years, many public prosecutors are making between $51,927 and $64,000 annually.

Opportunities

There are opportunities for advancement in larger offices, especially in urban areas. A state prosecutor

---

Noninterventionism

Some prosecutors' offices will make liberal use of alternatives such as placement in a community program in lieu of being charged with a criminal offense. The availability of these community programs is a function of how advocates of non-intervention have shaped the justice process in an effort to reduce stigma and labeling.

every postsentence agency performed his or its responsibility in strict accordance with the rules of law, precisely and narrowly laid down, the criminal law would be ordered but intolerable."[32]

Meanwhile, too much discretion can lead to abuses that result in the abandonment of law. Prosecutors are political creatures. They are charged with serving the people, but they must also be wary of their reputations. Losing too many high-profile cases might jeopardize their chances of reelection. Therefore, they may be unwilling to prosecute cases in which the odds of conviction are low. They are worried about *convictability*.[33]

◆ THE DEFENSE ATTORNEY

defense attorney
Legal counsel for the defendant in a criminal case, representing the accused person from arrest to final appeal.

The **defense attorney** is the counterpart of the prosecuting attorney in the criminal process. The accused has a constitutional right to counsel. If the defendant cannot afford an attorney, the state must provide one.

For many years, much of the legal community looked down on the criminal defense attorney and the practice of criminal law. This attitude stemmed from the kinds of legal work a defense attorney was forced to do—working with shady characters, negotiating for the release of known thugs and hoodlums, and often overzealously defending alleged criminals in criminal trials. Lawyers were reluctant

may also wish to seek a position as a federal prosecutor.

A position as a prosecutor is quite often used as a stepping-stone to other prestigious government and law careers. After leaving their position, former prosecutors might open up their own private practice, possibly with the intent of running a lucrative defense attorney business. Prosecutors can also seek appointments to prestigious and well-paying judge positions or choose to leave law practice for a political career.

Qualifications

The basic qualifications for becoming a prosecutor are the same as those for any successful career as an attorney. This means that in addition to the demanding education requirements of college and law school, a future lawyer will need to pass the bar exam of the state in which she wants to work.

Like other lawyers, prosecutors need to be comfortable and practiced at public speaking, and they also need well-developed analytical skills. There is also a political aspect to being a prosecutor because in some areas one must be elected or appointed to this position.

Education and Training

A bachelor's degree with an emphasis on building writing, analytical, and research skills is necessary. In addition to a four-year degree, taking the standardized Law School Admission Test (LSAT) is necessary in order to gain entry into a law school. Entry into law school is very competitive, and the educational requirements are challenging.

Sources: "Lawyer," *Occupational Outlook Handbook*, 2006–2007 edition (Bureau of Labor Statistics, U.S. Department of Labor), retrieved July 21, 2006, from http://www.bls.gov/oco/ocos053.htm; "Prosecutor" (*Court TV Careers in Justice*), retrieved July 22, 2006, from http://www.courttv.com/careers_justice/career_track/list/prosecutor.html; "New Research on Attorney Salaries at Public Sector and Public Interest Organizations" (National Association for Legal Career Professionals), retrieved August 4, 2006, from http://www.nalp.org/content/index.php?pid=191; "Princeton Review Career Profiles: Lawyer," retrieved July 22, 2006, from http://www.princetonreview.com/cte/profiles/dayInLife.asp?careerID=16.

to specialize in criminal law because they received comparatively low pay and often provided services without compensation. In addition, law schools in the past seldom offered more than one or two courses in criminal law and trial practice.

In recent years, however, with the implementation of constitutional requirements regarding the right to counsel, interest has grown in criminal law. Almost all law schools today have clinical programs that employ students as voluntary defense attorneys. They also offer courses in trial tactics, brief writing, and appellate procedures. In addition, legal organizations such as the American Bar Association, the National Legal Aid and Defenders Association, and the National Association of Criminal Defense Lawyers have assisted in recruiting able lawyers to do criminal defense work. As the American Bar Association has noted, "An almost indispensable condition to fundamental improvement of American criminal justice is the active and knowledgeable support of the bar as a whole."[34]

The Role of the Criminal Defense Attorney

The defense counsel is an attorney as well as an officer of the court. As an attorney, the defense counsel is obligated to uphold the integrity of the legal profession and to observe the requirements of the *Model Rules of Professional Conduct* in the defense of a client. The duties of the lawyer to the adversary system of justice are as follows:

> Our legal system provides for the adjudication of disputes governed by the rules of substantive, evidentiary, and procedural law. An adversary presentation counters the natural human tendency to judge too swiftly in terms of the

The National Legal Aid and Defenders Association (NLADA) is the nation's leading advocate for front-line attorneys and other equal justice professionals. Representing legal aid and defender programs, as well as individual advocates, NLADA is the oldest and largest national, nonprofit membership association serving the equal justice community. Check out its website by going to the Siegel/Senna Introduction to Criminal Justice 11e website: www.thomsonedu.com/criminaljustice/siegel.

Defense attorneys are sworn to represent their clients' interests no matter how unpopular the case or troubling the crime. They serve as an objective legal defender whose integrity cannot be questioned. Johnny Griffin III (shown here) was the attorney for terror suspect Umer Hayat. On April 25, 2006, U.S. District Judge Garland E. Burrell declared a mistrial in the case after the jury told the judge that it was hopelessly deadlocked. Hayat faced up to 16 years in prison if he had been convicted of the two counts against him, both related to making false statements to federal agents about his son Hamid Hayat attending an Al-Qaeda training camp in Pakistan. At left is Wazhma Mojaddidi, attorney for Hamid Hayat. Hayat eventually accepted a plea agreement with federal prosecutors rather than face a retrial. He was sentenced to time served, a $3,600 fine, and 36 months probation for pleading guilty to trying to smuggle $28,000 into Pakistan.

familiar that which is not yet fully known; the advocate, by his zealous preparation of facts and law, enables the tribunal to come to the hearing with an open and neutral mind to render impartial judgments. The duty of the lawyer to his client and his duty to the legal system are the same: To represent his client zealously within the boundaries of the law.[35]

The defense counsel performs many functions while representing the accused in the criminal process. Exhibit 10.1 lists some of the major duties of a defense attorney, whether privately employed by the accused, appointed by the court, or serving as a public defender.

Because of the way the U.S. system of justice operates, criminal defense attorneys face many role conflicts. They are viewed as the prime movers in what is essentially an adversary process. The prosecution and the defense engage in conflict over the facts of the case, with the prosecutor arguing the case for the state and the defense counsel using all the means at his or her disposal to aid the client. This system can be compared to a sporting event, in which the government and the accused are the players, and the judge and the jury are the referees.

As members of the legal profession, defense counsel must also be aware of their role as officers of the court. As attorneys, defense counsel are obligated to uphold the integrity of the legal profession and to rely on constitutional ideals of fair play and professional ethics to provide adequate representation for a client.

Ethical Issues

As an officer of the court, along with the judge, prosecutors, and other trial participants, the defense attorney seeks to uncover the basic facts and elements of the criminal act. In this dual capacity as both a defense advocate and an officer of the court, the attorney is often confronted with conflicting obligations to his or her client and profession. In a famous work, Monroe Freedman identified three of the most difficult problems involving the professional responsibility of the criminal defense lawyer:

1. Is it proper to cross-examine for the purpose of discrediting the reliability or credibility of an adverse witness whom you know to be telling the truth?

2. Is it proper to put a witness on the stand when you know he will commit perjury?

3. Is it proper to give your client legal advice when you have reason to believe that the knowledge you give him will tempt him to commit perjury?[36]

Other equally important issues confound a lawyer's ethical responsibilities. Lawyers are required to keep their clients' statements confidential—the attorney–client privilege. Suppose that a client confides that he is planning to commit a crime. What are the defense attorney's ethical responsibilities? The lawyer would have to counsel the client to obey the law. If the lawyer assisted the client in engaging in illegal behavior, the lawyer would be subject to charges of unprofessional conduct and criminal liability. If the lawyer believed that the danger was imminent, he would have to alert the police. The criminal lawyer needs to be aware of these troublesome situations to properly balance the duties of being an attorney with those of being an officer of the court and a moral person. These decisions are often difficult to make. What should an attorney do when her client reveals that he committed a murder and that an innocent person has been convicted of the crime and is going to be executed? Should the attorney do the moral thing and reveal the information before a terrible miscarriage of justice occurs? Or should the attorney do the professional thing and maintain her client's confidence?

EXHIBIT 10.1

Functions of the Defense Attorney

- ♦ Investigating the incident.
- ♦ Interviewing the client, police, and witnesses.
- ♦ Discussing the matter with the prosecutor.
- ♦ Representing the defendant at the various pretrial procedures, such as arrest, interrogation, lineup, and arraignment.
- ♦ Entering into plea negotiations.
- ♦ Preparing the case for trial, including developing tactics and strategy.
- ♦ Filing and arguing legal motions with the court.
- ♦ Representing the defendant at trial.
- ♦ Providing assistance at sentencing.
- ♦ Determining the appropriate basis for appeal.

In the aftermath of terrorist attacks and corporate scandals, the government is pressuring lawyers to breach their clients' confidences. In 2003 the Securities and Exchange Commission adopted a rule requiring lawyers to report potential fraud to corporate boards, the Internal Revenue Service is trying to make law firms disclose which clients bought questionable tax shelters, and the Justice Department has stated that conversations between lawyers and terrorism suspects are subject to eavesdropping.[37]

Because the defense attorney and the prosecutor have different roles, their ethical dilemmas may also differ. The defense attorney must maintain confidentiality and advise his or her client of the constitutional requirements of counsel, the privilege against self-incrimination, and the right to trial. The prosecutor represents the public and is not required to abide by such restrictions in the same way. In some cases, the defense counsel may be justified in withholding evidence by keeping the defendant from testifying at the trial. In addition, whereas prosecutors are prohibited from expressing a personal opinion on the defendant's guilt during summation of the case, defense attorneys are not barred from expressing their belief about a client's innocence.

PERSPECTIVES ON JUSTICE

Due Process

The defense attorney's obligation to her client is one of the purest illustrations of the due process perspective because it mandates fair and equitable treatment to those accused of a crime even if they are personally obnoxious to those representing them in court. The defense attorney cannot let her personal feelings interfere with her obligation to put on a spirited defense.

As a practical matter, therefore, ethical rules may differ because the state is bringing the action against the defendant and must prove the case beyond a reasonable doubt. This is also why a defendant who is found guilty can appeal, whereas a prosecutor must live with an acquittal, and why defense lawyers generally have more latitude in performing their duties on behalf of their clients. However, neither side should encourage unethical practices.[38]

It would be considered unethical for a prosecutor to withhold exculpatory evidence from the defense or for a defense lawyer to condone perjury by their client during cross examination.

ThomsonNOW Improve your grade on the exam with Personalized Study! For reinforcement resources and a mastery check of defense attorneys, go to www.thomsonedu.com/thomsonnow.

♦ THE RIGHT TO COUNSEL

Over the past decades, the rules and procedures of criminal justice administration have become extremely complex. Bringing a case to court involves a detailed investigation of the crime, knowledge of court procedures, the use of rules of evidence, and skills in criminal advocacy. Both the state and the defense must

indigent defendant
A defendant who lacks the funds to hire a private attorney and is therefore entitled to free counsel.

have this specialized expertise, particularly when an individual's freedom or life is at stake. Consequently, the right to the assistance of counsel in the criminal justice system is essential if the defendant is to have a fair chance of presenting a case in the adversary process.

One of the most critical issues in the justice system has been whether an **indigent defendant** has the right to counsel. Can an accused person who is poor and cannot afford an attorney have a fair trial without the assistance of counsel? Is counsel required at preliminary hearings? Should the convicted indigent offender be given counsel at state expense in appeals of the case? Questions such as these have arisen constantly in recent years. The federal court system has long provided counsel to indigent defendants on the basis of the Sixth Amendment to the U.S. Constitution, unless he or she waives this right. This constitutional mandate clearly applies to the federal courts, but its application to state criminal proceedings has been less certain.

In the landmark case of *Gideon v. Wainwright* (1963), the U.S. Supreme Court took the first major step on the issue of right to counsel by holding that state courts must provide counsel to indigent defendants in felony prosecutions.[39] Nine years later, in *Argersinger v. Hamlin* (1972), the Court extended the obligation to provide counsel to all criminal cases in which the penalty includes imprisonment—regardless of whether the offense is a felony or a misdemeanor.[40] These two major decisions apply to the Sixth Amendment right to counsel when presenting a defense at the trial stage of the criminal justice system.

In numerous Supreme Court decisions since *Gideon*, the states have been required to provide counsel for indigent defendants at virtually all other stages of the criminal process, beginning with the arrest and concluding with the defendant's release from the system.

The Sixth Amendment right to counsel and the Fifth Amendment guarantee of due process of law have been judicially interpreted together to require state-provided counsel in all types of criminal proceedings. The right to counsel begins at the earliest stages of the justice system, usually when a criminal suspect is interrogated while in police custody. *Miranda v. Arizona* (1966) held that any statements made by the accused when in custody are inadmissible at trial unless the accused has been informed of the right to counsel and, if indigent, the right to have an attorney appointed by the state.[41]

The Supreme Court also has extended the right to counsel to postconviction and other collateral proceedings, such as probation and parole revocation and appeal. When, for example, the court intends to revoke a defendant's probation and impose a sentence, the probationer has a right to counsel at the deferred sentence hearing.[42] When the state provides for an appellate review of the criminal conviction, the defendant is entitled to the assistance of counsel for this initial appeal.[43] The Supreme Court has also required states to provide counsel in other proceedings that involve the loss of personal liberty, such as juvenile delinquency hearings and mental health commitments.[44]

Areas still remain in the criminal justice system where the courts have not required assistance of counsel for the accused. These include preindictment lineups; booking procedures, including the taking of fingerprints and other forms of identification; grand jury investigations; appeals beyond the first review; disciplinary proceedings in correctional institutions; and postrelease revocation hearings. Nevertheless, the general rule is that no person can be deprived of freedom without representation by counsel if there is a chance that they will lose their liberty and be incarcerated in a correctional institution.

The Private Bar

The lawyer whose practice involves a substantial proportion of criminal cases is often considered a specialist in the field. And there is little question that having a preeminent private attorney can help clients prove their innocence. Just ask

O. J. Simpson, who was represented by the late Johnny Cochran, one of the nation's best-known attorneys. Recent research by Talia Roitberg Harmon and William Lofquist found that having a competent private attorney who puts on a rigorous defense is the single most important factor separating those exonerated in murder cases and those who are executed.[45]

Although lucky few defendants are able to afford the services of skilled and experienced private counsel, most criminal defendants are represented by lawyers who often accept many cases for minor fees. These lawyers may belong to small law firms or work alone, but a sizable portion of their practice involves representing those accused of crime. Other private practitioners occasionally take on criminal matters as part of their general practice. Criminal lawyers often work on the fringe of the legal business, and they may receive little respect from colleagues or the community as a whole.

All but the most eminent criminal lawyers are bound to spend much of their working lives in overcrowded, physically unpleasant courts, dealing with people who have committed questionable acts, and attempting to put the best possible construction on those acts. It is not the sort of working environment that most people choose. Sometimes a criminal lawyer is identified unjustifiably in the public eye with the client he or she represents. "How could someone represent a child killer and try to get him off?" is a question that many people may ask and few attorneys want to answer.

Another problem associated with the private practice of criminal law is that the fee system can create a conflict of interest. Private attorneys are usually paid in advance and do not expect additional funds whether their client is convicted or acquitted. Many are aware of the guilt of their client before the trial begins, and they earn the greatest profit if they get the case settled as quickly as possible. This usually means bargaining with the prosecutor instead of going to trial. Even if attorneys win the case at trial, they may lose personally because the time expended will not be compensated by more than the gratitude of their client. And many criminal defendants cannot afford even a modest legal fee and therefore cannot avail themselves of the services of a private attorney. For these reasons, an elaborate, publicly funded legal system has developed.

Legal Services for the Indigent

Justice Hugo Black, one of the greatest Supreme Court Justices of the twentieth century, acknowledged the need for public defenders when he wrote, in his dissent in *Betts v. Brady*, "A fair trial is impossible if an indigent is not provided with a free attorney."[46]

To satisfy the constitutional requirement that indigent defendants be provided with the assistance of counsel at various stages of the criminal process, the federal government and the states have had to evaluate and expand criminal defense services. Prior to the Supreme Court's mandate in *Gideon v. Wainwright*, public defense services were provided mainly by local private attorneys appointed and paid for by the court, called **assigned counsel**, or by limited **public defender** programs. In 1961, for example, public defender services existed in only 3 percent of the counties in the United States, serving only about one-quarter of the country's population.[47] The general lack of defense services for indigents traditionally stemmed from the following causes, among others:

assigned counsel
A private attorney appointed by the court to represent a criminal defendant who cannot afford to pay for a lawyer.

public defender
An attorney employed by the government to represent criminal defendants who cannot afford to pay for a lawyer.

◆ Until fairly recently, laws of most jurisdictions did not require the assistance of counsel for felony offenders and others.

◆ Only a few attorneys were interested in criminal law practice.

◆ The organized legal bar was generally indifferent to the need for criminal defense assistance.

◆ The caseloads of lawyers working in public defender agencies were staggering.

◆ Financial resources for courts and defense programs were limited.

However, since the *Gideon* case in 1963 and the *Argersinger* decision in 1972, the criminal justice system has been forced to increase public defender services. Today, about 3,000 state and local agencies are providing indigent legal services in the United States.

Providing legal services for indigent offenders is a huge undertaking. More than 4.5 million offenders are given free legal services annually. And although most states have a formal set of rules for determining who is indigent, and many require repayment to the state for at least part of their legal services (known as **recoupment**), indigent legal services still cost more than $1.5 billion annually.

Programs providing assistance of counsel to indigent defendants can be divided into three major categories: public defender systems, assigned counsel systems, and contract systems. Other approaches to the delivery of legal services include mixed systems, such as representation by both public defenders and the private bar; law school clinical programs; and prepaid legal services. Of the three major approaches, assigned counsel systems are the most common; a majority of U.S. courts use this method. However, public defender programs seem to be on the increase, and many jurisdictions use a combination of programs statewide.

PUBLIC DEFENDERS The first public defender program in the United States opened in 1913 in Los Angeles. Over the years, primarily as a result of efforts by judicial leaders and bar groups, the public defender program became the model for the delivery of legal services to indigent defendants in criminal cases throughout the country.

Most public defender offices can be thought of as law firms whose only clients are criminal offenders. However, they are generally administrated at one of two government levels: state or county. About one-third of the states have a statewide public defender's office, headed by a chief public defender who administers the system. In some of these states, the chief defender establishes offices in all counties around the state; in others, the chief defender relies on part-time private attorneys to provide indigent legal services in rural counties. Statewide public defenders may be organized as part of the judicial branch, as part of the executive branch, as an independent state agency, or as a private, non-profit organization.

ASSIGNED COUNSEL SYSTEM In contrast to the public defender system, the assigned counsel system involves the use of private attorneys appointed by the court to represent indigent defendants. The private attorney is selected from a list of attorneys maintained by the court and is reimbursed by the state for any legal services rendered to the client. Assigned counsels are usually used in rural areas, which do not have sufficient caseloads to justify a full-time public defender staff.

There are two main types of assigned counsel systems. In an *ad hoc* assigned counsel system, the presiding judge appoints attorneys on a case-by-case basis. In a *coordinated* assigned counsel system, an administrator oversees the appointment of counsel and sets up guidelines for the administration of indigent legal services. The fees awarded assigned counsels can vary widely, ranging from a low of $10 per hour for handling a misdemeanor out of court to a high of $100 per hour for a serious felony. Some jurisdictions may establish a maximum allowance per case of $750 for a misdemeanor and $1,500 for a felony. Average rates seem to be between $40 and $80 per hour, depending on the nature of the case. Proposals for higher rates are pending. Restructuring the attorney fee system is undoubtedly needed to maintain fair standards for payment.

The assigned counsel system, unless organized properly, suffers from such problems as unequal assignments, inadequate legal fees, and the lack of supportive or supervisory services. Other

recoupment
Process by which the state later recovers some or all of the cost of providing free legal counsel to an indigent defendant.

Public defenders are assigned to indigent defendants who cannot afford their own defense. Murder suspect John Mark Karr listens with his attorney, deputy public defender Haydeh Takasugi, during an extradition hearing in Los Angeles Superior Court on August 22, 2006. Karr made national headlines when he confessed to murdering JonBenet Ramsey, but DNA evidence showed that he could not have committed the crime.

disadvantages are the frequent use of inexperienced attorneys and the tendency to use the guilty plea too quickly. Some judicial experts believe that the assigned counsel system is still no more than an ad hoc approach that raises serious questions about the quality of representation. However, the assigned counsel system is simple to operate. It also offers the private bar an important role in providing indigent legal services because most public defender systems cannot represent all needy criminal defendants. Thus, the appointed counsel system gives attorneys the opportunity to do criminal defense work.

CONTRACT SYSTEM The **contract system** is a relative newcomer in providing legal services to the indigent. It is being used in a small percentage of the counties around the United States. In this system, a block grant is given to a lawyer or law firm to handle indigent defense cases. In some instances, the attorney is given a set amount of money and is required to handle all cases assigned. In other jurisdictions, contract lawyers agree to provide legal representation for a set number of cases at a fixed fee. A third system involves representation at an estimated cost per case until the dollar amount of the contract is reached. At that point, the contract may be renegotiated, but the lawyers are not obligated to take new cases.

> **contract system**
> Provision of legal services to indigent defendants by private attorneys under contract to the state or county.

The contract system is often used in counties that also have public defenders. Such counties may need independent counsel when a conflict of interest arises or when there is a constant overflow of cases. It is also used in sparsely populated states that cannot justify the structure and costs of full-time public defender programs. Experts have found that contract attorneys are at least as effective as assigned counsel and are cost-effective.[48]

The per-case cost in any jurisdiction for indigent defense services is determined largely by the type of program offered. In most public defender programs, funds are obtained through annual appropriations. Assigned counsel costs relate to legal charges for the appointed counsel, and contract programs negotiate a fee for the entire service. No research currently available indicates which is the most effective way to represent the indigent on a cost-per-case basis. However, Lawrence Spears reports that some jurisdictions have adopted the contract model with much success. Advantages include the provision of comprehensive legal services, controlled costs, and improved coordination in counsel programs.[49]

MIXED SYSTEMS A mixed system uses both public defenders and private attorneys in an attempt to draw on the strengths of both. In this approach, the public defender system operates simultaneously with the assigned counsel system or contract system to offer total coverage to the indigent defendant. This need occurs when the caseload increases beyond the capacity of the public defender's office. In addition, many counties supply independent counsel to all codefendants in a single case to prevent a conflict of interest. In most others, separate counsel will be provided if a codefendant requests it or if the judge or the public defender perceives a conflict of interest.

Other methods of providing counsel to the indigent include the use of law school students and prepaid legal service programs (similar to comprehensive medical insurance). Most jurisdictions have a student practice rule of procedure. Third-year law school students in clinical programs provide supervised counsel to defendants in nonserious offenses. In *Argersinger v. Hamlin*, Supreme Court Justice William Brennan suggested that law students are an important resource in fulfilling constitutional defense requirements.[50]

COSTS OF DEFENDING THE POOR Over the past decade, the justice system has faced extreme pressure to provide counsel for all indigent criminal defendants. However, inadequate funding has made implementation of this Sixth Amendment right an impossible task. The chief reasons for underfunded defender programs are caseload problems, lack of available attorneys, and legislative restraints. Increasing numbers of drug cases, mandatory sentencing, and overcharging have put tremendous stress on defender services.

The system is also overloaded with appeals by indigent defendants convicted at the trial level whose representation involves filing complex briefs and making oral arguments. Such postconviction actions often consume a great deal of time and result in additional backlog problems. Death penalty litigation is another area in which legal resources for the poor are strained.

The indigent defense crisis is a chronic problem. In some jurisdictions, attorneys are just not available to provide defense work. Burnout from heavy caseloads, low salaries, and poor working conditions are generally the major causes for the limited supply of attorneys interested in representing the indigent defendant. Some attorneys refuse to accept appointments in criminal cases because the fees are too low.

Lack of government funding is the most significant problem today. Although the entire justice system is often underfunded, the indigent defense system is usually in the worst shape. Ordinarily, providing funding for indigent criminal defendants is not the most politically popular thing to do. Yet indigent defense services are a critical component of the justice system. If there is growing disparity in the resources allocated to police, courts, and correctional agencies, then few cases will go to trial, and most will have to be settled by informal processing, such as plea bargaining or diversion.[51]

According to Robert Spangenberg and Tessa Schwartz, noted experts on public defense programs, only 3 percent of justice expenditures are devoted to the indigent defense system. All too often, the limited criminal justice resources available are used to place more police officers on the streets and build more prisons, while ignoring prosecution, courts, and public defense.[52] As the country entered the twenty-first century, the resources spent on public defense were not much higher than before.

Current funding for defender programs is ordinarily the responsibility of state and local governments. As a result of an amendment to the Crime Control Act of 1990, however, federal funds are also available through the Drug Control Act of 1988.[53] No effort was made to increase available funds in the 1994–1995 federal crime legislation, but the Anti-Terrorism Act of 1996 authorized $300 million to improve the federal judiciary's public defender program.

Public Versus Private Attorneys

Do criminal defendants who hire their own private lawyers do better in court than those who depend on legal representatives provided by the state? Although having private counsel has some advantages, national surveys indicate that state-appointed attorneys do well in court. According to data compiled by the federal government,

◆ Conviction rates for indigent defendants and those with their own lawyers were about the same in federal and state courts. About 90 percent of the federal defendants and 75 percent of the defendants in the most populous counties were found guilty regardless of the type of their attorneys.

◆ Of those found guilty, however, those represented by publicly financed attorneys were incarcerated at a higher rate than those defendants who paid for their own legal representation: 88 percent compared with 77 percent in federal courts and 71 percent compared with 54 percent in the most populous counties.

◆ On average, sentence lengths for defendants sent to jail or prison were shorter for those with publicly financed attorneys than those who hired counsel. In federal district court, those with publicly financed attorneys were given just under five years on average and those with private attorneys just over five years. In large state courts, those with publicly financed attorneys were sentenced to an average of two and a half years and those with private attorneys to three years.[54]

The data indicate that private counsel may have a slightly better track record in some areas (such as death penalty cases) but that court-appointed lawyers do quite well.

◆ THE DEFENSE LAWYER AS A PROFESSIONAL ADVOCATE

The problems of the criminal bar are numerous. Private attorneys are often accused of sacrificing their clients' interests for pursuit of profit. Many have a bad reputation in the legal community because of their unsavory clientele and reputation as shysters who hang out in court hoping for referrals. Attorneys who specialize in criminal work base their reputation on their power and influence. A good reputation is based on the ability to get obviously guilty offenders acquitted on legal technicalities, to arrange the best deal for clients who cannot hope to evade punishment, and to protect criminals whose illegal activities are shocking to many citizens. Consequently, the private criminal attorney is not often held in high esteem by his or her colleagues.

Public defenders are often young attorneys who are seeking trial practice before going on to high-paying jobs in established law firms. They are in the unenviable position of being paid by the government yet acting in the role of the government's adversary. Generally, they find themselves at the bottom of the legal profession's hierarchy because, for limited wages, they represent clients without social prestige. Forced to work under bureaucratic conditions, public defenders can do only routine processing of their cases. Large caseloads prevent them from establishing more than a perfunctory relationship with their clients. To keep their caseload under control, they may push for the quickest and easiest solution to a case—a plea bargain.

Assigned counsel and contract attorneys may also be young lawyers just starting out and hoping to build their practice by taking on indigent cases. Because their livelihood depends on getting referrals from the court, public defender's office, or other government bodies, they risk the problem of conflict of interest. If they pursue too rigorous a defense or handle cases in a way not approved by the presiding judge or other authorities, they may be removed from the assigned counsel lists.

Very often, large firms contribute the services of their newest members for legal aid to indigents, referred to as **pro bono** work. Although such efforts may be made in good spirit, they mean that inexperienced lawyers are handling legal cases in which a person's life may be at stake.

pro bono
The practice by private attorneys of taking the cases of indigent offenders without fee as a service to the profession and the community.

The Informal Justice System

What has emerged is a system in which plea bargaining predominates because little time and insufficient resources are available to give criminal defendants a full-scale defense. Moreover, because prosecutors are under pressure to win their cases, they are often more willing to work out a deal than pursue a case trial. After all, half a loaf is better than none. Defense attorneys also often find it easier to encourage their clients to plead guilty and secure a reduced sentence or probation instead of seeking an acquittal and risking a long prison term.

These conflicts have helped erode the formal justice process, which is based on the adversary system. Prosecutors and defense attorneys meet in the arena of the courtroom to do battle over the merits of the case. Through the give-and-take of the trial process, the truth of the matter becomes known. Guilty defendants are punished, and the innocent go free. Yet the U.S. legal system seldom works that way. Because of the pressures faced by defense attorneys and prosecutors, the defense and the prosecution more often work together in a spirit of cooperation to get the case over with rather than fighting it out, wasting each other's time, and risking an outright loss. In the process of this working relationship, the personnel in the courtroom—judge, prosecutor, defense attorney—form working groups that leave the defendant on the outside. Criminal defendants may find that everyone they encounter in the courtroom seems to be saying "plead guilty," "take the deal," "let's get it over with."

The informal justice system revolves around the common interest of its members to move the case along and settle matters. In today's criminal justice system, defense attorneys share a common history, goals, values, and beliefs with their colleagues in the prosecution. They are alienated by class and social background from the clients they defend. Considering the reality of who commits crime, who are its victims, and who defends, prosecutes, and tries the case, it should not be surprising that the adversary system has suffered.

The Competence of Defense Lawyers

The presence of competent and effective counsel has long been a basic principle of the adversary system. With the Sixth Amendment's guarantee of counsel for virtually all defendants, the performance of today's attorneys has come into question.

Inadequacy of counsel can occur in a variety of instances. The attorney may refuse to meet regularly with his or her client, neglect to cross-examine key government witnesses, or fail to investigate the case properly. A defendant's plea of guilty might be based on poor advice—for example, when the attorney may have misjudged the admissibility of evidence. When codefendants have separate counsel, conflicts of interest between defense attorneys may arise. On an appellate level, the lawyer may decline to file a brief, instead relying on a brief submitted for one of the co-appellants. Such problems as these are occurring with increasing frequency.

Even a legally competent attorney sometimes makes mistakes that can prejudice a case against his or her client. In *Taylor v. Illinois* (1988), a defense lawyer sprung a surprise witness against the prosecution.[55] The judge ruled the witness out of order (invoking the *surprise witness rule*), thereby depriving the defendant of valuable testimony and evidence. The Supreme Court affirmed the conviction despite the defense attorney's error in judgment because the judge had correctly ruled that surprising the prosecution was not legally defensible. The key issue is the level of competence that should be required of defense counsel in criminal cases.

reasonable competence standard
Minimally required level of functioning by a defense attorney such that defendants are not deprived of their rights to counsel and to a fair trial.

In recent years, the courts have adopted a **reasonable competence standard**, but differences exist in the formulation and application of this standard. For example, is it necessary for defense counsel to answer on appeal every nonfrivolous issue requested by his or her convicted client? What if counsel does not provide the court with all the information at the sentencing stage and the defendant believes that counsel's performance is inadequate? Whether counsel should be considered incompetent in such circumstances is a question that requires court review.

The concept of attorney competence was clearly defined by the Supreme Court in the case of *Strickland v. Washington* (1984).[56] Strickland had been arrested for committing a string of serious crimes, including murder, torture, and kidnapping. Against his lawyer's advice, Strickland pleaded guilty and threw himself on the mercy of the trial judge at a capital sentencing hearing. He also ignored his attorney's recommendation that he exercise his right to have an advisory jury at his sentencing hearing.

In preparing for the hearing, the lawyer spoke with Strickland's wife and mother but did not otherwise seek character witnesses. A psychiatric examination was not requested because, in the attorney's opinion, Strickland did not have psychological problems. The attorney also did not ask for a presentence investigation because he believed that such a report would contain information damaging to his client.

Although the presiding judge had a reputation for leniency in cases in which the defendant confessed, he sentenced Strickland to death. Strickland appealed on the grounds that his attorney had rendered ineffective counsel, citing his failure to seek psychiatric testimony and present character witnesses.

The case eventually went to the Supreme Court, which upheld Strickland's sentence. The justices found that a defendant's claim of attorney incompetence must have two components. First, the defendant must show that the counsel's performance was deficient and that such serious errors served to eliminate the presence of counsel guaranteed by the Sixth Amendment. Second, the defendant must show that the deficient performance prejudiced the case to such an extent that the defendant was deprived of a fair trial (that is, a trial with valid results). In *Strickland*, the Court found insufficient evidence that the attorney had acted beyond the boundaries of professional competence. Although the strategy he adopted might not have been the best one possible, it certainly was not unreasonable, considering minimum standards of professional competence.

The Court recognized the defense attorney's traditional role as an advocate of the defendant's cause, which includes such duties as consulting on important decisions, keeping the client informed of important developments, bringing knowledge and skill to the trial proceeding, and making the trial a reliable adversary proceeding. But the Court found that a mechanical set of rules to define competency would be unworkable.

Relations Between Prosecutor and Defense Attorney

In the final analysis, the competence of the prosecutor and the defense attorney depends on their willingness to work together in the interest of the client, the criminal justice system, and the rest of society. However, serious adversarial conflicts have arisen between them in recent years.

The prosecutor, for instance, should exercise discretion in seeking to **subpoena** other lawyers to testify about any relationship with their clients. Although not all communication between a lawyer and his or her client is privileged, confidential information entrusted to a lawyer is ordinarily not available for prosecutorial investigation. Often, however, overzealous prosecutors try to use their subpoena power against lawyers whose clients are involved in drug or organized crime cases to obtain as much evidence as possible. Prosecutors interested in confidential information about defendants have subpoenaed lawyers to testify against them. Court approval should be needed before a lawyer is forced to give information about a client. Otherwise, the defendant is not

subpoena
A court order requiring a witness to appear in court at a specified time and place.

Despite being locked in an adversarial procedure, the prosecution and defense must cooperate during the trial process. Here, Assistant District Attorney Freda Black, holding a piece of evidence, looks over shared witness data with District Attorney Jim Hardin (center), and one of the defendant's attorneys, David Rudolf, in Durham, North Carolina. Michael Peterson was charged with first-degree murder in the death of his wife, Kathleen. Peterson was subsequently found guilty of murder on March 10, 2003, and sentenced to life in prison.

© AP Images/Harry Lynch

receiving effective legal counsel under the Sixth Amendment. In addition, prosecutors should refrain from using their grand jury subpoena power to obtain information from private investigators employed by the defense attorney. Judicial remedies for violations of these rules often include suppression of subpoenaed evidence and dismissal of a criminal indictment.

By the same token, some criminal defense lawyers ignore situations in which a client informs them of his or her intention to commit perjury. The purpose of the defense attorney's investigation is to learn the truth from the client. The defense attorney also has a professional responsibility to persuade the defendant not to commit perjury, which is a crime.

It is the duty of the prosecutor to seek justice and not merely to obtain a conviction; this goal also applies to the criminal defense attorney. As legal scholar David G. Bress so aptly put it, "A defense attorney does not promote the attainment of justice when he secures his client's freedom through illegal and improper means."[57]

Often, the public image of prosecutors and defense attorneys is shaped by television programs, movies, and newspaper stories. You may hear of a prosecutor who takes a campaign donation and ignores a politician's crime. A defense attorney may use improper influence in representing a client. Unfortunately, corruption is still a fact of life in the justice system. Doing everything possible to deter such behavior is an important feature of a fair justice system.

ThomsonNOW Improve your grade on the exam with Personalized Study! For reinforcement resources and a mastery check of defense lawyers, go to www.thomsonedu. com/thomsonnow.

ETHICAL CHALLENGES IN CRIMINAL JUSTICE: A WRITING ASSIGNMENT

You are a defense attorney. Your client is on trial for a burglary. During an interview he admits to killing three people and burying their bodies near where he lives. He takes you to the graves to verify his claims. The police and prosecutor seem totally unaware of these crimes. Write an essay describing how you would/should handle this disclosure: keep it confidential, call the cops, and so on. Consider the legal, moral, and practical issues associated with your decision.

Doing Research on the Web

Before you answer, you might want to read a little more about the confidentiality issue. Try these works: "Commentary to ABA Model Rules of Professional Conduct," "Balancing Life and Practice," and "Defending Attorney–Client Privilege." You can access all three by going to the Siegel/Senna Introduction to Criminal Justice 11e website: www.thomsonedu.com/criminaljustice/siegel.

SUMMARY

◆ The prosecutor and the defense attorney are the major officers of justice in the judicial system.

◆ The prosecutor, who is the people's attorney, has discretion to decide the criminal charge and disposition.

◆ The prosecutor's daily decisions have a significant impact on police and court operations.

◆ To improve their efficiency, prosecutors' offices have created priority programs such as antirape and white-collar prosecution efforts.

◆ The prosecutor retains a great deal of discretion in processing cases.

◆ Political, social, and legal factors all shape a prosecutor's charging decisions.

- Prosecutors work closely with both police and the community.
- The role of the defense attorney in the criminal justice system has grown dramatically during the past few decades.
- Today, providing defense services to the indigent criminal defendant is an everyday practice. Under landmark decisions of the U.S. Supreme Court, particularly *Gideon v. Wainwright* and *Argersinger v. Hamlin*, all defendants who can face imprisonment for any offense must be afforded counsel at trial.
- Methods of providing counsel include assigned counsel systems, in which an attorney is selected by the court to represent the accused, and public defender programs, in which public employees provide legal services.
- Many ethical issues face defense attorneys, such as whether they should keep their clients' statements confidential even though they know they are lying or whether they should defend criminals whom they know are guilty.
- Lawyers doing criminal defense work have discovered an increasing need for their services, not only at trial, but also at the pre- and postjudicial stages of the criminal justice system.
- The issue of defense lawyer competence has become an important one for judicial authorities.

KEY TERMS

prosecutor, 326
attorney general, 329
district attorney, 329
community prosecution, 331
grand jury, 332
diversion, 335

defense attorney, 336
indigent defendant, 340
assigned counsel, 341
public defender, 341
recoupment, 342
contract system, 343

pro bono, 345
reasonable competence
 standard, 346
subpoena, 347

ThomsonNOW™ Maximize your study time by using ThomsonNOW's diagnostic study plan to help you review this chapter. The Study Plan will

- help you identify areas on which you should concentrate;
- provide interactive exercises to help you master the chapter concepts; and
- provide a post-test to confirm you are ready to move on to the next chapter.

CRITICAL THINKING QUESTIONS

1. Should attorneys disclose information given them by their clients concerning participation in earlier unsolved crimes?

2. Should defense attorneys cooperate with prosecutors if it means that their clients will go to jail?

3. Should prosecutors have absolute discretion over which cases to proceed on and which to drop? Do you believe prosecutors should have a great deal of discretion? Why?

4. Should potential clients have access to their attorney's track record in court?

5. Does the assigned counsel system present an inherent conflict of interest because attorneys are hired and paid by the institution they are to oppose?

6. Which kinds of cases do you think are most likely to be handled informally?

7. Explain the following: "It is the duty of the prosecutor to seek justice, not merely a conviction."

8. What are the differences between community prosecution and the traditional approach to prosecution?

NOTES

1. To read more about Eliot Spitzer and his campaign, go to http://www.oag.state.ny.us/bio.html and http://www.spitzer2006.com.

2. *Berger v. United States*, 295 U.S. 78, 88, 55 S.Ct. 629, 633, 79 L.Ed. 1341 (1935).

3. See Bennett Gershman, "Why Prosecutors Misbehave," *Criminal Law Bulletin* 22 (1986): 131–43. See also Joan Jacoby, "The American Prosecutor—from Appointive to Elective Status," *Prosecutor* 31 (1997): 25.

4. American Bar Association, *Model Rules of Professional Conduct* (Chicago: 1983), Rule 3.8. See also Stanley Fisher, "In Search of the Virtuous Prosecutor: A Conceptual Framework," *American Journal of Criminal Law* 15 (1988): 197.

5. Stanley Fisher, "Zealousness and Overzealousness: Making Sense of the Prosecutor's Duty to Seek Justice," *Prosecutor* 22 (1989): 9. See also Bruce Green, "The Ethical Prosecutor and the Adversary System," *Criminal Law Bulletin* 24 (1988): 126–45.

6. Judith McFarlane, Ann Malecha, Julia Gist, Kathy Watson, Elizabeth Batten, Iva Hall, and Sheila Smith, "Protection Orders and Intimate Partner Violence: An 18-Month Study of 150 Black, Hispanic, and White Women," *American Journal of Public Health* 94 (2004): 613–18.

7. Michael Benson, Francis Cullen, and William Maakestad, "Local Prosecutors and Corporate Crime," *Crime and Delinquency* 36 (July 1990): 356–72.

8. Heather Jacobson and Rebecca Green, "Computer Crime," *American Criminal Law Review*, 39 (2002): 273–326; Identity Theft and Assumption Act of 1998 (18 U.S.C. §1028(a)(7)).

9. American Prosecutors Research Institute, *Environmental Crime Prosecution: Results of a National Survey*, National Institute of Justice Research in Brief (Washington, D.C.: National Institute of Justice, 1994), pp. 1–12 (www.ncjrs.org/txtfiles/ENVIR.txt), accessed on October 31, 2003.

10. "NDAA Establishes Environmental Center," *National District Attorneys Association Bulletin* 10 (October 1991): 1.

11. Marcia Chaiken and Jan Chaiken, *Priority Prosecutors of High-Rate Dangerous Offenders* (Washington, D.C.: National Institute of Justice, 1991).

12. Bureau of Justice Statistics, *The Criminal Justice and Community Response to Rape* (Rockville, Md.: National Criminal Justice Reference Service, 1994).

13. Donald Rebovich, "Expanding the Role of Local Prosecution," *National Institute of Justice Journal Research in Action* 28 (1994): 21–24.

14. Michael Powell and David Segal, "In New York, a Grisly Traffic in Body Parts, Illegal Sales Worry Dead's Kin, Tissue Recipients," *Washington Post*, January 28, 2006, p. A3; William Sherman, "Clients Flee Biz Eyed in Ghoul Probe," *New York Daily News*, October 13, 2005.

15. Mark Cohen, "Environmental Crime and Punishment: Legal/Economic Theory and Empirical Evidence on Enforcement of Federal Environmental Statutes," *Journal of Criminal Law and Criminology* 82 (1992): 1054–1109.

16. Grace Wong, "Kozlowski Gets Up to 25 Years" (http://money.cnn.com/2005/09/19/news/newsmakers/kozlowski_sentence/index.htm).

17. American Bar Association, *Standards for Criminal Justice: Prosecution Function and Defense Function*, 3rd ed. (Washington, D.C.: 1993). See also American Bar Association, *Standards for Criminal Justice: Providing Defense Sources*, 3rd ed. (Washington, D.C.: 1993).

18. Eric Holden, "Community Prosecution," *Prosecutor* 34 (2000): 31.

19. Douglas Gansler, "Implementing Community Prosecution in Montgomery County, Maryland," *Prosecutor* 34 (2000): 30.

20. Kenneth C. Davis, *Discretionary Justice* (Baton Rouge: Louisiana State University Press, 1969), p. 180. See also James B. Stewart, *The Prosecutor* (New York: Simon and Schuster, 1987).

21. Barbara Boland, *The Prosecution of Felony Arrests* (Washington, D.C.: Government Printing Office, 1983).

22. Leslie Griffin, "The Prudent Prosecutor," *Georgetown Journal of Legal Ethics* 14 (2001): 259–308.

23. *United States v. Armstrong*, 517 U.S. 456 at 464 (1996).

24. Newman Baker, "The Prosecutor—Initiation of Prosecution," *Journal of Criminal Law, Criminology, and Police Science* 23 (1933): 770–71.

25. Rodney F. Kingsworth, Randall C. Macintosh, and Sandra Sutherland, "Criminal Charge or Probation Violation? Prosecutorial Discretion and Implication for Research in Criminal Court Processing," *Criminology* 40 (2002): 553–77.

26. Frank W. Miller, *Prosecution: The Decision to Charge a Suspect with a Crime* (Boston: Little, Brown, 1970). See also Harvey Wallace, "A Prosecutor's Guide to Stalking," *Prosecutor* 29 (1995): 26–30.

27. Boland, *The Prosecution of Felony Arrests*.

28. John Worrall, Jay Ross, and Eric Mccord, "Modeling Prosecutors' Charging Decisions in Domestic Violence Cases," *Crime and Delinquency* 52 (2006): 472–503.

29. American Bar Association, *Standards for Criminal Justice: Prosecution Function and Defense Function*, Standard 3.8, p. 33.

30. Michael Tonry and Richard Frase, *Sentencing and Sanctions in Western Countries* (London: Oxford University Press, 2001).

31. Robert Davis, Barbara Smith, and Bruce Taylor, "Increasing the Proportion of Domestic Violence Arrests That Are Prosecuted: A Natural Experiment in Milwaukee," *Criminology and Public Policy* 2 (2003): 263–82.

32. Charles D. Breitel, "Control in Criminal Law Enforcement," *University of Chicago Law Review* 27 (1960): 427.

33. Cassia Spohn, Dawn Beichner, and Erika Davis-Frenzel, "Prosecutorial Justifications for Sexual Assault Case Rejection: Guarding the 'Gateway to Justice,'" *Social Problems* 48 (2001): 206–35.

34. American Bar Association, *Report of Standing Committee on Legal Aid and Indigent Defendants* (Chicago: 1991).

35. See American Bar Association, *Model Rules of Professional Conduct* (Chicago: 1994), Rule 12.

36. Monroe H. Freedman, "Professional Responsibility of the Criminal Defense Lawyer: The Three Hardest Questions," *Michigan Law Review* 64 (1966): 1468.

37. Jonathan Glater, "Lawyers Pressed to Give Up Ground on Client Secrets," *New York Times*, August 10, 2003, p. 1.

38. Bennett Brummer, *Ethics Resource Guide for Public Defenders* (Chicago: American Bar Association, February 1992).

39. 372 U.S. 335, 83 S.Ct. 792, 9 L.Ed.2d 799 (1963).

40. 407 U.S. 25, 92 S.Ct. 2006, 32 L.Ed.2d 530 (1972).

41. 384 U.S. 436, 86 S.Ct. 1602, 16 L.Ed.2d 694 (1966).

42. *Mempa v. Rhay*, 389 U.S. 128, 88 S.Ct. 254, 19 L.Ed.2d 336 (1967).

43. *Douglas v. California*, 372 U.S. 353, 83 S.Ct. 814, 9 L.Ed.2d 811 (1963).

44. *In re Gault*, 387 U.S. 1, 875 S.Ct. 1428, 18 L.Ed.2d 527 (1967); *Specht v. Patterson*, 386 U.S. 605, 87 S.Ct. 1209, 18 L.Ed.2d 326 (1967).

45. Talia Roitberg Harmon and William Lofquist, "Too Late for Luck: A Comparison of Post-*Furman* Exonerations and Executions of the Innocent," *Crime and Delinquency* 51 (2005): 498–520.

46. See *Betts v. Brady*, 316 U.S. 455, 62 S.Ct. 1252, 86 L.Ed. 1595 (1942). Justice Black subsequently wrote the majority opinion in *Gideon v. Wainwright*, guaranteeing defendants' right to counsel and overruling the *Betts* case.

47. See F. Brownell, *Legal Aid in the United States* (Chicago: National Legal Aid Defender Association, 1961). For an interesting study of the Cook County, Illinois, Office of Public Defenders, see Lisa

McIntyre, *Public Defenders: Practice of Law in Shadows of Dispute* (Chicago: University of Chicago Press, 1987).

48. Pauline Houlden and Steven Balkin, "Quality and Cost Comparisons of Private Bar Indigent Defense Systems: Contract vs. Ordered Assigned Counsel," *Journal of Criminal Law and Criminology* 76 (1985): 176–200. See also John Arrango, "Defense Services for the Poor," *American Bar Association Journal on Criminal Justice* 12 (1998): 35.

49. Lawrence Spears, "Contract Counsel: A Different Way to Defend the Poor—How It's Working in North Dakota," *American Bar Association Journal on Criminal Justice* 6 (1991): 24–31.

50. 407 U.S. 25, 92 S.Ct. 2006, 32 L.Ed.2d 530 (1972).

51. Timothy Murphy, "Indigent Defense and the War on Drugs: The Public Defender's Losing Battle," *American Bar Association Journal on Criminal Justice* 6 (1991): 14–20.

52. Robert Spangenberg and Tessa J. Schwartz, "The Indigent Defense Crisis Is Chronic," *Criminal Justice Journal* 9 (1994): 13–16; *Sourcebook of Criminal Justice Statistics: 1998* (Washington, D.C.: U.S. Department of Justice, 1999).

53. See Drug Control Act of 1988, 42 U.S.C. §375 (G)(10).

54. Data compiled by the Bureau of Justice Statistics http://www.ojp.usdoj.gov/bjs/id.htm#conviction), accessed on August 8, 2003.

55. *Taylor v. Illinois*, 484 U.S. 400, 108 S.Ct. 646, 98 L.Ed.2d 798 (1988).

56. *Strickland v. Washington*, 466 U.S. 688, 104 S.Ct. 2052, 80 L.Ed.2d 674 (1984).

57. David G. Bress, "Professional Ethics in Criminal Trials," *Michigan Law Review* 64 (1966): 1493; John Mitchell, "The Ethics of the Criminal Defense Attorney," *Stanford Law Review* 32 (1980): 325.

Pretrial Procedures

Chapter Outline

Chapter Objectives

After reading this chapter, you should be able to:

1. Understand the concept of grand juries and preliminary hearings.
2. Know the role and actions of pretrial services.
3. Discuss the advantages of bail.
4. Describe the various types of bail systems.
5. Discuss the likelihood of making bail.
6. Recount the history of bail reform.
7. Describe the difference between preventive detention and release on recognizance.
8. Explain what is meant by the term *plea bargain*.
9. Identify the different types of pleas and how they are used.
10. Explain the role of the prosecutor, defense attorney, and judge in the plea negotiation.
11. Comment on the success of plea-bargain reform.
12. Discuss pretrial diversion.

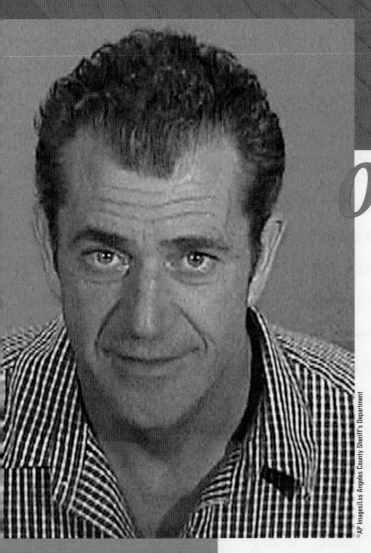

O n July 28, 2006, Hollywood star Mel Gibson made headlines around the world, not because of the release of one of his films, but because he was stopped for drunk driving along the Pacific Coast Highway in Malibu, California. After his arrest, Gibson was alleged to have made virulent anti-Semitic remarks to the officer who pulled him over. His career in danger, a remorseful Gibson soon sought forgiveness for his crude behavior, apologized, and said that the comments were "blurted out in a moment of insanity."

Gibson announced that he was entering a recovery program to battle alcoholism, and he asked to meet with Jewish leaders to help him "discern the appropriate path for healing." To get the matter over with, Gibson arranged a plea deal in which he agreed to serve three years of probation, attend one year of AA meetings, and pay $1,200 in fines and penalties. He also checked himself into a rehab facility on his own free will.[1] ◆

Should a famous personage such as Mel Gibson be allowed to bargain his way out of court? Or was his treatment fair considering the totality of the circumstances? What more should a judge do—throw him in prison? These are some of the questions that surround the pretrial stage of the justice process.

The plea bargain is just one of a series of events that are critical links in the chain of justice. These include arraignments, grand jury investigations, bail hearings, plea-bargaining negotiations, and predisposition treatment efforts. **Pretrial procedures** are critically important components of the justice process because the great majority of all criminal cases are resolved informally at this stage and never come before the courts. Although the media like to focus on the elaborate jury trial with its dramatic elements and impressive setting, formal criminal trials are relatively infrequent. Consequently, understanding the events that take place during the pretrial period is essential to grasping the reality of criminal justice policy.

Cases are settled during the pretrial stage in a number of ways. Prosecutors can use their discretion to drop cases before formal charges are filed because of insufficient evidence, office policy, witness conflicts, or similar problems. Even if charges are filed, the prosecutor can decide not to proceed against the defendant (**nolle prosequi**) because of a change in the circumstances of the case.

In addition, the prosecution and the defense almost always meet to try to arrange a nonjudicial settlement for the case. Plea bargaining, in which the defendant exchanges a guilty plea for some consideration, such as a reduced sentence, is commonly used to terminate the formal processing of the case. The prosecution or the defense may believe, for example, that a trial is not in the best interests of the victim, the defendant, or society because the defendant is incapable of understanding the charges or controlling her behavior. In this instance, the defendant may have a competency hearing before a judge and be placed in a secure treatment facility until ready to stand trial. Or the prosecutor may waive further action so that the defendant can be placed in a special treatment program, such as a detoxification unit at a local hospital.

◆ PROCEDURES FOLLOWING ARREST

After arrest, the accused is ordinarily taken to the police station, where the police list the possible criminal charges against him and obtain other information for the booking process. This may include recording a description of the suspect and the circumstances of the offense. The suspect may then be fingerprinted, photographed, and required to participate in a lineup.

An individual arrested on a misdemeanor charge is ordinarily released from the police station on his own recognizance to answer the criminal charge before the court at a later date. He is usually detained by the police until it is decided whether a criminal complaint will be filed. The **complaint** is the formal written document identifying the criminal charge, the date and place where the crime occurred, and the circumstances of the arrest. The complaint is sworn to and signed under oath by the complainant, usually a police officer. The complaint will request that the defendant be present at an initial hearing held soon after the arrest is made. In some jurisdictions, this may be referred to by other names, such as arraignment. The defendant may plead guilty at the initial hearing, and the case may be disposed of immediately. A defendant who pleads not guilty to a minor offense has been informed of the formal charge, provided with counsel if he is unable to afford a private attorney, and asked to plead guilty or not guilty as charged. A date in the near future is set for trial, and the defendant is generally released on bail or on his own recognizance to await trial.

When a felony or a more serious crime is involved, the U.S. Constitution requires an intermediate step before a person can be tried. This involves proving to an objective body that there is probable cause to believe that a crime has taken place and that the accused should be tried on the matter. This step of the formal

---

pretrial procedures
Legal and administrative actions that take place after arrest and before trial, including grand jury indictments, preliminary hearings, bail, and plea negotiation.

nolle prosequi
Decision by a prosecutor to drop a case after a complaint has been made because of, for example, insufficient evidence, witness reluctance to testify, police error, or office policy.

The Pretrial Services Resource Center is an independent, nonprofit clearinghouse for information on pretrial issues and a technical assistance provider for pretrial practitioners, criminal justice officials, academics, and community leaders nationwide. To reach its website, go to the Siegel/Senna Introduction to Criminal Justice 11e website: www.thomsonedu.com/criminaljustice/siegel.

complaint
A sworn written statement addressed to a court or judge by the police, prosecutor, or individual alleging that an individual has committed an offense and requesting indictment and prosecution.

charging process is ordinarily an indictment from a grand jury or an information issued by a lower court.

An **indictment** is a written accusation charging a person with a crime. It is drawn up by a prosecutor and submitted to a grand jury, which—after considering the evidence presented by the prosecutor—votes to endorse or deny the indictment. In jurisdictions that do not use the grand jury system, the prosecutor will draw up an **information**, a charging document that is brought before a lower court judge in a **preliminary hearing** (sometimes called a **probable cause hearing**). The purpose of this hearing is to require the prosecutor to present the case so that the judge can determine whether the defendant should be held to answer for the charge in a felony court.

After being indicted, the accused is brought before the trial court for **arraignment**, during which the judge informs the defendant of the charge, ensures that the accused is properly represented by counsel, and determines whether he should be released on bail or some other form of release pending a hearing or trial.

The defendant who is arraigned on an indictment or information can ordinarily plead guilty, not guilty, or **nolo contendere**, which is equivalent to a guilty plea but cannot be used as evidence against the defendant in a civil case on the same matter. In cases in which a guilty plea is entered, the defendant admits to all elements of the crime, and the court begins a review of the person's background for sentencing purposes. A not guilty plea sets the stage for a trial on the merits of the case or for negotiations, known as plea bargaining, between the prosecutor and the defense attorney.

In addition to these steps in the pretrial phase, the defendant is also considered for bail so that he may remain in the community to prepare his criminal defense. Even at this early stage, some may enter court-based treatment programs.

◆ BAIL

Bail is a form of security, usually a sum of money that is put up or exchanged to secure the release of an arrested person before the trial begins. The bail amount serves as a bond, ensuring that the released criminal defendant will return for trial. Failure to appear results in the forfeiting of the bail. Whether a defendant can be expected to appear at the next stage of the criminal proceedings is a key issue in determining bail.[2] Bail cannot be used to punish an accused, and it cannot be denied or revoked at the indulgence of the court. Bail is a critical stage in the justice process and a key ingredient of a fair and equitable adjudication process: It enables people charged with a crime to be free in the community in order to prepare a defense to the state's criminal charges. It also prevents an innocent person from spending months if not years behind bars awaiting trial only to be freed after a not guilty verdict is rendered.

The Legal Right to Bail

Bail is not a new practice. Under English common law, criminal defendants were eligible to be released before trial. Up through the thirteenth century, however, the county shire reeve or sheriff controlled the release of defendants awaiting trial. The sheriffs were given discretion to determine who would be held and who released and how much bail was required. Because sheriffs sometimes exploited their power, Parliament issued the Statute of Westminster in 1275; it set out the offenses that were bailable and those that were not. Under the new law, the sheriff still retained the authority to determine the amount of bail.

English bail practices were continued in the original colonies. After the Revolution, Congress passed the Judiciary Act of 1789, which set out conditions for bail and limited judicial discretion in setting bail amounts. As the Judiciary Act states, "Upon all arrests in criminal cases, bail shall be admitted, except where punishment may be by death, in which cases it shall not be admitted but by the

indictment
A written accusation returned by a grand jury, charging an individual with a specified crime after determination of probable cause.

information
A formal charging document, similar to an indictment, based on probable cause as determined at a preliminary hearing.

preliminary hearing (probable cause hearing)
Hearing before a magistrate to determine if the government has sufficient evidence to show probable cause that the defendant committed the crime.

arraignment
Initial trial court appearance, at which the accused is read the charges, advised of his or her rights, and asked to enter a plea.

nolo contendere
A plea of "no contest"—the defendant submits to sentencing without any formal admission of guilt that could be used against him or her in a subsequent civil suit.

To read about how nolo contendere pleas are taken, check out the guidelines of the U.S. District Court of the Middle District of Alabama. You can access these at Siegel/Senna Introduction to Criminal Justice 11e website: www.thomsonedu.com/criminaljustice/siegel.

bail
The monetary amount required for pretrial release, normally set by a judge at the initial appearance. The purpose of bail is to ensure the return of the accused at subsequent proceedings.

Bail hearings are generally held in court, but there are always exceptions. At his bail hearing, carjacking suspect John Powell, 30, hospitalized with a gunshot wound to the head, lies on his bed at Boston Medical Center after his arraignment. Judge Edward Redd (left) arraigned Powell in private before opening the room to the media. At center is Court Officer Michael McCusker. At right are defense attorney Beth Eisenberg and intern Jason Benzahn, from the Roxbury Defenders League.

supreme or a circuit court, or by a justice of the supreme court, or a judge of a district court, who shall exercise their discretion therein."[3]

Bail was also incorporated into the Eighth Amendment of the U.S. Constitution, which prohibits "excessive bail." The excessive bail clause may be interpreted to mean that the sole purpose of bail is to ensure that the defendant returns for trial. Bail may not be used as a form of punishment or to coerce or threaten a defendant. In most cases, a defendant has the right to be released on reasonable bail. Many jurisdictions also require a bail review hearing by a higher court in cases in which the initial judge set what might be considered excessive bail.

The U.S. Supreme Court's interpretation of the Eighth Amendment's provisions on bail was set out in the 1951 case of *Stack v. Boyle*.[4] In that case, the Court found bail to be a traditional right to freedom before trial that permits unhampered preparation of a defense and prevents the criminal defendant from being punished prior to conviction. The Court held that bail is excessive when it exceeds an amount reasonably calculated to ensure that the defendant will return for trial. The Court indicated that bail should be in the amount that is generally set for similar offenses. Higher bail can be imposed when evidence supporting the increase is presented at a hearing in which the defendant's constitutional rights can be protected. Although *Stack* did not mandate an absolute right to bail, it did set guidelines for state courts to follow: If a crime is bailable, the amount set should not be frivolous, unusual, or beyond a person's ability to pay.

Making Bail

In practice, a majority of criminal defendants are released on bail prior to trial.[5] The most recent surveys of pretrial release practices show that about two-thirds of felony defendants were released prior to the final disposition of their case. As might be expected, defendants charged with the most serious violent offenses were less likely to be released than those charged with less serious public order or drug offenses. Nonetheless, more than half of all violent criminals are released before trial. As might be expected, defendants charged with murder (8 percent) are the least likely to be released prior to case disposition, followed by defendants whose most serious arrest charge was robbery (42 percent), motor vehicle theft (44 percent), burglary (49 percent), or rape (55 percent).

When and how are these decisions made? Bail is typically considered at a court hearing conducted shortly after a person has been taken into custody. At the hearing, such issues as crime type, flight risk, and dangerousness will be considered before a bail amount is set. In jurisdictions with pretrial release programs, program staff often interview arrestees detained at the jail prior to the first hearing, verify the background information, and present recommendations to the court at arraignment. Prior record is an important factor: Less than half of defendants with an active criminal justice status, such as parole (31 percent) or probation (44 percent), at the time of arrest were released, compared to 69 percent of these with no active status. Some jurisdictions have developed bail schedules to make amounts uniform based on the crime and the defendant's criminal history.

Alternative Bail Release Mechanisms

Although bail is typically granted during a court hearing, there are other stages in the system in which bail may be granted:

♦ *Police field citation release.* An arresting officer releases the arrestee on a written promise to appear in court made at or near the actual time and location of the arrest. This procedure is commonly used for misdemeanor charges and is similar to issuing a traffic ticket.

♦ *Police station house citation release.* The determination of an arrestee's eligibility and suitability for release and the actual release of the arrestee are deferred until after he or she has been removed from the scene of an arrest and brought to the station house or police headquarters.

♦ *Police/pretrial jail citation release.* The determination of an arrestee's eligibility and suitability for citation release and the actual release of the arrestee are deferred until after he or she has been delivered by the arresting department to a jail or other pretrial detention facility for screening, booking, and admission.

♦ *Pretrial/court direct release by pretrial bail program.* To streamline release processes and reduce the length of stay in detention, pretrial program courts may authorize pretrial programs to release defendants without direct judicial involvement. When court rules delegate such authority, the practice is generally limited to misdemeanor charges, but felony release authority has been granted in some jurisdictions.

♦ *Police/court bail schedule.* An arrestee can post bail at the station house or jail according to amounts specified in a bail schedule. The schedule is a list of all bailable charges and a corresponding dollar amount for each. Schedules may vary widely from jurisdiction to jurisdiction.

Types of Bail

There are a variety of ways or mechanisms to secure bail, depending on the jurisdiction, the crime, and the defendant:

♦ *Full cash bail.* The defendant pays the full bail amount out of pocket. In some jurisdictions, property can be pledged instead of cash.

♦ *Deposit bail.* The defendant deposits a percentage of the bail amount, typically 10 percent, with the court. When the defendant appears in court, the deposit is returned, sometimes minus an administrative fee. If the defendant fails to appear, he or she is liable for the full amount of the bail.

♦ *Surety bail.* The defendant pays a percentage of the bond, usually 10 percent, to a bonding agent, who posts the full bail. The fee paid to the bonding agent is not returned to the defendant if he or she appears in court. The bonding agent is liable for the full amount of the bond should the defendant fail to appear. Bonding agents often require posting collateral to cover the full bail amount.

♦ *Conditional bail.* The defendant is released after promising to obey some specified conditions in lieu of cash. For example, she promises to attend a treatment program prior to trial.

If you want to understand how a bail bond agency operates, go to Action Immigration Bonds. To reach its website, go to the Siegel/Senna Introduction to Criminal Justice 11e website: www.thomsonedu.com/criminaljustice/siegel.

The Professional Bail Agents of the United States is an organization designed to help bail bondspersons be more competent and effective. You can access its site by going to the Siegel/Senna Introduction to Criminal Justice 11e website: www.thomsonedu.com/criminaljustice/siegel.

Bail Bondsman/Bail Enforcement Agent

Duties and Characteristics of the Job

A bail bondsman provides collateral or cash in order to help a defendant meet bail if she cannot pay the full amount. In return, the defendant must provide a portion of the bail, usually 10 percent of the total, that the bondsman gets to keep as a fee. The deal is contingent upon the defendant making all scheduled court appearances. If the defendant does not meet this requirement, the deal has been broken, and the bail bondsman can revoke bail.

There are several different types of bondsmen; the most common include surety, professional, and runner. Surety bondsmen are licensed insurance agents; they represent a company that pledges the collateral for bail, and they receive a salary from their insurance company. In contrast, professional bondsmen are more likely to be self-employed; they put up their own money for bail and take payment in the form of fees. Finally, runner bondsmen work for bail bondsmen; they keep track of defendants and make sure that they appear in court. All three kinds of bondsmen need to be licensed by the state in which they work. A bondsman's ability to write bonds is limited by bail laws and how much collateral he can pledge to the clerk of the court.

A bail enforcement agent is a person who assists the professional bail agent in presenting the defendant in court when required, who assists in the apprehension and surrender of the defendant to the court if he absconds, or who keeps the defendant under necessary surveillance before trial.

Job Outlook

A few states do not use the surety bail system; however, a clear majority of states do, so the need for bail bondsmen will continue. Because bail bondsmen are self-employed businesspeople, they can offer services wherever they are needed. The demand for bail bondsmen's services fluctuates according to the crime rate, with more opportunities existing in areas where the crime rate is high.

Salary

Professional bail bondsmen make their living off the fees they charge clients, so more clients mean more income. Surety bondsmen are paid by their employer. Bail enforcement agents make about $25,000 per year to start. But they receive 10 percent of the bond if it is violated, so they make approximately $10,000 per every $100,000 worth of bail jumpers they arrest.

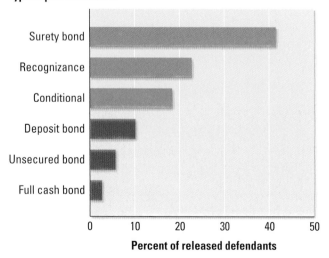

FIGURE 11.1

Pretrial Release by Type of Bail Recevied

Type of pretrial release

Percent of released defendants

♦ *Unsecured bond.* The defendant is released with no immediate requirement of payment. However, if the defendant fails to appear, he is liable for the full amount.

♦ *Release on recognizance.* Eligible defendants are released without bail upon their promise to return for trial.

As Figure 11.1 shows, surety bond is now the most common type of bail form used with felony defendants, followed by release on recognizance and conditional bail. Relatively few defendants pay full cash bail out of pocket.

Pretrial Detention

The criminal defendant who is not eligible for bail or release on recognizance is subject to pretrial detention in the local county jail. The jail has long been a trouble spot for the criminal justice system. Conditions tend to be poor and rehabilitation nonexistent.

Opportunities

Opportunities for advancement are limited for this profession. A runner bondsman can work toward becoming a professional or surety bondsman. Professional bondsmen can raise their salary by increasing the amount of cash they pledge to post bail, which increases the number of clients they can have at one time.

Qualifications

Although specific requirements vary by state, in general a bail bondsman must be a U.S. citizen at least 18 or 21 years old (depending on the state), have a high school diploma, and be a resident of the state in which she wishes to work. Future bail bondsmen must also pass a thorough background check, and in many states a conviction or a guilty plea for certain kinds of felonies and misdemeanors makes one ineligible for the position.

In order to work as a bondsman, certain educational and licensing requirements must be met. Once a future bail bondsman successfully earns her license, she must renew it annually. Although this process might not sound very hard, it is not cheap. Classes, licensing, and other fees can cost several hundred dollars, and professional bondsmen may have to pledge several thousand dollars to the court in order to write bonds.

Education and Training

The completion of certain educational requirements, usually in the form of preparatory classes, is generally required before one can apply for a bail bondsman license. Surety bondsmen will have to get more education because they will become licensed insurance agents. This training usually includes information on bail law, ethics, and the workings of the criminal justice system. Even after obtaining a license, bail bondsmen generally have yearly continuing education requirements they have to meet in order to keep working.

Sources: "Bail Bonds" (Oklahoma Insurance Department), retrieved August 1, 2006, from http://www.oid.state.ok.us/www2.oid.state.ok.us/ Divisions/BailBonds.asp; Philadelphia County, "Bail Bonds Posted by Professional Bondsmen" (Joint General Court Regulation No. 2006-02 [2006]), retrieved August 1, 2006, from http://origin-www.courts. state.pa.us/judicial-council/local-rules/philadelphia/philadel_chg_ 052206.pdf; South Carolina Department of Insurance, "Professional/ Surety Bailbond Questions and Answers (2005-06)," retrieved August 1, 2006, from https://www.doi.sc.gov/Eng/Public/Agents/bailbondfaq .aspx; South Carolina Department of Insurance, "Professional Bail Bondsmen/Runner (2005-06)," retrieved August 1, 2006, from https://www.doi.sc.gov/Eng/Public/Agents/ProBB.aspx.

In terms of the number of persons affected each year, pretrial custody accounts for more U.S. incarceration than does imprisonment after sentencing. On any given day in the United States, more than 600,000 people are held in more than 3,500 local jails. Over the course of a year, many times that number pass through the jailhouse door. More than 50 percent of those held in local jails have been accused of crimes but not convicted; they are **pretrial detainees**. In the United States, people are detained at a rate twice that of neighboring Canada and three times that of Great Britain. Hundreds of jails are overcrowded, and many are under court orders to reduce their populations and improve conditions. The national jail-crowding crisis has worsened over the years.

Jails are often considered the weakest link in the criminal justice process. They are frequently dangerous, harmful, decrepit, and filled with the poor and friendless. The costs of holding a person in jail range up to more than $100 per day ($36,000 per year). In addition, detainees are often confined with those convicted of crimes and those who have been transferred from other institutions because of overcrowding. Many felons are transferred to jails from state prisons to ease crowding. It is possible to have in close quarters a convicted rapist, a father jailed for nonpayment of child support, and a person awaiting trial for a crime that he did not commit. Thus, jails contain a mix of inmates, which can lead to violence, brutality, and suicide.

What happens to people who do not get bail or who cannot afford to put up bail money? Traditionally, they find themselves more likely to be convicted and

pretrial detainees
People who either are denied bail or cannot afford to post bail before trial and are kept in secure confinement.

Jails can be overcrowded and dangerous. Sometimes it takes a court order to improve conditions. Prisoners at Marion County Lockup in Indianapolis sleep on the floor. At least 19 of the Indiana's 92 counties have jail populations that are near or beyond their intended capacities. Many have been using some form of early release to reduce the number of inmates. Despite early releases, crowding at the Marion County Lockup is under new scrutiny as its population continues to soar.

then getting longer prison sentences than those who commit similar crimes but who were released on bail. A federally sponsored study of case processing in the nation's largest counties found that about 63 percent of all defendants granted bail were convicted; in contrast, 78 percent of detainees were convicted.[6] Detainees are also more likely to be convicted of a felony offense than releasees and, therefore, are eligible for a long prison sentence instead of the much shorter term of incarceration given misdemeanants. People being held in jails are in a less attractive bargaining position than those released on bail, and prosecutors, knowing their predicament, may be less generous in their negotiations. It is for these reasons that bail reform advocates have tried so hard to eliminate whenever possible the detention of nondangerous criminal defendants.

Bail Reform

Most states place no precise limit on the amount of bail that a judge may impose. People charged with the most serious crimes usually receive the highest amount of bail. As Table 11.1 shows, about 40 percent of all defendants are given bail amounts of under $10,000, and about one-third are asked to put up more than $25,000. As Figure 11.2 shows, as bail amounts increase, so does the likelihood of pretrial detention.

These data trouble experts who believe that the bail system is discriminatory because defendants who are financially well off can make bail, whereas indigent defendants languish in pretrial detention in the county jail. In addition, keeping a person in jail imposes serious financial burdens on local and state governments— and, in turn, on taxpayers, who must pay for the cost of confinement. These factors have given rise to bail reform programs that depend on the defendant's personal promise to appear in court for trial (recognizance), instead of on financial ability to meet bail. These reforms have enabled many deserving but indigent offenders to go free, but another trend has been to deny people bail on the grounds that they are a danger to themselves or to others in the community.

Bail has been heavily criticized as one of the most unacceptable aspects of the criminal justice system. Some view it as discriminatory because it works against the poor, who have a much tougher time making bail. Others argue that it is costly because the government must pay to detain those offenders who are unable to make bail but who would otherwise remain in the community. Another problem is the legal effect of detention. About 60 percent of released offenders are eventually convicted as compared to more than 80 percent of detainees. Once they are convicted, detainees receive somewhat longer sentences than people released before trial.

The bail system can be dehumanizing because innocent people who cannot make bail suffer in the nation's deteriorated jail system. There have also been charges that the system can be corrupted. Powerful ties often exist between bonding agents and the court, with the result that defendants are steered toward

TABLE 11.1

Bail Amount Set for Felony Defendants

Number of defendants	Under $5,000	$5,000– $9,999	$10,000– $24,999	$25,000– $49,999	$50,000 or more
31,894	25%	18%	22%	13%	21%

Source: Thomas Cohen and Brian Reaves, *Felony Defendants in Large Urban Counties, 2002* (Washington, D.C.: Bureau of Justice Statistics, 2006).

particular bonding agents. Charges of kickbacks and cooperation accompany such arrangements.

RELEASE ON RECOGNIZANCE Because of these and other problems, efforts have been made to reform and even eliminate money bail and reduce the importance of bonding agents. Until the early 1960s, the justice system relied primarily on money bonds as the principal form of pretrial release. Many states now allow defendants to be released on their own recognizance without any money bail. **Release on recognizance (ROR)** was pioneered by the Vera Institute of Justice in an experiment called the Manhattan Bail Project, which began in 1961 with the cooperation of the New York City criminal courts and local law students.[7] It came about because defendants with financial means were able to post bail to secure pretrial release while indigent defendants remained in custody. The project found that if the court had sufficient background information about the defendant, it could make a reasonably good judgment about whether the accused would return to court. When release decisions were based on such information as the nature of the offense, family ties, and employment record, most defendants returned to court when released on their own recognizance. The results of the Vera Institute's initial operation showed a default rate of less than 0.7 percent. The bail project's experience suggested that releasing a person on the basis of verified information more effectively guaranteed appearance in court than did money bail. Highly successful ROR projects were set up in major cities around the country, including Philadelphia and San Francisco. By 1980, more than 120 formal programs were in operation, and today they exist in almost every major jurisdiction.[8]

The success of ROR programs in the early 1960s resulted in bail reforms that culminated with the enactment of the federal Bail Reform Act of 1966, the first change in federal bail laws since 1789.[9] This legislation sought to ensure that release would be granted in all noncapital cases in which sufficient reason existed to believe that the defendant would return to court. The law clearly established the presumption of ROR that must be overcome before money bail is required, authorized 10-percent deposit bail, introduced the concept of conditional release, and stressed the philosophy that release should be under the least restrictive method necessary to ensure court appearance.

During the 1970s and early 1980s, the pretrial release movement was hampered by public pressure over pretrial increases in crime. As a result, more recent federal legislation, the Bail Reform Act of 1984, mandated that no defendants shall be kept in pretrial detention simply because they cannot afford money bail, established the presumption for ROR in all cases in which a person is bailable, and formalized restrictive preventive detention provisions. The 1984 act required that community safety, as well as the risk of flight, be considered in the release decision. Consequently, such criminal justice factors as the seriousness of the charged offense, the weight of the evidence, the sentence that may be imposed upon conviction, court appearance history, and prior convictions are likely to influence the release decisions of the federal court.

Bail reform is considered one of the most successful programs in the recent history of the criminal justice system. Yet it is not without critics, who suggest that emphasis should be put on controlling the behavior of serious criminals instead of on making sure that nondangerous defendants are released before their trials. Criminal defendants released without bail and those who commit crimes awaiting trial fuel the constant debate over pretrial release versus community protection. Although some experts believe that all people—even noncitizens accused of crimes—enjoy the right to bail, others view it as a license to abscond or to commit more crimes.[10]

FIGURE 11.2

Probability of Release by Bail Amount

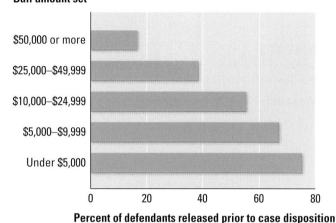

Source: Thomas Cohen and Brian Reaves, *Felony Defendants in Large Urban Counties, 2002* (Washington, D.C.: Bureau of Justice Statistics, 2006).

release on recognizance (ROR)
A pretrial release in which a defendant with ties to the community is not required to post bail but promises to appear at all subsequent proceedings.

To see the provisions of the Bail Reform Act of 1984, go to the website of the Wheat Law Library, University of Kansas. You can access it by going to the Siegel/Senna Introduction to Criminal Justice 11e website: www.thomsonedu.com/criminaljustice/siegel.

Preventive Detention

Whereas bail reform efforts are typically aimed at liberalizing bail, there are also efforts to tighten bail restrictions on the most dangerous offenders. The reason is the fear that serious criminals may re-offend while in the community. These fears are not unfounded. As Figure 11.3 shows, a significant number of all people arrested are actually out on bail or some other form of pretrial release at the time of their arrest, including about 10 percent of rapists and more than 15 percent of robbers.

Looking at this association another way, many serious felons released on bail commit new crimes while awaiting trial. As Figure 11.4 shows, more than 20 percent of people arrested for murder and released on bail are arrested on new charges. We call these people **avertable recidivists**—their crimes could have been prevented if they had not been given discretionary release and instead been kept behind bars! Overall, 18 percent of released defendants were re-arrested for a new offense allegedly committed while they awaited disposition of their original case. About two-thirds of these defendants, 12 percent of all released defendants, were charged with a new felony. Those released after being charged with burglary (24 percent), murder (23 percent), motor vehicle theft (23 percent), and drug offenses (21 percent) had higher pretrial re-arrest rates than

FIGURE 11.3

Percentage of Criminal Defendants Out on Bail at the Time of Their Arrest

Crime committed while on pretrial release

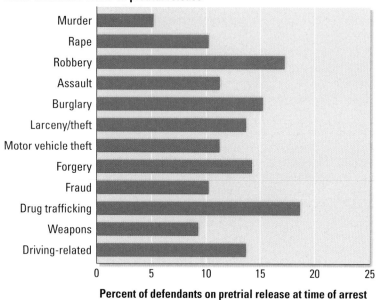

Percent of defendants on pretrial release at time of arrest

Source: Thomas Cohen and Brian Reaves, *Felony Defendants in Large Urban Counties, 2002* (Washington, D.C.: Bureau of Justice Statistics, 2006).

FIGURE 11.4

Percentage of People Out on Bail Who Commit New Crimes and Who Are Arrested, by Charge and Arrest Type

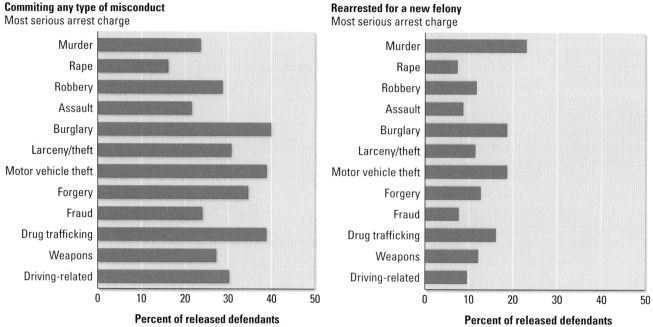

Source: Thomas Cohen and Brian Reaves, *Felony Defendants in Large Urban Counties, 2002* (Washington, D.C.: Bureau of Justice Statistics, 2006).

defendants originally charged with rape (8 percent) or fraud (10 percent).

Today, about one-third of released defendants are either re-arrested for a new offense, fail to appear in court as scheduled, or commit some other violation that results in the revocation of their pretrial release. Those re-arrested tend to be on bail longer, have a serious prior record, abuse drugs, have a poor work record, and be disproportionately young, male, and members of minority groups.

One response to the alleged failure of the bail system to protect citizens is the adoption of preventive detention statutes. These laws require that certain dangerous defendants be confined before trial for their own protection and that of the community. Preventive detention is an important manifestation of the crime control perspective on justice because it favors the use of incapacitation to control the future behavior of suspected criminals. Often, the key question is whether preventive detention is punishment before trial.

The most striking use of preventive detention can be found in the federal Bail Reform Act of 1984, which contrasted sharply with previous laws.[11] Although the act does contain provisions for ROR, it allows judges to order preventive detention if they determine "that no condition or combination of conditions will reasonably assure the appearance of the person as required and the safety of any other person and the community."[12]

A number of state jurisdictions have incorporated elements of preventive detention into their bail systems. Although most of the restrictions do not constitute outright preventive detention, they serve to narrow the scope of bail eligibility. These provisions include exclusion of certain crimes from bail eligibility, definition of bail to include appearance in court and community safety, and limitations on right to bail for those previously convicted.

Preventive detention has also been a source of concern for civil libertarians who believe it violates the due process clause of the Constitution, because it means that a person will be held in custody before proven guilty. In two important cases, the Supreme Court disagreed with this analysis. In *Schall v. Martin*, the Court upheld the application of preventive detention statutes to juvenile defendants on the grounds that such detention is useful to protect the welfare of the minor and society as a whole.[13] In 1987 the Court upheld the Bail Reform Act's provision on preventive detention for adults in the case of *United States v. Salerno* when it ruled that the Bail Reform Act's denial of bail to dangerous defendants did not violate the 8th Amendment.[14]

PERSPECTIVES ON JUSTICE

Crime Control

The fact that some people arrested on murder charges are later released on bail chagrins those who believe in the crime control perspective. The fact that more than 20 percent of these releasees commit felonies while on bail reinforces the view that incapacitation of known criminals is the most effective crime control policy.

avertable recidivist
A person whose crime would have been prevented if he or she had not been given discretionary release and instead been kept behind bars.

PERSPECTIVES ON JUSTICE

Crime Control

Doesn't preventive detention amount to punishing an individual before he has been brought to trial and found guilty? Even if the defendant is later found not guilty at trial, it is better to err on the side of caution and community safety. Denying defendants the right to bail because they are presumed to be dangerous is at the heart of the crime control perspective.

♦ PRETRIAL SERVICES

In our overburdened court system, it is critical to determine which defendants can safely be released on bail pending trial.[15] In many jurisdictions, specialized pretrial services help courts deal with this problem. Hundreds of pretrial programs have been established in rural, suburban, and urban jurisdictions, typically housed in probation departments, court offices, and local jails, or handled by independent county contractors.

These programs provide a number of critical services, including the following:

♦ Gathering and verifying information about arrestees, including criminal history, current status in the criminal justice system, address, employment, and drug and alcohol use history, which judicial officers can then take into account in making release/detention decisions.

◆ Assessing each arrestee's likelihood of failure to appear and chances of being re-arrested.

◆ Providing supervision for defendants conditionally released and notifying the court of any failure to comply with release conditions.

PERSPECTIVES ON JUSTICE

Due Process and Noninterventionism

Due process advocates bemoan the fact that bail is one of the few decision points in the justice system where money is the deciding factor. Why should one person be detained for months or years because he cannot make bail while a more affluent person can simply write a check? Noninterventionists would argue that a jail experience can be extremely damaging to the future chances of young offenders.

Virtually all larger jurisdictions in the United States have pretrial release in one form or another. Court-administered programs make up the greatest percentage of pretrial programs, although most newer programs are located within probation departments. The general criteria used to assess eligibility for release look at the defendant's community ties and prior criminal justice involvement. Many jurisdictions have conditional and supervised release and third-party custody release, in addition to release on a person's own recognizance.

Some pretrial services programs are now being aimed at special needs. One type focuses on defendants suffering from mental illness; almost three-quarters of pretrial services programs now inquire about mental health status and treatment as a regular part of their interview, and about one-quarter report having implemented special supervision procedures for defendants with mental illness. Another area of concern is domestic violence; about one-quarter of all pretrial programs have developed special risk-assessment procedures for defendants charged with domestic violence offenses, and about one-third have implemented special procedures to supervise defendants charged with domestic violence offenses.

◆ CHARGING THE DEFENDANT

Charging a defendant with a crime is a critical stage in the pretrial process. The charge is selected by the prosecutor depending on the facts of the case, strength of the evidence, availability of witnesses, and so on. The process varies depending on whether it occurs via a grand jury or a preliminary hearing.

The Indictment Process—The Grand Jury

The grand jury was an early development of English common law. Under the Magna Carta (1215), no "freeman" could be seized and imprisoned unless he had been judged by his peers. To determine fairly who was eligible to be tried, a group of freemen from the district where the crime was committed would be brought together to examine the facts of the case and determine whether the charges had merit. Thus, the grand jury was created as a check against arbitrary prosecution by a judge who might be a puppet of the government.

The concept of the grand jury was brought to the American colonies by early settlers and later incorporated into the Fifth Amendment, which states that "no person shall be held to answer for a capital, or otherwise infamous crime, unless on a presentment or indictment of a grand jury." Today, the use of the grand jury is diminishing. Relatively few states require a grand jury indictment to begin all felony proceedings; most allow the prosecutor the option of calling a grand jury or proceeding with a preliminary hearing. The federal government employs both the grand jury and the preliminary hearing systems.

The grand jury today has two roles. First, it has the power to act as an independent investigating body. In this capacity, it examines the possibility of criminal activity within its jurisdiction. These investigative efforts are directed toward general, not individual, criminal conduct. After completing its investigation, the grand jury issues a report called a **presentment**, which contains its findings and also usually a recommendation of indictment.

The grand jury's second and better-known role is accusatory in nature. In this capacity, the grand jury acts as the community's conscience in determining

presentment
The report of a grand jury investigation, which usually includes a recommendation of indictment.

whether an accusation by the state (the prosecution) justifies a trial. The grand jury relies on the testimony of witnesses called by the prosecution through its subpoena power. After examining the evidence and the testimony of witnesses, the grand jury decides whether probable cause exists for prosecution. If it does, an indictment, or **true bill**, is affirmed. If the grand jury fails to find probable cause, a **no bill** (meaning that the indictment is ignored) is passed. In some states, a prosecutor can present evidence to a different grand jury if a no bill is returned; in other states, this action is prohibited by statute.

A grand jury is ordinarily made up of 16 to 23 individuals, depending on the requirements of the jurisdiction. This group theoretically represents a county. Selection of members varies from state to state, but for the most part, they are chosen at random (for example, from voting lists). To qualify to serve on a grand jury, an individual must be at least 18 years of age, must be a U.S. citizen, must be a resident of the jurisdiction for one year or more, and must possess sufficient English-speaking skills for communication.

The grand jury usually meets at the request of the prosecution. Hearings are closed and secret. The prosecuting attorney presents the charges and calls witnesses who testify under oath to support the indictment. Usually, the accused individuals are not allowed to attend the hearing unless they are asked to testify by the prosecutor or the grand jury.

REFORMING THE GRAND JURY? The grand jury usually meets at the request of the prosecution, and hearings are closed and secret. The defense attorney, defendant, and general public are not allowed to attend. The prosecuting attorney presents the charges and calls witnesses who testify under oath to support the indictment. This process has been criticized as being a rubber stamp for the prosecution because the presentation of the evidence is shaped by the district attorney, who is not required by law to reveal information that might exonerate the accused.[16]

In the case of *United States v. Williams* (1992), the Supreme Court ruled that no supervisory power in the federal courts requires presentation to a grand jury of **exculpatory evidence** (evidence that can clear a defendant from blame or fault).[17] Some legal scholars find that the *Williams* decision conflicted with the grand jury's historical purpose of shielding criminal defendants from unwarranted and unfair prosecution and overrode the mandate that it be both informed and independent. An alternative might be to change the rule of criminal procedure so that prosecutors would be obliged to present exculpatory evidence to the grand jury even if it might result in the issuance of no indictment.[18] Another alternative put forth by defense lawyers is to open the grand jury room to the defense and to hold the government to the same types of constitutional safeguards required to protect defendants that are now used at trial.[19]

Because the grand jury is often controlled solely by the state prosecutor, some legal experts believe that the system should provide the defendant with more due process protection. The American Bar Association publication *Grand Jury Policy and Model Act* suggests the following changes in state grand jury statutes: Witnesses should have their own attorneys when they give testimony, prosecutors should be required to present evidence that might show that a suspect is innocent, witnesses should be granted constitutional privileges against self-incrimination, and grand jurors should be informed of all the elements of the crimes being presented against the suspect.[20]

The Indictment Process—The Preliminary Hearing

The preliminary hearing is used in about half the states as an alternative to the grand jury. Although the purpose of preliminary hearings and grand jury hearings is the same—to establish whether probable cause is sufficient to merit a trial—the procedures differ significantly.

The preliminary hearing is conducted before a magistrate or lower court judge and, unlike the grand jury hearing, is open to the public unless the defendant

true bill
The action by a grand jury when it votes to indict an accused suspect.

no bill
The action by a grand jury when it votes not to indict an accused suspect.

exculpatory evidence
Includes all information that is material and favorable to the accused defendant because it casts doubt on the defendant's guilt or on the evidence the government intends to use at trial.

To get the latest news on grand juries, go to Susan Brenner's "Federal Grand Jury" site. You can access it by going to the Siegel/Senna Introduction to Criminal Justice 11e website: www.thomsonedu.com/criminaljustice/siegel.

Preliminary hearings, an alternative to the grand jury, are designed to determine whether sufficient evidence exists to bring criminal defendants to trial. Here, Kris and Sarah Everson talk with their public defendant Kalpesh Patel as they wait for their preliminary hearing on May 3, 2006, in Independence, Missouri. The couple was charged with stealing by deceit after crafting a hoax about having sextuplets, allegedly to collect thousands of dollars in gifts from neighbors and co-workers.

requests otherwise. Present at the preliminary hearing are the prosecuting attorney, the defendant, and the defendant's counsel, if already retained. The prosecution presents its evidence and witnesses to the judge. The defendant or the defense counsel then has the right to cross-examine witnesses and to challenge the prosecutor's evidence.

After hearing the evidence, the judge decides whether there is sufficient probable cause to believe that the defendant committed the alleged crime. If so, the defendant is bound over for trial, and the prosecuting attorney's information (same as an indictment) is filed with the superior court, usually within 15 days. When the judge does not find sufficient probable cause, the charges are dismissed, and the defendant is released from custody.

WAIVING THE PRELIMINARY HEARING A unique aspect of the preliminary hearing is the defendant's right to waive the proceeding. In most states, the prosecutor and the judge must agree to this waiver. A waiver has advantages and disadvantages for both the prosecutor and the defendant. In most situations, a prosecutor will agree to a waiver because it avoids revealing evidence to the defense before trial. However, if the state believes it is necessary to obtain a record of witness testimony because of the possibility that a witness or witnesses may be unavailable for the trial or unable to remember the facts clearly, the prosecutor might override the waiver. In this situation, the record of the preliminary hearing can be used at the trial.

The defendant will most likely waive the preliminary hearing for one of three reasons: (1) he has already decided to plead guilty, (2) he wants to speed up the criminal justice process, or (3) he hopes to avoid the negative publicity that might result from the hearing. However, the preliminary hearing is of obvious advantage to the defendant who believes that it will result in a dismissal of the charges. In addition, the preliminary hearing gives the defense the opportunity to learn what evidence the prosecution has. Figure 11.5 outlines the significant differences between the grand jury and the preliminary hearing processes.

Arraignment

After an indictment or information is filed following a grand jury or preliminary hearing, an arraignment takes place before the court that will try the case. At the arraignment, the judge informs the defendant of the charges against her and appoints counsel if one has not yet been retained. According to the Sixth Amendment, the accused has the right to be informed of the nature and cause of the accusation. Thus, the judge at the arraignment must make sure that the defendant clearly understands the charges.

After the charges are read and explained, the defendant is asked to enter a plea. If a plea of not guilty or not guilty by reason of insanity is entered, a trial date is set. When the defendant pleads guilty or nolo contendere, a date for sentencing is arranged. The magistrate then either sets bail or releases the defendant on personal recognizance.

The Plea

Ordinarily, a defendant in a criminal trial will enter one of three pleas: guilty, not guilty, or nolo contendere.

GUILTY On June 6, 2005, Oscar-winning actor Russell Crowe was staying at the Mercer Hotel in New York City when he had trouble reaching his wife, Danielle Spencer, in Australia. He took out his frustration on Nestor Estrada, who was on

FIGURE 11.5

Charging the Defendant with a Crime

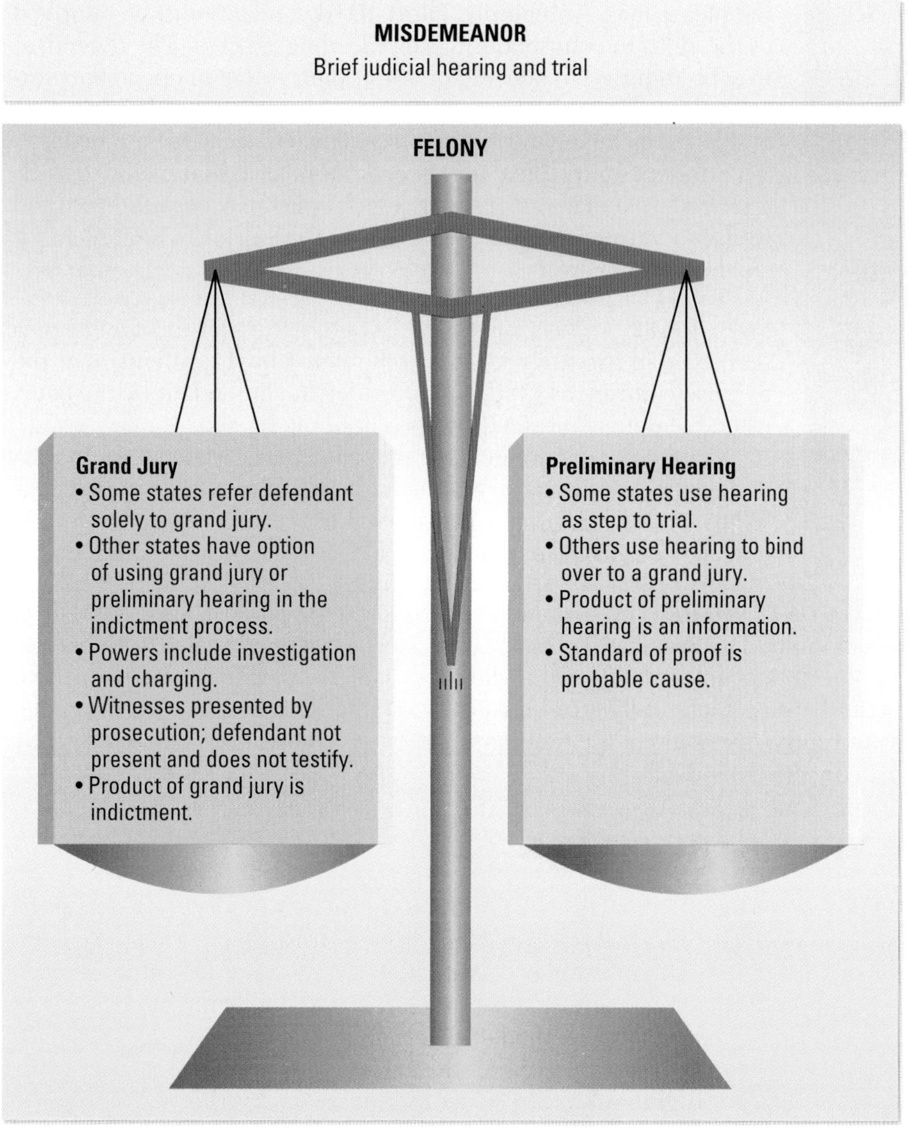

> **MISDEMEANOR**
> Brief judicial hearing and trial
>
> **FELONY**
>
> **Grand Jury**
> - Some states refer defendant solely to grand jury.
> - Other states have option of using grand jury or preliminary hearing in the indictment process.
> - Powers include investigation and charging.
> - Witnesses presented by prosecution; defendant not present and does not testify.
> - Product of grand jury is indictment.
>
> **Preliminary Hearing**
> - Some states use hearing as step to trial.
> - Others use hearing to bind over to a grand jury.
> - Product of preliminary hearing is an information.
> - Standard of proof is probable cause.

the night desk, by hurling a telephone at his head. Estrada was taken to a nearby hospital and treated for cuts to his cheek, while Crowe was taken into custody and charged with felony second-degree assault and fourth-degree criminal possession of a weapon (the telephone). Eager to get the matter over with (and retain his ability to work in the United States), Crowe pleaded guilty to third-degree assault. Manhattan Criminal Court Judge Kathryn Freed sentenced Crowe to a conditional discharge and required him to pay a $160 court surcharge.[21]

The Crowe case is certainly not unique. More than 90 percent of defendants appearing before the courts plead guilty prior to the trial stage. A guilty plea has several consequences. It functions not only as an admission of guilt but also as a surrender of the entire array of constitutional rights designed to protect a criminal defendant against unjustified conviction, including the right to remain silent, the right to confront witnesses against him or her, the right to a trial by jury, and the right to be proven guilty by proof beyond a reasonable doubt. Once a plea is made, it cannot be rescinded or withdrawn even if a change is made in the law that might have made conviction more problematic.[22]

As a result, judges must follow certain procedures when accepting a plea of guilty. First, the judge must clearly state to the defendant the constitutional

guarantees automatically waived by this plea. Second, the judge must believe that the facts of the case establish a basis for the plea and that the plea is made voluntarily. Third, the defendant must be informed of the right to counsel during the pleading process. The defendant may be required to allocute or admit their crime in open court. Finally, the judge must inform the defendant of the possible sentencing outcomes, including the maximum sentence that can be imposed.

After a guilty plea has been entered, a sentencing date is arranged. In a majority of states, a guilty plea may be withdrawn and replaced with a not guilty plea at any time prior to sentencing if good cause is shown.

NOT GUILTY At the arraignment or before the trial, a not guilty plea is entered in two ways: (1) it is orally stated by the defendant or the defense counsel, or (2) it is entered for the defendant by the court when the defendant stands mute before the bench.

Once a plea of not guilty is recorded, a trial date is set. In misdemeanor cases, trials take place in the lower court system, whereas felony cases are normally transferred to the superior court. At this time, a continuance or issuance of bail is once again considered.

Russell Crowe, following his arrest for throwing a telephone at hotel employee Nestor Estrada of the Mercer Hotel in New York after he received poor phone service. Crowe later pleaded guilty to third-degree assault, and Manhattan Judge Kathryn Freed sentenced him to a conditional discharge, meaning that he must avoid all criminal acts for a year or else face jail time. The actor was also given a $160 court surcharge. As part of the deal, Crowe received no jail time and no probation.

NOLO CONTENDERE The plea nolo contendere ("no contest") is essentially a plea of guilty. This plea has the same consequences as a guilty plea, with one exception: It may not be held against the defendant as proof in a subsequent civil matter because technically no admission of guilt has been made. This plea is accepted at the discretion of the trial court and must be voluntarily and intelligently made by the defendant.

◆ PLEA BARGAINING

One of the most common practices in the criminal justice system today, and a cornerstone of the informal justice system, is plea bargaining.[23] Plea bargaining is a relatively recent development, taking hold late in the nineteenth century. During the first 150 years after the nation's birth, the trial by jury was viewed as the fairest and most reliable method of determining the truth in a criminal matter. Not surprisingly, the Constitution does not mention plea bargaining, nor does the Bill of Rights address the issue. However, by the middle of the nineteenth century, plea negotiations steadily became the dominant method of case disposition in the United States. During this evolution, the prevailing view of criminal case processing switched from being a dispute between two parties that could be resolved through a trial to a conflict between the state and an individual, controlled by police involvement and prosecutorial discretion. As this change evolved, the court process switched from dispensing individual, carefully considered justice via trials to mass justice dispensed through guilty pleas.[24] At first, judges were reluctant to accept pleas, preferring trials to sharing their power with prosecutors (who make the deal). However, plea bargaining became more attractive at the turn of the twentieth century, when the mechanization of manufacture and transportation prompted a flood of complex civil cases, which persuaded judges that criminal cases had to be settled quickly lest the court system break down.[25] Today, more than 90 percent of criminal convictions are estimated to result from negotiated pleas of guilty. And, as Figure 11.6 shows, most defendants are likely to plead guilty in even the most serious felony cases.

The data shows that plea bargains benefit both the prosecution, which is assured a conviction, and the defendant, who is rewarded with a lenient sentence.[26] For example, people who plead guilty to murder are much less likely to get the death penalty or a life sentence than those who are convicted at trial.

The Nature of the Bargain

Plea bargaining is the exchange of prosecutorial and judicial concessions for pleas of guilty (see Exhibit 11.1). Normally, a bargain can be made between the prosecutor and the defense attorney in four ways: (1) the initial charges may be reduced to those of a lesser offense, thus automatically reducing the sentence imposed; (2) in cases in which many counts are charged, the prosecutor may reduce the number of counts; (3) the prosecutor may promise to recommend a lenient sentence, such as probation; and (4) when the charge imposed has a negative label attached (for example, child molestation), the prosecutor may alter the charge to a more socially acceptable one (such as assault) in exchange for a plea of guilty. In a jurisdiction where sentencing disparities exist between judges, the prosecutor may even agree to arrange for a defendant to appear before a lenient judge in exchange for a plea; this practice is known as judge shopping.

Bargains are rarely a one-shot deal and may be negotiated many times as evidence becomes known and the case unfolds.[27] They are negotiated until the defense believes that it has gotten the best deal for its client and the prosecutor believes that, considering the totality of the circumstances, it has been able to dispense a fair amount of punishment. The defense attorney conducts the bargain as a form of negotiation, putting forth information that will convince the prosecutor that the case is very strong and the chances of an acquittal are quite high. If the defense attorney can magnify the strength of her case, the chances of a favorable plea outcome will increase.

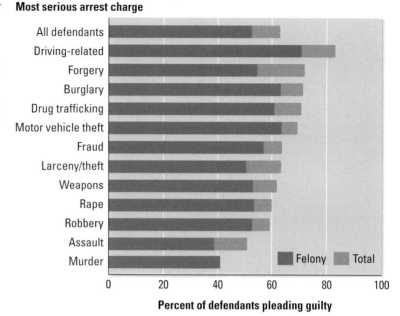

FIGURE 11.6

Plea Rate by Most Serious Arrest Charge

Most serious arrest charge

Percent of defendants pleading guilty

Source: Thomas Cohen and Brian Reaves, *Felony Defendants in Large Urban Counties, 2002* (Washington, D.C.: Bureau of Justice Statistics, 2006).

To gain more insight on plea bargaining, go to MyLawyer.com. You can access it by going to the Siegel/Senna Introduction to Criminal Justice 11e website: www.thomsonedu.com/criminaljustice/siegel.

Pros and Cons of Plea Bargaining

Plea bargaining is so widespread that it is recognized as one of the major elements of the criminal justice system. Despite its prevalence, its merits are hotly debated. Those opposed to the widespread use of plea bargaining assert that it is coercive in its inducement of guilty pleas, that it encourages the unequal exercise of prosecutorial discretion, and that it complicates sentencing as well as the job of correctional authorities. There is the danger that plea bargaining encourages defendants to waive their constitutional right to a trial. Prosecutors are given too much leeway to convince defendants to plea bargain, thus circumventing law.[28] Plea bargaining then raises the danger that an innocent person will be convicted of a crime if the individual believes that she has little chance of an acquittal because she is poor, a member of an ethnic minority, or both.

Others argue that plea bargaining is unconstitutional and that it results in cynicism and disrespect for the justice process.[29] Some argue that plea bargaining is objectionable because it encourages defendants to waive their constitutional right to trial, and others contend that sentences tend to be less severe when a defendant enters a guilty plea than when the case proceeds to trial. This aspect of plea negotiations convinces the general public that plea bargaining allows the defendant to beat the system and further tarnishes the criminal process.

Proponents of plea bargaining contend that the practice ensures the flow of guilty pleas essential to administration efficiency. It allows the system the flexibility to individualize justice and inspires respect for the system because it is

---

EXHIBIT 11.1

To Plea or Not to Plea?

Although almost all cases are settled with a plea, a few proceed to a full-blown trial. What factors influence the decision to plea or not to plea?

◆   Court-appointed lawyers may want to gain trial experience. They convince their clients not to accept favorable bargains, fearing that the case will be settled out of court and they will lose the opportunity to try the case.

◆   Both the prosecution and defense may be overly optimistic about their abilities and skills.

◆   The lawyers' overconfidence in their abilities may cloud their judgment, causing them to either refuse to offer a bargain in the case of the prosecution or refuse to accept in the case of the defense.

◆   Some defendants falsely assume that they are so charismatic and appealing that a jury will never reach a conviction.

Source: Stephanos Bibas, "Plea Bargaining Outside the Shadow of Trial," *Harvard Law Review* 117 (2004): 2464–2543.

---

associated with certain and prompt punishment. Proponents contend that plea bargaining benefits both the state and the defendant in the following ways:

◆   The overall costs of the criminal prosecution are reduced.

◆   The administrative efficiency of the courts is greatly improved.

◆   The prosecution can devote more time to more serious cases.

◆   The defendant avoids possible detention and an extended trial and may receive a reduced sentence.

◆   Resources can be devoted more efficiently to cases that need greater attention.[30]

In recent years, efforts have been made to convert plea bargaining into a more visible, understandable, and fair dispositional process. Some jurisdictions have developed safeguards and guidelines to prevent violations of due process and to ensure that innocent defendants do not plead guilty under coercion. Such safeguards include the following:

◆   Uniform plea practice.

◆   Time limits on plea negotiations.

◆   Presence of defense counsel to advise defendant.

◆   Open discussions about the plea between prosecutor and defense attorney.

◆   Full information regarding offender and offense.

◆   Judicial questioning of defendant before accepting the plea.

◆   Judicial supervision of the plea.

Plea negotiations are unlikely to be eliminated or severely curtailed in the near future. Supporters of the total abolition of plea bargaining are in the minority. As a result of abuses, however, efforts are being made to improve plea-bargaining operations. Such reforms include development of uniform plea practices, representation of counsel during plea negotiations, and establishment of time limits on plea negotiations.

Legal Issues in Plea Bargaining

The U.S. Supreme Court has reviewed the propriety of plea bargaining in several decisions. Some of its more important findings are discussed here.

EFFECTIVE ASSISTANCE OF COUNSEL Defendants are entitled to the effective assistance of counsel to protect them from pressure and influence during plea negotiations. In *Hill v. Lockhart* (1985), the Supreme Court ruled that to prove ineffectiveness, the defendant must show a "reasonable probability that, but for counsel's errors, he would not have pleaded guilty and would have insisted on going to trial."[31]

VOLUNTARINESS Guilty pleas must be voluntary, and the prosecutor cannot threaten or coerce a defendant into pleading guilty. In *Boykin v. Alabama* (1969), the Court held that an affirmative action (such as an oral statement) that the plea was made voluntarily must exist on the record before a trial judge may accept a guilty plea.[32] This is essential because a guilty plea basically constitutes a waiver of the defendant's Fifth Amendment privilege against self-incrimination and Sixth Amendment right to a jury trial. However, a prosecutor can apprise the defendant of the consequences of going to trial. For example, the prosecutor can let the defendant know that the death penalty will be sought in a murder case if a trial is required. The Court ruled in *Brady v. United States* (1970) that a guilty plea is not invalid simply because it is entered to avoid the possibility of the death penalty.[33]

How far can prosecutors go to convince a defendant to plead guilty? The Supreme Court ruled in the 1978 case of *Bordenkircher v. Hayes* that a defendant's due process rights are not violated when a prosecutor threatens to reindict the accused on more serious charges if the defendant does not plead guilty to the original offense.[34] Although the threat of reindictment seems coercive, the Supreme Court did not see it that way and gave the prosecutor the upper hand in the bargaining process.

PROMISES MUST BE KEPT In *Santobello v. New York* (1971), the Court held that the promise of the prosecutor must be kept and that a prosecutor's breaking of a plea-bargaining agreement required a reversal for the defendant.[35]

Not only must the prosecutor keep her word in a plea-bargain agreement, but the defendant must as well. In *Ricketts v. Adamson* (1987), the Court ruled that defendants must also keep their side of a bargain to receive the promised offer of leniency.[36] An example of defendant cooperation can be observed in a recent New York appellate case, *People v. Hicks* (2002).[37] In *Hicks*, a defendant pleaded guilty to sex-related crimes in exchange for a promised lenient sentence. A condition of the plea included that he truthfully answer all questions asked by probation officers when they investigated the case. After he told the investigators that he was not really guilty and that the children initiated sexual contact with him, the trial judge imposed a more severe sentence. Hicks appealed the longer sentence, but his request was turned down by the appellate court, which ruled that the defendant violated his promise to be truthful, thereby negating the plea-bargain agreement.

NEED FOR GUILT When the question arose about whether a guilty plea may be accepted by a defendant maintaining her innocence, the Supreme Court, in *North Carolina v. Alford* (1970), said that such action was appropriate when a defendant was seeking a lesser sentence. In other words, a defendant could plead guilty without admitting guilt.[38]

USE OF STATEMENTS In *United States v. Mezzanatto* (1995), the Supreme Court declared that statements made by the defendant during plea bargaining can be used at trial for impeachment purposes. This means that a prosecutor can refuse to plea bargain with a defendant unless the defendant agrees that any statements made during the negotiations can be used to impeach him at trial. Therefore, if the plea negotiations break down and the defendant testifies in his own behalf at trial, anything he said during the negotiation process can be used to rebut his testimony. In its decisions, the Court narrowly interpreted Rule 410 of the

CONCEPT SUMMARY 11.1

Control over Plea Negotiation

Case	Decision
BOYKIN V. ALABAMA (1969)	The defendant must make an affirmative statement that the plea is voluntary before the judge can accept it.
BRADY V. UNITED STATES (1970)	Avoiding the possibility of the death penalty is not grounds to invalidate a guilty plea.
NORTH CAROLINA V. ALFORD (1970)	Accepting a guilty plea from a defendant who maintains his or her innocence is valid.
SANTOBELLO V. NEW YORK (1971)	The promise of a prosecutor that rests on a guilty plea must be kept in a plea-bargaining agreement.
BORDENKIRCHER V. HAYES (1978)	A defendant's constitutional rights are not violated when a prosecutor threatens to reindict the accused on more serious charges if he or she is not willing to plead guilty to the original offense.
HILL V. LOCKHART (1985)	To prove ineffectiveness of defense counsel, the defendant needs to show a reasonable probability that, except for counsel's errors, the defendant would not have pleaded guilty.
RICKETTS V. ADAMSON (1987)	The defendant is required to keep his or her side of the bargain to receive the promised offer of leniency, because plea bargaining rests on an agreement between the parties.
UNITED STATES V. MEZZANATTO (1995)	A defendant who wants to plea bargain in federal court can be required to agree that if he testifies at trial, his statements during the plea-bargain negotiations can be used against him.

Federal Rules of Evidence, which says that statements made during plea bargaining are inadmissible at trial. Although the ruling applies only to federal trials, it is likely to be adopted by many state court systems that watch Supreme Court decisions and follow suit.[39]

Repeated actions by the Supreme Court show that plea bargaining is a constitutionally accepted practice in the United States. Concept Summary 11.1 summarizes the major Supreme Court decisions regulating plea-bargaining practices.

The Role of the Prosecutor in Plea Bargaining

The prosecutor in the U.S. system of criminal justice has broad discretion in the exercise of his responsibilities. Such discretion includes deciding whether to initiate a criminal prosecution, determining the nature and number of the criminal charges, and choosing whether to plea bargain a case and under what conditions. Plea bargaining is one of the major tools the prosecutor uses to control and influence the criminal justice system (the other two are the decision to initiate a charge and the ability to take the case to trial). Few states have placed limits on the discretion of prosecutors in plea-bargaining situations. Instead, in making a plea-bargaining decision, the prosecutor is generally free to weigh competing alternatives and factors, such as the seriousness of the crime, the attitude of the victim, the police report of the incident, and applicable sentencing provisions. Such factors as the offense, the defendant's prior record and age, and the type, strength, and admissibility of evidence are considered important in the plea-bargaining decision.[40] The attitude of the complainant is also an important factor in the decision-making process. For example, in victimless cases, such as heroin possession, the police attitude is most often considered, whereas in victim-related crimes, such as rape, the attitude of the victim is a primary

Plea bargains are used in some of the most notorious violent cases. Gary Leon Ridgway initials the plea agreement in the King County Courthouse in Seattle where he pleaded guilty to 48 murders. Ridgway added a confession read out by the prosecutor in open court: "I killed so many women I have a hard time keeping them straight." Ridgway pleaded guilty as part of a plea bargain with prosecutors in which his life would be spared. Should a murderer escape serious punishment by admitting his guilt?

concern. Prosecutors in low-population or rural jurisdictions not only use more information while making their decisions but also seem more likely than their urban counterparts to accept bargains, a finding that suggests case pressure alone is not the incentive for most plea bargains.[41]

Plea bargaining frequently occurs in cases in which the government believes the evidence is weak, as when a key witness seems unreliable or unwilling to testify. Bargaining permits a compromise settlement in a weak case when the criminal trial outcome is in doubt.

Some jurisdictions have established guidelines to provide consistency in plea-bargaining cases. They may require the district attorney to define the kinds and types of cases and offenders that may be suitable for plea bargaining. In other jurisdictions, approval to plea bargain may be required. Other controls might include procedures for internally reviewing decisions by the chief prosecutor and the use of written memorandums to document the need and acceptability for a plea bargain in a given case. In some cases pleas may be offered on a "take it or leave it" basis. In each case, a special prosecutor, whose job it is to screen cases, sets the bargaining terms. If the defense counsel cannot accept the agreement, there is no negotiation, and the case must go to trial. Only if complications arise in the case, such as witnesses changing their testimony, can negotiations be reopened.[42]

The prosecutor's role in plea bargaining is also important on a statewide or system-wide basis because it involves exercising leadership in setting policy. The most extreme example of a chief prosecutor influencing the plea-negotiation process occurred when the prosecutor attempted to eliminate plea bargaining. In Alaska, such efforts met with resistance from assistant prosecutors and others in the system, particularly judges and defense attorneys.[43]

The Role of the Defense Counsel in Plea Bargaining

Both the U.S. Supreme Court and such organizations as the American Bar Association have established guidelines for the court receiving a guilty plea and for the defense counsel representing the accused in plea negotiations.[44] No court should accept a guilty plea unless the defendant has been properly advised by counsel and the court has determined that the plea is voluntary and has a factual basis. The court has the discretion to reject a plea if it is inappropriately offered. The defense counsel—a public defender or a private attorney—is required to play an advisory role in plea negotiations. The defendant's counsel is expected to be aware of the facts of the case and of the law and to advise the defendant of the available alternatives. The defense attorney is basically responsible for making certain that the accused understands the nature of the plea-bargaining process and the guilty plea. This means that the defense counsel should explain to the defendant that, by pleading guilty, she is waiving certain rights that would be available if the case went to trial. In addition, the defense attorney has the duty to keep the defendant informed of developments and discussions with the prosecutor regarding plea bargaining. While doing so, the attorney for the accused cannot misrepresent evidence or mislead the client into making a detrimental agreement. The defense counsel is not only ethically but also constitutionally required to communicate all plea-bargaining offers to a client even if counsel believes the offers to be unacceptable.[45]

In reality, most plea negotiations occur in the chambers of the judge, in the prosecutor's office, or in the courthouse hallway. Under these conditions, it is often difficult to assess the actual roles played by the prosecutor and the defense attorney. Even so, it is fundamental that a defendant not be required to plead guilty until advised by counsel and that a guilty plea should not be made unless it is done with the consent of the accused.

The Role of the Judge in Plea Bargaining

One of the most confusing problems in the plea-bargaining process has been the proper role of the judge. Should the judge act only in a supervisory capacity or enter into the negotiation process? The leading national legal organization, the ABA, is opposed to judicial participation in plea negotiations.[46] According to ABA standards, judges should not be a party to arrangements for the determination of a sentence, whether as a result of a guilty plea or a finding of guilty based on proof. Furthermore, judicial participation in plea negotiations creates the impression in the mind of the defendant that she could not receive a fair trial, lessens the ability of the judge to make an objective determination of the voluntariness of the plea, is inconsistent with the theory behind the use of presentence investigation reports, and may induce an innocent defendant to plead guilty because she is afraid to reject the disposition desired by the judge.[47] In addition to the ABA, the Federal Rules of Criminal Procedure prohibit federal judges from participating in plea negotiations.[48]

Although these learned legal bodies frown on judicial involvement, most states still permit the judge to participate in the negotiation procedure. This approach allows the judge to work closely with prosecutors in securing the conviction of potentially dangerous offenders and shaping sentencing outcomes. When John Kramer and Jeffrey Ulmer examined sentencing practices in Pennsylvania, they found that judges were willing to work with the prosecutor as long as the agreed-upon sentence did not "shock their conscience."[49] As one judge commented, when asked about a negotiated plea agreement in which the prosecutor agreed not to seek a mandatory five-year prison sentence,

> When a district attorney comes in and says, "Judge, the defendant is willing to plead to 4–8 years and I think that the public is better off with that than me running the risk of losing this case because I think we have some evidentiary problems. The witness against him is a convicted felon that told two different stories." What are you going to do? Sounds like the best deal to me for everybody [is to accept the plea].

Despite the legal ethics of such a view, especially when evidence is questionable or tainted, there seems little question that judges are willing to work with prosecutors for the sake of crime control at the expense of due process.

The Victim and Plea Bargaining

What role should victims play in plea bargaining? Crime victims are not empowered at the pretrial stage of the criminal process and should not play a role in the plea negotiations. Statutes do not require that the prosecutor defer to the victim's wishes, and there are no legal consequences for ignoring the victim in a plea-bargaining decision. Even the ABA's *Model Uniform Victims of Crime Act* suggests only that the prosecutor "confer" with the victim.[50] Nonetheless, many prosecutors do confer with crime victims, and some critics have suggested that the system today is too victim-driven—that is, in too many cases prosecutors seek approval for the plea from a victim or family member.

Plea-Bargaining Reform

In recent years, efforts have been made to convert plea bargaining into a more visible, understandable, and fair dispositional process. Many jurisdictions have developed safeguards and guidelines to prevent violations of due process and to ensure that innocent defendants do not plead guilty under coercion. Such safeguards include the following:

1. The judge questions the defendant about the facts of the guilty plea before accepting the plea.

2. The defense counsel is present and can advise the defendant of her rights.

3. The prosecutor and the defense attorney openly discuss the plea.

4. Full and frank information about the defendant and the offenses is made available at this stage of the process. In addition, judicial supervision ensures that plea bargaining is conducted in a fair manner.

What would happen if plea bargaining were banned outright, as its critics advocate? Numerous jurisdictions throughout the United States have experimented with bans on plea bargaining. In 1975 Alaska eliminated the practice. Honolulu, Hawaii, has also attempted to abolish plea bargaining. Other jurisdictions, including Arizona, Delaware, the District of Columbia, and Iowa, have sought to limit the use of plea bargaining.[51] In theory, eliminating plea bargains means that prosecutors in these jurisdictions give no consideration or concessions to a defendant in exchange for a guilty plea.

In reality, however, in these and most jurisdictions, sentence-related concessions, charge-reduction concessions, and alternative methods for prosecution continue to be used in one fashion or another.[52] When plea bargaining is limited or abolished, the number of trials may increase, the sentence severity may change, and more questions regarding the right to a speedy trial may arise. Discretion may also be shifted further up the system. Instead of spending countless hours preparing for and conducting a trial, prosecutors may dismiss more cases outright or decide not to prosecute them after initial action has been taken. Candace McCoy's study of plea reform in California investigated legislative efforts to eliminate the state's plea-bargaining process. Instead of achieving a ban on plea bargaining, the process shifted from the superior to the municipal courts. McCoy found that the majority of defendants pled guilty after some negotiations and that the new law accelerated the guilty plea process. McCoy suggests an alternative model of plea-bargaining reform that includes emphasizing public scrutiny of plea bargaining, adhering to standards of professionalism, and making a greater commitment to due process procedures.[53]

ThomsonNOW Improve your grade on the exam with Personalized Study! For reinforcement resources and a mastery check of plea bargaining, go to www.thomsonedu.com/thomsonnow.

♦ PRETRIAL DIVERSION

Another important feature of the early court process is placing offenders into noncriminal diversion programs before their formal trial or conviction. Pretrial diversion programs were first established in the late 1960s and early 1970s, when it became apparent that a viable alternative to the highly stigmatized criminal sentence was needed. In diversion programs, formal criminal proceedings against an accused are suspended while that person participates in a community treatment program under court supervision. Diversion helps the offender avoid

Drug courts are often active in the diversion process. In Austin, Texas, a judge presides over the weekly meeting of the Drug Diversion Court, a year-long program for defendants who have been arrested for felony possession of a controlled substance. The program relies on frequent drug screening, offers classes and treatment referrals, and can result in dismissal of charges if the defendant completes the program successfully.

the stigma of a criminal conviction and enables the justice system to reduce costs and alleviate prison overcrowding.

Many diversion programs exist throughout the United States. These programs vary in size and emphasis but generally pursue the same goal: to constructively bypass criminal prosecution by providing a reasonable alternative in the form of treatment, counseling, or employment programs.

The prosecutor often plays the central role in the diversion process. Decisions about nondispositional alternatives are based on the nature of the crime, special characteristics of the offender, whether the defendant is a first-time offender, whether the defendant will cooperate with a diversion program, the impact of diversion on the community, and consideration for the opinion of the victim.[54]

Diversion programs can take many forms. Some are separate, independent agencies that were originally set up with federal funds but are now being continued with county or state assistance. Others are organized as part of a police, prosecutor, or probation department's internal structure. Still others are a joint venture between the county government and a private, nonprofit organization that carries out the treatment process.

First viewed as a panacea that could reduce court congestion and help treat minor offenders, diversion programs have come under fire for their alleged failures. Some national evaluations have concluded that diversion programs are no more successful at avoiding stigma and reducing recidivism than traditional justice processing.[55] The most prominent criticism is that they help *widen the net* of the justice system. By this, critics mean that the people placed in diversion programs are the ones most likely to have otherwise been dismissed after a brief hearing with a warning or small fine.[56] Instead of limiting contact with the system, the diversion programs increase it. Not all justice experts agree with this charge, and some have championed diversion as a worthwhile exercise of the criminal justice system's rehabilitation responsibility. Although diversion may not be a cure-all for criminal behavior, it is an important effort that continues to be made in most jurisdictions across the United States. Even if diversion programs were no more successful than traditional court processing, they are certainly less expensive to operate and help reduce court crowding and trial delays.[57]

ETHICAL CHALLENGES IN CRIMINAL JUSTICE: A WRITING ASSIGNMENT

Critics argue that the U.S. practice of holding terrorist suspects at Guantanamo in Cuba is the ultimate use of preventive detention. Currently, terrorism suspects can be detained as enemy combatants, held as material witnesses, or detained for immigration violations. In June 2006, three prisoners at the Guantanamo Bay detention center committed suicide, and those opposed to the practice renewed calls for closing the facility. Write an essay on the practice of detaining terror suspects without trial. Is it justified, or does it violate age-old concepts of due process and equal protection?

Doing Research on the Web

Before you start your essay, you may want to read this op-ed piece by Michael Ignatieff: "Lesser Evils." Other helpful works include Pamela M. von Ness, "Guantanamo Bay Detainees: National Security or Civil Liberty," and Robert M. Chesney, "The Sleeper Scenario: Terrorism-Support Laws and the Demands of Prevention." You can access all three of these articles by going to the Siegel/Senna Introduction to Criminal Justice 11e website: www.thomsonedu.com/criminaljustice/siegel.

SUMMARY

♦ Many important decisions about what happens to a defendant are made prior to trial.

♦ Hearings, such as before the grand jury and the preliminary hearing, are held to determine if probable cause exists to charge the accused with a crime. If so, the defendant is arraigned, enters a plea, is informed of his constitutional rights (particularly the right to the assistance of counsel), and is considered for pretrial diversion.

♦ The use of money bail and other alternatives, such as release on recognizance, allows most defendants to be free pending their trial.

♦ Bail reform has resulted in the use of release on recognizance to replace money bail for nondangerous offenders.

♦ Preventive detention has been implemented because many believe that significant numbers of criminals violate their bail and commit further crimes while on pretrial release.

♦ Research indicates that most cases never go to trial but are bargained out of the system.

♦ Bargains can be made for a plea of guilty in exchange for a reduced sentence, dropping charges, lowering the charge, or substituting a more socially acceptable charge for one with negative connotations.

♦ People who plead guilty generally get lighter sentences than those who go to trial.

♦ The U.S. Supreme Court has shaped the legal contours of the plea system. For example, it has ruled that bargains must be kept on both sides.

♦ Although plea bargaining has been criticized, efforts to control it have not met with success.

♦ Diversion programs offering a criminal defendant the ability to enter a treatment program instead of a criminal trial continue to be used throughout the United States.

KEY TERMS

pretrial procedures, 354
nolle prosequi, 354
complaint, 354
indictment, 355
information, 355
preliminary hearing (probable
   cause hearing), 355

arraignment, 355
nolo contendere, 355
bail, 356
pretrial detainees, 360
release on recognizance
   (ROR), 361
avertable recidivist, 363

presentment, 364
true bill, 365
no bill, 365
exculpatory evidence, 365

ThomsonNOW Maximize your study time by using ThomsonNOW's diagnostic study plan to help you review this chapter. The Study Plan will

♦ help you identify areas on which you should concentrate;

♦ provide interactive exercises to help you master the chapter concepts; and

♦ provide a post-test to confirm you are ready to move on to the next chapter.

CRITICAL THINKING QUESTIONS

1. Should criminal defendants be allowed to bargain for a reduced sentence in exchange for a guilty plea? Should the victim always be included in the plea-bargaining process?

2. Should those accused of violent acts be subjected to preventive detention instead of bail, even though they have not been convicted of a crime? Is it fair to the victim to have his alleged attacker running around loose?

3. What purpose does a grand jury or preliminary hearing serve in adjudicating felony offenses? Should one of these methods be abandoned? If so, which one?

4. Why should pretrial services be provided for defendants?

5. Should a suspect in a terrorist case be allowed bail? Wouldn't that give him license to carry out his plot?

NOTES

1. CNN, "Mel Gibson Pleads No Contest in DUI Case," August 17, 2006.
2. Christopher Stephens, "Bail," *Georgetown Law Journal* 90 (2002): 1395–1416.
3. The Judiciary Act of 1789 (http://www.constitution.org/uslaw/judiciary_1789.htm), accessed on May 23, 2006.
4. *Stack v. Boyle*, 342 U.S. 1, 72 S.Ct. 1, 96 L.Ed. 3 (1951).
5. Data in this section come from Thomas Cohen and Brian Reaves, *Felony Defendants in Large Urban Counties, 2002* (Washington, D.C.: Bureau of Justice Statistics, 2006).
6. Ibid.
7. *Vera Institute of Justice, 1961–1971: Programs in Criminal Justice* (New York: Vera Institute of Justice, 1972).
8. Chris Eskridge, *Pretrial Release Programming* (New York: Clark Boardman, 1983), p. 27.
9. Public Law 89–465, 18 U.S.C., Sec. 3146 (1966).
10. Ellis M. Johnston, "Once a Criminal, Always a Criminal? Unconstitutional Presumptions for Mandatory Detention of Criminal Aliens," *Georgetown Law Journal* 89 (2001): 2593–2636.
11. 18 U.S.C., Sec. 3142 (1984).
12. Fred Cohen, "The New Federal Crime Control Act," *Criminal Law Bulletin* 21 (1985): 330–37.
13. *Schall v. Martin*, 467 U.S. 253, 104 S.Ct. 2403, 81 L.Ed.2d 207 (1984).
14. *United States v. Salerno*, 481 U.S. 739, 107 S.Ct. 2095, 95 L.Ed.2d 697 (1987).
15. This section leans on John Clark and D. Alan Henry, *Pretrial Services Programming at the Start of the 21st Century: A Survey* (Washington, D.C.: Bureau of Justice Assistance, 2003).
16. Ric Simmons, "Reexamining the Grand Jury: Is There Room for Democracy in the Criminal Justice System?" *Boston University Law Review* 82 (2002): 1–76.
17. *United States v. Williams*, 504 U.S. 36, 38 (1992).
18. Suzanne Roe Neely, "Preserving Justice and Preventing Prejudice: Requiring Disclosure of Substantial Exculpatory Evidence to the Grand Jury," *American Criminal Law Review* 39 (2002): 171–200.
19. John Gibeaut, "Indictment of a System," *ABA Journal* 87 (2001): 34.
20. American Bar Association, *Grand Jury Policy and Model Act* (Chicago: 1982). See also Deborah Day Emerson, *Grand Jury Reform: A Review of Key Issues* (Washington, D.C.: Institute of Justice, 1983).
21. ABC News Online, "Crowe Released After Court Hearing" (http://www.abc.net.au/news/newsitems/200506/s1385947.htm), accessed on August 20, 2006.
22. Kirke D. Weaver, "A Change of Heart or a Change of Law? Withdrawing a Guilty Plea Under Federal Rule of Criminal Procedure 32(e)," *Journal of Criminal Law and Criminology* 92 (2001): 273–306.
23. F. Andrew Hessick and Reshma Saujani, "Plea Bargaining and Convicting the Innocent: The Role of the Prosecutor, the Defense Counsel, and the Judge," *BYU Journal of Public Law* 16 (2002): 189–243.
24. Mike McConville and Chester Mirsky, *Jury Trials and Plea Bargaining: A True History* (Oxford, England: Hart, 2005).
25. George Fisher, "Plea Bargaining's Triumph," *Yale Law Journal* 109 (2000): 857–1058.
26. Matthew Durose and Patrick Langan, *Felony Sentencing in State Courts, 2000* (Washington, D.C.: Bureau of Justice Statistics, 2003).
27. Debra Emmelman, "Trial by Plea Bargain: Case Settlement as a Product of Recursive Decisionmaking," *Law and Society Review* 30 (1996): 335–61.
28. William Stuntz, "Plea Bargaining and Criminal Law's Disappearing Shadow," *Harvard Law Review* 117 (2004): 2548–69.
29. Fisher, "Plea Bargaining's Triumph."
30. Fred Zacharis, "Justice in Plea Bargaining," *William and Mary Law Review* 39 (1998): 1211–40.
31. *Hill v. Lockhart*, 474 U.S. 52, 106 S.Ct. 366, 88 L.Ed.2d 203 (1985).
32. *Boykin v. Alabama*, 395 U.S. 238, 89 S.Ct. 1709, 23 L.Ed.2d 274 (1969).
33. *Brady v. United States*, 397 U.S. 742, 90 S.Ct. 1463, 25 L.Ed.2d 747 (1970).
34. *Bordenkircher v. Hayes*, 434 U.S. 357, 98 S.Ct. 663, 54 L.Ed.2d 604 (1978).
35. *Santobello v. New York*, 404 U.S. 257, 92 S.Ct. 495, 30 L.Ed.2d 427 (1971).
36. *Ricketts v. Adamson*, 483 U.S. 1, 107 S.Ct. 2680, 97 L.Ed.2d 1 (1987).

37. *People v. Hicks*, NY2d (July 1, 2002), 2002 NYSlipOp 05513.
38. *North Carolina v. Alford,* 400 U.S. 25, 91 S.Ct. 160, 27 L.Ed.2d 162 (1970).
39. *United States v. Mezzanatto*, 116 S.Ct. 1480, 134 L.Ed.2d 687 (1995).
40. Stephen P. Lagoy, Joseph J. Senna, and Larry J. Siegel, "An Empirical Study on Information Usage for Prosecutorial Decision Making in Plea Negotiations," *American Criminal Law Review* 13 (1976): 435–71.
41. Ibid., p. 462.
42. Barbara Boland and Brian Forst, *The Prevalence of Guilty Pleas* (Washington, D.C.: Bureau of Justice Statistics, 1984), p. 3. See also Gary Hengstler, "The Troubled Justice System," *American Bar Association Journal* 80 (1994): 44.
43. National Institute of Law Enforcement and Criminal Justice, *Plea Bargaining in the United States* (Washington, D.C.: Georgetown University, 1978), p. 8.
44. See American Bar Association, *Standards Relating to Pleas of Guilty,* 2nd ed. (Chicago: 1988). See also *North Carolina v. Alford*, 400 U.S. 25, 91 S.Ct. 160, 27 L.Ed.2d 162 (1970).
45. Keith Bystrom, "Communicating Plea Offers to the Client," in *Ethical Problems Facing the Criminal Defense Lawyer,* ed. Rodney Uphoff (Chicago: American Bar Association, Section on Criminal Justice, 1995), p. 84.
46. American Bar Association, *Standards Relating to Pleas of Guilty,* Standard 3.3; National Advisory Commission on Criminal Justice Standards and Goals, *Task Force Report on Courts* (Washington, D.C.: Government Printing Office, 1973), p. 42.
47. American Bar Association, *Standards Relating to Pleas of Guilty,* p. 73. See also Alan Alschuler, "The Trial Judge's Role in Plea Bargaining," *Columbia Law Review* 76 (1976): 1059.
48. Federal Rules of Criminal Procedure, 11 (C) (1) (amended December 1, 2002).
49. John Kramer and Jeffrey Ulmer, "Downward Departures for Serious Violent Offenders: Local Court 'Corrections' to Pennsylvania's Sentencing Guidelines," *Criminology* 40 (2002): 897–933.
50. American Bar Association, *Model Uniform Victims of Crime Act* (Chicago: 1992).
51. National Institute of Law Enforcement and Criminal Justice, *Plea Bargaining in the United States,* pp. 37–40.
52. Gary Blankenship, "Debating the Pros and Cons of Plea Bargaining," *Florida Bar News* 30 (July 15, 2003): 6–7.
53. Candace McCoy, *Politics and Plea Bargaining: Victims' Rights in California* (Philadelphia: University of Pennsylvania Press, 1993).
54. National District Attorneys Association, *National Prosecution Standards,* 2nd ed. (Alexandria, Va.: 1991), p. 130.
55. Franklyn Dunford, D. Wayne Osgood, and Hart Weichselbaum, *National Evaluation of Diversion Programs* (Washington, D.C.: Government Printing Office, 1982).
56. Sharla Rausch and Charles Logan, "Diversion from Juvenile Court: Panacea or Pandora's Box?" in *Evaluating Juvenile Justice*, ed. James Kleugel (Beverly Hills, Calif.: Sage, 1983), pp. 19–30.
57. See Malcolm Feeley, *Court Reform on Trial* (New York: Basic Books, 1983).

The Criminal Trial

Chapter Outline

Chapter Objectives

After reading this chapter, you should be able to:

1. Understand the concept of a jury trial.
2. Know what it means to confront witnesses.
3. Recognize the term *speedy trial*.
4. Explain the concept of the pro se defense.
5. Discuss what a fair trial means.
6. Argue the right of the press to attend trials.
7. Discuss the issues surrounding the broadcast of criminal trials.
8. Know the difference between a challenge for cause and a peremptory challenge.
9. Identify the different ways that evidence is presented in criminal trials.
10. Explain the concept of proof beyond a reasonable doubt.

On January 18, 2002, Sara Jane Olson was sentenced to 20 years to life in prison for her role in a failed bomb plot to kill Los Angeles police officers in 1975. Then known as Kathy Soliah, a member of the radical Symbionese Liberation Army (SLA), Olson escaped capture and fled to Minnesota, where she led a quiet life. She married a doctor, raised a family, and became an upstanding member of the community who engaged in many charitable works. Then, in a segment of the TV show "America's Most Wanted," pictures of Soliah and another SLA fugitive, James Kilgore, were broadcast, and the FBI offered a $20,000 reward for information leading to Soliah's capture. Identified by someone who watched the show, she peacefully surrendered to the police on June 16, 1999, after being pulled over a few blocks from her home.

During trial, Olson's defense attorneys suffered one setback after another. They argued that she could not hope to get a fair hearing in light of the events of the 9/11 terrorist attack. The judge sided with the prosecutors, who said that international acts of terrorism have no bearing on any case in the court system, even one involving domestic terrorism. The judge also ruled that prosecutors could present evidence of the Symbionese Liberation Army's history of criminal acts, even though she was not accused of participating in them. The judge said that all the acts were relevant because they showed the deadly intentions of the group. ◆

On November 6, 2002, Sara Jane Olson, along with three other former members of the Symbionese Liberation Army, agreed to plead guilty to murder in the shotgun slaying of a bank customer during a 1975 holdup. They were charged with first-degree murder but agreed to plead guilty to second-degree murder in a deal with prosecutors to avoid a possible sentence of life in prison. Olson received a six-year sentence for the crime, which she will have to serve after completing her earlier sentence. To read more about the Olson case, go to the Court TV website, which you can reach by going to the Siegel/Senna Introduction to Criminal Justice 11e website: www.thomsonedu. com/criminaljustice/siegel.

adjudication
The determination of guilt or innocence—a judgment concerning criminal charges.

bench trial
The trial of a criminal matter by a judge without a jury.

The Olson case illustrates the difficulty of getting a fair trial in a highly charged political environment. Might she have been found not guilty if the September 11 terrorist acts had never taken place? Can such high-profile cases ever hope to get fair and unbiased juries? The Olson case aptly illustrates the moral and legal dilemmas that are raised when such issues as pretrial publicity and televised trials are considered. It also raises issues about the purpose of prosecuting and punishing criminal defendants. This middle-aged mother hardly presents a danger to society. Given that Sarah Jane Olson had rehabilitated herself, were her prosecution and trial merely a cruel afterthought? Then again, should she be rewarded with lenient treatment because she was able to escape capture and elude the authorities for 25 years? Her sterling record as a wife and mother could have been accomplished only because she evaded the grasp of the law at the time her crimes were committed. Should a rapist be freed merely because he escaped capture for 20 years?[1]

The center point of the **adjudication** process is the criminal trial, an open and public hearing designed to examine the facts of the case brought by the state against the accused. Although trials are relatively rare events and most cases are settled by a plea bargain, the trial is an important and enduring fixture in the criminal justice system. By its very nature, it is a symbol of the moral authority of the state. The criminal trial is the symbol of the administration of objective and impartial justice. Regardless of the issues involved, the defendant's presence in a courtroom is designed to guarantee that he will have a hearing conducted under rules of procedure in an atmosphere of fair play and objectivity and that the outcome of the hearing will be clear and definitive. If the defendant believes that his constitutional rights and privileges have been violated, he may appeal the case to a higher court, where the procedures of the original trial will be examined. If, after examining the trial transcript, the appellate court rules that the original trial employed improper and unconstitutional procedures, it may order that a new hearing be held or order that the charges against the defendant be dismissed.

Most formal trials are heard by a jury, although some defendants waive their constitutional right to a jury trial and request a **bench trial**, in which the judge alone renders a verdict. In this situation, which occurs daily in the lower criminal courts, the judge may initiate a number of formal or informal dispositions, including dismissing the case, finding the defendant not guilty, finding the defendant guilty and imposing a sentence, or continuing the case indefinitely. Bench trials may also occur in serious felonies. In a 2003 case, James C. Kopp, the accused killer of Dr. Barnett A. Slepian, an abortion provider in Buffalo, New York, waived his right to a jury trial and requested a bench trial. Kopp, who had admitted that he shot and killed Slepian with an assault rifle in 1998, was warned by the trial judge that he was giving up the most logical defense tactic—that is, having his lawyers appeal to the emotions and religious principles of a jury.[2] Kopp proceeded nonetheless, was found guilty, and was given a long prison sentence.

The decision that the judge makes often depends on the seriousness of the offense, the background and previous record of the defendant, and the judgment of the court about whether the case can be properly dealt with in the criminal process. Instead of holding a trial, the judge may simply continue the case without a finding, which means the verdict is withheld without a finding of guilt to induce the accused to improve her behavior in the community. If the defendant's behavior does improve, the case is ordinarily closed within a specific amount of time.

◆ LEGAL RIGHTS DURING TRIAL

Underlying every trial are constitutional principles, complex legal procedures, rules of court, and interpretation of statutes, all designed to ensure that the accused will receive a fair trial.

The Right to Be Competent at Trial

To stand trial, a criminal defendant must be considered mentally competent to understand the nature and extent of the legal proceedings. If a defendant is considered mentally incompetent, his trial must be postponed until treatment renders him capable of participating in his own defense. Can state authorities force a mentally unfit defendant to be treated so that he can be tried? In *Riggins v. Nevada* (1992), the U.S. Supreme Court ruled that forced treatment does not violate a defendant's due process rights if it was medically appropriate and, considering less intrusive alternatives, was essential for the defendant's own safety or the safety of others.[3] In a 2003 case, *Sell v. United States*, the Court set out four rules that guide the use of forced medication:[4]

1. A court must find that important governmental interests are at stake. Courts must consider each case's facts in evaluating this interest because special circumstances may lessen its importance. A criminal defendant's refusal to take drugs may mean they can be sentenced to a lengthy confinement in an institution. Their incarceration would diminish the risks of freeing someone who has committed a serious crime. Their incarceration would also enhance public safety.

2. The court must conclude that forced medication will significantly further state interests. It must find that medication is substantially likely to render the defendant competent to stand trial and substantially unlikely to have side-effects that will interfere significantly with the defendant's ability to assist counsel in conducting a defense.

3. The court must conclude that involuntary medication is necessary to further state interests and find that alternative, less intrusive treatments are unlikely to achieve substantially the same results.

4. The court must conclude that administering the drugs is medically appropriate.

The Right to Confront Witnesses

The Sixth Amendment states that "In all criminal prosecutions, the accused shall enjoy the right . . . to be confronted with the witnesses against him." The **confrontation clause** is essential to a fair criminal trial because it restricts and controls the admissibility of hearsay evidence. Secondhand evidence, which depends on a witness not available in court, is ordinarily limited; in-court statements by a witness or victim of a crime is usually required. The Framers of the Constitution sought face-to-face accusations in which the defendant has a right to see and cross-examine all witnesses. The idea that it is always more difficult to tell lies about people to their face than behind their back underlies the focus of the confrontation clause. A witness in a criminal trial may have more difficulty repeating his or her testimony when facing the accused in a trial than in providing information to the police during an investigation. The accused has the right to confront any witnesses and challenge their assertions and perceptions: Did they really see what they believe? Are they biased? Can they be trusted? What about the accuracy of their testimony? Generally speaking, the courts have been nearly unanimous in their belief that the right to confrontation and cross-examination is an essential requirement for a fair trial.[5]

This face-to-face presence was reviewed by the Supreme Court in a case involving a child as a witness in criminal proceedings. In *Coy v. Iowa* (1988), the Supreme Court limited the protection available to child sex victims at the trial stage.[6] In *Coy*, two girls were allowed to be cross-examined behind a screen that separated them from the defendant. The Court ruled that the screen violated the defendant's right to confront witnesses and overturned his conviction. However, in her supporting opinion, Justice Sandra Day O'Connor made it clear that ruling out the protective screen did not bar the states from using videotapes or closed-circuit television. Although Justice O'Connor recognized that the Sixth Amendment

confrontation clause
The constitutional right of a criminal defendant to see and cross-examine all the witnesses against him or her.

Crawford v. Washington

Michael Crawford was convicted of assault after he stabbed Kenneth Lee at Lee's apartment. Crawford claimed that Lee had attempted to rape his wife. Both Crawford and his wife, Sylvia, who was present during the assault, initially provided substantially similar accounts of the attack to police. When questioned again several hours later, however, the Crawfords' stories were different from their initial accounts and from each other's. The distinguishing factor was whether Lee had a weapon. Michael Crawford thought Lee had a weapon in his hand when he stabbed him:

Q: Okay. Did you ever see anything in [Lee's] hands?

A: I think so, but I'm not positive.

Q: Okay, when you think so, what do you mean by that?

A: I coulda swore I seen him goin' for somethin' be-fore, right before everything happened. He was like reachin', fiddlin' around down here and stuff . . . and I just . . . I don't know, I think, this is just a possibility, but I think, I think that he pulled some-thin' out and I grabbed for it and that's how I got cut . . . but I'm not positive. I, I, my mind goes blank when things like this happen. I mean, I just, I remember things wrong, I remember things that just doesn't, don't make sense to me later.

However, during Sylvia's interrogations, she stated that Lee grabbed for a weapon after Crawford stabbed him.

Q: Did Kenny do anything to fight back from this assault?

A: (pausing) I know he reached into his pocket . . . or somethin' . . . I don't know what.

Q: After he was stabbed?

A: He saw Michael coming up. He lifted his hand . . . his chest open, he might [have] went to go strike his hand out or something and then (inaudible).

Q: Okay, you, you gotta speak up.

A: Okay, he lifted his hand over his head maybe to strike Michael's hand down or something and then he put his hands in his . . . put his right hand in his right pocket . . . took a step back. . . . Michael proceeded to stab him . . . then his hands were like . . . how do you explain this . . . open arms . . . with his hands open and he fell down . . . and we ran (describing subject holding hands open, palms toward assailant).

Q: Okay, when he's standing there with his open hands, you're talking about Kenny, correct?

A: Yeah, after, after the fact, yes.

Q: Did you see anything in his hands at that point?

A: (pausing) um um (no).

Crawford's defense attorney used the marital privilege at trial to prevent his wife from testifying against his client. However, the state introduced her second statement at trial to undermine Craw-ford's self-defense argument, and Crawford was convicted.

Crawford appealed his conviction, claiming that his Sixth Amendment right to confront a witness against him in court was violated when his wife's

right to confront witnesses was violated, she indicated that an exception to a lit-eral interpretation of the confrontation clause might be appropriate.

In *Maryland v. Craig* (1990), the Supreme Court carved out an exception to the Sixth Amendment confrontation clause by deciding that alleged child abuse victims could testify by closed-circuit television if face-to-face confrontation would cause them trauma.[7] In allowing the states to take testimony via closed-circuit television, the Supreme Court found that circumstances exist in child sex abuse cases that override the defendant's right of confrontation.

As a result of these decisions, the confrontation clause does not appear to guarantee criminal defendants the absolute right to a face-to-face meeting with witnesses at their trial. Instead, according to *Maryland v. Craig*, it reflects a preference for such a guarantee. *Craig* signals that the Court is willing to com-promise a defendant's right to confront his or her accuser to achieve a social objective, the prosecution of a child abuser. However, as the Law in Review feature indicates, the spirit of the confrontation clause is still in effect.

The Right to a Jury Trial

It is not by accident that of all the rights guaranteed to the people by the Consti-tution, only the right to a jury trial in criminal cases appears in both the original

statement was admitted at trial. Under the Supreme Court's decision in *Ohio v. Roberts*, statements of nontestifying accomplices are not admitted at trial unless they are sufficiently reliable and trustworthy— e.g., if the statements "interlock" or are virtually identical. When the case got to the State of Washington Supreme Court, it upheld the conviction on the grounds that the differences between the two statements were minor.

Upon further appeal, the U.S. Supreme Court ordered a new trial. Justice Scalia, writing the opinion, noted that the Framers of the Constitution had included the confrontation clause because they recognized that out-of-court statements used in evidence in criminal trials were very damaging even if they were unreliable. Mrs. Crawford had given at least two different versions of events to police, one of which was not before the jury and may have led them to believe that she had not seen the actual attack. Her statement to the police may have been tainted because they were pressuring her to talk, something that could have been brought out at trial. Her statement seemed less than reliable. The Court concluded that the confrontation clause in the Sixth Amendment was designed to protect defendants by allowing them to challenge a witness's version of events and that denying Mr. Crawford the opportunity was clearly an error.

The *Crawford* decision will make it tougher for prosecutors to prove their cases. They cannot use evidence that is "testimonial" in nature unless the actual witness testifies at trial. However, the decision does not precisely define what *testimonial* means, which has allowed courts across the country to determine that issue for themselves. For example, if someone calls 911 and makes a complaint, can the recording be used if the caller is not available to testify? These issues will be dealt with in further legal actions.

Critical Thinking

The Crawford case concluded that the use at trial of out-of-court statements made to police by an unavailable witness violated a criminal defendant's Sixth Amendment right to confront witnesses. Should this rule be applied to terror cases where a witness believes that his appearance in court will jeopardize his life and the lives of his family? Should an exception be made for cases with extraordinary circumstances?

InfoTrac College Edition Research

To read an in-depth analysis of *Crawford v. Washington*, see Miguel A. Mendez, "*Crawford v. Washington*: A Critique," *Stanford Law Review* 57 (2004): 569–610.

Source: *Crawford v. Washington,* 541 U.S. 36; 124 S. Ct. 1354; 158 L. Ed. 2d 177 (2004).

Constitution and the Bill of Rights. Although they may have disagreed on many points, the Framers did not question the wisdom of the jury trial.

Today, the criminal defendant has the right to choose whether the trial will be before a judge or a jury. Although the Sixth Amendment guarantees the defendant the right to a jury trial, the defendant can and often does waive this right. A substantial proportion of defendants, particularly those charged with misdemeanors, are tried before the court without a jury.

The major legal issue surrounding jury trial has been whether all defendants, those accused of misdemeanors as well as felonies, have an absolute right to a jury trial. Although the Constitution is silent on this point, the U.S. Supreme Court has ruled that all defendants in felony cases have this right. In *Duncan v. Louisiana* (1968), the Court held that the Sixth Amendment right to a jury trial is applicable to all states, as well as to the federal government, and that it can be interpreted to apply to all defendants accused of serious crimes.[8] The *Duncan* ruling was based on the premise that in the state court system, as in the federal judicial system, a general grant of jury trial for serious offenses is a fundamental right, essential for preventing miscarriages of justice and for ensuring that fair trials are provided for all defendants.[9] The *Duncan* decision did not settle

In some cases, especially those involving capital crimes, juries not only decide guilt but also make recommendations during the sentencing phase of the trial. Here jury members from the Scott Peterson trial read a statement during a news conference in Redwood City, California. In the Peterson case, the jury returned with a sentence recommendation of death. Peterson was convicted of two counts of murder in the deaths of his wife, Laci Peterson, and their unborn child.

whether all defendants charged with crimes in state courts are constitutionally entitled to jury trials. It seemed to draw the line at only those charged with serious offenses, leaving the decision to grant jury trials to defendants in minor cases to the discretion of the individual states.

In *Baldwin v. New York* (1970), the Supreme Court departed from the distinction of serious versus minor offenses and decided that a defendant has a constitutional right to a jury trial when facing a possible prison sentence of six months or more, regardless of whether the crime committed was a felony or a misdemeanor.[10] When the possible sentence is six months or less, the accused is not entitled to a jury trial unless it is authorized by state statute. In most jurisdictions, the more serious the charge, the greater likelihood of trial—and of a trial by jury.

The Supreme Court has used six months' potential imprisonment as the dividing line between petty offenses for which the Sixth Amendment gives no right to jury trial and serious offenses that enjoy such a legal right. In *Lewis v. United States* (1996), the Court faced the unusual problem of multiple petty offenses that, when added together, could lead to imprisonment in excess of six months.[11] The defendant argued that he was constitutionally entitled to a jury trial. But the Supreme Court said there was no Sixth Amendment right to a jury trial for a string of petty offenses tried together, even when the potential total sentence could exceed six months. The Court's reasoning was that the legislature was responsible for the design of an offense with a maximum possible penalty, and the prosecutor has the right to exercise discretion to join different offenses in one trial without defeating the legislative intent to distinguish between petty and serious offenses.

In sum, the Sixth Amendment guarantees the right to a jury trial. The accused can waive this right and be tried by a judge, who then becomes the fact finder as well as the determiner of the law.

Other important issues related to the defendant's rights in a criminal jury trial include the right to a jury of twelve people and the right to a unanimous verdict.

JURY SIZE   The size of the jury has been a matter of great concern. Can a defendant be tried and convicted of a crime by a jury of fewer than twelve persons? Traditionally, twelve jurors have deliberated as the triers of fact in criminal cases involving misdemeanors or felonies. However, the Constitution does not specifically require a jury of twelve persons. As a result, in *Williams v. Florida* (1970), the Supreme Court held that a six-person jury in a criminal trial does not deprive a defendant of the constitutional right to a jury trial.[12] The Court made it clear that the twelve-person panel is not a necessary ingredient of the trial by jury and upheld a Florida statute permitting the use of a six-person jury in a robbery trial. The majority opinion in the Williams case traced the Court's rationale for its decision:

> We conclude, in short, as we began: the fact that a jury at common law was composed of precisely twelve is a historical accident, unnecessary to effect the purposes of the jury system and wholly without significance "except to mystics."[13]

Justice Byron R. White, writing further for the majority, said this:

> In short, while sometime in the 14th century the size of the jury came to be fixed generally at 12, that particular feature of the jury system appears to have been a historical accident, unrelated to the great purpose which gave rise to the jury in the first place.[14]

On the basis of this decision, many states are using six-person juries in misdemeanor cases, and some states, such as Florida, Louisiana, and Utah, use them in felony cases (except in capital offenses). In the *Williams* decision, Justice White emphasized that "We have an occasion to determine what minimum number can still constitute a jury, but do not doubt that six is above the minimum."[15]

The six-person jury can play an important role in the criminal justice system because it promotes court efficiency and also helps implement the defendant's right to a speedy trial. However, the Supreme Court has ruled that a jury composed of fewer than six people is unconstitutional and that if a **six-person jury** is used in serious crimes, its verdict must be unanimous.[16] *Williams v. Florida*, decided more than 30 years ago, offered a welcome measure of relief to an overburdened crime control system. Today, jury size can be reduced for all but the most serious criminal cases.

six-person jury
According to the U.S. Supreme Court, the smallest legally acceptable jury.

UNANIMOUS JURY In addition to the convention of twelve-person juries in criminal trials, tradition had been that the jurors' decision must be unanimous. However, in *Apodaca v. Oregon* (1972), the Supreme Court held that the Sixth and Fourteenth amendments do not prohibit criminal convictions by less than unanimous jury verdicts in noncapital cases.[17] In the *Apodaca* case, the Court upheld an Oregon statute requiring only ten of twelve jurors to convict the defendant of assault with a deadly weapon, burglary, and grand larceny.

Nonunanimous verdicts are not unusual in civil matters, but much controversy remains regarding their place in the criminal process. Those in favor of less than unanimous verdicts argue, as the Court stated in *Apodaca*, that unanimity does not materially contribute to the exercise of commonsense judgment. Some also believe that it would be easier for the prosecutor to obtain a guilty plea if the law required only a substantial majority to convict the defendant. Today, the unanimous verdict remains the rule in the federal system and all but two state jurisdictions. Unanimity is required in six-person jury trials.

The Right to Counsel at Trial

Through a series of leading U.S. Supreme Court decisions (*Powell v. Alabama* in 1932, *Gideon v. Wainwright* in 1963, and *Argersinger v. Hamlin* in 1972), the right of a criminal defendant to have counsel in state trials has become fundamental in the U.S. criminal justice system.[18] Today, state courts must provide counsel at trial to indigent defendants who face the possibility of incarceration.

The historical development of the law regarding right to counsel reflects the gradual process of decision making in the Supreme Court. It also reiterates the relationship between the Bill of Rights, which protects citizens against federal encroachment, and the Fourteenth Amendment, which provides that no state shall deprive any person of life, liberty, or property without due process of law. A difficult constitutional question has been whether the Fourteenth Amendment incorporates the Bill of Rights and makes its provisions binding on individual states.

In 1932's *Powell v. Alabama* (also known as the "Scottsboro boys" case), nine young black men were charged in an Alabama court with raping two young white women. They were tried and convicted without the benefit of counsel. The U.S. Supreme Court concluded that the presence of a defense attorney is so vital to a fair trial that the failure of the Alabama trial court to appoint counsel was a denial of due process of law under the Fourteenth Amendment. In this instance, due process meant the right to counsel for defendants accused of a capital offense.

More than 30 years later, in *Gideon v. Wainwright*, the Supreme Court in a unanimous and historic decision stated that although the Sixth Amendment does not explicitly lay down a rule binding on the states, the right to counsel is so fundamental to a fair trial that states are obligated to abide by it under the Fourteenth Amendment's due process clause. Thus, the Sixth Amendment requirement regarding the right to counsel in the federal court system is also binding on the states.

The *Gideon* decision made it clear that a person charged with a felony in a state court has an absolute constitutional right to counsel. But whereas some states applied the *Gideon* ruling to all criminal trials, others did not provide a defendant with an attorney in misdemeanor cases. Then, in 1972, in the momentous decision of *Argersinger v. Hamlin*, the Supreme Court held that no person can be imprisoned for any offense—whether classified as a petty offense, a misdemeanor, or a felony—unless he or she is offered representation by counsel at trial. The decision extended this right to virtually all defendants in state criminal prosecutions.

What about a case in which incarceration is not on the table but could be an issue later on? In *Alabama v. Shelton* (2002), the Court ruled that a defendant must be represented by counsel if he receives a probation sentence in which a prison or jail term is suspended but can later be imposed if the rules of probation are violated. In other words, if the sentence contains even a threat of future incarceration, the defendant must be afforded the right to counsel at trial.[19] In its decision, the Court stated the following: "We hold that a suspended sentence that may end up in the actual deprivation of a person's liberty may not be imposed unless the defendant was accorded 'the guiding hand of counsel' in the prosecution for the crime charged."[20] *Shelton* may be interpreted as saying any person who is currently in jail on the basis of a probation violation and who did not have legal representation at trial is being held unconstitutionally.

The time line in Figure 12.1 tracks the more than 200 years it has taken to establish what the U.S. Constitution stated in 1791: "In all criminal prosecutions, the accused shall enjoy the right . . . to have the assistance of counsel for his defense."

PERSPECTIVES ON JUSTICE

Due Process

Tremendous indigent defense caseload increases have far outpaced increases in funding. Underfunding is the major problem for virtually all of the public defender offices in America. Yet the emergence and growth of professional criminal defense attorneys for indigent defendants are among the most important contemporary developments in the criminal justice system. Today, criminal defendants are granted the right to an attorney at almost all stages of the legal process. The success of indigent defenders is attributable to the use of the due process model.

FIGURE 12.1

Historical Time Line of Right Counsel

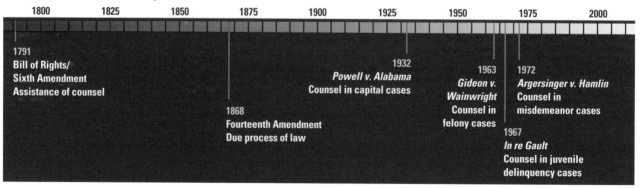

The Right to Self-Representation

Are criminal defendants guaranteed the right to represent themselves—that is, to act as their own lawyers? Prior to the 1975 Supreme Court decision in *Faretta v. California*, defendants in most state courts and in the federal system claimed the right to proceed **pro se**, or for themselves, by reason of federal and state statutes and on state constitutional grounds.[21] This permitted defendants to choose between hiring counsel or conducting their own defense. Whether a constitutional right to represent oneself in a criminal prosecution existed remained an open question until the *Faretta* decision.

pro se
To present one's own defense in a criminal trial: self-representation.

The defendant, Anthony Faretta, was charged with grand theft in Los Angeles County. Before his trial, he requested that he be permitted to represent himself. The judge told Faretta that he believed this would be a mistake but accepted his waiver of counsel. The judge then held a hearing to inquire into Faretta's ability to conduct his own defense and subsequently ruled that Faretta had not made an intelligent and knowing waiver of his right to assistance of counsel. As a result, the judge appointed a public defender to represent Faretta, who was brought to trial, found guilty, and sentenced to prison. He appealed, claiming that he had a constitutional right to self-representation.

Upon review, the U.S. Supreme Court recognized Faretta's pro se right on a constitutional basis, while making it conditional on a showing that the defendant could competently, knowingly, and intelligently waive his right to counsel. The Court's decision was based on the belief that the right of self-representation is supported by the Sixth Amendment, as well as by English and colonial jurisprudence from which the amendment emerged. Thus, in forcing Faretta to accept counsel against his will, the California trial court deprived him of his constitutional right to conduct his own defense.

Today, a defendant in a criminal trial is able to waive the right to the assistance of counsel. Generally, however, the courts have encouraged defendants to accept counsel so that criminal trials may proceed in an orderly and fair manner. When defendants ask to be permitted to represent themselves and are found competent to do so, the court normally approves their requests. However, these defendants are almost always cautioned by the court against self-representation. When pro se defendants' actions are disorderly and disruptive, the court can terminate their right to represent themselves.

No ruling, similar to *Faretta*, has been made that a defendant has a federal constitutional right to prosecute his own criminal appeal. In *Martinez v. Court of Appeals of California* (2000), the U.S. Supreme Court indicated that historical and practical differences between trials and appeals convinced it that due process does not require a recognition of the right to self-representation in criminal appeals.[22]

The Right to a Speedy Trial

The requirement of the right to counsel at trial in virtually all criminal cases often causes delays in the formal processing of defendants through the court system. Counsel usually seeks to safeguard the interests of the accused and in doing so may employ a variety of legal devices (pretrial motions, plea negotiations, trial procedures, and appeals) that require time and extend the decision-making period in a particular case. The involvement of counsel, along with inefficiencies in the court process—such as the frequent granting of continuances, poor scheduling procedures, and the abuse of time by court personnel—has made the problem of delay in criminal cases a serious constitutional issue. According to the American Bar Association's *Standards Relating to Speedy Trial*, "Congestion in the trial courts of this country, particularly in urban centers, is currently one of the major problems of judicial administration."[23]

The Sixth Amendment guarantees a criminal defendant the right to a speedy trial in federal prosecutions. This right was made applicable to the states by the decision in *Klopfer v. North Carolina* (1967).[24] In this case, the defendant, Klopfer, was charged with criminal trespass. His original trial ended in a mistrial, and he sought to determine if and when the government intended to retry him. The prosecutor asked the court for a *nolle prosequi with leave*, a legal device discharging the defendant but allowing the government to prosecute him in the future. The U.S. Supreme Court held that the government's attempt to postpone Klopfer's trial indefinitely without reason denied him the right to a speedy trial guaranteed by the Sixth and Fourteenth amendments.

In *Klopfer*, the Supreme Court emphasized the importance of the speedy trial in the criminal process, stating that this right was "as fundamental as any of the rights secured by the Sixth Amendment."[25] Its primary purposes are the following:

◆   To improve the credibility of the trial by seeking to have witnesses available for testimony as early as possible.

◆   To reduce the anxiety for the defendant in awaiting trial, as well as to avoid pretrial detention.

◆   To avoid extensive pretrial publicity and questionable conduct of public officials that would influence the defendant's right to a fair trial.

◆   To avoid any delay that could affect the defendant's ability to defend himself or herself.

Since the Klopfer case in 1967, the Supreme Court has dealt with the speedy trial guarantee on numerous occasions. One example is the 1992 case of *Doggett v. United States*, in which the Court found that a delay of eight-and-a-half years between indictment and arrest was prejudicial to the defendant and required a dismissal of the charges.[26]

Because of court backlogs, the government has been forced to deal with the problem of how to meet the constitutional requirement of a speedy trial. In 1967 the President's Commission on Law Enforcement and the Administration of Justice suggested that nine months would be a reasonable period of time in which to litigate the typical criminal felony case through appeal. The process from arrest through trial would take four months, and the decision of an appeals court an additional five months.[27] In 1973 the National Advisory Commission on Criminal Justice Standards and Goals recommended that the period from the arrest of the defendant in a felony prosecution to the beginning of the trial should generally not be longer than 60 days and that the period from arrest to trial in a misdemeanor prosecution should be no more than 30 days.[28]

Today, most states and the federal government have statutes fixing the period of time during which an accused must be brought to trial. These requirements ensure that a person's trial cannot be unduly delayed and that the suspect cannot be held in custody indefinitely. The federal Speedy Trial Act of 1974 established the following time limits:

◆   An information or indictment charging a person with a crime must be filed within 30 days of the time of arrest.

◆   The arraignment must be held within 10 days of the time of the information or indictment.

◆   The trial must be held within 60 days of the arraignment.[29]

This means that the accused must be brought to trial in the federal system within 100 days of arrest. Other special provisions of the Speedy Trial Act include the gradual phasing in of time standards, the use of fines against defense counsels for causing delays, and the allocation of funds with which to plan speedy trial programs in the federal judicial districts. The Speedy Trial Act was amended in 1979 to more precisely define what constitutes the guarantee of a speedy trial and to encourage state jurisdictions to adopt similar procedures. Many state speedy trial statutes provide even shorter time limits when a defendant is detained in jail.

Long delays have been a central feature of the U.S. justice system. Many states have found that dramatic results can be achieved in reducing such extreme delays by establishing special courts to deal with, for example, drug-related crimes or homicide. These courts aim to get cases to trial within 60 days of a defendant's initial appearance. The results often include shortened disposition time, reduced case backlogs, increased convictions, and lowered pretrial jail costs. The success of speedy trial courts also enhances the quality of justice for defendants and the public by getting victims and witnesses to attend court proceedings and to give reliable and accurate testimony.

The Right to Press Coverage

Recently, one of the most controversial issues involving the conduct of a trial has been the apparent conflict between the constitutional guarantees of fair trial and freedom of the press. When there is widespread pretrial publicity, can an accused defendant get a fair trial as guaranteed by the Fifth, Sixth, and Fourteenth amendments? Think about the intense media coverage of the O. J. Simpson double-murder trial, the Oklahoma City bombing case, and the Michael Jackson child molestation case. It is now common for both the prosecution and the defense to use the media to reflect their side. Press conferences, leaked news stories, and daily television and radio coverage can all contribute to a media sideshow. Even jury sequestration has not always been successful because many of the jurors have prior knowledge of the case. In the end, the media can play a critical role in both the initial conviction and the subsequent acquittal on retrial of the defendant.

Some critics have suggested that the media should be prohibited from reporting about ongoing criminal trials. However, such an approach would inhibit the role of the press under the First Amendment. Public information about criminal trials, the judicial system, and other areas of government is an indispensable characteristic of a free society. At the same time, trial by the media violates a defendant's right to a fair trial. Still, publicity is essential to preserving confidence in the trial system, even though this principle may occasionally clash with the defendant's right to a fair trial.

There have been a number of specific points of contention between the press who want to report on a case and the judiciary who are concerned that publicity will taint the trial process. The clash can begin even before a trial takes place if a judge attempts to stifle press coverage or prohibit newspapers from printing articles about the case. The U.S. Supreme Court dealt with the fair trial–free press issue in *Nebraska Press Association v. Stuart* (1976).[30] The Court ruled unconstitutional a trial judge's gag order prohibiting the press from reporting about a confession implicating the defendant in the crime. The Court ruled that "prior restraints on speech and publication are the most serious and least tolerable infringement on First Amendment rights."[31]

In *Press-Enterprise Co. v. Superior Court* (1986), the Court said that the press had a right to attend preliminary hearings unless there existed a "substantial probability" that the defendant's right to a fair trial would be prejudiced by the resulting publicity.[32] According to the Court, preliminary hearings have traditionally been open to the public and should remain so. The *Press-Enterprise* case clearly established the First Amendment right of access to criminal trials.[33]

In the most critical free press–fair trial case, the Supreme Court has also interpreted the First Amendment to mean that members of the press (and the public) have a right to attend trials. The most important case on this issue is *Richmond Newspapers Inc. v. Commonwealth of Virginia* (1980).[34] Here, the Supreme Court clearly established that criminal trials must remain public.

In the future, the question of access of the press to nontrial judicial and administrative hearings may become significant. Should the press have the right to attend and report on deportation hearings involving illegal immigrants or

CONCEPT SUMMARY 12.1

Decisions Affirming the Defendant's Constitutional Rights at Trial

Constitutional right	Decision
Confrontation of witnesses	*Coy v. Iowa; Maryland v. Craig*
Jury trial	*Duncan v. Louisiana*
Right to counsel	*Gideon v. Wainwright*
Self-representation	*Faretta v. California*
Speedy trial	*Klopfer v. North Carolina*
Fair trial, free press	*Nebraska Press Association v. Stuart*
Public trial	*Richmond Newspapers Inc. v. Commonwealth of Virginia*

quasi-military hearings involving suspected terrorists? Procedures at these new and different types of hearings must still be mapped out.[35]

Concept Summary 12.1 summarizes the decisions guaranteeing the defendant's constitutional rights at trial.

TELEVISING CRIMINAL TRIALS Today, many state courts permit televised coverage of trials, often at the judge's discretion; the use of television cameras, video recorders, and still photography is banned in the federal court system.[36] Televising criminal proceedings could have significant advantages. Judges would be better prepared, the public would be informed about important legal issues, and the proceedings would serve an educational function, offsetting the simplistic views offered by television programs and feature films. On the other hand, televising trials can have some drawbacks. Broadcasting can feed the media frenzy that has turned some high-profile cases into three-ring circuses. Lawyers might be encouraged to show off for the camera rather than prepare a sound legal defense. And then again, so may witnesses and possibly the judge and defendant as well. Security may become an issue. Witnesses are already reluctant to testify in high-profile cases against organized crime figures and drug cartels. How would they react if forced to testify while their face is broadcast around the world? The same would apply to jurors fearful of retaliation. Under these circumstances, trial judges may be inclined to ban cameras from the very cases that the public is most interested in viewing.[37]

Regardless of the kind of crime committed, a defendant is always permitted to have family, close associates, and legal counsel at his or her trial. Still, the Supreme Court has held, in *Chandler v. Florida* (1981), that subject to certain safeguards, a state may allow electronic media coverage by television stations and still photography of public criminal proceedings over the objection of the defendant in a criminal trial.[38] The Supreme Court did not maintain in *Chandler* that the media had a constitutional right to televise trials; it left it up to state courts to decide whether they wanted trials televised in their jurisdictions.

The controversy surrounding the televising of trials has prompted bar and media groups to develop standards in an attempt to find an acceptable middle ground between the First and Sixth Amendment rights concerning public trials. The defendant has a constitutional right to a public trial, and the media must be able to exercise their First Amendment rights. Above all, the court must seek to protect the rights of the accused to a fair trial by an unbiased jury.

The Images of Justice feature discusses further the topic of televised trials.

ThomsonNOW Improve your grade on the exam with Personalized Study! For reinforcement resources and a mastery check of legal rights during trials, go to www. thomsonedu.com/thomsonnow.

◆ THE TRIAL PROCESS

The trial of a criminal case is a formal process conducted in a specific and orderly fashion in accordance with rules of criminal law, procedure, and evidence. Unlike what transpires in popular television programs involving lawyers—where witnesses are often asked leading and prejudicial questions and where judges go far beyond their supervisory role—the modern criminal trial is a complicated and often time-consuming technical affair. It is a structured adversarial proceeding in which both the prosecution and defense follow specific procedures and argue the merits of their cases before the judge and jury.

Each side seeks to present its own case in the most favorable light. When possible, the prosecutor and the defense attorney object to evidence that they consider damaging to their position. The prosecutor uses direct testimony, physical evidence, and a confession, if available, to convince the jury that the accused is guilty beyond a reasonable doubt. The defense attorney rebuts the government's case with his or her own evidence, makes certain that the rights of the criminal defendant under the federal and state constitutions are considered during all phases of the trial, and determines whether an appeal is appropriate if the client is found guilty. The defense attorney uses his or her skill at cross-examination to discredit government witnesses: Perhaps they have changed their statements from the time they gave them to the police, perhaps their memory is faulty, perhaps their background is unsavory, and so on. From the beginning of the process to its completion, the judge promotes an orderly and fair administration of the criminal trial.

Although each jurisdiction in the United States has its own trial procedures, all jurisdictions conduct criminal trials in a generally similar fashion. The basic steps of the criminal trial, which proceed in an established order, are described in this section and outlined in Figure 12.2 on page 396.

Jury Selection

Jurors are selected randomly in both civil and criminal cases from tax assessment, driver's license, or voter registration lists within each court's jurisdiction. Advocates of more diverse jury pools contend that such lists often do not accurately reflect a state's ethnic composition. As a result, some jurisdictions are requiring that their pool of prospective jurors include people drawn from welfare and unemployment rolls.

Few states impose qualifications on those called for jury service, but many states do mandate a residency requirement.[39] Most jurisdictions also prohibit convicted felons from serving on juries, as well as others exempted by statute, such as public officials, medical doctors, and attorneys. The initial list of persons chosen—called **venire** or *jury array*—provides the state with a group of capable citizens able to serve on a jury. Many states, by rule of law, review the venire to eliminate unqualified persons and to exempt those who by reason of their profession are not allowed to be jurors. The jury selection process begins with those remaining on the list.

The court clerk, who handles the administrative affairs and documents related to the trial, randomly selects enough names (sometimes from a box) to fill the required number of places on the jury. In most cases, the jury in a criminal trial consists of twelve persons, with two alternate jurors standing by to serve should one of the regular jurors be unable to complete the trial. There is little uniformity in the amount of time served by jurors, with the term ranging from one day to months, depending on the nature of the trial.

Once the prospective jurors are chosen, they undergo a process known as **voir dire** (French for "to tell the truth"), in which they are questioned by both the prosecution and the defense to determine their appropriateness to sit on the jury. They are examined under oath by the government, the defense, and sometimes the judge about their background, occupation, residence, and possible

venire
The group called for jury duty from which jury panels are selected.

voir dire
The process in which a potential jury panel is questioned by the prosecution and the defense to select jurors who are unbiased and objective.

Should Criminal Trials Be Televised?

On January 18, 2002, a federal judge refused to allow TV cameras into the trial of Zacarias Moussaoui, who was on trial for being part of the 9/11 conspiracy. Judge Leonie N. Brinkema, in a 13-page ruling, denied the request of the Court TV cable channel to broadcast the trial of Moussaoui, who was charged with six terrorism conspiracy counts. In her ruling, Brinkema wrote that she had no authority to reject a federal court ban on cameras in courtrooms. Even if she did, she would not, she wrote, because "given the issues raised in this indictment, any societal benefits from photographing and broadcasting these proceedings are heavily outweighed by the significant dangers worldwide broadcasting of this trial would pose to the orderly and secure administration of justice." Her ruling embraced concerns raised by prosecutors that broadcasting the trial would intimidate witnesses, endanger court officers, and provide Moussaoui with a platform to vent his political beliefs. Moussaoui's lawyers favored televising the trial, with restrictions. They argued that the broadcasts would give their client an added layer of protection in getting a fair trial on charges that could result in the death penalty. The decision outraged some commentators, who felt that the American people were cheated by the decision. Writing in *Newsweek*, Anna Quindlen said that

> [T]he events of September 11 have left a nation of victims, and the number who bear witness should not be determined by the square footage of a courtroom. Let the world see how well the American justice system works. The point of public trials in the first place was to let the people in. In the 21st century, letting the people in means letting the cameras in.

The Supreme Court has upheld the public's right of access to the judicial system but has stopped short of saying the right to a public trial means the right to a televised trial. As Justice David H. Souter testified in 1996 before a Senate subcommittee, "The day you see cameras come into our courtroom, it's going to

roll over my dead body." Until recently, the Justices did not even allow live audio broadcasting of arguments, although they did permit archival audiotaping. In the landmark case of *Bush v. Gore*—the case that awarded George W. Bush the presidency after the 2000 election—the Justices finally relented and permitted the real-time audio transmission of the final arguments. Sociologist Hedieh Nasheri points out that *Bush v. Gore* was a good first step, but many Americans wondered why the Justices were prepared to be heard but not seen. Today's television cameras require no special lighting, she argues in her book *Crime and Justice in the Age of Court TV*, and can be placed discreetly behind walls so as not to interfere with courtroom proceedings. *Bush v. Gore* was a wonderful civics lesson, but it was somewhat incomplete because the television cameras were excluded. One option, she notes, is the Sunshine in the Courtroom Act, which was pending in the 108th Congress (2003–2005). This bill would give judges in federal trial and appeals courts discretion to permit cameras in their courtrooms, but it would require them to afford witnesses the option of having their faces and voices obscured.

Although federal court rules specifically prohibit the televising of any federal criminal trial, state courts are more flexible. All states now allow some judicial proceedings to be broadcast, and 38 states permit the showing of state criminal trials.

What are the pros and cons of televising criminal trials? Lawyers who represent the news media often point out valid arguments for using cameras in the courtroom:

◆ Televised trials would encourage participants to do a better job.

◆ In a democratic society, the public should have access to all trials, even those of a scandalous nature.

◆ TV coverage can contribute to educating the public about the justice system.

---

challenge for cause
Dismissal of a prospective juror by either the prosecution or the defense because he or she is biased, he or she has prior knowledge about a case, or for other reasons that demonstrate the individual's inability to render a fair and impartial judgment.

knowledge of or interest in the case. Detailed questionnaires are also used for this purpose. A juror who acknowledges any bias for or prejudice against the defendant (if the defendant is a friend or relative, for example, or if the juror has already formed an opinion about the case) is **challenged for cause** and replaced with another. Thus, any prospective juror who declares that he or she cannot be impartial and render a verdict solely on the evidence to be presented at the trial may be removed by either the prosecution or the defense. Because no limit is normally placed on the number of challenges for cause, it often takes considerable time to select a jury for controversial and highly publicized criminal cases.

Conversely, some defense lawyers and judges believe that televised trials should be restricted because they are only a form of entertainment and suppress the search for truth. Others question whether the public interest outweighs the defendant's ability to obtain a fair trial. In any case, resistance to the idea remains firm. The U.S. Judicial Conference, the policy-making body for the federal courts, says that cameras in courtrooms raise privacy concerns for witnesses in sensitive cases and put traditionally low-profile, but powerful, federal judges at risk.

One advocate of cameras in the courtroom is lawyer Ronald Goldfarb, who in his book *TV or Not TV* argues that the proper line between entertainment and education, between exploitation and information, between the negative consequences of televised and nontelevised trials is not clear, nor can it be measured with scientific objectivity. So even though visibility on TV may be a yet-unmeasured risk to trial fairness, it is one worth taking. Televising trials keeps the legal system in the "sunlight" and ensures that judges, lawyers, and even witnesses act honestly. Allowing cameras in the courtroom helps the public's perception of the trial as a fair process. The public is more suspicious of the outcome if the trial is held behind closed doors. Goldfarb dismisses critics by stating that "[m]uch of the current criticism of televised trials amounts to killing the messenger while ignoring the message" (p. 164). The media are not at fault for showing that trials are sometimes unfair and boring, or that lawyers may be bullies or incompetent; that is the nature of the trial process and not the media coverage. Instead, he argues, live and inconspicuous television might improve upon some shortcomings of ordinary press coverage of the courts: "One can bribe a reporter, but not a camera" (p. 172).

Goldfarb proposes a regulated system of total media coverage. He foresees cameras in every courtroom, with the broadcast of every trial available for viewing on a publicly run TV station or through the Internet.

However, he would also allow for the right to oppose broadcast by a number of people involved in the trial.

Critical Thinking

Three major concerns arise in TV criminal trials: (1) jurors and potential jurors are exposed to media coverage that may cause prejudgment; (2) in-court media coverage, especially cameras and TV, can increase community and political pressure on participants and even cause grandstanding by participants; and (3) media coverage can erode the dignity and decorum of the courtroom. In a democratic society, shouldn't the public have access to all trials through the TV medium, regardless of these concerns?

InfoTrac College Edition Research

Televising courtroom dramas in criminal trials has resulted in a boom of lawyer-centered talk shows as well as Court TV. Does the public debate the legal, political, and social issues through these trials? Use InfoTrac College Edition to do research on high-profile criminal trials such as the O. J. Simpson case. Focus on such issues as a defendant's right to a public trial and the rights of the press under the First Amendment.

Sources: Hedieh Nasheri, *Crime and Justice in the Age of Court TV* (New York: LFB Scholarly Publishing, 2002); Ronald Goldfarb, *TV or Not TV: Television, Justice, and the Courts* (New York: New York University Press, 1998); Anna Quindlen, "Lights, Camera, Justice for All," *Newsweek*, January 21, 2002, p. 64; "Judge Won't Allow Televising Terror Trial," *Quill* 90 (March 2002): 8.

PEREMPTORY CHALLENGES In addition to challenges for cause, both the prosecution and the defense are allowed peremptory challenges, which enable the attorneys to excuse jurors for no particular reason or for undisclosed reasons. For example, a prosecutor might not want a bartender as a juror in a drunk-driving case, believing that a person with that occupation would be sympathetic to the accused. Or the defense might excuse a prospective male juror because the attorney prefers to have a predominantly female jury. The number of peremptory challenges permitted is limited by state statute and often varies by case and jurisdiction.

The **peremptory challenge** has been criticized by legal experts who question the fairness and propriety with which it has been used.[40] In 1986, *Batson v.*

peremptory challenge
Dismissal of a prospective juror by either the prosecution or the defense for unexplained, discretionary reasons.

FIGURE 12.2
The Steps in a Jury Trial

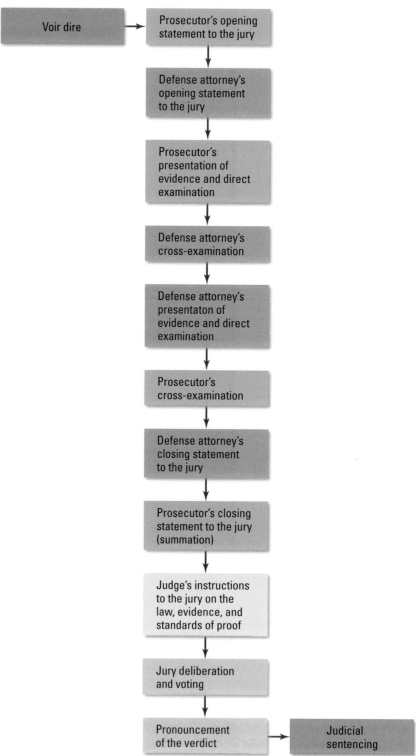

Source: Marvin Zalman and Larry Siegel, *Criminal Procedure: Constitution and Society* (St. Paul, Minn: West Publishing, 1991), P. 655.

CONCEPT SUMMARY 12.2
U.S. Supreme Court Decisions Regarding the Peremptory Challenge

Court case	Decision
Batson v. Kentucky (1986)	The Supreme Court ruled that the Fourteenth Amendment barred prosecutors from using peremptory challenges to remove jurors because of their race.
Powers v. Ohio (1991)	The Supreme Court concluded that a defendant has the standing to object to race-based exclusion of jurors by the use of peremptory challenges on the grounds of equal protection, even if the defendant is not of the same race as the challenged jurors.
Edmonson v. Leesville Concrete Co. (1991)	The Court held that the *Batson* ruling applies to attorneys in civil lawsuits. A private party in a civil action may not use peremptory challenges to exclude jurors on the basis of race.
Georgia v. McCollum (1992)	On the basis of *Batson*, the Court prohibited the exercise of race-based peremptory challenges by defense attorneys in criminal cases.
J. E. B. v. Alabama (1994)	The Supreme Court held that the equal protection clause of the Fourteenth Amendment bars discrimination in jury selection on the basis of sex. Discrimination in jury selection, whether based on race or gender, causes harm to the litigants, the community, and the individual jurors who are wrongfully excluded from participation in the judicial process.

Kentucky held that the use of peremptory challenges by prosecutors in criminal cases, if based on race, violated the Constitution. Before Batson's criminal trial began, the prosecutor used his peremptory challenges to remove four blacks from the venire. Consequently, an all-white jury was selected. The U.S. Supreme Court held that although defendants have no right to a jury composed of members in whole or in part of their own race, the Fourteenth Amendment's equal protection clause guarantees that the state will not exclude jury members on account of race or under the false assumption that members of the defendant's own race cannot render a fair verdict. Such a practice would discriminate against the jury members and undermine public confidence in the jury system.

Since the *Batson* decision, the issue of racial discrimination in the use of peremptory challenges has been raised by defendants in numerous cases. In *Powers v. Ohio* (1991), the Court ruled that the equal protection clause prohibits a prosecutor from using the peremptory challenge to exclude qualified and unbiased persons from a jury solely by reason of race even when the defendant is a member of a *different* racial group. In *Georgia v. McCollum*, the Supreme Court found that the defense, as well as the prosecution, may not seek to exclude potential jurors strictly on the basis of race. Race-based peremptory challenges to potential jurors in civil lawsuits have also been declared unconstitutional.[41]

In 1994 the Supreme Court, in *J. E. B. v. Alabama*, ruled that prosecutors and defense attorneys may not use peremptory challenges to strike men or women from juries solely on the basis of gender. Such discrimination also violates the equal protection clause of the Fourteenth Amendment, the Court said.[42] The decisions on peremptory challenges can be found in Concept Summary 12.2. Some state courts have ruled that peremptory challenges cannot be based on religion. Someday, states may rule that they cannot be based on age or disability.[43]

IMPARTIAL JURIES The Sixth Amendment provides for the right to a speedy trial by an impartial jury, but the concept of an impartial jury has always been controversial. Research indicates that jury members often have little in common

Circuit Judge Ric Howard talks to attorneys and baliffs before releasing members of the jury pool for John Evander Couey's trial at the Lake County Courthouse in Tavares, Florida, on July 13, 2006. Convicted sex offender Couey was accused of kidnapping, raping, and burying alive 9-year-old Jessica Lunsford. The judge halted the trial because of the difficulty in finding jurors who had not been exposed to media reports or other discussions of the case. The Sixth Amendment ensures the right to a trial by an impartial jury of one's peers, and it is a judge's responsibility to ensure that juries are fair and impartial.

with their criminal peers. Moreover, remaining impartial may be a struggle. Studies of jury deliberations indicate that the dynamics of decision making often involve pressure to get the case over with and convince recalcitrant jurors to join the majority. Nevertheless, jurors also appear to take cases seriously and to reach decisions not too different from those made by legal professionals.[44] Judges, for instance, often agree with jury decisions. However, jurors often have problems understanding judicial instructions and legal rule making in criminal trials, and this may cause confusion in determining the appropriate verdict.

The Supreme Court has sought to ensure compliance with the constitutional mandate of impartiality by eliminating racial discrimination in jury selection. For instance, in *Ham v. South Carolina* (1973), the Court held that the defense counsel of a black civil rights leader was entitled to question each juror on the issue of racial prejudice.[45] In *Taylor v. Louisiana* (1975), the Court overturned the conviction of a man by an all-male jury because a Louisiana statute allowed women but not men to exempt themselves from jury duty.[46]

The issue of racial composition of the jury is particularly acute in cases involving the death penalty. In *Turner v. Murray* (1986), the Court ruled that a defendant accused of an interracial crime in which the death penalty is an option can insist that prospective jurors be informed of the victim's race and be questioned on the issue of their bias. A trial judge who refuses this line of questioning during voir dire risks having the death penalty vacated, but not having the conviction reversed.[47] These and other, similar decisions have had the effect of providing safeguards against jury bias.

Jury selection can be even more difficult in capital punishment cases, when jurors are asked about their views on the death penalty. In *Lockhart v. McCree* (1986), the Supreme Court decided that jurors who strongly oppose capital punishment may be disqualified from determining a defendant's guilt or innocence in capital cases.[48] The *Lockhart* decision raises certain questions, however. Juries are not supposed to represent only one position or another. An impartial jury of one's peers is rooted in the idea that the defendant should be judged by a cross-section of members of the local community. Their views should not be disproportionate on any one issue. Consequently, a ruling such as *Lockhart* could theoretically result in higher conviction rates in murder cases.

The Supreme Court has not yet fully answered all of the important questions regarding impartiality in the role and qualifications of jurors in criminal cases.

Another safeguard against bias, used in highly publicized and celebrated cases, is to sequester jury members, once selected, for the duration of the trial, isolating them from contact with the outside world. Sequestration is discretionary with the trial judge, and most courts believe that "locking a jury up" is needed only in sensational cases.

Opening Statements

Once the jury has been selected and has heard the criminal complaint read by the court clerk, the prosecutor and the defense attorney may each make an opening statement to the jury. The purpose of the prosecutor's statement is to introduce the judge and jury to the particular criminal charges, to outline the facts, and to describe how the government will prove the defendant guilty beyond a reasonable doubt. The defense attorney reviews the case and indicates how the defense intends to show that the accused is not guilty of the charge. The defense attorney's opening statement ordinarily follows that of the prosecution.

The opening statement gives the jury a concise overview of the evidence that is to follow. In the opening statement, neither attorney is allowed to make prejudicial remarks or inflammatory statements or to mention irrelevant facts. However, both are free to identify what they will eventually prove by way of evidence—witnesses, physical evidence, and expert testimony. The actual content of the statement is left to the discretion of the trial judge. As a general rule, the opening statements used in jury trials are important because they provide the finders of fact (the jury) with an initial summary of the case. Opening statements are less effective and are infrequently used in bench trials, however, where juries are not employed. Most lower court judges have handled hundreds of similar cases and do not need the benefit of an opening statement.

Presentation of the Prosecutor's Evidence

Following the opening statements, the government begins its case by presenting evidence to the court through its witnesses. Those called as witnesses, such as police officers, victims, or experts, provide testimony via direct examination. During **direct examination**, the prosecutor questions the witness to reveal the facts believed pertinent to the government's case. Testimony involves what the witness saw, heard, or touched and does not include opinions. However, a witness's opinion can be given in certain situations, such as when describing the motion of a vehicle or indicating whether a defendant appeared to act intoxicated or insane. Witnesses may also qualify to give opinions because they are experts on a particular subject relevant to the case; for example, a psychiatrist may testify about a defendant's mental capacity at the time of the crime.

direct examination
The initial questioning of one's own (prosecution or defense) witness during a trial.

After the prosecutor finishes questioning a witness, the defense may cross-examine the same witness by asking questions that seek to clarify the defendant's role in the crime. The right to cross-examine witnesses is an essential part of a trial, and except in extremely unusual circumstances (such as a person's being hospitalized), witness statements will not be considered unless they are made in court and open for question. In the case of *Lee v. Illinois* (1986), the U.S. Supreme Court ruled that a confession made to police by a codefendant in a criminal trial cannot be used in court unless the person making the confession is available for cross-examination.[49] If desired, the prosecutor may seek a second direct examination after the defense attorney has completed **cross-examination**. This allows the prosecutor to ask additional questions about information brought out during cross-examination. Finally, the defense attorney may question or cross-examine the witness once again. All witnesses for the trial are sworn in and questioned in the same basic manner.

cross-examination
The questioning of a prosecution witness by the defense, or of a defense witness by the prosecution.

CONCEPT SUMMARY 12.3

Types of Trial Evidence

♦ *Testimonial evidence.* Given by police officers, citizens, and experts, this is the most basic form of evidence. Witness must state, under oath, what they heard, saw, or experienced.

♦ *Real evidence.* Consists of the exhibits that can be taken into the jury room for review by the jury. A revolver that may have been in the defendant's control at the time of a murder, tools in the possession of a suspect charged with a burglary, and a bottle allegedly holding narcotics are all examples of real, or physical, evidence. Photographs, maps, diagrams, and crime scene displays are further types of real evidence.

♦ *Documentary evidence.* Includes writings, government reports, public records, business or hospital records, fingerprint identification, and DNA profiling.

♦ *Circumstantial (indirect) evidence.* Such evidence is often inferred or indirectly used to prove a fact in question. For example, in a murder case, evidence that carpet fibers found on the body match the carpet in the defendant's home may be used at trial to link the two, even though they do not provide direct evidence that the suspect actually killed the victim.

Types of Evidence at a Criminal Trial

real evidence
Any object, such as a weapon or a photograph, produced for inspection at a trial: physical evidence.

In addition to testimonial evidence given by police officers, citizens, and experts, the court acts on real (nonverbal) evidence.[50] **Real evidence** may include exhibits such as a revolver that may have been in the defendant's control at the time of a murder, tools found in the possession of a suspect charged with a burglary, a bottle allegedly holding narcotics, or blood samples from a murder victim. The criminal court judge will also review documentary evidence, such as writings, government reports, public records, and business or hospital records.

In general, the primary test for the admissibility of evidence in either a criminal or civil proceeding is its relevance. The court must ask itself whether the gun, shirt, or photograph, for instance, has relevant evidentiary value in determining the issues of the case. Ordinarily, evidence that establishes an element of the crime is acceptable to the court. For example, in a prosecution for possession of drugs, evidence that shows the defendant to be a known drug user might be relevant.

circumstantial (indirect) evidence
Indirect evidence from which a fact may be inferred.

Circumstantial (indirect) evidence is also often used in trial proceedings. Such evidence is often inferred or used indirectly to prove a fact in question. On the issue of malice in a criminal murder trial, for instance, circumstantial evidence could be used to prove the defendant's state of mind. Circumstantial evidence bearing on or establishing the facts in a crime is ordinarily admissible, but evidence that is prejudicial, remote, or unrelated to the crime should be excluded by the court. In general, the admissibility of such evidence remains governed by constitutional law, such as the right to be free from unreasonable search and seizure, the privilege against self-incrimination, and the right to counsel.

In recent years, a considerable amount of real evidence has come from video recordings. Courtroom use of videotape originated with undercover surveillance operations. Today, citizens are being filmed regularly. Security cameras are mounted everywhere. The widespread availability of cameras makes evidentiary videotape widely available and an important part of the technology of criminal evidence collection.[51]

Concept Summary 12.3 illustrates the different types of evidence presented at trial.

Motion for a Directed Verdict

Once the prosecution has provided all the government's evidence against a defendant, it will inform the court that it rests the people's case. The defense attorney at this point may enter a motion for a **directed verdict**. This is a procedural device by which the defense attorney asks the judge to order the jury to return a verdict of not guilty. In essence, the defense attorney argues that the prosecutor's case against the defendant is insufficient to prove the defendant guilty beyond a reasonable doubt. The judge must rule on the motion and will either sustain it or overrule it, depending on whether he or she believes that the prosecution has proved all the elements of the alleged crime. If the motion is sustained, the trial is terminated. If it is rejected, the case continues with the defense portion of the trial.

The defense usually makes a motion for a directed verdict so that a finding of guilt can later be appealed to a higher court. If the judge refuses to grant the motion, this decision can be the focus of an appeal charging that the judge did not use proper procedural care in making his or her decision. In some cases, the judge may reserve decision on the motion, submit the case to the jury, and consider a decision on the motion before the jury verdict.

Presentation of Evidence by the Defense Counsel

The defense attorney has the option of presenting many, some, or no witnesses on behalf of the defendant. In addition, the defense attorney must decide if the client should take the stand and testify in his or her own behalf. In a criminal trial, the defendant is protected by the Fifth Amendment right against self-incrimination, which means that a person cannot be forced by the state to testify against himself or herself in a criminal trial. However, defendants who choose to tell their side of the story can be subject to cross-examination by the prosecutor.

After the defense concludes its case, the government may then present **rebuttal evidence**. This normally involves bringing evidence forward that was not used when the prosecution initially presented its case. The defense may examine the rebuttal witnesses and introduce new witnesses in a process called **surrebuttal**. After all the evidence has been presented to the court, the defense attorney may again submit a motion for a directed verdict. If the motion is denied, both the prosecution and the defense prepare to make closing arguments, and the case on the evidence is ready for consideration by the jury.

Closing Arguments

The attorneys use closing arguments to review the facts and evidence of the case in a manner favorable to each of their positions. At this stage of the trial, both the prosecution and the defense are permitted to draw reasonable inferences and to show how the facts prove or refute the defendant's guilt. Both attorneys have a relatively free hand in arguing about the facts, issues, and evidence, including the applicable law. They cannot comment on matters not in evidence, however, or on the defendant's failure to testify in a criminal case. Normally, the defense attorney makes a closing statement first, followed by the prosecutor. Either party can elect to forgo the right to make a final summation to the jury. Because the prosecution gives the opening statement first and makes the closing argument last, some experts believe that the government has a decided advantage over the defense.

Instructions to the Jury

In a criminal trial, the judge will instruct, or charge, the jury members on the principles of law that ought to guide and control their decision on the defendant's innocence or guilt. Included in the charge

directed verdict
A judge's order directing a jury to acquit a defendant because the state has not proven the elements of the crime or otherwise has not established guilt according to law.

rebuttal evidence
Evidence presented by the prosecution at the conclusion of the defense case, with the permission of the court, to rebut or disprove defense evidence.

surrebuttal evidence
Evidence presented by the defense to refute the prosecution's rebuttal evidence.

After all evidence is presented, both the prosecution and defense have opportunities during closing arguments to summarize their cases and to show the jury that either the defendant was guilty as charged, or that the state's evidence was insufficient to convict. Los Angeles Deputy District Attorney Todd Hicks gives his closing argument on February 9, 2006, during the child molestation trial of retired Catholic priest Michael Wempe, after three weeks of testimony by eight past molestation victims. Wempe was later sentenced to three years in state prison.

©AP images/Nick Ut

Jury Nullification

In 1735, John Peter Zenger, editor of the *New York Weekly Journal*, was charged with printing libelous statements about the governor of the Colony of New York, William Cosby. Despite the fact that Zenger clearly printed the alleged libels and the trial judge gave the jury clear instructions for a finding of guilt, the jury found Zenger not guilty on all charges. The Zenger case is one of the most famous examples of jury nullification in the nation's history.

Jury nullification refers to a jury's refusal to render a verdict according to the law and fact regardless of the evidence presented. Instead, the jury can base its verdict on other grounds that need not be stated publicly. Nullification is possible because jurors cannot be punished for their decision, no matter how outlandish, and the defendant cannot be tried twice for the same crime. If they could, then the jury's quixotic decision could be nullified by a second trial.

In another famous case that possibly involved jury nullification, the O. J. Simpson murder trial, jurors were told by the defense attorneys that police carelessness and misconduct, motivated by racism, introduced an element of reasonable doubt against the prosecution's case. Judge Lance Ito allowed the defense great leeway to make that argument, and the jury seemed to buy it. However, it cannot be known for sure whether the jury considered O. J. guilty and then nullified their verdict or truly believed him innocent of the act as he claimed.

Juries can nullify the facts and evidence for a number of reasons:

◆ Classic jury nullification occurs when jury members believe that the law is unjust, such as when a jury refuses to convict defendants for a drug offense because members believe that drugs should be legalized.

◆ Another form of classic nullification is when the jury believes the law is just but the punishment is excessive. For example, a person being tried for murder is acquitted because the only punishment is death or life in prison, and jury members consider these options too harsh.

◆ "As applied" jury nullification refers to the situations where the jury does not object to the law as such, but acquits because it believes that the law is being unjustly applied—for instance, when a jury refuses to convict antiwar protestors of trespassing on government property.

◆ "Symbolic" nullification occurs when the jury does not object to the law or its application, but acquits to send a political message. The jury may have acquitted O. J. Simpson to send the message that the jury thought that the police officers who handled the case were racist cops and not to be believed.

Jury nullification is a controversial issue. Although supporters argue that it can be used only to acquit

is information about the elements of the alleged offense, the type of evidence needed to prove each element, and the burden of proof required for a guilty verdict. Although the judge commonly provides the instruction, he or she may ask the prosecutor and the defense attorney to submit instructions for consideration; the judge then uses discretion in determining whether to use any of their instructions. The instructions that cover the law applicable to the case are particularly important because they may serve as the basis for a subsequent appeal.

A good example of an improper jury instruction that voided a conviction occurred in *Sullivan v. Louisiana* (1993).[52] In this murder case, the defendant's lawyer argued that there was reasonable doubt concerning the identity of the killer. The trial judge in his instructions said that reasonable doubt must have a "substantial" basis that would give rise to a "grave uncertainty" that the defendant was the killer. The Supreme Court declared that this instruction violated the Fifth Amendment due process clause because using the word *substantial* downplayed the duty of the state to prove all the elements of a crime beyond a reasonable doubt. Thus, even the use of one word can create further confusion in interpreting the reasonable doubt standard.

The Verdict

Once the charge is given to the jury members, they retire to deliberate on a verdict. The verdict in a criminal case is usually required to be unanimous. A review

and not to convict because a judge can set aside a conviction that is clearly irresponsible, many magistrates are reluctant to tamper with jury decisions. Thus, safeguards are not absolute, and a jury that dislikes a defendant has the ability to convict an innocent defendant through nullification. Another argument for nullification is that it is an important safeguard against government oppression. The jury should not allow a person to be convicted unless his peers, and not the government, agree with the verdict. This approach suggests that the function of the jury is to serve as a safety valve against unjust application of the law. Jury nullification, the argument goes, can be used to protect the rights of disempowered groups who are at the mercy of governmental control.

Nullification has its supporters, but others view it as an abuse of power. What happens if a racist jury finds a minority-group member guilty despite overwhelming evidence of her innocence? Although a judge has the power to set aside a jury verdict, many are loathe to do so out of respect for the jury process. Conversely, would it not be an abuse of power if a jury, motivated by racial bias, found a person accused of a hate crime not guilty despite overwhelming evidence of his guilt?

Critical Thinking

1. You are on a jury considering the guilt of a terrorism suspect. At trial, the prosecution presents conclusive evidence linking him to many heinous prior acts. There is no question he is a terrorist. However, the evidence linking him to the current crime, a bombing that took 20 lives, is shaky. Despite your reasonable doubt, would you convict him anyway?

2. You are a juror in a high-profile case. The prosecution presents ironclad evidence of guilt in the trial of an African American accused of rape. During the trial you see a news story showing evidence that the lead detective had been a member of a skinhead group when he was a teenager. He is now married, has three kids, and has been a detective for eight years. Would you find the defendant guilty?

InfoTrac College Edition Research

To learn more about the history of jury nullification, read Stanton D. Krauss, "An Inquiry into the Right of Criminal Juries to Determine the Law in Colonial America," *Journal of Criminal Law and Criminology* 89 (1998): 111–215.

Sources: Arie Rubenstein, "Verdicts of Conscience: Nullification and the Modern Jury Trial," *Columbia Law Review* 106 (2006): 959–93; David Pepper, "Nullifying History: Modern-Day Misuse of the Right to Decide the Law," *Case Western Reserve Law Review* 50 (2000): 599–643.

of the case by the jury may take hours or even days. The jurors are always sequestered during their deliberations, and in certain lengthy and highly publicized cases, they are kept overnight in a hotel until the verdict is reached. In less sensational cases, the jurors may be allowed to go home, but they are cautioned not to discuss the case with anyone.

The rules of procedure for most jurisdictions permit only two possible verdicts in a criminal trial: *guilty* and *not guilty*. In a criminal trial, the government has the responsibility to convince the judge or jury that the defendant is guilty. If the government fails, the defendant is then found "not guilty." Contrary to what is often observed on television or in the movies, where a person accused of a crime is found "innocent," criminal courts do not make such a determination. Remember that a person can be judged to have committed the crime (i.e., the person is not innocent) but found not guilty because he acted in self-defense, was entrapped, or had a mental defect. Sometimes a jury may consider a person guilty but render a verdict of not guilty. How can that be? In this instance, jurors are practicing **jury nullification**, a topic discussed in the Analyzing Criminal Justice Issues feature.

If a verdict cannot be reached, the trial may result in a hung jury. If the prosecution still wants a conviction, it must bring the defendant to trial again.

If found not guilty, the defendant is released from the criminal process. If the defendant is found guilty, the judge normally orders a presentence investigation by the probation department before imposing a sentence. Prior to sentencing,

jury nullification
A jury's refusal to render a verdict according to the law and fact regardless of the evidence presented.

Paralegal

Duties and Characteristics of the Job

Paralegals assist lawyers by conducting much of the preparation for trials. A paralegal's exact duties will vary according to the needs of the office for which she works. However, a paralegal's work will typically include assisting with or carrying out client interviews, drafting legal documents, reviewing pertinent case law, summarizing legal proceedings, and doing some standard office work. Although a paralegal's work may at first be relatively simple, after some experience paralegals are usually given more responsibilities and more complex tasks. Paralegals working outside the law office setting will have similar duties, but also additional ones that reflect the specialty of their employer.

Paralegals do much of the same work as a lawyer, but there are definite limits to what they can do. For example, paralegals cannot advise on legal issues. Although most paralegals have general legal knowledge, it is becoming more common, especially for long-term or career paralegals, to choose a field of specialization.

A clear majority of paralegals will work for law firms, but some will find positions with the government, with corporations, or in community service. A paralegal working for government, a corporation, or in community service can expect a normal 40-hour workweek, but a paralegal working in a law firm will be expected to put in many hours of overtime during busy periods. Increasingly, paralegals are choosing the option of self-employment and working freelance.

Job Outlook

The paralegal profession is expected to grow rapidly in the near future for several reasons, most prominently the fact that some organizations need legal expertise but do not want the extra expense of hiring a lawyer.

Salary

The mean annual salary for paralegals is $43,510. However, the majority of paralegals earn between $32,470 and $52,470 a year. Paralegals who work for private firms will often receive bonuses for good work.

Opportunities

The number of people entering the profession has been steadily increasing, so those entering the paralegal field should expect competition for desirable jobs.

---

the defense attorney will probably submit a motion for a new trial, alleging that legal errors occurred in the trial proceedings. The judge may deny the motion and impose a sentence immediately, a practice common in misdemeanor offenses. In felony cases, however, the judge sets a date for sentencing, and the defendant is either released on bail or held in custody until that time.

The Sentence

Imposing the criminal sentence is normally the responsibility of the trial judge. In some jurisdictions, the jury may determine the sentence or make recommendations for leniency for certain offenses. Often, the sentencing decision is based on information and recommendations given to the court by the probation department after a presentence investigation of the defendant. The sentence itself is determined by the statutory requirements for the particular crime, as established by the legislature. In addition, the judge ordinarily has a great deal of discretion in sentencing. The different criminal sanctions available include fines, probation, imprisonment, and commitment to a state hospital, as well as combinations of these.

The Appeal

Defendants have three possible avenues of appeal: the direct appeal, federal court review, and postconviction remedy.[53] Both the direct appeal and federal court review provide the convicted person with the opportunity to appeal to a

A great deal of research is being conducted on criminal sanctions. One of the best sources of information is the Sentencing Project. You can reach its website by going to the Siegel/Senna Introduction to Criminal Justice 11e website: www.thomsonedu.com/criminaljustice/siegel.

Opportunities for advancement within the field come mainly in the form of supervisory positions, which entail more responsibilities and higher pay. Ultimately, many paralegals will use their knowledge and skills to earn a law degree and become a lawyer or judge. They can also move on to better-paying careers where legal experience is useful, such as insurance claims adjuster.

Qualifications

Much of a paralegal's work is focused on conducting legal research, so skills that aid this process are critical. Because much of this research can now be done using computer programs, databases, and the Internet, up-to-date computer skills provide a distinct advantage. Those with knowledge and experience in a specialized legal field will also be in demand, especially for government and corporate positions. Real-world work experience and internship experience can also increase the chances of employment.

Relevant educational experience and certification are useful for gaining employment. Although one can work as a paralegal without certification, it provides a hiring advantage. Various groups such as the National Association of Legal Assistants provide certification if the applicant can pass rigorous exams.

Education and Training

There are multiple ways of entering the field. Most paralegals enter their profession with training from a two-year paralegal program approved by the American Bar Association. However, it is possible for people with a liberal arts degree to enter the field by working in legal offices and learning skills on the job. Others with bachelor's degrees enter certification programs or complete a combination bachelor's/paralegal degree. The entrance requirements for these programs will vary. Classes in political science may provide useful knowledge for future paralegals. Finally, paralegals must always keep up-to-date on changes in the law in their area of specialization.

Sources: "Paralegal," *Occupational Outlook Handbook,* 2006–2007 edition (Bureau of Labor Statistics, U.S. Department of Labor), retrieved July 22, 2006, from http://www.bls.gov/oco/ocos114.htm; "Occupational Employment and Wages, May 2005" (Bureau of Labor Statistics, U.S. Department of Labor), retrieved July 22, 2006, from http://www.bls.gov/news.release/ocwage.toc.htm; "Paralegal" (*Court TV Careers in Justice*), retrieved July 21, 2006, from http://www.courttv.com/careers_justice/career_track/list/paralegal.html; "Princeton Review Career Profiles: Paralegal," retrieved July 22, 2006, from http://www.princetonreview.com/cte/profiles/dayInLife.asp?careerID=105).

higher state or federal court on the basis of an error that affected the conviction in the trial court. Extraordinary trial court errors, such as the denial of the right to counsel or the inability to provide a fair trial, are subject to the "plain error" rule of the federal courts.[54] "Harmless errors," such as the use of innocuous identification procedures or the denial of counsel at a noncritical stage of the proceeding, would not necessarily result in overturning a criminal conviction.

A postconviction remedy—often referred to as a "collateral attack"—is the primary means by which state prisoners can have their conviction or sentence reviewed in federal court. It takes the form of a legal petition, such as for a writ of habeas corpus. A writ of habeas corpus (meaning "you should have the body") seeks to determine the validity of detention by asking the court to release the person or give legal reasons for the incarceration.

In most jurisdictions, direct criminal appeal to an appellate court is a matter of right. This means that the defendant has an automatic right to appeal a conviction based on errors that may have occurred during the trial proceedings. A substantial number of criminal appeals are the result of disputes over points of law, such as the introduction at the trial of illegal evidence detrimental to the defendant or statements made during the trial that were prejudicial to the defendant. Through objections made at the pretrial and trial stages of the criminal process, the defense counsel preserves specific legal issues on the record as the basis for appeal. Much of the background work for such appeals may be handled by paralegals, the subject of the Careers in Criminal Justice box.

Although the defendant has an automatic right to an appeal in the first instance, all further appeals are discretionary, including an appeal "all the way to the U.S. Supreme Court." Because an appeal is an expensive, time-consuming, and technical process, involving a review of the lower court record, the research and drafting of briefs, and the presentation of oral arguments to the appellate court, the defendant has been granted the right to counsel at this stage of the criminal process. In *Douglas v. California* (1963), the Supreme Court held that an indigent defendant has a constitutional right to the assistance of counsel on a direct first appeal.[55] If the defendant appeals to a higher court, the defendant must have private counsel or apply for permission to proceed in forma pauperis, meaning that the defendant may be granted counsel at public expense if the court believes that the appeal has merit.

The right of appeal normally does not extend to the prosecution in a criminal case. At one extreme are states that grant no right of appeal to the prosecution in criminal cases. At the other, some jurisdictions permit the prosecution to appeal in those instances that involve the unconstitutionality of a statute or a motion granting a new trial to the defendant. However, the prosecutor cannot bring the defendant to trial again on the same charge after an acquittal or a conviction, as this would violate the defendant's right to be free from double jeopardy under the Fifth Amendment. The purpose of the double jeopardy guarantee is to protect the defendant from a second prosecution for the same offense.

After an appeal has been fully heard, the appeals court renders an opinion on the procedures used in the case. If an error of law is found, such as an improper introduction of evidence or an improper statement by the prosecutor that was prejudicial to the defendant, the appeals court may reverse the decision of the trial court and order a new trial. If the lower court's decision is upheld, the case is finished, unless the defendant seeks a discretionary appeal to a higher state or federal court.

Over the past decade, criminal appeals have increased significantly in almost every state and the federal courts. Criminal case appeals make up a majority of the state appellate and federal caseload, which includes prisoner petitions and ordinary criminal appeals. Today, a substantial number of these appeals involve drug-related cases. As new scientific evidence is created, especially the use of DNA, the number of appeals may increase. In an important 2006 case, *House v. Bell*, the U.S. Supreme Court expanded the ability of death row inmates to challenge their convictions in federal court based on DNA evidence produced long after their trials. *House* is the first case in which the Court considered the new evidentiary technology of DNA evidence when re-examining a death sentence. In its 5–3 decision, the Court held that new evidence, including DNA test results, raised sufficient doubt to merit a new hearing in federal court for Tennessee death row inmate Paul House, who had been on death row for more than 20 years for the rape and murder of his neighbor. The Court recognized that because DNA tests, not available at the time of his conviction, pointed the finger at the victim's husband, House was entitled to a new trial. In his opinion, Justice Kennedy wrote that "all the evidence, old and new, incriminating and exculpatory must be taken into account . . . the court's function is not to make an independent factual determination about what likely occurred, but rather to assess the likely impact of the evidence on reasonable jurors."[56]

Take a look at Massachusetts' appeal petition in the famous Louise Woodward child abuse case. You can reach it by going to the Siegel/Senna Introduction to Criminal Justice 11e website: www.thomsonedu.com/criminaljustice/siegel.

ThomsonNOW Improve your grade on the exam with Personalized Study! For reinforcement resources and a mastery check of the trial process, go to www.thomsonedu.com/thomsonnow.

♦ EVIDENTIARY STANDARDS

The standard required to convict a defendant at the trial stage of the criminal process is proof beyond a reasonable doubt. This requirement dates back to early

Why is it important to have proof beyond a reasonable doubt in criminal cases? Joe Amrine (left), who spent 16 years on Missouri's death row before being exonerated, talks with first-year law student Nicole Waggner before speaking to students at Saint Louis University Law School. Amrine was released from prison in July 2003 after DNA testing did not implicate him in the stabbing death of inmate Gary Barber in 1985. Without high standards of proof, mistakes like the ones made in Amrine's case would be all too common.

U.S. history and, over the years, has become the accepted measure of persuasion needed by the prosecutor to convince the judge or jury of the defendant's guilt. Many twentieth-century U.S. Supreme Court decisions reinforced this standard by making "beyond a reasonable doubt" a constitutional due process requirement.[57]

The reasonable doubt standard is an essential ingredient of the criminal justice process. It is the prime instrument for reducing the risk of convictions based on factual errors. The underlying premise of this standard is that it is better to release a guilty person than to convict someone who is innocent. In applying the reasonable doubt standard to juvenile trials, in *In re Winship* (1970), the Supreme Court noted the following:

> If the standard proof for a criminal trial were preponderance of evidence rather than proof beyond a reasonable doubt, there would be a smaller risk of factual errors that result in freeing guilty persons, but a far greater risk of factual errors that result in convicting the innocent.[58]

Because the defendant is presumed innocent until proven guilty, this standard forces the prosecution to overcome the presumption of innocence with the highest standard of proof. Unlike the civil law, where a mere preponderance of the evidence is the standard, the criminal process requires proof beyond a reasonable doubt for each element of the offense. These and other evidentiary standards of proof are defined and compared in Concept Summary 12.4.

Over the years, the courts have struggled to define many of the standards of evidence, particularly reasonable doubt. The Federal Judicial Center's model standard states it best:

> Proof beyond a reasonable doubt is proof that leaves you firmly convinced of the defendant's guilt. There are very few things in this world that we know with absolute certainty, and in criminal cases the law does not require proof that overcomes every possible doubt. If, based on your consideration of the evidence, you are firmly convinced that the defendant is guilty of the crime charged, you must find him guilty. If, on the other hand, you think there is a real possibility that he is not guilty, you must give him the benefit of the doubt and find him not guilty.[59]

CONCEPT SUMMARY 12.4

Evidentiary Standards of Proof: Degrees of Certainty

Standard	Definition	Where used
Absolute certainty	No possibility of error; 100 percent certainty	Not used in civil or criminal law
Beyond a reasonable doubt; moral certainty	Conclusive and complete proof, without leaving any reasonable doubt as to the guilt of the defendant; allowing the defendant the benefit of any possibility of innocence	Criminal trial
Clear and convincing evidence	Prevailing and persuasive to the trier of fact	Civil commitments, insanity defense
Preponderance of evidence	Greater weight of evidence in terms of credibility; more convincing than an opposite point of view	Civil trial
Probable cause	U.S. constitutional standard for arrest and search warrants, requiring existence of facts sufficient to warrant that a crime has been committed	Arrest, preliminary hearing, motions
Sufficient evidence Reasonable suspicion	Adequate evidence to reverse a trial; rational, reasonable belief that facts warrant investigation of a crime on less than probable cause	Appellate review Police investigations
Less than probable cause	Mere suspicion; less than reasonable to conclude that criminal activity exists	Prudent police investigation when safety of an officer or others is endangered

ETHICAL CHALLENGES IN CRIMINAL JUSTICE: A WRITING ASSIGNMENT

Write a critical essay addressing the following ethical scenario: You are a superior court judge. A local television station has asked you to allow cameras to be placed in the jury room while the jurors consider whether to recommend the death penalty in a high-profile murder trial. The station argues that the recording would serve an important purpose and shed light on the death penalty process. The prosecutor is opposed to this tactic and believes it would disrupt jury deliberations, invade the jurors' privacy, and inhibit some jurors from giving their opinions. It is one thing, she argues, to have cameras in the courtroom; it is quite another to have them in the jury room. Should jury deliberations be turned into a kind of TV reality show? What would you decide to do?

Doing Research on the Web

The following articles may help you write your essay: Debra Rosenberg, "Death Penalty: Cameras Report, the Jury Decides," and Mary Alice Robbins,

"Texas Court Considers Whether to Allow Filming of Deliberations." For an opposing view, read Martin Kimel, "Justice Filmed Is Justice Distorted." You can access all three of these articles by going to the Siegel/Senna Introduction to Criminal Justice 11e website: www.thomsonedu.com/criminaljustice/siegel.

SUMMARY

◆ The jury trial is the centerpiece of the criminal justice system because it provides every defendant with the right to be judged by his peers and not the government.

◆ A defendant may choose between a trial before a judge alone or a trial by jury. In either case, the purpose of the trial is to adjudicate the facts, ascertain the truth, and determine the guilt or innocence of the accused.

◆ Criminal trials represent the adversary system at work. The state uses its authority to seek a conviction, and the defendant is protected by constitutional rights, particularly those under the Fifth and Sixth amendments.

◆ When they involve serious crimes, criminal trials are complex legal affairs. Each jurisdiction relies on rules and procedures that have developed over many years to resolve legal issues.

◆ During trials, criminal defendants are afforded particular rights guaranteed by the Constitution and applied by the U.S. Supreme Court.

◆ These include the right to confront witnesses, to be competent at trial, to have a fair jury and public trial, to have a speedy trial, to be represented by counsel, and to represent oneself if competent and informed.

◆ The right to have or not have trials televised is still open to debate, although many notorious cases have been broadcast.

◆ An established order of steps is followed throughout a criminal trial, beginning with the selection of a jury, proceeding through opening statements and the introduction of evidence, and concluding with closing arguments and a verdict.

◆ For a defendant to be found guilty at trial, the allegations must be proven beyond a reasonable doubt.

◆ The trial is the central test of the facts and law involved in a criminal case.

KEY TERMS

adjudication, 382
bench trial, 382
confrontation clause, 383
six-person jury, 387
pro se, 389
venire, 393

voir dire, 393
challenge for cause, 394
peremptory challenge, 395
direct examination, 399
cross-examination, 399
real evidence, 400

circumstantial (indirect) evidence, 400
directed verdict, 401
rebuttal evidence, 401
surrebuttal evidence, 401
jury nullification, 403

ThomsonNOW™ Maximize your study time by using ThomsonNOW's diagnostic study plan to help you review this chapter. The Study Plan will

◆ help you identify areas on which you should concentrate;

◆ provide interactive exercises to help you master the chapter concepts; and

◆ provide a post-test to confirm you are ready to move on to the next chapter.

CRITICAL THINKING QUESTIONS

1. What are the steps involved in the criminal trial?

2. What are the pros and cons of a jury trial versus a bench trial?

3. What are the legal rights of the defendant in a trial process?

4. Should people be denied the right to serve as jurors without explanation or cause? In other words, should the peremptory challenge be maintained?

5. "In the adversary system of criminal justice, the burden of proof in a criminal trial to show that the defendant is guilty beyond a reasonable doubt is on the government." Explain the meaning of this statement.

6. What is testamentary evidence?

NOTES

1. James Sterngold, "A Radical's Tale: Compassion Then Led to Prison Now," *New York Times*, December 14, 2001, p. A24; James Sterngold, "70s Radical Is Sentenced, Then Arraigned in New Case," *New York Times*, January 19, 2002, p. A10.

2. Thomas J. Lueck, "Man Who Killed Abortion Provider Asks for Trial by Judge," *New York Times*, March 12, 2003, p. A12.

3. *Riggins v. Nevada*, 504 U.S. 127 (1992).

4. *Sell v. United States*, No. 02–5664, June 16, 2003.

5. *Pointer v. State of Texas*, 380 U.S. 400, 85 S.Ct. 1065, 13 L.Ed.2d 923 (1965).

6. 487 U.S. 1012, 108 S.Ct. 2798, 101 L.Ed.2d 867 (1988).

7. 497 U.S. 836, 110 S.Ct. 3157, 111 L.Ed.2d 666 (1990).

8. 391 U.S. 145, 88 S.Ct. 1444, 20 L.Ed.2d 491 (1968).

9. Ibid., at 157–58, 88 S.Ct., at 1451–52.

10. 399 U.S. 66, 90 S.Ct. 1886, 26 L.Ed.2d 437 (1970).

11. See *Blanton v. City of Las Vegas*, 489 U.S. 538, 109 S.Ct. 1289, 103 L.Ed.2d 550 (1989). See also *Lewis v. United States*, 116 S.Ct. 2163 (1996).

12. 399 U.S. 78, 90 S.Ct. 1893, 26 L.Ed.2d 446 (1970).

13. Ibid., at 102–3, 90 S.Ct., at 1907.

14. Ibid., at 101, 90 S.Ct., at 1906.

15. Ibid., at 102, 90 S.Ct., at 1907.

16. *Ballew v. Georgia*, 435 U.S. 223, 98 S.Ct. 1029, 55 L.Ed.2d 234 (1978); *Burch v. Louisiana*, 441 U.S. 130, 99 S.Ct. 1623, 60 L.Ed.2d 96 (1979).

17. 406 U.S. 404, 92 S.Ct. 1628, 32 L.Ed.2d 184 (1972).

18. 287 U.S. 45, 53 S.Ct. 55, 77 L.Ed. 158 (1932); 372 U.S. 335, 83 S.Ct. 792, 9 L.Ed.2d 799 (1963); Yale Kamisar, "*Gideon v. Wainwright*: A Quarter Century Later," *Pace Law Review* 10 (1990): 343; 407 U.S. 25, 92 S.Ct. 2006, 32 L.Ed.2d 530 (1972).

19. *Shelton v. Alabama*, 122 U.S. 1764 (2002).

20. *Shelton*, quoting *Argersinger v. Hamlin*, 407 U.S. 25, 40 (1972).

21. 422 U.S. 806, 95 S.Ct. 2525, 45 L.Ed.2d 562 (1975).

22. 120 S.Ct. 684 (2000).

23. See American Bar Association, *Standards Relating to Speedy Trial* (New York: Institute of Judicial Administration, 1986), p. 1.

24. 386 U.S. 213, 87 S.Ct. 988, 18 L.Ed.2d 1 (1967).

25. Ibid., at 223, 87 S.Ct., at 993.

26. *Doggett v. United States*, 505 U.S. 647, 112 S.Ct. 2686, 120 L.Ed.2d 520 (1992).

27. President's Commission on Law Enforcement and the Administration of Justice, *Task Force Report: The Courts* (Washington, D.C.: Government Printing Office, 1967), pp. 86–87. See also B. Mahoney and others, *Implementing Delay Reduction and Delay Prevention: Programs in Urban Trial Courts* (Williamsburg, Va.: National Center for State Courts, 1985); *The State of Criminal Justice: An Annual Report, 1994* (Chicago: American Bar Association, 1994).

28. National Advisory Commission on Criminal Justice Standards and Goals, *Courts* (Washington, D.C.: 1973), pp. xx–xxi. See also

Gregory S. Kennedy, "Speedy Trial," *Georgetown Law Journal* 75 (1987): 953–64.

29. 18 U.S.C.A. § 3161 (Supp. 1975). For a good review of this legislation, see Marc I. Steinberg, "Right to Speedy Trial: The Constitutional Right and Its Applicability to the Speedy Trial Act of 1974," *Journal of Criminal Law and Criminology* 66 (1975): 229. See also Thomas Schneider and Robert Davis, "Speedy Trial and Homicide Courts," *American Bar Association Journal of Criminal Justice* 9 (1995): 24.

30. 427 U.S. 539, 96 S.Ct. 2791, 49 L.Ed.2d 683 (1976).

31. Ibid., at 547, 96 S.Ct., at 2797.

32. *Press-Enterprise Co. v. Superior Court* 478 U.S. 1, 106 S.Ct. 2735, 92 L.Ed.2d 1 (1986).

33. 478 U.S. 1, 106 S.Ct. 2735, 92 L.Ed.2d 1 (1986).

34. 448 U.S. 555, 100 S.Ct. 2814, 65 L.Ed.2d 1 (1980).

35. Dale Edwards, "If It Walks, Talks and Squawks Like a Trial, Should It Be Covered Like One? The Right of the Press to Cover INS Deportation Hearings," *Communication Law & Policy* 10 (2005): 217–39.

36. T. Dyk and B. Donald, "Cameras in the Supreme Court," *American Bar Association Journal* 75 (1989): 34.

37. James Morton, "Court TV—The Cameras Are Switched on Again," *Journal of Criminal Law* 68 (2004): 451–53.

38. 449 U.S. 560, 101 S.Ct. 802, 66 L.Ed.2d 740 (1981).

39. Conference of State Court Administrators, *State Court Organization, 1987* (Williamsburg, Va.: National Center for State Courts, 1988).

40. George Hayden, Joseph Senna, and Larry Siegel, "Prosecutorial Discretion in Peremptory Challenges: An Empirical Investigation of Information Use in the Massachusetts Jury Selection Process," *New England Law Review* 13 (1978): 768.

41. *Powers v. Ohio*, 499 U.S. 400, 111 S.Ct. 1364, 113 L.Ed.2d 411 (1991); *Georgia v. McCollum*, 505 U.S. 42, 112 S.Ct. 2348, 120 L.Ed.2d 33 (1992).

42. *J. E. B. v. Alabama*, ex rel. T. B., 511 U.S. 142, 114 S.Ct. 1419, 128 L.Ed.2d 89 (1994).

43. "Peremptory Challenges Can't Be Based on Religion," *Lawyers Weekly USA*, February 13, 1995, p. 1.

44. For a review of jury decision making, see John Baldwin and Michael McConville, "Criminal Juries," in *Crime and Justice*, vol. 2, ed. Norval Morris and Michael Tonry (Chicago: University of Chicago Press, 1980), pp. 269–320. See also Reid Hastie, ed., *Inside the Juror* (New York: Cambridge University Press, 1993).

45. 409 U.S. 524, 93 S.Ct. 848, 35 L.Ed.2d 46 (1973).

46. 419 U.S. 522, 95 S.Ct. 692, 42 L.Ed.2d 690 (1975).

47. 476 U.S. 28, 106 S.Ct. 1683, 90 L.Ed.2d 27 (1986). See James Gobert, "In Search of an Impartial Jury," *Journal of Criminal Law and Criminology* 79 (1988): 269.

48. 476 U.S. 162, 106 S.Ct. 1758, 90 L.Ed.2d 137 (1986).

49. 476 U.S. 530, 106 S.Ct. 2056, 90 L.Ed.2d 514 (1986).

50. See *John Strong, McCormick on Evidence*, 5th edition (St. Paul, Minn: West Group, 2006), Chapter 1.

51. Deborah Mahan, "Forensic Image Processing," *American Bar Association Journal of Criminal Justice* 10 (1995): 2.

52. *Sullivan v. Louisiana*, 508 U.S. 275, 113 S.Ct. 2078, 124 L.Ed.2d 182 (1993).

53. Bureau of Justice Statistics, *Report to the Nation on Crime and Justice*, 2nd ed. (Washington, D.C.: Government Printing Office, 1988), p. 88.

54. *Chapman v. California*, 386 U.S. 18, 87 S.Ct. 824, 17 L.Ed.2d 705 (1967).

55. 372 U.S. 353, 83 S.Ct. 814, 9 L.Ed.2d 811 (1963).

56. *House v. Bell*, No. 04–8990, January 2006.

57. Barry Scheck, Peter Newfeld, and Jim Dugen, *Actual Innocence* (New York: Doubleday, 2000).

58. Benjamin Austin, "Right to Jury Trial," *Georgetown University Law Review* 85 (1997): 1240.

59. *Model Jury Standards for Criminal Trial* (Washington, D.C.: Federal Judicial Center, 1987). See also Michael Higgins, "Not So Plain English," *American Bar Association Journal* 84 (1998): 40.

CHAPTER 13

Punishment and Sentencing

Chapter Outline

Chapter Objectives

After reading this chapter, you should be able to:
1. Understand the concept of criminal punishment.
2. Know the different stages of punishment used throughout history.
3. Recognize the differences between concurrent sentences and consecutive sentences.
4. Explain the various reasons for criminal sanctions.
5. Discuss the concept of indeterminate sentencing.
6. Recognize why determinate sentencing was instituted.
7. Describe the role of sentencing guidelines.
8. Know what is meant by "three strikes and you're out."
9. Understand the concept of mandatory sentencing.
10. Know the arguments for and against capital punishment.
11. Describe the legal issues in capital sentencing.
12. Discuss the issue of whether the death penalty deters murder.

©FBI/AFP/Getty Images

*O*n July 15, 2002, Samantha Runnion, age five, was kidnapped while playing in front of her California home. The police received an anonymous tip and found her body soon afterward. She had been raped and murdered. A playmate of Samantha's gave the police a good description of her attacker. Alejandro Avila was arrested and charged with four felonies—one count of kidnapping, two of forcible lewd acts on a child, and one of murder. Avila had been charged in a previous child molestation case but had not been convicted. After Avila's arrest, prosecutors cited "special circumstances" in the killing, kidnapping, and sexual assault on a minor, a standard that would allow them to seek the death penalty. Tony Ruckauckas, the Orange County district attorney, told reporters that he would consult with the victim's family and members of his staff before coming to a decision on whether Avila, if convicted, should be put to death. But he further said that "Anyone who commits this kind of crime in Orange County will either die in prison of natural causes or will be executed." The district attorney's office also let it be known that DNA evidence found at the crime scene linked Avila to the crime. Ruckauckas told reporters that the evidence was "very, very compelling, and we are satisfied that we have the right person."[1] Avila was convicted of the crime, and on May 16, 2005, the jury recommended that he receive the death penalty. On July 22, 2005, the judge in the case formally sentenced Avila to death. ◆

Although such terrible incidents are relatively rare, the Runnion case raises important issues for the criminal justice system. First, the suspect's name and picture were broadcast almost instantly after his arrest, along with statements testifying to the incriminating evidence that had been gathered at the crime scene. Does such pretrial publicity make it virtually impossible for a suspect in a high-profile murder case to get a fair trial? In this age of pervasive media exposure, should limits be placed on press coverage? Or does this violate the Constitution's guarantee of free speech and press?

The Runnion case also illustrates the system's growing dependence on technology to solve crimes. How did the district attorney conclude that Avila was the real culprit? Because of DNA matches found at the crime scene. Is it fair to convict someone of a crime based primarily on relatively new technologies that have not been proven over years of use? Avila may face the death penalty in the case. Should a person be executed based on a DNA match?

The Runnion case shows the complex issues surrounding the application of capital punishment in the United States. The district attorney told the press that he would consult with the family before making the decision to seek the death penalty. Should family members, justifiably emotional after their loss, be part of the decision to take the defendant's life? Why should a murder suspect's fate rest in the hands of the victim's family? Would the outcome be altered if the victim did not have any living family members? What role does public opinion play in the distribution of the death penalty? Samantha Runnion was a beautiful girl. Her death caused understandable public outrage. But should her killer be treated more harshly than another person who killed someone less vulnerable and less attractive? Should not all crime victims be considered equal? Finally, should the death penalty have been employed if Samantha's killer suffered from some mental defect that caused him to have uncontrollable violent sexual urges? The U.S. Supreme Court has ruled that the death penalty cannot be used with people who are insane at the time they committed their offense. But what about people who are not legally insane but still suffer from severe psychological problems? Skeptics might suggest that all killers must suffer from psychological deficits. Should they be immune from capital punishment?

Historically, a full range of punishments has been inflicted on criminal defendants, including physical torture, branding, whipping, and, for most felony offenses, death. During the Middle Ages, the philosophy of punishment was to "torment the body for the sins of the soul."[2] People who violated the law were considered morally corrupt and in need of strong discipline. If punishment were harsh enough, it was assumed, they would never repeat their mistakes. Punishment was also viewed as a spectacle that taught a moral lesson. The more gruesome and public the sentence, the greater the impact it would have on the local populace.[3] Harsh physical punishments would control any thoughts of rebellion and dissent against the central government and those who held political and economic control. Such barbaric use of state power is no longer tolerated in the United States.

Today, the major issue regarding criminal punishment involves both its nature and extent: Are too many people being sent to prison?[4] Do people get widely different sentences for similar crimes?[5] Is there discrimination in sentencing based on race, gender, or social class?[6] These are but a few of the most significant issues in the sentencing process.

◆ THE HISTORY OF PUNISHMENT

The punishment and correction of criminals have changed considerably through the ages, reflecting custom, economic conditions, and religious and political ideals.[7]

In earlier times, punishment was quite severe. Brutal public punishments which included beheading and burning were designed to teach the value of obedience to authority. Even kings, such as Charles I of England, were not immune from death. Following his conviction on charges of treason during the English Civil War of 1642–1648, Charles was beheaded on January 30, 1649.

From Exile to Fines, Torture to Forfeiture

In early Greece and Rome, the most common state-administered punishment was banishment, or exile. Only slaves were commonly subjected to harsh physical punishment for their misdeeds. Interpersonal violence, even attacks that resulted in death, was viewed as a private matter. These ancient peoples typically used economic punishments, such as fines, for such crimes as assault on a slave, arson, or housebreaking.

During the Middle Ages (the sixth to fifteenth centuries), there was little law or governmental control. Offenses were settled by blood feuds carried out by the families of the injured parties. When possible, the Roman custom of settling disputes by fine or an exchange of property was adopted as a means of resolving interpersonal conflicts with a minimum of bloodshed. After the eleventh century, during the feudal period, forfeiture of land and property was common punishment for persons who violated law and custom or who failed to fulfill their feudal obligations to their lord. The word *felony* comes from the twelfth century, when the term *felonia* referred to a breach of faith with one's feudal lord.

During this period the main emphasis of criminal law and punishment was on maintaining public order. If in the heat of passion or while intoxicated a person severely injured or killed his neighbor, freemen in the area would gather to pronounce a judgment and make the culprit do penance or pay compensation called *wergild*. The purpose of the fine was to pacify the injured party and ensure that the conflict would not develop into a blood feud and anarchy. The inability of the peasantry to pay a fine led to the use of corporal punishment, such as whipping or branding, as a substitute penalty.

The development of the common law in the eleventh century brought some standardization to penal practices. However, corrections remained an amalgam of fines and brutal physical punishments. The criminal wealthy could buy their way out of punishment and into exile, but capital and corporal punishment were used to control the criminal poor, who were executed and mutilated at ever-increasing rates. Execution, banishment, mutilation, branding, and flogging were used on a whole range of offenders, from murderers and robbers to vagrants and Gypsies.

The trial and execution of William Wallace are depicted by Mel Gibson in the film *Braveheart*. Wallace's execution was a textbook case of medieval punishment. You can read about it by linking through the Siegel/Senna Introduction to Criminal Justice 11e website: www.thomsonedu.com/criminaljustice/siegel.

sanctions
Social control mechanisms designed to enforce society's laws and standards.

punishment
Pain, suffering, loss, or sanction inflicted on a person because he or she committed a crime or offense.

poor laws
Seventeenth-century English laws under which vagrants and abandoned and neglected children were bound to masters as indentured servants.

Punishments became unmatched in their cruelty, featuring a gruesome variety of physical tortures that were often part of a public spectacle, presumably so that the sadistic **sanctions** would act as deterrents. But the variety and imagination of the tortures inflicted on even minor criminals before their death suggest that retribution, sadism, and spectacle were more important than any presumed deterrent effect.

Public Work and Transportation to the Colonies

By the end of the sixteenth century, the rise of the city and overseas colonization provided tremendous markets for manufactured goods and spurred the need for labor. **Punishment** of criminals changed to meet the demands created by these social conditions. Instead of being tortured or executed, many offenders were made to do hard labor for their crimes. **Poor laws**, developed at the end of the sixteenth century, required that the poor, vagrants, and vagabonds be put to work in public or private enterprises. Houses of correction were developed to make it convenient to assign petty law violators to work details. In London a workhouse was developed at Brideswell in 1557. Its use became so popular that by 1576 Parliament ordered a Brideswell-type workhouse to be built in every county in England. Many convicted offenders were pressed into sea duty as galley slaves. Galley slavery was considered a fate so loathsome that many convicts mutilated themselves to avoid servitude on the high seas.

The constant shortage of labor in the European colonies also prompted authorities to transport convicts overseas. In England an Order in Council of 1617 granted a reprieve and stay of execution to people convicted of robbery and other felonies who were strong enough to be employed overseas. Similar measures were used in France and Italy to recruit galley slaves and workers.

Transporting convicts to the colonies became popular. It supplied labor, cost little, and was profitable for the government because manufacturers and plantation owners paid for convicts' services. The Old Bailey Court in London supplied at least 10,000 convicts between 1717 and 1775. Convicts would serve a period as workers and then become free again.

The American Revolution ended the transportation of felons to North America, although the practice continued in Australia and New Zealand. Between 1787 and 1875, when the practice was finally abandoned, more than 135,000 felons were transported to Australia.

Although transportation in lieu of a death sentence may at first glance seem advantageous, transported prisoners endured enormous hardships. Those who were sent to Australia suffered incredible physical abuse, including severe whippings and mutilation. Many of the British prison officials placed in charge of the Australian penal colonies could best be described as sociopaths or sadists.

The Rise of the Prison

Between 1776, when the American colonies declared their independence from the British Crown, and the first decades of the nineteenth century, the population of Europe and the United States increased rapidly. Transportation of convicts to North America was no longer an option. The increased use of machinery made industry capital-intensive, not labor-intensive. As a result, there was less need for unskilled laborers in England, and many workers could not find suitable employment.

The gulf between poor workers and wealthy landowners and merchants widened. The crime rate rose significantly, prompting a return to physical punishment and increased use of the death penalty. During the latter part of the eighteenth century, 350 types of crime in England were punishable by death. Although many people sentenced to death for trivial offenses were spared the gallows, the use of capital punishment was common in England during the mid-eighteenth century. Prompted by the excessive use of physical and capital punishment, legal philosophers argued that physical punishment should be replaced by periods of confinement and incapacitation. Jails and workhouses were commonly used to hold petty offenders, vagabonds, the homeless, and debtors. However, these institutions were not meant for hard-core criminals. One solution to imprisoning a growing criminal population was to keep prisoners in abandoned ships anchored in rivers and harbors throughout England. The degradation under which prisoners lived in these ships inspired John Howard, the sheriff of Bedfordshire, in 1777 to write *The State of the Prisons*, which inspired Parliament to pass legislation mandating the construction of secure and sanitary structures to house prisoners.

By 1820, long periods of incarceration in walled institutions called reformatories or **penitentiaries** began to replace physical punishment in England and the United States. These institutions were considered liberal reforms during a time when harsh physical punishment and incarceration in filthy holding facilities were the norm. Incarceration has remained the primary mode of punishment for serious offenses in the United States since it was introduced in the early nineteenth century. Ironically, in America's high-tech society, some of the institutions constructed soon after the Revolutionary War are still in use today. In recent times, prison as a method of punishment has been supplemented by a sentence to community supervision for less serious offenders, and the death penalty is reserved for those considered to be the most serious and dangerous.

penitentiary
A state or federal correctional institution for the incarceration of felony offenders for terms of one year or more: prison.

ThomsonNOW™ Improve your grade on the exam with Personalized Study! For reinforcement resources and a mastery check of the history of punishment, go to www.thomsonedu.com/thomsonnow.

♦ THE GOALS OF MODERN SENTENCING

When a notorious criminal, such as serial killer Jeffrey Dahmer or Ted Bundy, receives a long prison sentence or the death penalty for a particularly heinous crime, each person has a distinct reaction. Some are gratified that a truly evil person "got just what he deserved"; many people feel safer because a dangerous person is now "where she can't harm any other innocent victims"; others hope that the punishment serves as a warning to potential criminals that "everyone gets caught in the end"; some may feel sorry for the defendant: "He got a raw deal—he needs help, not punishment"; and still others hope that "when she gets out, she'll have learned her lesson." And when an offender is forced to pay a large fine, someone says, "What goes around comes around."

Each of these sentiments may be at work when criminal sentences are formulated. After all, sentences are devised and implemented by judges, many of whom are elected officials and share the general public's sentiments and fears. The objectives of criminal sentencing today can usually be grouped into six distinct areas: general deterrence, incapacitation, specific deterrence, retribution/just desert, rehabilitation, and equity/restitution.

General Deterrence

One of the goals of sentencing is **general deterrence**. Sentencing for the purposes of general deterrence is designed to give a signal to the community at large: Crime does not pay. By severely punishing those people convicted of crime, others who are merely contemplating criminality will be deterred or dissuaded from their planned actions.

By punishing an offender severely, the state can demonstrate its determination to control crime. However, the need to deter crime must be balanced against the need to dispense fair justice. Too lenient a sentence might encourage criminal conduct; too severe a sentence might reduce the system's ability to dispense fair and impartial justice and may encourage criminality. For example, if the crime of rape were punished with death, rapists might be encouraged to kill their victims to dispose of the one person who could identify them. Because they would already be facing the death penalty for rape, they would have nothing more to lose. Maintaining a balance between fear and justice is an ongoing quest in the justice system.

general deterrence
A crime control policy that depends on the fear of criminal penalties.

EXPECTED PUNISHMENT The general deterrence concept relies on the fact that people will forgo criminal activity if they expect to be punished for their crimes. As the likelihood of getting punished increases, crime rates should go down. Similarly, if punishments become more severe, they should have a greater deterrent power.

Some justice experts attribute the recent decline in the crime rates to the fact that criminal penalties have been toughened for many crimes. Once arrested, people have a greater chance of being convicted today than in the past. This is referred to as "expected punishment" or the number of days in prison that a typical criminal can expect to serve per each crime committed.[8] Expected punishment is affected by such factors as the chances of getting caught and convicted as well as the type and length of sentence received. According to the National Center for Policy Analysis (NCPA), crime rates dropped dramatically during the past two decades because expected punishment rose:

♦ For murder, it nearly tripled from 14 months to 41 months.

♦ For rape, it tripled to 128 days.

♦ For robbery, it increased by 70 percent to 59 days.

♦ For serious assault, it more than doubled to 18 days.

♦ For burglary, it more than doubled from 4 days to 9 days.

Despite these increases, expected punishment is still low because most criminals are never apprehended and many who are apprehended have their cases dropped. Still others are given probation instead of prison sentences. The NCPA figures that for every 100 burglaries, only about 7 are cleared by arrest, and less than 2 convicted burglars are sentenced to prison.[9] Putting it another way, about 2,000,000 burglaries are reported to the police each year, about 200,000 burglars are arrested, about 100,000 are convicted, and about 42,000 are sent to prison. Therefore, for every 50 reported burglaries, only 1 burglar is incarcerated (of course, some burglars commit multiple crimes). Such inefficiency limits the deterrent effect of punishment.

The percentage of convicted offenders who now receive a prison sentence is once again on a decline (see Table 13.1). Deterrence advocates would argue that this trend portends an eventual crime rate increase because sentencing leniency will cause expected punishments to drop.

incapacitation
The policy of keeping dangerous criminals in confinement to eliminate the risk of their repeating their offense in society.

Incapacitation

The **incapacitation** of criminals is a justifiable goal of sentencing because inmates will not be able to repeat their criminal acts while they are under state control. For some offenders, this means a period in a high-security state prison where behavior is closely monitored. According to this strategy, choosing the type of sentence and fixing its length involve determining how long a particular offender needs to be incarcerated to ensure that society is protected.

To some critics, incapacitation strategies seem of questionable utility because little association seems to exist between the number of criminals behind bars and the crime rate. Although the prison population jumped between 1980 and 1990, the crime rate also increased. This indicates that crime rates may have little to do with incarceration trends and that reductions in crime are related to other factors such as population makeup, police effectiveness, declining drug use, and a strong economy.[10]

TABLE 13.1

Trends in the Percentage of Convicted Felons Who Receive a Prison Sentence

Percentage of Convicted Felons Who Received a Prison Sentence			
	1994	**1998**	**2002**
All offenses	45	44	41
Murder	95	94	91
Robbery	77	76	71
Aggravated assault	48	46	42
Burglary	53	54	46
Larceny	38	40	36
Drug trafficking	48	45	42

Source: Matthew Durose and Patrick Langan, *Felony Sentences in State Courts, 2002* (Washington, D.C.: Bureau of Justice Statistics, 2004).

It is also possible that incarceration can have a short-term effect that diminishes as more and more people are put in prison. Think of it this way: If only one person could be locked up at a time, chances are that this would be the most dangerous chronic offender in the entire country. The crime reduction benefit of locking up just that single person would be significant. If we could incarcerate only two, the second inmate would be slightly less dangerous. Each time a person is added to the prison population, the crime reduction benefit is somewhat less than the inmate who came before. We now have 1.3 million people behind bars. The millionth inmate is far less dangerous than the first, and the incarceration benefits of locking her up are insignificant.[11]

In contrast, those who favor an incapacitation policy claim that the crime reducing effect of putting people in prison has just taken a little longer than expected. The number of people and percentage of the general population behind bars escalated rapidly between 1990 and 2006, and the crime rate fell. This correlation, they argue, is not a mere coincidence but a true incapacitation effect.

Specific Deterrence

Experiencing harsh criminal punishments should convince convicted offenders that crime does not pay and that **recidivism** is not in their best interests. The suffering caused by punishment should inhibit future law violations. A few research efforts have found that punishment can have significant specific deterrence on future criminality, but these studies are balanced by research that has failed to find specific deterrence effects. For example, a number of research studies have found little association between severity of punishment for past spousal abuse and re-arrest on subsequent charges. Abusers seem just as likely to recidivate if their case is dismissed, if they are given probation, or if they are sent to jail.[12] The effect of **specific deterrence** is further undermined by data showing that most inmates (more than 80 percent) who are released from prison have had prior convictions and that the great majority (68 percent) will reoffend soon after their release. The specific deterrent goal of sentencing is weakened by the fact that a prison stay seems to have little effect on reoffending.[13]

recidivism
Repetition of criminal behavior: habitual criminality.

specific deterrence
Punishment severe enough to convince convicted offenders never to repeat their criminal activity.

Retribution/Just Desert

According to the retributive goal of sentencing, the essential purpose of the criminal process is to punish deserving offenders—fairly and justly—in a manner that is proportionate to the gravity of their crimes.[14]

Offenders are punished simply and solely because they deserve to be disciplined for what they have done: "the punishment should fit the crime."[15] It would be wrong to punish people to set an example for others or to deter would-be criminals, as the general deterrence goal demands. Punishment should be no more or less than the offender's actions deserve. It must be based on how **blameworthy** the person is; this is referred to as the concept of **just desert**.[16]

According to this view, punishments must be equally and fairly distributed to all people who commit similar illegal acts. Determining just punishments can be difficult because there is generally little consensus about the treatment of criminals, the seriousness of crimes, and the proper response to criminal acts. Nonetheless, an ongoing effort has been made to calculate fair and just sentences by creating guidelines to control judicial decision making.

blameworthy
A person who is deserving of blame or punishment because of evil or injurious behavior.

just desert
The view that those who violate the rights of others deserve punishment commensurate with the seriousness of the crime.

Rehabilitation

Can criminal offenders be effectively treated so that they can eventually readjust to society? It may be fair to offer offenders an opportunity for rehabilitation instead of harsh criminal punishments. In a sense, society has failed criminal offenders, many of whom have grown up in disorganized neighborhoods and dysfunctional families. They may have been the target

PERSPECTIVES ON JUSTICE

Justice Perspective

The just desert basis of criminal sentencing is at the heart of the justice perspective, which maintains that people should be punished fairly, equally, and in proportion to the severity of their crimes.

felony
A more serious crime that carries a penalty of incarceration in a state or federal prison, usually for one year or more.

wergild
During the Middle Ages, the compensation paid to the victim by a defendant found guilty of a crime.

equity
Sanction designed to compensate victims and society for the losses caused by crime: restitution.

A key purpose of the criminal law is to provide the victims of crime with restitution for their losses. If a society is to be equitable, it is only fair that if criminals benefit from their crimes, they must repay society for its losses. Former Georgia schools superintendent Linda Schrenko walks toward the Richard B. Russell Federal Building to face sentencing on July 12, 2006, in Atlanta. Schrenko was sentenced to eight years in prison and ordered to pay more than $414,000 in restitution for her role in an embezzlement scheme that helped pay for her face lift and campaign for governor.

©AP Images/Gregory Smith

of biased police officers and, once arrested and labeled, placed at a disadvantage at home, at school, and in the job market.[17] Therefore, society is obligated to help these unfortunate people who, through no fault of their own, experience social and emotional problems that are often the root of their criminal behavior.

The rehabilitation aspect of sentencing is based on a prediction of the future needs of the offender, not on the gravity of the current offense. For example, if a judge sentences a person convicted of a **felony** to a period of community supervision, the judge's actions reflect her belief that the offender can be successfully treated and presents no future threat to society. The rehabilitation goal of sentencing has also been criticized by those who find little conclusive evidence exists that correctional treatment programs can prevent future criminality.[18] Although the rehabilitative ideal has been undermined by such attacks, surveys indicate that the general public still supports the treatment goal of sentencing.[19] Many people express preferences for programs that are treatment oriented, such as early-childhood intervention and services for at-risk children, rather than those that espouse strict punishment and incarceration policies.[20] And evidence is growing that offender rehabilitation can be effective if the proper methods are used.[21]

Equity/Restitution

Because criminals gain from their misdeeds, it seems both fair and just to demand that they reimburse society for its losses caused by their crimes. In the early common law, **wergild** and fines represented the concept of creating an equitable solution to crime by requiring the convicted offender to make restitution to both the victim and the state. Today, judges continue to require that offenders pay victims for their losses.

The **equity** goal of punishment means that convicted criminals must pay back their victims for their loss, the justice system for the costs of processing their case, and society for any disruption they may have caused. In a so-called victimless crime, such as drug trafficking, the social costs might include the expense of drug enforcement efforts, drug treatment centers, and care for infants born to drug-addicted mothers. In predatory crimes, the costs might include the services of emergency room doctors, lost workdays and productivity, and treatment for long-term psychological problems. To help defray these costs, convicted offenders might be required to pay a fine, forfeit the property they acquired through illegal gain, do community service work, make financial restitution to their victim, and reimburse the state for the costs of the criminal process. Because the criminals' actions helped expand their personal gains, rights, and privileges at society's expense, justice demands that they lose rights and privileges to restore the social balance.

Each factor that influences sentencing decisions is illustrated in Figure 13.1.

Imposing the Sentence

Regardless of the factors that influence the sentence, it is generally imposed by the judge, and sentencing is one of the most crucial functions of judgeship. Sentencing authority may also be exercised by the jury, or it may be mandated by statute (for example, a mandatory prison sentence for a certain crime).

In most felony cases, except when the law provides for mandatory prison terms, sentencing is usually based on a variety of information available to the judge. Some jurisdictions allow victims to make impact statements that are considered at sentencing hearings. Most judges also consider a presentence investigation report by the probation department in making a sentencing decision. This report is a social and personal history, as well as an evaluation

FIGURE 13.1
The Goals Behind Sentencing Decisions

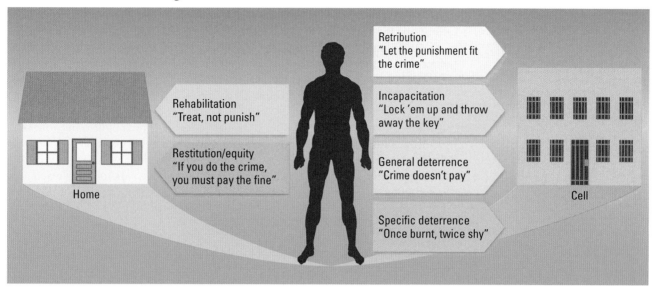

of the defendant's chances for rehabilitation within the community. Some judges give the presentence investigation report great weight; others may dismiss it completely or rely on only certain portions.

When an accused person is convicted of two or more charges, he must be sentenced on each charge. If the sentences are *concurrent*, they begin the same day and are completed when the longest term has been served. For example, a defendant is convicted of burglarizing an apartment and assaulting its occupant. He is sentenced to 3 years on a charge of assault and 10 years for burglary, with the sentences to be served concurrently. After he spends 10 years in prison, the sentences would be completed.

In contrast, receiving a **consecutive sentence** means that on completion of the sentence for one crime the offender begins serving time for the second of multiple crimes. If the defendant in the above example had been sentenced consecutively, he would serve 3 years on the assault charge and then 10 years for the burglary. Therefore, the total term on the two charges would be 13 years.

Concurrent sentences are the norm. Consecutive sentences are requested for the most serious criminals and for those who are unwilling to cooperate with authorities. Figure 13.2 shows the difference between a consecutive and concurrent sentence.

FIGURE 13.2
Consecutive Versus Concurrent Sentences

Example: In state X
1. Rape is punishable by 10 years in prison
2. Possession of a handgun by 3 years
3. Possession of heroin by 4 years

Consecutive sentence
Rape + possession of a handgun + possession of heroin
10 + 3 + 4 = 17 years
(each sentence must be served individually)

Concurrent sentence
Rape + possession of a handgun + possession of heroin
10 years
(all sentences served simultaneously)

consecutive sentence
Incarceration for more than one offense such that each sentence begins only after the previous one has been completed.

concurrent sentence
Incarceration for more than one offense such that all sentences begin on the same day and are completed after the longest term has been served.

◆ SENTENCING MODELS

When a convicted offender is sentenced to prison, the statutes of the jurisdiction in which the crime was committed determine the penalties that may be imposed by the court. Over the years, a variety of sentencing structures have been used in the United States. They include indeterminate sentences, determinate sentences, and mandatory sentences.

Indeterminate Sentences

indeterminate sentence
A term of incarceration with a stated minimum and maximum length; the prisoner is eligible for parole after serving the minimum.

determinate sentence
A fixed term of incarceration.

In the 1870s, prison reformers such as Enoch Wines and Zebulon Brockway called for creation of **indeterminate sentences**, tailored to fit individual needs. Offenders, the argument went, should be placed in confinement only until they were rehabilitated, and then they should be released on parole. Criminals were believed to be sick, not bad. They could be successfully treated in prison. Instead of holding that "the punishment should fit the crime," reformers believed that "the treatment should fit the offender."

The indeterminate sentence is still the most widely used type of sentence in the United States. Convicted offenders are typically given a light minimum sentence that must be served and a lengthy maximum sentence that is the outer boundary of the time that can be served. For example, the legislature might set a sentence of a minimum of 3 years and a maximum of 20 years for burglary. Thus, the convicted offender must be sentenced to no less than 3 years but no more than 20 years in prison. Under this scheme, the actual length of time served by the offender is controlled both by the judge and the correctional agency. A judge could sentence a burglar to a term of between 3 and 20 years. The inmate could then be paroled from confinement soon after serving the minimum sentence if the correctional authorities believe that she is ready to live in the community. If the inmate accumulates good time, she could be released in 18 months; a troublesome inmate would be forced to do all 20 years.

The basic purpose of the indeterminate sentence is to individualize each sentence in the interests of rehabilitating the offender. This type of sentencing allows for flexibility not only in the type of sentence to be imposed but also in the length of time to be served.

Most jurisdictions that use indeterminate sentences employ statutes that specify minimum and maximum terms but allow judicial discretion to fix the actual sentence within those limits. The typical minimum sentence is at least one year; a few state jurisdictions require at least a two-year minimum sentence for felons.[22]

Determinate Sentences

The indeterminate sentence has come under attack in recent years for a variety of reasons. It is alleged to produce great disparity in the way that people are treated in the correctional system. It is possible for one offender to serve 1 year, and another 20 years, for similar crimes. Further, the indeterminate sentence is believed to take control of sentencing out of the hands of the judiciary and place it within the framework of corrections, especially when the minimum sentence is short. Every time an inmate who is granted early release via discretionary parole and commits a violent crime, the call goes up to get tough on prison inmates. In contrast, many inmates feel cheated by the system when they are denied parole despite having a good prison record. The protections of due process maintained in the courtroom are absent in the correctional setting. Dissatisfaction with the disparity and uncertainty of indeterminate sentencing has prompted some states and the federal government to abandon it in favor of determinate sentencing models or structured sentencing models.

Determinate sentences, the first kind used in the United States, are still being used today. In its current form, a determinate sentence is a fixed term of years, the maximum set in law by the legislature, to be served in its entirety by the offender sentenced to prison for a particular crime. For example, if the law provides for a sentence of up to 20 years for robbery, the judge might sentence a repeat offender to a 15-year term. Another, less experienced felon might receive a more lenient sentence of 5 years.

Amy Grossberg is embraced by a correctional officer as she walks out of Baylor Women's Correctional facility in New Castle, Delaware on May 11, 2000. Grossberg, who pleaded guilty along with her college sweetheart to killing their newborn son in a Delaware motel, was released eight months early from her 2½-year sentence because of credit for time served before her guilty plea and for good behavior. "Good time" laws give inmates an incentive to obey institutional rules and enter institutional treatment programs. They also help prison officials maintain order and control the inmate population.

©AP Images/Roberto Borea

GOOD TIME Although determinate sentences provide a set term of years to be served without benefit of parole, the time spent in prison is reduced by the implementation of "time off for good behavior." This concept was first used in 1817 in New York, and it was quickly adopted in most other jurisdictions. **Good time** is still in use today. Inmates can accrue standard good time at a rate ranging from 10 to 15 days per month. In addition, some correctional authorities grant earned sentence reductions to inmates who participate in treatment programs, such as educational and vocational training, or who volunteer for experimental medical testing programs. More than half of a determinate sentence can be erased by accumulating both standard and earned good time.

Good-time laws allow inmates to calculate their release date at the time they enter prison by subtracting the expected good time from their sentence. However, good time can be lost if inmates break prison rules, get into fights, or disobey correctional officers. In some jurisdictions, former inmates can be returned to prison to serve the balance of their unexpired sentence when their good time is revoked for failing to conform to conditions set down for their release (for example, not reporting to a postrelease supervisor or abusing drugs).

good time
Reduction of a prison sentence by a specified amount in exchange for good behavior within the institution.

Structured Sentences

Coinciding with the development of determinate sentencing has been the development of sentencing guidelines to control and structure the process and make it more rational. Guidelines are usually based on the seriousness of a crime and the background of an offender: The more serious the crime and the more extensive the offender's criminal background, the longer the prison term recommended by the guidelines. Guidelines might require that all people convicted of robbery who had no prior offense record and who did not use excessive force or violence be given an average of a five-year sentence; those who used force and had a prior record will have three years added to their sentence. By eliminating judicial discretion, structured sentences are designed to reduce racial and gender disparity.[23]

Within this basic framework are many different approaches to using guidelines. Some coexist with discretionary parole release, whereas others replace parole with mandatory release from prison once the statutory guideline sentence has been fulfilled. Some deal with all crimes and others only with felonies. Some set narrow sentencing ranges, and some set broad ones.[24] Some states provide for a wide range of sentences, whereas others prescribe a narrow range. Some states link use of guidelines to the availability of correctional resources, whereas others do not take resources into account. There are states that address only confinement and those that incorporate a range of intermediate sentencing options. Finally, there are states whose guidelines incorporate an appellate review process for all sentences and those with no appellate review.[25]

THE MINNESOTA GUIDELINES Guidelines can be formulated in a number of ways. One method is to create a grid with prior record and current offense as the two coordinates and then set out specific punishments. Figure 13.3 shows Minnesota's guidelines. As prior record and offense severity increase, so does recommended sentence length. After a certain point, probation is no longer an option, and the defendant must do prison time. A burglar with no prior convictions can expect to receive probation or a 12-month sentence for a house break-in; an experienced burglar with six or more prior convictions can get 30 months for the same crime, and probation is not an option.

If an offender is sent to prison, the sentence consists of two parts: a *term of imprisonment* equal to two-thirds of the total executed sentence and a *supervised release* term equal to the remaining one-third. The amount of time the offender serves in prison may be extended by the commissioner of corrections if the offender violates disciplinary rules while in prison or violates conditions of supervised release. This extension period could result in the offender serving the entire sentence in prison.[26]

Check out the Minnesota Sentencing Guidelines. You can reach them by going to the Siegel/Senna Introduction to Criminal Justice 11e website: www.thomsonedu.com/criminaljustice/siegel.

FIGURE 13.3
Sentencing Guidelines Grid

SEVERITY LEVEL OF CONVICTION OFFENSE (Common offenses listed in italics)		CRIMINAL HISTORY SCORE						
		0	**1**	**2**	**3**	**4**	**5**	**6 or more**
Murder, 2nd Degree (intentional murder; drive-by shootings)	**XI**	306 *261– 367*	326 *278– 391*	346 *295– 415*	366 *312– 439*	386 *329– 463*	406 *346– 480*	426 *363– 480*
Murder, 3rd Degree Murder, 2nd Degree (unintentional murder)	**X**	150 *128– 180*	165 *141– 198*	180 *153– 216*	195 *166– 234*	210 *179– 252*	225 *192– 270*	240 *204– 288*
Criminal Sexual Conduct, 1st Degree [2] *Assault, 1st Degree*	**IX**	86 *74–103*	98 *84–117*	110 *94–132*	122 *104– 146*	134 *114– 160*	146 *125– 175*	158 *135– 189*
Aggravated Robbery, 1st Degree Criminal Sexual Conduct, 2nd Degree (c),(d),(e),(f),(h) [2]	**VIII**	48 *41–57*	58 *50–69*	68 *58–81*	78 *67–93*	88 *75–105*	98 *84–117*	108 *92–129*
Felony DWI	**VII**	36	42	48	54 *46–64*	60 *51–72*	66 *57–79*	72 *62–86*
Criminal Sexual Conduct, 2nd Degree (a) & (b)	**VI**	21	27	33	39 *34–46*	45 *39–54*	51 *44–61*	57 *49–68*
Residential Burglary Simple Robbery	**V**	18	23	33	33 *29–39*	38 *33–45*	43 *37–51*	48 *41–57*
Nonresidential Burglary	**IV**	12[1]	15	18	21	24 *21–28*	27 *23–32*	30 *26–36*
Theft Crimes (More than $2,500)	**III**	12[1]	13	15	17	19 *17–22*	21 *18–25*	23 *20–27*
Theft Crimes ($2,500 or less) Check Forgery ($200–$2,500)	**II**	12[1]	12[1]	13	15	17	19	21 *18–25*
Sale of Simulated Controlled Substance	**I**	12[1]	12[1]	12[1]	13	15	17	19 *17–22*

Presumptive commitment to state imprisonment. First Degree Murder is excluded from the guidelines by law and continues to have a mandatory life sentence. See section II.E. Mandatory Sentences for policy regarding those sentences controlled by law, including minimum periods of supervision for sex offenders released from prison.

Presumptive stayed sentence; at the discretion of the judge, up to a year in jail and/or other non-jail sanctions can be imposed as conditions of probation. However, certain offenses in this section of the grid always carry a presumptive commitment to state prison. See sections II.C. Presumptive Sentence and II.E. Mandatory Sentences.

Source: Minnesota Sentencing Guideline Commission.

FEDERAL GUIDELINES The federal guidelines use a somewhat different cookbook approach to determine sentences. A magistrate must first determine the base penalty that a particular charge is given in the guidelines. For example, the federal guidelines give a base score (20) and mitigation factors for robbery. The base level can be adjusted upward if the crime was particularly serious or violent. Seven points could be added to the robbery base if a firearm was discharged during the crime, or five points if the weapon was simply in the offender's possession. Similarly, points can be added to a robbery if a large amount of money was taken, a victim was injured, a person was abducted or restrained to aid an escape, or the object of the robbery was to steal weapons or drugs. Upward adjustments can also be made if the defendant was a ringleader in the crime, obstructed justice, or used a professional skill or position of trust (such as doctor, lawyer, or politician) to commit the crime. Offenders designated as career criminals by a court can likewise receive longer sentences.

Once the total score is computed, judges determine the sentence by consulting a sentencing table that converts scores into months to be served. Offense levels are set out in the vertical column, and the criminal history (ranging from one to six prior offenses) is displayed in a horizontal column, forming a grid that contains the various sentencing ranges (similar to the Minnesota guideline grid). By matching the applicable offense level and the criminal history, the judge can determine the sentence that applies to the particular offender.

You can read about federal sentencing guidelines by linking through the Siegel/Senna Introduction to Criminal Justice 11e website: www.thomsonedu.com/criminaljustice/siegel.

GUIDELINES EVALUATED Although applauded by some, guidelines have also created controversy. One important criticism is that guidelines are biased against African Americans and Hispanics despite their stated goal of removing discrimination from the sentencing process. One recent research effort found that in some federal jurisdictions, Hispanic defendants are often perceived as "villains" instead of "victims" in drug-trafficking cases and receive sentences that are longer than those given to other minority-group members.[27] The most notorious element of the federal guidelines is the one mandating that the possession of crack cocaine be punished far more severely than possession of powdered cocaine. Critics charge that this amounts to racial bias because African Americans are much more likely to be charged with possessing crack cocaine than Caucasians, who are more commonly charged with possessing powder cocaine.[28] The disparity in sentencing seems ludicrous to critics because there is no pharmacological difference between crack cocaine and powdered cocaine. However, the former can be broken into bits and sold relatively cheaply on the street, whereas the latter is usually bought and sold more discreetly indoors.[29]

Some jurisdictions give enhanced sentences if defendants have a prior juvenile conviction or if they are on juvenile probation or parole at the time of an arrest. African American offenders are more likely than white offenders to have a prior record as a juvenile and therefore receive harsher sentences for their current crime.[30] Some defense attorneys oppose the use of guidelines because they result in longer prison terms, prevent judges from considering mitigating circumstances, and reduce the use of probation. Even the widely heralded federal guidelines have had and will continue to have some dubious effects. The use of probation has diminished and the size of the federal prison population is increasing because guideline sentences are tougher and defendants have little incentive to plea bargain. The guidelines require incarceration sentences for petty offenders who in pre-guideline days would have been given community release. Many of these petty offenders might be better served with cheaper alternative sanctions.[31] Evidence also exists that judges in different courts interpret elements of the guidelines differently—for example, assigning different crime-seriousness scores—so that the effect is to create jurisdictional differences in the way that guidelines are applied.[32]

Legal Challenges

Until recently, some guidelines were *voluntary/advisory sentencing guidelines* (sometimes called descriptive guidelines), which merely suggest rather than mandate sentences to judges. Others were *presumptive sentencing guidelines* (sometimes called prescriptive guidelines), which required judges to use the guidelines to shape their sentencing decisions.[33]

Two recent Supreme Court cases have put a moratorium on the use of presumptive guidelines. First, in *Blakely v. Washington* the Court found that Washington state's sentencing guidelines were a violation of a defendant's Sixth Amendment rights because they allow a judge to consider aggravating factors that would enhance the sentence.[34] The Court ruled that this amounts to a finding of fact without the benefit of a jury trial or personal admission. In *Blakely*, the sentencing judge, acting alone, decided that the offense involved "deliberate cruelty" and enhanced Blakely's sentence. Proving a state of mind such as "deliberate cruelty" must be determined by a jury "beyond a reasonable doubt" and not by a judge applying guidelines. Then, in *United States v. Booker*, the Court ruled that as practiced, the federal guidelines were unconstitutional. The Court ruled that judges should consider the guideline ranges but must also be permitted the right to alter sentences in consideration of other factors; sentences could then be subject to appellate review if they were unreasonable.[35]

These cases did not in essence outlaw guidelines, but required changes in the way they are administered. State and federal courts are now addressing these issues and creating mechanisms for the proper administration of the guidelines, especially if the case involves sentencing enhancement. This work is now ongoing. Since these cases were decided, the future of guidelines seems hazy. However, a recent (2006) report by the Federal Sentencing Commission found that even though federal courts interpreted the *Booker* decision in different ways, the majority of federal cases continue to be sentenced within the range of existing sentencing guidelines. National data show that sentencing in conformance with the sentencing guidelines is 85.9 percent. This conformance rate remained stable throughout the year that followed *Booker*. So even though the guidelines are now advisory rather than mandatory, they still have a great deal of impact on sentencing decisions.[36] Sentencing guidelines are still being used in Minnesota and other states, with modifications being made to how upward adjustments are being used.

Mandatory Sentences

Another effort to limit judicial discretion and at the same time get tough on crime has been the development of the mandatory sentence. For example, some states prohibit people convicted of certain offenses, such as violent crimes, and chronic offenders (recidivists) from being placed on probation. They must serve at least some time in prison. Other statutes bar certain offenders from being considered for parole. Mandatory sentencing legislation may impose minimum and maximum terms, but typically it requires a fixed prison sentence.

Mandatory sentencing generally limits the judge's discretionary power to impose any disposition but that authorized by the legislature. As a result, it limits individualized sentencing and restricts sentencing disparity. Mandatory sentencing provides equal treatment for all offenders who commit the same crime, regardless of age, sex, or other individual characteristics.

More than 35 states have replaced discretionary sentencing with fixed-term mandatory sentences for such crimes as the sale of hard drugs, kidnapping, gun possession, and arson. The results have been mixed. Many offenders who in the past might have received probation are now being incarcerated, helping to increase the size of the correctional population to record levels. Mandatory sentences have also failed to eliminate racial disparity from the sentencing process.[37] Some state courts have ruled such practices unconstitutional.

mandatory sentence
A statutory requirement that a certain penalty be set and carried out in all cases on conviction for a specified offense or series of offenses.

If you'd like to read more on mandatory sentencing, note that the Sentencing Project has news publications and a search engine on its website. You can reach it by going to the Siegel/Senna Introduction to Criminal Justice 11e website: www.thomsonedu.com/criminaljustice/siegel.

Three-Strikes Laws

Three-strikes (and-you're-out) laws provide lengthy terms for any person convicted of three felony offenses. Of those in use, the most well known is California's Penal Code Section 667, a three-strikes law aimed at getting habitual criminals off the street. Anyone convicted of a third felony must do a minimum term of twenty-five years to life; the third felony does not have to be serious or violent. The Federal Crime Act of 1994 also adopted a three-strikes provision, requiring a mandatory life sentence for any offender convicted of three felony offenses; 26 states have so far followed suit and passed some form of the three-strikes law.

Although welcomed by conservatives looking for a remedy for violent crime, the three-strikes policy is controversial because a person convicted of a minor felony can receive a life sentence.

Three-strikes laws have undeniable political appeal to legislators being pressured by their constituents to "do something about crime." Yet even if these laws are possibly effective against crime, any effort to deter criminal behavior through tough laws is not without costs. Criminologist Marc Mauer, a leading opponent of the three-strikes law, finds that the approach may satisfy the public's hunger for retribution but makes little practical sense. First, "three-time losers" are on the brink of aging out of crime; locking them up for life should have little effect on the crime rate. In addition, current sentences for chronic violent offenders are already severe, yet they seem to have had little influence on reducing national violence rates. A three-strikes policy also suffers because criminals typically underestimate their risk of apprehension while overestimating the rewards of crime. Given their inflated view of the benefits of crime, coupled with a seeming disregard of the risks of apprehension and punishment, it is unlikely that a three-strikes policy can have a measurable deterrent effect on the crime rate.

Even if such a policy could reduce the number of career offenders on the street, the drain in economic resources that might have gone for education and social welfare ensures that a new generation of young criminals will fill the offending shoes of their incarcerated brethren. Mauer also suggests that a three-strikes policy will enlarge an already overburdened prison system, driving up costs and, presumably, reducing resources available to house non-three-strikes inmates. Mauer warns too that African Americans face an increased risk of being sentenced under three-strikes statutes, expanding the racial disparity in sentencing. More ominous is the fact that police officers may be put at risk because two-time offenders would violently resist arrest, knowing that they face a life sentence.

Because of its use with petty offenders, there are ongoing legal challenges to the use of three-strikes laws, and their future is still uncertain. However, on March 6, 2003, the U.S. Supreme Court in *Lockyer v. Andrade* upheld the three-strikes sentence of Leandro Andrade, a man sentenced to prison in California for 50 years for stealing $153 worth of videotapes. It also upheld the conviction of Gary Ewing, who appealed a prior 25-year sentence for stealing a set of golf clubs. In both cases the Court ruled that the challenged sentences were not so grossly disproportionate as to violate the Eighth Amendment's prohibition against cruel and unusual punishment.[38] These cases solidified the legality of three-strikes laws.

Truth in Sentencing

Truth-in-sentencing laws, another get-tough measure designed to fight a rising crime rate, require offenders to serve a substantial portion of their prison sentence behind bars.[39] Parole eligibility and good-time credits are restricted or eliminated. The movement was encouraged by the Violent Offender Incarceration and Truth-in-Sentencing Incentive Grants Program, part of the federal government's 1994 Crime Act, which offered funds to support the state costs associated with creating longer sentences. To qualify for federal funds, states must require persons convicted of a violent felony crime to serve not less than 85 percent of the

truth in sentencing
Sentencing reform sponsored by the federal government mandating that any defendant who has pled guilty to or has been found guilty of a felony shall be required to serve a minimum prison term of 85 percent of the sentence imposed by the court.

ThomsonNOW™ Improve your grade on the exam with Personalized Study! For reinforcement resources and a mastery check of sentencing models, go to www.thomsonedu. com/thomsonnow.

prison sentence. Today, more than half the states and the District of Columbia meet the federal Truth-in-Sentencing Incentive Grant Program eligibility criteria. Eleven states adopted truth-in-sentencing laws in 1995, one year after the 1994 Crime Act. To qualify for TIS federal funding, offenders must serve 85 percent of their sentence for qualifying crimes, and today a majority of states qualify for this money.

◆ HOW PEOPLE ARE SENTENCED

The federal government conducts surveys on sentencing practices in state and federal courts.[40] The most recent survey found that more than one million adults are convicted of felonies in a single year. What happens after conviction? About two-thirds (69 percent) of all felons convicted in state courts were sentenced to a period of confinement—41 percent to state prisons and 28 percent to local jails. The remaining third were sentenced to straight probation with no jail or prison time to serve. Felons sentenced to a state prison had an average sentence of 4½ years but were likely to serve only half of that sentence—just 2¼ years—before release. Besides being sentenced to incarceration or probation, 36 percent or more of convicted felons were also ordered to pay a fine, pay victim restitution, receive treatment, perform community service, or comply with some other additional penalty. A fine was imposed on at least 25 percent of convicted felons. As Table 13.2 shows, violent offenders average about 5 years incarceration (about 7 years if sent to prison), and property offenders are typically sentenced to about 2 years (3.5 years if sent to prison).

As Figure 13.4 shows, the number of convicted offenders being sent to prison today is slightly lower than a decade ago, illustrating the increasing popularity of cost-effective community sentencing. As might be expected, people who commit more serious violent crimes are more likely to receive a prison sentence.

What Factors Affect Sentencing?

What factors influence judges when they decide on criminal sentences? Crime seriousness and the offender's prior record are certainly considered. State sentencing codes usually include various factors that can legitimately influence the length of prison sentences, including the following:

◆   The severity of the offense.

◆   The offender's prior criminal record.

TABLE 13.2
Lengths of Felony Sentences Imposed by State Courts

| Most Serious Conviction Offense | Average Maximum Sentence Length (in Months) for Felons Sentenced to: | | | |
| | Incarceration | | | Probation |
	Total	Prison	Jail	
All offenses	36	53	7	38
Violent offenses	62	84	8	43
Property offenses	28	41	7	37
Drug offenses	32	48	6	36
Weapons offenses	28	38	7	35
Other offenses	23	38	6	37

Source: Matthew Durose and Patrick Langan, *Felony Sentences in State Courts, 2002* (Washington, D.C.: Bureau of Justice Statistics, 2004).

♦ Whether the offender used violence.

♦ Whether the offender used weapons.

♦ Whether the crime was committed for money.

Research shows a strong correlation between these legal variables and the type and length of sentence received. For example, judges seem less willing to use discretion in cases involving the most serious criminal charges such as terrorism, but employ greater control in low-severity cases.[41] As Figure 13.5 shows, people with prior convictions are much more likely to receive prison time than those convicted of similar offenses without a prior record.

Besides these legally appropriate factors, sentencing experts suspect that judges may be influenced by the defendant's age, race, gender, and income. Considerations of such variables would be a direct violation of constitutional due process and equal protection, as well as of federal statutes such as the Civil Rights Act. Limiting judicial bias is one of the reasons that states have adopted determinate and mandatory sentencing statutes. Do extralegal factors influence judges when they make sentencing decisions?

FIGURE 13.4

Percentage of Convicted Felons Receiving a Prison Sentence

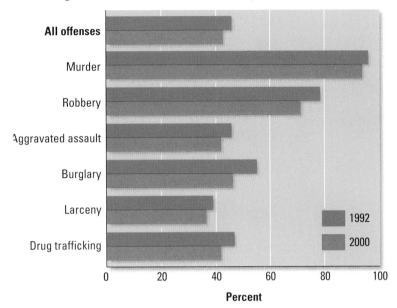

Source: Matthew Durose and Patrick Langan, *Felony Sentences in State Courts, 2002* (Washington, D.C.: Bureau of Justice Statistics, 2004).

JUSTICE CONTEXT There is evidence that the context of justice may influence sentencing outcomes. Judges in courts that have smaller caseloads seem to sentence more severely than judges in larger courts. Similarly, counties that have greater jail capacity seem to send more defendants to jail. The relationship between judge and defendant characteristics may influence sentences: Minority judges tend to be more lenient with minority defendants and are much less likely to incarcerate them than are white judges.[42]

SOCIAL CLASS Evidence supports an association between social class and sentencing outcomes. Members of the lower class may expect to get longer prison sentences than more affluent defendants. One reason is that poor defendants may be unable to obtain quality legal representation or to make bail, factors that influence sentencing.[43]

Not all research efforts have found a consistent class–crime relationship, however, and the relationship may be more robust for some crime patterns than for others.[44]

GENDER Does a defendant's gender influence how he or she is sentenced? Some theorists believe that women benefit from sentence disparity because the criminal justice system is dominated by men who have a paternalistic or protective attitude toward women; this is referred to as the **chivalry hypothesis**. Others argue that female criminals can be the victim of bias because their behavior violates what men believe is proper female conduct.[45]

Most research indicates that women receive more favorable outcomes the further they go in the criminal justice system.[46] They are more likely to receive preferential treatment from a judge at sentencing than they are from the police officer making the arrest or the prosecutor seeking the indictment.[47] Favoritism crosses both racial and ethnic lines, benefiting African American, white, and Hispanic women.[48] Gender bias may be present because judges perceive women as better risks than men. Women have been granted more lenient pretrial release

chivalry hypothesis
The idea that female defendants are treated more leniently in sentencing (and are less likely to be arrested and prosecuted in the first place) because the criminal justice system is dominated by men who have a paternalistic or protective attitude toward women.

FIGURE 13.5

Sentence by Prior Record

Defendants convicted of a violent felony

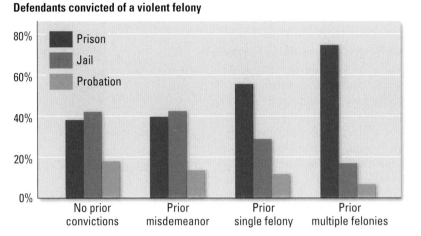

Defendants convicted of a nonviolent felony

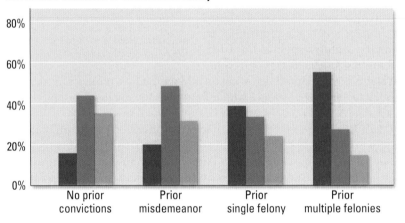

Source: Thomas Cohen and Brian Reaves, *Felony Defendants in Large Urban Counties, 2002*
(Washington, D.C.: Bureau of Justice Statistics, 2006).

conditions and lower bail amounts than men. Women are also more likely to
spend less time in pretrial detention.[49] Women with dependent children are the
ones most likely to receive leniency, probably because judges are reluctant to
incarcerate a child's most essential caregiver.[50]

AGE   Another extralegal factor that may play a role in sentencing is age. Judges
may be more lenient with elderly defendants and more punitive toward younger
ones.[51] Although sentencing leniency may be a result of judges' perception that
the elderly pose little risk to society, such practices are a violation of the civil
rights of younger defendants.[52] However, some judges may wish to protect the
youngest defendants, sparing them the pains of a prison experience.[53]

VICTIM CHARACTERISTICS   Victim characteristics may also influence sentencing. Victims may be asked to make a **victim impact statement** before the sentencing judge. This gives victims an opportunity to tell of their experiences and
describe their ordeal. In the case of a murder trial, the surviving family members
can recount the effect that the crime has had on their lives and well-being.[54] The
effect of victim and witness statements on sentencing has been the topic of some
debate. Some research finds that victim statements result in a higher rate of

victim impact statement
A written statement that
describes the harm or loss
suffered by the victim of an
offense, considered by the court
when the offender is sentenced.

incarceration, but other efforts find that victim and witness statements are insignificant.[55]

A victim's personal characteristics may influence sentencing. Sentences may be reduced when a victim has negative personal characteristics or qualities. For example, rapists whose victims are described as prostitutes or substance abusers or who have engaged in risky behaviors, such as hitchhiking or going to bars alone, receive much shorter sentences than those who assault women without such characteristics.[56] Sentences may also be tailored to the needs of the offender, especially when he has severe psychological deficits. In making the decision, a judge may rely on the opinion of a forensic psychologist, who may be asked to clinically evaluate the defendant before sentencing.

RACE No issue concerning personal factors in sentencing is more important than the suspicion that race influences outcomes. Racial disparity in sentencing has been suspected because a disproportionate number of African American inmates are in state prisons and on death row. The war on drugs has been concentrated in African American communities, and politically motivated punitive sentencing policies aimed at crack cocaine have had a devastating effect on young African American men. If, charges Michael Tonry, such punitive measures are allowed to continue or are even expanded, an entire cohort of young African Americans may be placed in jeopardy.[57] Because this issue is so important, it is the focus of the Race, Gender, and Ethnicity in Criminal Justice feature on page 434.

ThomsonNOW Improve your grade on the exam with Personalized Study! For reinforcement resources and a mastery check of how people are sentenced, go to www.thomsonedu.com/thomsonnow.

♦ CAPITAL PUNISHMENT

The most severe sentence used in the United States is capital punishment, or execution. More than 14,500 confirmed executions have been carried out in America under civil authority, starting with the execution of Captain George Kendall in 1608. Most of these executions were for murder and rape. However, federal, state, and military laws have conferred the death penalty for other crimes, including robbery, kidnapping, treason (offenses against the federal government), espionage, and desertion from military service.

In recent years, the U.S. Supreme Court has limited the death penalty to first-degree murder and only then when aggravating circumstances, such as murder for profit or murder using extreme cruelty, are present.[58] The federal government still has provisions for granting the death penalty for espionage by a member of the armed forces, treason, and killing during a criminal conspiracy, such as drug trafficking. Some states still have laws assessing capital punishment for such crimes as aircraft piracy, ransom kidnapping, and the aggravated rape of a child, but it remains to be seen whether the courts will allow criminals to be executed today for any crime less than aggravated first-degree murder. The death penalty for murder is used in 38 states and by the federal government. However, some states such as New York and Illinois have put moratoriums on the use of the death penalty for legal and other reasons.

In 2005, 60 inmates were executed, 1 more than in 2004. As Figure 13.6 shows, the number of executions has been in decline since 1998–99. The recent (2005)

FIGURE 13.6
Yearly Executions in the United States

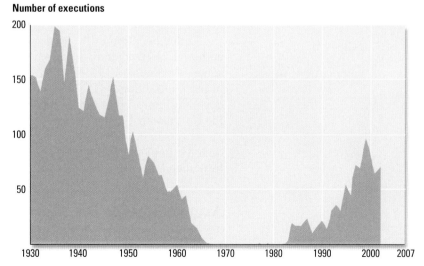

Source: Thomas Bonczar and Tracy Snell, *Capital Punishment, 2004* (Washington, D.C.: Bureau of Justice Statistics, 2005).

Forensic Psychologist

Duties and Characteristics of the Job

Forensic psychologists apply the knowledge and scientific methods from the field of psychology in legal settings. Their skills can be applied to various areas of the justice system, such as evaluation of the mental health of parolees, running inmate mental health programs, and providing counseling to victims. Perhaps the most well-known task of a forensic psychologist is consulting with law enforcement at all levels in order to apprehend criminals. In these cases, the forensic psychologist might create a psychological model of a suspect to predict her behavior.

Forensic psychologists also work in the court system. They often consult with attorneys to assess an individual's mental health to determine how his mental state relates to the trial. For example, they can act as expert witnesses and testify on the extent to which a victim was harmed by the crime, or whether a defendant should be considered mentally sound and able to stand trial. They may help in crafting sentences based on the clinical needs of the criminal defendant. Forensic psychologists are also involved in policy matters, such as reviewing laws and lobbying. They may also conduct research and teach.

Job Outlook

The outlook for employment as a psychologist is good, and the number of employment opportunities is expected to grow in the near future. The recognition of the importance of psychological factors in behavior and functioning is leading to an increasing demand for psychological services from qualified individuals.

Salary

Like other psychologists, a forensic psychologist's mean annual salary is $74,250. The majority of these psychologists make between $51,520 and $93,870 per year. Some will earn around $33,150, but others will earn more than $111,620 per year.

Opportunities

The number of educational institutions that offer graduate programs in forensic science is relatively small, so entry into a program is competitive.

rise in the murder rate may encourage death penalty advocates to lobby for more frequent executions to deter would-be killers.

In 2005, 60 persons in 16 states were executed—19 in Texas; 5 each in Indiana, Missouri, and North Carolina; 4 each in Ohio, Alabama, and Oklahoma; 3 each in Georgia and South Carolina; 2 in California; and 1 each in Connecticut, Arkansas, Delaware, Florida, Maryland, and Mississippi. Of those executed, the overwhelming majority were white (41) and male (59). All were given lethal injections.[59]

Lethal injection is the predominant method of death, although 9 states still authorize electrocution; 4 states, lethal gas; 3 states, hanging; and 3 states, firing squad (see Figure 13.7). All told, there are more than 3,300 people on death row in the United States (Figure 13.8 on page 436). Although the death penalty is generally approved of in the United States, it fares less well abroad, as shown in the International Justice feature on page 438.

No issue in the criminal justice system is more controversial or emotional than the implementation of the death penalty. Opponents and proponents have formulated a number of powerful arguments in support of their positions.

Arguments for the Death Penalty

Supporters have a number of arguments for retaining the death penalty in the United States.

INCAPACITATION Supporters argue that death is the "ultimate incapacitation" and the only one that can ensure that convicted killers can never be pardoned,

Qualifications

The primary qualifier for a position as a forensic psychologist is education. A forensic psychologist will have to gain entrance into a select number of master's or doctorate programs. A master's degree will prepare future forensic psychologists for entry-level work in places such as police departments, prisons and jails, and mental health centers. The two most advanced programs are a doctorate of philosophy of psychology (Ph.D.) and a doctorate of psychology (Psy.D.) in forensic psychology. Students should choose their track based on their interests and future goals.

In some states a forensic psychologist will need to be certified to perform certain jobs. However, many states do not have this requirement, so it is best to check with the state in which one plans to work.

Education and Training

A significant amount of schooling is required for a forensic psychologist. A master's program will prepare future forensic psychologists for entry-level

positions, whereas those who wish to advance will need to earn a doctorate. A forensic psychologist can earn either a Ph.D. or Psy.D. The two programs have two different focuses depending on the career goals of a future forensic psychologist. A doctorate program will primarily prepare students for administrative or management positions in law enforcement and health organizations, and provide services such as mediation and research for organizations. Psy.D. training prepares students for an applied focus in jobs such as providing mental health treatment and being an expert court witness.

Sources: "Forensic Psychology Programs" (Alliant International University, 2004), retrieved from http://www2.alliant.edu/cas/forensic/general.htm; "Psychologists," *Occupational Outlook Handbook*, 2006–2007 edition (Bureau of Labor Statistics, United States Dept of Labor), retrieved June 29, 2006, from http://www.bls.gov/oco/ocos056.htm; "Occupational Employment and Wages, May 2005" (Bureau of Labor Statistics, U.S. Department of Labor), retrieved June 29, 2006, from http://www.bls.gov/oes/current/oes_nat.htm; "Occupational Employment and Wages, May 2005: Psychologists, All Other" (Bureau of Labor Statistics, U.S. Department of Labor), retrieved June 29, 2006, from http://www.bls.gov/oes/current/oes193039.htm.

FIGURE 13.7
Methods of Execution

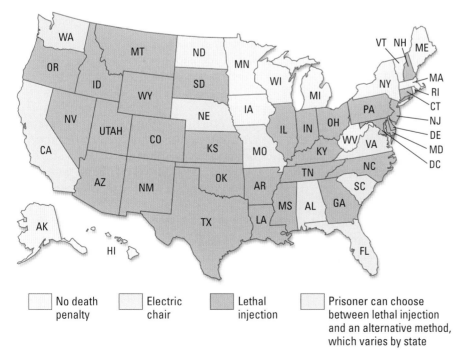

No death penalty   Electric chair   Lethal injection   Prisoner can choose between lethal injection and an alternative method, which varies by state

Source: Death Penalty Information Center.

Race and Criminal Sentencing

Although critics of U.S. race relations may think otherwise, research on sentencing has failed to show a definitive pattern of racial discrimination. Some research does indicate that a defendant's race has a direct impact on sentencing outcomes, but other efforts show that the influence of race on sentencing is less clear-cut than anticipated. It is possible that the disproportionate number of minority-group members in prison is a result of crime and arrest patterns and not racial bias by judges when they hand out criminal sentences; racial and ethnic minorities commit more crime, the argument goes, so they are more likely to constitute a disproportionate share of the prison population.

Why does the critical issue of racial disparity remain so murky? One reason may be that if disparity is a factor in sentencing, its cause might lie outside of judicial sentencing practices. Research efforts show that minority defendants suffer discrimination in a variety of court actions that affect sentencing: They are more likely to be detained before trial than whites and, upon conviction, are more likely to receive jail sentences rather than fines. Prosecutors are less likely to divert minorities from the legal system than whites who commit the same crimes; minorities are less likely to win appeals than are white appellants. Pauline Brennan's research shows that minorities are more likely to receive harsher sentences than whites not because of judicial bias but because of social inequality: Minorities have less money for bail and attorneys, have fewer ties to the community, and are more likely to have a prior record; each of these factors affects sentencing.

It is also possible that some research efforts miss a racial effect because they use invalid measures of race. Some may combine Anglo and Hispanic cases into a single category of "white" defendants and then compare them with the sentencing of black defendants. Darrell Steffensmeier and Stephen Demuth's analysis of sentencing in Pennsylvania found that Hispanics are punished considerably more severely than non-Hispanic Anglos and that combining the two groups masks the ethnic differences in sentencing.

Where Race and Sentencing Collide

The relationship between race and sentencing may be difficult to establish because of external factors that shroud the association. Consider the following.

NONLINEAR ASSOCIATION

Minority defendants may be punished more severely for some crimes and under some circumstances, but they are treated more leniently for others. Sociologist Darnell Hawkins explains this phenomenon as a matter of "appropriateness":

> Certain crime types are considered less "appropriate" for blacks than for whites. Blacks who are charged with committing these offenses will be treated more severely than blacks who commit crimes that are considered more "appropriate." Included in the former category are various white collar offenses and crimes against political and social structures of authority. The latter groups of offenses would include various forms of victimless crimes associated with lower social status (e.g., prostitution, minor drug use, or drunkenness). This may also include various crimes against the person, especially those involving black victims.

Race may have an impact on sentencing because some race-specific crimes are punished more harshly than others. African Americans receive longer sentences for drug crimes than whites because (a) they are more likely to be arrested for crack possession and sales and (b) crack dealing is more severely punished by state and federal laws than other drug crimes. Whites are more likely to use marijuana and methamphetamines, so prosecutors are more willing to plea-bargain and offer shorter jail terms.

THE VICTIM'S RACE

Racial bias has also been linked to victim–offender status. Minority defendants are sanctioned more severely if their victim is white than if their target is a fellow minority-group member; minorities who kill whites are more likely to get the death penalty than those who kill other minorities. Judges may base sentencing decisions on the race of the victim and not the race of the defendant. For example, Charles Crawford, Ted Chiricos, and Gary Kleck found that African American defendants are more likely to be prosecuted under habitual offender statutes if they commit crimes where there is a greater likelihood of a white victim (larceny and burglary) than if they commit violent crimes that are largely intraracial. When there is a perceived "racial threat," punishments are enhanced.

FINANCIAL EFFECTS

Tracy Nobiling, Cassia Spohn, and Miriam DeLone have found that racial status influences sentencing partially because minority-group members have a lower income than whites and are more likely to be unemployed. Judges may possibly view their status as "social dynamite," considering them more dangerous and more likely to recidivate than white offenders.

Being poor also affects sentencing in other ways. Defendants who can afford bail receive more lenient sentences than those who remain in pretrial detention, and minority defendants are less likely to make bail because they suffer a higher degree of income inequality. That is, minorities earn less on average and are therefore less likely to be able to make bail. Sentencing outcome is also affected by the defendant's ability to afford a private attorney and put on a vigorous legal defense that makes use of highly paid expert witnesses. These factors place minority-group members at a disadvantage in the sentencing process and result in sentencing disparity.

The Persistent Problem of Race

Although efforts to limit racial disparity have been ongoing, some studies still find that minorities receive longer sentences and more punitive treatment than white defendants. When Shawn Bushway and Anne Morrison Piehl studied sentencing outcomes in Maryland, they found that, on average, African Americans have 20 percent longer sentences than whites, even when holding constant age, gender, and recommended sentence length. Stephanie Bontrager, William Bales, and Ted Chiricos studied the effect of a Florida law that allows judges to withhold adjudication of guilt for persons who have either pled guilty or been found guilty of a felony in order to shield them from the stigma of a criminal conviction and enable them to retain all their civil rights; the law applies only to persons who will be sentenced to probation. They found that Hispanics and blacks are significantly less likely to have adjudication withheld than whites, especially if they come from a disadvantaged background. So the nagging issue of racial disparity in sentencing still haunts the justice process.

Critical Thinking

Do you believe that sentences should be influenced by the fact that one ethnic or racial group is more likely to commit a particular crime? For example, critics have called for changes in the way that federal sentencing guidelines are designed, asking that the provisions that punish crack possession more heavily than powdered cocaine possession be repealed because African Americans are more likely to use crack and whites powdered cocaine. Do you approve of such a change?

InfoTrac College Edition Research

Use the terms "race" and "sentencing" as key words to find out more about the relationship between these two factors.

Sources: Sara Steen, Rodney Engen, and Randy Gainey, "Images of Danger and Culpability: Racial Stereotyping, Case Processing, and Criminal Sentencing," *Criminology* 43 (2005): 435–68; Stephanie Bontrager, William Bales, and Ted Chiricos, "Race, Ethnicity, Threat and the Labeling of Convicted Felons," *Criminology* 43 (2005): 589–622; Pauline Brennan, "Sentencing Female Misdemeanants: An Examination of the Direct and Indirect Effects of Race/Ethnicity," *Justice Quarterly* 23 (2006): 60–95; Ojmarrh Mitchell, "A Meta-Analysis of Race and Sentencing Research: Explaining the Inconsistencies," *Journal of Quantitative Criminology* 21 (2005): 439–66; Shawn Bushway and Anne Morrison Piehl, "Judging Judicial Discretion: Legal Factors and Racial Discrimination in Sentencing," *Law and Society Review* 35 (2001): 733–65; Barbara Koons-Witt, "The Effect of Gender on the Decision to Incarcerate Before and After the Introduction of Sentencing Guidelines," *Criminology* 40 (2002): 97–129; Marian R. Williams and Jefferson E. Holcomb, "Racial Disparity and Death Sentences in Ohio," *Journal of Criminal Justice* 29 (2001): 207–18; Rodney Engen and Randy Gainey, "Modeling the Effects of Legally Relevant and Extra-legal Factors Under Sentencing Guidelines: The Rules Have Changed," *Criminology* 38 (2000): 1207–30; Darrell Steffensmeier and Stephen Demuth, "Ethnicity and Judges' Sentencing Decisions: Hispanic–Black–White Comparisons," *Criminology* 39 (2001): 145–78; Tracy Nobiling, Cassia Spohn, and Miriam DeLone, "A Tale of Two Counties: Unemployment and Sentence Severity," *Justice Quarterly* 15 (1998): 459–86; Travis Pratt, "Race and Sentencing: A Meta-analysis of Conflicting Empirical Research Results," *Journal of Criminal Justice* 26 (1998): 513–25; Charles Crawford, Ted Chiricos, and Gary Kleck, "Race, Racial Threat, and Sentencing of Habitual Offenders," *Criminology* 36 (1998): 481–511; Jon'a Meyer and Tara Gray, "Drunk Drivers in the Courts: Legal and Extra-legal Factors Affecting Pleas and Sentences," *Journal of Criminal Justice* 25 (1997): 155–63; Darnell Hawkins, "Race, Crime Type and Imprisonment," *Justice Quarterly* 3 (1986): 251–69.

FIGURE 13.8
Persons Under Sentence of Death

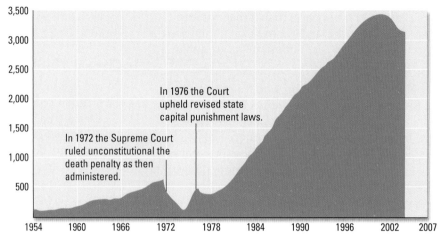

Source: Thomas Bonczar and Tracy Snell, *Capital Punishment, 2004* (Washington, D.C.: Bureau of Justice Statistics, 2005).

be paroled, or escape. Most states that do not have capital punishment provide the sentence of "life in prison without the chance of parole." However, 48 states grant their chief executive the right to grant clemency and commute a life sentence and may give lifers eligibility for various furlough and release programs.

Death penalty advocates believe that the potential for recidivism is a serious enough threat to require that murderers be denied further access to the public. Stephen Markman and Paul Cassell analyzed the records of 52,000 state prison inmates serving time for murder and found that 810 had previously been convicted of homicide and that these recidivists had killed 821 people following their first convictions.[60] More than 250 inmates on death row today have prior homicide convictions. If they had been executed for their first offense, at least 250 innocent people would still be alive.[61]

DETERRENT Proponents of capital punishment argue that executions serve as a strong deterrent for serious crimes. Although capital punishment would probably not deter the few mentally unstable criminals, it could have an effect on the cold, calculating murderer, such as the hired killer or someone who kills for profit. The fear of death may also convince felons not to risk using handguns during armed robberies.

Proponents argue that the deterrent effect of an execution can produce a substantial decline in the murder rate.[62] Some supporters use a commonsense approach, not relying on scientific analysis. They argue, for example, that homicide rates increased dramatically in the 1960s and 1970s, when executions were halted by the courts and death penalty laws were subsequently abolished. Proponents also maintain that even if homicide rates increase after the death penalty is adopted in a state, murder rates may have been much higher if capital punishment had never been legislated.[63]

Other proponents rely on more scientific analysis of data. In one assessment of 16 well-publicized executions, Steven Stack found that they may have saved 480 lives by immediately deterring potential murderers.[64] In a more recent survey, he concluded that well-publicized executions of criminals in California reduced the homicide rate 12 percent during the month of the execution.[65]

MORALLY CORRECT Advocates of capital punishment justify its use on the grounds that it is morally correct because it is mentioned in the Bible and other religious works. Although the U.S. Constitution forbids "cruel and unusual punishments," this prohibition would not include the death penalty because capital punishment was widely used at the time that the Constitution was drafted. The original intent of the Founders was to allow the states to use the death penalty. Capital punishment may be cruel, but it is not unusual.

The death penalty is morally correct because it provides the greatest justice for the victim and helps alleviate the psychic pain of the victim's family and friends. It has even been accepted by criminal justice experts who consider themselves humanists, people who are concerned with the value and dignity of human beings. As the noted humanist David Friedrichs argues, a civilized society has no choice but to hold responsible those who commit horrendous crimes. The death penalty makes a moral statement: Some behavior is so unacceptable to a community of human beings that one who engages in such behavior forfeits his right to live.[66]

PROPORTIONAL Putting dangerous criminals to death also conforms to the requirement that the punishment must be proportional to the seriousness of the crime. Because the United States uses a system of escalating punishments, it follows that the most serious punishment should be used to sanction the most serious crime. Before the brutality of the death penalty is considered, the cruelty with which the victim was treated should not be forgotten.

REFLECTS PUBLIC OPINION Those who favor capital punishment charge that a majority of the public believes that criminals who kill innocent victims should forfeit their own lives. Public opinion polls show that up to 67 percent of the public favors the death penalty, almost double the percentage of 20 years ago (though the numbers have declined somewhat in the last 5 years from a high of 75 percent).[67] Public approval is based on the rational belief that the death penalty is an important instrument of social control, can deter crime, and is less costly than maintaining a murderer in prison for life.[68] The 67-percent approval rating could underestimate public opinion. Research by Alexis Durham and his associates found that almost everyone (95 percent) would give criminals the death penalty under some circumstances, and the most heinous crimes are those for which the public is most likely to approve capital punishment.[69]

UNLIKELY CHANCE OF ERROR The many legal controls and appeals currently in use make it almost impossible for an innocent person to be executed or for the death penalty to be used in a racist or capricious manner. Although some unfortunate mistakes may have been made in the past, the current system makes it virtually impossible to execute an innocent person. Federal courts closely scrutinize all death penalty cases and rule for the defendant in an estimated 60 percent to 70 percent of the appeals. Such judicial care should ensure that only those who are both truly guilty and deserving of death are executed.

In sum, those who favor the death penalty see it as a traditional punishment for serious crimes, one that can help prevent criminality, one that is in keeping with the traditional moral values of fairness and equity, and one that is highly favored by the public.

Arguments Against the Death Penalty

Arguments for the death penalty are matched by those that support its abolition.

POSSIBILITY OF ERROR Critics of the death penalty believe that capital punishment has no place in a mature democratic society.[70] They point to the finality of the act and the real possibility that innocent persons can be executed.

The Death Penalty Abroad

The United States is not alone in using the death penalty, although the trend has been to abolish its use. According to the latest data from watchdog group Amnesty International, over half the countries in the world have now abolished the death penalty in law or practice. Amnesty International's latest information shows the following:

◆ Eighty-six countries and territories have abolished the death penalty for all crimes.

◆ Eleven countries have abolished the death penalty for all but exceptional crimes such as wartime crimes.

◆ Twenty-seven countries can be considered abolitionist in practice: They retain the death penalty in law but have not carried out any executions for the past 10 years or more and are believed to have a policy or established practice of not carrying out executions, making a total of 124 countries that have abolished the death penalty in law or practice.

◆ Seventy-two other countries and territories retain and use the death penalty, but the number of countries that actually execute prisoners in any one year is much smaller.

Progress Toward Worldwide Abolition

Since 1990, more than 40 countries have abolished the death penalty for all crimes. They include countries in Africa (recent examples include Liberia and Côte d'Ivoire), the Americas (Canada, Paraguay, and Mexico), Asia and the Pacific (Bhutan and Samoa), and Europe and Central Asia (Armenia, Bosnia-Herzegovina, Cyprus, Serbia and Montenegro, Turkey, and Turkmenistan).

Moves to Reintroduce the Death Penalty

Once abolished, the death penalty is seldom reintroduced. Since 1985, more than 50 countries have abolished the death penalty in law or, having previously abolished it for ordinary crimes, have gone on to abolish it for all crimes. During the same period only four abolitionist countries have reintroduced the death penalty. One of them—Nepal—has since abolished the death penalty again; one, the Philippines, resumed executions but later stopped. There have been no executions in the other two (Gambia and Papua New Guinea).

Death Sentences and Executions

During 2005, at least 2,148 people were executed in 22 countries, and at least 5,186 people were sentenced to death in 53 countries. These were only minimum figures; the true figures were certainly higher.

In 2005, 94 percent of all known executions took place in China, Iran, Saudi Arabia, and the United States.

Based on the available public reports, Amnesty International estimated that at least 1,770 people were executed in China during the year, although the true figures were believed to be much higher. A Chinese legal expert was recently quoted as stating the

---

Examples of people wrongfully convicted of murder abound. Critics point to miscarriages of justice such as the case of Rolando Cruz and Alejandro Hernandez, who, wrongfully convicted of murder, were released in 1995 after spending more than a decade on death row in the Illinois prison system. Three former prosecutors and four deputy sheriffs who worked on the case were charged with fabricating evidence against the pair.[71] Cruz and Hernandez are certainly not alone. Jeffrey Blake went to prison for a double murder in 1991 and spent seven years behind bars before his conviction was overturned in 1998. The prosecution's star witness conceded that he had lied on the stand, forcing Blake to spend a quarter of his life in prison for a crime he did not commit.[72] These wrongful convictions would have been even more tragic if the defendants had been executed for their alleged crimes. A congressional report cited 48 cases in the past two decades in which people who served time on death row were released because of new evidence proving their innocence. One Maryland man served nine years on death row before DNA testing proved that he could not have committed the crime.[73] These findings show that, even with the best intentions, grave risk exists that an innocent person can be executed.[74] In Illinois, 17 men on death row were freed within the past two decades, causing the governor to impose a moratorium on executions there because of the high number of mistaken convictions.[75]

figure for executions is approximately 8,000, based on information from local officials and judges, but official national statistics on the application of the death penalty remained classified as a state secret.

Iran executed at least 94 people and Saudi Arabia at least 86. There were 60 executions in the United States.

Executions of Juveniles

International human rights treaties prohibit anyone under 18 years old at the time of the crime from being sentenced to death. The International Covenant on Civil and Political Rights, the American Convention on Human Rights, and the U.N. Convention on the Rights of the Child all have provisions to this effect. More than 100 countries have laws specifically excluding the execution of juvenile offenders or may be presumed to exclude such executions by being parties to one or another of the above treaties. However, a small number of countries continue to execute juvenile offenders. Seven countries since 1990 are known to have executed prisoners who were under 18 years old at the time of the crime—Iran, Nigeria, Pakistan, Congo, Saudi Arabia, the United States, and Yemen. Since 1994, there have been 20 executions of juvenile offenders, including 13 in the United States (before the practice was prohibited in 2005).

Critical Thinking

1. The movement toward abolition in the United States is encouraged by the fact that so many nations have abandoned the death penalty. Should we model our own system of punishments after other nations, or is our crime problem so unique that it requires the use of capital punishment?

2. Do you believe that someone who joins a terrorist group and trains to kill Americans deserves the death penalty even if she has never actually killed anyone?

InfoTrac College Edition Research

Are there really innocent people on death row? To find out, read Peter Vilbig, "Innocent on Death Row," *New York Times Upfront*, September 18, 2000, p. 10. The death penalty remains a controversial issue around the world. To learn more, read Stefanie Grant, "A Dialogue of the Deaf? New International Attitudes and the Death Penalty in America," *Criminal Justice Ethics* 17 (1998): 19.

Sources: Amnesty International's most recent data on the death penalty can be found at http://web.amnesty.org/pages/deathpenalty-index-eng, accessed on June 7, 2006; "Nigeria: Stoning Sentence Stands," *New York Times*, September 9, 2002, late edition, p. A6; "Saudi Arabia Executes Man for Sorcery" (Amnesty International Death Penalty News), March 2000; "USA Set to Break a Global Consensus—Execution of Child Offender Due" (Amnesty International News Release), October 22, 2001; "China 'Striking Harder' Than Ever Before" (Amnesty International News Release), June 7, 2001; "Saudi Brothers Beheaded for Raping," *New York Times*, July 20, 2001, p. 3; Larry Rohter, "In Caribbean, Support Growing for Death Penalty," *New York Times*, October 4, 1998; "Chechen Pair Executed in Public," *Boston Globe*, September 19, 1997, p. 9; "Saudi Beheadings Over 100 for 1997," *Boston Globe*, September 28, 1997, p. A29.

According to classic research by Michael Radelet and Hugo Bedeau, about 350 wrongful murder convictions were handed down in the twentieth century, of which 23 led to executions. They estimate that about three death sentences are returned every two years in cases in which the defendant has been falsely accused. More than half the errors stem from perjured testimony, false identifications, coerced confessions, and suppression of evidence. In addition to the 23 who were executed, 128 of the falsely convicted served more than 6 years in prison, 39 served more than 16 years in confinement, and 8 died while serving their sentence.[76] Radelet and Bedeau's view is that even though the system attempts to be especially cautious in capital cases, unacceptable mistakes can occur. Although death penalty sentences are carefully reviewed, relatively few stays of execution are granted (about 2 out of 50). Obviously, there is room for judicial error.[77] Some states have placed a moratorium on executions until the possibility of error can be investigated.

UNFAIR USE OF DISCRETION Critics also frown on the tremendous discretion used in seeking the death penalty and the arbitrary manner in which it is imposed. Of the approximately 10,000 persons convicted each year on homicide charges, only 250 to 300 are sentenced to death, and an equal number receive a sentence of probation or community supervision only. Many convicted

Does capital punishment present ethical problems that make its use morally dubious? Read what the American Civil Liberties Union has to say about this issue. You can access its website by going to the Siegel/Senna Introduction to Criminal Justice 11e website: www.thomsonedu.com/criminaljustice/siegel.

Critics maintain that the death penalty should be abolished because of the possibility of error. Rolando Cruz (right) and friend Doug Cook embrace following a forum at Northwestern University Law School in Chicago. Cruz, who was freed after spending 12 years on death row for a murder he didn't commit, joined his attorneys in speaking at the forum. Such errors convince abolitionists that capital punishment is just too risky.

©AP Images/Beth A. Keiser

www You can get more information about and from the Capital Jury Project by linking through the Siegel/Senna Introduction to Criminal Justice 11e website: www.thomsonedu.com/criminaljustice/siegel.

murderers have not committed first-degree murder and are therefore ineligible for execution, but many serious criminals who could have received the death penalty are not sentenced to death because of prosecutorial discretion. Some escape death by cooperating or giving testimony against their partners in the crime. A person who commits a particularly heinous crime and knows full well that she will receive the death penalty if convicted may be the one most likely to plea bargain to avoid capital punishment. Is it fair to spare the life of a dangerous killer who cooperates with the prosecutor while executing another who does not?

Abolitionists also argue that juries use inappropriate discretion when making capital punishment recommendations. The ongoing Capital Jury Project has been interviewing members of juries involved in making death penalty decisions and finds that many are motivated by ignorance and error. Read more about the project in the Analyzing Criminal Justice Issues feature.

RELIANCE ON PERJURED TESTIMONY Critics fear that prosecutors may rely on perjured testimony in order to get convictions in capital cases. The real criminal may accuse an innocent person or even one of her partners in crime to save her own skin. Some may lie for money or to get a special deal for another crime. Lying is easier in capital cases than in any other type because the victim is dead and unable to dispute the testimony in court.[78]

VICIOUS CRIMINALS OFTEN GOING FREE Some vicious criminals who grievously injure victims during murder attempts are spared the death penalty because a physician's skill saved the victim. Some notable cases come to mind. Lawrence Singleton used an axe to cut off the arms of a woman he raped, yet he served only eight years in prison because the victim's life was saved by prompt medical care. (After being released from prison, Singleton killed a female companion in 1997.) "David," a boy severely burned in a murder attempt, lives in fear because his assailant, his father, Charles Rothenberg, was paroled from prison after serving a short sentence.[79] Although these horrific crimes received national attention and the intent to kill the victim was present, the death penalty could not be applied because of the availability of effective medical treatment. Areas that have superior medical resources have lower murder rates than less well-equipped areas. For example, ambulance response time can reduce the death rate by expeditiously transporting victims to an appropriate treatment center.[80] It makes little sense to punish someone for an impulsive murder while sparing the lives of those who intentionally maim and torture victims who happen by chance to live because of prompt medical care.

MISPLACED VENGEANCE Although critics acknowledge that the general public approves of the death penalty, they maintain that prevailing attitudes reflect a primitive desire for revenge and not just desert. Public acceptance of capital punishment has been compared with the approval of human sacrifices practiced by the Aztecs in Mexico 500 years ago.[81] It is ironic that many death penalty advocates also oppose abortion on the grounds that it is the taking of human life.[82] The desire to be vengeful and punitive outweighs their concern about taking life.

WEAK PUBLIC SUPPORT One reason that we still retain the death penalty is that politicians routinely overestimate public support for capital punishment.[83] Abolitionists claim that public support is not as strong as death penalty advocates believe. When surveys ask about a choice of punishments, such as life without parole, support for the death penalty declines from 80 percent to 50 percent.[84]

The Capital Jury Project

The Capital Jury Project (CJP), begun by sociologist William Bowers in 1990, has sent research teams to 15 states to interview jurors in death penalty cases. The interviews, which run for more than three hours, are taped and coded for analysis.

CJP findings show that the decision making in capital cases often strays from legal and moral guidelines. Some jurors express overwhelming racial prejudice in making their decisions. Others say that they have decided on the punishment before the trial is completed and the defendant is found guilty.

Others are confused about the law and are influenced by factual misconceptions. For example, many believe that prison terms are far shorter than they are, and many underestimate the time served for murder by 10 years or more. Many jurors mistakenly believe that the death penalty is mandatory in cases in which it is not, and others reject capital punishment in situations in which the law clearly mandates its use. The greater the factual errors, however, the most likely the juror will vote for death.

Many capital jurors are unwilling to accept primary responsibility for their punishment decisions. They vote for the death penalty in the mistaken belief that most defendants will never be executed, absolving them of responsibility. They often place responsibility for the defendant's punishment elsewhere, such as with the judge or other jurors. For example, one female juror who had recommended death told CJP interviewers that she had voted only to go along with the other jurors and that she had never believed the man should be executed. "I really had no thought about it," she said. "It wasn't my choice to make. It was a judgment call. It really doesn't mean a whole lot what I say because it's ultimately up to the judge." These feelings were most often expressed in states where the law allows judges to override a jury's decisions and either impose or reject a capital sentence.

Recent research by Wanda Foglia on CJP data from Pennsylvania found that many jurors made up their minds before the sentencing stage and were confused by or misunderstood judicial instructions. Most admitted discussing the death penalty during jury deliberations before the defendant was even found guilty. Some based their decisions on legally irrelevant concepts, such as whether the defendant would be dangerous in the future. Disturbingly, many jurors seem to make more than one error in their decision making. They misunderstand the judge, ignore relevant facts, underestimate life sentences, and make up their minds without considering all the evidence.

Critical Thinking

The Capital Jury Project clearly shows that instead of being a precise and objective decision-making process, the imposition of the death penalty is often a legal crapshoot. Considering this finding, would you advocate that the death penalty be abolished? Or, considering the right to appeal and to have the case reviewed by an appellate court, would you advocate that capital punishment be retained?

InfoTrac College Edition Research

To read more about how capital jurists make their decisions, go to Margaret Gonzalez-Perez, "A Model of Decisionmaking in Capital Juries," *International Social Science Review* (Fall–Winter 2001): 79.

Sources: Wanda Foglia, "They Know Not What They Do: Unguided and Misguided Discretion in Pennsylvania Capital Cases," *Justice Quarterly* 20 (2003): 187–212; William J. Bowers, "The Capital Jury Project: Rationale, Design, and Preview of Early Findings," *Indiana Law Journal* 70 (1995): 1043–1102; William J. Bowers, Marla Sandys, and Benjamin Steiner, "Foreclosed Impartiality in Capital Sentencing: Jurors' Predispositions, Guilt Trial Experience, and Premature Decision Making," *Cornell Law Review* 83 (1998): 1476–1556; Margaret Vandiver, "Race in the Jury Room: A Preliminary Analysis of Cases from the Capital Jury Project," paper presented to the American Academy of Criminal Justice Sciences, March 1997.

Public opinion is influenced by such factors as the personal characteristics of the offender and the circumstances of the offense. Therefore, the public does not support death in many cases of first-degree murder.[85] There are also race-based divisions for the use of capital punishment: Although whites support its use, it is far less popular in the minority community.[86]

NO DETERRENT EFFECT Those opposed to the death penalty also find little merit in the argument that capital punishment deters crime. They charge that insufficient evidence exists that the threat of a death sentence can convince potential murderers to forgo their criminal activity. Most murders involve people who knew each other, very often friends and family members. Given that murderers are frequently under the influence of alcohol or drugs at the time of the crime or are suffering severe psychological turmoil, no penalty will likely be a deterrent. Most research concludes that the death penalty is not an effective deterrent.[87] For example, Keith Harries and Derral Cheatwood studied differences in homicide rates in 293 contiguous counties within the United States and found higher violent crime rates in counties that routinely employed the death penalty than in those in which the use of the death penalty was rare.[88]

HOPE OF REHABILITATION The death sentence also rules out any hope of offender rehabilitation. Evidence indicates that convicted killers make good parole risks. Convicted murderers are model inmates and, once released, commit fewer crimes than other parolees. The general public, including people who sit on juries, could be overestimating the dangerousness of people who commit murder. One recent study found that capital jurors predicted an 85-percent likelihood that the defendant would commit a future violent crime and a 50-percent likelihood that the defendant would commit a new homicide if he had been given a sentence of life imprisonment. In reality, those people given a life sentence for capital murder have a less than 1-percent (0.2-percent) chance of committing another homicide over a 40-year term. The risk of their committing an assault is about 16 percent.[89]

RACIAL, GENDER, AND OTHER BIAS Capital punishment may be tarnished by gender, racial, and ethnic and other biases. Evidence suggests that homicides with male offenders and female victims are more likely to result in a death sentence than homicides involving female offenders and male victims.[90] Homicides involving strangers are more likely to result in a death sentence than homicides involving nonstrangers and acquaintances.

Prosecutors are more likely to recommend the death sentence for people who kill white victims than they are in any other racial combination of victim and criminal—for example, whites who kill blacks.[91] Not surprisingly, since the death penalty was first instituted in the United States, a disproportionate number of minorities have been executed. Charges of racial bias are supported by the disproportionate numbers of African Americans who have received the death sentence, are currently on death row, and who have been executed (53.5 percent of all executions). Although white victims account for approximately one-half of all murder victims, 81 percent of all capital cases involve white victims. Furthermore, as of October 2002, 12 people have been executed in cases in which the defendant was white and the murder victim black, compared with 178 black defendants executed for murders with white victims.[92]

Racism was particularly blatant when the death penalty was invoked in rape cases. Of those receiving the death penalty for rape, 90 percent in the South and 63 percent in the North and West were black.[93] Today, about 40 percent of the inmates on death row are African Americans, a number disproportionate to their representation in the population.

CAUSES MORE CRIME THAN IT DETERS Some critics fear that the introduction of capital punishment will encourage criminals to escalate their violent behavior, consequently putting police officers at risk. For example, a suspect who kills someone during a botched robbery may be inclined to fire away upon encountering police rather than surrender peacefully. The killer faces the death penalty already, so what does he have to lose? Geoffrey Rapp studied the effect of capital punishment on the killings of police and found that, all other things being equal, the greater number of new inmates on death row, the greater the number of police officers killed by citizens.[94] Rapp concludes that the death penalty seems to create an extremely dangerous environment for law enforcement officers because it does not deter criminals and it may lull officers into a false sense of security. They come to believe that the death penalty will deter violence directed against them, which causes them to let down their guard.

BRUTALITY Abolitionists believe that executions are unnecessarily cruel and inhuman and come at a high moral and social cost. U.S. society does not punish criminals by subjecting them to the same acts they themselves committed. Rapists are not sexually assaulted, and arsonists do not have their house burned down. Why, then, should murderers be killed?

Robert Johnson has described the execution process as a form of torture in which the condemned are first tormented psychologically by being made to feel powerless and alone while on death row. Suicide is a constant problem among those on death row.[95] The execution itself is a barbaric affair marked by the smell of burning flesh and stiffened bodies. The executioners suffer from delayed stress reactions, including anxiety and a dehumanized personal identity.

The brutality of the death penalty may produce more violence than it prevents—the so-called **brutalization effect**.[96] Executions may increase murder rates because they raise the general violence level in society and because violence-prone people identify with the executioner, not with the target of the death penalty. When someone gets in a conflict with such individuals or challenges their authority, he executes them in the same manner the state executes people who violate its rules.[97] The brutalization effect was encountered by John Cochran and his associates when they studied the influence of a well-publicized execution in Oklahoma. After the execution, murders of strangers increased by one per month.[98] Follow-up research by William Bailey finds that the brutalization effect extends to other types of murder (for example, nonstranger murder) and that a vicarious brutalization effect may occur in which people in a state that does not practice capital punishment are influenced by news reports of executions in death penalty states.[99]

Because of its brutality, many enlightened nations have abandoned the death penalty with few ill effects. Abolitionists point out that such nations as Denmark and Sweden abandoned the death penalty long ago and that 40 percent of the countries with a death penalty have active abolitionist movements.[100] Ironically, citizens of countries that have eliminated the death penalty sometimes find themselves on death row in the United States. For example, a Paraguayan citizen, Angel Francisco Breard, age 32, was executed in Virginia, for murder and attempted rape, despite a plea from the International Court of Justice that he be spared and intense efforts by the Paraguayan government to stay the execution.[101]

EXPENSE Some people complain that they do not want to support "some killer in prison for 30 years." Abolitionists counter that legal appeals drive the cost of executions far higher than the cost of years of incarceration. If the money spent on the judicial process were invested, the interest would more than pay for the lifetime upkeep of death row inmates. For example, a study of 508 men and 9 women on death row in California found that because of numerous appeals, the median time between conviction by a jury, sentencing by a judge, and execution was 14 years. The cost of processing appeals is extremely costly, and the annual budget for the state's public defender staff of 45 lawyers who represent inmates in death cases is $5 million.[102]

At least 30 states now have a sentence of life in prison without parole, and this can more than make up for an execution. Being locked up in a hellish prison without any chance of release (barring a rare executive reprieve) may be a worse punishment than a quick death by lethal injection. If vengeance is the goal, life without parole may eliminate the need for capital punishment.

Legal Issues in Capital Punishment

The constitutionality of the death penalty has been a major concern to both the nation's courts and its social scientists. In 1972 the U.S. Supreme Court, in

brutalization effect
The belief that capital punishment creates an atmosphere of brutality, reinforces the view that violence is an appropriate response to provocation, and thus encourages rather than deters the criminal use of violence.

The Supreme Court has banned the death penalty for the mentally challenged. But sometimes the line defining normal intelligence is hard to draw. Death row inmate Travis Walters, 23, is shown at Central Prison in Raleigh, North Carolina. Walters received federal disability payments for mental retardation from age 13 until police say he walked into a Lumberton, North Carolina fast-food restaurant in 1998 and shot a supervisor in the head. Although a judge originally ruled that Walters was not retarded, a recent appellate court case took Walters off death row.

©AP Images/The Charlotte Observer/Jeff Siner

Furman v. Georgia,[103] decided that the discretionary imposition of the death penalty was cruel and unusual punishment under the Eighth and Fourteenth amendments of the Constitution. The Supreme Court did not completely rule out the use of capital punishment as a penalty; rather, it objected to the arbitrary and capricious manner in which it was imposed. After *Furman*, many states changed statutes that had allowed jury discretion in imposing the death penalty. Then, in July 1976, the Supreme Court ruled on the constitutionality of five state death penalty statutes. In the first case, *Gregg v. Georgia*,[104] the Court found valid the Georgia statute holding that a finding by the jury of at least one "aggravating circumstance" out of ten is required in pronouncing the death penalty in murder cases. In the Gregg case, for example, the jury imposed the death penalty after finding beyond a reasonable doubt two aggravating circumstances: (1) the offender was engaged in the commission of two other capital felonies, and (2) the offender committed the offense of murder for the purpose of receiving money and other financial gains (for example, an automobile).[105] The Gregg case signaled the return of capital punishment as a sentencing option.

The Court, by allowing the death penalty, has implied that it cannot be barred by the Eighth Amendment's rule against "cruel and unusual punishments." However, in a recent case, *Hill v. McDonough* (2006), the Court gave a death row inmate the opportunity to appeal his sentence on the grounds that the method now used to give a lethal injection may cause severe pain that is constitutionally unacceptable.[106] Although the case hinged on a technicality, it opens the door for an eventual Eighth Amendment challenge to lethal injections.

Although the Court has generally supported the death penalty, it has also placed some limitations on its use. The Court's rulings have promoted procedural fairness in the capital sentencing process. In *Ring v. Arizona*, the Court found that juries, not judges, must make the critical findings that send convicted killers to death row. The Court reasoned that the Sixth Amendment's right to a jury trial would be "senselessly diminished" if it did not allow jurors to decide whether a person deserves the death penalty.[107] The Court has also limited who may be eligible for death:

1. The Court has limited the crimes for which the death penalty can be employed, ruling, for example, that it is not permissible to punish rapists with death.[108] Only people who commit intentional or felony murder may be executed.

2. People who are mentally ill may not be executed.[109] In a 2002 case, *Atkins v. Virginia*, the Court ruled that execution of mentally retarded criminals is "cruel and unusual punishment" prohibited by the Eighth Amendment.[110]

3. In *Roper v. Simmons* (2005), the Court set a limit of 18 years as the age of defendants who could be sentenced to death.[111] The Court said that executing people for crimes they committed as young teens violates "the evolving standards of decency that mark the progress of a maturing society" and that U.S. society regards juveniles as less responsible than adult criminals. Although 19 states had allowed the execution of juvenile murderers prior to *Simmons*, only Texas, Virginia, and Oklahoma have executed any in the past decade.

DEATH-QUALIFIED JURIES One area of interest is the **death-qualified jury**, in which any person opposed in concept to capital punishment is removed during voir dire. Defense attorneys are opposed to death qualification because it bars from serving on juries those citizens who oppose the death penalty and who may be more liberal and less likely to convict defendants. Death qualification creates juries that are nonrepresentative of the 20 percent of the public that opposes capital punishment.

> **death-qualified jury**
> A jury formed to hear a capital case, with any person opposed in principle to capital punishment automatically excluded.

In *Witherspoon v. Illinois* (1968), the Supreme Court upheld the practice of excusing jurors who are opposed to the death penalty.[112] The Court has made it easier to convict people in death penalty cases by ruling that jurors can be excused if their views on capital punishment are deemed by a trial judge to "prevent or substantially impair the performance of their duties."[113] The Court has also ruled that jurors can be removed because of their opposition to the death penalty at the guilt phase of a trial, even though they would not have to consider the issue of capital punishment until a separate sentencing hearing. In *Lockhart v. McCree* (1986), the Court also ruled that removing anti–capital punishment jurors does not violate the Sixth Amendment provision that juries represent a fair cross section of the community and does not unfairly tip the scale toward juries that are prone to convict people in capital cases.[114] So it appears that, for the present, prosecutors will be able to excuse jurors who feel that the death penalty is wrong or immoral.

RACIAL BIAS In one of the most important death penalty cases, *McKlesky v. Kemp*, the Court upheld the conviction of a black defendant in Georgia, despite social science evidence that black criminals who kill white victims have a significantly greater chance of receiving the death penalty than white offenders who kill black victims. The Court ruled that the evidence of racial patterns in capital sentencing was not persuasive without a finding of racial bias in the specific case in question.[115] Many observers believe that *McKlesky* presented the last significant legal obstacle that death penalty advocates had to overcome and that, as a result, capital punishment will be a sentence in the United States for years to come. (Warren McKlesky was executed in 1991.)

Although the Court was not swayed by charges of racial bias in the decision to prosecute, it has ruled that jury selection cannot be tainted by racial bias. In 2003 the Court ruled against selecting biased juries in the case of *Miller-El v. Cockrell*. Thomas Miller-El, who is an African American, was convicted of capital murder and sentenced to death in 1986. He appealed, arguing that prosecutors excluded African Americans from the jury in Dallas County, Texas. The lower courts refused to consider his claim. The Supreme Court disagreed, noting that the prosecution had used its peremptory challenge to eliminate

91 percent of the eligible African Americans. Also, the stated reasons given by the prosecutor for eliminating the African American jurors—ambivalence about the death penalty, hesitancy to vote to execute defendants capable of being rehabilitated, and the jurors' own family history of criminality—applied to some white jurors who were not challenged and who did serve on the jury. The Court noted that the prosecutor used underhanded techniques to limit or eliminate African Americans (the so-called Texas shuffle) and used disparate questioning of potential jurors based on race. Furthermore, a memo instructed prosecutors to eliminate jurors based on race, religion, and ethnic background.[116]

Does the Death Penalty Deter Murder?

The key issue in the capital punishment debate is whether it can lower the murder rate and save lives. Despite its inherent cruelty, capital punishment might be justified if it proved to be an effective crime deterrent that could save many innocent lives. Abolitionists claim it has no real deterrent value; advocates claim it does. Who is correct?

Considerable empirical research has been carried out on the effectiveness of capital punishment as a deterrent. In particular, studies have tried to discover whether the death sentence serves as a more effective deterrent than life imprisonment for capital crimes such as homicide. Three methods have been used:

1. Immediate-impact studies, which calculate the effect a well-publicized execution has on the short-term murder rate.

2. Time-series analysis, which compares long-term trends in murder and capital punishment rates.

3. Contiguous-state analysis, which compares murder rates in states that have the death penalty with murder rates of a similar state that has abolished capital punishment.

Using these three methods over a 60-year period, most researchers have failed to show any deterrent effect of capital punishment.[117] These studies show that murder rates do not seem to rise when a state abolishes capital punishment any more so than they decrease when the death penalty is adopted. The murder rate is also similar both in states that use the death penalty and neighboring states that have abolished capital punishment. Finally, little evidence shows that executions can lower the murder rate. For example, a test of the deterrent effect of the death penalty in Texas found no association between the frequency of execution during the years 1984–1997 and murder rates.[118]

Only a few studies have found that the long-term application of capital punishment may reduce the murder rate.[119] However, these have been disputed by researchers who have questioned the methodology used and indicate that the deterrent effects that the studies uncover are an artifact of the statistical techniques used in the research.[120]

The general consensus among death penalty researchers today is that the threat of capital punishment has little effect on murder rates. It is still unknown why capital punishment fails as a deterrent, but the cause may lie in the nature of homicide. Murder is often a crime of passion involving people who know each other, and many murders are committed by people under the influence of drugs and alcohol—more than 50 percent of all people arrested for murder test positive for drug use. People involved in interpersonal conflict with friends, acquaintances, and family members and who may be under the influence of drugs and alcohol are not likely to be capable of considering the threat of the death penalty.

Murder rates have also been linked to the burdens of poverty and income inequality. Desperate adolescents who get caught up in the cycle of urban violence and become members of criminal groups and gangs may find that their life situation gives them little choice except to engage in violent and deadly behavior. They have few chances to ponder the deterrent impact of the death penalty.

The failure of the "ultimate deterrent" to deter the "ultimate crime" has been used by critics to question the value of capital punishment.

Despite the less than conclusive empirical evidence, many people still hold to the efficacy of the death penalty as a crime deterrent, and recent U.S. Supreme Court decisions seem to justify its use. Even if the death penalty were no greater a deterrent than a life sentence, some people would still advocate its use on the grounds that it is the only way to permanently rid society of dangerous criminals who deserve to die.

ThomsonNOW Improve your grade on the exam with Personalized Study! For reinforcement resources and a mastery check of capital punishment, go to www.thomsonedu.com/thomsonnow.

ETHICAL CHALLENGES IN CRIMINAL JUSTICE: A WRITING ASSIGNMENT

Carla B. is a 36-year-old white female convicted of killing her husband of 12 years, Jack B., a wealthy and prominent attorney. The police report shows that in order to inherit his substantial trust fund, Carla gave her husband a large dose of a sleeping sedative and, when he felt uncomfortable and dizzy, offered to take him to the emergency room at the local hospital. After he passed out in the car, she slid the comatose man into the driver's seat and then rolled the vehicle down an embankment. After watching the car burst into flames, she walked to her own car, which she had hidden earlier, and drove home. When police came to report the accident, she told the officers that Jack had gone to get some groceries, and she was wondering why he had taken so long. At first, she expressed shock over his death and burst into tears. Later, forensic evidence and an eyewitness to the event helped investigators unravel her plot.

The investigators found that Carla suspected her husband was going to divorce her because he had discovered that she was having an extramarital affair with her tennis instructor. Carla had incurred large debts and bank loans, which she kept secret from her husband, because she had been buying gifts for her young paramour. These included leasing a new car and putting a down payment on a condo. Carla had a taste for luxury and travel but few occupational skills, which made divorce out of the question.

This is Carla's first conviction. She is a highly educated woman with a degree in French literature from an Ivy League university. She comes from a loving and devoted family. Her parents and sisters, though in shock, are willing to stand beside her. She has two young children who are currently living with relatives; they also seem devoted to their mother. She has done charitable work and is well liked. She has no prior history of violence or mental instability. Psychiatric reports show that she is unlikely to commit further crimes.

At the sentencing hearing, Carla is filled with remorse and states that her greed overcame her reasoning. She is currently on a suicide watch at the county jail because she has told her counselor that she "does not deserve to live"; her anguish seems genuine.

As the sentencing judge, her fate is solely in your hands. You can recommend death, life in prison, a prison sentence, or even probation. State law requires that you provide a written document stating the reasons for your sentencing decision. Please state them here.

Doing Research on the Web

Before you write your essay, you may want to look at the following websites:

1. Amnesty International: The Death Penalty
2. The Capital Jury Project
3. The Death Penalty Information Center: Costs of the Death Penalty

You can link to all of these sites by going to the Siegel/Senna Introduction to Criminal Justice 11e website: www.thomsonedu.com/criminaljustice/siegel.

SUMMARY

◆ Punishment and sentencing have gone through various phases throughout the history of Western civilization.

◆ Initially, punishment was characterized by retribution and the need to set sentences for convicted offenders. The prison developed as a place of reform.

◆ At the end of the nineteenth century, individualized sentencing was created and became widely accepted. The concept of rehabilitation was used to guide sentencing.

◆ During the 1970s, experts began to become disenchanted with rehabilitation and concepts related to treating the individual offender. There was less emphasis on treatment and more on the legal rights of offenders. A number of states returned to the concept of punishment in terms of mandatory and fixed sentences.

◆ The philosophy of sentencing has thus changed from a concentration on rehabilitation to a focus on incapacitation and deterrence, where the goal is to achieve equality of punishment and justice in the law and to lock up dangerous criminals for as long as possible.

◆ Sentencing in today's criminal justice system is primarily based on deterrence, incapacitation, retribution, and rehabilitation. Traditional dispositions include fines, probation, and incarceration, with probation being the most common choice.

◆ Although sentences are getting shorter and fewer people are sent to prison per crime, people are serving a greater proportion of their sentences than they did a decade ago. Consequently, prison populations are not dropping despite a decrease in the crime rate.

◆ Most states use indeterminate sentences, which give convicted offenders a short minimum sentence after which they can be released on parole if they are considered rehabilitated.

◆ A number of states have developed determinate sentences, which eliminate parole and attempt to restrict judicial discretion so that convicted criminals are given a single sentence that they must serve without parole.

◆ Efforts have been made to control judicial discretion and reduce sentencing disparity. Methods for making dispositions more uniform include sentencing guidelines that create uniform sentences based on offender background and crime characteristics.

◆ Jurisdictions that use either determinate or indeterminate sentences also allow inmates to be released early on good behavior.

◆ Social and personal factors continue to influence sentencing. Some evidence suggests that young males, especially if they are members of a minority group, are more likely to receive longer sentences than older, Caucasian females.

◆ The death penalty continues to be the most controversial sentence, with more than half the states reinstituting capital punishment laws since the 1972 *Furman v. Georgia* decision.

◆ Although little evidence exists that the death penalty deters murder, supporters still view it as necessary in terms of incapacitation and retribution and cite the public's support for the death penalty and the low chance of error in its application.

◆ Opponents point out that mistakes can be made, that capital sentences are apportioned in a racially biased manner, and that the practice is cruel and barbaric.

◆ Nonetheless, the courts have generally supported the legality of capital punishment, and it has been used more frequently in recent years.

◆ The death penalty is used abroad, though it has been abolished in many nations.

KEY TERMS

sanctions, 416
punishment, 416
poor laws, 416
penitentiary, 417
general deterrence, 417
incapacitation, 418
recidivism, 419
specific deterrence, 419

blameworthy, 419
just desert, 419
felony, 420
wergild, 420
equity, 420
consecutive sentence, 421
concurrent sentence, 421
indeterminate sentence, 422

determinate sentence, 422
good time, 423
mandatory sentence, 426
truth in sentencing, 427
chivalry hypothesis, 429
victim impact statement, 430
brutalization effect, 443
death-qualified jury, 445

ThomsonNOW Maximize your study time by using ThomsonNOW's diagnostic study plan to help you review this chapter. The Study Plan will

♦ help you identify areas on which you should concentrate;

♦ provide interactive exercises to help you master the chapter concepts; and

♦ provide a post-test to confirm you are ready to move on to the next chapter.

CRITICAL THINKING QUESTIONS

1. Discuss the sentencing dispositions in your jurisdiction. What are the pros and cons of each?

2. Compare the various types of incarceration sentences. What are the similarities and differences? Why are many jurisdictions considering the passage of mandatory sentencing laws?

3. Discuss the issue of capital punishment. In your opinion, does it serve as a deterrent? What new rulings has the U.S. Supreme Court made on the legality of the death penalty?

4. Why does the problem of sentencing disparity exist? Do programs exist that can reduce disparate sentences? If so, what are they? Should all people who commit the same crime receive the same sentence? Explain.

5. Should convicted criminals be released from prison when correctional authorities are convinced they are rehabilitated? Why or why not?

NOTES

1. Nick Madigan, "Man Accused of Killing Girl in California Postpones Plea," *New York Times*, July 22, 2002, p. 1.
2. Michel Foucault, *Discipline and Punish* (New York: Vintage, 1978).
3. Graeme Newman, *The Punishment Response* (Philadelphia: Lippincott, 1978), p. 13.
4. Peter Greenwood with Allan Abrahamse, *Selective Incapacitation* (Santa Monica, Calif.: RAND, 1982).
5. Kathleen Auerhahn, "Selective Incapacitation and the Problem of Prediction," *Criminology* 37 (1999): 703–34.
6. Kathleen Daly, "Neither Conflict Nor Labeling Nor Paternalism Will Suffice: Intersections of Race, Ethnicity, Gender, and Family in Criminal Court Decisions," *Crime and Delinquency* 35 (1989): 136–68.
7. Among the most helpful sources for this section are Benedict Alper, *Prisons Inside-Out* (Cambridge, Mass.: Ballinger, 1974); Gustave de Beaumont and Alexis de Tocqueville, *On the Penitentiary System in the United States and Its Applications in France* (Carbondale: Southern Illinois University Press, 1964); Orlando Lewis, *The Development of American Prisons and Prison Customs, 1776–1845* (Montclair, N.J.: Patterson-Smith, 1967); Leonard Orland, ed., *Justice, Punishment, and Treatment* (New York: Free Press, 1973); J. Goebel, *Felony and Misdemeanor* (Philadelphia: University of Pennsylvania Press, 1976); George Rusche and Otto Kircheimer, *Punishment and Social Structure* (New York: Russell and Russell, 1939); Samuel Walker, *Popular Justice* (New York: Oxford University Press, 1980); Newman, *The Punishment Response*; David Rothman, *Conscience and Convenience* (Boston: Little, Brown, 1980); George Ives, *A History of Penal Methods* (Montclair, N.J.: Patterson-Smith, 1970); Robert Hughes, *The Fatal Shore* (New York: Knopf, 1986); Leon Radzinowicz, *A History of English Criminal Law*, vol. 1 (London: Stevens, 1943), p. 5.
8. *Crime and Punishment in America, 1999*, Report 229 (Washington, D.C.: National Center for Policy Analysis, 1999).
9. Ibid.
10. Tomislav Kovandzic and Lynne Vieraitis, "The Effect of County-Level Prison Population Growth on Crime Rates," *Criminology & Public Policy* 5 (2006): 213–44.
11. Raymond Liedk, Anne Morrison Piehl, and Bert Useem, "The Crime-Control Effect of Incarceration: Does Scale Matter?" *Criminology & Public Policy* 5 (2006): 245–76.
12. Christopher D. Maxwell, Joel H. Garner, and Jeffrey A. Fagan, *The Effects of Arrest in Intimate Partner Violence: New Evidence from the Spouse Assault Replication Program* (Washington, D.C: National Institute of Justice, 2001); Robert Davis, Barbara Smith, and Laura Nickles, "The Deterrent Effect of Prosecuting Domestic Violence Misdemeanors," *Crime and Delinquency* 44 (1998): 434–42.
13. Patrick Langan and David Levin, *Recidivism of Prisoners Released in 1994* (Washington, D.C.: Bureau of Justice Statistics, 2002).
14. Charles Logan, *Criminal Justice Performance Measures for Prisons* (Washington, D.C.: Bureau of Justice Statistics, 1993), p. 3.
15. Alexis Durham, "The Justice Model in Historical Context: Early Law, the Emergence of Science, and the Rise of Incarceration," *Journal of Criminal Justice* 16 (1988): 331–46.
16. Andrew von Hirsh, *Doing Justice: The Choice of Punishments* (New York: Hill and Wang, 1976).
17. Shawn Bushway, "The Impact of an Arrest on the Job Stability of Young White American Men," *Journal of Research in Crime and Delinquency* 35 (1998): 454–79.
18. Charles Logan and Gerald Gaes, "Meta-Analysis and the Rehabilitation of Punishment," *Justice Quarterly* 10 (1993): 245–64.
19. Richard McCorkle, "Research Note: Punish and Rehabilitate? Public Attitudes Toward Six Common Crimes," *Crime and Delinquency* 39 (1993): 240–52; D. A. Andrews, Ivan Zinger, Robert Hoge, James Bonta, Paul Gendreau, and Francis Cullen, "Does Correctional Treatment Work? A Clinically Relevant and Psychologically Informed Meta-analysis," *Criminology* 28 (1990): 369–404.
20. Francis Cullen, John Paul Wright, Shayna Brown, Melissa Moon, and Brandon Applegate, "Public Support for Early Intervention Programs: Implications for a Progressive Policy Agenda," *Crime and Delinquency* 44 (1998): 187–204.
21. Lawrence W. Sherman, David P. Farrington, Doris Layton MacKenzie, Brandon Walsh, Denise Gottfredson, John Eck, Shawn Bushway, and Peter Reuter, *Evidence-Based Crime*

Prevention (London: Routledge and Kegan Paul, 2002). See also Arnulf Kolstad, "Imprisonment as Rehabilitation: Offenders' Assessment of Why It Does Not Work," *Journal of Criminal Justice* 24 (1996): 323–35.

22. Paula M. Ditton and Doris James Wilson, *Truth in Sentencing in State Prisons* (Washington, D.C.: Bureau of Justice Statistics, 1999).

23. Jo Dixon, "The Organizational Context of Criminal Sentencing," *American Journal of Sociology* 100 (1995): 1157–98.

24. Ibid.

25. Robin Lubitz and Thomas Ross, *Sentencing Guidelines: Reflections on the Future* (Washington, D.C.: National Institute of Justice, June 2001).

26. Ibid.

27. Lisa Pasko, "Villain or Victim: Regional Variation and Ethnic Disparity in Federal Drug Offense Sentencing," *Criminal Justice Policy Review* 13 (2002): 307–28.

28. Michael Tonry, "Racial Politics, Racial Disparities, and the War on Crime," *Crime and Delinquency* 40 (1994): 475–94.

29. Louis F. Oberdorfer, "Mandatory Sentencing: One Judge's Perspective, 2002," *American Criminal Law Review* 40 (2003): 11–19.

30. Joan Petersilia and Susan Turner, *Guideline-Based Justice: The Implications for Racial Minorities* (Santa Monica, Calif.: RAND, 1985).

31. Elaine Wolf and Marsha Weissman, "Revising Federal Sentencing Policy: Some Consequences of Expanding Eligibility for Alternative Sanctions," *Crime and Delinquency* 42 (1996): 192–205.

32. Paula Kautt, "Location, Location, Location: Interdistrict and Intercircuit Variation in Sentencing Outcomes for Federal Drug-Trafficking Offenses," *Justice Quarterly* 19 (2002): 633–72.

33. Michael Tonry, *Reconsidering Indeterminate and Structured Sentencing Series: Sentencing and Corrections: Issues for the 21st Century* (Washington, D.C.: National Institute of Justice, 1999).

34. *Blakely v. Washington*, 124 S.Ct. 2531 (2004).

35. *United States v. Booker*, No. 04–104, decided January 12, 2005.

36. United States Sentencing Commission, *Final Report on the Impact of* United States v. Booker *on Federal Sentencing, March 2006* (http://www.ussc.gov/booker_report/Booker_Report.pdf), accessed on June 19, 2006.

37. Henry Scott Wallace, "Mandatory Minimums and the Betrayal of Sentencing Reform: A Legislative Dr. Jekyll and Mr. Hyde," *Federal Probation* 57 (1993): 9–16.

38. *Lockyer v. Andrade*, 538 U.S. 63 (2003), 270 F.3d 743; *Ewing* v. *California*, 538 U.S. 11 (2003).

39. Ditton and Wilson, *Truth in Sentencing in State Prisons.*

40. Matthew Durose and Patrick Langan, *Felony Sentences in State Courts, 2002* (Washington, D.C.: Bureau of Justice Statistics, 2004).

41. Brent Smith and Kelly Damphouse, "Terrorism, Politics, and Punishment: A Test of Structural–Contextual Theory and the Liberation Hypothesis," *Criminology* 36 (1998): 67–92.

42. Brian Johnson, "The Multilevel Context of Criminal Sentencing: Integrating Judge- and County-Level Influences," *Criminology* 44 (2006): 259–98.

43. For a general look at the factors that affect sentencing, see Susan Welch, Cassia Spohn, and John Gruhl, "Convicting and Sentencing Differences Among Black, Hispanic, and White Males in Six Localities," *Justice Quarterly* 2 (1985): 67–80.

44. Stewart D'Alessio and Lisa Stolzenberg, "Socioeconomic Status and the Sentencing of the Traditional Offender," *Journal of Criminal Justice* 21 (1993): 61–77.

45. Cecilia Saulters-Tubbs, "Prosecutorial and Judicial Treatment of Female Offenders," *Federal Probation* 57 (1993): 37–41.

46. Fernando Rodriguez, Theodore Curry, and Gang Lee, "Gender Differences in Criminal Sentencing: Do Effects Vary Across Violent, Property, and Drug Offenses?" *Social Science Quarterly* 87 (2006): 318–39.

47. Janet Johnston, Thomas Kennedy, and I. Gayle Shuman, "Gender Differences in the Sentencing of Felony Offenders," *Federal Probation* 87 (1987): 49–56; Cassia Spohn and Susan Welch, "The Effect of Prior Record in Sentencing Research: An Examination of the Assumption That Any Measure Is Adequate," *Justice Quarterly* 4 (1987): 286–302; David Willison, "The Effects of Counsel on the Severity of Criminal Sentences: A Statistical Assessment," *Justice System Journal* 9 (1984): 87–101.

48. Cassia Spohn, Miriam DeLone, and Jeffrey Spears, "Race/Ethnicity, Gender and Sentence Severity in Dade County, Florida: An Examination of the Decision to Withhold Adjudication," *Journal of Crime and Justice* 21 (1998): 111–32.

49. Ellen Hochstedler Steury and Nancy Frank, "Gender Bias and Pretrial Release: More Pieces of the Puzzle," *Journal of Criminal Justice* 18 (1990): 417–32.

50. Barbara Koons-Witt, "The Effect of Gender on the Decision to Incarcerate Before and After the Introduction of Sentencing Guidelines," *Criminology* 40 (2002): 97–129.

51. Dean Champion, "Elderly Felons and Sentencing Severity: Interregional Variations in Leniency and Sentencing Trends," *Criminal Justice Review* 12 (1987): 7–15.

52. Darrell Steffensmeier, John Kramer, and Jeffery Ulmer, "Age Differences in Sentencing," *Justice Quarterly* 12 (1995): 583–601.

53. Darrell Steffensmeier, Jeffery Ulmer, and John Kramer, "The Interaction of Race, Gender, and Age in Criminal Sentencing: The Punishment Cost of Being Young, Black, and Male," *Criminology* 36 (1998): 763–98.

54. *Payne v. Tennessee*, 111 S.Ct. 2597, 115 L.Ed.2d 720 (1991).

55. Robert Davis and Barbara Smith, "The Effects of Victim Impact Statements on Sentencing Decisions: A Test in an Urban Setting," *Justice Quarterly* 11 (1994): 453–69; Edna Erez and Pamela Tontodonato, "The Effect of Victim Participation in Sentencing on Sentence Outcome," *Criminology* 28 (1990): 451–74.

56. Rodney Kingsworth, Randall MacIntosh, and Jennifer Wentworth, "Sexual Assault: The Role of Prior Relationship and Victim Characteristics in Case Processing," *Justice Quarterly* 16 (1999): 276–302.

57. Michael Tonry, *Malign Neglect: Race, Crime, and Punishment in America* (New York: Oxford University Press, 1995), 105–09.

58. *Coker v. Georgia*, 433 U.S. 584, 97 S.Ct. 2861, 53 L.Ed.2d 982 (1977).

59. Thomas Bonczar and Tracy Snell, *Capital Punishment, 2004* (Washington, D.C.: Bureau of Justice Statistics, 2005).

60. Stephen Markman and Paul Cassell, "Protecting the Innocent: A Response to the Bedeau–Radelet Study," *Stanford Law Review* 41 (1988): 121–70.

61. Thomas Bonczar and Tracy Snell, *Capital Punishment 2002* (Washington, D.C.: Bureau of Justice Statistics, 2003), p. 2.

62. Stephen Layson, "United States Time-Series Homicide Regressions with Adaptive Expectations," *Bulletin of the New York Academy of Medicine* 62 (1986): 589–619.

63. James Galliher and John Galliher, "A 'Commonsense' Theory of Deterrence and the 'Ideology' of Science: The New York State Death Penalty Debate," *Journal Criminal Law and Criminology* 92 (2002): 307.

64. Steven Stack, "Publicized Executions and Homicide, 1950–1980," *American Sociological Review* 52 (1987): 532–40. For a study challenging Stack's methods, see William Bailey and Ruth Peterson, "Murder and Capital Punishment: A Monthly Time-Series Analysis of Execution Publicity," *American Sociological Review* 54 (1989): 722–43.

65. Steven Stack, "The Effect of Well-Publicized Executions on Homicide in California," *Journal of Crime and Justice* 21 (1998): 1–12.

66. David Friedrichs, "Comment—Humanism and the Death Penalty: An Alternative Perspective," *Justice Quarterly* 6 (1989): 197–209.

67. Kathleen Maguire and Ann L. Pastore, eds., *Sourcebook of Criminal Justice Statistics* (2002) (http://www.albany.edu/sourcebook), accessed on November 13, 2003.

68. For an analysis of the formation of public opinion on the death penalty, see Kimberly Cook, "Public Support for the 428 Part Three Courts and Adjudication Death Penalty: A Cultural Analysis," paper presented at the annual meeting of the American Society of Criminology, San Francisco, November 1991.

69. Alexis Durham, H. Preston Elrod, and Patrick Kinkade, "Public Support to the Death Penalty: Beyond Gallup," *Justice Quarterly* 13 (1996): 705–36.

70. Hugo Bedeau, *Death Is Different: Studies in the Morality, Law, and Politics of Capital Punishment* (Boston: Northeastern University Press, 1987); Keith Otterbein, *The Ultimate Coercive Sanction* (New Haven, Conn.: HRAF, 1986).

71. "Illinois Ex-Prosecutors Charged with Framing Murder Defendants," *Criminal Justice Newsletter* 28 (1997): 3.

72. Jim Yardley, "Convicted in Murder Case, Man Cleared 7 Years Later," *New York Times*, October 29, 1998, p. A3.

73. House Subcommittee on Civil and Constitutional Rights, *Innocence and the Death Penalty: Assessing the Danger of Mistaken Executions* (Washington, D.C.: Government Printing Office, 1993).

74. David Stewart, "Dealing with Death," *American Bar Association Journal* 80 (1994): 53.

75. Editorial, "The Innocence Protection Act," *America* 187 (September 23, 2002): 2–3.

76. Michael Radelet and Hugo Bedeau, "Miscarriages of Justice in Potentially Capital Cases," *Stanford Law Review* 40 (1987): 121–81.

77. Stewart, "Dealing with Death."

78. Samuel Gross, "The Risks of Death: Why Erroneous Convictions Are Common in Capital Cases," *Buffalo Law Review* 44 (1996): 469–500.

79. "A Victim's Progress," *Newsweek*, June 12, 1989, p. 5.

80. William Doerner, "The Impact of Medical Resources on Criminally Induced Lethality: A Further Examination," *Criminology* 26 (1988): 171–77.

81. Elizabeth Purdom and J. Anthony Paredes, "Capital Punishment and Human Sacrifice," in *Facing the Death Penalty: Essays on Cruel and Unusual Punishment*, ed. Michael Radelet (Philadelphia: Temple University Press, 1989), pp. 152–53.

82. Kimberly Cook, "A Passion to Punish: Abortion Opponents Who Favor the Death Penalty," *Justice Quarterly* 15 (1998): 329–46.

83. John Whitehead, Michael Blankenship, and John Paul Wright, "Elite Versus Citizen Attitudes on Capital Punishment: Incongruity Between the Public and Policy Makers," *Journal of Criminal Justice* 27 (1999): 249–58.

84. Kathleen Maguire and Ann Pastore, *Sourcebook of Criminal Justice Statistics, 1995* (Washington, D.C.: Government Printing Office, 1996), p. 183.

85. Gennaro Vito and Thomas Keil, "Elements of Support for Capital Punishment: An Examination of Changing Attitudes," *Journal of Crime and Justice* 21 (1998): 17–25.

86. John Cochran and Mitchell B. Chamlin, "The Enduring Racial Divide in Death Penalty Support," *Journal of Criminal Justice* 34 (2006): 85–99.

87. William Bowers and Glenn Pierce, "Deterrence or Brutalization: What Is the Effect of Executions?" *Crime and Delinquency* 26 (1980): 453–84.

88. Keith Harries and Derral Cheatwood, *The Geography of Executions: The Capital Punishment Quagmire in America* (Lanham, Md.: Rowman and Littlefield, 1997).

89. Jonathan R. Sorensen and Rocky L. Pilgrim, "An Actuarial Risk of Assessment of Violence Posed by Murder Defendants," *Journal of Criminal Law and Criminology* 90 (2000): 1251–71.

90. Marian Williams and Jefferson Holcomb, "Racial Disparity and Death Sentences in Ohio," *Journal of Criminal Justice* 29 (2001): 207–18.

91. Jon Sorenson and Danold Wallace, "Prosecutorial Discretion in Seeking Death: An Analysis of Racial Disparity in the Pretrial Stages of Case Processing in a Midwestern County," *Justice Quarterly* 16 (1999): 559–78.

92. Data from the American Civil Liberties Union website (http://www.aclu.org/capital/unequal/10389pub20030226.html), accessed on August 14, 2003.

93. Lawrence Greenfield and David Hinners, *Capital Punishment, 1984* (Washington, D.C.: Bureau of Justice Statistics, 1985).

94. Geoffrey Rapp, "The Economics of Shootouts: Does the Passage of Capital Punishment Laws Protect or Endanger Police Officers?" *Albany Law Review* 65 (2002): 1051–84.

95. Robert Johnson, *Death Work: A Study of the Modern Execution Process* (Pacific Grove, Calif.: Brooks/Cole, 1990).

96. William Bailey, "Disaggregation in Deterrence and Death Penalty Research: The Case of Murder in Chicago," *Journal of Criminal Law and Criminology* 74 (1986): 827–59.

97. Gennaro Vito, Pat Koester, and Deborah Wilson, "Return of the Dead: An Update on the Status of *Furman*-Commuted Death Row Inmates," in *The Death Penalty in America: Current Research*, ed. Robert Bohm (Cincinnati: Anderson, 1991), pp. 89–100; Gennaro Vito, Deborah Wilson, and Edward Latessa, "Comparison of the Dead: Attributes and Outcomes of *Furman*-Commuted Death Row Inmates in Kentucky and Ohio," in *The Death Penalty in America: Current Research*, ed. Robert Bohm (Cincinnati: Anderson, 1991), pp. 101–12.

98. John Cochran, Mitchell Chamlin, and Mark Seth, "Deterrence or Brutalization? An Impact Assessment of Oklahoma's Return to Capital Punishment," *Criminology* 32 (1994): 107–34.

99. William Bailey, "Deterrence, Brutalization, and the Death Penalty: Another Examination of Oklahoma's Return to Capital Punishment," *Justice Quarterly* 36 (1998): 711–34.

100. Joseph Schumacher, "An International Look at the Death Penalty," *International Journal of Comparative and Applied Criminal Justice* 14 (1990): 307–15.

101. David Stout, "Clemency Denied, Paraguayan Is Executed," *New York Times*, April 15, 1998, p. A2.

102. Don Terry, "California Prepares for Faster Execution Pace," *New York Times*, October 17, 1998, p. A7.

103. *Furman v. Georgia*, 408 U.S. 238, 92 S.Ct. 2726, 33 L.Ed.2d 346 (1972).

104. *Gregg v. Georgia*, 428 U.S. 153, 96 S.Ct. 2909, 49 L.Ed.2d 859 (1976).

105. Ibid., at 205–207, 96 S.Ct. at 2940–2941.

106. *Hill v. McDonough*, No. 05–8794 (2006).

107. *Ring v. Arizona*, No. 01–488 (2002).

108. *Coker v. Georgia*, 430 U.S. 349, 97 S.Ct. 1197, 51 L.Ed.2d 393 (1977).

109. *Ford v. Wainwright*, 477 U.S. 399 (1986).

110. *Atkins v. Virginia*, No. 00–8452 (2002).

111. *Roper v. Simmons*, No. 03–0633 (2005).

112. *Witherspoon v. Illinois*, 391 U.S. 510, 88 S.Ct. 1770, 20 L.Ed.2d 776 (1968).

113. *Wainwright v. Witt*, 469 U.S. 412, 105 S.Ct. 844, 83 L.Ed.2d 841 (1985).

114. *Lockhart v. McCree*, 476 U.S. 162, 106 S.Ct. 1758, 90 L.Ed.2d 137 (1986).

115. *McKlesky v. Kemp*, 428 U.S. 262, 96 S.Ct. 2950, 49 L.Ed.2d 929 (1976).

116. *Miller-El v. Cockrell, Director, Texas Department of Criminal Justice, Institutional Division*, No. 01–7662, decided February 25, 2003.

117. Walter C. Reckless, "Use of the Death Penalty," *Crime and Delinquency* 15 (1969): 43; Thorsten Sellin, "Effect of Repeal and Reintroduction of the Death Penalty on Homicide Rates," in *The Death Penalty*, ed. Thorsten Sellin (Philadelphia: American Law Institute, 1959); Robert H. Dann, "The Deterrent Effect of Capital Punishment," *Friends Social Service Series* 29 (1935): 1; William Bailey and Ruth Peterson, "Murder and Capital Punishment: A Monthly Time-Series Analysis of Execution Publicity," *American Sociological Review* 54 (1989): 722–43; David Phillips, "The Deterrent Effect of Capital Punishment," *American Journal of Sociology* 86

(1980): 139–48; Sam McFarland, "Is Capital Punishment a Short-Term Deterrent to Homicide? A Study of the Effects of Four Recent American Executions," *Journal of Criminal Law and Criminology* 74 (1984): 1014–32; Richard Lempert, "The Effect of Executions on Homicides: A New Look in an Old Light," *Crime and Delinquency* 29 (1983): 88–115.

118. Jon Sorenson, Robert Wrinkle, Victoria Brewer, and James Marquart, "Capital Punishment and Deterrence: Examining the Effect of Executions on Murder in Texas," *Crime and Delinquency* 45 (1999): 481–93.

119. Isaac Ehrlich, "The Deterrent Effect of Capital Punishment: A Question of Life or Death," *American Economic Review* 65 (1975): 397.

120. For a review, see William Bailey, "The General Prevention Effect of Capital Punishment for Non-Capital Felonies," in *The Death Penalty in America: Current Research*, ed. Robert Bohm (Cincinnati: Anderson, 1991), pp. 21–38.

Corrections

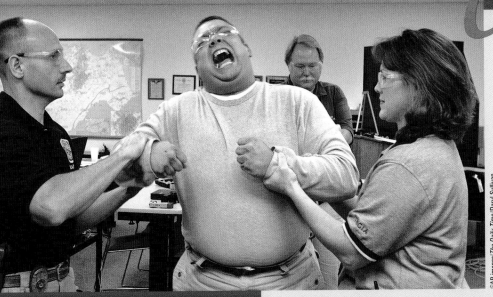

PART FOUR

©AP images/*The Daily Time*/Daryl Sullivan

Could an enlightened nation such as the United States be subduing correctional inmates with painful jolts of electricity? Hard to believe, but the use of stun belts, which deliver up to 50,000 volts of electricity, has become a somewhat routine practice in U.S. correctional institutions. Critics of the practice, such as Amnesty International, have called for the abolition of the device, which they view as a form of torture. Although the use of stun belts may be troubling to some, the correctional system has also developed restorative programs that seek to reintegrate the offender back into society with a minimum of coercion and harm. ◆

THE CONTEMPORARY correctional system, which controls and treats more than four million people, is immense and intricate. The chapters in this section attempt to describe its operations, philosophies, and programs. Chapter 14 looks at community sentences such as probation, alternative sanctions, and restorative justice. Chapters 15 and 16 cover secure correctional institutions, including prisons and jails. A number of important issues are analyzed, ranging from the development of new-generation jails to the reentry of prisoners into society.

CHAPTER 14

Community Sentences: Probation, Intermediate Sanctions, and Restorative Justice

Chapter Outline

Chapter Objectives

After reading this chapter, you should be able to:
1. Understand the concept of community sentencing.
2. Know how probation developed.
3. Recognize the different types of probation sentences.
4. Identify the rules of probation.
5. Discuss the issue of probation revocation.
6. Describe the effectiveness of probation.
7. Understand the concept of alternative sanctions.
8. Know the various alternative sanctions, from fines to community incarceration.
9. Describe the concept of the punishment ladder.
10. Explain the principles of restorative justice.
11. Discuss the challenges faced by restorative justice.
12. List the various types of restorative justice programs in use.

*F*lorida teacher Debra Lafave (shown in the picture) made headlines when she was accused of having had a sexual affair with one of her 14-year-old students. After a plea arrangement fell through, prosecutors decided not to pursue criminal charges. Lafave's risque behavior made national headlines, but it was certainly not unique; there have been numerous incidents involving sexual activity between teachers and younger students that have received far less publicity and media attention. One case that fell under the radar involved Elizabeth Stow, an English and reading teacher at Western High School in Tulare, California, who on April 4, 2005, was arrested on charges that she had had sexual relations with underage students.[1]

In June of that year she accepted a nolo contendere plea and was sentenced to a 29-condition probation term of 5 years. As part of the sentence, she was required to serve 364 days in jail, perform community service, and pay restitution fines. Stow and her sentence received mixed reactions from the people involved. As the judge in the case stated during the sentencing hearing, "You were the adult. You were the teacher. You were the role model. You let us down." Not surprisingly, her attorney defended the sentence: "She held a position of trust. She violated that. I won't sugar coat that, but it would have been a shame if she was sentenced to prison." The prosecutor saw things differently: "It sends a horrible message. It chips away at the security of schools."

In addition to her having to spend part of her sentence behind bars, Stow's probation also required that she do the following:

♦ Not have unsupervised, intentional contact with children under 18.

♦ Not have contact with any of the victims.

♦ Stay away from the schools the victims attend or the homes where they live.

♦ Complete a six-month outpatient counseling program.

- ◆ *Seek placement in a substance abuse program. If told she doesn't need one, the judge wants a written explanation.*

- ◆ *Read a 147-page teacher sexual misconduct code.*

- ◆ *Prepare a teaching curriculum to avoid teacher–student sexual relationships.*

- ◆ *Pay restitution for any of the victims' counseling.*

- ◆ *Send letters of apology to the victims and their families.*

- ◆ *Abstain from possession of pornographic material.*

- ◆ *Not obtain a post office box without the permission of the probation department.* ◆

These cases illustrate the difficulty of reaching appropriate sentences in the criminal justice system. Although some people may believe that they should have been sentenced to a long prison term, others felt that their exposure and humiliation were punishment enough. Stow's treatment, in particular, reflects the evolution of punishment, which has produced the widespread use of community sentencing, including probation, alternative sanctions, and restorative justice.

The core value of community sentencing is that many convicted in criminal courts are deserving of a second chance; most present little threat to society. If they can be reintegrated into the community and given the proper treatment, they are unlikely to recidivate. Considering these circumstances, it seems foolish to incarcerate them in an overcrowded and dangerous prison system, which inmates describe as "criminal universities" where deviant identities are reinforced.[2] It may be both more effective and less costly to have them remain in the community under the supervision of a trained court officer where they can receive treatment that will help them turn their lives around. Rehabilitation would be aided immensely if those who commit crimes could be made to understand the problems that their actions caused their family, friends, and community.

Considering the potential benefits and cost-effectiveness of a community sentence, it is not surprising that the number of community sentences is at an all-time high. There are now a great variety of community sentences, including traditional probation and probation plus (also called **alternative sanctions** or **intermediate sanctions**), which typically involves probation and a fine, forfeiture, restitution, shock probation, split sentencing, intensive probation supervision (IPS), house arrest, electronic monitoring (EM), or residential community corrections (RCC). These programs are designed to provide greater control over an offender and to increase the level of sanction without resorting to a prison sentence. In addition, restorative justice programs are being implemented that involve offenders in new forms of treatment typically designed to reintegrate them back into society.

Both traditional probation and the newer forms of community sentences have the potential to become reasonable alternatives to many of the economic and social problems faced by correctional administrators. They are less costly than jail or prison sentences, they help the offender maintain family and community ties, they can be structured to maximize security and maintain public safety, they can be scaled in severity to correspond to the seriousness of the crime, and they can feature restoration and reintegration instead of punishment and ostracism. No area of the criminal justice system is undergoing more change and greater expansion than community sentencing.

alternative sanctions
Community sentences featuring probation as well as additional requirements such as restitution, fines, home confinement, or electronic monitoring, designed to provide more control and sanctions than traditional probation but less than secure incarceration in jail or prison.

intermediate sanctions
A group of punishments falling between probation and prison—community-based sanctions including house arrest and intensive supervision.

◆ THE HISTORY OF PROBATION

The roots of probation can be traced back to the traditions of English common law. During the Middle Ages, judges wishing to spare deserving offenders from the pains of the then commonly used punishments of torture, mutilation, and death used their power to grant clemency and stays of execution. The common-law practice of **judicial reprieve** allowed judges to suspend punishment so that convicted offenders could seek a pardon, gather new evidence, or demonstrate that they had reformed their behavior. Similarly, the practice of **recognizance** enabled convicted offenders to remain free if they agreed to enter into a debt obligation with the state. The debt would have to be paid only if the offender was caught engaging in further criminal behavior. **Sureties** were sometimes required—these were people who made themselves responsible for the behavior of an offender after he was released.

Early U.S. courts continued the practice of indefinitely suspending sentences of criminals who seemed deserving of a second chance, but it was John Augustus of Boston who is usually credited with originating the modern probation concept.[3] As a private citizen, Augustus began in 1841 to supervise offenders released to his custody by a Boston judge. Over an 18-year period, Augustus supervised approximately 2,000 probationers and helped them get jobs and establish themselves in the community. Augustus had an amazingly high success rate, and few of his charges became involved in crime again.

In 1878 Augustus's work inspired the Massachusetts legislature to pass a law authorizing the appointment of a paid probation officer for the city of Boston. In 1880 probation was extended to other jurisdictions in Massachusetts, and by 1898 the probation movement had spread to the superior (felony) courts.[4] The Massachusetts experience was copied by Missouri (1887), by Vermont (1898), and soon after by most other states. In 1925 the federal government established a probation system for the U.S. district courts. The probation concept soon became the most widely used correctional mechanism in the United States.[5]

◆ PROBATION TODAY

Preserving Augustus's vision, the philosophy of probation today rests on the assumption that the typical offender is not actually a dangerous criminal or a menace to society but someone who has the ability and potential to reform. If offenders are institutionalized instead of being granted community release, the prison community becomes their new reference point; they are forced to interact with hardened criminals, and the "ex-con" label prohibits them from making successful adjustments to society.

Why Probation?

Probation provides offenders with the opportunity to prove themselves, gives them a second chance, and allows them to be closely supervised by trained personnel who can help them reestablish proper forms of behavior in the community. Even dangerous offenders who might normally be sent to a penal institution can be successfully rehabilitated in the community if given the proper balance of supervision, treatment, and control.

Probation is a criminal sentence mandating that a convicted offender be placed and maintained in the community under the supervision of a duly authorized agent of the court. Once on probation, the offender is subject to certain rules and conditions that must be followed. The probation sentence is managed by a probation department that supervises the offender's behavior and treatment

judicial reprieve
In medieval England, a judge's suspension of punishment, enabling a convicted offender to seek a pardon, gather new evidence, or demonstrate reformed behavior.

recognizance
The medieval practice of letting convicted offenders remain free if they agreed to enter a debt relation with the state to pay for their crimes.

sureties
During the Middle Ages, people who made themselves responsible for people given release or a reprieve.

probation
A sentence entailing the conditional release of a convicted offender into the community under the supervision of the court (in the form of a probation officer), subject to certain conditions for a specified time.

Rehabilitation and Noninterventionism

Probation is at the heart of both the rehabilitation perspective and the noninterventionist perspective. It rests on the assumption that the average offender is not a dangerous criminal or a menace to society and can be rehabilitated without further risk to the community. When offenders are institutionalized, the prison community becomes their new reference point. They are forced to interact with hardened criminals, and the "ex-con" label prohibits them from making successful adjustments to society. Probation provides offenders with the opportunity to prove themselves, gives them a second chance, and allows them to be closely supervised by trained personnel who can help them re-establish proper forms of behavior in the community.

revocation

Removing a person from probation (or parole) in response to a violation of law or of the conditions of probation (or parole).

Probation is not unique to the United States. Read about probation in England at the website of the Probation Service—South Yorkshire. To reach this website, go to the Siegel/Senna Introduction to Criminal Justice 11e website: www.thomsonedu.com/criminaljustice/siegel.

and carries out other tasks for the court. Although the term has many meanings, probation usually indicates a nonpunitive form of sentencing for convicted criminal offenders and delinquent youth, emphasizing maintenance in the community and treatment without institutionalization or other forms of punishment.

Probation is not limited to minor or petty criminals. A significant proportion of people convicted of felony offenses receive probation, including about 4 percent of murderers and 16 percent of rapists.[6]

Probation usually involves suspension of the offender's sentence in return for the promise of good behavior in the community under the supervision of the probation department. As practiced in all 50 states and by the federal government, probation implies a contract between the court and the offender in which the former promises to hold a prison term in abeyance while the latter promises to adhere to a set of rules or conditions mandated by the court. If the rules are violated, and especially if the probationer commits another criminal offense, probation may be revoked. **Revocation** means that the contract is terminated and the original sentence is enforced. If an offender on probation commits a second offense that is more serious than the first, she may also be indicted, tried, and sentenced on the second offense. However, probation may be revoked simply because the rules and conditions of probation have not been met; it is not necessary for an offender to commit another crime.

Each probationary sentence is for a fixed period of time, depending on the seriousness of the offense and the statutory law of the jurisdiction. Probation is considered served when offenders fulfill the conditions set by the court for that period of time. They can then live without state supervision.

Awarding Probation

Probationary sentences may be granted by state and federal district courts and state superior (felony) courts. In some states, juries may recommend probation if the case meets certain legally regulated criteria (for example, if it falls within a certain class of offenses as determined by statute). Even in those jurisdictions that allow juries to recommend probation, judges have the final say in the matter

A judge may impose special conditions of probation depending on the circumstances of the case. Here, Kevin Kelly looks back toward his family as he waits for his sentencing hearing to begin at the Prince William County Courthouse in Manassas, Virginia. Kelly, a father of 13 who allowed his youngest daughter to die in a sweltering van, was given probation, but will spend one night in jail every February 21st for the next seven years. Kelly was convicted of involuntary manslaughter and reckless endangerment. Passers-by found Frances Kelly, 21 months, strapped into her car seat inside the family's van, which was parked at their Manassas home.

©AP Images/*Mansfield News Journal*/Dave Polcyn

and may grant probation at their discretion. In nonjury trials, probation is granted solely by judicial mandate. Some states have attempted to shape judicial discretion by creating guidelines for granting probation.

In most jurisdictions, all juvenile offenders are eligible for probation, as are most adults. Some state statutes prohibit probation for certain types of adult offenders, usually those who have engaged in repeated and serious violent crimes, such as murder or rape, or those who have committed crimes for which mandatory prison sentences have been legislated.

As Table 14.1 shows, in more than half of all cases a probationary sentence is imposed without an incarceration sentence being formulated or threatened; this is referred to as *straight probation*, or a probation-only sentence. The threat here is that if the probationer commits another crime, there may not be any more "second chances."

It is also common for the judge to formulate a prison sentence and then suspend it if the offender agrees to obey the rules of probation while living in the community (a **suspended sentence**). The term of a probationary sentence may extend to the limit of the suspended prison term, or the court may set a time limit that reflects the sentencing period. For misdemeanors, probation usually extends for the entire period of the jail sentence, but felonies are more likely to warrant probationary periods that are shorter than the suspended prison sentence. If the probationer violates the rules of probation or commits another crime, his probation can be revoked, and he may be required to begin serving his incarceration sentence.

About 10 percent of offenders, such as Elizabeth Stow, receive some form of split sentence in which they must first serve a jail term before being released on probation. In about 10 percent of all cases, the imposition of the sentence to probation is suspended. This step is usually taken to encourage the defendant to pursue a specific rehabilitation program, such as treatment for alcohol abuse. If the program is successfully completed, further legal action is not usually taken.

The Extent of Probation

The United States has approximately 2,000 adult probation agencies. Slightly more than half are associated with a state-level agency, while the remainder are organized at the county or municipal level of government. About 30 states combine probation and parole supervision into a single agency.

About four million adults are under federal, state, or local probation.[7] Among offenders on probation, slightly less than half (49 percent) were convicted of felonies, and the rest misdemeanors and other offenses. In 1980, 1.1 million people were on probation, so the number of probationers has quadrupled in two decades; probation (Figure 14.1) today makes up more than half of the entire correctional population. Some states, such as California and Texas, are maintaining hundreds of thousands of probationers in their caseloads. Without probation, the correctional system would rapidly become overcrowded, overly expensive, and unmanageable.

Eligibility for Probation

Several criteria are used in granting probation. The statutes of many states determine the factors that a judge should take into account. Some jurisdictions limit the use of probation in serious felony cases and for specific crimes with penalties that are controlled by mandatory sentencing laws. However, the granting of probation to serious felons is common. More than half of all probationers were convicted on felony offenses.

TABLE 14.1

How Probationary Sentences Are Imposed, by Percentage

Status of Probation	1995	2000	2004
Direct Imposition	48	56	56
Split Sentence	15	11	8
Sentence Suspended	26	25	24
Imposition Suspended	6	7	10
Other	4	1	1

Source: Lauren Glaze and Seri Pala, *Probation and Parole in the United States, 2004* (Washington, D.C.: Bureau of Justice Statistics, 2005).

suspended sentence
A sentence of incarceration that is not carried out if the offender agrees to obey the rules of probation while living in the community.

The most recent data on the extent of probation are provided by the Bureau of Justice Statistics. To reach this section of the Bureau of Justice website, go to the Siegel/Senna Introduction to Criminal Justice 11e website: www.thomsonedu.com/criminaljustice/siegel.

FIGURE 14.1

The Growth of the Correctional Population

Probationers Now Make Up More Than Half of the 7 Million People Under Correctional Care

Number of prisoners (millions)

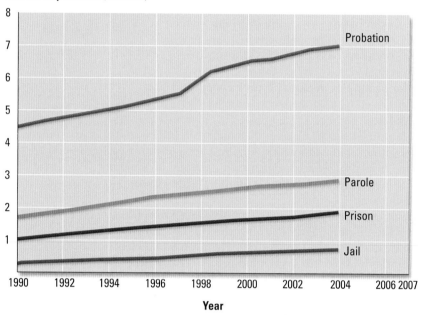

Source: Lauren Glaze and Seri Pala, *Probation and Parole in the United States, 2004* (Washington, D.C.: Bureau of Justice Statistics, 2005).

Some states have attempted to control judicial discretion by creating guidelines for granting probation. Judges often follow these guidelines, but probation decision making is varied: An individual offender granted probation in one jurisdiction might not be if tried in another. Probation is most often granted by a discretionary decision based on the beliefs and attitudes of the presiding judge and the probation staff.

Probation Rules

When probation is fixed as a sentence, the court sets down certain conditions or rules that must be followed in order for the offender to qualify for community treatment. Some rules are standard and are applied in every probation case (for example, "Do not leave the jurisdiction"), but the sentencing judge usually has broad discretion to set specific conditions on a case-by-case basis. A presiding judge may not impose capricious or cruel conditions, such as requiring an offender to make restitution out of proportion to the seriousness of the criminal act.[8]

However, judges may legally impose restrictions tailored to fit the probationer's individual needs, to protect society from additional harm, or both. Some probationers may find these special rules overly restrictive and in violation of constitutional protections and have filed legal actions to get the rules overturned.[9] It has become common for judges to try to impose rules that require probationers to broadcast their crimes in order to (a) shame them into compliance and (b) deter others from committing crimes. In this instance a judge may require someone convicted of soliciting a prostitute to appear on a "John List" in the local newspaper or for a drunk driver to take out an ad apologizing for her behavior. Although some believe that such rules will deter crime, others argue that exotic and public penalties might backfire and give the message that crime is more common than it really is and that the government might be acting like a "bully" when it punishes the guy next door in an embarrassing fashion.[10]

Some probationers may be forced to obey exotic conditions, but most are asked to enter a treatment program as part of their probationary sentence.

A Los Angeles gang police officer questions a gang member caught associating with another member and violating his probation rules on August 4, 2006, in Los Angeles, California. Violation of probation rules can mean revocation and incarceration.

Alcohol- or drug-abuse treatment and testing and mental health counseling are the most commonly required conditions.

Administration of Probation Services

Probation services are organized in a variety of ways, depending on the state and the jurisdiction in which they are located. Some states have a statewide probation service, but each court jurisdiction actually controls its local department. Other states maintain a strong statewide authority with centralized control and administration. Thirty states combine probation and parole services in a single unit; some combine juvenile and adult probation departments, whereas others maintain these departments separately.

The typical probation department is situated in a single court district, such as juvenile, superior, district, or municipal court. The relationship between the department and court personnel (especially the judge) is extremely close.

In the typical department, the chief probation officer (CPO) sets policy, supervises hiring, determines training needs, and may personally discuss with or recommend sentencing to the judge. In state-controlled departments, some of the CPO's duties are mandated by the central office—e.g., training guidelines may be determined at the state level. If, on the other hand, the department is locally controlled, the CPO is invested with great discretion in his or her management.

The line staff, or the probation officers (POs), may be in direct and personal contact with the entire supervisory staff, or they may be independent of the CPO and answer mainly to the assistant chiefs. Line staff perform the following major functions:

1. Supervise or monitor cases assigned to them to ensure that the rules of probation are followed.
2. Attempt to rehabilitate their cases through specialized treatment techniques.
3. Investigate the lives of convicted offenders to enable the court to make intelligent sentencing decisions.
4. Occasionally collect fines due the court or oversee the collection of delinquent payments, such as child support.
5. Interview complainants and defendants to determine whether criminal action should be taken, whether cases can be decided informally, whether diversion should be advocated, and so on. This last procedure, called *intake*, is common in juvenile probation.

Probation Officer

Duties and Characteristics of the Job

Probation officers—who, in some states, may be referred to as community supervision officers—monitor offenders' behavior through personal contact with the offenders and their families. Officers may also arrange for offenders to get substance abuse rehabilitation or job training. Probation officers usually work with either adults or juveniles exclusively. Only in small, usually rural, jurisdictions do probation officers counsel both adults and juveniles.

Another part of the probation officer's job involves working in the courts. Officers investigate the background of offenders brought before the court, write presentence reports, and make sentencing recommendations for each offender; review sentencing recommendations with offenders and their families before submitting the recommendations to the court; and testify in court regarding their findings and recommendations. Probation officers also attend hearings to update the court on an offender's probation compliance status and on the offender's efforts at rehabilitation. Occasionally, probation officers in the federal court system work as pretrial services officers, conducting pretrial investigations and making bond recommendations for defendants.

The number of cases a probation officer has depends on both the counseling needs of offenders and the risks they pose to society. Higher-risk offenders and those who need more counseling usually command more of an officer's or specialist's time and resources. Those who work with these offenders handle fewer cases. Caseloads also vary by agency jurisdiction. Consequently, officers may handle 20 to more than 300 active cases at a time.

Probation officers and specialists usually work a standard 40-hour week, but they may be required to work longer or to be on call 24 hours a day to supervise and assist offenders at any time. In addition, meeting with offenders who are on probation or parole may require extensive travel or fieldwork. However, this burden may be eased somewhat for workers whose agencies allow them to telecommute from home via computers and other equipment and to make use of other technology, such as electronic devices worn by offenders that allow probation officers to monitor their activities.

Probation officers may find their jobs stressful for a variety of reasons. They work with convicted criminals, some of whom may be dangerous. In the course of supervising offenders, officers and specialists usually interact with many other individuals, including family members and friends of their clients, who may be angry, upset, or uncooperative. Officers and specialists may also be required to collect and transport urine samples of offenders for drug testing.

Although stress makes these jobs difficult at times, the work can be rewarding. Many probation officers gain personal satisfaction from counseling members of their community and helping them become productive citizens.

Job Outlook

Jobs for probation officers are more plentiful in urban areas. There are also more jobs in states that have numerous men and women on probation, such as California and Texas, which currently have the largest such populations.

Many states have their own probation professional organization. You can access the website for the New York State Probation Officers Association by linking through the Siegel/Senna Introduction to Criminal Justice 11e website: www.thomsonedu. com/criminaljustice/siegel.

For more about a career as a probation officer, see the Careers in Criminal Justice feature.

How probation officers carry out these tasks may be a function of their self-image and professional orientation. Some POs view themselves as "social workers" and maintain a treatment orientation; their goal is to help offenders adjust in the community. Others are "law enforcers" who are more concerned with supervision, control, and public safety. An officer's style is influenced by both personal values and the department's general policies and orientation toward the goals of probation.[11] New York City probation officers are now authorized to carry handguns under a new departmental policy intended to enhance the supervision of their clients, the majority of whom are felons. Arming the officers became necessary when the department began to require officers to spend more time visiting their clients in their neighborhoods and homes. Other departments have armed their officers as the number of probationers increase and duties become more dangerous.[12]

Salary

Median annual earnings of probation officers and correctional treatment specialists are $39,600. The middle 50 percent earn between $31,500 and $52,100. The lowest 10 percent earn less than $26,310, and the highest 10 percent earn more than $66,660. Officers and specialists who work in urban areas usually have higher earnings than those working in rural areas.

Opportunities

Employment of probation officers is projected to grow through 2008. Vigorous law enforcement is expected to result in a continuing increase in the prison population. Overcrowding in prisons has also swelled the probation population as judges and prosecutors search for alternative forms of punishment, such as electronic monitoring and day reporting centers.

In addition to openings due to growth, many other openings will result from the need to replace workers who leave the occupation permanently, including the large number expected to retire over the next several years.

Qualifications

Prospective probation officers must be in good physical condition and be emotionally stable. Most agencies require applicants to be at least 21 years old and, for federal employment, no older than 37. Those convicted of felonies may not be eligible for employment in these occupations.

Probation officers need strong writing skills and computer skills because of the large number of reports they must prepare. Job candidates should also be knowledgeable about laws and regulations pertaining to corrections.

Education and Training

Educational requirements for probation officers vary by state, but a bachelor's degree in social work or criminal justice is usually required. In addition, some states require probation officers to have one year of work experience in a related field or one year of graduate study in criminal justice, social work, or psychology. Most probation officers must complete a training program sponsored by their state government or the federal government and then work as trainees for about six months. Candidates who successfully complete the training period obtain a permanent position. Some states require applicants to take a certification test during or after training. Applicants usually must also pass written, oral, psychological, and physical examinations.

Agencies that employ probation officers have several levels of officers and specialists, as well as supervisors. A graduate degree—such as a master's degree in criminal justice, social work, or psychology—may be helpful for advancement.

Source: Andrew Alpert, "Probation Officers and Correctional Treatment Specialists," *Occupational Outlook Quarterly* 45 (2001): 28; Donald Evans, "Seeking to Develop a Best Value Probation Service," *Corrections Today* 68 (2006): 84–85; United States Department of Labor, "Probation Officers and Correctional Treatment Specialists" (http://www.bls.gov/oco/ocos265.htm).

Duties of Probation Officers

Staff officers in probation departments are usually charged with five primary tasks: presentence investigation, intake, diagnosis, treatment supervision, and risk classification.

PRESENTENCE INVESTIGATION   In the investigative stage, the supervising probation officer accumulates important information on the background and activities of the offender who is being considered for probation. This **presentence investigation** serves as the basis for sentencing and controls whether the convicted defendant will be granted community release or sentenced to secure confinement. In the event that the offender is placed on probation, the investigation becomes useful as a tool to shape treatment and supervision efforts.

The style and content of presentence investigations may vary among jurisdictions and also among individual POs within the same jurisdiction. Some

presentence investigation
An investigation performed by a probation officer after the conviction of a defendant, with the report containing information about the defendant's background, education, previous employment, and family; his or her own statement concerning the offense; his or her prior criminal record; interviews with neighbors or acquaintances; and his or her mental and physical condition (that is, information that would not be made public record in the case of a guilty plea or that would be inadmissible as evidence at a trial but could be influential and important at the sentencing stage).

intake
The process by which a probation officer settles cases at the initial appearance before the onset of formal criminal proceedings.

departments require voluminous reports covering every aspect of the defendant's life; other departments, which may be rule oriented, require that officers stick to the basic facts, such as the defendant's age, race, sex, and previous offense record.

At the conclusion of most presentence investigations, a recommendation is made to the presiding judge that reflects the department's sentencing posture on the case at hand. This is a crucial aspect of the report because the probation department's recommendation is followed by the sentencing judge in most cases.

INTAKE Probation officers who conduct **intake** interviews may be looking to settle the case without the necessity of a court hearing. The probation officer will work with all parties involved in the case—offender, victim, police officer, etc.—to design an equitable resolution of the case. If the intake process is successful, the probation officer may settle the case without further court action, recommend restitution or other compensation, or recommend unofficial or informal probation. If an equitable solution cannot be found, the case is filed for a court hearing.

DIAGNOSIS In order to select appropriate treatment modes, probation officers, using their training in counseling, social work, or psychology, analyze the probationer's character, attitudes, and behavior. The goal of diagnosis is to develop a personality profile that may be helpful in treating the offender. An effective diagnosis integrates all that has been learned about the individual, organized in such a way as to provide a means for the establishment of future treatment goals.

TREATMENT SUPERVISION After the diagnosis has been completed, the probation staff is asked to carry out the treatment supervision, a program of therapy designed to help the client deal with the problems that resulted in her antisocial behavior. In years past, the probation staff had primary responsibility for supervision and treatment, but today's large caseloads limit opportunities for hands-on treatment; most probation treatment efforts rely on community resources. A probation officer who discovers that a client has a drinking problem may place her in a detoxification program. A spousal abuser may be required to enroll in an anger management or drug treatment program, make a personal apology to the victim, or have no contact with his ex-wife.[13] In the case of juvenile delinquency, a PO may work with teachers and other school officials to help a young offender stay in school. The need for treatment is critical, and the vast size of probation caseloads, especially the large numbers of narcotics abusers, can provide a formidable challenge to community-based substance abuse programs.[14]

Effective supervision is critical for another reason: It protects the probation department from civil liability. Failure to supervise probationers adequately and to determine whether they are obeying the rules of probation can result in the officer and the department being held legally liable for civil damages. If a probationer with a history of child molestation attacks a child while working as a school custodian, the probationer's case supervisor can be held legally responsible for failing to check on the probationer's employment activities.[15]

risk classification
Categorizing probationers so that they may receive an appropriate level of treatment and control.

RISK CLASSIFICATION **Risk classification** is the process of categorizing probationers and then assigning them to a level and type of supervision on the basis of their particular needs and the risks they present to the community. For example, some clients may receive frequent (intensive) supervision in which they are contacted by their supervising probation officer almost every day, whereas other minor offenders are assigned to minimum monitoring by a PO.

A number of risk-assessment approaches are used, but most employ such objective measures as the offender's age, employment status, drug abuse history, prior felony convictions, and number of address changes in the year prior to sentencing. Efforts are under way to create more effective instruments that use subjective information obtained through face-to-face interviews and encounters.[16]

Does classification make a dramatic difference in the success of probation? Although there is little clear-cut evidence that classification has a substantial impact on reducing recidivism, its use has become commonplace, and administrators believe that it may be a useful tool in case management and treatment delivery.[17] The classification of offenders aids the most important goal of supervision: reducing the risk that the probationer presents to the community. In addition, classification ensures that the most serious cases get the most intensive supervision and that resources are not wasted on cases with relatively few treatment needs.[18]

How Successful Is Probation?

Probation is the most commonly used alternative sentence for a number of reasons. It is humane, it helps offenders maintain community and family ties, and it is cost-effective. Incarcerating an inmate costs more than $20,000 per year, but probation costs only about $2,000 per year.[19]

Although unquestionably inexpensive, is probation successful? If most probation orders fail, the costs of repeated criminality would certainly outweigh the cost savings of a probation sentence. Overall, most probation orders do seem successful. National data indicate that about 60 percent of probationers successfully complete their probationary sentence and about 40 percent are either re-arrested, violate probation rules, or abscond.[20] Most revocations occur for technical violations that occur during the first three months of the probation sentence.[21] A 40-percent failure rate seems high, but even the most serious criminals who receive probation are less likely to recidivate than those who are sent to prison for committing similar crimes.[22]

> ### PERSPECTIVES ON JUSTICE
> #### *Rehabilitation Versus Crime Control*
> The revocation of probation represents the inherent conflict between its rehabilitation and crime control aspects. On the one hand, probation is viewed as a second chance that enables deserving offenders to rehabilitate themselves in the community. On the other hand, probationers are convicted offenders who must obey stringent rules unless they want to be sent to prison. Rehabilitation advocates may not want to pull the revocation trigger unless it is absolutely necessary, whereas those who espouse a crime control approach may be less charitable to breaches of probation rules.

FELONY PROBATION A significant issue involving eligibility for probation is community supervision of convicted felons. Many people believe that probation is given to minors or first offenders who are deserving of a break. This is not the case. Many serious criminal offenders are given probation sentences, including people convicted on homicide, rape, or robbery charges.

Although originally conceived as a way to provide a second chance for young offenders, probation today is also a means of reducing the population pressures on an overcrowded and underfunded correctional system. So there are two distinct sides to the probation, one involving the treatment and rehabilitation of nondangerous offenders deserving of a second chance and the other the supervision and control of criminals who might well otherwise be incarcerated.

Although probationers are less likely to recidivate than former prison inmates, the fact that many felons who commit violent offenses are granted probation is an issue of some concern. Tracking the outcome of felony probation was the goal of Joan Petersilia and her colleagues at the RAND Corporation, a private think tank, when they traced 1,672 men convicted of felonies who had been granted probation in Los Angeles and Alameda counties in California.[23] In this now-classic study, Petersilia found that 1,087 (65 percent) were re-arrested; of those re-arrested, 853 (51 percent) were convicted; and of those convicted, 568 (34 percent) were sentenced to jail or prison. Of the probationers who had new charges filed against them, 75 percent were charged with burglary, theft, robbery, and other predatory crimes; 18 percent were convicted of serious, violent crimes.

The RAND researchers found that probation is by far the most common sentencing alternative to prison, used in about 60 to 80 percent of all criminal convictions. However, what is disturbing is that the crimes and criminal records of about 25 percent of all probationers are indistinguishable from those of offenders who go to prison.

To read more about the RAND Corporation, go to its website, which you can access by going to the Siegel/Senna Introduction to Criminal Justice 11e website: www.thomsonedu.com/criminaljustice/siegel.

WHO FAILS ON PROBATION, AND WHY? Who is most likely to fail on probation? Young males who are unemployed or who have a very low income, a prior criminal record, and a history of instability are most likely to be re-arrested. In contrast, probationers who are married with children, have lived in the area for two or more years, and are adequately employed are the most likely to be successful on probation.[24] Recent research (2005) shows, surprisingly, that males convicted on sexual offenses seem to do quite well on probation.[25] Among female probationers, those who have stable marriages, are better educated, and are employed full or part time are more likely to complete probation orders successfully than male probationers or women who are single, less educated, and unemployed. Prior record is also related to probation success: Clients who have a history of criminal behavior, prior probation, and previous incarceration are the most likely to fail.[26]

Probationers bring with them a lot of emotional baggage that may reduce their chances of successful rehabilitation. Many are felons who have long histories of offending; more than 75 percent of all probationers have had prior convictions. Others suffer from a variety of social and psychological disabilities. Surveys indicate that almost 20 percent suffer from mental illness.[27] Whether mentally ill or mentally sound, probationers are likely to have grown up in households in which family members were incarcerated, and to have lived part of their lives in foster homes or state institutions. Many had parents or guardians who abused drugs; they also suffered high rates of physical and sexual abuse. They are now unemployed or underemployed, and almost half are substance abusers. Considering their harsh and abusive backgrounds and their current economic distress and psychological stresses and strains, it comes as no surprise that many find it difficult to comply with the rules of probation and forgo criminal activity.

Legal Rights of Probationers

What are the legal rights of probationers? How has the U.S. Supreme Court set limits on the probation process? A number of important legal issues surround probation, one set involving the civil rights of probationers and another involving the rights of probationers during the revocation process.

CIVIL RIGHTS The U.S. Supreme Court has ruled that probationers have a unique status and therefore are entitled to fewer constitutional protections than other citizens:

♦ *Minnesota v. Murphy* (1984).[28] In *Murphy*, the Supreme Court ruled that the probation officer–client relationship is not confidential, as physician–patient or attorney–client relationships are. If a probationer admits to committing a crime to his or her probation supervisor, the information may be passed on to the police or district attorney. Furthermore, the *Murphy* decision held that a probation officer could even use trickery or psychological pressure to get information and turn it over to the police.

♦ *Griffin v. Wisconsin* (1987).[29] In *Griffin*, the Court held that a probationer's home may be searched without a warrant on the grounds that probation departments "have in mind the welfare of the probationer" and must "respond quickly to evidence of misconduct."

♦ *United States v. Knights* (2001).[30] In *Knights*, the Court upheld the legality of a warrantless search of a probationer's home for the purposes of gathering criminal evidence. The Court ruled that the home of a probationer who is suspected of a crime can be searched without a warrant if the search was based on (a) reasonable suspicion that he had committed another crime while on probation and (b) that a condition of his previous probation was that he would submit to searches. The Court reasoned that the government's interest in preventing crime, combined with Knights's diminished expectation of privacy, required only a *reasonable suspicion* to make the search fit within the protections of the Fourth Amendment.

REVOCATION RIGHTS During the course of a probationary term, a violation of the rules or terms of probation or the commitment of a new crime can result in probation being revoked, at which time the offender may be placed in an institution. Revocation is not often an easy decision, because it conflicts with the treatment philosophy of many probation departments.

When revocation is chosen, the offender is notified, and a formal hearing is scheduled. If the charges against the probationer are upheld, the offender can then be placed in an institution to serve the remainder of the sentence. Most departments will not revoke probation unless the offender commits another crime or seriously violates the rules of probation.

Because placing a person on probation implies that probation will continue unless the probationer commits some major violation, the defendant has been given certain procedural due process rights at this stage of the criminal process. In four significant decisions, the U.S. Supreme Court provided procedural safeguards to apply at proceedings to revoke probation (and parole):

♦ *Mempa v. Rhay* (1967). The Court unanimously held that a probationer was constitutionally entitled to counsel in a revocation-of-probation proceeding where the imposition of sentence had been suspended.[31]

♦ *Morrissey v. Brewer* (1972). The Court required an informal inquiry to determine whether there was probable cause to believe that an arrested parolee had violated the conditions of parole, as well as a formal revocation hearing with minimum due process requirements. Because the revocations of probation and parole are similar, the standards in the *Morrissey* case affected the probation process as well.[32]

♦ *Gagnon v. Scarpelli* (1973). The Court held that both probationers and parolees have a constitutionally limited right to counsel in revocation proceedings.[33] This means that during a probation revocation hearing, the defendant must be given counsel if he or she requires it for an effective defense. A judge may deny counsel under some circumstances, such as when probation will be continued despite the violation. The Gagnon case can be viewed as a step forward in the application of constitutional safeguards to the correctional process. The provision of counsel helped give control over the unlimited discretion exercised in the past by probation and parole personnel in revocation proceedings.

♦ *United States v. Granderson* (1994). The Court helped clarify what can happen to a probationer whose community sentence is revoked. Granderson was eligible for a six-month prison sentence but instead was given sixty months of probation. When he tested positively for drugs, his probation was revoked. The statute he was sentenced under required that he serve one-third of his original sentence in prison. When the trial court sentenced him to twenty months, he appealed. Was his original sentence six months or sixty months? The Supreme Court found that it would be unfair to force a probationer to serve more time in prison than he would have if originally incarcerated and ruled that the proper term should have been one-third of the six months, or two months.[34]

If during a hearing a judge rules that the conditions of probation have been violated, probation may be revoked. Here, actor Nick Nolte turns to address the prosecutor during a progress hearing on Nolte's probation on an earlier driving under the influence case, in a Malibu, California, courtroom. Judge Lawrence Mira determined that an anonymous tip that Nolte was drinking and driving was unfounded and refused to find the actor in violation of probation.

The Future of Probation

A number of initiatives are now ongoing or being suggested that may help shape the future of probation:

1. At least twenty-five states now impose some form of fee on probationers to defray the cost of community corrections. Massachusetts initiated **day fees**,

day fees
Fees imposed on probationers to offset the costs of probation.

which are based on the probationer's wages (the usual fee is between one and three days' wages each month).[35] Texas requires judges to impose supervision fees unless the offender is truly unable to pay; fees make up more than half of each probation department's annual budget.[36]

HotSpot probation
A program using community supervision teams to monitor offenders.

2. Maryland's **HotSpot probation** initiative involves having police officers, probation agents, neighbors, and social service professionals form community probation supervision teams. Using a team approach, they provide increased monitoring of offenders through home visits, drug testing, and regular meetings. They also work with the offenders to ease reentry through the creation of offender work crews that aid in community clean-ups, work on vacant houses, and participate in other projects. Recent evaluations find that the recidivism rates of Hot Spot probationers were not significantly different from those of traditional probationers, but the initiative seems to have a great deal of utility and warrants further study.[37]

3. Some experts suggest that probation caseloads be organized around areas rather than clients. Research shows that probationers' residences are concentrated in certain locations. In the future, probation officers may be assigned cases based on where they live in order to develop a working knowledge of community issues and develop expertise on how to best serve their clients' interests and needs.[38]

ThomsonNOW™ Improve your grade on the exam with Personalized Study! For reinforcement resources and a mastery check of modern probation, go to www.thomsonedu.com/thomsonnow.

Probation is unquestionably undergoing dramatic changes. In many jurisdictions, traditional probation is being supplemented by *intermediate sanctions*, the penalties that fall between traditional community supervision and confinement in jail or prison. These new correctional services are discussed in the following section.

♦ INTERMEDIATE SANCTIONS

In 2005 Jennifer Wilbanks became notorious for running away just before her wedding and claiming to have been abducted. When the truth was revealed, she pled guilty to charges of filing a false police report. At her hearing, after she told

Intermediate sanctions are a particularly useful sanction for people who pose little threat to the community. Here, famed runaway bride Jennifer Wilbanks (right) leaves the Gwinnett County jail with her attorney, Lydia Sartain, in Lawrenceville, Georgia. Wilbanks pleaded no contest earlier that week to a felony charge and was sentenced to probation, community service, and a fine. Wilbanks made national headlines when a case of pre-marital jitters caused her to flee before her wedding. She then filed a false kidnapping claim to cover up her behavior.

the court that "I'm truly sorry for my actions and I just want to thank Gwinnett County and the city of Duluth," the judge, Ronnie Batchelor, sentenced her to 2 years of probation and 120 hours of community service. He also ordered her to continue mental health treatment and to pay the sheriff's office $2,550 in addition to the $13,250 she had previously agreed to pay the city of Duluth, Georgia, to help cover the overtime costs incurred in searching for her.[39]

Wilbanks's sentence reflects the growing trend of adding additional sanctions to traditional probation sentences; in her case, it was monetary fines and community service. These programs can be viewed as "probation plus" because they add restrictive penalties and conditions to traditional community service orders, which usually favor treatment and rehabilitation over control and restraint.[40]

Community sentencing has traditionally emphasized offender rehabilitation. The probation officer has been viewed as a caseworker or counselor whose primary job is to help the offender adjust to society. Offender surveillance and control have seemed more appropriate for law enforcement, jails, and prisons than for community corrections.[41]

But since 1980 a more conservative justice system has moved toward social control. Although the rehabilitative ideals of probation have not been abandoned, new programs have been developed that add a control dimension to community corrections. Being more punitive than probation, intermediate sanctions can be sold to conservatives, but they still remain attractive to liberals as alternatives to incarceration.[42]

Intermediate sanctions include programs typically administered by probation departments: intensive probation supervision, house arrest, electronic monitoring, restitution orders, shock probation or split sentences, and residential community corrections.[43] Some experts also include high-impact shock incarceration, or boot camp experiences, within the definition of intermediate sanctions, but these programs are typically operated by correctional departments (and are discussed separately in Chapter 15). Intermediate sanctions also involve sentences administered independently of probation staffs: fines and forfeiture, pretrial programs, and pretrial and posttrial residential programs. Intermediate sanctions therefore range from the barely intrusive, such as restitution orders, to the highly restrictive, such as house arrest accompanied by electronic monitoring and a stay in a community correctional center.

Advantages of Intermediate Sanctions

What are the advantages of creating a system of intermediate sanctions? Primary is the need to develop alternatives to prisons and jails, which have proved to be costly, ineffective, and injurious. Little evidence exists that incapacitation is either a general deterrent to crime or a specific deterrent against future criminality. Some correctional systems have become inundated with new inmates. Even states that have extensively used alternative sanctions have experienced rapid increases in their prison populations. The pressure on the correctional system if alternative sanctions were not an option is almost inconceivable. Other nations have embraced alternative sanctions and, despite rising crime rates, have not experienced the explosion in the prison population that has occurred in the United States. This issue is explored further in the International Justice feature.

Intermediate sanctions also have the potential to save money. Although they are more expensive than traditional probation, they are far less costly than incarceration. If those offenders given alternative sanctions would have otherwise been incarcerated, the extra cost would be significant. In addition, offenders given intermediate sanctions generate income, pay taxes, reimburse victims, perform community service, and provide other cost savings that would be nonexistent had they been incarcerated. Intermediate sanctions are not likely to pay an immediate corrections dividend because many correctional costs are fixed, but they may reduce the need for future prison and jail construction.

INTERNATIONAL JUSTICE

Alternatives to Incarceration Abroad

Although the crime rate has been declining in the United States for nearly a decade, get-tough measures such as "three strikes and you're out" have resulted in a steadily increasing prison population. Western European countries have crime rates similar to those of the United States, but their incarceration rates are much lower. European criminal penalties are not nearly as harsh as those in the United States.

This disparity in punishment has not been lost on researchers such as legal scholar Michael Tonry, who has explored the differences between the United States and other Western democracies. Tonry points out that crime trends seem to have an important impact on U.S. incarceration policies. As the crime rate goes up, so does the media coverage of crime stories. Political figures, especially those running for office, feed off the media coverage and make crime an election focus. Because these events fuel public anxiety, there is an outcry for punitive measures to be taken against criminals. Politicians are happy to oblige their constituents and pass tough sanctions against criminals to show their sensitivity to the voters.

Western European nations have taken a different approach to crime control. When rates of crime rose in European democracies, lawmakers focused on making punishment fair as opposed to harsh. Instead of mandatory sentencing, individual circumstances and the reasons for committing a crime are considered. Western European lawmakers also focus on punishments that are utilitarian and effective in reducing crime, not punitive and retributive. They often rely on community sentences such as day fines, which are based on the offender's earnings and economic circumstances. The money collected from day fines not only punishes the offender but also serves to benefit society. Western European judges have also been more likely to sentence offenders to community service. First created in the United States, community service has quickly become the sentence of choice for minor crimes in European nations. Whereas community service hours can number in the thousands for a U.S. criminal, European sentences often limit the number of hours to 240.

Because of the focus on the individual, probation in Europe covers a range of services, so it resembles intermediate sanctions in the United States. Electronic monitoring programs have become common and are viewed as one of the most promising alternatives to incarceration specifically adopted for the relief of the problem of prison overcrowding. Projects using electronic monitoring are well-established in the penal and correctional systems in England, Sweden, and the Netherlands. Pilot projects can be observed in Belgium, France, Germany, Italy, Portugal, Switzerland, and Spain.

Community programs vary from country to country and involve crimes of varying severity. The Dutch have early-help programs: If an accused person is held longer than six hours in a police cell, the probation department is notified. At the other extreme, probation services in England provide supervision of life-sentenced inmates conditionally released to the community. In between these two extremes are various services such as sentencing reports, diversion programs, work with inmates in custody (e.g., prerelease planning), supervision of released inmates, and supervision of offenders released from court on probation orders.

Some countries that do not yet have probation are attempting to establish probation-like programs without specific probation statutes. Slovakia, with conditional sentences, and Bulgaria, with conditional sentences and conditional release programs, are attempting these strategies. It has not been easy to convince judicial authorities in these countries to establish community sentencing, but efforts are being made. There is also the issue of where in the criminal justice system probation services should be located. The current discussion focuses on whether to make probation a part of the penitentiary system or the courts, or have it be an independent directorate in a ministry of justice.

Critical Thinking

Incarceration sentences in Europe are substantially shorter than those in the United States. No European country has implemented mandatory sentences or truth-in-sentencing laws. Almost all efforts to control or reduce judicial discretion have been met with disapproval. Michael Tonry points out that this may be because Western European judges and prosecutors are career civil servants, free from political concerns. Not having to worry about an upcoming election allows them to focus on what they believe is just, not what is politically expedient. Would you encourage such practices in the United States? Why or why not?

InfoTrac College Edition Research

To learn more about community sentences abroad, read Donald G. Evans, "Ontario's New Probation Supervision Model," *Corrections Today* 60 (1998): 126; Donald G. Evans, "'What Works' in the United Kingdom," *Corrections Today* 60 (1998): 124.

Sources: Rita Haverkamp, Markus Mayer, and René Lévy, "Electronic Monitoring in Europe," *European Journal of Crime, Criminal Law & Criminal Justice* 12 (2004): 36–45; Donald Evans, "Probation in Europe: Current Developments," *Corrections Today* 65 (2003): 87; Michael Tonry, "Why Are U.S. Incarceration Rates So High?" *Crime and Delinquency* 45 (1999): 419–38; Michael Tonry, "Parochialism in U.S. Sentencing Policy," *Crime and Delinquency* 45 (1999): 48–66.

Intermediate sanctions also help meet the need for developing community sentences that are fair, equitable, and proportional.[44] It seems unfair to treat both a rapist and a shoplifter with the same type of probationary sentence, considering the differences in their crimes. As Figure 14.2 illustrates, intermediate sanctions can form the successive steps of a meaningful ladder of scaled punishments outside of prison, thereby restoring fairness and equity to nonincarceration sentences.[45]

Burglars may be ordered to make restitution to their victims, and rapists can be placed in a community correctional facility while they receive counseling at a local psychiatric center. This feature of intermediate sanctions allows judges to fit the punishment to the crime without resorting to a prison sentence. Intermediate sentences can be designed to increase punishment for people whose serious or repeat crimes make a straight probation sentence inappropriate yet for whom a prison sentence would be unduly harsh and counterproductive.[46]

In the broadest sense, intermediate sanctions can serve the needs of a number of offender groups. The most likely candidates are convicted criminals who would normally be sent to prison but who either pose a low risk of recidivism or are of little threat to society (such as nonviolent property offenders). Used in this sense, intermediate sanctions are a viable solution to the critical problem of prison overcrowding.

Intermediate sanctions can also reduce overcrowding in jails by providing alternatives to incarceration for misdemeanants and cut the number of pretrial detainees, who currently make up about half the inmate population.[47] Some forms of bail already require conditions, such as supervision by court officers and periods of home confinement (conditional bail), that are a form of intermediate sanction.

Intermediate sanctions can also potentially be used as halfway-back strategies for probation and parole violators. Probationers who violate the conditions of their community release could be placed under increasingly more intensive supervision before incarceration is required. Parolees who pose the greatest risk of recidivism might receive conditions that require close monitoring or home confinement. Parole violators could be returned to a community correctional center instead of a walled institution.

Fines

Fines are monetary payments imposed on offenders as an intermediate punishment for their criminal acts. They are a direct offshoot of the early common-law practice of requiring compensation be paid to the victim and the state (*wergild*) for criminal acts. Fines are still commonly used in Europe, where they are often the sole penalty, even in cases involving chronic offenders who commit fairly serious crimes.[48]

In the United States, fines are most commonly used in cases involving misdemeanors and lesser offenses. Fines are also frequently used in felony cases when the offender benefited financially. Fines may be used as a sole sanction or combined with other punishments, such as probation or confinement. To increase the force of the financial punishment, judges commonly levy other monetary sanctions along with fines, such as court costs, public defender fees, probation and treatment fees, and victim restitution. However, evidence suggests that many offenders fail to pay fines and that courts are negligent in their efforts to collect unpaid fees.

In most jurisdictions, little guidance is given to the sentencing judge directing the imposition of the fine. Judges often have inadequate information on the

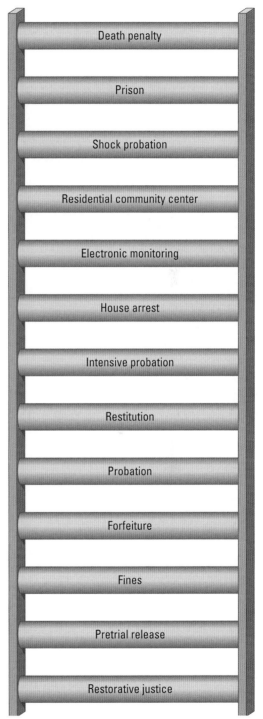

FIGURE 14.2
The Punishment Ladder

- Death penalty
- Prison
- Shock probation
- Residential community center
- Electronic monitoring
- House arrest
- Intensive probation
- Restitution
- Probation
- Forfeiture
- Fines
- Pretrial release
- Restorative justice

fine
A sum imposed as punishment for an offense.

©AP Images/George Nikitin

Even the rich and powerful pay fines, though the amount may be somewhat higher than those paid by the average criminal. Former Ukrainian Prime Minister Pavlo Lazarenko leaves a San Francisco federal building on Friday, August 25, 2006, after being sentenced to nine years in prison and $10 million in fines for money laundering, wire fraud, and extortion. Lazarenko was the first former head of government to be tried in the United States since the 1992 trial of Manuel Noriega of Panama for cocaine trafficking, racketeering, and money laundering.

day fine
A fine geared to an offender's net daily income, as well as the number of dependents and the seriousness of the crime, in an effort to make sentences more equitable.

forfeiture
The seizure of personal property by the state as a civil or criminal penalty.

offender's ability to pay, resulting in defaults and contempt charges. Because the standard sanction for nonpayment is incarceration, many offenders held in local jails are confined for nonpayment of criminal fines. Although the U.S. Supreme Court in *Tate v. Short* (1971) recognized that incarcerating a person who is financially unable to pay a fine discriminates against the poor, many judges continue to incarcerate offenders for noncompliance with financial orders.[49] Research indicates that, given the facts of a case, judges do seem to use fines in a rational manner: Low-risk offenders are the ones most likely to receive fines instead of a jail sentence; the more serious the crime, the higher the amount of the fine. Offenders who are fined seem less likely to commit new crimes than those who receive a jail sentence.[50]

DAY FINES   Because judges rely so heavily on offense seriousness to fix the level of fines, financial penalties may have a negative impact on success rates. The more serious the offense and the higher the fine, the greater the chances that the offender will fail to pay the fine and risk probation revocation. To overcome this sort of problem, some jurisdictions began experimenting with **day fines**.[51]

A concept originated in Europe, the first day fines pilot program in the United States was designed and operated by the Vera Institute of Justice in Staten Island, New York, between 1987 and 1989. Since then, similarly structured fine systems have been tried experimentally in Arizona, Connecticut, Iowa, and Oregon; a number of states including Alaska use day fines.[52]

Day fines are geared to an offender's net daily income. In an effort to make them equitable and fairly distributed, fines are based on the severity of the crime, weighted by a daily-income value taken from a chart similar to an income tax table. The number of the offender's dependents is also taken into account. The day fine concept means that the severity of punishment is based on the offender's ability to pay. Day fines hold the promise of becoming an equitable solution to the problem of setting the amount of a fine for differently situated offenders. However, there is little conclusive evidence on whether the day fine program works as intended.[53]

Forfeiture

Another intermediate sanction with a financial basis is criminal (*in personam*) and civil (*in rem*) **forfeiture**. Both involve the seizure of goods and instrumentalities related to the commission or outcome of a criminal act. The difference is that criminal forfeiture proceedings target criminal defendants and can only follow a criminal conviction. In contrast, civil forfeiture proceedings target property used in a crime and do not require that formal criminal proceedings be initiated against a person or that he is proven guilty of a crime.[54] For example, federal law provides that after arresting drug traffickers, the government may seize the boats they used to import the narcotics, the cars they used to carry the drugs overland, the warehouses in which the drugs were stored, and the homes paid for with the drug profits. On conviction, the drug dealers lose permanent ownership of these instrumentalities of crime.

Forfeiture is not a new sanction. During the Middle Ages, "forfeiture of estate" was a mandatory result of most felony convictions. The Crown could seize all of a felon's real and personal property. Forfeiture derived from the common-law concept of "corruption of blood" or "attaint," which prohibited a felon's family from inheriting or receiving his property or estate. The common law mandated that descendants could not inherit property from a relative who may have attained the property illegally: "[T]he Corruption of Blood stops the Course of Regular Descent, as to Estates, over which the Criminal could have no Power, because he never enjoyed them."[55]

Forfeiture was reintroduced to U.S. law with the passage of the Racketeer Influenced and Corrupt Organization (RICO) Act and the Continuing Criminal Enterprises Act, both of which allow the seizure of any property derived from illegal enterprises or conspiracies. Although these acts were designed to apply to ongoing criminal conspiracies, such as drug or pornography rings, they are now being applied to a far-ranging series of criminal acts, including white-collar crimes. More than 100 federal statutes use forfeiture of property as a punishment.

Although law enforcement officials at first applauded the use of forfeiture as a hard-hitting way of seizing the illegal profits of drug law violators, the practice has been criticized because the government has often been overzealous in its application. Million-dollar yachts have been seized because someone aboard possessed a small amount of marijuana; this confiscatory practice is referred to as **zero tolerance**. This strict interpretation of the forfeiture statutes has come under fire because it is often used capriciously, the penalty is sometimes disproportionate to the crime involved, and it makes the government a "partner in crime."[56] It is also alleged that forfeiture unfairly targets a narrow range of offenders. While it has been routine for government employees involved in corruption to forfeit their pensions, employees of public companies are exempt from such punishment.[57] There is also the issue of conflict of interest. Because law enforcement agencies can use forfeited assets to supplement their budgets, they may direct their efforts to cases that promise the greatest payoff instead of ones that have the highest law enforcement priority.[58]

zero tolerance
A practice in which criminal defendants forfeit homes, cars, and so on for the slightest law violation.

Restitution

Another popular intermediate sanction is **restitution**, which can take the form of requiring offenders to either pay back the victims of crime (monetary restitution) or serve the community to compensate for their criminal acts (**community service restitution**).[59] Restitution programs offer offenders a chance to avoid a jail or prison sentence or a lengthier probation period. It may help them develop a sense of allegiance to society, better work habits, and some degree of gratitude for being given a second chance. Restitution serves many other purposes, including giving the community something of value without asking it to foot the bill for an incarceration stay and helping victims regain lost property and income.

If **monetary restitution** is called for, the probation department typically makes a determination of victim loss and develops a plan for paying fair compensation. To avoid the situation in which a wealthy offender can fill a restitution order by merely writing a check, judges will sometimes order that compensation be paid out of income derived from a low-paid social service or public works job.

Community service orders usually require duty in a public nursing home, shelter, hospital, drug treatment unit, or works program. Some young vandals may find that they must clean up the damage they caused to a school or park. Judges sometimes have difficulty gauging the length of community service orders. One suggestion is that the maximum order should be no more than 240 hours and that this should be considered the equivalent of a 6- to 12-month jail term.[60] Whether these terms are truly equivalent remains a matter of personal opinion.

Judges and probation officers have embraced the concept of restitution because it appears to benefit the victim, the offender, the criminal justice system, and society.[61] Financial restitution is inexpensive to administer, helps avoid stigma, and provides compensation for victims of crime. Offenders ordered to do community service work have been placed in schools, hospitals, and nursing homes. Helping them avoid a jail sentence can mean saving the public thousands

restitution
Criminal sanction that requires the offender to repay the victim or society or both for damage caused by the criminal act.

community service restitution
Criminal sanction that requires the offender to work in the community at such tasks as cleaning public parks or helping handicapped children as an alternative to incarceration.

monetary restitution
Criminal sanction that requires the offender to compensate the victim for property damage, lost wages, medical costs, or other losses.

of dollars that would have gone to maintaining them in a secure institution, frees up needed resources, and gives the community the feeling that equity has been returned to the justice system.

Does restitution work? Most reviews rate it as a qualified success. A recent evaluation of community service in Texas found that nearly three-fourths of offenders with community service orders met their obligations and completed community service work.[62] The Texas experience is not atypical; most restitution clients successfully complete their orders and have no subsequent contact with the justice system.[63]

Shock Probation and Split Sentencing

shock probation
A sentence in which offenders serve a short term in prison to impress them with the pains of incarceration before they begin probation.

split sentence
Giving a brief term of incarceration as a condition of probation.

Shock probation and **split sentences** are alternative sanctions designed to allow judges to grant offenders community release only after they have sampled incarceration. The case of Elizabeth Stow, the California teacher whose probation order was detailed in the opening vignette, illustrates the use of split sentencing.

These sanctions are based on the premise that if offenders are given a taste of incarceration sufficient to shock them into law-abiding behavior, they will be reluctant to violate the rules of probation or commit another crime.

In a number of states and in the federal court system, a jail term can be a condition of probation, known as split sentencing. About 10 percent of probationers are now given split sentences. The shock probation approach involves resentencing an offender to probation after a short prison stay. The shock comes because the offender originally received a long maximum sentence but is then eligible for release to community supervision at the discretion of the judge (usually within 90 days of incarceration).

Shock probation and split sentencing have been praised as ways to limit prison time, reintegrate the client quickly into the community, maintain family ties, and reduce prison populations and the costs of corrections. An initial jail sentence probably makes offenders more receptive to the conditions of probation because it amply illustrates the problems they will face if probation is violated. However, shock probation and split sentencing have been criticized by those who believe that even a brief period of incarceration can interfere with the purpose of probation, which is to provide the offender with nonstigmatizing, community-based treatment. Even a short-term commitment subjects probationers to the destructive effects of institutionalization, disrupts their life in the community, and stigmatizes them for having been in jail.

Intensive Probation Supervision

intensive probation supervision (IPS)
A type of intermediate sanction involving small probation caseloads and strict daily or weekly monitoring.

Intensive probation supervision (IPS) programs are another important form of intermediate sanctions (these programs are also referred to as intensive supervision programs). IPS programs, which have been implemented in some form in about 40 states and today include about 100,000 clients, involve small caseloads of 15 to 40 clients who are kept under close watch by probation officers.[64]

The primary goal of IPS is decarceration: Without intensive supervision, clients would normally be sent to already overcrowded prisons or jails. The second goal is control: High-risk offenders can be maintained in the community under much closer security than traditional probation efforts can provide. A third goal is reintegration: Offenders can maintain community ties and be reoriented toward a more productive life while avoiding the pains of imprisonment.

In general, IPS programs rely on a great degree of client contact to achieve the goals of decarceration, control, and reintegration. Most programs have admissions criteria based on the nature of the offense and the offender's criminal background. Some programs exclude violent offenders; others will not take substance abusers. In contrast, some jurisdictions do not exclude offenders based on their prior criminal history.

IPS programs are used in several ways. In some states, IPS is a direct sentence imposed by a judge; in others, it is a postsentencing alternative used to divert offenders from the correctional system. A third practice is to use IPS as a case management tool to give the local probation staff flexibility in dealing with clients. Other jurisdictions use IPS in all three ways, in addition to applying it to probation violators to bring them halfway back into the community without resorting to a prison term.

THE EFFECTIVENESS OF IPS PROGRAMS Evaluations indicate that IPS programs are generally successful, deliver more services than would normally be received by probationers, are cost-effective, and produce recidivism rates equal to or better than those of offenders who have been confined. However, evaluations have so far not been definitive, often ignoring such issues as whether the program meets its stated goals, whether IPS is more attractive than other alternative sanctions, and which types of offenders are particularly suited for IPS. For example, IPS seems to work better for offenders with good employment records than it does for the underemployed or unemployed. Younger offenders who commit petty crimes are the most likely to fail on IPS. Ironically, people with these characteristics are the ones most likely to be included in IPS programs.[65]

Indications also exist that the failure rate in IPS caseloads is high, in some cases approaching 50 percent. IPS clients may even have a higher re-arrest rate than other probationers.[66] It should come as no surprise that IPS clients fail more often because, after all, they are more serious criminals who might otherwise have been incarcerated and are now being watched and supervised more closely than other probationers. Probation officers may also be more willing to revoke the probation of IPS clients because they believe that the clients are a risk to the community and, under normal circumstances, would have been incarcerated. Why risk the program to save a few bad apples?

Although evidence that it can significantly reduce offending rates is still insufficient, IPS might be an attractive alternative to traditional correctional methods if it can be restricted to offenders who most likely would have been incarcerated without the availability of the IPS program. IPS may also be more effective if it is combined with particular treatment modalities such as cognitive–behavioral treatment that stresses such life skills as problem solving, social skills, negotiation skills, management of emotion, and values enhancement.[67]

After thoroughly reviewing the impact of IPS, Betsy Fulton and her associates concluded that IPS programs are among the most popular alternatives to imprisonment in the United States and that although IPS has not provided a solution to prison crowding, it is useful for those not meriting imprisonment but at high risk for probation.[68]

House Arrest

The **house arrest** concept requires convicted offenders to spend extended periods of time in their own home as an alternative to an incarceration sentence. For example, persons convicted on a drunk-driving charge might be sentenced to spend between 6 P.M. Friday and 8 A.M. Monday and every weekday after 5:30 P.M. in their home for six months. Current estimates indicate that more than 10,000 people are under house arrest.

As with IPS programs, a great deal of variation exists in house arrest initiatives. Some are administered by probation departments, and others are simply judicial sentences monitored by surveillance officers. Some check clients 20 or more times a month (such as the Florida Community Control Program), but others do only a few curfew checks. Some use 24-hour confinement, whereas others allow offenders to attend work or school.

No definitive data exist indicating that house arrest is an effective crime deterrent, and sufficient evidence is not available to conclude that it has utility as a device to lower the recidivism rate. One evaluation of the Florida program found that nearly 10 percent of the house arrest sample had their probation revoked for technical violations within 18 months of their sentencing.[69] Another

house arrest
A sentence that requires convicted offenders to spend extended periods of time in their own home as an alternative to incarceration.

Fans wait for rapper Lil' Kim to be released from the Federal Detention Center in Philadelphia. The rapper, who was sentenced in September 2006 to a year and a day in prison for lying about a shootout outside a hip-hop radio station, was released after serving nearly 10 months. She was ordered to remain under house arrest for 30 days after her release.

©AP Images/Joseph Kaczmarek

evaluation of the same program found that recidivism rates were almost identical to a matched sample of inmates released from secure correctional facilities; four out of five offenders in both forms of correction recidivated within five years.[70]

Although these findings are troublesome, the advantages of house arrest in reducing costs and overcrowding in the correctional system probably make further experimentation inevitable. There may also be some unanticipated benefits. Older offenders find house arrest rather than a traditional incarceration sentence to be especially appealing because it allows them to stay clear of the perceived dangerous prison environment and keep their family relations intact. Those with health problems can maintain better access to health care while in the community, especially if they have their own insurance. Furthermore, the state is relieved of the economic burden of paying for the inmate's health care needs when she is on a community-based sanction such as house arrest as opposed to incarceration in a prison.[71]

Electronic Monitoring

For house arrest to work, sentencing authorities must be assured that arrestees are actually at home during their assigned times. Random calls and visits are one way to check on compliance with house arrest orders. However, one of the more interesting developments in the criminal justice system has been the introduction of **electronic monitoring (EM)** devices to manage offender obedience to home confinement orders.[72]

electronic monitoring (EM)

Electronic equipment that enables probation officers to monitor the location of those under house arrest or other forms of supervision.

Electronically monitored offenders wear devices around their ankles, wrists, or necks that send signals to a control office. Two basic types of systems are used: active and passive. Active systems constantly monitor offenders by continuously sending a signal to the central office. If offenders leave their home at an unauthorized time, the signal is broken, and the failure is recorded. In some cases, the control officer is automatically notified electronically through a beeper. Passive systems usually involve random phone calls generated by computers to which the offenders have to respond within a particular time (such as 30 seconds). In addition to probationers, EM can be used at the front end of the system with bailees and at the back end with parolees.

More than 150,000 offenders are being monitored at home.[73] Roughly estimated, about 20 percent of community-based supervision in the United States now involves electronic monitoring, and equipment is provided by approximately 20 private companies. In England and Wales, about 20 percent of 50,000 offenders who started pre- or post-release supervision are electronically monitored; in Sweden, approximately 25 percent of all prisoners are placed on electronic monitoring.[74]

Electronic monitoring supporters claim that EM has the benefits of relatively low cost and high security while helping offenders avoid the pains of imprisonment in overcrowded, dangerous state facilities. Electronic monitoring is capital-intensive, not labor-intensive. Because offenders are monitored by computers, an initial investment in hardware rules out the need for hiring many more supervisory officers to handle large numbers of clients. EM can also benefit from rapidly expanding technological advances. Today, more than 1,000 probationers are now being tracked by global positioning satellite (GPS) systems. Veridian Information Solutions has developed a software system called VeriTracks, which records the GPS data of its wearer (typically every 10 or 15 minutes) and then at night creates a log of the position of the EM client. The position coordinates are then stored in a database application and compared the next morning with crime incident data reported by law enforcement agencies. Crime-mapping software can then be used to pinpoint whether monitored offenders were in the vicinity of a reported crime close to the time it was committed.[75]

The public, not surprisingly, supports EM as a cost-effective alternative to prison sentences that have proven ineffective.[76] EM can be used as part of a pretrial diversionary program, to enhance probation, or as a postincarceration security measure.[77] Surveys of offenders find that they find EM preferable to incarceration.[78] EM can be a welcome addition to the galaxy of intermediate sanctions, providing the judiciary with an enhanced supervision tool.[79]

IS EM EFFECTIVE?   Does EM help reduce recidivism? Some evaluations find that offenders monitored on EM misunderstand its purpose and are as likely to recidivate as are those released without such supervision.[80] However, a number of recent studies have produced more positive results. Kevin Courtright and his associates examined the cost-saving potential of using house arrest with EM as an alternative to incarceration for a drunk-driving population in a Pennsylvania county and found that the program saved money and avoided new construction costs, without widening the net of social control.[81] Kathy Padgett and her associates evaluated data on more than 75,000 offenders placed on home confinement in Florida from 1998 to 2002 and concluded that EM significantly reduced the likelihood of technical violations, reoffending, and absconding. Probationers placed on home confinement with EM had been involved in significantly more serious crimes than those placed on home confinement without EM, indicating that the procedure is being used with the appropriate offender population.[82]

Despite these encouraging results, some civil libertarians are troubled by the fact that EM can erode privacy and liberty. Should U.S. citizens be watched over by a computer? What are the limits of EM? Can it be used with mental patients? HIV carriers? Suicidal teenagers? Those considered high-risk future offenders?

Residential Community Corrections

residential community corrections (RCC)
An intermediate sanction, as well as a parole or pretrial option, in which convicted offenders are housed in a nonsecure facility from which they go to work, attend school, or participate in treatment activities and programs.

The most secure intermediate sanction is a sentence to a **residential community corrections (RCC)** facility. Such a facility has been defined as "a freestanding nonsecure building that is not part of a prison or jail and houses pretrial and adjudicated adults. The residents regularly depart to work, to attend school, and/or participate in treatment activities and programs."[83]

Traditionally, the role of community corrections was supplied by the nonsecure halfway house, designed to reintegrate soon-to-be-paroled prison inmates back into the community. Inmates spent the last few months in the halfway house, acquiring suitable employment, building up cash reserves, obtaining an apartment, and developing a job-related wardrobe.

The traditional concept of community corrections has expanded. Today, the community correctional facility is a vehicle to provide intermediate sanctions as well as a prerelease center for those about to be paroled from the prison system. For example, RCC has been used as a direct sentencing option for judges who believe that particular offenders need a correctional alternative halfway between traditional probation and a stay in prison. Placement in an RCC center can be used as a condition of probation for offenders who need a nonsecure community facility that provides a more structured treatment environment than traditional probation. It is commonly used in the juvenile justice system for youths who need a more secure environment than can be provided by traditional probation yet who are not deemed a threat to the community and do not require a secure placement.

Probation departments and other correctional authorities have been charged with running RCC centers that serve as a pre-prison sentencing alternative. In addition, some RCC centers are operated by private, nonprofit groups that receive referrals from the county or district courts and from probation or parole departments. One such program, Portland House, a private residential center in Minneapolis, operates as an alternative to incarceration for young adult offenders. The 25 residents regularly receive group therapy and financial, vocational, educational, family, and personal counseling. Residents may work to earn a high school equivalency degree. With funds withheld from their earnings at work-release employment, residents pay room and board, family and self-support, and income taxes. Portland House appears to be successful. It is significantly cheaper to run than a state institution, and the recidivism rate of clients is much lower than that of those who have gone through traditional correctional programs.[84]

RCC facilities have also been used as residential pretrial release centers for offenders who are in immediate need of social services before their trial and as halfway-back alternatives for both parole and probation violators who might otherwise have to be imprisoned. In this capacity, RCC programs serve as a base from which offenders can be placed in outpatient psychiatric facilities, drug and alcohol treatment programs, job training, and so on. Some programs make use of both inpatient and outpatient programs to provide clients with specialized treatment, such as substance abuse management.[85]

One recent development has been the use of RCC facilities as **day reporting centers (DRCs)**.[86] Day reporting centers provide a single location to which a variety of clients can report for supervision and treatment. Used in Delaware, Georgia, Utah, and other jurisdictions, DRCs employ existing RCC facilities to service nonresidential clients. They can be used as a step up for probationers who have failed in the community and a step down in security for jail or prison inmates.[87] The Atlanta Day Reporting Center, opened in June 2001, was developed as a joint project by the Georgia Parole Board and the Georgia Department of Corrections. It provides 125 probationers and parolees with structured daily programs in general equivalency diploma (GED) preparation, substance abuse recovery, and cognitive skills training. Although offenders return to their homes at night, the center intensifies training and support and therefore affords many of the well-documented benefits of traditional halfway houses.[88]

More than 2,000 state-run community-based facilities are in use today. In addition, up to 2,500 private, nonprofit RCC programs operate in the United States. About half also have inmates who have been released from prison (halfway houses) and use the RCC placement to ease back into returning to society. The remainder are true intermediate sanctions, including about 400 federally sponsored programs.

Despite the thousands of traditional and innovative RCC programs in operation around the United States, relatively few efforts have been made to evaluate their effectiveness. Those evaluations that do exist suggest that many residents

day reporting center (DRC)
A nonresidential, community-based treatment program.

CONCEPT SUMMARY 14.1		
Intermediate Sanctions		
	Goal	**Problems**
Fines	Monetary sanction	Overburdens the poor
Forfeiture	Monetary sanction, equity	Can be overreaching
Restitution	Pay back victim	Does not reduce recidivism
Shock incarceration and split sentence	"Taste of bars" as a deterrent	Can cause labeling and stigma
Intensive probation	Small caseloads, more supervision	High failure rate
House arrest	Avoids jail	Lacks treatment possibility
Electronic monitoring	Supervision by computer	Technology-dependent, no treatment
Residential community corrections	Less secure than prison	Expensive, high failure rate

do not complete their treatment regimen in RCC facilities because of violating the rules or committing new offenses. Those who do complete the program have lower recidivism rates than the unsuccessful discharges.[89] California's Substance Abuse and Crime Prevention Act (SACPA) allows adults convicted of nonviolent drug possession offenses to participate in community-based drug treatment programs. A recent evaluation of the program found that SACPA clients were likely to be re-arrested for drug crimes, undercutting the effectiveness of the treatment initiative.[90] One explanation for the failure may have been that the sudden influx of offenders simply overwhelmed the treatment resources of an already strained community treatment system; many clients were simply "undertreated."

One reason that it is so difficult to assess RCC facilities is that programs differ considerably with respect to target population, treatment alternatives, and goals. Whereas some are rehabilitation oriented and operate under loose security, others are control oriented and use such security measures as random drug and alcohol testing. Although critics question their overall effectiveness, RCC facilities appear to work for some types of offenders, and some treatment orientations seem to work better than others. Instead of being used as a last-resort community alternative before sentence to a jail or prison, RCC placement might work better with first-time offenders who have relatively little experience with the criminal or juvenile justice systems.[91]

Can Intermediate Sanctions Work?

Intermediate community-based sanctions hold the promise of providing cost-effective crime control strategies without widening the net of the criminal justice system (see Concept Summary 14.1). They reduce overreliance on incarceration and exploding correctional construction costs.[92] Intermediate sanctions are now routinely being used in conjunction with probation. Nonetheless, indications are that, as currently situated, intermediate sanctions are no more effective in reducing recidivism than traditional forms of probation. Because of the more intense monitoring involved, intermediate sanctions may result in more offenders being discovered to have committed technical violations.[93] Revocation for technical reasons helps increase instead of decrease the correctional population, an outcome in opposition to the stated goals of alternative sentencing.[94]

Some criminal justice professionals welcome the use of intermediate sanctions as a practical alternative to prison, whereas others are skeptical about the ability of community sentences to significantly reduce the correctional population. John DiIulio and Charles Logan argue that it is a myth that prison crowding can be reduced, that new construction can be avoided, and that annual operating costs can be cut if greater advantage is taken of intermediate sanctions. The great majority of those offenders under correctional supervision, they argue, have already been on probation and will eventually be supervised in the community. In other words, most convicted criminals are already experiencing an intermediate sanction for at least some part of their sentence. Of inmates currently in state prisons, 67 percent were given probation as an intermediate sanction one or more times on prior convictions, and over 80 percent have had prior convictions resulting in either probation or incarceration. On any day of the week, conclude DiIulio and Logan, you will find three times as many convicts under alternative supervision as you will find under the watchful eye of a warden. And most of those in the warden's custody are probably there at least partly because they did not do well under some prior alternative.[95]

In contrast to this view, Michael Tonry and Mary Lynch suggest that intermediate sanctions can be a useful correctional tool. Not everyone who commits a crime is the same, and all should not receive identical punishments. Clients for intermediate sanction programs might be chosen from those already incarcerated, eliminating the threat of net widening. It might be possible, they suggest, to establish exchange rates that create equivalent sentences for prison and community alternatives, such as three days in home confinement instead of one day in jail. Although intermediate sanctions are not a panacea for all offenders (as Tonry and Lynch put it, "There is no free lunch"), they conclude that for offenders who do not present unacceptable risks of violence, well-managed intermediate sanctions offer a cost-effective way to keep them in the community.[96]

PERSPECTIVES ON JUSTICE

Noninterventionism

The premise of alternative sanctions is attractive, but there is still little evidence that they reduce recidivism. Increased monitoring and surveillance almost guarantee a higher probation failure rate. The more intensive monitoring results in more offenders committing technical violations. Revocation for technical reasons helps increase, not decrease, the correctional population, an outcome in opposition to the stated goals of alternative sentencing. In this sense, alternative sentencing programs may work counter to the noninterventionist philosophy that underpins traditional probation. Instead of resocializing offenders, they may help to widen the net.

♦ RESTORATIVE JUSTICE

Some crime experts believe that, ironically, instead of reducing crime and recidivism, policies based on getting tough on crime can cause crime rates to fluctuate higher and offenders to commit more crime. Punishment does not work because it destroys the offender's dignity and peace of mind. Instead, **restorative justice** advocates suggest a policy based on restoring the damage caused by crime and creating a system of justice that includes all the parties harmed by the criminal act—the victim, offender, community, and society.[97]

restorative justice
A perspective on justice that views the main goal of the criminal justice system to be a systematic response to wrongdoing that emphasizes healing the wounds of victims, offenders, and communities caused or revealed by crime; it stresses noncoercive and healing approaches whenever possible.

John Braithwaite's influential book *Crime, Shame, and Reintegration* helps define restoration. According to Braithwaite, a law violator must be made to realize that while his actions have caused harm, he is still a valuable person who can be reaccepted by society, a process he called *reintegrative shaming*. To be reintegrative, shaming must be brief and controlled and then followed by ceremonies of forgiveness, apology, and repentance.[98]

The Concept of Restoration

According to the restorative view, crimes can seem quite different, ranging from a violent assault to a white-collar fraud scheme. Nonetheless, they all share one common trait: They bring harm to the community in which they occur. The traditional justice system does little to involve the community in the justice process.

What has developed is a system of coercive punishments, administered by bureaucrats, that is inherently harmful to offenders and reduces the likelihood

EXHIBIT 14.1

The Basic Principles of Restorative Justice

- ◆ Crime is an offense against human relationships.
- ◆ Victims and the community are central to justice processes.
- ◆ The first priority of justice processes is to assist victims.
- ◆ The second priority is to restore the community, to the degree possible.
- ◆ The offender has personal responsibility to victims and to the community for crimes committed.
- ◆ The offender will develop improved competency and understanding as a result of the restorative justice experience.
- ◆ Stakeholders share responsibilities for restorative justice through partnerships for action.

Source: Anne Seymour, "Restorative Justice/Community Justice," in *National Victim Assistance Academy Textbook*, ed. Grace Colman, Mario Gaboury, Morna Murray, and Anne Seymour (Washington, D.C.: National Victim Assistance Academy, 2001, updated July 2002), Chapter 4.

they will ever become productive members of society. This system relies on punishment, stigma, and disgrace. What is needed instead is a justice policy that repairs the harm caused by crime and includes all parties having suffered from that harm, including the victim, the community, and the offender. The principles of this approach are set out in Exhibit 14.1.

An important aspect of achieving these goals is for the offender to accept accountability for her actions and responsibility for the harm that her actions have caused. Only then can she be restored as a productive member of her community. **Restoration** involves turning the justice system into a healing process rather than a distributor of retribution and revenge.

Most people involved in offender–victim relationships know one another or were related in some way before the criminal incident took place. Instead of treating one of the involved parties as a victim deserving sympathy and the other as a criminal deserving punishment, it is more productive to address the issues that produced conflict between these people. Instead of taking sides and choosing whom to isolate and punish, society should try to reconcile the parties involved in conflict.[99] The effectiveness of justice ultimately depends on the stake that a person has in the community (or a particular social group). If a person does not value his membership in the group, he will be unlikely to accept responsibility, show remorse, or repair the injuries caused by his actions.

The Process of Restoration

The restoration process begins by redefining crime in terms of a conflict among the offender, the victim, and affected constituencies (families, schools, workplaces, and so on). Therefore, it is vitally important that the resolution take place within the context in which the conflict originally occurred and not be transferred to a specialized institution that has no social connection to the community or group from which the conflict originated. In other words, most conflicts are better settled in the community than in a court.

By maintaining ownership or jurisdiction over the conflict, the community is able to express its shared outrage about the offense. Shared community outrage is directly communicated to the offender. The victim is also given a chance to voice his or her story, and the offender can directly communicate his or her need for social reintegration and treatment.

restoration
A vision of justice that attempts to heal the rift between criminal and victim to provide healing instead of punishment.

The website for the Center for Restorative Justice and Peacemaking provides links and information on the ideals of restoration and programs based on its principles. You can check it out by linking through the Siegel/Senna Introduction to Criminal Justice 11e website: www.thomsonedu.com/criminaljustice/siegel.

Restoration programs involve an understanding among all the parties involved in a criminal act: the victim, offender, and community. Although processes differ in structure and style, they generally include the following:

◆ An element in which the offender is asked to recognize that he caused injury to personal and social relations, and a determination and acceptance of responsibility (ideally accompanied by a statement of remorse).

◆ A commitment to both material reparation (for example, monetary restitution) and symbolic reparation (for example, an apology).

◆ A determination of community support and assistance for both victim and offender.

The intended result of the process is to repair the injuries suffered by the victim and the community while ensuring the reintegration of the offender.

Restoration Programs

Negotiation, mediation, consensus building, and peacemaking have been part of the dispute-resolution process in European and Asian communities for centuries.[100] Native American and Native Canadian people have long used the type of community participation in the adjudication process (for example, sentencing circles, sentencing panels, and elders panels) that restorative justice advocates are now embracing.[101]

In some Native American communities, people accused of breaking the law will meet with community members; victims, if any; village elders; and agents of the justice system in a **sentencing circle**. Each member of the circle expresses his or her feelings about the act that was committed and raises questions or concerns. The accused can express regret about his or her actions and a desire to change the harmful behavior. People may suggest ways that the offender can make things up to the community and those whom he or she harmed. A treatment program, such as Alcoholics Anonymous, can be suggested, if appropriate.

Restorative justice policies and practices are now being adopted around the world. Legislation in 19 states includes reference to the use of victim–offender mediation. There are more than 1,400 victim–offender mediation programs in North America and Europe.[102] What forms do these programs take?

SCHOOLS Some schools have adopted restorative justice practices to deal with students who are involved in drug and alcohol abuse, without having to resort to more punitive measures such as expulsion. Schools in Colorado, Minnesota, and elsewhere are trying to involve students in relational rehabilitation programs, which strive to improve the person's relationships with key figures in the community who may have been harmed by his or her actions.[103]

POLICE Restorative justice has also been implemented when crime is first encountered by police. The new community policing models are an attempt to bring restorative concepts into law enforcement. Restorative justice relies on the fact that criminal justice policy makers need to listen and respond to the needs of those who are to be affected by their actions, and community policing relies on policies established with input and exchanges between officers and citizens.[104]

In addition, police may be included in family group conference (FGC) programs. Developed in New Zealand, FGCs are conferences in which victims are invited to meet offenders and their families, with the police and a justice coordinator present, to discuss the crime and its outcome.[105] Victims are thereby given a voice to tell of the impact of the crime and ask the offender: Why were they victimized? Will they be victimized again? How will the offender put things right? In New Zealand, victims have the right to attend the mandated FGC and to tell offenders face to face about the personal impact of the crime.

---

sentencing circle
In native communities, a group of citizens, leaders, victims, and so on who meet to deal with conflicts between people in an equitable way.

To learn more about sentencing circles, read the description and analysis provided by the National Institute of Justice. To reach this section of the NIJ website, go to the Siegel/Senna Introduction to Criminal Justice 11e website: www.thomsonedu.com/criminaljustice/siegel.

Restorative Cautioning in England

After an arrest is made, police in England and Wales have four possible procedures they may follow: (1) take no further action, (2) give an informal warning, (3) administer a formal police caution, or (4) decide to prosecute by sending the case to the Crown Prosecution Service. If the officer in charge decides to formally caution the suspect, the case will terminate at the police level. The formal caution, usually given by a senior officer, involves forcefully reminding the offender not to reoffend. Although the formal caution results in termination of the case, it is recorded in the National Police Computer and can be disclosed to courts in subsequent criminal cases.

English police forces are now experimenting with a form of restorative cautioning. This uses a trained police facilitator with a script to encourage an offender to take responsibility for repairing the harm caused by the offense. Sometimes the victim is present, in which case the meeting is called a restorative conference; usually, however, the victim is not present. Traditional cautioning, on the other hand, lasts only a few minutes, requires no special training, and focuses on the officer explaining the possible consequences of future offending.

In 2004 the Home Office conducted a study that attempted to evaluate the effectiveness of restorative cautioning. It compared resanctioning rates from the Thames Valley police force, where restorative cautioning is standard policy, with rates from two police forces in similar jurisdictions—Sussex and Warwickshire— where traditional cautioning is used. Resanctioning is defined as an offender receiving either a conviction or a police disposition.

In order to test the impact of restorative cautioning, the study looked at resanctioning rates over a 24-month period using the records of 29,000 offenders from the three police forces. The study showed that resanctioning rates in Thames Valley were statistically significantly lower than in the other two jurisdictions. Although resanctioning rates declined in all three jurisdictions, Thames Valley had significantly lower rates than Sussex for all three years as well as significantly lower rates than Warwickshire for the first two years of the study. Restorative cautioning also seemed to provide many positive outcomes for both victims and offenders regardless of its impact on resanctioning:

◆ It helped offenders understand the impact of crime.

◆ It provided symbolic and material reparation to victims.

◆ It offered a sense of resolution in the case.

Critical Thinking

1. How would the cautioning system work in the United States? Is it too lenient, is it too formal, or would it be an effective program?

2. Would restorative justice measures work with felony offenders such as rapists and drug abusers? Can we really forgive their misdeeds? Should they be given the privilege of remaining in the community while they receive treatment? Should they be punished for their criminal activity and not merely restored to the community?

InfoTrac College Edition Research

To learn more about policing in England, use it in a keyword search on InfoTrac College Edition.

Sources: Aidan Wilcox, Richard Young, and Carolyn Hoyle, "Two-Year Resanctioning Study: A Comparison of Restorative and Traditional Cautions" (British Home Office, 2004) (http://www.homeoffice. gov.uk/rds/pdfs04/rdsolr5704.pdf); Lynette Parker, "Evaluating Restorative Programmes: Reports from Two Countries" (Restorative Justice.org, June 2005) (http://www.restorativejustice.org/editions/ 2005/june05/evaluations), accessed on June 1, 2006.

COURTS In the court system, restorative programs typically involve diverting the formal court process. Restoration programs encourage meeting and reconciling the conflicts between offenders and victims via victim advocacy, mediation programs, and sentencing circles, in which crime victims and their families are brought together with offenders and their families in an effort to formulate a sanction that addresses the needs of each party. Victims are given a chance to voice their stories, and offenders can help compensate them financially or provide some service (for example, fixing damaged property).[106] The goal is to enable offenders to appreciate the damage they have caused, to make amends, and to be reintegrated back into society.

The International Justice feature describes the "restorative cautioning" program used in England.

The Challenge of Restorative Justice

Although restorative justice holds great promise, there are also some concerns.[107] One issue is whether programs reach out to all members of the community. Research indicates that entry into programs may be tilted toward white offenders and more restrictive to minorities, a condition that negates the purpose of the restorative movement.[108]

Restorative justice programs must be wary of the cultural and social differences that can be found throughout the heterogeneous society of the United States.[109] What may be considered restorative in one subculture may be considered insulting and damaging in another.[110] Similarly, so many diverse programs call themselves restorative that evaluating them is difficult. Each one may be pursuing a unique objective. In other words, no single definition has been derived of what constitutes restorative justice.[111]

Possibly the greatest challenge to restorative justice is the difficult task of balancing the needs of offenders with those of their victims. If programs focus solely on the reconciliation of the victim's needs, they may risk ignoring the offender's needs and increasing the likelihood of reoffending. Sharon Levrant and her colleagues suggest that restorative justice programs featuring short-term interactions with victims fail to help offenders learn prosocial ways of behaving. Restorative justice advocates may falsely assume that relatively brief interludes of public shaming will change deeply rooted criminal predispositions.[112]

In contrast, programs focusing on the offender may turn off victims and their advocates. Some victim advocacy groups have voiced concerns about the focus of restorative justice programs. Some believe that victims' rights are threatened by certain features of the restorative justice process, such as respectful listening to the offender's story and consensual dispositions. These features seem opposed to a victim's claim of the right to be seen as a victim, to insist on the offender being branded a criminal, to blame the offender, and not to be "victimized all over again by the process." Many victims do want an apology if it is heartfelt and easy to get. But some want, even more, to put the traumatic incident behind them, to retrieve stolen property being held for use at trial, and to be assured that the offender will receive treatment that he is thought to need if he is not to victimize someone else. For victims such as these, restorative justice processes can seem unnecessary at best.[113]

These are a few of the obstacles that restorative justice programs must overcome for them to be successful and productive. Yet, because the method holds so much promise, criminologists are conducting numerous demonstration projects to find the most effective means of returning the ownership of justice to the people and the community.

ThomsonNOW™ Improve your grade on the exam with Personalized Study! For reinforcement resources and a mastery check of restorative justice, go to www.thomsonedu.com/thomsonnow.

ETHICAL CHALLENGES IN CRIMINAL JUSTICE: A WRITING ASSIGNMENT

Two local teens have been convicted for a hate crime. It seems that while at a party they observed a 17-year-old Hispanic male kissing a 15-year-old white girl. Enraged, they dragged the boy outside and beat him severely, yelling out ethnic slurs during the attack. The victim suffered multiple contusions and a fractured arm. The attackers have no prior arrests or convictions. Would you recommend that they be placed in a restorative justice program? If so, why? What program would you recommend? If not, state your reasons for barring them from the program.

Doing Research on the Web

To learn more about restorative justice and to do research on recent developments in the field, go to Restorative Justice Online, a comprehensive, nonpartisan website devoted to restorative justice principles, practice, programs, and theory. As well, note that the National Institute of Justice maintains an online resource designed to promote the understanding of restorative justice. A third source is the Centre for Restorative Justice at Simon Fraser University. You can access all three of these sources by going to the Siegel/Senna Introduction to Criminal Justice 11e website: www.thomsonedu.com/criminaljustice/siegel.

SUMMARY

◆ Probation can be traced to the common-law practice of granting clemency to deserving offenders.

◆ The modern probation concept was developed by John Augustus of Boston, who personally sponsored 2,000 convicted inmates over an 18-year period.

◆ Today, probation is the community supervision of convicted offenders by order of the court. It is a sentence reserved for defendants whom the magistrate views as having potential for rehabilitation without needing to serve prison or jail terms.

◆ Probation is practiced in every state and by the federal government and includes both adult and juvenile offenders.

◆ In the decision to grant probation, most judges are influenced by their personal views and the presentence reports of the probation staff.

◆ Once on probation, the offender must follow a set of rules or conditions, the violation of which may lead to revocation of probation and reinstatement of a prison sentence. These rules vary from state to state but usually involve such demands as refraining from using alcohol or drugs, obeying curfews, and terminating past criminal associations.

◆ Probation officers are usually organized into countywide departments, although some agencies are statewide and others are combined parole–probation departments.

◆ Probation departments have instituted a number of innovative programs designed to bring better services to their clients. These include restitution and diversionary programs, intensive probation, and residential probation.

◆ In recent years, the U.S. Supreme Court has granted probationers greater due process rights. Today, when the state wishes to revoke probation, it must conduct a full hearing on the matter and provide the probationer with an attorney when that assistance is warranted.

◆ To supplement probation, a whole new family of intermediate sanctions has been developed. These range from pretrial diversion to residential community corrections. Other widely used intermediate sanctions include fines and forfeiture, house arrest, and intensive probation supervision.

◆ Electronic monitoring involves a device worn by an offender under home confinement. Although some critics complain that EM smacks of a "Big Brother Is Watching You" mentality, it would seem an attractive alternative to a stay in a dangerous, deteriorated, secure correctional facility.

◆ A stay in a community correctional center is one of the most intrusive alternative sentencing options. Residents may be eligible for work and educational release during the day but will attend group sessions in the evening. Residential community correction is less costly than more secure institutions, while being equally effective.

◆ It is too soon to determine whether alternative sanction programs are successful, but they provide a hope of being lost-cost, high-security alternatives to traditional corrections. Alternatives to incarceration can help reduce overcrowding in the prison system and spare nonviolent offenders the pains of a prison experience. Although alternatives may not be much more effective than prison sentences in reducing recidivism rates, they are far less costly and can free up needed space for more violent offenders.

◆ A promising approach to community sentencing is the use of restorative justice programs.

◆ Restorative justice programs stress healing and redemption, not punishment and deterrence. Restoration means that the offender accepts accountability for her actions and responsibility for the harm that her actions have caused. Restoration involves turning the justice system into a healing process instead of a distributor of retribution and revenge.

◆ Restoration programs are being used around the nation and involve mediation and sentencing circles.

KEY TERMS

ThomsonNOW Maximize your study time by using ThomsonNOW's diagnostic study plan to help you review this chapter. The Study Plan will

◆ help you identify areas on which you should concentrate;

◆ provide interactive exercises to help you master the chapter concepts; and

◆ provide a post-test to confirm you are ready to move on to the next chapter.

CRITICAL THINKING QUESTIONS

1. What is the purpose of probation? Identify some conditions of probation, and discuss the responsibilities of the probation officer.

2. Discuss the procedures involved in probation revocation. What are the rights of the probationer?

3. Is probation a privilege or a right? Explain.

4. Should a convicted criminal make restitution to the victim? Why or why not? When is restitution inappropriate?

5. Should offenders be fined based on the severity of what they did or according to their ability to pay? Is it fair to gear day fines to wages? Why or why

not? Should offenders be punished more severely if they are financially successful? Explain.

6. Does house arrest involve a violation of personal freedom? Does wearing an ankle bracelet smack of "Big Brother"? Would you want the government monitoring your daily activities? Could this be expanded, for example, to monitor the whereabouts of AIDS patients? Explain.

7. Do you agree that criminals can be restored through community interaction? Considering the fact that recidivism rates are so high, are traditional sanctions a waste of time and restorative ones the wave of the future?

NOTES

1. Luis Hernandez, "Ex-Teacher Gets a Year in Sex Case: Elizabeth Stow Avoids Prison But Not Jail for Sex with Teens," *Visalia Times Delta*, November 19, 2005 (http://www.visaliatimesdelta.com/apps/pbcs.dll/article?AID=/20051119/NEWS01/511190317/1002/NEWS17), accessed on May 29, 2006.

2. Arnulf Kolstad, "Imprisonment as Rehabilitation: Offenders' Assessment of Why It Does Not Work," *Journal of Criminal Justice* 24 (1996): 323–35.

3. For a history of probation, see Edward Sieh, "From Augustus to the Progressives: A Study of Probation's Formative Years," *Federal Probation* 57 (1993): 67–72.

4. Ibid.

5. David Rothman, *Conscience and Convenience* (Boston: Little, Brown, 1980), pp. 82–117.

6. Matthew Durose and Patrick A. Langan, *State Court Sentencing of Convicted Felons, 1998* (Washington, D.C.: Bureau of Justice Statistics, February 2001).

7. Data in this section come from Lauren E. Glaze and Seri Pala, *Probation and Parole in the United States, 2004* (Washington, D.C.: Bureau of Justice Statistics, 2005).

8. *Higdon v. United States*, 627 F.2d 893 (9th Cir. 1980).

9. *United States v. Lee*, No. 01–4485, January 7, 2003; *United States v. Lee*, PICS N. 03–0023.

10. Brian Netter, "Avoiding the Shameful Backlash: Social Repercussions for the Increased Use of Alternative Sanctions," *Journal of Criminal Law & Criminology* 96 (2005): 187–215.

11. Todd Clear and Edward Latessa, "Probation Officers' Roles in Intensive Supervision: Surveillance Versus Treatment," *Justice Quarterly* 10 (1993): 441–62.

12. Paul von Zielbauer, "Probation Dept. Is Now Arming Officers Supervising Criminals," *New York Times*, August 7, 2003, p. 5.

13. Karl Hanson and Suzanne Wallace-Carpretta, "Predictors of Criminal Recidivism Among Male Batterers," *Psychology, Crime & Law* 10 (2004): 413–27.

14. David Duffee and Bonnie Carlson, "Competing Value Premises for the Provision of Drug Treatment to Probationers," *Crime and Delinquency* 42 (1996): 574–92.

15. Richard Sluder and Rolando Del Carmen, "Are Probation and Parole Officers Liable for Injuries Caused by Probationers and Parolees?" *Federal Probation* 54 (1990): 3–12.

16. Patricia Harris, "Client Management Classification and Prediction of Probation Outcome," *Crime and Delinquency* 40 (1994): 154–74.

17. Anne Schneider, Laurie Ervin, and Zoann Snyder-Joy, "Further Exploration of the Flight from Discretion: The Role of Risk/Need Instruments in Probation Supervision Decisions," *Journal of Criminal Justice* 24 (1996): 109–21.

18. Todd Clear and Vincent O'Leary, *Controlling the Offender in the Community* (Lexington, Mass.: Lexington, 1983), pp. 11–29, 77–100.

19. Joan Petersilia, "An Evaluation of Intensive Probation in California," *Journal of Criminal Law and Criminology* 82 (1992): 610–58.

20. Glaze and Pala, *Probation and Parole in the United States, 2004.*

21. M. Kevin Gray, Monique Fields, and Sheila Royo Maxwell, "Examining Probation Violations: Who, What, and When," *Crime and Delinquency* 47 (2001): 537–57.

22. Cassia Spohn and David Holleran, "The Effect of Imprisonment on Recidivism Rates of Felony Offenders: A Focus on Drug Offenders," *Criminology* 40 (2002): 329–59.

23. Joan Petersilia, Susan Turner, James Kahan, and Joyce Peterson, *Granting Felons Probation: Public Risks and Alternatives* (Santa Monica, Calif.: RAND, 1985).

24. Kathryn Morgan, "Factors Influencing Probation Outcome: A Review of the Literature," *Federal Probation* 57 (1993): 23–29.

25. Michelle Meloy, "The Sex Offender Next Door: An Analysis of Recidivism, Risk Factors, and Deterrence of Sex Offenders on Probation," *Criminal Justice Policy Review* 16 (2005): 211–36.

26. Kathryn Morgan, "Factors Associated with Probation Outcome," *Journal of Criminal Justice* 22 (1994): 341–53.

27. Paula M. Ditton, *Mental Health and Treatment of Inmates and Probationers* (Washington, D.C.: Bureau of Justice Statistics, 1999).

28. *Minnesota v. Murphy*, 465 U.S. 420, 104 S.Ct. 1136, 79 L.Ed.2d 409 (1984).

29. *Griffin v. Wisconsin*, 483 U.S. 868, 107 S.Ct. 3164, 97 L.Ed.2d 709 (1987).

30. *United States v. Knights*, 122 S.Ct. 587 (2001).

31. *Mempa v. Rhay*, 389 U.S. 128, 88 S.Ct. 254, 19 L.Ed.2d 336 (1967).

32. *Morrissey v. Brewer*, 408 U.S. 471, 92 S.Ct. 2593, 33 L.Ed.2d 484 (1972).

33. *Gagnon v. Scarpelli*, 411 U.S. 778, 93 S.Ct. 1756, 36 L.Ed.2d 656 (1973).

34. *United States v. Granderson*, 114 Ct. 1259, 127 L.Ed.2d 611 (1994).

35. "Law in Massachusetts Requires Probationers to Pay 'Day Fees,'" *Criminal Justice Newsletter*, September 15, 1988, p. 1.

36. Peter Finn and Dale Parent, *Making the Offender Foot the Bill: A Texas Program* (Washington, D.C.: National Institute of Justice, 1992).

37. Nicole Leeper Piquero, "A Recidivism Analysis of Maryland's Community Probation Program," *Journal of Criminal Justice* 31 (2003): 295–308.

38. Todd R. Clear, "Places Not Cases? Re-thinking the Probation Focus," *Howard Journal of Criminal Justice* 44 (2005): 172–84.

39. Ariel Hart, "Runaway Bride Enters Plea And Is Sentenced to Probation," *New York Times*, June 3, 2005, p. A14.

40. Todd Clear and Patricia Hardyman, "The New Intensive Supervision Movement," *Crime and Delinquency* 36 (1990): 42–60.

41. Richard Lawrence, "Reexamining Community Corrections Models," *Crime and Delinquency* 37 (1991): 449–64.

42. Clear and Hardyman, "The New Intensive Supervision Movement."

43. For a thorough review of these programs, see James Byrne, Arthur Lurigio, and Joan Petersilia, eds., *Smart Sentencing: The Emergence of Intermediate Sanctions* (Newbury Park, Calif.: Sage, 1993).

44. Norval Morris and Michael Tonry, *Between Prison and Probation: Intermediate Punishments in a Rational Sentencing System* (New York: Oxford University Press, 1990).

45. Michael Tonry and Richard Will, *Intermediate Sanctions* (Washington, D.C.: National Institute of Justice, 1990).

46. Ibid., p. 8.

47. Michael Maxfield and Terry Baumer, "Home Detention with Electronic Monitoring: Comparing Pretrial and Postconviction Programs," *Crime and Delinquency* 36 (1990): 521–56.

48. Sally Hillsman and Judith Greene, "Tailoring Fines to the Financial Means of Offenders," *Judicature* 72 (1988): 38–45.

49. *Tate v. Short*, 401 U.S. 395, 91 S.Ct. 668, 28 L.Ed.2d 130 (1971).

50. Margaret Gordon and Daniel Glaser, "The Use and Effects of Financial Penalties in Municipal Courts," *Criminology* 29 (1991): 651–76.

51. "'Day Fines' Being Tested in New York City Court," *Criminal Justice Newsletter*, September 1, 1988, pp. 4–5.

52. Pennsylvania Department of Corrections, "Day Fines, 2003" (http://www.cor.state.pa.us/stats/lib/stats/Day_Fines.pdf), accessed on June 10, 2005.

53. Doris Layton MacKenzie, "Evidence-Based Corrections: Identifying What Works," *Crime and Delinquency* 46 (2000): 457–72.

54. John L. Worrall, "Addicted to the Drug War: The Role of Civil Asset Forfeiture as a Budgetary Necessity in Contemporary Law Enforcement," *Journal of Criminal Justice* 29 (2001): 171–87.

55. C. Yorke, *Some Consideration on the Law of Forfeiture for High Treason*, 2nd ed. (London, England: printed by Mr. Thomas Cadell, 1746), p. 26, cited in David Fried, "Rationalizing Criminal Forfeiture," *Journal of Criminal Law and Criminology* 79 (1988): 329.

56. Fried, "Rationalizing Criminal Forfeiture," 436.

57. James B. Jacobs, Coleen Friel, and Edward O'Callaghan, "Pension Forfeiture: A Problematic Sanction for Public Corruption," *American Criminal Law Review* 35 (1997): 57–92.

58. Worrall, "Addicted to the Drug War."

59. For a general review, see Burt Galaway and Joe Hudson, *Criminal Justice, Restitution, and Reconciliation* (New York: Criminal Justice Press, 1990); Robert Carter, Jay Cocks, and Daniel Glazer, "Community Service: A Review of the Basic Issues," *Federal Probation* 51 (1987): 4–11.

60. Morris and Tonry, *Between Prison and Probation*, pp. 171–75.

61. Frederick Allen and Harvey Treger, "Community Service Orders in Federal Probation: Perceptions of Probationers and Host Agencies," *Federal Probation* 54 (1990): 8–14.

62. Gail Caputo, "Community Service in Texas: Results of a Probation Survey," *Corrections Compendium* 30 (2005): 8–12.

63. Sudipto Roy, "Two Types of Juvenile Restitution Programs in Two Midwestern Counties: A Comparative Study," *Federal Probation* 57 (1993): 48–53.

64. Jodi Brown, *Correctional Populations in the United States, 1996* (Washington, D.C.: Bureau of Justice Statistics, 1999), p. 39.

65. James Ryan, "Who Gets Revoked? A Comparison of Intensive Supervision Successes and Failures in Vermont," *Crime and Delinquency* 43 (1997): 104–18.

66. Peter Jones, "Expanding the Use of Noncustodial Sentencing Options: An Evaluation of the Kansas Community Corrections Act," *Howard Journal* 29 (1990): 114–29; Michael Agopian, "The Impact of Intensive Supervision Probation on Gang-Drug Offenders," *Criminal Justice Policy Review* 4 (1990): 214–22.

67. Angela Robertson, Paul Grimes, and Kevin Rogers, "A Short-Run Cost–Benefit Analysis of Community-Based Interventions for Juvenile Offenders," *Crime and Delinquency* 47 (2001): 265–84.

68. Betsy Fulton, Edward Latessa, Amy Stichman, and Lawrence Travis, "The State of ISP: Research and Policy Implications," *Federal Probation* 61 (1997): 65–75.

69. S. Christopher Baird and Dennis Wagner, "Measuring Diversion: The Florida Community Control Program," *Crime and Delinquency* 36 (1990): 112–25.

70. Linda Smith and Ronald Akers, "A Comparison of Recidivism of Florida's Community Control and Prison: A Five-Year Survival Analysis," *Journal of Research in Crime and Delinquency* 30 (1993): 267–92.

71. Brian Payne and Randy Gainey, "The Influence of Demographic Factors on the Experience of House Arrest," *Federal Probation* 66 (2002): 64–70.

72. Robert N. Altman, Robert E. Murray, and Evey B. Wooten, "Home Confinement: A '90s Approach to Community Supervision," *Federal Probation* 61 (1997): 30–32.

73. Jennifer Lee, "Some States Track Parolees by Satellite," *New York Times*, January 31, 2002, p. A3.

74. Ralph Gable and Robert Gable, "Electronic Monitoring: Positive Intervention Strategies," *Federal Probation* 69 (2005): 21–25.

75. Cecil Greek, "The Cutting Edge," *Federal Probation* 66 (2002): 51–53; Veridian's website (http://www.veridian.com), accessed on November 18, 2003.

76. Preston Elrod and Michael Brown, "Predicting Public Support for Electronic House Arrest: Results from a New York County Survey," *American Behavioral Scientist* 39 (1996): 461–74.

77. Peter Ibarra and Edna Erez, "Victim-centric Diversion? The Electronic Monitoring of Domestic Violence Cases," *Behavioral Sciences & the Law* 23 (2005): 259–76.

78. Brian Payne and Randy Gainey, "The Electronic Monitoring of Offenders Released from Jail or Prison: Safety, Control, and Comparisons to the Incarceration Experience," *Prison Journal* 84 (2004): 413–35.

79. Joseph Papy and Richard Nimer, "Electronic Monitoring in Florida," *Federal Probation* 55 (1991): 31–33.

80. Payne and Gainey, "The Electronic Monitoring of Offenders Released from Jail or Prison"; Mary Finn and Suzanne Muirhead-Steves, "The Effectiveness of Electronic Monitoring with Male Parolees," *Justice Quarterly* 19 (2002): 293–313.

81. Kevin E. Courtright, Bruce L. Berg, and Robert J. Mutchnick, "The Cost Effectiveness of Using House Arrest with Electronic Monitoring for Drunk Drivers," *Federal Probation* 61 (1997): 19–22.

82. Kathy Padgett, William Bales, and Thomas Blomberg, "Under Surveillance: An Empirical Test of the Effectiveness and Consequences of Electronic Monitoring," *Criminology & Public Policy* 5 (2006): 61–91.

83. Edward Latessa and Lawrence Travis III, "Residential Community Correctional Programs," in James Byrne, Arthur Lurigio, and Joan Petersilia, eds., *Smart Sentencing: The Emergence of Intermediate Sanctions* (Newbury Park, Calif.: Sage, 1993).

84. Updated with personal correspondence, Portland House personnel, September 4, 2006.

85. Harvey Siegal, James Fisher, Richard Rapp, Casey Kelliher, Joseph Wagner, William O'Brien, and Phyllis Cole, "Enhancing Substance Abuse Treatment with Case Management," *Journal of Substance Abuse Treatment* 13 (1996): 93–98.

86. Dale Parent, *Day Reporting Centers for Criminal Offenders—A Descriptive Analysis of Existing Programs* (Washington, D.C.: National Institute of Justice, 1990).

87. David Diggs and Stephen Pieper, "Using Day Reporting Centers as an Alternative to Jail," *Federal Probation* 58 (1994): 9–12.

88. Information on the Atlanta program can be found at http://www.pap.state.ga.us/2001%20Annual%20Report%20Web/ day_reporting_centers.htm (accessed on November 18, 2003).

89. David Hartmann, Paul Friday, and Kevin Minor, "Residential Probation: A Seven-Year Follow-Up of Halfway House Discharges," *Journal of Criminal Justice* 22 (1994): 503–15.

90. David Farabee, Yih-Ing Hser, Douglas Anglin, and David Huang, "Recidivism Among an Early Cohort of California's Proposition 36 Offenders," *Criminology & Public Policy* 3 (2004): 563–83.

91. Banhram Haghighi and Alma Lopez, "Success/Failure of Group Home Treatment Programs for Juveniles," *Federal Probation* 57 (1993): 53–57.

92. Richard Rosenfeld and Kimberly Kempf, "The Scope and Purposes of Corrections: Exploring Alternative Responses to Crowding," *Crime and Delinquency* 37 (1991): 481–505.

93. For a thorough review, see Michael Tonry and Mary Lynch, "Intermediate Sanctions," in *Crime and Justice: A Review of Research*, vol. 20, ed. Michael Tonry (Chicago: University of Chicago Press, 1996), pp. 99–144.

94. Francis Cullen, "Control in the Community: The Limits of Reform?" paper presented at the International Association of Residential and Community Alternatives, Philadelphia, November 1993.

95. John DiIulio and Charles Logan, "The Ten Deadly Myths About Crime and Punishment in the U.S.," *Wisconsin Interest* 1 (1992): 21–35.

96. Tonry and Lynch, "Intermediate Sanctions."

97. Kathleen Daly and Russ Immarigeon, "The Past, Present and Future of Restorative Justice: Some Critical Reflections," *Contemporary Justice Review* 1 (1998): 21–45.

98. John Braithwaite, *Crime, Shame, and Reintegration* (Melbourne, Australia: Cambridge University Press, 1989).

99. Gene Stephens, "The Future of Policing: From a War Model to a Peace Model," in *The Past, Present, and Future of American Criminal Justice*, ed. Brendan Maguire and Polly Radosh (Dix Hills, N.Y.: General Hall, 1996), pp. 77–93.

100. Kay Pranis, "Peacemaking Circles: Restorative Justice in Practice Allows Victims and Offenders to Begin Repairing the Harm," *Corrections Today* 59 (1997): 74–78.

101. Carol LaPrairie, "The 'New' Justice: Some Implications for Aboriginal Communities," *Canadian Journal of Criminology* 40 (1998): 61–79.

102. Robert Coates, Mark Umbreit, and Betty Vos, "Restorative Justice Systemic Change: The Washington County Experience," *Federal Probation* 68 (2004): 16–23.

103. David R. Karp and Beau Breslin, "Restorative Justice in School Communities," *Youth and Society* 33 (2001): 249–72.

104. Paul Jesilow and Deborah Parsons, "Community Policing as Peacemaking," *Policing and Society* 10 (2000): 163–83.

105. Donald J. Schmid, *Restorative Justice in New Zealand* (Wellington, New Zealand: Fullbright New Zealand, 2001).

106. Gordon Bazemore and Curt Taylor Griffiths, "Conferences, Circles, Boards, and Mediations: The 'New Wave' of Community Justice Decision Making," *Federal Probation* 61 (1997): 25–37.

107. John Braithwaite, "Setting Standards for Restorative Justice," *British Journal of Criminology* 42 (2002): 563–77.

108. Nancy Rodriguez, "Restorative Justice, Communities, and Delinquency: Whom Do We Reintegrate?" *Criminology & Public Policy* 4 (2005): 103–30.

109. Braithwaite, "Setting Standards for Restorative Justice."

110. David Altschuler, "Community Justice Initiatives: Issues and Challenges in the U.S. Context," *Federal Probation* 65 (2001): 28–33.

111. Lois Presser and Patricia Van Voorhis, "Values and Evaluation: Assessing Processes and Outcomes of Restorative Justice Programs," *Crime and Delinquency* 48 (2002): 162–89.

112. Sharon Levrant, Francis Cullen, Betsy Fulton, and John Wozniak, "Reconsidering Restorative Justice: The Corruption of Benevolence Revisited?" *Crime and Delinquency* 45 (1999): 3–28.

113. Michael E. Smith, *What Future for "Public Safety" and "Restorative Justice" in Community Corrections?* (Washington, D.C.: National Institute of Justice, 2001).

CHAPTER 15

Corrections: History, Institutions, and Populations

Chapter Outline

Chapter Objectives

After reading this chapter, you should be able to:

1. Describe the history of penal institutions.
2. Know the differences between the Auburn (congregate) system and the Pennsylvania (isolate) system.
3. Understand the history of penal reform.
4. Explain the concept of the jail.
5. Discuss the issue of the new-generation jails.
6. Describe different levels of prison security.
7. Discuss the super-maximum-security prison.
8. Know what is meant by the term *penal harm*.
9. Discuss the benefits and drawbacks of boot camps.
10. Explain the current trends in the prison population.

he fact that prison can be a dangerous place was graphically demonstrated on August 23, 2003, when ex-priest John Geoghan, a convicted pedophile, was strangled by Joseph L. Druce, 38 (shown at left), a fellow inmate inside a maximum-security Massachusetts prison. Geoghan, who was accused of molesting more than 150 boys in his parishes over three decades, had been serving a nine-year sentence for fondling a boy in a public swimming pool in 1991. Druce, who was serving a life sentence without parole for strangling a trucker whom he believed was gay, later told investigators that he had plotted to murder Geoghan for at least a month. He had come up with a plan to jam the priest's cell door shut with part of a book, tie him up with a T-shirt, and use stretched-out socks to strangle him.

Druce represents an all-too-familiar figure in the U.S. prison system. Named Darrin Smiledge at birth, Druce was an unplanned child who by age nine was obsessed with sex and violent fantasies, often venting his rage on smaller children. In 1999, he changed his name to Joseph L. Druce, allegedly because he hated his mother.[1] Mental health professionals who evaluated Druce found that he suffered from a personality disorder as a child and from severe attention deficit disorder. Bullying people half his strength was a pattern that apparently started when Druce attended the Lakeside School in Peabody, Massachusetts, an alternative facility for children. "If there is a child in a group who is weaker than Darrin," one psychologist wrote, "he will focus his provocative behavior and teasing toward that child." ♦

Although the Geoghan case is unusual, it is not atypical. Despite ongoing efforts to improve security, violence is an ever-present occurrence in the prison system. Many prisoners come from troubled backgrounds. Many have serious emotional problems and grew up in abusive households. A majority are alcohol- and drug-dependent at the time of their arrest. Is it realistic to expect that a significant portion of these troubled individuals will successfully adjust to society after a lengthy stay in an overcrowded and dangerous penal institution?

Today, the correctional system has branches in the federal, state, and county levels of government. Felons may be placed in state or federal penitentiaries (prisons), which are usually isolated, high-security structures. Misdemeanants are housed in county jails, sometimes called reformatories or houses of correction. Juvenile offenders have their own institutions, sometimes euphemistically called schools, camps, ranches, or homes. Typically, the latter are nonsecure facilities, often located in rural areas, that provide both confinement and rehabilitative services for young offenders.

Other types of correctional institutions include ranches and farms for adult offenders and community correctional settings, such as halfway houses, for inmates who are about to return to society. Today's correctional facilities encompass a wide range, from maxi-maxi-security institutions, such as the federal prison in Florence, Colorado, where the nation's most dangerous felons are confined, to low-security camps that house white-collar criminals convicted of such crimes as insider trading and mail fraud.

One of the great tragedies of the current era is that correctional institutions, whatever form they take, do not seem to correct. Instead, they have become a revolving door through which too many of their residents return time and again. More than half of all inmates will be back in prison within six years of their release. Correctional institutions are, in most instances, overcrowded, understaffed, outdated warehouses for social outcasts and to some skeptics seem better suited for control, punishment, and security than rehabilitation and treatment.

Despite the apparent lack of success of penal institutions, great debate continues over the direction of their future operations. Some penal experts maintain that prisons and jails are not places for rehabilitation and treatment but should be used to keep dangerous offenders apart from society and give them the "just deserts" for their crimes.[2] In this sense, prison success would be measured by such factors as physical security, length of incapacitation, relationship between the crime rate and the number of incarcerated felons, and inmates' perceptions that their treatment was fair and proportionate. The dominance of this correctional philosophy is illustrated by the three-strikes presumptive and mandatory sentencing structures, which are used in such traditionally progressive states as California, Illinois, and Massachusetts; the number of people under lock and key, which has risen rapidly in the past few years even though the crime rate has declined; and commentators taking note that the crime rate has declined as the prison population increases.

All too often, building prisons and putting people behind bars are used to energize political campaigns and not to provide effective and efficient treatment. Political candidates who advocate inmate rehabilitation soon find themselves on the defensive among voters.[3] Although punishment has its political appeal, many penal experts still maintain that if properly funded and effectively directed, correctional facilities can still provide successful offender rehabilitation.[4] Many examples of the treatment philosophy still flourish in prisons: Educational programs allow inmates to get college credits, vocational training has become more sophisticated, counseling and substance abuse programs are almost universal, and every state maintains some type of early-release and community correctional programs. Correctional rehabilitation is still an important element of the justice system, and there are numerous opportunities for a career in counseling (see the Careers in Criminal Justice feature on page 494).

The American Correctional Association is a multidisciplinary organization of professionals representing all facets of corrections and criminal justice, including federal, state, and military correctional facilities and prisons; county jails and detention centers; probation and parole agencies; and community corrections and halfway houses. It has more than 20,000 members. To learn about what the association does, check out its website, which you can reach by going to the Siegel/Senna Introduction to Criminal Justice 11e website: www. thomsonedu.com/criminaljustice/ siegel.

Although this debate is ongoing, there is little question that the correctional system is vast and, despite a drop in the crime rate, still growing. The total number of state and federal inmates has increased from 400,000 in 1982 to more than 1,300,000 today.

◆ THE HISTORY OF CORRECTIONAL INSTITUTIONS

The original legal punishments were typically banishment or slavery, restitution, corporal punishment, and execution. The concept of incarcerating convicted offenders for long periods of time as a punishment for their misdeeds did not become the norm of corrections until the nineteenth century.[5]

Although the use of incarceration as a routine punishment began much later, some early European institutions were created specifically to detain and punish criminal offenders. Penal institutions were constructed in England during the tenth century to hold pretrial detainees and those waiting for their sentence to be carried out.[6] During the twelfth century, King Henry II constructed a series of county jails to hold thieves and vagrants prior to the disposition of their sentence. In 1557 the workhouse in Brideswell was built to hold people convicted of relatively minor offenses who would work to pay off their debt to society. Those who had committed more serious offenses were held there pending execution.

Le Stinche, a prison in Florence, Italy, was used to punish offenders as early as 1301.[7] Prisoners were enclosed in separate cells, classified on the basis of gender, age, mental state, and crime seriousness. Furloughs and conditional release were permitted, and—perhaps for the first time—a period of incarceration replaced corporal punishment for some offenses. Although Le Stinche existed for 500 years, relatively little is known about its administration or whether this early example of incarceration was unique to Florence.

The first penal institutions were foul places devoid of proper care, food, or medical treatment. The jailer, usually a **shire reeve** (sheriff)—an official appointed by the king or a noble landholder as chief law enforcement official of a county—ran the jail under a fee system, whereby inmates were required to pay

shire reeve
In early England, the chief law enforcement official in a county—the forerunner of today's sheriff.

van Gogh, Prisoner's Round (detail), 1890. Pushkin Museum of Fine Arts, Moscow. Scala/Art Resource, New York.

"Prisoners Exercising" by Vincent van Gogh. Painted in 1890, this work captures the despair of the nineteenth-century penal institution. The face of the prisoner near the center of the picture looking at the viewer is van Gogh's.

Correctional Counselor

Duties and Characteristics of the Job

Correctional counselors' responsibility is to review the situation of individual offenders and, based on this review, determine the most effective method of rehabilitation. They will create, enact, manage, and sometimes evaluate programs designed to improve the psycho-social functions of offenders, with the goal of ultimately making them capable of successfully reintegrating into society when they are released. Correctional counselors must also provide counseling and educational sessions, survey the needs of offenders, and prepare reports for court. Counselors' specific duties vary by employer; they can remain general caseworkers, or they can pick a specialization such as substance abuse or juvenile rehabilitation.

Correctional counselors will most often work in an office setting. In contrast, in some institutions correctional counselors will also fulfill correctional officer duties as well. Not surprisingly, being a correctional counselor can be stressful, considering the population being served, the often serious nature of their problems, and the pressure for immediate results.

Job Outlook

As a whole, the employment of counselors is expected to grow at a faster than average rate in the near future. Additionally, due to the recent trend toward the expansion of the prison system, opportunities for employment as a correctional counselor are good.

Salary

Correctional counselors' median salary is $39,540. Like other counselors, the majority of corrections counselors will make between $27,600 and $49,690. Positions at the federal level will generally pay a higher salary. Those with graduate-level education are also more likely to have higher salaries and opportunities for advancement.

Opportunities

Generally, counselor positions in federal prisons and maximum-security prisons are higher paying and more prestigious. There is greater competition for these desirable positions, so the qualifications are more demanding. A master's degree and a year of experience in a state or local prison are usually required. However, in

---

for their own food and services. Those who could not pay were fed scraps until they starved to death:

> In 1748 the admission to Southwark prison was eleven shillings and four pence. Having got in, the prisoner had to pay for having himself put in irons, for his bed, of whatever sort, for his room if he was able to afford a separate room. He had to pay for his food, and when he had paid his debts and was ready to go out, he had to pay for having his irons struck off, and a discharge fee. . . . The gaolers [jailers] were usually "low bred, mercenary and oppressive, barbarous fellows, who think of nothing but enriching themselves by the most cruel extortion, and have less regard for the life of a poor prisoner than for the life of a brute."[8]

Jail conditions were deplorable because jailers ran them for personal gain. The fewer the services provided, the greater their profit. Early jails were catchall institutions that held not only criminal offenders awaiting trial but also vagabonds, debtors, the mentally ill, and assorted others.

From 1776 to 1785, a growing inmate population that could no longer be transported to North America forced the English to house prisoners on **hulks**, abandoned ships anchored in harbors. The hulks became infamous for their degrading conditions and brutal punishments but were not abandoned until 1858. The writings of John Howard, the reform-oriented sheriff of Bedfordshire, drew attention to the squalid conditions in British penal institutions. His famous book, *The State of the Prisons* (1777), condemned the lack of basic care given English inmates awaiting trial or serving sentences.[9] Howard's efforts to create humane standards in the British penal system resulted in the Penitentiary Act, by which Parliament established a more orderly penal system, with periodic inspections, elimination of the fee system, and greater consideration for inmates.

hulk
Mothballed ship used to house prisoners in eighteenth-century England.

certain cases additional education, such as clinical training, can take the place of experience. Specialized positions such as working with drug addiction or violent offenders can also lead to a higher-paying position.

Good workers who continue their education will find opportunities for advancement to higher-paying positions such as case management coordinator.

Qualifications

In addition to educational requirements, for many entry-level jobs some previous work experience will be necessary. This can be in related jobs such as substance abuse counseling or corrections case work; however, some educational degrees may fulfill this requirement. The ability to speak another language is also an advantage. Personality characteristics and skills such as the desire to help others and the ability to communicate well are important.

Due to the settings and populations that counselors work with, a future counselor will need to pass a background check and gain security clearance of the appropriate level. Additionally, certain states require certification.

Education and Training

Prospective correctional counselors should have a bachelor's degree in a field such as social work, criminal justice, or psychology. However, additional education at the master's level in these fields may be necessary to advance in the field or to get certain positions. Correctional counselors' education and work experience should familiarize them with the criminal justice system and prepare them for determining how to reduce a client's chances of recidivism as well as how to deal with unwilling clients.

Sources: "Counselors," *Occupational Outlook Handbook,* 2006–2007 edition (Bureau of Labor Statistics, U.S. Department of Labor), retrieved June 29, 2006, from http://www.bls.gov/oco/ocos067.htm; "Occupational Employment and Wages, May 2005" (Bureau of Labor Statistics, U.S. Department of Labor), retrieved June 29, 2006, from http://www.bls.gov/oes/current/oes_nat.htm; "Occupational Employment and Wages, May 2005: Counselors, All Other" (Bureau of Labor Statistics, U.S. Department of Labor), retrieved June 29, 2006, from http://www.bls.gov/oes/current/oes211019.htm; S. E. Lambert and D. Regan, "Corrections Counselor/Corrections Caseworker," *Great Careers for Criminal Justice Majors* (New York: McGraw-Hill, 2001), pp. 196–99, 203–05.

The Origin of Corrections in the United States

Although Europe had jails and a variety of other penal facilities, correctional reform was first instituted in the United States. The first American jail was built in James City in the Virginia colony in the early seventeenth century. However, the modern American correctional system had its origin in Pennsylvania under the leadership of William Penn.

At the end of the seventeenth century, Penn revised Pennsylvania's criminal code to forbid torture and the capricious use of mutilation and physical punishment. These penalties were replaced with imprisonment at hard labor, moderate flogging, fines, and forfeiture of property. All lands and goods belonging to felons were to be used to make restitution to the victims of their crimes, with restitution being limited to twice the value of the damages. Felons who owned no property were assigned by law to the prison workhouse until the victim was compensated.

Penn ordered that a new type of institution be built to replace the widely used public forms of punishment—stocks, pillories, gallows, and branding irons. Each county was instructed to build a house of corrections similar to today's jails. County trustees or commissioners were responsible for raising money to build the jails and providing for their maintenance, although they were operated by the local sheriff. Penn's reforms remained in effect until his death in 1718, when the criminal penal code was changed back to open public punishment and harsh brutality.

Identifying the first American prison is difficult. Alexis Durham has described the 1773 opening of the Newgate Prison of Connecticut on the site of an abandoned copper mine. However, Newgate, which closed in the 1820s, is often ignored by correctional historians.[10] In 1785, Castle Island prison was opened in Massachusetts and operated for about 15 years.

The Pennsylvania System

The origin of the modern correctional system is usually traced to eighteenth-century developments in Pennsylvania. In 1776 postrevolutionary Pennsylvania again adopted William Penn's code, and in 1787 a group of Quakers led by Benjamin Rush formed the Philadelphia Society for Alleviating the Miseries of Public Prisons. The aim of the society was to bring some degree of humane and orderly treatment to the growing penal system. The Quakers' influence on the legislature resulted in limiting the use of the death penalty to cases involving treason, murder, rape, and arson. Their next step was to reform the institutional system so that the prison could serve as a suitable alternative to physical punishment.

The only models of custodial institutions at that time were the local county jails that Penn had established. These facilities were designed to detain offenders, to securely incarcerate convicts awaiting other punishment, or to hold offenders who were working off their crimes. The Pennsylvania jails placed men, women, and children of all ages indiscriminately in one room. Liquor was often freely sold.

Under pressure from the Quakers to improve these conditions, the Pennsylvania legislature in 1790 called for the renovation of the prison system. The eventual result was the creation of a separate wing of Philadelphia's **Walnut Street Jail** to house convicted felons (except those sentenced to death). Prisoners were placed in solitary cells, where they remained in isolation and did not have the right to work.[11] Quarters that contained the solitary or separate cells were called the **penitentiary house**, as was already the custom in England.

The new Pennsylvania prison system took credit for a rapid decrease in the crime rate—from 131 convictions in 1789 to 45 in 1793.[12] The prison became known as a school for reform and a place for public labor. The Walnut Street Jail's equitable conditions were credited with reducing escapes to none in the first four years of its existence (except for 14 on opening day). However, the Walnut Street Jail was not a total success. Isolation had a terrible psychological effect on inmates, and eventually inmates were given in-cell piecework on which they worked up to eight hours a day. Overcrowding undermined the goal of solitary confinement of serious offenders, and soon more than one inmate was placed in each cell. Despite these difficulties, similar institutions were erected in New York (Newgate in 1791) and New Jersey (Trenton in 1798).

The Auburn System

As the nineteenth century got under way, both the Pennsylvania and the New York prison systems were experiencing difficulties maintaining the ever-increasing numbers of convicted criminals. Initially, administrators dealt with the problem by increasing the use of pardons, relaxing prison discipline, and limiting supervision.

In 1816, New York built a new prison at Auburn, hoping to alleviate some of the overcrowding at Newgate. The Auburn Prison design became known as the **tier system** because cells were built vertically on five floors of the structure. It was also referred to as the **congregate system** because most prisoners ate and worked in groups. In 1819, construction began on a wing of solitary cells to house unruly prisoners. Three classes of prisoners were then created. One group remained continually in solitary confinement as a result of breaches of prison discipline, the second group was allowed labor as an occasional form of recreation, and the third and largest class worked and ate together during the day and was separated only at night.

The philosophy of the **Auburn system** was crime prevention through fear of punishment and silent confinement. The worst felons were to be cut off from all contact with other prisoners, and although they were treated and fed relatively

---

Walnut Street Jail
The birthplace of the modern prison system and of the Pennsylvania system of solitary confinement.

penitentiary house
A correctional institution for those convicted of major crimes.

tier system
A type of prison in which cells are located along corridors in multiple layers or levels.

congregate system
A prison system, originated in New York, in which inmates worked and ate together during the day and then slept in solitary cells at night.

Auburn system
A prison system, developed in New York during the nineteenth century, based on congregate (group) work during the day and separation at night.

well, they had no hope of pardon to relieve their solitude or isolation. For a time, some of the worst convicts were forced to remain alone and silent during the entire day. This practice, which led to mental breakdowns, suicides, and self-mutilations, was abolished in 1823.

The combination of silence and solitude as a method of punishment was not abandoned easily. Prison officials sought to overcome the side effects of total isolation while maintaining the penitentiary system. The solution adopted at Auburn was to keep convicts in separate cells at night but allow them to work together during the day under enforced silence. Hard work and silence became the foundation of the Auburn system wherever it was adopted. Silence was the key to prison discipline. It prohibited the formulation of escape plans, it prevented plots and riots, and it allowed prisoners to contemplate their infractions.

The Development of Prisons

Why did prisons develop at this time? One reason was that during this period of enlightenment, a concerted effort was made to alleviate the harsh punishments and torture that had been the norm. The interest of religious groups, such as the Quakers, in prison reform was prompted in part by humanitarian ideals. Another factor was the economic potential of prison industry, viewed as a valuable economic asset in times of short labor supply.[13]

The concept of using harsh discipline and control to retrain the heart and soul of offenders was the subject of an important book on penal philosophy, *Discipline and Punish* (1978), by French sociologist Michel Foucault.[14] Foucault's thesis is that as societies evolve and become more complex, they create increasingly more elaborate mechanisms to discipline their recalcitrant members and make them docile enough to obey social rules. In the seventeenth and eighteenth centuries, discipline was directed toward the human body itself, through torture. However, physical punishment and torture turned some condemned men into heroes and martyrs. Prisons presented the opportunity to rearrange, not diminish, punishment—to make it more effective and regulated. In the development of the nineteenth-century prison, the object was to discipline the offender psychologically: "[T]he expiation that once rained down on the body must be replaced by a punishment that acts in the depths of the heart."[15]

Regimentation became the standard mode of prison life. Convicts did not simply walk from place to place; instead, they went in close order and single file, each looking over the shoulder of the preceding person, faces inclined to the right, feet moving in unison. The lockstep prison shuffle was developed at Auburn and is still used in some institutions today.[16]

When discipline was breached in the Auburn system, punishment was applied in the form of a rawhide whip on the inmate's back. Immediate and effective, Auburn discipline was so successful that when 100 inmates were used to build the famous Sing Sing Prison in 1825, not one dared try to escape, although they were housed in an open field with only minimal supervision.[17]

In 1818, Pennsylvania took the radical step of establishing a prison that placed each inmate in a single cell for the duration of his sentence. Classifications were abolished because each cell was intended as a miniature prison that would prevent the inmates from contaminating one another.

The new Pennsylvania state prison, called the Western Penitentiary, had an unusual architectural design. It was built in a semicircle, with the cells positioned along its circumference. Built back to back, some cells faced the boundary wall while others faced the internal area of the circle. Its inmates were kept in solitary confinement almost constantly, being allowed out for about an hour a day for exercise. In 1829 a second, similar penitentiary using the isolate system was built in Philadelphia and was called the Eastern Penitentiary.

Supporters of the **Pennsylvania system** believed that the penitentiary was truly a place to do penance. By removing the sinner from society and allowing the prisoner a period of isolation in which to consider the evils of crime, the

Pennsylvania system
A prison system, developed in Pennsylvania during the nineteenth century, based on total isolation and individual penitence.

CONCEPT SUMMARY 15.1

Early Correctional Systems

Prison	Structure	Living conditions	Activities	Discipline
Auburn system	Tiered cells	Congregate	Group work	Silence, harsh punishment
Pennsylvania system	Single cells set in semicircle	Isolated	In-cell work, Bible study	Silence, harsh punishment

The Eastern State Penitentiary, in Philadelphia, became the most expensive and most copied building of its time. It is estimated that more than 300 prisons worldwide are based on its wagon-wheel or radial floor plan. Some of America's most notorious criminals were held in this penitentiary's vaulted, sky-lit cells, including Al Capone. After 142 years of consecutive use, Eastern State Penitentiary was abandoned in 1971. For more information, visit its website, which you can reach by going to the Siegel/Senna Introduction to Criminal Justice 11e website: www.thomsonedu.com/criminaljustice/siegel.

Pennsylvania system reflected the influence of religion and religious philosophy on corrections. Its supporters believed that solitary confinement with in-cell labor would make work so attractive that upon release the inmate would be well suited to resume a productive existence in society.

The Pennsylvania system eliminated the need for large numbers of guards or disciplinary measures. Isolated from one another, inmates could not plan escapes or collectively break rules. When discipline was a problem, however, the whip and the iron gag were used.

Many fiery debates occurred between advocates of the Pennsylvania system and adherents of the Auburn system. Those supporting the latter claimed that it was the cheapest and most productive way to reform prisoners. They criticized the Pennsylvania system as cruel and inhumane, suggesting that solitary confinement was both physically and mentally damaging. The Pennsylvania system's devotees argued that their system was quiet, efficient, humane, and well ordered, providing the ultimate correctional facility.[18] They chided the Auburn system for tempting inmates to talk by putting them together for meals and work and then punishing them when they did talk. Finally, the Auburn system was accused of becoming a breeding place for criminal associations by allowing inmates to get to know one another.

The Auburn system eventually prevailed and spread throughout the United States. Many of its features are still used today. Its innovations included congregate working conditions, the use of solitary confinement to punish unruly inmates, military regimentation, and discipline. In Auburn-like institutions, prisoners were marched from place to place. Their time was regulated by bells telling them to wake up, sleep, and work. The system was so like the military that many of its early administrators were recruited from the armed services.

Although the prison was viewed as an improvement over capital and corporal punishment, it quickly became the scene of depressed conditions. Inmates were treated harshly and routinely whipped and tortured. Prison brutality flourished in these institutions, which had originally been devised as a more humane correctional alternative. In these early penal institutions, brutal corporal punishment took place indoors where, hidden from public view, it could become even more savage (see Concept Summary 15.1).[19]

Prisons in the Late Nineteenth Century

The prison of the late nineteenth century was remarkably similar to that of today. The congregate system was adopted in all states except Pennsylvania. Prisons were overcrowded, and the single-cell principle was often ignored. The prison, like the police department, became the scene of political intrigue and efforts by political administrators to control the hiring of personnel and dispensing of patronage.

Prison industry developed and became the predominant theme around which institutions were organized. Some prisons used the **contract system**, in which officials sold the labor of inmates to private businesses. Sometimes

contract system
System whereby officials sold the labor of prison inmates to private businesses, for use either inside or outside the prison.

the contractor supervised the inmates inside the prison itself. Under the **convict-lease system**, the state leased its prisoners to a business for a fixed annual fee and gave up supervision and control. Finally, some institutions had prisoners produce goods for the prison's own use.[20]

The development of prison industry quickly led to the abuse of inmates, who were forced to work for almost no wages, and to profiteering by dishonest administrators and business owners. During the Civil War era, prisons were major manufacturers of clothes, shoes, boots, furniture, and the like. Beginning in the 1870s, opposition by trade unions sparked restrictions on interstate commerce in prison goods.

The National Congress of Penitentiary and Reformatory Discipline, held in Cincinnati in 1870, heralded a new era of prison reform. Organized by penologists Enoch Wines and Theodore Dwight, the congress provided a forum for corrections experts from around the nation to call for the treatment, education, and training of inmates. Overseas, another penal reform was being developed in which inmates could earn early release and serve out their sentence in the community; this was called **parole**.

One of the most famous people to attend the congress, Zebulon Brockway, warden of the Elmira Reformatory in New York, advocated individualized treatment, the indeterminate sentence, and parole.

The reformatory program initiated by Brockway included elementary education for illiterates, designed library hours, lectures by faculty members of the local Elmira College, and a group of vocational training shops. From 1888 to 1920, Elmira administrators used military-like training to discipline the inmates and organize the institution. The military organization could be seen in every aspect of the institution: schooling, manual training, sports, supervision of inmates, and even parole decisions.[21] The cost to the state of the institution's operations was to be held to a minimum.

Although Brockway proclaimed Elmira to be an ideal reformatory, his achievements were limited. The greatest significance of his contribution was the injection of a degree of humanitarianism into the industrial prisons of that day (although accusations were made that excessive corporal punishment was used and that Brockway personally administered whippings).[22] Many institutions were constructed across the nation and labeled reformatories based on the Elmira model, but most of them continued to be industrially oriented.[23]

Prisons in the Twentieth Century

The early twentieth century was a time of contrasts in the U.S. prison system.[24] At one extreme were those who advocated reform, such as the Mutual Welfare League, led by Thomas Mott Osborne. Prison reform groups proposed better treatment for inmates, an end to harsh corporal punishment, the creation of meaningful prison industries, and educational programs. Reformers argued that prisoners should not be isolated from society and that the best elements of society—education, religion, meaningful work, and self-governance—should be brought to the prison. Osborne went so far as to spend a week in New York's notorious Sing Sing Prison to learn firsthand about its conditions.

In time, some of the more rigid prison rules gave way to liberal reform. By the mid-1930s, few prisons required inmates to wear the red-and-white-striped convict suit; nondescript gray uniforms were substituted. The code of silence ended, as did the lockstep shuffle. Prisoners were allowed "the freedom of the yard" to mingle and exercise an hour or two each day.[25] Movies and radio appeared in the 1930s. Visiting policies and mail privileges were liberalized.

A more important trend was the development of specialized prisons designed to treat particular types

convict-lease system
Contract system in which a private business leased prisoners from the state for a fixed annual fee and assumed full responsibility for their supervision and control.

parole
The early release of a prisoner from incarceration subject to conditions set by a parole board.

PERSPECTIVES ON JUSTICE

Crime Control

Prison reform challenged the crime control orientation of prisons. Opposed to the reformers were conservative prison administrators and state officials who believed that stern disciplinary measures were needed to control dangerous prison inmates. They continued the time-honored system of regimentation and discipline. Although the whip and the lash were eventually abolished, solitary confinement in dark, bare cells became a common penal practice.

Elmira Reformatory, training course in drafting, 1909. Inmates stand at drafting tables as guards watch and a supervisor sits at a fenced-off desk at the front of the hall. Elmira was one of the first institutions to employ education and training programs.

of offenders. In New York, for example, the prisons at Clinton and Auburn were viewed as industrial facilities for hard-core inmates, Great Meadow was an agricultural center for nondangerous offenders, and Dannemora was a facility for the criminally insane. In California, San Quentin housed inmates considered salvageable by correctional authorities, and Folsom was reserved for hard-core offenders.[26]

Prison industry also evolved. Opposition by organized labor helped put an end to the convict-lease system and forced inmate labor. By 1900, a number of states had restricted the sale of prisoner-made goods on the open market. The worldwide Great Depression, which began in 1929, prompted industry and union leaders to further pressure state legislators to reduce competition from prison industries. A series of ever more restrictive federal legislative initiatives led to the Sumners-Ashurst Act (1940), which made it a federal offense to transport interstate commerce goods made in prison for private use, regardless of the laws of the state receiving the goods.[27] The restrictions imposed by the federal government helped to severely curtail prison industry for 40 years. Private entrepreneurs shunned prison investments because they were no longer profitable. The result was inmate idleness and make-work jobs.[28]

Despite some changes and reforms, the prison in the mid-twentieth century remained a destructive total institution. Although some aspects of inmate life improved, severe discipline, harsh rules, and solitary confinement were the way of life in prison.

Prisons in the Modern Era

The modern era has been a period of change and turmoil in the nation's correctional system. Three trends stand out. First, between 1960 and 1980, came the prisoners' rights movement. After many years of indifference (the so-called **hands-off doctrine**), state and federal courts ruled in case after case that institutionalized inmates had rights to freedom of religion and speech, medical care, procedural due process, and proper living conditions. Inmates won rights unheard of in the nineteenth and early twentieth centuries. Since 1980, however, an increasingly conservative judiciary has curtailed the growth of inmate rights.

hands-off doctrine
The judicial policy of not interfering in the administrative affairs of prisons.

Second, violence within the correctional system became a national concern. Well-publicized riots at New York's Attica Prison and the New Mexico State Penitentiary drew attention to the potential for death and destruction that lurks in every prison. Prison rapes and killings have become commonplace. The locus of control in many prisons has shifted from the correctional staff to violent inmate gangs. In reaction, some administrators have tried to improve conditions and provide innovative programs that give inmates a voice in running the institution. Another reaction has been to tighten discipline and build new super-maximum-security prisons to control the most dangerous offenders. The problem of prison overcrowding has made attempts to improve conditions extremely difficult.

Third, the view that traditional correctional rehabilitation efforts have failed has prompted many penologists to reconsider the purpose of incarcerating criminals. Between 1960 and 1980, it was common for correctional administrators to cling to the **medical model**, which viewed inmates as sick people who were suffering from some social malady that prevented them from adjusting to society. Correctional treatment could help cure them and enable them to live productive lives once they returned to the community. In the 1970s, efforts were also made to help offenders become reintegrated into society by providing them with new career opportunities that relied on work release programs. Inmates were allowed to work outside the institution during the day and return in the evening. Some were given extended furloughs in the community. Work release became a political issue when Willie Horton, a furloughed inmate from Massachusetts, raped a young woman. Criticism of the state's "liberal" furlough program helped Vice President George Bush defeat Massachusetts Governor Michael S. Dukakis for the U.S. presidency in 1988. In the aftermath of the Horton case, a number of states, including Massachusetts, restricted their furlough policies.

Prisons have come to be viewed as places for control, incapacitation, and punishment, instead of sites for rehabilitation and reform. Advocates of the "no-frills" or penal harm movement believe that if prison is a punishing experience, would-be criminals will be deterred from crime and current inmates will be encouraged to go straight. Nonetheless, efforts to use correctional institutions as treatment facilities have not ended, and such innovations as the development of private industries on prison grounds have kept the rehabilitative ideal alive.

Although historians sometimes find the conditions in early prisons to be severe, some modern administrators have sought to copy the harsh regimes in an effort to convince inmates that their institution is no country club and that they had better not return. This no-frills movement and its relation to housing terror suspects is the subject of the Analyzing Criminal Justice Issues feature.

medical model
The view that convicted offenders are victims of their environment who need care and treatment to be transformed into valuable members of society.

PERSPECTIVES ON JUSTICE

Noninterventionism

The alleged failure of correctional treatment coupled with constantly increasing correctional costs has prompted advocates of the nonintervention perspective to develop alternatives to incarceration, such as intensive probation supervision, house arrest, and electronic monitoring. The idea is to move as many nonviolent offenders as possible out of the correctional system by means of community-based programs. These efforts have been compromised by a growing get-tough stance in judicial and legislative sentencing policy, including mandatory minimum sentences for gun crimes and drug trafficking.

◆ JAILS

The nation's jails are institutional facilities with five primary purposes: (1) they detain accused offenders who cannot make or are not eligible for bail prior to trial, (2) they hold convicted offenders awaiting sentence, (3) they serve as the principal institution of secure confinement for offenders convicted of misdemeanors, (4) they hold probationers and parolees picked up for violations and waiting for a hearing, and (5) they house felons when state prisons are overcrowded. Today, the **jail** is a multipurpose correctional institution. Its main functions are set out in Exhibit 15.1 on page 504.

A number of formats are used to jail offenders. About 15,000 local jurisdictions maintain short-term police or municipal lockups that house offenders for no more than 48 hours before a bail hearing can be held. Thereafter, detainees are kept in the county jail. In some jurisdictions, such as Massachusetts and

jail
A county correctional institution used to hold people awaiting trial or sentencing, as well as misdemeanor offenders sentenced to a term of less than one year.

Penal Harm and the War on Terror

According to the penal harm movement, punishment is a planned governmental act in which a law violator is harmed. Although some may consider punishment for the sake of harming someone immoral, those who advocate this position find it justifiable because the person who is suffering is an offender who has harmed others. Penal harm has dominated correctional thinking for the past 30 years. The incarceration rate per 100,000 citizens has doubled during this period, and sentencing reform has meant more people behind bars than ever before. Parole has been limited. Some of the elements of penal harm include the following:

◆ Requiring inmates to do hard labor.

◆ Providing only rationed and/or unappetizing food.

◆ Forcing inmates to live in small and overcrowded cells.

◆ Using long isolation, even in a dark "hole" for punishment.

◆ Doing little to alleviate sleep deprivation.

◆ Frequent use of humiliating security procedures such as strip searches.

◆ Limiting or denying visits, correspondence, and recreation.

One aspect of the penal harm movement is the no-frills approach to prison. Its advocates want to return to the early days of corrections, when prisons were places of harsh punishment and strict confinement. Some correctional administrators believe that such a system may not have been as bad as reformers suggest and that prisons should still be places of punishment only. If inmate privileges and treatment programs were curtailed, they argue, then the return rate would not be so high. Who would recidivate and chance a return to a harsh penal environment without TV or sports facilities?

Inmates in some states have suffered reduced visiting hours, removal of televisions and exercise gear, and substitution of cold sandwiches for hot meals. Some correctional administrators are charging fees for jail services, just like in the original eighteenth-century institutions. Some have taken out the televisions from inmates' cells and charge inmates for haircuts and even for medical care co-payments.

In some jails, inmates are forced to wear stun belts while on work details. After detonation, the belts give fleeing inmates an 8-second, 50,000-volt jolt of electricity, which renders them helpless for up to 10 minutes. Developed by Stun Tech Inc., more than 1,000 belts have been sold to law enforcement and correctional agencies. Amnesty International has asked Congress to ban the belts, in part because they can be used for torture. Amnesty charges that the belts are "cruel, inhuman, and degrading." Advocates of the no-frills movement claim to be responding to the public's desire to get tough on crime. They are tired of hearing that some prison inmates get free education, watch cable TV, or get special educational programs. Some of the efforts to restrict inmates' rights include the following:

◆ The Alabama Department of Corrections (DOC) introduced no-frills chain gangs in each of the state's three prisons in 1994. Inmates in the gangs do not have telephones or visitation privileges, and recreation is limited to basketball on the weekends. Chain-gang crews include primarily parole violators and repeat offenders, especially offenders who are former gang members. After six months of good behavior, chain-gang members return to the general population and are given standard inmate privileges.

◆ The Arizona DOC, supplementing the legislature's ban on weightlifting equipment, reduced the amount of property and clothing that inmates may keep in their cells, the number of items for sale in the store, the number and types of movies and television programs that inmates may watch, and the frequency of telephone calls.

◆ The Kansas DOC introduced a formal incentive program in which incoming inmates have to earn a range of privileges, including television, handicrafts, use of outside funds, canteen expenditures, personal property, and visitation. Under a three-level system, new inmates who spend their first 120 days (Incentive Level I) without disciplinary reports and participate in educational programs or work assignments earn increased privileges (Incentive Level II). After another 120 days

New Hampshire, a house of corrections holds convicted misdemeanants, and a county jail holds pretrial detainees.

Jails are typically a low-priority item in the criminal justice system. Because they are usually administered on a county level, jail services have not been sufficiently regulated, and a unified national policy has not been developed to

of similar behavior, additional privileges are made available (Incentive Level III). Inmates are reduced one level for misbehavior. Furloughs were the only privilege that the DOC banned permanently for all inmates.

♦ Complementing the action of the state's governor, the commissioner of corrections in Wisconsin reduced the amount of personal property that inmates may own, established limits on the amount of personal clothing and electronic equipment that they may keep, and introduced monitoring of telephone calls.

No Frills and Terrorism

The controversy swirling around the penal harm movement has morphed from the treatment of prisoners in the United States to the handling of suspected terrorists. What has proven to be one of the more controversial aspects of the war against terror has been the use of no-frills facilities to detain suspected Al-Qaeda and Taliban operatives at the joint military prison and interrogation center in Guantanamo Bay, Cuba. There are now two facilities at the base, Camp Delta and Camp Iguana.

Camp Delta is a high-security facility. Each of its detention units is 8 feet long, 6 feet 8 inches wide, and 8 feet tall and is constructed with metal mesh material on a solid steel frame. Approximately 24 units make up a detention block. A unit has indoor plumbing, a flush toilet, a metal bed frame raised off the floor, and a sink with running water. There are two recreation/exercise areas per detention block at Camp Delta, and inmates are allowed out to exercise, pray, and get fresh air. Among the notorious inmates housed there are Khalid Sheik Mohammed, who served as the number-three Al-Qaeda leader before he was captured in Pakistan in 2003, and Abu Zubaydah, a critical link between Osama bin Laden and Al-Qaeda cells around the world. Before entering Guantanamo, they were being held in even more secret CIA-run facilities.

Camp Iguana was originally a low-security detention facility dedicated to juvenile detainees aged between 13 and 15. It now holds detainees who are deemed not to be enemy combatants, or who are to be transferred to their home country.

The facility has drawn criticism because the detainees are being held without trial, and charges of torture and deprivation have abounded. According to reports, detainees are kept in isolation most of the day, are blindfolded when moving from place to place within the camp, and are forbidden to talk in groups of more than three. There have been allegations that inmates are being subjected to sleep deprivation, so-called truth drugs, beatings, being locked in confined and cold cells, and being forced to maintain uncomfortable postures. At first, the government's position was that detainees were not entitled to the protections of the Geneva Convention. However, on June 29, 2006, the U.S. Supreme Court ruled in *Hamdan v. Rumsfeld* that the military commissions established by executive order to try detainees are unlawful and violate the U.S. Uniform Code of Military Justice; the inmates are in fact covered by the Geneva Convention. On July 7, 2006, the Department of Defense issued an internal memo stating that prisoners will in the future be entitled to protection under the Geneva Convention.

Critical Thinking

Should terror detainees be entitled to a higher level of care and custody, or do their evil deeds justify their being held under "no frills" conditions? Can they ever really be "rehabilitated"? And if not, what should be done with them if you believe that the conditions at Guantanamo are too harsh?

InfoTrac College Edition Research

To read more about the Guantanamo Bay detention facilities, go to Maggie Ardiente, "Everything But the Truth: Allegations of Abuse and Torture at Guantanamo Bay," *Humanist* 66 (2006): 16–18.

Sources: *CBS News,* "White House Does About-Face On Gitmo," July 11, 2006 (http://www.cbsnews.com/stories/2006/07/11/politics/main1790470.shtml); Amnesty International, "Guantánamo Bay—A Human Rights Scandal" (accessed on September 6, 2006); Peter Finn, "No-Frills Prisons and Jails: A Movement in Flux," *Federal Probation* 60 (1996): 35–49; W. Wesley Johnson, Katherine Bennett, and Timothy Flanagan, "Getting Tough on Prisoners: Results from the National Corrections Executive Survey, 1995," *Crime and Delinquency* 43 (1997): 24–41; Peter Kilborn, "Revival of Chain Gangs Takes a Twist," *New York Times,* March 11, 1997, p. A18.

mandate what constitutes adequate jail conditions. Many jails have consequently developed into squalid, crumbling holding pens.

Jails are considered to be holding facilities for the county's undesirables, not correctional institutions that provide meaningful treatment. They may house indigents who, looking for a respite from the winter's cold, commit a minor offense;

EXHIBIT 15.1

Jail Functions and Services

♦ Receive individuals pending arraignment and hold them awaiting trial, conviction, or sentencing.

♦ Readmit probation, parole, and jail-bond violators and absconders.

♦ Temporarily detain juveniles pending transfer to juvenile authorities.

♦ Hold mentally ill persons pending their movement to appropriate health facilities.

♦ Hold individuals for the military, for protective custody, for contempt, and for the courts as witnesses.

♦ Release convicted inmates to the community on completion of their sentence.

♦ Transfer inmates to federal, state, or other authorities.

♦ House inmates for federal, state, or other authorities because of crowding of their facilities.

♦ Relinquish custody of temporary detainees to juvenile and medical authorities.

♦ Sometimes operate community-based programs as alternatives to incarceration.

♦ Hold inmates sentenced to short terms (generally under one year).

Source: Paige M. Harrison and Allan J. Beck, *Prison and Jail Inmates at Midyear 2005* (Washington, D.C.: Bureau of Justice Statistics, 2006).

the mentally ill who will eventually be hospitalized after a civil commitment hearing; and substance abusers who are suffering the first shocks of confinement. The jail rarely holds "professional" criminals, most of whom are able to make bail.[29] Instead, the jail holds the people considered detached from and disreputable in local society and who are frequently arrested because they are considered offensive by the local police. A recent survey in New York City found that on any given day more than 2,800 people with serious mental illness were being confined in jail, constituting about 20 percent of the total inmate population.[30] The purpose of the jail is to manage these persons and keep them separate from the rest of society. By intruding in their lives, jailing them increases their involvement with the law.

Jail Populations

According to the most recent statistics, about 750,000 offenders are confined in jail facilities. This represents an increase of about 50 percent in a decade despite a declining crime rate.[31] About half of the jailed inmates are awaiting formal charges (arraignment), bail, or trial. The remaining half are convicted offenders who are serving time, are awaiting parole or probation revocation hearings, or have been transferred from a state prison because of overcrowding.

A national effort has been made to remove as many people from local jails as possible through the adoption of both bail reform measures and pretrial diversion. Nonetheless, jail populations have been steadily increasing between 4 and 5 percent per year, due in part to the increased use of mandatory jail sentences for such common crimes as drunk driving. Jail populations also respond to prison overcrowding. Correctional departments sometimes use local jails to house inmates for whom there is no room in state prisons.

Who Are Jail Inmates?

Not surprisingly, the makeup of jail inmates reflects the arrest statistics. Males still predominate and, as Figure 15.1 shows, constitute about 90 percent of the jail population. Jail inmates tend to be older than the typical arrestee because of the movement to remove juveniles from adult jails. A majority of local jail inmates are either black or Hispanic (Figure 15.2). African Americans are nearly five times more likely than whites, nearly three times more likely than Hispanics, and over nine times more likely than persons of other races to have been in jail.

Although removing juveniles from adult jails has long been a national priority, over 50,000 youths are still being admitted to adult jails each year. About 7,000 persons under age 18 are housed in adult jails on a given day. Almost 90 percent of these young inmates have been convicted or are being held for trial as adults in criminal court.

WOMEN IN JAIL Although the jail population is predominantly male, the number of women in jail is growing at a faster pace (Figure 15.1). On average, the adult female jail population has grown 6 percent annually since 1990, whereas the adult male inmate population has grown about 4 percent. The female-to-male jail inmate ratio reflects developments in the crime rate; that is, female crime rates are increasing at a faster pace than male crime rates.

Female jail inmates face many challenges. Most come from significantly disadvantaged backgrounds. Many have suffered abuse and severe economic disadvantage. One recent study of 100 female inmates found extremely high rates of lifetime trauma exposure (98 percent), current mental disorders (36 percent), and drug/alcohol problems (74 percent).[32]

Given this background, how can female inmates survive jail and avoid recidivism? Employment seems to be a key issue. Those who have worked recently before their incarceration are the ones most likely to have other survival

FIGURE 15.1
Jail Populations by Age and Gender

Number of jail inmates (one-day count)

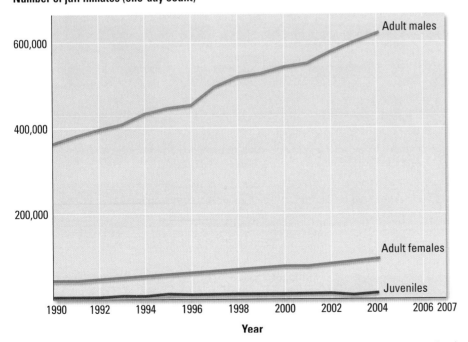

Source: Bureau of Justice Statistics Correctional Surveys (The National Probation Data Survey, National Prisoner Statistics, Survey of Jails, and The National Parole Data Survey) as presented in *Correctional Populations in the United States, 1997; Prison and Jail Inmates at Midyear; and Census of Jails 1999.*

FIGURE 15.2

Incarcerations Rates by Race and Ethnicity

Number of jail inmates per 100,00

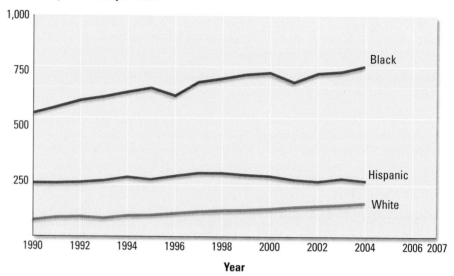

Note: U.S. resident population estimates for sex, race, and Hispanic origin were made using a U.S. Census Bureau Internet release, December 23, 1999, with adjustments for census undercount. Estimates for 2000–2004 are based on the 2000 Census and then estimated for July 1 of each year.

Source: Bureau of Justice Statistics Correctional Surveys (The National Probation Data Survey, National Prisoner Statistics, Survey of Jails, and The National Parole Data Survey) as presented in *Correctional Populations in the United States, 1997; Prison and Jail Inmates at Midyear;* and *Census of Jails 1999.*

Conditions in female institutions can be harsh and uncomfortable. Female prisoners on a chain gang pick up trash on Route 129 on November 3, 2005, during a Butler County Sheriff's Department detail in Hamilton, Ohio. Chain gangs were instituted by Sheriff Richard Jones because he believes the jail was too comfortable for inmates. Would you consider the sheriff's program part of the "no frills" movement?

©AP Images/David Kohl

PERSPECTIVES ON JUSTICE

Due Process

The racial disparity in the jail population is a red flag for those who advocate the due process perspective. If justice were fair, they maintain, this disproportionality would diminish or end.

skills and assets: They are more likely to have a high school education, to have a skill, and to have a driver's license and access to a car.[33] One recent interview study of female inmates at the Baltimore City Detention Center found that their median income in the 30 days prior to arrest was $145. Those who earned as little as $400–$799 were much more likely to gain stable housing after their release and have a better chance of making it on the outside.[34]

A strong association also exists between prior physical and sexual abuse and jail inmate status. About 13 percent of males and 47 percent of female inmates report either physical or sexual abuse.[35] Not surprisingly, about 16 percent of those in local jails report having had either a mental condition or an overnight stay in a mental hospital at least once in their lives.[36]

Jail Conditions

Jails are the oldest and most deteriorated institutions in the criminal justice system. Because they are usually run by the county government (and controlled by a sheriff), persuading taxpayers to support increased funding for improved facilities is difficult. In fact, jails are usually administered under the concept of custodial convenience, which involves giving inmates minimum standards of treatment and benefits while controlling the cost of jail operations. Jail employees are often underpaid, ill-trained, and lacking in professional experience.

A number of factors lead to overcrowded and ineffective jails. One is the concerted effort being made to reduce or control particular crime problems, including substance abuse, spousal abuse, and driving while intoxicated (DWI). A number of jurisdictions have passed legislation requiring that people arrested on suspicion of domestic violence be held in confinement for a number of hours to cool off before becoming eligible for bail. Other jurisdictions have attempted to deter drunk driving by passing mandatory jail sentences for people convicted of DWI. Such legislation can quickly result in overcrowded jails.[37]

New-Generation Jails

To relieve overcrowding and improve effectiveness, a jail building boom has been under way. Many of the new jails are using modern designs to improve effectiveness; these are referred to as new-generation jails.[38] Traditional jails are constructed and use what is referred to as the linear or intermittent surveillance model. Jails of this design are rectangular, with corridors leading to either single- or multiple-occupancy cells arranged at right angles to the corridor. Correctional officers must patrol to see into cells or housing areas, and when they are in a position to observe one cell, they cannot observe others. Unobserved inmates are essentially unsupervised.

A group of inmates await arraignment in a crowded jail holding cell. Critics complain that jails are overcrowded and understaffed. Proponents of the new generation jail hope to alleviate these conditions through better design and management.

©A. Ramey/PhotoEdit

The new-generation jails allow for continuous observation of residents. There are two types: direct and indirect supervision. Direct supervision jails contain a cluster of cells surrounding a living area or pod, which contains tables, chairs, TVs, and so on. A correctional officer is stationed within the pod. The officer has visual observation of inmates and maintains the ability to relate to them on a personal level. By being in the pod, the officer has an increased awareness of the inmates' behaviors and needs. This results in creating a safer environment for both staff and inmates. Because interaction between inmates is constantly and closely monitored, dissension can be quickly detected before it escalates. During the day, inmates stay in the open area (dayroom) and typically are not permitted to go into their rooms except with the permission of the officer in charge. The officer controls door locks to cells from the control panel. In case of trouble or if the officer leaves the station for an extended period of time, command of this panel can be switched to a panel at a remote location, known as central control. The officer usually wears a device that permits immediate communication with central control in case of trouble, and the area is also covered by a video camera monitored by an officer in the central control room.

Indirect supervision jails use similar construction, but the correctional officer's station is located inside a secure room. Microphones and speakers inside the living unit permit the officer to hear and communicate with inmates. Although these institutions have not yet undergone extensive evaluation, research shows that they may help reduce postrelease offending in some situations.[39]

♦ PRISONS

The Federal Bureau of Prisons and every state government maintain closed correctional facilities, also called **prisons**, penitentiaries, or reformatories.[40] Corrections is a vast and costly system. According to the Bureau of Justice Statistics, local governments, state governments, and the federal government spend more than $50 billion per year on corrections, an amount that has risen a whopping 946 percent since 1977.[41]

There are now more than 1,600 public and private adult correctional facilities housing state prisoners. In addition, more than 100 public and private federal facilities house federal inmates.

Usually, prisons are organized or classified on three levels—maximum, medium, and minimum security—and each has distinct characteristics.

Maximum-Security Prisons

Housing the most famous criminals and providing the basis of many films and novels, **maximum-security prisons** are probably the institutions most familiar to the public. Famous "max prisons" have included Sing Sing, Joliet, Attica, Walpole, and the most fearsome prison of all, the now-closed federal facility on Alcatraz Island known as The Rock.

A typical maximum-security facility is fortress-like, surrounded by stone walls with guard towers at strategic places. These walls may be 25 feet high, and sometimes inner and outer walls divide the prison into courtyards. Barbed-wire or electrified fences are used to discourage escapes. High security, armed guards, and stone walls give the inmate the sense that the facility is impregnable and reassure the citizens outside that convicts will be completely incapacitated.

Inmates live in interior, metal-barred cells that contain their own plumbing and sanitary facilities and are locked securely by either key or electronic device. Cells are organized in sections called blocks, and in large prisons, a number of cell blocks make up a wing. Thus, an inmate may be officially located in, for example, Block 3 of E Wing. During the evening, each cell block is sealed off from the others, as is each wing.

Every inmate is assigned a number and a uniform on entering the prison system. Unlike the striped, easily identifiable uniforms of old, the maximum-security

ThomsonNOW Improve your grade on the exam with Personalized Study! For reinforcement resources and a mastery check of jails, go to www.thomsonedu.com/thomsonnow.

prison
A state or federal correctional institution for the incarceration of felony offenders for terms of one year or more; penitentiary.

maximum-security prison
A correctional institution that houses dangerous felons and maintains strict security measures, including high walls, guard towers, and limited contact with the outside world.

The administrative goal of a maximum security prison is safety and control. Here a correction officer delivers a meal to a maximum security cell inmate at the Holman Unit in Atmore, Alabama. Some inmates are so dangerous that they are kept in segregation from the rest of the inmate population.

© A. Ramey/PhotoEdit, Inc.

inmate today wears khaki attire not unlike military fatigues. Dress codes may be strictly enforced in some institutions, but closely cropped hair and other strict features are vestiges of the past.

During the day, the inmates engage in carefully controlled activities: meals, workshops, education, and so on. Rule violators may be confined to their cells, and working and shared recreational activities are viewed as privileges.

The byword of the maximum-security prison is security. Guards and other correctional workers are made aware that each inmate may well be dangerous and that, as a result, the utmost in security must be maintained. In keeping with this philosophy, prisons are designed to eliminate hidden corners where people can congregate, and passages are constructed so that they can be easily blocked off to quell disturbances. Some states have constructed **super-maximum-security prisons** (supermax prisons) to house the most predatory criminals. These high-security institutions can be independent correctional centers or locked wings of existing prisons.[42] Some supermax prisons lock inmates in their cells 22 to 24 hours a day, never allowing them out unless they are shackled.[43] The Analyzing Criminal Justice Issues discusses supermax prisons.

> **PERSPECTIVES ON JUSTICE**
>
> ### Due Process
>
> Critics of supermax prisons believe that they are a direct threat to inmate due process rights because they deprive inmates of basic human rights such as human contact. They also eliminate the chance for rehabilitation.

super-maximum-security prison
A prison designed, constructed, and maintained to provide the greatest possible control of the most dangerous prisoners.

Medium-Security Prisons

Although **medium-security prisons** are similar in appearance to maximum-security prisons, the security and atmosphere within them are neither so tense nor so vigilant. Medium-security prisons are also surrounded by walls, but there may be fewer guard towers or other security precautions. In these institutions, visitor privileges may be more extensive, and personal contact may be allowed, whereas in a maximum-security prison visitors may be separated from inmates by Plexiglas or other barriers (to prohibit the passing of contraband). Most prisoners are housed in cells, but individual honor rooms in medium-security prisons are used to reward those who make exemplary rehabilitation efforts. Finally, medium-security prisons promote greater treatment efforts, and the relaxed atmosphere allows freedom of movement for rehabilitation workers and other therapeutic personnel.

medium-security prison
A correctional institution that houses nonviolent offenders, characterized by a less tense and vigilant atmosphere and more opportunities for contact with the outside world.

Ultramaximum-Security Prisons

Many states have created supermax (also called ultramax) prisons, either as stand-alone facilities or as secure units within lower-security prisons. In all, there are now more than 30 facilities that can be labeled as supermax. They contain a total of 20,000 beds and account for about 2 percent of the total state prison population.

The first federal maxi-prison, in Marion, Illinois, was infamous for its tight security and isolated conditions. Marion has been supplanted by a new 484-bed facility in Florence, Colorado. This new prison has the most sophisticated security measures in the United States, including 168 video cameras and 1,400 electronically controlled gates. Inside the cells, all furniture is unmovable; the desk, bed, and TV stand are made of cement. All potential weapons, including soap dishes, toilet seats, and toilet handles, have been removed. The cement walls are 5,000-pound quality, and steel bars are placed so they crisscross every eight inches inside the walls. Cells are angled so that inmates can see neither one another nor the outside scenery (see Figure 15.A). This cuts down on communications and denies inmates a sense of location in order to prevent escapes.

Getting out of the prison seems impossible. Six guard towers are situated at different heights to prevent air attacks. To get out, the inmates would have to pass through seven three-inch-thick steel doors, each of which can be opened only after the previous one has closed. If a guard tower is ever seized, all controls are switched to the next station. If the whole prison is seized, it can be controlled from the outside. The only way out appears to be via good works and behavior, through which an inmate can earn transfer to another prison within three years.

The threat of transfer to a maxi-maxi institution is used to deter inmate misbehavior in less restrictive institutions. Civil rights watchdog groups charge that these maxi-maxi prisons violate the United Nations standards for the treatment of inmates. They are typically located in rural areas, which makes staffing difficult in the professional areas of dentistry, medicine, and counseling. Senior officers prefer not working in these institutions, leaving the most difficult inmates in the hands of the most inexperienced correctional officers.

Benefits and Drawbacks

The development of the ultramax prison represents a shift from previous correctional policy, which favored dispersing the most troublesome inmates to different prisons to prevent them from joining forces or planning escapes. The supermax model finds that housing the most dangerous inmates in an ultrasecure facility eases their control while reducing violence levels in the general prison population.

A number of experts have given supermax prisons mixed reviews. They seem to achieve some correctional benefits of security and quality of life but also create problems for staff and inmates. One survey by Leena Kurki and Norval Morris found that although conditions vary from state to state, many supermax prisons subject inmates to nearly complete isolation and deprivation of sensory stimuli. Although the long-term effects of such conditions on inmates is still uncertain, Kurki and Morris believe that such conditions are likely to have an extremely harmful effect, especially on those who suffer from preexisting mental illness or those with subnormal intelligence.

Some recent research by Daniel Mears and his colleagues finds that supermax prisons produce a mixed bag of results. Mears and Jamie Watson conducted surveys of correctional officials and found that supermax prisons may actually enhance the quality of life of inmates and consequently improve their mental health. Supermax prisons increase privacy, reduce danger, and even provide creature comforts such as TV sets that are unavailable in general population prisons. Staff report less stress and fear because they have to contend with fewer disruptive inmates.

On the other hand, Mears and Watson found that supermax prisons also bring some unintended negative consequences. Staff may have too much control over inmates, a condition that damages staff–inmate relationships. Long hours of isolation may be associated with mental illness and psychological disturbances. Supermax inmates seem to have a more difficult time readjusting upon release. A stay in a supermax prison inhibits reintegration into other prisons, communities, and families. In another study, Mears and Jennifer Castro surveyed wardens and found that although they seem to favor supermax prisons, they also express concern that the general public believes that supermax institutions are inhumane, that they drain limited funds away from state budgets, and that they produce increases in litigation and court interventions as well as increased recidivism and reentry failure among released inmates.

According to Mears and his associates, for supermax prisons to be effective they must achieve a number of hard-to-reach goals: identifying the most disruptive inmates, placing enough of them in supermax confinement, and reducing their misbehavior upon return to the general population. As well, other inmates must take their place as being disruptive, and so on. Failure to meet these requirements, Mears and company believe, undermines the overall effectiveness of the supermax concept.

FIGURE A

Typical Cell in a Super-Maximum Security Prison

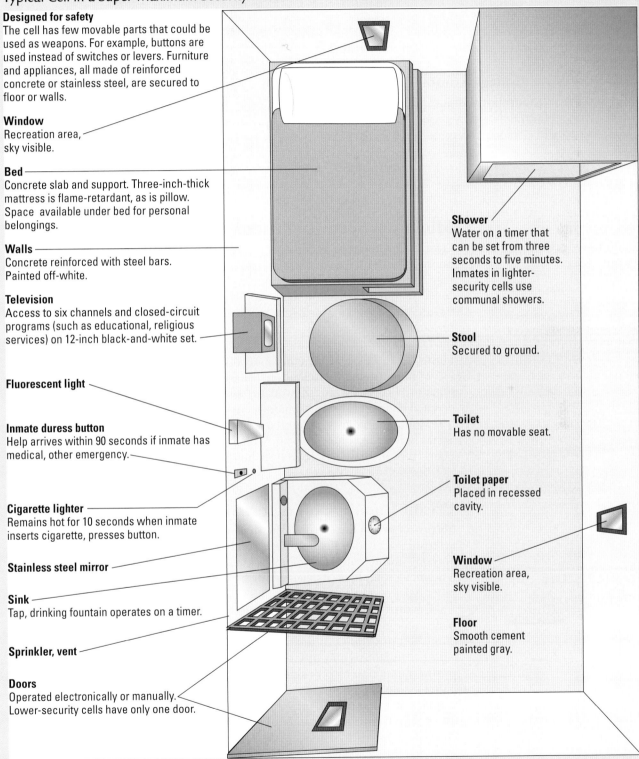

Designed for safety
The cell has few movable parts that could be used as weapons. For example, buttons are used instead of switches or levers. Furniture and appliances, all made of reinforced concrete or stainless steel, are secured to floor or walls.

Window
Recreation area, sky visible.

Bed
Concrete slab and support. Three-inch-thick mattress is flame-retardant, as is pillow. Space available under bed for personal belongings.

Walls
Concrete reinforced with steel bars. Painted off-white.

Television
Access to six channels and closed-circuit programs (such as educational, religious services) on 12-inch black-and-white set.

Fluorescent light

Inmate duress button
Help arrives within 90 seconds if inmate has medical, other emergency.

Cigarette lighter
Remains hot for 10 seconds when inmate inserts cigarette, presses button.

Stainless steel mirror

Sink
Tap, drinking fountain operates on a timer.

Sprinkler, vent

Doors
Operated electronically or manually. Lower-security cells have only one door.

Shower
Water on a timer that can be set from three seconds to five minutes. Inmates in lighter-security cells use communal showers.

Stool
Secured to ground.

Toilet
Has no movable seat.

Toilet paper
Placed in recessed cavity.

Window
Recreation area, sky visible.

Floor
Smooth cement painted gray.

Source: Louis Winn, United States Penitentiary, Administrative Maximum. Florence, Colorado.

(continued)

Critical Thinking

Ultramaximum-security prisons are reminiscent of the old Pennsylvania system, which made use of solitary confinement and high security. Is such an approach inhumane in this more enlightened age? Why or why not?

InfoTrac College Edition Research

To read about the conditions in the new super-maximum-security prisons, read "Cruel and Unusual Punishment," *Harper's*, July 2001, p. 92.

Sources: Daniel Mears and Jamie Watson, "Towards a Fair and Balanced Assessment of Supermax Prisons," *Justice Quarterly* 23 (2006): 232–70; Daniel Mears and Jennifer Castro, "Wardens' Views on the Wisdom of Supermax Prisons," *Crime and Delinquency* 52 (2006): 398–431; Leena Kurki and Norval Morris, "The Purpose, Practices, and Problems of Supermax Prisons," in *Crime and Justice: An Annual Edition*, ed. Michael Tonry (Chicago: University of Chicago Press, 2001), pp. 385–422; Richard H. Franklin, "Assessing Supermax Operations," *Corrections Today* 60 (1998): 126–28; Chase Riveland, *Supermax Prison: Overview and General Considerations* (Longmont, Colo.: National Institute of Corrections, 1998); Federal Bureau of Prisons, *State of the Bureau, 1995* (Washington, D.C.: Government Printing Office, 1996); Dennis Cauchon, "The Alcatraz of the Rockies," *USA Today*, November 16, 1994, p. 6A.

Minimum-Security Prisons

minimum-security prison
A correctional institution that houses white-collar and other nonviolent offenders, characterized by few security measures and liberal furlough and visitation policies.

Operating without armed guards or walls, **minimum-security prisons** usually house the most trustworthy and least violent offenders. White-collar criminals may be their most common occupants. Inmates are allowed a great deal of personal freedom. Instead of being marched to activities by guards, they are summoned by bells or loudspeaker announcements and assemble on their own. Work furloughs and educational releases are encouraged, and vocational training is of the highest level. Dress codes are lax, and inmates are allowed to grow beards or mustaches or demonstrate other individual characteristics.

Minimum-security facilities may have dormitories or small private rooms for inmates. Prisoners are allowed to own personal possessions that might be deemed dangerous in a maximum-security prison, such as radios.

Minimum-security prisons have been criticized for being like country clubs. Some federal facilities for white-collar criminals even have tennis courts and pools (they are called derisively "Club Fed"). Yet they remain prisons, and the isolation and loneliness of prison life deeply affect the inmates.

Prison Inmate Characteristics

Surveys of prison inmates indicate that, as might be expected, the personal characteristics of prison inmates reflect common traits of arrestees. Most inmates are currently incarcerated for committing a violent crime, and the proportion of violent inmates has been rising at a much faster pace than inmates incarcerated for other types of crime (see Figure 15.3).

Inmates tend to be young, single, poorly educated, disproportionately male, and minority-group members. Many were either underemployed or unemployed prior to their arrest. Many have incomes of less than $10,000 and suffer drug abuse and other personal problems. Gender differences in the prison population are considerable. Women are underrepresented in prison, and not solely because they commit less serious crimes. The Uniform Crime Reports arrest statistics indicate that the overall male-female arrest ratio is about 3.5 male offenders to 1 female offender; for violent crimes, the ratio is closer to 6 males to 1 female. Yet men are about 14 times more likely than women to be in a state or federal prison. There is also considerable racial disparity in the inmate population. Today, black males outnumber white males and Hispanic males among inmates with sentences of more than one year. More than 40 percent of all prison inmates are black men, and a significant

FIGURE 15.3

Trends in the Prison Population by Offense

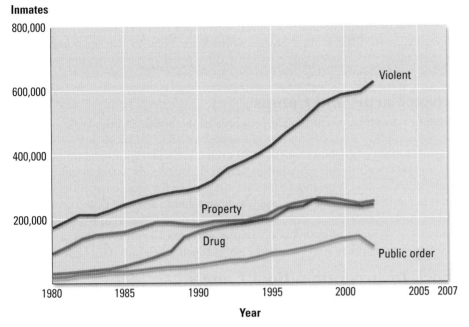

Source: *Correctional Populations in the United States, Annual,* and *Prisoners in 2004.*

portion of the entire black male population is now behind bars. For example, about 8 percent of black males aged 25 to 29 are now in prison, compared to 2.5 percent of Hispanic males and about 1 percent of white males in the same age group. These race-based differences in the incarceration rate are maintained over the life course (see Table 15.1).

SUBSTANCE ABUSE A strong association exists between substance abuse and inmate status. One study of 400 Texas inmates found that almost 75 percent suffered from lifetime substance abuse or dependence.[44] About 80 percent of inmates report having used drugs sometime during their life, and more than 60 percent are regular users. About half of the inmates report being either drunk, high, or both when they committed the crime that landed them in prison. Considering this background, it should come as no surprise that more inmates die from HIV-related disease than from prison violence.[45] (See Chapter 16.)

PHYSICAL ABUSE Like jail inmates, prison inmates also report a long history of physical abuse and mental health problems. About 19 percent report some form of physical abuse, including 57 percent of female offenders.[46] In addition, about 16 percent of state prison inmates report having some form of mental problems.[47] Mentally ill inmates are more likely to be arrested for violent offenses and to have suffered a variety of personal and emotional problems than the general inmate population. The picture that emerges is that prisons hold those people who face the toughest social obstacles in society. Only a few members of the educated middle class wind up behind bars, and these people are usually held in low-security, "country club" institutions.

TABLE 15.1

Percentage of Prisoners by Race

	1995	2003	2004
Total	100	100	100
Hispanic	17.6	19.0	19.2
White	33.5	35.0	34.3
Black	45.7	44.1	40.7
Other	3.2	1.9	2.9
Two or more races	—	—	2.9

Sources: Paige M. Harrison and Allen J. Beck, *Prisoners in 2004* (Washington, D.C.: Bureau of Justice Statistics, 2005).

ThomsonNOW Improve your grade on the exam with Personalized Study! For reinforcement resources and a mastery check of prisons, go to www.thomsonedu.com/ thomsonnow.

♦ ALTERNATIVE CORRECTIONAL INSTITUTIONS

In addition to prison and jails, a number of other correctional institutions are operating around the United States. Some have been in use for a long time, whereas others have been more recently developed as part of an innovative or experimental program.

Prison Farms and Camps

Prison farms and camps are found primarily in the South and the West and have been in operation since the nineteenth century. Today, about 40 farms, 40 forest camps, 80 road camps, and more than 60 similar facilities (vocational training centers, ranches, and so on) exist in the nation. Prisoners on farms produce dairy products, grain, and vegetable crops that are used in the state correctional system and other governmental facilities, such as hospitals and schools. Forestry camp inmates maintain state parks, fight forest fires, and do reforestation work. Ranches, primarily a Western phenomenon, employ inmates in cattle raising and horse breeding, among other activities. Road gangs repair roads and state highways.

Shock Incarceration/Boot Camps

A recent approach to correctional care that is gaining popularity around the United States is **shock incarceration** or **boot camps**. Such programs typically include youthful, first-time offenders and feature military discipline and physical training. The concept is that short periods (90 to 180 days) of high-intensity exercise and work will shock the inmate into going straight. Tough physical training is designed to promote responsibility and improve decision-making skills, build self-confidence, and teach socialization skills. Inmates are treated with rough intensity by drillmasters, who may call them names and punish the entire group for the failure of one of its members. Discipline is so severe that some critics warn that it can amount to "cruel and unusual punishment" and generate costly inmate lawsuits.[48]

The programs operating around the United States vary widely.[49] Some programs include educational and training components, counseling sessions, and

shock incarceration
A short prison sentence served under military discipline at a boot camp facility.

boot camp
A short-term militaristic correctional facility in which inmates, usually young first-time offenders, undergo intensive physical conditioning and discipline.

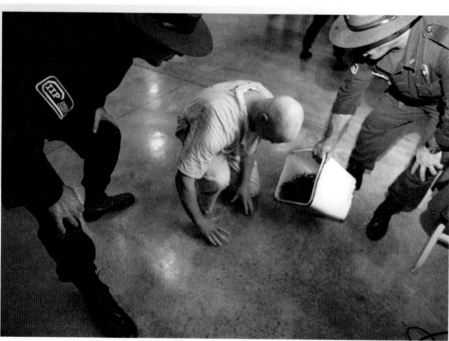

Boot camps use strict discipline regimes, which some critics find demeaning to inmates. Here at the Prison Boot Camp in Illinois, one correctional officer bangs the metal waste basket against the cement floor. Two officers yell at the new inmate, demanding that he hurry and gather his newly-cut hair into the basket. They hurl a barrage of non-profane insults at him. Profanity by correctional officers as well as inmates is forbidden at the boot camp.

©Jacksonville Courier/Zuzana Killiam/The Image Works

treatment for special-needs populations, whereas others devote little or no time to therapeutic activities. Some receive program participants directly from court sentencing, whereas others choose potential candidates from the general inmate population. Some allow voluntary participation and others voluntary termination.[50]

Supporters believe that the shock incarceration programs can provide some important correctional benefits. New York houses inmates in these programs in separate institutions and provides most, but not all, graduates with extensive follow-up supervision. Although recidivism rates for these programs in New York are similar to those of traditional prisons, indications are that both inmates and staff view shock incarceration as a positive experience.[51] It is estimated that the New York program has saved taxpayers hundreds of millions of dollars because boot camps are cheaper to build and maintain than traditional prisons. Other evaluations have found that a boot camp experience can improve inmates' attitudes and can have the potential for enhancing their postcorrection lifestyle.[52]

Shock incarceration has the advantage of being a lower-cost alternative to overcrowded prisons because inmates are held in nonsecure facilities and sentences are short. Both staff and inmates seem excited by the programs, and even those who fail on parole report that they felt the shock incarceration was a valuable experience.[53] If shock incarceration is viewed as an exciting or helpful experience by its graduates, however, they could be encouraged to recidivate, given that the threat of the prison experience has been weakened.

EVALUATING SHOCK INCARCERATION Is shock incarceration a correctional panacea or another fad doomed to failure? The results so far are mixed. The costs of boot camps are no lower than those of traditional prisons, but because sentences are shorter they do provide long-term savings. Some programs suffer high failure-to-complete rates, which makes program evaluations difficult (even if graduates are successful, success could be achieved because troublesome cases drop out and are placed back in the general inmate population). Those evaluations that exist indicate that the recidivism rates of inmates who attend shock programs are in some cases no lower than for those released from traditional correctional experiences.[54]

Many of these evaluations have been conducted by Doris Layton Mackenzie and her associates. As a group, these studies find little evidence that boot camps can help lower recidivism rates.[55] One recent analysis of multiple programs in multiple settings found little evidence that boot camps can be effective.[56] Because of these sketchy results, the future of the boot camp approach is clouded. Recently (2005), the federal government announced the termination of its boot camp program.[57]

Even though these results are disappointing, it is possible that boot camps can be effective with some offenders by using a combination of treatment modalities. Older residents with ties to the community seem to do much better than younger, more impulsive clients who maintain deviant friends.[58] There is also evidence that how the boot camp experience is managed may shape its effect. A recent study of boot camp graduates shows that recidivism rates are significantly lowered if the graduates are placed in residential aftercare program upon their release.[59]

Community Correctional Facilities

One of the goals of correctional treatment is to help reintegrate the offender into society. Placing offenders in a prison makes them more likely to adopt an inmate lifestyle than to reassimilate conventional social norms. As a result, the **community treatment** concept began to take off in the 1960s. State and federal correctional systems created community-based correctional models as an alternative to closed institutions. Many are **halfway houses** to which inmates are transferred just before their release into the community. These facilities are designed to bridge the gap between institutional living and the community. Specialized

community treatment
Correctional treatment services, such as a halfway house, located within the community.

halfway house
A community-based correctional facility that houses inmates before their outright release so that they can become gradually acclimated to conventional society.

treatment may be offered, and the residents use the experience to cushion the shock of reentering society.

Commitment to a community correctional center may also be used as an intermediate sanction and the sole mode of treatment. An offender may be assigned to a community treatment center operated by the state department of corrections. Or the corrections department can contract with a private community center. This practice is common in the treatment of drug addicts and other nonviolent offenders whose special needs can be met in a self-contained community setting that specializes in specific types of treatment.

Halfway houses and community correctional centers can look like residential homes and, in many instances, were originally residences. In urban centers, older apartment buildings can be adapted for the purpose. Usually, these facilities have a central treatment theme—such as group therapy or reality therapy—that is used to rehabilitate and reintegrate clients.

Another popular approach in community-based corrections is the use of ex-offenders as staff members. These individuals have made the transition from the closed institution to living in society and can be invaluable in helping residents overcome the many hurdles they face in proper readjustment.

Despite the encouraging philosophical concept presented by the halfway house, evaluation of specific programs has not led to a definite endorsement of this type of treatment.[60] One significant problem has been a lack of support from community residents, who fear the establishment of an institution housing what they perceive as dangerous offenders in their neighborhood. Court actions and zoning restrictions have been brought in to some areas to foil efforts to create halfway houses.[61] As a result, many halfway houses are located in rundown neighborhoods in the worst areas of town—certainly a condition that must influence the attitudes and behavior of the inmates. Furthermore, the climate of control exercised in most halfway houses, where rule violation can be met with a quick return to the institution, may not be one that the average inmate can distinguish from his former high-security penal institution.

Despite these problems, the promise held by community correctional centers, coupled with their low cost of operations, has led to their continued use into the new millennium.

Private Prisons

On January 6, 1986, the U.S. Corrections Corporation opened in Marion, Kentucky, the first private state prison—a 300-bed minimum-security facility for inmates who are within three years of parole.[62] Today, more than 264 privately operated facilities are under contract with state or federal authorities to house prisoners, an increase of 140 percent since 1995. The number of inmates held in these facilities has risen 459 percent, from 16,663 inmates in June 1995 to more than 100,000 today.[63] Private prisons now play an important correctional role in the United States, Australia, and the United Kingdom.[64]

There are a number of different models of private correctional facilities. In some instances, a private corporation will finance and build an institution and then contract with correctional authorities to provide services for convicted criminals. Sometimes the private concern will finance and build the institution and then lease it outright to the government. This model has the advantage of allowing the government to circumvent the usually difficult process of getting voters to approve a bond issue and raising funds for prison construction. Another common method of private involvement is with specific service contracts; for example, a private concern might be hired to manage the prison health care system, food services, or staff training.

How have private prisons fared? Some evaluations of **recidivism** among inmates released from private and public facilities find that recidivism rates are equal and/or lower among the private prison group than the state prison inmates.[65] Inmates released from private prisons who reoffend commit less serious

recidivism
Repetition of criminal behavior; habitual criminality.

offenses than those released from public institutions. Private and state institutions cost about the same to operate, but private prisons seem cheaper to construct.[66]

These findings help support the concept of the private correctional institution. Nonetheless, some experts question reliance on private prisons, believing that their use raises a number of vexing problems. Will private providers be able to effectively evaluate programs, knowing that a negative evaluation might cause them to lose their contract? Will they skimp on services and programs to reduce costs? Might they not skim off the easy cases and leave the hard-core inmates to the state's care? And will the need to keep business booming require widening the net to fill empty cells? Must they maintain state-mandated liability insurance to cover inmate claims?[67]

Private corrections firms also run into opposition from existing state correctional staff and management who fear the loss of jobs and autonomy. Moreover, the public may be skeptical about an untested private concern's ability to provide security and protection. Private corrections also face administrative problems. How will program quality be controlled? To compete on price, a private facility may have to cut corners to beat out the competition. Determining accountability for problems and mishaps will be difficult when dealing with a corporation that is a legal fiction and protects its officers from personal responsibility for their actions.

LEGAL ISSUES Unresolved legal problems can emerge quickly: Can privately employed guards patrol the perimeter and use deadly force to stop escape attempts? Do private correctional officers have less immunity from lawsuits than state employees? In *Richardson v. McKnight* the U.S. Supreme Court held that prison guards employed by a private firm are not entitled to a qualified immunity from suit by prisoners charging a section 1983 violation. Emphasizing that a private firm was systematically organized to manage the prison, the Court majority said that "[o]ur examination of history and purpose . . . reveals nothing special enough about the job or about its organizational structure that would warrant providing these private prison guards with a governmental immunity."[68]

The case of *Correctional Services Corp. v. Malesko* (2001) helped define the rights and protections of inmates in private correctional facilities. John Malesko had a heart condition but was forced to walk the stairs instead of being allowed to take an elevator. When he suffered a heart attack, he sued the Correctional Services Corp., which was operating the prison. He alleged that under the Federal Civil Rights Act, the denial of proper medial care violated his civil rights. Citizens are generally allowed to seek damages against federal agents who violate their civil rights. However, the Supreme Court ruled that although Malesko could sue an individual employee of the private correctional corporation for allegedly violating his or her constitutional rights, he could not sue the correctional corporation itself. This decision shields the private prison corporation from suits brought under federal civil rights statutes. The *Malesko* decision confirms the concerns of some critics who view the private prison as an insidious expansion of state control over citizens: a state-supported entity that has more freedom to exert control than the state itself.[69]

What does the future hold for the private prison industry? In the abstract, an efficiently run private correctional enterprise may be an attractive alternative to a costly public correctional system, but legal, administrative, and cost issues need to be resolved before private prisons can become widespread.[70] A balance must be reached between the need for a private business to make a profit and the integrity of a prison administration that must be concerned with such complex issues as security, rehabilitation, and dealing with highly dangerous people in a closed environment.[71] And, unlike state institutions, private prisons, like all private enterprise systems, must conform to the whims of the marketplace. The private prison industry expanded rapidly during a time when mushrooming inmate populations strained the capacities of existing public institutions to house the inmate population. Now that the demand has leveled off, so has the need for private prisons. In addition, government regulation of the industry has produced conditions in which private interests have been molded into mirror images of their public-sector counterparts. There has also been an anti-privatization movement conducted by faith-based groups competing for funding that has further limited the growth of private prisons.[72]

◆ CORRECTIONAL POPULATIONS

The U.S. prison population has had a number of cycles of growth and decline.[73] Between 1925 and 1939, it increased about 5 percent a year, reflecting the nation's concern for the lawlessness of that time. The incarceration rate reached a high of 137 per 100,000 U.S. population in 1939. During World War II, the prison population declined by 50,000, as potential offenders were drafted into the armed services. By 1956, the incarceration rate had dropped to 99 per 100,000 population.

The late 1950s saw a steady increase in the prison population until 1961, when 220,000 people were in custody, a rate of 119 per 100,000. From 1961 to 1968, with the escalation of the Vietnam War, the prison population declined by about 30,000. The incarceration rate remained fairly stable until 1974, when the current dramatic rise began. Between 1995 and 2004, the number of state and federal prisoners grew 24 percent, reaching more than 1,400,000 in 2004.

However, the most recent data indicate that the prison population has finally begun to stabilize (Figure 15.4). Whether this is a short-term correction or a long-term trend remains to be seen.[74]

Going to Prison During Your Lifetime

The prison boom means that a significant portion of people will one day be behind bars. Today, more than six million adult residents are serving time or have previously served time.[75] This means that one in thirty adults has been confined in prison at sometime during his or her life. The number of current or former inmates increased by 3.8 million men and women between 1974 and 2002.

Significant racial differences exist in the likelihood of going to prison. About 16.6 percent of adult African American males are current or former inmates, compared with 7.7 percent of Hispanic males and 2.6 percent of white males. Among African American males 35 to 44 years of age, 22 percent are current or former prisoners, compared with 10 percent of Hispanic males and 3.5 percent of white males in the same age group. The lifetime chances of going to prison are six times higher for men (11.3 percent) than women (1.8 percent). If the current rates of incarceration were to continue indefinitely, an African American male in the United States would have about a 1 in 3 chance of going to prison during his lifetime; a Hispanic male, a 1 in 6 chance; and a white male, a 1 in 17 chance. Making the same assumptions, African American females (5.6 percent) would be almost as likely to go to prison as white males (5.9 percent); Hispanic females (2.2 percent) and white females (0.9 percent) would have much lower lifetime chances of imprisonment.

Explaining Prison Population Trends

Why did the prison population grow so rapidly over the past decade despite the fact that the crime rate fell? One reason may be politicians responding to the general public's more punitive response to criminal offenders, creating the penal harm movement. Public concern about drugs and violent crime has not been lost on state lawmakers. Mandatory sentencing laws,

FIGURE 15.4
Incarceration Rate

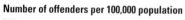

Number of offenders per 100,000 population

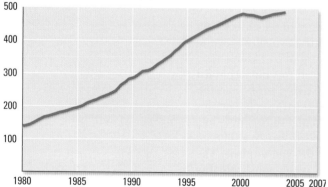

Source: *Correctional Populations in the United States, Annual,* and *Prisoners in* 2004.

which have been implemented by a majority of states and the federal government, increase eligibility for incarceration and limit the availability for early release via parole.

Although fewer people are going to prison and the length of prison sentences have declined, structural changes in criminal codes and crime rates have also helped produce an expanding correctional population. The amount of time served in prison has increased because of such developments as truth-in-sentencing laws that require inmates to serve at least 85 percent of their sentence behind bars.[76] As Table 15.2 shows, the percentage of the imposed prison sentence served behind bars has risen dramatically over the past decade.

The conviction rate is increasing for crimes that are traditionally punished with a prison sentence, such as robbery and burglary. In addition, get-tough policies have helped curtail the use of parole and have reduced judicial discretion to impose nonincarceration sentences.[77] Some states have implemented laws mandating that violent juveniles be waived or transferred to the adult court for treatment.[78] Thousands of juveniles are being tried as adults each year and may end up in adult prisons.

Also swelling the prison population is an increasing number of ex-inmates who have failed on community release. Today, about one-third of new admissions to prison are parole or other conditional-release violators, up more than 10 percent since 1990.

The recent stabilization in the prison population may signal that the effect of a declining crime rate has overcome harsh sentencing policies. As costs skyrocket, some states are spending more on prisons than on higher education. The public may begin to question the wisdom of a strict incarceration policy. There may also be fewer criminals to incarcerate. The waning of the crack cocaine epidemic in large cities may hasten this decline because street crimes will decline and fewer offenders will be eligible for the long penalties associated with the possession of crack.[79] In the final analysis, changes in the correctional population may depend on the faith that judges and legislators place in incarceration as a crime control policy. As long as policy makers believe that incarcerating predatory criminals can bring down crime rates, the likelihood of a significant decrease in the institutional population seems remote. If little evidence exists that this costly system lowers crime rates, less costly and equally effective alternatives may be sought.

TABLE 15.2
Percentage of Sentence Served by Inmates

	1994	1998	2002
All offenses	38	47	51
Murder	47	52	63
Robbery	44	51	58
Aggravated assault	46	57	66
Burglary	35	45	49
Larceny	37	45	52
Drug trafficking	32	41	45

Source: Matthew Durose and Patrick Langan, *Felony Sentences in State Courts, 2002* (Washington, D.C.: Bureau of Justice Statistics, 2004).

ThomsonNOW Improve your grade on the exam with Personalized Study! For reinforcement resources and a mastery check of correctional populations, go to www.thomsonedu.com/thomsonnow.

ETHICAL CHALLENGES IN CRIMINAL JUSTICE: A WRITING ASSIGNMENT

In supermax prisons, prisoners are generally kept in their cells for 20 to 22 hours per day, most often in solitary confinement. They receive their meals through "food ports" in the doors of their cells. They are given no work and are prevented from recreational activities; many do not even have access to a TV set. When supermax inmates are allowed to exercise, it is in a small, enclosed area kept under constant surveillance, usually with closed-circuit television cameras; prisoners have no privacy. Cell walls, and sometimes plumbing, are often soundproofed to prevent communication between the inmates.

Write an essay addressing the utility of supermax prisons. Address these issues: Do their existing conditions violate constitutional principles? Do they represent the core values of U.S. society?

Doing Research on the Web

A number of sites address supermax prisons. Go to Supermaxed.com and/or PrisonCentral.org: Supermax Homepage.

For an essay on the psychological effects of supermax prisons, read "Psychological Death Row: Supermaximum Security Prisons, Sensory Deprivation and Effects of Solitary Confinement."

For an essay critical of the supermax movement, read "The Prison Inside the Prison: Control Units, Supermax Prisons, and Devices of Torture."

You can access all of these sources by going to the Siegel/Senna Introduction to Criminal Justice 11e website: www.thomsonedu.com/criminaljustice/siegel.

SUMMARY

◆ Today's correctional institutions can trace their development to European origins.

◆ Punishment methods developed in Europe were modified and improved by American colonists, most notably William Penn. He replaced the whip and other methods of physical punishment with confinement in county institutions or penitentiaries.

◆ Later, as needs grew, the newly formed states created their own large facilities. Discipline was harsh within them, and most enforced a code of silence.

◆ At Auburn Prison, New York developed the system of congregate working conditions during the day and isolation at night.

◆ Pennsylvania adopted an isolate system that required inmates to be locked into their cells for the duration of their sentence. Although this was a secure system, it drove many inmates mad.

◆ The congregate system, developed in New York, has been adopted by the present U.S. penal system.

◆ Correctional rehabilitation programs began to develop in the late nineteenth century.

◆ Parole developed abroad but was imported to the United States and became the predominant type of prison release.

◆ A number of correctional reforms have been instituted over the centuries, including the development of specialized prisons.

◆ A number of institutions currently house convicted offenders. Jails are used for misdemeanants and minor felons. Because conditions are so poor in jails, they have become a major trouble spot for the criminal justice system. New-generation jails have improved security and reduced violence.

◆ Federal and state prisons—classified as minimum, medium, and maximum security—house most of the nation's incarcerated felons.

◆ The poor track record of prisons has spurred the development of new correctional models, specifically the boot camp, the halfway house, and the community correctional center.

◆ The success of these institutions has been challenged by research efforts indicating that their recidivism rates are equal to those of state prisons.

◆ One newer development has been the correctional institution operated by private companies, which receive a fee for their services. There are more than 240 of these institutions around the nation.

◆ The prison population has skyrocketed in the past few years, but recent data indicate that the boom may be leveling off.

◆ A significant percentage of the U.S. public will serve a prison sentence during their lifetime. Significant racial discrepancies exist in the likelihood of going to prison.

KEY TERMS

shire reeve, 493
hulk, 494
Walnut Street Jail, 496
penitentiary house, 496

tier system, 496
congregate system, 496
Auburn system, 496
Pennsylvania system, 497

contract system, 498
convict-lease system, 499
parole, 499
hands-off doctrine, 500

ThomsonNOW™ Maximize your study time by using ThomsonNOW's diagnostic study plan to help you review this chapter. The Study Plan will

◆ help you identify areas on which you should concentrate;

◆ provide interactive exercises to help you master the chapter concepts; and

◆ provide a post-test to confirm you are ready to move on to the next chapter.

CRITICAL THINKING QUESTIONS

1. Would you want a community correctional center to be built in your neighborhood? Why or why not?

2. Should pretrial detainees and convicted offenders be kept in the same institution? Explain.

3. What can be done to reduce correctional overcrowding?

4. Should private companies be allowed to run correctional institutions? Why or why not?

5. What are the drawbacks of shock incarceration?

NOTES

1. Michael S. Rosenwald, "Court Records Show Druce's Troubled, Deviant Life," *Boston Globe*, August 28, 2003, p. A1.

2. See David Fogel, *We Are the Living Proof*, 2nd ed. (Cincinnati: Anderson, 1978); Andrew von Hirsch, *Doing Justice: The Choice of Punishments* (New York: Hill and Wang, 1976); R. G. Singer, *Just Deserts—Sentencing Based on Equality and Desert* (Cambridge, Mass.: Ballinger, 1979).

3. Thomas Stucky, Karen Heimer, and Joseph Lang, "Partisan Politics, Electoral Competition and Imprisonment: An Analysis of States Over Time," *Criminology* 43 (2005): 211–47.

4. Francis Cullen, "The Twelve People Who Saved Rehabilitation: How the Science of Criminology Made a Difference," *Criminology* 43 (2005): 1–42.

5. Among the most helpful sources in developing this section were Mark Colvin, *Penitentiaries, Reformatories, and Chain Gangs* (New York: St. Martin's, 1997); David Duffee, *Corrections: Practice and Policy* (New York: Random House, 1989); Harry Allen and Clifford Simonsen, *Correction in America*, 5th ed. (New York: Macmillan, 1989); Benedict Alper, *Prisons Inside-Out* (Cambridge, Mass.: Ballinger, 1974); Harry Elmer Barnes, *The Story of Punishment*, 2nd ed. (Montclair, N.J.: Patterson-Smith, 1972); Gustave de Beaumont and Alexis de Tocqueville, *On the Penitentiary System in the United States and Its Applications in France* (Carbondale: Southern Illinois University Press, 1964); Orlando Lewis, *The Development of American Prisons and Prison Customs, 1776–1845* (Montclair, N.J.: Patterson-Smith, 1967); Leonard Orland, ed., *Justice, Punishment, and Treatment* (New York: Free Press, 1973); J. Goebel, *Felony and Misdemeanor* (Philadelphia: University of Pennsylvania Press, 1976); Georg Rusche and Otto Kircheimer, *Punishment and Social Structure* (New York: Russell and Russell, 1939); Samuel Walker, *Popular Justice* (New York: Oxford University Press, 1980); Graeme Newman, *The Punishment Response* (Philadelphia: J. B. Lippincott, 1978); David Rothman, *Conscience and Convenience* (Boston: Little, Brown, 1980).

6. F. Pollock and F. Maitland, *History of English Law* (London, England: Cambridge University Press, 1952).

7. Marvin Wolfgang, "Crime and Punishment in Renaissance Florence," *Journal of Criminal Law and Criminology* 81 (1990): 567–84.

8. Margaret Wilson, *The Crime of Punishment*, Life and Letters Series, no. 64 (London, England: Jonathan Cape, 1934), p. 186.

9. John Howard, *The State of Prisons*, 4th ed. (1792; reprint, Montclair, N.J.: Patterson-Smith, 1973).

10. Alexis Durham III, "Newgate of Connecticut: Origins and Early Days of an Early American Prison," *Justice Quarterly* 6 (1989): 89–116.

11. Lewis, *Development of American Prisons and Prison Customs*, p. 17.

12. Ibid., p. 29.

13. Dario Melossi and Massimo Pavarini, *The Prison and the Factory: Origins of the Penitentiary System* (Totowa, N.J.: Barnes and Noble, 1981).

14. Michel Foucault, *Discipline and Punish* (New York: Vintage, 1978).

15. Ibid., p. 16.

16. David Rothman, *The Discovery of the Asylum* (Boston: Little, Brown, 1970).

17. Orland, *Justice, Punishment, and Treatment*, p. 143.

18. Ibid., p. 144.

19. Walker, *Popular Justice*, p. 70.

20. Ibid., p. 71.

21. Beverly Smith, "Military Training at New York's Elmira Reformatory, 1880–1920," *Federal Probation* 52 (1988): 33–41.

22. Ibid.

23. See Z. R. Brockway, "The Ideal of a True Prison System for a State," in *Transactions of the National Congress on Penitentiary*

and Reformatory Discipline (reprint, Washington, D.C.: American Correctional Association, 1970), pp. 38–65.

24. This section leans heavily on Rothman, *Conscience and Convenience.*

25. Ibid., p. 23.

26. Ibid., p. 133.

27. 18 U.S.C. 1761.

28. Barbara Auerbach, George Sexton, Franlin Farrow, and Robert Lawson, *Work in American Prisons: The Private Sector Gets Involved* (Washington, D.C.: National Institute of Justice, 1988), p. 72.

29. John Irwin, *The Jail: Managing the Underclass in American Society* (Berkeley: University of California Press, 1985).

30. Correctional Association of New York, *Prison and Jails: Hospitals of Last Resort* (New York: 1998).

31. Paige M. Harrison and Allen Beck, *Prison and Jail Inmates at Midyear 2005* (Washington, D.C.: Bureau of Justice Statistics, 2006).

32. Bonnie Green, Jeanne Miranda, Anahita Daroowalla, and Juned Siddique, "Trauma Exposure, Mental Health Functioning, and Program Needs of Women in Jail," *Crime & Delinquency* 51 (2005): 133–51.

33. Sonia Alemagno and Jill Dickie, "Employment Issues of Women in Jail," *Journal of Employment Counseling* 42 (2005): 67–74.

34. Rachel McLean, Jacqueline Robarge, and Susan Sherman, "Release from Jail: Moment of Crisis or Window of Opportunity for Female Detainees?" *Journal of Urban Health* 83 (2006): 382–93.

35. Caroline Wolf Harlow, *Prior Abuse Reported by Inmates and Probationers* (Washington, D.C.: Bureau of Justice Statistics, 1999).

36. Paula M. Ditton, *Mental Health and Treatment of Inmates and Probationers* (Washington, D.C.: Bureau of Justice Statistics, 1999).

37. Fred Heinzlemann, W. Robert Burkhart, Bernard Gropper, Cheryl Martorana, Lois Felson Mock, Maureen O'Connor, and Walter Philip Travers, *Jailing Drunk Drivers: Impact on the Criminal Justice System* (Washington, D.C.: National Institute of Justice, 1984).

38. Brandon Applegate, Ray Surette, and Bernard McCarthy, "Detention and Desistance from Crime: Evaluating the Influence of a New Generation of Jail on Recidivism," *Journal of Criminal Justice* 27 (1999): 539–48.

39. Ibid.

40. Data in this section come from Paige M. Harrison and Allen J. Beck, *Prisoners in 2004* (Washington, D.C.: Bureau of Justice Statistics, 2005).

41. Sidra Lee Gifford, *Justice Expenditure and Employment in the United States, 1999* (Washington, D.C.: Bureau of Justice Statistics, 2002).

42. Human Rights Watch, *Cold Storage: Super-Maximum Security Confinement in Indiana* (New York: 1997); Jamie Fellner, *Red Onion State Prison: Super-Maximum Security Confinement in Virginia* (New York: Human Rights Watch, 1999).

43. "Suit Alleges Violations in California's 'Super-Max' Prison," *Criminal Justice Newsletter*, September 1, 1993, p. 2.

44. Roger Peters, Paul Greenbaum, John Edens, Chris Carter, and Madeline Ortiz, "Prevalence of DSM–IV Substance Abuse and Dependence Disorders Among Prison Inmates," *American Journal of Drug and Alcohol Abuse* 24 (1998): 573–80.

45. Craig Hemmens and James Marquart, "Fear and Loathing in the Joint: The Impact of Race and Age on Inmate Support for Prison AIDS Policies," *Prison Journal* 78 (1998): 133–52.

46. Harlow, *Prior Abuse Reported by Inmates and Probationers*, p. 1.

47. Ditton, *Mental Health and Treatment of Inmates and Probationers*, p. 1.

48. James Anderson, Laronistine Dyson, and Jerald Burns, *Boot Camps: An Intermediate Sanction* (Lanham, Md.: University Press of America, 1999), pp. 1–17.

49. Doris Layton Mackenzie, Robert Brame, David McDowall, and Claire Souryal, "Boot Camp Prison and Recidivism in Eight States," *Criminology* 33 (1995): 327–57.

50. Ibid., 328–29.

51. "New York Correctional Groups Praise Boot Camp Programs," *Criminal Justice Newsletter*, April 1, 1991, pp. 4–5.

52. Velmer Burton, James Marquart, Steven Cuvelier, Leanne Fiftal Alarid, and Robert Hunter, "A Study of Attitudinal Change Among Boot Camp Participants," *Federal Probation* 57 (1993): 46–52.

53. Doris Layton Mackenzie, "Boot Camp Prisons: Components, Evaluations, and Empirical Issues," *Federal Probation* 54 (1990): 44–52.

54. Jeanne Stinchcomb and W. Clinton Terry III, "Predicting the Likelihood of Rearrest Among Shock Incarceration Graduates: Moving Beyond Another Nail in the Boot Camp Coffin," *Crime and Delinquency* 47 (2001): 221–42.

55. Doris Layton MacKenzie, David Wilson, and Suzanne Kider, "Effects of Correctional Boot Camps on Offending," *Annals of the American Academy of Political and Social Science* 578 (2001): 126–43; Doris Layton Mackenzie and James Shaw, "The Impact of Shock Incarceration on Technical Violations and New Criminal Activities," *Justice Quarterly* 10 (1993): 463–87.

56. MacKenzie, Wilson, and Kider, "Effects of Correctional Boot Camps on Offending."

57. Vanessa St. Gerard, "Federal Prisons to Eliminate Boot Camps" *Corrections Today*, 67 (2005): 13–16.

58. Brent B. Benda, Nancy J. Toombs, and Mark Peacock, "Distinguishing Graduates from Dropouts and Dismissals: Who Fails Boot Camp?" *Journal of Criminal Justice* 34 (2006): 27–38.

59. Megan Kurlychek and Cynthia Kempinen, "Beyond Boot Camp: The Impact of Aftercare on Offender Reentry," *Criminology & Public Policy* 5 (2006): 363–88.

60. Correctional Research Associates, *Treating Youthful Offenders in the Community: An Evaluation Conducted by A. J. Reiss* (Washington, D.C.: Correctional Research Associates, 1966).

61. Kevin Krajick, "Not on My Block: Local Opposition Impedes the Search for Alternatives," *Corrections Magazine* 6 (1980): 15–27.

62. "Many State Legislatures Focused on Crime in 1995, Study Finds," *Criminal Justice Newsletter*, January 2, 1996, p. 2.

63. *Census of State and Federal Correctional Facilities, 2000* (Washington, D.C.: Bureau of Justice Statistics, 2003).

64. Richard Harding, "Private Prisons," in *Crime and Justice: An Annual Edition*, ed. Michael Tonry (Chicago: University of Chicago Press, 2001), pp. 265–347.

65. William Bales, Laura Bedard, Susan Ouinn, David Ensley, and Glen Holley, "Recidivism of Public and Private State Prison Inmates in Florida," *Criminology & Public Policy* 4 (2005): 57–82; Lonn Lanza-Kaduce, Karen Parker, and Charles Thomas, "A Comparative Recidivism Analysis of Releases from Private and Public Prisons," *Crime and Delinquency* 45 (1999): 28–47.

66. Charles Thomas, "Recidivism of Public and Private State Prison Inmates in Florida: Issues and Unanswered Questions," *Criminology & Public Policy* 4 (2005): 89–99; Travis Pratt and Jeff Maahs, "Are Private Prisons More Cost-Effective Than Public Prisons? A Meta-Analysis of Evaluation Research Studies," *Crime and Delinquency* 45 (1999): 358–71.

67. Ira Robbins, *The Legal Dimensions of Private Incarceration* (Chicago: American Bar Association, 1988).

68. *Richardson v. McKnight*, 521 U.S. 399 (1997).

69. Ahmed A. White, "Rule of Law and the Limits of Sovereignty: The Private Prison in Jurisprudential Perspective," *American Criminal Law Review* 38 (2001): 111–47.

70. Lawrence Travis, Edward Latessa, and Gennaro Vito, "Private Enterprise and Institutional Corrections: A Call for Caution," *Federal Probation* 49 (1985): 11–17.

71. Patrick Anderson, Charles Davoli, and Laura Moriarty, "Private Corrections: Feast or Fiasco," *Prison Journal* 65 (1985): 32–41.

72. Richard Culp, "The Rise and Stall of Prison Privatization: An Integration of Policy Analysis Perspectives," *Criminal Justice Policy Review* 16 (2005): 412–42.

73. Data in this section come from Bureau of Justice Statistics, *Prisoners, 1925–1981* (Washington, D.C.: Government Printing Office, 1982).

74. Harrison and Beck, *Prisoners* in 2004.

75. Thomas Bonzcar, *Prevalence of Imprisonment in the U.S. Population, 1974–2001* (Washington, D.C.: Bureau of Justice Statistics, 2003).

76. Todd Clear, *Harm in American Penology: Offenders, Victims and Their Communities* (Albany: State University of New York Press, 1994).

77. Daniel Nagin, "Criminal Deterrence Research: A Review of the Evidence and a Research Agenda for the Outset of the 21st Century," in *Crime and Justice: An Annual Review*, vol. 23, ed. Michael Tonry (Chicago: University of Chicago Press, 1997), pp. 1–42.

78. For more on this issue, see Marcy Rasmussen Podkopacz and Barry Feld, "The End of the Line: An Empirical Study of Judicial Waiver," *Journal of Criminal Law and Criminology* 86 (1996): 449–92.

79. Andrew Lang Golub, Farrukh Hakeem, and Bruce Johnson, *Monitoring the Decline in the Crack Epidemic with Data from the Drug Use Forecasting Program: Final Report* (Washington, D.C.: National Institute of Justice, 1996).

CHAPTER 16

Prison Life: Living in and Leaving Prison

Chapter Objectives

After reading this chapter, you should be able to:
1. Understand the experience of living in prison.
2. Describe the various elements of the inmate social code.
3. Recognize the differences between the prison culture today and at mid-twentieth century.
4. Know what is meant by the make-believe family.
5. Discuss the problems of women in prison.
6. Recognize the recent changes in correctional law.
7. Describe the role of prison rehabilitation efforts.
8. Know about the problems faced by correctional officers.
9. Understand the different forms of parole.
10. Show how the problem of reentry has influenced the correctional system.

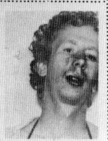

©AP Images/Chicago Police Department

K

athy Boudin served 20 years in prison at the Bedford Hills Correctional Facility for her role in the October 20, 1981, robbery of a Brinks truck at the Nanuet Mall in Rockland County, New York. During the robbery, Peter Paige, a Brinks employee, was killed. Boudin, a member of the 1960s radical group the Weathermen, drove the getaway truck in what was considered a revolutionary act by members of the Black Revolutionary Army. After the police closed in, Boudin surrendered, but two officers were killed in the resulting shootout with the other robbers. Although at trial it was determined she was unarmed and unaware that the conspirators would use violence, under New York's felony murder law Boudin was liable for any death that occurred during the course of the robbery. However, Boudin could not be held legally responsible for the killings of the officers because she had already surrendered and was in custody.

While in prison, Boudin was considered an exemplary prisoner who worked with AIDS patients, supported incarcerated parents and their children, and taught educational programs for inmates. She earned a master's degree and started on a doctorate. After twice being denied parole, she was granted release on August 20, 2003. Her victims' surviving relatives treated the decision with bitterness, questioning whether she was at all remorseful. Her supporters endorsed her release, proclaiming that she was ashamed and contrite about her earlier life. Barbara Hanson Treen, a former member of the New York State Division of Parole who got to know Boudin, told the media the following:

Kathy is really an example of the best that prison could provide for people. . . . People are so much more complex than that one crime that defines them. The best thing for people coming home is to treat them with dignity, as individual human beings, and to get them ready.[1]

Three other surviving participants in the robbery, including Boudin's estranged husband, David Gilbert, cannot be considered for parole before 2056. A fourth defendant, Abdul Majid, is up for parole in 2015. A fifth defendant, Kuwasi Balagoon, died in prison in 1986. ◆

Boudin's release illustrates the fact that most inmates, even those involved in notorious crimes, do not serve their entire sentence in prison but are released on parole or other early-release mechanisms. It also illustrates how many inmates try to turn their lives around while inside prison walls, entering treatment programs and even earning graduate degrees. Unfortunately, most inmates are not rehabilitated, and a majority return to prison soon after their release. The spotty record of correctional rehabilitation is not surprising considering the overcrowded correctional system. A significant percentage of facilities are old, decrepit, archaic structures. Twenty-five prisons still in operation were built before 1875, 79 between 1875 and 1924, and 141 between 1925 and 1949. Some of the first prisons ever constructed, such as the Concord Reformatory in Massachusetts, are still in operation.

Although a majority of prisons are classified as medium security, more than half of all inmates are being held in large, maximum-security institutions. Despite the continuous outcry by penologists against the use of fortress-like prisons, institutions holding 1,000 or more inmates still predominate. Prison overcrowding is a significant problem. The U.S. prison system now holds more than 1.3 million people. Many institutions are operating above stated capacity. Recreation and workshop facilities have been turned into dormitories housing 30 or more inmates in a single room. Most prison experts agree that a minimum of 60 square feet is needed for each inmate, but many prisons fail to reach this standard.

This giant, overcrowded system designed to reform and rehabilitate offenders is instead undergoing a crisis of massive proportions. Institutions are so overcrowded that meaningful treatment efforts are often a matter of wishful thinking; recidivism rates are shockingly high. Inmates are resentful of the deteriorated conditions, and correctional officers fear that the institution is ready to explode. Some may resort to violence themselves. And, rather than rehabilitate their residents, penal institutions seem to exacerbate their criminal tendencies. It is popular to describe the typical prison as a "school for crime" in which young offenders are taught by older cons to become sophisticated criminals. The "school for crime" may not be some form of urban myth. Rather than deter people from future criminality, research shows that a prison stay may actually reinforce and/or encourage their criminal offending.[2] This lack of success is not lost on the general public: Although it might surprise some "get-tough" politicians, the general public is not ready to embrace a prison building boom.[3] Why spend millions on prisons if they really do not work?

◆ MEN IMPRISONED

total institution
A regimented, dehumanizing institution, such as a prison, in which like-situated people are kept in social isolation, cut off from the world at large.

According to prevailing wisdom, prisons in the United States are **total institutions**. This means that inmates locked within their walls are segregated from the outside world, kept under constant scrutiny and surveillance, and forced to obey strict official rules to avoid facing formal sanctions. Their personal possessions are taken from them, and they must conform to institutional dress and personal appearance norms. Many human functions are strictly curtailed—heterosexual relationships and sex, friendships, family relationships, education, participation in groups, and even smoking become privileges of the past. For example, Vermont and other states have decided to ban cigarettes from prisons.[4]

Living in Prison

Inmates quickly learn what the term *total institution* means. When they arrive at the prison, they are stripped, searched, shorn, and assigned living quarters. Before they get there, though, their first experience occurs in a classification or reception center, where they are given a series of psychological and other tests and are evaluated on the basis of their personality, background, offense history, and treatment needs. Based on the classification they are given, they will be assigned to a permanent facility. Hard-core, repeat, and violent offenders will go to the maximum-security unit; offenders with learning disabilities may be assigned to an institution that specializes in educational services; mentally disordered offenders will be held in a facility that can provide psychiatric care; and so on. Some states such as California have instituted rigorous classification instruments designed to maximize the effectiveness of placements, thereby cutting down on the cost of incarceration. If classification could be conducted in an efficient and effective manner, nondangerous offenders would not needlessly be kept in expensive high-security facilities.[5]

Once they arrive at the long-term facility, inmates may be granted a short orientation period and then given a permanent cell assignment in the general population. Because of overcrowding, they may be sharing with one or more others a cell designed for a single inmate. All previous concepts of personal privacy and dignity are soon forgotten. Personal losses include the deprivation of liberty, goods, services, heterosexual relationships, autonomy, and security.[6] Inmates may be subject to verbal and physical attack and threats, with little chance of legal redress. Younger inmates, gay men, and bisexual men are selected most often to be targets of sexual assaults.[7] Although the criminal law applies to inmates as to any other citizens, it is rarely enforced within prison walls.[8] Therefore, part of living in prison involves learning to protect oneself and developing survival instincts.

Inmates in large, inaccessible prisons may find themselves physically cut off from families, friends, and associates. Visitors may find it difficult to travel great distances to see them. Mail is censored and sometimes destroyed.

Adjusting to Prison

Inmates may go through a variety of attitude and behavior changes, or cycles, as their sentence unfolds. During the early part of their prison stay, inmates may become easily depressed while considering the long duration of the sentence and the loneliness and dangers of prison life. They must learn the ins and outs of survival in the institution: Which persons can be befriended, and which are best avoided? Who will grant favors and for what repayment? Some inmates will request that regular payments be made to them in exchange for protection from rape and beatings. To avoid victimization, inmates must learn to adopt a lifestyle that shields them from victimization.[9] They must discover areas of safety and danger. Some learn how to fight back to prove they are not people who can be taken advantage of. Whereas some kill their attackers and get even longer sentences, others join cliques that provide protection and the ability to acquire power within the institution.

Inmates may find that some prisoners have formed cliques, or groups, based on ethnic backgrounds or personal interests. They are likely to encounter Mafia-like or racial terror groups that must be dealt with. Inmates may be the victim of homosexual attacks. They may find that power in the prison is shared by terrified guards and inmate gangs. The only way to avoid being beaten and raped may be to learn how to beat and rape.[10] If they are weak and unable to defend themselves, new inmates may find that they are considered "punks." If they ask a correctional officer for help, they can be labeled "snitches." After that, they may spend the rest of their sentence in protective custody, sacrificing the "freedom of the yard" and rehabilitation services for personal protection.[11]

Because so many inmates are now returnees, however, their adjustment to prison is relatively painless. They may have only recently left.

COPING BEHAVIOR Despite all these hardships, many inmates learn to adapt to the prison routine. Each prisoner has his own method of coping: He may stay alone, become friends with another inmate, join a group, or seek the advice of treatment personnel. Inmates may soon learn that their lifestyle and activities can contribute to their being victimized by more aggressive inmates. The more time they spend in closely guarded activities, the less likely they are to become the victims of violence; the more they isolate themselves from others who might protect them, the greater is their vulnerability to attack; the more visitors they receive, the more likely they are to be attacked by fellow inmates jealous of their relationship with the outside world.[12]

New inmates must learn to deal with the demands and needs of correctional personnel. These relationships will determine whether the inmates do "hard time" or "easy time." For example, when inmates housed in open institutions are sent out to work on roads or to do farm work, they may be forced to wear stun belts for security. Once confined in a stun belt, the inmate can receive a shock of 50,000 volts and three to four milliamps for a period of eight seconds. Although not fatal, the shock is very painful, and victims are immediately incapacitated. Burns, which may take months to heal, may develop where the electrodes touch the skin above the left kidney. Critics charge that stun guns are brutal and can be used by correctional workers to terrorize or torture inmates whom they dislike or find offensive.[13]

Regardless of adaptation style, the first stage of an inmate's prison cycle is marked by a growing awareness that he can no longer depend on his traditional associates for help and support and that, for better or worse, the institution is a new home to which he must adjust. Unfortunately for the goal of rehabilitation, the predominant emotion that inmates must confront is boredom. The absence of anything constructive to do, the forced idleness, is what is often so frustrating and so damaging.[14]

CONFLICT AND HUSTLING Part of new inmates' early adjustment involves becoming familiar with and perhaps participating in the black market, the hidden economy of the prison—the hustle. Hustling provides inmates with a source of steady income and the satisfaction that they are beating the system.[15] Hustling involves sales of such illegal commodities as drugs (uppers, downers, pot), alcohol, weapons, or illegally obtained food and supplies. When prison officials crack down on hustled goods, it merely serves to drive up the price—giving hustlers greater incentive to promote their activities. Drugs and other contraband are smuggled into prison by visitors, carried in by inmates who are out on furlough or work release programs, or bought from corrupt prison officials. Control of the prison drug trade is often the spark that creates violence and conflict.

Inmates must also learn to deal with the racial conflict that is a daily fact of life. Prisoners tend to segregate themselves, and if peace is to reign in the institution, they learn to stay out of one another's way. Often, racial groupings are exact; for example, Hispanics will separate themselves according to their national origin (Mexican, Puerto Rican, Colombian, and so on). Because racial disparity in sentencing is common in many U.S. courts, prisons are one place where minorities often hold power.

Inmates may find that the social support of inmate peers can make incarceration somewhat less painful. They may begin to take stock of their situation and enter into educational or vocational training programs, if they are available. Many turn to religion and take Bible classes. They heed the inmate grapevine to determine what the parole board considers important in deciding to grant community release. They may become more politically aware in response to the influence of other inmates, and the personal guilt they may have felt may be shifted to society at large. (Why should they be in prison when those equally guilty go free?) They learn the importance of money and politics. Eventually, they may be called on by new arrivals to aid them in adapting to the system.

Even in the harsh prison environment, inmates may learn to find a niche for themselves. They may be able to find a place, activity, or group in which they can feel comfortable and secure.[16] An inmate's niche is a kind of insulation from the pains of imprisonment, enabling him to cope and providing him with a sense of autonomy and freedom. Finding a niche may insulate inmates from attack, and research indicates that prison victimization may be less prevalent than commonly believed. Not surprisingly, the relatively few victims of prison violence seem less psychologically healthy, more fearful, and less able to avoid the pains of imprisonment.[17]

Not all inmates learn to cope. Some may repeatedly violate institutional rules. One reason is that in both the United States and abroad, many inmates suffer from serious psychological and emotional problems. A review of inmate mental health in 12 countries, including the United States, found that almost 4 percent of male inmates suffered from psychotic illnesses, 10 percent were diagnosed with major depression, and 65 percent had a personality disorder, including 47 percent with antisocial personality disorder. Prisoners were several times more likely to have psychosis and major depression, and about ten times more likely to have antisocial personality disorder than the general population.[18] The prevalence of psychological problems in the inmate population makes coping problematic.

Predicting who will become an institutional troublemaker is difficult, but rule-breaking behavior has been associated with being a younger inmate with a low intelligence quotient (IQ), possessing numerous juvenile convictions, being a repeat offender, and having victimized a stranger. Inmates who have limited intelligence and maintain low self-control may not be able to form adaptive coping mechanisms and manage the stress of being in prison.[19]

Prison Culture

For many years, criminal justice experts maintained that inmates formed their own world with a unique set of norms and rules, known as the **inmate subculture**.[20] A significant aspect of the inmate subculture was a unique **inmate social code**, unwritten guidelines that expressed the values, attitudes, and type of behavior that older inmates demanded of younger ones. Passed on from one generation of inmates to another, the inmate social code represented the values of interpersonal relations within the prison.

National attention was first drawn to the inmate social code and subculture by Donald Clemmer's classic book *The Prison Community*, in which he presented a detailed sociological study of life in a maximum-security prison.[21] Referring to thousands of conversations and interviews, as well as to inmate essays and biographies, Clemmer was able to identify a unique language, or argot, that prisoners use. In addition, Clemmer found that prisoners tend to group themselves into cliques on the basis of such personal criteria as sexual preference, political beliefs, and offense history. He found complex sexual relationships in prison and concluded that many heterosexual men will turn to homosexual relationships when faced with long sentences and the loneliness of prison life.

inmate subculture
The loosely defined culture that pervades prisons and has its own norms, rules, and language.

inmate social code
The informal set of rules that governs inmates and shapes the inmate subculture.

Inmates must learn how to adapt to the prison culture. Some are able to participate in activities, such as the baseball players shown here, while others fearful of victimization may spend most of their time alone in protective custody.

©AP Images/Eric Risberg

> **EXHIBIT 16.1**
>
> ## *Elements of the Inmate Social Code*
>
> 1. *Don't interfere with inmates' interests.* Within this area of the code are maxims concerning serving the least amount of time in the greatest possible comfort. For example, inmates are warned never to betray another inmate to authorities; in other words, grievances must be handled personally. Other aspects of the noninterference doctrine include "Don't be nosy," "Don't have a loose lip," "Keep off the other inmates' backs," and "Don't put another inmate on the spot."
> 2. *Don't lose your head.* Inmates are also cautioned to refrain from arguing, quarreling, or engaging in other emotional displays with fellow inmates. The novice may hear such warnings as "Play it cool" and "Do your own time."
> 3. *Don't exploit inmates.* Prisoners are warned not to take advantage of one another—"Don't steal from cons," "Don't welsh on a debt," and "Be right."
> 4. *Be tough and don't lose your dignity.* Although Rule 2 forbids conflict, once it starts, an inmate must be prepared to deal with it effectively and thoroughly. Maxims include "Don't cop out," "Don't weaken," and "Be tough; be a man."
> 5. *Don't be a sucker.* Inmates are cautioned not to make fools of themselves and support the guards or prison administration over the interest of the inmates—"Be sharp."
>
> Source: Gresham Sykes, *The Society of Captives: A Study of a Maximum Security Prison* (Princeton, N.J.: Princeton University Press, 1958).

prisonization
Assimilation into the separate culture in the prison that has its own rewards and behaviors.

Clemmer's most important contribution may have been his identification of the **prisonization** process. This he defined as the inmate's assimilation into the existing prison culture through acceptance of its language, sexual code, and norms of behavior. Those who become the most "prisonized" will be the least likely to reform on the outside.

Using Clemmer's work as a jumping-off point, a number of prominent sociologists have set out to more fully explore the various roles in the prison community. The most important principles of the dominant inmate subculture are listed in Exhibit 16.1.

Whereas some inmates violate the code and exploit their peers, the "right guy" is someone who uses the inmate social code as his personal behavior guide. He is always loyal to his fellow prisoners, keeps his promises, is dependable and trustworthy, and never interferes with inmates who are conniving against the officials.[22] The right guy does not go around looking for a fight, but he never runs away from one. He acts like a man.

DEVELOPING A PRISON CULTURE How do prison cultures develop? What are the forces that shape inmate roles? There are three views on the matter. First, some prison experts believe that the prison experience transforms people and forces them to accept the inmate culture. According to this deprivation model, inmate behavior is a product of the prison environment. Developed by experts such as Clemmer and Gresham Sykes, the "pains of imprisonment," which include loss of liberty, possessions, and freedom, alter people and cause them to change their values and behaviors.[23]

A second view, referred to as the importation perspective, suggests that an inmate's early socialization, which occurs before he enters prison, is what shapes his behavior and values. In other words, the prison culture is imported from the outside world.[24] Inmate culture is affected as much by the values of newcomers and events on the outside as it is by traditional inmate values. People who view violence as an acceptable alternative before entering prison are the ones most likely to adopt the inmate social code.[25]

A third view, referred to as the administrative control model, suggests that inmate culture is deeply influenced by the management style of the prison administration. Prisons managed with a formal organizational structure that features a strict division of labor, detailed rules, routines, and a strong leader at the top of the organization will have significantly less prison disorder.[26] When there is an administrative breakdown—for example, when the organizational structure of the prison is unsound—security cannot protect weaker inmates, and overall prison conditions and services deteriorate. Under these conditions, inmates band together for self-protection while prison misconduct increases as a result of organizational breakdown.[27] Research shows that administrative behaviors can influence inmate behaviors and that positive enforcements may have a more significant impact on inmate behaviors and attitudes than punitive measures.[28]

The effects of prisonization may be long term and destructive. Many inmates become hostile to the legal system, learning to use violence as a means of solving problems and to value criminal peers.[29] For some, this change may be permanent. For others, it is temporary, and they may revert to their normal life after release.

THE NEW INMATE CULTURE The importation of outside values into the inmate culture has had a dramatic effect on prison life. Although the old inmate subculture may have been harmful because its norms and values insulated the inmate from rehabilitation efforts, it did help create order within the institution and prevent violence among the inmates. People who violated the code and victimized others were sanctioned by their peers. An understanding developed between guards and inmate leaders: The guards would let the inmates have things their own way; the inmates would not let things get out of hand and draw the attention of the administration.

The old system may be dying or already dead in most institutions. The change seems to have been precipitated by the Black Power movement in the 1960s and 1970s. African American inmates were no longer content to fill a subservient role and challenged the power of established white inmates. As the Black Power movement gained prominence, racial tension in prisons created divisions that severely altered the inmate subculture. Older, respected inmates could no longer cross racial lines to mediate disputes. Predatory inmates could victimize others without fear of retaliation. Consequently, more inmates than ever are now assigned to protective custody for their own safety.

In the new culture, African American and Latino inmates are much more cohesively organized than whites.[30] Their groups sometimes form out of religious or political affiliations, such as the Black Muslims; out of efforts to combat discrimination in prison, such as the Latino group La Familia; or from street gangs, such as the Vice Lords or Gangster Disciples in the Illinois prison system and the Crips in California. Where white inmates have successfully organized, it is in the form of a neo-Nazi group called the Aryan Brotherhood. Racially homogenous gangs are so cohesive and powerful that they are able to supplant the original inmate code with one of their own.

To read about the California prison system, go to the California Department of Corrections and Rehabilitation website, which you can reach by going to the Siegel/Senna Introduction to Criminal Justice 11e website: www.thomsonedu.com/criminaljustice/siegel.

ThomsonNOW Improve your grade on the exam with Personalized Study! For reinforcement resources and a mastery check of the imprisonment of men, go to www.thomsonedu.com/thomsonnow.

♦ WOMEN IMPRISONED

Before 1960, few women were in prison. Women's prisons were relatively rare and were usually an outgrowth of male institutions. Only four institutions for women were built between 1930 and 1950. In comparison, 34 women's prisons were constructed during the 1980s as crime rates soared. At the turn of the twentieth century, female inmates were viewed as morally depraved people who flaunted conventional rules of female behavior. The treatment of white and

African American women differed significantly. In some states, white women were placed in female-only reformatories designed to improve their deportment. African American women were placed in male prisons, where they were subject to the chain gang and beatings.[31]

Although the number of women in prison is still far smaller than the number of men, their population has been increasing at a much faster pace. The female offender population has increased so rapidly for a number of reasons. Women have accelerated their crime rate at a higher rate than men. The get-tough policies that produced mandatory and determinate sentencing statutes also helped reduce the judicial discretion that has traditionally benefited women. As Meda Chesney-Lind points out, women have been swept up in the get-tough movement and no longer receive the benefits of male chivalry. The use of sentencing guidelines means that such factors as family ties and employment record, two elements that usually benefit women during sentencing, can no longer be considered by judges.[32] Chesney-Lind notes that judges seem willing once again to view female offenders as "depraved" and outside the ranks of "true womanhood."[33]

Female Institutions

State jurisdictions have been responding to the influx of female offenders into the correctional system by expanding the facilities for housing and treating them.[34] Women's prisons tend to be smaller than those housing male inmates.[35] Although some female institutions are strictly penal, with steel bars, concrete floors, and other security measures, the majority are nonsecure institutions similar to college dormitories and group homes in the community. Women's facilities, especially those in the community, commonly offer a great deal of autonomy to inmates and allow them to make decisions affecting their daily lives.

Like men's prisons, women's prisons suffer from a lack of adequate training and health, treatment, and educational facilities. Psychological counseling often takes the form of group sessions conducted by laypeople, such as correctional officers. Most trained psychologists and psychiatrists restrict themselves to such activities as conducting intake classifications and court-ordered examinations and prescribing mood-controlling medication. Although many female inmates are parents and had custody of their children before their incarceration, little effort is made to help them develop better parenting skills. And whereas most female (and male) inmates have at least one child, less than one-quarter get an annual visit. Who takes care of the children while their mothers are incarcerated? Most children of incarcerated women are placed with their father, grandparent, other relative, or a family friend. About 10 percent wind up in foster homes or state facilities.

Job-training opportunities are also a problem. Where vocational training exists, it is in areas with limited financial reward, hindering adjustment on release. Female inmates, many of whom were on the economic margin before their incarceration began, find little opportunity for improvement during their prison experience.[36] Surveys also indicate that the prison experience does little to prepare women to reenter the work force after their sentence has been completed. Gender stereotypes still shape vocational opportunities.[37] Female inmates are still being trained for "women's roles," such as child rearing, and not given the programming to make successful adjustments in the community.[38]

Female Inmates

Like their male counterparts, female inmates are young (most are under age 30), minority-group members, unmarried, undereducated (more than half are high school dropouts), and either unemployed or underemployed.

Many incarcerated women have also had a troubled family life. Significant numbers were at-risk children, products of broken homes and the welfare system. Over half had received welfare at sometime during their adult lives. They experienced a pattern of harsh discipline and physical abuse. Many claim to have been physically or sexually abused.

Female offenders are more likely than males to be convicted of a nonviolent crime and be incarcerated for a low-level involvement in drug offenses, such as driving a boyfriend to make a drug deal. The female offender may end up serving a longer sentence than the boyfriend simply because she is less likely to work out a plea arrangement.[39]

Not surprisingly, many female offenders display psychological problems, including serious psychopathology.[40] One recent survey found that 4 percent of incarcerated women in 12 nations including the United States had psychotic illnesses; 12 percent, depression; and 42 percent, a personality disorder, including 21 percent with antisocial personality disorder.[41]

A significant number of female inmates report having substance abuse problems. About three-fourths have used drugs at some time in their lives, and almost half have been involved with addictive drugs, such as cocaine, heroin, or PCP. Little difference exists in major drug use between male and female offenders when measured over their life span or at the time of their current arrest. The incarceration of so many women who are low-criminal risks yet face a high risk of exposure to HIV (human immunodeficiency virus, which causes AIDS) and other health issues because of their prior history of drug abuse presents a significant problem. One study of incarcerated women found that one-third of the sample reported that before their arrest they had traded sex for money or drugs. Twenty-four percent of the women reported trading sex for money or drugs "weekly or more often."[42] Such risky behavior significantly increases the likelihood of their carrying the AIDS virus or other sexually transmitted diseases.

The picture that emerges of the female inmate is troubling. After a lifetime of emotional turmoil, physical and sexual abuse, and drug use, it seems improbable that overcrowded, underfunded correctional institutions can forge a dramatic turnaround in the behavior of at-risk female inmates. Many have lost custody of their children, a trauma that is more likely to afflict those who are already substance abusers and suffer from depression.[43] Therefore, it should come as no surprise that many female inmates feel strain and conflict, psychological conditions related to violent episodes.[44]

SEXUAL EXPLOITATION Numerous reports have surfaced of female prisoners being sexually abused and exploited by male correctional workers who use either brute force or psychological coercion to gain sexual control over inmates.[45] Staff-on-inmate sexual misconduct covers a wide range of behaviors, from lewd remarks to voyeurism to assault and rape. Although more than 40 states and the District of Columbia have been forced to pass laws criminalizing some types of staff sexual misconduct in prisons, such misconduct persists despite efforts to correct problems and train staff.[46]

Criminologist Meda Chesney-Lind finds that the movement to eliminate gender inequality has triggered an increase in sexual abuse in male-dominated institutions. She cites the example of New York state, which created a policy of videotaping male inmates while they were being strip-searched. For the sake of gender equality, the state instituted a policy of also taping women's strip searches. The videotaping was done while male officers were in the vicinity, and the female inmates sued and won damages when they suspected that the videos were being watched by prison officials. Such sexually charged situations are particularly damaging to women who have a history of sexual and physical abuse. Because male correctional officers are now commonly assigned to women's prisons, major scandals have erupted involving the sexual exploitation and rape of female inmates. Few, if any, of these incidents are reported, and perpetrators rarely go to trial. Institutional workers cover for one another, and women who file complaints are offered little protection from vengeful guards.[47]

Adapting to the Female Prison

Daily life in women's prisons differs somewhat from that in male institutions. For one thing, unlike male inmates, women usually do not present an immediate physical danger to staff and fellow inmates. Relatively few engage in violent behavior, and incidents of inmate-initiated sexual aggression, so common in male institutions, are rare in women's prisons.[48] Research conducted in the California prison system finds that few female inmates either experience the violent atmosphere common in male institutions or suffer the racial and ethnic conflict and divisiveness.[49] Female inmates seem to receive more social support from both internal sources (e.g., inmate peers and correctional staff) and external sources (e.g., families and peers), a factor that may help lessen the pains of prison life, help them adjust, and improve the social climate within female institutions.[50]

Although the rigid, anti-authority inmate social code found in many male institutions does not exist in female institutions, life in a female prison is not a bed of roses.[51] When Mark Pogrebin and Mary Dodge interviewed former female inmates who had done time in a western state, they discovered that an important element of prison life for many women is dealing with fear and violence. Some reported that violence in women's prisons is common and that many female inmates undergo a process of socialization fraught with danger and volatile situations.[52] For women, confinement may produce severe anxiety and anger because of separation from families and loved ones and the inability to function in normal female roles. Unlike men, who direct their anger outward, female prisoners may turn to more self-destructive acts to cope with their problems. Female inmates are more likely than males to maim themselves and attempt suicide. For example, one common practice among female inmates is self-mutilation, or carving. This ranges from simple scratches to carving the name of their boyfriend on their body or even complex statements or sentences ("To mother, with hate").[53]

MAKE-BELIEVE FAMILIES Another form of adaptation to prison used by women is the make-believe family. This group contains masculine and feminine figures acting as fathers and mothers; some even act as children and take on the role of brother or sister. Formalized marriages and divorces may be conducted. Sometimes one inmate holds multiple roles so that a "sister" in one family may "marry" and become the "wife" of another inmate. About half of all female inmates are members of make-believe families.[54]

Why do make-believe families exist? Experts suggest that they provide the warm, stable relationships otherwise unobtainable in the prison environment. People both in and out of prison have needs for security, companionship, affection, attention, status, prestige, and acceptance that can be filled only by having primary-group relationships. Friends fill many of these needs, but the family better represents the ideal or desire for these things in a stable relationship.

The Race, Gender, and Ethnicity in Criminal Justice feature has more on this topic.

ThomsonNOW Improve your grade on the exam with Personalized Study! For reinforcement resources and a mastery check of the imprisonment of women, go to www.thomsonedu.com/thomsonnow.

◆ CORRECTIONAL TREATMENT METHODS

Almost every prison facility uses some mode of treatment for inmates. This may come in the form of individual or group therapy programs or educational or vocational training. Despite good intentions, rehabilitative treatment within prison walls is extremely difficult to achieve. Trained professional treatment personnel usually command high salaries, and most institutions do not have sufficient budgets to adequately staff therapeutic programs. Usually, a large facility may have a single staff psychiatrist or a few social workers. Another problem revolves around the philosophy of *less eligibility*, which has been interpreted to mean that prisoners should always be treated less well than the most underprivileged law-abiding citizen. Translated into today's terms, less eligibility usually involves this question: Why should inmates be treated to expensive programs

World Apart–Life in a Female Prison

Christina Rathbone has dedicated her journalistic career to both exposing myths about women's prisons and telling the life story of women behind bars. She is appalled at the conditions that they are forced to endure, their exploitation by correctional officers, and their struggles to maintain ties to family and friends. Rather than violent and aggressive, the typical female inmate she encounters is more likely to be a 35-year-old single mother with three children serving a five-year mandatory sentence for a first-time, nonviolent drug offense.

A great deal of her research was conducted in a women's prison in Massachusetts, MCI-Framingham. There, after years of battling authorities for access, she was able to meet and interview female inmates in the visitors' rooms. She finds that unlike the men's prisons in the state, where most inmates are serving time for violent crimes, almost two-thirds of incarcerated women—63 percent—are serving time for nonviolent offenses. Most are drug and alcohol addicts; about one-third are seriously mentally ill; more than 70 percent are mothers.

Rathbone finds the female inmates are cut off from their families and provided with little help in maintaining contact with their children. Behind prison walls, they are offered a minimum of education and job-training programs. Therefore, it is not surprising that more than 60 percent of the women in Framingham receive some kind of mental health services. The truth, Rathbone finds, is that the air in a woman's prison is filled more with despair than depravity.

Rathbone also finds that women's prisons have not changed as much as we would like to believe since they were opened more than 100 years ago. When MCI-Framingham first opened its doors in 1877, the prison held just 3 women convicted of violent acts and more than 240 being held for nonviolent crimes, including a majority imprisoned for being drunk or promiscuous. Many were sentenced to incarceration for being "lewd," "stubborn," "intemperate," or "idle." At the time, living and sleeping with a man outside marriage was punishable by prison terms of up to five years. The first inmates were almost exclusively poor first-generation immigrants; the law applied to some people more than others.

Despite their shortcomings, the creation of women's prisons such as Framingham was considered an improvement over prior practices—for example, women were simply sent to the basements or attics of men's prisons, where they had no opportunities for exercise or education. Rape—at the hands of both guards and male inmates—was common. Women's prisons had programs that taught inmates how to read, gave them job training, and instructed them in "domestic skills" such as knitting and sewing.

Rathbone spent more than four years investigating the prison, including her legal fight to gain access to inmates. Even then she was harassed, made to wait hours to enter the visitors' area, and subject to random searches. She met Denise, a 32-year-old crack addict serving time for an illegal drug purchase. Denise was terrified when she arrived in prison and was befriended by older, more experienced inmates. She despaired for her nine-year-old son, Pat, who had been left in the care of his abusive father. Denise's fears were well founded; by the time she left prison, Pat had been incarcerated for petty theft.

Denise's story is not unique. Framingham inmates are the daughters of abuse and abandonment. Some are given long sentences for acting as drug mules and traffickers for their boyfriends, who go free. Others have been ignored by their parents and forced to fend for themselves on the streets. Many of the inmates engage in sexual relationships with correctional officers even though it is a felony under state law. Some are seeking favors and special treatment, whereas others are simply bored and looking for ways to pass the time. Those who do not wish such intimacies can still be victimized: Inmates are defenseless against sexual abuse and rape. Relatively few cases are prosecuted, and even fewer offenders are convicted.

Rathbone calls for the reform of women's prisons. Sentences should be geared to the special status of women. Mothers should have better access to their children. Meaningful programming is needed. Women must be protected from predatory guards. Despite the problems, Rathbone is convinced that dedicated and sensitive prison administrators can make a substantial difference.

Critical Thinking

1. Considering the culture and custom in a women's prison, should female inmates be treated differently than men, or would that be a violation of equal protection under the law?

2. If you ran the corrections department in your state, would you allow male guards to work in a women's prison?

InfoTrac College Edition Research

Use "female inmates" and "women's prisons" in a key word search on InfoTrac.

Sources: Cristina Rathbone, *World Apart: Women, Prison, and Life Behind Bars* (New York: Random House, 2005); Cristina Rathbone, "Locked In," *Boston Globe*, May 29, 2005.

denied to the average honest citizen? Enterprising state legislators use this argument to block expenditures for prison budgets, and some prison administrators may agree with them.

Finally, correctional treatment is hampered by the ignorance surrounding the practical effectiveness of one type of treatment program over another. What constitutes proper treatment has not yet been determined, and studies evaluating treatment effectiveness have suggested that few, if any, of the programs currently used in prisons produce significant numbers of rehabilitated offenders.

The following is a description of a selected number of therapeutic methods that have been used nationally in correctional settings.

Counseling and Treatment

Prison inmates typically suffer from a variety of cognitive and psychosocial deficits, such as poor emotional control, social skills, and interpersonal problem solving. These deficits are often linked to long-term substance abuse. Modern counseling programs help them to better control emotions (understanding why they feel the way they do, learning how not to get too nervous or anxious, solving their problems creatively), to communicate effectively with others (understanding what people tell them and communicating clearly when they write), to deal with pressing legal concerns (keeping out of legal trouble and avoiding breaking laws), to efficiently manage general life issues (finding a job, dealing with difficult coworkers, being a good parent), and to develop and maintain supportive social relationships (getting along with others, making others happy, making others proud).[55] To achieve these goals, correctional systems use a variety of intensive individual and group techniques, including behavior modification, aversive therapy, milieu therapy, reality therapy, transactional analysis, and responsibility therapy. Under the Bush administration, faith-based rehabilitation efforts have flourished, and some have shown to be positive influences on inmate behavior.[56]

DRUG TREATMENT   Most prisons have programs designed to help inmates suffering from alcohol and substance abuse issues. One approach is to provide abusers with methadone as a substitute for heroin; some evaluations have shown this method to be effective.[57] Because substance abuse is so prevalent among correctional clients, some correctional facilities have been reformulated into treatment-dispensing total institutions called "therapeutic communities." This is the topic of the Analyzing Criminal Justice Issues feature.

Treating the Special-Needs Inmate

special-needs inmate
A correctional client who requires special care and treatment, such as someone who is elderly, mentally ill, drug-addicted, or AIDS-infected.

One of the challenges of correctional treatment is caring for **special-needs inmates**. These individuals can have a variety of social problems. Some are mentally ill but have been assigned to prison because the state has toughened its insanity laws. Others suffer mental problems developed during their imprisonment. An additional 1 to 6 percent of the inmate population is mentally retarded. Treating the mentally ill inmate has required the development and use of new therapies in the prison environment. Although some critics warn of the overuse of "chemical straitjackets"—psychotropic medications—to keep disturbed inmates docile, prison administrators have been found to have a genuine concern for these special-needs inmates.[58]

ELDERLY INMATES   Restrictive crime control policies have also produced another special-needs group—elderly inmates who require health care, diets, and work and recreational opportunities that are different from those of the general population. Some correctional systems have responded to the growing number of elderly inmates by creating facilities tailored to their needs.[59] There are about 40,000 inmates age 55 and older in the correctional system. In 1990, there were 49 people older than 55 for every 100,000 residents; by 1996, the number had jumped to 69, and today it is more than 141.[60]

Therapeutic Communities

Because drug abuse is so prevalent among inmates, some institutions have been organized into therapeutic communities (TCs) in order to best serve their clientele. The TC approach to substance abuse treatment uses a psychosocial, experiential learning process that relies on positive peer pressure within a highly structured social environment. The community itself, including staff and program participants, becomes the primary method of change. Everyone works together as members of a "family" in order to create a culture where community members confront one another's negative behavior and attitudes and establish an open, trusting, and safe environment; TC relies on mutual self-help. The TC approach encourages personal disclosure rather than the isolation of the general prison culture. Participants view staff as role models and rational authorities rather than as custodians or treatment providers.

Therapeutic communities have several distinctive characteristics:

1. They present an alternative concept of inmates that is usually much more positive than prevailing beliefs.

2. Their activities embody positive values, help to promote positive social relationships, and start a process of socialization that encourages a more responsible and productive way of life.

3. Their staff, some of whom are recovering addicts and former inmates, provide positive role models.

4. They provide transition from institutional to community existence, with treatment occurring just prior to release and with continuity of care in the community.

Theraputic communities are also viewed as a viable alternative for treating the numerous polyproblem inmates, who suffer from a variety of social and personal ills such as mental health and substance abuse issues.

Evaluations of TC programs have been positive. There is evidence that those inmates who successfully complete programs have significantly lower five-year recidivism rates than nonattendees and are more likely to seek treatment once they return to the community. TC programs seem to work as well for female offenders as they do for male inmates.

The Residential Substance Abuse Treatment (RSAT)

Residential Substance Abuse Treatment (RSAT) is a good example of a therapeutic community program

that has been implemented to help substance abusing inmates in the state of Idaho. It consists of 9–12 months of rigorous drug treatment provided by a private contractor. Clients are low-risk offenders who have a habitual substance abuse problem, a desire to change, a positive attitude, and also legitimate resources on the outside to assist them when they are released.

During their treatment, participants are to better themselves by learning to think before they act in order to change their ways of decision making. They are required to write down their thoughts and feelings, expressing why they engage in destructive behavior and how they expect to change their ways with more constructive choices. Participants work on their social, behavioral, and vocational skills as well. Clients are also part of a 12-step model similar to the programs used by Alcoholics and/or Narcotics Anonymous, group counseling, individual counseling, group meetings, and physical activity.

Critical Thinking

How does the use of a program such as Residential Substance Abuse Treatment jibe with the no-frills movement? Should inmates in a therapeutic community receive treatment and counseling privileges denied to those who have not yet been in trouble with the law?

 InfoTrac College Edition Research
Use the term "therapeutic community" in a key word search on InfoTrac.

Sources: James Inciardi, Steven Martin, and Clifford Butzin, "Five-Year Outcomes of Therapeutic Community Treatment of Drug-Involved Offenders After Release from Prison," *Crime and Delinquency* 50 (2004): 88–107; Clayton Mosher and Dretha Phillips, "The Dynamics of a Prison-Based Therapeutic Community for Women Offenders: Retention, Completion, and Outcomes," *Prison Journal* 86 (2006): 6–31; Mary Stohr, Craig Hemmens, Diane Baune, Jed Dayley, Mark Gornik, Kirstin Kjaer, and Cindy Noon, *Residential Substance Abuse Treatment for State Prisoners: Breaking the Drug-Crime Cycle Among Parole Violators* (Washington, D.C.: National Institute for Justice, 2003); *Therapeutic Communities in Correctional Settings*, "Appendix B: Revised TCA Standards for TCs in Correctional Settings" (Washington, D.C.: Office of National Drug Control Policy, 1999) (http://www.whitehousedrugpolicy.gov/national_assembly/publications/therap_comm/toc.html), accessed on June 10, 2005; William Burdon, David Farabee, Michael Prendergast, Nena Messina, and Jerome Cartier, "Prison-Based Therapeutic Community Substance Abuse Programs—Implementation and Operational Issues," *Federal Probation* 66 (2002): 3–9; Roger Peters, Michelle LeVasseur, and Redonna Chandler, "Correctional Treatment for Co-occurring Disorders: Results of a National Survey," *Behavioral Sciences & the Law* 22 (2004): 563–84.

Research indicates that older prisoners tend to be loners who may experience symptoms of depression or anxiety. They suffer from an assortment of physical and health problems associated with aging, including arthritis, ulcers, prostate problems, hypertension, and emphysema. Because many have had a long-term history of smoking and alcohol consumption, they may suffer incontinence as well as heart, respiratory, and degenerative diseases. After reviewing available evidence, one study came to the following conclusions:

♦   The proportion of state and federal inmates 55 years of age and older is steadily increasing. The number of inmates older than 75 will continue to increase in the future if current sentencing practices remain in place.

♦   The older inmate is most likely an unmarried white man with children, who did not graduate from high school.

♦   Older offenders are most likely to be incarcerated for violent crimes, often perpetrated against family members in the home.

♦   Older inmates are likely to report one or more chronic health problems. Cigarette and alcohol use is common.

♦   Most states and the Federal Bureau of Prisons have implemented limited provisions to accommodate older inmates with special needs.[61]

THE DRUG-DEPENDENT INMATE   Another special-needs group in prison is drug-dependent inmates. Although most institutions attempt to provide drug and alcohol treatment, these efforts are often inadequate.

The ideal drug treatment has yet to be identified, but experimental efforts around the country use counseling sessions, instruction in coping strategies, employment counseling, and strict security measures featuring random urinalysis.

THE AIDS-INFECTED INMATE   The AIDS-infected prisoner is another acute special-needs inmate. Two groups of people at high risk of contracting HIV are intravenous drug users who share needles and males who engage in homosexual sex. Both are common in prison. Because drug use is common and syringes scarce, many high-risk inmates share drug paraphernalia, increasing the danger of HIV infection.[62]

Although the numbers are constantly changing, the rate of HIV infection among state and federal prisoners has stabilized at around 2 percent. Correctional administrators have found it difficult to arrive at effective policies to confront AIDS. All state and federal jurisdictions do some AIDS testing, but only 18 states and the Federal Bureau of Prisons conduct mass screenings of all inmates. Most states test inmates only if there are significant indications that they are HIV-positive. About 40 percent of all state prison inmates have never been tested for AIDS.

Most correctional systems are now training staff about AIDS. Educational programs for inmates are often inadequate because administrators are reluctant to give them information on the proper cleaning of drug paraphernalia and safe sex (because both drug use and homosexual sex are forbidden in prison).

INMATES WITH FAMILIES   Many inmates are married, and a stay in prison strains relationships with both spouses and children. To help inmates deal with the disruption caused by a prison sentence, some institutions allow **conjugal visits**, which are private family visits designed to maintain and strengthen family bonds.[63]

Private family visits are typically 48 hours or more in length and provide inmates and their families the opportunity to interact in a private setting. Programs make use of quarters that are separate from the rest of the inmate population to ensure privacy. Private family visits are currently allowed in California, Mississippi, New York, and Washington. In addition, 4,500 such visits took place in Canada last year. Although proponents believe that conjugal visits are an ideal method of maintaining family bonds, critics point out that they may cause resentment among the

To read how corrections departments are trying to treat drug-dependent inmates in the prison setting, read "Promising Strategies to Reduce Substance Abuse." You can access this article by going to the Siegel/Senna Introduction to Criminal Justice 11e website: www.thomsonedu.com/criminaljustice/siegel.

conjugal visit
A prison program that allows inmates to receive visits from spouses for the purpose of maintaining normal interpersonal relationships.

unmarried inmate population and result in pregnancies and children whom inmates are ill equipped to support or raise.

Educational and Vocational Programs

Besides treatment programs stressing personal growth through individual analysis or group process, inmate rehabilitation is pursued through vocational and educational training. Although these two kinds of training sometimes differ in style and content, they can overlap when, for example, education involves practical, job-related study. Educational programs are critical in prison because about 41 percent of inmates in the nation's state and federal prisons have not completed high school or its equivalent, in comparison to the 18 percent of the general population age 18 or older that have not finished school.[64]

Many female inmates have families, and correctional authorities have designed programs that help them maintain family ties. In May 2006 at the California Institution for Women in Corona, Laticia Casio connects with her son Joseph in anticipation of a Mother's Day visit during a program where children throughout California are reunited with their incarcerated mothers.

The first prison treatment programs were educational. A prison school was opened at the Walnut Street Jail in Philadelphia in 1784. Elementary courses were offered in New York's prison system in 1801 and in Pennsylvania's in 1844. A school system was established in Detroit's House of Corrections in 1870, and Elmira Reformatory opened a vocational trade school in 1876. Today, most institutions provide some type of educational program. At some prisons, inmates can obtain a high school diploma or a general educational development (GED) certificate through equivalency exams. Other institutions provide a classroom education, usually staffed by certified teachers employed full time at the prison or by part-time teachers who also teach full time at nearby public schools.

The number of hours devoted to educational programs and the quality and intensity of these efforts vary greatly. Some are full-time programs employing highly qualified and concerned educators, whereas others are part-time programs without any real goals or objectives. Although worthwhile attempts are being made, prison educational programs often suffer from inadequate funding and administration. However, the picture is not totally bleak. In some institutions, programs have been designed to circumvent the difficulties inherent in the prison structure. They encourage volunteers from the community and local schools to tutor willing and motivated inmates. Some prison administrators have arranged flexible schedules for inmate students and actively encourage their participation in these programs. In several states, statewide school districts serving prisons have been created. Forming such districts can make better-qualified staff available and provide the materials and resources necessary for meaningful educational programs.

Recent surveys indicate how prevalent and successful prison-based educational programs have become. About 26 percent of state prison inmates said they had completed the GED while serving time in a correctional facility. And although the percentage of state prison inmates who reported taking education courses while confined fell from 57 percent in 1991 to 52 percent at last count (1997), the number who participated in an educational program since admission increased from 402,500 inmates in 1991 to 550,000 in 2002.[65]

Prison education is also important in Europe. Go to the website of the European Prison Education Association to read about its efforts. You can get there by linking through the Siegel/Senna Introduction to Criminal Justice 11e website: www.thomsonedu.com/criminaljustice/siegel.

Vocational Services

Every state correctional system also has some job-related services for inmates. Some have elaborate training programs within the institution, whereas others have instituted prerelease and postrelease employment services. Inmates who hope to obtain parole need to participate in prison industry. Documenting a history of stable employment in prison is essential if parole agents are to convince prospective employers that the ex-offender is a good risk. Postrelease employment is usually required for parole eligibility.[66]

BASIC PRISON INDUSTRIES Prisoners are normally expected to work within the institution as part of their treatment program. Aside from saving money for the institution, prison work programs are supposed to help inmates develop good habits and skills. Most prominent among traditional prison industries are those designed to help maintain and run the institution and provide services for other public or state facilities, such as mental hospitals. These include the following:

♦ *Food services*. Inmates are expected to prepare and supply food for prisoners and staff. These duties include baking bread, preparing meat and vegetables, and cleaning and maintaining kitchen facilities.

♦ *Maintenance*. The buildings and grounds of most prisons are cared for by inmates. Electrical work, masonry, plumbing, and painting are all inmate activities. Requiring less skills are such duties as garbage collection, gardening, and cleaning.

♦ *Laundry*. Most prisons have their own inmate-run laundries. Prison laundries will often also furnish services to other state institutions.

♦ *Agriculture*. In western and southern states, many prisons farm their own land. Dairy herds, crops, and poultry are all managed by inmates. The products are used in the prison and in other state institutions.

VOCATIONAL TRAINING Most institutions also provide vocational training programs. In New York, Corcraft is the manufacturing division of the department of correctional services, which employs 2,500 inmates. Corcraft products include inmate and officers' clothing and uniforms, cleaning supplies, furniture, and prescription eyeglasses, which must be used by the corrections department or sold to other state agencies and local governments. By law, Corcraft products and services cannot be sold on the open market to private organizations or individuals. The products of most of these programs save the taxpayers money, and the programs provide the inmates with practical experience. Many other states offer this type of vocational programming.

Despite the promising aspects of such programs, they have also been seriously criticized. Inmates often have trouble finding skill-related, high-paying jobs on their release; equipment in prisons is often secondhand, obsolete, and hard to come by; some programs are thinly disguised excuses for prison upkeep and maintenance; and unions and other groups resent the intrusion of prison labor into their markets.

WORK RELEASE To supplement programs stressing rehabilitation via in-house job training or education, more than 44 states have attempted to implement **work release** or **furlough** programs. These allow deserving inmates to leave the institution and hold regular jobs in the community.

Inmates enrolled in work release may live at the institutions at night while working in the community during the day. However, security problems (for example, contraband smuggling) and the usual remoteness of prisons often make this arrangement difficult. More typical is the extended work release, where prisoners are allowed to remain in the community for significant periods of time. To help inmates adjust, some states operate community-based prerelease centers where inmates live while working. Some inmates may work at their previous jobs, whereas others seek new employment.

Like other programs, work release has its good and bad points. Inmates are sometimes reluctantly received in the community and find that certain areas of employment are closed to them. Citizens are often concerned about prisoners "stealing" jobs or working for lower than normal wages. However, such practices are prohibited on the federal level by statute (Public Law 89–176), which controls the federal work release program.

To read more about Corcraft, visit its website, which you can reach by linking through the Siegel/Senna Introduction to Criminal Justice 11e website: www.thomsonedu.com/criminaljustice/siegel.

work release (furlough)
A prison treatment program in which inmates leave the institution to work in the community, sometimes returning to prison or another supervised facility at night.

However, inmates gain many benefits from work release, including the ability to maintain work-related skills, to foster community ties, and to make an easier transition from prison to the outside world. For those who have learned a skill in the institution, work release offers an excellent opportunity to test out a new occupation. For others, the job may be a training situation in which new skills are acquired. A number of states have reported that few work release inmates abscond while in the community.

VOCATIONAL TRAINING FOR FEMALE OFFENDERS Critics have charged that educational and vocational programs are especially deficient in female institutions, which typically have offered only remedial-level education or occasional junior college classes. Female inmates are not being provided with the tools needed to succeed on the outside because the limited vocational training stresses what is considered traditional women's work: cosmetology, secretarial work, and food services.

Today, 47 states have instituted some sort of vocational training programs for women; the other states provide supplemental services for their few female inmates. Although the traditional vocation of sewing is the most common industrial program, correctional authorities are beginning to teach data processing, and female inmates are involved in such other industries as farming, printing, telemarketing, and furniture repair. Clearly, greater efforts are needed to improve the quality of work experiences for female inmates.

PRIVATE PRISON ENTERPRISE Opposition from organized labor ended the profitability of commercial prison industries, but a number of efforts have been made to vary the type and productivity of prison labor.[67] The federal government helped put private industry into prisons when it approved the Free Venture Program in 1976. Seven states, including Connecticut, Minnesota, and South Carolina, were given grants to implement private industries within prison walls. This successful program led to the Percy Amendment (1979), federal legislation that allowed prison-made goods to be sold across state lines if the projects complied with strict rules, such as making sure that unions were consulted and preventing manufacturers from undercutting the existing wage structure.[68] The new law authorized a number of Prison Industry Enhancement pilot projects. These were certified as meeting the Percy Amendment operating rules and were therefore free to ship goods out of state. By 1987, 15 projects had been certified.

Today, private prison industries have used a number of models. One approach, the state-use model, makes the correctional system a supplier of goods and services to state-run institutions. Like Corcraft in New York, the California Prison Industry Authority (PIA) is an inmate work program that provides work assignments for approximately 7,000 inmates and operates 70 service, manufacturing, and agricultural industries in 23 prisons. These industries produce a variety of goods and services, including flags, printing services, signs, binders, eyewear, gloves, office furniture, clothing, and cell equipment. PIA products and services are available to government entities, including federal, state, and local government agencies. Court-ordered restitutions or fines are deducted from the wages earned by PIA inmates and are transferred to the Crime Victims' Restitution Fund. PIA inmates receive wages between 30 and 95 cents per hour, before deductions.[69]

In another approach, the free enterprise model, private companies set up manufacturing units on prison grounds or purchase goods made by inmates in shops owned and operated by the corrections department. In the corporate model, a semi-independent business is created on prison grounds, and the profits go to the state government and inmate laborers.[70] Despite widespread publicity, the partnership between private enterprise and the prison community has been limited to a few experimental programs. However, it is likely to grow in the future.

You can access the California Prison Industry Authority by linking through the Siegel/Senna Introduction to Criminal Justice 11e website: www. thomsonedu.com/criminaljustice/siegel.

Some treatment programs allow inmates to help themselves. James Lucas (second from right) and fellow inmates listen as Case Manager Phelicia Jones (left) gives advice during a class at the San Francisco County Jail in San Bruno, California. The group was participating in Roads to Recovery, a class designed to rid substance abusing inmates of their dependencies. The class is funded by the Inmate Welfare Fund.

www Staffed primarily by ex-prisoners, the Fortune Society is a nonprofit community-based organization dedicated to educating the public about prisons, criminal justice issues, and the root causes of crime. It also helps ex-prisoners and at-risk youth break the cycle of crime and incarceration through a broad range of services. You can check out its website by going through the Siegel/Senna Introduction to Criminal Justice 11e website: www.thomsonedu.com/criminaljustice/siegel.

POSTRELEASE PROGRAMS A final element of job-related programming involves helping inmates obtain jobs before they are released and keep them once they are on the outside. A number of correctional departments have set up employment services designed to ease the transition between institution and community. Employment program staff assess inmates' backgrounds to determine their abilities, interests, goals, and capabilities. They also help them create job plans essential to receiving early release (parole) and successfully reintegrating into the community. Some programs maintain community correctional placements in sheltered environments that help inmates bridge the gap between institutions and the outside world. Services include job placement, skill development, family counseling, and legal and medical assistance.

Inmate Self-Help

Recognizing that the probability of failure on the outside is acute, inmates have attempted to organize self-help groups to provide the psychological tools needed to prevent recidivism.[71] Membership in these programs is designed to improve inmates' self-esteem and help them cope with common problems such as alcoholism, narcotics abuse, and depression.

Some groups are chapters of common national organizations, such as Alcoholics Anonymous. Other groups are organized along racial and ethnic lines. For example, in prisons stretching from California to Massachusetts are chapters of the Chicanos Organizados Pintos Aztlan, the Afro-American Coalition, and the Native American Brotherhood. These groups try to establish a sense of community so that members will work together for individual betterment. They hold literacy, language, and religion classes and offer counseling, legal advice, and prerelease support. Ethnic groups seek ties with outside minority organizations, such as the National Association for the Advancement of Colored People (NAACP), the Black Muslims, the Urban League, La Raza, and the American Indian Movement, as well as the religious and university communities.

Another type of self-help group assists inmates in finding the strength to make it on the outside. The best known is the Fortune Society, which claims more than 7,000 members. Staffed by ex-offenders, the Fortune Society provides counseling, education, and vocational training to parolees. The group also helps supervise offenders in the community in alternatives to incarceration programs. The staffers run a substance abuse treatment unit that provides individual and group counseling to clients sent by the New York City Department of Probation, provide HIV-prevention information, and work as an advocate group to improve prison conditions.[72]

Can Rehabilitation Work?

Despite the variety and number of treatment programs in operation, questions remain about their effectiveness. In their oft-cited research, Robert Martinson and his associates found that a majority of treatment programs were failures.[73] Through a national study they discovered that, with few exceptions, rehabilitative efforts seemed to have no appreciable effect on recidivism. The research produced a "nothing works" view of correctional treatment.

The research by Martinson and his colleagues was followed by efforts showing that some high-risk offenders were more likely to commit crimes after they had been placed in treatment programs than before the onset of rehabilitation efforts.[74] A slew of reviews have claimed that correctional treatment efforts aimed at youthful offenders provide little evidence that rehabilitation can take place within correctional settings. Evidence is scant that treatment efforts—even those that include vocational, educational, and mental health services—can consistently lower recidivism rates.[75]

The so-called failure of correctional treatment has helped promote a conservative view of corrections in which prisons are considered places of incapacitation and punishment, not treatment centers. Current policies stress eliminating the nonserious offender from the correctional system while increasing the probability that serious, violent offenders will be incarcerated and serve longer sentences. This view supports the utility of mandatory and determinate sentences for serious offenders and the simultaneous use of intermediate sanctions, such as house arrest, restitution, and diversion, to limit the nonserious offender's involvement in the system.

In the decades since Martinson's work was published there has been considerable debate over the effectiveness of correctional treatment. Even some of the most carefully crafted treatment efforts, using the most up-to-date rehabilitation modalities such as cognitive-behavioral therapy, have failed to show that treatment has a positive impact on inmates who return to the community.[76]

Despite these challenges to the efficacy of rehabilitation, many experts still believe strongly in the rehabilitative ideal.[77] They view it as not only humanistic but cost effective as well: Even though treatment programs may be expensive, if they reduce crime the savings in suffering and loss will more than offset their costs.[78]

Some evaluations of education, vocation, and work programs indicate that they may be able to lower recidivism rates and increase postrelease employment.[79] Research shows that inmates who have completed higher levels of education find it easier to gain employment upon release and consequently are less likely to recidivate over long periods.[80] The programs that have produced positive results both in the community and inside correctional institutions contain the following elements:

♦ Teach interpersonal skills.

♦ Provide individual counseling.

♦ Make use of behavioral modification techniques.

♦ Use cognitive-behavioral therapy.

♦ Stress improving moral reasoning.

♦ Combine in-prison therapeutic communities with follow-up community treatment.[81]

It is also possible that a combination of efforts rather than a single approach can have beneficial results—such as combining institutional treatment with postrelease aftercare.[82] So although not all programs are successful for all inmates, many treatment programs are effective, and some participants, especially younger clients, have a better chance of success on the outside than those who forgo treatment.[83]

ThomsonNOW Improve your grade on the exam with Personalized Study! For reinforcement resources and a mastery check of correctional treatment methods, go to www.thomsonedu.com/thomsonnow.

♦ GUARDING THE INSTITUTION

Control of a prison is a complex task. On one hand, a tough, high-security environment may meet the goals of punishment and control but fail to reinforce positive behavior changes. On the other hand, too liberal an administrative stance can lower staff morale and place inmates in charge of the institution.

For many years, prison guards were viewed as ruthless people who enjoyed their positions of power over inmates, fought rehabilitation efforts, were racist, and had a "lock psychosis" developed from years of counting, numbering, and checking on inmates. This view has changed in recent years. Correctional officers are now viewed as public servants who are seeking the security and financial rewards of a civil service position.[84] Most are in favor of rehabilitation efforts and do not hold any particular animosity toward the inmates. The correctional officer has been characterized as a "people worker" who must be prepared to deal with the problems of inmates on a personal level and also as a member of a complex bureaucracy who must be able to cope with its demands. Consequently, most state jurisdictions now require at least a high school diploma or GED as a hiring prerequisite for correctional officer positions. Some states, such as Minnesota, require an associate's or bachelor's degree. Another 12 states give monetary incentives to correctional officers as encouragement to continue their education after they are hired. For example, Florida will pay up to $1,560 per year, whereas Massachusetts provides an incentive of $1,500 per year for an associate's degree, $2,500 for a bachelor's degree, and $3,000 for a master's degree.[85] For more on a career as a correctional officer, read the Careers in Criminal Justice feature.

Corrections officers play a number of roles within the institution. They supervise cell houses, dining areas, shops, and other facilities as well as perch up on the walls, armed with rifles to oversee the yard and prevent escapes. Corrections officers also sit on disciplinary boards and escort inmates to hospitals and court appearances.

The greatest problem faced by correctional officers is the duality of their role: maintainers of order and security and advocates of treatment and rehabilitation. Added to this basic dilemma is the changing inmate role. In earlier times, corrections officers could count on inmate leaders to help them maintain order, but now they are faced with a racially charged atmosphere in which violence is a way of life. Today, correctional work is filled with danger, tension, boredom, and little evidence that efforts to help inmates lead to success. Research indicates that next to a police officer, the correctional worker has the most high-risk job in the United States and abroad.[86] And, unlike police officers, correctional officers apparently do not form a close-knit subculture with unique values and a sense of intergroup loyalty. Correctional officers experience alienation and isolation from inmates, the administration, and one another. This sense of alienation seems greatest in younger officers. Evidence exists that later in their careers officers enjoy a revival of interest in their work and take great pride in providing human services to inmates.[87] Not surprisingly, some research efforts have found that correctional officers perceive significant levels of stress related to such job factors as lack of safety, inadequate career opportunities, and work overload.[88] However, those who have high levels of job satisfaction, good relations with their coworkers, and high levels of social support seem to be better able to deal with the stress of the correctional setting.[89]

Many state prison authorities have developed training programs to prepare guards for the difficulties of prison work. Guard unions have also been formed to negotiate wages and working conditions with corrections departments.

Female Correctional Officers

The issue of female correctional officers in male institutions comes up repeatedly. Today, an estimated 5,000 women are assigned to all-male institutions.[90] The employment of women as guards in close contact with male inmates has spurred many questions of privacy and safety and a number of legal cases. In one important case, *Dothard v. Rawlinson* (1977), the U.S. Supreme Court upheld Alabama's refusal to hire female correctional officers on the grounds that it would put them in significant danger from the male inmates.[91] Despite such setbacks, women now work side by side with male officers in almost every state, performing the same duties. Research indicates that discipline has not suffered because of the inclusion of women in the guard force. Sexual assaults have been rare, and more negative attitudes have been expressed by the female guards' male peers than by inmates. Most commentators believe that the presence of

female guards can have an important beneficial effect on the self-image of inmates
and improve the guard-inmate working
relationship.

Little research has been conducted
on male correctional officers in female prisons, although almost every institution housing female offenders employs male officers.
What research there is indicates that male
officers are generally well received, and
although there is evidence of sexual exploitation and privacy violations, female
inmates generally believe that the presence
of male correctional officers helps create a
more natural environment and reduces tension. Both male and female inmates are
concerned about opposite-sex correctional
workers intruding on their privacy, such as
being given assignments in which they may

Violence is a constant threat in the prison environment and administrators must be vigilant in order to maintain order. Here, prison guard Tatum Lodish opens a gate in the Berks County Prison near Reading, Penn-sylvania. Lodish graduated with a bachelor's degree in criminal justice and the intention of working with troubled teenagers. Now she uses her education behind prison walls.

observe inmates dressing or bathing or in which they may come into physical contact, such as during searches or pat-downs. Ironically, female correctional officers
may find that an assignment to a male institution can boost their career. Recent
restrictions on male staff in women's prisons, in the wake of well-publicized sex
scandals, have forced administrators to assign women officers to the dormitory
areas, the least desirable areas in which to work. Women officers are not similarly
restricted in male-only facilities.[92]

The difficulties faced by correctional officers, both male and female, have
been captured in a new book called *Newjack* (slang for a rookie officer), which is
the subject of the Images of Justice feature on page 548.

◆ PRISON VIOLENCE

On August 9, 1973, Stephen Donaldson, a Quaker peace activist, was arrested
for trespassing after participating in a pray-in at the White House. Sent to a
Washington, D.C., jail for two nights, Donaldson was gang-raped approximately
60 times by numerous inmates. Donaldson later became president of Stop Prisoner Rape, a nonprofit organization that advocates for the protection of inmates
from sexual assault and offers support to victims.[93]

Conflict, violence, and brutality are sad but ever-present facts of institutional
life. Violence can involve individual conflict: inmate versus inmate, inmate versus
staff, staff versus inmate. Although surveys show that prison administrators deny
or downplay its occurrence, sexual assault is a common threat.[94] Research has
shown that prison rapes usually involve a victim who is viewed as weak and sub-
missive and a group of aggressive rapists who can dominate the victim through
their collective strength.[95] Sexual harassment leads to fights, social isolation, fear,
anxiety, and crisis. Nonsexual assaults may stem from an aggressor's desire to
shake down the victim for money and personal favors, may be motivated by racial
conflict, or may simply be used to establish power within the institution. Surveys
indicate that at least 20 percent of all inmates are raped during their prison stay.[96]
The problem is so severe that Congress enacted the Prison Rape Reduction Act
of 2003, which established three programs in the Department of Justice:

1. A program dedicated to collecting national prison rape statistics, gathering
   data, and conducting research.

2. A program dedicated to the dissemination of information and procedures
   for combating prison rape.

3. A program to assist in funding state programs.[97]

Check out the Stop Pris-
oner Rape website, which
you can access by linking
through the Siegel/Senna Introduction to Criminal Justice 11e
website: www.thomsonedu.com/
criminaljustice/siegel.

Correctional Officer

Duties and Characteristics of the Job

The primary job of a correctional officer is to supervise individuals awaiting trial in jail or who are serving time in prison after being convicted. Duties include supervising inmates and submitting reports on inmate behavior, maintaining order within the population by enforcing institutional rules and policies, and ensuring order in the institution by searching for contraband or settling disputes between inmates. Certain specially trained correctional officers handle especially dangerous situations such as forced cell moves or riots.

At the local level, such as in a county or municipal jail, a correctional officer who performs these tasks is referred to as a detention officer. Bailiffs are also considered correctional officers, and they maintain the order and safety in a courtroom. Although correctional officers will tend to work a standard 5-day, 40-hour workweek, odds are they will work overtime on weekends, holidays, and nights as well because jails and prisons must be staffed at all hours. Working environments will vary in quality because some institutions are kept modern and up-to-date and some may be older and less comfortable.

Job Outlook

Although opportunities exist for employment at the local level, a majority of correctional officer positions are at state and federal prisons. There are also a smaller number of jobs available with private institutions.

Correctional officers are needed in all penitentiary and courthouse settings. However, many correctional institutions, especially prisons, are in rural areas, so certain job opportunities will be available only in these settings.

Salary

Median annual salary for a correctional officer is $33,600. The majority of correctional officers earn between $26,500 and $44,200 a year. At the extremes, a small percentage of correctional officers will earn around $22,630, and the highest paid will earn more than $54,820. However, those who work at the federal level will generally have a higher salary than those at the state level, and those at the state level will have higher salaries than those at the local level.

Violence can also involve large groups of inmates, such as the famous Attica riot in 1971, which claimed 39 lives, or the New Mexico State Penitentiary riot of February 1980, in which the death toll was 33. More than 300 prison riots have occurred since the first one in 1774, 90 percent of them since 1952.[98]

A number of factors can spark such damaging incidents. They include poor staff-inmate communications, destructive environmental conditions, faulty classification, and promised but undelivered reforms. The 1980 New Mexico State Penitentiary riot drew national attention to the problem of prison riots. The prison was designed for 800 prisoners but held 1,135. Conditions of overcrowding, squalor, poor food, and lack of medical treatment abounded. The state government had been called on to improve guard training, physical plant quality, and relief from overcrowding but was reluctant to spend the necessary money.

Although revulsion over the violent riots in New Mexico and the earlier riot at Attica led to calls for prison reform, prison violence has continued unabated. About 75–100 inmates are killed by their peers each year in U.S. prisons, 6 or 7 staff members are murdered, and some 120 suicides are recorded.

Individual Violence

A number of explanations are offered for individual violence by prisoners:[99]

1. Before they were incarcerated, many inmates were violence-prone individuals who always used force to get their own way. Many are former gang members who upon entering the institution quickly join inmate gangs.[100] In many instances, street gangs maintain prison branches that unite new

Opportunities

Thanks to a growing demand for correctional officers, combined with high rates of turnover within the field, prospects for employment are very favorable. A good correctional officer with the proper education and training has the potential to be promoted to correctional sergeant and to other administrative and supervisory positions.

Qualifications

Being a correctional officer is a stressful and potentially dangerous job, so being properly qualified for the position is important. Exact qualifications will vary depending on what level of government one works in and what type of setting the position is in. A majority of correctional institutions will look for several characteristics from potential employees: Correctional officers should be U.S. citizens, at least 18 to 21 years old, and be able to pass a background check and a drug test. A potential correctional officer must also be in good physical and mental health, meet education requirements (see following), and be able to work in a challenging environment where good judgment and quick thought are necessary. Tests may be administered to judge whether an applicant meets these qualifications.

Education and Training

Although only a high school diploma may be necessary to become a correctional officer, a bachelor's degree, especially in a field such as criminology, sociology, or criminal justice, will make career advancement easier and can greatly increase annual salary. After hiring and training, there may be a period of on-the-job training with an experienced officer.

At the federal level, a bachelor's degree or three years of experience in a related field is necessary for employment. Federal corrections officers will have at least 200 hours of on-the-job training and a period of training at the Federal Bureau of Prisons.

Sources: "Correctional Officers," *Occupational Outlook Handbook*, 2006–2007 edition (Bureau of Labor Statistics, United States Dept. of Labor), retrieved May 25, 2006, from http://www.bls.gov/oco/ocos156.htm; S. E. Lambert and D. Regan, "Corrections Officer," *Great Careers for Criminal Justice Majors* (New York: McGraw-Hill, 2001), pp. 193–96.

---

inmates with their former violence-prone peers. Having this connection supports and protects gang members while they are in prison, and it assists in supporting gang members' families and associates outside the wall.[101] Gang violence is a significant source of prison conflict.

2. Many inmates suffer from personality disorders. Recent research shows that among institutionalized offenders, psychopathy is the strongest predictor of violent recidivism and indifferent response to treatment.[102] In the crowded, dehumanizing world of the prison, it is not surprising that people with extreme psychological distress may resort to violence to dominate others.[103]

3. The prison experience itself causes people to become violent. Inhuman conditions, including overcrowding, depersonalization, and the threat of sexual assault, are violence-producing conditions. Overcrowding has been linked to self-directed violence: Suicide levels are higher in overcrowded institutions.[104] Even in the most humane prisons, life is a constant put-down, and prison conditions are a threat to the inmate's sense of self-worth; violence is an expected consequence of these conditions. Violence levels are not much different in high- and low-security prisons, indicating that the prison experience itself, and not the level of control, produces violence.[105]

4. Violence may result because prisons lack effective mechanisms to enable inmate grievances against either prison officials or other inmates to be handled fairly and equitably. Prisoners who complain about other inmates are viewed as "rats" or "snitches" and are marked for death by their enemies.

Newjack

The daily operations of criminal justice are not only portrayed on TV and in the movies but are also the focus of the print media. The number of novels focusing on police work is incalculable, but there is also an extensive true-crime literature. One unique addition to this literature (*Newjack: Guarding Sing Sing*) was recently produced by Ted Conover, a well-known author (*Whiteout, Coyotes*) who wanted to write about what it meant to be a correctional officer in a maximum-security prison.

He soon found out that a civilian (especially a writer) would not be allowed to enter a prison and be given needed access to inmates and correctional personnel. So he applied to become a correctional officer, was given a position, and underwent seven weeks of preparation at the Correctional Officer Training Academy in Albany, New York. After graduation he was ready, so he thought, to become a newjack, a rookie correctional officer. He was assigned as a gallery officer who oversaw a prison pod in Sing Sing. This infamous 170-year-old institution, one of the first built in the United States, is the kind of maximum-security institution where men instantly size each other up to see who can be dominated and who will dominate.

On his first day on the job, Conover was asked to stand before a camera, holding a piece of paper showing his name and Social Security number. When he asked why, Conover was told that the pictures were "hostage shots" and were kept on file in case a correctional officer is injured or taken hostage, at which time the photographs are released to the press. He at first laughed but then realized that "hostage shots" are not all that funny and that correctional officers can be injured or killed at any moment. It

comes as no surprise that although some of his colleagues were hardworking and sincere, others were brutal and vicious.

Conover soon learned that correctional officers cannot show a trace of fear because it attracts abuse from inmates and the loss of respect of fellow officers. Inmates will grant respect if the correctional officer is firm but willing to make an exception to the rules once in a while. Too many exceptions, and the respect vanishes as the residents start taking advantage. Inmates are described as the "lowest of the low," and officers describe themselves as "warehousers" and "baby-sitters." Some recollect what they call the "good old days" when they could beat up inmates at will; some suggest that a correctional officer can still beat up an inmate with immunity in some isolated institutions.

Conover felt the aggression, frustration at the procedures, and perpetually tense interaction between inmates and correctional personnel that permeated the institution. Officers bragged about how at some institutions unruly inmates are savagely beaten and how they would not mind doing the same at Sing Sing. Horrified at first, Conover realized that he himself has a violent side, which he never before knew existed, and he learned the tricks that could be used to protect himself when his aggression emerged. To avoid brutality charges, he learned to yell "stop resisting" as he roughed up an inmate; he was shown how logbooks can be fudged to conceal undeserved discipline. He considered some of his duties demeaning and ugly, especially body cavity searches. He was attacked and punched in the head by an inmate and forced to wrestle with powerful muscle-bound men. For all this he earned about $23,000 per year.

Similarly, complaints or lawsuits filed against the prison administration may result in the inmate being placed in solitary confinement—"the hole."

5. Inmates resort to violence in order to survive. They lack physical security and adequate mechanisms for resolving complaints, and the code of silence promotes individual violence by inmates who might otherwise be controlled.

Collective Violence

Two distinct theories have been put forth to explain the cause of collective violence. The first, called the **inmate balance theory**, suggests that riots and other forms of collective action occur when prison officials make an abrupt effort to take control of the prison and limit freedoms. Crackdowns occur when officials perceive that inmate leaders have too much power and take measures to control their illicit privileges, such as gambling or stealing food.[106] According to the **administrative control theory**, collective violence may be caused by prison mismanagement, lack of strong security, and inadequate control by prison officials. Poor management may inhibit conflict management and set the stage for

inmate balance theory
The view that riots and other forms of collective prison violence occur when officials make an abrupt effort to take control of the prison and limit freedoms.

administrative control theory
The view that collective violence in prison may be caused by mismanagement, lack of strong security, and inadequate control by prison officials.

Conover experienced what he considered to be the essence of correctional life: unending tedium interrupted by a sudden adrenaline rush when an incident occurs. He began to understand why correctional officers develop a feeling that they are in confinement themselves. It is a consequence of dealing all day and night with men who can do almost nothing for themselves on their own and who depend on their gallery officer to take care of their most personal needs. Instead of feeling tough and in control, at the end of the day the correctional officer feels like a waiter who has served 100 tables or a mother with too many dependent children. Because of their dependence, the inmates are often made to feel like infants, and those who do not take it well may revert to violence to ease their frustrations. The potential for violence in the prison setting is so great that it makes even routine assignments seem dangerous. Yet Conover was astonished that there were not even more violent incidents considering that 1,800 rapists, murderers, and assaulters were trapped together in a hellish environment.

Conover did find that some inmates were intelligent and sensitive. One prisoner pointed out that the United States is now planning prisons that will be built in 12 years. By planning that far into the future, he told Conover, the government is planning on imprisoning people who are now children. Instead of spending millions on future prisons, why not spend thousands on education and social services to ensure that these children will not be just statistics? Conover could not think of an adequate answer.

Probably most disturbing was the effect the institution had on Conover's personal life. Although he got to go home to his wife and children, he could not leave his prison experiences at the gate. Prison gets into your skin, he said. If you stayed long enough, "some of it seeped into your soul." His wife was troubled by the changes she saw in him and begged him to quit. He in turn implored her to let him finish out the year. If a man such as Conover experienced such personal stress knowing that he was a writer incognito on temporary assignment, what must the stress be like for professional officers who do not share the luxury of having another career waiting over the horizon?

Critical Thinking

Can a writer truly experience what it must be like to be a prison guard when he is only playing a role, one that he can step out of any time he chooses? If a writer wanted to experience college life and enrolled at your school, would he truly begin to understand what it means to be a student?

InfoTrac College Edition Research

How do correctional officers perceive their job? Are they different from law enforcement personnel? To find out, read Charles Mesloh, Ross Wolf, and Mark Henych, "Perceptions of Misconduct: An Examination of Ethics at One Correctional Institution," *Corrections Compendium* 25 (2003): 1–9.

Source: Ted Conover, *Newjack: Guarding Sing Sing* (New York: Random House, 2000).

violence. Repressive administrations give inmates the feeling that nothing will ever change, that they have nothing to lose, and that violence is the only means for change.

Overcrowding caused by the rapid increases in the prison population has also been linked to prison violence. As the prison population continues to climb, unmatched by expanded capacity, prison violence may increase.

Future prison officials could lean on technology to control the prison environment. This issue is discussed in the Criminal Justice and Technology feature.

ThomsonNOW™ Improve your grade on the exam with Personalized Study! For reinforcement resources and a mastery check of prison violence, go to www.thomsonedu.com/thomsonnow.

◆ PRISONERS' RIGHTS

Before the early 1960s, it was accepted that on conviction an individual forfeited all rights not expressly granted by statutory law or correctional policy; inmates were civilly dead. The U.S. Supreme Court held that convicted offenders should expect to be penalized for their misdeeds and that part of their punishment was the loss of rights that free citizens take for granted.

Technocorrections—Contemporary Correctional Technology

Contemporary technological forces are converging with the forces of law and order to create techno-corrections. The correctional establishment—the managers of the jail, prison, probation, and parole systems—and their sponsors in elected office are seeking more cost-effective ways to increase public safety as the number of people under correctional supervision continues to grow. A correctional establishment that takes advantage of all the potential offered by the new technologies to reduce the costs of supervising criminal offenders and minimize the risk they pose to society will define the field of technocorrections.

A few recent advances, some of which have been deployed and others of which are in the development stage, are discussed following.

Ground-Penetrating Radar

Special Technologies Laboratories (STL) has developed a new technology called ground-penetrating radar (GPR), which is able to locate tunnels that inmates use to escape. GPR works almost like an old-fashioned Geiger counter, held in the hand and swept across the ground by an operator. Instead of detecting metal, however, the GPR system detects changes in ground composition, including voids, such as those created by a tunnel.

Heartbeat Monitoring

The weakest security link in any prison has always been the sally port, where trucks unload their supplies and where trash and laundry are taken out of the facility. Over the years, inmates have hidden in loads of trash, old produce, laundry—any possible container that might be exiting the facility. Now escapes can be prevented by monitoring inmates' heartbeats. The Advanced Vehicle Interrogation and Notification System (AVIAN), being marketed by Geo Vox Security, works by identifying the shock wave generated by the beating heart, which couples to any surface the body touches. The system takes all the frequencies of movement, such as the expansion and contraction of an engine or rain hitting the roof, and determines if a pattern is present similar to a human heartbeat.

Satellite Monitoring

Pro Tech Monitoring Inc., of Palm Harbor, Florida, has developed a system to monitor offenders by satellite using cellular technology combined with the federal government's global positioning system of satellites. While in the community, each offender wears an ankle bracelet and carries a three-pound portable tracking device (smart box), programmed with information on his or her geographical restrictions. For instance, a sex offender may be forbidden to come within five miles of his victim's home or workplace, or a pedophile may be barred from getting close to a school. A satellite monitors the geographic movements of the offender, either in real time or by transmitting the information to the smart box for later retrieval. The smart box and the ankle bracelet sound an alarm when boundaries are breached, alerting potential victims.

Pulsed Radar

Special Technologies Laboratories has developed the GPR-X, ground-penetrating radar that transmits energy into the ground and, by measuring the time it takes for that energy to be reflected, detects changes in ground material. GPR-X can detect contraband buried in the recreation yard, for instance, or a tunnel being built under the prison.

Sticky Shocker

This less-than-lethal projectile uses stun gun technology to temporarily incapacitate a person at standoff range. The Sticky Shocker is a low-impact, wireless projectile fired from compressed gas or powder launchers and is accurate to within 10 meters.

Back-Scatter Imaging System for Concealed Weapons

This system uses a back-scatter imager to detect weapons and contraband. The major advantage of this device over current walk-through portals is that it can detect nonmetallic as well as metallic weapons. It uses low-power X-rays equal to about five minutes of exposure to the sun at sea level. Although these X-rays penetrate clothing, they do not penetrate the body.

Body Scanning Screening System

This is a stationary screening system to detect nonmetallic weapons and contraband in the lower body cavities. It uses simplified magnetic resonance imaging (MRI) as a noninvasive alternative to X-ray and physical body cavity searches. The stationary screening system makes use of first-generation medical MRI.

Transmitter Wristbands

Developed by Technology Systems International, these broadcast a unique serial number via radio frequency every two seconds so that antennas throughout the prison can pick up the signals and pass the data via a local area network to a central monitoring station computer. The bands can sound an alert when a prisoner gets dangerously close to the perimeter fence or when an inmate does not return from a furlough on time. They can even tag gang members and notify guards when rivals get into contact with one another.

Personal Health Status Monitor

Correctional authorities are now developing a personal health status monitor that, in its initial form, will use acoustics to track the heartbeat and respiration of a person in a cell. The monitor does not need to be located on the person of the inmate but (because it is the size of two packs of cigarettes) can be placed on the ceiling or just outside a cell. The device is similar to ones that are installed inside the cribs of infants in hospitals.

Advanced health status monitors are now being developed that can monitor more than five vital signs at once and, based on the combination of findings, produce an assessment of an inmate's state of health. Although this more advanced version of the personal health status monitor may take another decade to develop, the current version will be able to help save lives that would otherwise be lost to suicide and will be available in the near future.

All-in-One Drug Detection Spray

For the past several years, Mistral Security of Bethesda, Maryland, has marketed drug detection sprays for marijuana, methamphetamines, heroin, and cocaine. A specially made piece of paper is wiped on a surface. When sprayed with one of the aerosol sprays, it changes color within 15 seconds if as little as 4 to 20 micrograms of drugs are present. A new detection device is being developed that uses a single spray that will test for all drugs at once. The test paper will turn different colors depending on which drugs the spray contacts, and several positive results will be possible with a single use of the spray.

Radar Vital Signs Monitor, Radar Flashlight

Researchers at Georgia Tech have developed a handheld radar flashlight that can detect the respiration of a human in a cell from behind a 20-centimeter hollow-core concrete wall or an eight-inch cinderblock wall. It instantly gives the user a bar-graph readout that is viewed on the apparatus itself. Other miniature radar detectors give users heartbeat and respiration readings. The equipment is expected to be a useful tool in searches for people who are hiding, because the only thing that successfully blocks its functioning is a wall made of metal or conductive material in the direction it is pointed. The radars can also be used in telemedicine and for individuals to whom electrodes would be difficult to apply. Future applications for this technology include advanced lie detectors and using the human heartbeat as a biometric for personnel identification.

Personal Alarm Location System

Prison employees can carry a tiny transmitter linking them with a computer in a central control room. In an emergency, they can hit an alarm button and transmit to a computer that automatically records whose distress button has been pushed. An architectural map of the facility instantly appears onscreen showing the exact location of the staff member.

Although sensors are placed only inside the prison, the Personal Alarm Location System (PALS) works up to 300 feet outside prison walls. It locates within a range of four meters inside the room in which the duress button is pushed and also locates signals in between floors. The PALS system also has an option that tracks the movement of employees who have pressed their duress buttons. If an officer moves after hitting the duress button, the red dot that represents him or her on the computer screen will move as well. The PALS system is being used in six correctional institutions in the United States and Canada and is scheduled to be adopted in more.

Future Technology

Not yet employed but in the planning stage are the following technological breakthroughs:

♦ *Angel chip.* This microchip would be implanted underneath the skin of the user and would contain vital and identifying information. To avoid future legal entanglements, it is being developed by Sun Microsystems with the assistance of the American Civil Liberties Union.

(continued)

♦ *Noninvasive body cavity scanner.* Eliminating the necessity of a physical search, this machine uses magnetic resonance imaging technology to scan body cavities.

♦ *Noninvasive drug detection.* This is a swab or patch that, when placed on the skin, absorbs perspiration and detects the presence of illegal drugs.

Critical Thinking

Should the use of technology for prison security be unrestricted, or must it follow the same legal guidelines guaranteeing privacy that apply in the outside world? That is, do inmates lose their First Amendment rights when they enter prison?

InfoTrac College Edition Research

To read more about the issues surrounding the use of prison technology, go to Ann H. Crowe, "Electronic Supervision: From Decision-Making to Implementation," *Corrections Today* 64, no. 5 (August 2002): 130.

Sources: Mark Robert, "Big Brother Goes Behind Bars," *Fortune,* September 30, 2002, p. 44; Tony Fabelo, "'Technocorrections': The Promises, the Uncertain Threats," *Sentencing and Corrections: Issues for the 21st Century* (Washington, D.C.: National Institute of Justice, 2000); Irwin Soonachan, "The Future of Corrections: Technological Developments Are Turning Science Fiction into Science Fact," *Corrections Today* 62 (2000): 64–66; Steve Morrison, "How Technology Can Make Your Job Safer," *Corrections Today* 62 (2000): 58–60; Nolin Renfrow, "The Evolution of Corrections Technology." *Corrections Today* 67 (2005): 8.

One reason that inmates lacked rights was that state and federal courts were reluctant to intervene in the administration of prisons unless the circumstances of a case clearly indicated a serious breach of the Eighth Amendment protection against cruel and unusual punishment. This judicial policy is referred to as the **hands-off doctrine.** The courts used three basic justifications for their neglect of prison conditions:

hands-off doctrine
The judicial policy of not interfering in the administrative affairs of prisons.

1.   Correctional administration was a technical matter best left to experts instead of to courts ill equipped to make appropriate evaluations.

2.   Society as a whole was apathetic to what went on in prisons, and most individuals preferred not to associate with or know about the offender.

3.   Prisoners' complaints involved privileges, not rights. Prisoners were considered to have fewer constitutional rights than other members of society.[107]

As the 1960s drew to a close, the hands-off doctrine was eroded. Federal district courts began seriously considering prisoners' claims concerning conditions in the various state and federal institutions and used their power to intervene on behalf of the inmates. In some ways, this concern reflected the spirit of the times, which saw the onset of the civil rights movement, a movement that was subsequently paralleled in such areas as student rights, public welfare, mental institutions, juvenile court systems, and military justice.

Beginning in the late 1960s, such activist groups as the NAACP Legal Defense Fund and the American Civil Liberties Union's National Prison Project began to search for appropriate legal vehicles to bring prisoners' complaints before state and federal courts. The most widely used device was the federal Civil Rights Act, 42 U.S.C. 1983:

> Every person who, under color of any statute, ordinance, regulation, custom, or usage of any State or Territory subjects, or causes to be subjected, any citizen of the United States or other person within the jurisdiction thereof to the deprivation of any rights, privileges, or immunities secured by the Constitution and laws shall be liable to the party injured in an action at law, suit in equity, or other proper proceeding for redress.

The legal argument went that, as U.S. citizens, prison inmates could sue state officials if their civil rights were violated—for example, if they were the victims of racial or religious discrimination.

The U.S. Supreme Court first recognized the right of prisoners to sue for civil rights violations in cases involving religious freedom brought by the Black Muslims. This well-organized group had been frustrated by prison administrators who feared its growing power and desired to place limits on its recruitment activities. In the 1964 case of *Cooper v. Pate*, however, the Supreme Court ruled that inmates who were being denied the right to practice their religion were entitled to legal redress under 42 U.S.C. 1983.[108] Although *Cooper* applied to the narrow issue of religious freedom, it opened the door to providing other rights for inmates.

The subsequent prisoners' rights crusade, stretching from 1960 to 1980, paralleled the civil rights and women's movements. Battle lines were drawn between prison officials, who hoped to maintain their power and resented interference by the courts, and inmate groups and their sympathizers, who used state and federal courts as a forum for demanding better living conditions and personal rights. Each decision handed down by the courts was viewed as a victory for one side or the other. This battle continues today.

Substantive Rights

Through a slow process of legal review, the courts have granted inmates a number of **substantive rights** that have significantly influenced the entire correctional system. The most important of these rights are discussed in the following sections.

substantive right
A specific right, such as the right to medical care or freedom of religion.

ACCESS TO COURTS, LEGAL SERVICES, AND MATERIALS Without the ability to seek judicial review of conditions causing discomfort or violating constitutional rights, the inmate must depend solely on the slow and often insensitive administrative mechanism of relief within the prison system. Therefore, the right of easy access to the courts gives inmates hope that their rights will be protected during incarceration. Courts have held that inmates are entitled to have legal materials available and be provided with assistance in drawing up and filing complaints. Inmates who help others, so-called **jailhouse lawyers**, cannot be interfered with or harassed by prison administrators. Here are some of the key rulings on this issue:

jailhouse lawyer
An inmate trained in law or otherwise educated who helps other inmates prepare legal briefs and appeals.

♦ *DeMallory v. Cullen* (1988). An untrained inmate paralegal is not a constitutionally acceptable alternative to law library access.[109]

♦ *Lindquist v. Idaho State Board of Corrections* (1985). Seven inmate law clerks for a prison population of 950 were sufficient legal representation because they had a great deal of experience.[110]

♦ *Smith v. Wade* (1983). An inmate who has been raped can have access to the state court to sue a correctional officer for failing to protect the inmate from aggressive inmates.[111]

♦ *Bounds v. Smith* (1977). State correctional systems are obligated to provide inmates with either adequate law libraries or the help of people trained in the law.[112]

FREEDOM OF THE PRESS AND OF EXPRESSION Correctional administrators traditionally placed severe limitations on prisoners' speech and expression. For example, they have read and censored inmate mail and restricted their reading material. With the lifting of the hands-off doctrine, courts have consistently ruled that only when a compelling state interest exists can prisoners' First Amendment rights be modified. Correctional authorities must justify the limiting of free speech by showing that granting it would threaten institutional security. In a 2001 case, *Shaw v. Murphy*, the Court ruled that inmates do not have a right to correspond with other inmates even if they are requesting legal advice. If prison administrators believe that such correspondence undermines prison security, the First Amendment rights of inmates can be curtailed.[113] Here are some related decisions:

♦ *Turner v. Safley* (1987). Prisoners do not have a right to receive mail from one another. Inmate-to-inmate mail can be banned if the reason is "related to legitimate penological interests."[114]

♦ *Ramos v. Lamm* (1980). The institutional policy of refusing to deliver mail in a language other than English is unconstitutional.[115]

♦ *Procunier v. Martinez* (1974). Censorship of a prisoner's mail is justified only when there exists substantial government interest in maintaining the censorship to further prison security, order, and rehabilitation, and the restrictions are not greater or more stringent than is demanded by security precautions.[116]

♦ *Nolan v. Fitzpatrick* (1971). Prisoners may correspond with newspapers unless their letters discuss escape plans or contain contraband or otherwise objectionable material.[117]

FREEDOM OF RELIGION Freedom of religion is a fundamental right guaranteed by the First Amendment. In general, the courts have ruled that inmates have the right to assemble and pray in the religion of their choice but that religious symbols and practices that interfere with institutional security can be restricted. Administrators can draw the line if religious needs become cumbersome or impossible to carry out for reason of cost or security. Granting special privileges can also be denied on the grounds that they will cause other groups to make similar demands. Here are some key cases:

♦ *Mumin v. Phelps* (1988). If there is a legitimate penological interest, inmates can be denied special privileges to attend religious services.[118]

♦ *O'Lone v. Estate of Shabazz* (1987). Prison officials can assign inmates work schedules that make it impossible for them to attend religious services as long as no reasonable alternative exists.[119]

♦ *Rahman v. Stephenson* (1986). A prisoner's rights are not violated if the administration refuses to use the prisoner's religious name on official records.[120]

In an important 2005 case, *Cutter v. Williamson*, the Supreme Court ruled that the Religious Land Use and Institutionalized Persons Act of 2000, which

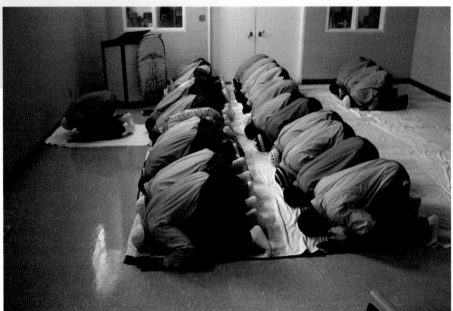

Federal court rulings allow inmates the opportunity to participate in religious services in their own faith. Here Muslims attend Juma, Friday's group prayer, in a gathering room reserved for prisoner activities at a state prison in Virginia.

©Andrew Lichtenstein/Corbis

was intended to protect the rights of prisoners, is not an unconstitutional government promotion of religion.[121] Writing for the majority, Ruth Bader Ginsburg stated that "[i]t confers no privileged status on any particular religious sect, and singles out no bona fide faith for disadvantageous treatment." *Cutter* allows inmates to practice their own religion unless these practices clearly undermine prison security and safety.

MEDICAL RIGHTS In early prisons, inmates' right to medical treatment was restricted through the "exceptional circumstances doctrine." Using this policy, the courts would hear only those cases in which the circumstances disregarded human dignity, while denying hearings for less serious cases. The cases that were allowed access to the courts usually represented a situation of total denial of medical care.

To gain their medical rights, prisoners have resorted to class action suits (for example, suits brought on behalf of all individuals affected by similar circumstances, in this case poor medical attention). In the most significant case, *Newman v. Alabama* (1972), the entire Alabama prison system's medical facilities were declared inadequate.[122] The Supreme Court cited the following factors as contributing to inadequate care: insufficient physician and nurse resources, reliance on untrained inmates for paramedical work, intentional failure in treating the sick and injured, and failure to conform to proper medical standards. The Newman case forced corrections departments to upgrade prison medical facilities.

It was not until 1976, in *Estelle v. Gamble*, that the Supreme Court clearly mandated an inmate's right to have medical care.[123] J. W. Gamble had hurt his back in a Texas prison and filed suit because he contested the type of treatment he had received and questioned the lack of interest that prison guards had shown in his case. The Supreme Court said that "[d]eliberate indifference to serious medical needs of prisoners constitutes the 'unnecessary and wanton infliction of pain,' proscribed by the Eighth Amendment."[124] Gamble was allowed to collect monetary damages for his injuries.

The *Gamble* decision means that lower courts can decide, on a case-by-case basis, whether "deliberate indifference" to an inmate's medical needs occurred and to what damages the inmate is entitled. Yet, when budgets are tight, correctional systems may be forced to cut back on medical care. Private health care providers are now relied on in many prisons, and because states are often required by law to accept the lowest bid for service, companies bid low amounts and make money by either denying treatment or by providing the minimum possible care. The right to medical care goes only so far.[125]

CRUEL AND UNUSUAL PUNISHMENT The concept of **cruel and unusual punishment** is founded in the Eighth Amendment. The term itself has not been specifically defined by the Supreme Court, but the Court has held that treatment constitutes cruel and unusual punishment when it

- ♦ Degrades the dignity of human beings.[126]

- ♦ Is more severe (disproportional) than the offense for which it has been given.[127]

- ♦ Shocks the general conscience and is fundamentally unfair.[128]

- ♦ Is deliberately indifferent to a person's safety and well-being.[129]

- ♦ Punishes people because of their status, such as race, religion, and mental state.[130]

- ♦ Is in flagrant disregard of due process of law, such as punishment that is capriciously applied.[131]

State and federal courts have placed strict limits on disciplinary methods that may be considered inhumane. Corporal punishment all but ended after the

cruel and unusual punishment
Treatment that degrades human dignity, is disproportionately severe, or shocks the general conscience; prohibited by the Eighth Amendment to the U.S. Constitution.

practice was condemned in *Jackson v. Bishop* (1968).[132] Although the solitary confinement of disruptive inmates continues, its prolonged use under barbaric conditions has been held in violation of the Eighth Amendment. Courts have found that inmates placed in solitary have the right to adequate personal hygiene, exercise, mattresses, ventilation, and rules specifying how they can earn their release.

In *Hope v. Pelzer et al.* (2002), the Supreme Court ruled that correctional officials who knowingly violate the Eighth Amendment rights of inmates can be held liable for damages.[133]

OVERALL PRISON CONDITIONS   Prisoners have long had the right to the minimal conditions necessary for human survival, such as food, clothing, shelter, and medical care to sustain human life. A number of attempts have been made to articulate reasonable standards of prison care and to make sure they are carried out. Courts have held that although people are sent to prison for punishment, it does not mean that prison should be a punishing experience.[134] In the 1994 case of *Farmer v. Brennan*, the Court ruled that prison officials are legally liable if, knowing that an inmate faces a serious risk of harm, they disregard that risk by failing to take measures to avoid or reduce it. Furthermore, prison officials should be able to infer the risk from the evidence at hand; they need not be warned or told.[135]

Although inmates retain the right to reasonable care, if a legitimate purpose exists for the use of governmental restrictions, they may be considered constitutional. For example, it might be possible to restrict reading material, allow strip searches, and prohibit inmates from receiving packages from the outside if the restrictions are legitimate security measures. If overcrowded conditions require it, inmates may be double-bunked in cells designed for a single inmate.[136]

Courts have also reviewed entire correctional systems to determine whether practices are unfair to inmates. In a critical case, *Estelle v. Ruiz*, the Texas Department of Corrections was ordered to provide new facilities to alleviate overcrowding; to abolish the practice of using inmate trustees; to lower the inmate-to-staff ratio; to improve treatment services, such as medical, mental health, and occupational rehabilitation programs; and to adhere to the principles of procedural due process in dealing with inmates.[137] A court-ordered master was appointed to oversee the changes and served from 1981 to 1990, when the state was deemed in compliance with the most critical of the court-ordered reforms.[138] A period of tension and violence followed this decision, in part perhaps because the staff and administration felt that the court had undermined their authority. It took more than 18 years for the case to be settled.

Because of the large numbers of lawsuits filed by inmates, the federal government has moved to limit inmate access to the courts. The Prison Litigation Reform Act (PLRA) of 1996 limited the number of prison cases in federal court by providing that "no action shall be brought with respect to prison conditions" by an inmate in either state or federal prison "until such administrative remedies as are available are exhausted."[139] The PLRA includes a new form of "three strikes and you're out": If a prisoner has filed three suits that are dismissed because they fail to state a claim for relief (or are frivolous), he or she is barred from filing future actions unless in imminent danger of serious physical harm. Although such measures are designed to limit litigation, the overcrowding crisis likely will prompt additional litigation requesting overall prison relief.

◆ LEAVING PRISON

At the expiration of their prison term, most inmates return to society and try to resume their life there. For some inmates, their reintegration into society comes by way of parole, the planned community release and supervision of incarcerated offenders before the expiration of their full prison sentences. In states where determinate sentencing statutes have eliminated discretionary parole, offenders are released after having served their determinate sentence, less time off for good behavior and other credits designed to reduce the term of incarceration. Their release may involve supervision in the community, and rule violations can result in return to prison for the balance of their unexpired sentence.

In a few instances, inmates are released after their sentence has been commuted by a board of pardons or directly by a governor or even the president of the United States. About 15 percent of prison inmates are released after serving their entire maximum sentence without any time excused or forgiven. And despite the efforts of correctional authorities, about 7,000 inmates escape every year from state and federal prisons (the number of escapes is declining, due in part to better officer training and more sophisticated security measures).[140]

Regardless of the method of their release, former inmates face the formidable task of having to readjust to society. This means regaining legal rights they may have lost on their conviction, reestablishing community and family ties, and finding employment. After inmates have been in prison, these goals are often difficult to achieve.

Parole

The decision to **parole** is determined by statutory requirement. In some states parole is granted by a parole board, a duly constituted body of men and women who review inmate cases and determine whether offenders have reached a rehabilitative level sufficient to deal with the outside world. The board also dictates what specific parole rules parolees must obey. In other jurisdictions, the amount of time a person must remain in prison is a predetermined percentage of the inmate's sentence, assuming that there are no infractions or escape attempts. With **mandatory parole release**, the inmate is released when the unserved portion of the maximum prison term equals the inmate's earned good time (less time served in jail awaiting trial). In some states, sentences can be reduced by more than half with a combination of statutory and earned good time. If the conditions of their release are violated, mandatory releasees can have their good time revoked and be returned to the institution to serve the remainder of their unexpired term. The remaining inmates are released for a variety of reasons, including expiration of their term, commutation of their sentence, and court orders to relieve overcrowded prisons.

The Parole Board

In those states that have maintained discretionary parole, the authority to release inmates is usually vested in the parole board. State parole boards have four primary functions:

1. To select and place prisoners on parole.

2. To aid, supervise, and provide continuing control of parolees in the community.

3. To determine when the parole function is completed and to discharge parolees.

4. To determine whether parole should be revoked if violations of conditions occur.

Most parole authorities are independent agencies with their own staff and administration, and a few parole boards are part of the state department of corrections. Arguments for keeping the board within a corrections department usually include improved communication and the availability of more intimate knowledge about offenders.

Most boards are relatively small, usually numbering fewer than 10 members. Their size, coupled with their large caseloads and the varied activities they are expected to perform, can prevent board members from becoming as well acquainted with the individual inmates as might be desired.

parole
The early release of a prisoner from incarceration subject to conditions set by a parole board.

mandatory parole release
A release date determined at the beginning of the confinement period based on a percentage of the inmate's sentence to be served. Inmates can have their expected time served increased if they violate prison rules or conditions.

The United States Parole Commission maintains a website, which you can access by going to the Siegel/Senna Introduction to Criminal Justice 11e website: www.thomsonedu.com/criminaljustice/siegel.

Parole Hearings

The actual (discretionary) parole decision is made at a parole-granting hearing. At this hearing the full board or a selected subcommittee reviews information, may meet with the offender, and then decides whether the parole applicant has a reasonable probability of succeeding outside of prison. Each parole board has its own way of reviewing cases. In some, the full board meets with the applicant; in others, only a few members do that. In a number of jurisdictions, a single board member can conduct a personal investigation and submit the findings to the full board for a decision.

When parole is discretionary, most parole boards will look at the inmate's crime, institutional record, and willingness to accept responsibility before making the release decision. Letters may be solicited from the inmate's friends and family members. In some jurisdictions, victims may appear and make statements of the losses they suffered. By speaking directly to the applicant, the board can also promote and emphasize the specific types of behavior and behavior changes it expects to see if the inmate is to eventually qualify for or effectively serve parole. Inmates who maintain their innocence may find that denying responsibility for their crimes places their release date in jeopardy. The requirement that they admit guilt or culpability is especially vexing for those inmates who are actually innocent and who actively refuse to accept their institutional label of "convicted criminal."[141]

The inmate's specific rights at a parole-granting hearing also vary from jurisdiction to jurisdiction. In about half of the parole-granting jurisdictions, inmates are permitted counsel or are allowed to present witnesses on their behalf; other jurisdictions do not permit these privileges. Because the federal courts have declared that the parole applicant is not entitled to any form of legal representation, the inmate may have to pay for legal services when this privilege is allowed. In almost all discretionary parole-granting jurisdictions, the reasons for the parole decision must be given in writing, and in about half of the jurisdictions, a verbatim record of the hearing is made.

In the case of *Pennsylvania Board of Probation and Parole v. Scott*, the U.S. Supreme Court held that the exclusionary rule for illegally obtained evidence does not apply to parole revocation proceedings. The Court reasoned that the social costs of excluding incriminating evidence outweigh any benefits of protecting parolees from invasion of their privacy. *Scott* thus allows evidence to be used in a parole revocation hearing that would be excluded from a criminal prosecution.[142]

The Parolee in the Community

Once released into the community, a parolee is given a standard set of rules and conditions that must be obeyed. As with probation, the offender who violates these rules may have parole revoked and be sent back to the institution to serve the remainder of the sentence. Once in the community, the parolee is supervised by a trained staff of parole officers who help the offender search for employment and monitor the parolee's behavior and activities to ensure that the conditions of parole are met.

Parole is generally viewed as a privilege granted to deserving inmates on the basis of their good behavior while in prison. Parole has two conflicting sides, however. On one hand, the paroled offender is allowed to serve part of the sentence in the community, an obvious benefit for the deserving offender. On the other hand, because parole is a privilege and not a right, the parolee is viewed as a dangerous criminal who must be carefully watched and supervised. The conflict between the treatment and enforcement aspects of parole has not been reconciled by the criminal justice system, and the parole process still contains elements of both.

To overcome these roadblocks to success, the parole officer may have to play a much greater role in directing and supervising clients' lives than the probation officer. In some instances, parole programs have become active in creating new postrelease treatment-oriented programs designed to increase the chances of parole success. For example, the Kansas Parole Department has adopted a restorative justice approach and is now having parolees work in community service settings upon their release. Jobs may include work at soup kitchens, homeless shelters, and halfway houses. Reports indicate that the program is quite successful.[143] In other instances, parole agencies have implemented law enforcement-oriented services that work with local police agencies to identify and apprehend parolees who may have been involved in criminal activity. The California Department of Corrections has established the Special Service Unit, which among its other tasks acts as a liaison with local police agencies in helping them solve major crimes when inmates or state parolees are the known or suspected offenders.[144]

INTENSIVE SUPERVISION PAROLE To aid supervision, some jurisdictions are implementing systems that classify offenders on the basis of their supervision needs. Typically, a point or guideline system (sometimes called a salient factor score) based on prior record and prison adjustment divides parolees into three groups: (1) those who require intensive surveillance, (2) those who require social services instead of surveillance, and (3) those who require limited supervision.

In some jurisdictions, parolees in need of closer surveillance are placed on **intensive supervision parole (ISP)**. These programs use limited caseload sizes, treatment facilities, the matching of parolee and supervisor by personality, and shock parole (which involves immediate short-term incarceration for parole violators to impress them with the seriousness of a violation). ISP clients are required to attend more office and home visits than routine parolees. ISP may also require frequent drug testing, a term in a community correctional center, and electronic monitoring in the home. More than 17,000 parolees are under intensive supervision, 1,400 of whom are monitored electronically by computer.

Evaluations of ISP programs have produced mixed results. Some show that they may actually produce a higher violation rate than traditional parole supervision because limiting caseload size allows parole officers to supervise their clients more closely and spot infractions more easily.[145] Some recent research shows that under some conditions a properly run ISP program can significantly reduce recidivism upon release. The key factors may be parole officer orientation (a balance between social service and law enforcement seems to work best) and a supportive organizational environment in which the program is being run.[146]

intensive supervision parole (ISP)
A form of parole characterized by smaller caseloads and closer surveillance; it may include frequent drug testing or, in some cases, electronic monitoring.

The Effectiveness of Parole

According to Joan Petersilia,

> Persons released from prison face a multitude of difficulties. They remain largely uneducated, unskilled, and usually without solid family support systems—to which are added the burdens of a prison record. Not surprisingly, most parolees fail, and rather quickly—rearrests are most common in the first six months after release.[147]

Despite all efforts to treat, correct, and rehabilitate incarcerated offenders, a majority still return to prison shortly after their release. A federal study of more than 270,000 prisoners released in 15 states in 1994 provides data that underscore the problem. Of the total number of releasees, 67.5 percent were re-arrested within three years of leaving prison for a felony or serious misdemeanor.[148] About 47 percent were reconvicted for a new crime and 25 percent resentenced to prison for a new crime. Within three years, about 52 percent were back in prison, serving time for a new prison sentence or for a technical violation of their release, such as failing a drug test, missing an appointment with their parole officer, or being arrested for a new crime. Who was most likely to fail on parole or other release mechanisms? Released prisoners with the highest re-arrest rates were robbers, burglars, larcenists, motor vehicle thieves, those in prison for possessing or selling stolen property, and those in prison for possessing, using, or selling illegal weapons. Ironically, those who might be considered the most dangerous criminals—murderers and rapists—had the lowest recidivism rates.

Who failed on parole, and who succeeded? Not surprisingly, characteristics of those who violate parole and return to prison include maintaining criminal peer associations, carrying weapons, abusing alcohol, and harboring aggressive feelings.[149] In contrast, those who are employed, have stable living arrangements, and are receiving some type of drug and/or alcohol program intervention are far less likely to fail on parole.[150]

The cost of recidivism is acute. The 272,111 offenders discharged in 1994 had accumulated 744,000 charges within three years of release. Put another way, about a quarter of a million U.S. citizens are victimized each year by people released on parole in just 15 states. Another federal survey of 156,000 parole violators serving time in the nation's prison system estimated that these offenders had committed at least 6,800 murders, 5,500 rapes, 8,800 assaults, and 22,500 robberies while under supervision in the community an average of 13 months.[151]

The Problems of Parole

Parole failure is still a significant problem, and a growing portion of the correctional population consists of parolees who failed on the outside. Why has the phenomenon of parole failure remained so stubborn and hard to control? One reason may be the nature of the prison experience itself. The psychological and economic problems that lead inmates to recidivism are rarely addressed by a stay in prison. Despite rehabilitation efforts, the typical ex-convict is still the same undereducated, unemployed, substance-abusing lower-class male he was when arrested. Being separated from friends and family, not sharing in conventional society, associating with dangerous people, and adapting to a volatile lifestyle probably have done little to improve offenders' personality or behavior. And when they return to society, it may be to the same destructive neighborhood and social groups that prompted their original law-violating behavior.

A significant portion of all inmates commit crimes while on parole. As a result, the problem of reentry back into society has become a critical issue for the justice system. While on parole after serving two years for burglary, robbery, and drug possession, Christopher DiMeo (right) is believed to have killed three jewelers during a robbery spree in New York and Connecticut. DiMeo was arrested without incident when he surrendered in an Atlantic City, New Jersey motel.

©AP Images/*The Press of Atlantic City*/Michael Ein

It seems naïve to think that incarceration alone can help someone overcome these lifelong disabilities. By their very nature, prisons seek to impose and maintain order and conformity instead of helping inmates develop such skills as independence and critical thinking, factors that may be essential once the inmate is forced to cope outside the prison's walls.[152]

Some private groups have attained funding to provide postrelease counseling and support. One promising Virginia program, Women Inspired to Transform (WIT), uses volunteers to teach female returnees about anger management, job interviewing, communication, relationships, and parenting.[153] Yet the large number of parolees strains the system of public and private providers and has made the problem of returning inmates a national issue. Crime experts believe that the large numbers of former inmates returning to their neighborhoods can destabilize areas and increase existing crime rates. This issue is further explored in the Analyzing Criminal Justice Issues feature.

Parole failure can also be tied to the releasee's own personal deficits. Most research efforts indicate that a long history of criminal behavior, an antisocial personality, and childhood experiences with family dysfunction are all correlated with postrelease recidivism.[154] Many releasees have suffered from a lifetime of substance abuse or dependence disorder.[155] A history of physical and sexual abuse has also been linked to recidivism.[156] Other parolees have substance abuse and mental health problems, and more than 10 percent exhibit both mental illness and substance abuse. One study of 400 Texas inmates found that almost 75 percent suffered from lifetime substance abuse or dependence disorder.[157]

SOCIAL AND ECONOMIC CONSEQUENCES The prison experience probably does little to improve offenders' personality or behavior. And when offenders return to society, it may be to the same destructive neighborhoods and social groups that they left for prison. Some ex-inmates may have to prove that the prison experience has not changed them: Taking drugs or being sexually aggressive may show friends that they have not lost their "heart."[158]

Ex-inmates may find their home life torn and disrupted. Wives of inmates report that they must face the shame and stigma of having an incarcerated spouse while withstanding a barrage of calls from jealous husbands on the inside who try to monitor their behavior and control their lives. Family visits to the inmate become traumatic and strain interpersonal relationships because they often involve strip searches and other invasions of privacy.[159] One study of youthful ex-offenders trying to make it on the outside found that many experience delayed emotional and cognitive development because of early drug use. Most have never learned to use problem-solving or coping skills outside of the correctional setting, and most remain drug dependent.[160] Sensitive to these problems, some states have instituted support groups designed to help inmates' families adjust to their loneliness and despair.[161]

Even if familial and spousal support is present, former inmates soon find that imprisonment reduces their income and employment opportunities.[162] By law, ex-convicts are denied the right to work in certain occupations. And even if a criminal record does not automatically prohibit employment, many employers are reluctant to hire people who have served time. Why would someone hire an ex-con when other applicants are available? Many find that it is difficult to get jobs because potential employers are unconvinced that reform is possible or doubt that former inmates have the people skills that will enable them to succeed in the workplace. Some business owners are concerned about customers' reactions if they know that an employee is an ex-inmate.[163] If ex-offenders lie about their prison experience and are later found out, they can be dismissed for misrepresentation. The stress of economic deprivation, in turn, can lead to family breakup and to less involvement with children.[164] Research shows that former inmates who gain and keep meaningful employment are more likely to succeed on parole than those who are unemployed or underemployed.[165]

When Prisoners Return–The Problems of Reentry

Because of America's two-decade-long imprisonment boom, more than 500,000 inmates are now being released back into the community each year. As criminologist Joan Petersilia warns, there are a number of unfortunate consequences to this release back into the community because many of those being released have not received adequate treatment and are unprepared for life in conventional society. The risks they present to the community include increases in child abuse, family violence, the spread of infectious diseases, homelessness, and community disorganization. Many have no way to cope and wind up in homeless shelters. A recent (2006) study of shelters in New York City found that 23 percent of the occupants had been released from New York prisons and jails in the past two years.

The increased reentry risks can be tied to legal changes in how people are released from prison. In the past, offenders were granted early release only if a parole board believed they were rehabilitated and had ties to the community—such as a family or a job. Inmates were encouraged to enter treatment programs to earn parole. Changes in sentencing laws have resulted in the growth of mandatory release and limits on discretionary parole. People now serve a fixed sentence, and the discretion of parole boards has been blunted. Inmates may be discouraged from seeking involvement in rehabilitation programs (they do not influence the chance of parole), and the lack of incentive means that fewer inmates leaving prison have participated in programs to address work, education, and substance use deficiencies. Nor does the situation improve upon release. Many inmates are not assigned to supervision caseloads once back in the community. About 200,000 released inmates go unsupervised each year, three-quarters of whom have been released after completing their maximum sentence and are therefore not obligated to be supervised.

Petersilia argues that most leave prison with no savings, no immediate entitlement to unemployment benefits, and few employment prospects. Upon release, some find that they are no longer welcome in subsidized public housing complexes due to the U.S. Department of Housing and Urban Development's "one strike and you're out" policy, where all members of the household are evicted if one member is involved in crime. A year after release, as many as 60 percent of former inmates are not employed in the regular labor market, and there is increasing reluctance among employers to hire ex-offenders. Ex-offenders are commonly barred from working in the fields in which most jobs are being created, such as child care, education, security, nursing, and home health care. More jobs are also now unionized, and many unions exclude ex-offenders.

Being barred from work opportunities produces chronic unemployment, a status closely related to drug and alcohol abuse. Losing a job can lead to substance abuse, which in turn is related to child and family violence. Mothers released from prison have difficulty finding services such as housing, employment, and child care, and this causes stress for them and their children. Children of incarcerated and released parents may suffer confusion, sadness, and social stigma, and these feelings often result in difficulties in school, low self-esteem, aggressive behavior, and general emotional dysfunction. If the parents are negative role models, children fail to develop positive attitudes about work and responsibility. Children of incarcerated parents are five times more likely to serve time in prison than are children whose parents are not incarcerated.

Prisoners have significantly more physical and mental health problems than the general population. More than three-fourths of the inmates leaving prison report a history of drug and/or alcohol abuse in the next year. Inmates with mental illness (about 16 percent of all inmates) are also increasingly being imprisoned—and then released. Even when public mental health services are available, many mentally ill individuals fail to use

The specter of recidivism is especially frustrating to the U.S. public. It is so difficult to apprehend and successfully prosecute criminal offenders that it seems foolish to grant them early release so they can prey on more victims. This problem is exacerbated when the parolee is a chronic, frequent offender. Research indicates that many of these returning prisoners are less prepared for reintegration and less connected to community-based social structures than in the past.[166] There seems to be a strong association between prior and future offending: The parolees most likely to fail on release are the ones who have failed in the past; chronic offenders are the ones most likely to reoffend. Because of these issues, some state jurisdictions are creating programs that ease the reentry process.

them because they fear institutionalization, deny they are mentally ill, or distrust the mental health system. The situation will become increasingly serious as more and more parolees are released back into the disorganized communities whose deteriorated conditions may have motivated their original crimes.

Fear of a prison stay has less of an effect on behavior than ever before. As the prison population grows, the negative impact of incarceration may be lessening. In neighborhoods where "doing time" is more the rule than the exception, it becomes less of a stigma and more of a badge of acceptance. However, it also becomes a way of life from which some ex-convicts do rebound. Teens may encounter older men who have gone to prison and have returned to begin their lives again. With the proper skills and survival techniques, prison is considered "manageable." Although a prison stay is still unpleasant, it has lost its aura of shame and fear. By becoming commonplace and mundane, the "myth" of the prison experience has been exposed and its deterrent power reduced.

The Effect on Communities

Parole expert Richard Seiter notes that when there were only a few hundred thousand prisoners, and a few thousand releasees per year, the issues surrounding the release of offenders did not overly challenge communities. Families could house ex-inmates, jobsearch organizations could find them jobs, and community social service agencies could respond to their individual needs for mental health or substance abuse treatment. Today, the sheer number of reentering inmates has taxed the communities to which they are returning. Charis Kubrin and Eric Stewart have found that communities that already face the greatest social and economic disadvantages are ones that produce the highest recidivism rates. Obviously, the influx of returning inmates can magnify their problems.

Research shows that high rates of prison admissions produce high crime rates. Clearly, the national policy of relying on prison as a deterrent to crime may produce results that policy makers had not expected or wanted.

Critical Thinking

1. All too often, government leaders jump on the incarceration bandwagon as a panacea for the nation's crime problem. Is it a "quick fix" whose long-term consequences may be devastating for the nation's cities, or are these problems counterbalanced by the crime-reducing effect of putting large numbers of high-rate offenders behind bars?

2. If you agree that incarceration undermines neighborhoods, can you think of some other, indirect ways that high incarceration rates help increase crime rates?

InfoTrac College Edition Research

Alternatives to prison are now being sought because high incarceration may undermine a community's viability. What do you think? For some interesting developments, check out these articles: Joe Loconte, "Making Criminals Pay: A New York County's Bold Experiment in Biblical Justice," *Policy Review* 87 (January–February 1998): 26; and Katarina Ivanko, "Shifting Gears to Rehabilitation," *Corrections Today* 59 (April 1997): 20.

Sources: Stephen Metraux and Dennis Culhane, "Recent Incarceration History Among a Sheltered Homeless Population," *Crime and Delinquency* 52 (2006): 504–17; Charis Kubrin and Eric Stewart, "Predicting Who Reoffends: The Neglected Role of Neighborhood Context in Recidivism Studies," *Criminology* 44 (2006): 165–97; Joan Petersilia, *When Prisoners Come Home: Parole and Prisoner Reentry* (New York: Oxford University Press, 2003); Joan Petersilia, "Hard Time Ex-Offenders Returning Home After Prison," *Corrections Today* 67 (2005): 66–72; Joan Petersilia, "When Prisoners Return to Communities: Political, Economic, and Social Consequences," *Federal Probation* 65 (2001): 3–9; Richard Seiter, "Prisoner Reentry and the Role of Parole Officers," *Federal Probation* 66 (2002).

LOSING RIGHTS One reason that ex-inmates find it so difficult to make it on the outside is the legal restrictions they are forced to endure.[167] These may include bars on certain kinds of employment, limits on obtaining licenses, and restrictions on their freedom of movement. Surveys have found that a significant number of states still restrict the activities of former felons.[168] Some of the more important findings are listed in Exhibit 16.2.

In general, states have placed greater restrictions on former felons, part of the get-tough movement. However, courts have considered individual requests by convicted felons to have their rights restored. It is common for courts to look at such issues as how recently the criminal offense took place and its relationship to the particular right before deciding whether to restore it.

EXHIBIT 16.2

Rights Lost by Convicted Felons

- ◆ Forty-seven jurisdictions restrict the right to vote; 38 of these allow for restoration.

- ◆ Forty-eight jurisdictions allow for termination of parental rights.

- ◆ Twenty-nine states consider a felony conviction to be legal grounds for divorce.

- ◆ Forty-seven states deny convicted felons the right to serve on juries; 37 allow restoration of the right.

- ◆ Forty jurisdictions prevent convicted felons from holding public office; 31 allow for restoration of the right.

- ◆ Federal law prevents ex-convicts from owning guns. Forty-four states employ additional legal measures to prevent felons from possessing firearms. Twelve states allow for restoration of the right.

- ◆ Forty-six states require that felons register with law enforcement agencies. This requirement is up sharply in recent years; in 1986, only eight states required felons to register. All states require criminal registration of sex offenders.

- ◆ Civil death, or the denial of all civil rights, is still practiced in two states.

Sources: Kevin Buckler and Lawrence Travis, "Reanalyzing the Prevalence and Social Context of Collateral Consequences Statutes," *Journal of Criminal Justice* 31 (2003): 435–53; Kathleen Olivares, Velmer Burton, and Francis Cullen, "The Collateral Consequences of a Felony Conviction: A National Study of State Legal Codes 10 Years Later," *Federal Probation* 60 (1996): 10–17.

ThomsonNOW Improve your grade on the exam with Personalized Study! For reinforcement resources and a mastery check of parole and life after prison, go to www.thomsonedu.com/thomsonnow.

A number of experts and national commissions have condemned the loss of rights of convicted offenders as a significant cause of recidivism. Consequently, courts have generally moved to eliminate the most restrictive elements of post-conviction restrictions.[169]

MAKING GOOD Although most inmates recidivate soon after they are released, some do not and somehow are able to turn their lives around. What helps them go straight when so many others fail? One reason may be tied to the social and economic support that inmates receive on the outside. Maintaining family ties and gaining steady employment may help. Parolees who had a good employment record before their incarceration and who are able to find jobs after their release are the ones most likely to avoid recidivating.[170]

Some inmates undergo a cognitive change while inside. When justice expert Shadd Maruna interviewed a group of serious criminals to understand how they were able to reform their lives, he found that going straight was a long process, not an instantaneous event.[171] Those who do well after prison have undergone a long-term cognitive change in which they begin to see themselves as a new person or have a new outlook on life. They begin to try to understand their past and develop insights into why they behaved the way they did and why and how things went wrong. Those who leave a life of crime begin to feel a sense of fulfillment in engaging in productive behaviors and in so doing become agents of their own change. They start feeling in control of their future and have a newfound purpose in life. Instead of running from the past, they view their prior history as a learning experience, finding a silver lining in an otherwise awful situation.

Maruna finds that ex-offenders who desist from crime almost always attribute their deviant pasts to environmental factors outside of their control.[172] Similarly, they believe that their radical change in lifestyle—from convict to conventional success story—stems from outside forces over which they have little control. Often, success is linked to some person or persons who, being forgiving and generous, can see past the ex-offender's mistakes. They give the ex-offender an opportunity to finally become his or her true self (a good productive person). This kindness does not go unappreciated. As a way of trying to give something back to the society from which they have taken so much, they make every effort to go straight, to become the man or woman their benefactor believed they could be.

ETHICAL CHALLENGES IN CRIMINAL JUSTICE: A WRITING ASSIGNMENT

Considering the reentry failure rate, some experts believe that early release from prison is bound to fail and to create greater opportunities for crime. The solution is to keep people in prison as long as possible through mandatory minimum sentencing and "truth in sentencing" policies. Comment on the failure of correctional treatment to make a dent in the recidivism rate. Come up with a "five-point plan" to ease reentry and reduce recidivism.

Doing Research on the Web

1. Read the following two articles from the Urban Institute's website: "Reentry and Prison Work Programs" and "Prisoner Reentry in Perspective."

2. To find out about government programs regarding reentry, read this section of the Office of Justice Programs website: "Learn About Reentry."

3. The state of Michigan offers reentry assistance and programming. Check out the "Michigan Prisoner Reentry Initiative."

4. Prison administrators are beginning to pay more attention to communications and other technologies that have been developed for correctional facilities. In some cases, technology has been used for security purposes; in others, it has been used to keep down costs. Check out Justnet: Justice Technology Information Network, which has abundant information on correctional technology.

You can access all of these sites by going to the Siegel/Senna Introduction to Criminal Justice 11e website: www.thomsonedu.com/criminaljustice/siegel.

SUMMARY

- On entering a prison, offenders must make tremendous adjustments to survive. Usual behavior patterns or lifestyles are radically changed. Opportunities for personal satisfaction are reduced. Passing through a number of adjustment stages or cycles, inmates learn to cope with the new environment.

- Inmates also learn to obey the inmate social code, which dictates proper behavior and attitudes. If inmates break the code, they may be unfavorably labeled.

- Inmates must learn how to deal with sexual and physical predators.

- Inmates are eligible for a large number of treatment devices designed to help them readjust to the community once they are released.

- A number of treatment programs have offered inmates individualized and group psychological counseling. Some make use of the therapeutic community idea.

- There are many educational programs at the high school and even college levels.

- There are vocational training programs. Work furloughs have also been used.

- Violence is common in prisons. Women often turn their hatred inward and hurt themselves, and male inmates engage in collective and individual violence against others. The Attica and New Mexico riots are examples of the most serious collective prison violence.

- In years past, society paid little attention to the incarcerated offender. The majority of inmates confined in jails and prisons were basically deprived of the rights guaranteed them under the Constitution.

- Today, however, the judicial system is actively involved in the administration of correctional institutions. Inmates can now take their grievances to courts and seek due process and equal protection under the law.

- The courts have recognized that persons confined in correctional institutions have rights—which include access to the courts and legal counsel, the exercise of religion, the rights to correspondence and visitation, and the right to adequate medical treatment.

◆ Most inmates return to society before the completion of their prison sentence. The majority earn early release through time off for good behavior or other sentence-reducing mechanisms.

◆ In addition, inmates are paroled before the completion of their maximum term.

◆ Most state jurisdictions maintain an independent parole board whose members decide whether to grant parole. Their decision making is discretionary and is based on many factors, such as the perception of the needs of society, the correctional system, and the client.

◆ Once paroled, the client is subject to control by parole officers who ensure that the conditions set by the board (the parole rules) are maintained. Parole can be revoked if the offender violates the rules of parole or commits a new crime.

◆ At one time most inmates were released on discretionary parole, but today changes in sentencing provisions have resulted in a significant increase in mandatory parole releases.

◆ Ex-inmates have a tough time adjusting on the outside, and the recidivism rate is disturbingly high. One reason is that many states restrict their rights and take away privileges granted to other citizens.

KEY TERMS

total institution, 526
inmate subculture, 529
inmate social code, 529
prisonization, 530
special-needs inmate, 536
conjugal visit, 538

work release (furlough), 540
inmate balance theory, 548
administrative control theory, 548
hands-off doctrine, 552
substantive right, 553
jailhouse lawyer, 553

cruel and unusual punishment, 555
parole, 557
mandatory parole release, 557
intensive supervision
 parole (ISP), 559

ThomsonNOW™ Maximize your study time by using ThomsonNOW's diagnostic study plan to help you review this chapter. The Study Plan will

◆ help you identify areas on which you should concentrate;

◆ provide interactive exercises to help you master the chapter concepts; and

◆ provide a post-test to confirm you are ready to move on to the next chapter.

CRITICAL THINKING QUESTIONS

1. What are the benefits and drawbacks of conjugal visits?

2. Should women be allowed to work as guards in male prisons? What about male guards in female prisons? Why or why not?

3. Should prison inmates be allowed a free college education while noncriminals are forced to pay tuition? Why or why not? Do you believe in less eligibility for prisoners? Explain.

4. Define parole, including its purposes and objectives. How does it differ from probation?

5. What is the role of the parole board?

6. Should a former prisoner have all the civil rights afforded the average citizen? Explain. Should people be further penalized after they have paid their debt to society? Why or why not?

NOTES

1. Darryl McGrath, "Brinks Case Decision: Ex-Militant's Parole Buoys Son, Angers Bereaved," *Boston Globe*, September 1, 2003, p. 1.

2. Ros Burnett and Shadd Maruna, "So 'Prison Works,' Does It? The Criminal Careers of 130 Men Released from Prison Under Home Secretary, Michael Howard," *Howard Journal of Criminal Justice* 43 (2004): 390–404.

3. Barbara Sims and Eric Johnston, "Examining Public Opinion About Crime and Justice: A Statewide Study" *Criminal Justice Policy Review* 15 (2004): 270–94.

4. Vanessa O'Connell, "Bans on Smoking in Prison Shrink a Coveted Market," *Wall Street Journal*, August 27, 2003, pp. A1–3.

5. Richard Berk, Heather Ladd, Heidi Graziano, and Jong-Ho Baek, "A Randomized Experiment Testing Inmate Classification Systems," *Criminology and Public Policy* 2 (2003): 215–42.

6. Gresham Sykes, *The Society of Captives: A Study of a Maximum Security Prison* (Princeton, N.J.: Princeton University Press, 1958).

7. Christopher Hensley, Mary Koscheski, and Richard Tewksbury, "Examining the Characteristics of Male Sexual Assault Targets in a Southern Maximum-Security Prison," *Journal of Interpersonal Violence* 20 (2005): 667–79.

8. David Eichenthal and James Jacobs, "Enforcing the Criminal Law in State Prisons," *Justice Quarterly* 8 (1991): 283–303.

9. John Wooldredge, "Inmate Lifestyles and Opportunities for Victimization," *Journal of Research in Crime and Delinquency* 35 (1998): 480–502.

10. David Anderson, *Crimes of Justice: Improving the Police, Courts, and Prison* (New York: Times Books, 1988).

11. Robert Johnson, *Hard Time: Understanding and Reforming the Prison* (Monterey, Calif.: Brooks/Cole, 1987), p. 115.

12. Wooldredge, "Inmate Lifestyles and Opportunities for Victimization."

13. Lawrence Hinman, "Stunning Morality: The Moral Dimensions of Stun Belts," *Criminal Justice Ethics* 17 (1998): 3–6.

14. Kevin Wright, *The Great American Crime Myth* (Westport, Conn.: Greenwood, 1985), p. 167.

15. Sandra Gleason, "Hustling: The Inside Economy of a Prison," *Federal Probation* 42 (1978): 32–39.

16. Hans Toch, *Living in Prison* (New York: Free Press, 1977), pp. 179–205.

17. Angela Maitland and Richard Sluder, "Victimization and Youthful Prison Inmates: An Empirical Analysis," *Prison Journal* 77 (1998): 55–74.

18. Seena Fazel and John Danesh, "Serious Mental Disorder in 23,000 Prisoners: A Systematic Review of 62 Surveys," *Lancet* 359 (2002): 545–61.

19. Leonore Simon, "Prison Behavior and Victim-Offender Relationships Among Violent Offenders," paper presented at the annual meeting of the American Society of Criminology, San Francisco, November 1991.

20. John Irwin, "Adaptation to Being Corrected: Corrections from the Convict's Perspective," in *Handbook of Criminology*, ed. Daniel Glazer (Chicago: Rand McNally, 1974), pp. 971–93.

21. Donald Clemmer, *The Prison Community* (New York: Holt, Rinehart, and Winston, 1958).

22. Gresham Sykes and Sheldon Messinger, "The Inmate Social Code," in *The Sociology of Punishment and Corrections*, ed. Norman Johnston et al. (New York: Wiley, 1970), pp. 401–08.

23. Gresham Sykes, *The Society of Captives*.

24. John Irwin and Donald Cressey, "Thieves, Convicts, and the Inmate Culture," *Social Problems* 10 (1962): 142–55.

25. Mark Kellar and Hsiao-Ming Wang, "Inmate Assaults in Texas County Jails," *Prison Journal* 85 (2005): 515–34; Brent Paterline and David Petersen, "Structural and Social Psychological Determinants of Prisonization," *Journal of Criminal Justice* 27 (1999): 427–41.

26. John DiIulio, *Governing Prisons: A Comparative Study of Correctional Management* (New York, Free Press, 1987).

27. B. Useem and M. Reisig, "Collective Action in Prisons: Protests, Disturbances, and Riots," *Criminology* 37 (1999): 735–59.

28. Beth Huebner, "Administrative Determinants of Inmate Violence: A Multilevel Analysis," *Journal of Criminal Justice* 31 (2003): 107–17.

29. Paterline and Petersen, "Structural and Social Psychological Determinants of Prisonization," 439.

30. James B. Jacobs, ed., *New Perspectives on Prisons and Imprisonment* (Ithaca, N.Y.: Cornell University Press, 1983).

31. Nicole Hahn Rafter, *Partial Justice* (New Brunswick, N.J.: Transaction, 1990), pp. 181–82.

32. Meda Chesney-Lind, "Patriarchy, Prisons, and Jails: A Critical Look at Trends in Women's Incarceration," paper presented at the International Feminist Conference on Women, Law, and Social Control, Mont Gabriel, Quebec, Canada, July 1991.

33. Meda Chesney-Lind, "Vengeful Equity: Sentencing Women to Prison," in *The Female Offender: Girls, Women, and Crime*, ed. Meda Chesney-Lind (Thousand Oaks, Calif.: Sage, 1997).

34. Elaine DeCostanzo and Helen Scholes, "Women Behind Bars, Their Numbers Increase," *Corrections Today* 50 (1988): 104–06.

35. This section synthesizes the findings of a number of surveys of female inmates, including DeCostanzo and Scholes, "Women Behind Bars"; Ruth Glick and Virginia Neto, *National Study of Women's Correctional Programs* (Washington, D.C.: Government Printing Office, 1977); Ann Goetting and Roy Michael Howsen, "Women in Prison: A Profile," *Prison Journal* 63 (1983): 27–46; Meda Chesney-Lind and Noelie Rodrigues, "Women Under Lock and Key: A View from Inside," *Prison Journal* 63 (1983): 47–65; Contact Inc., "Women Offenders," *Corrections Compendium* 7 (1982): 6–11.

36. Merry Morash, Robin Harr, and Lila Rucker, "A Comparison of Programming for Women and Men in U.S. Prisons in the 1980s," *Crime and Delinquency* 40 (1994): 197–221.

37. Pamela Schram, "Stereotypes About Vocational Programming for Female Inmates," *Prison Journal* 78 (1998): 244–71.

38. Morash, Harr, and Rucker, "A Comparison of Programming for Women and Men in U.S. Prisons in the 1980s."

39. Polly Radosh, "Reflections on Women's Crime and Mothers in Prison: A Peacemaking Approach," *Crime and Delinquency* 48 (2002): 300–16.

40. Rebecca Jackson, Richard Rogers, Craig Neuman, and Paul Lambert, "Psychopathy in Female Offenders: An Investigation of Its Underlying Dimensions," *Criminal Justice and Behavior* 29 (2002): 692–705.

41. Fazel and Danesh, "Serious Mental Disorder in 23,000 Prisoners."

42. Gary Michael McClelland, Linda Teplin, Karen Abram, and Naomi Jacobs, "HIV and AIDS Risk Behaviors Among Female Jail Detainees: Implications for Public Health Policy," *American Journal of Public Health* 92 (2002): 818–26.

43. Christine Grella and Lisa Greenwell, "Correlates of Parental Status and Attitudes Toward Parenting Among Substance-Abusing Women Offenders," *Prison Journal* 86 (2006): 89–113.

44. Lee Ann Slocum, Sally Simpson, and Douglas Smith, "Strained Lives and Crime: Examining Intra-individual Variation in Strain and Offending in a Sample of Incarcerated Women," *Criminology* 43 (2005): 1067–1110.

45. "Sex Abuse of Female Inmates Is Common, Rights Group Says," *Criminal Justice Newsletter*, December 16, 1996, p. 2.

46. General Accounting Office, *Women in Prison: Sexual Misconduct by Correctional Staff* (Washington, D.C.: Government Printing Office, 1999).

47. Chesney-Lind, "Vengeful Equity."

48. Candace Kruttschnitt and Sharon Krmpotich, "Aggressive Behavior Among Female Inmates: An Exploratory Study," *Justice Quarterly* 7 (1990): 370–89.

49. Candace Kruttschnitt, Rosemary Gartner, and Amy Miller, "Doing Her Own Time? Women's Responses to Prison in the Context of the Old and New Penology," *Criminology* 38 (2000): 681–718.

50. Shanhe Jiang and L. Thomas Winfree Jr., "Social Support, Gender, and Inmate Adjustment to Prison Life," *Prison Journal* 86 (2006): 32–55.

51. Edna Erez, "The Myth of the New Female Offender: Some Evidence from Attitudes Toward Law and Justice," *Journal of Criminal Justice* 16 (1988): 499–509.

52. Mark Pogrebin and Mary Dodge, "Women's Accounts of Their Prison Experiences: A Retrospective View of Their Subjective Realities," *Journal of Criminal Justice* 29 (2001): 531–41.

53. Robert Ross and Hugh McKay, *Self-Mutilation* (Lexington, Mass.: Lexington, 1979).

54. Alice Propper, *Prison Homosexuality* (Lexington, Mass.: Lexington, 1981).

55. Dianna Newbern, Donald Dansereau, and Urvashi Pitre, "Positive Effects on Life Skills Motivation and Self-Efficacy: Node-Link Maps in a Modified Therapeutic Community," *American Journal of Drug and Alcohol Abuse* 25 (1999): 407–10.

56. Charles Mcdaniel, Derek Davis, and Sabrina Neff, "Charitable Choice and Prison Ministries: Constitutional and Institutional Challenges to Rehabilitating the American Penal System," *Criminal Justice Policy Review* 16 (2005): 164–89.

57. Kate Dolan, James Shearer, Bethany White, Zhou Jialun, John Kaldor, and Alex Wodak, "Four-Year Follow-Up of Imprisoned Male Heroin Users and Methadone Treatment: Mortality, Reincarceration and Hepatitis C Infection," *Addiction* 100 (2005): 820–28.

58. Ira Sommers and Deborah Baskin, "The Prescription of Psychiatric Medication in Prison: Psychiatric Versus Labeling Perspectives," *Justice Quarterly* 7 (1990): 739–55.

59. Judy Anderson and R. Daniel McGehee, "South Carolina Strives to Treat Elderly and Disabled Offenders," *Corrections Today* 53 (1991): 124–27.

60. Paige M. Harrison and Allen Beck, *Prisoners in 2004* (Washington, D.C.: Bureau of Justice Statistics, 2005); Paige Harrison and Allen Beck, *Prison and Jail Inmates at Midyear 2005* (Washington, D.C.: Bureau of Justice Statistics, 2006).

61. Catherine Lemieux, Timothy Dyeson, and Brandi Castiglione, "Revisiting the Literature on Prisoners Who Are Older: Are We Wiser?" *Prison Journal* 82 (2002): 432–56.

62. Will Small, S. Kain, Nancy Laliberte, Martin Schechter, Michael O'shaughnessy, and Patricia Spittal, "Incarceration, Addiction and Harm Reduction: Inmates Experience Injecting Drugs in Prison," *Substance Use & Misuse* 40 (2005): 831–43.

63. Charles Sullivan, "Private Family Visits Are a Matter of Logic," *Corrections Today* 65 (2003): 18–19.

64. Caroline Wolf Harlow, *Education and Correctional Populations* (Washington, D.C.: Bureau of Justice Statistics, 2003).

65. Harlow, *Education and Correctional Populations*.

66. Howard Skolnik and John Slansky, "A First Step in Helping Inmates Get Good Jobs After Release," *Corrections Today* 53 (1991): 92.

67. This section leans heavily on Barbara Auerbach, George Sexton, Franklin Farrow, and Robert Lawson, *Work in American Prisons: The Private Sector Gets Involved* (Washington, D.C.: National Institute of Justice, 1988).

68. Public Law 96–157, Sec. 827, codified as 18 U.S.C., Sec. 1761(c).

69. Courtesy of the Prison Industry Authority, 560 East Natoma Street, Folsom, CA 95630–2200.

70. Diane Dwyer and Roger McNally, "Public Policy, Prison Industries, and Business: An Equitable Balance for the 1990s," *Federal Probation* 57 (1993): 30–35.

71. This section leans heavily on Mark Hamm, "Current Perspectives on the Prisoner Self-Help Movement," *Federal Probation* 52 (1988): 49–56.

72. For more information, contact the Fortune Society, 39 West 19th Street, New York, NY 10011, (212) 206–7070. The e-mail address is info@fortunesociety.org.

73. Douglas Lipton, Robert Martinson, and Judith Wilks, *The Effectiveness of Correctional Treatment: A Survey of Treatment Evaluation Studies* (New York: Praeger, 1975).

74. Charles Murray and Louis Cox, *Beyond Probation: Juvenile Corrections and the Chronic Delinquent* (Beverly Hills, Calif.: Sage, 1979).

75. Steven Lab and John Whitehead, "An Analysis of Juvenile Correctional Treatment," *Crime and Delinquency* 34 (1988): 60–83.

76. James Wilson and Robert Davis, "Good Intentions Meet Hard Realities: An Evaluation of the Project Greenlight Reentry Program," *Criminology & Public Policy* 5 (2006): 303–38.

77. Francis Cullen and Karen Gilbert, *Reaffirming Rehabilitation* (Cincinnati: Anderson, 1982).

78. Michael Caldwell, Michael Vitacco, and Gregory Van Rybroek, "Are Violent Delinquents Worth Treating? A Cost-Benefit Analysis," *Journal of Research in Crime and Delinquency* 43 (2006): 148–68.

79. David Wilson, Catherine Gallagher, and Doris MacKenzie, "A Meta-analysis of Corrections-Based Education, Vocation, and Work Programs for Adult Offenders," *Journal of Research in Crime and Delinquency* 37 (2000): 347–68.

80. Mary Ellen Batiuk, Paul Moke, and Pamela Wilcox Rountree, "Crime and Rehabilitation: Correctional Education as an Agent of Change—A Research Note," *Justice Quarterly* 14 (1997): 167–80.

81. David Wilson, Leana Bouffard, and Doris Mackenzie, "A Quantitative Review of Structured, Group-Oriented, Cognitive-Behavioral Programs for Offenders," *Criminal Justice and Behavior* 32 (2005): 172–204; Mark Lipsey and David Wilson, "Effective Intervention for Serious Juvenile Offenders: A Synthesis of Research," in *Serious and Violent Juvenile Offenders: Risk Factors and Successful Interventions*, eds. Rolf Loeber and David Farrington (Thousand Oaks, Calif.: Sage, 1998).

82. Megan Kurlychek and Cynthia Kempinen, "Beyond Boot Camp: The Impact of Aftercare on Offender Reentry," *Criminology & Public Policy* 5 (2006): 363–88.

83. David Farrington and Brandon Welsh, "Randomized Experiments in Criminology: What Have We Learned in the Last Two Decades?" *Journal of Experimental Criminology* 1 (2005): 9–38.

84. Lucien X. Lombardo, Guards Imprisoned (New York: Elsevier, 1981); James Jacobs and Norma Crotty, "The Guard's World," in *New Perspectives on Prisons and Imprisonment*, ed. James Jacobs (Ithaca, N.Y.: Cornell University Press, 1983), pp. 133–41.

85. "Correctional Officer Education and Training," *Corrections Compendium* 28 (2003): 11–13.

86. Claire Mayhew and Duncan Chappell, "An Overview of Occupational Violence," *Australian Nursing Journal* 9 (2002): 34–35.

87. John Klofas and Hans Toch, "The Guard Subculture Myth," *Journal of Research in Crime and Delinquency* 19 (1982): 238–54.

88. Ruth Triplett and Janet Mullings, "Work-Related Stress and Coping Among Correctional Officers: Implications from the Organizational Literature," *Journal of Criminal Justice* 24 (1996): 291–308.

89. Stephen Owen, "Occupational Stress Among Correctional Supervisors," *Prison Journal* 86 (2006): 164–81; Eugene Paoline, Eric Lambert, and Nancy Hogan, "A Calm and Happy Keeper of the Keys: The Impact of ACA Views, Relations with Coworkers, and Policy Views on the Job Stress and Job Satisfaction of Correctional Staff," *Prison Journal* 86 (2006): 182–205.

90. Peter Horne, "Female Correction Officers," *Federal Probation* 49 (1985): 46–55.

91. *Dothard v. Rawlinson*, 433 U.S. 321 (1977).

92. Dana Britton, *At Work in the Iron Cage: The Prison as Gendered Organization* (New York: New York University Press, 2003), Chapter 6.

93. Christopher D. Man and John P. Cronan, "Forecasting Sexual Abuse in Prison: The Prison Subculture of Masculinity as a Backdrop for 'Deliberate Indifference,'" *Journal of Criminal Law and Criminology* (2001): 127–66.

94. Christopher Hensley and Richard Tewksbury, "Wardens' Perceptions of Prison Sex," *Prison Journal* 85 (2005): 186–97.

95. Christopher Hensley, Mary Koscheski, and Richard Tewksbury, "Examining the Characteristics of Male Sexual Assault Targets in a Southern Maximum-Security Prison," *Journal of Interpersonal Violence* 20 (2005): 667–79.

96. Jesse Walker, "Rape Behind Bars," *Reason* 35 (2003): 10–12.

97. S. 1435[108]: Prison Rape Elimination Act of 2003; Public Law No. 108–79.

98. David Duffee, *Corrections, Practice, and Policy* (New York: Random House, 1989), p. 305.

99. Randy Martin and Sherwood Zimmerman, "A Typology of the Causes of Prison Riots and an Analytical Extension to the 1986 West Virginia Riot," *Justice Quarterly* 7 (1990): 711–37.

100. David Allender and Frank Marcell, "Career Criminals, Security Threat Groups, and Prison Gangs," *FBI Law Enforcement Bulletin* 72 (2003): 8–12.

101. Terri Compton and Mike Meacham, "Prison Gangs: Descriptions and Selected Intervention," *Forensic Examiner* 14 (2005): 26–31.

102. Grant Harris, Tracey Skilling, and Marnie Rice, "The Construct of Psychopathy," in Michael Tonry, ed., *Crime and Justice: An Annual Edition* (Chicago: University of Chicago Press, 2001), 197–265.

103. For a series of papers on the position, see A. Cohen, G. Cole, and R. Baily, eds., *Prison Violence* (Lexington, Mass.: Lexington, 1976).

104. Meredith Huey and Thomas McNulty, "Institutional Conditions and Prison Suicide: Conditional Effects of Deprivation and Overcrowding," *Prison Journal* 85 (2005): 490–514.

105. Scott Camp and Gerald Gaes, "Criminogenic Effects of the Prison Environment on Inmate Behavior: Some Experimental Evidence," *Crime & Delinquency* 51 (2005): 425–42.

106. Bert Useem and Michael Resig, "Collective Action in Prisons: Protests, Disturbances, and Riots," *Criminology* 37 (1999): 735–60.

107. National Advisory Commission on Criminal Justice Standards and Goals, *Corrections* (Washington, D.C.: Government Printing Office, 1973), p. 18.

108. *Cooper v. Pate*, 378 U.S. 546 (1964).

109. *DeMallory v. Cullen*, 855 F.2d 422 (7th Cir. 1988).

110. *Lindquist v. Idaho State Board of Corrections*, 776 F.2d 851 (9th Cir. 1985).

111. *Smith v. Wade*, 461 U.S. 30, 103 S.Ct. 1625 (1983).

112. *Bounds v. Smith*, 430 U.S. 817 (1977).

113. *Shaw v. Murphy*, 99–1613 (2001).

114. *Turner v. Safley*, 482 U.S. 78, 107 S.Ct. 2254 (1987) at 2261.

115. *Ramos v. Lamm*, 639 F.2d 559 (10th Cir. 1980).

116. *Procunier v. Martinez*, 411 U.S. 396 (1974).

117. *Nolan v. Fitzpatrick*, 451 F.2d 545 (1st Cir. 1971). See also *Washington Post Co. v. Kleindienst*, 494 F.2d 997 (D.C. Cir. 1974).

118. *Mumin v. Phelps*, 857 F.2d 1055 (5th Cir. 1988).

119. *O'Lone v. Estate of Shabazz*, 482 U.S. 342, 107 S.Ct. 2400 (1987).

120. *Rahman v. Stephenson*, 626 F.Supp. 886 (W.D. Tenn. 1986).

121. *Cutter v. Wilkinson*, 03–9877 (2005).

122. *Newman v. Alabama*, 92 S.Ct. 1079, 405 U.S. 319 (1972).

123. *Estelle v. Gamble*, 429 U.S. 97 (1976).

124. Ibid.

125. "Pennsylvania's State Prisons Changing Way They Treat Inmates," *Health and Medicine Week*, August 11, 2003, pp. 259–61.

126. *Trop v. Dulles*, 356 U.S. 86, 78 S.Ct. 590 (1958). See also *Furman v. Georgia*, 408 U.S. 238, 92 S.Ct. 2726, 33 L.Ed.2d 346 (1972).

127. *Weems v. United States*, 217 U.S. 349, 30 S.Ct. 544, 54 L.Ed. 793 (1910).

128. *Lee v. Tahash*, 352 F.2d 970 (8th Cir. 1965).

129. *Estelle v. Gamble*, 429 U.S. 97 (1976).

130. *Robinson v. California*, 370 U.S. 660 (1962).

131. *Gregg v. Georgia*, 428 U.S. 153 (1976).

132. *Jackson v. Bishop*, 404 F.2d 571 (8th Cir. 1968).

133. *Hope v. Pelzer et al.*, No. 01–309, June 27, 2002.

134. *Bell v. Wolfish*, 99 S.Ct. 1873–1974 (1979). See also "*Bell v. Wolfish*: The Rights of Pretrial Detainees," *New England Journal of Prison Law* 6 (1979): 134.

135. *Farmer v. Brennan*, 144 S.Ct. 1970 (1994).

136. *Rhodes v. Chapman*, 452 U.S. 337 (1981). For further analysis of *Rhodes*, see Randall Pooler, "Prison Overcrowding and the Eighth Amendment: The Rhodes Not Taken," *New England Journal on Criminal and Civil Confinement* 8 (1983): 1–28.

137. *Estelle v. Ruiz*, No. 74–329 (E.D. Texas 1980).

138. "Ruiz Case in Texas Winds Down: Special Master to Close Office," *Criminal Justice Newsletter*, January 15, 1990, p. 1.

139. Prison Litigation Reform Act of 1995, Pub. L. No. 104–134 (codified as amended in scattered titles and sections of the U.S.C.). See also H.R. 3019, 104th Cong., 2d sess. (1996).

140. *Prison Escape Survey* (Lincoln, Neb.: Corrections Compendium, 1991).

141. Kathryn Campbell and Myriam Denov, "The Burden of Innocence: Coping with a Wrongful Imprisonment," *Canadian Journal of Criminology and Criminal Justice* 46 (2004): 139–64.

142. Duncan N. Stevens, "Off the *Mapp*: Parole Revocation Hearings and the Fourth Amendment," *Journal of Criminal Law and Criminology* 89 (1999): 1047–60.

143. Gregg Etter and Judy Hammond, "Community Service Work as Part of Offender Rehabilitation," *Corrections Today* 63 (2001): 114–17.

144. Brian Parry, "Special Service Unit: Dedicated to Investigating and Apprehending Violent Offenders," *Corrections Today* 63 (2001): 120.

145. Thomas Hanlon, David N. Nurco, Richard W. Bateman, and Kevin E. O'Grady, "The Response of Drug Abuser Parolees to a Combination of Treatment and Intensive Supervision," *Prison Journal* 78 (1998): 31–44; Susan Turner and Joan Petersilia, "Focusing on High-Risk Parolees: An Experiment to Reduce Commitments to the Texas Department of Corrections," *Journal of Research in Crime and Delinquency* 29 (1992): 34–61.

146. Mario Paparozzi and Paul Gendreau, "An Intensive Supervision Program That Worked: Service Delivery, Professional Orientation, and Organizational Supportiveness," *Prison Journal* 85 (2005): 445–66.

147. Joan Petersilia, "When Prisoners Return to Communities: Political, Economic, and Social Consequences," *Federal Probation* 65 (2001): 3–9.

148. Patrick A. Langan and David J. Levin, *Recidivism of Prisoners Released in 1994* (Washington, D.C.: Bureau of Justice Statistics, 2002).

149. Brent Benda, "Gender Differences in Life-Course Theory of Recidivism: A Survival Analysis," *International Journal of Offender Therapy and Comparative Criminology* 49 (2005): 325–42.

150. Pamela Schram, Barbara Koons-Witt, Frank Williams, and Marilyn Mcshane, "Supervision Strategies and Approaches for Female Parolees: Examining the Link Between Unmet Needs and Parolee Outcome," *Crime and Delinquency* 52 (2006): 450–71.

151. Robyn L. Cohen, *Probation and Parole Violators in State Prison, 1991: Survey of State Prison Inmates, 1991* (Washington, D.C.: Bureau of Justice Statistics, 1995).

152. Stephen Duguid, *Can Prisons Work? The Prisoner as Object and Subject in Modern Corrections* (Toronto: University of Toronto Press, 2000).

153. Stacy Adams, "Richmond Program Helps Former Female Inmates," *Crisis* (113) 2006: 8.

154. James Bonta, Moira Law, and Karl Hanson, "The Prediction of Criminal and Violent Recidivism Among Mentally Disordered Offenders: A Meta-analysis," *Psychological Bulletin* 123 (1998): 123–42.

155. Roger Peters, Paul Greenbaum, John Edens, Chris Carter, and Madeline Ortiz, "Prevalence of DSM-IV Substance Abuse and Dependence Disorders Among Prison Inmates," *American Journal of Drug and Alcohol Abuse* 24 (1998): 573–80.

156. Catherine Hamilton, Louise Falshaw, and Kevin D. Browne, "The Link Between Recurrent Maltreatment and Offending Behavior," *International Journal of Offender Therapy and Comparative Criminology* 46 (2002): 75–95.

157. Peters, Greenbaum, Edens, Carter, and Ortiz, "Prevalence of DSM-IV Substance Abuse and Dependence Disorders Among Prison Inmates."

158. J. E. Ryan, "Who Gets Revoked? A Comparison of Intensive Supervision Successes and Failures in Vermont," *Crime and Delinquency* 43 (1997): 104–18.

159. Laura Fishman, *Women at the Wall: A Study of Prisoners' Wives Doing Time on the Outside* (New York: State University of New York Press, 1990).

160. Bonnie Todis, Michael Bullis, Miriam Waintrup, Robert Schultz, and Ryan D'ambrosio, "Overcoming the Odds: Qualitative Examination of Resilience Among Formerly Incarcerated Adolescents," *Exceptional Children* 68 (2001): 119–40.

161. Leslee Goodman Hornick, "Volunteer Program Helps Make Inmates' Families Feel Welcome," *Corrections Today* 53 (1991): 184–86.

162. Jeffrey Fagan and Richard Freeman, "Crime and Work," in *Crime and Justice: A Review of Research*, vol. 25, ed. Michael Tonry (Chicago: University of Chicago Press, 1999), pp. 211–29.

163. Rachelle Giguere and Lauren Dundes, "Help Wanted: A Survey of Employer Concerns About Hiring Ex-Convicts," *Criminal Justice Policy Review* 13 (2002): 396–408.

164. John Hagan and Ronit Dinovitzer, "Collateral Consequences of Imprisonment for Children, Communities, and Prisoners," in *Crime and Justice: A Review of Research*, vol. 26, ed. Michael Tonry and Joan Petersilia (Chicago: University of Chicago Press, 1999), pp. 89–107.

165. Hanlon, Nurco, Bateman, and O'Grady, "The Response of Drug Abuser Parolees to a Combination of Treatment and Intensive Supervision."

166. Jeremy Travis and Joan Petersilia, "Reentry Reconsidered: A New Look at an Old Question," *Crime and Delinquency* 47 (2001): 291–313.

167. Hanlon, Nurco, Bateman, and O'Grady, "The Response of Drug Abuser Parolees to a Combination of Treatment and Intensive Supervision."

168. Kevin Buckler and Lawrence Travis, "Reanalyzing the Prevalence and Social Context of Collateral Consequences Statutes," *Journal of Criminal Justice* 31 (2003): 435–53; Kathleen Olivares, Velmer Burton, and Francis Cullen, "The Collateral Consequences of a Felony Conviction: A National Study of State Legal Codes 10 Years Later," *Federal Probation* 60 (1996): 10–17.

169. See, for example, *Bush v. Reid*, 516 P.2d 1215 (Alaska, 1973); *Thompson v. Bond*, 421 F.Supp. 878 (W.D. Mo., 1976); *Delorne v. Pierce Freightlines Co.*, 353 F.Supp. 258 (D. Or., 1973); *Beyer v. Werner*, 299 F.Supp. 967 (E.D. N.Y., 1969).

170. Hanlon, Nurco, Bateman, and O'Grady, "The Response of Drug Abuser Parolees to a Combination of Treatment and Intensive Supervision."

171. Shadd Maruna, *Making Good: How Ex-Convicts Reform and Rebuild Their Lives* (Washington, D.C.: American Psychological Association, 2000).

172. Shadd Maruna, "Going Straight: Desistance from Crime and Self-Narratives of Reform," *Narrative Study of Lives* 5 (1997): 59–93.

PART FIVE

The History and Nature of the Juvenile Justice System

athaniel Abraham was 11 years old when he fired a shot from a .22-caliber rifle, fatally wounding Ronnie Lee Greene, Jr. As the trial began, Abraham's defense attorney told jurors that the shooting was a "very tragic, tragic accident" and that Abraham had the developmental abilities of a boy 6 to 8 years old at the time of the killing. He argued that Abraham was not capable of forming the intent to kill, as is required for a first-degree murder conviction. The prosecutor retorted that Abraham bragged to friends about the killing. Prosecutors also noted that Abraham had had 22 scrapes with police and that his mother had tried to have him ruled incorrigible in juvenile court.

After Abraham's conviction for murder, prosecutors sought a blended sentence of incarceration in a juvenile facility until age 21, followed by imprisonment in an adult facility. However, the sentencing judge ordered him to be held in juvenile detention until age 21, when he would be released. "While there is no guarantee Nathaniel will be rehabilitated at 21, it is clear 10 years is enough to accomplish this goal," said Judge Eugene Moore at the sentencing hearing. In August of 2006, Abraham, now 20 years old, entered a Michigan halfway house from which he will be transitioned back into society. ◆

THE ABRAHAM case, while extreme, is representative of the difficult choices that agents of the juvenile justice system are continually asked to make: How should troubled children be treated? What can be done to save dangerous young offenders? Should youthful law violators be given unique treatment because of their age, or should they be treated in a similar fashion to an adult committing the same crime? In this section, the juvenile justice system

The Juvenile Justice System

Chapter Objectives

After reading this chapter, you should be able to:

1. Understand why the juvenile justice system developed.
2. Discuss the differences between delinquents and status offenders.
3. Recognize the problems associated with the child-saving movement.
4. Describe the efforts to create the first juvenile court.
5. Know the similarities and differences between adult justice and juvenile justice.
6. Understand the legal rights of children.
7. Describe the various stages in the juvenile justice process.
8. Discuss the concept of deinstitutionalizaton.
9. Describe the various juvenile institutions.
10. Understand the argument for abolishing the juvenile court.

ee Boyd Malvo, the 17-year-old identified as one of the two snipers who went on a shooting spree in the Washington, D.C., area in October 2002, was an enigma to those who knew him. Some described him as "unremarkable" and others as "caring and very respectful." To his classmates at a Bellingham, Washington, high school, Malvo, a Jamaican native, seemed quiet and studious.[1] The prosecutor in the sniper case announced after Malvo's arrest that he would be tried as an adult and eligible for the death penalty. On October 28, 2006, Malvo confessed to still another murder—the 2002 Killing of Jerry Taylor on a golf course in Tucson, Arizona. ◆

On December 23, 2003, Malvo was spared capital punishment and sentenced instead to life in prison without the possibility of parole. Like the Nathaniel Abraham case, the Malvo case is indicative of the difficulties facing the juvenile justice system. Independent yet interrelated with the adult criminal justice system, the juvenile justice system is primarily responsible for dealing with juvenile and youth crime, as well as with incorrigible and truant children and runaways. First conceived at the turn of the twentieth century, the juvenile justice system was viewed as a quasi-social welfare agency that was to act as a surrogate parent in the interests of the child; this is referred to as the **parens patriae** philosophy. Today, some authorities still hold to the original social welfare principles of the juvenile justice system and argue that it is primarily a treatment agency that acts as a wise parent, dispensing personalized, individual justice to needy children who seek guidance and understanding. They recognize that many children who are arrested and petitioned to juvenile court come from the lowest economic classes. These at-risk children have grown up in troubled families, attend inadequate schools, and live in deteriorated neighborhoods. They are deserving of care and concern, not punishment and control.

> **parens patriae**
> The power of the state to act on behalf of a child and provide care and protection equivalent to that of a parent.

In contrast to this view, those with a crime control orientation suggest that the juvenile justice system's parens patriae philosophy is outdated. They point to nationally publicized incidents of juvenile violence, such as the D.C. sniper case and the shootings at Columbine High School in Colorado, as indicators that serious juvenile offenders should be punished and disciplined instead of treated and rehabilitated. They note that juveniles 17 years and under commit almost 10 percent of all murders in the United States.[2] Not surprisingly, they applaud when court rulings enhance the state's ability to identify and apprehend youthful law violators. For example, in 1995 the U.S. Supreme Court held in *Vernonia School District v. Acton* that a public school athlete in middle or high school can be required to submit to random drug testing even though the student did not engage in suspicious behavior.[3] On June 27, 2002, the Court, in *Board of Education of Independent School District No. 92 of Pottawatomie County et al. v. Earls et al.,* ruled permissible a school drug testing policy that established random, suspicionless urinalysis testing of any students participating in extracurricular competitive activities.[4] These and similar rulings encourage those who want the state to be given a free hand to deal with juveniles who are disruptive at school and in the community.

It remains to be seen whether the juvenile justice system will continue on its path toward identification and control or return to its former role of a treatment-dispensing agency. Some call for a new approach to the juvenile justice system, using the balanced and restorative justice model, which relies on offender–victim reconciliation, personal accountability, and community-based program developments.[5]

◆ THE HISTORY OF JUVENILE JUSTICE

The modern practice of legally separating adult and juvenile offenders can be traced to two developments in English custom and law: poor laws and chancery court. Both were designed to allow the state to take control of the lives of needy but not necessarily criminal children.[6] They set the precedent for later American developments.

> **poor laws**
> Seventeenth-century English laws under which vagrants and abandoned and neglected children were bound to masters as indentured servants.

As early as 1535, the English passed statutes known as **poor laws**, which in part mandated the appointment of overseers who placed destitute or neglected children with families who then trained them in agricultural, trade, or domestic services; this practice was referred to as *indenture*. The Elizabethan poor laws of 1601 created a system of church wardens and overseers who, with the consent of the justices of the peace, identified vagrant, delinquent, and neglected children and took measures to put them to work. Often this meant placing them in poorhouses or workhouses or, more commonly, apprenticing them until their adulthood. The indenture, or involuntary apprentice, system set the precedent, which continues today, of allowing the government to take control of youths who have committed no illegal acts but who are deemed unable to care for themselves.

In contrast, **chancery courts** were concerned primarily with protecting the property rights and welfare of more affluent minor children who could not care for themselves—children whose position and property were of direct concern to the monarch. They dealt with issues of guardianship and the use and control of property. Chancery courts operated under the parens patriae philosophy, which held that children were under the protective control of the state and that its rulers were justified in intervening in their lives.[7] In the famous English case *Wellesley v. Wellesley,* a duke's children were taken from him in the name of parens patriae because of his scandalous behavior.[8]

The concept of parens patriae came to represent the primacy of the state and its power to act in "the best interests of the child." The idea that the state was legally obligated to protect the immature, the incompetent, the neglected, and the delinquent subsequently became a major influence on the development of the U.S. juvenile justice system in the twentieth century.

Care of Children in Early America

The forced apprenticeship system and the poor laws were brought from England to colonial America. Poor laws were passed in Virginia in 1646 and in Connecticut and Massachusetts in 1678, and continued in place until the early nineteenth century. They mandated care for wayward and destitute children. However, those youths who committed serious criminal offenses were tried in the same courts as adults.

To accommodate dependent youths, local jurisdictions developed almshouses, poorhouses, and workhouses. Crowded and unhealthy, these accepted the poor, the insane, the diseased, and vagrant and destitute children. Middle-class civic leaders, who referred to themselves as **child savers**, began to develop organizations and groups to help alleviate the burdens of the poor and immigrants by sponsoring shelter care for youths, educational and social activities, and the development of settlement houses. In retrospect, their main focus seems to have been on extending governmental control over a whole range of youthful activities that previously had been left to private or family control, including idleness, drinking, vagrancy, and delinquency.[9]

The Child-Saving Movement

The child savers were responsible for creating a number of programs for indigent youths, including the New York House of Refuge, which began operations in 1825.[10] Its creation was effected by prominent Quakers and influential political leaders, such as Cadwallader Colden and Stephen Allen. In 1816 they formed the Society for the Prevention of Pauperism, which was devoted to the concept of protecting indigent youths who were at risk of leading a life of crime by taking them off the streets and reforming them in a family-like environment.[11]

The first House of Refuge constructed in New York City was the product of these reform efforts. Although the program was privately managed, the state legislature began providing funds partly through a head tax on arriving transatlantic passengers and seamen, plus the proceeds from license fees for New York City's taverns, theaters, and circuses. These revenue sources were deemed appropriate, given that supporters blamed immigration, intemperance, and commercial entertainment for juvenile crime.

The reformatory opened on January 1, 1825, with only six boys and three girls. However, within the first decade of its

chancery courts
English courts assigned with the protection of the property rights of minor children.

child savers
Civic leaders who focused their attention on the misdeeds of poor children to control their behavior.

Boys on the steps of an abandoned tenement building in New York City, 1889. The child savers were concerned that, if left alone, children such as these would enter a life of crime. Critics accused them of class and race discrimination and thought they sought to maintain control over the political system.

©The Granger Collection, New York

operation, 1,678 youths were admitted. Most were sent because of vagrancy and petty crimes and were sentenced or committed indefinitely until they reached adulthood. Originally, the institution accepted inmates from across the state, but when a Western House of Refuge was opened in Rochester, New York, in 1849, residents of the original reformatory came only from the eastern quarters.

Once a resident, a large part of the adolescent's daily schedule was devoted to supervised labor, which was regarded as beneficial to education and discipline. Inmate labor also supported operating expenses for the reformatory. Male inmates worked in shops that produced brushes, cane chairs, brass nails, and shoes. Female inmates sewed uniforms, did laundry, and carried out other domestic work. A badge system was used to segregate inmates according to their behavior. Although students received rudimentary educational skills, greater emphasis was placed on evangelical religious instruction; non-Protestant clergy were excluded. The reformatory had the authority to commit inmates to indenture agreements with private employers. Most males became farmworkers; most females became domestic laborers.

The Reform Movement Spreads

When the House of Refuge opened, the majority of children admitted were wayward youth placed there because of vagrancy or neglect. Children were put in the institution by court order, sometimes over parents' objections. Their length of stay depended on need, age, and skill. Critics complained that the institution was run like a prison, with strict discipline and absolute separation of the sexes. Such a harsh program drove many children to run away, and the House of Refuge was forced to take a more lenient approach. Despite criticism, the concept enjoyed expanding popularity. In 1826 the Boston City Council founded the House of Reformation for juvenile offenders.[12] The courts committed children found guilty of criminal violations, or found to be beyond the control of their parents, to these schools. Because the child savers considered parents of delinquent children to be as guilty as convicted offenders, they sought to have the reform schools establish control over the children. Refuge managers believed that they were preventing poverty and crime by separating destitute and delinquent children from their parents and placing them in an institution.[13]

The child savers also influenced state and local governments to create independent correctional institutions to house minors. The first of these reform schools opened in Westboro, Massachusetts, in 1848 and in Rochester, New York, in 1849. Other states soon followed suit—Ohio in 1850 and Maine, Michigan, and Rhode Island in 1860. Children lived in congregate conditions and spent their days working at institutional jobs, learning a trade when possible, and receiving some basic education. They were racially and sexually segregated, discipline was harsh and often involved whipping and isolation, and the physical care was of poor quality.

Children's Aid Society
A group created by Charles Loring Brace to place indigent city children with farm families.

In 1853 New York philanthropist Charles Loring Brace helped develop the **Children's Aid Society** as an alternative for dealing with neglected and delinquent youths. Brace proposed rescuing wayward youths from the harsh environment of the city and providing them with temporary shelter and care. He then sought to place them in private homes in rural communities where they could engage in farming and agricultural work outside the harsh influence of the city.

Although some placements proved successful, others resulted in the exploitation of children in a strange environment with few avenues of escape.

Establishment of the Juvenile Court

As the nation expanded, it became evident that private charities and public organizations were not caring adequately for the growing number of troubled youths. The child savers lobbied for an independent, state-supported juvenile court, and their efforts prompted the development of the first comprehensive juvenile court, in Illinois in 1899. The Illinois Juvenile Court Act set up an independent court to handle criminal law violations by children under 16 years of age, as well as to care for neglected, dependent, and wayward youths. The act also created a probation department to monitor youths in the community and to direct juvenile court judges to place serious offenders in secure schools for boys and industrial schools for girls. The ostensible purpose of the act was to separate juveniles from adult offenders and provide a legal framework in which juveniles could get adequate care and custody. By 1925, most states had developed juvenile courts. The enactment of the Juvenile Court Act of 1899 was a major event in the history of the juvenile justice movement in the United States.

Although the efforts of the child savers to set up independent juvenile courts were originally seen as liberal reforms, modern scholars commonly view them as attempts by members of the upper classes to control and punish those in the lower classes.[14] Thus, according to this revisionist approach, the reformers applied the concept of parens patriae for their own purposes, including the continuance of middle- and upper-class values, the control of the political system, and the furtherance of a child labor system consisting of lower-class workers with marginal skills.

The Development of Juvenile Justice

The juvenile court movement quickly spread across the United States. In its early form it provided youths with quasi-legal, quasi-therapeutic, personalized justice. The main concern was the "best interests of the child," not strict adherence to legal doctrine, constitutional rights, or due process of law. The court was paternalistic, not adversarial. For example, attorneys were not required. Hearsay evidence, inadmissible in criminal trials, was commonly employed in the adjudication of juvenile offenders. Children were encouraged to admit their guilt in open court in violation of their Fifth Amendment rights. Verdicts were based on a "preponderance of the evidence" instead of "beyond a reasonable doubt." Juvenile courts functioned as quasi–social service agencies.

REFORM SCHOOLS Youngsters found delinquent in juvenile court could spend years in a state training school. Although priding themselves as nonpunitive, these early reform schools were generally aimed at punishment and based on the concept of reform through hard work and discipline. In the second half of the nineteenth century, the emphasis shifted from massive industrial schools to the cottage system. Juvenile offenders were housed in a series of small cabins, each one holding 20 to 40 children, run by "cottage parents" who attempted to create a homelike atmosphere. The first cottage system was established in Massachusetts, the second in Ohio. The system was generally applauded for being a great improvement over the industrial training schools. The general movement was away from punishment and toward rehabilitation by attending to the needs of the individual and by implementing complex programs of diagnosis and treatment.[15] In the 1950s, the influence of such therapists as Karen Horney and Carl Rogers promoted the introduction of psychological treatment in juvenile corrections. Group counseling techniques became standard procedure in most institutions.

JUVENILE JUSTICE 1960–1980 In the 1960s and 1970s the U.S. Supreme Court radically altered the juvenile justice system when it issued a series of decisions that established the right of juveniles to receive due process of law.[16] The Court ruled that juveniles had the same rights as adults in important areas of trial process, including the right to confront witnesses, notice of charges, and the right to counsel. Figure 17.1 illustrates some of the most important legal cases bringing procedural due process to the juvenile justice process.

Also during this period Congress passed the Juvenile Justice and Delinquency Prevention Act of 1974 (JJDP Act), which established the federal Office of Juvenile Justice and Delinquency Prevention (OJJDP).[17] This legislation was enacted to identify the needs of youths and to fund programs in the juvenile justice

FIGURE 17.1
Supreme Court Cases That Have Shaped Procedures in the Juvenile Justice System

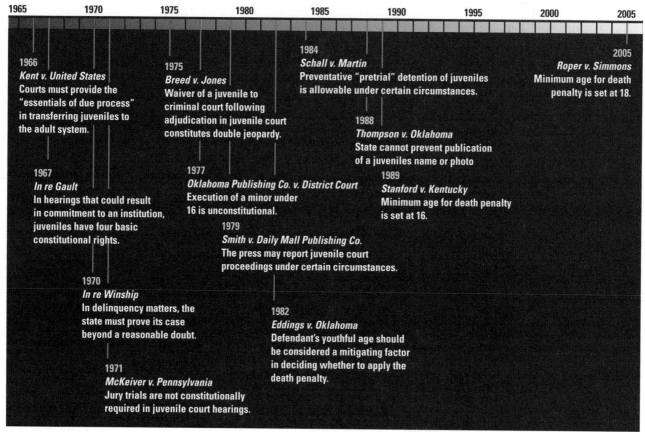

Source: Howard Snyder and Melissa Sickmund, *Juvenile Offenders and Victims: 2006 National Report* (Washington, D.C.: Office of Juvenile Justice and Delinquency Prevention, 2006), p. 101.

status offender
A noncriminal youth who falls under the jurisdiction of the juvenile court by reason of the fact he has engaged in behavior prohibited to minors, such as being truant from school, running away from home, and being habitually disobedient and ungovernable.

system. Some of the most important provisions of the act were to insulate juveniles from contact with more dangerous and/or older offenders. In practice, this meant that juveniles who were being held by the state for noncriminal actions such as cutting school or running away from home (referred to as **status offenders**) could not be detained in the same institutions with delinquent youth who had committed actual crimes. The *deinstitutionalization of status offenders and nonoffenders* provision of the JJDP act mandated that juveniles not charged with conduct that would be crimes for adults "shall not be placed in secure detention facilities or secure correctional facilities." In addition, delinquents were expected to be removed from facilities housing adults and, failing that, were prohibited from having any sight or sound contact with adult inmates in custody because they were awaiting trial on criminal charges or had been convicted of a crime. The sight and sound provision requires that juvenile and adult inmates cannot see one another and that no conversation among them is possible.

JUVENILE JUSTICE 1980–2000 During the last two decades of the twentieth century, public concern over juvenile crime helped reshape the philosophy of the juvenile justice system. The media picked up on stories of violent juvenile gangs, school shootings, and juvenile predators. Media frenzy helped fuel legislative change. States began to pass laws that made it easier to exclude from juvenile court jurisdiction juveniles who commit serious crimes such as violent acts or drug trafficking. Some states gave prosecutors greater discretion to prosecute cases directly in criminal court rather than juvenile court, and others passed laws making it easier to transfer juvenile offenders to the criminal justice system,

CONCEPT SUMMARY 17.1

Shifting Philosophies of Juvenile Justice

♦ Before 1899: Juveniles treated similarly to adult offenders. No distinction by age or capacity to commit criminal acts.

♦ 1899–1950s: Children treated differently, beginning with the Illinois Juvenile Court Act of 1899. By 1925, juvenile court acts established in virtually every state. Parens patriae philosophy dominates.

♦ 1950–1970: Recognition by experts that the rehabilitation model and the protective nature of parens patriae had failed to prevent delinquency.

♦ 1970–1980: Introduction of constitutional due process into the juvenile justice system. Experimentation with diversion and concern about stigma and labeling. Juvenile Justice and Delinquency Prevention Act of 1974 enacted.

♦ 1980–2000: Rising juvenile crime rates coupled with the perceived failure of rehabilitation to control delinquency lead to a shift to a crime control and punishment philosophy similar to that of the adult criminal justice system. Focus on expanding the crime control capabilities of the juvenile justice system so that it resembles the adult system.

♦ 2000–today: Balanced approach. Attempt to provide treatment to needy youths and get tough with dangerous repeat offenders. Restorative justice.

where they could be treated as adults. Many states increased sentencing length and severity for juvenile offenders. There was also an effort to make juvenile proceedings more open, an effort that included making juvenile records and court proceedings, historically kept confidential, more easily accessible to the public. The victims' rights movement invaded the juvenile court so that the victims of juvenile crime were now being heard during court proceedings. In sum, as a reaction to a rising tide of juvenile crime, the juvenile justice system was modified to look and act more like the adult system.[18]

The various stages in juvenile justice history are set out in Concept Summary 17.1.

♦ JUVENILE JUSTICE TODAY

Today, in most jurisdictions the juvenile justice system is attempting to reconcile its philosophical contradictions by adopting a more balanced vision: addressing the treatment needs of juveniles with the community's need for protection. There is much interest in restorative justice programming, a direction that seems particularly useful to younger offenders.

The contemporary juvenile court has jurisdiction over two distinct categories of offenders—delinquents and status offenders.[19] Juvenile delinquency refers to children who fall under a jurisdictional age limit, which varies from state to state, and who commit an act in violation of the penal code. Status offenders include noncriminal youths who fall under the jurisdiction of the juvenile court because they have engaged in behavior prohibited to minors, such as being truant from school, running away from home, and being habitually disobedient and ungovernable. They are commonly characterized in state statutes as persons or **children in need of supervision** (PINS or CHINS). Most states distinguish such behavior from delinquent conduct to lessen the effect of any stigma on children as a result of their involvement with the juvenile court. In addition, juvenile

The Office of Juvenile Justice and Delinquency Prevention (OJJDP) is an excellent resource for information on the juvenile justice system. To reach its website, go to the Siegel/Senna Introduction to Criminal Justice 11e website: www.thomsonedu.com/criminaljustice/siegel.

ThomsonNOW Improve your grade on the exam with Personalized Study! For reinforcement resources and a mastery check of the history of juvenile justice, go to www.thomsonedu.com/thomsonnow.

children in need of supervision (CHINS)
A legal term used in some states to designate juvenile status offenders.

CONCEPT SUMMARY 17.2

Similarities and Differences Between Juvenile and Adult Justice Systems

Similarities	Differences
♦ Discretion used by police officers, judges, and correctional personnel.	♦ The primary purpose of juvenile procedures is protection and treatment; with adults, the aim is to punish the guilty.
♦ Right to receive *Miranda* warning.	♦ Jurisdiction is determined by age in the juvenile system; by the nature of the offense in the adult system.
♦ Protection from prejudicial lineups or other identification procedures.	♦ Juveniles can be apprehended for acts that would not be criminal if committed by an adult (status offenses).
♦ Procedural safeguards when making an admission of guilt.	♦ Juvenile proceedings are not considered criminal; adult proceedings are.
♦ Advocacy roles of prosecutors and defense attorneys.	♦ Juvenile court proceedings are generally informal and private; adult court proceedings are more formal and are open to the public.
♦ Right to counsel at most key stages of the court process.	♦ Courts cannot release to the press identifying information about a juvenile, but they must release such information about an adult.
♦ Availability of pretrial motions.	♦ Parents are highly involved in the juvenile process but not in the adult process.
♦ Plea negotiation or plea bargaining.	♦ The standard of arrest is more stringent for adults than for juveniles.
♦ Right to a hearing and an appeal.	♦ Juveniles are released into parental custody; adults are generally given bail.
♦ Standard of proof beyond a reasonable doubt.	♦ Juveniles have no constitutional right to a jury trial; adults do. Some states extend this right to juveniles by statute.
♦ Pretrial detention possible.	♦ Juveniles can be searched in school without probable cause or a warrant.
♦ Detention without bail if defendant considered dangerous.	♦ A juvenile's record is generally sealed when the age of majority is reached; an adult's record is permanent.
♦ Determinate sentencing in some states.	♦ A juvenile court cannot sentence juveniles to county jails or state prisons, which are reserved for adults.
♦ Probation as a sentencing option.	♦ The U.S. Supreme Court has prohibited the execution of any person who committed his or her crime before the age of 18.
♦ Community treatment as a sentencing option.	

courts generally have jurisdiction over situations involving conduct directed at (rather than committed by) juveniles, such as parental neglect, deprivation, abandonment, and abuse.

The states have also set different maximum ages below which children fall under the jurisdiction of the juvenile court. Most states include all children under 17 years of age, but a few others set the age limit at 16 (Georgia, Michigan, and Illinois, for example) and 15 (Connecticut, New York, and North Carolina).

CONCEPT SUMMARY 17.3

Comparison of Terms Used in Adult and Juvenile Justice Systems

	Juvenile term	Adult term
The person and the act	Delinquent child	Criminal
	Delinquent act	Crime
Preadjudicatory stage	Take into custody	Arrest
	Petition	Indictment
	Agree to a finding	Plead guilty
	Deny the petition	Plead not guilty
	Adjustment	Plea bargain
	Detention facility	Jail
	Child care shelter	Jail
Adjudicatory stage	Substitution	Reduction of charges
	Fact-finding hearing	Trial
	Adjudication	Trial
Postadjudicatory stage	Dispositional hearing	Sentencing hearing
	Disposition	Sentence
	Commitment	Incarceration
	Training school	Prison
	Community resdential facility	Halfway house
	Aftercare	Parole

States may retain jurisdiction over minors until their disposition orders have been served, even if that means that they are in their twenties.

Because of the "get-tough" approach instituted in the 1990s, some states now exclude certain classes of offenders or offenses from the juvenile justice system. Youths who commit serious violent offenses such as rape or murder may be automatically excluded from the juvenile justice system and treated as adults on the premise that they stand little chance of rehabilitation within the confines of the juvenile system. Juvenile court judges may also transfer, or waive, repeat offenders whom they deem untreatable by the juvenile authorities.

The juvenile justice system has evolved into a parallel yet independent system of justice with its own terminology and rules of procedure. Concept Summary 17.2 describes the basic similarities and differences between the juvenile and adult justice systems, and Concept Summary 17.3 points out how the language used in the juvenile court differs from that used in the adult system.

The juvenile justice system is responsible for processing and treating almost two million cases of youthful misbehavior annually. Each state's system is unique, so it is difficult to give a precise accounting of the justice process. Moreover, depending on local practice and tradition, case processing often varies from community to community within a single state. Therefore, the following sections provide a general description of some of the key processes and decision points within juvenile justice. Figure 17.2 illustrates a model of the juvenile justice process.

FIGURE 17.2

FIGURE 17.2
The Stages of the Juvenile Justice System

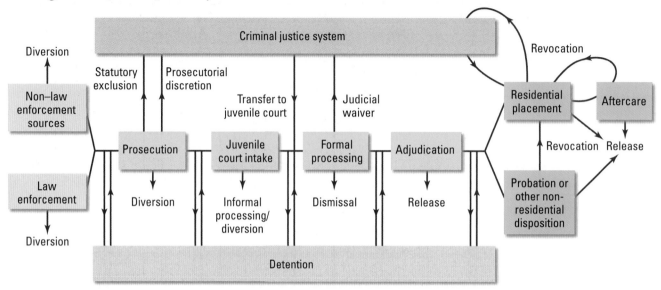

Source: Howard Snyder and Melissa Sickmund, *Juvenile Offenders and Victims: 2006 National Report* (Washington, D.C.: Office of Juvenile Justice and Delinquency Prevention, 2006), p. 105.

◆ POLICE PROCESSING OF THE JUVENILE OFFENDER

According to the Uniform Crime Reports, police officers arrest more than 1.6 million juveniles under age 18 each year, including about 500,000 under age 15; about 390,000 juveniles are arrested for serious and/or violent crimes. The number of juvenile arrests has been in decline (for example, more than 2 million youths were arrested in 1995, including 677,000 serious and/or violent crime arrests), an indication that—like the adult crime problem—juvenile delinquency has diminished during the past decade.[20]

Most larger police departments have separate juvenile detectives who handle delinquency cases and focus their attention on the problems of youth. In addition to conducting their own investigations, they typically take control of cases after an arrest is made by a uniformed officer.

Most states do not have specific statutory provisions distinguishing the arrest process for children from that for adults. However, some jurisdictions give broad arrest powers to the police in juvenile cases by authorizing the officer to make an arrest whenever it is believed that the child's behavior falls within the jurisdiction of the juvenile court. Consequently, police may arrest youths for behavior considered legal for adults, including running away, curfew violations, and being in possession of alcohol.

Use of Discretion

When a juvenile is found to have engaged in delinquent or incorrigible behavior, police agencies are charged with the decision to release or to detain the child and refer her to juvenile court. Because of the state's interest in the child, the police generally have more discretion in the investigatory and arrest stages of the juvenile process than they do when dealing with adult offenders.

This discretionary decision—to release or to detain—is based not only on the nature of the offense but also on police attitudes and the child's social and personal conditions at the time of the arrest. The following is a partial list of

TABLE 17.1
Police Handling of Arrested Juveniles

Population Group	Total	Handled Within Department and Released	Referred to Juvenile Court Jurisdiction	Referred to Welfare Agency	Referred to Other Police Agency	Referred to Criminal or Adult Court
Number	660,974	133,664	467,288	2,461	8,808	48,753
Percentage	100.0	20.2	70.7	0.4	1.3	7.4

Source: *Uniform Crime Reports, 2005* (Washington, D.C.: U.S. Government Printing Office, 2006), Table 68.

factors believed to be significant in police decision making regarding juvenile offenders:

♦ The type and seriousness of the child's offense.

♦ The ability of the parents to be of assistance in disciplining the child.

♦ The child's past contacts with police.

♦ The degree of cooperation obtained from the child and parents and the child's demeanor, attitude, and personal characteristics.

♦ Whether the child denies the allegations in the petition and insists on a court hearing.

Research indicates that most police decisions involve discretion.[21] Table 17.1 shows how police officers dispose of juveniles who are arrested. About 20 percent were handled informally by the police and released, whereas 70 percent were petitioned to the juvenile court. Although about 2 percent were sent to some other agency, either police or welfare, 7 percent were sent to the prosecutor's office for processing in adult court. Clearly, how police perceive the qualities of the case affects its final outcome.[22]

Legal Rights

Once a juvenile has been taken into custody, the child has the same Fourth Amendment right to be free from unreasonable searches and seizures as an adult does. Children in police custody can be detained prior to trial, interrogated, and placed in lineups. However, because of their youth and inexperience, children are generally afforded more protections than adults. Police must be careful that the juvenile suspect understands his constitutional rights and, if there is some question, must provide access to a parent or guardian to protect the child's legal interests. In the past, police often questioned juveniles in the absence of their parents or an attorney. Any incriminatory statements or confessions made by juveniles could be placed in evidence at their trials. That is no longer permissible, and children have the same (or more) *Miranda* rights as adults, a right that was confirmed in the case of *Fare v. Michael C.* (1979).[23] Today, police will interrogate a juvenile without an adult present only if they believe that the youth is unquestionably mature and experienced enough to understand her legal rights.

To read more about a police juvenile division, go to the website of the Pasadena, Texas, Police Department, which you can access by going to the Siegel/Senna Introduction to Criminal Justice 11e website: www.thomsonedu.com/criminaljustice/siegel.

Police in Schools

Because a great deal of juvenile crime occurs on school grounds, police departments have been stationing officers within schools. These police officers are generally referred to as school resource officers (SROs). The increased presence of law enforcement officers within schools raises the question of the legal rights of students within the educational environment. The issue of student privacy relates not only to police but also to school officials, who often assume quasi-police powers over children. Both police officers and school officials may wish to search students to determine whether they are in possession of contraband, such as drugs or weapons; search their lockers and desks; and question them about illegal activities.

In *New Jersey v. T.L.O.* (1985), the U.S. Supreme Court held that a school official had the authority to search a student's purse even though no warrant was issued and no probable cause existed that a crime had been committed, only a suspicion that T.L.O. had violated school rules.[24] This case involved an assistant principal's search of the purse of a 14-year-old female student who had been observed smoking a cigarette in a school lavatory. The assistant principal found cigarette-rolling papers when a pack of cigarettes was removed from the purse. A further search revealed marijuana and several items indicating marijuana selling. As a result, T.L.O. was adjudicated as a delinquent. The Supreme Court held that the Fourth Amendment protections against unreasonable searches and seizures apply to students but that the need to maintain an orderly educational environment modified the usual Fourth Amendment requirements of warrants and probable cause. The Court relaxed the usual probable cause standard and found the search to be reasonable. It declared that the school's right to maintain discipline on school grounds allowed it to search students and their possessions as a safety precaution. The Court, which had guarded the warrant requirement and its exceptions in the past, now permitted warrantless searches in school, based on the lesser standard of "reasonable suspicion." This landmark decision did not deal with other thorny issues, however, such as the search and seizure of contraband from a student's locker or desk.

SEARCHING FOR DRUGS Faced with crime by students in public schools, particularly illicit drug use, school administrators have gone to extreme measures to enforce drug control statutes and administrative rules. Some urban schools are using breathalyzers, drug-sniffing dogs, hidden video cameras, and routine searches of students' pockets, purses, lockers, and cars. In general, courts consider such searches permissible when they are not overly offensive and when reasonable grounds are found to suspect that the student may have violated the law. School administrators are walking a tightrope between a student's constitutional right to privacy and school safety.

In 1995 the U.S. Supreme Court held in *Vernonia v. Acton* that public school athletes in middle and high school may be required to submit to random drug testing without violating their Fourth Amendment rights. James Acton, a seventh-grader, was kept off a football team because his parents refused to sign a urinalysis consent form. The Supreme Court held that such testing is constitutional even though the student does not engage in suspicious behavior.[25]

In 2002, the parents of Lindsey Earls sued school officials in Tecumseh, Oklahoma, challenging their policy of drug testing all high school students who participate in extracurricular activities. Lindsey was forced to provide a urine sample before she sang in the high school choir and participated on an academic scholarship team. In *Board of Education of Pottawatomie County v. Earls*, the Court upheld the school's drug testing policy. It found that even though "urination is an excretory function traditionally shielded by great privacy," the method the school used was sufficient to protect the student's dignity (a faculty monitor "waits outside the closed restroom stall for the student to produce a sample and must listen for the normal sounds of urination in order to guard against tampered specimens and to insure an accurate chain of custody"). The ruling suggested that the need to reduce student drug use was sufficiently compelling to warrant this minor invasion of a student's privacy.[26]

◆ **THE JUVENILE COURT PROCESS**

After the police have determined that a case warrants further attention, they will bind it over to the prosecutor's office, which then has the responsibility for channeling the case through the juvenile court. The juvenile court plays a major role in controlling juvenile behavior and delivering social services to children in need.

One of the best sources of information on juveniles and the law is the National Center for Youth Law (NJDA). Visit its website by linking through the Siegel/Senna Introduction to Criminal Justice 11e website: www.thomsonedu.com/criminaljustice/siegel.

ThomsonNOW™ Improve your grade on the exam with Personalized Study! For reinforcement resources and a mastery check of police processing of the juvenile offender, go to www.thomsonedu.com/thomsonnow.

A great number of cases are settled during the intake process—without the need for a juvenile court hearing. Katherine Lester is led away from the Tuscola County courthouse by her father, Terry, after her preliminary hearing on June 29, 2006, in Caro, Michigan. The 17-year-old flew to the Middle East without her parents' knowledge to meet a man she met through the Internet. Lester, prosecutors, and her parents reached an agreement in court that she would not be charged as a runaway.

The Intake Process

After police processing, the juvenile offender is typically remanded to the local juvenile court's **intake** division. Court intake officers, probation personnel, or both review and screen the child and the family to determine if the child needs to be handled formally or whether the case can be settled without the necessity of costly and intrusive official intervention. Their report helps the prosecutor decide whether to handle the case informally or bind it over for trial. The intake stage represents an opportunity to place a child in informal programs both within the court and in the community. The intake process is also critically important because more than half of the referrals to the juvenile courts never go beyond this stage.

intake
The process by which a probation officer reviews cases at the initial court appearance, before the onset of formal criminal proceedings: the screening.

The Detention Process

After a juvenile is formally taken into custody, either as a delinquent or as a status offender, the prosecutor usually makes a decision to release the child to the parent or guardian or to detain the child in a secure shelter pending trial.

Detention has always been a controversial area of juvenile justice. Far too many children have been routinely placed in detention while awaiting court appearances. Status offenders and delinquents have been held in the same facility, and in many parts of the country, adult county jails have been used to detain juvenile offenders. The JJDP Act of 1974 emphasized reducing the number of children placed in inappropriate detention facilities, yet the practice continues, albeit less frequently. As a result, detention is used less today than it has been in the past for most crimes except property offenses (see Figure 17.3).

detention
Temporary care of a child alleged to be a delinquent or status offender who requires secure custody pending court disposition.

LEGAL ISSUES Most state statutes ordinarily require a hearing on the appropriateness of detention if the initial decision is to keep the child in custody. At this hearing, the child has a right to counsel and may be given other procedural due process safeguards, notably the privilege against self-incrimination and the right

FIGURE 17.3

Detention Rate Trends by Crime Type

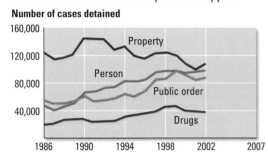

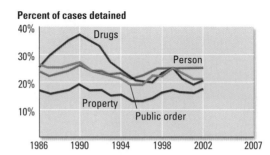

Source: Howard Snyder and Melissa Sickmund, *Juvenile Offenders and Victims: 2006 National Report* (Washington, D.C.: Office of Juvenile Justice and Delinquency Prevention, 2006), p. 168.

to confront and cross-examine witnesses. Most state juvenile court acts provide criteria to support a decision to detain the child. These include the need to protect the child, whether the child presents a serious danger to the public, and the likelihood that the juvenile will return to court for adjudication. Whereas in adult cases the sole criterion for pretrial release may be the offender's availability for trial, juveniles may be detained for other reasons, including their own protection. Normally, the finding of the judge that the child should be detained must be supported by factual evidence. In the 1984 case of *Schall v. Martin*, the U.S. Supreme Court upheld the right of the states to detain a child before trial to protect his welfare and the public safety.[27]

REFORMING DETENTION   An ongoing effort has been made to reform detention. The most important reform has been to remove status offenders from lockups containing delinquents. After decades of effort, almost all states have passed laws requiring that status offenders be placed in nonsecure shelters, not secure detention facilities, thereby reducing their contact with more dangerous delinquent youths.

Another serious problem is the detention of youths in adult jails. The practice is common in rural areas where relatively few separate facilities are available for young offenders.[28] The OJJDP has given millions of dollars in aid to encourage the removal of juveniles from adult lockups. These grants have helped jurisdictions develop intake screening procedures, specific release or detention criteria, and alternative residential and nonresidential programs for juveniles awaiting trial. By 1980, amendments to the act mandating the absolute removal of juveniles from jails had been adopted. Despite such efforts, many states are not complying with the removal provisions, and thousands of youths are annually detained in adult jails. Whatever the actual number jailed today, placing young offenders in adult jails continues to be a significant problem in the juvenile justice system. Juveniles detained in adult jails often live in squalid conditions and are subject to physical and sexual abuse. The practice is widely condemned, but eliminating the confinement of juveniles in adult institutions remains a difficult task.[29] Many youths who commit nonserious acts are still being held in adult jails—for example, runaways who are apprehended in rural areas. Minority juveniles may be spending greater amounts of time in jail than white offenders for the same offense.[30] This is troubling, but the fact that a smaller percentage of juvenile cases now involve detention indicates that reforms may be working.

With offices based at Eastern Kentucky University and at Michigan State University, the National Juvenile Detention Association (NJDA) exists exclusively to advance the science, processes, and art of juvenile detention services through the overall improvement of the juvenile justice profession. Check it out by linking through the Siegel/Senna Introduction to Criminal Justice 11e website: www.thomsonedu.com/criminaljustice/siegel.

Bail

If a child is not detained, the question of bail arises. Federal courts have not found it necessary to rule on the issue of a juvenile's constitutional right to bail because liberal statutory release provisions act as appropriate alternatives. Although only a few state statutes allow release on money bail, many others have juvenile code provisions that emphasize the release of the child to the parents as an acceptable substitute. A constitutional right to bail that on its face seems to benefit a child may have unforeseen results. For example, money bail might impose a serious economic strain on the child's family while conflicting with the protective and social concerns of the juvenile court. Considerations of economic liabilities and other procedural inequities have influenced the majority of courts confronting this question to hold that juveniles do not have a right to bail.

Plea Bargaining

Before trial, juvenile prosecutors may attempt to negotiate a settlement to the case. For example, if the offender admits to the facts of the petition, she may be offered a placement in a special community-based treatment program in lieu of a term in a secure facility. Or a status offense petition may be substituted for one of delinquency so that the adolescent can avoid being housed in a state training school and instead be placed in a more treatment-oriented facility.

If a bargain can be reached, the child will be asked to admit in open court that he did in fact commit the act of which he stands accused. State juvenile courts tend to minimize the stigma associated with the use of adult criminal standards by using other terminology, such as "agree to a finding" or "accept the petition" instead of "admit guilt." When the child makes an admission, juvenile courts require the following procedural safeguards: The child knows of the right to a trial, the plea or admission is made voluntarily, and the child understands the charges and consequences of the plea.

Waiver of Jurisdiction

Prior to the development of the first modern juvenile court, in Illinois in 1899, juveniles were tried for violations of the law in adult criminal courts. The consequences were devastating. Many children were treated as criminal offenders and often sentenced to adult prisons. Although the subsequent passage of state legislation creating juvenile courts eliminated this problem, the juvenile justice system did recognize that certain forms of conduct require that children be tried as adults. Today, most jurisdictions provide by statute for **waiver**, or transfer, of juvenile offenders to the criminal courts. The decision of whether to waive a juvenile to the adult, or criminal, court is made in a transfer hearing.

The **transfer** of a juvenile to the criminal court is often based on statutory criteria established by the state's juvenile court act, so waiver provisions vary considerably among jurisdictions. Most commonly considered are the child's age and the nature of the offense alleged in the petition. Some jurisdictions require that the child be older than a certain age (typically, 14) before he or she can be waived. Some mandate that the youth be charged with a felony before being tried as an adult, whereas others permit waiver of jurisdiction to the criminal court regardless of the seriousness of the offense (for example, when a child is a petty albeit chronic offender).

waiver
The transfer of a juvenile offender to criminal court for prosecution as an adult.

transfer
The process of sending a case from the juvenile court to an adult court.

LEGAL CONTROLS Because of the nature of the waiver decision and its effect on the child in terms of status and disposition, the U.S. Supreme Court has imposed procedural protections for juveniles in the waiver process. In *Kent v. United States* (1966), the Court held that the waiver proceeding is a critically important stage in the juvenile justice process and that juveniles must be afforded minimum requirements of due process of law at such proceedings, including the right to legal counsel.[31] Then, in *Breed v. Jones* (1975), the Court held that the prosecution of juveniles as adults in the California Superior Court violated the double jeopardy clause of the Fifth Amendment if they previously had been tried on the same charge in juvenile court.[32] The Court concluded that jeopardy attaches when the juvenile court begins to hear evidence at the adjudicatory hearing; this requires that the waiver hearing take place prior to any adjudication.

FIGURE 17.4

Waiver Rates and Trends

Cases judicially waived to criminal court

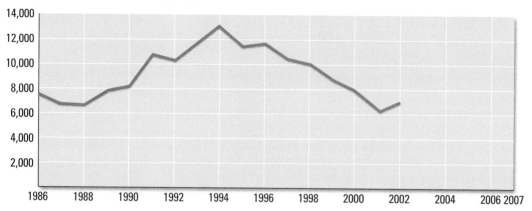

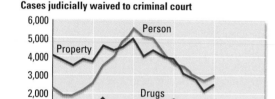

Cases judicially waived to criminal court

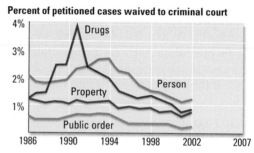

Percent of petitioned cases waived to criminal court

Source: Howard Snyder and Melissa Sickmund, *Juvenile Offenders and Victims: 2006 National Report* (Washington, D.C.: Office of Juvenile Justice and Delinquency Prevention, 2006), p. 186.

YOUTHS IN ADULT COURTS All states allow juveniles to be tried as adults in criminal courts in one of four ways:

1. *Concurrent jurisdiction.* The prosecutor has the discretion of filing charges for certain offenses in either juvenile or criminal court.

2. *Excluded offenses.* State laws exclude from juvenile court jurisdiction certain offenses that are either very minor, such as traffic or fishing violations, or very serious, such as murder or rape.

3. *Judicial waiver.* After a formal hearing at which both prosecutor and defense attorney present evidence, a juvenile court judge may decide to waive jurisdiction and transfer the case to criminal court. This procedure is also known as binding over or certifying juvenile cases to criminal court.

4. *Reverse waiver.* State laws mandate that certain offenses be tried in adult court. However, a judge may decide that a case should be tried in juvenile court.

Nearly every state has provisions for handling juveniles in adult criminal courts, and the trend is to make the waiver broader.[33] In more than 30 states, once a juvenile is tried in adult court, she is no longer eligible for juvenile justice on any subsequent offense. To get tough on juvenile crime, these efforts have limited the judge's ability to consider the individual circumstances that apply in each case.

As Figure 17.4 shows, the use of waiver has declined significantly during the past 15 years. This trend probably reflects the influence of a declining crime rate coupled with the ability of the juvenile justice system to handle more serious cases.

SHOULD THE WAIVER PROCESS BE MAINTAINED? Although the percentage of waived cases may be in decline, the problem of youths processed in adult courts is still a serious one. What is accomplished by treating juveniles like adults? There are experts who support waiver and those who are opposed to it.

Against Waiver Some experts criticize waiver because in the final tally, juveniles whose cases are waived to criminal court are sentenced more leniently than they would have been in juvenile court. This outcome contradicts the purpose of waiver. In many states, even when juveniles are tried in criminal court and convicted on the charges, they may still be sentenced to a juvenile or youthful offender institution instead of an adult prison. Some studies show that only a small percentage of juveniles tried as adults are incarcerated for periods longer than the terms served by offenders convicted of the same crime in the juvenile court. Others have found that waived juveniles serve more time behind bars.[34] Waived youth spend more time in juvenile detention awaiting trial. In the end, what began as a get-tough measure has had the opposite effect, while costing taxpayers more money.[35]

Transfer decisions are not always carried out fairly or equitably, and evidence suggests that minorities are waived at a rate that is greater than their representation in the population.[36]

Some critics view waiver as inefficient, ineffective, and philosophically out of step with the original concept of the juvenile court. They believe that youths transferred to the criminal system are more likely to commit new offenses, especially if they have spent time in jail or prison. They also reoffend more quickly and more frequently. Furthermore, no evidence exists that youths who are transferred are more mature or responsible than others their age or less amenable to treatment.[37] Exacerbating this problem is that a significant portion of younger teens are mentally incompetent to stand trial, if the same criteria are employed with adults who are mentally ill.[38]

Little in the way of national policy has been offered on how to treat juveniles once they are waived or provide them with treatment different from the adult offender. Their position is summed up in this statement by Shay Bilchick, director of the Child Welfare League of America:

> [T]oo many communities are failing to determine which offenders are beyond the reach of the juvenile justice system and failing to provide programs to hold those youths accountable in a timely manner, for the duration and intensity needed. As we increasingly transfer juveniles blindly, we are failing both our youths and our communities. We deserve better.[39]

For Waiver Supporters view the waiver process as a sound method of getting the most serious juvenile offenders off the streets while ensuring that rehabilitation plays a less critical role in the juvenile justice system. They point to data showing that minors are involved in serious violent crimes and that society must be protected from predatory youths. When the juvenile justice system was first formulated early in the twentieth century, it was aimed at treating petty offenders and not the gun-toting super-predators of the twenty-first century.

Youths are most likely to be transferred to criminal court if they have injured someone with a weapon or if they have a long juvenile court record.[40] Also, even if transferred, juveniles are typically not placed in an adult facility until they are at least 18. Until then, they are detained in juvenile facilities or special institutions for younger offenders. Their position is aptly summed up by this statement made by U.S. representative Lamar Smith of Texas:

> It is common sense public policy when states pass laws that allow or require violent juveniles to be transferred to adult courts. I strongly believe that we can no longer tolerate young people who commit violent crimes simply because of their age. Young people have the ability to decide between right and wrong, as the vast majority do every day.
>
> But those youths who choose to prey on other juveniles, senior citizens, merchants or homeowners will be held responsible. If that choice results in confinement in an adult prison system, perhaps youths who have a propensity to commit violent crimes will think twice before acting.[41]

The Trial

There are typically two judicial hearings in the juvenile court process. The first, usually called an **initial appearance**, is similar to the arraignment in the adult system. The child is informed of the charges against him, attorneys are appointed, bail is reviewed, and in many instances cases are settled with an admission of the facts, followed by a community sentence. If the case cannot be settled at this initial stage, it is bound over for trial.

During the **adjudication** or trial process, often called the **fact-finding hearing** in juvenile proceedings, the court hears evidence on the allegations stated in the delinquency petition. In its early development, the juvenile court did not emphasize judicial rule making similar to that of the criminal trial process. Absent were such basic requirements as the standard of proof, rules of evidence, and similar adjudicatory formalities. Proceedings were to be nonadversarial, informal, and noncriminal. However, the juvenile trial process was the target of criticism because judges were handing out punishments to children without affording them legal rights. This changed in 1967 when the U.S. Supreme Court's landmark *In re Gault* decision radically altered the juvenile justice system.[42]

The *Gault* decision completely altered the juvenile trial process. Instead of dealing with children in a benign and paternalistic fashion, the courts were forced to process juvenile offenders within the framework of appropriate constitutional procedures. And though *Gault* was technically limited to the adjudicatory stage, it has spurred further legal reform throughout the juvenile system. Today, the right to counsel, the privilege against self-incrimination, the right to treatment in detention and correctional facilities, and other constitutional protections are applied at all stages of the juvenile process, from investigation through adjudication to parole. *Gault* ushered in an era of legal rights for juveniles.

After *Gault*, the Supreme Court continued its trend toward legalizing and formalizing the juvenile trial process with the decision in *In re Winship* (1970), which held that a finding of delinquency in a juvenile case must be made with the same level of evidence used in an adult case: beyond a reasonable doubt.[43]

Although the informality of the traditional juvenile trial court was severely altered by *Gault* and *Winship*, the trend of increased rights for juveniles was somewhat curtailed when the Supreme Court held in *McKeiver v. Pennsylvania* (1971) that children do not have the same right to a jury trial as an adult.[44] The Court reasoned that juries were not an essential element of justice and, if used in juvenile cases, would end confidentiality.

Once an adjudicatory hearing has been completed, the court is normally required to enter a judgment against the child. This may take the form of declaring the child delinquent or a ward of the court or possibly even suspending judgment to avoid the stigma of a juvenile record. Following the entering of a judgment, the court can begin its determination of possible dispositions for the child.

In all, about 1.6 million cases are adjudicated in juvenile courts each year. As Figure 17.5 shows, there was a rapid expansion of juvenile court caseloads between 1960 and the mid-1990s, a development that followed crime rate increases. Now that the crime rate has leveled off, so has the number of youths entering the juvenile justice system.

There has also been a movement to create alternatives to the traditional juvenile court adjudication process. One approach has been the development of teen courts to supplement the traditional juvenile court process. These use peer juries and prosecutors to try minor cases and create appropriate community sentences. In 2006, there were over 1,100 youth court programs in operation in 49 states and the District of Columbia.

Disposition and Treatment

At the **dispositional hearing**, the juvenile court judge imposes a sentence on the juvenile offender based on her offense, prior record, and family background.

---

initial appearance
The first hearing in juvenile court.

adjudication
The juvenile court hearing at which the juvenile is declared a delinquent or status offender, or no finding of fact is made.

fact-finding hearing
The trial in the juvenile justice system.

You can access the transcript of the *In re Gault* case by going to the Siegel/Senna Introduction to Criminal Justice 11e website: www.thomsonedu.com/criminaljustice/siegel.

One group that has struggled to upgrade the juvenile court system is the National Council of Juvenile and Family Court Judges (NCJFCJ). Check out this important organization, which you can learn about by linking through the Siegel/Senna Introduction to Criminal Justice 11e website: www.thomsonedu.com/criminaljustice/siegel.

You can access the transcript of the *McKeiver v. Pennsylvania* case by going to the Siegel/Senna Introduction to Criminal Justice 11e website: www.thomsonedu.com/criminaljustice/siegel.

---

dispositional hearing
A court hearing to determine the appropriate treatment for a youth found to be a delinquent.

FIGURE 17.5

Trends in Juvenile Court Caseloads

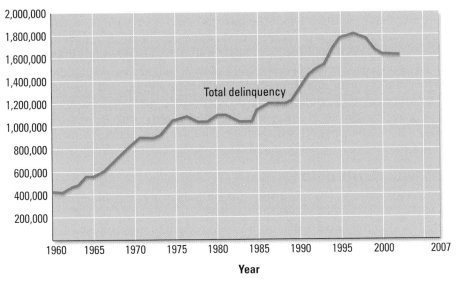

Number of cases

Total delinquency

Year

Source: Howard Snyder and Melissa Sickmund, *Juvenile Offenders and Victims*: *2006 National Report*
(Washington, D.C.: Office of Juvenile Justice and Delinquency Prevention, 2006), p. 158.

Participants are sworn in at Onslow County's Teen Court annual training session in Jacksonville, North Carolina. Teen Court offers an alternative system of justice, where first-time juvenile offenders have an opportunity to take responsibility for their offenses through community-based sentencing options. To participate, they must admit to their involvement in the forbidden/ illegal act.

Normally, the judge has broad discretionary power to issue a range of dispositions from dismissal to institutional commitment. In theory, the dispositional decision is an effort by the court to serve the best interests of the child, the family, and the community. In many respects, this postadjudicative process is the most important stage in the juvenile court system because it represents the last opportunity for the court to influence the child and control her behavior.

To ensure that only relevant and appropriate evidence is considered by the court during trial, most jurisdictions require a separate hearing to consider the disposition. The bifurcated hearing process ensures that the adjudicatory hearing is used solely to determine the merits of the allegations, whereas the dispositional hearing determines whether the child is in need of rehabilitation.

In theory, the juvenile court seeks to provide a disposition that represents an individualized treatment plan for the child. This decision is normally based on the presentence investigation of the probation department, reports from social agencies, and possibly a psychiatric evaluation. The judge generally has broad discretion in dispositional matters but is limited by the provisions of the state's juvenile court act. Typical juvenile court dispositions are suspended judgment, probation, placement in a community treatment program, and commitment to the state agency responsible for juvenile institutional care.

In addition, the court may place the child with parents or relatives, make dispositional arrangements with private youth-serving agencies, or order the child committed to a mental institution.

Juvenile Sentencing

Over the past decade, juvenile justice experts and the general public have become aroused about the serious juvenile crime rate in general and about violent acts committed by children in particular. As a result, some law enforcement officials and conservative legislators have demanded that the juvenile justice system take a more serious stand with dangerous juvenile offenders. In the past two decades, many state legislatures have responded by toughening their juvenile codes. Some jurisdictions have passed mandatory or determinate incarceration sentences for juveniles convicted of serious felonies. The get-tough approach even called for the use of the death penalty for minors transferred to the adult system.[45] Over the years, however, numerous commentators have called for the abolition of the death penalty for minors, arguing that it is a sad misuse of the principles that govern the legal system, and in the 2005 case *Roper v. Simmons*, the U.S. Supreme Court ruled that no one could be executed for a crime committed before he or she was 18 years old.[46]

However, many jurisdictions have not abandoned rehabilitation as a primary dispositional goal and still hold to the philosophy that placements should be based on the least-detrimental alternative. This view requires that judges employ the least-intrusive measures possible to safeguard a child's growth and development.[47]

A second reform has been the concerted effort to remove status offenders from the juvenile justice system and restrict their entry into institutional programs.

Juvenile sentencing is a critical element of the juvenile justice process. Jeffrey Lee Parson (right) walks out of a U.S. federal courthouse in Seattle, Washington, with his lawyers, Carol Koller (left) and Nancy Tenney, following his sentencing in the Blaster Internet worm case. A federal judge took pity on the Minnesota teen, sentencing him to just a year and a half for unleashing a variant of the Blaster Internet worm that crippled more than 48,000 computers.

Because of the development of numerous diversion programs, many children who are involved in truancy and incorrigible behavior and who ordinarily would have been sent to a closed institution are now being placed in community programs. There are far fewer status offenders in detention or institutions than ever before.

A third reform effort has been to standardize dispositions in juvenile court. As early as 1977, Washington passed one of the first determinate sentencing laws for juvenile offenders. It uses a guideline format similar in structure to the one used in Minnesota for adult offenders (discussed in Chapter 13).[48] All children found to be delinquent are evaluated on a point system based on their age, prior juvenile record, and type of crime committed. Minor offenders are handled in the community. Those committing more serious offenses are placed on probation. Children who commit the most serious offenses are subject to standardized institutional penalties. As a result, juvenile offenders who commit such crimes as rape or armed robbery are being sentenced to institutionalization for two, three, and four years. This approach is different from the indeterminate sentencing under which children who had committed a serious crime might be released from institutions in less than a year if correctional authorities believe that they have been rehabilitated.

ThomsonNOW Improve your grade on the exam with Personalized Study! For reinforcement resources and a mastery check of the juvenile court process, go to www.thomsonedu. com/thomsonnow.

◆ THE JUVENILE CORRECTIONAL PROCESS

After disposition in juvenile court, delinquent offenders may be placed in some form of correctional treatment. Although many are placed in the community, more than 100,000 are now in secure facilities.

Probation

Probation is the most commonly used formal sentence for juvenile offenders, and many states require that a youth fail on probation before being sent to an institution (unless the criminal act is serious). Probation involves placing the child under the supervision of the juvenile probation department for the purpose of community treatment. Conditions of probation are normally imposed on the child by either statute or court order. There are general conditions, such as those that require the child to stay away from other delinquents or to obey the law. More specific conditions of probation include requiring the child to participate in a vocational training program, to attend school regularly, to obtain treatment at a child guidance clinic, or to make restitution. Restitution can be in the form of community service—for example, a youth found in possession of marijuana might be required to work 50 hours in a home for the elderly. Monetary restitution requires delinquents to pay back the victims of their crimes. Restitution programs have proven successful and have been adopted around the country.[49]

Juvenile probation is a major component of the juvenile justice system. Juvenile courts place more than 80 percent of adjudicated delinquents on some form of probation. It is the most widely used method of community treatment. The cost savings of community treatment, coupled with its nonpunitive intentions, are likely to keep probation programs growing.

Institutionalization

The most severe of the statutory dispositions available to the juvenile court involves commitment of the child to an institution. The committed child may be sent to a state training school or private residential treatment facility. These are usually minimum-security facilities with small populations and an emphasis on treatment and education. As Table 17.2 indicates, there are almost 3,000 juvenile facilities in the United States holding slightly more than 100,000 youths in custody. Most are public institutions that are administered by state or county authorities. There are also more than 1,700 privately run facilities that hold more than 30,000 youths.

TABLE 17.2
Juvenile Facilities

	Facilities		Juvenile Offenders	
	Number	Percentage	Number	Percentage
Total	2,964	100	102,388	100
Public	1,182	40	70,243	69
State	513	17	41,138	40
Local	669	23	29,105	28
Private	1,773	60	31,992	31

Note: The total includes 9 tribal facilities holding 153 juvenile offenders.
Source: Melissa Sickmund, *Juvenile Residential Facility Census, 2002* (Washington, D.C.: Office of Juvenile Justice and Delinquency Prevention, 2006).

FIGURE 17.6
Trends in Juvenile Institutionalization

Offenders in juvenile facilities

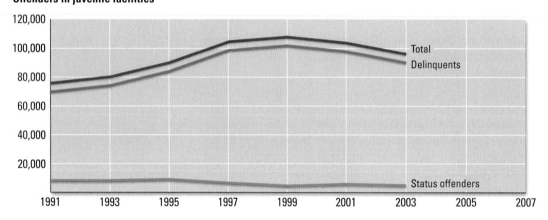

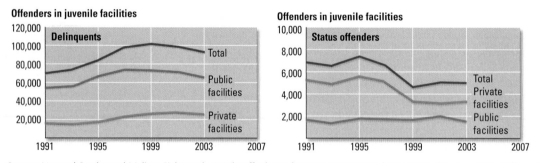

Source: Howard Snyder and Melissa Sickmund, *Juvenile Offenders and Victims: 2006 National Report* (Washington, D.C.: Office of Juvenile Justice and Delinquency Prevention, 2006), p. 199.

As Figure 17.6 shows, the number of incarcerated juveniles peaked in the mid-1990s and has trended downward ever since, a development that most likely reflects the recent drop in both juvenile crime and juvenile arrests.

Most state statutes vary when determining the length of the child's commitment. Jurisdictions usually have the ability to commit youths up to their majority age, which can range from 15 to 17. Once a juvenile has been committed by a court, there is a great deal of difference in the way that the states determine the

FIGURE 17.7
Custody Rates per 100,000 Juveniles

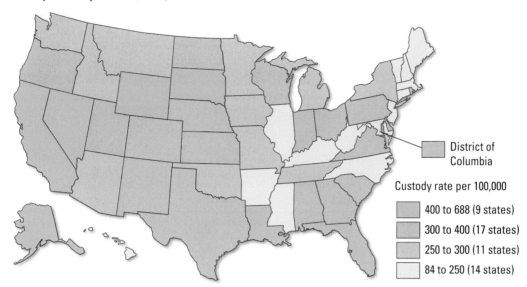

District of
Columbia

Custody rate per 100,000

400 to 688 (9 states)

300 to 400 (17 states)

250 to 300 (11 states)

84 to 250 (14 states)

Source: Melissa Sickmund, *Juvenile Residential Facility Census, 2000* (Washington, D.C.: Office of Juvenile Justice and Delinquency Prevention, 2006), p. 201.

juvenile's placement, length of stay, and eventual release. In some states, the agency that runs the state's juvenile correctional facilities determines the place of confinement, the level of security, treatment methods, the length of stay, and conditions of release. In other states, the juvenile court judge may make some or all of these decisions. Some states allow judges to pass down definite periods of confinement similar to a determinate sentence in adult court, whereas others use purely indeterminate sentences in which the juvenile is released when the correctional agency believes he is rehabilitated. In some states, the juvenile court judge makes or at least reviews the release decision, and in other states a juvenile parole board operates independently of the court and the secure correctional system.[50] As a result of these varying procedures and practices, the per capita juvenile institutionalization rate varies widely. As Figure 17.7 shows, some state have custody rates of over 600 children per 100,000, and others have as low as 84. Across the United States, about 326 juveniles are institutionalized per 100,000 population.[51]

The typical resident of a juvenile facility is a 15-to-16-year-old white male incarcerated for an average stay of five months in a public facility or six months in a private facility. Private facilities tend to house younger youths, while public institutions provide custodial care for older youths, including a small percentage of youths between 18 and 21 years of age. Most incarcerated youths are person, property, or drug offenders.

MINORITIES IN JUVENILE INSTITUTIONS Minority youths are incarcerated at a rate two to five times that of white youths.[52] Research has found that this overrepresentation is not a result of differentials in arrest rates but often stems from disparity at early stages of case processing.[53] Minority youths accused of delinquent acts are less likely than white youths to be diverted from the court system into informal sanctions and are more likely to receive sentences involving incarceration.

As Table 17.3 shows, although more than half the juvenile institutional population is made up of minority youths, decreases in the minority institutional

The Council of Juvenile Correctional Administrators (CJCA) is dedicated to the improvement of juvenile correctional services and practices. You can visit its website by linking through the Siegel/Senna Introduction to Criminal Justice 11e website: www.thomsonedu.com/criminaljustice/siegel.

TABLE 17.3
Juvenile Offenders in Custody

Race/Ethnicity	Number	Percentage	Percentage Change 1997–2003
Total	96,655	100	–8
White	37,347	39	–5
Minority	59,308	61	–10
Black	36,740	38	–12
Hispanic	18,422	19	–5
Native American	1,771	2	10
Asian	1,462	2	–34
Other/mixed	913	1	62

Note: The total may not equal 100% because of rounding.
Source: Howard Snyder and Melissa Sickmund, *Juvenile Offenders and Victims: 2006 National Report* (Washington, D.C.: Office of Juvenile Justice and Delinquency Prevention, 2006).

population have actually outstripped the reduction in the white resident population. For example, during this period the number of black youths in juvenile facilities declined 10 percent, compared to a 5-percent reduction in the white population. However, the disproportionate confinement of minority youth remains a topic of national concern, and although these recent findings are encouraging, a great deal of work is still ahead.

Deinstitutionalization

Some experts in delinquency and juvenile law question the policy of institutionalizing juvenile offenders. Many believe that large institutions are too costly to operate and only produce more sophisticated criminals. This dilemma has produced a number of efforts to remove youths from juvenile facilities and replace large institutions with smaller, community-based facilities. In a reform effort, Massachusetts closed all its state training schools more than 20 years ago (subsequently, however, public pressure caused a few secure facilities to be reopened). Many other states have established small residential facilities operated by juvenile care agencies to replace larger units.

Despite the daily rhetoric about crime control, public support for community-based programs for juveniles still exists. Although such programs are not panaceas, many experts still recommend more treatment and less incarceration for juvenile offenders. Some states, including Maryland, Pennsylvania, Utah, and Vermont have dramatically reduced their reform school populations while setting up a wide range of intensive treatment programs for juveniles. Many large, impersonal, and expensive state institutions with unqualified staff and ineffective treatment programs have been eliminated.

STATUS OFFENDERS An ongoing effort has been made for almost 30 years to deinstitutionalize status offenders (DSO).[54] This means removing noncriminal youths from institutions housing delinquents to prevent them from interacting with violent or chronic offenders.

Since its inception, the DSO approach has been hotly debated. Some have argued that early intervention is society's best hope of forestalling future delinquent behavior and reducing victimization. Other experts maintain that legal control over status offenders is a violation of youths' rights. Still others have viewed status-offending behavior as a symptom of some larger trauma or problem that requires attention. These diverse opinions still exist today.

Since Congress passed the JJDP Act in 1974, all 50 states have complied with some aspect of the deinstitutionalization mandate. Millions of federal, state, and local dollars have been spent on the DSO movement. Vast numbers of programs have been created around the country to reduce the number of juveniles in secure confinement. However, what remains to be done is to study the effect that DSO has had on juveniles and the justice system.

Aftercare

Aftercare marks the final stage of the formal juvenile justice process. Its purpose is to help youths make the transition from residential or institutional settings back into the community. Effective aftercare programs provide adequate supervision and support services to help juvenile offenders avoid criminal activity. Examples of programs include electronic monitoring, counseling, treatment and community service referrals, education, work training, and intensive parole supervision.

Most juvenile aftercare involves parole. A juvenile parole officer provides the child with counseling, school referral, vocational training, and other services. Children who violate the conditions of parole may have their parole revoked and be returned to the institution. Unlike the adult postconviction process, where the U.S. Supreme Court has imposed procedural protections during probation and parole revocations, juveniles do not have such due process rights. State courts have also been reluctant to grant juveniles rights in this area, and those that have generally refuse to require that the whole array of rights be made available as they are to adult offenders. Since the *Gault* decision, however, many states have adopted administrative regulations requiring juvenile agencies to incorporate due process, such as proper notice of the hearing and the right to counsel in postconviction proceedings.

ThomsonNOW Improve your grade on the exam with Personalized Study! For reinforcement resources and a mastery check of the juvenile correctional process, go to www. thomsonedu.com/thomsonnow.

◆ PREVENTING DELINQUENCY

Although the juvenile justice system has been concerned with controlling delinquent behavior, important efforts are being made to prevent delinquency before it occurs. **Delinquency prevention** refers to intervening in a young person's life prior to him or her engaging in delinquency in the first place. In the past, delinquency prevention was the responsibility of treatment-oriented agencies such as the YMCA (Young Men's Christian Association), Boys and Girls Clubs of America, and other private and public agencies. Today, many community-based treatment programs involve a combination of juvenile justice and treatment agencies. Much of this effort is conducted by social workers whose specialty is working with troubled youth. The Careers in Criminal Justice feature describes this occupation.

delinquency prevention
Intervening in a young person's life to help him or her avoid involvement in delinquent activities.

Community Strategies

Comprehensive community-based delinquency prevention programs are made up of a range of different types of interventions and typically involve an equally diverse group of community and government agencies that are concerned with the problem of juvenile delinquency. Today, these are being supplemented with a systematic approach or comprehensive planning model to develop preventive interventions. This includes an analysis of the delinquency problem, an identification of available resources in the community, the development of priority delinquency problems, and the identification of successful programs in other communities and tailoring them to local conditions and needs.[55] Not all comprehensive community-based prevention programs follow this model, but evidence

Social Worker

Duties and Characteristics of the Job

Social workers aid individuals or families who are disadvantaged or facing particular challenges. Social workers pick a specialization within one of several larger categories. Public health social workers help individuals and families dealing with the consequences of a serious illness. Child, family, and health social workers aid families dealing with issues of social functioning, such as child abuse or truancy. Clinical social workers help families deal with issues related to mental health and substance abuse through a rehabilitation program.

Other social workers take positions where they aren't dealing with the public; instead, they teach in higher education or provide psychotherapy in private practices. There are also policy writers and advocates who attempt to find legislative solutions to social problems and lobby for funding.

Social work is a demanding profession both intellectually and emotionally. Although social workers traditionally work a 40-hour office week, working overtime or during evening hours to attend meetings or meet clients is not unusual. Limited budgets often mean that a social worker will be handling many cases at one time. Emotionally, the job can be challenging because the social worker often deals with people in difficult situations that can have disappointing outcomes.

Job Outlook

The prospects for employment as a social worker are good because jobs are expected to grow faster than average in the near future, and in many places there are more jobs than there are applicants. Because of the impending retirement of the baby boom generation, there are many job opportunities in hospices and nursing homes for social workers specializing in elderly care. Additionally, although the growth of hospital social workers will be slow, there is and will continue to be a growing number of opportunities for social workers with a substance abuse specialization because many drug offenders are sent to treatment programs rather than incarcerated. The employment offerings by school and private social service agencies will also increase.

Salary

Social workers' salary varies according to their specialization. Social workers who specialize in medical and public health have an average salary of $42,690; child, family, and school $38,780; mental health and substance abuse $36,920; and all others $42,720. Those with more education and specialized experience can advance their careers and increase their salaries.

Some community delinquency prevention strategies combine the efforts of law enforcement with those of treatment-oriented agencies. An unusual one is located in the city of Lowell, Massachusetts: the Venerable Khon Sao, a Buddhist monk, teaches Young Cambodian youths, many of them gang members, how to meditate at a Buddhist temple. In conjunction with the police department, the temple has begun a program that teaches the fundamentals of Buddhist thought two evenings a week to the teens. In the classes, the youths learn how to pray, meditate, and act peacefully.

©Spencer Platt/Getty Images

Opportunities

A majority of social worker positions are in urban and suburban areas; potential social workers will find more competition for a limited number of jobs in urban areas. Because there will be higher competition for these jobs in urban areas, those with more education and/or some specialized experience stand better chances of getting desirable positions and career advancement. It may be considerably easier to find a job in a rural area, because educational requirements will be less stringent. Those who leave social work often successfully pursue careers in related fields such as counseling.

Qualifications

The ability to meet the challenging education requirements and certification is the primary qualification necessary to become a social worker. Personal characteristics such as sensitivity, responsibility, and the ability to work independently are also very important. Potential social workers must have at least a bachelor's degree in social work to start at entry-level positions, and additional education for higher degrees will prepare them for more advanced duties, such as clinical assessments and supervisory positions. In addition to being educated, social workers have to meet the particular licensing requirements of the state where they are seeking employment. Additional credentials are helpful and can be obtained through the National Association of Social Workers. Knowledge of a second language is also helpful.

Education and Training

For entry-level positions, a bachelor's degree in social work (B.S.W.) or a similar degree such as sociology is necessary. Those who wish to advance further should earn a master's degree in social work (M.S.W.) or a doctorate (Ph.D. or D.S.W.). Those who wish to ascend to the highest-level positions in a social work organization or design new social work policies or programs should pursue a Ph.D. The education of social workers is never truly complete; they must keep up on recent developments through attending conferences and reading the most recent literature.

Sources: "Social Worker," *Occupational Outlook Handbook*, 2006–2007 edition (Bureau of Labor Statistics, U.S. Department of Labor), retrieved June 27, 2006, from http://www.bls.gov/oco/ocos060.htm; "Occupational Employment and Wages, May 2005" (Bureau of Labor Statistics, U.S. Department of Labor), retrieved June 28, 2006, from http://www.bls.gov/oes/current/oes_nat.htm; "Social Worker," *Princeton Review Career Profiles*, retrieved June 27, 2006, from http://www.princetonreview.com/cte/profiles/dayInLife.asp?careerID=143.

---

suggests that this approach will produce the greatest reductions in juvenile delinquency.[56]

Many jurisdictions are developing new intervention programs for at-risk teenage youths. Some are treatment-oriented programs that rely on rehabilitation ideals. For example, the federal Children at Risk program was set up to help improve the lives of young people at high risk for delinquency, gang involvement, substance abuse, and other problem behaviors. It was delivered to a large number of young people in poor and high-crime neighborhoods in five cities across the country. It involved a wide range of preventive measures, including case management and family counseling, family skills training, tutoring, mentoring, after-school activities, and community policing. The program was different in each neighborhood. A study of all five cities showed that one year after the program ended, the young people who received the program, compared with a control group, were less likely to have committed violent delinquent acts and used or sold drugs. Some of the other beneficial results for those in the program included less association with delinquent peers, less peer pressure to engage in delinquency, and more positive peer support.[57]

Other large-scale comprehensive community-based delinquency prevention programs include Communities That Care (CTC) and the SafeFutures Initiative.[58] Both programs are funded by OJJDP. The CTC strategy emphasizes the reduction of risk factors for delinquency and the enhancement of protective factors against delinquency for different developmental stages from birth through adolescence.[59] CTC follows a rigorous, multilevel planning process that includes drawing upon interventions that have previously demonstrated success and tailoring them to the needs of the community.[60]

The SafeFutures Initiative operates much like CTC—for example, by emphasizing the reduction of risk factors for delinquency and protective factors against delinquency, using what works, and following a rigorous planning model to implement different interventions. It also aims to build or strengthen existing collaborations among the many community groups and government departments working to prevent delinquency. However, unlike CTC, the SafeFutures Initiative is targeted only at youths, those who are both at high risk for delinquency and adjudicated offenders. An important part of the SafeFutures Initiative is the Juvenile Mentoring Program (JUMP), which links at risk youth with adult mentors.

Enforcement Strategies

Although these community-based programs are primarily treatment oriented, many new programs combine treatment with enforcement. Some important ones are now targeting teenage gun use. Easy availability of guns is a significant contributor to teen violence. Research indicates a close relationship among gun use, control of drug markets, and teen violence. Gang-related homicides almost always involve firearms. Unless significant efforts are made to control the spread of handguns, teenage murder rates should continue to rise.

At least 35 states have adopted legislation dealing with guns and children, including measures that require schools to expel or suspend students for possessing weapons on school grounds.[61] At the federal level, laws have also been passed to restrict the possession, sale, and transfer of guns to juveniles. The Gun-Free Schools Act of 1994 requires local educational agencies receiving financial assistance to expel for one year any student who brings a firearm to school. The Youth Handgun Safety Act (part of the Omnibus Violent Crime Control and Law Enforcement Act of 1994) prohibits the possession or private transfer of a handgun to a juvenile. Although this legislation was enacted by the federal government, it is the state and local officials who can deal most effectively with juvenile gun violations.

♦ KEEP THE JUVENILE COURT?

Over the past century, the juvenile court has struggled to provide treatment for juvenile offenders while guaranteeing them constitutional due process. The juvenile court system has been transformed from a rehabilitative to a quasi-criminal court. Many states are toughening juvenile codes. With limited resources and procedural deficiencies, significant change is unlikely in the near future.

The system has been so overwhelmed by violent juvenile crime and family breakdown that some judges and politicians have suggested abolishing the juvenile system. Even those experts who want to retain an independent juvenile court have called for its restructuring. Crime control advocates want to reduce the court's jurisdiction over juveniles charged with serious crimes and enhance the prosecutor's ability to try them in adult courts. In contrast, child advocates suggest that the court scale back its judicial role and transfer its functions to community groups and social service agencies.[62] Despite these differing opinions, the juvenile court will likely remain a critical societal institution; there are few viable alternatives. This issue is addressed in the Analyzing Criminal Justice Issues feature.

www To read about the prosecution of juvenile gun offenders, read the OJJDP publication "Prosecution of Juvenile Firearm Offenders," which you can access by going to the Siegel/Senna Introduction to Criminal Justice 11e website: www.thomsonedu.com/criminaljustice/siegel.

www Parenting Resources for the 21st Century links parents and other adults responsible for the care of a child with information on issues covering the full spectrum of parenting. It also provides information on delinquency prevention in the community. Check out this organization by linking through the Siegel/Senna Introduction to Criminal Justice 11e website: www.thomsonedu.com/criminaljustice/siegel.

ThomsonNOW   Improve your grade on the exam with Personalized Study! For reinforcement and a mastery check of the debate over retaining the juvenile court, go to www.thomsonedu.com/thomsonnow.

Should the Juvenile Court Be Abolished?

In an important work, *Bad Kids: Race and the Transformation of the Juvenile Court,* legal expert Barry C. Feld makes the controversial suggestion that the juvenile court system should be discontinued or replaced by an alternative method of justice. He says that the current structure of juvenile court makes it almost impossible to fulfill or achieve the purpose for which it was originally intended.

Feld maintains that the juvenile court was intended to create a process that was more lenient than that used against adult criminals. Although a worthwhile goal, the juvenile court system was doomed to failure even from the beginning because it was thrown into the role of providing child welfare while at the same time being an instrument of law enforcement, two missions that are often at cross-purposes. During its history, various legal developments have further undermined its purpose. Most notable was the *In re Gault* ruling, which led to juveniles receiving legal protections similar to those given to adults and to children being treated like adults. The juvenile court's vision of leniency was further undercut by fear and racism created by postwar migration and economic trends, which led to the development of large enclaves of poor and underemployed African Americans living in northern cities. Then, in the 1980s, the sudden rise in gang membership, gun violence, and homicide committed by juveniles further undermined the juvenile court mission and resulted in legislation that created mandatory sentences for juvenile offenders and mandatory waivers to adult courts. As a result, the focus of the juvenile court has been on dealing with the offense instead of treating the offender. In Feld's words, the juvenile court has become a "deficient second-rate criminal court." The welfare and rehabilitative purposes of the juvenile court have been subordinated to its role of law enforcement agent.

Can juvenile court be reformed? Feld maintains that it is impossible because of the court's conflicting purposes and shifting priorities. The money spent on serving the court and its large staff would be better spent on child welfare, which would target a larger audience and prevent antisocial acts before they occur. In lieu of juvenile court, youths who violate the law should receive full procedural protections in the criminal court system. The special protections given youths in the juvenile court could be provided by altering the criminal law and recognizing age as a factor in the creation of criminal liability. Because youths have had a limited opportunity to develop self-control, their criminal liability should also be limited.

Is Feld's dour assessment of the juvenile court valid? Not so, according to John Johnson Kerbs, who suggests that Feld's assumptions may not be wedded to the reality of the U.S. legal system. First, Kerbs finds that it is naïve to assume that the criminal courts can provide the same or greater substantive and procedural protections as the juvenile court. Many juvenile court defendants are indigent, especially those coming from the minority community, and they may not be able to obtain adequate legal defense in the adult system. Second, Feld's assumption that criminal courts will take a defendant's age into close consideration may be illusory. In this get-tough era, criminal courts likely will provide harsher sentences, and the brunt of these draconian sentences will fall squarely on the shoulders of minority youths. Research efforts routinely show that African American adults are unduly punished in adult courts. Sending juvenile offenders to these venues will most likely further enmesh them in an already unfair system. Finally, Kerbs finds that the treatment benefits of the juvenile courts should not be overlooked or abandoned. Ample research, he maintains, shows that juvenile courts can create lower recidivism rates than criminal courts. Although the juvenile court is far from perfect and should be improved, it would be foolish to abandon a system that is aimed at helping youths find alternatives to crime for one that produces higher recidivism rates, lowers future prospects, and has a less than stellar record of providing due process and equal protection for the nation's most needy citizens.

Critical Thinking

Should the juvenile court be abolished? Given that the trend has been to transfer the most serious criminal cases to the adult court, is there still a purpose for an independent juvenile court? Should the juvenile court be reserved for nonserious first-time offenders?

InfoTrac College Edition Research

Before you make up your mind about the future of juvenile court, read Joseph V. Penn, "Justice for Youth? A History of the Juvenile and Family Court," *Brown University Child and Adolescent Behavior Letter* 17, no. 9 (September 2001): 1.

Sources: Barry C. Feld, *Bad Kids: Race and the Transformation of the Juvenile Court* (New York: Oxford University Press, 1999); John Johnson Kerbs, "(Un)equal Justice: Juvenile Court Abolition and African Americans," *Annals of the American Academy of Political and Social Science,* 564 (1999): 109–25.

ETHICAL CHALLENGES IN CRIMINAL JUSTICE: A WRITING ASSIGNMENT

You are a juvenile court judge. John M. has been arrested for robbery and rape. His victim, a young neighborhood girl, was seriously injured in the attack and needed extensive hospitalization; she is now in counseling. The charges are serious, and even though John is only 14 years old, he can be waived to the adult court and tried as an adult. Under existing state law, a hearing must be held to determine whether there is sufficient evidence that John cannot be successfully treated in the juvenile justice system and therefore warrants transfer to the adult system; the final decision on the matter is yours alone.

At the waiver hearing, you discover that John is the oldest of three siblings living in a single-parent home. He has had no contact with his father for more than 10 years. His psychological evaluations show hostility, anger toward females, and great feelings of frustration. His intelligence is above average, but his behavioral and academic records are poor. John is a loner with few friends. This is his first formal involvement with the juvenile court. Previous contact was limited to an informal complaint for disorderly conduct at age 13, which was dismissed by the court's intake department. During the hearing, John verbalizes what you interpret to be superficial remorse for his offenses.

In your essay, discuss whether you would waive John to the adult court or treat him as a juvenile, and give the reasons for your decision.

Doing Research on the Web

To read more about juvenile waiver decisions, try the following:

1. Go to the website of the Center for Policy Analysis and read "Juvenile Waiver of Counsel."

2. Go the Office of Juvenile Justice and Delinquency Prevention website and use its search engine to find out more about waiver.

You can link to both of these sites by going through the Siegel/Senna Introduction to Criminal Justice 11e website: www.thomsonedu.com/criminaljustice/siegel.

SUMMARY

◆ The juvenile justice system is concerned with delinquent children, as well as with those who are beyond the care and protection of their parents.

◆ The juvenile justice system was established at the turn of the twentieth century after decades of effort by child-saving groups. These reformers sought to create an independent category of delinquent offenders and to keep their treatment separate from adults.

◆ Juveniles involved in antisocial behavior come under the jurisdiction of juvenile or family court systems.

◆ These courts belong to a system of juvenile justice agencies, including law enforcement, child care, and institutional services. Representatives from different disciplines, such as lawyers, social workers, and psychiatrists, all play major roles in the judicial process.

◆ In recent years the juvenile court system has become more legalistic by virtue of U.S. Supreme Court decisions that have granted children procedural safeguards. The child has a right to counsel and is generally given other procedural due process safeguards, notably the privilege against self-incrimination and the right to confront and cross-examine witnesses.

◆ The juvenile justice process consists of a series of steps: the police investigation, the intake procedure in the juvenile court, the pretrial procedures used for juvenile offenders, and the adjudication, disposition, and postdisposition procedures.

♦ Youths who are considered dangerous are detained in secure facilities. A major effort has been made to remove juveniles from detention in adult jails and to make sure that status offenders are not placed in secure detention facilities.

♦ Those who are held for trial are generally released to their parents, on bail or through other means.

♦ An issue related to bail is preventive detention, which refers to the right of a judge to deny persons release before trial on the grounds that they may be dangerous to themselves or others.

♦ Each year, thousands of youths are transferred to adult courts because of the serious nature of their crimes. This process, known as waiver, is an effort to remove serious offenders from the juvenile process and into the more punitive adult system. Today, virtually all jurisdictions provide for waiver of juvenile offenders to the criminal courts.

♦ Juveniles alleged to be delinquent have virtually all the rights given a criminal defendant at trial—except possibly the right to a trial by jury. In addition, juvenile proceedings are generally closed to the public.

♦ Types of dispositional orders in juvenile court include dismissal, fine, probation, and institutionalization. Legislatures have begun to take a tougher position with regard to the sentencing of some juvenile offenders.

♦ In recent years a number of states have made drastic changes in juvenile sentencing laws, moving away from the indeterminate sentence and embracing more determinate forms of disposition.

♦ The future of the juvenile justice system is in doubt. A number of state jurisdictions are revising their juvenile codes to restrict eligibility in the juvenile justice system and to eliminate the most serious offenders.

KEY TERMS

parens patriae, 574
poor laws, 574
chancery courts, 575
child savers, 575
Children's Aid Society, 576
status offender, 578

children in need of
    supervision (CHINS), 579
intake, 585
detention, 585
waiver, 587
transfer, 587

initial appearance, 590
adjudication, 590
fact-finding hearing, 590
dispositional hearing, 590
delinquency prevention, 597

ThomsonNOW™ Maximize your study time by using ThomsonNOW's diagnostic study plan to help you review this chapter. The Study Plan will

♦ help you identify areas on which you should concentrate;

♦ provide interactive exercises to help you master the chapter concepts; and

♦ provide a post-test to confirm you are ready to move on to the next chapter.

CRITICAL THINKING QUESTIONS

1. Should status offenders be treated by the juvenile court? Explain. Should they be placed in confinement for running away or cutting school? Why or why not?

2. Should a juvenile ever be waived to adult court if the child will face the risk of being incarcerated with adult felons? Why or why not?

3. Do you support the Supreme Court's decision prohibiting the death penalty for children? Explain.

4. Should juveniles be given mandatory incarceration sentences for serious crimes, as adults are? Explain.

5. Is it fair to deny juveniles a jury trial? Why or why not?

6. Do you think the trend toward treating juveniles like adult offenders is desirable? Explain.

NOTES

1. Jeordan Legon, "Teen Sniper Suspect Remains a Mystery," *CNN News*, April 28, 2003 (http://www.cnn.com/2002/US/ 10/28/ sproject.sniper.malvo.profile/index.html), accessed on November 27, 2003.

2. Federal Bureau of Investigation, *Crime in the United States, 2005* (Washington, D.C.: Government Printing Office, 2006); Howard Snyder and Melissa Sickmund, *Juvenile Offenders and Victims: 2006 National Report* (Washington, D.C.: Office of Juvenile Justice and Delinquency Prevention, 2006). Hereafter cited as *2006 National Report*.

3. *Vernonia School District v. Acton*, 515 U.S. 646, 115 S.Ct. 2386, 132 L.Ed.2d (1995).

4. *Board of Education of Independent School District No. 92 of Pottawatomie County v. Earls et al.* (No. 01–332), 2002.

5. Gordon Bazemore, "What's 'New' About the Balanced Approach?," *Juvenile and Family Court Journal* 48 (1997): 1–21. See also Office of Justice Programs, *Balanced and Restorative Justice for Juveniles—A Framework for Juvenile Justice in the 21st Century* (Washington, D.C.: Office of Juvenile Justice and Delinquency Prevention, 1997).

6. Material in this section depends heavily on Sanford J. Fox, "Juvenile Justice Reform: A Historical Perspective," *Stanford Law Review* 22 (1970): 1187–1205; Lawrence Stone, *The Family, Sex, and Marriage in England: 1500–1800* (New York: Harper and Row, 1977); Philippe Aries, *Century of Childhood: A Social History of Family Life* (New York: Vintage, 1962); Douglas R. Rendleman, "Parens Patriae: From Chancery to the Juvenile Court," *South Carolina Law Review* 23 (1971): 205–29; Anthony Platt, "The Rise of the Child-Saving Movement: A Study in Social Policy and Correctional Reform," *Annals of the American Academy of Political and Social Science* 381 (1979): 21–38; Anthony M. Platt, *The Child Savers: The Intervention of Delinquency* (Chicago: University of Chicago Press, 1969); Robert S. Pickett, *House of Refuge: Origins of Juvenile Reform in New York State, 1815–1857* (Syracuse, N.Y.: Syracuse University Press, 1969).

7. Douglas Besharov, *Juvenile Justice Advocacy: Practice in a Unique Court* (New York: Practicing Law Institute, 1974), p. 2. See also Jay Albanese, *Dealing with Delinquency—The Future of Juvenile Justice* (Chicago: Nelson-Hall, 1993).

8. 4 Eng.Rep. 1078 (1827).

9. Platt, *The Child Savers*, pp. 11–38.

10. Anne Meis Knupfer, *Reform and Resistance: Gender, Delinquency, and America's First Juvenile Court* (London: Routledge, 2001).

11. This section is based on material from the New York State Archives, *The Greatest Reform School in the World: A Guide to the Records of the New York House of Refuge: A Brief History 1824–1857* (Albany, N.Y.: 2001); Sanford J. Fox, "Juvenile Justice Reform: A Historical Perspective," *Stanford Law Review* 22 (1970): 1187.

12. Pickett, *House of Refuge*.

13. Robert Mennel, "Origins of the Juvenile Court: Changing Perspectives on the Legal Rights of Juvenile Delinquents," in Juvenile Justice Philosophy, ed. Frederick Faust and Paul Brantingham (St. Paul, Minn.: West, 1974), pp. 69–70.

14. Platt, *The Child Savers*, p. 116.

15. LaMar T. Empey, *American Delinquency: Its Meaning and Construction* (Homewood, Ill.: Dorsey, 1978), p. 515.

16. *Kent v. United States*, 383 U.S. 541, 86 S.Ct. 1045, 16 L.Ed.2d 84 (1966); *In re Gault*, 387 U.S. 1, 87 S.Ct. 1428, 18 L.Ed.2d 527 (1967); *In re Winship*, 397 U.S. 358, 90 S.Ct. 1068, 25 L.Ed.2d 368 (1970); *Breed v. Jones*, 421 U.S. 519, 95 S.Ct. 1779, 44 L.Ed.2d 346 (1975).

17. Public Law 93–415 (1974).

18. *2006 National Report*, pp. 96–97.

19. For a comprehensive view of juvenile law, see, generally, Joseph J. Senna and Larry J. Siegel, *Juvenile Law: Cases and Comments*, 2nd ed. (St. Paul, Minn.: West, 1992).

20. Federal Bureau of Investigation, *Crime in the United States*, 2004, p. 220.

21. Joan McCord, Cathy Spatz-Widom, and Nancy A. Crowell, eds., *Juvenile Crime, Juvenile Justice* (Panel on Juvenile Crime: Prevention, Treatment, and Control) (Washington, D.C.: National Academy Press, 2001), p. 163.

22. FBI, *Uniform Crime Reports, 2004* (Washington, D.C.: U.S. Government Printing Office, 2005), Table 68 (http://www.fbi.gov/ ucr/cius_04/persons_arrested/table_64–68.html), accessed on June 24, 2006.

23. *Fare v. Michael C.*, 442 U.S. 707 (1979).

24. *New Jersey v. T.L.O.*, 469 U.S. 325 (1985).

25. *Vernonia School District v. Acton* (1995).

26. *Board of Education of Independent School District No. 92 of Pottawatomie County, et al., Petitioners v. Lindsay Earls et al.*, 122 S. Ct. 2559 (2002).

27. *Schall v. Martin*, 467 U.S. 253, 104 S.Ct. 2403, 81 L.Ed.2d 207 (1984).

28. See Juvenile Justice and Delinquency Prevention Act of 1974, 42 U.S.C., Sec. 5633.

29. Ira Schwartz, Linda Harris, and Laurie Levi, "The Jailing of Juveniles in Minnesota," *Crime and Delinquency* 34 (1988): 131. See also Barry Krisberg and Robert DeComo, *Juveniles Taken into Custody—1991* (San Francisco: National Council on Crime and Delinquency, 1993), p. 25.

30. Schwartz, Harris, and Levi, "The Jailing of Juveniles in Minnesota," 134.

31. 383 U.S. 541, 86 S.Ct. 1045, 16 L.Ed.2d 84 (1966).

32. 421 U.S. 519, 528, 95 S.Ct. 1779, 1785, 44 L.Ed.2d 346 (1975).

33. Alan Karpelowitz, *State Legislative Priorities—1995* (Denver, Colo.: National Conference of State Legislatures, 1995), p. 10.

34. Dale Parent et al., *Key Issues in Criminal Justice: Transferring Serious Juvenile Offenders to Adult Courts* (Washington, D.C.: National Institute of Justice, 1997).

35. Barry Feld, "The Juvenile Court Meets the Principle of the Offense: Legislative Changes in Juvenile Waiver Statutes," *Journal of Criminal Law and Criminology* 78 (1987): 471–533. See also John Kramer, Henry Sontheimer, and John Lemmon, "Pennsylvania Waiver to Adult Court," paper presented at the annual meeting of the American Society of Criminology, San Francisco, November 1991. The authors confirm that juveniles tried in adult courts are generally male, age 17 or older, and disproportionately minorities.

36. Charles M. Puzzanchera, *Delinquency Cases Waived to Criminal Court, 1989–1998* (Washington, D.C.: Office of Juvenile Justice and Delinquency Prevention, 2001); James Howell, "Juvenile Transfers to Criminal Court," *Juvenile and Family Justice Journal* 6 (1997): 12–14.

37. Jeffrey Fagan and Franklin Zimring, eds., *The Changing Borders of Juvenile Justice: Transfer of Adolescents to the Criminal Court* (Chicago: University of Chicago Press, 2000).

38. Thomas Grisso and Robert Schwartz, *Juveniles' Competence to Stand Trial: A Comparison of Adolescents' and Adults' Capacities as Trial Defendants* (Philadelphia: MacArthur Foundation Research Network on Adolescent Development and Juvenile Justice, 2003).

39. Shay Bilchik, "Sentencing Juveniles to Adult Facilities Fails Youths and Society," *Corrections Today* 65 (2003): 21.

40. *2006 National Report*.

41. Lamar Smith, "Sentencing Youths to Adult Correctional Facilities Increases Public Safety," *Corrections Today* 65 (2003): 20.

42. 387 U.S. 1, 87 S.Ct. 1428, 18 L.Ed.2d 527 (1967).

43. 397 U.S. 358, 90 S.Ct. 1068, 25 L.Ed.2d 368 (1970).

44. 403 U.S. 528, 91 S.Ct. 1976, 29 L.Ed.2d 647 (1971).

45. Victor Streib, *Death Penalty for Juveniles* (Bloomington: Indiana University Press, 1987).

46. Biko Agozino, "The Crisis of Authoritarianism in the Legal Institutions," *Journal of Contemporary Criminal Justice* 19 (2003): 315–50; *Roper v. Simmons* 543 U.S. 551 (2005).

47. See Joseph Goldstein, Anna Freud, and Albert Solnit, *Beyond the Best Interest of the Child* (New York: Free Press, 1973).

48. See Michael Serrill, "Police Write a New Law on Juvenile Crime," *Police Magazine* (September 1979): 47. See also A. Schneider and D. Schram, *Assessment of Juvenile Justice Reform in Washington State*, vols. 1–4 (Washington, D.C.: Institute of Policy Analysis, 1983); T. Castellano, "Justice Model in the Juvenile Justice System—Washington State's Experience," *Law and Policy* 8 (1986): 479.

49. Anne Schneider, *Guide to Juvenile Restitution* (Washington, D.C.: Department of Justice, 1985).

50. *Following Commitment, How Are Placement, Length of Stay, and Release Decisions Made?* (Pittsburgh: National Center for Juvenile Justice, April 18, 2003).

51. Melissa Sickmund, *Juvenile Residential Facility Census, 2002* (Washington, D.C.: Office of Juvenile Justice and Delinquency Prevention, 2006) (http://www.ncjrs.gov/pdffiles1/ojjdp/211080.pdf), accessed on June 26, 2006.

52. Melissa Sickmund and Yi-chun Wan, "Census of Juveniles in Residential Placement Databook" (http://www.ojjdp.ncjrs.org/ojstatbb/cjrp), accessed on November 25, 2003.

53. *2006 National Report*.

54. National Conference of State Legislatures, *A Legislator's Guide to Comprehensive Juvenile Justice, Juvenile Detention, and Corrections* (Denver, Colo.: 1996).

55. J. David Hawkins, Richard F. Catalano, and associates, *Communities That Care: Action for Drug Abuse Prevention* (San Francisco, Calif.: Jossey-Bass, 1992).

56. Richard F. Catalano, Michael W. Arthur, J. David Hawkins, Lisa Berglund, and Jeffrey J. Olson, "Comprehensive Community- and School-Based Interventions to Prevent Antisocial Behavior," in *Serious and Violent Juvenile Offenders: Risk Factors and Successful Interventions*, ed. Rolf Loeber and David P. Farrington (Thousand Oaks, Calif.: Sage, 1998).

57. Adele V. Harrell, Shannon E. Cavanagh, and Sanjeev Sridharan, *Evaluation of the Children at Risk Program: Results 1 Year after the End of the Program* (Washington, D.C.: NIJ Research in Brief, 1999).

58. Hawkins, Catalano, and Associates, *Communities That Care*; Elaine Morley, Shelli B. Rossman, Mary Kopczynski, Janeen Buck, and Caterina Gouvis, *Comprehensive Responses to Youth at Risk: Interim Findings from the SafeFutures Initiative* (Washington, D.C.: Office of Juvenile Justice and Delinquency Prevention, 2000).

59. Catalano, Arthur, Hawkins, Berglund, and Olson, "Comprehensive Community- and School-Based Interventions to Prevent Antisocial Behavior," 281.

60. James C. Howell and J. David Hawkins, "Prevention of Youth Violence," in *Youth Violence: Crime and Justice: A Review of Research*, vol. 24, ed. Michael Tonry and Mark H. Moore (Chicago: University of Chicago Press, 1998), pp. 303–04.

61. Office of Justice Programs, *Reducing Youth Gun Violence* (Washington, D.C.: Office of Juvenile Justice and Delinquency Prevention, 1996).

62. Fox Butterfield, "Justice Besieged," *New York Times*, July 21, 1997, p. A16.

APPENDIX
The Constitution of the United States

Preamble

We the People of the United States, in Order to form a more perfect Union, establish Justice, insure domestic Tranquility, provide for the common defence, promote the general Welfare, and secure the Blessings of Liberty to ourselves and our Posterity, do ordain and establish this Constitution for the United States of America.

Article I

SECTION 1 All legislative Powers herein granted shall be vested in a Congress of the United States, which shall consist of a Senate and House of Representatives.

SECTION 2 The House of Representatives shall be composed of Members chosen every second Year by the People of the several States, and the Electors in each State shall have the Qualifications requisite for Electors of the most numerous Branch of the State Legislature.

No Person shall be a Representative who shall not have attained to the Age of twenty five Years, and been seven Years a Citizen of the United States, and who shall not, when elected, be an Inhabitant of that State in which he shall be chosen.

Representatives and direct Taxes shall be apportioned among the several States which may be included within this Union, according to their respective Numbers, which shall be determined by adding to the whole Number of free Persons, including those bound to Service for a Term of Years, and excluding Indians not taxed, three fifths of all other Persons. The actual Enumeration shall be made within three Years after the first Meeting of the Congress of the United States, and within every subsequent Term of ten Years, in such Manner as they shall by Law direct. The Number of Representatives shall not exceed one for every thirty Thousand, but each State shall have at Least one Representative; and until such enumeration shall be made, the State of New Hampshire shall be entitled to choose three, Massachusetts eight, Rhode Island and Providence Plantations one, Connecticut five, New York six, New Jersey four, Pennsylvania eight, Delaware one, Maryland six, Virginia ten, North Carolina five, South Carolina five, and Georgia three.

When vacancies happen in the Representation from any State, the Executive Authority thereof shall issue Writs of Election to fill such Vacancies.

The House of Representatives shall choose their Speaker and other Officers; and shall have the sole Power of Impeachment.

SECTION 3 The Senate of the United States shall be composed of two Senators from each State, chosen by the Legislature thereof, for six Years; and each Senator shall have one Vote.

Immediately after they shall be assembled in Consequence of the first Election, they shall be divided as equally as may be into three Classes. The Seats of the Senators of the first Class shall be vacated at the Expiration of the second Year, of the second Class at the Expiration of the fourth Year, and of the third Class at the Expiration of the sixth Year, so that one third may be chosen every second Year; and if Vacancies happen by Resignation, or otherwise, during the Recess of the Legislature of any State, the Executive thereof may make temporary Appointments until the next Meeting of the Legislature, which shall then fill such Vacancies.

No Person shall be a Senator who shall not have attained to the Age of thirty Years, and been nine Years a Citizen of the United States, and who shall not, when elected, be an Inhabitant of that State for which he shall be chosen.

The Vice-President of the United States shall be President of the Senate, but shall have no Vote, unless they be equally divided.

The Senate shall choose their other Officers, and also a President pro tempore, in the Absence of the Vice-President, or when he shall exercise the Office of President of the United States.

The Senate shall have the sole Power to try all Impeachments. When sitting for that Purpose, they shall be on Oath or Affirmation. When the President of the United States is tried the Chief Justice shall preside: And no Person shall be convicted without the Concurrence of two thirds of the Members present.

Judgment in Cases of Impeachment shall not extend further than to removal from Office, and disqualification to hold and enjoy any Office of honor, Trust or Profit under the United States: but the Party convicted shall nevertheless be liable and subject to Indictment, Trial, Judgment, and Punishment, according to Law.

SECTION 4 The Times, Places and Manner of holding Elections for Senators and Representatives, shall be prescribed in each State by the Legislature thereof; but the Congress may at any time by Law make or alter such Regulations, except as to the Places of choosing Senators.

The Congress shall assemble at least once in every Year, and such Meeting shall be on the first Monday in December, unless they shall by Law appoint a different Day.

SECTION 5 Each House shall be the Judge of the Elections, Returns and Qualifications of its own Members, and a Majority of each shall constitute a Quorum to do Business; but a smaller Number may adjourn from day to day, and may be authorized to compel the Attendance of absent Members, in such Manner, and under such Penalties as each House may provide.

Each House may determine the Rules of its Proceedings, punish its Members for disorderly Behaviour, and, with the Concurrence of two thirds, expel a Member.

Each House shall keep a Journal of its Proceedings, and from time to time publish the same, excepting such Parts as may in their Judgment require Secrecy; and the Yeas and Nays of the Members of either House on any question shall, at the Desire of one fifth of those Present, be entered on the Journal.

Neither House, during the Session of Congress, shall, without the Consent of the other, adjourn for more than three days, nor to any other Place than that in which the two Houses shall be sitting.

SECTION 6 The Senators and Representatives shall receive a Compensation for their Services, to be ascertained by Law, and paid out of the Treasury of the United States. They shall in all Cases, except Treason, Felony and Breach of the Peace, be privileged from Arrest during their Attendance at the Session of their respective Houses, and in going to and returning from the same; and for any Speech or Debate in either House, they shall not be questioned in any other Place.

No Senator or Representative shall, during the Time for which he was elected, be appointed to any civil Office under the Authority of the United States, which shall have been created, or the Emoluments whereof shall have been increased during such time; and no Person holding any Office under the United States, shall be a Member of either House during his Continuance in Office.

SECTION 7 All Bills for raising Revenue shall originate in the House of Representatives; but the Senate may propose or concur with Amendments as on other Bills.

Every Bill which shall have passed the House of Representatives and the Senate, shall, before it become a Law, be presented to the President of the United States; If he approve he shall sign it, but if not

he shall return it, with his Objections to that House in which it shall have originated, who shall enter the Objections at large on their Journal, and proceed to reconsider it. If after such Reconsideration two thirds of that House shall agree to pass the Bill, it shall be sent, together with the Objections, to the other House, by which it shall likewise be reconsidered, and if approved by two thirds of that House, it shall become a Law. But in all such Cases the Votes of both Houses shall be determined by Yeas and Nays, and the Names of the Persons voting for and against the Bill shall be entered on the Journal of each House respectively. If any Bill shall not be returned by the President within ten Days (Sundays excepted) after it shall have been presented to him, the Same shall be a Law, in like Manner as if he had signed it, unless the Congress by their Adjournment prevent its Return, in which Case it shall not be a Law.

Every Order, Resolution, or Vote to which the Concurrence of the Senate and House of Representatives may be necessary (except on a question of Adjournment) shall be presented to the President of the United States; and before the Same shall take Effect, shall be approved by him, or being disapproved by him, shall be repassed by two thirds of the Senate and House of Representatives, according to the Rules and Limitations prescribed in the Case of a Bill.

SECTION 8 The Congress shall have Power To lay and collect Taxes, Duties, Imposts and Excises, to pay the Debts and provide for the common Defence and general Welfare of the United States; but all Duties, Imposts and Excises shall be uniform throughout the United States;

To borrow Money on the credit of the United States;

To regulate Commerce with foreign Nations, and among the several States, and with the Indian Tribes;

To establish an uniform Rule of Naturalization, and uniform Laws on the subject of Bankruptcies throughout the United States;

To coin Money, regulate the Value thereof, and of foreign Coin, and fix the Standard of Weights and Measures;

To provide for the Punishment of counterfeiting the Securities and current Coin of the United States;

To establish Post Offices and post Roads;

To promote the Progress of Science and useful Arts, by securing for limited Times to Authors and Inventors the exclusive Right to their respective Writings and Discoveries;

To constitute Tribunals inferior to the supreme Court;

To define and punish Piracies and Felonies committed on the high Seas, and Offences against the Law of Nations;

To declare War, grant Letters of Marque and Reprisal, and make Rules concerning Captures on Land and Water;

To raise and support Armies, but no Appropriation of Money to that Use shall be for a longer Term than two Years;

To provide and maintain a Navy;

To make Rules for the Government and Regulation of the land and naval Forces;

To provide for calling forth the Militia to execute the Laws of the Union, suppress Insurrections and repel Invasions;

To provide for organizing, arming, and disciplining, the Militia, and for governing such Part of them as may be employed in the Service of the United States, reserving to the States respectively, the Appointment of the Officers, and the Authority of training the Militia according to the discipline prescribed by Congress;

To exercise exclusive Legislation in all Cases whatsoever, over such District (not exceeding ten Miles square) as may, by Cession of particular States, and the Acceptance of Congress, become the Seat of the Government of the United States, and to exercise like Authority over all Places purchased by the Consent of the Legislature of the State in which the Same shall be, for the Erection of Forts, Magazines, Arsenals, dock-Yards, and other needful Buildings;—And

To make all Laws which shall be necessary and proper for carrying into Execution the foregoing Powers, and all other Powers vested by this Constitution in the Government of the United States, or in any Department or Officer thereof.

SECTION 9 The Migration or Importation of such Persons as any of the States now existing shall think proper to admit, shall not be prohibited by the Congress prior to the Year one thousand eight hundred and eight, but a Tax or duty may be imposed on such Importation, not exceeding ten dollars for each Person.

The privilege of the Writ of Habeas Corpus shall not be suspended, unless when in Cases of Rebellion or Invasion the public Safety may require it.

No Bill of Attainder or ex post facto Law shall be passed.

No Capitation, or other direct, Tax shall be laid, unless in Proportion to the Census or Enumeration herein before directed to be taken.

No Tax or Duty shall be laid on Articles exported from any State.

No Preference shall be given by any Regulation of Commerce or Revenue to the Ports of one State over those of another: nor shall Vessels bound to, or from, one State be obliged to enter, clear, or pay Duties in another.

No Money shall be drawn from the Treasury, but in Consequence of Appropriations made by Law; and a regular Statement and Account of the Receipts and Expenditures of all public Money shall be published from time to time.

No Title of Nobility shall be granted by the United States: And no Person holding any Office of Profit or Trust under them, shall, without the Consent of the Congress, accept of any present, Emolument, Office, or Title, of any kind whatever, from any King, Prince, or foreign State.

SECTION 10 No State shall enter into any Treaty, Alliance, or Confederation; grant Letters of Marque and Reprisal; coin Money; emit Bills of Credit; make any Thing but gold and silver Coin a Tender in Payment of Debts; pass any Bill of Attainder, ex post facto Law, or Law impairing the Obligation of Contracts, or grant any Title of Nobility.

No State shall, without the Consent of the Congress, lay any Imposts or Duties on Imports or Exports, except what may be absolutely necessary for executing its inspection Laws: and the net Produce of all Duties and Imposts, laid by any State on Imports or Exports, shall be for the Use of the Treasury of the United States; and all such Laws shall be subject to the Revision and Control of the Congress.

No State shall, without the Consent of Congress, lay any Duty of Tonnage, keep Troops, or Ships of War in time of Peace, enter into any Agreement or Compact with another State, or with a foreign Power, or engage in War, unless actually invaded, or in such imminent Danger as will not admit of delay.

Article II

SECTION 1 The executive Power shall be vested in a President of the United States of America. He shall hold his Office during the Term of four Years, and, together with the Vice-President, chosen for the same Term, be elected, as follows:

Each State shall appoint, in such Manner as the Legislature thereof may direct, a Number of Electors, equal to the whole Number of Senators and Representatives to which the State may be entitled in the Congress; but no Senator or Representative, or Person holding an Office of Trust or Profit under the United States, shall be appointed an Elector.

The Electors shall meet in their respective States, and vote by Ballot for two Persons, of whom one at least shall not be an Inhabitant of the same State with themselves. And they shall make a List of all the Persons voted for, and of the Number of Votes for each; which List they shall sign and certify, and transmit sealed to the Seat of Government of the United States, directed to the President of the Senate. The President of the Senate shall, in the Presence of the Senate and House of Representatives, open all the Certificates, and the Votes shall then be counted. The Person having the greatest Number of Votes shall be the President, if such Number be a Majority of the whole Number of Electors appointed; and if there be more than one who have such Majority, and have an equal Number of Votes, then the House of Representatives shall immediately choose by Ballot one of them for President; and if no Person have a Majority, then from the five highest on the List the said House shall in like Manner choose the President. But in choosing the President, the Votes shall be taken by States, the Representation from each State having one Vote; A quorum for this Purpose shall consist of a Member or Members from two thirds of the States, and a Majority of all the States shall be necessary to a Choice. In every Case, after the Choice of the President, the Person having the greatest Number of Votes of the Electors shall be the Vice-President. But if there should remain two or more who have equal Votes, the Senate shall choose from them by Ballot the Vice-President.

The Congress may determine the Time of choosing the Electors, and the Day on which they shall give their Votes; which Day shall be the same throughout the United States.

No Person except a natural born Citizen, or a Citizen of the United States, at the time of the Adoption of this Constitution, shall be eligible to the Office of President; neither shall any Person be eligible to that Office who shall not have attained to the Age of thirty five Years, and been fourteen Years a Resident within the United States.

In Case of the Removal of the President from Office, or of his Death, Resignation, or Inability to discharge the Powers and Duties of the said Office, the same shall devolve on the Vice-President, and the Congress may by Law provide for the Case of Removal, Death, Resignation or Inability, both of the President and Vice-President declaring what Officer shall then act as President, and such Officer shall act accordingly, until the Disability be removed, or a President shall be elected.

The President shall, at stated Times, receive for his Services, a Compensation, which shall neither be increased nor diminished during the Period for which he shall have been elected, and he shall not receive within that Period any other Emolument from the United States, or any of them.

Before he enter on the Execution of his Office, he shall take the following Oath or Affirmation: "I do solemnly swear (or affirm) that I will faithfully execute the Office of President of the United States, and will to the best of my Ability, preserve, protect and defend the Constitution of the United States."

SECTION 2 The President shall be Commander in Chief of the Army and Navy of the United States, and of the Militia of the several States, when called into the actual Service of the United States; he may require the Opinion, in writing, of the principal Officer in each of the executive Departments, upon any Subject relating to the Duties of their respective Offices, and he shall have Power to grant Reprieves and Pardons for Offenses against the United States, except in Cases of Impeachment.

He shall have Power, by and with the Advice and Consent of the Senate, to make Treaties, provided two thirds of the Senators present concur; and he shall nominate, and by and with the Advice and Consent of the Senate, shall appoint Ambassadors, other public Ministers and Consuls, Judges of the supreme Court, and all other Officers of the United States, whose Appointments are not herein otherwise provided for, and which shall be established by Law; but the Congress may by Law vest the Appointment of such inferior Officers, as they think proper, in the President alone, in the Courts of Law, or in the Heads of Departments.

The President shall have Power to fill up all Vacancies that may happen during the Recess of the Senate, by granting Commissions which shall expire at the End of their next Session.

SECTION 3 He shall from time to time give to the Congress Information of the State of the Union, and recommend to their Consideration such Measures as he shall judge necessary and expedient; he may, on extraordinary Occasions, convene both Houses, or either of them, and in Case of Disagreement between them, with Respect to the Time of Adjournment, he may adjourn them to such Time as he shall think proper; he shall receive Ambassadors and other public Ministers; he shall take Care that the Laws be faithfully executed, and shall Commission all the Officers of the United States.

SECTION 4 The President, Vice-President and all civil Officers of the United States, shall be removed from Office on Impeachment for, and Conviction of, Treason, Bribery, or other high Crimes and Misdemeanors.

Article III

SECTION 1 The judicial Power of the United States, shall be vested in one supreme Court, and in such inferior Courts as the Congress may from time to time ordain and establish. The Judges, both of the supreme and inferior Courts, shall hold their Offices during good Behaviour, and shall, at stated Times, receive for their Services a Compensation which shall not be diminished during their Continuance in Office.

SECTION 2 The judicial Power shall extend to all Cases, in Law and Equity, arising under this Constitution, the Laws of the United States, and Treaties made, or which shall be made, under their Authority;—to all Cases affecting Ambassadors, other public Ministers and Consuls;—to all Cases of admiralty and maritime Jurisdiction;—to Controversies to which the United States shall be a Party;—to Controversies between two or more States;—between a State and Citizens of another State;—between Citizens of different States;—between Citizens of the same State claiming Lands under Grants of different States, and between a State, or the Citizens thereof, and foreign States, Citizens or Subjects.

In all Cases affecting Ambassadors, other public Ministers and Consuls, and those in which a State shall be Party, the supreme Court shall have original Jurisdiction. In all the other Cases before mentioned, the supreme Court shall have appellate Jurisdiction, both as to Law and Fact, with such Exceptions, and under such Regulations as the Congress shall make.

The Trial of all Crimes, except in Cases of Impeachment, shall be by Jury; and such Trial shall be held in the State where the said Crimes shall have been committed; but when not committed within any State, the Trial shall be at such Place or Places as the Congress may by Law have directed.

SECTION 3 Treason against the United States shall consist only in levying War against them, or in adhering to their Enemies, giving them Aid and Comfort. No Person shall be convicted of Treason unless on the Testimony of two Witnesses to the same overt Act, or on Confession in open Court.

The Congress shall have Power to declare the Punishment of Treason, but no Attainder of Treason shall work Corruption of Blood, or Forfeiture except during the Life of the Person attainted.

Article IV

SECTION 1 Full Faith and Credit shall be given in each State to the public Acts, Records, and judicial Proceedings of every other State. And the Congress may by general Laws prescribe the Manner in which such Acts, Records and Proceedings shall be proved, and the Effect thereof.

SECTION 2 The Citizens of each State shall be entitled to all Privileges and Immunities of Citizens in the several States.

A Person charged in any State with Treason, Felony, or other Crime, who shall flee from Justice, and be found in another State, shall on Demand of the executive Authority of the State from which he fled, be delivered up, to be removed to the State having Jurisdiction of the Crime.

No Person held to Service or Labour in one State, under the Laws thereof, escaping into another, shall, in Consequence of any Law or Regulation therein, be discharged from such Service or Labour, but shall be delivered up on Claim of the Party to whom such Service or Labour may be due.

SECTION 3 New States may be admitted by the Congress into this Union; but no new State shall be formed or erected within the Jurisdiction of any other State; nor any State be formed by the Junction of two or more States, or Parts of States, without the Consent of the Legislatures of the States concerned as well as of the Congress.

The Congress shall have Power to dispose of and make all needful Rules and Regulations respecting the Territory or other Property belonging to the United States; and nothing in this Constitution shall be so construed as to Prejudice any Claims of the United States, or of any particular State.

SECTION 4 The United States shall guarantee to every State in this Union a Republican Form of Government, and shall protect each of them against Invasion; and on Application of the Legislature, or of the Executive (when the Legislature cannot be convened) against domestic Violence.

Article V

The Congress, whenever two thirds of both Houses shall deem it necessary, shall propose Amendments to this Constitution, or, on the Application of the Legislatures of two thirds of the several States, shall call a Convention for proposing Amendments, which, in either Case, shall be valid to all Intents and Purposes, as Part of this Constitution, when ratified by the Legislatures of three fourths of the several States, or by Conventions in three fourths thereof, as the one or the other Mode of Ratification may be proposed by the Congress; Provided that no Amendment which may be made prior to the Year One thousand eight hundred and eight shall in any Manner affect the first and fourth Clauses in the Ninth Section of the first Article; and that no State, without its Consent, shall be deprived of its equal Suffrage in the Senate.

Article VI

All Debts contracted and Engagements entered into, before the Adoption of this Constitution, shall be as valid against the United States under this Constitution, as under the Confederation.

This Constitution, and the Laws of the United States which shall be made in Pursuance thereof; and all Treaties made, or which shall be made, under the Authority of the United States, shall be the supreme Law of the Land; and the Judges in every State shall be bound thereby, any Thing in the Constitution or Laws of any State to the Contrary notwithstanding.

The Senators and Representatives before mentioned, and the Members of the several State Legislatures, and all executive and judicial Officers, both of the United States and of the several States, shall be bound by Oath or Affirmation, to support this Constitution; but no religious Test shall ever be required as a Qualification to any Office or public Trust under the United States.

Article VII

The Ratification of the Conventions of nine States shall be sufficient for the Establishment of this Constitution between the States so ratifying the Same.

Done in Convention by the Unanimous Consent of the States present the Seventeenth Day of September in the Year of our Lord one thousand seven hundred and Eighty seven and of the Independence of the United States of America the Twelfth IN WITNESS whereof We have hereunto subscribed our Names,

Amendment 1 [1791]

Congress shall make no law respecting an establishment of religion, or prohibiting the free exercise thereof; or abridging the freedom of speech, or of the press; or the right of the people peaceably to assemble, and to petition the Government for a redress of grievances.

Amendment 2 [1791]

A well regulated Militia, being necessary to the security of a free State, the right of the people to keep and bear Arms, shall not be infringed.

Amendment 3 [1791]

No Soldier shall, in time of peace be quartered in any house, without the consent of the Owner, nor in time of war, but in a manner to be prescribed by law.

Amendment 4 [1791]

The right of the people to be secure in their persons, houses, papers, and effects, against unreasonable searches and seizures, shall not be violated, and no Warrants shall issue, but upon probable cause, supported by Oath or affirmation, and particularly describing the place to be searched, and the persons or things to be seized.

Amendment 5 [1791]

No person shall be held to answer for a capital, or otherwise infamous crime, unless on a presentment or indictment of a Grand Jury, except in cases arising in the land or naval forces, or in the Militia, when in actual service in time of War or public danger; nor shall any person be subject for the same offence to be twice put in jeopardy of life or limb; nor shall be compelled in any criminal case to be a witness against himself, nor be deprived of life, liberty, or property, without due process of law; nor shall private property be taken for public use, without just compensation.

Amendment 6 [1791]

In all criminal prosecutions, the accused shall enjoy the right to a speedy and public trial, by an impartial jury of the State and district wherein the crime shall have been committed, which district shall have been previously ascertained by law, and to be informed of the nature and cause of the accusation; to be confronted with the witnesses against him; to have compulsory process for obtaining witnesses in his favor, and to have the Assistance of Counsel for his defence.

Amendment 7 [1791]

In Suits at common law, where the value in controversy shall exceed twenty dollars, the right of trial by jury shall be preserved, and no fact tried by a jury, shall be otherwise re-examined in any Court of the United States, than according to the rules of the common law.

Amendment 8 [1791]

Excessive bail shall not be required, nor excessive fines imposed, nor cruel and unusual punishments inflicted.

Amendment 9 [1791]

The enumeration in the Constitution, of certain rights, shall not be construed to deny or disparage others retained by the people.

Amendment 10 [1791]

The powers not delegated to the United States by the Constitution, nor prohibited by it to the States, are reserved to the States respectively, or to the people.

Amendment 11 [Jan. 8, 1798]

The Judicial power of the United States shall not be construed to extend to any suit in law or equity, commenced or prosecuted against one of the United States by Citizens of another State, or by Citizens or Subjects of any Foreign State.

Amendment 12 [Sept. 25, 1804]

The Electors shall meet in their respective states, and vote by ballot for President and Vice-President, one of whom, at least, shall not be an inhabitant of the same state with themselves; they shall name in their ballots the person voted for as President, and in distinct ballots the person voted for as Vice-President, and they shall make distinct lists of all persons voted for as President, and of all persons voted for as Vice-President, and of the number of votes for each, which list they shall sign and certify, and transmit sealed to the seat of the government of the United States, directed to the President of the Senate;—The President of the Senate shall, in the presence of the Senate and House of Representatives, open all the certificates and the votes shall then be counted;—The person having the greatest number of votes for President, shall be the President, if such number be a majority of the whole number of Electors appointed; and if no person have such majority, then from the persons having the highest numbers not exceeding three on the list of those voted for as President, the House of Representatives shall choose immediately, by ballot, the President. But in choosing the President, the votes shall be taken by states, the representation from each state having one vote; a quorum for this purpose shall consist of a member or members from two-thirds of the states, and a majority of all the states shall be necessary to a choice. And if the House of Representatives shall not choose a President whenever the right of choice shall devolve upon them, before the fourth day of March next following, then the Vice-President shall act as President, as in the case of the death or other constitutional disability of the President.—The person having the greatest number of votes as Vice-President, shall be the Vice-President, if such number be a majority of the whole number of Electors appointed, and if no person have a majority, then from the two highest numbers on the list, the Senate shall choose the Vice-President; a quorum for the purpose shall consist of two-thirds of the whole number of Senators, and a majority of the whole number shall be necessary to a choice. But no person constitutionally ineligible to the office of President shall be eligible to that of Vice-President of the United States.

Amendment 13 [Dec. 18, 1865]

SECTION 1 Neither slavery nor involuntary servitude, except as a punishment for crime whereof the party shall have been duly convicted, shall exist within the United States, or any place subject to their jurisdiction.

SECTION 2 Congress shall have power to enforce this article by appropriate legislation.

Amendment 14 [July 28, 1868]

SECTION 1 All persons born or naturalized in the United States, and subject to the jurisdiction thereof, are citizens of the United States and of the State wherein they reside. No State shall make or enforce any law which shall abridge the privileges or immunities of citizens of the United States; nor shall any State deprive any person of life, liberty, or property, without due process of law; nor deny to any person within its jurisdiction the equal protection of the laws.

SECTION 2 Representatives shall be apportioned among the several States according to their respective numbers, counting the whole number of persons in each State, excluding Indians not taxed. But when the right to vote at any election for the choice of electors for President and Vice-President of the United States, Representatives in Congress, the Executive and Judicial officers of a State, or the members of the Legislature

thereof, is denied to any of the male inhabitants of such State, being twenty-one years of age, and citizens of the United States, or in any way abridged, except for participation in rebellion, or other crime, the basis of representation therein shall be reduced in the proportion which the number of such male citizens shall bear to the whole number of male citizens twenty-one years of age in such State.

SECTION 3 No person shall be a Senator or Representative in Congress, or elector of President and Vice-President, or hold any office, civil or military, under the United States, or under any State, who, having previously taken an oath, as a member of Congress, or as an officer of the United States, or as a member of any State legislature, or as an executive or judicial officer of any State, to support the Constitution of the United States, shall have engaged in insurrection or rebellion against the same, or given aid or comfort to the enemies thereof. But Congress may by a vote of two-thirds of each House, remove such disability.

SECTION 4 The validity of the public debt of the United States, authorized by law, including debts incurred for payment of pensions and bounties for services in suppressing insurrection or rebellion, shall not be questioned. But neither the United States nor any State shall assume or pay any debt or obligation incurred in aid of insurrection or rebellion against the United States, or any claim for the loss or emancipation of any slave; but all such debts, obligations and claims shall be held illegal and void.

SECTION 5 The Congress shall have power to enforce, by appropriate legislation, the provisions of this article.

Amendment 15 [March 30, 1870]

SECTION 1 The right of citizens of the United States to vote shall not be denied or abridged by the United States or by any State on account of race, color, or previous condition of servitude.

SECTION 2 The Congress shall have power to enforce this article by appropriate legislation.

Amendment 16 [Feb. 25, 1913]

The Congress shall have power to lay and collect taxes on incomes, from whatever source derived, without apportionment among the several States, and without regard to any census or enumeration.

Amendment 17 [May 31, 1913]

SECTION 1 The Senate of the United States shall be composed of two Senators from each State, elected by the people thereof, for six years; and each Senator shall have one vote. The electors in each State shall have the qualifications requisite for electors of the most numerous branch of the State legislatures.

SECTION 2 When vacancies happen in the representation of any State in the Senate, the executive authority of such State shall issue writs of election to fill such vacancies: Provided, That the legislature of any State may empower the executive thereof to make temporary appointments until the people fill the vacancies by election as the legislature may direct.

SECTION 3 This amendment shall not be so construed as to affect the election or term of any Senator chosen before it becomes valid as part of the Constitution.

Amendment 18 [Jan. 29, 1919; repealed Dec. 5, 1933]

SECTION 1 After one year from the ratification of this article the manufacture, sale, or transportation of intoxicating liquors within, the importation thereof into, or the exportation thereof from the United States and all territory subject to the jurisdiction thereof for beverage purposes is hereby prohibited.

SECTION 2 Congress and the several States shall have concurrent power to enforce this article by appropriate legislation.

SECTION 3 This article shall be inoperative unless it shall have been ratified as an amendment to the Constitution by the legislatures of the several States, as provided in the Constitution, within seven years from the date of the submission hereof to the States by the Congress.

Amendment 19 [Aug. 26, 1920]

SECTION 1 The right of citizens of the United States to vote shall not be denied or abridged by the United States or by any State on account of sex.

SECTION 2 Congress shall have power to enforce this article by appropriate legislation.

Amendment 20 [Feb. 6, 1933]

SECTION 1 The terms of the President and Vice-President shall end at noon on the 20th day of January, and the terms of Senators and Representatives at noon on the third day of January, of the years in which such terms would have ended if this article had not been ratified; and the terms of their successors shall then begin.

SECTION 2 The Congress shall assemble at least once in every year, and such meeting shall begin at noon on the third day of January, unless they shall by law appoint a different day.

SECTION 3 If, at the time fixed for the beginning of the term of the President, the President elect shall have died, the Vice-President elect shall become President. If a President shall not have been chosen before the time fixed for the beginning of his term, or if the President elect shall have failed to qualify, then the Vice-President elect shall act as President until a President shall have qualified; and the Congress may by law provide for the case wherein neither a President elect nor a Vice-President elect shall have qualified, declaring who shall then act as President, or the manner in which one who is to act shall be selected, and such person shall act accordingly until a President or Vice-President shall have qualified.

SECTION 4 The Congress may by law provide for the case of the death of any of the persons from whom the House of Representatives may choose a President whenever the right of choice shall have devolved upon them, and for the case of the death of any of the persons from whom the Senate may choose a Vice-President whenever the right of choice shall have devolved upon them.

SECTION 5 Sections 1 and 2 shall take effect on the 15th day of October following the ratification of this article.

SECTION 6 This article shall be inoperative unless it shall have been ratified as an amendment to the Constitution by the legislatures of three-fourths of the several States within seven years from the date of its submission.

Amendment 21 [Dec. 5, 1933]

SECTION 1 The eighteenth article of amendment to the Constitution of the United States is hereby repealed.

SECTION 2 The transportation or importation into any State, Territory, or possession of the United States for delivery or use therein of intoxicating liquors, in violation of the laws thereof, is hereby prohibited.

SECTION 3 This article shall be inoperative unless it shall have been ratified as an amendment to the Constitution by conventions in the several States, as provided in the Constitution, within seven years from the date of the submission hereof to the States by the Congress.

Amendment 22 [March 1, 1951]

SECTION 1 No person shall be elected to the office of the President more than twice, and no person who has held the office of President, or acted as President, for more than two years of a term to which some other person was elected President shall be elected to the office of the President more than once. But this Article shall not apply to any person holding the office of President when this Article was proposed by the Congress, and shall not prevent any person who may be holding the office of President, or acting as President, during the term within which this Article becomes operative from holding the office of President or acting as President during the remainder of such term.

SECTION 2 This article shall be inoperative unless it shall have been ratified as an amendment to the Constitution by the legislatures of three-fourths of the several States within seven years from the date of its submission to the States by the Congress.

Amendment 23 [April 3, 1961]

SECTION 1 The District constituting the seat of Government of the United States shall appoint in such manner as the Congress may direct:

A number of electors of President and Vice-President equal to the whole number of Senators and Representatives in Congress to which the District would be entitled if it were a State, but in no event more than the least populous State; they shall be in addition to those appointed by the States, but they shall be considered, for the purposes of the election of President and Vice-President, to be electors appointed by a State; and they shall meet in the District and perform such duties as provided by the twelfth article of amendment.

SECTION 2 The Congress shall have power to enforce this article by appropriate legislation.

Amendment 24 [Feb. 4, 1964]

SECTION 1 The right of citizens of the United States to vote in any primary or other election for President or Vice-President, for electors for President or Vice-President, or for Senator or Representative in Congress, shall not be denied or abridged by the United States or any State by reason of failure to pay any poll tax or other tax.

SECTION 2 The Congress shall have power to enforce this article by appropriate legislation.

Amendment 25 [Feb. 10, 1967]

SECTION 1 In case of the removal of the President from office or his death or resignation, the Vice-President shall become President.

SECTION 2 Whenever there is a vacancy in the office of the Vice-President, the President shall nominate a Vice-President who shall take the office upon confirmation by a majority vote of both houses of Congress.

SECTION 3 Whenever the President transmits to the President pro tempore of the Senate and the Speaker of the House of Representatives his written declaration that he is unable to discharge the powers and duties of his office, and until he transmits to them a written declaration to the contrary, such powers and duties shall be discharged by the Vice-President as Acting President.

SECTION 4 Whenever the Vice-President and a majority of either the principal officers of the executive departments, or of such other body as Congress may by law provide, transmit to the President pro tempore of the Senate and the Speaker of the House of Representatives their written declaration that the President is unable to discharge the powers and duties of his office, the Vice-President shall immediately assume the powers and duties of the office as Acting President.

Thereafter, when the President transmits to the President pro tempore of the Senate and the Speaker of the House of Representatives his written declaration that no inability exists, he shall resume the powers and duties of his office unless the Vice-President and a majority of either the principal officers of the executive department, or of such other body as Congress may by law provide, transmit within four days to the President pro tempore of the Senate and the Speaker of the House of Representatives their written declaration that the President is unable to discharge the powers and duties of his office. Thereupon Congress shall decide the issue, assembling within forty-eight hours for that purpose if not in session. If the Congress, within twenty-one days after receipt of the latter written declaration, or, if Congress is not in session, within twenty-one days after Congress is required to assemble, determines by two-thirds vote of both Houses that the President is unable to discharge the powers and duties of his office, the Vice-President shall continue to discharge the same as Acting President; otherwise, the President shall resume the powers and duties of his office.

Amendment 26 [June 30, 1971]

SECTION 1 The right of citizens of the United States, who are eighteen years of age or older, to vote shall not be denied or abridged by the United States or any state on account of age.

SECTION 2 The Congress shall have power to enforce this article by appropriate legislation.

Amendment 27 [May 7, 1992]

No law, varying the compensation for the services of Senators and Representatives, shall take effect until an election of Representatives shall have intervened.

Glossary

accountability system A system that makes police supervisors responsible for the behavior of the officers in their command.

actus reus An illegal act, or failure to act when legally required.

adjudication (adult) The determination of guilt or innocence; a judgment concerning criminal charges.

adjudication (juvenile) The juvenile court hearing at which the juvenile is declared a delinquent or status offender, or no finding of fact is made.

administrative control theory The view that collective violence in prison may be caused by mismanagement, lack of strong security, and inadequate control by prison officials.

Al-Qaeda (Arabic for "the base") an international fundamentalist Islamist organization comprising independent and collaborative cells whose goal is reducing Western influence upon Islamic affairs.

alternative sanctions Community sentences featuring probation plus additional requirements such as restitution, fines, home confinement, or electronic monitoring, designed to provide more control and sanctions than traditional probation but less than secure incarceration in jail or prison.

anomie The absence or weakness of rules, norms, or guidelines as to what is socially or morally acceptable.

appellate courts Courts that reconsider cases that have already been tried to determine whether the lower court proceedings complied with accepted rules of criminal procedure and constitutional doctrines.

arraignment Initial trial court appearance at which the accused is read the charges, advised of his or her rights, and asked to enter a plea.

arrest Taking a person into legal custody for the purpose of restraining the accused until he or she can be held accountable for the offense at court proceedings.

arrest warrant Written court order authorizing and directing that an individual be taken into custody to answer criminal charges.

assigned counsel A private attorney appointed by the court to represent a criminal defendant who cannot afford to pay for a lawyer.

attorney general The chief legal officer and prosecutor of each state and of the United States.

Auburn system A prison system, developed in New York during the nineteenth century, based on congregate (group) work during the day and separation at night.

avertable recidivist A person whose crime would have been prevented if he or she had not been given discretionary release and instead been kept behind bars.

bail The monetary amount required for pretrial release, normally set by a judge at the initial appearance; the purpose of bail is to ensure the return of the accused at subsequent proceedings.

beats Designated police patrol areas.

bench trial The trial of a criminal matter by a judge without a jury.

biometrics Automated methods of recognizing a person based on a physiological or behavioral characteristic.

blameworthy A person who is deserving of blame or punishment because of evil or injurious behavior.

blue curtain The secretive, insulated police culture that isolates officers from the rest of society.

booking The administrative record of an arrest listing the offender's name, address, physical description, date of birth, employer, time of arrest, offense, and name of arresting officer; it also includes photographing and fingerprinting of the offender.

boot camp A short-term militaristic correctional facility in which inmates, usually young first-time offenders, undergo intensive physical conditioning and discipline.

broken windows model Role of the police as maintainers of community order and safety.

brutalization effect The belief that capital punishment creates an atmosphere of brutality, reinforces the view that violence is an appropriate response to provocation, and thus encourages rather than deters the criminal use of violence.

bus sweep Police investigation technique in which officers board a bus or train without suspicion of illegal activity and question passengers, asking for identification and seeking permission to search their baggage.

career criminals Persistent repeat offenders who organize their lifestyle around criminality.

challenge for cause Dismissal of a prospective juror by either the prosecution or the defense because he or she is biased, has prior knowledge about a case, or for other reasons that demonstrate the individual's inability to render a fair and impartial judgment.

chancery courts English courts assigned with the protection of the property rights of minor children.

child savers Civic leaders who focused their attention on the misdeeds of poor children to control their behavior.

children in need of supervision A legal term used in some states to designate juvenile status offenders.

Children's Aid Society Group created by Charles Loring Brace to place indigent city children with farm families.

chivalry hypothesis The idea that female defendants are treated more leniently in sentencing (and are less likely to be arrested and prosecuted in the first place) because the criminal justice system is dominated by men who have a paternalistic or protective attitude toward women.

chronic offenders As defined by Marvin Wolfgang, Robert Figlio, and Thorsten Sellin, delinquents arrested five or more times before the age of 18 who commit a disproportionate amount of all criminal offenses.

circumstantial (indirect) evidence Indirect evidence from which a fact may be inferred.

civil law All law that is not criminal, including tort, contract, personal property, maritime, and commercial law.

cleared An offense is cleared by arrest or solved when at least one person is arrested or charged with the commission of the offense and is turned over to the court for prosecution. If the following questions can all be answered "yes," the offense can then be cleared "exceptionally": (1) Has the investigation definitely established the identity of the offender? (2) Is there enough information to support an arrest, charge, and turning over to the court for prosecution? (3) Is the exact location of the offender known so that the subject could be taken into custody now? (4) Is there some reason outside law enforcement control that precludes arresting, charging, and prosecuting the offender?

collective efficacy A condition of mutual trust and cooperation that develops in neighborhoods that have a high level of formal and informal social control.

community-oriented policing (COP) Programs designed to bring police and the public closer together and create a more cooperative working environment between them.

community policing A law enforcement program that seeks to integrate officers into the local community to reduce crime and gain good community relations. It typically involves personalized service and decentralized policing, citizen empowerment, and an effort to reduce community fear of crime, disorder, and decay.

community prosecution A prosecutorial philosophy that emphasizes community support and cooperation with other agencies in preventing crime as well as a less centralized and more proactive role for local prosecutors.

community service restitution Criminal sanction that requires the offender to work in the community at such tasks as cleaning public parks or helping handicapped children as an alternative to incarceration.

community treatment Correctional treatment services located within the community such as the halfway house.

complaint A sworn written statement addressed to a court or judge by the police, prosecutor, or individual alleging that an individual has committed an offense and requesting indictment and prosecution.

concurrent sentence Incarceration for more than one offense such that all

sentences begin on the same day and are completed after the longest term has been served.

confrontation clause The constitutional right of a criminal defendant to see and cross-examine all the witnesses against him or her.

congregate system A prison system, originated in New York, in which inmates worked and ate together during the day and then slept in solitary cells at night.

conjugal visit A prison program that allows inmates to receive visits from spouses for the purpose of maintaining normal interpersonal relationships.

consecutive sentence Incarceration for more than one offense such that each sentence begins only after the previous one has been completed.

constable In early English towns, an appointed peacekeeper who organized citizens for protection and supervised the night watch.

contract system (court) Provision of legal services to indigent defendants by private attorneys under contract to the state or county.

contract system (prison) System whereby officials sold the labor of prison inmates to private businesses, for use either inside or outside the prison.

convict-lease system Contract system in which a private business leased prisoners from the state for a fixed annual fee and assumed full responsibility for their supervision and control.

corporate crime Crimes committed by a corporation or by individuals who control the corporation or other business entity for such purposes as illegally increasing market share, avoiding taxes, or thwarting competition.

court of last resort A court that handles the final appeal on a matter—in the federal system, the U.S. Supreme Court.

courtroom work group All parties in the adversary process working together in a cooperative effort to settle cases with the least amount of effort and conflict.

courts of general jurisdiction Courts that try felony cases and more serious civil matters.

courts of limited jurisdiction Courts that handle misdemeanors and minor civil complaints.

crime control perspective A model of criminal justice that emphasizes the control of dangerous offenders and the

protection of society through harsh punishment as a deterrent to crime.

criminal justice system The various sequential stages through which offenders pass, from initial contact with the law to final disposition, and the agencies charged with enforcing the law at each of these stages.

criminal law The body of rules that defines crimes, sets out their punishments, and mandates the procedures for carrying out the criminal justice process.

criminal negligence Liability that can occur when a person's careless and inattentive actions cause harm.

criminal procedure The rules and laws that define the operation of the criminal proceedings. Procedural law describes the methods that must be followed in obtaining warrants, investigating offenses, effecting lawful arrests, conducting trials, introducing evidence, sentencing convicted offenders, and reviewing cases by appellate courts.

criminology The scientific study of the nature, extent, cause, and control of criminal behavior.

critical criminology The view that crime results from the imposition by the rich and powerful of their own moral standards and economic interests on the rest of society.

cross-examination The questioning of a prosecution witness by the defense, or of a defense witness by the prosecution.

cruel and unusual punishment Treatment that degrades human dignity, is disproportionately severe, or shocks the general conscience; it is prohibited by the Eighth Amendment to the U.S. Constitution.

culture of poverty The view that people in the lower class of society form a separate culture with its own values and norms that are in conflict with those of conventional society.

curtilage Grounds or fields attached to a house.

cyber crime Illegal behavior that targets the security of computer systems and/or the data accessed and processed by computer networks.

cyber terrorism Internet attacks against an enemy nation's technological infrastructure.

cynicism The belief that most people's actions are motivated solely by personal needs and selfishness.

data mining Using sophisticated computer software to conduct analysis of behavior patterns in an effort to identify crime patterns and link them to suspects.

day fees Fees imposed on probationers to offset the costs of probation.

day fine A fine geared to an offender's net daily income, as well as number of dependents and the seriousness of the crime, in an effort to make sentences more equitable.

day reporting center (DRC) Nonresidential, community-based treatment program.

deadly force Police killing of a suspect who resists arrest or presents a danger to an officer or the community.

death-qualified jury A jury formed to hear a capital case, with any person opposed in principle to capital punishment automatically excluded.

decriminalization Reducing the penalty for a criminal act without legalizing it.

defense attorney Legal counsel for the defendant in a criminal case, representing the accused person from arrest to final appeal.

deinstitutionalization The movement to remove as many offenders as possible from secure confinement and treat them in the community.

delinquency prevention Intervening in a young person's life to help him or her avoid involvement in delinquent activities.

demeanor The way in which a person outwardly manifests his or her personality.

denial-of-service attack Extorting money from an Internet service user by threatening to prevent the user from having access to the service.

Department of Homeland Security (DHS) A federal agency created to coordinate national efforts to prevent terrorist attacks from occurring within the United States, to respond if an attack takes place, and to reduce or minimize the damage from attacks that do happen.

detention Temporary care of a child alleged to be a delinquent or status offender who requires secure custody pending court disposition.

determinate sentence A fixed term of incarceration.

deterrent Preventing crime before it occurs by means of the threat of criminal sanctions.

developmental theories A view of crime holding that as people travel through the life course their experiences along the way influence behavior patterns. Behavior changes at each stage of the human experience.

differential association theory The view that criminal acts are related to a person's exposure to antisocial attitudes and values.

direct examination The initial questioning of one's own (prosecution or defense) witness during a trial.

directed verdict A judge's order directing a jury to acquit a defendant because the state has not proven the elements of the crime or otherwise has not established guilt according to law.

Director of National Intelligence (DNI) Government official charged with coordinating data from the nation's primary intelligence-gathering agencies.

discretion The use of personal decision making and choice in carrying out operations in the criminal justice system.

disinhibition Unrestricted behavior resulting from a loss of inhibition produced by an external influence, such as drugs or alcohol, or from a brain injury.

displacement An effect that occurs when criminals move from an area targeted for increased police presence to another that is less well protected.

dispositional hearing A court hearing to determine the appropriate treatment for a youth found to be a delinquent.

district attorney The county prosecutor who is charged with bringing offenders to justice and enforcing the criminal laws of the state.

diversion The use of a noncriminal alternative to trial, such as referral to treatment or employment programs.

DNA profiling The identification (or elimination) of criminal suspects by comparing DNA samples (genetic material) taken from them with specimens found at crime scenes.

double marginality According to Nicholas Alex, the social burden that African American police officers carry by being both minority-group members and law enforcement officers.

drug courts Specialty courts with jurisdiction over cases involving illegal substances, often providing treatment alternatives for defendants.

due process perspective A model of criminal justice that emphasizes individual rights and constitutional safeguards against arbitrary or unfair judicial or administrative proceedings.

electronic monitoring (EM) Electronic equipment that enables probation officers to monitor the location of those under house arrest or other forms of supervision.

equity Sanction designed to compensate victims and society for the losses caused by crime: restitution.

etailing fraud Illegally buying or selling merchandise on the Internet.

ex post facto law A law that makes an act criminal after it was committed or retroactively increases the penalty for a crime.

exclusionary rule The principle that prohibits using illegally obtained evidence in a trial.

exculpatory evidence Includes all information that is material and favorable to the accused defendant because it casts doubt on the defendant's guilt or on the evidence the government intends to use at trial.

excuse defenses A defense in which a person states that his or her mental state was so impaired that he or she lacked the capacity to form sufficient intent to be held criminally responsible.

exigent Emergency or immediate circumstance.

expressive crimes Criminal acts that serve to vent rage, anger, or frustration.

fact-finding hearing The trial in the juvenile justice system.

Federal Bureau of Investigation (FBI) The arm of the Justice Department that investigates violations of federal law, gathers crime statistics, runs a comprehensive crime laboratory, and helps train local law enforcement officers.

felony A more serious crime that carries a penalty of incarceration in a state or federal prison, usually for one year or more.

fine A sum imposed as punishment for an offense.

focal concerns Central values and goals that, according to Walter Miller, differ by social class.

foot patrol Police patrol that takes officers out of cars and puts them on a walking beat to strengthen ties with the community.

forfeiture The seizure of personal property by the state as a civil or criminal penalty.

gang tactical detail A police unit created to combat neighborhood gang problems by targeting known offenders who have shown a propensity toward gang violence or criminal activity.

general deterrence A crime control policy that depends on the fear of criminal penalties.

globalization The process of creating transnational markets, politics, and legal systems in order to develop a global economy.

good faith exception The principle that evidence may be used in a criminal trial even though the search warrant used to obtain it was technically faulty, so long as the police acted in good faith when they sought the warrant from a judge.

good time Reduction of a prison sentence by a specified amount in exchange for good behavior within the institution.

grand jury A group of citizens chosen to hear charges against persons accused of crime and to determine whether there is sufficient evidence to bring the persons to trial.

grass eater A term used for a police officer who accepts payoffs when everyday duties place him or her in a position to be solicited by the public.

halfway house A community-based correctional facility that houses inmates before their outright release so that they can become gradually acclimated to conventional society.

hands-off doctrine The judicial policy of not interfering in the administrative affairs of prisons.

hate crimes Criminal acts directed toward a particular person or members of a group targeted because of their racial, ethnic, religious, or gender characteristics.

hearsay evidence Testimony that is not firsthand but relates information told by a second party.

hot pursuit A legal doctrine that allows police to search premises where they suspect a crime has been committed without a warrant when delay would endanger their lives or the lives of others and lead to the escape of the alleged perpetrator.

HotSpot probation A program using community supervision teams to monitor offenders.

hot spots of crime The view that a significant portion of all police calls in metropolitan areas typically radiate from a relatively few locations: bars, malls, the bus depot, hotels, and certain apartment buildings.

house arrest A sentence that requires convicted offenders to spend extended periods of time in their own home as an alternative to incarceration.

hue and cry In medieval England, a call for mutual aid against trouble or danger.

hulk Mothballed ship used to house prisoners in eighteenth-century England.

hundred In medieval England, a group of 100 families responsible for maintaining order and trying minor offenses.

identity theft Using the Internet to steal someone's identity and/or impersonate the victim in order to conduct illicit transactions such as committing fraud using the victim's name and identity.

in presence requirement A police officer cannot arrest someone for a misdemeanor unless the officer sees the crime occur. To make an arrest for a crime he did not witness, the officer must obtain a warrant.

incapacitation The policy of keeping dangerous criminals in confinement to eliminate the risk of their repeating their offense in society.

indeterminate sentence A term of incarceration with a stated minimum and maximum length; the prisoner is eligible for parole after serving the minimum.

indictment A written accusation returned by a grand jury, charging an individual with a specified crime after determination of probable cause.

indigent defendant A poor defendant who lacks the funds to hire a private attorney and is therefore entitled to free counsel.

inevitable discovery rule The principle that evidence can be used in court even though the information that led to its discovery was obtained in violation of the *Miranda* rule if a judge finds it would have been discovered anyway by other means or sources.

information A formal charging document, similar to an indictment, based on probable cause as determined at a preliminary hearing.

initial appearance The first hearing in juvenile court.

inmate balance theory The view that riots and other forms of collective prison violence occur when officials make an abrupt effort to take control of the prison and limit freedoms.

inmate social code The informal set of rules that governs inmates and shapes the inmate subculture.

inmate subculture The loosely defined culture that pervades prisons and has its own norms, rules, and language.

instrumental crimes Criminal acts intended to improve the financial or social position of the criminal.

intake The process by which a probation officer settles cases at the initial court appearance, before the onset of formal criminal proceedings; also, the screening process in which a juvenile is referred to the juvenile court, referred elsewhere, or released.

intensive probation supervision (IPS) A type of intermediate sanction involving small probation caseloads and strict daily or weekly monitoring.

intensive supervision parole (ISP) A form of parole characterized by smaller caseloads and closer surveillance; may include frequent drug testing or, in some cases, electronic monitoring.

intermediate sanctions A group of punishments falling between probation and prison; community-based sanctions including house arrest and intensive supervision.

internal affairs Unit that investigates allegations of police misconduct.

jail A county correctional institution used to hold people awaiting trial or sentencing, as well as misdemeanor offenders sentenced to a term of less than one year.

jailhouse lawyer An inmate trained in law or otherwise educated who helps other inmates prepare legal briefs and appeals.

judicial reprieve In medieval England, a judge's suspension of punishment, enabling a convicted offender to seek a pardon, gather new evidence, or demonstrate reformed behavior.

jury nullification A jury's refusal to render a verdict according to the law and fact regardless of the evidence presented.

just desert The view that those who violate the rights of others deserve punishment commensurate with the seriousness of the crime.

justice of the peace Official appointed to act as the judicial officer in a county.

justification A defense for a criminal act claiming that the criminal act was reasonable or necessary under the circumstances.

Knapp Commission A public body that conducted an investigation into police corruption in New York City in the early 1970s and uncovered a widespread network of payoffs and bribes.

latent trait theories A view that human behavior is controlled by a master trait, present at birth or soon after, which influences and directs their behavior.

Law Enforcement Assistance Administration (LEAA) Agency funded by the federal Safe Streets and Crime Control Act of 1968 that provided technical assistance and hundreds of millions of dollars in aid to local and state justice agencies between 1969 and 1982.

left realism A branch of conflict theory that accepts the reality of crime as a social problem and stresses its impact on the poor.

legislature The branch of government in a state invested with power to make and repeal laws.

liberal feminist theory An ideology holding that women suffer oppression, discrimination, and disadvantage as a result of their sex. Calls for gender equality in pay, opportunity, child care, and education.

life course The course of social and developmental changes through which an individual passes as he or she travels from birth through childhood, adolescence, adulthood, and finally old age.

lineup Placing a suspect in a group for the purpose of being viewed and identified by a witness.

low-visibility decision making Decision making by police officers that is not subject to administrative review—for example, when a decision is made not to arrest someone or not to stop a speeding vehicle.

mala in se In common law, offenses that are from their own nature evil, immoral, and wrong. Mala in se offenses include murder, theft, and arson.

mandatory parole release A release date determined at the beginning of the confinement period based on a percentage of the inmate's sentence to be served. Inmates can have their expected time served increased if they violate prison rules or conditions.

mandatory sentence A statutory requirement that a certain penalty be set and carried out in all cases on conviction for a specified offense or series of offenses.

masculinity hypothesis The view that women who commit crimes have biological and psychological traits similar to those of men.

maximum-security prison A correctional institution that houses dangerous felons and maintains strict security measures, including high walls, guard towers, and limited contact with the outside world.

meat eater A term used to describe a police officer who actively solicits bribes and vigorously engages in corrupt practices.

medical model The view that convicted offenders are victims of their environment who need care and treatment to be transformed into valuable members of society.

medium-security prison A correctional institution that houses nonviolent offenders, characterized by a less tense and vigilant atmosphere and more opportunities for contact with the outside world.

mens rea A guilty mind: the intent to commit a criminal act.

Metropolitan Police Act In 1829, when Sir Robert Peel was home secretary, the first Metropolitan Police Act was passed and the Metropolitan Police Force was established to replace the local watch and constable system in the London area.

minimum-security prison A correctional institution that houses white-collar and other nonviolent offenders, characterized by few security measures and liberal furlough and visitation policies.

Miranda **rights** According to the case of *Miranda v. Arizona*, the right of a suspect to refuse to answer questions after an arrest and to have an attorney provided to protect civil rights and liberties.

Missouri Plan A method of judicial selection that combines a judicial nominating commission, executive appointment, and nonpartisan confirmation elections.

Mollen Commission An investigative unit set up to inquire into police corruption in New York City in the 1990s.

monetary restitution Criminal sanction that requires the offender to compensate the victim for property damage, lost wages, medical costs, or other losses.

National Crime Victimization Survey (NCVS) The NCVS is the nation's primary source of information on criminal victimization. Each year, data are obtained from a national sample that measure the frequency, characteristics, and consequences of criminal victimization by such crimes as rape, sexual assault, robbery, assault, theft, household burglary, and motor vehicle theft.

National Incident-Based Reporting System (NIBRS) A new form of crime data collection created by the FBI requiring local police agencies to provide at least a brief account of each incident and arrest within 22 crime patterns, including the incident, victim, and offender information.

neighborhood-oriented policing (NOP) A philosophy of police suggesting that problem solving is best done at the neighborhood level, where issues originate, not at a far-off central headquarters.

neurotransmitters Chemical substances that carry impulses from one nerve cell to another. Neurotransmitters are found in the space (synapse) that separates the transmitting neuron's terminal (axon) from the receiving neuron's terminal (dendrite).

no bill The action by a grand jury when it votes not to indict an accused suspect.

nolle prosequi The decision by a prosecutor to drop a case after a complaint has been made because of, for example, insufficient evidence, witness reluctance to testify, police error, or office policy.

nolo contendere A plea of "no contest"; the defendant submits to sentencing without any formal admission of guilt that could be used against him or her in a subsequent civil suit.

nonintervention perspective A model of criminal justice that favors the least-intrusive treatment possible: decarceration, diversion, and decriminalization.

obitiatry Helping people take their own lives: assisted suicide.

order maintenance (peacekeeping) Maintaining order and authority without the need for formal arrest; "handling the situation"; keeping things under control by means of threats, persuasion, and understanding.

overload hypothesis The theory that police workload influences discretion so that as workload increases, less time and attention can be devoted to new cases, especially petty crimes.

parens patriae The power of the state to act on behalf of a child and provide care and protection equivalent to that of a parent.

parental efficacy Parenting that is supportive, effective, and noncoercive.

parole The early release of a prisoner from incarceration subject to conditions set by a parole board.

Part I crimes Those crimes in the FBI's former Crime Index, which was composed of offenses used to gauge fluctuations in the overall volume and rate of crime. The offenses included were the violent crimes of murder and non-negligent manslaughter, forcible rape, robbery, and aggravated assault and the property crimes of burglary, larceny-theft, motor vehicle theft, and arson.

Part II crimes All other crimes reported to the FBI not included in the former Crime Index. These were less serious crimes and misdemeanors, excluding traffic violations.

particularity The requirement that a search warrant state precisely where the search is to take place and what items are to be seized.

peacemaking criminology A branch of conflict theory that stresses humanism, mediation, and conflict resolution as means to end crime.

penitentiary A state or federal correctional institution for the incarceration of felony offenders for terms of one year or more: prison.

penitentiary house A correctional institution for those convicted of major crimes.

Pennsylvania system A prison system, developed in Pennsylvania during the nineteenth century, based on total isolation and individual penitence.

penumbral crimes Criminal acts defined by a high level of noncompliance with the stated legal standard, an absence of stigma associated with violation of the stated standard, and a low level of law enforcement or public sanction.

peremptory challenge Dismissal of a prospective juror by either the prosecution or the defense for unexplained, discretionary reasons.

phishing Illegally acquiring personal information, such as bank passwords and credit card numbers, by masquerading as a trustworthy person or business in what appears to be an official electronic communication, such as an e-mail or an instant message. The term *phishing* comes from the lures used to "fish" for financial information and passwords.

plain view doctrine Evidence that is in plain view of police officers may be seized without a search warrant.

plea negotiations/plea bargaining Discussions between defense counsel and prosecution in which the accused agrees to plead guilty in exchange for certain considerations, such as reduced charges or a lenient sentence.

police brutality Actions such as using abusive language, making threats, using force or coercion unnecessarily, prodding with nightsticks, and stopping and searching people to harass them.

police styles The working personalities adopted by police officers that can range from being a social worker in blue to a hard-charging crime fighter.

poor laws Seventeenth-century English laws under which vagrants and abandoned and neglected children were bound to masters as indentured servants.

preliminary hearing (probable cause hearing) Hearing before a magistrate to determine if the government has sufficient evidence to show probable cause that the defendant committed the crime.

presentence investigation A postconviction investigation, performed by a probation officer attached to the trial court, of the defendant's background, education, employment, family, acquaintances, physical and mental health, prior criminal record, and other factors that may affect sentencing.

presentment The report of a grand jury investigation, which usually includes a recommendation of indictment.

pretrial detainees People who either are denied bail or cannot afford to post bail before trial and are kept in secure confinement.

pretrial diversion Informal, community-based treatment programs that are used in lieu of the formal criminal process.

pretrial procedures Legal and administrative actions that take place after arrest and before trial, including grand jury indictments, preliminary hearings, bail, and plea negotiation.

prison A state or federal correctional institution for the incarceration of felony offenders for terms of one year or more: penitentiary.

prisonization Assimilation into the separate culture in the prison that has its own rewards and behaviors.

pro bono The practice by private attorneys of taking the cases of indigent offenders without fee as a service to the profession and the community.

pro se To present one's own defense in a criminal trial: self-representation.

proactive policing An aggressive law enforcement style in which patrol officers take the initiative against crime instead of waiting for criminal acts to occur. For example, they stop motor vehicles to issue citations and aggressively arrest and detain suspicious persons.

probable cause The evidentiary criterion necessary to sustain an arrest or the issuance of an arrest or search warrant; a set of facts, information, circumstances, or conditions that would lead a reasonable person to believe that an offense was committed and that the accused committed that offense.

probable cause hearing If a person is taken into custody for a misdemeanor, a hearing is held to determine if probable cause exists that he committed the crime.

probation A sentence entailing the conditional release of a convicted offender into the community under the supervision of the court (in the form of a probation officer), subject to certain conditions for a specified time.

problem-oriented policing (POP) A style of police management that stresses proactive problem solving instead of reactive crime fighting.

profile (profiling) The practice of police targeting members of particular racial or ethnic groups for traffic and other stops because they believe that members of that group are more likely to be engaged in criminal activity even though the individual being stopped has not engaged in any improper behavior.

prosecutor The public official who presents the government's case against a person accused of a crime.

psychopath A person whose personality is characterized by a lack of warmth and feeling, inappropriate behavioral responses, and an inability to learn from experience; also called sociopath or antisocial personality.

public defender An attorney employed by the government to represent criminal defendants who cannot afford to pay for a lawyer.

public order crimes Behaviors considered illegal because they run counter to existing moral standards. Obscenity and prostitution are considered public order crimes.

public safety doctrine A suspect can be questioned in the field without a *Miranda* warning if the information the police seek is needed to protect public safety.

public safety or strict liability crime A criminal violation—usually one that endangers the public welfare—that is defined by the act itself, irrespective of intent.

punishment Pain, suffering, loss, or sanction inflicted on a person because he or she committed a crime or offense.

racial threat theory The view that young minority males are subject to greater police control—e.g., formal arrest—when their numbers increase within the population.

radical feminism A branch of conflict theory that focuses on the role of capitalist male dominance in female criminality and victimization.

real evidence Any object, such as a weapon or a photograph, produced for inspection at a trial: physical evidence.

reasonable competence standard Minimally required level of functioning by a defense attorney such that defendants are not deprived of their rights to counsel and to a fair trial.

rebuttal evidence Evidence presented by the prosecution at the conclusion of the defense case, with the permission of the court, to rebut or disprove defense evidence.

recidivism Repetition of criminal behavior: habitual criminality.

recognizance Medieval practice of letting convicted offenders remain free if they agreed to enter a debt relation with the state to pay for their crimes.

recoupment Process by which the state later recovers some or all of the cost of providing free legal counsel to an indigent defendant.

rehabilitation perspective A model of criminal justice that sees crime as an expression of frustration and anger created by social inequality that can be controlled by giving people the means to improve their lifestyle through conventional endeavors.

release on recognizance (ROR) A pretrial release in which a defendant with ties to the community is not required to post bail but promises to appear at all subsequent proceedings.

residential community corrections (RCC) An intermediate sanction, as well as a parole or pretrial option, in which convicted offenders are housed in a nonsecure facility from which they go to work, attend school, or participate in treatment activities and programs.

restitution Criminal sanction that requires the offender to repay the victim or society or both for damage caused by the criminal act.

restoration A vision of justice that attempts to heal the rift between criminal and victim to provide healing instead of punishment.

restorative justice A perspective on justice that views the main goal of the criminal justice system to be a systematic response to wrongdoing that emphasizes healing the wounds of victims, offenders, and communities caused or revealed by crime. It stresses noncoercive and healing approaches whenever possible.

revocation Removing a person from probation (or parole) in response to a violation of law or of the conditions of probation (or parole).

risk classification Assigning probationers to a level and type of supervision based on their particular needs and the risks they pose for the community.

routine activities theory The view that crime is a product of three everyday factors: motivated offenders, suitable targets, and a lack of capable guardians.

sanctions Social control mechanisms designed to enforce society's laws and standards.

search incident to a lawful arrest An exception to the search warrant rule; limited to the immediate surrounding area.

search warrant An order, issued by a judge, directing officers to conduct a search of specified premises for specified objects or persons and to bring them before the court.

self-report survey A research approach that questions large groups of subjects, typically high school students, about their own participation in delinquent or criminal acts.

sentencing circle In native communities, a group of citizens, leaders, victims, and so on who meet to deal with conflicts between people in an equitable way.

sheriff The chief law enforcement officer in a county.

shire reeve In early England, the chief law enforcement official in a county: the forerunner of today's sheriff.

shock incarceration A short prison sentence served under military discipline at a boot camp facility.

shock probation A sentence in which offenders serve a short term in prison to impress them with the pains of incarceration before they begin probation.

six-person jury According to the U.S. Supreme Court, the smallest legally acceptable jury.

slave patrols Vigilante groups that enforced discipline on slaves and apprehended runaway slaves seeking freedom.

social capital Positive relations with individuals and institutions that foster self-worth and inhibit crime.

social control The ability of society and its institutions to control, manage, restrain, or direct human behavior.

social control theory The view that most people do not violate the law because of their social bonds to family, peer group, school, and other institutions. If these bonds are weakened or absent, they become free to commit crime.

social learning theory The view that human behavior is learned through observation of human social interactions, either directly from those in close proximity or indirectly from the media.

social reaction (labeling) theory The view that society produces criminals by stigmatizing certain individuals as deviants, a label that they come to accept as a personal identity.

social structure The stratifications, classes, institutions, and groups that characterize a society.

specific deterrence Punishment severe enough to convince convicted offenders never to repeat their criminal activity.

split sentence Giving a brief term of incarceration as a condition of probation.

stalking The willful, malicious, and repeated following, harassing, or contacting of another person. It becomes a criminal act when it causes the victim to feel fear for his or her safety or the safety of others.

stare decisis To stand by decided cases: the legal principle by which the decision or holding in an earlier case becomes the standard by which subsequent similar cases are judged.

status offender A noncriminal youth who falls under the jurisdiction of the juvenile court by reason of the fact he or she has engaged in behavior prohibited to minors, such as being truant from school, running away from home, and being habitually disobedient and ungovernable.

sting operation Organized groups of detectives who deceive criminals into openly committing illegal acts or conspiring to engage in criminal activity.

stop and frisk The situation in which police officers who are suspicious of an individual run their hands lightly over the suspect's outer garments to determine if the person is carrying a concealed weapon—also called a threshold inquiry or pat-down.

strain The emotional turmoil and conflict caused when people believe they cannot achieve their desires and goals through legitimate means.

subpoena A court order requiring a witness to appear in court at a specified time and place.

substantive criminal law A body of specific rules that declare what conduct is criminal and prescribe the punishment to be imposed for such conduct.

substantive right A specific right, such as the right to medical care or freedom of religion.

super-maximum-security prison A high-security prison in which inmates are kept in solitary confinement up to 23 hours per day.

sureties During the Middle Ages, people who made themselves responsible for people given release or a reprieve.

surrebuttal evidence At the end of rebuttal, the defense may be allowed to refute the evidence presented by the prosecution with its own surrebuttal evidence.

suspended sentence A sentence of incarceration that is not carried out if the offender agrees to obey the rules of probation while living in the community.

terrorism Premeditated, politically motivated violence perpetrated against noncombatant targets by subnational groups or clandestine agents.

three strikes laws Sentencing codes that require that an offender receive a life sentence after conviction for a third felony. Some states allow parole after a lengthy prison stay—for example, 25 years.

threshold inquiry A term used to describe a stop and frisk.

tier system A type of prison in which cells are located along corridors in multiple layers or levels.

time-in-rank system The promotion system in which a police officer can advance in rank only after spending a prescribed amount of time in the preceding rank.

torts The law of personal injuries.

total institution A regimented, dehumanizing institution, such as a prison, in which like-situated people are kept in social isolation, cut off from the world at large.

transfer The process of sending a case from the juvenile court to an adult court.

true bill The action by a grand jury when it votes to indict an accused suspect.

truth in sentencing Sentencing reform sponsored by the federal government mandating that any defendant who has pled guilty to or has been found guilty of a felony shall be required to serve a minimum prison term of 85 percent of the sentence imposed by the court.

tything (tithing) During the Middle Ages, a group of about 10 families responsible for maintaining order among themselves and dealing with disturbances, fire, wild animals, or other threats.

Uniform Crime Reports (UCRs) The official crime data collected by the FBI from local police departments.

venire The group called for jury duty from which jury panels are selected.

vice squads Police officers assigned to enforce morality-based laws, such as those regarding prostitution, gambling, and pornography.

victim impact statement A written statement that describes the harm or loss suffered by the victim of an offense; the court considers the statement when the offender is sentenced.

victim precipitation The role of the victim in provoking or encouraging criminal behavior.

victimless crime A crime typically involving behavior considered immoral or in violation of public decency that has no specific victim, such as public drunkenness, vagrancy, or public nudity.

vigilantes In the old west, members of a vigilance committee or posse called upon to capture cattle thieves or other felons.

voir dire The process in which a potential jury panel is questioned by the prosecution and the defense to select jurors who are unbiased and objective.

waiver The voluntary and deliberate relinquishing of a known right, such as those guaranteed under the Fifth and Sixth amendments; also, the transfer of a juvenile offender to criminal court for prosecution as an adult.

Walnut Street Jail The birthplace of the modern prison system and of the Pennsylvania system of solitary confinement.

warez The efforts of organized groups to download and sell copyrighted software in violation of its license.

watch system In medieval England, men organized in church parishes to guard at night against disturbances and breaches of the peace under the direction of the local constable.

"wedding cake" model of justice A view of justice that divides the criminal process into four layers based on the seriousness and notoriety of the crime. The top layer gets the full interest of the law, whereas the bottom layer receives only superficial attention.

wergild During the Middle Ages, the compensation paid to the victim by a defendant found guilty of crime.

white-collar crime Crimes that involve the violation of rules that control business enterprise; they can include employee pilferage, bribery, commodities law violations, mail fraud, computer fraud, environmental law violations, embezzlement, Internet scams, extortion, forgery, insurance fraud, price fixing, and environmental pollution.

widening the net To enmesh more offenders for longer periods in the criminal justice system—a criticism of pretrial diversion programs.

work release (furlough) A prison treatment program in which inmates leave the institution to work in the community, sometimes returning to prison or another supervised facility at night.

writ of certiorari An order of a superior court requesting that a record of an inferior court (or administrative body) be brought forward for review or inspection.

zero tolerance A practice in which criminal defendants forfeit homes, cars, and so on for the slightest law violation.

Name Index

Subject Index

Photo Credits

This page constitutes an extension of the copyright page. We have made every effort to trace the ownership of all copyrighted material and to secure permission from copyright holders. In the event of any question arising as to the use of any material, we will be pleased to make the necessary corrections in future printings. Thanks are due to the following authors, publishers, and agents for permission to use the material indicated.

Chapter Opener Pages: **3**: © AP Images/ Evan Vucci; **45**: © Erik S. Lesser/Getty Images; **87**: © Royalty Free/Corbis; **159**: © AP Images/Khampha Bouaphanh; **191**: © Julia Gaines/NewsDay. Reprinted by permission of *Los Angeles Times*; **225**: right, © AP Images/Louis Lanzano **225**: left, © Seth Wenig/Reuters/Corbis; **267**: inset, © AP Photo/Detroit Police Department **267**: © Reuters/Carlos Barria/ Landov; **297**: © April Saul/*The Philadelphia Inquirer*; **325**: © Ted Thai/ Time & Life Pictures/Getty Images; **353**: © AP Images/Los Angeles County Sheriff's Department; **381**: © AP Images/Nick Ut; **413**: © FBI/AFP/Getty Images; **455**: © AP Images/*Tampa Tribune*/Victor Junco; **491**: © AP Images/*The Worcester Telegram & Gazette*/Mark Ide; **525**: © AP Images/ Chicago Police Department; **573**: © Mark Wilson/Getty Images

Chapter 1. 6: left, © Bettmann/Corbis right, © Bettmann/Corbis **15**: © Sara D. Davis/Getty Images **22**: © AP Images/ Leslie Mazoch **24**: © Don Murray-Pool/ Getty Images **30**: © Carl De Souza/AFP/ Getty Images

Chapter 2. 50: © Andrew Lichtenstein/ The Image Works **51**: © AP Images/Bill Haber **60**: © Associated Press/AP Images/ Antelope Valley Press, Kelly Lacefield **65**: © AP Images/ Saurabh Das **78**: © AP Images/Kiichiro Sato

Chapter 3. 90: © AP Images/Tuno de Vieira, Diario do Nordeste **93**: © Associated Press/AP Images **99**: © Larry W. Smith/ AFP/Getty Images **102**: © AP Images/Daily Press, Sangjib Min **106**: © Lara Jo Regan/ Getty Images **110**: © AP Images/Louis Lanzano

Chapter 4. 132: © Pierre Barbier/Roger Viollet/Getty Images **136**: © AP Images/ The Patriot Ledger/Amelia Kunhardt **138**: © AP Images/DeWitt County Sheriff's Department, HO **141**: © AP Images/*The Northwestern*/Shu-Ling Zhou **147**: © AP Images/Jeff Roberson **153**: © AP Images/ Brennan Linsley

Chapter 5. 162: © Claudet/Getty Images **164**: © Bettmann/Corbis **165**: © Associated Press/AP Images **168**: © AP Images/John M. Galloway **172**: © Larry Downing/ Reuters/Landov **180**: © AP Images/*The Plain Dealer*/C. H. Pete Copeland

Chapter 6. 194: © AP Images/*West Bend Daily News*/Nathan Pier **198**: © AP Images/ Nick Ut **203**: © AP Images/M. Spencer Green **204**: © Gilles Mingasson/Getty Images **208**: © AP Images/Jim Mone **214**: © AP Images/Independent-Mail/Sefton Ipock

Chapter 7. 228: © Lynsey Addario/ Corbis **232**: © AP Images/Mel Evans **240**: © Shannon Stapleton REUTERS/Landov **247**: © UPI Photo/KTVITV/Landov **253**: © AP Images/Richard Drew

Chapter 8. 269: © AP Images/*Tribune-Review*/Sean Stipp **273**: © AP Images/ Rainier Ehrhardt **282**: © AP Images/*East Valley Tribune* **286**: © AP Images/Broward Sheriff's Office **289**: © AP Images/Oakland County Sheriff, HO

Chapter 9. 300: © AP Images/Steve Pope **307**: © AP Images/Dana Verkouteren **308**: © AP Images/Manuel Balce Ceneta **311**: © AP Images/Elaine Thompson **317**: © *Syracuse Newspapers*/The Image Works

Chapter 10. 329: © AP Images/Louis Lanzano **332**: © Stephen Chernin/Getty Images **338**: © AP Images/Rich Pedroncelli **342**: © AP Images/Mario Anzuoni **347**: © AP Images/Harry Lynch

Chapter 11. 356: © AP Images/Matthew West **360**: © AP Images/*Indianapolis Star*/Mike Fender **366**: © AP Images/Ed Zurga **368**: © AP Images/Louis Lanzano **373**: © Elaine Thompson/Reuters/Pool/ Landov **376**: © Bob Daemmrich/The Image Works

Chapter 12. 386: © Lou Dematteis/ AFP/Getty Images **398**: © AP Images/ Bruce Ackerman **401**: © AP Images/Nick Ut **407**: © UPI Photo/Bill Greenblatt/ Landov

Chapter 13. 415: The Granger Collection, New York **420**: © AP Images/Gregory Smith **422**: © AP Images/Roberto Borea **440**: © AP Images/Beth A. Keiser **444**: © AP Images/*The Charlotte Observer*/Jeff Siner

Chapter 14. 458: © AP Images/*Mansfield News Journal*/Dave Polcyn **461**: © Robert Nickelsberg/Getty Images **467**: © AP Images/Reed Saxon **468**: © AP Images/ John Bazemore **472**: © AP Images/George Nikitin **476**: © AP Images/Joseph Kaczmarek

Chapter 15. 493: van Gogh, Vincent: Prisoner's Round (detail), 1890. Pushkin Museum of Fine Arts, Moscow. Scala/Art Resource, New York **500**: American Correctional Association **506**: © AP Images/David Kohl **507**: © A. Ramey/ PhotoEdit **509**: © A. Ramey/PhotoEdit, Inc. **514**: © *Jacksonville Courier*/Zuzana Killiam/The Image Works

Chapter 16. 529: © AP Images/Eric Risberg **539**: © Tim Rue/Corbis **542**: © AP Images/Marcio Jose Sanchez **545**: © AP Images/Kalim A. Bhatti **554**: © Andrew Lichtenstein/Corbis **560**: © AP Images/ *The Press of Atlantic City*/Michael Ein

Chapter 17. 575: The Granger Collection, New York **585**: © Bill Pugliano/Getty Images **591**: © AP Images/*The Daily News*/Randy Davey **592**: © AP Images/ Elaine Thompson **598**: © Spencer Platt/ Getty Images

Part Opener 1: © AP Images/Peter Cosgrove

Part Opener 157: © AP Images/Joseph Kaczmarek

Part Opener 295: © Denver Rocky Mountain/Corbis-Sygma

Part Opener 453: © AP Images/*The Daily Times*/Daryl Sullivan

Part Opener 571: © AP Images/Charlie Cortez

TO THE OWNER OF THIS BOOK:

We hope that you have found *Introduction to Criminal Justice,* Eleventh Edition useful. So that this book can be improved in a future edition, would you take the time to complete this sheet and return it? Thank you.

School and address: _____

_____

Department: _____

Instructor's name: _____

1. What I like most about this book is:_____

_____

_____

2. What I like least about this book is: _____

_____

_____

3. My general reaction to this book is: _____

_____

_____

4. The name of the course in which I used this book is: _____

_____

5. Were all of the chapters of the book assigned for you to read? _____

    If not, which ones weren't? _____

6. In the space below, or on a separate sheet of paper, please write specific suggestions for improving this book and anything else you'd care to share about your experience in using this book.

_____

_____

_____

_____

_____

_____

BUSINESS REPLY MAIL
FIRST-CLASS MAIL   PERMIT NO. 34   BELMONT CA

POSTAGE WILL BE PAID BY ADDRESSEE

Attn: Carolyn Henderson Meier,
Criminal Justice Editor

Wadsworth/Thomson Learning
10 Davis Dr
Belmont CA 94002-9801

FOLD HERE

OPTIONAL:

Your name: _____ Date: _____

May we quote you, either in promotion for *Introduction to Criminal Justice,* Eleventh
Edition, or in future publishing ventures?

Yes: _____   No: _____

Sincerely yours,

Larry J. Siegel and Joseph J. Senna